INDEX TO JAZZ

Jazz Recordings 1917-1944

by ORIN BLACKSTONE

Issued in four volumes
(1945-1948)
by alphabetical division

GREENWOOD PRESS, PUBLISHERS
WESTPORT, CONNECTICUT

Library of Congress Cataloging in Publication Data
Blackstone, Orin.
   Index to jazz.

   Reprint of the ed. published by Record Changer,
Fairfax, Va.
   1. Jazz music--Discography. I. Title.
ML156.4.J3B6 1978   016.7899'12   77-27076
ISBN 0-313-20178-1

Copyright © 1945, 1947, 1948 by Gordon Gullickson

Reprinted with the permission of Mrs. Donald W. Olivier

Reprinted in 1978 by Greenwood Press, Inc.
51 Riverside Avenue, Westport, CT. 06880

Printed in the United States of America

10 9 8 7 6 5 4 3 2 1

CONTENTS

Volume I,   A–E

Volume II,   F–L

Volume III, M–R

Volume IV,   S–Z

INDEX TO JAZZ

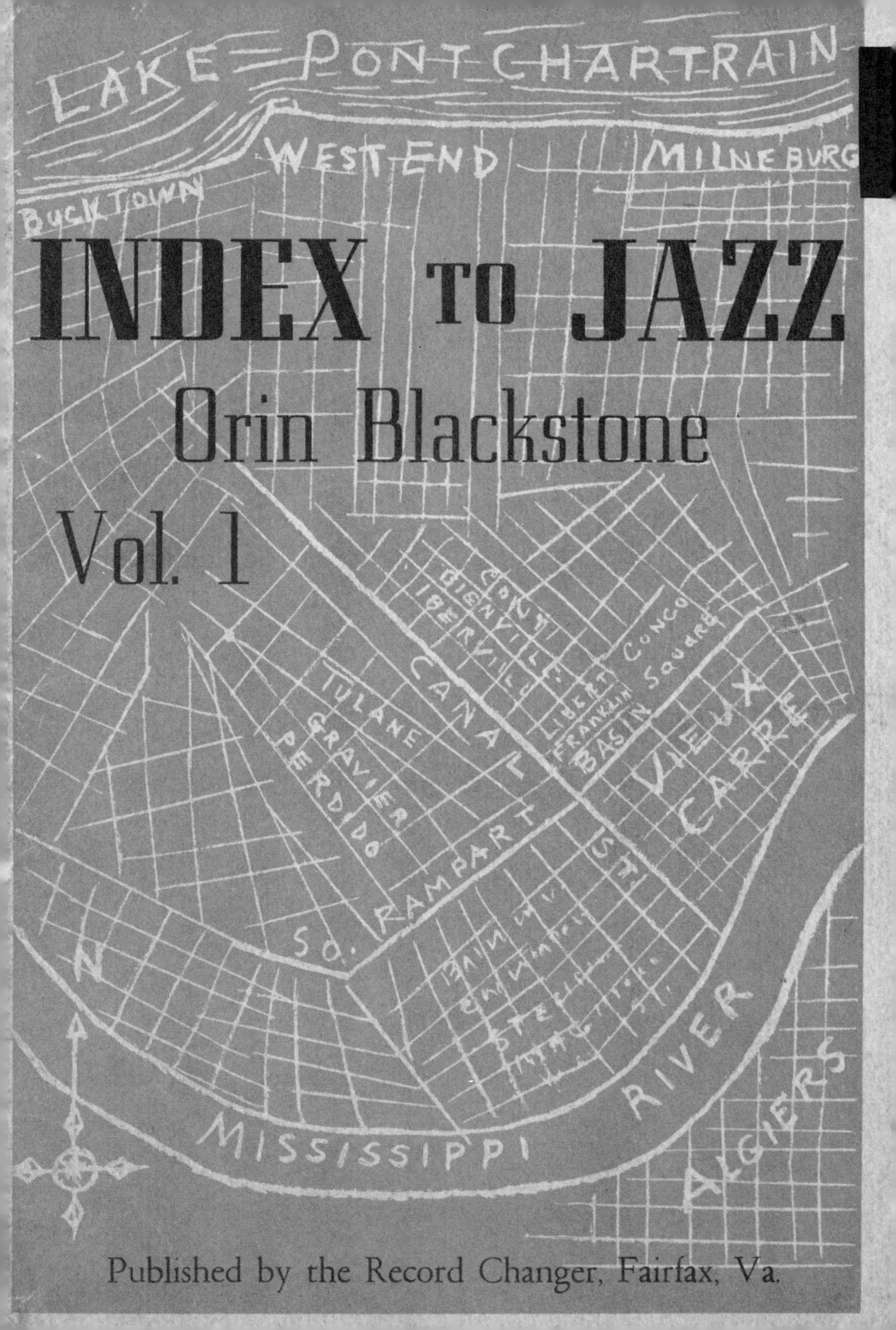

Orin Blackstone

Vol. 1

Published by the Record Changer, Fairfax, Va.

Hey GETCHA RECORD CHANGER!
YA CAN'T COLLECT RECORDS WITHOUT A RECORD CHANGER

- It's a fact. You can't collect jazz records,—and for that matter, you can't obtain a well-rounded perspective of jazz music,—without a subscription to the Record Changer.
- The Record Changer is the one, the only, the original advertising medium for jazz record collectors. In the past 38 issues of the magazine more than 46,000 collector's items have been offered for sale, auction or trade. More than 12,000 items have been advertised in the "Wanted" section.
- Some of the greatest articles ever printed on jazz music have appeared in the Record Changer by these writers: Nesuhi Ertegun, Roy Carew, John M. Phillips, Eugene Williams, Tom Williston, William Love, William Russell, Charles Wilford, E. S. Stewart, R. E. Stearns, John Steiner, Jazzbo Brown, Jelly Roll Morton, Leslie Smith, Ralph Sturges, Ernest Borneman, Thurman and Mary Grove, Albert McCarthy, Paul Eduard Miller, Ralph Gleason, Fred Ramsey, Herman Rosenberg, Don Fowler, Sterling Brown, Roger Pryor Dodge, Jeff Aldam, Graham McInnes, Bill Riddle, R. H. Pflug-Felder, and George Montgomery.
- Don Anderson's cover drawings alone are worth more than the price of the magazine.
- 1945 is our fourth year of continuous publication,—the longest run of any magazine ever devoted to jazz music.
- Our subscription rate is lower than that of any other comparable publication. Drop us a card.

Sirs:

Send me the current issue of the Record Changer.
On receipt I will send you my subscription.

THE RECORD CHANGER
Fairfax, Virginia
$1.50 (U. S. Money) 12 Issues Per Year

Introduction

This is the beginning of an attempt to put into a single list all the records of interest to jazz collectors. Covering the period from 1917 through 1944, it represents an expansion of material contained in *Hot Discography* and *Rhythm on Record* with information drawn from periodicals, catalogues, private lists and from direct sources.

Collectors are urged to help complete it by checking and correcting personnels and supplying missing details such as master numbers, recording dates and locations, as well as additional titles.

Because it was conceived as an index, this list follows a rigid alphabetical arrangement according to the artists' names under which the records originally were issued.

Purely commercial dance or vocal records have been avoided where possible, but many non-hot items are included because of the apparent importance of setting down complete discographies of interesting names. The less worthwhile records may be eliminated from a final list after they have been discussed among collectors and rejected. It is not the purpose of this index to evaluate in any way the records listed except that they be of interest to the jazz collector.

The records themselves are listed generally in the order in which they were *issued*, so that the catalogue number appears first, then the title with master number and, finally, any reissue numbers. Principal exceptions are reissues with different masters, which are usually listed under their reissue numbers immediately below the originals. Since additional masters mean additional records to most jazz collectors, such items are given a separate listing even in the case of identical catalogue numbers.

The numerical method of listing has presented problems in denoting proper personnels and dates when various titles were issued without regard to the time of their recording. But these problems were overcome where possible in order to keep the book in line as an index for the casual collector as well as the more experienced.

Intended as a further means of quick reference are the Label-serial number discographies for important artists who are represented on records issued under other names. These summaries, with cross references to record numbers only, appear in alphabetical order also.

Source of all the information is given where possible. But some of it is uncertain and there are many gaps, especially as to personnels. That is why the assistance of readers is earnestly solicited in the assembling of accurate data for final revision. Special thanks are due already to John Hammond for his valuable help.

The index in its present form will be issued in four sections. This first section covers the material from "A" through "E."

—ORIN BLACKSTONE

ABBREVIATIONS

RECORDS

Ae	Aeolian Vocalion	KP	Keith Prowse
Aj	Ajax	Li	Lincoln
Ap	Apex	Ma	Master
Au	Autograph	Mad	Madison
Ba	Banner	Max	Maxsa
BB	Bluebird	Me	Melotone
Bea	Beacon	MW	Montgomery Ward
BN	Blue Note	Nor	Nordskog
Br	Brunswick	OdF	French Odeon
BrE	English Brunswick	OdG	German Odeon
BrF	French Brunswick	OK	Okeh
BS	Black Swan	Or	Oriole
Bu	Buddy	OrE	English Oriole
Bwy	Broadway	PaE	English Parlophone
Ca	Cameo	PaF	French Parlophone
Cap	Capitol	Pana	Panachord
Ch	Champion	Para	Paramount
CI	Collectors Item	Pat	Pathe
Cl	Clarion	PatA	Pathe Actuelle
Clax	Claxtonola	PatF	French Pathe
Co	Columbia	Pe	Perfect
Com	Commodore	Ph	Philharmonic
Cq	Conqueror	Pu	Puritan
Cr	Crown	Re	Regal
De	Decca	Ro	Romeo
DeE	English Decca	RZ	Regal Zonophone
DeF	French Decca	Sa	Salabert
Di	Diva	SA	Solo Art
Do	Domino	SD	Steiner-Davis
El	Elite		
Elec	Electradisk	Se	Session
Em	Emerson	Si	Silvertone
Ex	Excelsior	Sig	Signature
FR	Firestone	Su	Sunshine
Ge	Gennett	Sw	Swing
GG	Grey Gull	Tele	Telefunken
GrF	French Gramophone	Tri	Triangle
Ha	Harmony	UHCA	United Hot Clubs
Harmo	Harmograph	Ul	Ultraphone
Her	Herwin	VD	Van Dyke
HMV	His Master's Voice	Ve	Velvet Tone
HoW	Hit of Week	Vi	Victor
HRS	Hot Record Society	Vo	Vocalion
Hy	Hytone	VoE	English Vocalion
Im	Imperial	Vr	Variety
Je	Jewel	Vs	Varsity
Key	Keynote		

SOURCES

DB	Down Beat (George Hoefer)	JR	Jazz Record
Dis	Discography (British magazine)	JRB	Jazz Record Book
HD	Hot Discography	JT	Jazz Tempo
HJ	Hot Jazz	RC	Record Changer
JAZZ	Magazine (W. C. Love)		(Eugene Williams)
JI	Jazz Information	RR	Rhythm on Record
JM	Jazz Music (British magazine)	Te	Tempo

A

ABNEY, BEN (blues with piano):
   BB 6496. Dirty Double Crosser/What Makes Your Heart So Hard

ADDISON, BERNARD AND HIS RHYTHM (Freddie Jenkins and one other trumpet; Albert Nicholas, clarinet; Joe Turner, piano; Bernard Addison, guitar; Joe Watts, bass; Adrian Rollini, drums.--JI 2/16/40, 9/20/40:   1935
   BB 6144. Lovely Liza Lee/(rev., The Little Ramblers)
   BB 6174. I Can't Dance/Toledo Shuffle
(See also Freddie Jenkins' Harlem Seven)

ADKINS, KATHERINE (acc. by W.M. Gill, piano):
   OK 8363. Individual Blues/Did She Fall

ADRIAN'S RAMBLERS (Pat Circicello, trumpet; Charles Barnet, tenor sax; Jimmy Dorsey, clarinet; Adrian Rollini, bass sax; Fulton McGrath, piano; Carl Kress, guitar; Gene Krupa, drums.--HD):   1934
   Br 6786. Get Goin'/Keep on Doin' What You're Doin'   -BrE 01750

(Max Kaminsky, trumpet; Milton Myaner, clarinet; Bud Freeman, tenor sax; Adrian Rollini, bass sax; Roy Bargy, piano; Carl Kress guitar; Mel Clark, bass; Stanley King, drums.--HD):
   Br 6877. Why Don't You Practice What You Preach   -BrE 01775
      "   I've Got a Warm Spot   -BrE 01831
   Br 6889. The Better to Love You (15167)   -BrE 01831
      "   I Wish I Were Twins (15168)   -BrE 01775

ADRIAN'S TAP ROOM GANG (Wingy Mannone, trumpet and vocal; Joe Marsala, clarinet and alto sax; Adrian Rollini, bass sax and vibraphone; Putney Dandridge, piano and vocal; Carmen Mastren, guitar; Sid Weiss, drums; Jeanne Burns, vocal.--HD):
   Vi 25072. I Got a Need for You   -BB 8382,   HMV JF-43
     "   Weather Man (92265)

   Vi 25085. Jazz o' Jazz(92268)/Nagasaki(92266)   -BB 8397,   HMV JF-44

   Vi 25208. Bouncin' in Rhythm (92263)   -HMV JF-39
     "   Honeysuckle Rose (92267)   -BB 8382,

ALABAMA HARMONIZERS:
   VD 74287. St. Louis Blues/Woman Down in Memphis

ALABAMA HARMONY BOYS (trumpet, trombone, clarinet, saxophone, piano, traps):
   Si 5139. Chicken Supper Strut/Sweet Patootie

ALABAMA RASCALS (probably Darnell Howard, clarinet; James Blythe, piano; trumpet; trombone, guitar, tenor sax, bass, drums):
   Pe 0205. Georgia Grind (11612-2)/Ruckus Juice Shuffle(11619-1) -Or 8136, Ro 5136
   Pe 0206. Endurance Stomp (11629)/(rev., Black Diamond Twins)   -Ro 5137
   Pe 0240. Jockey Stomp(11622-2)/Stomp That Thing(11628-2).   -Vo 1736*- Me 12689
   Me 70163. The Dirty Dozen's Cousins(19995)/Nancy Jane(20000)
(*Issued under name of Memphis Night Hawks, q.v. for additional titles)

ALABAMA RED PEPPERS (Red Nichols, trumpet; Miff Mole, trombone; Fud Livingston or Jimmy Dorsey, clarinet; Arthur Schutt, piano; Eddie Lang, guitar; Vic Berton, drums):
   Ro 494. A Good Man Is Hard to Find
   Ca 8109. San (2788)   -Ro 532
   Ca 8129. Red Head Blues (2833)   -Ro 552
   Ca 8130. The Drag (2834)   -Li 2784,   Ro 553
   Ca 8132. The New Twister (2835)   -Ro 555
   Ca 8204. Riverboat Shuffle (3070)   -Ro 634
   Ca 8205. Eccentric (3021)   -Ro 635
(See also Kentucky Hot Hoppers)

ALABAMA WASHBOARD STOMPERS:
   Vo 1546. If I Could Be With You/Pig Meat Stomp
   Vo 1586. I Want a Little Girl/You're Lucky to Me
   Vo 1587. Rockin' Chair/Who Stole the Lock
   Vo 1630. Corrine Corrina/Porter's Love Song
   Vo 1635. I Need Lovin'/You Can't Stop Me from Lovin' You
   Vo 1697. Pepper Steak/You Can Depend on Me

ALMO GARDEN JAZZERS:
   Ch 15132. St. Louis Hop/Messin' Around

ALBERT, DON AND HIS ORCHESTRA:
   Vo 3401. True Blue Lou/Rockin' and Swingin'
   Vo 3411. Sheik of Araby/You Don't Love Me
   Vo 3423. Deep Blue Melody/On the Sunny Side of the Street
   Vo 3491. Liza/Tomorrow

ALDERSON, MOZELLE (vocal, acc. by Judson Brown, piano):
    Br 7159. Tight in Chicago/Tight Whoopee

ALEXANDER, HILDA (and Mamie McClure):
    Br 7069. He's Tight Like This/(rev., Jabbo Smith Rhythm Aces)

ALEXANDER, ORA:
    Co 14626. Men Sure Are Deceiving/Sweetest Daddy in Town

ALEXANDER, TEXAS (vocal; principally with piano and guitar accompaniment, some by Lonnie Johnson* and Eddie Lang#):
    OK 8498. Section Gang Blues (81224b)/Levee Camp Moan Blues(81225b)
    OK 8511. Corn Bread Blues(81223)/Long Lonesome Day(81213)
    OK 8526. Farm Hand Blues/Range in My Kitchen Blues
    OK 8542. Sabine River Blues(81243)/Mama I Heard You Brought It Back(81235)
    OK 8563. Bell Cow Blues(400449)*/Boe Hog Blues(400456)*
    OK 8571. Rolling Mill Blues/Peaceful Blues
    OK 8578. Death Bed Blues(400441)*/Bad Luck Child(400455)*
    OK 8591. Bantam Rooster Blues(400444)*/Deep Blue Sea Blues(400445)*
    OK 8603. West Texas Blues(400443)*/Don't You Wish Your Baby(400448)*
    OK 8624. Sitting on a Log(400454)*/No More Women Blues(400446)*
    OK 8640. Penitentiary Moan Blues/Blue Devil Blues
    OK 8658. Work Ox Blues(401330)*#/Frisco Train Blues(401347)#, plus cornet
    OK 8673. Tell Me Woman Blues(301346)#, plus cornet/The Risin' Sun(401331)*#
    OK 8688. Evil Women Blues/St. Louis Fair Blues(401348)#
    OK 8705. Gold Tooth blues(402645)/Ninety-Eight Degree Blues(402640)
    OK 8731. Awful Moaning Blues, I & II
    OK 8745. Double Crossing Blues/Johnny Behren's Blues
    OK 8751. Rolling Mill Blues/Peaceful Blues
    OK 8764. Broken Yo Yo/When You Get Thinking
    OK 8785. Thirty Day Blues(403360)/Water Bound Blues(402642)
    OK 8801. Yellow Girl Blues(400442)*/I Am Calling Blues(401349)#
    OK 8813. Rolling and Stumbling Blues/She's So Fair
    Vo 02856. Justice Blues/Easy Rider Blues

ALEXANDER, VAN AND HIS ORCHESTRA:
    Vs 8065. In the Mood(7856-5-33)/Angry(7857-34)
    Vs 8317. Cherry (US 1711)/Slap Jack (US 1712)
    BB 10049. I Cried for You/No Star Is Lost
    BB 10073. On the Road to Mandalay/Night and Day
    BB 10271. Tony's Wife/Thou Swell
    BB 10278. Way Down Yonder in New Orleans/Adios Muchachos
    BB 10330. The Jumpin' Jive/Ragtime Cowboy Joe
    BB 10338. Stumbling/La Rosita

ALL STAR BAND (Benny Goodman, Hymie Schertzer, Eddie Miller, Adrian Rollini, saxes; Charlie Spivak, Bunny Berigan, Sonny Dunham, trumpets; Tommy Dorsey, Jack Teagarden, trombones; Carmen Mastren, guitar; Bob Haggart, bass; Bob Zurke, piano; Ray Bauduc, drums):
    Vi 26144. Blue Lou/The Blues(sub.Harry James for Spivak)

ALL STAR JAM BAND (Joe Marsala, clarinet; Pete Brown, alto sax; Bobby Hackett, cornet; Ray Biondi, guitar; Joe Bushkin, piano; George Wettling, drums; Artie Shapiro, bass):
    Com C-528. For He's a Jolly Good Fellow(M775)/Let's Get Happy(M777) ---Marsala
        doubles on tenor, Brown on trumpet, Hackett on guitar, Bushkin
        on celeste, and Biondi on violin

ALL STAR ORCHESTRA (Some of these feature Jimmy McPartland, cornet; Benny Goodman, clarinet):
    Vi 21149. Chloe
    Vi 21212. My Melancholy Baby/I Just Roll Along
    Vi 21326. I Must Be Dreaming(41511)/(rev., Roger Wolfe Kahn)
    Vi 21423. Oh Baby/Add a Little Wiggle
    Vi 21605. I'm More Than Satisfied(43384)/(rev., Eddie South)
    Vi 21667. She Didn't Say Yes/There's a Rainbow Around My Shoulder
    Vi 22054. My Dream Memory/(rev., Gus Arnheim)
    Vi 22073. Waiting at the End of the Road
    Vi 22104. Steppin' Along/Too Wonderful for Words
    Vi 22197. I'll Close My Eyes/Deep in My Arms

ALL STAR RHYTHM BOYS (See Joe Venuti groups):
    Ha 1346. Pardon Me Pretty Baby/Little Buttercup   -Ve 2422
    Ha 1420. Sensation/(rev., Tennessee Music Men)

ALLEN, ED (trumpet; for work see following:
    Blue Grass Foot Warmers: Ha 206, 248.
    Bessie Smith: Co 14435, 14451.
    Willie Smith: De 7073, 7074, 7086, 7090, BrE 02388.
    Clarence Williams: uncertain.

ALLEN, FLETCHER AND HIS ORCHESTRA (Fletcher Allen, Charles Lisee, Alix Combelle, saxes; Pierre Allier, trumpet; Ray Stokes, piano; Marcel Bianchi, guitar; Rovira bass; Pierre Fouad, drums):
   Sw   29. Swingin' in Paris (OSW 21)/Fletcher's Stomp (OSW 22)
   Sw   36. What'll I Do (OSW 20)/(Rev., Benny Carter)

HENRY ALLEN

For records under other names see:
- LOUIS ARMSTRONG: OK 8756, 8774, 41350,41375, Co 2688, De 1347,1353,1369,1408, 1635,1636,1560,1653, 1661, 2267, 3283.
- BUSTER BAILEY: Vo 2887.
- BILLY BANKS: Pe 15615, 15620, 15642.
- BLUE LU BARKER: De 7713 et al.
- JACK BLAND: Me 12510, 12513.
- LEE BROWN: De 7710, 7775.
- IDA COX: Ok 6405.
- PUTNEY DANDRIDGE: Vo 3006,3007,3024,3082, 3083, 3291, 3304, 3315, 3351, 3352.
- DIXIE JAZZ BAND: Or 1726, 1728.
- COLEMAN HAWKINS: PaE R1685, R1766.
- FLETCHER HENDERSON: Vo 2527, 2583, 3322; Vi 24699; De 157, 158, 213, 214,342, 555; BB 5682; CoE CB678, CB727, CB701; PaE R1792, 1743, 1766, 2031, 1717.
- J.C. HIGGINBOTHAM: OK 8772.
- SPIKE HUGHES: DeE F3639, 3836, 3972, 3717, 5101.
- FRANKIE HALF PINT JAXON: De 7786, 7795, 7806, 7733, 7742.
- LAZY LEVEE LOUNGERS: Co 2243.
- LOU AND HIS GINGER SNAPS: Ba 6536, 6540.
- BENNY MORTON: Co 2902, 2924.
- JELLY ROLL MORTON: Vi 23402,23424; General 1703,1704,1706,1707,1710,1711.
- KING OLIVER: Vi 38134, 23009; BB 6778, 10707.
- WALTER PICHON: Vi 38544.
- DON REDMAN: Br 6211, 6237, 6745.
- RHYTHMAKERS: Ba 32502, 32530.
- LUIS RUSSELL: OK 8734,8766,8780,8811,8830, 8849; Vo 1579; Me 12000; Vi 22793, 22789, 22815.
- ZUTTY SINGLETON: De 18093.
- VICTORIA SPIVEY: Vi 38546, 38570.
- SWEET PEAS: Vi 38565.
- EVA TAYLOR: Me 13228.
- FATS WALLER: Vi 38110, 38119.
- CLARENCE WILLIAMS: Uncertain.
- TEDDY WILSON: Br 7840, 7844.

ALLEN, HENRY AND HIS ORCHESTRA (Henry Allen,Otis Johnson,trumpets; James Archey, trombone; Albert Nicholas, Charlie Holmes, Greely Walton, saxes; Luis Russell, piano; Will Johnson, guitar; Bass Hill, bass; Paul Barbarin, drums.--HD):
   Vi 23006. Roamin'(62343)
               Patrol Wagon Blues(62345)   -GrF 7171, HMV 6377
   Vi 23338. Singing Pretty Songs(62344)   HMV 4985
           I Fell in Love With You(62346)   -GrF 7171, HMV 6426

HENRY ALLEN AND HIS NEW YORKERS (omit Johnson; Greely Walton; sub. J.C. Higginbotham, trombone; George Foster, bass.--HD):
   Vi 38073. It Should Be You(55133)   -BB 10235, HMV 6487, GrF 6949
           Biffly Blues(55134)

HENRY ALLEN AND HIS ORCHESTRA (add Theo Hill, sax):
   Vi 38080. Feeling Drowsy(53929)   -BB 10702, HMV 4070
           Swing Out(53930)   -HMV 6500,
   BB 10702. Swing Out (second master)
   Vi 38088. Funny Feathers Blues(55853),Victoria Spivey, vocal)   -BB 6588
           How Do They Do It That Way(55854),Victoria Spivey, vocal)
   Vi 38107. Make a Country Bird Fly Wild(55852)
           Pleasin' Paul(55855)   -BB 10235

(Add Otis Johnson,trumpet; sub William Blue,clarinet & alto sax for Nicholas):
   Vi 38140. Sugar Hill Function(58581)/You Might Get Better(58582)   -HMV 8409
   Vi 38121. Everybody Shout(58583)/Dancing Dave(58584)   -BB 6588

(Henry Allen, Pee Wee Irwin, trumpets; Dicky Wells, trombone; Hilton Jefferson, clarinet and alto sax; Ben Webster, tenor sax; Horace Henderson, piano; Lawrence Lucie, guitar; John Kirby, bass; Walter Johnson, drums.--HD):
   Pe 15933. Why Don't You Practice What You Preach(15148)
                      -Me 13016, Ba 33054, Vo 3016, Or 2898
          "   Don't Let Your Love Go Wrong(15149)   "   "   "   "
   Pe 15948. I Never Slept a Wink Last Night(15147)-Me 13045, Ba 33081, Or 2915
          "   I Wish I Were Twins(15146)

FILL IN THE GAPS

There are several sections of this list in which no personnel changes are noted for large groups of records. This is not intended as a claim that there are no changes, but rather that information to the contrary was not available. Recording musicians who can expand and correct the information shown in this Index are urged to contact us. Collectors with hunches on unknown personnels are likewise invited to send us their observations, together with whatever substantiation they can offer. Address: Orin Blackstone, 1016 Eleonore St., New Orleans 15, Louisiana.

PAGE NO.	RECORDING GROUP	LABEL	SERIAL NUMBER	WAS SHOWN:	SHOULD HAVE BEEN SHOWN:

PAGE NO.	RECORDING GROUP	L A B E L	SERIAL NUMBER	WAS SHOWN:	SHOULD HAVE BEEN SHOWN:

(Omit Irwin; sub Keg Johnson, trombone; Elmer James, bass; omit Webster; add Buster Bailey, clarinet.--HD):
    Pe 15970. Pardon My Southern Accent(15472)/How's About Tomorrow Night(15474)
                                                                             -Me 13096, Or 2942
    Pe 15994. Rug Cutter's Swing/There's a House in Harlem
                                                    -Me 13145, Ba 33178, VoE 8, Co 35676

(Add Irwin, trumpet; sub. George Washington, trombone; Luis Russell, piano; Daniel Balker, guitar; Pop Foster, bass; Barbarin, drums.--HD):
    Pe 16071. Believe It Beloved(16671)/It's Written All Over Your Face(16672)
                                                       -Me 13304, Ba 33337, Ro 2461, Or 3087
    Pe 16080. Smooth Sailing(16681)/Whose Honey Are You(16682)   -Me 13322

(Henry Allen, trumpet; Dicky Wells, trombone; Cecil Scott, clarinet; Chu Berry, tenor sax; Horace Henderson piano; Bernard Addison, guitar; John Kirby, bass; Walter Johnson, drums):   (April 29,1935)
    Vo 2956. Get Rhythm in Your Feet   -BrE 02079
    "   I'll Never Say Never Again
    Vo 2965. Body and Soul(17396)   -Co 36282
    "   Rosetta(17395)   -Co 35954

(Sub. J.C. Higginbotham, trombone; Albert Nicholas, clarinet; Cecil Scott, tenor sax; Lawrence Lucie, guitar; Elmer James, bass; Kaiser Marshall, drums.--HD):
    Vo 2997. I Wished on the Moon
    "   Roll Along Prairie Moon   -VoE S29
    Vo 2998. Truckin'   -Pana 25809
    "   Dinah Lou
    Vo 3097. Red Sails in the Sunset
    "   I Found a Dream   -Pana 25809
    Vo 3098. On Treasure Island/Take Me Back to My Boots and Saddle

(Add Willie Humphries, alto sax; omit Nicholas; sub. Norman Lester, piano; Cozy Cole, drums.--HD):
    Vo 3214. I'll Bet You Tell That to All the Girls/Lost
    Vo 3215. The Touch of Your Lips(18903)/Every Minute of the Hour(18910)

(Happy Caldwell, tenor sax; Teddy Wilson, piano):
    Vo 3244. You(19300)/Would You(19303)
    Vo 3245. Tormented(19301)/Nothin's Blue But the Sky(19302)

(Henry Allen, trumpet; J. C. Higginbotham, trombone; Tab Smith, alto sax; Joe Garland, tenor sax; Edgar Hayes, piano; Lawrence Lucie, guitar; Elmer James, bass O'Neil Spencer, drums.):   (June 19, 1936)
    Vo 3261. Take My Heart(19451)/On the Beach at Bali Bali(19454)
    Vo 3262. Chloe(19452)/You're Not the Kind(19453)

(Sub. Rudy Powell, clarinet; Cecil Scott, tenor sax; Cozy Cole, drums; omit Higginbotham):
    Vo 3292. Am I Asking Too Much(19660)/Until Today(19661)
    Vo 3302. When Did You Leave Heaven(19659)
            Algiers Stomp(19662)   -VoE S29
    Vo 3305. Out Where the Blues Begin/Darling Not Without You
    Vo 3306. I'll Sing a Thousand Love Songs/Picture Me Without You
    Vo 3339. Whatcha Gonna Do/Midnight Blue
    Vo 3340. Lost in My Dreams(20050)/Sitting on the Moon(20051)
    Vo 3377. Did You Mean It(20267)/In the Chapel in the Moonlight(20268)
    Vo 3389. Here's Love in Your Eye(20269)/When My Dream Boat Comes Home (20270)

(Billy Kyle, piano):
    Vo 3422. Let's Put Our Heads Together/I Adore You.
    Vo 3432. He Ain't Got Rhythm(20459)/This Year's Kisses(20460)

(Henry Allen, trumpet; Buster Bailey, clarinet; Tab Smith, alto sax; Sonny Fredericks, tenor sax; Billy Kyle, piano; Danny Barker, guitar; John Williams, bass; Alphonse Steele, drums.--HD):
    Vo 3490. Good Night My Lucky Day/There's a Kitchen Up in Heaven
    Vo 3524. I Was Born to Swing/After Last Night With You
    Vo 3564. Sticks and Stones(21070)/A Love Song of Long Ago(21073)
    Vo 3574. Meet Me in the Moonlight/Don't You Care What Anyone Says
    Vo 3594. The Merry Go Round Broke Down/You'll Never Go to Heaven
    Vo 3607. The Miller's Daughter Marianne/Till the Clocks Strike Three
    Vo 3690. Love or Infatuation/Can I Forget You
    Vo 3704. Have You Ever Been in Love/I Owe You

RED ALLEN AND HIS ORCHESTRA (Lil Armstrong, piano; Henry Allen, trumpet; Benny Morton, trombone; Edmond Hall, clarinet; Bernard Addison, guitar; Pop Foster, bass; Zutty Singleton, drums):
   De 18092. Down in Jugle Town(67839a)/Canal Street Blues(67840)

(Henry Allen, trumpet; J.C. Higginbotham, trombone; Edmond Hall, clarinet; Kenneth Kersey, piano; Billy Taylor, bass; Jimmy Hoskins, drums):
   OK 6281. K.K. Boogie(CO 30270)/Ol' Man River (CO 30273)
   OK 6357. A Sheridan Square(30894)/Indiana(30896)

ALLEN-HAWKINS AND THEIR ORCHESTRA (Henry Allen, trumpet; Dicky Wells, trombone; Hilton Jefferson, alto sax; Coleman Hawkins, tenor sax; Horace Henderson, piano; Bernard Addison, guitar; John Kirby, bass; Walter Johnson, drums.--HD):   1933
   Pe 15802. Stringin' Along on a Shoestring(13618)/Shadows on the Swanee(13619)
                      -Ba 32829, Me 12759, Or 2739, BrE 01776
   Pe 15808. The River's Takin' Care of Me(13616)/Ain'tcha Got Music(13617)
                      -Me 12769, Or 2746, BrF 500371, BrE 02005

(Sub. Benny Morton, trombone; Bob Ysaguire, bass; Manzie Johnson, drums; omit Jefferson; add Edward Inge, clarinet.--HD):   1933
   Pe 15851. You're Gonna Lose Your Gal(14283)/My Galveston Gal(14285)
                   -Me 12842, Ba 32901, Ro 2170, BrE 01664
      Pe 15858. Hush My Mouth(14282) -Me 12858, Or 2806, Ba 32915, BrF 500374, BrE 01709
    "   Dark Clouds(14284)   "   "   "   "   "   BrE 01664

ALLISON, GEORGE (and Willie White; blues with piano):
   Para 12960. I'll Be Mean to You Blues/How I Feel My Love

ALSTON, OVIE AND HIS ORCHESTRA:
   Vo 4448. Ja Da/Junk Man's Serenade

ALTIER, DANNY AND HIS ORCHESTRA (Muggsy Spanier, cornet; Danny Altier, alto sax; Morry Bercov, clarinet; Floyd O'Brien, trombone; Jess Stacy, piano; George Wettling, drums; Pat Pattison, bass; unknown guitar.--JI 1/24/41; DB 8/1/43):
   Vo 15740. I'm Sorry Sally/My Gal Sal

AMMONS, ALBERT (piano solos):
   SA 12000. Bass Goin' Crazy(R2092)/Monday Struggle(R 2093)
   SA 12001. Boogie Woogie/Mecca Flat Blues
   SA 12002. St. Louis Blues/(rev., Meade Lux Lewis)
   BN   2. Boogie Woogie Stomp(441-5)/Boogie Woogie Blues(442-8)
   BN   4. Chicago in Mind(GM 535)/Twos and Fews(GM 537), with Meade Lux Lewis
   BN   21. Suitcase Blues(1007)/Bass Goin' Crazy(1014)
   Vo 4606. Boogie Woogie Prayer, I & 2(23890-91), with Meade Lux Lewis and Pete
               Johnson   -Co 35960
   Vo 4608. Shout for Joy(23894)/rev., Meade Lux Lewis)   -Co 35961
   Vo 5186. Cafe Society Rag(25026), with Lewis and Johnson/(rev., Pete Johnson
               Boogie Woogie Boys)
(following are duets with Pete Johnson):
   Vi 27504. Cuttin' the Boogie/Barrel House Boogie
   Vi 27505. Boogie Woogie Man/Walkin' the Boogie
   Vi 27506. Sixth Avenue Express/Pine Creek
   Vi 27507. Foot Pedal Boogie/Movin' the Boogie

ALBERT AMMONS AND HIS RHYTHM KINGS (Albert Ammons, piano; Israel Crosby, bass; Jimmy Hoskins, drums; Ike Perkins, guitar; Guy Kelly, trumpet; Dalbert Bright, clarinet
   De   749. Nagasaki   -BrE 02187
      "   Boogie Woogie Stomp   -De 3386,
   De   975. Early Mornin' Blues(90573a)   -De 3512, BrE 02336
      "   Mile-or-No Bird Rag(90574a)

(Albert Ammons, piano; Hot Lips Page, trumpet; Vic Dickenson, trombone; Don Byas, tenor sax; Israel Crosby, bass; Sidney Catlett, drums):
   Com C-1516. Jammin' the Boogie/Bottom Blues

ANDERSON, BILLY (vocal, with piano probably by Cow Cow Davenport):
   Co 14216. Lonely Billy Blues/Adam and Eve
   Co 14247. Cow Cow Blues/Married Man Blues

ANDERSON, CHARLES (second couplings acc. by Charles Avery, piano):
   OK 8124. Comic Yodle Song/Sing 'em Blues
   OK 8208. Walkin' Blues/Dirty Mistreatin' Blues

ANDERSON, IVY AND HER BOYS FROM DIXIE:
   Vr   591. All God's Chillun Got Rhythm/Old Plantation

ANDREWS SISTERS (acc. by Frank Froeba, piano; Vic Schoen, Bobby Hackett, trumpets; Don Watt, clarinet; Dave Barbour, guitar; Al Philburn, trombone; Haig Stephens, bass; Stan King, drums):
   De 1562. Nice Work If You Can Get It(62810)/Bei Mir Bist du Schon(62811)

(Sub. John McGee, trumpet for Hackett; Tony Zimmer, clarinet, George Mazza, trombone; Sammy White, drums):
    De 1744. Shortenin' Bread(63314a)/Ooh Boom!(63317a)

ANDREWS, ED (guitar solos):
    OK 8137. Barrel House Blues/Time Ain't Gonna Make Me Stay

ARCADIA PEACOCK ORCHESTRA OF ST. LOUIS:
    OK 40044. Dream Boat/Tripping Along
    OK 40052. She Wouldn't Do What I Asked Her(8511b)/Ain't You Ashamed(8510b)
    OK 40254. Let Me Be the First to Kiss You Good Morning/Where's My Sweetie
    OK 40264. Spring Has Come/Ah Ah Archie
    OK 40272. Dog on the Piano(8763b),piano by Ed Ward/(rev.,Arcadian Serenaders)
    OK 40372. I Wouldn't Be Crying Now(9016a)/Waitin' for the Moon(9017a)
    OK 40440. Little Boy Blues(8765a)/(rev., Arcadian Serenaders)

ARCADIAN SERENADERS (Wingy Mannone, trumpet; Cliff Holman, clarinet; Avery Lopeser, trombone; John Riddick, piano; Slim Hill, banjo; Felix Guarino, drums.--
JI 1/24/41; DB 8/1/41):   St. Louis 1926:
    OK 40272. Fidgety Feet(8778a)/(rev., Arcadia Peacock Orchestra)
    OK 40378. San Sue Strut(8775a)/Bobbed Haired Bobbie(8777a)
    OK 40440. Who Can Your Regular Be Blues(8776a)/(rev.,Arcadia Peacock Orch.)

(Sub. Sterling Bose, trumpet; Bob Marvin, banjo; Holman doubles on sax?)
    OK 40503. The Co-ed(9407a)/Just a Little Bit Bad(9413a)
    OK 40517. You Gotta Know How(9409a)/Angry(9414a)
    OK 40538. Back Home in Illinois(9408a)/Carry It on Down(9410a)
    OK 40562. Yes Sir Boss(9411a),solo by Riddick/Original Dixieland(9412a)

ARKANSAS TRAVELERS (directed by Sam Lanin and sometimes featuring Red Nichols, trumpet, and his associates):
    OK 40124. Georgia Blues(s72553c)/Lost My Baby Blues(s72554a)
    OK 40183. She Loves Me/Any Way the Wind Blows
    OK 40236. Copenhagen(72980c)/Those Panama Mamas(72981b)
    OK 40267. Homebound(rev., Okeh Syncopators)
    OK 40277. How I Love That Girl/I'll See You in My Dreams
    OK 40426. Row Row Rosie

    OK 40640. Breezin' Along With the Breeze(74180b)   -PaE 5635
    "   When the Red Red Robin Comes Bob Bob Bobbin' Along(74181a)
    OK 40674. Ting-a-Ling the Bells'll Ring(74508a)/(rev., Lloyd Turner)
    OK 40700. Give Me a Ukelele(80148a)/(rev., Harry Raderman)
    OK 40724. Take in the Sun Hang Out the Moon(80226c)/(rev., Mike Markel)

    OK 40727. Brown Sugar   -PaE 5761
    "   I Can't Get Over a Girl Like You

    PaE R3438. There Ain't No Land Like Dixieland
    PaE R3488. How Long Has This Been Goin' on
    PaE R3528. Away Down South in Heaven

(Red Nichols, cornet: Miff Mole, trombone; Jimmy Dorsey, clarinet and alto sax;
Arthur Schutt, piano; Vic Berton, crums.--1927 HD):   1927
    Ha   332. Washboard Blues(143260)/Boneyard Shuffle(143262)   -Ve 1332
    Ha   383. That's No Bargain(1436   -Ve 1383
    "   (rev., the Emperors)
    Ha   421. Ja Da(144119)/Sensation(144120)   -Di 2421
    Ha   459. Stompin' Fool(144121)   -Di 2459
    "   (rev., Original Indiana Five)

(sub. Fud Livingstone, clarinet):
    Ha   505. Birmingham Breakdown(14467)/I Ain't Got Nobody(144669)   -Di 2505
    Ha   601. Red Head Blues(144668)   -Di 2601
    "   (rev., Washingtonians)

ARMSTRONG, LIL AND HER SWING BAND (Joe Thomas, trumpet; Buster Bailey, clarinet; Chu Berry, tenor sax; Teddy Cole, piano; Huey Long, guitar; John Frazier, bass
Lil Armstrong, vocal.--HD):   1937
    De 1059. My Hi De Ho Man   -BrE 02372
    "   Doin' the Suzie Q   -De 3883,
    De 1092. Or Leave Me Alone(90967b)/Brown Gal(90969a)   -BrE 02395, F505086
    De 1182. Just for a thrill/It's Murder

(Sub. Robert Carroll, tenor sax; James Sherman, piano; Arnold Adams,guitar; Wellman Braud, bass; George Foster, drums.--HD):
    De 1272. I'm Knocking at the Cabin Door/Sit Down Strike for Rhythm
    De 1299. Bluer Than Blue/Born to Swing   -BrE 02465,BrF 505104

COMMODORE
Recent Releases

★ ★

(10-INCH RECORDS—$1.00 PLUS TAX)

★ ★

554—EDDIE HEYWOOD AND HIS ORCHESTRA
T'AINT ME   SAVE YOUR SORROW

Eddie Heywood, piano; "Doc" Cheatham, trumpet; Vic Dickenson, trombone; Lem Davis, alto sax; Al Lucas, bass; Jack Parker, drums.

★ ★

555—KANSAS CITY SIX
I GOT RHYTHM   JO JO

Lester Young, tenor sax; Dickey Wells, trombone; Bill Coleman, trumpet; Joe Bushkin, piano; John Simmons, bass; Joe Jones, drums.

★ ★

556—GEORGE BRUNIS AND HIS JAZZ BAND
TIN ROOF BLUES   ROYAL GARDEN BLUES

George Brunis, trombone; "Wild Bill" Davison, trumpet; Pee Wee Russell, clarinet; Eddie Condon, guitar; Gene Schroeder, piano; Bob Casey, bass; George Wettling, drums.

★ ★

(12-Inch Records—$1.50 Plus Tax)

★ ★

1518—MIFF MOLE AND HIS NICKSIELAND BAND
ST. LOUIS BLUES   PEG O' MY HEART

Miff Mole, trombone; Bobby Hackett, trumpet; Pee Wee Russell, clarinet; Ernie Caceres, baritone sax; Eddie Condon, guitar; Gene Schroeder, piano; Bob Casey, bass; Joe Grauso, drums.

★ ★

1519—MUGGSY SPANIER AND HIS RAGTIMERS
MEMPHIS BLUES   SWEET SUE, JUST YOU

Muggsy Spanier, cornet; Pee Wee Russell, clarinet; Miff Mole, trombone; "Boomie" Richman, tenor sax; Eddie Condon, guitar; Gene Schroeder, piano; Bob Haggart, bass; George Wettling, drums.

COMMODORE MUSIC SHOP
136 East 42nd Street, Call MUrray Hill 2-7967, New York City

(Sub. Shirley Clay,trumpet; Prince Robinson, tenor sax; Manzie Johnson, drums.--HD):
De 1388. Lindy Hop/When I Went Back Home   -BrE 02553
De 1502. Let's Call It Love/You Mean So Much to Me   -BrE 02578

(Frank Froeba, piano; Sammy Weiss, drums; Haig Stephens, bass; Dave Barbour, guitar;Tony Zimmer,tenor;Ralph Muzzillo,Johnny McGee,trumpets;Al Philburn, trombone,--JM 6/43):   Feb., 1938
De 1722. Happy Today, Sad Tomorrow   -BrE 02597
         You Shall Reap What You Sow   -BrE 02633

De 1904. Let's Get Happy Together   -BrE 02597
         Oriental Swing   -BrE 02633

(Renald Jones, trumpet; J.C. Higginbotham,trombone; Buster Bailer,clarinet; Lil Armstrong,piano; Wellman Braud, bass; O'Neill Spencer, drums.--JRB):   1938
De 2234. Safely Locked Up in My Heart(64604)/Harlem Sat.Night(64606) -BrE 02732
De 2542. Everything's Wrong,Ain't Nothing Right/Knock Kneed Sal   -BrE 2824

(LIL ARMSTRONG AND HER DIXIELANDERS (Jonah Jones,trumpet; Don Stovall,alto; Russell Johns, tenor; Lil Armstrong,piano;Wellman Braud,bass; Manzie Johnson, drums. --JM 6/43):
De 7739. Sixth Street(67331a)/My Secret Flame(67334a)
De 7803. Riffin' the Blues(67332a)/Why Is a Good Man So Hard to Find(6733a)

LOUIS ARMSTRONG

SEE ALSO:
BABY MACK: 8313.
JOSEPHINE BEATTY: Ge 5594, 5626.
PERRY BRADFORD: Vo 15165.
BUTTERBEANS AND SUSIE: OK 8355.
BLANCHE CALLOWAY: OK 8279.
L.D. CHRISTIAN: OK 8596, 8607, 8650, 8660.
CLUB ALABAM: Do 426 (reissue)
CLUB WIGWAM: Do 3458 (Henderson reissue)
JOHNNY DODDS: Br 3567, Vo 15632.
SEGER ELLIS: OK 41255, 41290, 41291.
GLEN GRAY: De 2395.
FLETCHER HENDERSON: Para 20367; Re 9739, 9753, 9767, 9774, 9775, 9789, 9803;
       Apex 8309, 8316; Vo 14926, 14935, 15030; Pat 36156, 36157, 36214; Co 228, 249, 292, 383, 395, 509.
BERTHA HILL: OK 8273, 8312 8339, 8420, 8437, 8453.
WILMOUTH HOUDINI: Uncertain.
GRANT and WILSON: Para 12317, 12324, 12337.
MARGARET JOHNSON: OK 8185, 8193.
MAGGIE JONES: Co 14050, 14055, 14059, 14063.
LILL'S HOT SHOTS: Vo 1037.
VIRGINIA LISTON: OK 8173, 8187.
KING OLIVER: Ge 5132, 5133, 5134, 5135, 5184, 5274, 5275, 5276; Para 12088, 20292; OK 4906, 4918, 4933, 4975, 8148, 8235, 40000, 40034; Co 13003,14003.
MA RAINEY: Para 12238, 12252.
RED ONION JAZZ BABIES: Ge 5626, 5627; Si 5024.
ROSELAND DANCE ORCHESTRA: Do 3445 (reissue)
SOUTHAMPTON SOCIETY ORCHESTRA: Pe 14395.
SOUTHERN SERENADERS: Ha 4, 5.
BESSIE SMITH: Co 14064, 14056, 14079, 14090, 14083, 14095.
CLARA SMITH: Co 14058, 14064, 14073, 14077.
TRIXIE SMITH: Para 12256, 12262.
VICTORIA SPIVEY: OK 8713.
ERSKINE TATE: Vo 1027.
EVA TAYLOR: OK 8342, 40330.
HOCIEL THOMAS: OK 8258, 8289, 8326, 8297, 8346.
SIPPIE WALLACE: OK 8212, 8301, 8328, 8345, 8470, 8449.
NOLAN WELSH: OK 8372.
HAL WHITE: Do 3444 (Henderson reissue)
CLARENCE WILLIAMS: OK 8171, 8181, 8215, 8245, 8254,8267,8272,40260,40321.
SAM HILL: Or 303, 347, 374 (Henderson reissues)

ARMSTRONG, LOUIS AND HIS HOT FIVE (Louis Armstrong, trumpet and vocal: Kid Ory, trombone; Johnny Dodds,clarinet and alto sax; Lil Hardin, piano; Johnny St. Cyr, banjo):
OK 8261. Yes I'm in the Barrel(9485a)/Gut Bucket Blues(9486a)   -Co 36152
OK 8299. Oriental Strut(9536a)/You're Next(9537a)   -HRS 10, Co 36155
OK 8300. Heebie Jeebies(9534a)   -Co 35660
         Muskrat Ramble(9538a)   -Co 36153
OK 8318. Come Back Sweet Papa(9503a)/Georgia Grind(9533a)

15

```
OK  8320. My Heart(9484a)                                    -Co 36154, OdG 60259
          Cornet Chop Suey(9535a)                    -HRS 2,  "           "
                                                                    October, 1926
OK  8343. Don't Forget to Mess Around(9729a)/I'm Gonna Gitcha(9730a)
OK  8357. Droppin' Shucks(9731a)/Who'sit(9732a)
OK  8379. Big Fat Ma and Skinny Pa(9777a)/Sweet Little Papa(9779a)
OK  8396. The King of the Zulus(9776a)/Lonesome Blues(9778a)(See also OK 41581)
                                                                            1927
OK  8423. Big Butter and Egg Man from the West(9892a)/Sunset Cafe Stomp(9893a)
OK  8436. Jazz Lips(9890a)
     "    Skid-Dat-De-Dat(9891a)                                       -Co 36153
OK  8447. You Made Me Love You(9980a)/Irish Black Bottom(9981a)
```

LOUIS ARMSTRONG AND HIS HOT SEVEN (Same personnel with Baby Dodds, drums; Pete
Biggs, bass):

```
    OK  8474. Wild Man Blues(80848c)                    -Vo 3193, PaE 3492
              Gully Low Blues(80877d)                             PaE R113
    OK  8482. Willie the Weeper(80847c)                 -Vo 3381, PaE 2393
         "    Alligator Crawl (80854b)                           -PaE 2185
    OK  8496. Melancholy Blues(80862a)                PaE R2162,  Vo 3137
              Keyhole Blues(80876b)
    OK  8503. Potato Head Blues(80855c)      -UHCA 59, Co 35660, PaE R2185
              Put 'em Down Blues(81302b)(Hot Five)               -UHCA 60
    OK  8519. Weary Blues(80863a) (Hot Five)         -Vo 3216, PaE 2393
              That's When I'll Come Back to You(80884b)         -PaE R113
    Co 35661. S.O.L. Blues(81126b)                              -PaE 2774
    Co 35663. Twelfth Street Rag(80864a)
    Co 35838. Ory's Creole Trombone(81310d)/The Last Time(81317a)   -PaE 2792
```

(Louis Armstrong, trumpet; Earl Hines, piano; Boyd Atkins, soprano sax; Stomp
Evans, baritone sax; Honore Dutrey, trombone; Rip Bassett, banjo):
Co 36376. Chicago Breakdown(80851c)/Don't Jive Me(400966c)(Hot Five,see below)
LOUIS ARMSTRONG AND HIS HOT FIVE, original personnel, except Lonnie Johnson*:

```
    OK  8535. Hotter Than That(82055b)*                        -Vo 3237
              Savoy Blues(82056a)*                    -PaE 2127, Vo 3217
    OK  8551. Got No Blues(82038b)                     -Vo 3204, PaE 2449
         "    I'm Not Rough(82040b)*                             -Vo 3237
    OK  8566. Struttin' With Some Barbecue(82037b)
              Once in Awhile(82039b)*                           -PaE 2242
```

(Louis Armstrong, trumpet; Fred Robinson, trombone; Jimmy Strong, clarinet and
tenor sax; Earl Hines, piano; Mancy Cara, banjo; Zutty Singleton, drums):
                                                                         1928
```
    OK  8597. Fireworks(400960b)                -OK 41078,-Vo 3148, PaE 2282
              West End Blues(400967b)     -Co 36377,   "  -Vo 3204, PaE 448
    OK  8609. A Monday Date(400962b)                    -Co 36375, PaE R2135
         "    Sugar Foot Strut(400968b)                 -Vo 3148, PaE R2449
    OK  8631. Skip the Gutter(400961a)/Knee Drops(400991b)  -OK 41157,PaE R2438
    OK  8641. Two Deuces(400973b)                                -PaE R2282
              Squeeze Me(400974b)              PaE 2774,-Co 35661, PaE R2242
```

LOUIS ARMSTRONG AND HIS SAVOY BALLROOM FIVE(Same personnel,with Don Redman,alto):

```
 *  OK  8649. Heah Me Talkin' to Ya?(402224a)-Co 36378, Vo 3303, PaE 1767, F22246
              Tight Like This(402226c)            "         "   PaE 1591,  "
    OK  8657. Save It Pretty Mama(402170c)-Co 35662, Vo 3381, OK 41180,OdF 165617
              St. James Infirmary(402225a)                       "
```

(For starred(*) titles only: Louis Armstrong, trumpet; J.C. Higginbotham, trombone; Charlie Holmes, alto sax; Albert Nicholas, clarinet and alto sax; Theo Hill,tenor sax; Luis Russell,piano; Eddie Condon,banjo; Lonnie Johnson, guitar, Pop Foster, bass; Paul Barbarin, drums):

```
    OK  8669. I Can't Give You Anything But Love(401690c)*
                  -UHCA 36, OK 41204, OdF 165683, PaF 22382,PaE 753
         "    No One Else But You (402168b)
                  -Vo 3085, Co 35662, OK 41204, OdF 165683, PaF 22382, E540
    OK  8669. I Can't Give You Anything But Love(401690a)*
    OK  8680. Mahogany Hall Stomp(401691b)*             -PaE R571, Co 35879
              Beau Koo Jack(402169c)            -Vo 3085, PaE R2066,  "
    Vo 3055. Mahogany Hall Stomp(401691)*
    (Omit Redman):
    OK  8690. No(402153a)                       -OK 41241, Vo 3205,PaE R1767
              Basin Street Blues(402154a)   -Cq 9124,   "  Vo 3008,PaE R531
```

(For starred(*) title only: Louis Armstrong, trumpet; Jack Teagarden, trombone; Happy Caldwell, tenor sax; Joe Sullivan, piano; Ed Lang, guitar; Kaiser Marshall, drums):
March 5, 1929

OK 8703. Knockin' a Jug(401689b)* -Co 35663, OdF 165913, PaE R1064, UHCA 35
  "   Muggles (402200b)   -Co 36377,   PaE R840, Vo 3194

LOUIS ARMSTRONG AND HIS ORCHESTRA (Louis Armstrong, trumpet; Homer Hobson, trumpet; Fred Robinson, trombone; Jimmy Strong, clarinet and tenor sax/ Bert Curry, Crawford Wethington, alto saxes; Carroll Dickerson, violin; Gene Anderson, piano; Mancy Cara, banjo; Pete Biggs, bass; Zutty Singleton, drums.--HD): 1929

OK 8714. Ain't Misbehavin'(402534b)
                              -Vo 3040, OK 41276, OdF 165814, PaF 22497, PaE R462
  "   Black and Blue(402535b)
                              -Vo 3115, OK 41276, OdF 165814, PaF 22497, PaE R1573
OK 8717. That Rhythm Man(402540c) -OK 41281, Vo 3205, OdF 165815, PaE R1494
  "   Sweet Savannah Sue(402541b)   "   Vo 3136,   "   PaE R 1573
OK 8729. Some of These Days(402923c)
  "   When You're Smiling(402924b)   -PaE R671

(Louis Armstrong, trumpet; Henry Allen, Otis Johnson, trumpets; J.C. Higginbotham, trombone; Albert Nicholas, clarinet and alto sax; Charlie Holmes, alto sax; Theo Hill, tenor sax; Luis Russell, piano; Wil Johnson, guitar; Pop Foster, bass; Paul Barbarin, drums.--HD): 1930

OK 8756. I Ain't Got Nobody(403493a)   -Vo 3102, PaE 1261
  "   Rockin' Chair(403496c)   -Co 2688, Vo 3039, PaE 785
OK 8774. Dallas Blues(403494c)   -Vo 3025, PaE 973
  "   Bessie Couldn't Help It(403714b)   PaE 698
OK 8800. Dinah(404001c), see personnel next below -Cq 9554, Vo 3009, PaE 1159
  "   Tiger Rag(404002b),   "   "   "   "   PaE 942
OK 41298. Some of These Days(402943), personnel above -Vo 3202, OdF 165844, PaE 520
  "   When You're Smiling(402947)   "   "   "   PaE 1286
OK 41350. After You've Gone(403454b)   -PaE 607, -Co 2727,   Vo 3643
  "   St. Louis Blues(40349") -Cq 9124, Vo 3008, OdF 165975, PaE 618
OK 41375. Song of the Islands(403681a), three violins added -Vo 3026, Pa 909
  "   Blue Turning Grey Over You(403715b)-OK 4678,Vo3124,OdF 238995,PaE 1494

(Louis Armstrong, Edward Anderson, trumpets; Henry Hicks, trombone; Bobby Holmes, clarinet and alto sax; Theodore McCord, alto sax; Castor McCord, tenor sax; Joe Turner, piano; Bernard Addison, guitar; Levat Hutchinson, bass;. Willie Lynch, drums.--HD):

OK 41415. My Sweet(403896d)   -Vo 3308, OdF 238287, Pa 1718
  "   I Can't Believe That You're in Love With Me(403897a)
                                               -Vo 3308, OdF 238287, Pa 1261
OK 41423. Indian Cradle Song(403999a)   -Vo 3370, OdF 238120, PaE 2066
  "   Exactly Like You(404000b)   -Vo 3040, OdF 238120, PaE 2042

LOUIS ARMSTRONG AND HIS SEBASTIAN NEW COTTON CLUB ORCHESTRA (Louis Armstrong, trumpet; Lawrence Brown, trombone; Les Hite, alto sax; Jimmie Prince, piano; Lionel Hampton, drums, and others.--HD):

OK 41442. I'm a Ding Dong Daddy(404403a)-Vo 3370,OdF 238184,PaF 80345,PaE 796
  "   I'm in Market For You(404404c)-Vo 3301, "   "   PaE 778
OK 41448. Confessin'(404405a)   -Vo 3059, OdF 238227, PaF 80444, PaE 909
  "   If I Could Be With You(404406a)   PaE 1100

(Trumpet solos with Earl Hines* and Buck Washington# piano accompaniment):
OK 41454. Weather Bird(402199a)*   -HRS 18, Co 36375, OdF 238456, PaE 1194
  "   Dear Old Southland(403895a)#   Co 36282, "   PaE 1718

(Previous personnel, except Lawrence Brown):
OK 41463. Memories of You(404412d)   -Vo 3180, PaE 854
  "   You're Lucky to Me(404413c)   PaE 865
OK 41468. Memories of You(404412e)
OK 41468. Body and Soul(404411d)/(rev.,Harlem Music Masters)-Vo 3072,Co2707, PaE 1355
OK 41478. The Peanut Vendor(404419b)   -Vo 3194, PaE 865
  "   You're Driving Me Crazy(404418b)   -PaE 866, -Vo 3216
OK 41486. Just a Gigolo(404420a)   PaE 1863
  "   Shine(404421c)   -Co 2707, Vo 3102, PaE 1100
Co 2688. Sweethearts on Parade(404417a)   -Vo 3337

LOUIS ARMSTRONG AND HIS ORCHESTRA (Louis Armstrong, Zilmer Randolph, trumpets; Preston Jackson, trombone; Lester Boone, George James, alto saxes; Albert Washington, tenor sax; Charlie Alexander, piano; Mike McKendrick, banjo; John Lindsay, bass; Tubby Hall, drums): 1931

OK 41497. Walkin' My Baby Back Home(404422b)   -Vo 3217, PaE 2365
  "   I Surrender Dear (404423b)   -Vo 3203, PaE 1863

```
OK 41498.  Blue Again(404425a)                              -Vo 3115, PaE 2365
    "      When Your Lover Has Gone(404873a)                -Vo 3114, PaE 1034
OK 41501.  Little Joe(404870c)                              -Vo 3301, PaE 1013
    "      Them There Eyes(404872c)                         -Vo 3337, PaE 1286
OK 41504.  When It's Sleepy Time Down South(404424b)-Vo 3203,PaF 85031,PaE 1034
    "      I'll Be Glad When You're Dead(404871a)   -Vo 3072,    "    ,PaE  992
                                                                         1932
OK 41530.  Wrap Your Troubles in Dreams(405060)      -Vo 3172, PaF 85232,PaE 2135
    "      Star Dust(405061)                         -Co 2574,     "    PaE 1591
OK 41530.  Star Dust(405061a?)
OK 41534.  Chinatown My Chinatown(405059) -Vo 3039, Co 2574,PaF 85294,PaE 1159
    "      I Got Rhythm(405065)  -PaE 1207,-Vo 3643, Co 2590        PaE 1591
OK 41538.  You Can Depend on Me(405062)    -Vo 3055, Co 2590,PaF 85294,PaE 1355
    "      The Lonesome Road(405064)       -Vo 3026         PaF 85295
OK 41541.  Lazy River(405058)                     -Vo 3114,PaF 85296,PaE 1127
    "      Georgia on My Mind(405063)             -Vo 3073,
OK 41550.  Between Devil & Deep Blue Sea(405130a) -Vo 3136, Co 2600, PaE 1170
    "      Kickin' the Gong Around(405131a)       -Vo 3073,     "
OK 41552.  Home(405132)                           -Vo 3125, Co 2606, PaE 2042
    "      All of Me(405133)                              "     "   PaE 1894
OK 41557.  Love You Funny Thing(405154b)                   -Co 2631, PaE 1260
    "      New Tiger Rag(405155c)                 -Vo 3124.     "    PaE 1894
OK 41560.  Keepin' Out of Mischief Now(405166b)
                                       -Vo 3181, Co 2646, OdF 250230,PaE 1260
    "      Lawd You Made the Night Too Long(405167b)
                                       -Vo 3181, Co 2646, OdF 250230,PaE 1207
OK 41581.  The King of the Zulus(17344)/Lonesome Blues(17343), see OK 8396.
(Featuring Louis Armstrong,Louis Bacon, trumpets; Charlie Green, trombone; Elmer
Williams, tenor sax; Elmer James,bass; Chick Webb,drums.--JRB):  December, 1932
     Vi 24200.  That's My Hone(74820)          -BB 6644,BB 10236,HMV  B6315
           "    Hobo You Can't Ride This Train(74821) -BB 6501
     Vi 24204.  I Hate to Leave You Now(74822)          -BB 10236, HMV B6335
           "    You'll Wish You'd Never Been Born(74823)
(Louis Armstrong, Elmer Whitlock, Zilmer Randolph, trumpets; Keg Johnson, trom-
bone; Scoville Brown, George Oldham, alto saxes; Bud Johnson, tenor sax; Teddy
Wilson, piano;Mike McKendrick,banjo; Bill Oldham,bass; Yank Porter,drums.--HD):
                                                              January, 1933
     Vi 24232.  High Society(74895)              -BB 6771, HMV B6345
           "    Mahogany Hall Stomp(75106)       -BB 5086, HMV B6368
     Vi 24233.  Hustlin' and Bustlin' for Baby(74893)
                                     -Elec 2067, BB 5173, 7506, HMV 4978, GrF K6942
           "    I Gotta Right to Sing the Blues(74892)
                                     -Elec 2067, BB 5173, 6771, HMV 6368,    "
     Vi 24245.  I've Got the World on a String(74891) -BB 6910, GrF K6941, HMV 6345
           "    Sittin' in the Dark (74894)           -BB 7506         "
     Vi 24257.  He's a Son of the South(74896)     -BB 5086,          HMV 4976
           "    Some Sweet Day(75102)              -BB 6590, BB 10237,    "
     Vi 24351.  Basin Street Blues(75103)          -BB 5408,          HMV 4979
           "    Mighty River(75477, see below)     -BB 5409, BB 10703,    "
     Vi 24369.  Honey Do(75104)                    -BB 7787,
           "    Snow Ball(75105)                   -BB 5408, BB 10255, HMV 4968
     Vi 24320.  Dusky Stevedore(75424)             -BB 5408,          HMV 6387
           "    St.Louis Blues(75480)              -BB 5280, MW 4886, HMV 4975
     Vi 24321.  Mississippi Basin(75421)           -BB 6501,          HMV 6387
           "    Sweet Sue(75478)                   -BB 5280, MW 4886, HMV 4975
     Vi 24335.  Honey Don't You Love Me Any More(75420)-BB 7787,      HMV 4977
           "    There's a Cabin in the Pines(75476)   -BB 6910,
     Vi 24425.  I Wonder Who(75479)                -BB 6644,          HMV 4989
           "    Don't Play Me Cheap                -BB 5409, BB 10237,    "
(Unknown personnel):
     Vi 36084.  You Rascal You; When It's Sleepy Time Down South*; Nobody's Sweet-
           heart(74878)/When You're Smiling; St.James Infirmary;Dinah(74877)
(Previous personnel):
     BB  5363.  Laughin' Louie(75422)                      -HMV X4432
           "    Tomorrow Night(75423)
     BB 10225.  Swing You Cats(75107), Jan.1933 personnel.
    *BB 10703.  When It's Sleepy Time Down Douth(dubbed from Vi 36084 above)
```

18

(Louis Armstrong, Jack Hamilton, Leslie Thomson, trumpets; L. Guimaraes, trombone; Peter Duconge, clarinet and alto sax; Henry Tyree, alto sax; Alfred Pratt, tenor sax; Herman Chittison, piano; M.Jefferson, guitar; O.Arago, bass; O.Tines, drums.--HD)   Paris, October, 1934

```
BrF 500490. St. Louis Blues(1483-1)/Super Tiger Rag(1479)
BrF 500490. St. Louis Blues(1483-2)
BrF 500491. On the Sunny Side of the Street, I & II (1481/1482)
BrF 500492. Song of the Vipers(1484)/Will You Won't You Be My Baby(1480)
```

(Louis Armstrong, Leonard Davis, Gus Atkins, Louis Bacon, trumpets; James Archey, Harry White, trombones; Henry Jones, Bingie Madison, Charlie Holmes, alto saxes; Greely Walton, tenor sax; Luis Russell, piano; Will Blair, guitar; Pop Foster, bass; Paul Barbarin, drums.--HD):   1935-36

```
De  579. I'm in the Mood for Love(60021f)       -De 3796,  DeE 5785
 "       Got a Bran' New Suit(60024e)                      -DeE 5836
De  580. You Are My Lucky Star(60022e)                     -DeE 5785
 "       La Cucuracha(60023e)                              -DeE 5835
De  622. Old Man Mose(60156d)                              -DeE 5895
 "       Falling in Love With You(60158d)                  -DeE 5961
De  623. I've Got My Fingers Crossed(60155d)/I'm Shooting High(60157c)DeE 5869
De  648. Red Sails in the Sunset(60227a)                   -DeE 5836
 "       On Treasure Island(60228a)                        -DeE 5835
De  666. Thanks a Million(60249b)/Solitude(60251a)
De  666. Thanks a Million(60249a)/Solitude(60251b)         -DeE 5868
De  672. Shoe Shine Boy(60250a)/I Hope Gabriel Likes My Music(60252b)DeE 5936
De  685. The Music Goes Round and Around(60362a)           -DeE 5895
 "       Rhythm Saved the World(60363a)                    -DeE 5961
```

(For next coupling only: Louis Armstrong, Bunny Berigan, Bob Mayhew, trumpets; Al Philburn, trombone; Phil Waltzer, alto sax; Paul Ricci, tenor sax; Sid Trucker, baritone sax; Fulton McGrath, piano; Dave Barbour, guitar; Pete Peterson, bass; Stan King, drums.--HD):   1937

```
De  698. I'm Putting All My Eggs in One Basket(60438a)/Yes Yes, My My(60439a)
                                                 -DeE 5915, BrF 505050
```

(Previous personnel):

```
De  797. I Come from a Musical Family(61058a)/Somebody Stole My Break(61075a)
                                                           -DeE 5996
De  824. Mahogany Hall Stomp(61111a)(coupled with 60363a above) -De 3793 ,DeE 6324
De  835. Lyin' to Myself(61106a)/Ev'ntide(61107a)          -DeE 6040, BrF 505067
De  866. Swing That Music(61108a)/Thankful(61109a)         DeE 6066
```

LOUIS ARMSTRONG with Jimmy Dorsey and His Orchestra (George Thow, Toots Camarata, trumpets; Bobby Byrne, Joe Yukl, Don Matteson, trombones; Jimmy Dorsey, Fud Livingstone, Jack Stacy, Skeets Herfurt, saxes; Bobby Van Eps, piano; Roc Hillman, guitar; Slim Taft; bass; Ray McKinley, drums):

```
De  906. Dipper Mouth(DLA 542a)                  -De 3796, DeE 6202
 "       If We Never Meet Again(61059a, above)
De  949. The Skeleton in the Closet(DLA 539a)/Hurdy Gurdy Man(DLA 541a)DeE 6146
De 1049. When Ruben Swings the Cuban(DLA 540a)             -DeE 6324
 "       Red Nose(61110a, see personnel above)
De 15027. Pennies from Heaven, I & II                      -BrE 0134
```

LOUIS ARMSTRONG with the Polynesians (Lionel Hampton, drums):

```
De  914. To You Sweetheart Aloha(DLA 581a)/On a Cocoanut Island(DLA 582a)
                                                           -DeE 6082
```

LOUIS ARMSTRONG with Andy Iona and His Islanders:

```
De 1216. On a Little Bamboo Bridge(62070a)/Hawaiian Hospitality(62071a)
                                                           -DeE 6393
```

LOUIS ARMSTRONG and the Mills Brothers:

```
De 1245. Carry Me Back to Old Virginny(62116a)/Darling Nelly Gray(62117b)
                                                           -BrE 02446
De 1245. Darling Nelly Gray(62117a)
De 1360. The Old Folks at Home(62323a)/(rev.,Mills Brothers alone) -BrE 02461
De 1495. In the Shade of the Old Apple Tree(62322a)/(rev.,Mills Bros.,alone)
```

LOUIS ARMSTRONG AND HIS ORCHESTRA (Louis Armstrong, Louis Bacon, Shelton Hemphill, Henry Allen, trumpets; George Matthews, George Washington, Jack Higginbotham, trombones; Peter Clark, Charlie Holmes, Albert Nicholas, Bingie Madison, saxes; Russell, Blair, Foster, Barbarin.--HD):

```
De 1347. Public Melody No.1(62328a)                          -BrF 505118
  "      Red Cap(62330a)                                     -DeE   6583
De 1353. She's the Daughter of a Planter(62335a)/Cuban Pete(62337a)
De 1369. Yours and Mine(62329a)                              -BrF 505118
         Sun Showers(62339a)
De 1408. Alexander's Ragtime Band(62336a)                    -DeE  6583
  "      I've Got a Heart Full of Rhythm(62338a)
De 1560. Once in a While(DLA 1084a)                          -DeE  6613
  "      On the Sunny Side of the Street(DLA 1085a)   -De 3794,   "
De 1635. Jubilee(DLA 1133a)
  "      True Confession(DLA 1137a)                          -DeE  6619
De 1636. Satchel Mouth Swing(DLA 1132a)            -De 3794
  "      I Double Dare You(DLA 1136a)                        -DeE  6619
De 1653. The Trumpet Player's Lament(DLA 1135a)
         Sweet as a Song(DLA 1139a)                          -DeE  6655
De 1661. Struttin' With Some Barbecue(DLA 1134a)   -De 3795
  "      Let That Be a Lesson to You(DLA 1138a)              -DeE  6655
```
(Omit Bacon,Allen, Matthews, Washington, Nicholas; sub. Rupert Cole for P.Clark.
--JM 12):   May 13, 1938
```
De 1822. So Little Time(63775a)                              -DeE  6716
  "      Mexican Swing(63776a)                               -DeE  7428
De 1841. On the Sentimental Side(63809a)/It's Wonderful(63810a)   -DeE  6780
De 1842. Something Tells Me(63811a)                          -DeE  6765
  "      Love Walked In(63812a)                              -DeE  6716
```
LOUIS ARMSTRONG and the Mills Brothers: June, 1938
```
  De 1876. The Flat Foot Floogee(63950a)/(rev.,Mills Bros.,alone)  -BrE 02622
  De 1892. The Song Is Ended(63967a)/My Walking Stick(63968a)
```
(Vocal, with Decca Mixed Chorus):
```
  De 1913. Shadrack(63982a)/Jonah and the Whale(63985c)      -DeE  6835
  De 2085. Going to Shout All Over God's Heaven(63983a)/Nobody Knows de Trouble
                  I've Seen(63894a)                          -DeE  6912
```
(Monologue with Harry Mills, organ):
```
  De15043. Elder Eatmore's Sermon on Throwing Stones/Elder Eatmore's Sermon o'
           Generosity
```
LOUIS ARMSTRONG AND HIS ORCHESTRA (Louis Armstrong, Bob Cusamano, Johnny McGee, trumpets; Al Philburn, trombone; Sid Stoneburn, clarinet; Nat Jaffe, piano; Dave Barbour, guitar;Haig Stephens,bass; Sam Weiss,drums.--JM 12): June 24, 1938
```
  De 1937. Naturally(64227a)
           I've Got a Pocketful of Dreams(64228a)            -DeE  6915
  De 2042. I can't give you Anything But Love(64229a)/Ain't Misbehavin'(64230b)
                                                             -DeE  6954
  De 2230. As Long As You Live(63777a)/When the Saints Go Marching In (63778a)
           (for personnel see May 13, 1938)                  -DeE  7056
```
(Louis Armstrong, Shelton Hemphill, Henry Allen, Otis Johnson, trumpets; Wilbur de Paris, George Washington, J.C. Higginbotham, trombones; Charlie Holmes,Rupert Cole, Albert Nicholas, Bingie Madison, saxes/ Russell, Blair, Foster; Sidney Catlett, drums.--JM 12):   January, 1939
```
  De 2267. Jeepers Creepers(64907a)/What Is This Thing Called Swing(64908a)
                                                             -DeE  6990
```
(Sub. Joe Garland, tenor, for Nicholas)   April, 1939
```
  De 2405. Hear Me Talkin' to Ya(65344a)                     -DeE  7110
    "      Save It Pretty Mama(65345a)              -De 3516,     "
  De 2480. West End Blues(65346a)                   -De 3793, DeE 7127
    "      If It's Good(65462a)
  De 2538. Savoy Blues(65347a)/Me and Brother Bill(65463a)   DeE  7177
  De 2615. Confessin'(65460a)                       -De 3795, DeE 7213
    "      Our Monday Date(65461a)
```
(Sub. Bernard Flood, trumpet for Johnson):   June 15, 1939
```
  De 2729. Baby Won't You Please Come Home(65824a)/Shanty Boat on the Mississi-
                  ppi(65826a)                                -DeE  7388
```
                                                             December 18, 1939
```
  De 2934. You're a Lucky Guy(66985a)/You're Just No Account(66986a)  -DeE 7567
  De 3011. Poor Old Joe(66984a)
    "      Bye and Bye(66987)                                -De 3946
```

```
                                                                March 14, 1940
     De 3092. You've Got Me Voodoo'd(67322a)/Harlem Stomp(67323a)    -DeE 7598
     De 3105. Wolverine Blues(67324a)                                 -DeE 8099
      "      Swing That Music DLA 543a), with Dorsey Orchestra
```

LOUIS ARMSTRONG and the Mills Brothers:
```
     De 3151. W.P.A.(67519a)
      "      Marie(67531a)                                    -De 3291, BrE 03065
     De 3180. Boog-It(67520aa)                                        -BrE 03150
      "      Cherry(67530a)                                           -BrE 03065
```

LOUIS ARMSTRONG and orchestra, previous personnel: May 1, 1940
```
     De 3204. You Run Your Mouth,I'll Run My Business(67649a)/Cain and Abel(67651a)
                                                                      -DeE 7849
     De 3235. Sweethearts on Parade(67648a)/Cut Off My Legs and Call Me Sh(67650a)
     De 3283. Hep Cats' Ball(67321a)/Lazy 'Sippi' Steamer(67325a)     -DeE 7700
```
(Louis Armstrong, trumpet; Prince Robinson, clarinet and tenor sax; George Washington, trombone; Luis Russell, piano; Lawrence Lucie, guitar; John Williams, bass; Sidney Catlett, drums.--):   March 10, 1941
```
     De 3700. I Cover the Waterfront(68797a)/Long Long Ago(68799a)
     De 3756. Hey Lawdy Mama(68997a)/New Do You Call That a Buddy(68999a)
     De 3825. Everything's Been Done Before(68796a)/In the Gloaming(68798b)
     De 3900. I'll Get Mine Bye and Bye(68998a)/Yes Suh!(69000c)
```
(Armstrong, Hemphill, Gene Prince, Frank Galbraith, trumpets; Herman Greene, Henderson Chambers, George Washington, trombones; Cole, Carl Frye, Robinson, Garland, saxes; Russell, Lucie, Catlett; Hayes Alvis, bass.--JM 12):   November 16, 1941
```
     De 4106. Leap Frog(93788a)/I Used to Love You(93789b)            -DeE 8163
     De 4140. When It's Sleepy Time Down South(93787a)/You Rascal You(93790a)
```
(Sub. Flood, trumpet, for Prince; James Whitney, trombone, for Greene; John Simmons, bass.):   Los Angeles, April 17, 1942
```
     De 4229. Cash for Your Trash(DLA 2974a)/I Never Knew(DLA 2977a)
     De 4327. Among My Souvenirs(DLA 2975a)/Coquette(DLA 2976a)
```

ARMSTRONG, MAY (blues vocal):
     Br 7010. Joe Boy Blues/Nobody Can Take His Place

ARMSTRONG, SHELLY:
     Ch 50008. How Long How Long Blues/You Don't Mean Me No Good
     De 7350. New B & O Blues/Prison Bound Blues

ARODIN, SIDNEY, clarinet (see following:
     Halfway House Dance Orchestra,
     Monk Hazel and His Bienville Roof Orchestra,
     Jones-Collins Astoria Eight,
     Wingy Mannone and His Orchestra,
     Johnnie Miller's New Orleans Frolickers,
     New Orleans Rhythm Kings (Decca),
     Louis Prima's Band

ATLANTA MERRYMAKERS:
     Mad 1935. Black Stomp(3572)

ATLANTA SYNCOPATORS:
     Mad 50015. Beale Street Blues/Lead Pipe Blues
     Mad 50040. John Henry Blues

AUSTIN AND HIS MUSICAL AMBASSADORS:
     Para 12359. Don't Forget to Do the Mess Around/(rev., Hottentots)

AULD, GEORGE AND HIS ORCHESTRA:
     Vs 8212. With the Wind and Rain in Your Hair(1380)/Sweet Sue(US 1381)

LOVIE AUSTIN'S BLUES SERENADERS

For accompaniments see the following:
     VIOLA BARTLETTE: Para 12322, 12351, 12363, 12369.
     IDA COX: Para 12044, 12045, 12056, 12063, 12064, 12085, 12086, 12087, 12202,
              12212, 12220, 12228, 12237, 12255, 12282, 12291, 12298, 12307, 12325,
              12334, 12344, 12353, 12361, 12381, 12384.
     JULIA DAVIS: Para 12248.
     EDMONIA HENDERSON: Para 12084, 12095, 12203, 12239.
     EDNA HICKS.
     OZIE McPHERSON: Para 12327, 12350.
     MA RAINEY: Para 12080, 12081, 12082, 12083, 12200, 12215, 12227, 12257.
     ETHEL WATERS: Para 12214, 12230, 12313.

Watch for this

Exciting Four-Way *Esquire* Jazz Program

The February Jazz Issue of Esquire ❶

Announcing the winners for Esquire's 1945 All-American Jazz Band, and Esquire's All-American New Stars—selected by a board of 22 leading jazz critics and writers. This great issue of Esquire also gives you Barry Ulanov's "The Blues for the Times" ... and many other jazz-minded articles and stories. At your newsstand January 15.

Esquire's 1945 Jazz Book ❷
Published by A. S. Barnes & Co.*

A brand-new Esquire Jazz Book, edited by Paul Eduard Miller. Here are comments by the 22 experts on their choices for Esquire's All-American Jazz Band, lists of their favorite records, and biographies of about 100 musicians named; additional biographies of some 50 New Orleans musicians; lists of all important jazz records and events of the year; wartime hints to record collectors; a complete history of New Orleans jazz; articles by Leonard Feather, Paul Eduard Miller, George Hoefer, and James Crenshaw; and 24 full pages of hot jamming photos. On sale about January 12 at newsstands, book and department stores, record shops, PX and ships' stores. $1.

Two Concerts ❸
By Members of Esquire's All-American Jazz Band
Wednesday, January 17, in Los Angeles and New Orleans

• Duke Ellington and his band *plus* six winners in Esquire's All-American Band. At the Philharmonic Auditorium, Los Angeles. Gross proceeds to Volunteer Army Canteen Service.

• Louis Armstrong and other All-American Band winners *plus* New Orleans jazz old-timers, celebrating 50 years of New Orleans jazz. Municipal Auditorium, New Orleans. Sponsored by the National Jazz Foundation.

1½-Hour ❹
Broadcast of the Concerts Over Blue Network
January 17, from 10:30 to 12 PM Central War Time

Hear this great broadcast over the Blue Network from Los Angeles, from New Orleans, plus 15 minutes of Benny Goodman and his quintet and Mildred Bailey in a studio broadcast from New York. Featured will be playing by musicians simultaneously from all three cities. The show will be broadcast to the Armed Forces overseas, and shortwaved to South America.

*A. S. Barnes and Co. is the parent company of Smith and Durrell, publishers of the Record Book, the Jazz Record Book, and Panassié's the Real Jazz.

© ESQUIRE, INC., 1944

AUSTIN, LOVIE AND HER BLUES SERENADERS (Tommy Ladnier, cornet; Jimmy O'Bryant,
clarinet; Lovie Austin, piano; unknown drums):
    Para 12255. Steppin' on the Blues(10004)/Traveling Blues(10005)
    Para 12277. Peepin' Blues(2097)/(rev., O'Bryant Washboard Band)
    Para 12278. Charleston Mad(2094)/Charleston South Carolina(2095)
    Para 12283. Heebie Jeebies(2096)/Mojo Blues(2098)

(Sub. Johnny Dodds, clarinet):
    Para 12300. Don't Shake It No More/Rampart Street Blues
    Para 12313. Too Sweet for Words(2222),see Bobby's Revelers/(rev.,Ethel Waters)
    Para 12361. Jackass Blues(317-11096)/Frog Tongue Stomp(318-11097)
    Para 12380. Chicago Messa Round(2621)/Galion Stomp(2622)
    Para 12391. In the Alley Blues(2623)/Merry Makers Twine(2624)

AVERY, CHARLES (piano solo):
    Para 12896. Dearborn Street Breakdown(21438)/(rev., Meade Lux Lewis)
    (See also; Li'l Johnson Vo 1299; Charles Anderson OK 8208; Red Nelson De 7136, 7154.)

B

BABY BONNIE (acc. by Lovell Bolan, piano):
    Ge 5616. Backbiting Moan(12057)/Black Bottom Blues(12103),C.Carpenter,cornet

(Acc. by Fats Browne, piano, and Theodore Carpenter, cornet):
    Ge 5644. Longing Blues(12133)/Home Sweet Home Blues(12134)   -Bu 8023

BABY MACK (acc. by Louis Armstrong, cornet; Richard M. Jones, piano):
    OK 8313. You've Got to Go Home on Time(9512)/What Kind o'Man Is That(9513)

BACON, LOUIS, trumpet: See Armstrong, Ellington, Webb.

LOUIS BACON'S JAZZ MEN (Louis Bacon, trumpet and vocal; Henry Mason, trumpet;
Johnny Russell, clarinet; Alfred Siegrist, piano; June Cole, bass; Tommy Benford,
drums.--DB 11/1/41):   Zurich, 1941
    Swiss Decca -----. Bacon's Blues/Blues for Panassie
    Swiss Decca -----. Low Down Trumpet Blues/Fidgety Feet

BAILEY'S DIXIE DUDES:
    Ge 5562. Aunt Eliza/I Want to See My Tennessee
    Ge 5577. I'm Satisfied/(rev., Willie Creager)
    Ge 5606. Go Long Mule(9187)/Oh! How I Love My Darling(9188)

BUSTER BAILEY

For records under other names see: HENRY ALLEN, LIL ARMSTRONG, LOVIE AUSTIN'S
BLUES SERENADERS (accompaniments), MILDRED BAILEY, CHU BERRY, BLUE RHYTHM BAND,
PUTNEY DANDRIDGE, FLETCHER HENDERSON, LIONEL HAMPTON, W.C.HANDY, BILLIE HOLIDAY,
BOB HOWARD, NOBLE SISSLE, BESSIE SMITH, STUFF SMITH, WILLIE (The Lion) SMITH, MA
RAINEY, JOHNNY TEMPLE, CLARENCE WILLIAMS, TEDDY WILSON.

BAILEY, BUSTER AND HIS SEVEN CHOCOLATE DANDIES (Henry Allen, trumpet; J.C. Higginbotham, trombone; Buster Bailey, clarinet; Benny Carter, alto sax; Charlie Beal,
piano; Danny Barker, guitar; Elmer James, bass; Walter Johnson, drums.--JRB):
    Vo 2887. Call of the Delta(16445-1)/Shanghai Shuffle(16446-1)
                                -Co 35677, PaE 2612, DeE 5492, BrF 500525

BUSTER BAILEY AND HIS RHYTHM BUSTERS (Buster Bailey, clarinet; Pete Brown, alto
sax; Frank Newton, trumpet; James McLin, guitar; Don Frye, piano;John Kirby,bass;
O'Neil Spencer, drums.):   1937
    Vr 668. Afternoon in Africa(M 644)/Dizzy Debutante(M 645)   -Vo 3846

(sub. Charles Shavers, trumpet; Billy Kyle, piano):
    Vo 4089. Sloe Jam Fizz/Planter's Punch
    Vo 4564. Light Up(M 941)/Man With a Horn Goes Berserk(M 942)
    Vo 5510. Chained to a Dream(M 940)/(rev., Rex Stewart)

BUSTER BAILEY SEXTET (Charles Chavers, trumpet; Billy Kyle, piano;Russell Procope,
alto sax; John Kirby, bass; Buster Bailey, clarinet; O'Neil Spencer, drums):
    Vs 8333. The Blue Room(US 1760)/Am I Blue(US 1762)   -El 1762; Ph 84
    Vs 8337. Should I(US 1759)/April in Paris(US 1761)

(Sub. Benny Carter, alto; Zutty Singleton, drums):
    Vs 8358. Fable of the Rose/Seems Like a Month of Sundays
    Vs 8365. Eccentric Rag/Pinetop's Boogie Woogie   -El 6, Ph 82

BAILEY, KID (vocal with guitars):
    Br 7114. Mississippi Bottom Blues/Rowdy Blues

23

BAILEY, MILDRED, vocalist, with orchestra (see also):
BENNY GOODMAN: Co 2892, 2907.
RED NORVO
PAUL WHITEMAN: Vi 22828, 22876, 22879, 22883, 24088.

Vi 22874.	Too Late(70623)	-HMV 4084,	BB 7873
"	Home(70630)	"	BB 7763
Vi 22880.	Concentratin'(70625)		-HMV 4110
"	Lies		
Vi 22891.	Georgia on My Mind(70624) (rev., Gene Austin)	-HMV 4110,	BB 6945
Vi 22942.	Strangers(71911)	-HMV 4193	
"	Stop the Sun, Stop the Moon(71910)		BB 7763
Vi 24117.	Rockin' Chair		-BB 6945
"	Love Me Tonight		
Vi 24137.	Dear Old Mother Dixie/(rev., Wayne King)		-BB 7873

(acc. by Casa Loma Orchestra):
   Br 6184. You Call It Madness
   "   Wrap Your Troubles in Dreams   -BrE 1210
   Br 6190. Blues in My Heart
   "   When It's Sleepy Time Down South   -BrE 1210

(acc. by Dorsey Brothers, geaturning Bunny Berigan):   1933
   Br 6558. Is That Religion(13208)/Harlem Lullaby(13209) -BrE 01544,F500269
   Br 6587. Lazy Bones(13428)/Cabin in the Pines(13427) -BrE 01564,F500305
   Br 6655. Snowball(13956)/Shouting in That Amen Corner(13955)-BrE 01593,F500335
   Br 6680. Give Me Liberty(14159)/Doin' Uptown Lowdown(14160)-BrE 01631,BrF 9500
   Br 7542. I Can't Make a Man(14157), see Dorsey Brothers)

(Unknown accompaniment)
   Br 8088. Please Be Kind/Week-end
   Br 8171. After Dinner Speech
   Br 8202. Jump Jump's Here/Garden

MILDRED BAILEY AND HER SWING BAND (Gordon Griffin, trumpet; Chu Berry, tenor sax; Teddy Wilson, piano; Artie Bernstein, bass; Dick McDonough, guitar; Eddie Dougherty, drums.):   1935
   Vo 3056. I'd Love to Take Orders from You(18090)/I'd Rather Listen to your
              Eyes(18091)   -BrE 02121,F500620
   Vo 3057. Someday Sweetheart(18092)/When Day Is Done(18093)
                                 -BrE 02106,F500619, OK 3057

MILDRED BAILEY AND HER ALLEY CATS (Bunny Berigan, trumpet; Johnny Hodges,alto sax; Teddy Wilson, piano; Grachan Moncur, bass.):   1936
   PaE R2201. Honeysuckle Rose(60202)/Willow Tree(60201)   -De 18108
   PaE R2257. Squeeze Me(60203)/Downhearted Blues(60204)   -De 18109

MILDRED BAILEY AND HER ORCHESTRA (Teddy Wilson, piano; John Kirby, bass; Dave Barbour, guitar; Cozy Cole, drums; Francis Love, tenor sax; Artie Shaw,clarinet; Harry Finkleman(Ziggy Elman), trumpet):   1936
   Vo 3367. For Sentimental Reasons(20217)/It's Love I'm After(20218) -VoE S51
   Vo 3378. Long About Midnight/More Than You Know   -VoE S42

(Roy Eldridge, trumpet; Scoops Carey, alto sax; Herbie Haymer, tenor sax; Teddy Cole, piano; Johnny Collins, guitar; Truck Parham, bass; Zutty Singleton, drums.--HD):   1937
   Vo 3449. My Last Affair(C 1751)   -VoE S67
   "   Trust in Me(C 1752)   -VoE S115
   Vo 3456. Where Are You   -VoE S84, BrF 500708
   "   You're Laughing at Me   -VoE S100

(Bill Hyland, Stew Pletcher, E. Sauter, trumpet; Alex Mastren, trombone; Hank D'Amico, F. Simeone, H. Haymer, saxes; Red Norvo, xylophone; Joe Liss, piano; Dave Barbour, guitar; Peterson, bass; Maurice Purtill, drums.--HD):
   Vo 3508. Never in a Million Years/There's a Lull in My Life
   Vo 3553. Rockin' Chair   -VoE S88
   "   Little Joe

(Including Herschel Evans, tenor sax):
   Vo 3615. If You Ever Should Leave Me
   "   Heaven Help This Heart of Mine   -VoE S115
   Vo 3626. It Is the Natural Thing to Do/The Moon Got in My Eyes
   Vo 3712. Bob White/Just a Stone's Throw from Heaven
   Vo 3758. Loving You(LA 1446)/Right or Wrong(LA 1447)

(Jimmy Blake,trumpet; Hank D'Amico, clarinet; Chu Berry, tenor sax; Teddy Wilson, piano; Allen Reuss, guitar; Dave Tough, drums; D.W. Peterson, bass.--JRB): 1938
   Vo 3931. I See Your Face Before Me(22265)/Thanks for the Memory(22266)
   Vo 3982. From the Land of the Sky Blue Water/Lover Come Back to Me

(Unknown):
   Vo 4016. I Can't Face the Music
   Vo 4036. At Your Beck and Call/Bewildered
   Vo 4083. Rock It for Me/I Let a Song Go Out of My Heart
   Vo 4109. Moonshine Over Kentucky/If You Were in My Place
   Vo 4139. Washboard Blues/'Round My Old Deserted Farm
   Vo 4224. Small Fry(23179)/Born to Swing(23181)
   Vo 4253. As Long As You Live/So Help Me
   Vo 4282. Now It Can Be Told/I Haven't Changed a Thing
   Vo 4345. Love Is Where You Find It/I Used to Be Color Blind
   Vo 4408. My Reverie/What Have You Got That Gets Me
   Vo 4432. Old Folks/Have You Forgot
   Vo 4474. My Melancholy Baby(22906)/The Lonesome Road(22908)
   Vo 4548. The Say(23810)/I Go for That(23812)

(Charles Shavers, trumpet; Buster Bailey, clarinet; Russell Procope, alto sax; Billy Kyle, piano; Red Norvo,xylophone;John Kirby,bass;O'Ne'l Spencer,drums: 1939
   Vo 4619. Begin the Beguine/I Cried for You
   Vo 4632. What Shall I Say(23988)/Blame It on My Last Affair(23811),unknown
   Vo 4708. Tain't What You Do/Slumber
   Vo 4785. Three Little Fishies

MILDRED BAILEY AND HER OXFORD GREYS (Mary Lou Williams, piano; Floyd Smith, guitar; Johnny Williams, bass; Eddie Dougherty, drums)*:
   Vo 4800. Down Hearted Blues/Gulf Coast Blues*
   Vo 4801. St. Louis Blues(23516)/Arkansas Blues(W24230)*
   Vo 4802. Barrle House Music(W24229)-/You Don't Know My Mind Blues(W24232)*
   Vo 4815. And the Angels Sing
   Vo 4845. Tit Willow/The Lamp Is Low
   Vo 4939. Moon Love/It Seems Like Old Times
   Vo 4966. Guess I'll Go Back Home(W24764)/The Little Man Who Wasn't(W24820)
   Vo 5006. You're the Moment in My Life/You and Your Love
   Vo 5086. Ghost of a Chance/I'm Forever Blowin' Bubbles
   Vo 5209. Don't Dally With the Devil(25372)/Sometimes I feel Like(25374)
   Vo 5236. I've Gone Off the Deep End/I Shoulda Stood in Bed
   Vo 5268. There'll Be Some Changes Made*/Prisoner of Love*

(Next two couplings with Alec Wilder Octet):
   Vo 5277. Blue Rain/All the Things You Are
   Co 35348. Hold On/Nobody Knows the Trouble I've Seen
   Co 35370. Little High Chairman/Wham
   Co 35409. A Bee Gezindt/After All I've Been to You

(Featuring Roy Eldridge, trumpet; Teddy Wilson, piano):
   Co 35463. Fools Rush In/From Another World
   Co 35532. Tennessee Fish Fry/How Can I
   Co 35589. I'll Pray for You/Blue
   Co 35626. I'm Nobody's Baby/Give Me Time
   Co 35921. Easy to Love(WCO 26415)/Don't Take Your Love from Me(WCO 26464)
   Co 35943. Rockin' Chair/There'll Be Some Changes Made

(**MILDRED BAILEY** with Delta Rhythm Boys:
   De 3661. Jenny/When That Man Is Dead and Gone
   De 3691. Georgia on My Mind(68819)/I'm Afraid of Myself(68822)
   De 3755. Rockin' Chair/Sometimes I'm Happy

(*Acc. by Herman Chittison, piano; Dave Barbour, guitar; Frenchy Covett, bass; Jimmy Hoskins, drums.): 1941
   De 3888. Ev'rything Depends on You(69361)/All Too Soon(69363)*
   De 3953. It's So Peaceful in the Country(69412)/LoverCome Back to Me(69562)*

(Acc. by Harry Sosnik's Orchestra):
   De 4252. Sometimes/Wherever You Are
   De 4267. I Think of You/More Than You Know

BAIRD, MAYNARD AND HIS ORCHESTRA:
   Vo 1516. Postage Stomp/I Can't Stop Loving You
   Vo 15834. Sorry/Just for You

BAKER, VIOLA (Piano acc. by Fannie Goosby:)
   OK 8141. Sweet Man Blues/What's the Use Blues(Piano acc. by Eddie Heywood)

BAKER, WILLIE (guitar acc.):
   Ge 6846. Crooked Woman Blues/Rag Baby

BALTIMORE BELL HOPS (Russell Smith, Bobby Stark, Rex Stewart, trumpets; Benny Morton, Claude Jones, trombones; Russell Procope, Harvey Boone, Coleman Hawkins, saxes; Fletcher Henderson, piano; Clarence Haliday, guitar; John Kirby, bass; Walter Johnson, drums.--HD): 1931
   Co 2449. Hot and Anxious(151443)/Comin' and Goin'(151444)

BANKS, BILLY AND BLUE RHYTHM BOYS (Wardell Jones, Shelton Hamph¹ll, Edward Anderson, trumpets; Harry White, Henry Hicks, trombones; Theodore McCord, Crawford Wethlington, Castor McCord, saxes; Edgar Hayes, piano; Benny James, banjo; Hayes Alvis, bass; Willie Lynch, drums.--HD): **1931**
  Pe 15505. Low Down on the Bayou(10626)/Futuristic Jungleism(10628) -DeE 2728
  Pe 15605. Cabin in the Cotton/Scat Song
  Pe 15606. Heat Waves(11363)/Minnie the Moocher's(11752) -Or 2469, Ba 32444
(Henry Allen, trumpet; Pee Wee Russell, clarinet and tenor sax; Joe Sullivan, piano; Eddie Condon, banjo; Jack Bland, guitar; Al Morgan, bass; Zutty Singleton drums.--HD): **1932**
  Pe 15615. Bugle Call Rag(11716)/Spider Crawl(11719)
       -Or 2483, Ba 32459, Ro 1856, BrF 500198, BrE 01590, UHCA 109
(Billy Banks and Harlem Hot Shots):
  Pe 15620. Oh Peter(11717)/Margie(11718) -Ro 1861, UHCA 110, BrE 01561
  Co 35841. Oh Peter(2nd master, under name of "Rhythmakers)
  Pe 15642. Who's Sorry Now(11881)/Bald Headed Mama(11883) -Or 2521,VoE 9,UHCA 112
(For first group see also; Earl Jackson's Musical Champions; (Mills) Blue Rhythm Boys; Mills'Music Makers; Baron Lee's Blue Rhythm Band. Second group:(Jack Bland) Rhythmakers)

BILLY BANKS' RHYTHMAKERS (Same as second group):
  HRS 17. Take It Slow and Easy(11882)/(rev.,Pee Wee Russell Rhythmakers)

BILLY BANKS AND HIS ORCHESTRA (Unknown personnel):
  Vi 23399. Mighty Sweet/You Wonderful Thing
  Vi 24027. Minnie the Moocher's Wedding Day/The Scat Song
  Vi 24148. It Don't Mean a Thing/Oh You Sweet Thing

BAQUET, GEORGE (clarinet), see:
  JELLY ROLL MORTON: Vi 38075, 38078, 38093, 38113.
  BESSIE SMITH: Co 13000.

BARBECUE JOE AND HIS HOT DOGS (Wingy Mannone):
  Ge 7320. Up the Country   -Ch 16127, 40054
  "   Weary Blues   ", 40055
  Ch 16192. Shake That Thing   -BrE 02504,Ch 40054
  "   Big Butter and Egg Man   -Ch 40055
  Ch 16153. (See Wingy Mannone)

BARKER, BLUE LU (mostly accompanied by Danny Barker's Fly Cats(Benny Carter,trumpet; Buster Bailey,clarinet; Sam Price,piano; Danny Barker,guitar;Wellman Braud, bass.--JRB):
  De 7506. He Caught That B & O/Don't You Make Me High
  De 7538. New Orleans Blues(64433)/That Made Him Mad(64770)
  De 7560. I Got Ways Like the Devil/You're Going to Leave the Old Home Him
  De 7588. Georg's Grind/Nix on Those Lush Heads
(Charles Shavers, trumpet.--JI 10/24/39):
  De 7648. You Ain't Had No Blues/Marked Woman
  De 7683. Midnight Blues/Never Brag About Your Man
  De 7695. He's So Good/You Been Holding Out Too Long
  De 7709. Handy Andy/Deep Blue Sea Blues
(Henry Allen, trumpet.--JI 4/5/40):
  De 7713. Down in the Dumps/Jitterbug Blues
  De 7770. Lu's Blues/I don't Dig You Jack
  De 7813. Scat Skunk(65433)/(rev., Cow Cow Davenport)

BARKER, TOM (Frank Trumbauer) AND HIS ORCHESTRA:
  PaA 34119. What's the Use

BARNES, FAE (acc. by Sam Clark, guitar):
  Para 12099. You Don't Know My Mind(1720)/Good Bye Blues(12099)
(Acc. by Fletcher Henderson Orchestra):
  Para 12209. The Gouge of Armour Avenue(1801)/The Chicago Gouge(1802)
(Acc. by Don Redmond):
  BS 14153. Do It a Long Time Papa/Just Want a Daddy

BARNES, WALTER AND HIS ROYAL CREOLIANS (Cicero Thomas. George Thigpen, trumpets; Ed Burke, Bradley Bullett, trombones; Walter Barnes, Lucius Wilson (tenor), Irby Gage,Wilson Underwood,sax and clarinet; Plunker Hall, banjo; Bill Winston, drums; Paul Johnson, piano; Louis Thompson, bass.--1928,--DB 6/1/40): **1928**
  Br 4187. How Long How Long Blues/My Kinda Love
  Br 4244. It's Tight Like That/rev., Jabbo Smith
  Br 4480. Birmingham Bertha/If You're Thinking of Me
  Br 7072. Third Rail/Buffalo Rhythm
  -- -----. Beau Koo Jack

BARNET, CHARLES AND HIS ORCHESTRA (Charles Barnet, Les Cooper, Don Morres, George Bone, Jack Henderson, saxes; Gordon Griffin,Toots Camarata,Eddie Myers, trumpets; Russ Jenner, Bill McVeigh, trombones; Billy Miller, piano; Buford Turner, guitar; Pete Peterson, bass; Rudy de Julius, drums.--RR): **1935**

```
        Pe 15834. Buckin' the Wind/What Is Sweeter                    -Or 2778
        Pe 15912. Infatuation/Buggerfingers
        Pe 15923. I Lost Another Sweetheart(14987)/Emaline(14988)     -Me 12992
        Me 60703. Cross Parch/The Swing Waltz
        Me 60712. My First Thrill(19241)/Too Good to be True(19244)
        Ro  2150. I Want You/I'm no Angel
(Unknown personnel):
        BB  5814. Don't Be Afraid/I'm Keeping Those Keepsakes
        BB  5815. Nagasaki                                            -HMV X4495
         "        Fare Thee Well Annabelle                            -RZ MR 1762
        BB  5816. Growling                                            -HMV X4495
         "        On a Holiday
        BB  6432. Long Ago and Far Away/Where Is My Heart
        BB  6433. When I'm With You/But Definitely
        BB  6448. Empty Saddles/I'm an Old Cowhand
        BB  6487. Always/Until the Real Thing Comes Along
        BB  6488. A Star Fell Out of Heaven/When Did You Leave Heaven
        BB  6504. Bye Bye Baby/Make Believe Ballroom
        BB  6593. Sing Baby Sing/The Milkman's Matinee
        BB  6594. It's Love I'm After/You Do the Darndest Things Baby
        BB  6605. Did You Mean It/(rev., Wingy Mannone)
        BB  6619. Rainbow on the River/(rev., Amanda Randolph)
        BB  6967. Sailboat in the Moonlight/He Walked Right In
        BB  6973. Love Is a Merry Go Round/The First Time I Saw You
        BB  6975. You're Looking for Romance/In Your Own Little Way
(Robert Burnet, John Mendell, Charles Huffine, trumpets; Ben Hall, Don Ruppers-
berg, Bill Robertson, trombones;   Charlie Barnet, Kurt Bloom, Gene Kinney, Donald
McCook, James Lemare, saxes; Nat Jaffe, piano; Bus Etri, guitar; Phil Stevens,
bass; Wesley Dean, drums.--JRB):                                          1939
        BB 10119. I Get Along Without You Very Well/I'm Prayin' Humble
        BB 10131. Knockin' at the Famous Door/Tin Roof Blues
        BB 10153. A New Moon and an Old Serenade/The Gal from Joe's
        BB 10162. Where Can She Be?
        BB 10172. Jump Session/Swing Street Strut
        BB 10182. Class Will Tell/Some Like It Hot
        BB 10191. In a Mizz/Night Song
        BB 10206. Asleep or Awake/S'posin'
(Sub. Bill Miller, piano; add Charlie Shavers, trumpet):
        BB 10210. Scotch and Soda/Echoes of Harlem
        BB 10227. Strange Enchantment/Only a Rose
        BB 10285. Midweek Function/I Never Knew
        BB 10294. Lazy Bug
        BB 10341. Ebony Rhapsody/Lament for a Lost Love
        BB 10361. For Tonight/What's New
(Sub. Ray Michaels, drums; Bill May, John Owens, trumpets, for Mendell, Huffine;
omit Shavers):
        BB 10373. Cherokee/The All Night Record Man
        BB 10389. Love Grows on the White Oak Tree/The Last Jump
        BB 10439. Lilacs in the Rain/Pigtails
(Sub. Skippy Martin, sax, for Lemare; add Lyman Vunk, trumpet):
        BB 10453. The Duke's Idea/The Count's Idea
        BB 10479. Cuban Boogie Woogie/Two Hearts Are Better Than One
        BB 10511. Night Glow/A Lover is Blue
        BB 10530. The Right Idea/Ogoun Badagris
        BB 10543. Somebody Told Me/Between 18th & 19th on Chestnut Street
        BB 10549. Now You Know/Night After Night
        BB 10568. Thank Your Stars/I Kinda Like You
(Sub. Cliff Leeman, drums; Spud Murphy, trombone. for Hall  Noni Bernardi, James
Lemare, saxes, for Martin, McCook):
        BB 10584. Comanche War Dance/Tarpin' at the Tappa
        BB 10602. Clap Hands Here Comes Charlie/Southland Shuffle
        BB 10610. It's a Wonderful World/Busy As a Bee
        BB 10618. 720 in the Books/So Far So Good
        BB 10637. From Another World/Ev'ry Sunday Afternoon
        BB 10644. Castle of Dreams/You've Got Me Out on a Limb
        BB 10662. A Lover's Lullaby/You've Got Me Voodoo'd
        BB 10669. Where Was I/'Deed I do
        BB 10696. The Fable of the Rose/The Breeze and I
(Sub. Skippy Martin, sax, for Bernardi):
        BB 10721. Afternoon of a Moax/Wanderin' Blues
        BB 10734. You and Who Else/When the Spirit Moves Me
        BB 10737. No Name Jive, I & II
        BB 10743. Six Lessons from Madame La Zonga/Lament for May
        BB 10751. All This and Heaven Too/Where Do You Keep Your Heart
        BB 10774. Leapin' at the Lincoln/Dark Avenue
        BB 10778. And So Do I¼It's the Last Time I'll Fall in Love
        BB 10785. Rockin' in Rhythm/The Reverie of a Moax
        BB 10794. Tangleweed 'Round My Heart/Flying Home
        BB 10804. Wrong Idea/(rev., Dorsey Family)
```

```
     BB 10817. At a Dixie Roadside Diner/That's for Me
(Sub. Leo White, sax, for Martin; Bernie Priven, Sam Skolnick, trumpets, for Bur-
nett, Owens):
     BB 10825. I Don't Want to Cry Any More/Pompton Turnpike
     BB 10846. Peaceful Valley/Reminiscing
     BB 10862. The Sergeant Was Shy/Ring Dem Bells
     BB 10885. Wings Over Manhattan, I & II
     BB 10888. Wild Mab of the Fish Pond/Night and Day
     BB 10918. Isola Bella/Whatcha Know Joe
     BB 10934. I Hear a Rhapsody/The Moon Is Cryin' for Me
     BB 10944. Southern Fried/Redskin Rhumba
     BB 10975. I Can't Forget to Remember/Scrub Me Mama With a Boogie Beat
     BB 11004. He's a Latin from Staten
     BB 11014. Lumby/Phyllysse
     BB 11037. Charleston Alley
              Good for Nothing Joe                                  -BB 30-0823
     BB 11051. Afraid to Say Hello/Conga del Moaxo
     BB 11081. The Captain and His Men/Birmingham Breakdown
     BB 11093. Haunted Town
              Buffy Boy                                             -BB 30-0823
     BB 11111. Blue Juice/Harmony Haven
     BB 11141. Nowhere/You're My Thrill
     BB 11165. Consider Yourself Kissed/Little John Ordinary
     BB 11194. Little Dip/Ponce de Leon
     BB 11265. Spanish Kick/Lois
     BB 11281. Swingin' on Nothin'/Harlem Speaks
     BB 11292. Murder at Peyton Hall
     BB 11321. You Were There/Mother Fuzzy
     BB 11327. Isle of Pines/Blues in the Night
     BB 11396. Fifty Million Nickels/Macumba
     BB 11417. I'm Comin' Virginia/I'll Remember April              -BB 30-0826
(Charles Barnet, Harry Carrel, Kurt Bloom, Ernie Diven, saxophones; Jack Foven,
Jimmy Milazzo, Frank Newton, trumpets; John D'Augustino, Bob Fisher, trombones;
Joe Dale, drums; Ludwig Flato, piano; George Cuomo, guitar; Harry Sulkin, bass):
     Vr   627. Shame on You/If You're Ever in My Arms Again
     Vr   633. Surrealism (add Josef Myrow, piano)/Everheard in a Cocktail Lounge
(See also California Ramblers, Vr 577, 603)
(Unknown personnel):
     De 18363. Smiles/That Real Romance
     De 18378. I Like to Riff/Shady Lady
     De 18507. Things Ain't What They Used to Be/The Victory Walk
     De 18541. I Don't Want Anybody at All/That Old Black Magic
     De 18547. Oh Miss Jaxson/Washington Shirligig
     De 18585. Strollin'/Sittin' Home Waitin' for You
     De 18601. Saltin' Away My Sweet Dreams/My Heart Isn't In It
BARREL HOUSE ANNIE (Blues with piano and guitar):
     Vo 03542. Must Get Mine in Front/Ain't Gonna Give It Away
BARREL HOUSE BUCK (Blues with instrumental acc.):
     De  7013. I Got to Go Blues/Lamp Post Blues
     De  7030. Mean to Me/Mercy Mercy Blues
BARREL HOUSE FIVE (Natty Dominique, trumpet; Jimmy Blythe, piano; Jasper Taylo-
traps; clarinet,--JM 12):
     Para 12851. Hot Livin'(325a)/Mama Stayed Out(326a)           -QRS 7059, Bwy 5058
     Para 12875. Endurance Stomp(1595)/Some Do and Some Don't(1596) -QRS 7019*
     Para 12942. Nobody's Business(327)/Scufflin' Blues(332a)     -QRS 7057
                *Issued under name of South Street Ramblers.
BARREL HOUSE PETE (Piano solos):
     Co 14308. Rollin' Stone(145562)/Pussy(145563)
BARROW, RAY (piano solo)
     Para 12803. Walking Blues(20242)                             -Bwy 1161*
          *Broadway issue under name of Axel Christensen and coupled with his "Synco-
     phonic" (20243)
BARTLETTE, VIOLA (acc. by Lovie Austin's Blues Serenaders(Buster Bailey,clarinet;
Lovie Austin, piano; drums; cornet):
     Para 12322. Go Back Where You Stayed Last Night(2300)/Tennessee Blues(2301)
     Para 12351. You Never Can Tell
     Para 12363. Out Bound Train Blues/You Don't Mean Me No Good
(Johnny Dodds, clarinet; Lovie Austin, piano; trumpet;trombone;guitar; drums):
     Para 12369. Sunday Morning Blues(2545)/Walk Easy Cause My Papa's Here(2548), acc.
              by Cobbs Paramount Syncopators, including Johnny Dodds, clarinet.
```

COUNT BASIE

See also:
SAM DONAHUE: OK 6334.
JONES-SMITH: Vo 3459, 3441.
KANSAS CITY FIVE & SEVEN: Key 1302, 1303.
BENNIE MOTEN'S KANSAS CITY ORCHESTRA
WALTER PAGE: Vo 1463.
BENNY GOODMAN: Co 35404, 35810, 35901, 35938, 36039.

BASIE, COUNT, piano solos (with Fred Green, guitar; Walter Page, bass; Joe Jones, drums):
```
    De  2355.  How Long How Long Blues(64731)/Boogie Woogie(64735)
    De  2498.  The Dirty Dozens/When the Sun Goes Down
    De  2722.  Hey Lawdy Mama(64733)/The Fives(64734)
    De  2780.  Oh Red/Fare Then Honey Fare Thee Well
    De  3071.  Dupree Blues/Red Wagon
```

COUNT BASIE AND HIS ORCHESTRA (Joe Keys, Carl Smith, Buck Clayton, trumpets; George Hunt, Dan Minor, trombones; Jack Washington, Caughey Roberts, alto saxes; Herschel Evans, Lester Young, tenor saxes; Count Basie, piano; Walter Page, bass; Joe Jones, drums.--JRB):

1936
```
    De  1121.  Swingin' at the Daisy Chain               -De 3708, BrE 02379
         "     Pennies from Heaven
    De  1141.  Roseland Shuffle                          -BrE 02515
         "     Honeysuckle Rose                          -BrE 02496
    De  1228.  Glory of Love(62080)/Boo Hoo(62079)       -BrE 02427
    De  1252.  Boogie Woogie/Exactly Like You            -BrE 02521
```

(Keys, Smith replaced by Ed Lewis, Bobby Moore, trumpets; Eddie Durham, trombone, added; Roberts, replaced by Earl Warren, alto sax, 1937):
```
    De  1363.  One O'Clock Jump(62332)                   -De 3708, BrE 02466
         "     John's Idea(62334)                        -De 3518,
    De  1379.  Smarty(62331)/Listen My Children(62333)   -BrE 02490
    De  1446.  Our Love Was Meant to Be(62512)           -BrE 02543
         "     Good Morning Blues(62511)                 -De 18125, BrE 02496
    De  1538.  Time Out(62513)                           -BrE 02543
         "     Let Me Dream(62685)
    De  1581.  I Keep Remembering
         "     Out the Window(Benny Morton, trombone)    -De 3946, BrE 02595
    De  1682.  Georgiana/Blues in the Dark               -BrE 02581
```
(Sub. Baby Hicks, trumpet, for Moore):
1938
```
    De  1728.  Every Tub                                 -BrE 02595
         "     Now Will You Be Good
    De  1770.  Topsy(62514)/Don't You Miss Your Baby?(62684)
    De  1880.  Sent for You Yesterday/Swinging the Blues -BrE 02619
```
(Sub. Harry Edison, trumpet, for Hicks; Benny Morton, trombone, for Hunt; add Dicky Wells, trombone):
1938
```
    De  1965.  Blue and Sentimental(63919a)              -De 3882
         "     Doggin' Around(63920a)                    -De 18125
    De  2004.  Stop Beatin' Around Mulberry Bush/London Bridge Is Falling Down
    De  2030.  Mama Don't Want No Peas an' Rice(63918)/Texas Shuffle(64473)
    De  2212.  Dark Rapture
         "     Jumpin' at the Woodside                   -De 3709
    De  2224.  Panassie Stomp/Do You Wanna Jump, Children?
    De  2249.  My Heart Belongs to Daddy(64851)/Sing for Your Supper(64852)
    De  2284.  The Blues I Like to Hear(64748)/Blame It on My Last Affair(64981)
    De  2325.  Shorty George(64747)
         "     Thursday(64983)                           -De 3709
```
(Omit Morton; Add Lester "Shad" Collins, trumpet):
1939
```
    De  2406.  Cherokee, I & II(64979/80)
    De  2631.  You Can Depend on Me(64978)/Oh Lady Be Good(64985)
    De  2922.  Jive at Five(64982)/Evil Blues(64984)
```
(Sub. Buddy Tate, tenor sax, for Evans):
```
    Vo  4734.  What Goes Up Must Come Down(W24238)/Don't Worry 'Bout Me(W24243)
    Vo  4747.  Rock-a-Bye Basie(W24239)/Baby Don't Tell on Me(W24240)
    Vo  4748.  If I Could Be With You(W24241)/Taxi War Dance(W24242)
    Vo  4784.  And the Angels Sing(W24337)/If I Didn't Care(W24338)
```

29

```
Vo  4860. Miss Thing, I & II(W24340/41)
Vo  4886. Jump for Me(W24244)/12th Street Rag(W24339)
Vo  4967. You Can Count on Me(WC2632)/You and Your Love(WC2633)
Vo  5010. How Long Blues(WC2634)/Sub-Deb Blues(WC2635)
Vo  5036. Moonlight Serenade(W24978)/I Can't Believe That You're(W24980)
Vo  5085. Clap Hands Here Comes Charlie/Pound Cake
Vo  5169. Nobody Knows(WC2596)/Song of the Islands(W24979)
```

COUNT BASIE KANSAS CITY SEVEN (Buck Clayton, trumpet; Dicky Wells, trombone; Lester Young, tenor sax; Count Basie, piano; Freddy Green, guitar; Walter Page, bass; Joe Jones, drums.--JRB):   1939
```
    Vo  5118. Dickie's Dream(25296)/Lester Leaps In(25297)
```
COUNT BASIE AND HIS ORCHESTRA (Buck Clayton, Ed Lewis, Al Killian, Harry Edison, trumpets; Vic Dickerson, Dicky Wells, Dan Minor, trombones; Earl Warren, Tab Smith, Jack Washington, Lester Young, Buddy Tate, saxes; Count Basie, Green, Page, Jones):   1940
```
    OK  5629. Blow Top(wco26870)/Gone With What Wind(wco26871)
    OK  5673. Super Chief(wco26872)/You Can't Run Around(wco26873)
(Omit Tab Smith):
    OK  5732. Evenin'(wc3254)/Moten Swing(wc3257)
    OK  5773. It's Torture(wc3258)/I Want a Little Girl(wc3259)
    OK  5816. The World Is Mad, I & II (wc3255/6)
(Add Tab Smith; sub Don Byas, tenor sax, for Lester Young):                    1940
    OK  5862. The Apple Jump(wco26276)/Blues(wco26661)
    OK  5884. All or Nothing at All(29006)/The Moon Fell in the River(29007)
    OK  5897. What's Your Number(29008)/Draftin' Blues(29009)
    OK  5922. Five o'Clock Whistle(29087)/My Wandering Man(29089),P.Bascomb,tenor
    OK  5963. Love Jumped Out(29088)/It's the Same Old South(29246)      "     "
    OK  5987. Stampede in G. Minor(29247)/Who Am I?(29248)
    OK  6010. Volcano/Rockin' the Blues
    OK  6047. Music Makers/It's Square But It Rocks
    OK  6071. Tuesday at Ten(29584)/Undecided Blues(29585)
    OK  6095. Broadway(29090),Paul Bascomb,tenor sax/The Jitters(29583)
    OK  6122. I'll Forget(29522)/Beau Brummel(29535)
    OK  6157. Wiggle Woogie(29534)/Jump the Blues Away(29581)
(Coleman Hawkins, tenor sax*):
    OK  6180. I Do Mean You(c3677)/Feedin' the "Bean"(c3680)*
    OK  6221. Down Down/You Betcha My Life
    OK  6244. 9:20 Special(c3678)*/Goin' to Chicago(c3681)
    OK  6267. You Lied to Me(29533)/Tune Town Shuffle(30522)
    OK  6319. Meeting You/One Two Three Oh Lary
    OK  6365. H and J(c3679)/Diggin' for Dex(30834)
    OK  6330. Basie Boogie/Let Me See
    OK  6440. Fiesta in Blue/Take Me Back Baby
    OK  6449. Moon Nocturne/Something New
    OK  6475. King Joe, I & II(31373/4), with Paul Robeson
    OK  6508. Platterbrains/In the Dark
    OK  6527. Tom Thumb/My Old Flame
    OK  6564. Harvard Blues/Comin' Out Party
    OK  6584. Down for Double/More Than You Know
    OK  6626. Blue Shadows and White Gardenias/'Ay Now
    OK  6634. One o'clock Jump
(Lewis, Collins, Clayton, Edison, trumpets; Minor, Morton, Wells, trombones, Warren, Washington, Young, Tate, saxes; Basie, Green, Jones, Page):
    Co  35321. I Left My Baby(wco26277)/Riff Interlude(wco26278)
    Co  35338. Hollywood Jump(wco26282)/Someday Sweetheart(wco26283)
    Co  35357. Between the Devil and the Deep Blue Sea(wco26280)/Ham'n Eggs(wco26281)
(Sub. Al Killian, trumpet, for Collins; Vic Dickerson,trombone, for Morton):
    Co  35448. Louisiana(wco26658)/Easy Does It(wco26659)
    Co  35500. Let's Make Hey While the Moon Shines(wco26657)/Somebody Stole My Gal
    Co  35521. I Never Knew(wco26655)/Tickle Toe(wco26656)         (wco26662)
    Co  36601. Basie Blues/I'm Gonna Move to the Outskirts of Town
    Co  36647. It's Sand Man/Ride On
    Co  36675. Rusty Dusty Blues(hco888)/All of Me(81644)
    Co  36685. For the Good of Your Country/Time on My Hands
```
COUNT BASIE AND HIS ALL-AMERICAN RHYTHM SECTION (Count Basie, piano; Joe Jones, drums; Freddy Green, guitar; Walter Page, bass; plus Buck Clayton, trumpet, and Don Byas, tenor sax, in starred(*) titles):
```
    Co  36709. Sugar Blues(hco876)*/Bugle Blues(hco875)*
    Co  36710. Royal Garden Blues(hco874)*/How Long Blues(hco873)
    Co  36711. St.Louis Blues(hco880*/Cafe Society Blues(hco878)
    Co  36712. Farewell Blues(hco877)/Way Back Blues(hco879)
```
BAT THE HUMMING BIRD (Cow Cow Davenport), piano solo:
```
    Vs  6068. Slow Drag(reissue of Para 12800)
```
BAXTER, HELEN (acc. by Lemuel Fowler, piano):
```
    Co  A3922. You Got Everything a Sweet Mama Needs But Me(31026)/(rev.,Irene Gibbons)
    OK  8080. Satisfied Blues(s71633b)/Daddy Ease It to Me(s71634b)
```

BAYERSDORFFER, JOHNNY AND HIS JAZZOLA NOVELTY ORCHESTRA (Johnny Bayersdorffer, trumpet; Steve Loyocano, banjo; Nuncio Scaglioni, clarinet; Tom Brown, trombone; Johnnie Miller, piano; Leo Adde(or Ray Bauduc),drums,Chink Martin,sousaphone):
New Orleans, 1924
OK 40133. I Wonder Where My Easy Rider's Riding Now(8570a)/Waffle Man's Call (8571a)

BAYLOR, BERLYN:
Ch 40000. Clarinet Marmalade/Riverboat Shuffle

BAYSTATE BROADCASTERS:
VD 81843. St.James Infirmary/(rev., New Orleans Pepsters)   -GG 1843

BEALE STREET FIVE:
Ca 553. Meanest Gal in Town/(rev., Johnny Johnson)
Li -----. St. Louis Gal/(rev., University Sextette)

BEALE STREET ROUNDERS:
Vo 1555. I'm Sitting on Top/Talking About Your Yo Yo

BEALE STREET WASHBOARD BAND (Herb Morand, trumpet; Johnny Dodds, clarinet; Baby Dodds, washboard; Frank Melrose,piano.--DB 3/1/41):
Chicago, 1930
Vo 1403. Forty and Tight(3936a)/Piggly Wiggly(3937a)
(Also issued on Pe 196, Or 8120, Ro 5120, Cq 7980 under Rampart Street Washboard Band)

BEAMAN, LOTTIE (blues vocals):
Para 12201. Red River Blues/Honey Blues (with Pruitt Twins)
Para 12235. Mama Can't Lose(piano,banjo acc.)/Regular Man Blues(banjo acc.)
(Acc. by Jimmie Blythe, piano):
Para 12254. Sugar Daddy Blues(1902)/Low Down Painful Blues(1903)
Br 7147. Going Away Blues/Rollin' Log Blues

BEASLEY, HELEN (blues vocals):
Br 7077. Rambling Mind Blues/Tia Juana Blues

BEATTY, JOSEPHINE (Alberta Hunter), accompanied by Red Onion Jazz Babies:
Ge 5594. Everybody Loves My Baby(9167)   -Ge 3048
Texas Moaner Blues(9176a)
Ge 5626. Nobody Knows the Way I Feel Dis Mornin'(9246)   -Ge 3044, Si 4030
Early Every Morn(9247a)   -Bu 8024,

SIDNEY BECHET

For other records see:
LOUIS ARMSTRONG: De 18090, 18091.
JOSEPHINE BEATTY: Ge 5626.
ROSETTA CRAWFORD: OK 8096.
GET HAPPY BAND: Co 14091.
GRANT AND WILSON: De 7500.
HAITIAN ORCHESTRA: Baldwin 581, 1012, 1013; Vs 8360, 8399, 8405.
MARGARET JOHNSON: OK 8107, 8193.
TOMMY LADNIER: BB 10086, 10089.
VIRGINIA LISTON: OK 8122, 8173, 8187.
SARA MARTIN: OK 8090, 8099, 8154.
JELLY ROLL MORTON JAZZMEN: BB 10429, 10434.
PORT OF HARLEM SEVEN: BN 6, 7.
RED ONION JAZZ BABIES: Ge 5627
NOBLE SISSLE: Br 6073,6129; De 153,154,766,778,788,847; Vr 552,648.
MAMIE SMITH: OK 4926.
TRIXIE SMITH: De 7469, 7489, 7528, 7617.
SOUTHERN RAG-A-JAZZ BAND: Si 3592, 3607, 3625.
EVA TAYLOR: OK 4927, 40330.
SIPPIE WALLACE: OK 8212, 8197.
CLARENCE WILLIAMS: OK 3055, 4925, 4966, 4975, 4933, 8129, 8171, 8215, 8245, 40006, 40260, 40321.

BECHET, SIDNEY AND NEW ORLEANS FEETWARMERS (Tommy Ladnier, trumpet; Teddy Nixon, trombone; Sidney Bechet, soprano sax and clarinet; Henry Duncan, piano; Wilson Myers, bass; Morris Morland, drums):
New York, Sept. 15,1932
Vi 23358. I Want You Tonight(73399)/Lay Your Racket(73501)   -BB 10472
Vi 23360. Sweetie Dear(73398)/Maple Rag(73502)   -BB 7614
Vi 24150. I Found a New Baby(73400)   -BB 10022, HMV 4991
Shag(73503)   HMV 4944

SIDNEY 'POPS' BECHET, with Noble Sissle's Swingsters (Clarence Brereton, trumpet; Gil White, tenor sax; Harry Brooks, piano; Jimmy Miller, guitar; Jimmy Jones,bass; Wilbur Kirk, drums.--JI 11/22/40):
1938
De 2129. Blackstick(63264)
When the Sun Sets Down South(63265)   -De 3865
De 7429. Sweet Patootie(63266)
Viper Mad(63263)   -De 3521

BOB THIELE

announces publication of the new

JAZZ

PUBLISHED ON THE FIRST OF EVERY MONTH

This is the magazine you have been waiting for —intelligent articles, by credited critics, about jazz music—previously unpublished photographs—special record releases for subscribers—a column for record collectors—other features too numerous to mention.

SUBSCRIBE NOW!

FIRST ISSUE AVAILABLE DECEMBER 1, 1944

25c PER COPY   **$2.75 PER YEAR**

JAZZ

139 East 57th Street   New York City

SIDNEY BECHET AND HIS ORCHESTRA (Sidney Bechet, soprano sax and clarinet; Ernie Caceres, baritone and tenor sax; Dave Bowman, piano; Leonard War, guitar; Ed Robinson, bass; Zutty Singleton, drums.--JI 11/22/40): 1938
   Vo 4537. Hold Tight(M925)/Jungle Drums(M926)
   Vo 4575. What a Dream(M924)/Chant in the Night(M927)

SIDNEY BECHET QUINTET (Sidney Bechet, soprano sax; Meade Lux Lewis, piano; Teddy Bunn, guitar; John Williams, bass; Sidney Catlett, drums): 1930
   BN 6. Summertime(GM 533-14)/(rev., Port of Harlem Seven)

BECHET'S BLUE NOTE QUARTET (Bechet, Bunn, Catlett; Pop Foster, bass):
   BN 13. Lonesome Blues(RS 709-b)/Dear Old Southland(RS 710-a)
   BN 502. Bechet's Steady Rider(RS 711-a)/Saturday Night Blues(RS 712-a)

(Sidney Bechet, soprano sax and clarinet; Sonny White, piano; Charlie Howard, guitar; Wilson Myers, bass; Kenny Clarke, drums):--JI 11/22/40   New York 2/5/40
   BB 8509. Sidney's Blues(046835)/Make Me a Pallet on the Floor(051226), Bechet, Jackson (Cliff), Wellman Braud, Sidney Catlett:"Bechet Rhythm"
   BB 10623. Indian Summer(046832)/Preachin' Blues(046834)

(Sidney Bechet, soprano sax and clarinet; Sidney deParis, trumpet; Sandy Williams, trombone; Cliff Jackson, piano; Bernard Addison, guitar; Wellman Braud, bass; Sidney Catlett, drums.):   New York, June 4, 1940
   Vi 26640. Shake It and Break It(051222)/Wild Man Blues(051224)
   Vi 26663. Old Man Blues(051223)/Nobody Knows the Way I Feels Dis Mornin'
   (051225)
(Rex Stewart, trumpet; Sidney Bechet, clarinet and soprano sax; Earl Hines, piano; John Lindsay, bass; Baby Dodds, drums.):   Chicago, Sept. 6, 1940
   Vi 26746. Blue for You, Johnny(053432)/Ain't Misbehavin'(053433)
   Vi 27204. One o'Clock Jump(046833), see 2/5/40 group/Blues in Thirds(053431),
   Vi 27240. Save It Pretty Mama(053434)/Stompy Jones(053435) (Bechet, Hines, Dodds

PROFESSOR SIDNEY BECHET (with Dr.Henry Levine and His Barefooted Dixieland Philharmonic):
   Vi 27302. Muskrat Ramble/(rev., Dinah Shore)

FEETWARMERS (Sidney Bechet, clarinet and soprano sax; Henry Allen, trumpet; J.C. Higginbotham, trombone; Wellman Braud, bass; James Toliver, piano; James Heard, drums):
   Vi 27337. Egyptian Fantasy/Slippin' and Slidin'
   Vi 27386. Coal Black Shine/Baby Won't You Please Come Home

(Sidney Bechet, soprano sax; Lem Johnson, tenor sax; Gus Aiken, trumpet; Sandy Williams, trombone; Cliff Jackson, piano; Wilson Myers, bass; Arthur Herbert, drums):
   Vi 27447. When It's Sleepy Time Down South/I Ain't Gonna Give Nobody None O'
   (this Jelly Roll
BECHET ONE MAN BAND (playing clarinet; soprano and tenor saxes; piano; bass; drums):
   Vi 27485. Blues of Bechet/The Sheik of Araby

(Previous personnel):
   Vi 27574. Swing Parade/I Know That You Know

(Sidney Bechet, clarinet and soprano sax; Charlie Shavers, trumpet; Willie "The Lion" Smith, piano; Everett Barksdale, guitar; Wellman Braud, bass; Manzie Johnson, drums):   New York, Sept., 1941
   Vi 27600. Texas Moaner/Limehouse Blues
   Vi 27663. Laughin' in Rhythm/Rip Up the Joint(see personnel below)
   Vi 27707. Rose Room/Lady Be Good(personnel unknown)
   Vi 27904. I'm Coming Virginia/Georgia Cabin

(Bechet, Smith and Barksdale):
   Unissued. Strange Fruit/You're the Limit

(Sidney Bechet, soprano sax and clarinet; Henry Goodwin, trumpet; Vic Dickerson, trombone; Don Donaldson, piano; Ernest Williamson, bass; Manzie Johnson, drums):
   Vi 20-1510. The Mooche/Blues in the Air   New York, 10/14/41):

BECHET-SPANIER BIG FOUR (Sidney Bechet, soprano sax and clarinet; Muggsy Spanier, cornet; Carmen Mastren, guitar; Wellman Braud, bass.): 1940
   HRS 2000. Sweet Lorraine(R2774)/Lazy River(R2775)
   HRS 2001. Four or Five Times(R2773)/China Boy(R2776)
   HRS 2002. If I Could Be With You(R2801)/That's a Plenty(R2802)
   HRS 2003. Squeeze Me(R2803)/Sweet Sue(R2804)

BIX BEIDERBECKE

For other records see:
BIX AND RHYTHM JUGGLERS: Ge 5654.
BROADWAY BELL HOPS: Ha 504, 508.
HOAGY CARMICHAEL: Vi 22864, 23013, 25371, 38139.
CHICAGO LOOPERS: Pat 36729, HRS 1
JEAN GOLDKETTE: Vi 20270, 20981, 20273, 20300, 20466, 20469, 20471, 20472, 20491, 20493, 20588, 20675, 20926, 20994, 25354, Special "Oldsmobile" Victor.
RUSSELL GRAY: OK 40938 (doubtful)
JAZZ HARMONIZERS: Cx 40366, 40375, 40339(reissues of Gennett Wolverines)
BENNY MEROFF: OK 40912
NEW ORLEANS LUCKY SEVEN: OK 8544.
WILLARD ROBISON: Pat 36724.
SIOUX CITY SIX: Ge 5569.
TRAM-BIX-LANG: OK 40916.
FRANKIE TRUMBAUER: OK 40772, 40822, 40843, 40871, 40879, 40903, 40926, 40966, 40979, 41044, 41019, 41039, 41100, 41145, 41128,(41209, 41231, 41286, PaE 420), PaE 2176, 2645.
PAUL WHITEMAN: Vl21103, 21214, 21218, 21228, 21240, 21274, 21301, 21338, 21365, 21389, 21398, 21438, 21453, 21464, 24078, 24105, 25238, 25675, 26415, 25366-70, 27685, 27686, 27688, 27689, 35877, 35912, 35934; HMV 5509;Co 1441,1444, 1478,1491,1496,1505,1723,1822,1877,1945,50068,50096,50103,50140.
WOLVERINES: Ge 5408, 5453, 5454, 5542, 5565, 20062; BrE 02205.

BEIDERBECKE, BIX (piano solo):
  OK 40916. In a Mist(81426b)/(rev.,Tram-Bix-Lang)   -PaE 3504, Vo 3150

BIX BEIDERBECKE AND HIS GANG (Box Beiderbecke, cornet; Billy Rank, trombone; Don Murray,clarinet; Adrian Rollini, bass sax; Frank Signorelli, piano; Howdy Quicksell, banjo; Chauncey Morehouse, drums):   1927
  OK 40923. At the Jazz Band Ball(81518b)   -Vo 3042, PaE 3465,2711, Co 36156
    "   Jazz Me Blues(81520a)   PaE 127, 2580
  OK 41001. Sorry(81569a)   -Vo 3149, PaE 2054,3503
    "   Since My Best Gal Turned Me Down(81572b)
                                    -Vo 3149, PaE 2711,3503

(Bix Beiderbecke, cornet; Billy Rank, trombone; Izzy Friedman, clarinet; Min Leibrook, bass sax; Lennie Hayton, piano; Harry Gale, drums):   1928
  OK 41030. Somebody Stole My Gal(600616b)   -Br 8242
    "   Thou Swell(400617c)   PaE 2355, Co 35665
  OK 41088. Ol' Man River(400994a)   -PaE 2328, Co 35666, UHCA 25
    "   Wa Da da(400995a)   -PaE 2286,   "   UHCA 26
  OK 41173. Rhythm King(401138b)   -Br 8242, PaE 2269
    "   Louisiana(401139a)   PaE 2833, Co 35665
  PaE R2833.Margie(401140a)

BIX BEIDERBECKE AND HIS ORCHESTRA (Bix Beiderbecke, cornet; Benny Goodman, clarinet; Joe Venuti, violin; Ed Lang, guitar; Jimmy Dorsey, sax; Ray Ludwig, trumpet; Gene Krupa, drums):   New York, Sept. 8, 1930
  Vi 23008. I Don't Mind Walkin' in Rain(63631)/I'll Be a Friend with Pleasure
                                                           (63632-2)
  Vi 23008. I'll Be a Friend With Pleasure(63632-3)/(same coupling as above)
                                                         -Vi 26415
  Vi 23018. Deep Down South(63630)   -HMV 8841,Vi 25370

BELL, ANNA (Acc. by Clarence Williams Orchestra):
  QRS 7008. Kitchen Woman Blues(173)/Lock Step Blues(174)

BEN'S BAD BOYS (Ben Pollack's Orchestra,):   1928
  Vi 21971. Yellow Dog Blues/Wang Wang Blues

BENNETT, ELOISE (acc. by Irene Eadie, piano):
  Para 12412. Effervescent Daddy/Love Me Mr. Strange Man

BENNETT, RALPH AND HIS SEVEN ACES:
  Me 12479. Love Me Tonight/Isn't It Romantic?(12239)
  Me 12491. High Society(12225)/Sing(12269)

BENNETT'S SWAMPLANDERS:
  Co 14557. Big Ben(150767)/You Can't Be Mine and Someone Else's Too(150768)
  Co 14662. Jet Black Blues/(rev., New Orleans Wildcats)

BENTLEY,GLADYS (with piano and guitar):
  OK 8612. Moanful Wailin' Blues/How Long How Long Blues
  OK 8643. How Much Can I Stand/Wild Geese Blues
  OK 8707. Red Beans and Rice/Big Gorilla Man

BUNNY BERIGAN

For other records see:
  ALL STAR BAND: Vi 26144.
  LOUIS ARMSTRONG: De 698.
  MILDRED BAILEY: Br 6558, 6587, 6655, 6680; PaE 2201, 2257.
  DORSEY BROTHERS: BrE 1386; Br 6409, 6537, 7542.
  TOMMY DORSEY: Vi 25508, 25513, 25519, 25516, 25523, 25534, 25532, 25539
  BUD FREEMAN: PaE 2210, 2285.
  GENE GIFFORD: Vi 25041, 25065.
  BENNY GOODMAN: Vi 25081, 25136, 25090, 25145, 25268.
  BILLIE HOLIDAY: Vo 3276, 3288, 3333, 3334.
  BOB HOWARD: De 689.
  JAM SESSION AT VICTOR: Vi 25569.
  HAL KEMP
  DICK McDONOUGH: Me 60908 et al.
  GLENN MILLER: Co 3051, 35881.
  MOUND CITY BLUE BLOWERS
  RED NORVO: Co 3026, 3059, 3079.
  ADRIAN ROLLINI: Me 12815 12855, Or 2784.
  FRANKIE TRUMBAUER: HMV BD119, Vi 24834.
  PAUL WHITEMAN

BERIGAN, BUNNY AND HIS ORCHESTRA:
  Vo 15875. A Tree Was a Tree   -Me 12611
  "   The Girl in the Little Green Hat   -Me 12593
  Vo 15884. Tony's Wife(13213)/Stormy Weather(13236)
  Vo 15887. Sweetheart Darlin'(13289)/Pettin' in the Park(13298)
  Vo 15891. Remember My Forgotten Man/The Shadow Waltz

BUNNY BERIGAN AND HIS BOYS (Bunny Berigan, trumpet; Forrest Crawford, tenor sax;
Joe Bushkin, piano; Dave Barbour, guitar; Martin Stuhlmaker, bass; Dave Tough,
drums.--HD):   1936
  Vo 3178. I'd Rather Lead a Band/Let Yourself Go
  Vo 3179. It's Been So Long(18718)/Swing Mr. Charlie(18721)

(Add Jack Teagarden, trombone; Shaw, clarinet; sub. Eddie Condon, guitar):
  Vo 3224. A Melody from the Sky/A Little Bit Later On
  Vo 3225. I Can't Get Started(19013)   -Br 7949
  "   Rhythm Saved the World(19015)   , VoE S26

(Sub. Jack Lacey, trombone; Slats Long, clarinet, Cozy Cole, drums):
  Vo 3253. But Definitely(19417)/When I'm With You(19419)
  Vo 3254. If I Had My Way/
           I Nearly Let Love Go Slipping   -VoE S26

BUNNY BERIGAN AND HIS BLUE BOYS (Bunny Berigan, trumpet; Eddie Miller, clarinet
and tenor sax; Edgar Sampson, alto; Cliff Jackson, piano; Grachan Moncur, bass;
Ray Bauduc, drums):   February, 1936
  PaE R2316. I'm Coming Virginia(60231)/Blues(60232)   -De 18116
  PaE R2327. You Took Advantage of Me(60229)/Chicken & Waffles(60230) -De 18117

BUNNY BERIGAN AND HIS ORCHESTRA (Bunny Berigan, L. Brown, Henry Greenwald, trum-
pets; Ford Leary, trombone; Mat Mattlock, clarinet; Hymie Schertzer, Arthur
Dollinger, saxes; Leo Burness, piano; Tom Morgan, guitar; Arnold Fiskin, bass;
Manny Berger, drums; Johnny Hauser, vocal.--HD):
  Br 7784. That Foolish Feeling/Where Are You
  Br 7823. One in a Million/Who's Afraid of Love
  Br 7832. Blue Lou/Goona Goo   -VoE S68
  Br 7847. Big Boy Blue/I'm Gonna Kiss Myself Goodbye   -VoE S47
  Br 7858. Dixieland Shuffle/Let's Do It   -VoE S75

(Bunny Berigan, Cliff Natale, Sid Lipkins, trumpets; Ford Leary, Frank D'Annolfo,
trombones; Henry Freeman, George Auld, Clyde Rounds, Frank Langome, saxes; George
Wettling, drums; Arnold Fishkind, bass; Tom Morgan, guitar; Joe Lippman, piano):
  Vi 25557. All Dark People Are Light On Their Feet/(rev., T.Dorsey)   1938
  Vi 25562. You Can't Run Away from Love/Cause My Baby Says It's So

(Sub. Sid Pearlmutter, sax, for Langome):
  Vi 25587. The Image of You/I'm Happy Darling Dancing With You
  Vi 25588. Swanee River/Love Is a Merry Go Round
  Vi 25593. The First Time I Saw You/(rev., Roy Fox)

(Sub. Irving Goodman, trumpet for Natale; Morey Samuel, Sonny Lee, trombones,
for Leary, D'Annolfo; Joe Dixon for Freeman):
  Vi 25609. All God's Chillun Got Rhythm/The Lady from Fifth Avenue

35

```
Vi 25613. Roses in December                                   -HMV 5368
        Let's Have Another Cigarette
Vi 25616. Frankie and Johnnie/Mother Goose
Vi 25622. Mahogany Hall Stomp/(rev., Shefter's Rhythm Octet)
```

(Sub. Mike Doty for Pearlmutter,Al George for Samuel, Hank Wayland for Fishkind):
```
Vi 25646. Let 'er Go/Turn on That Red Hot Heat
Vi 25653. A Study in Brown/Caravan                            -HMV 8632
Vi 25664. Ebb Tide/Gee But It's Great to Meet a Friend
Vi 25667. Sweet Varsity Sue/Why Talk About Love
Vi 25677. Mama I Wanna Make Rhythm/Have You Ever Been in Heaven
Vi 25688. I'd Love to Play a Love Scene/I Want a New Romance
Vi 25690. Miles Apart/Strange Loneliness
Vi 25728. I Can't Get Started/The Prisoner's Song
```

(Sub. Fulton McGrath, piano, for Lippman; Dave Tough, drums, for Wettling):
```
Vi 25776. Heigh-Ho/Piano Tuner Man
Vi 25781. Outside of Paradise/Serenade to the Stars
Vi 25811. Sophisticated Swing/Down Stream
Vi 25816. An Old Straw Hat/Lovelight in the Starlight
Vi 25820. Rinka Tinka Man/I Dance Alone
```

(Sub. Nat Lebovsky,trombone, for Lee; John Blowers, drums; Dick Wharton,guitar):
```
Vi 25833. I Got a Guy/Moon Shine Over Kentucky
Vi 25848. Azure/(rev., Tommy Dorsey)
Vi 25858. Never Felt Better Never Had Less/'Round the Old Deserted Farm
Vi 25868. It's the Little Things That Count/Somewhere
Vi 25872. Wacky Dust/Wearing of the Green
Vi 25877. And So Forth
Vi 25881. The Pied Piper/Ten Easy Lessons
Vi 26001. Russian Lullaby
Vi 26055. Why Doesn't Somebody Tell Me These Things/When a Prince of a Fella
Vi 26061. Father Dear Father/Let This Be a Warning to You
```

(Bunny Berigan, Steve Lipkins, Irving Goodman, trumpets; G. Bohn, Gus Bivona, Clyde Rounds, George Auld, saxes; Ray Coniff, N. Lebovsky, trombones; Hank Wayland, bass; Dick Wharton, guitar; Joe Bushkin, piano; Buddy Rich, drums):
```
Vi 26068. High Society/Livery Stable Blues
Vi 26077. Button Button/Rockin' Rollers Jubilee
Vi 26086. Simple and Sweet/I Won't Tell a Soul I Love You
```

(Sub. Johnny Napton, trumpet, for Lipkins; Murray Williams, sax, for Bohn, Bob Jenney, trombone, for Lebovsky; Lippman for Bushkin):
```
Vi 26113. Jelly Roll Blues/'Deed I Do
Vi 26116. Sobbin' Blues/I Cried for You
```

BUNNY BERIGAN AND HIS MEN (Bunny Berigan, Irving Goodman, trumpets; Ray Coniff, trombone; Murray Williams, Gus Bivona, George Auld saxes; Lippman,Wayland,Rich):
```
Vi 26121. Flashes/Davenport Blues
Vi 26122. Candlelights/In the Dark
Vi 26123. In a Mist/Walkin' the Dog
```

BUNNY BERIGAN AND HIS ORCHESTRA (A. George, Sonny Lee, trombones; Joe Dixon, Mike Doty, Clyde Rounds, George Auld,saxes; Tom Morgan, guitar; George Wettling, drums; Lippman, Wayland; Berigan, Napton, Goodman):
```
Vi 26138. Black Bottom/Trees
Vi 26152. In a Little Spanish Town/Can't Help Lovin' That Man
Vi 26196. Patty Cake/Ya Had It Comin' to You
```

(Berigan, Napton, J. Koven, G. Johnson, trumpets; Bivona, D. Ladice, H. Saltman, L. Walsh, saxes; Coniff, Jenney, trombones; Bushkin, Wayland; Allen Reuss, guitar; E. Jenkins, drums):
```
Vi 26244. Jazz Me Blues/There'll Be Some Changes Made
Vi 26338. Gangbuster's Holiday/Little Gate's Special
Vi 26753. Ain't She Sweet/Ay-sy-ay
Vi 27258. Peg o' My Heart/Night Song
Vi 36208. I Can't Get Started/The Prisoner's Song(see 25728 for personnel)
```

(Unknown personnel):
```
El 5005. 'Tis Autumn(w111)                                    -Ph 63
         Two in Love(w112)                                    -Ph 62
El 5006. I Got It Bad(w109)                                   -Ph 64
         White Cliffs of Dover(w110)                          -Ph 62
El 5019. Somebody Else Is Taking My Place(w139)               -Ph 64
         Me and My Melinda(w140)                              -Ph 61
El 5020. Skylark(w137)                                        -Ph 61
         My Little Cousin(w138)                               -Ph 63
```

CHU BERRY

For other records see:
HENRY ALLEN: Vo 2956, 2965.
LIL ARMSTRONG: De 1059, 1092, 1182.
MILDRED BAILEY: Vo 3056, 3057.
CAB CALLOWAY:
BENNY CARTER: CoE 628, 636.
CHOCOLATE DANDIES: PaE 1792; Co 2875, OK 41568.
PUTNEY DANDRIDGE: Vo 2935, 2982, 3122, 3123.
FLETCHER HENDERSON: Vo 3211, 3213, 3485, 3487, 3511, 3534, 3627, 3641;Vi 25297, 25317, 25334, 25339, 25373, 25375, 25379.
TEDDY HILL: Me 13351, 13364.
GENE KRUPA: Vi 25263, 25276.
RED NORVO: Co 3026, 3059, 3079.
BESSIE SMITH: OK 8945, 8949.
TEDDY WILSON: Br 7550, 7554, 7663, 7684.

BERRY, CHU AND HIS STOMPY STEVEDORES (Hot Lips Page, trumpet; George Mathews, trombone; Buster Bailey, clarinet; Cozy Cole, drums; Horace Henderson,piano;Israel Crosby, bass; Lawrence Lucie, guitar; Chu Berry, tenor sax.--HD): 1937
    Vr   532. Now You're Talking My Language(M293)/Too Marvelous for Words(M295)
    Vr   587. Indiana(M294)/Limehouse Blues(M296)

(Chu Berry, tenor sax; Irving Randolph, trumpet; Keg Johnson, trombone; Bennie Payne,piano; Dave Barbour, guitar; Milton Hinton, bass; Leroy Maxey, drums.--HD):
    Vr   657. My Secret Love Affair(M624)/Ebb Tide(M625)   -Vo 3793

CHU BERRY AND HIS 'LITTLE JAZZ' ENSEMBLE (Chu Berry, tenor sax; Roy Eldridge, trumpet; Clyde Hart, piano; Danny Barker, guitar; Artie Shapiro, bass; Sidney Catlett; drums.--): 1938
    Com 516. Sitting In (p23699-2)/Forty Six West Fifty Two(p23702-1)
    Com 1502. Stardust(xp23700-1a)/Body and Soul(xp23701-1)

CHU BERRY AND HIS JAZZ ENSEMBLE (Chu Berry, tenor sax; Hot Lips Page, trumpet; Clyde Hart, piano; Al Casy, guitar; Al Morgan, bass; Harry Jaeger, drums.): 1941
    Com 541. Blowing up a Breeze(R4178)/Monday at Minton's(R4180)
    Com 1508. On the Sunny Side of the Street(R4179)/Gee Ain't I Good to You(R4181)

BERTON, VIC AND HIS ORCHESTRA (Vic Berton, drums; Mat Matlock, clarinet; Jimmy Granader, alto sax and clarinet; Pee Wee Russell, tenor sax and clarinet*; Spencer Clark, bass sax; Henry Levine, Ronald Garcia, Sterling Bose, trumpets; Art Foster, Wally Barron,trombones; Irving Brodsky, piano; Dan Calker, guitar; Merle Klein, bass; Chick Bullock, vocals.--RR): 1935
    Vo 2915. Dardanella   -BrF 500557
    "   Jealous   -BrF 500558
    Vo 2944. Mary Lou(17175)*   -BrF 500559
    "   Lonesome and Sorry(17178)*   -BrF 500560
    Vo 2964. In Blinky Winky Chinky Chinatown(17176)*
    "   A Smile Will Go a Long, Long Way (16787)
    Vo 2974. Blue(17177)*   -BrF 500560
    "   Taboo   -BrF 500558
    Co 3074. Devil's Kitchen/I've Been Waiting
    Co 3092. Imitations of You/Two Rivers Flow Through Harlem

BERTRAND'S (JIMMY) WASHBOARD WIZARDS (Johnny Dodds, clarinet; Jimmy Bertrand, washboard; Jimmy Blythe, piano; trumpet, except in first coupling.--JAZZ I,9): 1927
    Vo 1035. Little Bits(64)/Struggling(66)   -OrE 1008
    Vo 1060. Idle Hour Special(31)/47th Street Stomp(33)
    Vo 1099. I'm Goin' Huntin'(16)/If You Want to Be My Sugar Papa(18)
    Vo 1100. Easy Come Easy Go(12)/The Blues Stampede(14)

(Johnny Dodds, clarinet, Jimmy Bertrand, washboard; James Blythe, piano):
    Vo 1180. My Baby/Oriental Man

(Probably Omer Simeon, clarinet; Punch Miller, trumpet):
    Vo 1280. Isabella/I Won't Give You None

BIG ACES (Langston Curl, John Nesbitt, trumpets; Claude Jones, trombone; Don Redman,Milton Senior, George Thomas, Prince Robinson, saxes; Todd Rhodes, piano; Dave Wilburn, banjo; Bob Escudero, bass; Cuba Austin, drums.--HD): 1928
    OK 41136. Cherry(40117la)/(rev.,Little Aces)   PaE 365, OdF 165125
            (See McKinney's Cotton Pickers)

BIG BILL (Broonzy), blues singer:
```
  Pe  0217. Worryin' You Off My Mind, I & II
  Pe  0335. Hobo Blues/Wanta See My Baby
  Me 13049. Mistreatin' Mama Blues/Long Tail Mama
  Me 13311. Prowlin' Ground Hog/See See Rider
  Me 51265. Something Good/C & A Rider
  Me 60355. Ash Hauler/Brickbats in My Bed
  Me 61259. Detroit Special/Falling Rain
  Me 70157. These Ants Keep Biting Me/Black Maria Blues
  Me 70254. Black Widow Spider/Oh Babe
  Me 70354. Cherry Hill/Seven Leven
  Me 70368. Married Life's a Pain/Pneumonia Blues
  Me 70664. You Do Me Any Old Way/Let's Reel and Rock
  Me 80158. Hattie Blues/It's Too Late Now
  Ro 60757. Big Bill's Milk Cow No. 2/Bull Cow No. 3
  Vo 03075. Let Me Be Your Winder/Louise Louise Blues
  Vo 03147. Evil Hearted Me/My Gal Is Gone
  Vo 03252. Hattie Blues/It's Too Late Now
  Vo 03304. Made a Date With An Angel/I Want My Hands on It
  Vo 03400. Play Your Hand/Somebody Got to Go
  Vo 04095. I'll Start Cutting on You/Get Ready Tonight
  Vo 04149. New Shake 'em on Down                            -Cq 9073
            Night Time Is the Right Time No. 2
  Vo 04205. Trucking Little Woman/Why Did You Do That to Me
  Vo 04280. The Mill Man Blues/It's Your Time Now
  Vo 04378. Sad Penc'l Blues/Unemployment Stomp
  Vo 04429. WPA Rag/Living on Easy Street
  Vo 04486. Rider Rider Blues/Trucking Little Woman No. 2
  Vo 04532. Good Time Tonight/Hell Ain't but a Mile
  Vo 04591. Trouble and Lying Woman/Let Me Dig It
  Vo 04706. Just a Dream/Baby I Done Got Wise
  Vo 04760. Mary Blues/Just Got to Hold You Tight           -Cq 9278
  Vo  4938. Woodie Woodie/Please Be My So and So            -Cq 9309
  Vo 05043. Just Wondering/That's All Right Baby
  Vo 05096. Too Many Drivers/Preachin' the Blues
  Vo 05149. Cotton Choppin' Blues/Tell Me What I Done
  Vo 05205. Oh Yes/Fightin' Little Rooster
  Vo 05259. Just a Dream No. 2/My Last Goodbye to You
  Vo 05311. I'm Still Your Sweetheart/Let's Have a Little Fun
  Vo 05360. Don't You Want to Ride/Dreamy Eyed Baby
  Vo 05404. Don't You Be No Fool/J'vin' Mr. Fuller Blues
  Vo 05452. Looking for My Baby/Plow Hand Blues
  Vo 05514. Leap Year Blues/Make My Get Away
  Vo 05563. I've Got to Dig You/When I Had Money
  OK 05601. I.C. Blues/What Is That She Got
  OK 05641. Down and Lost in Mind/Messed Up in Love
  OK 05698. Lone Wolf Blues/Looking Up at Down              -Cq 9761
  OK 05758. Medicine Man Blues/Midnight Steppers
  OK 05869. Hit the Right Lick/Merry Go Round Blues
  OK 05919. I Wonder What's Wrong/You Better Cut That Out
  OK 05983. Bed Time Blues/Serenade Blues                   -Cq 9759
  OK 06031. Lonesome Road Blues/My Gal Is Gone
  OK 06080. I'll Never Dream Again/That Number of Mine
  OK 06116. Getting Older Every Day/Rockin' Chair Blues     -Cq 9794
  OK 06427. All by Myself/Double Trouble
  OK 06630. She's Gone With the Wind/Why Should I Spend My Money
  OK 06651. Hard Hearted Woman/I'M Gonna Move to the Outskirts of Town
  OK 06688. I Feel So Good/Tell Me Baby
  OK 06705. Night Watchman/What's Wrong
  Cq  8671. Big Bill Blues/March Box
  Cq  9284. You Can't Sell 'em in Here/Baby Don't You Remember
  Cq  9929. Green Grass Blues
  Cq  9932. Conversation With the Blues
  BB  5535. Mississippi River Blues/Friendless Blues
  BB  6188. Keep Your Hands Off Her/Sun Gonna Shine in My Door Some Day
```

BIG BILL AND THOMPS:
Para 12656. House Rent Stomp/Big Bill

BIG BOY BENN (blues with instrumental acc.):
Vs 8031. Mama Keep Your Yes Ma'am Clean/Mistreated the Only Friend You Had

BARNEY BIGARD

For other records see:
DUKE ELLINGTON: Almost all except earliest.
ELLINGTONIA: HRS 1003, 1004.
GOTHAM STOMPERS: Va 541, 620.
JOHNNY HODGES: Vr 576, 586, Vo 3948.

BOB HOWARD
FRANKIE 'HALF PINT' JAXON: De 7619, 7638.
JELLY ROLL MORTON: Vi 20252, 20296, 38108, 38601.
KING OLIVER: Vo 1014, 1007,1033,1059,1049,1112,1114.
RUSSELL'S HOT SIX: Vo 1010.
LUIS RUSSELL'S HEEBIE JEEBIE STOMPERS: OK 8424, 8454.
REX STEWART: Sw 56; Vo 5448, 5510; HRS 2004, 2005.
OZIE WARE: Vi 21777.
COOTIE WILLIAMS: Vo 3890, 3922, 4061, 4086, 4324, 4425, 4574, 4636, 5618,5690;
   OK 6336.
ALBERT WYNN: OK 8350.

BIGARD, BARNEY AND HIS JAZZOPATERS (Cootie Williams, trumpet; Juan Tizol,trombone;
Barney Bigard, clarinet; Harry Carney, baritone sax; Duke Ellington, piano; Fred
Guy, guitar; Billy Taylor, bass; Sonny Greer drums.--JAZZ L,5-6):   12/19/36
   Vr 515. Caravan(LO 373)/Stompy Jones(LO 374)   -Vo & OK 3809
   Vr 525. Clouds in My Heart(LO371)/Frolic Sam(LO372)   -Vo & OK 3813

(Sub. Rex Stewart for Williams):   4/29/37
   Vr 564. Four and One-Half Street(M434)/Solace(M433)   -Vo & OK 3820

                                                                         6/16/37
   Vr 596. Get It Southern Style(M525)/If You're Ever in My Arms(M528) -Vo 3828
   Vr 626. Moonlight Fiesta(M526)/Sponge Cake and Spinach(M527)   -Vo 3834

                                                                         4/29/37
   Vr 655. Demi-Tasse(M435)/Jazz a la Carte(M436)   -Vo & OK 3842

BARNEY BIGARD AND HIS ORCHESTRA (Same personnel):   1/19/38
   Vo 3985. Drummer's Delight(M724)/If I Thought You Cared(M725)
                                                                         1938
   Vo 5378. Barney Goin' Easy(WM1036)/Minuet in Blues(WM1117)
   Vo 5422. Early Mornin'(WM1105)/Lost in Two Flats(WM1118)
   Vo 5595. Mardi Gras Madness(WM1141)/Watch the Birdie(WM1142)
   OK 5663. Just Another Dream(WM1037)/Honey Hush(WM1119)
   Vo 4928. Utt-da-zay(WM1034)/Chew Chew Chew(WM1035),acc. the Quintones.

(Ray Nance, trumpet; Juan Tizol, trombone; Barney Bigard, clarinet; Ben Webster,
tenor sax; Duke Ellington, piano; Jimmy Blanton, bass; Sonny Greer, drums.--JAZZ
5-6):   11/11/40
   BB 10981. Charlie the Chulo(053621)/A Lull at Dawn(053623)   -HMV 9185
   BB 11098. Lament for a Javanette(053622)/Ready Eddy(053624)   -HMV 9215

(Sub. Jimmy Bryant,bass;Harry Carney,sax,for Webster;): Hollywood, Sept. 29, 1941
   BB 11581. Brown Suede(061688)/'C' Blues(061690)   -HMV 9314
   Unissues. Noir Bleu(061689)/June(061691)

BIGEOU, ESTHER (Blues singer, orchestra acc.):
   OK 8025. Stingaree Blues(s70294a)/If That's What You Want Here It Is(s70319)
   OK 8026. The Memphis Blues/The St. Louis Blues
   OK 8029. Nervous Blues/(rev., Clarence Williams)

(Acc. by Rickett's Stars):
   OK 8053. Aggravatin' Papa(s71322b)/(rev., Kitty Brown)
   OK 8054. Four O'Clock Blues/(rev., Tim Brymn)

(Acc. by Clarence Williams, piano):
   OK 8056. Outside of that He's All Right(s71341)/Gulf Coast Blues(s71342b)
   OK 8057. I'm Through With You(s71329c)/Beale Street Mama(s71330b)
   OK 8058. Beale Street Blues/(rev., Sara Martin)
   OK 8065. The Hesitating Blues/(rev., Sara Martin)
   OK 8125. You Ain't Treatin' Me Right/Panama Limited Blues

(acc. by Piron's New Orleans Orchestra):
   OK 8118. West Indies Blues(s72175b)/That Twa-Twa Tune(s72131b)(piano,C.Wms.)

BILLY AND JESSE (vocal duet):
   Br 7099. Put Your Mind on It/Strewin' Your Mess

BINNEY, JACK (Jack Pettis) AND HIS ORCHESTRA:
   PaA 34076. Freshman Hop/Bag o' Blues

BIRMINGHAM BLUE BUGLERS:
   Ge 5498. I Need You/Dancin' Blues

BIRMINGHAM BLUETETTE (orchestra):
   Herwin 92019. Back Home Blues(2116)/Old Man Blues(2601)

BIX AND HIS RHYTHM JUGGLERS (Bix Beiderbecke, cornet; Tom Dorsey, trombone; Don
Murray, clarinet; Paul Mertz, piano; Tom Gargano, drums.--DB 2/15/40):
                                                                                  Richmond, Ind., March,1925
  Ge 5654. Toddlin' Blues(12140)   -BrE 02501, HRS 23, Se 6
            Davenport Blues(12141)   -BrE 02206, HRS 22,   "
  Unissues. Magic Blues/Nobody Knows What It's All About

BLACK BIRDS OF PARADISE (orchestra)   October, 1927
  Ge 6210. Bugahoma Blues/Tishomingo Blues
  Ge 6211. Sugar/Muddy Water

BLACK DIAMOND SERENADERS
  Pe 14692. Ace in the Hole/(rev., G. Moyer)

BLACK DIAMOND TWINS (Jimmy Blythe and Buddy Burton, piano duet):
  Pe 0206. Block and Tackle/(rev., Alabama Rascals)

BLACK DOMINOES (orchestra)
  Ge 5263. Black Sheep Blues(8532)/Land of Cotton Blues(8531)
  Ge 5347. Back o' Town Blues(8669)/Dancin' Dan(8670)

BLACK PIRATES (orchestra):
  Bwy 1230. My Old Girl's My New Girl Now(20950)/Roll Up the Carpets(20952)

BLACK, TEDDY AND HIS ORCHESTRA:
  Pe 15498. How the Time Can Fly/Begging for Love   -Melodee 303

BLIND BLAKE (vocal with guitar):
  Para 12387. West Coast Blues/Morning Blues
  Para 12431. Stonewall Street Blues/Too Tight
  Para 12479. One Time/Dry Bone Shuffle
  Para 12497. Bad Feeling Blues/That Will Never Happen
  Para 12673. Doggon' My Mama/Hot Potatoes
  Para 12695. Bootleg Rum Dum Blues/Low Down Loving Gal
  Para 12710. Cold Hearted Mama Blues/Back Door Slam Blues
  Para 12754. Notoriety Woman Blues/Walkin' Across the Country
  Para 12794. Slippery Rag/Hookworm Blues
  Para 12810. Poker Woman Blues/Doing a Stretch
  Para 12863. Fightin' the Jug/(rev., Charles Spand)
  Para 12904. Ice Man Blues/Chump Man Blues
  Para 12918. Baby Lou Blues(L23)/Cold Love Blues(L24)

BLAKE, EUBIE AND HIS ORCHESTRA
  Vi 18791. Baltimore Buzz/Bandana Days   HMV 1297
  Vi 22735. Little Girl/My Blue Days Blew Over
  Vi 22737. Thumpin' and Bumpin'/(Rev., Snooks & Memphis Ramblers)
  Re 9199. Jimmie, I Love But You
  Em 10434. Sounds of Africa/Baltimore Buzz
  Em 10450. Ma/Sweet Lady
  Cr 3086. When Your Lover Has Gone(1240)/(rev., Adrian Schubert
  Cr 3090. Please Don't Talk About Me(1234)/I'm No Account Any More(1239)
  Cr 3111. One More Time/Two Little Blue Little Eyes
  Cr 3130. St. Louis Blues/Nobody's Sweetheart
  Cr 3193. River Stay Away from My Door/Life Is Just a Bowl of Cherries

BLAND, JACK AND HIS RHYTHMAKERS(Henry Allen, trumpet; Pee Wee Russell, clarinet;
Happy Caldwell, tenor sax; Tommy Dorsey, trombone; Frank Froeba, piano;Eddie Con-
don, banjo; Jack Bland, guitar; Pop Foster, bass; Zutty Singleton, drums.) 1932
  Pe 15689. A Shine on Your Shoes(12453)/It's Gonna be You(12454 -Me 12510,UHCA 111
  Pe 15694. Who Stole the Lock(12452)/Someone Stole Gabriel's Horn(12455)
              -Me 12513, Ro 1966, Or 2593, Ba 32605, BrF 500317, 01737,UHCA 104
  Co 35841. Who Stole the Lock (second master, under name of "Rhythmakers")

BLOOM, RUBE (Piano solos):
  Pe 15097. Rainbow 'Round My Shoulder/Sonny Boy
  OK 40842. Doll Dance   -PaE 3385
    "   March of the Dolls
  OK 40901. Silhouette   -Co 1195, PaE 3446
    "   Dancing Tambourine
  OK 40931. My Blue Heaven   -PaE 3508
    "   Sapphire   -Co 1195, PaE 111
  OK 40988. Losing You/Mine All Mine
  OK 41073. That Futuristic Rag   PaE 162
    "   Serenata
  OK 41117. Because My Baby Don't Mean Maybe(400848)   -PaE 208
    "   I Can't Give You Anything But Love(401049)
  Ha   164. Spring Fever   -PaE 3385
    "   Soliloquy   -PaE 3508

V' 25060. On the Green/Penthouse Romance
V' 25227. One Finger Joe/Aunt Jemima's Birthday
(Also accompaniments for: Chick Endor, Vo 15352; Esther Walker, Br 3008; Margaret Young, Br 2736, Ruth Etting, Beth Challis, Lillian Morton, Noble Sissle)

RUBE BLOOM AND HIS BAYOU BOYS (Phil Napoleon, trumpet; Tommy Dorsey, trombone; Benny Goodman, clarinet; Adrian Rollini, bass sax; Rube Bloom, piano.--HD):<u>1930</u>
  Co 2103. The Man from the South(149771)   -CoE DC57
          St. James Infirmary(149772)   -CoE CB75

Co 2186. Mysterious Mose(150156)/Bessie Couldn't Help It(150157)
Co 2218. On Revival Day(150531)/There a Wah-wah Gal in Ague Caliente(150532)

BLUE BELLE (Blues with piano and guitar):
  OK 8704. Mean Bloodhound Blues/Death Valley Moan

BLUE CHIPS:
  Me 60955. Chipp'n' the Rock of Blues/Oh Monah
  Me 61161. Froggy Bottom/Nit Wit Serenade
  Me 61162. Let's Get Drunk and Truck/Rattlesnakin' Daddy

BLUE GRASS FOOT WARMERS (Clarence Williams, piano; Ed Allen, cornet; Jasper Taylor, washboard; clarinet):
  Ha 206. Senorita Mine(142306)/How Could I Be Blue(142329)
  Ha 248. Charleston Hound(142307)/Old Folks' Shuffle(142330)

BLUE HARMONY BOYS:
  Para 12901. Good Feeling Blues/Sweet Miss Stella Blues

BLUE JAY BOYS (See also Blythe's Blue Boys):
  De 7224. Endurance Stomp/Tack It Down
  De 7225. Pleasure Mad(13688)/Some Do and Some Don't(13690)
  De 7240. Brown Skin Mama/My Baby

BLUE RYTHM BAND

See:
  BLUE RIBBON BOYS: Pe 15468.
  KING CARTER: Co 2439, 2504, 2638.
  EARL JACKSON: Pe 15481, 15505; Me 12164, 12080.
  BARON LEE: Vo 1617, 1646; Pe 15605, 15606, 15621, 15629, 15634, 15652, 15676, 15696, 15822.
  MILLS BLUE RHYTHM BAND: Vi 22763, 22800, 24442, 24482; BB 5688; VoE s6; CoE CB734; Co 2963, 2994, 3020, 3038, 3044, 3071, 3078, 3083, 3087, 3111, 3135, 3134, 3147, 3148, 3156, 3157, 3158, 3162; PaE 2366; Br 7534; Vr 503, 546, 604, 624.
  MILLS BLUE RHYTHM BOYS: Br 6156, 6199.
  MILLS MUSIC MASTERS: Me 12091, 12059.
  CHUCK RICHARD: Vo 2877, 2867, BrE 02009.

BLUE RHYTHM BOYS (Wardell Jones, Shelton Hemphill, Edward Anderson, trumpets;Harry White, Henry Hicks, trombones; Theodore McCord, Crawford Wethington, Castor McCord, saxes; Edgar Hayes,piano; Benny James,banjo; Hayes Alvis,bass; Willie Lynch, drums.--HD):   <u>1931</u>
  Br 6143. Blue Flame/Blue Rhythm   -BrE 01177,BrF9137
  Br 6299. Savage Rhythm   -BrE 01227,BrF 500152
        I'm Sorry I Made You Blue

BLUE RHYTHM ORCHESTRA:
  Pe 14531. Santa Claus Blues

BLUE RIBBON BOYS (See Blue Rhythm Boys personnel):
  Pe 15468. Poor Minnie the Moocher/Star Dust   -Ba 32166, Ro 1631

BLUE RIBBON SYNCOPATORS (George West, piano; Herbert Diemer, sax; Harry Tate, trumpet; Gilbert Roberts, banjo; Hurley Diemer, drums.--JI 8/9/40):
  OK 40349. Blues in A Minor/My Gal My Pal
  Co 14215. Scratch/Memphis Sprawler
  Co 14235. Whale Dip/Blue Ribbon Blues

BLUES CHASERS:
  Pe 14428. Sweet Georgia Brown(rev., Lou Gold)
  Pe 14432. Charleston/What a Smile Can Do

always

ask to hear

▽

▽

▽

▽

Signature
RECORDS

JAMES BLYTHE

For other records see:
ALABAMA RASCALS: Pe 0205, 0240, 0206, Me 70163.
BARREL HOUSE FIVE: Para 12851, 12875, 12942.
LOTTIE BEAMAN: Para 12254.
BERTRAND'S WASHBOARD WIZARDS: Vo 1035, 1060, 1099, 1100, 1280.
BLACK DIAMOND TWINS: Pe 0206.
CHICAGO FOOTWARMERS: OK 8533, 8548, 8599, 8613, 8792.
J.C. COBB: Vo 1204, 1263, 1269, 1449.
DIXIE FOUR: Para 12661, 12674.
DIXIELAND THUMPERS: Para 12525.
DIXIELAND JUG THUMPERS: Para 12594.
MEMPHIS NIGHT HAWKS: Vo 1736, 1744, 2593.
MIDNIGHT ROUNDERS: Vo 1218, 1237.
SODARISA MILLER: Para 12231, 12276, 12306.
MONETTE MOORE: Para 12210.
O'BRYANT WASHBOARD BAND: Para 12260,12246,12265,12277,12288,12297,12308,12329, 12346.
PARAMOUNT PICKERS: Para 12779.
MA RAINEY: Para 12438, 12352.
PRISCILLA STEWART: Para 12205, 12224,12240,12253,12286,12360,12402.

BLYTHE,JAMES (piano solos):   1924-25
  Para 12207. Chicago Stomps(1750)/Armour Avenue Struggle(1751)
  Para 12304. Fat Meat and Greens(2201)/Jimmie Blues(2202)
  Para 12370. Mr. Freddie Blues/Lovin's Been Here and Gone
  Vo 1181. Alley Rat/Sweet Papa

BLYTHE AND BURTON (James Blythe and Buddy Burton,piano duets.--):   1928
  Ge 6502. Block and Tackle Blues(See Black Diamone Twins)/Dustin' the Keys

JAMES BLYTHE AND JIM CLARK:
  Ch 16451. Bow to Your Papa/Don't Break Down

BLYTHE'S SINFUL FIVE (James Blythe, piano;cornet; sax; violin; banjo; drums):
  Para 12346. Pump Tillie(2420)/(rev., O'Bryant Washboard Band)

BLYTHE'S WASHBOARD BAND(Johnny Dodds, clarinet;James Blythe, piano; washboard):
  Para 12368. Bohunkus Blues(2541)/Buddy Burton's Jazz(2542)

JIMMIE BLYTHE AND HIS RAGAMUFFINS (Freddie Keppard, trumpet; Johnny Dodds, clarinet; James Blythe, piano; trombone; traps):   1926
  Para 12376. Messin' Around(2602-1)/Adam's Apple(2603)   -Sig 906
  Para 12376. Messin' Around(2602-2)

BLYTHE WASHBOARD RAGAMUFFINS (with Dodds):
  Para 12428. Ape Man(2749)/Your Folks(2750)

JIMMY BLYTHE'S OWLS (Johnny Dodds, clarinet; James Blythe, piano; Jimmy Bertrand, washboard; Natty Dominique, cornet; banjo):   1927
  Vo 1135. Pout'in' Papa/Weary Way Blues
  Vo 1136. Have Mercy!/Hot Stuff

BLYTHE'S BLUE BOYS (Johnny Dodds, clarinet; Natty Dominique, trumpet; James Blythe, piano; Jimmy Bertrand, washboard):
  Ch 15344. The Weary Way Blues(See State Street Ramblers)/There'll Come a Day

(James Blythe, piano; Natty Dominique, cornet; Jimmy Bertrand, washboard;sax; clarinet and bass in some numbers):
  Ch 15551. Pleasure Mad   -Ch 40025
          Some Do and Some Don't   -Ch 40062
  Ch 15615. Endurance Stomp   -Ch 40025
          Tack It Down   -Ch 40062
  Ch 15676. Orintnal Man/Brown Skin Mama (no cornet)   -Ch 40023
  Ch 40115. My Baby/Tell Me Cutie
        (See Also Blue Jay Boys)

BOBBY'S REVELERS (Lovie Austin's Blues Serenaders):
  Si 3537. Too Sweet for Words/(rev., Mamie Jones)

BOGAN, LUCILLE (acc. by piano):
  OK 8071. Chirpin' the Blues/Triflin' Blues
  OK 8074. Lonesome Daddy Blues/Don't Mean You No Good Blues
  Para 12459. Levee Blues/Sweet Petunia

(Next four sides with Will Ezell, piano):
      Para 12504. Jim Tampa Blues(725)with Charlie Jackson/Kind Stella Blues(726)
      Para 12577. Cravin' Whiskey Blues(961)/Nice and Kind(962)
          Br 7051. New Way Blues/Pay Roll Blues
          Br 7083. Pot Hound Blues/Coffee Grindin' Blues
          Br 7145. New Georgia Grind/Whiskey Selling Woman
          Br 7163. They Ain't Walking No More/Dirty Treatin' Blues
          Br 7186. Black Angel Blues/Tricks Ain't Walking No More
          Br 7210. Alley Boogie/Sloppy Drunk Blues
                       (See also: Bessie Jackson)

    BOLDEN, LELA (acc. by A. J. Piron, violin; Steve Lewis, piano;):
       OK 8139. Southern Woman Blues/Seawall Special Blues   Recorded in New Orleans

    BONANO, SHARKEY, trumpet (See Following):
        BROWNLEE'S ORCHESTRA OF NEW ORLEANS
        JOHNNIE MILLER'S NEW ORLEANS FROLICKERS
        MONK HAZEL'S BIENVILLE ROOF ORCHESTRA
        SHARKEY'S NEW ORLEANS BOYS
        SHARKEY AND HIS SHARKS OF RHYTHM

    BOONE'S JUMPING JACKS:
        De 8590. I'm for It/Take Me Back
        De 8644. Messy/Please Be Careful

    BOOTS (DOUGLAS) AND HIS BUDDIES (Theodore Gilders, Percy Bush, Douglas Byers, Chas.
    Anderson, trumpets; Johnnie Shields, trombone; Alva Brooks, Wee Demry, Baker Mill-
    ens, Dave Ellis, saxes; A. J. Johnson, piano; Jeff Vant, guitar; Walter McHenry,
    bass; Boots Douglas, drums.--TEMPO 9/38)   Recorded in San Antonio
        BB 6063. Wild Cherry/Rose Room
        BB 6081. Riffs/I Love You Truly
        BB 6132. Anytime/How Long, Part 1
        BB 6301. Georgia/How Long, Part 2
        BB 6307. Coquette/Marie
        BB 6333. Swing/Vamp
        BB 6357. Sweet Girl/(rev., King Garcia)   -BB 10043
        BB 6862. Jealous/I like You Best of All
        BB 6880. When the Time Has Come/Haunting Memories
        BB 6941. Swanee River Blues/Rhythmic Rhapsody
        BB 6968. Sleepy Gal/(rev., Tampa Red)
        BB 7005. San Anton' Tamales/(rev., Tiny Parham)   -BB 10044
        BB 7187. Blues of Avalon/The Raggle Taggle
        BB 7217. The Goo/The Weep
        BB 7236. The Sad/(rev., Tampa Red)
        BB 7241. Ain't Misbehavin'/(rev., Renolds)
        BB 7245. The Happy/(rev., Munro's Orchestra)
        BB 7269. The Somebody/(rev., Tampa Red)
        BB 7556. Deep South/Chubby
        BB 7596. Gone/True Blue Lou
        BB 7669. Lonely Moments/(rev., Art Kassel)
        BB 7944. Do Re Mi/A Salute to Harlem
        BB 10036. Careless Love/East Commerce Stomp
        BB 10106. Boots Stomp/I Don't Stand a Ghost of a Chance With You
        BB 10113. Remember/Lonesome Road Stomp

    BOOZE, BEA (Blues with rhythm accompaniment):
        De 8619. If I'm a Fool/Uncle Sam Come and Get Him
        De 8621. War Rationing Papa/Let's Be Friends
        De 8629. If I Didn't Love You/I Love to Georgia Brown So Slow
        De 8633. Catchin' As Catch Can/See See Rider Blues

STERLING BOSE
(Trumpet)

    See:
        ARCADIAN SERENADERS: OK 40503, 40517, 40538, 40562.
        VIC BERTON: Vo 2915, 2944, 2964, 2974; Co 3074, 3092.
        CLOVERDALE COUNTRY CLUB ORCHESTRA: OK 41551.
        BOB CROSBY
        TOMMY DORSEY: Vi 25144, 25159, 25145, 25236, 25172, 25191, 25183, 25206, 25216, 25217,
            25214, 25246, 25201, 25220.
        GOLDKETTE: Vi 21805, 21889.
        BENNY GOODMAN: Vi 25391, 25387, 25411, 25406.
        BOBBY HACKETT: Vo 4806, 4877.
        JOE HAYMES
        JOHNNY MERCER: De 142.
        MOUND CITY BLUE BLOWERS: Ch 40098 et al.
        RAY NOBLE
        ORIGINAL CRESCENT CITY JAZZERS: OK 40101.

BEN POLLACK: Pe 15325, 15432.
GIL RODIN; Cr 3016, 3017, 3045, 3046.
JACK TEAGARDEN: Cr 3051; Co 2558.
BOB ZURKE.

BOSWELL, CONNIE (Acc. by Ben Pollack Orchestra feat. Muggsy Spanier, trumpet:
De 1160. Serenade in the Night/Where Are You?
De 1161. When the Poppies Bloom Again/Trust in Me
De 1420. Whispers in the Dark/That Old Feeling
De 1421. Afraid to Dream/The Loveliness of You
De 1433. Yours and Mine/Am I in Love?
De 1434. Blossoms on Broadway/Love or Infatuation

BOSWELL SISTERS (Vartha, Connie and Vet):
Vi 19639. Nights When I'M Lonely/I'm Gonna Cry
OK 41444. Heebie Jeebies/My Future Just Passed
OK 41470. Don't Tell Her/Gee But I'd Like to
Br 6083. Wha'd Ja Do to Me/When I Take My Sugar to Tea -Br 80011, BrE 01113
Br 6109. Roll on Mississippi Roll On   -Br 80012, BrE 01136
"   Shout Sister Shout   BrE 01416
Br 6151. It's You   -BrE 01181
"   It's the Girl   -Br 80014,
Br 6170. I Can't Write the Words   -BrE 01395
"   Makin' Faces at the Man in the Moon
Br 6173. Shine on Harvest Moon/Heebies Jeebies   -Br 80013, BrE 01218
Br 6218. An Evening in Caroline   -BrE 01251
"   River Stay Away from My Door   -Br 80014,
Br 6231. I Thank You Mr. Moon/Nothing Is Sweeter Than You   -BrE 01272
Br 6257. Put That Sun Back in the Sky/Was That the Human Thing -BrE 01284
Br 6271. Everybody Loves My Baby   -Co 36520, BrE 01295
"   Stop the Sun Stop the Moon
Br 6291. There'll Be Some Changes Made   -Co 36521, BrE 01306
"   Between the Devil and the Deep Blue Sea
Br 6302. Got the South in My Soul/If It A'n't Love   -BrE 01330
Br 6335. Hand Me Down My Walkin' Cane   -Co 36520, BrE 01362
"   Doggone I've Done It   BrE 01893
Br 6405. Me Minus You/I'll Never Say
Br 6418. Charlie Two Step   -BrE 01403
"   Down Among the Sheltering Palms   -Co 36522, BrE 01347
Br 6442. It Don't Mean a Thing(12639)/Minnie the Moocher's Wedding day(12641)
                                                        -Vo 4546, BrE 01436
Br 6552. In a Second Hand Store
Br 6596. Gold Digger's Song/It's Sunday Down in Caroline   -BrE 01556
Br 6625. Puttin' It on/Swanee Mammy   -BrE 01576
Br 6650. Sophisticated Lady/That's How Rhythm Was Born   -BrE 01592
Br 6733. Song of Surrender/Coffee in the Morning   -BrE 01711
Br 6798. I Hate Myself/You Oughta Be in Pictures   -BrE 01751
Br 6929. Don't Let Your Love Go Wrong/Why Don't You Practice What -BrE 01832
Br 7302. Rock and Roll   -Co 36523, BrE 01957
"   If I Had a Million Dollars
Br 7348. Object of My Affection   -Co 36523, BrE 01961
"   It's Written All Over Your Face
Br 7412. Dinah   -Vo 4239, BrE 1926
"   Alexander's Ragtime Band   , BrE 1893
Br 7454. Way Back Home/Every Little Moment   -BrE 02033
Br 7467. St.Louis Blues(17646)/Travelin' All Alone(17645) -Vo 4495, BrE 02044
Br   Sing a Little Jingle/I Found a Million Dollar Baby   -BrE 01193
Br 6360. Old Yazoo   -BrE 01379
Br 6395. Sentimental Gentleman   -Co 36522, BrE 01397
"   Down on the Delta   -BrE 01403
Br   We Just Couldn't Say Goodbye   -BrE 01347
"   Crazy People   -BrE 01416
Br 6545. Forty-second Street/Shuffle Off to Buffalo   -BrE 01516
Br 6470. Mood Indigo   -Co 36521, BrE 01543
"   Louisiana Hayride   BrE 01625
Br 6951. Goin' Home/Lonesome Road   -BrE 01791
Br   Lullaby of Broadway/Fare Thee Well Annabelle   -BrE 02043
De 574. Cheek to Cheek/Top Hat White Tie and Tails   -BrE 02067
De 671. Music Goes Round and Around/I'm Gonna Sit Right Down   -BrE 02142
De 709. Let Yourself Go/I'm Puttin' All My Eggs in One Basket -BrE 02165

(With Victor Young Orchestra & Frank Munn):
Br 20100. Star Dust/I Surrender Dear   -BrE 0102

(Add Bing Crosby, Tom Dorsey, Mills Brothers):
Br 20102. Gems from George White's Scandals   -BrE 0108

(With Red Nichols, Arthur Jarrett et al):
Br 20107. California (medley)   -BrE 0118

```
          (Add Joe Venuti, Eddie Lang):
             Br 20110. New Orleans (medley)                            -BrE 0118

          (With Bing Crosby and Don Redman's Orchestra):
             Br 20109. Lawd You Made the Night Too Long                -BrE 0107

          BOYCE'S HARLEM SERENADERS:
             De  8585. 'Long About Three in the Morning(69801)/Get in the Groove(69802)
             De  8602. Harlem After Midnight/Good Old Hometown Blues

          BOYD, RAYMOND (piano and guitar acc):
             OK  8528. Unkind Mama/Blackbird Blues

          BRACKEN, JIMMY AND HIS TOE TICKLERS (Benny Goodman, clarinet; Jimmy McPartland,cor-
          net; Jack Teagarden, trombone; Gil Rodin, Larry Binyon, saxes; Vic Briedis, piano;
          Dick Morgan, banjo; Harry Goodman, bass; Ray Bauduc, drums.--HD):
             Re  8723. Icky Blues(8478)/Four or Five Times
             Re  8768. Makin' Friends(8543)/Tiger Rag(8476)
             Re  8813. Twelfth Street Rag(8762)/rev., Gil Rodin              -Do 4322
             Re  8826. After You've Gone
             Do  4274. Shirt Ta'l Stomp
                       It's T'ght Like That(8541)
                       (See also Whoopee Makers)                       -Ap 8950

          BRADFORD, MARY:
             Para 12617. Awful Lawdy Lawdy Blues/Loafing Blues

          (Acc. by Bennie Moten's Orchestra):
             OK  8102. Chattanooga Blues/Selma Bama Blues

          (Acc. by L. Wright, cornet; B. Moten, piano):
             OK  8123. Waco Texas Blues/(rev., Ada Brown)

          BRADFORD'S (PERRY) JAZZ PHOOLS (Louis Armstrong, cornet; Don Redman, alto sax; Jas.
          P. Johnson, Fats Waller, pianos; Perry Bradford,vocal;clarinet;trombone;others,-JI,
          1/26/40):
             Vo 15165. Lucy Long/I Ain't Gonna Play No Second Fiddle
              ?        Hateful Blues

          (Gus Aiken, trumpet; Bud Aiken, trombone; Garvin Bushell, clarinet; Brassfield, clar-
          inet and sax; "Speed", banjo; Bradford, piano.--JI 6/14/40):
             Para 12041. Fade Away Blues(1429)/Day Break Blues(1430)
             Para 20309. Hoola Boola Dance/Charleston S. C.           -Pu 11309, Cx 40309
                 (See also Lena Wilson, Para 12029, Sippie Wallace,OK 8232;Ethel Ridley, Vi
                                                                                    19111)
          PERRY BRADFORD AND HIS GANG( Johnny Dunn, cornet; Garvin Bushell, clarinet; Perry
          Bradford, piano; trombone; sax; banjo; others.--JI 1/26/40):
             OK  8416. Original Black Bottom Dance(74428)/Kansas City Blues(74429)
             OK  8324. Just Met a Friend(141992)/So's Your Old Man(141993)   -Co 14142
          (See also: Alberta Hunter, OK 8268, 3315, 8383, 8409; Laura Smith OK 8246, 8316;
          Mary Jackson Pe 12092; Louise Vant OK 8310, acc. by Perry Bradford's Mean Four;
          other Bradford records, mostly with Johnny Dunn, are Georgia Strutters, Gulf Coast
          Seven, Original Jazz Hounds)

          BRADLEY, MARIE (acc. by piano and violin):
             Para 12456. Down Home Moan(499)/Back to Town Blues(500)
             Para 12466. Mama's in a Strain(541)/Stormy Hailing Blues(540),with Will Ezell

          BRADLEY, VI AND RHYTHMETTES:
             Ch 40038. Star Dust

          BRADLEY, WILL AND HIS ORCHESTRA (Steve Lipkins, Joe Wiedman, Herbie Dell, trumpets;
          Will Bradley, Jim Emert, Bill Corti, trombones; Art Mendelssohn, Peanuts Hucko, Joe
          Huffman, Sam Sachelle, saxes; Ray McKinley, drums; Freddie Slack piano; Delman Kap-
          lan, bass; Bill Barford, guitar):
             Co 35333. Halleluhaj/Johnson Rag
             Co 35354. Love Nest/I'm Coming Virginia
             Co 35376. A Ghost of a Chance(co25689)/Jimtown Blues(co25801)
             Co 35399. I Get a Kick Outa Corn(co25899)/Gotta Get Home(co25900)
             Co 35414. Watching the Clock/It's a
             Co 35422. Flyin' Home(wco26545)/So Far So Good(wco26547)
             Co 35443. After I Say I'm Sorry/O Sole Mio
             Co 35464. Rhumboogie/This Is the Beginning of the End
             Co 35470. Secrets in the Moonlight(wco26734)/Polka Dots and Moonbeams(wco26737)
             Co 35485. A Young Man Sings

          (Sub. Nick Ciazza, sax, for Mucko; Al Mitchell, trumpet, for Dell;Steve Jordan,gui-
          tar; Doc Goldberg, bass):
             Co 35530. Beat Me Daddy Eight tothe Bar, I & II (co27329/30)
             Co 35545. Strange Cargo/Where Do You Keep Your Heart?
             Co 35566. In a Little Spanish Town(wco26736)/As Long As I Live(w26177),early
             Co 35597. Love Lies/Orchids for Remembrance                     (personnel)
             Co 35629. Deed I Do/Don't Let It Get You Down

                                            46
```

```
Co 35645. I Could Make You Care/One in a Lovetime
Co 35707. Celery Stalks at Midnight(co25688,original personnel)/Down the Road
              a Piece(co27872-trio: Slack,Goldberg,McKinley)
Co 35732. Scramble Two(wco26733)/Rock-a-bye the Boogie(wco28021)
Co 35743. Scrub Me Mama with a Boogie Beat(co28654)/There I Go(co28655)
Co 35764. The Moon Fell in the River/Somewhere
Co 35793. Dearest, Darest I(co28911)/Five o'Clock Whistle(co28914)
Co 35849. The Lonesome Road/You're Lucky to Me
Co 35871. I Should Have Known You Years Ago/ Three Ring Ragout
Co 35912. High on a Windy Hill/Love of My Life
Co 35922. Break It to Me Gently/This Little Icky Went to Town
Co 35939. Chicken Gumboogie/Stardust
Co 35963. Bounce Me Brother With a Solid Four/Southpaw Serenade
Co 35994. Boogie Woogie Conga(co29523)/I Need Somebody to Love(co29592)
Co 36014. It's Square But It Rocks/Prairieland Lullaby
Co 36044. I Boogied When I Should Have Woogied/That's Her Mason Dixon Line
Co 36052. Call Me a Taxi/Shadows in the Night
Co 36101. Think of Me(Bradley Quartet/Tea for Two( Bradley Quartet)
Co 36147. Flamingo/Swingin' Down the Lane
Co 36182. I'm Misunderstood/When You and I Were Young Maggie
Co 36225. Think of Me/Thinking of You
Co 36231. Boogie Woogie Piggy/Love Me a Little
Co 36248. Get Thee Behind Me Satan(co30464)/All That Meat,No Potatoes(co30729)
Co 36286. From the Land of the Sky Blue Water/In the Hall of the Mountain King
Co 36297. City Called Heaven/I'm Tired of Waiting for You
```

WILL BRADLEY'S SIX TEXAS HOT DOGS(Lee Castaldo, trumpet: Will Bradley, trombone;
Mahlon Clark, clarinet; Billy Maxted, piano; Ray McKinley, drums; Felix Giobbe,
bass (first title below only):
```
Co 36340. Basin Street Boogie(co30953)/Call It Anything It's Love(co30951)
Co 36372. Don't Let Julia Fool Ya(co31081)/Jack and Jill(co31082)
Co 36401. April in Paris/Stop and Ask Somebody
Co 36444. The Three B's/I Think of You
Co 36470. Sleepy Time Gal/Who Can I Turn To?
Co 36547. I Guess I'll Be On My Way/Seeing You Again Did Me No Good
Co 36719. Fry Me Cooke With a Can of Lard/Request for a Rhumba
Vo  5130. Memphis Blues(w26088)/Old Doc Yak(w26089)
Vo  5182. Speaking of Heaven/I Thought About You
Vo  5210. I'm Fit to Be Tied(w26213)/Make With the Kisses(w26212)
Vo  5237. Forevermore/Mean to Me
Vo  5262. Swingin' a Dream/This Changing World
```

WILL BRADLEY AND HIS BOOGIE WOOGIE BOYS (Will Bradley, trombone; Billy Butterfield,
trumpet; Bob Haggart, bass: Paul Ricci, clarinet; John Cuarnieri, piano; Billy Guss-
ak, drums):
    Beacon 7013. Jingle Bells Boogie Woogie/Cryin' the Boogie Blues

BRADSHAW, TINY AND HIS ORCHESTRA (featuring Happy Caldwell, tenor sax):
```
De  194. Darktown Strutters Ball/Sheik of Araby
De  236. I'm a Ding Dong Daddy/Ol' Man River
De  317. Mister Will You Serenade/She'll Be Coming Around the Mountain
De  456. I Ain't Got Nobody/Shout Sister Shout
```

BRADY'S (KING) CLARINET BAND:
    Ge 6393. Embarrassment Blues
       "   Lazybone Blues   -Ch 15455
            (See also; Ernest Michall Clarinet Band)

BRAGG, ARDELLA (blues acc. by Tiny Parham, piano):
Para 12398. Pig Meat Blues(3028)/Cane Break Blues(3029)
Para 12458. Doggin' Me/Wolf Man

ARDELLA BRAGG AND HER TEXAS BLUE BLOWERS (clarinet, piano and banjo):
Para 12429. That's Alright(2765)/What Makes You Treat Me This a Way(2766)

BRAGG, DOBBY (blues piano and vocals):
Para 12827. Single Tree Blues/Fire Detective Blues
Para 13004. We Can Sell That Thing/3,6, and 9
Para 13044. Conjur Man Blues/Little Sow Blues
Para 13083. Don't Look Strange at Me/Sail on Little Girl Sail On
       (See also Charlie McFadden: Para 12928, 13076, 13093)

BRAGG (J.H.) AND HIS RHYTHM FIVE (Alto sax, piano, banjo, drums, string bass):
Vo 3060. Pleading(sa2357)/Ethiopian Stomp(sa2358)
Vo 03174. Friskey Honey/Mama Don't 'low No Music in Here

BRILLHARDT'S ORCHESTRA (Probably Red Nichols and Leo McConville, trumpets; Arnold
Brillhardt and others, saxes; Arthur Schutt, piano; others):
Pe 14631. State Street Shuffle/(rev., Sam Lanin)

BROADWAY BANDITS (Pee Wee Irwin, **Art** Sylvester, Jerry Neary, trumpets;Jack Lacey, Red Ballard, trombones; Benny Goodman, clarinet; Toots Mondello, Hymie Schertzer, Dick Clark, Arthur Rollini, saxes; Frank Froeba, piano; Van Eps, guitar; Harry Goodman, bass; Sam Weiss, drums.--HD):
  ReZ MR1733. You're the Top(16347)/**All Through the Night**(16348)

BROADWAY BELL HOPS (Sam Lanin group featuring Bix Beiderbecke, cornet;Frank Trumbauer, alto sax; Joe Venuti, violin.-): <u>1927</u>
  Ha 504. There Ain't No Land Like Dixieland(144809)/There's a Cradle in Caroline(144810) -De 2504, Ve 1504
  Ha 508. Rainbow of Love(144811)/(rev., Harmonians) -D' 2508, Ve 1508

BROADWAY BROADCASTERS (To be heard in some of the following are:Jimmy McPartland, cornet*; Benny Goodman, clarinet#; and Jack Teagarden, trombone∅):
  Ca 498. Sobbin' Blues(819)/(rev., Varsity Eight)
  Ca 555. It Had to Be You(933)/(rev., Arthur Lange)
  Ca 606. Any Way the Wind Blows/(rev., Varsity Eight)
  Ca 613. My Best Girl
  Ca 678. Alabamy Bound/(rev., Lou Gold)
  Ca 738. Oh How I Miss You Tonight
  Ca 774. Breezin' Along
  Ca 775. Just a Little Drink
  Ca 836. No Man's Mamma (1702)/That Certain Party(1703)
  Ca 893. Let's Talk About My Sweetie/(rev., Carol'ners) -Li 2478
  Ca 912. Lonesome and Sorry(1875)/(rev., Bob Haring)
  Ca 939. Hot Henry
  Ca 955. Deep Henderson
  Ca 985. Birth of the Blues/Black Bottom
  Ca 1149. St. Louis Blues*#∅
  Ca 1239. Marvelous -Ro 470
  Ca 1933. Bye Bye Blackbird
              Rain -Ro 488
              You Only Want Me -Ro 495
              Wob-a-ly Walk(2887) -Li 2850, Ro 625
              South Bound -Ro 649
  Ca 8163. She's a Great Great Girl/(rev., Western Wanderers)
  Ca 8228. Lots o' Mamma(3127)*#/(rev., Sam Lanin) -Ro 650
  Ca 8245. Ready for the River/(rev., Dixie Daisies)
  Ca 8349. My Blackbirds Are Bluebirds Now(3387)#∅ / (rev.,Mills Merry Makers) -Ro 772
  Ca 9008. Adorable Dora(3416)*/(rev., Ernest Carl) -Li 3037
  Ca 9022. I'll Get By(3518)∅ /(rev., Bob Haring) -Li 3051, Ro 826
  Ca 9023. She's Funny That Way(3517)*/(rev., Washingtonians) -Ro 827
              My Castle in Spain(3702)/(rev., Society Night Club Orch) -Ro 904
  Ca 9036. Gypsy/(rev., Whoopee Makers)
  Ca 9056. Dream Train/(rev., Dixie Daisies)
  Ca 9057. If I Had You(3610) -Ro 961
  Ca 9084. I Want to Be Bad
  Ca 9130. Honey(3773)*#/(rev., Home Towners) -Ro 932
              Down Among the Sugar Cane -Ro 942
  Ca 9152. Do Something(3837)*#∅ /(rev., Caroliners) -Ro 960
              Orange Blossom Time(3880)#/(rev., Al Alberts) -Ro 989
              I'm in Seventh Heaven(4010)*#∅ /(rev., Al Alberts) -Ro 1043
  Pat 36876. Don't Be Like That/Everybody Loves My Baby -Pe 15057
  Br 4119. I Must Have That Man/(rev., Fletcher Henderson)
  Br 4124. Maybe This Is Love/Pompanola
              (See also Whoopee Makers)

BROADWAY RASTUS (Frank Melrose, piano solos):
  Para 12764. Rock My Soul(21227-1)/Whoopee Stomp(21228-2)

BROOKS' (HARVEY) QUALITY FOUR (L. Herriford, Paul Howard, saxes; Harvey Brooks, piano; H. "Tincan" Allen, drums.--JI 8/9/40):
  Hollywood 1008. Mistreatin' Daddy/Frankie and Johnny
  Hollywood 1021. If You'll Come Back/Nobody's Sweetheart
  Hollywood 1022. Who Will Get It/Down on the Farm

BROWN, ADA (acc. by George Mitchell, trumpet; Luis Russell, piano; Albert Nicholas, clarinet and alto sax; Barney Bigard, tenor sax; banjo.--JI 12/20/40):
  Vo 1009. Panama Limited Blues/Tia Juana Man

(Acc. by Bennie Moten's Orchestra):
  OK 8101. Evil Mama Blues(8458a)/Break o' Day Blues(8462a)
  OK 8123. Ill Natured Blues/(rev., Mary Bradford)

(Acc. by piano):
  OK 8694. Crazy 'bout My Lollypop/Down Home Dance

YOUR HELP IS NEEDED

No one person could profess to be an expert on all the records which will be inclosed in this list in its final form. There are many gaps in personnels; data are missing altogether on hundreds of records. This is only the basic list; the rest is up to collectors, all of whom are asked to share in perfecting a complete and accurate index to jazz. Send your corrections and additions to Orin Blackstone, 1016 Eleonore Street, New Orleans 15, Louisiana.

PAGE NO.	RECORDING GROUP	LABEL	SERIAL NUMBER	WAS SHOWN:	SHOULD HAVE BEEN SHOWN:

PAGE NO.	RECORDING GROUP	LABEL	SERIAL NUMBER	WAS SHOWN:	SHOULD HAVE BEEN SHOWN:

BROWN, ALBERTA:
   Co 14321. How Long/Lonely Blues

BROWN, AMANDA:
   PatA 032035. Got the World in a Jug/Do Right Blues

(Acc. by Porter Grainger, piano):
   Co A3876. Laughin' Cryin' Blues/Strut Long Papa
   Co A3921. M'chigan Water Blues/Tired o' Waitin' Blues

(Acc. by Fletcher Henderson, piano):
   Co A3901. Chirpin' the Blues/Tr'flin' Blues

BROWN, BESSIE
   Pe 12235. Papa De Da Da/Them Has Benn Blues
   Co 14029. Hoodoo Blues/How Can I Get It
   Br 3817. Chloe/Somebody Else May Be There
   Br 3922. Sm'le/Blue Ridge
   Br 4346. The Blues Singer from Alabam'/Ta'n't Nobody's Fault But My Own
   Br 4409. He Just Don't Appeal to Me/Song from a Cotton Field(acc.by jazz orch)

BESSIE BROWN AND GEORGE WILLIAMS (acc. by Fletcher Henderson, piano):
   Co A3974. Double Crossing Daddy/Satisfied Blues

BROWN, BILL (blues, acc. by trumpet, piano, banjo):
   Vs 6064. Goin' Away and Leavin' My Baby(15712)

BROWN, BILL AND HIS BROWNIES:
   Br 7003. Bill Brown Blues(86)   -Vo 1128
   "   Hot Lips(90)

   Br 7142. Zonky/What Kind of Rhythm Is That?

BROWN, CLEO (Cleo Brown, piano; Perry Botkin, guitar; Artie Bernstein, bass; Gene Krupa, drums.--HD):
   De   409. Lookie Look'e Here Comes Cookie/I'll Take the South   -BrE 02013
   De "410. Stuff Is Here and It's Mellow   -De 3683, BrE 02021
   "   You're a Heavenly Thing

(Piano solos):
   De   477. Boogie Woogie(with vocal)/Pelican Stomp

(Cleo Brown, piano;Mike McKendrick,guitar;Leonard Bibbs,bass; Gene Krupa, drums):
   De "486. Me and My Wonderful One   -BrE 02047
   "   Give a Broken Heart a Break   -BrE 02049
   De "512. Never Too Tired to Love   -BrE 02049
   "   Mama Don't Want No Peas and Rice   -BrE 02047

(Cleo Brown, piano; Bob Sherwood, guitar; Manny Stein, bass; Vic Berton, drums):
   De   632. When Hollywood Goes Black and Tan/When   -BrE 02123
   De   713. Breakin' in a New Pa'r of Shoes/You're My Fever -BrE 02147
   De   795. Latch On/Slow Poke   -BrE 02186
   De   846. Love in the First Degree/My Gal Mezzanine   -BrE 02271
   De 3386. Pinetop's Boogie Woogie (piano solo)

BROWN, ELIZA (cornet and piano acc.):
   Co 14471. Peddlin' Man/If Papa Has Outside Lovin'

BROWN, HENRY (piano solos):
   Para 12825. Henry Brown Blues(1425)/21st St.Stomp(1424).Ike Rodgers,trom.-Sig 909
   Para 12934. Blues Stomp(178),Ike Rodgers trombone/Blind Boy Blues(179)
   Para 12988. Deep Morgan Blues(180)/Eastern Chimes Blues(190)
   Br   7086. Stomp 'em Down to the Bricks/(rev., Rogers Biddle Street Boys)
        (See also: Edith Johnson, Para 12823; Mary Johnson, Br 7081; Alice
        Moore, Para 12868, Robert Peeples, Para 12995, Ike Rodgers,Para 12816)

BROWN, HI HENRY (blues):
   Vo 1692. Nut Factory Blues/Skin Man

BROWN, IDA:
   Ba 1343. Kiss Me Sweet/Jailhouse Blues

BROWN, JOE AND HIS BAND:
   De 8521. Red Bank Romp(68433)/Beaumont Street Blues(68434)

BROWN'S (JOE) ALABAMA BAND:
   BS 2041. Sal-o-may/How Many Times

BROWN, KITTY (acc. by piano):
    OK 8052. Ev'l Blues/(rev., Lizzie Miles)
    OK 8053. Mean Eyes(s71275),with Ricketts' Stars/(rev., Esther Bigeou)
    OK 8077. Deceitful Blues/I Don't Let No One Man Worry Me

KITTY BROWN AND LEROY MORTON (Piano and clarinet acc.):
    Para 12223. He's Never Gonna Throw Me Down(1782)/Keep on Going(1783)

BROWN, LEE (acc. by Henry Allen, trumpet, and others):
    De 7710. Rolling Stone/Howling Man Blues
    De 7775. Little Leg Woman/Lucille Blues

(trumpet, piano and bass):
    De 7726. Ripley Rumbling Blues/Midnight Dream

BROWN, LES AND HIS DUKE BLUE DEVILS (Les Brown, clarinet; Joe Gandreau,Herb Muse, altos; Dutch McMillan, Gus Brannon, tenors; Bob Thorne, William Irwin,Jack Atkins, trumpets: Joe Pilato, trombone; Coon Plyler, piano; Stacey McKee, guitar;Don Kramer, drums; Ken Dutton, bass):
    De   991. Papa Treetop Tall/Swing for Sale
    De 1231. Dance of the Blue Devils(62045)/Swamp Fire(62047)
    De 1238. Don't You Go Worryin' About Judgement Day/Rigamarole
    De 1296. Ramona/Don't You Care What Anyone Says
    De 1323. Feather Your Nest/Lazy River
    De 2045. Mutiny on the Band Stand/When You Wore a Tulip
    De 3155. Comanche War Dance/Mellow Bit of Rhythm
    De 3167. Love Your Magic Spell Is Everywhere/Walkin' and Swingin'

LES BROWN AND HIS ORCHESTRA:
    BB 7812. With You on My Mind/Why
    BB 7858. Star Dust/Boogie Woogie
    BB 10017. This Can't Be Love/Sing for Your Supper
    BB 10026. When Day Is Done/Sobbin' Blues
    BB 10114. Lightly and Politely/Darling Nelly Gray
    BB 10174. Duck Foot Waddle/Plumber's Revenge
    BB 10211. Out of the Night/Love for Sale
    BB 10226. Shangri-La/Love Your Magic Spell Is Everywhere
    BB 10314. Perisphere Shuffle/Trylon Stomp
    BB 10421. Cirib'irib'in/Oh Marie
    BB 10551. I've Got My Eyes on You/I Concentrate on You
    BB 10558. The Man Who Comes Around/That Old Gang of Mine
    BB 10787. Papoose/Rocket Ship to Mars
    BB 10827. Gravediggers Holiday/Blue Divel Jazz

(Bob Thorne, Eddie Bailey, Les Kriz, trumpets; Si Aentner, Ronnie Chase, Warren Brown, trombones; Steve Madrick, Wolffe Tennenbaum, Herb Muse, Eddie Scheer, Les Brown, saxes; Billy Rowland, piano; Joe Petrone, guitar; Johnny Knapper,bass;Eddie Julian, drums.--JRB):   1941
    OK 5937. Let's Be Buddies/Three at a Table for Two
    OK 5964. While the Music Plays On/Dig It
    OK 6011. Anvil Chorus/Between Friends
    OK 6049. Barbara Allen/Broomstreet
    OK 6085. Boogie Woogie Piggy/Little Miss Irish
    OK 6099. Celery Stalks at Midnight/Beau Night in Hotchkiss Corners
    OK 6199. Marche Slav
    OK 6293. Funiculi Funicula/Procession of the Sardar
    OK 6323. As If You Didn't Know/All That Meat and No Potatoes
    OK 6367. You Again/City Called Heaven
    OK 6377. Joltin' Joe Di Maggio/Nickel Serenade
    OK 6414. Nothing/I Got It Bad
    OK 6633. Evening Star
    OK 6696. When the Lights Go On Again/Mexican Hat Dance
    Co 36603. Here You Are/Sweet Eloise
    Co 36688. A Good Man Is Hard to Find/Bizet Has His Day
    Co 36724. Out of Nowhere/Sunday

BROWN, ORA (vocal with Will Ezell, piano):
    Para 12500. Restless Blues(701)/Jailhouse Moan(702)

BROWN, PETE AND HIS BAND (Pete Brown, alto sax and trumpet; Benny Carter, trumpet and alto sax; Joe Marsala, clarinet;Billy Kyle, piano; Bobby Hackett,guitar; Cozy Cole, drums; Hayes Alvis, bass):
    De 18118. Ocean Motion(65440)/Tempo di Jump(65439)

(Dizzy Gillespie, trumpet; Jim Hamilton, clarinet; Pete Brown, alto;Sam Price, piano; Charlie Drayton, bass; Roy Nathan, drums; Helen Humes, vocal):
    De 8613. Mound Bayou/Unlucky Woman
    De 8625. Cannon Ball/Gonna Buy Me a Telephone

BROWN, SAMMY(possibly Cripple Clarence Lofton, blues singing with piano):
    Ge 6337. The Jockey Blues   -Ch 15436

BROWN AND TERRY JAZZOLA BOYS:
   OK 8006. The Hesitatin' Blues/Darktown Strutters Ball

BROWNE, ALTA and Bertha Powell (Negro spiritual with piano accompaniment by Thomas Waller):
   Ge 3318. Nobody Knows de Trouble I See/(rev., Elkins Negro Ensemble)

BROWNLEE'S ORCHESTRA OF NEW ORLEANS (Harry Shields, clarinet: Norman Brownlee,piano, Tom Brown, trombone; Sharkey Bonano, cornet; Alonzo Crumby, drums;Behrman French, Banjo):   New Orleans, 1924
   OK 40337. Peculiar(8900a)/Dirty Rag(8901a)

BRUN, PHILLIPPE AND HIS SWING BAND (Phillippe Brun, Gus Deloof, Andre Cornille, trumpets; Jesse Breyere, Guy Paquinet, trombones; Max Blanc, Alix Combelle, Chas. Lisee, J. Helian, saxes; Stephane Grappelly, piano; Django Rheinhardt,guitar;Louis Vola, bass; Maurice Chaillou, drums):   Paris, 1937
   Sw   15. College Stomp/Harlem Swing
   Sw   26. Easy Going/Gabriel's Swing(Sub.Noel Chiboust,tenor sax,for Helian)

BRUNIES, ALBERT (ABBIE): See Halfway House Orchestra

BRUNIES, MERRITT AND HIS FRIARS INN ORCHESTRA (Merritt Brunies,Harry Brunies,trombone; Volly de Faut, clarinet and sax; Marty Freeman,piano;Bill Piley,drums.--HD):
                                                                                 1925
   Au   610. Angry/I Ween Over You
   Au   614. Up Jumped the Dev'l(85042)/Follow the Swallow(85043)
   OK 40526. Sugar Foot Stomp(9491a)/Want a Little Lovin'(9492b)   -OdG 60234
   OK 40576. Blue As the Blue Grass of Kentucky(9539a)/When Autumn Leaves are
   OK 40579. Flamin' Mamie(9541a)/Hangin' Around(9542a)   (Falling(9540b)
   OK 40593. Masculine Women! Feminine Men(9551a)/Someone's Stolen My Sweet Baby
                                                                            (9552a)
   OK 40618. Up Jumped the Dev'l(9549)   -OdG 60268

BRUNIS, GEORGE AND HIS JAZZ BAND (George Brunis, trombone;Wild Bill Davison,trumpet; Pee Wee Russell, clarinet; Eddie Condon, guitar; Gene Schroeder, Bob Casey, bass; George Wettling, drums):
   Com 546. Ugly Chile(a4680)/That Da Da Strain(a4682-2)

BRUNNER, EDDIE AND HIS ORCHESTRA (Bill Coleman, trumpet; Eddie Brunner, clarinet and tenor sax; Alix Combelle, Noel Chiboust, tenor saxes; Herman Chittison,piano; Oscar Alleman, guitar; Grasset, bass; Tommy Benford, drums.):   Paris, 1938
   Sw   30. I Double Dare You(osw28)/Montmarte Blues(osw30)
   Sw   41. Bagatelle(osw29)/Margie(osw31)

BRYANT, GLADYS (blues):
   Harmograph 2539. Darktown Flappers Ball/Triflin' Blues

(acc. by Porter Grainger, piano):
   Para 12026. Laughin' Crying Blues(1336)/You've Got to See Mama Every Night(1337)

(acc. by Henderson's Orchestra):
   Para 12031. Beale Street Mama/Tired o' Waiting Blues

BRYANT, JIMMY (See O'Bryant, Jimmy)

BRYANT, LAURA (acc. by Clarence Williams Orchestra):
   QRS ----. Dentist Chair Blues, I & II (322/3)

BRYANT, WILLIE AND HIS ORCHESTRA (Bobby Cheek, Richard Clark, Edward Battle, trumpets; John Haughton, Robert Horton, trombones; Glyn Pacque, Stanley Payne,alto saxes; Johnny Russell, Ben Webster, tenor saxes; Teddy Wilson, piano; Arnold Adams, guitar; Lou's Thompson, bass: Cozy Cole, drums; Willie Bryant, vocals,-HD):1934-35
   Vi 24847. Throwin' Stones at the Sun(87265)   -HMV JF-27
   "   Chimes at the Meetin'(87268)   -HMV X4476
   Vi 24858. It's Over Because We're Through   -HMV X4453
             A Viper's Moan   -HMV JF-27
   Vi 25038. Rigamarole(89817)   -HMV JF-29
             The Sheik(89819)   -HMV B8390,
   Vi 25045. Long About Midnight(89810)/Jerry the Junker'89820)   -HMV JF-37

(Add Benny Carter, trumpet):
   Vi 25129. Voice of Old Man River(92908)/Long Gone(92910)   -HMV JF-50
   Vi 25160. Steak and Potatoes(92909)/Liza(92911)   -HMV JF-52

(Sub. Jack Butler, Taft Jordan, trumpets, for Battle, Cheek; George Mathews, trombone, for Horton; Charles Fraser, sax, for Webster; Roger Ramirez, piano, for Wilson; omit Carter; Ernest Hill, bass, for Thompson):

```
     BB   6361. All My Life/The Right Somebody to Love
     BB   6362. Is It True What They Say About Dixie?/Moonrise on the Lowlands
     BB   6374. The Glory of Love
                Ride Red Ride                                    -HMV B8452.
     BB   6435. Mary Had a Little Lamb/Cross Patch
     BB   6436. I Like Bananas/I'm Grateful to You
     De   1772. Neglected/On the Alamo
     De   1881. You're Gonna Lose Your Gal/You'll Never Remember

BUBBLING OVER FIVE:
     OK  8737. Get Up off That Jazzophone/Don't Mistreat Your Good Boy Friend

BUCK (of Buck & Bubbles; piano solo):
     Co  2925. Old Fashioned Love/(rev., Joe Sullivan)

BUCKTOWN FIVE (Muggsy Spanier, cornet; Guy Garry, trombone; Volly de Faut, clari-
net; Mel Stitzel, piano; Marvin Saxbey, banjo.--JI 10/24/39):
     Ge  5405. Mobile Blues(11767)/Someday Sweetheart(11772)
     Ge  5418. Chicago Blues(11769)/Buddy's Habits(11771)
     Ge  5419. Steady Roll Blues(11766)/Really a Pain(11768)
     Ge  5518. Hot Mittens(11770)/rev., Happy Harmonists)            Cx 40353
                (See also Stomp Six)

BUFFALODIANS:
     Co   665. Deep Henderson/Here Comes Emaline
     Co   723. She's Still My Baby/Would Ja?

BUGLE CALL RAGGERS
     Ch 40063. New Jig Rhythm/Temptation Rag

BUMBLE BEE SLIM AND HIS THREE SHARKS:
     Vo 02773. Lost Confidence Blues/Wrecked Life Blues

BUMBLE BEE SLIM (acc. by Cripple Clarence Lofton,piano.--JI 1/24/41):
     Vo 02995. If the Blues Was Whiskey(c952)/Bricks in My Pillow(c950)
     Vo 03090. Policy Dream Blues(c951)/Big 80 Blues(c949)

BUMBLE BEE SLIM AND HIS RHYTHM RIFFERS:
     De  7121. I'll Take You Back(90305)/Sick and Tired to Singing the Blues(90306)

BUNCH, FRANK AND HIS FUZZY WUZZIES (trumpet, trombone, piano, clarinet, alto sax,
banjo, drums.):                                                            1927
     Ge  6293. Fourth Avenue Stomp/Congo Stomp

BUNN, TEDDY and Spencer Williams (guitar and piano with washboard and singing):
     Vi 23253. Tampa Twirl/Chicken and the Worm
     Vi 38592. Pattin' the Cat/It's Sweet Like So
     Vi 38602. Goose and Gander/Clean It Out
     Vi 38617. The New Goose and Gander/Blow It up

TEDDY BUNN,(guitar solos):
     BN   503. King Porter Stomp(rs713a)/Bachelor Blues(rs714a), with vocal
     BN   504. Blues Without Words(rs715b), with voacl/Guitar in High(rs716a)

BURKE, SONNY AND HIS ORCHESTRA (Bill Nichols, Paul Petrilla, John Forys,Max Krist-
man, Sam Donahue, saxes; Harry Gozzard, Bernie Mitchell, Al Sharaf, trumpets; Ken
Meisel, Ken Gaughey, trombones; Wayne Herdell, piano; John Jordan, guitar; Walter
Sherman, bass; Harold Hahn, drums):
     Vo  5139. The Last Jam Session(wc2688)/Tea for Two(wc2689)
     Vo  5397. If It Wasn't for the Moon/Easy Does It
     Vo  5459. Pick-a-Rib(25912)/I Never Purposely Hurt You(25913)

(omit Donahue; sub. Mitchell Paul, Louis LaRose,trumpets, for Mitchell, Sharaf):
     OK  5813. Jimmie Meets the Count(wc3275)/Blue Sonata(wc3278)
     OK  5873. Can I Be Sure(wc3276)/Carry Me Back to Old Virginny(wc3277)
     OK  5955. The Count Basically(28785)/More Than You Know(28786)
     OK  5989. Jumpin' Salty/Minor de Luxe

BURLESON, HATTIE (vocal with jazz band):
     Br  7042. Sadie's Servant Room Blues/Superstitious Blues
     Br  7054. Bye Bye Baby/Jim Nappy

BURNS, JEAN (vocal with Adrian's Tap Room Gang):
     BrE 02095. Monotony His Got Me Down/You're An Angel
     BrE 02342. Clownin' Around/Get the Gold

BURSE, CHARLIE AND HIS MEMPHIS MUDCATS:
     Vo 05070. It Makes No Difference Now/Memphis Highway Stomp
     Vo 05123. Magic Spell Blues(mem161)/Ain't Gonna Be No Doggone Afterwhile(m166)
```

```
Vo 05192. Scared to Death/It's Against the Rule
Vo 05299. What's the Matter With the Well/Good Potatoes on the Hill
Vo 05393. Brand New Day Blues/Too Much Beef
Vo 05551. Dawn of Day Blues/You Better Watch Out
```

BURSTON, CLARA (blues with piano):
```
Para 13003. Beggin' Man Blues/C.P. Blues
```

BUSHKIN, JOE (piano solos):
```
Com 532. Serenade in Thirds(r2957)/I Can't Get Started(r2958)
Com 534. Blue Chips(r2959)/In a Little Spanish Town(r2960)
```

BUSHKIN AND WILLIE The Lion SMITH (piano duets):
```
Com 520. The Lion and the Lamb/Three Keyboards (Jess Stacy, piano, added)
```

BUTLER, MARY
```
Br 7046. Bungalow Blues/Mary Blues
Br 7049. Electric Chair Blues/Mad Dog Blues
```

BUTTERBEANS AND SUSIE (vocal duets with Clarence Williams, piano, except as noted):
```
OK 8147. When My Man Shimmies(s72573b)/Get Yourself a Monkey Man(s72581b)
OK 8163. Construction Gang(s72817), Joe Oliver, cornet/A to Z Blues(s72820)
OK 8180. A Married Man's a Fool(s72574b),Butterbeans/I Can't Use You(s72821b)
OK 8182. Kiss Me Sweet(s72816b),Joe Oliver,cornet/(rev., Susie Edwards)
```

(Next eight sides with Eddie Heywood, piano):
```
OK 8192. Adam and Eve(8859a)/Consolation Blues(8861a)
OK 8199. That Same Dog/How Do You Expect to Get My Living?
OK 8202. Leaving Blues/Do Right Papa
OK 8209. I've Had Those Lonesome Journey Blues/Sue I Don't Want You No More

OK 8219. Brown Skin Gal(s73385b)/Hydrant Love(s73386b)
OK 8224. I'll Put You Under the Jail/If You Can't Bring It You've Got to Send
OK 8233. Don't Start Nothin'Here Tonight(Heywood)/You Ain't Talkin' To Me (It
OK 8241. Cold Storage Papa(s73452b)/Bow Legged Papa(s73453a)
OK 8303. Let the Door Knob Hit You/Your Folks Will Wear Black
OK 8307. Not Until Then, I & II
OK 8319. Mama Stayed Out the Whole Night Long/Tain't What You Used to Have
OK 8323. Love Me and the World Is Mine(Heywood)/Deacon Bite 'em in the Back
OK 8335. Not Today Sweet Mama/You Know Why       (Butterbeans & Grasshopper)
```

(First title below acc. by Armstrong Hot Five):
```
OK 8355. He Likes It Slow(9750a)/I Can't Do That(9749a), Lovie Austin, piano
```

(Eddie Heywood, piano; Robert Cheek, trumpet):
```
OK 8392. My Daddy's Got the Mojo but I Got the Say So&74357a)/Da Da Blues
OK 8432. Hard Luck Blues(74435a), Heywood)/Yes I've Been Cheatin(74436a) (74358b)
OK 8502. You're a No Account Triflin' Man/Oh Yeah!
OK 8520. Deal Yourself Another Hand(81475)/Jelly Roll Queen(81476)
OK 8556. Gonna Make You Sorry(81065),Heywood Trio/Tain't None o'Your Business
OK 8598. Watch Your Step/Been Some Changes Made              (81474)
OK 8614. I Ain't Scard of You(400958)/Fast Fadin' Papa(400959)
OK 8687. Get Yourself a Monkey Man/Get Away from My Window
OK 8701. Gonna Start Looking for a Man/Put Your Mind Right on It
OK 8769. Ain't Gonna Do That No More/Better Stop Knockin' Me Around
OK 8833. Elevator Papa Switchboard Mama/Times Is Hard
OK 8893. Broke Down Mama(480044),Heywood Harmony Sons/You Dirty Mistreater
OK 8950. Papa Ain't No Santa Claus/What It Takes to Bring You (480043),Heywood
```

BUTTERFIELD, ERSKINE AND HIS BLUE BOYS (Bill Graham, trumpet; Rolard DuPont, trombone; Sid Stoneburn, clarinet; Erskine Butterfield, piano; Frank Victor, guitar; Harry Clarke, bass; Sam Weiss, drums.--JRB):   1940
```
De 3042. Salt Butter/Tuxedo Junction
De 3043. Darn That Dream(67219)/Inconvenience(67222)
```

(Sub. Al Philburn, trombone; Sal Franzella, clarinet; Haig Stephens, bass; O'Neil Spencer, drums):
```
De 3209. Your Feet's Too Big/What's Cookin'?
De 3252. Down Home Blues/Nothin' to Do
```

(Sub. Stoneburn, clarinet; Vic Engle, drums):
```
De 3356. Boogie Woogie St. Louis Blues/Chocolate
De 3357. Pushin' the Conversation Along/Don't Leave Me Now
De 4360. Sleepy Town Train/You Made Me Care
De 4400. Birmingham Special/Jumpin' in a Julep Joint
```

(Jimmy Lytell, clarinet; Butterfield, piano; Carl Kress, guitar;Stephens,Weiss)1941
```
De 8510. Beale Street Mama(68354)/Whatcha Know Joe(68355)
De 8524. Stayin' at Home/Jivin' the Missouri Waltz
De 8539. All the Time/Paradiddle Joe
```

BIG NEWS

from

BASIN STREET

DOWN where jazz was born, things are happening NOW! Organized in the summer of 1944, the NATIONAL JAZZ FOUNDATION invites you to be among the first to share in a movement of prime importance to jazz enthusiasts everywhere.

Its purpose is to establish a National Museum of Jazz, to preserve and develop the history of jazz, to immortalize its creators, to foster and encourage contemporary jazzmen and their music.

You may become a sustaining member NOW by sending in the coupon below—or you may write for brochure with complete details. If you are a member of a jazz club in your community, have it affiliated with the Foundation. WRITE US TODAY!

NATIONAL JAZZ FOUNDATION, INC.
610 HIBERNIA BLDG.,   NEW ORLEANS 12, LA.

Here is my check for $3.00, for sustaining membership during the fiscal year 1944-45.

Name _____

Address _____

(Yank Lawson, Don Lipson, trumpets; Moe Zudecoff, trombone; Jerry Jerome, clarinet;
Tony Gottuse, guitar: piano, bass, drums same):
    De 8543. Blackberry Jam/Monday's Wash
    De 8551. Because of You/You Might Have Belonged to Another

(Graham, trumpet; Lytell, clarinet: Carmen Mastren, guitar; piano, bass, drums same):
    De 8552. I Dreamt I Dwelt in Harlem(69077)/Jelly Jelly(69079)
    De 8569. You Should Live So Long/Foo-Gee
    De 8576. Cheatin' on Me/You Done Lost Your Good Thing Now
    De 8588. Honey Dear(69859)/I Was a Fool to Let You Go(69860)
    De 8596. Mama Long and Tall/If Money Grew on Trees
    De 8600. The Devil Sat Down and Cried/Boogie de Concerto
    De 8620. Lovin' Man/Crazy Blues

C

CAHN-CHAPLIN ORCHESTRA:
    Ch 40112. You/All My Life
    Ch 40113. Christopher Columbus(60982)/Rhythm Saved the World(61056)

CALDWELL, HAPPY (tenor sax and clarinet, see:
    HENRY ALLEN: Vo 3244, 3245;
    LOUIS ARMSTRONG: OK 8703.
    BUSTER BAILEY
    JACK BLAND: Pe 15689, 15694;
    TINY BRADSHAW
    EDDIE CONDON: Vi 38046.
    LIONEL HAMPTON
    MEZZ MEZZROW: Vi 25636, 25612.
    BUBBER MILEY
    THOMAS MORRIS
    KING OLIVER
    CLARENCE WILLIAMS
    BERNIE YOUNG: Para 12088.

CALIFORNIA RAMBLERS (Collective personnel for 1923-1925 period: Ed Kirkeby, leader;
Arthur Hand, violin; Arnold Brillhardt, Bobby Davis, Jimmy Dorsey, Pete Pumiglio,
Fred Cusick, Fud Livingston, sax and clarinet; Adrian Rollini, Spencer Clark, bass
sax; Red Nichols, Frank Cush, Bill More, Roy Johnstone, Chelsea Qualey, trumpets;
Tommy Dorsey, trombone; Tommy Felline, banjo and guitar; Irving Brodsky, Jack Rusin,
piano; Stan King, Herbert Weil, drums, --RR):
    Co A3554. Smilin'(80126)/Bow Wow Blues(80136)
    Co A3635. Swanee Blue Bird(80326)/No Use Crying(80327)
    Co A3956. My Sweetie Went Away(81129)/I Love Me(81130)
    Co A3979. Louisville/That Big Blond Mama
    Co A3986. You've Got Me/If I Can't Get the Sweetie I Want
    Co A3994. Sittin' in a Corner/Tell All the Folks in Kentucky
    Co   9. Melancholy   -CoE 3391
    "   You Darling You   -CoE 3377
    Co   15. Moonlight Kisses/What Do You
    Co   39. Roamin' to Wyomin'(81355)   -CoE 3411
    "   Kaintucky(81363)   -CoE 3389
    Co   43. Arcady/(rev., Al Jolson)
    Co   49. Remembering/Linger Awhile
    Co   91. On Such a Night/Take a Little Step
    Co 103. Two Blues Eyes   -CoE 3404
    "   Monavanna
    Co 105. Lazy/I Must Have Company
    Co 127. Shine/It Had to Be You
    Co 153. You Know Me, Alabama/Where the Dreamy Wabash Flows
    Co 171. Charleston Cabin
    "   Please   -CoE 3537
    Co 179. Charley My Boy/Big Boy
    Co 199. Susquehanna Home/I Want to Be Happy
    Co 218. Back Where the Daffodils Grow/When I Was the Dandy
    Co 223. Eliza/I Want to See My Tennessee
    Co 236. Copenhagen(140115)/Gotta Getta Girl(140116)   -CoE 3555
    Co 249. Those Panama Mamas/Prince of Wails
    Co 278. Where's My Sweetie Hiding
    Co 293. Lady Be Good/Swanee Butterfly
    Co 340. Just a Little Drink/Dromedary
    Co 380. Sweet Georgia Brown/Everything Is Hotsy Totsy Now
    Co 419. Sonya/I'm Gonna Charleston Back to Charleston
    Co 449. I'm So in Love With You/Moon Deer
    Co 522. Show Me the Way to Go Home(141355)/Then I'll Be Happy(141350)

```
Co      527. Smile a Little Bit/Dreaming of a Castle in the Air
Co      610. I'd Climb the Highest Mountain/Under the Ukelele Tree
Co      638. No Foolin'/The Girl Friend                               -CoE 4461
Co      669. Ya Gotta Know How to Love/I'm Just Wild About Animal Crackers
Co      704. Me Too/She Belongs to Me
Co      834. Tell Me Tonight(143174)/Too Many Kisses in the Summer(143175)
Co      883. Stockholm Stomp(143234)/I Love the College Girls(143317) -CoE 4369
Co      992. Yes She Do/Pardon the Glove                              -CoE 4708
Co     1014. Pick Me Up and Lay Me Down/In Dear Old Dixieland
Co     1016. California
Co     1038. Lazy Weather/Vo-De-Do-De-o blues
Co     1148. Nothing Does Like It Used to Do/It Was Only a Sun Shower
Co     1275. Changes/Mine All Mine                                    -CoE 4876
Co     1314. What Do You Say(145516)/Singapore Sorrows(145529)
Co     1411. Anything to Make You Happy(145631)/Whisper Sweet and Low(146285)
Co     1504. Adoree/Who Wouldn't Be Blue
Co     1574. You're Just a Great Big Baby Doll(146439)/Bless You Sister(146818)
Co     1642. The Pay Off/(rev., Jan Garber)
Co     2208. I'm Needin' You(150423)/Washin' the Blues from My Soul(150424)
Co     2231. F'r Instance/I Love You So Much
Co     2351. The Peanut Vendor/Twenty Swedes Ran Through the Weeds
Co     2397. The King's Horses/Sleepy Town Express
Co     2569. Concentratin'/When I Wore My Daddy's Brown Derby
CoE    3404. Maybe
CoE    3410. Rememb'ring
CoE    3542. Charley My Boy
CoE    4793. Make My Cot
Para  20227. I Love Me/Who's Sorry Now
*Re    9740. Romany Days
Do     4011. Beale Street Blues/(rev., Missouri Jazz Band)
Do     4014. Delirium/Farewell Blues
Im     1385. Southern Rose
Pat    1597. Blue/Dancing Fool
PatA  11387. Them Ramblin' Blues
PatA  11571. Cause I Feel Low Down
Max    1519. Look at What I Got Now/I Want to Be Happy
Max    1520. Tessie Stop Teasing Me
Sa        8. Is She My Girl Friend?
Sa       37. Somebody Loves Me
Sa       85. Montmarte
Sa      114. Isn't She the Sweetest Thing?
Sa      166. Sonya/Alone at Last
Sa      168. Footloose
Sa      149. Ain't My Baby Grand?
Sa      283. Show Me the Way to Go Home
Sa      709. Are You Happy?
Sa      722. Vo-De-Do-De-O Blues
Vo    14275. Georgia Rose/The Sheik of Araby
Vo    14300. Eddie Leonard Blues/My Mammy Knows
Vo    14329. My Honey's Lovin' Arms/Who Believed in You
Vo    14384. Hot Lips/Nobody Lied
Vo    14411. Stuttering/I Wish I Knew                                 -Ae 1106
Vo    14436. Sister Kate/Lonesome Mama Blues                          -Ae 1106
Bell    319. Blue Eyed Sally/Where's My Sweetie Hiding
Arto   9138. Boo Hoo Hoo/California
Pu    11102. Granny/My Mammy Knows
Tri   11256. Down by the River/Trot Along
Em    10518. Lola Lo/(rev., Glantz)

(Group from Adrian's Tan Room Gang):
BB     6076. Simple Things in Life/Rhythm and Romance
BB     6077. Just We Two/(rev., Little Ramblers)
BB     6078. From the Top of Your Head/Without a Word of Warning
BB     6083. It's My Night to Howl
BB     6145. Thunder Over Paradise
BB     6156. Where Am I?/You Let Me Down
BB     6173. How Do I Rate With You?/You Took My Breath Away
BB     6189. With All My Heart/(rev., Little Ramblers)
BB     6190. I'll Never Forget I Love You/Beautiful Lady in Blue
BB     6191. I Feel Like a Feather in the Breeze/(rev., Little Ramblers)
BB     6238. Cling to Me/(rev., Little Ramblers)
BB     6239. So This Is Heaven
BB     6240. Hypnotized
BB     6253. It's Been So Long/Life Begins When You're In Love
BB     6254. Sing an Old Fashioned Song/Gotta Go to Work Again

(Charles Barnet, Dave Cotwals, Joe Estron,Kurt Bloom,Henry Galtman,saxes;Art Lom-
bardi,Frank Borati,Al Stuart,trumpets; Bob Fishel,Jimmy Curri,trombones; Tom Mor-
ganelli,guitar; Bob Elden,bass; Buddy Schutz,drums;John Niccolini, piano):
Vr      577. Down South Camp Meeting/Take My Word
Vr      603. Swingin' Down to Rio/Chris and His Gang
```

CALL, BOB (piano):
   Br 7137. Thirty-one Blues/(rev., Speckled Red)

(Piano acc. to Elzadie Robinson):
   Para 12573. St. Louis Cyclone/Santa Claus Crave

CALLICOTT, JOE (Vocal blues):
   Br 7166. Fare Thee Well Blues/Traveling Mama Blues

CALLOWAY, BLANCHE (acc. by Louis Armstrong,cornet; Richard M.Jones, piano):
   OK 8279. Lazy Woman's Blues(9458a)/Lonesome Lovesick(9459a)

BLANCHE CALLOWAY AND HER JOY BOYS (Andy Kirk's Clouds of Joy: Mary Lou Williams,
piano; Floyd Brady, trombone; Harry Lawson, Clarence Smith, Edgar Battle, trum-
pets; Lawrence Freeman, John Williams, John Harrington, saxes; Ben Thigpen,drums;
Andy Kirk,bass; Bill Dirvin,banjo; Billy Massey and Blanche Calloway,vocals,--DB
1/1/41):   1931
   Vi 22640. Casey Jones/(rev., McKinney Cotton Pickers)
   Vi 22641. There's Rhythm in the River
          " All I Need Is Lovin'   -BB 5334
   Vi 22659. Loveless Love/Getting Myself Ready for You
   Vi 22661. Sugar Blues   -BB 5334

(Unknown accompaniment):
   Vi 22717. It's Right Here for You/Misery
   Vi 22733. It Looks Like Susie/Without That Gal
   Vi 22736. Make Me Know It/(rev., McKinney Cotton Pickers)
   Vi 22866. Growling Dan/I Got What It Takes
   Vi 22896. Blue Memories/(rev., Julia Gerrity)
   Vi 22862. Concentratin' on You/Last Dollar
   Me 13191. I Need Lovin'/What's a Poor Girl Gonna Do?
   Me 13271. Catch On?/Growlin' Dan
   Vo 3112. I Gotta Swing/Louisiana Liza
   Vo 3113. Line-a Jive/You Ain't Livin' Right

CALLOWAY'S HOT SHOTS
   Vi 24037. Why Don't You Get Lost?/Sweet Birds

CALLOWAY, CAB AND HIS ORCHESTRA (R.Q.Dickerson,Lamar Wright,Reuben Reeves, trum-
pets; DePriest Wheeler, Harry White, trombones; William Blue, Andrew Brown, Wal-
ter Thomas, saxes; Jimmie Prince, piano; Charley Stamps, banjo; Smith, bass; Le-
Roy Maxey, drums.--HD):
   Br 6020. Some of These Days(35880) -Br 80017, Me 12639, BrE 01088,BrF 500094
          " Is That Religion
   Br 6074. Minnie the Moocher(36212)-Br 6511,Br 80015,Me 12887,BrE 1339, BrF 9036
          " Doin'the Rhumba(36213)   -Pe 15853, Me 12853, Or 2801,BrF 9036
   Br 6105. Nobody's Sweetheart(35881)
                 -Br 80018, Me 70605, Ba 33074, Me 13038, Pe 15941, BrF 9083, BrE 1161
          " St. James Infirmary(35882) -Br 80018, Me 70605,
   Br 6141. Black Rhythm(36803)/Six or Seven Times(36804) -Me 12695, BrE 01294,
                                                                      (BrF 500150
   Br 6196. You Rascal You(37221)   -Br 80017, BrF 500421
          " Bugle Call Rag(37220)   -Br 80016, Me 12802, BrE 1339, BrF 500150
   Br 6209. Between the Devil and the Deep Blue Sea   -BrE 1254, BrF 500172
          " Kickin'Gong Around(37268)
                 -Br 6511,80015, Ba 32945, Me 12888, BrE 1417, BrF 500172
   Br 6214. Trickeration/Ain't Got No Gal   -Pe 15727, Me 12609, BrE 1263
   Br 6272. The Scat Song/Cabin in the Cotton   -BrE 1313, BrF 500173
   Br 6292. Aw You Dog/Strictly Cullud Affair   BrF 9253
   Br 6321. Angeline(11913)   -Pe 15853, Or 2801, Me 12853, BrE 1387
          " Minnie the Moocher's Wedding Day   -BrE 1673, BrF 500421
(Sub. Adolphus Cheatham, Edwin Swayzee, trumpets, for Reeves, Dickerson, Arville
Harris, sax, for Blue; Bennie Payne, piano, for Prince;Al Morgan, bass; Morris
White, guitar):
   Br 6340. Reefer Man(11923)   -Me 12887, BrF 9301, BrE 1387
          " You Gotta Ho-De-Ho (11925)
                 -Pe 15873, Ba 32945, Me 12887, BrF 9301, BrE 1643
   Br 6400. Hot Toddy(12340)   -BrF 500195,BrE 1417
          " Old Yazoo(11912)
   Br 6424. Harlem Holiday   -Pe 15941, Me 13038, BrF 9339, BrE 01542
          " I've Got the World on a String
   Br 6435. Dixie Doorway(12550)/Wa-dee-dah(12586) -Or 2727, Ro 2100, Pe 15791
   Br 6450. Man from Harlem(12673)   -Me 12802, BrF 500386, BrE 1439
          " My Sunday Gal(12675)   BrE 1490
   Br 6460. I Gotta Right to Sing the Blues   -BrF 500420, BrE 1439
          " That's What I Hate About Love   -BrE 1490
   Br 6473. Sweet Rhythm   -BrE 1422
          " I Gotta Go Places and Do Things   -BrF 500355, BrE 1574

The Finest in Hot Jazz

BLUE NOTE

For Complete Catalog Write to
BLUE NOTE RECORDS
767 LEXINGTON AVENUE, NEW YORK CITY

BLUE NOTE
PRESENTS

PORT OF HARLEM SEVEN

SIDNEY BECHET ....Soprano Sax and Clarinet
FRANK NEWTON ....Trumpet
J. C. HIGGINBOTHAM....Trombone
MEADE "LUX" LEWIS........Piano
TEDDY BUNN ....Guitar
JOHN WILLIAMS ....Bass
SIDNEY CATLETT ....Drums

PETE JOHNSON BLUES TRIO

PETE JOHNSON ....Piano
ABE BOLAR ....Bass
ULYSSES LIVINGSTON.....Guitar

SIDNEY BECHET'S BLUE NOTE QUARTET

SIDNEY BECHET ....Clarinet and Soprano Sax
SIDNEY CATLETT ....DRUMS
TEDDY BUNN ....Guitar
GEORGE "POP" FOSTER.....Bass

EDMOND HALL CELESTE QUARTET

EDMOND HALL ....Clarinet
MEADE "LUX" LEWIS.......Piano
CHARLES CHRISTIAN......Guitar
ISRAEL CROSBY ....Bass

EDMOND HALL'S ALL STAR QUINTET

EDMOND HALL ....Clarinet
RED NORVO ....Vibraphone
JOHN WILLIAMS ....Bass
TEDDY WILSON ....Piano
CARL KRESS ....Guitar

EDMOND HALL'S BLUE NOTE JAZZ MEN

EDMOND HALL ....Clarinet
SIDNEY DE PARIS.........Trumpet
VIC DICKENSON ....Trombone
SIDNEY CATLETT ....Drums
JAMES P. JOHNSON........Piano
ARTHUR SHIRLEY ....Guitar
ISRAEL CROSBY ....Bass

JAMES P. JOHNSON'S BLUE NOTE JAZZ MEN

SIDNEY DE PARIS.........Trumpet
VIC DICKENSON ....Trombone
BEN WEBSTER ....Tenor Sax
SIDNEY CATLETT ....Drums
JAMES P. JOHNSON........Piano
ARTHUR SHIRLEY ....Guitar
JOHN SIMMONS ....Bass

ART HODES' BLUE NOTE JAZZ MEN

MAX KAMINSKY ....Trumpet
VIC DICKENSON ....Trombone
EDMOND HALL ....Clarinet
DANNY ALVIN ....Drums
ART HODES ....Piano
ARTHUR SHIRLEY ....Guitar
SID WEISS ....Bass

SIDNEY DE PARIS' BLUE NOTE JAZZ MEN

SIDNEY DE PARIS.........Trumpet
VIC DICKENSON ....Trombone
EDMOND HALL ....Clarinet
SIDNEY CATLETT ....Drums
JAMES P. JOHNSON........Piano
ARTHUR SHIRLEY ....Guitar
JOHN SIMMONS ....Bass

ALBERT AMMONS
PIANO IMPROVISATIONS

MEADE "LUX" LEWIS
PIANO IMPROVISATIONS

PETE JOHNSON
PIANO IMPROVISATIONS

JAMES P. JOHNSON
PIANO SOLOS

EARL "FATHER" HINES
PIANO IMPROVISATIONS

(Sub. Irving Randolph, trumpet, for Swayzee; Keg Johnson, Claude Jones, trombones, for White; Ben Webster, tenor, for Harris):

```
Br  6992. Chinese Rhythm/Weakness                        -BrF 500486, BrE 2011
Br  7386. Keep That Hi De Hi in Your Soul(b16589)-Br 7639,BrF 500539,BrE 01980
"         Good Sauce from the Gravy Bowl(b16587)
Br  7411. Moonlight Rhapsody/Avalon                              -BrE 01897
Br  7504. Miss Otis Regrets(c1C53)                       -BrF 500190
"         Nagasaki(c1055)                                               ,BrE 02060
Br  7530. Baby Won't You Please Come Home                -BrF 500591
"         I Ain't Got Nobody                                            ,BrE 02060
Br  7638. I Love to Sing(La1090)/Save Me Sister(La1092)        -BrF 500656
Br  7639. You're the Cure for What Ails Me/Keep That Hi De Hi in Your Soul
Br  7677. Love is the Reason/Jess's Naturally Lazy             -BrF 500669
Br  7685. When You're Smiling/Are You in Love With Me Again    -BrF 500670
Br  7748. Copper Colored Gal/Wedding of Mr. and Mrs. Swing     -BrF 500689
Br  7756. The Hi-Be-Ho Miracle Man/Frisco Flo
```

(Second personnel):

```
Pe 15366. Sweet Jennie Lee/(rev.,Caroliners)            --Re 10152, Cq  7769
Pe 15376. Happy Feet/(rev., Whoopee Makers)
Pe 15412. Vipers Drag(110274)/Yaller(110245)                      -Or 2185
Pe 15442. So Sweet(10429)/Dixie Vagabond(10428)                   -Je 6224
Pe 15457. Farewell Blues(10483)/Mood Indigo(10482)-Ba 32152, Ro 1609, Fi 224
Pe 15474. Creole Love Song/I'm Crazy About My Baby
Pe 15490. Blues in My Heart(10604-2 & 3)/Levee Low Down(10603)
Pe 15494. My Honey's Lovin' Arms/Nightmare                                Fi 304
Pe 15500. Basin Street Blues(10728)                      BrE 1574,-Or 2317
"         It Looks Like Susie(10726)                              -Or 2317
Pe 15507. Sweet Georgia Brown/(rev.,Whoopee Makers)  -BrF 500306,BrE 1792
Pe 15531. Star Dust(10865)/You Can't Stop Me from Lovin'(10866)-Or2361,Ro 1731
Pe 15541. Somebody Stole My Gal(10868)        -Or 2382, Rex 8627,Im 2743
"         You Dog(10867)
Pe 15551. Corrine Corrina/Down Hearted Blues         -Or 2396,Ba 32340
Pe 15572. Stack o' Lee Blues/Without Rhythm
Pe 15635. Old Man of the Mountain                       -Me 12487,Im 2780
"         This Time It's Love                                BrF 500214
Pe 15623. Dinah(11910)           -Me 12489,Or 2495,BrF 500214,BrE 01688
"         I'm Now Prepared to Tell the World(11914)     -Or 2495, Me 12489
Pe 15715. Eadie Was a Lady       -Me 12583,Ro 1997,BrF 500420,BrE 1643
"         Hot Water                                              BrE 1792
Pe 15704. Beale Street Mama(12588)           -Or 2607,Me 12554,BrE 01688
"         Strange As It Seems(11959)         -Or 2607, Me 12554
Ro  1933. Git Along(12339)/(rev., Will Osborne)         -Ro 2559, DeE F3272
Me 12488. Swanee Lullaby(11915)                              -BrF 500195
"         How Come You Do Me Like You Do(11911)
                                - - -
Vi 24414. Evenin'(77684)                                      -HMV B6437
"         Harlem Hospitality(77683)              -BB 5676,    "
Vi 24451. Father's Got His Glasses On(78506)     -BB 6819, HMV B6451
"         Lady With a Fan(78520)                 -GrF 7220,   "
Vi 24494. Little Town Gal(77697)                 -GrF 7220,   HMV B6456
"         Harlem Camp Meeting(78504)             -GrF 7221, BB 5677, HMV B6460
Vi 24511. The Scat Song(78867)/Cabin in Cotton  -GrF 7228       HMV B6465
Vi 24557. I Learned About Love(77685)                          -HMV B6451
"         Zah Zuh Zah(78505)                                   -HMV B6460
Vi    .   Minnie the Moocher(78866)
 '        Kickin' the Gong Around                              -HMV 4318
Vi 24592. Long About Midnight(81088)                           -HMV 4314
"         Jitter Bug(81090)                      BB 5676,  HMV   "
Vi 24659. Emaline(81095)                                       HMV 4315
"         Margie(81094)                                        HMV 4318
Vi 24690. Moon Glow(81089)                                     .
"         Hotcha Razz-Ma-Tazz(81093)                           HMV 4315
```

(Chu Berry, Walter Thomas, tenor saxes; Garvin Bushell, Andrew Brown, altos; Lamar Wright, Irving Randolph, Adolphus Cheatham, trumpets; Claude Jones, Keg Johnson, DePriest Wheeler, trombones; Morris White, guitar; Leroy Maxey, drums; Milton Hinton, bass; Bennie Payne, piano):

```
Vr   501. That Man Is Here Again/Swing Swing Swing         -Vo 3807
Vr   535. Don't Know If I'm Comin' or Goin'/Wake Up and Live
Vr   593. My Gal Mezzanine/Congo                           -Vo 3825
Vr   612. Peckin'/Manhattan Jam                            -Vo 3830
Vr   643. I'm Always in the Mood for You/She's Tall, Tan, Terrific -Vo 3787
Vr   644. Mama I Wanna Make Rhythm/Go South Young Man
Vr   651. Moon at Sea(m606)/Hi-De-Ho Romeo(m619)           -Vo 3789
Vo  3870. Doin' the Reactionary/One Big Union for Two
Vo  3896. Every Day's a Holiday(m690)/Jubilee(m691)
```

```
Vo  3995. Three Swings and Out/I Like My Music Hot
Vo  4019. Bugle Blues/Fooling With You
Vo  4045. Scronch/We're Breaking Up a Lovely Affair
Vo  4100. Azure/Peck a Doodle Doo
Vo  4144. Hoy Hoy/Rustle of Swing
Vo  4369. Shout Shout Shout
      "  Mister Paganini                                    -Cq 9091
Vo  4400. Miss Hallelujah Brown(m891)
      "  The Boogie Woogie(m893)                            -Cq 9091
Vo  4437. At the Clem Bake Carnival(m791)/Jive(m897)
Vo  4498. F.D.R. Jones/Angels With Dirty Faces
Vo  4511. I'm Madly in Love With You/Deep in a Dream
Vo  4538. Blue Interlude/Tee-um Tee-um Tahiti
Vo  4700. Ratamacue(m972)/Ad-De-Dey(m973)
Vo  4753. Minnie the Moocher/St.Louis Blues
Vo  4807. Floogie Walk/The Ghost of Smoky Joe
Vo  4905. Long Long Ago/Afraid of Love
Vo  5005. Trylon Swing(wm 1054)/The Jumpin' Jive(wm 1057)
Vo  5062. Crescendo in Drums/Utt da Zay
Vo  5126. For the Last Time I Cried Over You(wml065)/Twee-Twee-Tweet(wml066)
Vo  5195. I Ain't Gettin' Nowhere Fast(wml068)/Jiveformation Please(wml103)
Vo -5267. Tarzan of Harlem(wml102)/A Bee Gezindt(wml113)
Vo  5315. Chili Con Conga/Vuelva
Vo  5364. Sincere Love(wml115)/Do It Again(wml116)
```

(Sub. Dizzy Gillespie,Mario Bauza,trumpets,for Cheatham,Randolph; Hilton Jefferson, sax, for Bushell; add Jerry Blake, sax; Tyree Glenn,Quentin Jackson, trombones, for Jones, Wheeler; Cozy Cole, drums; Danny Barker, guitar):
```
Vo  5444. Chop Chop Charlie Chan(wc2984)/Boog It(wc2986)
Vo  5467. Paradiddle/Pickin' the Cabbage
Vo  5566. Who's Yehoodi?/Topsy Turvy
Vo  5591. Do I Care? No No/Hi-De-Ho Serenade
OK  5664. Fifteen Minute Intermission/Rhapsody in Rhumba
OK  5687. Come On With the Come On(wc3162)/A Ghost of a Chance(wc3163)
OK  5731. Calling All Bars(27295)/Papa's in Bed With His Britches on(27801)
OK  5774. Boo-Wah-Boo-Wah/Silly Old Moon
OK  5804. Are You Hep to the Jive?/Sunset
OK  5827. Lonesome Nights/Yo Eta Cansa
OK  5847. A Chicken Ain't Nothin' But a Bird/Make Yourself at Home
OK  5874. Feelin' Tip Top/The Worker's Train
OK  5911. Goin' Conga/North of the Mohawk Trail
OK  5950. Hot Air/Levee Lullaby
OK  6035. Are You All Reet?/Cupid's Nightmare
```

(Sub. Jonah Jones, trumpet, for Bauza):
```
OK  6109. Jonah Joins the Cab(29867)/Willow Weep for Me(c3519)
OK  6147. Geechy Joe/Special Delivery
OK  6192. Hep Cat's Love Song(29866)/Ebony Silhouette(c3522)
OK  6305. Take the A Train(30835)/Chattanooga Choo Choo(30836)
OK  6341. We Go Well Together/I See a Million People
OK  6422. Blues in the Night/Says Who
OK  6459. Mrs. Finnigan(31301)/My Coo-Coo Bird(31302)
OK  6501. Who Calls/Mermaid Song
OK  6547. Tappin' Off/Main Nain
OK  6616. Tain't No Good/I Want to Rock
OK  6717. I'll Be Around/Virginia Georgia and Caroline
OK  6720. Let's Go Joe(hco884)/A Smo-o-o-th One(31645)
        (See also: Missourians, Original Cotton Club Orchestra)
```

CAMPBELL, BUDDY AND HIS ORCHESTRA (some of the following feature Benny Goodman*, clarinet):
```
OK 41491. Hello Beautiful/It's a Lonesome Old Town
OK 41499. Roll on Mississippi*/Moonlight Saving Time
OK 41509. It's the Girl/All Dressed Up With a Broken Heart
OK 41516. Now That You're Gone/Life Is Just a Bowl of Cherries
OK 41524. Little Mary Brown*/Time on My Hands
OK 41527. Charlie Cadet/Lucille
OK 41532. Last Dollar/You Try Somebody Else
OK 41537. Now's the Time*/When I Wore My Daddy's Brown Derby*
OK 41543. Bend Down Sister*/I Wouldn't Change You for the World
OK 41540. I Wonder Who's Under/Hiding in the Shadows of the Moon
                       (See also: Roy Carroll)
```
CAMPBELL, FLOYD AND HIS GANG BUSTERS:
```
BB 10852. Blow My Blues Away/What You Want Poor Me to Do
```

CAMPBELL, GENE (vocal with guitar):
```
Br  7139. Bended Knee Blues/Mama You Don't Mean Me No Good Now
Br  7154. Western Plains Blues/Levee Camp Man Blues
Br  7161. Freight Train Yodeling Blues, I & II
Br  7170. Robbin' and Stealin' Blues/Wondering Blues
Br  7184. Wish I Could Die/Lazy Woman Blues
```

```
        Br  7197. Lonesome Nights Blues/Wedding Day Blues
        Br  7225. Overalls Papa Blues/Crooked Woman Blues
        Br  7226. "Tobby" Woman Blues/Turned Out Blues
```

CANDRIX, FUD AND HIS ORCHESTRA (Belgian swing, via Germany):
```
        Tele A2377. Cross Country Hop(22610)/Nagasaki(22611)
        Tele A2741. Milenberg Joys(23602)/Minuet for a Modern Miss(23601)
```

CANNON AND WOODS (vocal with guitar and banjo):
```
        Br  7138. Fourth and Beale/Last Chance Blues
```

CAPITOL JAZZMEN (Jack Teagarden,trombone; Joe Sullivan,piano; Jimmie Noone,clarinet; Dave Matthews, tenor sax; Billy May,trumpet; Dave Barbour,guitar; Artie Shapiro, bass; Zutty Singleton, drums):   November 16,1943;Hollywood
```
        Cap 10009. I'm Sorry I Made You Cry(107a),Tea.vocal/Clambake in B Flat(104a)
        Cap 10010. Casanova's Lament(105a),Teagarden,vocal/In My Solitude(106)
```

(Eddie Miller,tenor sax; Barney Bigard,clarinet; Pete Johnson,piano;Nappy LaMare, guitar; Shorty Sherock,trumpet; Les Robinson,alto sax;Hank Wayland, bass;Nick Fatool,drums.):   Jan.7, 1944
```
        Cap 10011. Sugar(171a)/Ain't Goin'No Place(172a), Peggy Lee vocal
        Cap 10012. Someday Sweetheart(173a),Stan Wrightsman,piano/Old Feeling(174a)
```
(For last title: Miller, Wrightsman(celeste), LaMare, Wayland,Fatool, with Peggy Lee, vocal)

CAPTIVATORS (Red Nichols group):
```
        Br  4308. I Used to Love Her in the Moonlight/Marching Home to You  -BrG 8257
        Br  4321. Building a Nest for Mary/(rev.,Copley Plaza Orchestra)-BrF1019,G8258
        Br  4591. Get Happy/Somebody to Love Me                             -BrF 8615
```

(personnel unknown):
```
        Me 12049. We're Friends Again/What Good Am I Without You
        Me 12235. River Stay 'way from My Door(37100)/I Idolize My Baby's Eyes(37101)
```

CARLISLE'S (BILL) ORCHESTRA
```
        Bwy 1359. Milenberg Joys/Clarinet Marmalade
```

CARLISLE, UNA MAE (vocal acc. by groups from John Kirby's and Benny Carter's orchestras):
```
        BB 10853. Now I Lay Me Down to Dream/Papa's in Bed With His Britches On
        BB 10898. You Made Me Love You/If I Had You
        BB 11033. Walkin' by the River/I Met You Then
        BB 11096. Beautiful Eyes/There'll Be Some Changes Made
        BB 11271. City Called Heaven/It Ain't Like That
        BB 11362. I'm the One Who Loves You/Coffee and Cakes
        BB 11507. Sweet Talk/So Long Shorty
```

(Ray Nance,trumpet; Bud Johnson,tenor sax; J.Wilson,guitar; E.Robinson, bass; Shadow Wilson, drums; Una Mae Carlisle, piano and vocal):   May 23, 1944
```
        Bea 7170. Without You Baby/Tain't Yours
```

CARMICHAEL, HOAGY AND HIS PALS (Hoagy Carmichael* or Emil Seidel#, piano;Byron Smart, trumpet; Gene Woods,Maurie Bennett, Dick Kent, saxes; Oscar Rossberg,trombone; Don Kimmell, banjo; Cliff Williams, drums; Paul Brown, bass and violin,--DB 4/15/40):
```
        Ge 6311. One Night in Havana*/Stardust#                             Jan.,1928
```

CARMICHAEL'S COLLEGIANS (personnel unknown):
```
        Ge 6474. March of the Hoodlums(13722)/Walkin' the Dog(13724b)-Ch 16453, 40001
```

HOAGY CARMICHAEL AND HIS ORCHESTRA (Bix Beiderbecke,Ray Ludwig,cornets; Jack Teagarden, Boyce Cullen,trombones;Jimmy Dorsey,clarinet; Bud Freeman,Arnold Brillhardt, Pee Wee Russell, saxes; Joe Venuti,violin;Eddie Lang,guitar;Chauncey Morehouse, drums; Min Le'brook tuba;Irving Brodsky, piano;Carmichael,vocal):New York, 9/15/30
```
        Vi 22864. Bessie Couldn't Help It(63655a)/(rev., Fess Williams)
        Vi 23013. Georgia on My Mind(63653b)             -Vi 25494, HMV 6133, 8549
                  One Night in Havana (no Bix)
```

(unknown personnel):
```
        Vi 23034. Lazy River/Just Forget
        Vi 24119. I Was Taken by Storm/After 12 o'clock
        Vi 24123. Mighty River/(rev., Joe Haymes)
        Vi 24182. Sing It Way Down Low/Thanksgiving
        Vi 24402. Lazy Bones/Snow Ball
        Vi 24484. Star Dust/Cosmics
        Vi 24505. One Morning in May/(rev., Don Bestor)
        Vi 24627. Moon Country/Judy
        Vi 25371. Bessie Couldn't Help It(63655b) (Second master of Vi 22864, with Bix)
```

(Bix Beiderbecke,cornet; Bubber Miley,trumpet; Benny Goodman, clarinet; Bud Freeman, Jimmy Dorsey, saxes; Tom Dorsey,trombone; Joe Venuti, violin; Eddie Lang, guitar; Irving Brodskey, piano; Harry Goodman, bass; Gene Krupa, drums): 5/21/30
   Vi 38139. Rockin' Chair(59800)   -Vi 25494
   "   Barnacle Bill the Sailor(62301a)   -Vi 25371

(Unknown personnel):
   Vi L-16009. Stardust, Still of the Night, Washboard Blues

(With Perry Botkin's Orchestra):
   Br 8255. Hong Kong Blues(1a1731)/Riverboat Shuffle(1a1732)
     (See also: Hitch's Happy Harmonists, Paul Whiteman Orchestra, Glen Gray,
                                     (De 2394

CARNEY, HARRY (alto and baritone saxes: See Teddy Wilson Br 7699,7702,7729,7862, 7877; Bigard, Ellington, Gotham Stompers, Hodges, Stewart, Cootie Williams, Joe Steele.

CAROLINA COTTON PICKERS:
   Ge 5016. Georgia Cabin Door
   Vo 03580. 'Deed I Do/Off and On Blues

CAROLINA DANDIES (Possibly featuring Jack Teagarden, trombone and vocal,--JI Dec. 15, 1939):
   Vi 22776. Come Easy, Go Easy Love/When I Can't Be With You

CAROLINERS (Some of these, particularly Ca 9042, reputed to feature Goodman, McPartland, Teagarden):
   Ro 492. Among My Souvenirs/Kiss of Spring
   Ro 657. Would You Miss Me If I Went Away(3135)/(rev.,Sam Lanin)   -Li 2882
   Ro 714. Blue Grass
   Ro 740. Blue Shadows(3348)/(rev., Dixie Daisies)   -Ca 9317
   Ro 759. It Goes Like This(3384)/(rev., Paul Mills)
   Ro 816. Dardanella/(rev., Detroiters)
   Ro 866. Good Little Bad Little You
   Ro 1053. My Sweetie Turned Sour on Me(4007)/(rev.,Buddy Fields)
   Ca 390. Oh Min
   Ca 8325. Got the Blues Blues/(rev., Dixie Daisies)
   Ca 8348. I Don't Care
   Ca 9042. Hungry for Love(3581)
   Li 2478. What,No Women?/(rev., Broadway Broadcasters)
   Li 2460. Sweet Child

CARPENTER, WINGY AND HIS WINGIES:
   De 7698. Look Out Papa Don't You Bend Down/Put Me Back in the Alley
   De 7711. Rhythm of the Dishes and Pans(67056)/Team Up(67058)
   De 8519. Preachin' Trumpet Blues/(rev., Bob Pope)
     (See also: Acc. for George Guesnon)

CARR, DORA (Blues singer, acc. by Clarence Williams, piano):
   OK 8130. Bring It On Home Blues(s72299a)/You Might Pizen Me(s72300a), duet
                                     (with Charles Davenport
   OK 8250. Cow Cow Blues,(piano by Charles Davenport)/Gonna Steal Somebody's Man
   OK 8306. Alabama Mistreater/You Got Another Thought Coming
   OK 8284. Fifth Street Blues/Black Girl Gets There Just the Same
     (See also; Davenport and Carr)

CARR, LEROY (Blues vocals, mostly with Scrapper Blackwell, guitar):
   Br 3107. Muddy Water/Southbound Blues
   Vo 1191. My Own Lonesome Blues/How Long How Long Blues
   Vo 1200. Tennessee Blues/Broken Spoke Blues
   Vo 1214. Mean Old Train Blues/Low Down Dirty Blues
   Vo 1232. Truthful Blues/You Reap What You Sow
   Vo 1241. Prison Bound Blues/How Long How Long Blues, #2
   Vo 1259. Think of Me Thinking of You/How About Me
   Vo 1261. Baby Don't You Love Me No More/Tired of Your Low Down Ways
   Vo 1279. You Don't Mean Me No Good/How Long How Long Blues, #3
   Vo 1290. Straight Alky Blues, I & 2
   Vo 1400. Naptown Blues/The Truth About the Thing
   Vo 1405. That's All Right for You/Wrong Man Blues
   Vo 1412. There Ain't Nobody Got I Like She's Got It/Gambler Blues
   Vo 1423. Just Worryin' Blues/Gettin' All Wet
   Vo 1432. Christmas in Jail Ain't That a Pain/Prison Cell Blues
   Vo 1435. Love Hides All Faults/New How Long How Long Blues
   Vo 1454. Workhouse Blues/The Dirty Dozen
   Vo 1585. Big House Blues/New How Long How Long Blues
   Vo 1593. Papa's on the House Top/Carried Water for the Elephant
   Vo 1605. Nineteen Thirty One Blues/Low Down Dog Blues
   Vo 02791. Barrel House Woman/Black Gal Blues
   Vo 02657. Blues Before Sunrise/Mean Mistreater Mama
   BB 7970. Big Four Blues/Vicksburg Blues #2

CARROLL, IRV AND HIS ORCHESTRA:
   Br 11390. Five Guys Named Moe/Go Home Little Girl Go Home

CARROLL, ROY AND HIS SANDS POINT ORCHESTRA (Benny Goodman, clarinet):
Ve	2318.	The Kings Horses(151326)		
Ve	2387.	Moonlight Saving Time(351015)		-Cl 5321
	"	Roll On Mississippi Roll On(351016)		
Vo	2402.	One More Time(351025)/Get Friendly		-Ha 1329
Ha	1397.	Too Late		-Cl 5446
	"	Bend Down Sister		

(Pseudonym for Casa Loma Orchestra):
   Ha 1271. Royal Garden Blues/Casa Loma Stomp

CARTER, ALICE (solos with piano):
   OK 8070. If You Want to Keep Your Daddy Home/Midnight Blues
   OK 8076. Bleeding Hearted Blues/I Just Want a Daddy

ALICE LESLIE CARTER (acc. by Jimmie Johnson's Jazz Boys, including June Clark, trumpet):
   Hytone 86. Dangerous Blues/I Want Some Lovin' Blues
   Hytone 95. Cry Baby Blues/The Also Ran Blues   Cleartone C-95
   Hytone 96. You'll Think of Me/Carol'na Shout
   Hytone 112. Decatur Street Blues/Got to Have My Daddy Blues

BENNY CARTER

See also:
   BUSTER BAILEY: Vo 2887.
   WILLIE BRYANT: Vi 25129, 25160.
   KING CARTER: Co 2439,2504,2638.
   CHOCOLATE DANDIES: OK 8728,Co 35679,2543,2875,OK 41568,PaE 1792,963.
   FLETCHER HENDERSON: Co 14392,1913,2329,2352,2586,2414; De 342,555.
   ALEX HILL: Vo 2826, 2848.
   SPIKE HUGHES: DeE 3563,3606,3639,5101,3836,3972,3717,3836.
   COLEMAN HAWKINS: Sw 1.
   WILLIE LEWIS: PatF 803,816,817.
   CHARLES JOHNSON: Vi 21247,21491; Em 10856.
   McKINNEY COTTON PICKERS: Vi38097,38102,22736,38112,38118,38142,22640,22932,23020,
      23024,22628,22811.
   MEZZ MEZZROW: Br 7551,6778; Vi 25202, 25019.
   CHICK WEBB: Br 6898, Vo 1607.

CARTER, BENNY AND HIS ORCHESTRA (Shad Collins, Leonard Davis, Bill Dillard, trumpets; George Washington, Wilbur DeParis, trombones; Benny Carter, alto sax and clarinet; Howard Johnson, alto sax; Chu Berry, tenor sax; Rodriguez, piano; Lawrence Lucie, guitar; Ernest Hill, bass; Sidney Catlett, drums.--HD)   April 1933
   CoE 628. Swing It(265090/Six Bells Stampede(265092)   -CoF 1304
   CoE 636. Synthetic Love(265091)/Love You're Not the One for Me(265093)

(Sub. Eddie Mallory,Richard Clark,trumpets, for Collins,Davis; J.C.Higginbotham, Fred Robinson, Keg Johnson, trombones; Carter Wayman, Carver, Johnny Russell, Glynn Pacque, saxes; Teddy Wilson, piano.--HD):   October, 1933
   CoE 698. Devil's Holiday(265160)   -Co 2898
   CoE 720. Lonesome Nights(265161)/Blue Lou(265163)   -OK 41567

(Sub. Russell Smith, Otis Johnson, Irving Randolph, trumpets; Bennie Morton, Keg Johnson, trombones; Carter, Ben Smith, Russell Procope, Ben Webster, saxes; Clarence Halliday, guitar; Elmer James, bass; Walter Johnson, drums):   Dec. 1934
Vo	2898.	Shoot the Works(16412)	-BrE 01981, BrF 500518
	"	Dream Lullaby(16413)	-BrE 02074, BrF 500517
Vo	2870.	Everybody Shuffle(16414)	-BrE 01981, BrF 500517
	"	Synthetic Love(16415)	-BrF 500518

(Max Goldberg, Tommy McQuarter, Duncan Whyte, trumpets; Ted Heath, Bill Mulraney, trombones; E.O.Pogson, Andy McDevitt, Buddy Featherstonehaugh, saxes; Pat Dodd, piano; George Elliott, guitar; Al Burke, bass; Ronnie Gubertini, drums;Carter,sax, clarinet and trumpet,--)   April-May 1936, England
VoE		4. Swingin' at the Maida Vale(S 103)/Nightfall(104)	
VoE	"	5. These Foolish Things	
		Swingin' the Blues(19482)	-Vo 3279
VoE	"	9. Big Ben Blues	-Br 7786
		I've Got Two Lips(19484)	-Vo 3279
VoE	"	11. Just a Mood	
		When Day Is Done	-Br 7786

(Sub. Leslie Thomson,trumpet,for Whyte; Lew Davis,trombone,for Mulraney; Freddy
Gardner, sax, for Pogson; Billy Munn, piano; Albert Harr's, guitar; Willy Morris,
bass; Kilcer, drums.--HD): 1936
    VoE   14. Accent on Swing/Scandal in A Flat
    VoE   16. I Gotta Go
    VoE „   When Lights Are Low(Quintet)   -Br 7853
    VoE „ 27. If Only I Could Read Your Mind   -Br 7853
               You Understand

(Tommy McQuarter, Duncan Whyte,trumpets; Ted Heath,Bill Mulraney, trombones;E.O.
Pogson,Andy McDevitt, Buddy Featherstonehaugh,George Evans,saxes; Eddie McClaulsv
piano; George Elliott, guitar; Al Burke, bass; Al Craig, drums; Carter, sax and
trumpet and clarinet,--HD): 1936
    VoE   57. Gin and Jive   -VoE 58
          „   There's a Small Hotel
    VoE   58. There's a Small Hotel(with vocal)
    VoE   69. I'm in the Mood for Swing/Nagasaki

(Quintet: Carter, sax and clarinet; Gene Rogers, piano; Bernard Addison,guitar;
Kilcer, drums.--HD):
    VoE   19. Tiger Rag/Waltzin' the Blues

(Quintet: Carter, sax and clarinet; McQuater, trumpet; Gerry Moore, piano;Har-
ris, Morris, Al Craig, drums):
    VoE   39. Carry Me Back to Old Virginny/Jingle Bells
    VoE   46. Royal Garden Blues/There'll Be Some Changes Made

(Featuring Coleman Hawkins, tenor sax; last four records: Carter, sax and trumpet; George Chisholm,trombone; Hawkins; Freddy Johnson piano.--HD)
    VoE   81. I'll Never Give In/New Street Swing   Holland, 1937
    VoE   94. Black Bottom/Rambler's Rhythm
    VoE 104. Somebody Loves Me/Blues in My Heart
    VoE 110. Mighty Like the Blues/I Ain't Got Nobody
    VoE 118. Lazy Afternoon/My Buddy   -DeF 118
    VoE 126. Skip It/Pardon Me Pretty Baby

(with Kai Ewans' Orchestra)   Denmark, 1937
    HMV X4699. Blue Interlude/When Lights Are Low
    HMV X4698. Bugle Call Rag/Memphis Blues

(Benny Carter, Fletcher Allen, alto saxes; Alix Combelle,Bertie King,tenor saxes; DeSota, piano;Django Rheinhardt, guitar; Len Harrison,bass;Robert Monmarche,
drums.--1938) Paris, 1938
    Sw   20. I'm Coming Virginia()SW 4)/Blue Light Blues(OSW 6)   -Vi 26221

(Benny Carter,trumpet and alto sax; Joe Thomas,Russell Smith,trumpets; T.Glenn,
and two other trombones; Jimmy Powell, Carl Frye, alto saxes; Ernie Powell,Sam-
my Davis, tenor saxes; Eddie Heywood, piano; Ulysses Livingston, guitar; Hayes
Alvis, bass; Keg Purnell, drums.--JRB 1939):
    Vo 4984. Plymouth Rock(WM 1046)/Melancholy Lullaby (WM 1048)
    Vo 5112. Savoy Stampede(WM 1047)/Scandal in A Flat(WM 1049)

(Add Eddie Mullins, Link Mills,trumpets,in place of Russell Smith; sub. Cass Mc-
Cord, sax, for Davis.--DB):
    Vo 5224. Vagabond Dreams (M1110)/Love's Got Me Down Again(M 1111)
    Vo 5294. Favor of a Fool/Riff Romp

(Sub. Russell Smith,trumpet,for Mullins;Eugene Simon,Vic Dickenson,James Archey,
trombones; Coleman Hawkins, Stanley Payne, for McCord):
    Vo 5399. Sleep(M 1126)/Slow Freight(M 1129)
    Vo 5458. Among My Souvenirs(M 1127)/Fash Fry(M1128)
    Vo 5420.
    Vo 5508. Shufflebug Shuffle(M 1109)/More Than You Know(M1112), Omit Hawkins
    OK 6001. Joe Turner Blues(28876)/Beale Street Blues(28877)

(Carter,alto and trumpet; Smith,Mills,Collins,trumpets; Milton Robinson,Madison
Vaughan, Fernando Arbelo, trombones; Frye,George Dorsey,Stafford Simon,Davis,
saxes; Sonny White, piano; same guitar, bass, drums.--JRB):
    De 3262. Pom Pom(67782)/Serenade to a Sarong(67784)
    De 3294. Night Hop(67781)/CK for Baby(67783)
    De 3545. By the Watermelon Vine Lindy Lou(68284)/I've Been in Love Before
    De 3588. The Last Kiss You Gave Me(68285)/Boogie Woogie (68286)   (68287)

(Russell Smith, Bob Williams, Sidney de Paris, trumpets; sub. Benny Morton,trom-
bone, for Arbelo; Simon, George Irish, Chauncey Haughton,George James, saxes;sub.
Everett Barksdale, guitar):
    BB 10962. The Very Thought of You/All of Me
    BB 10998. Cocktails for Two/Takin' My Time
    BB 11090. Babalu/There I've Said It Again

(Benny Carter, trumpet and alto; Adolphus Cheatham, Link Mills, Sidney De Paris, trumpets; Vic Dickenson, Joe Britton, James Archey, trombones; Ernest Purce, Edward Barefield, Frederick Williams, Ernie Powell, saxes; Sonny White, piano;Herb Thomas, guitar; Charles Drayton, bass; Alfred Taylor, drums.--JRB):   1941
  BB 11197. What a Difference a Day Made

(Cheatham,Mills, replaced by Jonah Jones, Purcell Smith;George Dorsey,Bill White, George Irish, Fred Mitchell, saxes; Ted Sturgis, bass; J. C. Heard, drums):
  BB 11197. Cuddle Up Huddle Up
  BB 11288. Midnight/My Favorite Blues
  BB 11341. Sunday/Back Bay Boogie

(Benny Carter, Porter Kilbert, Eugene Porter, Willard Brown, Bumps Myers, saxes; Claude Dunson, Vernon Porter, John Buckner, Freddie Webster, trumpets;Alton Moore, James J. Johnson, John Haughton, trombones: Humphrey Brannon, piano;Ulysses Livingston, guitar; Dillon Russell, bass; Oscar Bradley, drums):
  Cap 144. Poincianna(93a)/Hurry Hurry(95a)   (San Francisco,Oct.'43

(Sub. Karl George, John Carroll, Edwin Davis, Milton Fletcher, trumpets; Gerald Wiggins, piano; W. J. Edwards, guitar; Charles Drayton, bass; Max Roach,drums;add Batty Varsalona, trombone):   May 21, 1944
  Cap 165. I'm Lost/Just a Baby's Prayer at Twilight (10/25/43)

CARTER, BO (Blues with guitar):
  OK 8852. I'm an Old Bumble Bee/I've Got the Whole World in My Hand
  OK 8858. Times Is Tight Like That/Same Thing the Cats Fight About(duet with
  OK 8887. Pin in Your Cushion/I Love That Thing   (W. Jacobs
  OK 8889. Sorry Feeling Blues/Howling Tom Cat Blues
  OK 8897. Ram Rod Daddy/Ants in My Pants   -Vo 02359
  OK 8912. My Pencil Won't Write No More/Boot It
  BB 5912. Mashing That Thing/Who Broke the Latch?
  BB 8147. Some Day/Santa Claus
  BB 8397. The County Farm Blues/Arrangement for Me
  BB 8423. Border of New Mexico Blues/Lock the Lock
  BB 8459. Trouble oh Trouble/Baby Ruth
  BB 8495. Policy Blues/My Baby
  BB 8514. Tush Hog Blues/My Little Mind
  BB 8555. Honey/What You Want Your Daddy to Do?

CARTER, FRANCIS J. (Piano solos):
  OK 40693. I Wonder What's Become of Joe(80119a)/The Birth of the Blues(80120a)

CARTER, GEORGE (Blues with guitar):
  Para 12750. Rising River Blues(21153)/Hot Jelly Roll Blues(21154)

CARTER, KING AND HIS ROYAL ORCHESTRA (Wardell Jones, Shelton Hemphill,Edward Anderson, trumpets; Harry White, Henry Hicks, trombones; Charlie Holmes, Crawford Wethlington, Castor McCord, saxes; Edgar Hayes, piano; Benny James, banjo; Hayes Alvis, bass; O'Neil Spencer, drums; Benny Carter, leader.--HD):
  Co 2439. I'm Left With the Blues in My Heart(151455)   -PaE R1478
    "   Minnie the Moocher(151456)   -PaE R2345
  Co 2504. Moanin'(130477)/Blue Rhythm(151640)
  Co 2638. I Can't Get Along Without My Baby(130476)/Low Down on the Bayou
                                                              (151639)

CARY, CLARA (first side acc. by Tommy Ladnier, cornet):
  Vs 6067. Park No More Mama(14158)/Goin' Away Blues(14163)

CASA LOMA ORCHESTRA (Joe Hostetter, Frank Martinez, Bobby Jones, trumpets; Pee Wee Hunt, Russell Rauch, trombones; Glen Gray, Charles Hutchenrider, Pat Davis, saxes; Mel Jensen, violin; Joe Hall, piano; Gene Gifford, guitar; Stanley Dennis, bass; J. Briglia, drums.--HD):
  OK 41329. Love Is a Dreamer/Lady Luck
  OK 41339. Lucky Me/Happy Days Are Here Again
  OK 41403. China Girl(403755)   -PaE R1033
             San Sue Strut(403756)   -Co 2884, PaE R934
  OK 41476. Alexander's Ragtime Band(404568)/Put on Your Old Grey Bonnet(404571)
                                                      (-OdF 238743, PaE R982
  OK 41477. Overnight(404570)/Little Did I Know(404572)
  OK 41492. Casa Loma Stomp(404569)   Co 2615, PaE R890
  Co 2884. Royal Garden Blues(404573)   -PaE R1072
  Br 6085. When I Take My Sugar to Tea   -BrF 9057
             I Wanna Be Around My Baby All the Time
  Br 6092. I'm Crazy About My Baby
    "   White Jazz   -BrF 9057, BrE 1144, BrE 01657
  Br 6109. Alexander's Ragtime Band/Put on Your Old Gray Bonnet
  Br 6124. I Wanna Sing About You/Just a Blue Eyed Blonde
  Br 6150. Do the New York/Help Yourself to Happiness
  Br 6153. Take It From Me/It's the Girl
  Br 6187. Blue Kentucky Moon/Can't You See?

```
Br  6201. I Didn't Have You/Time on My Hands
Br  6242. Black Jazz/Maniac's Ball                    -BrF 9204, BrE 1279
Br  6252. Starlight(11177a)/Rain on the Roof(11179a)
Br  6256. Kiss by Kiss/One of Us Was Wrong
Br  6263. You're Still in My Heart(11316a)/Falling in Love With You(11319a)
Br  6289. Smoke Rings                                 -BrF 9249, BrE 1311
          In the Still of the Night
Br  6311. Lazy Day(11804b)/Evening(11806a)
Br  6318. Happy Go Lucky You/All of a Sudden
Br 20108. Four Indian Love Lyrics/Washboard Blues
      (See also: Glen Gray, O.K.Rhythm Kings, Bobby Gordon's Orchestra,Gene's
                                                                (Merrymakers)
```

CASTLE RECORD (Ned Dotson, cornet: George Phillips, trombone; Willy Pavia, clarinet; Monte Ballou, guitar; Bob Johnson, piano; Myron Shepler, bass; Alex Tyle, drums.):   Portland,Ore., 3/28/44.
```
          Jazz Band Ball/Ostrich Walk
          Jazz Band Ball/Sister Kate(Sub.Bob Scobey,cornet for Dotson,this side)
```

CATLETT, BIG SID QUARTET(Sidney Catlett, drums: Ben Webster, tenor sax; Marlowe Morris, piano; John Simmons, bass):
```
   Com  1515. Just a Riff/Memories of You
```

CELESTIN'S ORIGINAL TUXEDO JAZZ ORCHESTRA (Oscar Celestin and one other trumpet; August Rousseau, trombone; John Marrero, banjo; Paul Barnes, Sidney Carrere and one other, saxes; Abby Foster, drums: piano; bass)   Recorded in New Orleans
```
   Co   636. My Josephine(142015)/Station Calls(142016)
   Co 14200. I'm Satisfied You Love Me(142014)/Give Me Some More(142017)
   Co 14220. Dear Almanzoer(143953)/Papa's Got the Jim Jams(143954)
   Co 14259. As You Like It(143955)/Just for You Dear I'm Crying(143956)
   Co 14323. When I'm With You(145018)/It's Jam Up(145019)
   Co 14396. The Sweetheart of T.K.O.(147632)/Ta-ta Daddy(147633)
        (See also: Original Tuxedo Jazz Orchestra)
```

CELLAR BOYS (Frank Teschemacher, clarinet; piano; Bud Freeman, tenor sax; Wingy Mannone, trumpet; George Wettling, drums; Charlie Melrose, accordion):
```
   Vo  1503. Wailing Blues                                        -HRS 3
             Barrel House Stomp                                   -UHCA 62
   Br        Wailing Blues(5308b)/Barrel House Stomp(5309c)       -De T
```

CHARLESTON CHASERS (Red Nichols, trumpet; Miff Mole, trombone; Jimmy Dorsey,clarinet and alto sax; Arthur Schutt, piano; Eddie Lang, guitar; Joe Tarto, bass;Vic Berton, drums.--HD):   1927
```
   Co   446. Red Hot Henry Brown(140872)/Loud Speaking Papa(140873)
   Co   861. Someday Sweetheart(143258)                           -CoE 4419
     "      After You've Gone(143259)                             -CoE 4453
   Co   909. Davenport Blues(143534)                              -CoE 4453
     "      Wabash Blues(143537)                                  -CoE 4419
   Co  1076. Delirium(144169)/(rev., Ellington Washingtonians)    -CoE 4562
```

(Add Phil Napoleon, trumpet; sub. Fud Livingstone for Dorsey; Dick McDonough for Lang; bass;):   1928
```
   Co  1229. Five Pennies(144625)/Feelin' no Pain(144650)         -CoE 4797
   Co  1260. Sugar Foot Strut(144626)/Imagination(144649)         -CoE 4877
```

(Eddie Lang, guitar, returns):
```
   Co  1335. My Melancholy Baby(145726)/Mississippi Mud(145727)
```

(Original personnel):
```
   Co  1539. Farewell Blues(143530)/My Gal Sal(144168)
```

(Omit Nichols; sub. Dorsey for Livingstone; Frank Signorelli, piano; Dave Tough, drums; bass.--HD):
```
   Co  1891. Ain't Misbehavin'(148762)                            -CoE 5610
     "      Moanin' Low(148763)                                   -CoE 207
```

(Schutt, piano; Tarto, bass; Stanley King, drums;guitar;sax,clarinet, unknown):
```
   Co  1925. Red Hair and Freckles(148844)
     "      Lovable and Sweet(148845)                             -PaE R1522
```

(Benny Goodman, clarinet; Babe Rusin, tenor sax; rhythm section unknown):
```
   Co  1989. What Wouldn't I Do for That Man(149072)/Turn on Heat(149073)-CoE 16
```

(Sub. Tom Dorsey, trombone, for Mole; Jimmy Dorsey, clarinet and sax, for Goodman and Rusin; Schutt, piano; King, drums; bass.):   1930
```
   Co  2133. Cinderella Brown(150009)
     "      Sing You Sinners(150010)                              -CoE 95
```

(Goodman, clarinet; Signorelli, piano; banjo):
  Co 2219. Here Comes Emily Brown(150537)/Wasn't It Nice(150538)

(Dorsey, clarinet; Schutt, piano):
  Co 2309. Lovin' You the Way I Do(150846)   -CoE 205
   "   You're Lucky to Me(150847)

(Ruby Weinstein, Charlie Teagarden, trumpets; Glenn Miller, Jack Teagarden, trombones; Benny Goodman, clarinet; Sid Stoneberg, alto sax; Larry Binyon, tenor, Arthur Schutt, piano; Dick McDonough, guitar; Harry Goodman, bass; Gene Krupa, drums):
                                                                    1931
  Co 2415. Basin Street Blues(151292)   -OK 41577, PaE 1356
   "   Beale Street Blues(151293)   PaE 1431
          (See Kate Smith: Co 911)

CHATMAN, BO (vocal):
  Br 7048. East Jackson Blues/Good Old Turnip Greens
  Br 7185. Hard Times on Me Blues/Shakin' That Jelly

CHATMAN AND McCOY (vocal duet):
  Br 7080. Corrine Corrina/(rev., John Oscar)

CHESTER, BOB AND HIS ORCHESTRA (Alec Fila, Garner Clark, Al Stuart, trumpets, Seymour Shaffer, Sid Brantley, trombones; Manny Gershman, George Brodsky, altos; Bob Chester, Ed Scalzi, Harry Schuchman, tenors; Arthur Brennan, piano; Bobby Domenick guitar; Ray Leatherwood, bass; Lew Mann, drums,--JRB):
  BB 10378. Judy/Alla en el Rancho Grande
  BB 10396. You Tell Me Your Dream/Shoot the Sherbert to Me Herbert
  BB 10427. I Can't Tell You Why I Love You But I Do/Billy
  BB 10474. My Silent Mood/Stars Over the Campus
  BB 10489. Don't Make Me Laugh/I thought About You
  BB 10513. Aunt Hagar's Blues/57th Street Drag
  BB 10576. Make Love With a Guitar/Easy Does It
  BB 10614. With the Wind and the Rain in Your Hair/I Walk With Music
  BB 10633. I Hear Bluebirds/If It Weren't for You
  BB 10649. You Little Heart Breaker You/The Octave Jump
  BB 10686. We Met Each Other in a Dream/My Wonderful One, Let's Dance
  BB 10699. Secrets in the Moonlight/They Ought to Write a Book About You
  BB 10735. Orchids for Remembrance/The Moon Won't Talk
  BB 10752. Maybe/Pusin' the Conversation Along
  BB 10780. Chester's Choice/River Stay 'Way from My Door
  BB 10800. Rhumboogie/Rhythm on the River
  BB 10821. Now I Lay Me Down to Dream/Li'l Boy Love
  BB 10838. Don't Let It Get You Down/Practice Makes Perfect
  BB 10842. One Look at You/There Shall be No Night
  BB 10849. A Song of Old Hawaii/Take Care
  BB 10865. We Three/Off the Record
  BB 10890. You're Breaking My Heart All Over Again/Arise My Love
  BB 10904. May I Never Love Again/Buzz Buzz Buzz
  BB 10916. Old Old Castle in Scotland/Talkin' to My Heart
  BB 11172. Clap Your Hands on the Afterbeat/Time and Time Again
  BB 11259. A New Shade of Blue/You Were Meant for Me
  BB 11332. Wait Till the Sun Shines Nellie/I Can't Believe That You're in Love
  BB 11384. Clock Is Fast/Harlem Confusion
  BB 11521. Tanning Dr. Jekyll's Hyde/Moonlight Bay
  BB 11548. Keep the Home Fires Burning/Strictly Instrumental
  BB 11562. By the Light of the Silvery Moon/He's My Guy
  BB 11565. Isabella Kissed a Fella/Yesterday's Gardenias
  Hit 7088. How Blue the Night/It Could Happen to You
  Hit 7089. Where are You/Together

CHICAGOANS:
  Ca 8193. Sister Della's Fella/(rev.; Bob Haring)
  Pe 14794. Song of the Wanderer
  Pe 14795. Shanghai Dream Man

CHICAGO BLACK SWANS:
  Me 70465. Don't Tear My Clothes/You Drink Too Much

CHICAGO FIVE (Clarinet, piano, drums, guitar, bass, with Rob Robinson singing):
  BB 6543. I Ain't Gonna Do It/I'm a Gamblin' Man

CHICAGO FOOTWARMERS (Johnny Dodds, clarinet; Natty Dominique, trumpet; James Blythe, piano; Jimmy Bertrand, drums and washboard: John Lindsay, bass; Honore Dutrey, trombone):   1928
  OK 8533. Ballin' the Jack(82000)/Grandma's Ball(82001)
  OK 8548. My Baby(82076)/Oriental Man(82077)
  OK 8599. Get 'em Again Blues(400977)   -Co 35681
   "   Brush Stomp(400978)
  OK 8613. Brown Bottom Bess/Lady Love

PAGE NO.	RECORDING GROUP	L A B E L	SERIAL NUMBER	WAS SHOWN:	SHOULD HAVE BEEN SHOWN:

PAGE NO.	RECORDING GROUP	L A B E L	SERIAL NUMBER	WAS SHOWN:	SHOULD HAVE BEEN SHOWN:

(Ellington recording, q.v. for personnel):
   OK 8675. Chicago Stomp Down(81777)/Goin' to Town(401351)

(Original personnel):
   OK 8792. My Girl(400979)/Sweep 'em Clean(400986)

CHICAGO HOT FIVE:
   Vi 23285. Star Dust/You Can't Stop Me From Lovin' You
   Vi 23300. Wake 'em Up/Just One More Chance
   Vi 23326. Oh What a Thrill/You Can Depend on Me
           (See also: Ozie Ware, Vi 21777)

CHICAGO HOTTENTOTS(clarinet, possibly Johnny Dodds; piano and banjo):
   Vo 1008. All Night Shags/Put Me in the Alley

CHICAGO LOOPERS (Bix Beiderbecke, cornet; Frank Trumbauer, sax; Don Murray,clarinet; Arthur Schutt, piano; Carl Kress, guitar; Vic Berton, drums):New York,1926
   Pat 36729. Three Blind Mice(1)   -Pe 14910,HRS 1
              Clorinda(2)
   HRS   1. Three Blind Mice(2)
   Pat 36729. Clorinda(4)   -Pe 14910
           (See also: Willard Robison Orchestra)

CHICAGO RHYTHM KINGS (Muggsy Spanier, cornet; Frank Teschemacher, clarinet; Mezz Mezzrow, tenor sax; Jim Lannigan, tuba; Joe Sullivan, piano; Eddie Condon,banjo; Gene Krupa, drums; Red McKenzie, vocal--HD):   1928
   Br 4001. I've Found a New Baby/There'll Be Some Changes Made
                                                   -BrE 01739, BrF 500205
(Personnel unknown):
   BB 6371. Shanghai Honeymoon/Little Sandwich Wagon
   BB 6397. Sarah Jane/The Martins and the Coys
   BB 6400. She Shall Have Music/There Isn't Any Limit to My Love
   BB 6412. Stomping at the Savoy
   BB 6413. Where There's You There's Me
   BB 6564. Breeze
   BB 6690. Boston Tea Party/(rev., Frank Tanner)
   Vo 03208. It's Too Bad/You Battle Head Beetle Head

(Marty Marsala, cornet; Rod Cless, clarinet; Art Hodes, piano; Earl Murphy,bass; Jack Goss, guitar):   1940
   Sig 104. Song of the Wanderer(1604)/There'll Be Some Changes Made(1605)
   Sig 105. Sugar(1606)/Randolph Street Rag(1607)

CHICAGO STOMPERS (Piano, kazoo, banjo):
   Ch 40013. Wild Man Stomp(17628)/Stomp Your Stuff(17629)   -De 7424

CHICKASAW SYNCOPATORS (Early Lunceford: preaching in first title below by Moses Allen):
   Co 14301. Chickasaw Stomp(145373)/Memphis Rag(145374)

CHISHOLM, ANNA LEE (Blues singer. Acc. in first title probably by J. H. Shayne, piano):
   Para 12213. Georgia Sam Blues(8075-1)/Cool Kind Daddy Blues(8076-1)

CHISHOLM, GEORGE AND HIS JIVE FIVE (George Chisholm, trombone; Tommy McQuater,cornet; B. Winestone,tenor and clarinet; E.Macauley,piano; D.Barber, drums;T.Winters, bass):
   DeE F6867. Let's Go(DR 2985)/Archer Street Drag(DR 2988)

CHITTISON, HERMAN (Piano solos; first title under name of Ivory Chitison, with Banjo Ike):
   Vo 25011. Unlucky Blue(13553)/My Four Reasons(13554)
   BrE 01847. Honeysuckle Rose(1224wpp)/Bugle Call Rag(1249wpp)   -BrF 500438
   BrE 01960. Harlem Rhythm Dance(1227wpp)/Swingin'(1244½wpp)   -BrF 500439
   BrE 02022. You'll Be My Lover(1247wpp)   -BrF 500450
              Trees(1326wpp)
   BrF 500400. You Gave Me Everything But Love/Nagasaki
   BrF 500450. Stormy Weather
   BrF 500451. St.Louis Blues/Red Jill Rag
   BB 11333. Flamingo/The Man I Love

CHOCOLATE DANDIES (Langston Curl, John Nesbitt, trumpets; Claude Jones, trombone; Don Redman, Milton Senior, George Thomas, Prince Robinson, saxes; Todd Rhodes,piano; Dave Wilburn, banjo; Bob Escudero, tuba; Cuba Austin, drums; Lonnie Johnson, guitar.--HD):   1928
   OK 8627. Paducah(401218b)*
             Four or Five Times(401221a)   -PaE 365
   OK 8668. Star Dust(401219a)*/Birmingham Breakdown(401220b) -PaE 558

(Rex Stewart, trumpet; J.C. Higginbotham, trombone; Don Redman, sax; Bennie Carter, alto sax; Coleman Hawkins, tenor sax; Fats Waller, piano; and others.--HD):
                                                                                          1929
   OK 8728. That's How I Feel Today(402965c)/6 or 7 Times(402966d)   -PaE 542

(Bobby Stark, trumpet; Jimmy Harrison, trombone; Bennie Carter, clarinet and alto sax; Coleman Hawkins, tenor sax; Horace Henderson, piano; Genny Jackson, guitar; John Kirby, tuba):   December, 1930
   PaE R882. Goodbye Blues(404566a)/(rev., Dorsey Brothers)   -Co 35679
   PaE R963. Got Another Sweetie Now(404597b)/(rev.,Luis Russell)   -Co 36009
   PaE R1138. Dee Blues(404599)   -Co 2543, Co 36008
   PaE R1273. Cloudy Skies(404596b)/(rev., Luis Russell)   -Co 35679
   PaE R1645. Bugle Call Rag(404598)   -Co 2543, Co 36009

(Max Kaminsky, trumpet; Floyd O'Brien, trombone; Benny Carter alto sax and trumpet; Chu Berry, tenor sax; Teddy Wilson, piano; Lawrence Lucie, guitar;Bass Hill, bass; Sidney Catlett, drums):   1933
   PaE R1717. Once Upon a Time(265158)   -OK 41568, HRS 16

(Mezz Mezzrow, drums):
   PaE R1743. Krazy Kapers(265159)   -OK 41568, HRS 16
   PaE R1792. Blue Interlude(265156-2)/(Rev., Horace Henderson)
   PaE R1815. I Never Knew(265157)   -Co 2875

(KING OLIVER BAND: including Ward Pinkett, trumpet; Bingie Madison, sax.--Eugene Williams, RC 9/44)   April 15, 1931
    Vo 1610. Loveless Love(E36474A-b)/One More Time(E36475A-b)
    Vo 1617. When I Take My Sugar to Tea(E36476A-b)/That's My Stuff*
       *Last title is probably by Lloyd Smith's Gutbucketeers)

(Unknown personnel):
    Vo 1646. Levee Lowdown/Straddle the Fence

(Coleman Hawkins, tenor sax; Benny Carter, alto sax and piano*; Roy Eldridge,trumpet; John Kirby, bass; Bernard Addison, guitar; Sidney Catlett, drums):   1940
   Com   533. Smack/(rev., Coleman Hawkins)
   Com 1506. I Surrender Dear(R 2996)*/I Can't Believe That You're in Love With
                                                                              Me (R2997)

CHOO CHOO JAZZERS:
   Aj 17037. Hard Luck/He's Never Gonna Throw Me Down
   Aj 17055. Strut Yo' Puddy/Somebody's

CHRISTENSEN, AXEL (See Ray Barrow)

CHRISTIAN, BUDDY AND HIS JAZZ RIPPERS(Clarence Williams combination):
   Pe   118. The Skunk/South Rampart Street Blues   -Pat 7518

BUDDY CHRISTIAN'S FOUR CRY BABIES:
   OK 8332. Nina Lee/Jonah's Ridin' on His Mule

BUDDY CHRISTIAN'S CREOLE FIVE
   OK 8311. Sunset Blues/Texas Mule Stomp
   OK 8342. Sugar House Stomp(74059a)/(rev., Eva Taylor)

CHRISTIAN, LILLIE DELK (blues with banjo, John A. St.Cyr):
   OK 8317. Sweet Man(9573a)/Sweet Georgia Brown(9574a)

(Jimmie Noone, clarinet, added):
   OK 8356. Lonesome and Sorry(9717a)/Baby o'Mine(9718b)

(With Richard M. Jones' Jazz Wizards):
   OK 8475. It All Depends on You(80841a)/Ain't She Sweet(80842b)

(With Armstrong Hot Four: Louis Armstrong, trumpet; Jimmie Noone, clarinet; Earl Hines, piano; Mancy Cara, banjo):
   OK 8596. Too Busy(400955b)/Was It a Dream(400956a)
   OK 8607. You're a Real Sweetheart(900954b)/Last Night I Dreamed You Kisses Me
                                                                                       (400957a)
(With Louis Armstrong, trumpet; Jimmie Noone, clarinet; Earl Hines,piano; banjo):
   OK 8650. I Can't Give You Anything But Love(402206a)/Sweethearts on Parade
   OK 8660. Baby(402207b)/I Must Have That Man(402209b)   (402208a)

CHUBB-STEINBERG ORCHESTRA (including Wild Bill Davison,trumpet):   July, 1925
   Ge 3058. Mandy Make Up Your Mind(12230)/Steppin' in Society(12231)
   OK 40106. Walking Talking Dolly(8631b)/From One Till Two(8632a)
   OK 40107. Blue Evening Blues(8633b)/Horsey! Keep Your Tail Up(8634b)

CLAIRE, TED:
   Ge 5041. Four o'Clock Blues

CLARINET JOE AND HIS HOT FOOTERS (clarinet, piano and drums):
   Ha   8. Rabbit Foot Blues(140826)/What Kinda Man Is You(140827)   -Ve 1008

CLARK, BUDDY (vocal with orchestra; Bud Freeman, tenor sax; Morey Feld,drums;Jess Stacy, piano; Marty Marsala, trumpet; Brad Gowans, trombone; Pee Wee Russell;clarinet; Sid Weiss, bass):
   Vs 8230. Nothing But You(US 1457)/From Another World(US 1458)
   Vs 8233. I Walk With Music(US 1459)/This Is the Beginning of theEnd(US 1460)

CLARK, CARROLL (spirituals, acc. by Fletcher Henderson, piano):
   Co   128. I'm So Glad Trouble Don't Last Alway(81401)/Deep River(81402)

CLARK, GARNET AND HIS HOT CLUB FOUR (Bill Coleman, trumpet; George Johnson,clarinet and alto sax; Garnet Clark, piano; Django Rheinhardt, guitar; June Cole, bass.-):   Paris, 1935
  GrF K7618. Rosetta(OLA 730)/The Object of My Affection(OLA 732)
  GrF K7645. Star Dust(OLA 731)/I Got Rhythm(OLA 733), piano solo

CLARK, GERALD NITE OWLS (See Wilmouth Houdini

CLARK, JUNE, trumpet, see following:
   ELLINGTON: Br 3526 (Washingtonians)
   SARA MARTIN: OK 8270, 8283.
   ALICE LESLIE CARTER: Hytone 86, 95, 112.
   JOSEPHINE STEVENS
   LAVINIA TURNER
   LOUISE VANT
   CLARENCE WILLIAMS: Pe 15387, 15403, etc.

CLARKE, JIM (piano solos):
   Vo 1536. Fat Fanny Stomp/New Orleans Blues
          (See also: Jimmie Blythe and Jim Clark)

CLAY, SHIRLEY, trumpet, see following:
   LIL ARMSTRONG: De 1388, 1502.
   HARRY DIAL: Vo 1515, 1567, 1594.
   BENNY GOODMAN: Co 2867, et al.
   BERTHA HILL: OK 8376, 8437.
   EARL HINES: Vi 38042, 38048, et al.
   CLAUDE HOPKINS: Deccas.
   PRESTON JACKSON: Para 12400, 12411.
   RICHARD M. JONES: OK 8349, 8390, 8431; Vi 21345, etc.
   BEN POLLACK: Co 2879.
   DON REDMAN: Br 6368, 6528, 6412, 6622, et al.
   OMER SIMEON: Br 7115, 7127.

CLAY, SONNY AND HIS ORCHESTRA:
   Vo 1050. Slow Motion Blues/California Stomp
   Vo 15078. Jambled Blues/Bogaloosa Blues
   Vo 15641. In My Dreams/Devil's Serenade
   OrE 1000. Chicago Breakdown/Plantation Blues

CLAYTON, BUCK (trumpet, see: Count Basie, Billie Holiday, Harry James, Teddy Wilson)

CLAYTON, DOCTOR (Joe Clayton, blues singer, with piano):
   BB 8901. Doctor Clayton Blues/Gotta Find My Baby

CLIFFORD'S LOUISVILLE JUG BAND:
   OK 8221. Dancing Blues/I Don't Want You Blues
   OK 8238. Wakin' Up Blues/Struttin' the Blues
   OK 8248. Mammy o' Mine Blues/Louisville Blues

CLINTON, LARRY AND HIS ORCHESTRA (Toots Mondello, Babe Rusin, Tony Zimmers,Fletcher Hereford, sax; Charles Spivak, Ricky Traettino, Bob Cusamano, trumpets; Alex Polascy, Cliff Heather, trombones; Art Bernstein, bass; A.Brodsky, piano;Ken Benford, guitar; Ray Michaels, drums; Clinton, trumpet and leader):
   Vi 25697. The Big Dipper/Midnight in the Madhouse
   Vi 25704. I Cash Cloes/Swing Lightly

(R.Muzzillo, W.Kelly, B.Cusamano,trumpets; Babe Rusin, J.Sedola, F. Hereford, S. Stonburn, saxes; trombones and piano same; A. Whistler, bass; J. Chesleigh;guitar; Chauncey Morehouse, drums):
   Vi 25706. I've Got My Heart Set on You/True Confession
   Vi 25707. Abba Dabba/The Campbells Are Swingin'
   Vi 25721. Jubilee/Scrapin' the Toast
   Vi 25724. Lady be Good/The One Rose
   Vi 25734. Snake Charmer/Toy Trumpet
   Vi 25740. I Double Dare You/Two Dreams Get Together

```
Vi 25755. Military Madcaps/Shades of Hades
Vi 25768. Always and Always/Dr. Rhythm
Vi 25773. When the Heather Is in Bloom/At the Perfume Counter
Vi 25789. I Dreamt I Dwelt/Martha
Vi 25794. Look/You're an Education
Vi 25805. Dance of the Hours/Gavotte
Vi 25837. How to Win Friends/I Married an Angel
Vi 25841. Ferdinand the Bull/If It Rains
Vi 25849. I Can't Face the Music/You Go to My Head
Vi 25863. Strictly for the Persians/Wolverine Blues
Vi 25885. I'm Gonna Lock My Heart/There's a Brind New Picture
Vi 25897. Night Shades/Study in Blue
Vi 26006. My Reverie/Boogie Woogie Blues
Vi 26010. Change Partners/The Yam
Vi 26014. At Long Last Love/You Never Know
Vi 26018. Dipper Mouth/Milenberg Joys
Vi 26024. My Heart At Thy Sweet Voice/Pretty Girl Milking
Vi 26034. Fight On/Victory March
Vi 26042. Summer Souvenirs/Zig Zag
Vi 26046. Dodging the Dean/Heart and Soul
Vi 26056. Shadrach/Old Folks
Vi 26073. It Took a Million Years/Who Blew Out the Flame?
Vi 26076. Chant of the Jungle/Design for Dancing
Vi 26083. After Looking at You/I Kissed You in a Dream
Vi 26100. Most Gentlemen Don't/My Feart Belongs to Daddy
Vi 26108. Devil With the Devil/Jeepers Creepers
Vi 26112. Temptation/Variety Is the Spice of Life
Vi 26118. Are You in the Mood?/For Men Only
Vi 26127. Kerry Dancers/Lullaby
Vi 26131. I Go for That/It's a Lonely Trail
Vi 26137. Please Come Out of Your Dream/Study in Green
Vi 26141. Deep Purple/Study in Red
Vi 26151. I Get Along Without You/Masquerade Is Over
Vi 26158. Don't Look Now/I Want My Share
Vi 26161. I've Got a Little List/Sweet Little Buttercup
Vi 26174. Jitterbug/Over the Rainbow
Vi 26277. Boy Named Lem/Comes Love
Vi 26283. In a Persian Market/Poor Little Rich Girl
Vi 26303. I'll Remember/I Wanna Hat With Cherries
Vi 26308. Little Man Who Wasn't There/Parade of the Wooden Soldiers
Vi 26319. Hezekiah/Rockin' Chair
Vi 26341. Moon is Low/'s Wonderful
```

(Jimmy Sexton, Walter Smith, Snapper Lloyd,trumpets; George Mazza, Al George, Jimmy Skiles, trombones; Jack Henderson, Steve Benoric, George Berg, Ben Feman,saxes; Bill Straub, piano; George Rose, guitar; Hank Wayland, bass; Charlie Blake,drums.-JRB): 1939

```
Vi 26354. Satan in Stain/Golden Bantam
Vi 26414. Down Home Rag/Johnson Rag
Vi 26417. My Silent Mood/Toselli's Serenade
Vi 26435. Study in Scarlet/This Is My Song
Vi 26468. I Dream of Jeanie/Old Folks at Home
Vi 26481. Sunday/Study in Surrealism
Vi 26521. Bread and Butter/How High the Moon
Vi 26523. Kiss for You/Limehouse Blues
Vi 26534. From Another World/It Never Entered My Mind
Vi 26541. Tiny Old Town/You Oughta Hang Your Heart in Shame
Vi 26575. Lady Said "Yes"/Ten Mile Hop
Vi 26582. Missouri Scrambler/Study in Modernism
Vi 26626. Blue Lovebird/How Can I Ever Be Alone
Vi 26634. Nearness of You/When the Swallows Come Back to Capistrano
BB 10784. My Greatest Mistake/Feeling Like a Dream
BB 10801. Love Lies/I May Be Wrong
BB 10820. Boo-wah Boo-wah/Half Way Down the Street
BB 10836. Bolero in Blue/Shades of Twilight
BB 18050. A Brown Bird Singing/Dance of the Candy Fairy
BB 10868. Dig Me Honey/My Buddy
BB 10911. Semper Fidelis/Dance of the Flowers
BB 10927. Arab Dance/Dance of the Reed Flutes
BB 10999. Carnival of Venice/Cielito Lindo
BB 11018. Old Rockin' Chair/Nobody Knows the Trouble I've Seen
BB 11094. Sahara/Because of You
BB 11140. Estrellita/Essential to Me
BB 11224. Comin' Through the Rye/Tenement Symphony
BB 11240. Let Me Off Uptown/Jazz Me Blues
```

CLOVERDALE COUNTRY CLUB ORCHESTRA (with Jack Teagarden,trombone, Sterling Bose,trumpet):
    OK 41551. Chances Are(405143)/Carolina's Calling Me

CLUB ALABAM ORCHESTRA (probably Fletcher Henderson):
  Do   354. Jealous(11019)/(rev., Gotham Dance Orchestra)
  Do   370. The Grass Is Always Greener
  Do   371. Charley My Boy

(Henderson orchestra, with Louis Armstrong):
  Do   426. One of These Days(5712);   see Sam Hill Or 374.

CLUB AMBASSADORS (Jimmy Noone's Orchestra, with Zinky Cohn, piano):
  Br 7096. My Daddy Rocks Me   -Vo 2779*
          Apex Blues
                       (*under Noone's name)

CLUB WIGWAM ORCHESTRA (Fletcher Henderson's orchestra with Louis Armstrong, Elmer Chambers, Howard Scott, trumpets; Charlie Green, trombone; Buster Bailey, clarinet; Don Redman, alto sax; Coleman Hawkins, tenor sax; Charlie Dixon, guitar; Escudero, bass; Kaiser Marshall, drums; Henderson, piano.--HD):   1924
  Do 3458. Alabamy Bound(5835-3)/(rev., Missouri Jazz Band)
    (See also: Henderson Re 9789, Ba 1488, Im 1420; Sam Hill Or 347)

CLYDE, BILLY AND HIS ORCHESTRA:
  Ch 40102. Rose Room/Oh Baby
  Ch 40108. After You've Gone/Some of These Days

COBB, E. C. AND HIS CORN EATERS (Junie C. Cobb, piano (and trumpet?); Cecil Irwin, tenor sax (and clarinet?); Jimmy Bertrand, drums and xylophone; Tampa Red, guitar.-DB 9/1/42):
  Vi 38023. Barrel House Stomp/Transatlantic Stomp

COBB, JUNIE C. AND HIS GRAINS OF CORN (Thomas Gray, Jimmy Cobb, trumpets; Ed Atkins, trombone; Wood Fork, banjo; Jimmy Bertrand, drums; Cecil Irwin, tenor sax; George James, Scoville Brown, alto saxes; William Lyle, bass; James Blythe, piano; Junie C. Cobb, trumpet, sax, clarinet.--DB 9/1/42):
  Vo 1204. Endurance Stomp/Yearning and Blue
  Vo 1263. Shake That Jelly Roll/Don't Cry Honey
  Vo 1269. Smoke Shop Drag/Boot That Thing
  Vo 1449. Once or Twice/(rev., Six Jolly Jesters)

JUNIE COBB'S HOMETOWN BAND:
  Para 12382. East Coast Trot/Chicago Buzz
  Para 13002. Cornet Pleading Blues, I & 2

COBB, OLIVER AND HIS RHYTHM KINGS (possibly same as Junie C. Cobb, above):
  Br 7107. The Duck Yas Yas Yas/Hot Stuff

COLE, COZY ALL STARS (Cozy Cole, drums; Earl Hines, piano; Coleman Hawkins, tenor sax; Trummy Young, trombone; Joe Thomas, trumpet; Billy Taylor, bass; Teddy Walters, guitar.):   New York, Feb. 22, 1944
  Key 1300. Blue Moon(hlk17a)/Just One More Chance(hlk19)
  Key 1301. Father Cooperates(hlk18)/Thru for the Night(hlk20)

(Cozy Cole, drums; Johnny Guarnieri, piano; Teddy Walters, guitar; Billy Taylor, bass; Ben Webster, tenor sax; Ray Coniff, trombone; Lamar Wright, trumpet) 3/44
  Savoy 510. Body and Soul/Talk to Me

(Cozy Cole, drums; Coleman Hawkins, Foots Thomas, Bud Johnson, saxes; Johnny Guarnieri, piano; Emmet Berry, trumpet; Mack Shopnick, bass):
  Savoy 512. Ol' Man River/Wrap Your Troubles in Dreams

COLE'S (EDDIE) SOLID SWINGERS:
  De 7210. Honey Hush/Thunder
  De 7215. Bedtime/Stomping at the Panama

COLE'S (JAMES) WASHBOARD FOUR:
  Ch 40047. Runnin' Wild/Sweet Lizzie

COLE, KING TRIO (Nat Cole, piano; Oscar Moore, guitar; Wesley Prince, bass) with vocal
  De 8520. Sweet Lorraine/This Side Up
  De 8535. Honeysuckle Rose/Gone With the Draft
  De 8541. Babs/Early Morning Blues
  De 8556. Scotchin' with the Soda/Slow Down
  De 8571. Hit the Ramp/This'll Make You Laugh
  De 8592. Stop the Red Light's On/I Like to Riff
  De 8604. Are You Fer It?/Call the Police
  De 8630. Hit That Jive Jack/That Ain't Right
  Ex 8114. All for Lou/Vom Vim Veedle   -Cap 139
  Ex   104. I'm Lost/Pitchin' Up a Boogie
  Premier 100. My Lips Remember Your Kisses/ F. S. T.
  Cap   154. I Can't See for Lookin'/Straighten Up and Fly Right

COLE, LUCY (vocal blues, acc. by trumpet, clarinet and piano):
    Ch 15549. Empty Bed Blues, 1 & 2

BILL COLEMAN

See also:
    GARNET CLARK: GrF K7618, K7645.
    ALIX COMBELLE: Sw 11.
    COLEMAN HAWKINS: Sig 28102.
    TEDDY HILL: Me 13351, 13364.
    EDDY HOWARD: Co 35771, 35915.
    WILLIE LEWIS: PatF 803, 816, 817, 898, 914, 915, 1030.
    LOU AND GINGER SNAPS: Ba 6536, 6540.
    JOE MARSALA: General 1717, 3001.
    DON REDMAN: Br 6211, 6237.
    LOUIS RUSSELL: OK 8766.
    CECIL SCOTT: Vi 38098, 38117.
    FATS WALLER: Vi 24801, 24808, 24826, 24867, 24846, 24863, 24853.
    DICKY WELLS: Sw 6, 16, 27.

COLEMAN, BILL (trumpet solos; acc. by Herman Chittison, piano; D'Hellemmes, bass)
    Ul   1235. Georgia on My Mind/What's the Reason I'm Not Pleasing You   Paris '36
    GrF 7764. I'm in the Mood for Love(Ola849)/After You've Gone(Ola850)

COLEMAN, BILL AND HIS ORCHESTRA (Bill Coleman, trumpet; Edgar Currance, tenor sax
and clarinet; John Ferrier, piano; Oscar Allemand, guitar; D'Hellemmes, bass; William Diemer, drums.--):   Paris, Jan. 31, 1936
    GrF 7705. Joe Louis Stomp(OLA 851)/Coquette(OLA 852)

(Bill Coleman, trumpet; Stephane Grappelly, violin; Joseph Rheinhardt, guitar; Wilson Myers, bass; Ted Fields, drums.):   Paris, 1937
    Sw   9. Rose Room(OLA 1975)/The Merry Go Round Broke Down(OLA 1978)

(Bill Coleman, trumpet; Big Boy Goodie, tenor sax; Christian Wagner, clarinet and
alto sax; Emil Stern, piano; Django Rheinhardt, guitar; Simoens, bass; Jerry Mengo, drums.--):   1938
    Sw   14. I Ain't Got Nobody(OLA 1979)/Baby Won't You Please Come Home(OLA1980)

(Second personnel above):
    Sw   22. Bill Street Blues (OLA 1976)/After You've Gone(OLA 1977)

(Third personnel, above):
    Sw   32. Big Boy Blues(OLA 1981)/Swing Guitars(OLA 1982)

(Second personnel, above):
    Sw   42. Indiana (OLA 1974)/Bill Coleman Blues(OLA 1982), solo with Rheinhardt

COLLECTOR'S ITEM CATS (Bill Davison, cornet; Boyce Brown, alto sax; Mel Henke,
piano; Joe Kahn, drums; Walter Ross, bass):   February 12, 1940
    CI 102. On a Blues Kick/I Surrender Dear

COLLEGE SEVEN:
    Ch 15051. Smile a Little Bit/(rev., Silent Joe)

COLLINS, LEE (trumpet; see following):
    LIL JOHNSON: Vo 03331, 03374.
    RICHARD M. JONES: BB 6569.
    JONES-COLLINS: Vi 38576, BB 10952.
    JELLY ROLL MORTON: Au 606, 607.
    JIMMY O'BRYANT
    LuIS-RUSSELL: OK 8849.
    VICTORIA SPIVEY: Vo 3405.

COLLINS, SAM (Blues singing with guitar):
    Ge 6260. Pork Chop Blues/Dark Cloudy Blues

COLUMBIA PHOTO PLAYERS (including Tommy Dorsey*, trombone, in some numbers):
    Co 1985. Dance Away the Night/I Came to You
    Co 2048. Take Everything But You
    Co 2105. Mona
    Co 2131. Sweepin' the Clouds Away/In My Little Hope Chest
    Co 2149. The Free and Easy*/It Must Be You
    Co 2177. Leave It That Way/The Whole Darn Thing's for You
    Co 2187. I'm in the Market for You/My Future Just Passed
    Co 2196. Dust/Dark Night

COMBELLE, ALIX (Tenor sax and clarinet solos; acc. by Stephane Grappely, piano;
Django Theinhardt, Joseph Rheinhardt, Paul Ferret, guitars; Louis Vola, bass.--):
    Ul 1544. Crazy Rhythm(77522)/The Sheik or Araby(77523)   Paris, 1935

ALIX COMBELLE AND HIS ORCHESTRA (Alix Combelle, tenor sax; Bill Coleman,trumpet; David Martin, piano; Roger Chaput, guitar; Wilson Myers, bass; Jerry Mengo,drums)
    Sw   11. Alexander's Ragtime Band(ola 1956)/Hang Over Blues(01a1957)   **1937**

(omit Coleman):
    Sw   24. Avalon/Al's Idea(Combelle;Ray Stokes, piano; Pierre Fouad, drums)

ALIX COMBELLE'S HOT FOUR (Philippe Brun, cornet; Combelle,tenor sax;Joseph Rheinhardt, guitar; Louis Vola, bass.--HD):   **Paris, 1938**
    Sw   17. When You're Smiling/If I had You

CONDON, EDDIE AND HIS FOOTWARMERS (Jimmy McPartland, cornet; Jack Teagarden,trombone; Mezz Mezzrow, clarinet; Joe Sullivan, piano; Eddie Condon, banjo;Artie Miller, bass; Gene Krupa, drums.):   **1929**
  OK 41142. I'm Sorry I Made You Cry(401277a)   PaF 85378, UHCA 27,   OdF 165618
    "   Makin' Friends(401278a)   PaF 85378, UHCA 28,   PaE 2031
    (See also: McKenzie-Condon; Eddie's Hot Shots)

EDDIE CONDON'S QUARTET (Frank Teschemacher, clarinet and alto sax; Joe Sullivan, piano; Eddie Condon, banjo; Gene Krupa, drums.):   **New York, July, 1928**
  PaE 2932. Oh Baby(401034)/Indiana(401035)

EDDIE CONDON AND HIS ORCHESTRA (Max Kaminsky, trumpet; Floyd O'Brien,trombone;Bud Freeman, tenor sax; Pee Wee Russell, clarinet; Alex Hill or Joe Sullivan*,piano; Eddie Condon, banjo; Arthur Bernstein,bass; Sidney Catlett,drums.--HD):   **1933**
  BrF 500328. The Eel(14193c)   -Br 6743, BrE 2006
    "   Home Cooking(14196b)*   BrE 2005
  Co 35680. The Eel (second master)/Home Cooking(second master)
  BrF 500406. Tennessee Twilight(14194)   -UHCA 63, Co 36009, BrE 01690
    "   Madama Dynamite(14195)   -UHCA 64,

EDDIE CONDON AND HIS CHICAGOANS (Joe Sullivan, piano; Bud Freeman,tenor sax; Pee Wee Russell, clarinet;Max Kaminsky,trumpet; Brad Gowans,trombone; Clyde Newcomb, bass; Dave Tough, drums):   **New York, August 11, 1939**
  De 18040. Nobody's Sweetheart(66075a)/Friar's Point Shuffle(66074b)
  De 18041. Someday Sweetheart(66075a)/There'll Be Some Changes Made(66072a)

EDDIE CONDON AND HIS WINDY CITY SEVEN (Bobby Hackett,cornet; Pee Wee Russell,clarinet; Bud Freeman, tenor sax; George Brunis, trombone; Jess Stacy, Eddie Condon, guitar; George Wettling, drums; Artie Shapiro, bass):   **1938**
  Com   500. Love Is Just Around the Corner(22306)/Ja Da (22310)
  Com   502. Beat to the Socks(22307)/(rev., Bud Freeman Trio)

EDDIE CONDON AND HIS BAND (Sub. Vernon Brown, trombone; Joe Bushkin, piano;Lionel Hampton, drums):   **1939**
  Com   515. Sunday(p23706-1)/California Here I Come(p23707-2)

(Max Kaminsky,cornet; Brad Gowans,trombone;Wettling,drums: same clarinet, piano, bass, guitar):
  Com   530. Strut Miss Lizzie(p25707-1)/It's All Right Here for You(p25708-1)
  Com   531. I Ain't Gonna Give Nobody None of My Jelly Roll(p25706-1)/Ballin' the Jack(p25709-1)

(Sub.Marty Marsala,cornet; Brunis,trombone; "Maurice", piano):   **1940**
  Com   535. Oh Sister Ain't That Hot(p29055-2)/You're Some Pretty Doll(p29057-1)
  Com   536. Georgia Gr'nd(p29054-1b)/Dancing Fool(p29056-1)

(Sub. Max Kaminsky,cornet; Brad Gowans, trombone;Joe Sullivan,piano;Al Morgan,bass)
  Com   542. Don't Leave Me Daddy(r4305-3)/Fidgety Feet(r4306-4)

(Sub. Lou McGarrity, trombone; Gene Schroeder, piano; Bud Casey, bass0:
  Com   551. All the Wrongs You've Done to Me/Back in Your Own Back Yard

(Previous personnel):
  Com 1509. Tortilla B Flat(r4308-3)/Mammy o' Mine(r4307-1)
  Com 1510. More Tortilla B Flat(r4308-4)/Lonesome Tag Blues(r4308-1)
    (See also: Jam Session at Commodore)

CONNIE'S INN ORCHESTRA (Russell Smith, Bobby Stark, Rex Stewart, trumpets;Benny Morton, Claude Jones, trombones; Russell Procope, Harvey Boone, Coleman Hawkins, saxes; Fletcher Henderson, piano; Clarence Haliday,guitar; John Kirby,bass; Walter Johnson, drums.--HD):   **1931**
  Vi 22698. Roll On Mississippi Roll On(53067)/Moan You Moaners(53068)
  Vi 22721. Sugar Foot Stomp(53066)
    "   Singing the Blues(53069)   -HMV 4871
  Me 12145. Singin' the Blues
    "   I'm Crazy About My Baby   -BrF 500389, BrE 1176

(Sub. Edgar Sampson, sax, for Boone):
  Me 12215. The House of David Blues
    "   You Rascal You   -BrF 500191, BrE 1205
        BrE 1281
  Me 12239. Sugar Foot Stomp/Just Blues   -BrF 500153, BrE 1212

```
    Me 12340. Casa Loma Stomp(11445a)                      -BrF 500191, BrE 1319
        "       Goodbye Blues(11448a)

(Jimmy Harrison, trombone?):
    Cr  3093. After You've Gone/Star Dust
    Cr  3107. Tiger Rag(1232)                                  -Vs 8016
        "     Somebody Stole My Gal(1233)                      -Vs 8053
    Cr  3180. Blue Rhythm
              You Rascal You(1431)                             -Vs 8016
    Cr  3191. Sugar Foot Stomp                                 -HRS 4
        "     Low Down on the Bayou(1434)                      -Vs 8053
    Cr  3212. Milenberg Joys(1506)/Twelfth Street Rag(1503)    -Vs 8042
    Cr  2678. I Heard/Reefer Man
```

CONNOR, LOU AND HIS COLLEGIATES (Jimmy McPartland,cornet; Jack Teagarden, trombone; Benny Goodman, clarinet; Gil Rodin, Larry Binyon, saxes; Vic Briedis,piano; Dick Morgan, banjo;Harry Goodman,bass;Ray Bauduc,drums.--HD):   1929
    Or 1483. Four or Five Times(2061-1,2,3)/It's Tight Like That(2062-3,4)
              (See also: Kentucky Grasshoppers; Jimmy Bracken)

COOK, ANN, (blues, acc. by Louis Dumaine,cornet; Willie Joseph,clarinet;Leonard Mitchell, banjo; James Willigan, drums; William Rouse,piano):New Orleans,3/7/27
    Vi 20579. He's the Sweetest Black Man in Town/Mamma Cookie

COOK'S DREAMLAND ORCHESTRA (Freddie Keppard, Elwood Graham,cornets; Fred Garland, trombone; Jimmie Noone, clarinet; Clifford King, Joe Poston, Jerome Pasqual, tenor sax; Tony Spaulding, piano; Jimmy Bell, violin; Bill Newton, tuba; Bert Green, drums.--JI 11/8/40):   1923
    Ge 5360. So This Is Venice(11729a)/The One I Love(11732b)
    Ge 5373. Lonely Little Wall Flower(11728)/Moanful Man(11730)
    Ge 5374. Scissor Grinder Joe(11727b)/The Memphis Maybe Man(11731)

COOKIE'S GINGERSNAPS (Keppard,cornet; Noone, clarinet;trombone,piano,drums,sax, bass):   1926
    OK 8369. High Fever(9769a)/Here Comes the Hot Tamale Man(9770a)
    OK 8390. Messin' Around(9768a)/(rev., Jones' Jazz Wizards)
    OK 40675. Love Found You for Me(9771)/(rev., Arthur Sims)

COOK AND HIS DREAMLAND ORCHESTRA(featuring Keppard, trumpet):
    Co   727. Here Comes the Hot Tamale Man(142414)/Spanish Mama(142417)
    Co   813. Brown Sugar(142415)/High Fever(142416)
    Co   862. Sidewalk Blues(142981)/(rev., New Orleans Owls)

DOC COOK AND HIS 14 DOCTORS OF SYNCOPATION:
    Co 1070. Willie the Weeper(144318)/Slue Foot(144335)
    Co 1298. Alligator Crawl(144317)/Brainstorm(144334)
    Co 1430. Hum and Strum(145859)/I Got Worry(145861)

COOPER'S (AL) SAVOY SULTANS:
    De 2526. Jumpin' at the Savoy(65631a)/We'd Rather Jump Than Swing(65632a)
    De 2608. Draggin' My Heart Around/Stitches
    De 2819. Little Sally Water/Love Gave Me You
    De 2930. Jumpin' the Blues/When I Grow Too Old to Dream
    De 3142. Stop and Ask Somebody/Frenzy
    De 3274. Wishing and Crying for You/Sophisticated Jump
    De 7499. Jump Steady/Rhythm Doctor Man
    De 7502. Jeep's Blues/You Never Miss the Water Till the Well Runs Dry
    De 7525. The Thing(64360a)/Gett'n' in the Groove(64363a)
    De 7549. Looney/Someone Outside Is Taking Your Mind Off Me
    De 8540. Norfolk Ferry(68753a);See What I Mean?(68755a)
    De 8545. Jackie Boy/Second Balcony Jump
    De 8598. Boats/Fish for Supper
    De 8615. 'Ats in There/Let Your Conscience Be Your Guide

COOPER, ROB (Piano solos):
    BB 5459. West Dallas Drag
    BB 5947. West Dallas Drag No. 2/(rev., acc. to Joe Pullum)

COPELAND, MARTHA (Blues acc. by Eddie Heywood, Sr., piano):
    OK 8091. Daddy You've Done Put That Thing on Me/The Penetrating Blues
    OK 8112. The Pawn Shop Blues/The Down So Long Blues

(Some of the following acc. by Cliff Jackson, piano):
    Co 14161. Papa If You Can't Do No Better/Black Snake Blues
    Co 14189. Fortune Teller Blues/On Decoration Day
    Co 14196. Black Snake Blues/Mine's Just as Good as Yours
    Co 14208. Soul and Body/Sorrow Valley Blues
    Co 14227. Dyin' Crapshooter's Blues/Mister Brakesman

```
     Co 14237. Police Blues/Skeleton Key Blues
     Co 14248. Nobody Rocks Me Like My Baby Do/Hobo Bill
     Co 14262. Good Time Mama Blues/Shootin' Star Blues
     Co 14281. Bank Failure Blues/Second Hand Daddy

(with trio):
     Co 14310. Wylie Avenue Blues/Everybody Does It Now
     Co 14327. I Can't Give You Anything But Love/My Daddy Don't Do Nothin' Bad
     Co 14353. Something's Going Wrong/Desert Blues
     Co 14377. Mama's Well Done Gone Dry/I Ain't Your Hen

(First coupling below, duet with Sidney Easton):
     Vi 20548. Hard Headed Mama/When the Wind Makes Connection With Your Dry Goods
     Vi 20769. I Don't Care Who Ain't Got Nobody/Stole My Man

CORNELIUS, PAUL AND HIS ORCHESTRA:
     Ch 40084. I Found a New Baby/Sentimental Gentleman from Georgia

CORNELL AND HIS ORCHESTRA (Cornell Smelser,accordion; J.Dorsey, T.Dorsey,L.Hay-
ton, A. Rollini):                                                           1930
     OK 41386. Accordion Joe                                   -Od 36069
               Collegiate Love                    -PaE 758,
```

COTTON, BILLY AND HIS BAND:
     OK 41576. The Man from Harlem   -RZ 1501
          "   I Can't Dance   -RZ 1564

COTTON CLUB ORCHESTRA (R.Q. Dickerson, Harry Cooper, trumpets; DePriest Wheeler,
trombone; Dave Jones, Andrew Brown, saxes; Jimmie Prince, piano; Charley Stamps,
banjo; Smith, bass; LeRoy Maxey, drums.--HD)   1924-25
     Co 287. Down and Out Blues(140224)/Snag 'em Blues(140225)
     Co 374. Riverboat Shuffle/Original Two Time Man
     Co 14113. Everybody Stomp(141255)/Charleston Ball(141256)

COTTON PICKERS (First group by Original Memphis Five, probably comprising Phil
Napoleon, trumpet; Miff Mole, trombone; Jimmy Lytell, clarinet; Frank Signorelli,
piano; Jack Roth, drums):
     Br 2292. State Street Blues/Hot Lips
     Br 2338. I Wish I Could Shimmy Like My Sister Kate/Got to Coll My Doggies
     Br 2380. He May Be Your Man(9309)/Great White Way Blues(9312)   (Now
     Br 2382. Runnin' Wild(9487)/Loose Feet(9489)
     Br 2404. You Tell Her I Stutter(9868)/Way Down Yonder in New Orleans(9870)
     Br 2418. Snakes Hips/I Never Miss the Sunshine
     Br 2436. When Will the Sun Shine for Me(10421)/Down By the River(10426)
     Br 2461. Duck's Quack(10952)/My Sweetie Went Away(10955)
     Br 2486. Rampart Street Blues(11358)/Back O'Town Blues(11361)
     Br 2490. Mama Goes Where Papa Goes(11343)/Walk Jenny Walk(11347)
     Br 2507. Just Hot(11431)/Shufflin' Mose(11434)
     Br 2532. Blue Rose/Do Yo' Dooty Daddy

(Phil Napoleon, trumpet; Miff Mole, trombone; Chuck Miller, clarinet and sax;
Frankie Trumbauer, alto sax; Lucien Smith, saxes; Rube Bloom, piano; Mack Hugh,
banjo; Harry Lottman, drums.--HD):   1925
     Br 2766. Prince of Wails/Jimtown Blues
     Br 2818. Jacksonville Gal/Mishawaka Blues
     Br 2879. Down and Out Blues/Those Panama Mama

(Red Nichols, trumpet; Mickey Bloom, trumpet and mellophone; no other changes):
     Br 2937. Milenberg Joys/If You Hadn't Gone Away   1925-26
     Br 2981. Stomp Off Let's Go/Carolina Stomp (Omit Trumbauer)
     Br 3001. Fallin' Down/What Did I Tell Ya (Sub. Vic Berton, drums)
              (See also: Tennessee Tooters for above two groups)

(Phil Napoleon, trumpet; Tom Dorsey, trombone; Jimmy Dorsey, clarinet and alto
sax; Arthur Schutt or Frank Signorelli, piano; Stanley King, drums; bass;banjo.
--HD):   1928
     Br 4325. Kansas City Kitty   -BrF 81004
          "   Rampart Street Blues   -BrE 02505,
     Br 4404. Sugar Is Back in Town/Sweet Ida Joy(Ed Lang,guitar)   -BrF 1011
     Br 4440. St.Louis Gal/No Parking(Hoagy Carmichael, piano)   -BrF 1033
     Br 4446. Moanin'Low(Perry Botkin,guitar)/(rev., Al Goodman)   -BrF 1038
     Br 4447. He's a Good Man to Have Around/Shoo Shoo Boogy Boo

(Unknown personnel):
     Mad 1626. Hard Boiled Mama
     Mad 1653. Geraldine
     Ge 6380. Third Rail/What'll You Do (Andy Mansfield, director, 1928)

(J'mmy McPartland, cornet; Jack Teagarden, trombone; Benny Goodman, clarinet: Gil Rodin, alto sax; Larry Binyon, tenor sax; Vic Briedis, piano; Dick Morgan, banjo Harry Goodman, bass; Ray Bauduc, drums.--HD):
Ca 9048. St.Lou's Blues(2357)/Railroad Man(3591)   -Li 3077, Ro 852
Ca 9207. Some of These Days(3903)/Hot Heels(3912)   -Ro 1009
(See also: Whoopee Makers)
Vo 3262. Dere's Jazz in Dem Dere Horns/Woe Is Me

COTTON TOP MOUNTAIN SANCTIFIED SINGERS(Singing, with instrumental accompaniment, including trumpet):
Br 7100. Give Me That Old Time Religion/I Want Two Wings to Veil My Face
Br 7119. Christ Was Born on Christmas Morn/She's Coming 'Round the Mountain

COVINGTON, BLIND BEN (vocal):
Br 7121. Boodle-De-Bum-Bum/It's a Fight Like That

BOGUS BEN COVINGTON:
Para 12693. I Heard the Voice of a Pork Chop/Adam and Eve

COX, IDA (vocal blues, acc. by Lovie Austin and Her Blues Serenaders: Tommy Ladnier, trumpet; Lovie Austin, piano; Jimmy O'Bryant, clarinet):
Para 12044. Graveyard Dream Blues(1442)/Weary Way Blues(1443)   -Si 907

(Lovie Austin, piano):
Para 12045. Bama Bound Blues(1438)/Lov'n'Is the Thing I'm Wild About(1439)
Para 12053. Any Woman's Blues(1437)/Blue Monday Blues(1486)
Para 12056. I Love My Man Better Than I Love Myself(1487)/Chicago Bound Blues
                                                              (1503)
IDA COX AND HER BLUES SERENADERS (Same as Lovie Austin Serenaders, above):
Para 12063. I've Got the Blues for Rampart Street(1509)/Chattanooga bl(1496)*
Para 12064. Ida Cox's Lawdy Lawdy Blues(1488)/Moanin'Groan'n' Blues(1493)*
Para 12085. Mama Do Shee Blues(1594)/Worried Mama Blues(1595)
Para 12086. So Soon This Morn'ng Blues(1604)/Confidential Blues(1607)
Para 12087. Mail Man Blues(1605)/Bear Mash Blues(1626),acc by J.Crump
Para 12212. Last Time Blues(1705)/Blues Ain't Nothing Else But(1714)
Para 12202. Worried Any How Blues(1706)/Chicago Monkey Man Blues(1707)
Para 12220. Kentucky Man Blues(1840)/Death Letter Blues(1854)
Para 12228. Cherry Picking Blues(1841)/Wild Women Don't Have the Blues(1842)
Para 12237. Worried in Mind Blues(1943)/My Mean Man Blues(1855)
           (*Piano acc. only)

IDA COX (Acc. by the Pruitt Twins (banjo, guitar):
Para 12094. Mean Lovin' Man Blues(1696)/Down the Road Bound Blues(1697)

IDA COX AND HER FIVE BLUE SPELLS (Joe Smith or Ladnier, cornet; Charlie Green, trombone; Buster Bailey, clarinet; Fletcher Henderson,piano; Dixon,banjo):
Para 12251. Graveyard Bound Blues(2000)/Mississippi River Blues(2001)
Para 12258. Misery Blues(1999)/Blue Kentucky Blues(2003)
Para 12263. Those Married Man Blues(1998)/Georgia Hound Blues(2002)

(Acc. by Austin's Blues Serenaders (Joe Smith, cornet; Buster Bailey, clarinet; Lovie Austin, piano; Kaiser Marshall, drums.--HD):
Para 12282. Cold Black Ground Blues(2105)/Someday Blues(2106)
Para 12291. Black Crepe Blues(2103)/Fare Thee Well Poor Gal(2104)

(Johnny Dodds, clarinet):
Para 12298. Mistreatin' Daddy Blues(2242)/Southern Woman's Blues(2244)
Para 12307. Long Distance Blues(2243)/Lonesome Blues(2246)

(Acc. by Joe Smith, cornet; Lovie Austin, organ):
Para 12318. Coffin Blues(2293)/Rambling Blues(2294)
Para 12325. One Time Woman Blues(2299)/How Long Daddy(2287), banjo by C.Jackson

(Acc. by Austin Serenaders, above):
Para 12334. How Can I Miss You(2291)/I Ain't Got Nobody(2292)

(Joe Smith, cornet; Charlie Green, trombone; Buster Bailey, clarinet; Lovie Austin, piano; Kaiser Marshall, drums.--HD):
Para 12344. I'm Leaving Here Blues(2441)/Trouble Trouble Blues(2444)
Para 12353. Do Lawd Do(2443/Night and Day Blues(2445)

(Johnny Dodds, clarinet):
Para 12381. Don't Blame Me(2633)/Scuttle-De-Do(2634)

(Accompaniment by Jesse Crump, piano):
Para 12448. 'Fore Day Creep/Gypsy Glass Blues
Para 12502. Mercy Blues/Hard Oh Lawd
Para 12513. Pleading Blues/Lost Man Blues
Para 12540. Mojo Hand Blues/Alphonsia Blues
Para 12556. Seven Day Blues(20041)/Cold and Blue(20042)
Para 12582. Midnight Hour Blues/Give me a Break Blues

```
(With piano, banjo and cornet):
  Para 12664. Western Union Blues/Bone Orchard
  Para 12677. Booze Crazy Man Blues(20705)/Broadcasting Blues(20706)
  Para 12727. Sobbin' Tears Blues(20704)/Separated Blues(20713)

(Add sax):
  Para 12704. You Stole My Man/Worn Out Daddy Blues
  Para 12965. I'm So Glad/Jail House Blues
```

IDA COX AND HER ALL STAR BAND (Jimmy Johnson, piano; Charles Christian, guitar; Arthur Bernstein, bass; Lionel Hampton, drums; Ed Hall, clarinet; Hot Lips Page, trumpet; J.C. Higginbotham, trombone; Ida Cox, vocals):   1939
```
  Vo 05258. Pink Slip Blues(W26240)/Take Him Off My Mind(W26242)
  Vo 05298. Hard Times Blues(W26241)/Four Day Creep(W26239),F.Henderson,piano.
  Vo 05336. Deep Sea Blues(25509)/Death Letter Blues(25510)
```

(Red Allen, trumpet; J.C. Higginbotham,trombone; Edmund Hall, clarinet; Cliff Jackson, piano; Billy Taylor, bass; Jimmy Haskins, drums):
```
  OK  6405. Last Mile Blues(29277)/I Can't Quit That Man(29279)
```

CRAWFORD, ROSETTA (Acc. by King Bechet Trio: Sidney Bechet, clarinet,----):
```
  OK  8096. Down on the Levee Blues(s71945a)/Lonesome Woman's Blues(s71946b)
```

(Acc. by James P. Johnson's Hep Cats; Tommy Ladnier, trumpet; Mezz Mezzrow,clarinet; James P. Johnson, piano; Teddy Bunn, guitar; Elmer James, bass;Zutty Singleton, drums.--JRB):   1938
```
  De  7567. Stop It Joe/My Man Jumped Salty on Me
  De  7584. I'm Tired of Fattening Frogs for Snakes/Double Crossin' Papa
```

CRAWLEY, WILTON (clarinet, acc.by piano and Ed Lang, guitar*):
```
  OK  8479. Crawley Blues(80944)*/Irony Daddy Blues(80983)*
  OK  8492. Geechie River Blues(80945)*/She's Forty With Me(80984)*
  OK  8539. Crawley Clarinet Moan/Love Will Drive Me Crazy
  OK  8555. She's Nothing But Nice(82078)/Let's Pretend to Be Sweethearts(82081)
  OK  8589. I'm Forever Changing Sweethearts(401097)/Old Broke Up Shoes(400725)*
  OK  8619. Shadow of the Blues(401101)*/Tall Tillie's Too Tight(401096)*
  OK  8719. Wishing(400724)*/My Perfect Thrill(401100)*
```

WILTON CRAWLEY AND ORCHESTRA (including Jelly Roll Morton, piano, on Vi 38116,
```
  Vi 23292. Big Time Woman/She Saves Her Sweetest Smiles for Me       (38136):
  Vi 23344. I'm Her Papa/New Crawley Blues
  Vi 38116. Keep Your Business to Yourself(57567)/She's Got What(57568)-BB 5827
  Vi 38136. You Oughta See My Gal(57565)/Futuristic Blues(57566)
  Vi 38094. Snake Hip Dance/She's Driving Me Crazy
```

CREATH'S (CHARLES) JAZZ-O-MANIACS (Charles Creath, Leonard Davis,trumpets;Charlie Lawson, trombone; Sam Long, Thornton Blue, William Rollins, saxes; Cranston Hamilton, piano; Pete Patterson,banjo; Floyd Campbell,drums and vocal,--DB 5/15/40): St.Louis, 1924
```
  OK  8201. Pleasure Mad(8781a)/Market Street Blues(8782a)
  OK  8210. King Porter Stomp(9019a)/Every Man That Wears Bell Bottom Britches
  OK  8217. I Woke Up Cold in Hand/My Daddy Rocks Me (Ain't No Monkey Man(9020a)
```

(Sub. Zutty Singleton, drums; add Lonnie Johnson, violin and vocals):
```
  OK  8257. Grandpa's Spells/Down in Lover's Lane
  OK  8280. Market Street Stomp(9426a)/Won't Don't Blues(9427a)
  OK  8477. Butterfinger Blues(80823b)/Crazy Quilt(80824a)
```

CRIPPEN, KATIE (blues, acc. by Henderson's Novelty Orchestra):
```
  BS  2003. Play 'em for Mamma(p104-2)/Blind Man's Blues(p103-2)    -Pu 11054
  BS  2018. When It's Too Late/That's My Cup Blues
```

BING CROSBY

See also:
  LOUIS ARMSTRONG: De 15027.
  GUS ARNHEIM: Vi 22561, 22580, 22618, 22691, 22700.
  DORSEY BROTHERS: OK 41181, 41188.
  DUKE ELLINGTON: Vi 22528, Br 20105.
  IPANA TROUBADOURS: Co 1694.
  SAM LANIN: OK 41188, 41228.
  FRANKIE TRUMBAUER: OK 40979.
  PAUL WHITEMAN: Vi 20418,20508,20513,20627,20646,20679,20683,20751,20757,20828, 20882,20883,20973,21103,21218,21240,21274,21315,21365,21389,21398,21431,21438, 21453,21464,21678,24078,27685,35992,35934; Co 1401,1402,1441, 1444,1448,1465, 1491,1496,1505,1683,1701,1755,1771,1822,1845,1862,1877,1945, 1974, 1993,2010, 2023,2047,2098,2163,2164,2170,2171,50070,50098.
  WHITEMAN'S RHYTHM BOYS: Vi 20783, 21104, 21302, 27688; Co 1455, 1629, 1819, 2223.

CROSBY, BING (vocals):
```
Co    1773.  My Kinda Love/Till We Meet
Co    1851.  Baby Oh Where Can You Be/I Kiss Your Hand Madame
Co    2001.  Gay Love/Can't We Be Friends              -Ha 1428, Cl 5476
Vi   22701.  Just a Gigolo                             -BB 7118
 "           Wrap Your Troubles in Dreams              -BB 7102
Br    6080.  Out of Nowhere/If You Should Ever Need Me -Br 80043
Br    6120.  Just One More Chance                      -Br 80044
 "           Were You Sincere
Br    6140.  I Found a Million Dollar Baby/I'm Through With Love  -Br 80045
Br    6145.  Many Happy Returns/At Your Command
Br    6169.  Star Dust/Dancing in the Dark
Br    6179.  I Apologize/Sweet and Lovely
Br    6200.  Now That You're Gone                      -Br 80044
 "           A Faded Summer Love
Br    6203.  Goodnight Sweetheart/Too Late
Br    6226.  I'm Sorry Dear/Where the Blue of the Night
Br    6240.  Dinah                                     -Br 6485
 "           Can't We Talk It Over
Br    6248.  Snuggled on Your Shoulder/I Found You
Br    6259.  Starlight/How Long Will It Last
Br    6268.  My Woman/Love You Funny Thing
Br    6276.  Shine                                     - Br 6485
 "           Shadows on the Window
Br    6285.  Paradise/You're Still in My Heart
Br    6306.  Happy Go Lucky You/Lazy Day
Br    6320.  Sweet Georgia Brown                       -Br 6635
 "           Let's Try Again
Br    6329.  With Summer Coming On/Cabin in the Cotton
Br    6351.  Some of These Days                        -Br 6635
 "           Love Me Tonight
Br    6394.  Please/Waltzing in a Dream
Br    6406.  Here Lies Love/How Deep Is the Ocean
Br    6414.  Let's Put Out the Lights/Brother Can You Spare a Dime
Br    6427.  Someday We'll Meet Again/I'll follow You
Br    6454.  Just an Echo/A Ghost of a Chance
Br    6464.  Street of Dreams/It's Within Your Power
Br    6472.  I'm Young and Healthy/You're Getting to Be a Habit
Br    6477.  You're Beautiful Tonight
Br    6480.  Try a Little Tenderness/I'm Playing With Fire
Br    6491.  Linger a Little Longer/I've Got the World on a String
Br    6515.  What Do I Care It's Home/You've Got Me Crying Again
Br    6525.  My Honey's Lovin' Arms
Br    6535.  Stay on the Right Side Sister/Someone Stole Gabriel's Horn
Br    6594.  Moonstruck/Learn to Croon
Br    6599.  I've Got to Sing a Torch Song
 "           Shadow Waltz                              -Or 2971
Br    6601.  Blue Prelude                              -Cq 9553
 "           Down the Old Ox Road
Br    6610.  There's a Cabin in the Pines/I've Got to Pass Your House
Br    6623.  My Love/I Would If I Could
Br    6643.  Black Moonlight                           -Cq 9553
 "           Thanks
Br    6644.  The Day You Came Along/It Had to Be That Way
Br    6663.  The Last Round-Up/Home on the Range
Br    6694.  After Sundown/Beautiful Girl
Br    6695.  We'll Make Hay
 "           Temptation                                -Or 2971
Br    6696.  Our Big Love Scene/We're a Couple of Soldiers
Br    6724.  Let's Spend An Evening at Home/Did You Ever See a Dream Walking
Br    6794.  Shadows of Love/Little Dutch Mill
Br    6852.  Love Thy Neighbor/Riding Around in the Rain
Br    6853.  She Reminds Me of You/May I
Br    6854.  Once in a Blue Moon/Goodnight Lovely Little Lady
Br    6936.  Love in Bloom/Straight from the Shoulder
Br    6953.  Give Me a Heart to Sing to/I'm Hummin' I'm Whistlin'
Br   20102.  Gems from "George White's Scandals"
Br   20106.  "Face the Music" Medley
Br   20109.  Lawd You Made the Night Too Long
De     100.  I Love You Truly/Just a-Wearyin' for You
De     101.  Someday Sweetheart/Let Me Call you Sweetheart
De     179.  The Moon Was Yellow/The Very Thought of You
De     245.  Sweetheart Waltz/Two Cigarettes in the Dark
De     309.  With Every Breath I Take/Maybe I'm Wrong Again
De     310.  June in January/Love Is Just Around the Corner
De     391.  It's Easy to Remember/Swanee River
De     392.  Down By the River/Soon
```

De	543.	I Wished on the Moon/Two for Tonight
De	547.	I Wish I Were Aladdin/From the Top of Your Head
De	548.	Without a Word of Warning/Takes Two to Make a Bargain
De	616.	Boots and Saddles/Red Sails in the Sunset
De	617.	Moonburn/On Treasure Island
De	621.	Adeste Fidelis/Silent Night
De	631.	My Heart and I/Sailor Beware
De	756.	Lovely Lady/Would You
De	757.	Touch of Your Lips/Twilight on the Train
De	791.	Robins and Roses/We'll Rest at the End of the Trail
De	806.	I Got Plenty of Nuttin'/It Ain't Necessarily So
De	870.	Empty Saddles/Roundup Lullaby
De	871.	I Can't Escape from You/I'm an Old Cowhand
De	880.	Aloha Oe/Song of the Islands
De	886.	Hawaiian Paradise/South Sea Island Magic
De	905.	The House Jack Built for Jill/Shoe Shine Boy
De	912.	Beyond Compare/Me and the Moon
De	947.	Let's Call a Heart a Heart/Pennies from Heaven
De	948.	One Two Button Your Shoe/So Do I
De	1044.	Just One Word of Consolation/Dear Old Girl
De	1175.	Sweet Leilani/Blue Hawaii
De	1184.	I Have So Little to Give/Sweet Is the Word for You
De	1185.	Too Marvelous for Words/What Will I Tell My Heart?
De	1186.	Moonlight and Shadows/I Never Realized
De	1201.	The One Rose/Sentimental and Melancholy
De	1210.	In a Little Hula Heaven/Never in a Million Years
De	1234.	My Little Buckaroo/What Is Love?
De	1301.	Peckin'/(rev., Jimmy Dorsey)
De	1375.	Smarty/The Moon Got in My Eyes
De	1376.	All You Want to Do Is Dance/It's the Natural Thing to Do
De	1451.	I Still Love to Kiss You Goodnight/Remember Me?
De	1462.	Can I Forget You/Folks Who Live on the Hill
De	1518.	When You Dream About Hawaii/Sail Along Silvery Moon
De	1554.	Let's Waltz for Old Time's Sake/When the Organ Played Oh Promise Me
De	1565.	In the Mission by the Sea/There's a Gold Mine in the Sky
De	1616.	Dancing Under the Stars/Palace in Paradise
De	1648.	My Heart Is Taking Lessons/On the Sentimental Side
De	1649.	Moon of Manakoora/This Is My Night to Dream
De	1794.	Don't Be That Way/Little Lady Make-Believe
De	1819.	Let Me Whisper/Swing Low Sweet Chariot
De	1845.	Sweet Hawaiian Chimes/Little Angel
De	1874.	Darling Nellie Gray/When Mother Nature Sings Her Lullaby
De	1887.	Home on the Range/(rev., Connie Boswell)
De	1888.	It's the Dreamer in Me/Now It Can Be Told
De	1933.	Blues Serenade/I've Got a Pocketful of Dreams
De	1934.	Don't Let That Moon Get Away/Laugh and Call It Love
De	2001.	Silver on the Sage/Mexicali Rose
De	2123.	My Reverie/Old Folks
De	2147.	Summer Time/You Must Have Been a Beautiful Baby
De	2200.	Joobalai/You're a Sweet Little Headache
De	2201.	Funny Old Hills/I Have Eyes
De	2237.	When the Bloom Is on the Sage/It's a Lonely Trail
De	2257.	Just a Kid Named Joe/Lonesome Road
De	2273.	I Cried for You/Let's Tie the Old Forget-Me-Not
De	2289.	Between a Kiss and a Sigh/My Melancholy Baby
De	2315.	Ah Sweet Mystery of Life/Sweethearts
De	2359.	East Side of Heaven/Sing a Song of Sunbeams
De	2360.	Hang Your Heart on a Hickory Limb/That Sly Old Gentleman
De	2374.	Star Dust/Deep Purple
De	2385.	Little Sir Echo/Poor Old Rover
De	2400.	God Bless America/Star Spangled Banner
De	2413.	And the Angels Sing/S'posin'
De	2447.	Down by the Old Mill Stream/I'm Building a Sailboat of Dreams
De	2448.	If I Had My Way/Whistling in the Wildwood
De	2494.	Ida/El Rancho Grande
De	2535.	I Surrender Dear/It Must Be True
De	2626.	Neighbors in the Sky/Start the Day Right
De	2640.	Still the Bluebird Sings/An Apple for the Teacher
De	2641.	Go Fly a Kite/Man and His Dreams
De	2671.	Girl of My Dreams/What's New?
De	2676.	Home on the Range/Missouri Waltz
De	2680.	Thine Alone/When You're Away
De	2700.	In My Merry Oldsmobile/Medley of Gus Edward Song Hits
De	2775.	My Isle of Golden Dreams/To You Sweetheart Aloha
De	2874.	Maybe/Somebody Loves Me
De	2948.	Wrap Your Troubles in Dreams/Between 18th and 19th on Chestnut St.
De	2998.	Moon and the Willow Tree/Too Romantic
De	2999.	Just One More Chance/Sweet Potato Piper
De	3024.	If I Knew Then/Tumbling Tumbleweeds
De	3064.	Devil May Care/Singing Hills
De	3098.	Girl With Pigtails in Her Hair/Dream of Jeanie With Light Brown Hair

```
De  3118. Beautiful Dreamer/Yours Is My Heart Alone
De  3133. Marcheta/Sierra Sue
De  3161. April Played the Fiddle/I Haven't Time to Be a Millionaire
De  3162. Meet the Sun Half Way/Pessimistic Character
De  3257. Cynthia/I'm Waiting for Ships That Never Come In
De  3297. Ballad for Americans
De  3299. Song of Old Hawaii/Trade Winds
De  3300. Only Forever/When the Moon Comes Over Madison Square
De  3309. Rhythm on the River/That's for Me
De  3321. Can't Get Indiana Off My Mind/I Found a Million Dollar Baby
De  3354. Waltz You Saved for Me/Where the Blue of the Night
De  3388. Prairieland Lullaby/Legend of Old California
De  3450. Please/You Are the One
De  3477. When I Lost You/When You're a Long Long Way from Home
De  3540. Swing Low Sweet Chariot/Darling Nellie Gray
De  3565. Along the Santa Fe Trail/I'd Know You Anywhere
De  3584. Lone Star Trail/Nightingale Sang in Berkeley Square
De  3590. It Makes No Difference Now/New San Antonio Rose
De  3609. Did Your Mother Come from Ireland/Where the River Shannon Flows
De  3614. Chapel in the Valley/When Day Is Done
De  3636. It's Always You/You Lucky People You
De  3637. Birds of a Feather/You're Dangerous
De  3644. De Camptown Races/Dolores
De  3736. I Only Want a Buddy/My Buddy
De  3797. Aloha Kuu Ipo Aloha/Paradise Isle
De  3840. Brahms Lullaby/You and I
De  3856. Be Honest With Me/Goodbye Little Darlin'
De  3886. My Old Kentucky Home/Til Reveille
De  3887. Pale Moon/Who Calls?
De  3952. You Are My Sunshine/Ridin' Down the Canyon
De  3965. No Te Importe Saber/You're the Moment of a Lifetime
De  3970. Birth of the Blues/Waiter and the Porter and the Upstairs Maid
De  3971. I Ain't Got Nobody/Whistler's Mother-in-Law
De  4000. Dream Girl of Pi K.A./Sweetheart of Sigma Chi
De  4033. Clementine/Day Dreaming
De  4064. Do You Care?/Humpty Dumpty Heart
De  4065. Anniversary Waltz/Shepherd Serenade
De  4152. Dear Little Boy of Mine/Oh How I Miss You Tonight
De  4162. Deep in the Heart of Texas/Let's All Meet at My House
De  4173. Remember Hawaii/Sing Me a Song of the Islands
De  4183. Blues in the Night/Miss You
De  4184. I Don't Want to Walk Without You/Moonlight Cocktail
De  4193. Blue Shadows and White Gardenias/Skylark
De  4249. Lamplighter's Serenade/Mandy Is Two
De  4339. I'm Drifting Back to Dreamland/Singing Sands of Alamosa
De  4343. Conchita/Old Oaken Bucket
De  4367. Boy in Khaki/Hello Mom
De 18316. I'm Thinking Tonight of My Blue Eyes/I Want My Mama
De 18354. Got the Moon in My Pocket/Just Plain Lonesome
De 18360. Mary's a Grand Old Name/Waltz of Memory
De 18371. Walking the Floor Over You/When My Dream Boat Comes Home
De 18391. Nobody's Darlin' But Mine/When the White Azaleas Start Blooming
De 18432. Bombardier Song/My Great Great Grandfather
De 18511. Faith of our Fathers/God Rest Ye Merry Gentlemen
De 18513. Constantly/Moonlight Becomes You
De 18514. Ain't Got a Dime to My Name/Road to Morocco
De 18531. Darling Je Vous Aime Beaucoup/I Wonder What's Become of Sally
De 18561. If You Please/Sunday Monday or Always
```
BING CROSBY AND THE ANDREWS SISTERS:
```
De  2800. Cirbiribin/Yodelin' Jive
De 23277. Pistol Packin' Mama/Victory Polka
```
BING CROSBY AND FRED ASTAIRE:
```
De 18424. Happy Holiday/Be Careful It's My Heart
De 18425. Abraham/Easter Parade
De 18426. I've Got Plenty to Be Thankful For/Song of Freedom
De 18427. I'll Capture Your Heart/Lazy
De 18429. White Christmas/Let's Start the New Year Right
```
BING CROSBY AND CONNIE BOSWELL:
```
De  1483. Basin Street Blues/Bob White
De  3689. Tea for Two/Yes Indeed
```
BING CROSBY AND FRANCES LANGFORD:
```
De  2316. Gypsy Love Song/I'm Falling in Love With Someone
```
BING CROSBY AND JOHNNY MERCER:
```
De  1960. Small Fry/Mr.Crosby and Mr.Mercer
De  3182. Mister Meadowlark/On Behalf of the Visiting Firemen
```
BING CROSBY AND DIXIE LEE CROSBY:
```
De   907. Fine Romance/Way You Look Tonight
```
BING CROSBY AND THE MERRY MACS:
```
De  3423. Do You Ever Think of Me?/You Made Me Love You
```
BING CROSBY AND TRUDY ERWIN:
```
De 18564. Oh What a Beautiful Mornin'/People Will Say We're in Love
```
BING CROSBY AND MARY MARTIN:
```
De 18278. Lily of Laguna/Wait Till the Sun Shines Nellie
```

CROSBY'S (BOB) BOB CATS (Yank Lawson, trumpet; Bob Zurke, piano;Warren Smith,trombone; Eddie Miller, saxophone; Irving Fazola, clarinet; Nappy Lamare,guitar; Bob Haggart, bass; Ray Bauduc, drums):
```
    De   1593. Stumbling/Fidgety Feet                              -DeE 6704
    De   1680. You're Dirving Me Crazy/Can't We Be Friends
    De   1756. Big Crash from China                                -De 3683
      "        Coquette
    De   1865. March of the Bob Cats/Who's Sorry Now
    De   2011. Palesteena/Slow Mood
    De   2108. Big Foot Jump(63426)/Five Point Blues(63428)
```

(Sub. Billy Butterfield, trumpet):
```
    De   2206. Big Bass Viol(91515)/Speak to Me of Love(91514)
```

(Sterling Bose, trumpet):
```
    De   2209. Loopin' the Loop(91551)/(rev., Bob Crosby Orchestra)
    De   2416. Hang Your Heart on a Hickory Limb(91697)/Sing a Song of Sunbeams(91698)
    De   2482. Hindustan(64989)/Mournin' Blues(64991)
    De   2662. It Was a Lover and His Lass/Oh Mistress Mine
    De   2663. Blow Blow Thou Winter Winds/Sigh No More Ladies
    De   2789. Peruna(66663)/Washington and Lee Swing(66662)
```

(Sub. Joe Sullivan, piano; Billy Butterfield, trumpet):
```
    De   2825. Till We Meet Again(66601)/The Love Nest(66664)
```

(Sub. Jess Stacy, piano):
```
    De   3040. Do You Ever Think of Me(67172)/
      "        Jazz Me Blues(67175)                                -De 3523
    De   3055. So Far So Good/You Oughta Hang Your Heart in Shame
    De   3056. Mama's Gone Goodbye(67241)/A Vous Tout de Vey, a Vous?(67243)
    De   3080. Tech Triumph/V.M.I. Spirit
    De   3104. Adios, Americano/It's All Over Now
    De   3248. Spain(67173)/All By Myself(67174)
```

(Muggsy Spanier, cornet;Jess Stacy,piano; Floyd O'Brien, trombone; Hank d'Amico, clarinet; Miller, Lamare, Haggart, Bauduc):
```
    De   3431. Don't Call Me Boy(DLA 2136a)/You're Bound to Look Like a Monkey
    De   3576. Take Me Back Again(DLA2140a)/I'll Come Back(DLA2141a)   (DLA 2142b)
```

(Sub. Bobby Goodrich, trumpet):
```
    De   3808. I'll Keep Thinking of You(93640)/I've Nothing to Live for Now(93642)
    De   4357. I'll Be True to the One I Love/(rev., Bob Crosby's Orchestra)
    De   4398. A Precious Memory/Those Things I Can't Forget
    De   4403. Way Down Yonder in New Orleans/(rev., Bob Crosby's Orchestra
```

(Yank Lawson, trumpet; Matlock, clarinet):
```
    De  18355. It's a Long Long Way to Tipperary/Sweethearts on Parade
    De  18373. Tears on My Pillow/You'll Be Sorry
```

FOUR OF THE BOB CATS(Bob Zurke,piano;Eddie Miller,tenor sax; Bob Haffart,bass;Ray Bauduc, drums):
```
    De   2207. I Hear You Talkin(91516)/Call Me a Taxi(91517)
```

CROSBY, BOB AND HIS ORCHESTRA (Andy Ferretti, Yank Lawson, trumpets; Ward Silloway, Artie Foster, trombones; Mat Matlock,clarinet and alto sax; Gil Rodin, alto sax; Dean Kincaid, saxes; Eddie Miller, tenor sax; Gil Bowers, piano; Bob Haggart, bass; Nappy Lamare, guitar; Ray Bauduc, drums.):   1935
```
    De   478. In a Little Gypsy Tea Room                           -BrE 02041
      "        Flowers for Madame
    De   479. Beale Street Blues                                   -DeE 5896
      "        Dixieland Band                       -De 3335,      BrE 02041
    De   502. East of the Sun(39680)/
      "        And Then Some(39682)                                -DeE 5768
    De   508. I'm in the Mood for Love                             -DeE 5672
      "        Two Together                                        -DeE 5678
    De   544. Roll Along Prairie Moon/Tender Is the Night
    DeE 5820. I'm Sittin' High on a Hill Top/Thanks a Million
    De   614. At Your Service Madame(col34a)
      "        On Treasure Island(col33a)                          -DeE 5977
    De   615. Here's to Romance                                    -DeE 5870
      "        I Found a Dream
    De   629. A Little Bit Independent                             -DeE 5837
      "        No Other One                                        -DeE 5896
    De   633. One Night in Mote Carlo                              -DeE 5837
      "        Eeny Meeny Miney Mo                                 -DeE 5870
```

(Sub. Phil Hart, trumpet, for Ferretti; add Bernardi, saxes):
```
    De   727. Goody Goody                                          -DeE 5947
      "        What's the Name of That Song                        -DeE 5962
```

```
De   728. I Don't Want to Make History                              -DeE 5997
  "       So This Is Heaven                                         -DeE 5947
De   753. Christopher Columbus                                      -DeE 5962
  "       It's Great to Be in Love Again                            -DeE 5977
De   759. You're Tooty to Me
  "       Ooh Looka There, Ain't She Pretty                         -DeE 5997
De   825. Dixieland Shuffle/Muskrat Ramble          -De 3338,DeE 6067
De   836. Guess Who/Mary Had a Little Lamb                          -DeE 6255
De   841. Big Chief De Sota/Cross Patch                             -DeE 6041
De   896. Come Back Sweet Papa                      -De 3336,DeE 6083
  "       Pagan Love Song
De   903. My Kingdom for a Kiss/Through the Courtesy of Love
De   930. Peter Piper(61215)/Woman on My Weary Mind(61216)          -DeE 6229
```

(Sub Bob Zurke, piano; Zeke Zarchey, trumpet, for Hart; Smitty Smith, trombone, for Foster):
```
De  1094. Sugar Foot Strut                          -De 3337, DeE 6300
  "       Savoy Blues                                                       "
De  1170. Gin Mill Blues                            -Br 02515, DeE 6463
  "       If I Had You                                              -DeE 6416
```

(Sub. Mark Bennet, trombone, for Smith):
```
De  1196. Between Devil and Deep Blue Sea           -De 3335, DeE 6463
  "       Old Spinning Wheel                                        -DeE 6416
```

(Add Bill de Pauw, saxes):
```
De  1346. Whispers in the Dark(62340)/Stop You're Breaking (62341)-BrF 505105
De  1370. The Loveliness of You/You Can't Have Everything           -DeE 6514
```

(Add Billy Butterfield, trumpet):
```
De  1539. Foggy Day/Nice Work If You Can Get It
De  1552. Little Rock Getaway(DLA 1019)/Vieni Vieni(DLA 1030)       -DeE 6584
De  1555. Why Should I Care/I've Got a Strange New Rhythm           -DeE 6634
De  1556. I've Hitched My Wagon to a Star/Silhouetted in Moonlight  -DeE 6668
De  1566. Let's Give Love Another Chance/This Never Happened Before
De  1576. Be a Good Sport
  "       Sweet Someone                                             -DeE 6647
De  1580. Every Day's a Holiday
  "       Thrill of a Lifetime                                      -DeE 6647
De  1615. Big Apple - When My Dream Boat                            -DeE 6658
  "       Panama                                     -De 3040,              "
De  1657. Always and Always/More Than Ever
De  1658. In the Shade of the Old Apple Tree/It's Easier Said Than Done
De  1670. It's Wonderful/Just Strolling
De  1693. I Simply Adore You/Please Be Kind
De  1713. Jezebel/You're an Education
De  1725. Grand Terrace Rhythm/John Peel
De  1732. How Can You Gorget?/There's a Boy in Harlem
De  1747. At the Jazz Band Ball                     -De 3337
  "       Yancey Special
De  1850. Royal Garden Blues                        -BrF 505131,De 3339, DeE 6622
  "       Tea for Two
De  1962. Milk Cow Blues
  "       Squeeze Me                                -BrF 505131,De 3339, DeE 6622
De  2032. Louise Louise
  "       Wolverine Blues                           -De 3040
De  2142. What Have You Got That Gets Me,/You're Lovely Madame
De  2150. Two Sleepy People/Wait Til My Heart Finds Out
De  2151. Deep in a Dream/Hurry Home
```

(Gil Rodin, Eddie Miller, Joe Kearns, Matty Matlock, saxes; Irving Fazola, clarinet; Sterling Bose, Billy Butterfield, Zeke Zarchy, trumpets; Ward Silloway,Warren Smith,trombones; Nappy Lamare, guitar; Ray Bauduc, drums; Bob Haggart, bass; Bob Zurke, piano):
```
De  2205. I'm Free(91535)/Summertime(91550)
De  2208. Big Noise from Winnetka(91518),bass and drums/Honky Tonk Train(91536)
De  2209. My Inspiration(91543)/(rev., Bob Crosby's Bob Cats)
De  2210. Swingin' at the Sugar Bowl(91533)/I'm Prayin' Humble(91534)
De  2275. Diga Diga Do, I & 2(91538/9)
De  2282. Eye Opener(64933)/Skaters Waltz(64927)
De  2379. Stomp Off and Let's Go(64928)/Song of the Wanderer(64931)
De  2401. At a Little Hot Dog Stand(91689)/If I Didn't Care(91690)
De  2402. Don't Worry About Me(91683)/What Goes Up Must Come Down(91687)
De  2415. Strange Enchantment(91686)/That Sentimental Sandwich(91688)
De  2452. Only When You're in My Arms/When We're Alone
De  2464. I Never Knew Heaven Could Speak/Rose of Washington Square
De  2465. If I Were Sure of You/Lady's in Love With You
De  2537. When the Red Red Robin Comes(91695)/Them There Eyes(91696)
```

```
De  2569. Smokey Mary(64929)                                        -De 3336.
         South Rampart Street Parade(64930)
De  2652. Melancholy Mood/Oh You Crazy Moon
De  2657. Over the Rainbow/You and Your Love
De  2703. Cherry/Day In Day Out
De  2734. Blue Orchids(66221)/World Is Waiting for the Sunrise(66222)
De  2763. Lilacs in the Rain/What Used to Was Used to Was
De  2776. Can I Help It(66539)/The Little Man Who Wasn't There(66666)
De  2812. I Thought About You/Last Night
De  2824. Happy Birthday to Love(66792)/The Answer Is Love(66794)
De  2839. It's a Whole New Thing(66830)/Angry(66831)
De  2848. Boogie Woogie Maxixe(66220)/High Society(66701)
De  2924. Little Red Fox/Pinch Me
De  2935. Between 18th and 19th on Chestnut Street/I Wanna Wrap You Up
De  2978. Angel/Starlit Hour
De  2991. Gotta Get Home/I've Got My Eyes on You
De  2992. Air Mail Stomp/Ooh What You Said
De  3018. With the Wind and the Rain in Your Hair/You You Darlin'
De  3027. Leanin' on the Ole Top Rail/Shake Down the Stars
De  3039. Run Rabbit Run/Up the Chimney Go My Dreams
De  3054. Reminiscing Time/Tit Willow
De  3070. Angel in Disguise/Moments in the Moonlight
De  3079. My My/Say It
De  3090. Cecilia/They Ought to Write a Book About You
De  3091. From Another World/Over the Waves
De  3103. Believing/This Is the Beginning of the End
De  3138. For Dancers Only/Where the Blue of the Night Meets the Gold
De  3154. Fools Rush In(67335)/Sympathy(67475)
De  3179. I'm Nobody's Baby(67474)/Speak Easy(67476)
De  3233. Complainin'(66832)/Ja Da (67401)
De  3271. Shortenin' Bread(67403)/Embraceable You(67473)
De  3404. Down Argentina Way/Two Dreams Met

(Muggsy Spanier,* cornet ):
De  3417. You Forgot About Me/Gone But Not Forgotten
De  3434. I'd Know You Anywhere(DLA 2124)*/I've Got a One Track Mind(DLA2126)*
De  3445. Do You Know Why(DLA 2138a)*/Isn't That Just Like Love(DLA2139a)*
De  3451. Drummer Boy(DLA 2107a)*/Ain't Goin' Nowhere(67985)
De  3488. Cow Cow Blues(DLA2108a)*/Dry Bones(DLA 2125a)*
De  3605. Chick-ee-Chick(DLA 2308)/Blue Echoes(DLA 2309)
De  3611. Big Noise from Winnetka(DLA 2292)/Sunset at Sea(DLA 2347)
De  3623. I Yi Yi Yi Yi(DLA 2348)/Chica Chica Boom Chic(DLA 2349)
De  3668. Sweet Genevieve/Unt'l You Fall in Love
De  3694. The Mark Hop(DLA 2276)*/Burnin'the Candle at Both Ends(DLA 2277)*
De  3752. Far Away Music/Flamingo
De  3762. Much More Lovely(DLA 2311)/Well Well(93634)
De  3815. Call It Anything/Something I Dreamed No Doubt
De  3860. Do You Care?/Will You Still Be Mine?
De  3884. Slow Mood
De  3929. The Angels Came Through/Elmer's Tune
De  4009. Sinner Kissed an Angel/Two in Love
De  4027. I'm Trusting in You(DLA 2724)/From One Love to Another(DLA 2725)
De  4028. A Gay Ranchero/Something New
De  4049. My Imaginary Love/Week End in Havana
De  4137. It Was Only a Dream/Take It easy
De  4169. A Zoot Suit(DLA 2836)/BarrelHouse Bessie From Basin St.(DLA 2837)
De  4290. Don't Sit Under the Apple Tree/I'll Keep the Lovelight Burning
De  4305. You're a Darlin' Devil
De  4316. Last Call for Love/Poor You
De  4357. When You Think of Lovin' Baby Think of Me
De  4368. Over There/Pack Up Your Troubles
De  4374. Army Air Corps/Semper Paratus
De  4385. Marines' Hymn/Where Do We Go From Here?
De  4390. King Porter Stomp/Sugar Foot Stomp
De  4395. Anchors Aweigh/Caissons Go Rolling Along
De  4397. Russian Sailors' Dance/Vultee Special
De  4403. Big Tom
De  4415. Black Zephyr/Blue Surreal
De 15038. South Rampart Street Parade(DLA1090a)/Dogtown Bl(DLA1091a)-DeE 876

(Featuring Lawson, Matlock, O'Brien, Miller, Stacy):
De 15064. Chain Gang/Ec Stacy
De 18369. Brass Boogie, I & 2
```

CROSS, DAVID (vocal)
Br 7079 That's the Way She Likes It/Then My Gal's in Town

CROWLEY, TOM AND HIS ORCHESTRA:
BB 6079. Worries on My Mind/Doc'ology

CRUMP, JESSE (piano; see Ida Cox)

CUSTER, CLAY (Piano solo):
  OK 4809. The Rocks(s71290a)/(rev., Henry Lange)

D

DANDRIDGE, PUTNEY AND HIS ORCHESTRA (Roy Eldridge, trumpet: Chu Berry,tenor sax; Putney Dandridge, piano; Nappy Lamare, guitar; Artie Bernstein, bass; William Beason, drums.--HD):   1935
  Vo 2935. You're a Heavenly Thing(17173)/Mr. Bluebird(17174)
  Vo 2982. Chasing Shadows(17730),Harry Grey,piano
             When I Grow Too Old to Dream(17731)   -VoE 34

(Henry Allen,trumpet; Buster Bailey, clarinet and alto sax; Ben Webster, tenor sax; Teddy Wilson, piano; Lawrence Lucie, guitar; John Kirby, bass; Walter Johnson, drums; Putney Dandridge, vocal):   1936
  Vo 3006. Isn't This a Lovely Day(17935)/Cheek to Cheek(17936)
  Vo 3007. I'm in the Mood for Love(17934)/That's What You Think(17937)
  Vo 3024. Shine/Nagasaki
  Vo 3082. I'm on a See Saw/Double Trouble
  Vo 3083. Santa Claus Came in the Spring/Eeny Meeny Miney Mo

(Richard Clark, trumpet; Tom Macey, clarinet; Chu Berry, tenor sax; Teddy Wilson, piano; Cozy Cole, drums; Grachan Monchur, bass; probably Dave Barbour, guitar.--HD):   1936
  Vo 3122. No Other One/A Little Bit Independent
  Vo 3123. You Hit the Spot/You Took My Breath Away

(Bobby Stark, trumpet; Teddy McRae, tenor sax; Teddy Wilson, piano; John Trueheart, guitar; John Kirby, bass; Cozy Cole, drums.--HD):
  Vo 3252. It's a Sin to Tell a Lie/All My Life
  Vo 3269. Why Was I Born/Ol' Man River

(Wallace Jones, trumpet; Charles Frazier, saxes; Ram Ramirez, piano; Arnold Adam, guitar; Mack Walker, bass; Wilmore Jones, drums.--HD):
  Vo 3277. These Foolish Thing/Cross Patch
  Vo 3287. A Star Fell Out of Heaven/Mary Had a Little Lamb

(Henry Allen, trumpet; Joe Marsala, clarinet; James Sherman, piano; Eddie Condon, guitar; Wilson Myers, bass; Cozy Cole, drums.--HD):
  Vo 3291. Here Comes Your Pappy/If We Never Meet Again
  Vo 3304. Sing Baby Sing/You Turned the Tables on Me

(Sub. Clyde Hart, piano; John Kirby, bass):
  Vo 3315. When a Lady Meets a Gentleman   -VoE 34
             It's the Gypsy in Me
  Vo 3351. You're the Darnedest Thing/Easy to Love
  Vo 3352. The Skeleton in the Closet/High Hat, Piccolo and Cane

(Adolphus Cheatham,trumpet; Tom Macey, clarinet; Teddy Wilson, piano; Allen Reuss, guitar; Bass Hill, bass; Sidney Catlett, drums.--HD):
  Vo 3399. With Plenty of Money and You/In a Dancing Mood
  Vo 3409. Gee But You're Swell/That Foolish Feeling

COW COW DAVENPORT

See also:
  BILLY ANDERSON: Co 14216, 14247.
  BAT THE HUMMING BIRD: Vs 6068 (reissue)
  JOE BIRD: Vo ?.
  DORA CARR: OK 8130, 8250, 8306?
  GEORGIA GRINDER: Vo 02792 (reissue)
  HOUND HEAD HENRY: Vo 1208, 1209, 1210, 1288.
  HALF PINT JAXON: Vo 1226, 1257.
  LOVIN' SAM: Probably many Brunswicks
  IVY SMITH: Para 12436, 12447; Ge 7040, et al.
  JIM TOWEL: Br 7060.

DAVENPORT AND CARR (vocal duet acc. by Clarence Williams, piano):
  OK 8244. Good Woman's Blues(73660b)/He Don't Mean No Harm(73661b)

COW COW DAVENPORT, piano and vocals (Special Note: There is some relationship between the Paramount and Gennett records listed below that needs clarification.It seems likely that the same masters were used interchangeably. Some discographers, notably Albert J. McCarthy (Jazz Music, 5), indicate same masters for Champion known to have been used by Paramount, but Champion would seem to be reissue of Gennett):

```
    Para  12439. Jim Crow Blues/Goin' Home Rag, both with B.T. Wingfield, cornet
    Para  12452. New Cow Cow Blues(4088-2), with B. T. Wingfield, cornet      -SD 104
      "         Stealin' Blues(4095), with L. Pickett, violin                    "
    Para  12800. Chimes Blues(14978)*,solo/Slow Drag(14985)#, solo           -Bwy 5046
          *McCarthy gives 14979 as master number; my copy is as above.
          #Reissued under name of Bat the Humming Bird, Vs 6068.
```

CHARLIE DAVENPORT (piano and vocals):
```
    Ge   6829. Shadow Blues, with Ivy Smith/Giving It Away, with guitar acc.
    Ge   6838. Chimes Blues, piano solo                              -Ch 50033
      "        Struttin' the Blues                                   -Su  9517
    Ge   6869. Atlanta Rag(14986), piano solo            -Su 9517, Ch 50033
                Slow Drag (This may have been used for the Varsity reissue)
    Unissued.   Cow Cow Blues, piano solo
```

CHARLIE DAVENPORT AND IVY SMITH:
```
    Ch 50034. Now She Gives It Away/You Got Another Thought Coming
```

COW COW DAVENPORT (piano and vocals):   1927-28
```
    Vo   1198. Cow Cow Blues, piano solo/State Street Jive(with talking,Ivy Smith)
    Br  80022. Cow Cow Blues(c2063--second master)/State St.Jive(c2064,2nd master)
    Vo   1227. Alabama Mistreater/Dirty Ground Hog Blues
    Vo   1253. Chimin' Blues,piano solo/Alabama Strut,with talking, Ivy Smith)
    Vo   1282. Back in the Alley, piano solo/Mootch Piddle
    Vo   1291. Texas Shout, piano solo/We're Gonna Rub It
    Vo   1434. Slum Gullion Stomp, piano solo/Mama Don't Allow No Easy Riders Here.
                                                                      (piano solo
```

COW COW DAVENPORT AND SAM THEARD (vocal, with piano and guitar):
```
    Vo   1408. That'll Get It/I'm Gonna Tell You in Front
```

COW COW DAVENPORT (acc. by Sam Price, piano; Richard Fullbright, bass; Teddy Bunn,
guitar; Joe Bishop, fluegelhorn.):   April, 1938
```
    De   7462. I Ain't No Iceman(63764)/Railroad Blues(63766)
    De   7486. Don't You Loud Mouth Me(63763)/That'll Get It(63767)
    De   7813. The Mess Is Here(63765), with piano only/(rev., Blue Lu Barker)
```

DAVENPORT, JED AND HIS BEALE STREET JUG BAND (jug, harmonica, guitars):
```
    Vo   1504. Piccolo Blues/Jug Blues
```

DAVIS, JASPER AND HIS ORCHESTRA (Two trumpets, trombone, sax and clarinet, tuba,
piano, banjo, drums; vocals by Lizzie Miles):
```
    Ha    944. Georgia Gigolo(148465)/It Feels So Good(148468)
```

DAVIS, JULIA (acc. by Lovie Austin Blues Serenaders):
```
    Para 12248. Black Hand Blues(10003)/Ske Da De(10002)
```

DAVIS, MADLYN AND HER RED HOT SHAKERS (Cassino Simpson, piano; trumpet; guitar.—
Jazz 7):
```
    Para 12498. Climbin' Mountain Blues(699)/Worried Down With the Blues(700)
    Para 12528. Hurry Sundown Blues/Landlady's Footsteps
```

MADLYN DAVIS AND HER HOT SHOTS:
```
    Para 12615. Winter Blues/Kokola Blues
```

RED HOT SHAKIN' DAVIS:
```
    Para 12703. It's Red Hot/Too Black Bad
```

DAVIS, WALTER (Blues singing with piano or guitar):
```
    Vi  23282. What Made Me/That Stuff
    Vi  23291. Sunny Land Blues/You Don't
    Vi  23302. Davis Blues/ M. and O. Blues
    Vi  23308. Howlin' Wind Blues/Pleadin'
    Vi  23315. Strange Land Blues/Engineer's
    BB   5031. M. and O. Blues, 1 & 2
    BB   5982. Travelin' This Lonesome Road/Sad and Lonesome Blues
    BB   6410. Just Wondering/Fallin' Rain
    BB   6498. Think You Need a Shot/(rev., Tampa Red)
    BB   6971. What Else Can I Do?/Nightmare Blues
    BB   7064. Angel Child/West Coast Blues
    BB   7329. Streamline Woman/Holiday Blues
    BB   7512. I Hear My Baby Crying/Walking the Avenue
    BB   7589. Million Dollar Baby/When Nights Are Lonesome
    BB   7643. I Did Everything I Could/Candy Man
    BB   7693. Angel Child, part 2/13 Highway
    BB   7996. Pet Cream Blues/Easy Goin' Mama
    BB   8058. Everything Is O.K./Merry Blues
    BB   8227. New Orleans/Corrine
    BB   8261. Big Four/Airplane Blues
    BB   8282. Let Me in Your Saddle/Green and Lucky
```

```
BB   8312.  Bachelor Blues/I Love You More and More
BB   8343.  Just Another Day/Froggy Bottom
BB   8367.  Down and Out/Doctor Blues
BB   8393.  Sundown Blues/Cotton Farm Blues
BB   8434.  Jungle Blues/Nothing But You
BB   8470.  Call Your Name/Western Land
BB   8490.  Moonlight Is My Spread/Root Man Blues
BB   8510.  Come Back, Baby/No Place to Go
BB   8534.  If It Hadn't Been for You/The Way I Love You
BB   8574.  Four Feet Eleven/Hello Blues
BB   8860.  New Santa Claus/You Keep on Crying
BB   8961.  Biddle Street Blues/Frisco Blues
```

DAVIS, WILMER (Singer, acc. by Johnny Dodds, clarinet; piano; banjo):
    Vo 1034. Gut Struggle(85)/Rest Your Hips(87)

DAVISON, WILD BILL (Trumpet; See Chubb-Steinberg Orchestra: Ge 3058, OK 40106, 40107; Benny Meroff; Br 4709, OK 41171; Collectors Item 102; George Brunis, Com 546).

WILD BILL DAVISON AND HIS COMMODORES (Wild Bill Davison, trumpet; Pee Wee Russell, clarinet; George Brunis, trombone; Eddie Condon, guitar; Gene Schroeder, piano; Bob Casey, bass; George Wettling, drums):
    Com 1511. That's a Plenty(a4675)/Panama(a4676-1)

(Sub. Edmond Hall, clarinet):
    Com   549. Clarinet Marmalade(a4683)/Original Dixieland One-Step(a4684)

DEAN, JOE (piano and vocal):
    Vo 1544. Mexico Bound Blues/I'm So Glad I'm 21 Years Old Today

DEAN AND HIS KIDS (Harry James, Shorty Sherock, trumpets; Bruce Squires, trombone; O.P. Gates, saxes; Irving Fazola, clarinet; Al Beller, Roy Cohan,violins; Freddy Slack, piano; Joe Price, guitar; Thurman Teague, bass; Sammy Taylor,drums; Ben Pollack, drums and leader):
    Vo 3342. Spreadin' Knowledge Around   -VoE 55
               Zoom Zoom Zoom

DEAS, EDDIE AND HIS BOSTON BROWNIES:
    Vi 22841. Sings of the Highway/Jes Shufflin'
    Vi 22844. All I Care About Is You/Little Mary Brown

DeBERRY, JAMES AND HIS MEMPHIS PLAYBOYS:
    Vo 05084. Nummy Nimmy Not(MEM 134)/You Can Go(MEM 138)
    Vo 05247. Zugity Zugity Zomp/Insane Jealous Blues
    Vo 05349. You Played a Trick on Me(MEM 131)/Oh Liza (MEM 132)

DeDROIT, JOHNNY AND HIS NEW ORLEANS JAZZ ORCHESTRA (Johnny DeDroit, trumpet;Henry Raymond, clarinet; Rudolph Levy, sax; Russ Papalia, trombone; George Potter, banjo; Frank Cuny, piano; Paul DeDroit, drums.--Tempo 3/38)   New Orleans, 1923
    OK 40090. New Orleans Blues(8558a)/The Swing(8561a)
    OK 40150. Nobody Knows Blues(8557a)/Number Two Blues(8563b)
    OK 40192. Brown Eyes(8562a)/(rev., Jack Linx)

(Sub. Ellis Stratakos, trombone; Frank Froeba,piano,in all except first title):
    OK 40240. Panama(8556b)/Eccentric(s72943a)   New York, 1924
    OK 40285. Lucky Kentucky(s73093b)/When My Sugar Walks Down Street(s73094b)

DeLANGE, EDDIE AND HIS ORCHESTRA:
    BB   7837. Button/Jump Jump's Here
    BB   7855. What Are Little Girls Made Of?/New Shoes Blues
    BB 10027. Copenhagen/You Can't Kiss a Frigidaire
    BB 10035. Muskrat Ramble/(rev., Fats Waller)
    BB 10094. Livery Stable Blues/Cockeyed Mayor of Kaunakakai
    BB 10199. Beer Barrel Polka/Serenade to a Wild Cat
    BB 10356. WPA Polka/Broom Dance

DELTA FOUR (Roy Eldridge, trumpet: Joe Marsala, clarinet; Carmen Mastren, guitar; Sid Weiss, bass):   1936
    De   737. Swingin' on the Famous Door(60270)   -BrE 02273, De 3562
               Farewell Blues(60271)   De 3864

DePARIS BROTHERS ORCHESTRA (Sidney DeParis, trumpet; Wilbur deParis,trombone; Ed Hall, clarinet; Clyde Hart, piano; Specs Powell, drums; Billy Taylor, bass):
    Com   552. I've Found a New Baby/Black and Blue   Feb. 5, 1944
    Com   .Sunday at Ryan's/The Sheik

DEPPE, LOIS (baritone, acc. by Earl Hines, piano):
    Ge 20021. Southland(11669b)/Sometimes I Feel Like Motherless Child(11670a)
    Ge 20022. Isabel(11668a)/For the Last Time Call Me Sweetheart(11671a)

DEEPE'S SERENADERS (Vance Dixon, director; including Earl Hines, piano):
　　Ge 20012. Falling(11629)/Congaine(11630)

DEVINE'S WISCONSIN ROOF ORCHESTRA (Bill Carlson,director; three brass, three reeds, four rhythm):
　　Bwy 1140. New St.Louis Blues(20270)/Tiger Rag(20271)　　　　-Para 12599
　　Bwy 1141. Singapore Sorrows(20267)/Mississippi Mud(20268)
　　(See also: Wisconsin Roof Orchestra)

DeVRIES, LOUIS (trumpet and orchestra):
　　Ch 40083. St. Louis Blues/I Cover the Waterfront

DEXTER'S (FRED) PENNSYLVANIANS (including Floyd Bean,piano; Les Biegel,trumpet,--
DB 11/15/43)
　　Ch 16065. What's the Use/Cheer Up　　　　　　　　　　　　　　　　1929

DIAL, HARRY AND HIS BLUSICIANS (Shirley Clay and one other, trumpets: Omer Simeon, clarinet and alto sax; Harry Dial, drums; piano; tenor sax; banjo; bass):
　　Vo 1515. Funny Fumble/Don't Give It Away
　　Vo 1567. I Like What I Like Like It/It Must Be Love
　　Vo 1594. Poison/When My Baby Starts to Shake That Thing

DICKERSON'S (CARROLL) SAVOY ORCHESTRA
　　Br 3990. Missouri Squabble/Black Maria

DICKSON, PEARL (blues with guitars):
　　Co 14286. Twelve Pound Daddy/Little Rock Blues

DICKSON'S HARLEM ORCHESTRA:
　　Vi 23377. Jam Man/Jazz Rondo

DIXIE DAISIES (Jimmy McPartland, trumpet; Benny Goodman,clarinet; Jack Teagarden, trombone, in some of the following*)
　　Ca 230. Pipe Organ Blues/Beale Street Mama
　　Ca 299. Aggravatin' Papa/Yes Sir That's Lazy Bones
　　Ca 311. Lovin' Sam/What More Do You Want
　　Ca 312. Dee's Knees/Away Down East
　　Ca 325. Hotsy Totsy Town/(rev., Arthur Lange
　　Ca 403. Sam Jones Blues/St.Louis Gal
　　Ca 428. House of David Blues/Sweet Butter
　　Ca 461. If You Don't Give Me What I Want(750)/Mamma's Gonna Slow You Down(751)
　　Ca 476. Dancing Dan
　　Ca 612. Mama's the Boss/Sweet Temptation Man
　　Ca 630. Oh Flo/(rev., by Haring)
　　Ca 647. Everything You Do
　　Ca 2047. Louisville Lou/Papa Blues
　　Ca 8245. Got Everything/(rev., Broadway Broadcasters)
　　Ca 8317. There's a Rainbow Around My Shoulder/(rev.,Caroliners)　-Ro 740
　　Ca 8325. Somebody Sweet/(rev., Caroliners)
　　Ca 9004. Diga Diga Do(3502)*/Cause I'm in Love(3503)*　　　　-Ro 808
　　Ca 9035. Bugle Call Rag*　　　　　　　　　　　　　　　　　　　-Ro 839
　　　　　　St. Louis Blues*
　　Ca 9056. Remember I Love You/(rev., Broadway Broadcasters)
　　Ca 9261. You're All the World to Me(3999)/(rev.,Willard Young)　-Ro 1063
　　Ro 249. Tell Me Tonight
　　Ro 491. Sorry/(rev., Fletcher Henderson)
　　Ro 493. Smile
　　Ro 501. I Ain't Got Nobody
　　Ro 651. Brotherly Love(3125)/(rev., Bob Haring)
　　Ro 653. Down by the Congo
　　Ro 659. Peek-a-Boo Eyes(3162)/(rev., Miami Royal Orchestra)
　　Ro 714. Down in Argentine
　　Ro 720. Crazy Rhythm
　　Ro 739. Imagination
　　Ro 749. You're the One and Only One(3315)/(rev., Sam Lanin)
　　Ro 851. I'm Just Wondering Who
　　Ro 887. There's Something New About an Old Moon(3621)*
　　Ro 1006. It Took a Lot of Blue(3902)/(rev., Detroiters)
　　Ro 1067. You Broke My Heart
　　Ro 1082. In My Wedding Gown
　　Li 2765. Stay Out of the South(2794)/Rev., Georgians)
　　Li 3169. You're My Waterloo(3768)*/(rev., Al Alberts)

DIXIE FOUR (James Blythe, piano; drums; bass; guitar):
　Para 12661. Kentucky Stomp(20658)/St. Louis Man(20660)
　Para 12674. South Side Stomp/Five o'Clock Blues

DIXIE JAZZ BAND (This name was used by many groups, which are identified where possible):
    Or   271. How Could You Leave Me Now
    Or   291. Honey Don't You Shake Me Down/Copenhagen
    Or   315. Hot Sax/Doo Waka Doo
    Or   443. Milenberg Joys
    Or   462. I Wanna Go Home
    Or   517. Hot Aire
    Or   590. Say Mister Have You Met Rosie's Sister?
    Or   591. Poor Papa
    Or   625. Junk Bucket Blues
    Or   682. Jackass Blues(377)/My Pal Jerry(378)
    Or   685. Messin' Around
    Or   688. Black Bottom/(rev., Roy Collins)
    Or   691. Nervous Charlie Stomp
    Or   717. Old Folks Shuffle
    Or   799. St. Louis Shuffle
    Or   804. Stockholm Stomp
    Or   828. Coffee Pot Blues(682)/(rev.,Ted White)   (Indiana Five)
    Or   829. The Crawl(684)/(rev.,Billy James)   (Indiana Five)
    Or   883. Rosy Cheeks
    Or   926. Sugar(911)
    Or   927. Some of these Days
    Or   956. Lighthouse Blues
    Or 1022. Jelly Roll Blues/I Ain't Got Nobody
    Or 1046. Washington and Lee Swing
    Or 1100. Sorry(1275)/(rev., Yankee Ten)
    Or 1122. Chloe(1306)/(rev., Bob Green)
    Or 1127. Once Over Lightly(1308)/(rev.,Yankee Ten) (Jack Pettis)
    Or 1131. Candied Sweets(1314)/(rev.,Yankee Ten)   (Jack Pettis)
    Or 1172. Moten Stomp(1366)/My Blue Ridge Mountain Home(1363)
    Or 1230. Know Nothin'Blues(1517)/(rev.,Yankee Ten)   -Je 5291
    Or 1256. Try to Smile(1573)/(rev., Oriole Orchestra)
    Or 1275. Somebody's Making a Fuss Over Somebody(1589)/Mississippi Mud(1633)
    Or 1282. If I Can Ba-ba-baby You(1638)/(rev., Yankee Ten)
    Or 1287. Sluefoot/Jazz Holiday   -Je 5335
    Or 1313. Deep Hollow
    Or 1339. When Sweet Susie Goes Steppin'By(1755)/(rev.,Miami Orchestra)
    Or 1360. Baby's Coming Back/I Loved You Then   -Chal 919
    Or 1343. What-cha-call'em Blues(1753)/(rev., University Boys)
    Or 1363. High Hatt'n'Hattie(1804),Teagarden,McPartland,Goodman
    Or 1371. Cool Papa/West End Blues
    Or 1387. Sunday Afternoon
    Or 1396. Dixie Drag(1881), McPartland, Goodman & Miller)   -Je 5446
    Or 1416. Missouri Squabble/Louder and Funnier
    Or 1425. I'm Lost Without You(1928)/(rev., Yankee Ten)
    Or 1426. I Love My Best Girl Best
    Or 1447. Wide Open Gate(1974)/(rev., University Boys)
    Or 1450. Mystic Bengal Bay(1977)/(rev., Billy James)
    Or 1454. Kat's Kittens
    Or 1457. You Please Me(1995)/(rev., Yankee Ten)
    Or 1474. Pepper Pot(1991)/(rev., University Boys)
    Or 1476. She's My Sweet Patootie(2033)/(rev., Miami Orchestra)
    Or 1504. Geraldine(2086)/(rev., Ted White)
    Or 1505. What Do You Think of My Baby
    Or 1507. Let's Get Together(2092)/(rev., Ted White)   -Je 5540

(Jimmy McPartland,cornet;Jack Teagarden,trombone;Benny Goodman,clarinet; others):
    Or 1536. Pa's Old Hat(2172)/(rev., Billy James)
    Or 1537. Makin' Friends 2170, 4   -Chal 999, Je 5569

    Or 1576. Where Has Mammy Gone?(2233)/(rev., Ted White)
    Or 1582. I've Got the San Francisco Blues(2251)/(rev.,Oriole Orchestra)
    Or 1602. Breakaway(2276)/(rev., Tennessee Happy Boys)   -Je 5264

(McPartland, Teagarden, Goodman; Gil Rodin, sax):
    Or 1624. Twelfth Street Rag(2334, 6)/After You've Gone(2335, 5)
    Or 1668. It's So Good(2432, 5)/(rev., University Boys)
    Or 1690 St.Louis Blues(2109, 3)/(rev., Ted White)

    Or 1663. Moanin' Low/You're Gonna Regret
    Or 1683. Cuddle Up Closer

(Pseudonym for Luis Russell Orchestra: Henry Allen, Bill Coleman, trumpets; J.C. Higginbotham, trombone; Albert Nicholas, clarinet and alto sax; Charlie Holmes, alto sax; Theo Hill, tenor sax; Luis Russell, piano; Will Johnson, guitar; Pop Foster, bass; Paul Barbarin, drums.--HD]:
    Or 1726. The Way He Loves Is Just Too Bad(2533)
    Or 1728. Broadway Rhythm (2525)
                          (See also: Lou and His Ginger Snaps)

    Je 5677. Moanin' Low(2405)/My Sweetie Turned Sour on Me(2406)

DIXIE JAZZERS WASHBOARD BAND (trumpet; harmonica; guitar;piano;washboard):
    Pat 7539. Kansas City Shuffle(107619)/Black Cat Bones(107620)   -Pe 139

DIXIE JAZZ HOUNDS (trumpet; trombone; clarinet; piano; drums):
    Do   306. Mindin' My Business/Hula Lou
    Do   308. Lots o' mama/She Wouldn't Do What I Asked Her
    Do   328. 31st Street Blues(10059)/(rev., Six Black Diamonds)

DIXIE RHYTHM KINGS (Shirley Clay, and one other, trumpets; Omer Simeon, clarinet
and alto sax; Cecil Irsin,tenor sax; probably William Barbee,piano; bass; banjo;
drums.--JI 12/6/40):
    .Br 7115. The Chant/Congo Love Song
     Br 7127. Easy Rider/Story Book Ball
           (See also; Omer Simeon, Helen Savage)

DIXIE SERENADERS:
     Ch 40003. St. Louis Blues(18182)/Cho-king(18183)

DIXIE STOMPERS (Collective personnel: Joe Smith, Russell Smith, Rex Stewart,Tommy Ladnier, trumpets; Charlie Green, trombone; Buster Bailey, clarinet and alto;
Don Redman, alto sax; Coleman Hawkins, tenor sax; Fletcher Henderson, piano;Chas.
Dixon, banjo; Escudero, bass; Kaiser Marshall, drums.--HD):
    Ha - 70. Spanish Shawl(141301)/Clap Hands Here Comes Charley(141302)
    Ha   88. Florida Stomp(141303)/Get It Fixed(141422)
    Ha   92. Chinese Blues(141423)/Panama(141424)
    Ha   121. I Found a New Baby(141526)/(rev., Broadway Bell Hops)
    Ha   153. Nervous Charlie Stomp(141527)/Black Horse Stomp(141528)   -Ve 1153
    Ha   166. Tampeekoe(141832)/Jackass Blues(141959)
    Ha   179. Hi Diddle Diddle(141833)/(rev., Original Indiana Five)
   .Ha   197. Hard to Get Gertie(141834)/Static Strut(141960)
    Ha   209. Dynamite(141958)
    Ha   283. Alabama Stomp(142847)/(rev., WMCA Broadcasters)   -Ve 1283
    Ha   299. Brotherly Love(142846)/Off to Buffalo(142845)   -Ve 1299
    Ha   353. Ain't She Sweet(143333)/Snag It(143334)   -Ve 1353, D1 2353
    Ha   407. Wang Wang Blues(143638)/Wabash Blues(143637)   -Ve 1407, D1 2407
    Ha   451. Variety Stomp(lee135)/The St.Louis Blues(144136) -Ve 1451, D1 2451
    Ha   467. Have It Ready(143332)/St.Louis Shuffle(143639)   -Ve 1467
    Ha   526. Black Maria(144896)/Baltimore(144898)   -Ve 1526, D1 2526
    Ha   545. Corn Fed(144134)/Goose Pimples(144897)   -D1 2545
    Ha   636. Oh Baby(145975)/Feelin' Good(145976)   -Ve 1636, D1 2636
    Ha   974. I'm Feelin' Devilish(145977)/(rev., Bert Lown)   -Ve 1974, D1 2974

DIXIE SYNCOPATORS (Pseudonym for King Oliver's Orchestra; See also: Oliver, and
Helen Savage):
    Pe 15685. Farewell Blues/Sobbin' Blues

DIXIE WASHBOARD BAND (George Mitchell, trumpet; clarinet;sax;piano;washboard):
    Co 14128. Wait Till You See My Baby(141553)/Livin' High(141554)
    Co 14141. You for Me for You(142172)/My Own Blues(142173)
    Co 14171. King of the Zulus(142856),trombone,banjo added/Zulu Blues(142857)
    Co 14188. Dark Eyes(142852)/Gimme Blues(142853)
    Co 14239. Cushion Foot Stomp(143613)/Anywhere Sweetie Goes(143612)
                                        - - -
    Ba 1781. Boodle Am/New Baby

DIXIELAND JAZZ BAND (See Original Dixieland Jazz Band)

DIXIELAND JUG BLOWERS (Johnny Dodds, clarinet, starred(*) titles only; violin,
sax; banjo; jug):
    Vi 20403. Louisville Stomp/Florida Blues
    Vi 20415. Memphis Shake*/(rev., Jelly Roll Morton)
    Vi 20420. House Rent Rag*/Don't Give All the Lard Away
    Vi 20480. Carpet Alley*/Boodle Am Shake*
    Vi 20649. Hen Party Blues*
    Vi 20770. If You Can't Make It Easy/When I Stopped
    Vi 20854. I Never Did Want You/Only Mother Cares for Me
    Vi 20954. National Blues/Southern Shout
    Vi 21126. Garden of Joy Blues/You'd Better Leave Me Alone
    Vi 21473. Banjorene/Love Blues

DIXIELAND THUMPERS (Johnny Dodds, clarinet; Natty Dominique, trumpet; Jas.Blythe,
piano; washboard):
    Para 12525. There'll Come a Day(4762-856)/Weary Way Blues(4763-855)

DIXIELAND JUG THUMPERS (Same personnel as above):
    Para 12594. Oriental Man(20240)/Sock That Thing(20241)
           (See: Blythe's Blue Boys; State Street Ramblers)

DIXON, VANCE AND HIS PENCILS:
    Co 14608. Hot Peanuts/Laughing Stomp
    Co 14673. Pete the Dealer in Meat/Who Stole the Lock?   -OK 8891

Crescent RECORDS

Presents

KID ORY'S CREOLE JAZZ BAND

•

MUTT CAREY—Trumpet BUSTER WILSON—Piano
KID ORY—Trombone BUD SCOTT—Guitar
OMER SIMEON—Clarinet ED GARLAND—Bass
ALTON REDD—Drums

•

CRESCENT 1

SOUTH CREOLE SONG

CRESCENT 2

BLUES FOR JIMMY GET OUT OF HERE

PRICE $1.00 EACH, PLUS TAXES—READY FOR DELIVERY

Released by

JAZZ MAN RECORD SHOP

1221 Vine Street
HOLLYWOOD 38, CALIFORNIA

DIXON'S JAZZ MANIACS (Clarinet; piano; banjo):
  Para 12405. Tiger Rag/ D A D Blues
  Para 12446. Crazy Quilt(4090-466)/My Man Just Won't Don't(4091-465)

DIXON, MARY (Vocal, cornet and piano acc.; clarinet and piano* acc.):
  Co 14415. You Can't Sleep in My Bed(148109)/Daddy You Got Everything(148110)
  Co 14442. Old Forsaken Blues(148725)*/All Around Mama(148726)*
  Co 14459. Black Dog Blues/Fire and Thunder Blues
  Co 14532. Unhappy Blues/Daddy You're a Low Down Man

DIXON, TOM (guitar acc.):
  OK 8570. Worry Blues/Labor Blues

DIXON and CHANNEY:
  Para 12471. Sweet Petunia/(rev., Dodds and Parham)

DODD, DOROTHY (vocal):
  Hy 110. I've Got the Blues/I Ain't Gonna Do It

JOHNNY DODDS

See Also:
  LOUIS ARMSTRONG: OK 8320, 8261, 8318, 8300, 8299, 8343, 8357, 8396, 8379, 8436, 8423, 8447, 8482, 8474, 8503, 8496, 8519, 8566, 8551, 8535; Co 35663, 35661, 35838.
  LOVIE AUSTIN: Para 12380, 12391, 12361.
  VIOLA BARTLETTE: Para 12369.
  JIMMY BERTRAND: Vo 1035, 1180, 1100, 1099, 1060.
  BEALE STREET WASHBOARD BAND: Vo 1403.
  JIMMY BLYTHE: Para 12376, 12368, 12428; Vo 1136, 1135.
  BUTTERBEANS AND SUSIE: OK 8355.
  CHICAGO FOOTWARMERS: OK 8533, 8548, 8599, 8792, 8613.
  CHICAGO HOTTENTOTS: Vo 1008.
  JUNIE C. COBB: Para 12382.
  WILMER DAVIS: Vo 1034.
  DIXIELAND JUG BLOWERS: Vi 20415, 20420, 20480, 20649, 20954.
  DIXIELAND THUMPERS: Para 12525, 12594.
  EDMONIA HENDERSON: Vo 1015.
  FREDDIE KEPPARD: Para 12399.
  LILL'S HOT SHOTS: Vo 1037.
  JELLY ROLL MORTON: Vi 20772, 20948, 21345, 21064; BB 1C256.
  NEW ORLEANS BOOTBLACKS: Co 14337, 14465.
  NEW ORLEANS WANDERERS: Co 696, 735.
  KING OLIVER: Para 12088, 20292; Ge 5132, 5133, 5134, 5135, 5184; OK 4906, 4918, 4933, 4975, 8148, 8235, 40000, 40034; Co 13000, 14003.
  PARAMOUNT PICKERS: Para 12779.
  TEDDY PETERS: Vo 1006.
  STATE STREET RAMBLERS: Ge 6232, 6249.
  SIPPIE THOMAS: Vi 38502.
  HOCIEL THOMAS: OK 8258, 8289, 8326.

DODDS and PARHAM (Johnny Dodds, clarinet; Tiny Parham, piano):
  Para 12471. Oh Daddy(4332-3,548)   -SD 102
            (rev., Dixon and Chaney)
  Para 12483. Loveless Love(4413,635)/Nineteenth Street(4414,634)
  Para 12494. ?

JOHNNY DODDS' BLACK BOTTOM STOMPERS (Louis Armstrong, cornet; Johnny Dodds, clarinet; Kid Ory, trombone; Johnny St.Cyr, banjo; Earl Hines, piano; Baby Dodds, drums; sax):
  Br 3567. Wild Man Blues(25)   -BrE 02011, BrF 500165, Polk 9035
  Br 3567. Wild Man Blues(26)   -KP 103
  Br 3567. Melancholy(27)   -Vo 1128, BrE 02065, BrF 500165, Me 12064 (Jack Winn)
  Br 3567. Melancholy(28)   -KP 103

(Johnny Dodds, clarinet; two trumpets; trombone; banjo; bass; piano; drums):
  Br 3568. Come On and Stomp Stomp Stomp/After You've Gone   -Br 7124, Vo 1148
  Br 3997. When Erastus Plays His Old Kazoo(45)/Joe Turner Blues(42)

JOHNNY DODDS (clarinet solos with piano and guitar):
  Br 3574. Clarinet Wobble(01)/San(04)
  Br 3585. Oh Lizzie(07)/The New St.Louis Blues(09)

JOHNNY DODDS' TRIO (clarinet; bass; piano; drums):
  Vi 21554. Blue Clarinet Stomp(46055)
          Blue Piano Stomp(46056)   -BB 1C238

JOHNNY DODDS' WASHBOARD BAND AND ORCHESTRA OR HOT SIX (Johnny Dodds, clarinet;
Natty Dominique, trumpet; Lil Hardin, piano; bass; drums or washboard;trombone):
```
    Vi 21552.  Bull Fiddle Blues(46065)                     -BB 10239
        "      Blue Washboard Stomp(46066)                  -BB  8549
    Vi 23396.  Goober Dance(48799)                          -BB 10240
        "      Indigo Stomp(48869)                          -BB 10238
    Vi 38004.  Bucktown Stomp(46063)                        -BB  8549
        "      Weary City(46064)                            -BB 10239
    Vi 38038.  Pencil Papa(48794)/Sweet Lorraine(48841)
    Vi 38541.  Heah Me Talkin'(48798)/My Little Isabel(48842)  -BB 10241
    BB 10240.  Too Tight/(coupled with Goober Dance, above)
```
JOHNNY DODDS AND HIS CHICAGO BOYS (Johnny Dodds, clarinet; Charlie Shavers,trumpet; Lil Hardin, piano; Teddy Bunn, guitar; John Kirby, bass;O'Neil Spencer, drums):
```
    De  1676.  Melancholy(63190a)                           -De 3864
        "      Stack o'Lee Blues(63193)
    De  2111.  Wild Man Blues(63189a)                       -De 3519
        "      29th and Dearborn(63191a)
    De  7413.  Blues Galore(63192)/Shake Your Can(63194)
```
JOHNNY DODDS AND HIS ORCHESTRA (Richard Jones, piano; Nat Dominique,trumpet;Preston Jackson, trombone;Johnny Dodds,clarinet; Lonnie Johnson, guitar:Johnny Lindsay, bass; Baby Dodds, drums):
```
    De 18094.  Red Onion Blues(93032a)/Gravier Street Blues(93033a)   -BrE 03168
```
DONAHUE, SAM AND HIS ORCHESTRA:
```
    OK  6334.  It Counts a Lot(29298),Count Basie,piano/Lonesome(29298)
```
DORSEY BROTHERS AND THEIR ORCHESTRA (Fuzzy Farrar, Leo McConville, Mannie Klein, trumpets; Tom Dorsey,Glenn Miller, trombones; Arnold Brillhardt, Herbie Spencer, Jimmy Dorsey, saxes; Joe Raymond, Joe Venuti, violins; Arthur Schutt,piano;Eddie Lang, guitar; Hank Stern, bass; Stanley, King, drums.--HD):
```
    OK 40995.  Mary Ann(400082b)                            -PaE 181
        "      Persian Rug(400083c)                         -PaE 202
    OK 41007.  Coquette(400144b)                            -PaE 142
        "      Yale Blues(400145c)
    OK 41032.  Indian Cradle Song(400633c)                  -PaE 202
        "      My Melancholy Baby(400634c)                  -PaE 181
    OK 41050.  That's My Mammy(400698a)                     -PaE 215
        "      Dixie Dawn(400699c)                          -PaE 280
    OK 41065.  Evening Star(400740b)                        -PaE 215
        "      Forgetting You(400741a)         -OdF 165368
    OK 41083.  Was It a Dream, I & 2 (400871/72)  -OdF 165382, PaE 226
    OK 41124.  'Round Evening(401169b)
        "      Out of the Dawn(401170b)                     -PaE 256
    OK 41151   Sally of My Dreams(401385b)/Cross Roads(401387b) -OdF 165544, PaE 316
    OK 41158.  She's Funny That Way(401386a)/(rev.,Milt Shaw)  -PaE 331
    OK 41181.  Let's Do It(401561)                          -PaE 331
        "      The Spell of the Blues(401560)               -PaE 385
    OK 41188.  My Kinda Love(401562)                        -PaE 374
    OK 41210.  Mean to Me(401715b)                 -OdF 165685, PaE 374
        "      Button Up Your Overcoat(401716c)            , PaE 391
    OK 41220.  I'll Never Ask for More(401717)/(rev., Goofus Five)
    OK 41223.  Lover Come Back to Me, I & 2(401775/6), Justin Ring, director
    OK 41272.  Singin' in the Rain(402531)                  -PaE 433
        "      Your Mother and Mine(402532)
    OK 41279.  Maybe, Who Knows(402533c)/(rev.,Smith Ballew)  -PaE 464
```
(Sub. Charlie Margulies,Lou Garcia,William Moore,trumpets; Bud Freeman,sax for Spencer,--HD):
```
    OK 41471.  Fine and Dandy(404544)                       -PaE 993
        "      But I Can't Make a Man(404545)               -PaE 882
    Co  2581.  By the Sycamore Tree(152034)
        "      Ooh That Kiss(152036)                        -PaE 1287
    Co  2589.  Why Did It Have to Be Me(152035)/(rev., Joe Venuti)  -PaE 1239
```
(See also: Travellers, Sleepy Hall and His Collegians)

(Featuring Muggsy Spanier, cornet):
```
    Pe 15265.  Have a Little Faith in Me(9277)-Or 1827, Im 2279, Re 8926, Ro  1192
    Pe 15269.  Congratulations(9278)3        -Or 1828, Ba 0566, Ca 0166,  Re 8931
        "      Beside an Open Fireplace(9279-2)-Or 1846, Im 2263, Ro 1203, Ba 0589
```

(Bunny Berigan, trumpet; Tom Dorsey, trombone; Jimmy Dorsey, clarinet and alto;
Larry Binyon, tenor; Fulton McGrath, piano; Dick McDonough, guitar; Artie Bernstein, bass; Stanley King, drums.--HD):   <u>1933</u>
```
BrE  1386. Comeone Stole Gabriel's Horn                           -BrF 9332
Br   6409. Sentimental Over You(12363a)          -Co 36065, BrE 1386
 "         Sing(1238Qa)                                           -BrF 9332
Br   6537. Mood Hollywood/Shim Sham Shimmy  -Co 36066,BrF 500237, BrE 01505
```

(Sub. Mannie Klein, trumpet, for Berigan):
```
Br   6624. By Heck                         -Co 36065, BrF 500304, BrE 01575
 "         Old Man Harlem
```

(Add Berigan, trumpet, and a third sax):
```
Br   7542. She's Funny That Way(B14156)/I Can't Make a Man(B14157)
                                                -BrF 500360, BrE 01617
```

(Probably: Frank Guarente, Mannie Klein, Charlie Margulies, trumpets; Chuck Campbell, Lloyd Turner, Tom Dorsey, trombones; Jimmy Crossan, Lyall Bowen, Jimmy Dorsey, Larry Binyon saxes; Harry Bluestone, Serge Kostelarsky, Joe Venuti, violins; Harry Waller, viola; Fulton McGrath, piano; Dick McDonough, guitar; Artie Bernstein, bass; Stanley King, drums.--HD):
```
Br   6722. Fidgety/The Blue Room                  -BrF 9504, BrE 01713
Br   6938. Judy/Annie's Cousin Fanny              -BrF 500449, BrE 02006
```
'See also: Mildred Bailey)

(Probably includes: George Thow, Charlie Spivak, trumpets; Tommy Dorsey, Don Matteson, Joe Yukl, trombones; Jimmy Dorsey, Jack Stacy, Skeets Herfurt, saxes; Bobby Van Eps, piano; Roc Hillman, guitar; Delmar Kaplan, bass; Ray McKinley, drums.--JRB):
```
De    115. I'm Getting Sentimental Over You(38304)/Long May We Love(38307)
De    116. I Ain't Gonna Sin No More/I Can't Dance           (-BrE 02373
De    117. Annie's Cousin Fannie/Dr. Heckle and Mr. Jibe
De    118. By Heck(38302a)
 "         Basin Street Blues(38412b)                         -BrE 01892
De    119. Milenberg Joys                                     -BrE 02023
 "         St. Louis Blues                            -BrE 01892, De 3524
De    195. I Couldn't Be Mean to You/Lost in a Fog
De    196. How Can You Face Me?/Moon Was Yellow
De    206. Day Dreams/Out in the Cold Again
De    207. Breeze/Don't Let It Bother You
De    208. Heat Wave/Stop Look and Listen
De    258. Earful of Music/Your Head on My Shoulder
De    259. Okay Toots/When My Ship Comes In
De    260. Fun to be Fooled/Let's Take a Walk Around the Block
De    283. What a Difference a Day Made/What Can You Say in a Love Song
De    291. Dream Man/Hands Across the Table
De    296. Honeysuckle Rose, I & 2(38409/10)                  -BrE 01890
De    297. Missouri Misery/Sandman
De    311. Here Is My Heart/Love Is Just Around the Corner
De    314. Apache/It's Dark on Observatory Hill
De    318. All Through the Night/Anything Goes
De    319. I Get a Kick Out of You/You're the Top
De    320. Blame it on My Youth/You Didn't Know Me From Adam
De    321. I'd Like to Dunk You in My Coffee/If It's Love
De    335. Dancing With My Shadow/I Believe in Miracles
De    340. Church Bells Told/Home Ties
De    348. I'm Just a Little Boy Blue/New Deal in Love
De    357. Au Revoir L'Amour/Singing a Happy Song
De    358. I Was Lucky/Rhythm of the Rain
De    367. I'm Facing the Music/Tiny Little Ringerprints
De    368. Farmer Takes a Wife/I Threw a Bean Bag at the Moon
De    370. Lullaby of Broadway/Words Are in My Heart
De    371. Don't Be Afraid to Tell Your Mother/I'm Goin' Shoppin' With You
De    376. Dinah/Night Wind                                   -BrE 02373
De    445. Gracias/Mama
De    469. Dese Dem Dose/Weary Blues
De    476. Chasing Shadows/Every Single Little Tingle of My Heart
De    480. Every Little Moment(39540a)/I'll Never Say Never Again(39542a)
De    482. Footloose and Fancy Free(39539a)/You're All I Need(39541a)
De    515. I've Got Your Number/Tomorrow's Another Day
De    516. Top Hat White Tie and Tails/No Strings              -BrE 307
De    519. I Couldn't Believe My Eyes/My Very Good Friend the Milkman
De    520. You're So Darn Charming/You Saved My Life
De    559. On a Sunday Afternoon/You Are My Lucky Star
De    560. I've Got a Feelin' You're Foolin'
 "         Tailspin                                           -BrE 02023
De    561. Dipper Mouth/Gentleman Obviously Doesn't Believe
De   1304. Eccentric/You're Okah
De  15013. Solitude/Weary Blues                               -BrE 0135
```

JIMMY DORSEY

See also:
  ADRIAN'S RAMBLERS: Br 6786.
  ARKANSAS TRAVELERS: Ha 332, 383, 421, 459.
  HOAGY CARMICHAEL: Vi 22864, 23013.
  CHARLESTON CHASERS: Co 446,861,909,1076,1539,1891,2133,2309.
  COTTON PICKERS: Br 4325, 4404, 4440, 4446, 4447.
  DORSEY BROTHERS: All of above.
  SEGER ELLIS: OK 41255, 41290, 41291.
  JEAN GOLDKETTE: Vi 20466, 20469, 20675, 20671, 20672.
  SLEEPY HALL: Me 12211.
  HOTSY TOTSY GANG: Br 4014, 4044, 4112, 4122, 4838, 4200, 4498, 4482, 4559,
     4587, 4641, 4674, 4983, 4920, 4998, 4535.
  HOT AIR MEN: Co 2092, 2175.
  EDDIE LANG: OK 41410, 41253.
  TED LEWIS: Co 2088, 2113, 2181, 2144, 2336, 2217.
  LOUISIANA RHYTHM KINGS: Vo 15833, 15841; Br 4706, 4845, 4908, 4923, 4938,
     3953.
  MIFF MOLE: OK 40758,40784,40846,41232,41273,41445,41371; PaE 647.
  MOUND CITY BLUE BLOWERS: OK 41515, 41526.
  NAPOLEON'S EMPERORS: Vi 38069, 38057.
  RED NICHOLS: Br 3407, 3477, 3490, 3550, 3597, 3855,3961,4243,4286,4456,4724,
     4790,4839,6012,6058,20062,20091,20092,6133,6138,6149,6160, 6164,6191,6198,
     6234, 6266, 6312,6348,6219,6241,6767,6451,6461,6534,7358.
  ORIGINAL MEMPHIS FIVE: Co 2588, 2577.
  RED HEADS: Pe 14565,14568,14600,14639,14708,14717,14757,14738,14764.
  RED & MIFF'S STOMPERS: Ed 51854, 51878; Vi 20778.
  GIL RODIN: Cr 3016, 3017, 3045, 3046.
  JACK TEAGARDEN: Cr 3051; Br 6741,6716,6780.
  TRAVELLERS: OK 41259, 41260; Me 12131,12148,12230,12227.
  SIX HOTTENTOTS: Ba 1962, 1964, 6008, 6009, 1986; Do 3956.
  TRUMBAUER: OK 40772; Vi 21193, 21397.
  JOE VENUTI: OK 41251,41192,41263,41427,41434,41451; Vi 23039,23018,23015;OK
     41469,41506; Co 2488,2535,2589; PaE 1252,1063,2765,2782,2783;CoE 601,637.
  WABASH DANCE ORCHESTRA
  WE THREE: Pe 14673.

DORSEY, JIMMY (clarinet and alto sax solos, acc. by Leo McConville,Mannie Klein,
trumpets;Tom Dorsey,trombone; Larry Abbot, Lucien Smith,saxes; Arthur Schutt,pi-
ano; Tony Caluccio,banjo; Hank Stern,bass; Stanley King,drums.--HD):
  OK 41245. Beebe(400877), alto   -OdF 165757, PaE 449
       "   Praying the Blues(400878), clarinet -Co 36063,   PaE 511

(Acc. by Claude Ivy, piano; Alan Ferguson, guitar; Spike Hughes, bass; Bill Har-
ty, drums.--HD):   England, 1930
  DeE 1876. I'm Just Wild About Harry(MB1618)/After You've Gone(MB1619)
  DeE 1878. Tiger Rag(MB1620)/St. Louis Blues(MB1621)   -DeE 6142

(Alto sax, acc. by Dorsey Brothers):
  Br   6352. Beebe(12701)   -Co 36063
       "   Oodles of Noodles(12073)   -BrF 500204, BrE 1361

JIMMY DORSEY AND HIS ORCHESTRA (George Thow, Toots Camarato, trumpets; Bobby
Byrne, Joe Yukl, Don Mattison, trombones; Jimmy Dorsey, alto sax; Fud Living-
ston, tenor sax; Jack Stacy, Skeets Herferth, saxes; Bobby Van Eps,piano;Rock
Hillman, guitar; Slim Taft, bass; Ray McKinley, drums.--HD):
  De   570. Me and Marie/When Love Comes Your Way
  De   571. Picture of Me Without You/Why Shouldn't I?
  De   602. You Let Me Down/Where Am I?
  De   607. Dusk in Upper Sandusky/I'm a gambler   -BrE 02224
  BrE 02225. I'll Stand By/Broadway Cinderella
  De   655. Tap Dancer's Nightmare/Washington Grays   -BrE 02172
  De   762. Wah Hoo   -BrE 02188
       "   What's the Reason   -BrE 02274
  De   764. You/You Never Looked so Beautiful   -BrE 02240
  De   768. Is It True What They Say About Dixie   -BrE 02226
       "   Welcome Stranger   -BrE 02237
  De   776. Robins and Roses   -BrE 02226
       "   Sing Sing Sing   -BrE 02274
  De   782. It's No Fun   -BrE 02237
       "   Moonrise on the Lowlands
  De   808. I Love to Sing-a   -BrE 02292
       "   'Tain't No Use   -BrE 02188
  De   873. Ah Woo, Ah Woo to You/There's No Substitute for You   -BrE 02282
  De   882. In a Sent'mental Mood/Stompin' at the Savoy   -BrE 02354
  De   901. Boston Tea Party/It Ain't Right   -BrE 02334
  De   941. Don't Look Now/Parade of the Milk Bottle Caps   -BrE 02322

100

```
De   „950.  Let's Call a Heart a Heart                              -BrE 02318
             So Do I                                                 -BrE 02319
De   „951.  One Two Button Your Shoe                                 -BrE 02319
             Pennies from Heaven                                     -BrE 02318
De   1040.  Serenade to Nobody in Particular/Waddlin' at the Waldorf -BrE 02373
De   1086.  Chicken Reel/Funicul' Funicula                           -BrE 02364
```

(Joe Meyer, Toots Camarata, trumpets; Bobby Byrne, Bruce Squires, Don Matteson, trombones; Jimmy Dorsey, Fud Livingston, Charles Frazier, Leonard Whitney,:axes; Freddy Slack, piano; Roc Hillman, guitar; Jack Ryan, bass; Ray McKinley, drums.- JRB: 1937

```
De   1187.  Listen to the Mocking Bird(DLA 732)                      -BrE 02409
             The Love Bug Will Bite You (DLA 735)                    „
De   1200.  Hollywood Pastime
             Jamboree                                                -BrE 02423
De   1203.  Slap That Bass(DLA 758)/They Can't Take That(DLA 760)    -BrE 02433
De   1204.  Let's Call the Whole Thing Off/They All Laughed          -BrE 02434
De   1256.  All God's Ch'llun Got Rhythm                             -BrE 02423
             Mutiny in the Brass Section
De   1301.  Just Lately
De   1377.  All You Want to Do Is Dance                              -BrE 02528
             Moon Got in My Eyes                                     -BrE 02527
De   1378.  After You                                                -BrE 02527
   „        It's the Natural Thing to Do                             -BrE 02528
```

(Sub. Shorty Cherock, trumpet, for Meyer; Dave Matteson, sax for Livingston, beginning with second title,--JRB):

```
De   1508.  I Got Rhythm                                             -BrE 02481
   „        Flight of the Bumble Bee
De   1651.  Doctor Rhythm/On the Sentimental Side
De   1652.  My First Impression of You/Smoke from a Chimney
De   1660.  I Was Doing All Right/Love Is Here to Stay
De   1671.  How 'Dja Like to Love Me/I Fall in Love With You         -DeE  6740
De   1723.  Joseph Joseph
   „        Two Bouquets                                             -DeE  6692
De   1724.  At a Perfume Counter/Love Walked In
De   1733.  Don't Be That Way/It's the Dreamer in Me
De   1745.  Stop and Reconsider/Week End of a Private Secretary
De   1746.  I Can't Face the Music/Lost and Found
De   1784.  At Your Beck and Call/Who Do You Think I Saw Last Night?
De   1799.  Cowboy from Brooklyn/Popcorn Man
De   1809.  If You Were in My Place/I Let a Song Go Out of My Heart
De   1834.  I Hadn't Anyone Till You/There's a Far Away Look in Your Eye
```

(Sub. Ralph Muzzillo, trumpet, for Camarata; Sonny Lee, trombone, for Squires; Milton Yaner, alto, for Matteson; add Herbie Haymer, tenor.--JRB):   1938

```
De   1921.  Any Time at All/I Love You in Technicolor
De   1939.  Darktown Strutters Ball/Dusk in Upper Sandusky
De   1961.  I Haven't Changed a Thing/Killy-Ka-Lee
De   1970.  Garden of the Moon/Love Is Where You Find It
De   2002.  Change Partners/Yam
De   2213.  Kinda Lonesome/Room With a View
De   2293.  Let's Stop the Clock/Masquerade Is Over
De   2294.  Good for Nothin'/Romance Runs in the Fam'ly
De   2295.  Deep Purple
De   2322.  I Get Along Without You Very Well/It's Anybody's Moon
De   2332.  It's All Yours(65053)/Th'is Is It(65054)
De   2352.  All of Me/Our Love
De   2363.  Arkansas Traveler(63792)/You're So Desirable(65200)
De   2522.  Home in the Clouds/My Love for You
De   2523.  All I Remember Is You/Show Your Linen Miss Richardson
De   2536.  Romance/This Is No Dream
De   2553.  I Poured My Heart into a Song/Old Fashioned Tune Is Always New
De   2554.  Back to Back
De   2567.  Stairway to the Stars/Whisper While We Dance
De   2577.  Is It Possible?/Rendezvous Time in Paree
De   2579.  Begone/Lamp Is Low
De   2580.  All or Nothing at All/In the Middle of a Dream
De   2612.  Jumpin' Jive(65967)/Shoot the Meat Balls to Me(65662)
De   2650.  Go Fly a Kite/Man and His Dream
De   2702.  It's Funny to Everyone But Me/One Sweet Letter from You
De   2727.  So Many Times/Take a Tip from the Whippoorwill
De   2735.  Body and Soul(65880)/Dixieland Detour(65968)
De   2745.  Comes Love/Let's Make Memories Tonight
De   2761.  Are You Havin' Any Fun?/Melancholy Lullaby
De   2810.  My Prayer/You're the Greatest Discovery Since 1492
De   2813.  I Didn't Know What Time It Was/Love Never Went to College
De   2814.  If I Had You/Table in the Corner
```

(Sub. Sam Rubinowitch, alto, for Whitney; Buddy Schutz, drums, for McKinley;
Joe Lippman, piano, for Slack; add Sy Baker.--JRB):   1939
    De 2837. Tomorrow Night/You're a Lucky Guy
    De 2838. On a Little Street in Singapore/My Silent Mood
    De 2918. Rigamarole(66912)/Swamp Fire(66913)
    De 2925. Do It Again/Now You Know
    De 2961. Cherokee/Man and His Dream
    De 2980. Keep Knockin'/Major and Minor Stomp
    De 3150. Breeze and I/Little Curly Hair in a High Chair
    De 3152. Boog It/Six Lessons from Madame La Zonga
    De 3166. Let There By Love/Poor Ballerina
    De 3176. Fools Fall in Love/Latins Know How

(Nate Kazebier, Jimmy Campbell, Shorty Solomon, trumpets; Don Matteson, Al
Jordan, Sonny Lee, trombones; Dorsey, Herbie Haymer, Milt Yaner, Sam Rubinwitch,
Charlie Frazier, saxes; Jack Ryan, bass; Buddy Schutz, drums; Guy Smith, guitar;
Joe Lippman, piano):
    De 3197. How Can I Ever Be Alone?/Tennessee Fish Fry
    De 3198. Contrasts/Perfidia
    De 3215. I Can't Resist You/I Love to Watch the Moonlight
    De 3255. Devil May Care/Hear My Song, Violetta
    De 3259. If I Forget You(67854)/All This and Heaven Too(67856)
    De 3270. Shades of Twilight/Where Do You Keep Your Heart?
    De 3280. Blue/I Bought a Wooden Whistle
    De 3311. And So Do I/Let Me Dream
    De 3312. Dolimite/Hep-Tee-Hootie
    De 3322. Once in a Lovetime/While the Music Plays On
    De 3391. Talkin' to My Heart/Whispering Grass
    De 3395. On the Trail/Yesterthoughts
    De 3435. Bad Humor Man/You've Got Me This Way
    De 3446. Handful of Stars
    De 3570. I Hear a Rhapsody(68461)/The Memory of a Rose(68471)
    De 3585. High on a Windy Hill/I Understand
    De 3629. Amapola/Donna Maria
    De 3647. Turn Left(68463)/Turn Right(68654)
    De 3657. When the Sun Comes Out/Yours
    De 3698. Green Eyes/Maria Elena
    De 3710. In the Hush of the Night/My Sister and I
    De 3711. Minnie from Trinidad/La Rosita
    De 3721. Au Reet/Man, That's Groovy
    De 3737. Once and for All/The Things I Love
    De 3772. Aurora/Bar Babble
    De 3775. All Alone and Lonely/Blue Champagne
    De 3812. Be Fair/Rose and a Prayer
    De 3859. Isle of Pines/Time Was
    De 3861. I Got Rhythm
    De 3928. Embraceable You(69214)/Fingerbustin'(69215)
    De 3963. Jim(69594)/A New Shade of Blue(69595)
    De 3991. Moonlight Masquerade(69597)/Wasn't It You?(69599)
    De 4034. Tropical Magic/It Happened in Hawaii
    De 4044. Any Bonds Today?
    De 4047. The Magic of Magnolias(DLA 2792)/Day Dream(DLA 2793)
    De 4075. Charleston Alley(69596)/The Spirit's Got Me(69598)
    De 4102. I Said No/This Is No Laughing Matter
    De 4103. I Got It Bad/White Cliffs of Dover
    De 4122. Arthur Murray Taught Me Dancing in a Hurry/Not Mine
    De 4123. Everything I Love/Tangerine
    De 4132. If You Build a Better Mousetrap/I Remember You
    De 4142. Sinner Kissed an Angel/You Made Me Love You
    De 4165. Drop Me a Line/When the Roses Bloom Again
    De 4170. President's Birthday Ball
    De 4197. I'm Glad There Is You/Tomorrow's Sunrise
    De 4202. Romance
    De 4207. Heavenly Hideaway/Overture to Love
    De 4262. Tain't No Good, I & 2
    De 4263. Absent Minded Moon/Me and My Melinda
    De 4277. Always in My Heart/Last Night I Said a Prayer
    De 4288. Jersey Bounce/My Little Cousin
    De 4304. I Threw a Kiss in the Ocean/Sleepy Lagoon
    De 4312. Full Moon/If You Are But a Dream
    De 4356. Murderistic/What Makes Sammy Run?
    De 15041. Song of the Volga Boatman(63690a)/I Cried for You(1938 personnel)
    De 18362. On Echo Hill/Wonder When My Baby's Coming Home
    De 18372. My Devotion/Sorghum Switch
    De 18376. Take Me/This Is Worth Fighting For
    De 18385. Blue Skies/Someday Sweetheart
    De 18433. I've Got a Gal in Kalamazoo/Serenade in Blue
    De 18460. Brazil/Daybreak
    De 18462. Every Night About This Time/I'm Getting Tired So I Can Sleep
    De 18467. At the Cross Roads/Manhattan Serenade

```
De 18532. Let's Get Lost/Murder He Says
De 18545. I'll Find You/Only a Rose
De 18571. Star Eyes/The're Either Too Young or Too Old
De 18582. My First Love/When They Ask About You
De 18574. Besame Mucho/My Ideal
De 18611. I'm in Love With Someone/It's a Crying Shame
```

TOMMY DORSEY

```
See Also:
ALL STAR BAND: Vi 26144.
BIX RHYTHM JUGGLERS: Ge 5654.
JACK BLAND: Pe 15689, 15694.
RUBE BLOOM: Co 2103, 2186, 2218.
HOAGY CARMICHAEL: Vi 38139.
CHARLESTON CHASERS: Co 2133, 2219, 2309.
COTTON PICKERS: Br 4325, 4404, 4440, 4446, 4447.
DORSEY BROTHERS.
SEGER ELLIS: OK 41255, 41290, 41291.
JEAN GOLDKETTE: Vi 20466, 20675, 20469, 20471, 20472.
SLEEPY HALL: Me 12211.
JAM SESSION AT VICTOR: 25569.
ED LANG: OK 41410, 41253.
RED NICHOLS: Br 4701; Vi 23033, 23026.
ORIGINAL MEMPHIS FIVE: Co 2588, 2577.
JACK TEAGARDEN: Co 2558.
TRAVELLERS: OK 41259, 41260; Me 12137, 12148, 12230, 12227.
JOE VENUTI: OK 41051, 41056, 41192, 41263; Vi 23039, 23018, 23015.
```

TOM DORSEY, (trumpet solos, acc. by Arthur Schutt, piano; Eddie Lang,guitar;Tony Williams, bass; Stanley King, drums.--HD):
```
OK 41178. It's Right Here for You(401308c)              -PaE 449
         Tiger Rag(401309c)                             -PaE 462
```

TOM DORSEY AND HIS NOVELTY ORCHESTRA (Tom Dorsey, trumpet; Frank Signorelli, piano; Eddie Lang, guitar; Stanley King, drums.--HD):
```
OK 41422. Daddy Change Your Mind(401821b)/You Can't Cheat a Cheater(401822c)
                                                        (-OdF 238128
```

TOM DORSEY (trombone solo, acc. by Dorsey Brothers):
```
BrF 50024. Three Moods(12150)                           -BrE 1367
```

TOMMY DORSEY'S CLAMBAKE SEVEN (Sterling Bose, trumpet; Tommy Dorsey,trombone;Joe Dixon, clarinet; Sid Block, tenor sax; Dick Jones, piano; William Schaeffer,guitar; Gene Traxler, bass; Dave Tough, drums.--HD):   1936
```
Vi 25201. Rhythm in My Nursery Rhymes(98364)
          Music Goes Round and Round(98363)             -GrF 7664
Vi 25220. One Night in Monte Carlo(98389)/The Day I Let You Get Away(98390)
```

(Sub. Max Kaminsky,trumpet, for Bose; Carmen Mastren, guitar, for Schaeffer; Bud Freeman, sax, for Block, in second title):
```
Vi 25314. Rhythm Saved the World(99921)/At the Codfish Ball(101453)
```

(Sub. Pee Wee Irwin, trumpet, for Kaminsky; Johnny Mince, clarinet, for Dixon; Howard Smith, piano):
```
Vi 25568. Milkmen's Matinee(07807)/Twilight in Turkey(07804)  -HMV 8596
Vi 25577. Alibi Baby)07806)
          He's a Gypsy from Poughkeepsie(07805)         -GrF 7976
Vi 25605. If You Ever Should Leave(010559)/Posin'(010563)
Vi 25607. Don't Ever Change(010561)/Love Was Meant to Be(010562)
Vi 25610. Is This Gonna Be My Lucky Summer(010558)/Who'll Be the One This Sum-
                                                       (mer?(010560)
```

(Sub. Russ Isaacs, drums, for Tough):
```
Vi 25620. My Cabin of Dreams(011090)/Am I Dreaming?(011092)
Vi 25625. You're My Desire(011091)
          In My Meditations(011093)                     =HMV 5260
```

(Sub. Dave Tough, drums, for Isaacs):
```
Vi 25630. Stardust on the Moon(011353)/Having a Wonderful Time(011351)
Vi 25647. After You(011352)
          All You Want To Do Is Dance(011350)           -GrF 3021
Vi 25652. The Big Apple(011719)/(rev., Fats Waller)
Vi 25673. The Lady is a Tramp(013522)
          Tears(013523)                                 -GrF 3021
Vi 25676. Josephine(013524)/If the Man in the Moon(013525)
Vi 25695. Nice Work If You Can Get It(014679)/You're a Sweetheart(014680)
Vi 25821. Everybody's Doing It/When the Midnight Choo Choo Leaves
Vi 25899. As Long as You Live/A tisket a Tasket
Vi 26005. My Own/You're as Pretty as a Picture
Vi 26023. Chinatown/Sheik or Araby
```

```
Vi 26066.  Sailing at Midnight/You Must Have Been a Beautiful Baby
Vi 26119.  Do You Remember Last Night?/Thanks for Everything
Vi 26356.  Stop Kicking My Heart Around
Vi 26363.  It's a Hundred to One/Vol Vistu Gaily Star
Vi 26370.  Alla en el Rancho Grande/Shoot the Sherbert to Me Herbert
```

TOMMY DORSEY AND HIS ORCHESTRA (Andy Ferretti, Sterling Bose, Cliff Weston,trumpets; Tommy Dorsey, Joe Ortlando, Dave Jacobs, trombones; Sid Stoneburn, Nonie Bernardi, Clyde Rounds, Johnny Van Eps, saxes; Paul Mitchell, piano; Mac Cheikes, guitar; Gene Traxler, bass; Sam Weiss, drums.):   1935

```
    V" 25144.  Take Me Back to My Boots and Saddles(95141)
         "     On Treasure Island(95143)                           -HMV 308
    Vi 25145.  Santa Claus Is Comin' to Town(95144)/(rev.,Benny Goodman)
    V' 25158.  You Are My Lucky Star(95379)E.Powell,trumpet/I've Got a Feelin'
                                        (You're Foolin'(95380) -GrF 7647
    Vi 25159.  Weary Blues(95142)                                 -HMV   55
         "     Now You've Got Me Doing It(95503)                  -HMV 5022
    Vi 25172.  It's Written in the Stars(95518)/One Umbrella for Two(95519)
    Vi 25183.  At a Little Church Affair(98103)
               Don't Give Up the Ship(98101)                      -HMV   55
    Vi 25191.  Two Hearts Carved on a Lonesome Pine(98100)
               Alone(98102)                              -HMV 5029, GrF 7664
    Vi 25206.  Pagan Star(98104)/Weary(98368)
    Vi 25236.  I'm Gettin' Sentimental Over You(95145)            -HMV 8565
         "     I've Got a Note(95504)                             -HMV 8570
```

(Sub. Joe Bauer,trumpet, for Weston; Tom Macey, clarinet and sax,for Stoneburn):
```
    Vi 25214.  Love Will Live On(98391)/Then I Shan't Love You Any More(98392)
    Vi 25216.  I'm Shootin' High(98369)                           -GrF 7725
         "     That Lovely Night in Budapest(99040)
    Vi 25217.  I Picked a Flower(98378)/Please Believe in Me(98379)
    V' 25246.  If You Love Me(98857)/A Little Rendezvous in Honolulu(99039)
    Vi 25256.  Gotta Go to Work Again(99038)/Every Minute of the Hour(99041)
```

(Max Kaminsky, Sam Kolnick, Joe Bauer, trumpets; Tommy Dorsey, Ben Pickering,Walter Mercurio, trombones; Joe Dixon(clarinet), Fred Stulce, Clyde Rounds,Sid Block, saxes; Dick Jones. piano; William Schaefer, guitar; Gene Traxler, bass; D.Tough, drums;):
```
    Vi 25284.  Robins and Roses(99916)/You Started Me Dreaming(99918)
    Vi 25291.  You(99915)/You Never Looked So Beautiful(99917)
    Vi 25292.  It's You I'm Talkin' About(99919)/Will I Ever Know?
```

(Sub. Bob Bunch, sax, for Block):
```
    Vi 25320.  Star Dust(99949)/(rev., Benny Goodman)             -HMV 8468
    Vi 25326.  Royal Garden Blues(99950)/Ja-Da(101454)            -HMV 8517
```

(Sub. Carmen Mastren, guitar, for Schaeffer; Bud Freeman, for Bunch, sax):
```
    V' 25349.  On the Beach at Bali Bali(101261)/No Regrets(101262)
    Vi 25352.  You've Gotta Eat Your Spinach(101260)/San Francisco(101263)
```

Sub. Sid Lipkins, trumpet, for Kolnick; Les Jenkins, trombone, for Pickering):
```
    Vi 25363.  That's a Plenty(101264)
         "     There's a Small Hotel                              -HMV 8548
    Vi 25341.  Mary Had a Little Lamb(101846)/Did I Remember(101847)
    Vi 25446.  Another Perfect Night Is Ending(02171)/For Sentimental Reasons(02164)
    Vi 25447.  Close to Me(02168)/High Hat Piccolo and Cane(02166)
    V' 25467.  After You've Gone(02163)/(rev., Benny Goodman)
```

(Add Ray McKinney, trumpet)*
```
    Vi 25476.  Tea of the Terrace(03083)*/I'm in a Dancing Mood(03084)*
    Vi 25482.  Keepin' Out of Mischief Now(03085)*/There's Frost on the Moone(03248)*
    Vi 25474.  That Foolish Feeling(03247)*/Where Are You(03246)*
    Vi 25487.  Head Over Heels in Love(02165)/May I Have the Next Romance(02169)
    Vi 25496.  Maple Leaf Rag(02172)/Jamboree(03086)*
    Vi 25535.  Where Is My Heart(101844)/Long Ago and Far Away(101845)
```

(Sub. Bunny Berigan, trumpet, for Kaminsky; Artie Foster,trombone, for Jenkins):
```
    Vi 25508.  The Goona Goo(03898)/If My Heart Could-Only Talk(03899)
    Vi 25509.  Lookin' Around the Corner for You(04202)
               Mr. Ghost Goes to Town(04201)                      -HMV 5193
    Vi 25513.  How Could You(03991)/On a Little Bamboo Bridge(03990)
    Vi 25519.  Who'll Buy My Violets(03989)                       -HMV 5193
               Melody in F(03992)                                 -HMV 8578
```

(Sub. Edward Bone, trombone, for Foster; Bob Cusamano; Joe Welch, trumpet, for Lipkins):
```
    Vi 25516.  Dedicated to You(04535)
               You're Here You're There(04532)                    -HMV 5269
```

```
        Vi 25523. Marie(04534)                                -HMV 8570
                  Song of India(04533)            -Vi 20-1550, HMV 8565

(Sub. Ferrett', trumpet for Cusamano; Slats Long, clarinet, for Dixon):
        Vi 25532. In a Little Hula Heaven(04928)/Sweet Is the Word for You(04927)
        Vi 25534. I'll Dream My Way to Heaven(04929)/Thanks for Everything(04932)
        Vi 25539. Liebestraum(04933)                              -HMV 8578
                  Mendelssohn's Spring Song(04934)

(Sub. Pee Wee Irwin, trumpet, for Berigan; omit Welch; Johnny Mince, clarinet, for
Long; Mike Doty, sax, for Rounds):
        Vi 25544. Beginners Luck(06620)/They All Laughed(06619)
        Vi 25549. They Can't Take That Away from Me(06431)/I've Got Rain my Eyes
        Vi 25553. Jammin'(06675)/Turn Off the Moon(06674)              (06676)
        Vi 25556. Blue Danube(06622)/Black Eyes(06623)
        Vi 25557. Wanted(06621)/(rev., Bunny Berigan)
        Vi 25559. (See Jam Session at Victor)

(Howard Smith, piano):
        Vi 25570. Nola(7808)/Satan Takes a Holiday(7809)          -GrF 8022
        Vi 25573. Wake Up and Live(7807)/Sleep(02170),see above for personnel
        Vi 25581. Good Mornin'(010130)/Mountain Music(10129)
        Vi 25591. Love Is Never Out of Season(7897)/Our Penthouse on Third Avenue(8799)
        Vi 25596. Happy Birthday to Love(010343)/Strangers in the Dark(010344)

(Sub. A. Antonelli, sax, for Freeman, next coupling only):
        Vi 25600. Humoresque(010148)/Rollin' Home(010149)
        Vi 25603. You're Precious to Me(010342)/That Stolen Melody(010564)
        Vi 36207. Stop Look Listen(7810)/Beale St.Blues(010345)   -HMV 2938, GrF 1040
        Vi 36396. Deep River/Without a Song

(Sub. Russ Isaacs, drums, for Tough):
        Vi 25623. The Things I Want(011095)/Allegheny Al(011096)

(Sub. Walter Mercurio, trombone, for Bone; Skeets Herfurt, alto sax, for Doty; D.
Tough, drums):
        Vi 25635. Have You Got Any Castle Baby(011354)/You've Got Something (011355)
        Vi 25648. You and I Know(011711)/Goodbye Jonah(011712)
        Vi 25649. If You Were Someone Else/An Old Flame Never Dies(011710)
        Vi 25657. Night and Day(011356)/Smoke Gets in Your Eyes(011357)    -HMV 8681
        Vi 25663. In the Still of the Night(011354)/Who Knows(013355)      -GrF 8019
        Vi 25686. Once in a While(011363)/If It's the Last Thing(013356)
        Vi 25703. The Morning After(011362)/I May Be Wrong
        Vi 25733. I'm the One Who Loves You/Little White Lighthouse
        Vi 25741. Can't I/One I Love

(Sub. Lee Castaldo, trumpet, for Bauer; Dorsey, Kenkins, D'Annolfo, trombones):
        Vi 25750. Just a Simple Melody/ Little White Lies
        Vi 25692. Moan'n' in the Morning(014681)/Down With Love(014682)
        Vi 25693. Dipsy Doodle(014684)                          -HMV 8692, GrF 8125
                  Who (014683)
        Vi 25694. In a Mission by the Sea(014669)/Getting Some Fun Out of Live(014668)

(Sub. Hagen for D'Annolfo):
        Vi 25763. Big Dipper/Smoke from a Chimney
        Vi 25766. Just Let Me Look at You/You Couldn't Be Cuter
        Vi 25767. Beale Street Blues(17699)/Stop Look and Listen
        Vi 25774. Annie Laurie/More Than Ever
        Vi 25780. Oh Promise Me/Shine on Harvest Moon
        Vi 25795. Bewildered/Jezebel
        Vi 25799. How Can You Forget/There's a Boy in Harlem
        Vi 25803. Good Night Sweet Dreams/Moonlight on the Purple Sage
        Vi 25813. Comin' Thru the Rye/I Never Knew
        Vi 25815. Deed I Do/Yearning
        Vi 25824. Oh How I Hate to Get Up/What'll I Do
        Vi 25828. Says My Heart/You Leave Me Breathless
        Vi 25832. Cowboy from Booklyn,I'll Dream Tonight
        Vi 25848. I Hadn't Anyone Till You/(rev., Bunny Berigan)
        Vi 25856. My Walking Stick/Now It Can Be Told
        Vi 25862. Marching Along With Time/This Time It's Real
        Vi 25866. All Through the Night/Music Maestro Please
        Vi 25879. This Time It's Real
        Vi 25887. Barcarolle/Canadian Capers
        Vi 26012. I'll See You in My Dreams/Stop Beatin' Round
        Vi 26016. Copenhagen/Sweetheart of Sigma Chi
        Vi 26030. There's No Place Like Your Arms/Ya Got Me
        Vi 26054. Boogie Woogie/Weary Blues
        Vi 26062. Rainbow Round the Moon/Stompin' at the Stadium
        Vi 26072. Carolina Moon/(rev., Sammy Kaye)
```

(Tommy Dorsey, Les Jankins, E. Hagen, trombones; H. Schertzer, D. Kincaide, F. Stulce, J. Mince, A. Herfurt, saxes; A. Ferretti, L. Castaldo, G. Irwin, trumpets; G. Traxler, bass; C. Mastren, guitar; H. Smith, piano; M. Purtill, drums):
    Vi 26085. Lightly and Politely/Washboard Blues
    Vi 26097. Room With a View/Down Home Rag

(Sub. Zudecoff, Smithers, for Hagen, trombone; Shapiro, Lawson, trumpets, for Ferretti, Irwin; Babe Rusin, sax, for Herfurt):
    Vi 26105. Tin Roof Blues/Sweet Sue
    Vi 26115. Angels With Dirty Faces/Between a Kiss and a Sigh
    Vi 26126. Hawaiian War Chant/Midnight on the Trail
    Vi 26135. It's Easy to Blame the Weather/Davenport Blues
    Vi 26140. Old Curiosity Shop/What Do You Know
    Vi 26145. Old Black Joe/Cocktails for Two
    Vi 26148. I'm So Weary of It All/Never Again
    Vi 26149. It's All Yours/This Is It
    Vi 26154. Heaven Can Wait/You Taught Me to Love Again

(Sub. Ward Silloway, trombone, for Jenkins, Zudecoff; Stulce, Vince, Rusin, Herfurt, saxes; Ferretti, Irwin, Castaldo, trumpets; Tough, drums):
    Vi 26163. Hold Tight Hold Tight/Symphony in Riffs(personnel third above)
    Vi 26172. Honolulu/This Night
    Vi 26181. New Moon and Old Serenade/Peckin' With the Penguins
    Vi 26185. Blue Moon/Panama
    Vi 26195. Got No Time/Little Skipper
    Vi 26202. Only When You're in My Arms/Our Love
    Vi 26210. Asleep or Awake/If You Ever Change
    Vi 26226. You Grow Sweeter as the Years Go By/In the Middle of a Dream
    Vi 26234. This Is No Dream/To You
    Vi 26246. Dawn on the Desert/Why Begin Again

(Add Kincaide, sax; sub Yank Lawson, trumpet, for Castaldo):
    Vi 26259. The Lamp Is Low/Hymn to the Sun(Howard Smith, piano)
    Vi 26264. Is It Possible/Rendezvous Time in Paree
    Vi 26271. Back to Back/I Poured My Heart into a Song
    Vi 26281. All I Remember Is You/Well All Right
    Vi 26287. Oh You Crazy Moon/You Don't Know How Much You Can Suffer
    Vi 26294. Guess I'll Go Back Home/How Am I to Know
    Vi 26313. Go Fly a Kite/Man and His Dream
    Vi 26321. Tea for Two(add D. Jacobs, trombone)/Night in Sudan(C.Carroll, drums)
    Vi 26325. Running Through My Mind/Stop It's Wonderful
    Vi 26333. Let's disappear/La Rosita
    Vi 26339. Blue Orchids/Day in Day out
    Vi 26346. By the River St.Marie/March of the Toys
    Vi 26356. All in Favor Say Aye

(Sub. Schertzer, sax, for Herfurt; J.Blake, trumpet, for Irwin; C.Leeman, drums):
    Vi 26376. Night Glow/Stomp It Off(Herfurt for Kincaide, Mickey Bloom, trumpet,
    Vi 26386. Baby What Else Can I Do/So Many Times   (for Blake, no Jacobs)
    Vi 26390. Indian Summer/Lover Is Blue
    Vi 26401. All the Things You Are   -Vi 20-1561
    "   That Lucky Fellow
    Vi 26406. All in Fun/Heaven in My Arms
    Vi 26418. After All/Blue Rain
    Vi 26429. Easy Does It/Am I Proud
    Vi 26433. Careless/Darn That Dream

(Dorsey, Jacobs, Silloway, Smithers, trombones; Stulce, Mince Rusin, Herfurt, Kincaide, saxes; Ferretti, Lawson, Castaldo, trumpets; Mastren, Traxler, Smith, Tough):
    Vi 26437. Milenberg Joys, I & 2
    Vi 26439. Losers Weepers/Faithful to You
    Vi 26445. Deep Night/Starlit Hour
    Vi 26465. Angel/It's a Blue World
    Vi 26470. I Concentrate on You/I've Got My Eyes on You
    Vi 26500. Sweet Potato Piper/Too Romantic

(Sub. Irwin, trumpet, for Castaldo):
    Vi 26508. Lonesome Road, 1 & 2
    Vi 26518. The Sky Fell Down/After I Say I'm Sorry
    Vi 26525. Moments in the Moonlight/Shake Down the Stars
    Vi 26535. My My/Say It
    Vi 26539. I'll Be Seeing You   -Vi 20-1574
    "   Polka Dots and Moonbeams
    Vi 26555. This Is the Beginning of the End/Fable of the Rose
    Vi 26581. Charming Little Faker/Imagination
    Vi 26593. Devil May Care/Fools Rush In
    Vi 26596. It's a Lovely Day Tomorrow/You're Lonely and I'm Lonely
    Vi 26606. April Played the Fiddle/I Haven't Time to Be a Millionaire
    Vi 26609. Buds Won't Bud/I'm Nobody's Baby
    Vi 26616. Hear My Song Violetta/Yours Is My Heart Alone

```
Vi 26628. I'll Never Smile Again/Marcheta
Vi 26636. Hong Kong Blues/You Think of Everything
Vi 26653. All This and Heaven Too/Where Do You Keep Your Heart
Vi 26660. And So Do I/One I Love
Vi 26666. Only Forever/Trade Winds
Vi 26678. Call of the Canyon/Love Lies
Vi 26717. I Could Make You Care
Vi 26736. Our Love Affair/That's for Me
Vi 26738. Looking for Yesterday/I Wouldn't Take
Vi 26747. We Three/Tell Me at Midnight
Vi 26761. You're Breaking My Heart
Vi 26764. When You Awake
Vi 26770. I'd Know You Anywhere/You've Got Me This Way
Vi 26786. Make Me Know It/When I Saw You
Vi 26798. Do You Know Why/Isn't That Just Like Love
Vi 27208. Anything
     "    Another One of Them Things               -Vi 20-1553
Vi 27219. Not So Long Ago/You Say the Sweetest Things
Vi 27233. Star Dust/Swanee River
Vi 27249. Swing High/Swing Time Up in Harlem
Vi 27274. Oh Look at Me Now/You Might Have Belonged to Another
Vi 27317. Dolores/I Tries
Vi 27338. Do I Worry/Little Man With a Candy Cigar
Vi 27350. You Lucky People
Vi 27359. Everything Happens to Me/Whatcha Know Joe
Vi 27392. You Betcha My Life/I Love It
Vi 27421. Yes Indeed                               -Vi 20-1550
     "    Will You Be Mine
Vi 27461. Kiss the Boys Goodbye/I'll Never Let a Day Pass
Vi 27483. Nine Old Men/Love Me As I Am
Vi 27508. Ne'ani/This Love of Mine
Vi 27518. Royal Garden Blues/Getting Sentimental Over You
Vi 27519. Marie/Who
Vi 27520. Song of India/Star Dust
Vi 27521. Little White Lies/I'll Never Smile Again
Vi 27526. Loose Lid Special
Vi 27532. You and I/Free for All
Vi 27566. Blue Skies/Back Stage at the Ballet
Vi 27578. Swingin' on Nothin'/On the Alamo
Vi 27591. Hallelujah/Pale Moon
Vi 27597. None But the Lonely Heart/Eli Eli
Vi 27611. Two in Love/A Sinner Kissed an Angel
Vi 27617. That Solid Old Man/Fifty Million Sweethearts Can't Be Wrong
Vi 27621. The Skunk Song, 1 & 2
Vi 27638. Embraceable You/The Sunshine of Your Smile
Vi 27690. Violets for Your Furs/Somebody Loves Me
Vi 27701. Who Can I Turn to/I Think of You
Vi 27710. It Isn't a Dream Any More/How Do You Do Without Me
Vi 27749. Winter Weather/How About You
Vi 27782. What Is This Thing Called Love/Love Sends a Little Gift of Roses
Vi 27849. Poor You/Last Call for Love
Vi 27869. I'll Take Tallulah/Not So Quiet Please
Vi 27876. Moonlight on the Ganges/Snootie Little Cutie
Vi 27887. Well Git It/Somewhere a Voice Is Calling
Vi 27903. Just As Though You Were Here/Street of Dreams
Vi 27923. Be Careful It's My Heart/Take Me
Vi 27941. He's My Guy/Light a Candle in the Chapel
Vi 27947. A Boy in Khaki
     "    In the Blue of Evening                  -Vi 20-1530
Vi 27962. Blue Blazes/Manhattan Serenade
Vi 27974. There Are Such Things/Daybreak
Vi 20-1530.. It's Always You
Vi 20-1539. Dig Down Deep/You Took My Love
Vi 20-1552. It Started All Over Again/Mandy Make Up Your Mind
Vi 20-1553. The Night We Called it a Day
BB 10726. East of the Sun/Head on My Pillow
BB 10771. Whispering/Funny Little Pedro
BB 10810. Quiet Please/So What

DOUGLAS, DAISY:
   Co 14175. Down Hearted Blues/St. Louis Blues

DOUGLAS, RUSSELL (Tenor, acc. by piano and Ed Lang, guitar):
   OK 40747. In a Little Spanish Town/Thinking of You
   OK 40801. Somebody Said(80678b)/It All Depends on You(80679b)

DUBIN'S DANDIES (possibly a Rollini combination):
   Or 1761. What Do You Care(19087)
   Or 1786. Can't Stop Caring for you(19159)         -Ro 1151
   Or 1788. Can You Fry an Egg(19144)                -Ro 1153
   Or 1824. In Harlem's Araby(19268)                 -Ro 1187
   Or 1949. Every Highway Every Byway(19716)
   Or 2007. I've Got My Mind on You(19844)
```

DUDLEY, ROBERTA (acc. by Mutt Carey, cornet; Kid Ory, trombone; Dink Johnson, clarinet; Fred Washington, piano; Ed Garland, bass; Ben Borders, drums,-- JI, 8/9/40, 11/22/40): Los Angeles, 1921
   Nor 3001. When You're Alone/Krooked Blues   -Su 3001
   (See also: Spike's Seven Pods of Pepper, Ory's Sunshine Orchestra)

DUFFIE, SIDE WHEEL SALLY:
   Para 12519. Treat 'em Right Blues/Kind Papa Blues

DUFFY, AL FOUR (Al Duffy, violin; Jimmie Lytell, clarinet; Frank Victor, guitar; Joe Tarto, bass):
   De 1683. Ciribiribin/Marie Ah Marie
   De 2799. Fun'culi Funicula(63231a)/La Espagnole(63233a)

DUMAINE'S (LOUIS) JAZZOLA EIGHT (Louis Dumaine, cornet; Willie Joseph, clarinet; Earl Humphrey, trombone; Louis James, tenor sax; Morris Rouse, piano; Leonard Mitchell, banjo; Joe Howard, bass; James Willigan, drums.): New Orleans, 1927
   Vi 20580. Franklin Street/Red Onion Drag
   Vi 20723. Pretty Audrey/To-wa-bac-a-wa
   (See also: Ann Cook)

DUNHAM, SONNY AND HIS ORCHESTRA:
   BB 11253. Nickel Serenade/Hi Neighbor
   BB 11289. Memories of You/As We Walk into the Sunset
   BB 11514. You're Blase/Sweet talk

(Sonny Dunham, trumpet and trombone; Russell Johnson, drums; Herbert Sweet, piano; Lou Green, guitar; Charles Green, bass):
   Vs 8205. Just a Memory(US 1342)/Estrellita(US 1343)
   - - -
   Vs 8227. Little White Lies(US 1424)/Dark Eyes(US 1427)
   Vs 8234. Memories of You(US 1425)/Blue Skies(US 1426)
   - - -
   Hit 7073. When They Ask About You/I'll be Around
   Hit 7074. Holiday for String/Don't Worry Mom

DUNN, BLIND WILLIE (Ed Lang, guitar, acc. by Frank Signorelli, piano):
   OK 8633. Church Street Sobbin' Blues(401292c)/There'll Be Some Changes Made
                                                                (401293b) -PaE 1495

BLIND WILLIE DUNN AND LONNIE JOHNSON (guitar duets):
   OK 8637. Two Tone Stomp(401338)
       Have to Change Keys to Play These Blues(401339)   -PaE 1195
   OK 8743. Deep Minor Rhythm Stomp(403039a)/Hot Fingers(403043a)
      (See also: Lonnie Johnson, OK 8695, 8711, 8818)

BLIND WILLIE DUNN'S GIN BOTTLE FOUR:
   CK 8689. Jet Black Blues(401842b)/Blue Blood Blues(401843b)

DUNN, JOHNNY (cornet solos acc. by piano, banjo):
   Co 124. Dunn's Cornet Blues(81685)/You've Never Heard the Blues(81686)

JOHNNY DUNN'S ORIGINAL JAZZ HOUNDS: Includes Johnny Dunn, cornet; Cal Jones; Bud Aiken, trombones; Garvin Bushell, alto sax; George Wilson, Dan Wilson, pianos; Cokey Spivey, John Mitchell, guitars): 1923-24
   Co A3541. Bugle Blues(80113)/Birmingham Blues(80114)
   Co A3579. Put and Take(80214)/Moanful Blues(80215)
   Co A3729. Four o'Clock Blues(80529)/Hawaiian Blues(80530)
   Co A3839. Hallelujah Blues(80859)/Spanish Dreams(80860)
   Co A3878. Dixie Blues(80898)/Sugar Blues(80947)
   Co A3893. Vampin' Sal(80976)/Sweet Lovin' Mama(80975)
   Co 13004. I Promised Not to Holler But Hey Hey(81322)/Jazzin' Babies Blues
   Vo 1176. What's the Use of Being Along/Original Bugle Blues   (81321)

JOHNNY DUNN AND HIS BAND (Johnny Dunn, cornet; Santo Pecora, trombone; Jelly Roll Morton, piano; Omer Simeon, clarinet; Johnny Hodges, alto sax):
   Co 14306. Sergeant Dunn's Bugle Call Blues(145759)/Buffalo Blues(145761)
   Co 14358. Ham and Eggs(145760)/You Need Some Liv'n'(145762)
   (See also: Edith Wilson, Original Jazz Hounds, and Mam'e Smith)

DUPREE, CHAMPION JACK (blues with instrumental acc.):
   OK 05656. Warehouse Man Blues/Chain Gang Blues
   OK 05713. Black Woman Swing/Cabbage Greens No.1
   OK 05769. Gamblin' Man/New Low Down Dog
   OK 05823. Angola Blues/Cabbage Greens, No. 2
   OK 06068. My Baby's Gone/That's All Right
   OK 06104. Dupree Shake Dance/Gibing blues
   OK 06197. Weed Head Woman/Bad Health Blues

DURANTE (JIMMY) JAZZ BAND:
   Ge 9045. Why Cry Blues

DURHAM, DAVE AND THE DIXIELAND SWINGSTERS:
    BB 7899. Don't Try to Buy Your Way

DURHAM, EDDIE AND HIS BAND (Buster Smith, Willard Brown, Lem C. Johnson, saxophones; Joe Keys, trumpet, Conrad Frederick, piano; Eddie Durham, guitar; Aver-
ill Pollard, bass; Arthur Herbert, drums):
    De 8529. Fare Thee Honey Fare Thee Well(68338a)/Magic Carpet(68339a)
    De 18126. I Want a Little Girl(68336a)/Moten's Swing(68337a)

E

EASTON, AMOS (Bumble Bee Slim; vocal with piano):
    Vo 1694. M.and O.Blues, 1 & 2 (jc8588a/89a)

ECKSTEIN, BILLY AND THE DE LUXE ALL STAR BAND (Dizzie Gillespie, Al Killian,Fred-
die Webster, Shortie McConnell,trumpets; Trummy Young,Howard Scott,Claude Jones,
trombones; Bud Johnson, Jimmy Powell, Rudy Rutherford, Wardell Grey, Thomas Crump,
saxes; Oscar Pettiford, bass; Connie Wainwright,guitar; Clyde Hart, piano;Shadow
Wilson, drums.):   April 13, 1944
    DeLuxe 2000. Good Jelly Blues/I Stay in the Mood for You

EDDIE AND SUGAR LOU'S HOTEL TYLER ORCHESTRA (Tyler,Texas, colored band):
    Vo 1445. Yo Yo Blues/KWKH Blues
    Vo 1455. There'll Be Some Changes Made/I Never Miss the Sunshine
    Vo 1514. Eddie and Sugar Lou Stomp/Sweet Papa Will Be Gone
    Vo 1714. Sorrowful Blues/Sympathetic Blues
    Vo 1723. Love Song Blues/Cruel Mama Blues

EDDIE'S HOT SHOTS (Charlie Davis, trumpet; Jack Teagarden, trombone; Mezz Mezzrow
alto sax; Happy Caldwell, tenor sax; Joe Sullivan,piano; Eddie Condon, banjo; Geo.
Stafford, drums.--HD):   1929
    Vi 38046. That's a Serious Thing/I'm Gonna Stomp Mr. Henry Lee
                                                (-BB 10168, GrF 6952, HMV 4987
EDGEWATER CROWS:
    Me 70162. No Bonus Blues/Swinging Rhythm Around

EDINBORO, EDDIE AND HIS WASHBOARD BAND:
    Vo 1701. Dream Sweetheart/Lawd You Made the Night Too Long
    Vo 1702. Dinah/Nobody's Sweetheart

EDDIE EDINBOROUGH AND HIS NEW ORLEANS WILDCATS:
    Co 14613. Some of These Days(130454)/Wildcats Ball(151623)
    Co 14629. Brown Baby(151624)/Hot Stuff Red(151625)
                (See also: New Orleans Wildcats)

EDWARDS, CARRIE (blues with piano):
    Co 14562. Dirty Mistreater/Gettin' Lots of Lovin'

EDWARDS, MOANIN' BERNICE (piano and guitar acc.):
    Para 12620. South Bound Blues/Moaning Blues
    Para 12633. Mean Man Blues/Long Tall Mama
    Para 12713. Two Way Mind Blues/Jack of All Trades
    Para 12741. Born to Die Blues/Low Down Dirty Shame Blues
    Para 12766. High Powered Mama Blues/Hard Hustling Blues

EDWARDS, PIANO KID (vocal with piano):
    Para 13086. Gamblin' Man's Prayer Blues/Hard Luck Gamblin' Man
    Para 13051. Give Us Another Jug/Piano Kid Special

EDWARDS, SUSIE (acc. by Clarence Williams, piano):
    OK 8182. I Got Your Bath Water On(rev., Butterbeans and Susie)

EFFROS, BOB (trumpet solos):
    Br 4620. Tin Ear, acc. by Arthur Schutt/Sweet and Hot, acc. by F. Signorelli

ELDRIDGE, ROY AND HIS ORCHESTRA (Roy Eldridge, trumpet; Scoops Carey, alto sax;
Joe Eldridge, alto sax; Dave Young, tenor sax; Teddy Cole, piano; Johnny Collins,
guitar; Truck Parham, bass; Zutie Singleton, drums.--HD):   1937
    Vo 3458. Where the Lazy River Goes By/After You've Gone   -BrF 500711
    Vo 3479. Wabash Stomp(01793)/Florida Stomp(01794)   -VoE 82
    Vo 3577. That Thing/Heckler's Hop   -VoE 77

(Roy Eldridge, Robert Williams, trumpets; Eli Robinson, trombone; Prince Robinson, Joe Eldridge, Franz Jackson, saxes; Clyde Hart, piano; John Collins, guitar;
Ted Sturgis, bass; David Francis, drums):
    Vs 8084. It's My Turn Now(US 1005)/You're a Lucky Guy(US 1006)
    Vs 8107. Pluckin'the Bass(US 1007)/Gettin' Sentimental Over You(US 1008)
                                                            (-MW 10090

```
    (Sub. Kenneth Kersey, piano):
      Vs  8144. Who Told You I Cared(US 1191)/Does Your Heart Beat for Me(US 1192)
      Vs  8154. High Society(US 1189)           -Ph 81, El 5039, MW 10091
                Muskrat Ramble(US 1190)
```

ELGAR'S CREOLE ORCHESTRA (Charles Elgar, violin; Darnell Howard, alto sax; Wellman Braud, bass; others.--RR)
    Vo 15447. Cafe Capers/When Jenny Does Her Lowdown Dance
    Vo 15478. Brotherly Love/Nightmare   -Br 3404

DUKE ELLINGTON

See also:
  BARNEY BIGARD: All.
  CHICAGO FOOTWARMERS: OK 8675.
  GEORGIA SYNCOPATORS: Me 12444.
  SONNY GREER: Co 1868.
  ADELAIDE HALL: Br 6518.
  HARLEM FOOT WARMERS: OK 8720, 8746, 8760, 8836, 8840, 8869.
  HARLEM HOT CHOCOLATES: HoW 1045, 1046.
  HARLEM HOT SHOTS: Ro 1651 (reissue)
  HARLEM MUSIC MASTERS: OK 41468.
  JOHNNY HODGES: All.
  LONNIE JOHNSON HARLEM FOOTWARMERS: OK 8638.
  JUNGLE BAND: Br 4238,4309,4345,4492,4705,4760,4776,4783,4887,6038,4952.
  LOUISIANA RHYTHMAKERS: Me 12445, 12468(reissue)
  LUMBERJACKS: Ca 8352.
  MEMPHIS HOT SHOTS: Ha 1377.
  MILLS BROTHERS: Br 6519.
  MILLS TEN BLACKBERRIES: Ve 7082.
  WARREN MILLS: Vi 35962.
  PHILADELPHIA MELODIANS: PaE 883.
  SIX JOLLY JESTERS: Vo 1449, 15843.
  REX STEWART: All but Sw 56, 70.
  TEN BLACK BERRIES: Pe 15272, Ba 0594, Or 1854.
  JOE TURNER: Co 1813, 36157.
  OZIE WARE: Pat 3740, Ro 1042.
  WASHINGTONIANS: Bwy 11437; Ha 577,601; Ve 7072, 7088; Pat 36781, 36787; Ca
    9023,9094,9175,9195; Br 3526,4009.4044 4122.
  ETHEL WATERS: Br 6758, 6516.
  WHOOPEE MAKERS: Pe 15418; Pat 36899, 37059, 36923.
  COOTIE WILLIAMS. All but OK 6224, 6370, et seq.

```
ELLINGTON, DUKE (piano solos):                                       1928
   OK  8636. Black Beauty(401172b)                               -PaE 582
             Swampy River(401173b)                               -PaE 571
                                                                     1937
       Ma  102. Mood Indigo, Solitude/Sophisticated Lady,In a Sentimental Mood
                                                         -Br 7990. Co 36312
(With Jimmy Blanton, bass):                                          1939
   Co 35322. Blues(wml120)/Plucked Again(wml121)
                                                                     1940
   Vi 27221. Pitter Panther Patter(053504)/Sophisticated Lady(053506)
   Vi 27406. Body and Soul(053505)/Mr. J.B.Blues(053507)
                                                      New York, May 14, 1941
   Vi 27564. Dear Old Southland(065604)/Solitude(065605)
```

DUKE ELLINGTON'S WASHINGTONIANS (Harry Cooper, LeRoy Rutledge, trumpets; Charlie
Irvis, Jimmy Harrison, trombones; Otto Hardwicke, Don Redman, George Thomas,Prince
Robinson, saxes; Fred Guy, banjo; Bass Edwards, bass; Sonny Greer, drums;Elling-
ton, piano.--HD):   1926
    Ge 3291. If You Can't Hold the Man You Love/"Wanna Go Back Again"Bl. -Bu 8010

(Charlie Johnson, Bubber Miley,trumpets; Charlie Irvis,trombone;Otto Hardwicke,
Prince Robinson, saxes; same rhythm):
    Ge 3342. Animal Crackers   -Ch 15118, Bu 8063
            Lil' Farina
                             - - -
    Pat 7504. Georgia Grind/Parlor Social Stomp   -Pe 104
    Pat 36333. I'm Gonna Hang Around My Sugar(106250)/Trombone Blues(106251-1)
    Blu-Disc T-1004. Nashville Nightingale/My Rose Marie   -Pe 14514

(Bubber Miley,Louis Metcalf,trumpets; Joe"tricky Sam" Nanton,trombone;Rudy Jackson, tenor sax; Otto Hardwicke, clarinet and alto sax; Harry Carney,alto and baritone saxes; Duke Ellington, piano; Fred Guy,banjo; Wellman Braud,bass; S.Greer,
drums.--HD):   1927
    Co   953. East St.Louis Toodle-O(143705)/Hop Head(143706)   -CoE 4420
    Co 1076. Down in Our Alley Blues(143707)/(rev.,Charleston Chasers) -CoE 4562

THIS IS NOT THE LAST WORD

This is no bible of jazz music. Collectors who examine this list will find corrections to make, additions and deletions to suggest. This is only the rough draft of what is intended to be a co-operative effort of the entire jazz collecting world, a complete and objective guide to hot records. Please send your notes to Orin Blackstone, 1016 Eleonore St., New Orleans 15, Louisiana. Credit will be given each month in the Record Changer to all who contribute to the final list.

PAGE NO.	RECORDING GROUP	LABEL	SERIAL NUMBER	WAS SHOWN:	SHOULD HAVE BEEN SHOWN:

PAGE NO.	RECORDING GROUP	LABEL	SERIAL NUMBER	WAS SHOWN:	SHOULD HAVE BEEN SHOWN:

DUKE ELLINGTON AND HIS KENTUCKY CLUB ORCHESTRA (same personnel as above):
```
    Vo   1064. East St.Louis Toodle-O(10)              -BrF 5Q0247, BrE 01681
                Birmingham Breakdown(14)                             BrE 02299
    Br   3480. East St.Louis Toodle-O(72)/Birmingham Breakdown(41)-Vo1064,Br 80000
    Vo   1077. Immigration Blues(21)/The Creeper(23)            -OrE 1010
    Vo   1086. Song of the Cotton Field/New Orleans Low Down
    Vo   1153. Doin' the Frog(826)/Red Hot Band(824)
```

DUKE ELLINGTON AND HIS ORCHESTRA (Jabbo Smith, only trumpet, rest same as above):
                                                                Chicago,1927
```
    OK 40955. What Can a Poor Fellow Do?(81775a)    -OdF 165278, PaE 1549
              Black and Tan Fantasy(81776b)                     -PaE  648
    OK 40955. Black and Tan Fantasy(81776c)    -OdF 165278, PaF 85190,PaE 3492*
              *Issued under name of Louis Armstrong Washboard Beaters.
```

(Bubber Miley, Louis Metcalf, Arthur Whetsel, trumpets; Joe Nanton, trombone, Barney Bigard, tenor sax and clarinet; Harry Carney, alto and baritone saxes; Otto Hardwicke, alto sax; same rhythm):   1928
```
    OK 41013. Take It Easy(400030b)            -Br 7670? PaE 144, PaE 2304
              Jubilee Stomp(400031a)                    -Co 35766,
```

(Sub. Johnny Hodges, alto, for Hardwicke):
```
    OK  8602. Diga Diga Doo(400859b)/Doin' the New Low Down(400860c)
                                                        (-OK 41096,PaE  379
```
(Add Lonnie Johnson, guitar):
```
    OK  8623. The Mooche(401175a)                       -PaE 1615
              Hot and Bothered(401177a)                 -PaE  582
```
(Omit Metcalf, Johnson):
```
    OK  8662. The Blues With a Feelin'(401350d)         -Co 35955, PaE 2258
              Misty Mornin'(401352d)
```

(Miley, Metcalf, Nanton, Hardwicke, Carney, Jackson, Ellington, Guy, Braud, Green):
                                                                10/26/27
```
    Vi 21137. Creole Love Call(39370-1)/Black and Tan Fantasy(40155)  -Vi 24861
    Vi 21137. Creole Love Call(39370-2)
    Vi 21284. Washington Wabble(40156)              -BB 6782, HMV 4929
              Harlem River Quiver(41244)            -Vi 22791, HMV 4946
    Vi 21490. Blues I Love to Sing(39371)           -Vi 22985, BB 6531
              Blue Bubbles(41246)                           , BB 6415
```

(Add Whetsel, trumpet; sub Bigard for Jackson):
```
    Vi 21580. Black Beauty(43502)             -BB 6430,           HMV 6166
              Jubilee Stomp(43503)            -BB 6415, BB 10244
    Vi 21703. Got Everything But You(43504)   -BB 6531, BB 10244
              East St.Louis Toodle-oo(41245-2) -BB 6430
    Vi 20-1531. East St.Louis Toodle-oo(41245-1)
```

(Miley,Whetsel,Nanton,Hodges,Carney,Bigard; add F.Jenkins):   1928-29
```
    Vi 38007. Bandanna Babies(48166)           -BB 7182,           HMV 4957
              I Must Have That Man(48168)
    Vi 38008. Diga Diga Doo(48167)             -BB 6305.           HMV 4959
              I Can't Give You Anything but love(48102-2)
    BB  6280. I Can't Give You Anything but love(48102-1)
    Vi 38034. The Mooche(47799)/(rev.,King Oliver)   -Vi 24468, HMV 6354,HMV 4920
    Vi 38035. Flaming Youth(49652-2)                 -Vi 24057, HMV 6528
              Flaming Youth(49652-1)
       "      Doin' the Voom Voom(48655)             -Vi 24121,BB 7710
    Vi 38036. High Life(49654-1)               -BB 6269,           HMV 6294
       "      High Life(49654-2)
              Saturday Night Function(49653)   -Vi 24674
    Vi 38045. Japanese Dream(48373)                                -HMV 6353
              Harlemania(48374)                -BB 6306.           HMV 6351
```

DUKE ELLINGTON AND HIS COTTON CLUB ORCHESTRA (Cootie Williams, Arthur Whetsel, F. Jenkins, trumpets; Joe Nanton, trombone; Johnny Hodges, Harry Carney, Barney Bigard, saxes; same rhythm):   1929
```
    Vi 38053. The Dicty Glide(49767)           -BB 6269,           HMV 4920
              Stevedore Stomp(49770)           -BB 6306,           HMV 6106
    Vi 38058. Misty Mornin'(51972)             -BB 6565, BB 10245
              Saratoga Swing(51974),W.B.H.& rhythm
    Vi 38065. Hot Feet(49768)                  -BB 6335, MW 4989, HMV 4865
              Sloppy Joe(49769)                -BB 6396,
    Vi 38079. Cotton Club Stomp(51971)                 -BB 10242,  HMV 6292
              Arabian Lover(51973)             -BB 6782,           HMV 4395
```

(Add Juan Tizol, trombone; French horn in place of Freddie Jenkins):
```
    Vi 38089. Mississippi(55845)                       -Vi 24057, HMV 6355
              Swannee Shuffles(55848)          -BB 6614, Vi 24121
```

113

```
        Vi 38092. The Duke Steps Out(55846)              -BB 6727,         HMV 6292
           "      Haunted Nights(55847)                                    HMV 4960
    (Sub. Jenkins for French horn):
        Vi 38115. Breakfast Dance(57542)                 -BB 10243, HMV 6230
           "      March of the Hoodlums(57544)                             HMV 6404
        Vi 38129. Jazz Lips(57543)                       -BB 6396,         HMV 4939
           "      Double Check Stomp(59692),no Jenkins   -BB 6450,            "
        Vi 38130. My Gal Is Good for Nothing But Love(49693)/I Was Made to Love You
                                                         (59694) without Jenkins
                                                                              1930
        Vi 38143. Sweet Dreams of Love(62192)                              -HMV 6277
           "      Sweet Jazz o' Mine(62194-1)                              -HMV 6106
           "      Sweet Jazz o' Mine(62194-2)
        Vi 22528. Ring Dem Bells(61011-6)                -Vi 25076, HMV 5945
                  Three Little Words(61013)
     Vi 20-1532.  Ring Dem Bells(61011-3)
        Vi 22586. Nine Little Miles from Ten-Ten-Tennessee(64812)/What Good Am I With-
                                                              (out you?(64378)
        Vi 22587. Mood Indigo(64811)                     -Vi 20-1532, Vi 24486, HMV 4842
           "      When a Black Man's Blue(64380)
        Vi 22603. Blue Again(64379)/(rev., Bert Lown)
        Vi 22614. The River and Me(67798)                                  -HMV 4884
           "      Keep a Song in Your Soul(67799)        -BB 6305,             "
        Vi 22743. Limehouse Blues(68237)/Echoes of the Jungle(68238)-HMV 6066,GrF 6429
        Vi 22791. It's Glory(68239)                                        -HMV 6293
           "      Brown Berries (see Vi 21284 "Harlem River")
        Vi 22800. The Mystery Song(68240)/(rev.,Mills B.R.)-BB 6614,       HMV 6133
        Vi 22938. Dinah(71838)                                             -HMV 6175
           "      Bugle Call Rag(71839)                                    -HMV 6188
        Vi 23016. Hittin' the Bottle(63360)                                -HMV 4888
           "      That Lindy Hop(63361)                                    -HMV 6355
        Vi 23017. You're Lucky to Me(63362)                                -HMV 5954
           "      Memories of You(63363)                 -BB 6280,
        Vi 23022. Jungle Nights in Harlem(62193)         -BB 6335, MW 4989, HMV 6328
           "      Old Man Blues(61012-2)                 -BB 6450,         HMV 6353
           "      Old Man Blues(61012-6)
        Vi 23036. Sam and Delilah(67800)/(rev.,Bluejeans)                  -HMV 6175
        Vi 23041. Shout 'em Aunt Tillie(62195)           -BB 10242
           "      I'm So in Love With You(64813)
        Vi 26310. Rockin' in Rhythm(67401)/No Papa No(48103), see Vi 38008 for personnel
     Vi L-16006.  Mood Indigo, Hot and Bothered, Creole Love Call(71812-2)
     Vi L-16006.  Mood Indigo, Hot and Bothered, Creole Love Call(71812-3)
     Vi L-16007.  East St.Louis Toodle-oo, Lots O'Fingers, Black and Tan Fantasy(71836)
        Vi 36049. Creole Rhapsody, 1 & 2 (68231/33)

    (Add Louis Bacon, trumpet; Lawrence Brown, trombone; Otto Hardwicke, alto sax):
                                                                              1933-34
        Vi 24431. Rude Interlude(77025)/Dallas Doings(77026)   -HMV 6449,GrF 7181
    (Omit Tizol):
        Vi 24501. Dear Old Southland(77199)/Daybreak Express(77201) -HMV 6468,GrF 7229
           Unissued. Awful Sad(77200)
        Vi 24521. Stompy Jones(80145)/Blue Feeling(80150)                  -HMV 4992
        Vi 24755. Delta Serenade(80144)/Solitude(80149)
    (Omit Bacon, Hardwicke):
        Vi 24617. Cocktails for Two(79156)/Live and Love Tonight(79157)    -HMV 6497
        Vi 24622. Ebony Rhapsody(79155)                  -Vi 24674,HMV 4316
           "      I Met My Waterloo(79169) add Tizol, Hardwicke
    (Add Tizol):
        Vi 24651. Troubled Waters(79211)                                   -HMV 8410
           "      My Old Flame(79212)                                      -HMV 8404
           (For additional Victor records see next page)

    (Miley, Metcalf, Whetsel, Nanton, Bigard, Carney, Hodges, Ellington, Guy, Braud,
     Greer):                                                                  1928
        Br 3987. Yellow Dog Blues                 -Br 80049, BrF 500245, Br 6802
            "    Tishomingo Blues         -BrE 02503,
        Br 4122. The Mooche/(rev.,Hotsy Totsy Gang     -BrE 01235, Br 80002, Br 6812
    (Omit Metcalf):
        Br 4110. Louisiana                                                 -Br 6805
            "    Awful Sad                        -BrE 01616, Br 80050,
```

(Williams,Whetsel,Jenkins,Nanton,Tizol,Hodges,Bigard,Carney,rhythm): **1932**
Br 6093. Creole Rhapsody, 1 & 2 (E35939a/40a)   -Br 80047
Br 6732. Rockin' Chair(E35800a)   -BrE 01727

(Add Brown, Hardwicke):
Br 6265. It Don't Mean a Thing(11204a)/Rose Room(11265a)   -BrE 1292
Br 6288. Lazy Rhapsody(11205a)/Blue Tune(11223)   -BrF 500175,BrE 1299
Co 35834. Lazy Rhapsody(11205b)
Br 20105. St.Louis Blues(BX11263a)/Creole Love Call(BX11264a)-Co 55003,BrE 0116
Br 20105. St.Louis Blues(BX11263b)
Br 6317. Moon Over Dixie(11200a)   -BrF 500178,BrE 01827
          Baby When You Ain't There(11224a)   "   BrE 01681
Co 35835. Baby When You Ain't There(11224b)
Br 6336. The Sheik(11840a)/Blue Ramble(11866a)   -BrF 500179,BrE 1337
Co 35835. Blue Ramble(11866b)
Br 6355. Swampy River(11850a),featuring piano   -BrF 600180,BrE 01727
          Fast and Furious(11851a), featuring piano   "   ,BrE 01367
Br 6374. Blue Harlem(11839a)/Best Wishes(11852a)   -BrF 500207,BrE 1377
Co 35836. Best Wishes(11852b)
Br 6404. Jazz Cocktail(12343a)/Lightnin'(12344a)   -BrF 9327,BrE 1399
Co 35835. Lightnin'(12344b)
Br 6432. Ducky Wucky(12333a)/Swing Low(12346a)   -BrE 1426
Co 35683. Ducky Wucky(12333b)/Swing Low(12346b)
BrF 9331. Stars(12345)
Br 6467. Any Time Any Day Anywhere(12775a)/Eerie Moan(12855a) -BrE 1462
Br 6527. Slippery Horn(13078a)   -BrF 500243,BrE 1540
          Drop Me Off at Harlem(13081a)   "   BrE 1512
Co 35837. Drop Me Off at Harlem(13081b)

(Joe Garland, tenor, in place of Bigard):
Br 6571. Raisin' the Rent(13307a)   -BrF 500254,BrE 2076
     "   Happy As the Day Is Long(13306a)

(Bigard, tenor, in place of Garland):
Br 6600. Sophisticated Lady(13338a)
     "   Stormy Weather(13339a)   -BrF 500253,BrE 01527
Br 6607. Get Yourself a New Broom(13308a),Garland, tenor   BrE 01527
     "   Bundle of Blues(13337a)   -BrF 500300,BrE 01593
Co 35836. Bundle of Blues(13337b)
Br 6638. I'm Satisfied(13800a)   -BrF 500301,BrE 01973
     "   Jive Stomp(13801a)   "   ,BrE 01778
Br 6646. Harlem Speaks(13802a)   -BrF 500326,BrE 02004
     "   In the Shade of the Old Apple Tree(13803a)
CoE 591. Merry Go Round/(265049a)/Sophisticated Lady(265050)   -CoF 1232
Co 35837. Merry Go Round(265049)
CoE 625. I've Got the World on a String(265051)/Down a Carolina Lane(265052)

(Recorded in London, July, 1933)
De   323. Hyde Park(GB 6038)   -DeE 439
     "   Ain't Misbehavin'(GB 6040)   -De 3516,
De   800. Harlem Speaks(GB 6039)   -DeE 438
     "   Chicago(GB 6041)   -De 4203,
                                                                        1935
Br 6987. Solitude(15910a)   -Co 36317,-BrF 500484,BrE 02007
     "   Moonglow(15912a)   "   ,BrE 01901
Br 7310. Saddest Tale(15911a)   -BrF 500485,BrE 01901
     "   Sump'n 'Bout Rhythm(15913a)   "   ,BrE 01973

(Cootie Williams,Rex Stewart,Charlie Allen,trumpets; Lawrence Brown,Juan Tizol,
Joe Nanton, trombones; Johnny Hodges, Otto Hardwicke, Barney Bigard, Harry Car-
ney, saxes; Duke Ellington, piano; Fred Guy, guitar; Hayes Alvis, Billy Taylor,
bass; Sonny Greer, drums.--JAZZ I, 5-6):   **1935**
Unissued. Admiration(C883)
     "   Farewell Blues(C884)
     "   Let's Have a Jubilee(C885)
     "   Porto Rican Chaos(C886)
Br 7440. Merry Go Round(17408)/Admiration(17409)   -BrF 500563,BrE 02030
Br 7461. In a Sentimental Mood(17406)/Showboat Shuffle(17407)-Co 36112,BrE 02038
Unissued. Porto Rican Chaos(16974)
     "   Tough Truckin'(16975)
     (Indigo Echo(16976)

(Add Ben Webster, tenor sax):
Br 7514. Truckin'(17975)   -Co 36317, BrF 500606, BrE 2080
     "   Accent on Youth(17976)   ,   BrE 2096
Br 7526. Margie(16973)   -BrF 500607, BrE 2096
     "   Cotton(17974)   ,   BrE 2080

(Omit Webster; Sub. Whetsel for Allen):
Br 7546. Reminiscing in Tempo, 1 & 2(18072/3) -BrF 500608, Co 36114,BrE 2103
Br 7547. Reminiscing in Tempo, 3 & 4(18074/5) -BrF 500609, Co 36115,BrE 2104
Unissued. Cootie Concerto(C1195)
" Jumpy(C1196)
" Barney's Concerto(C1197)
" Farewell Blues(C1198)
" I Don't Know Why I Love You(C1199)
" Dinah Lou(C1200)
                                                                                                    Feb. 27, 1936
Br 7625. Isn't Love the Strangest Thing(18734)/No Greater Love(18735)-BrE 2194
Br 7627. Love Is Like a Cigarette(18738)   -BrF 500646,   BrE 02268
Br 7650. Clarinet Lament(18736),   -BrF 500653,   BrE 02222
" " Echoes of Harlem(18737)   Co 36283,
Br 7667. Oh Baby Maybe Someday(18740)/(rev.,Hudson-DeLange)   -BrE 02268
Br 7710. Shoe Shine Boy(19562)   -BrF 500683, VoE 22
" It Was a Sad Night in Harlem(19563)   "
Br 7734. In a Jam(19626)/Uptown Downbeat(19628)-BrF 500677, VoE 31
Br 7752. Trumpet in Spades(19564)   -BrF 500692, VoE 113
" " Yearning for Love(19565)   ", VoE 50
                                                                                   1937
Ma 101. I've Got to Be a Rug Cutter(M 179)   -Br 7989
" " The New East St.Louis Toodle-O(M 180)   -Co 36276,   "

(Add Freddie Jenkins, trumpet):
Ma 117. There's a Lull in My Life(M 379)/It's Swell of You(M 380)
Ma 123. New Birmingham Breakdown(M 177)/Scattin' at Kit Kat(M 178) -Br 7994
Ma 124. Can't Run Away from Love(M381)/Lady Who Couldn't Be(M 417) -Br 7995
Ma 131. Caravan(M 470)/Azure(M 471)   -Co 36120,Br 7997
Ma 137.All's God Chillun Got Rhythm(M519)/Alabamy Home(M521)   -Br 8001

(Williams,Steart,Danny Baker,trumpet; Taylor, bass):
Br 8004. Diminuendo in Blue(M 648)/Crescendo in Blue(M 649)   -Co 36125
Br 8029. Chatter Box(M 646)/Dusk in the Desert(M 651)
Br 9044. Harmony in Harlem(M 650)/Black Butterfly(L o376)
Br 8063. Stepping into Swing Society(M 713)/New Black and Tan Fantasy(M 715)
Br 8083. Riding on a Blue Note(M 751)/Lost in Meditation(M 752)
Br 8093. If You Were in My Place(M 770)/Scrounch(M 771)
Br 8099. Braggin' in Brass(M 773)   -Co 36276
" " Carnival in Caroline(M 774)
Br 8108. The Gal from Joe's(M753)/I Let Song Go Out of My Heart(M772)-Co36108
Br 8131. Swingtime in Honolulu(M 809)/I'm Slappin' Seventh Avenue(M 810)
Br 8168. Pyramid(M 834)/When My Sugar Walks Down the Street(M 835) -Co 36105
Br 8169. Dinah's in a Jam(M 811)/You Gave Me the Gate(M 832)
Br 8174. The Stevedore's Serenade(M 846)/La De Doody Doo(M 847)
Br 8186. Rose of the Rio Grande(M 833)   -Co 36279
" " A Gypsy Without a Song(M 845)
Br 8200. Watermelon Man(M 844)/Love in Swingtime(M 881)
Br 8204. Lambeth Walk(M 833)   -Co 36279
" " Prelude to a Kiss(M 884)
Br 8213. Exposition Swing(19627) see 1936 personnel/(rev.,Will Hudson

(Sub.Wallace Jones, trumpet, for Baker):
Br 8221. A Blues Serenade(M 880)/Hip Chic(M 885)
Br 8231. Buffet Flat(M 886)/Mighty Like the Blues(M 899)
Br 8256. Prologue to Black and Tan Fantasy(M 714)/Please Forgive Me (M 882)
Br 8293. Jazz Potpourri(M 947)/Battle of Swing(M 949)
Br 8297. Blue Light(M 958)/Slap Happy(M 961)   -Co 36128
Br 8306. Old King Dooji(M 959)/Boy Meets Horn(M 960)   -Co 36123
Br 8344. Pussy Willow(MW 997)/Subtle Lament(MW 998)
Unissued. Just Good Fun(MW 990)/Informal Blues(MW 991)
Br 8365. Portrait of the Lion(WM 1006)/Something to Live for(WM 1007)
Br 8380. Smorgasbord and Schnapps(WM 1000)/Solid Old Man(WM 1008)
Br 8405. Cotton Club Stomp(WM 1030)/In a Mizz(WM 1038)
Br 8411. Way Low(WM 1032)/You Can Count on Me(WM 1041)
                                                                                   1939
Co 35208. Goin' the Voom Voom(WM 1031a)/I'm Checkin' Out Goom Bye(WM 1039a)
Co 35214. Serenade to Sweden(WM 1033)/The Sergeant Was Shy(WM 1063)
Co 35240. A Lonely Co-ed(WM 1040a)/Bouncing Bouyancy(WM 1062a)
Co 35291. Lady in Blue(WM 999)/Little Posey(WM 1091a)
Co 35310. Grievin'(WM 1093a)/Tootin' Through the Roof(WM 1094a)
Co 35353. I Never Felt This Way Before(WM 1092a)/Weely(WM 1095a)
Co 35776. Country Gal(WM 1108a)/(rev., reissue of Jubilee Stomp(19264)

(Add Ben Webster, tenor sax; sub. Jimmy Blanton, bass):   1940
Co 35427. Solitude(WM 1135a)/Mood Indigo(WM 1137a)
Co 35556. Stormy Weather(WM 1136a)/Sophisticated Lady(WM 1138a)
Co 35640. Killin' Myself(WM 1106a)/Your Love Has Faded(WM 1107a)

```
Vi 26536. Jack the Bear(044888)/Morning Glory(044890)
Vi 26537. You You Darlin'(044887)/So Far So Good(044891)
Vi 26577. Ko-Ko(044889)/Conga Brava(049015)
Vi 26598. Concerto for Cootie(049016)            (Do Nothin')-Vi 20-1547
          Me and You(049017)
Vi 26610. Cotton Tail(049655)/Never No Lament(049656)
Vi 26644. Bojangles(053021)/A Portrait of Bert Williams(053022)
Vi 26677. Dusk(053020)/Blue Goose(053023)
Vi 26719. At a Dixie Roadside Diner(054607)/My Greatest Mistake(054624)
Vi 26731. Harlem Air Shaft(054606)/Sepia Panorama(054625)
Vi 26748. There Shall Be No Night(053427)/Five o'Clock Whistle(053429)
Vi 26788. In a Mellotone(053428)/Rumpus in Richmond(054609)
Vi 26796. The Flaming Sword(053552)/Warm Valley(053450)
Vi 27235. Across the Track Blues(053579)
          Chloe(053580)                                      -Vi 20-1547
Vi 27247. I Never Felt This Way Before(053581)/All Too Soon(054608)
```

(Stewart, Ray Nance, Wallace Jones, trumpets):
```
Vi 27326. Flamingo(053781)/The Girl in My Dreams Tries to Look Like You(053782)
                                                                          1941
Vi 27356. Jumpin' Punkins(055284)/Blue Serge(055286)
Vi 27380. The Sidewalks of New York(053780)/Take the "A" Train(055283)
Vi 27434. John Hardy's Wife(055285)/After All(055287)
Vi 27502. Bakiff(061283)/The Giddybug Gallop(061286)
Vi 27517. Jump for Joy/The Brown Skin Gal
Vi 27531. I Got It Bad And That Ain't Good(061319)/Chocolate Shake(061318)
Vi 27587. Just A-Settin' and A-Rockin'(061285)/Moon Over Cuba(061341)
Vi 27639. Rocks in My Bed(061685)/Bli-Blip(061686)
Vi 27700. Clementine(061338)/Five O'Clock Drag(061684)
```

(Sub. Alvin Raglin, bass, for Blanton):
```
Vi 27740. Chelsea Bridge(061687)/What Good Would It Do?(061942)
Vi 27804. Are You Sticking(061284)with Blanton/I Don't Know What Kind of Blues
                                                       (I Got(061943)
                                                                          1942
Vi 27856. The "C" Jam Blues(070683)/Moon Mist(070684)
Vi 27880. Raincheck(061941)/Perdido(070682)
```

(Sub. Chauncey Haughton for Bigard):
```
Vi 20-1505. Hayfoot Strawfoot(074781)/Sherman Shuffle(074784)
Vi 20-1528. A Slip of the Lip(074783)/Sentimental Lady(074782)
Vi 20-1556. Main Stem(072438)/Johnny Come Lately(072439)
Vi 20-1584. My Little Brown Book(072437)/Someone(071892)
    -     . What Am I Here For(071890)/I Don't Mind(071891)
```

Standard Radio Transcriptions (DB 2/15/43):
1. Frenesi, Until Tonight, West Indian Stomp, Love and I, John Hardy, I Hear a Rhapsody, Bounce, It's Sad But True, Madame Will Drop Her Shawl.
2. Clementine, Chelsea Bridge, Love Like This Can't Last, After All, The Girl in My Dreams Tries to Look Like You, Jumpin' Punkins, Frankie and Johnnie, Flamingo, Bakiff.
3. Stomp Caprice, Bugle Breaks, You and I, Have You Changed, Raincheck, Blue Serge, Moon Mist, I Don't Want to Set the World on Fire, Easy Street, Perdido.

ELLINGTONIA, IMPROVISATIONS IN (Rex Stewart, trumpet; Barney Bigard, clarinet; Django Reinhardt, guitar; Billy Taylor, bass):   Paris, 1938
```
HRS 1003. Low Cotton(R4098)/Montmarte(R4099)
HRS 1004. Finesse(R4100)/I Know That You Know(R4101)
    (Also issued under Rex Stewart and Feetwarmers, Swing 56 and 70)
```

ELLIS, SEGER (Acc. by Dorsey Brothers combination featuring Louis Armstrong):
```
OK 41255. S'posin'(402416b)/To Be in Love(402417c)
OK 41274. True Blue Lou(402283b)/(rev.,"My Song of the Nile" without Armstrong)
OK 41291. Ain't Misbehavin'(402881b)/There Was Nothing Else to De(402882b)
```

(Muggsy Spanier, cornet; Jimmy Dorsey, sax; Rube Bloom, piano):
```
BrE 1084. It's a Lonesome Old Town/My Love for You
```

ELMAN, ZIGGY AND HIS ORCHESTRA: (Jerry Jerome, Noni Bernardi, Toots Mondello, Art Rollini, sax; Ziggy, trumpet; Ben Heller, guitar; Art Bernstein, bass; John Guarneri, piano; Nick Fatool, drums):
```
BB 10096. Sugar/29th and Dearborn
BB 10103. Bublitchki/Fralich in Swing("And the Angels Sing")
BB 10316. You're Mine You/Zagg'n' With Zig
BB 10342. Let's Fall in Love/I'll Never Be the Same
BB 10413. You Took Advantage of Me/I'm Yours
BB 10490. Am I Blue/I Have Everything to Live For
BB 10563. Tootin' My Baby Back Home/What Used to Was Used to Was
BB 10663. I'm Through With Love/Something to Remember You By
BB 10855. Bye 'n Bye/Deep Night
BB 10741. Forgive My Heart/Love Is the Sweetest Thing
```

EMBASSY RHYTHM EIGHT
   Ch 40068. Hitchy Koo/He's a Rag Picker   -DeE 5435
   DeE 5467. Back Home in Tennessee/Where the Black Eyed Susans Grow

EMPERORS, THE (Phil Napoleon, trumpet; Frank Signorelli, piano, and others):
   Ha   383. Go Joe Go(143338)/(rev.,Arkansas Travelers)
   Ha   362. Clarinet Marmalade/Blues Serenade

ENGLISH, PEGGY (acc. by Red Nichols, trumpet; Eddie Lang, guitar; and others,---
JI 5/24/40):
   Vo 15504. How Long Must I Wait for You/High High High Up in the Hills
   Br 3752. Mine All Mine/What'll You Do (guitar, piano, violin, this coupling)

ENGLISH, CHARLIE (acc. by Tiny Parham and Bert Cobb):
   Para 12610. Transom Blues/Tuba Lawdy Blues

ERBY, JACK (vocal, piano acc.):
   Co 14151. Lonesome Jimmy Blues(142430)/Awfully Blue(142433)

ERWING BROTHERS ORCHESTRA:
   Vo 2564. The Erwing Blues(b796a)/Rhythm(b797a)

EUROPE'S (JIM) HELL FIGHTERS BAND (including Noble Sissle, piano and vocalist):
   PatF 22080. Arabian Nights/How Ya Gonna Keep 'em Down on the Farm   1919
   PatF 22081. Darktown Strutters Ball/Indianola
   PatF 22086. Hesitating Blues/Plantation Echoes
   PatF 22087. St. Louis Blues
   PatF 22103. Jazz Baby/When the Bees Make Honey
   PatF 22089. Mirandy/On Patrol in No Man's Land
   PatF 22104. All of No Man's Land Is Ours/Jazzola
   PatF 22147. Missouri Blues/My Chocolate Soldier

JIM EUROPE'S BAND or HARMONY KINGS:
   PatA 020928. Clarinet Marmalade   -PatF 22167,Pe 14110
                 Russian Rag
   PatA 020929. That Moaning Trombone/Memphis Blues   -Pe 14111
   PatA 022082. Ja Da/Broadway Hits
   Pe 11056. Roll Jordan Roll/Swing Low Sweet Chariot

EVANS, REDD AND HIS BILLY BOYS:
   Vo 4836. They Cut Down the Old Pine Tree(w24381)/Red Wing(w24382)

RED EVANS AND HIS ORCHESTRA (includes Teddy Wilson, piano):
   Vo 5173. Milenberg Joys(25189)/In the Baggage Coach Ahead(25190)

EVANS, ROY (acc. by J.P. Johnson, piano):
   Co 1559. Jazzbo Dan/Syncopated Yodelin' Man

(Novelty accompaniment):
   Co 2198. Ro-Ro-Rollin' Along/I Lost My Gal from Memphis
   Co 2469. Roll on You Mississippi/There Must be a Bright Tomorrow

EVERETTS, DOROTHY:
   Co 14444. Fat Mouth Blues/Macon Blues

WILL EZELL

See also:
   LUCILLE BOGAN: Para 12504, 12577.
   MARIE BRADLEY: Para 12466.
   ORA BROWN: Para 12500.
   ELZADIE ROBINSON: Para 12417, 12509, 12689, 12544, 12701, 12724, 12795.

EZELL, WILL (Piano solos):   1928
   Para 12549. Barrel House Man(4786-2,891)/West Coast Rag(4787-2,892)
   Para 12688. Old Mill Blues(20823-2)/Mixed Up Rag(20824-2)   -Sig 911
   Para 12729. Precious Fives(2106) with vocal/Crawlin' Spider Blues, with vocal
   Para 12753. Barrel House Woman(21142-1)/Heifer Dust(21145-2)   -Sig 910
   Para 12773. Bucket of Blood(21144)/Playing the Dozens(21146)
   Para 12855. Just Can't Stay Here(15649-1527)/Pitchin' Boogie(15650-1526),cornet
   Para 12914. Freakish Mistreater/Hot Spot Stuff, with cornet   (& banjo)

#

columbia re-issues
hot jazz albums

Set C-27—EDDIE SOUTH
Set C-28—KING LOUIS
Set C-29—JAZZ AS IT SHOULD BE
  PLAYED—Bix Beiderbecke
Set C-30—FLETCHER HENDERSON
Set C-31—BESSIE SMITH
Set C-38—THE DUKE—Duke Ellington
Set C-40—COMES JAZZ—
  Bud Freeman
Set C-41—EARL HINES
Set C-43—FRANK TESCHEMACHER

Set C-44—BOOGIE WOOGIE
Set C-46—HOT TROMBONES
Set C-51—DORSEY BROTHERS
Set C-57—LOUIS ARMSTRONG AND
  HIS HOT FIVE
Set C-61—TEDDY WILSON—BILLIE
  HOLIDAY
Set C-66—HOT TRUMPETS
Set C-73—LOUIS AND EARL—Louis
  Armstrong and Earl Hines

Your collection is incomplete if it lacks any one of these great classics.
See your dealer at once. He has them in stock.

columbia records

INDEX TO JAZZ
Orin Blackstone
Vol. II

Published by the Record Changer, Fairfax, Va.

columbia re-issues hot jazz albums

Set C-27—EDDIE SOUTH
Set C-28—KING LOUIS
Set C-29—JAZZ AS IT SHOULD BE PLAYED—Bix Beiderbecke
Set C-30—FLETCHER HENDERSON
Set C-31—BESSIE SMITH
Set C-38—THE DUKE—Duke Ellington
Set C-40—COMES JAZZ—Bud Freeman
Set C-41—EARL HINES
Set C-43—FRANK TESCHEMACHER
Set C-44—BOOGIE WOOGIE
Set C-46—HOT TROMBONES
Set C-51—DORSEY BROTHERS
Set C-57—LOUIS ARMSTRONG AND HIS HOT FIVE
Set C-61—TEDDY WILSON—BILLIE HOLIDAY
Set C-66—HOT TRUMPETS
Set C-73—LOUIS AND EARL—Louis Armstrong and Earl Hines

Your collection is incomplete if it lacks any one of these great classics. See your dealer at once. He has them in stock.

columbia records

Hey GETCHA RECORD CHANGER!
YA CAN'T COLLECT RECORDS WITHOUT A RECORD CHANGER

- It's a fact. You can't collect jazz records,—and for that matter, you can't obtain a well-rounded perspective of jazz music,—without a subscription to the Record Changer.
- The Record Changer is the one, the only, the original advertising medium for jazz record collectors. In the past 38 issues of the magazine more than 46,000 collector's items have been offered for sale, auction or trade. More than 12,000 items have been advertised in the "Wanted" section.
- Some of the greatest articles ever printed on jazz music have appeared in the Record Changer by these writers: Nesuhi Ertegun, Roy Carew, John M. Phillips, Eugene Williams, Tom Williston, William Love, William Russell, Charles Wilford, E. S. Stewart, R. E. Stearns, John Steiner, Jazzbo Brown, Jelly Roll Morton, Leslie Smith, Ralph Sturges, Ernest Borneman, Thurman and Mary Grove, Albert McCarthy, Paul Eduard Miller, Ralph Gleason, Fred Ramsey, Herman Rosenberg, Don Fowler, Sterling Brown, Roger Pryor Dodge, Jeff Aldam, Graham McInnes, Bill Riddle, R. H. Pflug-Felder, and George Montgomery.
- Don Anderson's cover drawings alone are worth more than the price of the magazine.
- 1945 is our fourth year of continuous publication,—the longest run of any magazine ever devoted to jazz music.
- Our subscription rate is lower than that of any other comparable publication. Drop us a card.

Sirs:
Send me the current issue of the Record Changer. On receipt I will send you my subscription.

THE RECORD CHANGER
Fairfax, Virginia
$2.00 (U. S. Money) 12 Issues Per Year

Introduction

With this second volume, the midway point has been reached in the effort to compile a complete listing, with pertinent data, of jazz collectors' records.

The response to the first volume, bringing many helpful suggestions as well as authoritative information from hundreds of collectors, offers real encouragement that the final objective, a single book embracing all the known jazz records of interest, may be achieved.

Some of the required personnels and other data may never be unearthed, of course, but progress is being made. The policy of setting down all the known records and recording groups will be continued, whether full information is currently available or not.

Looming as one of the major tasks in the final revision is the problem of drawing the line on what is to be included and what is to be left out. Several correspondents have objected to the long lists of dance records (one writer denying that Volume I was an "index" and that the records were "jazz"), but more have wanted them expanded to include their own favorites. This problem will have to be solved largely by the collectors themselves, with the prospect that a rather broad definition of jazz may have to be employed.

It should be pointed out here that these so-called commercial listings did not crowd out anything in the first volume. Special attention, for instance, was paid to the "race" items and it was only because they were not known to me that some were not listed.

As the work went forward on the second volume, it became increasingly difficult to adhere to a strict numerical arrangement of the records. In the Fletcher Henderson section, for example, it was impossible because Henderson apparently did not have many exclusive recording contracts during his career, and switched back and forth from one label to another with great frequency, thus forestalling any hope of simplifying his discography.

A compromise had to be made by dividing his list into three or four parts, grouped more or less chronologically. This perhaps will not completely satisfy anyone; so suggestions as to how to handle such a tangle will be highly welcome. This tends to reopen the whole question of which is more satisfactory: Numerical listings, which offer the advantage of quickly locating a given item, or chronological listings which better afford the study of an individual artist's work? It is now time, I think, for each collector to express his preference, unless he is content to prepare his own private discographies of favorite performers to suit himself.

Many discrepancies cropped up as the preparation of this index advanced. It has been found that the cross references do not always jibe. A reference, for instance, may be made in some artist's summary to a record in which he has no part, or to a record which is not listed. These errors are usually due to discovery of new information too late to rectify material already published or prepared for publication. Conversely, an artist may show up among the personnel of a record for which he has been given no earlier credit. These errors will be caught in final revision, but it might not be amiss for collectors to point them out and in the meanwhile I hope they will bear with me.

Some few mistakes in the first volume were typographical, and some listings were omitted entirely by oversight of the printer. These and other errors have been cited by collectors, of whom there are too many to be named here. But all corrections and additions will be fully acknowledged in the final revision. For the present, a blanket vote of thanks to them!

The original appeal for help is now being renewed, as Volume II opens up a wide field for further work.

—ORIN BLACKSTONE.

copyright, 1945, Gordon Gullickson.

EDDIE CONDON
CHU BERRY
BUD FREEMAN TRIO
EDMOND HALL SEXTET
GEORGE BRUNIS
BILLIE HOLIDAY
MEL POWELL
BOBBY HACKETT
"WILD BILL" DAVISON
THE THREE DEUCES
JESS STACY
COLEMAN HAWKINS
ROY ELDRIDGE
EDDIE HEYWOOD
BENNY CARTER
BEN WEBSTER
KANSAS CITY FIVE AND SIX
"BIG SID" CATLETT
JACK TEAGARDEN
JOE SULLIVAN
JOE BUSHKIN
De PARIS BROTHERS
JAM SESSIONS AT COMMODORE
ALBERT AMMONS

COMMODORE CLASSICS IN SWING

Ceiling Prices

C-1500 SERIES - $1.50

C- 500 SERIES - $1.00

Not including Federal, State and Local Taxes

F. O. B. New York City

★★★ SEND FOR OUR NEW COMPLETE CATALOGUE

COMMODORE MUSIC SHOP
136 EAST 42nd STREET   NEW YORK CITY

ABBREVIATIONS – RECORDS

Ae	Aeolian Vocalion	Key	Keynote
Aj	Ajax	KP	Keith Prowse
AM	American Music	Li	Lincoln
Ap	Apex	Ma	Master
Au	Autograph	Mad	Madison
Ba	Banner	Maj	Major
Bald	Baldwin	Max	Maxsa
BB	Bluebird	Me	Melotone
Bea	Beacon	Med	Medallion
BN	Blue Note	Mu	Musicraft
BP	Black Patti	MW	Montgomery Ward
Br	Brunswick	Na	National
BrE	English Brunswick	Nor	Nordskog
BrF	French Brunswick	OdF	French Odeon
BrG	German Brunswick	OdG	German Odeon
BS	Black Swan	OK	Okeh
Bu	Buddy	Or	Oriole
B&W	Black and White	OrE	English Oriole
Bwy	Broadway	PaA	American Parlophone
Ca	Cameo	PaE	English Parlophone
Cap	Capitol	PaF	French Parlophone
Ch	Champion	PaS	Spanish Parlophone
Chal	Challenge	Pana	Panachord
CI	Collectors Item	PanD	Dutch Panachord
Cl	Clarion	Para	Paramount
Cli	Climax	Pat	Pathe
Clax	Claxtonola	PatA	Pathe Actuelle
Co	Columbia	PatF	French Pathe
Com	Commodore	Pe	Perfect
Cq	Conqueror	Ph	Philharmonic
Cr	Crown	Po	Polk
De	Decca	Pu	Puritan
DeE	English Decca	Rad	Radiex
DeF	French Decca	Re	Regal
DeH	Dutch Decca	Ro	Romeo
Di	Diva	Roy	Royale
Do	Domino	RZ	Regal Zonophone
Ed	Edison	Sa	Salabert
El	Elite	Sav	Savoy
Elec	Electradisk	SA	Solo Art
Em	Emerson	SD	Steiner-Davis
Ex	Excelsior	Se	Session
FR	Firestone	Si	Silvertone
Ge	Gennett	Sig	Signature
GG	Grey Gull	Su	Sunshine
GrF	French Gramophone	Sup	Supertone
Gu	Guardsman	Sw	Swing
Ha	Harmony	Tele	Telefunken
Harmo	Harmograph	Tri	Triangle
Her	Herwin	UHCA	United Hot Clubs
HMV	His Master's Voice	Ul	Ultraphone
HoW	Hit of Week	VD	Van Dyke
HRS	Hot Record Society	Ve	Velvet Tone
Hy	Hytone	Vi	Victor
Im	Imperial	Vo	Vocalion
Je	Jewel	VoE	English Vocalion
JI	Jazz Information	Vr	Variety
JM	Jazz Man	Vs	Varsity
JR	Jazz Record		

SOURCES

DB	Down Beat (George Hoefer)	JM	Jazz Music (British magazine)
Dis	Discography (British magazine)	JR	Jazz Record
EW	Eugene Williams	JRB	Jazz Record Book
HD	Hot Discography	JT	Jazz Tempo
HJ	Hot Jazz	KH	Kenneth Hulsizer
JAZZ	Magazine (W. C. Love)	RC	Record Changer
JI	Jazz Information	RR	Rhythm on Record
		Te	Tempo

EXNER

Presents

The kind of Jazz Records you have dreamed about

HIGH FIDELITY RECORDINGS

of Classic Jazz Tunes played in authentic Jazz Style by some of the best of those semifabulous musicians who made JAZZ the envy and despair of a long line of would-be imitators.

DIPPERMOUTH BLUES   HIGH SOCIETY RAG
SAVOY BLUES   BALLIN' THE JACK

By

Kid Ory's Creole Band

Thomas "Papa Mutt" Carey . . Cornet	Albert "Buster" Wilson . . . Piano
Joe Darensbourg . . . Clarinet	Arthur "Bud" Scott . . . Guitar
Edward "Kid" Ory . . Trombone	Edward "Montule" Garland . . Bass
Alton Redd . . . . . Drums	

Also by

The Johnny Wittwer Trio

WOLVERINE BLUES   COME BACK SWEET PAPA
JOE'S BLUES   TIGER RAG

Joe Darensbourg . . Clarinet	Johnny Wittwer . . . . Piano
Keith Purvis . . . . . Drums	

(All these records will be issued as soon as pressings can be obtained. Pressings have been promised in June 1945. They will be available to retail stores for distribution. Previous inquiries have not been answered because exact information could not be supplied till we knew when pressings could be obtained.)

F. B. EXNER
509 OLIVE WAY, SEATTLE (1), WASHINGTON

F

FAIN, SAMMY, vocals (some supposedly accompanied by Eddie Lang, guitar, and/or Benny Goodman, clarinet):
```
Ha  1179.  You Brought a New Kind of Love/Rollin'
Ve  2250.  You're Drivin' Me Crazy/I'm Along
Di  2904.  The Things That Were Made
Di  2943.  To Be in Love/What a Day
Di  2993.  Ain't Misbehavin'
Di  3114.  Just Can't Be/Watching My Dreams Go
```

FARLEY, EDDIE AND HIS ORCHESTRA:
```
De  1165.  I Can't Break the Habit of you               -BrE 02411
 "         Nero
De  1168.  The Mood That I'm In/You're Everything Sweet
De  1237.  There's No Two Ways About It/To a Sweet Pretty Thing
De  1250.  I'm Bubbling Over(62109)/I Hum a Waltz(62110)
              (See also: Reilly-Farley)
```

FAURE, RENE, piano solos:
```
Vs  8236.  Honky Tonk Train Blues(1420)/Little Rock Getaway(1423)
```

FAZOLA, IRVING (Prestopnik), clarinet, see:
```
BOB CROSBY BOB CATS: De 1593-3248
BOB CROSBY ORCHESTRA: De 2205.
DEAN AND HIS KIDS: Vo 3342.
SEGER ELLIS
BILLY HOLIDAY: Vo 3333, 3334
GLENN MILLER: Br 8034, 8062.
BEN POLLACK: Br 7747, 7751, 7764; Vr 504, 556.
RHYTHM MANIACS: Vo 3655.
SHARKEY BONANO: Vo 3380, 3353.
MUGGSY SPANIER; De 4168, 4271.
JESS STACY: Vs 8121, 8132, 8140.
CLAUDE THORNHILL
```

FEATHER'S ALL STARS, LEONARD (Coleman Hawkins, tenor sax; Cootie Williams, trumpet; Edmond Hall, clarinet; Art Tatum, piano; Al Casey, guitar; Oscar Pettiford, bass; Big Sid Catlett, drums):   Dec. 4, 1943
```
Com  547.  Esquire Bounce(a4691-1)/Esquire Blues(a4694)
Com  548.  Mop Mop(a4692-1)/My Ideal(a4693-1)
```

FEATHERS AND FROGS, vocal (with piano, guitar and trumpet):
```
Para 12812. Sweet Black Dog/How Do You Get That Way?
```

FEATHERSTONHAUGH AND HIS COSMOPOLITANS, BUDDY (Buddy Featherstonhaugh, tenor sax; Harry Hayes, Fletcher Allen, alto saxes and clarinets; Charlie Johnson, Charles Price, Archie Craig, trumpets; Freddie Welsh, Lionel Guimaraes, trombones; Justo Barreto, piano; Alan Ferguson, guitar; German Araco, bass; Ollie Tines, Stanley Marshall, drums.--RR):   1933
```
DeE 3649. Royal Garden Blues(tbl022)/I've Got World on a String(gb6088)
```

FENWYCK, JERRY, vocals (with accompaniment possibly including Benny Goodman, clarinet):
```
Ha   1348.  Take It from Me
Ha   1352.  Do the New York
Ha   1384.  Faded Summer Love
Ha   1397.  By the Sycamore Tree
Ve   2475.  Now's the Time to Fall in Love
Cl   5281.  Two Hearts(151408)/(rev., Lou Gold)
Ve  10503.  With Love in My Heart(236012)/Who's Your Little Who-zis(236012)
```

FIELDS, ALFRED, vocal blues (instrumental acc.):
```
OK  05727.  Spongy Baby/Step Pepper Stepper
OK  06020.  Quit Your Jivin'/'29 Blues
OK  06129.  Mighty Blues/Money Green
```

FIELDS, BUDDY, AND HIS ORCHESTRA (Dorsey Brothers group):
```
Ro  1068.  Lovable and Sweet(4068-1)/(rev., Varsity Eight)
              (See also: University Boys, Oriole 1668).
```

FIELDS AND HIS ORCHESTRA, ERNIE:
  Vo 5073. Lard Stomp/T-Town Blues
  Vo 5157. Just Let Me Alone(w26070)/High Jivin'(w26072)
  Vo 5344. Blues at Midnight(w26071)/Blues in Your Heart(w26073)

FIELDS ORCHESTRA, HERBIE (Herbie Fields, alto, tenor and clarinet; Taft Jordan,trumpet; Johnny Mehegan, piano; Leonard Ware, guitar; Sid Catlett, drums; Rodney Richardson, bass):   April 14, 1944
  Sig   . Confessin'(voc., Taft Jordan)/These Foolish Things
  Sig   . You Can Depend on Me/Blues in C Minor

FINNELL AND HIS ROYAL STOMPERS, DOUGLAS:
  Br 7123. The Right String But the Wrong Yo Yo/Sweet Sweet Mama

ELLA FITZGERALD

For other records see:
  BENNY GOODMAN: Vi 25469, 25461.
  CHICK WEBB: Most.
  TEDDY WILSON: Br 7640, 7729.

FITZGERALD, ELLA (with the Mills Brothers:
  De 1148. Big Boy Blue/Dedicated to You
        ELLA FITZGERALD (vocal, acc. by Ted McRae, tenor sax; Tommy Fulford, piano; Ulysses Livingston, guitar; Beverley Peer, bass; Kenny Clarke, drums.--EW):
  De 4007. Jim(69784)/This Love of Mine(69785)   Oct.6,1941
        (Eddie Barefield, sax; Fulford, Livingston, Peer; W.Beason,drums.--EW)
  De 4073. I'm Thrilled(69906a)/Make Love to Me(69907a)   Nov.5,1941
  De 4082. Somebody Nobody Loves/You Don't Know What Love Is
  De 4291. Who Are You?(69905)/My Man(with her orchestra)
        ELLA FITZGERALD and The Four Keys (Bill Furness, piano; Slim Furness,guitar, Peck Furness, bass; Ernie Hatfield, vocal.--EW)   Mar.11,1942
  De 4315. When I Come Back Crying(70471)/I'm Gettin' Mighty Lonesome(70470)
        (Add Fulford, piano):   Apr.9,1942
  De 18347. All I Need Is You(70652)/Mama Come Home(70653)
  De 18472. Four Leaf Clover in Your Pocket/He's My Guy
  De 18530. My Heart and I Decided/I Must Have That Man(with her orchestra)

        ELLA FITZGERALD AND HER SAVOY EIGHT (Taft Jordan, trumpet; Sandy Williams, trombone; Pete Clark, alto and Baritone saxes; Ted McRae, tenor sax; Tommy Fulford, piano; John Trueheart, guitar; Beverley Peer, bass; Chick Webb, drums; Ella Fitzgerald, vocals.--HD):   1937
  De 1061. My Last Affair
   "   Darktown Strutters Ball(61422)   BrE 02366
  De 1062. Organ Grinder's Swing(61420a)
   "   Shine(61421a)   -BrE 02366
        (Sub. Louis Jordan, alto, for Clark; Bobby Johnson, guitar, for Trueheart.--HD):   May 24,1937
  De 1302. If You Ever Should Leave(62214a)/Everyone's Wrong(62215a) -BrE 02593
  De 1339. All Over Nothin' at All(62213)/Deep in the Heart of the South(62216)
                                                          -BrE 02451
                                                          Dec.21,1937
  De 1596. Bei Mir Bist du Schon(62896)   -BrE 02561
   "   It's My Turn Now(62897)   -De 2803,   "
                                                          Jan.25,1938
  De 1669. It's Wonderful(63225)/I Was Doing All Right(63226) -BrE 02605
                                                          May 3, 1938
  De 1806. This Time It's Real(63703a)/You Can't Be Mine(63705a)
  De 1846. Saving Myself for You(63709)/We Can't Go on This Way(63706)
  De 1967. If You Only Knew(63710)/What Do You Know About Love(63704)
        (Sub. Hilton Jefferson for Jordan.--EW)   Aug. 18,1938
  De 2202. Strictly from Dixie(64462)/Woe Is Me(64463)
        (Sub. John Trueheart for Johnson.--EW)
  De 2451. Don't Worry 'Bout Me/Once Is Enough for Me(65092; Mar.2,1939)
  De 2481. If Anything Happened to You/If You Ever Change Your Mind
  De 2581. If That's What You're Thinking/I Had to Live and Learn(65093;Mar.2,1939)
        ELLA FITZGERALD AND HER FAMOUS ORCHESTRA (Richard Vance,Bobby Stark, Taft Jordan, trumpets; G. Matthews, N. Storey, S. Williams, trombones; Hilton Jefferson, Garvin Bushell, Ted McRae, W. Carver, saxes; Fulford, Trueheart, Peer, Beason,--EW):   June 29,1939

```
De  2598. Stairway to the Stars(65904)/Out of Nowhere(65907)
De  2628. I Want the Waiter(65905)/That's All Brother(65906)
De  2721. Heart of Mine(63694)/My Last Goodbye(66134a; Aug.18,1939)

De  2769. Billy(66135)/Please Tell the Truth(66136)              Aug.18,1939

De  2816. You're Gonna Lose Your Gal(91836a)/My Wubba Dolly(91839a)  Oct.12,1939
De  2826. After I Say I'm Sorry(91837a)/Baby What Else Can I Do(91838a)
De  2904. Betcha Nickel(65903;June 29,1939)/Moon Ray

De  2988. Is There Somebody Else(67119)/Starlit Hour(67121)       Jan.26,1940
De  3005. I'm Not Complainin'(66137a; Aug.18,1939)/What's the Matter with Me
                                                                    (67122aa)
        (Sub. Irving Randolph, trumpet, for Stark; J.Haughton, trombone, for Storey;
        C. Houghton for Jefferson; E. Barefield for Bushell; Lonnie Simmons for Car-
        ver; R. Ramirez for Fulford.--EW):                        Feb.15,1940
De  3026. If It Weren't for You(67196)/Sing Song Swing(67197)
De  3078. Imagination(67198)/Sugar Blues(67120)
De  3186. Baby Won't You Please Come Home(67195a)/Lindy Hopper's Delight(91840a)

        (Sub. Fulford, piano, for Ramirez):
De  3199. I Fell in Love With a Dream(67706)/Shake Down the Stars(67700)
                                                                  Mar.20,1940
De  3236. Take It From the Top(67358a)/Jubilee Swing(67360a)

        (Sub. Pete Clark, sax, for Barefield; James Archey, Floyd Brady, John McCon-
        nell, new trombones.--EW):                                May 9,1940
De  3324. Deedle-de-dum(67699)/Gulf Coast Blues(67701)

        (G. Matthews, McConnell, Earl Hardy, trombones; Livingston, guitar.--EW):
                                                                  Sept.25,1940
De  3420. Five o'Clock Whistle(68146)/So Long(68147)

        (George Dorsey for C.Haughton.):                          Nov.9,1940
De  3490. Cabin in the Sky(68330)/Taking a Chance on Love(68329)
De  3441. Tea Dance(67359aa)/Louisville K-Y(68148b)
De  3608. The One I Love/Three Little Words
De  3612. Hello Ma! I Done It Again(68559aa)/Wishful Thinking(68560a)
De  3666. I'm the Lonesomest Gal in Town(68331)/The Muffin Man

        (Same, except C. Haughton for Dorsey):
De  3754. Keep Cool Fool(68894a)/No Nothing(68895a)

        (Same brass; C. Haughton,P.Clark, T.McRae, E.Williams,L.Simmons, reeds;same
        rhythm except Jesse Price, drums.--EW):                   July 31,1941
De   3968. I Got It Bad(dla2610)/Melinda the Mousie(dla2611)
De  18421. I Can't Believe That You're in Love With Me(dla2607)/Can't Help Lovin'
De  18530. I Must Have That Man(dla2608)/My Heart and I Decided  (Bat Man(dla2612)
De  18605. Once Too Often(71889)/Time Alone Will Tell(71890)

FIVE BIRMINGHAM BABIES (Reputedly a Rollini group):
Pat 036130. Hard Hearted Hannah/(rev.,Golden Gate Orchestra)      -Pe 14311
Pat 036218. Better Keep the Home Fires Burning/Pickin' on Your Baby
Pat 036236. Mamie/Where Do We Go from Boston
Pat 036266. Tiger Rag(rev., Fletcher Henderson)                   -Pe 14447
Pat 036352. Go Back Where You Stayed Last Night/(rev.,Bill Wirges) -Pe 14533
Pat 036432. What a Man/(rev., Van's Collegians)                   -Pe 14613
Pat 036454. Remember the Night/(rev., Sam Lanin)                  -Pe 14635
Pe  14350. Copenhagen/Deep Sea Blues
Pe  14416. You're in Wrong With the Right Baby/Just a Little Drink
Pe  14521. Dixie Stomp
Pe  14530. Indigo Blues(rev., Lou Gold)
Pe  14531. One Week from Now/(rev., Blue Rhythm Orchestra)
Pe  14560. What, No Women/(rev., Original Indiana Five)
Pe  14632. She's Not Too Hot

FIVE HARMANIACS (Blue blowing, washboard, strings):
Vi  20293. Coney Island Washboard/Sadie Green Vamp of New Orleans
Vi  20507. It Takes a Good Woman/What Makes My Baby Cry?

        (Blue Blowing, banjo, piano, drums, jug):
Br   7002. Sleepy Blues/Carolina Bound
Ge   6033. What Did Romeo Do?

FIVE HOT CHOCOLATES:
VD  71775. Alabama Shuffle

FIVE LITTLE CHOCOLATE DANDIES (See Chocolate Dandies)
```

FIVE MUSICAL BLACKBIRDS:
    Pat   7508. 18th Street Rag/(rev., Troy Harmonists)

FIVE RHYTHM KINGS:
    Vi 23269. Please Don't Talk About Me When I'm Gone/Minnie the Moocher
    Vi 23276. One More Time/Walkin' My Baby Back Home
    Vi 23279. You Rascal You/Call of the Freaks (under name of "The Rhythm Kings")

FLORENCE, NELLIE (vocal blues with guitar):
    Co 14342. Midnight Weeping Blues/Jacksonville Blues

FLOWERS, PAT (vocal blues, instrumental accompaniment):
    De 8587. After the Sun Goes Down/Beg Borrow and Steal

        (Piano solos, with string bass and traps):
    Hit 1010. Original Blues(t390-1)/Ain't Misbehavin'(t394)
    Hit 1011. Chopin E Minor Waltz(t389-1)/But Not for Me(t393)
    Hit 1012. Bach Prelude and Fugue(t396-2)/Canteen Honky Tonk Boogie(t392)
    Hit 1013. Blue Danube(t395-1)/Eight Mile Boogie(t391)

FLOYD, ELLZEE (vocal blues with piano):
    Br 7181. Snow Bound/Dry Spell Blues(Spider Carter)

FLOYD AND HIS SHADOWLAND ORCHESTRA, TROY (Don Albert, Willie Long, trumpet , Troy
Floyd, alto and clarinet; Siki Collins, alto and clarinet; Herschel Evans, tenor,
soprano and clarinet; Allen Van, piano; Braggs, guitar; Charlie Dixon, tuba and trombone; John Humphreys, drums.--JI 2/16/40):   Feb.16,1940
    OK 8571. Shadowland Blues, 1 & 2
    OK 8719. Dreamland Blues, 1 & 2 (402696/7)

FOOTE, BEA (vocal with orchestra):
    De 7457. Could Be You/Satisfied
    De 7535. Jive Lover/Try and Get it
    De 7554. Baby Ain't You Satisfied/I Want a Long Time Daddy

FORESYTHE, REGINALD (Piano solos):
    CoE 1407. Because It's Love   -CoE 1141
     "   St. Louis Blues   -Co 3088,   "

        REGINALD FORESYTHE AND ARTHUR YOUNG (Piano duets)
    CoE 1264. Camembert   -Co 3088
     "   Chromolithograph
    Vi 26224. Mood Indigo/Solitude
    Vi 26274. Tiger Rag/St. Louis Blues

        (Dick Ball, bass, and Max Bacon, drums, added):
    DeE 770. Anything Goes
    DeE 777. Rhumbas on Toast
    DeE 779. With the Duke
    DeE 797. Hits of 1935
    DeE 5636. Sweet Adeline
    DeE 5637. Roberta
    DeE 5715. Every Night at Eight
    DeE 5716. Big Broadcast of 1936/Casino de Paree
    DeE 5758. Cheek to Cheek/The Piccolino
    DeE 5759. Broadway Melody of 1936/Broadway Gondoliers
    DeE 5878. Modern Melodies
    DeE 5879. Follow the Sun/Tonight at 8:30

        THE NEW MUSIC OF REGINALD FORESYTHE (Reginald Foresythe, piano; Jimmy Wat-
son, Ivor Lamb, alto saxes; Alf Morgan, tenor sax; Ted Marshall,George Newman, clarinets; C. W. Harding, bassoon; Joe Gibson, bass; Don Whitelaw, drums--RR):
                                                                          1933
    CoE 675. Angry Jungle   -Co 2916
     "   Serenade for a Wealthy Widow
    CoE 726. Berceuse for an Unwanted Child
     "   Garden of Weed

        (Reginald Foresythe, piano; Cyril Clarke, Bill Apps, clarinets;Claude Hug-
hes, bassoon; Jimmy Watson, Bill Barclay, alto saxes; Jack Ambrose, tenor sax; Jack
Collier, bass;George Elrick,drums.--RR):   1933-34
    CoE 744. Bit
     "   The Duke Insists   -Co 3000
    CoE 787. Autocrat Before Breakfast/Volcanic

        (Reginald Foresythe, piano; Benny Goodman, Johnny Mince, clarinets; Sol
Schoenbach, bassoon; Toots Mondello, Hymie Schertzer, alto saxes; Dick
Clark, tenor sax; John Kirby, bass Gene Krupa, drums.--RR): New York, 1935
    Co 3012. Dodging a Divorcee/Lullaby   -CoE 1031
    Co 3060. Greener the Grass/Melancholy Clown   -CoE 1233

REGINALD FORESYTHE AND HIS ORCHESTRA (Reginald Foresythe, piano; Cyril Clarke, Dick Savage, clarinets; Harry Carr, Jimmy Watson, alto saxes; Eddie Farge, tenor sax; J. L. Brenchley, bassoon; Don Stuteley, bass; Jack Simpson, drums.--RR): 1935-36
DeE 5560. Landscape(tb1885)/Homage to Armstrong(tb1886)
DeE 5711. Tea for Two(tb1887)/Sweet Georgia Brown(tb1888)
DeE 6203. Swing for Roundabout(tb2617)/The Revolt of the Yes Men(tb2619)
DeE 6291. Anything You Like(tb2618)/Mead and Woad(tb2661)
DeE 6363. Aubade(tb2664)/Burlesque(tb2665)
DeE 6481. Meditation in Porcelain(tb2662)/Cross for Criss(tb2663)

FOSTER AND HARRIS (Ma Rainey's Boys):
Para 12709. Alley Crap Game/Crow Jane Alley

FOUR INSTRUMENTAL STARS (Joe Venuti, violin; Adrian Rollini, bass sax; Eddie Lang, guitar; Vic Berton, drums; Annette Hanshaw, vocals.--HD):
Pat 11485. I'm Somebody's Somebody(36664)/I Like What You Like(36665)

FOUR SPADES:
Co 14028. Squabblin' Blues/Makin' Up Blues

FOWLER, LEMUEL (Piano solos):
Co 3959. Satisfied Blues(81107)/Blues Mixture(81108)
(See also: Helen Baxter, Co 3922, OK 8080; Edna Hicks Vo 14659, Ge 5234, 5252, Co 14001; Maggie Jones Ge 5193, Co 14044; Sara Martin OK 8191;Clara Smith Co 14150)
FOWLER'S WASHBOARD WONDERS (clarinet, piano, washboard):
Co 14084. Chitterlin' Strut(140742)/Washboard Stomp(140743)

(Trumpet, sax and clarinet, piano, washboard):
Co 14096. Dodgin' My Man(140870)/Pig Foot Shuffle(140871)
Co 14101. Express Train Blues/Steppin' Old Fool
Co 14111. Salty Dog/Florida Blues
Co 14155. Frisky Feet/Jelly Roll Blues

FOWLER'S FAVORITES (Trumpet; trombone; tenor sax; alto and clarinet; banjo; piano; drums; tuba):
Co 14230. Percolatin' Blues(144427),vocal, Lem Fowler/Hot Strut(144428)

FRANKIE AND HER JAZZ DEVILS (vocal with trumpet, clarinet and piano):
Pat 7507. You Can't Guess How Good It Is/Those Creeping Sneaking Blues -Pe 107

FRANKO AND HIS LOUISIANIANS, FRANKIE (Punch Miller, trumpet and vocal; Omer Simeon, reeds; Fred Howard, tenor sax; Zinky Cohn, piano; Charlie du Caston, banjo; Bill Hilliard, tuba; Francois Moseley, drums.--EW): Nov.12,1930
Me 12009. Somebody Stole My Gal(c6179)/Golden Lily Blues(c6180)

BUD FREEMAN

See also:
ADRIAN: Br 6877, 6889.
HOAGY CARMICHAEL: Vi 22864, 23013, 38139.
CELLAR BOYS: Vo 1503.
BUDDY CLARK: Vs 8230, 8233.
EDDIE CONDON: BrF 500328, 500406; Com 500, 502, 1500; De 18040, 18041.
TOMMY DORSEY: Vi 25314, 25349 to 26072.
DORSEY BROTHERS: OK 41471, Co 2581, 2589.
GENE GIFFORD: Vi 25041, 25065.
BENNY GOODMAN: Br 4968, Vi 25827 to 26125.
TEDDY GRACE: De 3428, 3463.
JOE HAYMES
EDDY HOWARD: Co 35771, 35915.
JAM SESSION: Com 1500, 1501, 1504, 1505.
LOUISIANA RHYTHM KINGS: Vo 15915, 15828; Br 4706.
WINGY MANNONE: Vo 15728, 15797, 2989, 2990, 3023, 3058.
McKENZIE-CONDON: Ok 41011, 40971.
MEZZ MEZZROW: Vi 25202, 25019; BB 6320, 6319, 6321.
MIDNIGHT AIRDALES: Co 1981.
RED NICHOLS: Br 4778, 4925.
RAY NOBLE
BEN POLLACK: Or 2193, 2208, 1998, 2000, 2214; Re 10057.
JACK TEAGARDEN: Co 2558, 2802, 2913.
JOE VENUTI: CoE 686, 708.

FREEMAN AND HIS ORCHESTRA, BUD (Bud Freeman, tenor sax; Bud Jacobson,clarinet; John Mendell, trumpet; Floyd O'Brien, trombone; Dave North, piano; Herman Forest, banjo; John Mueller, bass; Gene Krupa, drums; Red McKenzie, vocal): 1929
OK 41168. Craze-ology(402151c)   -OdF 165581,UHCA 13
  "   Can't Help Lovin' Dat Man(402152b)   "   UHCA 14
  "   Can't Help Lovin' Dat Man(402152c)

BUD FREEMAN AND HIS WINDY CITY FIVE (Bunny Berigan, trumpet; Bud Freeman, tenor sax and clarinet; Claude Thornhill, piano; Eddie Condon, guitar; Grachan Moncur, bass; Cozy Cole, drums):   1936
PaE 2210. The Buzzard(60191a).   -De 18112
" Tillie's Downtown Now(60192b)
De 18112. Tillie's Downtown Now(60192a)
PaE 2285. What Is There to Say(60190a)/Keep Smilin'at Trouble(60193a)   -De 18113

BUD FREEMAN AND HIS TRIO(Bud Freeman, tenor sax; Jess Stacy, piano; George Wettling, drums):   1938
Com 501. You Took Advantage of Me(p22311)/Three's No Crowd(p22312)
Com 502. I Got Rhythm(p22313)/(rev., Eddie Condon)
Com 503. Keep Smiling at Trouble(p22719-2)/At Sundown(p22720-1)
Com 504. My Honey's Lovin' Arms(p22721-1)/I Don't Believe It(p22722-2)
Com 513. Exactly Like You/Blue Room
Com 514. Three Little Words(75957a)/Swingin' Without Mezz(75958a)

BUD FREEMAN AND HIS GANG(Bud Freeman, tenor sax; Dave Matthews, alto sax; Pee Wee Russell, clarinet; Bobby Hackett, cornet; Jess Stacy, piano; Eddie Condon, tenor guitar; Artie Shapiro, bass; Marty Marsala, drums):
Com 507. LIFE Spears a Jitterbug(p23235-1)/What's the Use(p23236-2)

(Sub. Dave Tough, drums):
Com 508. Tappin' the Commodore Till(p23233-1)/Memories of You(p23234)

BUD FREEMAN AND THE SUMMA CUM LAUDE ORCHESTRA (Bud Freeman, tenor sax; Pee Wee Russell, clarinet; Max Kaminsky, trumpet; Brad Gowans, valve trombone; Dave Bowman, piano; Eddie Condon, guitar; Clyde Newcomb, bass; Al Seidel, drums):   Sept.18,1939
De 2781. The Sail Fish(66604a)
" Satanic Blues(66606a)   -De 3525
De 2849. As Long As I Live(66603a)   -De 3885
" Sunday(66605a3)   -De 3865

(Pete Peterson, bass; Morey Feld, drums,for 67391-94 session)   Mar.25,1940
De 18064. Big Boy(67394a)/Copenhagen(67480a)
De 18065. Oh Baby(67391a)/Sensation(67477a)
De 18066. I Need Some Pettin'(67392a)/Tia Juana(67479a)
De 18067. Susie(67393a)/Fidgety Feet(67478a)

(Sub. Danny Alvin, drums):
BB 10370. I've Found a New Baby/Easy to Get
BB 10386. China Boy/The Eel

BUD FREEMAN AND HIS FAMOUS CHICAGOANS (Max Kaminsky, trumpet; Jack Teagarden, trombone; Pee Wee Russell, clarinet; Bud Freeman, tenor sax; Dave Bowman, piano; Eddie Condon, guitar; Mort Stuhlmaker, bass; Dave Tough,drums):
Co 35853. At the Jazz Band Ball(co27689)/Prince of Wails(co27691)   1940
Co 35854. Jack Hits the Road(co27684)/That Da Da Strain(co27687)
Co 35855. Muskrat Ramble(co27686)/47th and State(co27685)
Co 35856. Shimmeshawabble(co27688)/After Awhile(co27690)

FRENCH HOT BOYS (Andre Ekyan, alto sax and clarinet; Bari, alto sax*,. Jean Thiland, piano; Didier Mauprey, banjo; Charlie Barnes, drums):   1932
Sa 3166. China Boy(ss872)*/Some of These Days(ss873)

FRIARS SOCIETY ORCHESTRA (Paul Mares, trumpet; George Brunis, trombone; Leon Rappolo, clarinet; Jack Pettis, sax; Elmer Schoebel, piano; Lew Black, banjo; Steve Brown, bass; Frank Snyder, drums):   1921
Ge 4966. Farewell Blues(11179c)   -BrE 02211
" Oriental(11185)
Ge 4967. Discontented Blues(11180a)   -BrE 02213
" Bugle Call Blues(11181b)
Ge 4968. Tiger Rag(11183c)/Panama(11182b)   -BrE 02212
Ge 5009. Eccentric(11178b)/(rev., Husk O'Hare Orchestra)   -BrE 02211
(See also: New Orleans Rhythm Kings)

FROEBA AND HIS SWING BAND, FRANK (Slats Long, clarinet; Herbie Haymer, tenor sax; Jack Purvis, trumpet; Frank Froeba, piano; Clayton Duerr, guitar; Carroll Walrond, bass; Eddie Dougherty, drums.--RR):   1936
Co 3110. There'll Be a Great Day in the Morning/Music Goes 'Round and Around
Co 3131. Just to Be in Caroline/It Ain't Nobody's Bizness What I Do
Co 3151. Organ Grinder's Swing
Co 3152. Watcha Gonna Do When There Ain't No Swing/It All Begins and Ends with
    (You

FRANK FROEBA AND HIS ORCHESTRA (Frank Froeba, piano; Buddy Schutz, drums; Ralph Dunham, bass; Sam Rubinowitz, Joe Estren, alto saxes; Ed Apple, Kurt Bloom, tenors; Charles Colin, Frank Wysochanski, Charles Gognata, trumpets; Mack Zazmar, trombone):   Aug.19, 1937
De 1401. The Big Apple(62547a)/Josephine(62548a)
De 1418. Don't Save Your Love/Nothing Can Stop Me Now(62549)

```
            ('Frank Froeba,' piano; Bobby Hackett, trumpet; John Sadola, tenor sax; Milt
            Yaner, Sal Franzella, Don Watt, altos; Moe Zudicoff, trombone; Haig Steph-
            ens, bass; Al Seidel, drums):                                Oct.18, 1937
     De 1500. Tears in My Heart(62694)/My Swiss Hill Billy(62692)
     De 1525. Danger, Love at Work(62693)/Miles Apart(62695)
     De 1545. Who(62752a)/Goblins in the Steeple(62751a)                 Nov.4, 1937

FULCHER AND HIS ORCHESTRA, CHARLES:
    OK 4889. Black Cat Blues/Eskimo Song
    Co  316. The Georgia Stomp(140288)/Home Sweet Home Blues(140289)
    Co  551. My Pretty Girl/Blue for You
    Co 1706. Hey Hey/Voice of the Southland
                (See also: Thelma Terry)

            FULCHER'S DANCE TRIO:
    Co 1267. After Than/Daylight Breaking Blues

FULLER, BLIND BOY (vocals, mostly with Sonny Terry, harmonica):
    Vo 02956. Baby I Don't Have to Worry/Looking for My Woman
    Vo 02964. Ain't It a Crying Shame/I'm Climbin' on Top of the Hill
    Vo 03014. Somebody's Been Playing With That Thing
    Vo 03025. Evil Hearted Woman/My Brownskin Sugar Plum              -Me 60564
    Vo 03071. Black and Tan/Mama Let Me Lay It on You
    Vo 03084. I'm a Rattlesnakin' Daddy/Rag Mama Rag
    Vo 03098. Babe You Got to Do Better/Truckin' My Blues Away
    Vo 03123. Big Bed Blues/When Your Gal Packs up and Leaves
    Vo 03134. Cat Man Blues(19143)/Keep Away from My Woman(19138)     -Me 70156
    Vo 03179. She's Funny That Way/Walking My Troubles Away
    Vo 03234. Homesick and Lonesome Blues/Log Cabin Blues
    Vo 03254. If You Don't Give Me What I Want/Sweet Honey Hole
    Vo 03276. Mamie/New Oh Red                                        -Me 70556
    Vo 03302. Let Me Squeeze Your Lemon/My Baby Don't Mean Me No Good
    Vo 03324. Boots and Shoes/Truckin' My Blues Away No. 2
    Vo 03334. My Best Gal Gonna Leave Me/Wires All Down
    Vo 03351. Been Your Dog/Untrue Blues
    Vo 03408. New Louise Louise Blues/Snake Woman Blues
    Vo 03420. Death Valley/Throw Your Yas Yas Back in Jail
    Vo 03438. Stealing Bo-Hog/Worried and Evil Man Blues
    Vo 03457. Careless Love/I'm Going to Move
    Vo 03490. Mistreater You're Going to be Sorry/Shaggy Like a Bear
    Vo 03499. Hungry Calf Blues/Mojo Hidin' Woman
    Vo 04054. Looking for My Woman No. 2/Ten o'Clock Peeper
    Vo 04106. Mean and No Good Woman/Pistol Slapper Blues
    Vo 04137. I'm a Good Stem Winder/Meat Shakin' Woman
    Vo 04175. Painful Hearted Man/You've Got to Move It Out
    Vo 04237. Funny Feeling Blues/Mama Let Me Lay It on You No.2
    Vo 04315. Georgia Ham mama/Oozin' You Off My Mind
    Vo 04343. Oh Zee Zas Rag/Shake That Shimmy
    Vo 04391. Ain't No Gettin' Along/Bull Dog Blues
    Vo 04456. Break of Day Blues/Tom Cat Blues
    Vo 04510. Get Your Yas Yas Out/That's That Smells Like Fish
    Vo 04557. Flying Airplane Blues/You're Laughing Blues
    Vo 04603. Screamin' and Cryin' blues/She's a Truckin' Little Baby
    Vo 04675. Blacksnakin' Jiver/Long Time Trucker
    Vo 04732. Heart Ease Blues/Jivin' Woman Blues
    Vo 04782. Jitterbug Rag/Too Many Women Blues
    Vo 04843. Bye Bye Baby Blues/Steel Hearted Woman
    Vo 04897. Big House Bound/Stop Jivin' Me Mama
    Vo 05030. Big Leg Woman Gets My Pay/I Want Some of Your Pie
    Vo 05083. Baby Quit Your Low Down Ways/You've Got Something There
    Vo 05150. Woman You Better Wake Up
    Vo 05153. It Doesn't Matter Baby
    Vo 05218. Jivin' Big Bill Blues/Red's Got the Piccolo Blues
    Vo 05273. I Don't Care How Long/I'm a Stranger Here
    Vo 05324. Black Bottom Blues/Somebody's Been Talkin'
    Vo 05575. Shake It Baby/Worn Out Engine Blues
    Vo 05657. I Don't Want No Skinny Woman/Thousand Woman Blues
    Vo 05712. Bye Bye Baby/You Got to Have Your Dollar
    Vo 05756. Lost Lover Blues/When You Are Gone
    Vo 05785. Night Rambling Woman
    Vo 05933. Bus Rider Blues
    OK 06231. Passenger Train Blues/Good Feeling Blues

FULLER, BOB (Clarinet solos):
    Br  7006. Dallas Blues/I Ain't Got Nobody
    Co 14068. Too Bad Jim Blues/Black Cat Blues                  -Ha 580, Di 2580
    Co 14120. Pig Alley Stomp/Grand Opera Blues
    Ha   688. Nameless Blues/Ridiculous Blues
    Ba  7151. Alligator Crawl/Here 'Tis.
```

15

G

GAILLARD AND HIS FLAT FOOT FLOOGIE BOYS, SLIM: (Trumpet; sax; guitar; piano; drums; bass; vocals by Slim Gaillard):
   Vo 5138. Chicken Rhythm/A-Well-a-Take-'em-a-Joe
   Vo 5220. That's a Bringer(25363)/Early in the Morning(w26151)
   Vo 5301. Matzom Balls/It's You Only You
   Vo 5341. Chitlin' Switch Blues(w26152a)/Huh! Uh-Huh!(w26153a)
   Vo 5388. Swinging in the Key of C(25466)/Boot-ta-la-za(25467)
   Vo 5619. Baby Be Mine/Sploghm
   OK 6015. Bongo/Rhythm Mad

     (Add clarinet):
   OK 6088. Put Your Arms Around Me Baby(28697)/Hey Chef(28700)
   OK 6135. A Tip on the Numbers/Slim Slam Boogie
   OK 6260. Lookin' for a Place to Park/Hit That Mess
   OK 6295. Bassology/Ah Now
   OK 6382. Bingie Bingie/Champagne Lullaby
     (See also: Slim and Slam)

GAITHER, LITTLE BILL, (Blues with accompaniment including Honey Hill, piano; Baby Doo, guitar):
   Vo 05655. Love Crying Blues/Money Kills Love
   Vo 05714. Georgia Barrel House/It's Just a Woman's Way
   Vo 05770. Life of Leroy Carr/Tired of Your Trifling Ways
   Vo 05824. Wandering Rosa Lee/Love Trifling Blues
   OK 06044. Jealous Woman Blues/1940 Blues
   OK 06092. I'm Behind the 8-Ball Now/Uncle Sam Called the Roll
   OK 06128. Why Is My Baby So Nice to Me/I Got So Many Women
   OK 06164. You Done Ranked Yourself
     (See also: Leroy's Buddy)

GARBER AND HIS ORCHESTRA, JAN (Harry Goldfield, Paul Weirick, trumpets; Johnnie Cook, trombone; Bobbie Davis, Russ Hoffman, Tommy Christian, saxes; Steve Brodie, drums; Jack Gifford, Rudi Rudisell, pianos; George Hoge, banjo; Jan Garber, violin.--DB
   Co 1306. Sister Kate/Since My Best Gal Turned Me Down   (Oct.1, 1942):

     (Possibly Frank Teschemacher, clarinet):
   Co 2115. Puttin' on the Ritz

GARCIA AND HIS SWING BAND, LOUIS (KING):
   BB 6302. Love Is Like a Cigarette/It's Great to be in Love Again
   BB 6303. No Greater Love/Christopher Columbus
   BR 10043. Swing Mr. Charlie/(rev., Boots)   -ReZ 2103

GARDNER'S TEXAS UNIVERSITY TROUBADOURS, FRED:
   OK 41440. Loveless Love(404099a)/Papa's Gone(404100a)
   OK 41458. No Trumps(404101b)/Daniel's Blues(404102b)

GARDNER AND HIS ORCHESTRA, JACK:
   OK 40245. Ponjola/I Know She Does
   OK 40265. Blackin' Blues/Too Late Now
   OK 40339. Who? You'./ Who'd a Thunk It

GARNER, CORA (vocal blues):
   Co 14659. I ain't Going to Sell You None/Wouldn't Stop Doing It

GARNETT, BLIND LEROY (piano solos)   1930
   Para 12876. Chain 'em Down(1621)/Louisiana Glide(1622,
     (See also: James Wiggins, Para 12878)

GARY, SID (accompaniment possibly including Eddie Lang, guitar):
   Me 12069. At Last I'm Happy

GENE'S MERRYMAKERS (Casa Loma Orchestra):
   Pe 15601. Business in F/Business in Q   -Me 12365, DeE 3101
   Pe 15663. Clarinet Marmalade   -Me 12494, Ro 1927, BrF 500224,DeE 3397
   "   In the Shade of the Old Apple Tree   "   "   "   "
   Pe 15693. Milenberg Joys/Old Fashioned Love
   Pe 15698. Pink Elephants(12561)/Listen to the German Band(12562)   -Or 2604
   Pe 15767. It's Sunday Down in Caroline/Headin' for   -Me 12688
   Me 12491. High Society   -Ro 1927, DeE 3434
   "   Sing
   Me 12632. Casa Loma Stomp
   Me 12754. Seven Years With the Wrong Woman/Wheezy Anna   -Vo 4347
   Or 2753. Shame on You(13907)/There's a New Moon Over My Shoulder(13908)
   Or 2758. Shanghai Lil/Honeymoon Hotel

GEORGE'S HOT SHOTS:
   Vi 23739. We Do It Just the Same/Why Should I

GEORGE, HORACE (clarinet solo accompanied by Clarence Williams, piano):
   OK 8164. The Meal Is Low in the Barrel/Emancipation Day in Georgia (vocal with Charles and Effie Tyus assompanied by instrumental trio)

16

GEORGIA COTTON PICKERS (under direction of George Tynes; three reeds; trombone; trumpet; banjo; piano; drums; tuba):
```
Ha  1090. Cotton Pickers Shuffle(149795)/12th St.Rag(149794) -Ve 7090, Di 6064
Ha  1127. Snag It(149793)/Louisiana Bo Bo (149796)                    -Di 3127
Co 14577. She's Coming Back Some Cold Rainy Day/Diddle da diddle
```

GEORGIA GRINDER (Cow Cow Davenport), piano solos:
```
Ch 50033. Chimes Blues                                    -Reissue of Ge 6838
      "   Atlanta Rag                                     -Reissue of Ge 6869
Vo 02792. Southern Jack Chimes(15475)/Beale Street Drag(15476)
          (Latter two sides are reissues of Para 12800)
```

GEORGIA STRUTTERS (Perry Bradford group: trumpet; trombone; sax and clarinet; banjo; piano; drums):
```
Ha  231. Everybody Mess Aroun'(142512)/Georgia Grind(142513)
Ha  311. Wasn't It Nice(142854)/Original Black Bottom Dance)142855)
Ha  468. Rock Jennie Rock(144202)/It's right here for you (add tuba) -Di 2468
```

GEORGIA SYNCOPATORS (First title by Duke Ellington Orchestra, second by Noble Sissle):
```
Me 12444. I'm So in Love With You(10359-3)                 - Or 2528*
      "   Loveless Love(36122a)
          *Issued under name of Whoopee Makers.
```

GEORGIA TOM (vocal blues with Tampa Red, guitar):
```
Vo 1215. Grievin' Me Blues/It's Tight Like That
Vo 1246. Long Ago Blues/Lonesome Man Blues

         (Unknown accompaniment):
Ch 50054. Second Hand Love/Maybe It's the Blues
De  7362. Gee But It's Hard/Levee Bound Blues

         GEORGIA TOM AND JANE LUCAS:
De  7259. Terrible Operation Blues/Where Did You Stay Last Night
```

GEORGIA WASHBOARD STOMPERS:
```
De 7002. High Society/Everybody Loves My Baby
De 7003. Farewell Blues/Tiger Rag
De 7004. I Can't Dance/Who Broke the Lock Off the Henhouse Door
De 7005. Chinatown My Chinatown/Limehouse Blues
De 7006. After you've Gone/Alexander's Ragtime Band
De 7094. I'm Living in a Great Big Way/You're an Angel
De 7095. Lulu's Back in Town/Name it
De 7096. In the Middle of a Kiss/Every Little Moment
De 7097. Chasing Shadows/Lady in Red
BB 5089. Sophisticated Lady/Pretty
BB 5092. Nobody's Sweetheart/Bug a Boo
BB 5127. Dinah/(rev., Washboard Rhythm Kings)
```

GEORGIANS (Frank Guarente, trumpet; Johnny O'Donnel, clarinet; Arthur Johnson, saxophone; Ray Stilwell, or Archie Jones, or Russ Morgan, trombone; Russell Deppey, banjo; Arthur Schutt, piano; Chauncey Moorehouse, drums.--RR): 1923-25
```
Co 3775. Chicago/Sister Kate
Co 3804. Way Down Yonder in New Orleans/Nothing But
Co 3825. Aggravatin' Papa/Loose Feet
Co 3857. You've Got to See Mama Every Night
Co 3864. Farewell Blues/Snakes Hips
Co 3902. Old King Tut
     "   Barney Google                                    -CoE 3325
Co 3907. Long Lost Mama/Henpecked
Co 3987. Land of the Moon Blues/Mama Loves Papa
Co 3996. Somebody's Wrong/Mama Goes Where Papa Goes
Co   11. I'm Sitting Pretty(81272)                        -CoE 3379
     "   Learn to Do the Strut(81273)
Co   23. Home Town Blues                                  -CoE 3391
     "   You May Be Fast                                  -CoE 3387
Co   30. Shake Your Feet(81360)                           -CoE 3420
     "   Old Fashioned Love(81361)                        -CoE 3368
Co   40. I've Got a Cross Eyed Papa/You'd Better Keep Babyin' Baby -CoE 3412
Co   62. Lovey Come Back to Me/Dancing Dan
Co  102. Mindin' My Business/If You'll Come Back
Co  114. Don't Mind the Rain/Lazy
Co  136. New Kind of Man/Bringin' Home the Bacon
Co  142. Savannah/Doodle Do Do                            -CoE 3544
Co  252. My Best Girl/Everybody Loves My Baby
```

(Frank Guarente, trumpet; Ben Pickering, trombone and trumpet; Ernest White, saxophones, clarinet and trumpet; Eddie Bave, Rene de Pascal, saxes and clarinets; Joseph Murray, piano; B. Rundio, banjo and guitar; Jack Ryan, sousaphone; Eddie Noyes, drums and vocals.--RR): 1926

```
Co   523. Clap Hands Here Comes Charley/Spanish Shawl
Co   923. Frisco Bay/Cook a Doddle My Baby's Back
```

GERITY AND HER BOYS, JULIA:
```
Vi 22896. Sittin' on a Rubbish Can/(rev., Blanche Calloway)
```

GET HAPPY BAND (Sidney Bechet, clarinet and soprano sax; trumpet, trombone, alto
sax, banjo, piano, drums, bass):
```
Co 14091. Junk Bucket Blues(140773)/Harlem's Araby(140774)
Co 14099. On the Puppy's Tail/Puddlin' Papa
```

GIBBONS, IRENE (comedienne with jazz band):
```
Co  3834. That Da Da Strain(80724)/Last Go Round Bl(80838), acc. by Clarence
Co  3922. My Pillow and Me(80723)/(rev., Helen Baxter)         (Williams, piano
Co 14296. Longing(145652)/Let Me Forget(145653)
Co 14362. Jeannine/I'm Busy and You Can't Come In(Clarence Williams'Blue 5 with Lang)
```

GIBBS, ARTHUR AND HIS GANG (trumpet; trombone; saxes; clarinet; piano;banjo;drums;
violin):
```
Vi 19165. Charleston/Old Fashioned Love
```

GIBSON AND HER HOT THREE, CLEO (vocal with trumpet, piano and bass):
```
OK  8700. I've Got Ford Movements in My Hips(4023llb)/Nothing but Blues
                                                                 (4C2312b)
```

GIFFORD AND HIS ORCHESTRA, GENE (Bunny Berigan, trumpet; Morey Samuel, trombone;
Mat Matlock, clarinet; Bud Freeman, tenor sax; Claude Thornhill, piano; Dick Mc-
Donough, guitar; Pete Peterson, bass; Ray Bauduc, drums; Wingy Mannone, voc.):
```
                                                                         1935
Vi 25041. Nothin' But the Blues(89794)      -BB 10704, HMV 30,  HMV 8383
       "  New Orleans Twist(89795)                  "          "    HMV 8390
Vi 25065. Squareface(89796)                         -HMV 34,    HMV 8374
       "  Dizzy Glide(89797)                        "           HMV 8383
```

GILLUM AND HIS JAZZ BOYS, JAZZ:
```
BB  6445. Sarah Jane/I Want You By My Side
BB  8505. It Sure Had a Kick/Longest Train Blues
BB  8529. She Belongs to Me/Key to the Highway
```

GILMORE, GENE (blues with piano, traps, guitar):
```
De  7671. Brown Skin Woman/Charity Blues
```

GIRL FRIEND (vocal with instrumental accompaniment):
```
Vs  6045. Can't Get Enough/Good and Hot
```

GLASCOE, PERCY (clarinet solos):
```
Co 14088. Stomp 'em down/Steaming Blues
```

GLINN, LILLIAN (blues with jazz band):
```
Co 14275. Brown Skin Blues/Doggin' Me Blues
Co 14300. Come Home Daddy/All Alone and Blue
Co 14315. Shake It Down/Where Have All the Black Men Gone
Co 14330. Best Friend Blues/Man I Love Is Worth Talkin' About
Co 14360. Lost Letter Blues/Packing House Blues
Co 14421. Atlanta Blues/All the Week Blues
Co 14433. Black Man Blues(148226)/I'm a Front Door Woman(148212)
Co 14493. Moanin' Blues/Don't Leave Me Daddy
Co 14519. Shreveport Blues/Cravin' a Man Blues
Co 14617. Cannon Ball Blues/Wobble It
```

GOLDEN GATE ORCHESTRA:
```
Para 20294. The One I Love Belongs to Somebody Else(1637)/Tripping Along(1638)
Re    9758. Nobody Knows What a Red Head Mama Can Do/Doo Wacka Doo
Ba    6082. Jelly Roll Blues/I Ain't Got Nobody
Pe   14309. Ramblin' Blues
Pe   14441. Dusting the Donkey/(rev., Mayflower Serenaders)
```
   (Red Nichols, Jimmy Dorsey, Adrian Rollini):
```
Pe 14834. After You've Gone/(rev., Willard Robison)           -Pat 36653
Pe 14837. Vo Do Do De O Blues/(rev., Sam Lanin)
Ha   690. Dusky Stevedore/(rev., Astorites)
Ve  1704. Ready for the River/Cause I Feel Low Down
Ve  1937. Wishing and Waiting
Ve  1995. Shoo Shoo/Do I
Di  2760. Don't Be Like That(147130)/My Old Girl's My New Girl Now(147129)
Di  2839. Who Wouldn't Be Jealous of You(147910)/Weary River(147911)
Cl  5204. Fall in Love With Me(100457)
```
   (Reputedly featuring Miff Mole, Jimmy Dorsey, Red Nichols, Quicksell):
```
Ed 51491. Keep Smiling at Trouble(9947)/Oh Mabel(9948)
Ed 51580. Collegiate(10451)/(rev., Billy Wynne)
Ed 51590. Manhattan/Oh Say Can I See You Tonight
```

```
Ed 51591. Look Who's Here
Ed 51737. Shake(10930)/What a Man(10929)
Ed 51746. Static Strut/Could I
Ed 51820. Up and At 'em/Mee Too
Ed 51860. Sweet Thing/Cinderella
Ed 51897. Sidewalk Blues/Stockholm Stomp
Ed 52206. Third Rail/I Ain't Got Nobody
```

GOLDEN MELODY MEN (Shirley Clay, cornet; Preston Jackson, trombone; clarinet; piano; banjo):
    Challenge 803. Trombone Man(2650-2; reissue of Preston Jackson, Para 12411)

GOLDKETTE AND HIS ORCHESTRA, JEAN (including Joe Venuti, violin; Don Murray, saxex and clarinet):
```
Vi 19308. In the Evening                                    -HMV 1865
   "      Where the Lazy Daisies Grow
Vi 19313. My Sweetheart/(rev., Paul Biese)
Vi 19317. Cover Me Up With the Sunshine of Virginia/(rev., Benson Orchestra)
Vi 19327. Eileen/(rev., Benson Orchestra)
Vi 19345. Fox Trot Classique/(rev., Paul Whiteman)
Vi 19528. Honest and Truly, waltz/(rev., Ralph Williams)
Vi 19548. I Want to See My Tennessee/Remember
Vi 19600. It's the Blues/(rev., Coon-Sanders)
Vi 19664. Play Me Slow/What's the Use of Dreaming
```

    (Ray Ludwig, Fred Farrar, Jimmy McPartland, trumpets; Spiegel Wilcox, Bill Rank, trombones; Don Murray, Doc Ryker, Fud Livingston, saxes and clarinets; Joe Venuti, violin; Eddie Lang, guitar; Izzy Riskin, piano; Steve Brown, bass; Howdy Quicksell, banjo; Chauncey Moorehouse, drums.--DB 8/39):
```
Vi 19947. Dinah(34369; Jan.28,1926)/After I Say I'm Sorry(34368)
Vi 19962. Sorry and Blue/(rev., Troubadours)                -HMV 5081
Vi 19965. Behind the Clouds/(rev., International Novelty Orch.)
Vi 19975. Drifting Apart/(rev., C.Dornberger)
Vi 20031. Gimme a Little Kiss Will Ya Huh?(34798)    -HMV 5080, GrF 3564
   "      Lonesome and Sorry(34799)
Vi 20033. Roses/(rev., Ted Weems)                              GrF 3564
Vi 20256. Don't Be Angry With Me
Vi 20257. Kentucky Lullaby/I'd Love to Call You My Sweetheart
Vi 20268. There's a Little White House/Just a Bird's Eye View
```

    (Bix Beiderbecke, trumpet; Frankie Trumbauer, saxes, enter the band)
```
Vi 20270. Idolizing(36813)/Hush-a-Bye(36815), waltz            Oct.12,1926
Vi 20273. Sunday(36829)/I'd Rather Be the Girl in Your Arms(36814) Oct.15,1926
Vi 20300. Just One More Kiss/(rev., Art Landry)                -HMV 5470
```

    (Dorsey Brothers, next four sides):   Jan.28,1927
```
Vi 20466. I'm Looking Over a Four Leaf Clover(37580)/(rev., Roger Wolfe Kahn)
Vi 20469. Proud of a Baby Like You(37579)/(rev., Nat Shilkret)
Vi 20471. Hoosier Sweetheart(37584)/(rev., Nat Shilkret)       Jan.31,1927
Vi 20472. Look at the World and Smile(37586)/(rev.,George Olsen)  Feb.1,1927
Vi 20491. A Lane in Spain(37598)/(rev., Goodrich Orchestra)      Feb.3,1927
Vi 20493. Sunny Disposish(37599)/(rev., Roger Wolfe Kahn)        -HMV 5289
```

    (Danny Polo, clarinet*):   Feb.1,1927
```
Vi 20588. My Pretty Girl(37587)*                         -Vi 25283, HMV 5324
   "      Cover Me Up With Sunshine
Unissued. Stampede(37588)
```

    (Dorsey Brothers one side only):   Jan.31,1927
```
Vi 20675. I'm Gonna Meet My Sweetie Now(37583-2)/(rev., Shilkret)  -HMV 5363
Vi 20926. Slow River(38207-3; May 6, 1927)/(rev., Shildret)        -HMV 5397
Vi 25354. Slow River(38207-2)/I'm Gonna Meet My Sweetie Now(37583-3)
Unissued. Lily(38263)/Play It Red(38267)                           May 23,1927
Special Victor. In My Merry Oldsmobile(38264),waltz/In My Merry Olds.(38268)
Vi 20981. Blue River(40211)/(rev., Jacques Renard)                 Sept.15,1927
Vi 20994. Clementine(40212)/(rev., Jack Crawford)         -Vi 25283, HMV 5402
```

    (Personnel unknown for following; Dorsey Brothers may be heard in some titles; omit Bix Beiderbecke):
```
Vi 21150. So Tired(vocal, Hoagy Carmichael)/Just a Little Kiss from a Little
Vi 21166. My Ohio Home/Here Comes the Showboat
Vi 21527. Rosetta/For Old Time's Sake
Vi 21565. Just Imagine(46070)/(rev., Frankie Masters)          -HMV 5531
Vi 21590. That's Just My Way of Forgetting You(46097)/(rev.,Troubad.)-HMV 5566
Vi 21689. If I Lost You, waltz/(rev., Don Bestor)
```

    (Harold Stokes, director):
```
Vi 21800. That's What Puts the Sweet in Home Sweet Home/Sweethearts on Parade
Vi 21804. Withered Roses/(rev., Johnny Hamp)
```

JUMP

MEANS

JAZZ

JUMP RECORD CO.
P. O. Box 622—Hollywood Station
Hollywood 28, California

```
        (Sterling Bose, trumpet):
Vi 21805. My Blackbirds Are Bluebirds Now(48617)/Don't Be Like(48618)-HMV 5600
Vi 21853. She's Funny That Way/(rev., Nat Shilkret)           -HMV 5623
Vi 21889. Ya Comin' Up Tonight Huh?/Take a Good Look at Mine

        (Unknown personnel):
Vi 22027. Painting the Clouds With Sunshine/Tip Toe Thru the Tulips With Me
Vi 22077. Birmingham Bertha/(rev., Coon-Sanders)
Vi 22123. An Old Italian Love Song/(rev., Coon-Sanders)
```

GOODIE, FRANK 'BIG BOY' (trumpet, tenor sax and clarinet, accompanied by: Joseph and Django Rheinhardt, guitars; Stephane Grappelly, violin; Beck bass; J. Mengo, drums):
```
Ul 1527. St. Louis Blues/I Found a New Baby
```

GOODING AND HER THREE PEPPERS, SALLY:
```
Vr 554. Yours All Yours/Smile Up at the Sun
```

BENNY GOODMAN

See also:
ALL STAR ORCHESTRA
FRANK AUBURN
BIX BEIDERBECKE: Vi 23008, 23018.
BEN'S BAD BOYS: Vi 21971.
RUBE BLOOM: Co 2103, 2186, 2218.
JIMMY BRACKEN: Re 8723, 8768, 8813, 8826, Co 4274.
BROADWAY BANDITS: ReZ 1733.
BROADWAY BROADCASTERS: Co 1149,8228,8349,9023,9057,9130,9152; Ro 989, 1043.
BUDDY CAMPBELL: OK 41499, 41524, 41537, 41543.
CAPTIVATORS
HOAGY CARMICHAEL: Vi 38139.
CAROLINERS: Ca 9042.
ROY CARROLL: Ha 1397, 1329, 1379; Ve 2318, 2387.
CHARLESTON CHASERS: Co 1989, 2219, 2415.
RUSS COLUMBO
LOU CONNER'S COLLEGIATES: Or 1483, 1537.
COTTON PICKERS: Ca 9048, 9207.
DIXIE DAISIES: Ca 9004, 9035, Li 3169, Ro 887.
DIXIE JAZZ BAND: Or 1536, 1537, 1515, 1363, 1396, 1624, 1668, 1690.
D'ORSAY ORCHESTRA: Ha 1410, Ve 2466.
SAMMY FAIN
JERRY FENWYOK
BUDDY FIELDS: Ro 1068.
REGINALD FORESYTHE: Co 3012, 3060.
AL GOODMAN
GOODY AND HIS GOOD TIMERS: Pat 36902, 36903, 36924, Pe 15094.
COOT GRANT: Ca 9015.
JOHNNY GREEN: Br 6797, 6855.
HOT AIR MEN: Co 1850.
HOTSY TOTSY GANG: Br 4112, 4122, 4200.
LLOYD KEATING
KENTUCKY GRASSHOPPERS: Ba 6295, 6355, 6358, 6360, 6483, 8441.
GENE KRUPA: Vi 25263, 25276, PaE 2224, 2268.
CHESTER LEIGHTON
TED LEWIS: Co 2378, 2408, 2452, 2428, 2527, 2467, 2786.
LOUISIANA RHYTHM KINGS: Vo 15828.
LOUISVILLE RHYTHM KINGS: OK 41189, PaF 22305.
LUMBERJACKS: Ca 9030, Ro 867.
JIMMY McHUGH: Ha 763, 795, 823, 836.
MILLS MERRYMAKERS: Ha 1099, 1104, Ve 7121.
MILLS HOTSY TOTSY GANG: Br 4554, 4559, 4587, 4838, 4983, 4998.
MILLS MUSICAL CLOWNS: Pat 36944, 36955.
MODERNISTS: Me 13159.
NEW ORLEANS RAMBLERS: Me 12130, 12133.
RED NICHOLS: Br 4363,4373,4456,4790,4877,4885,4925,4944,4957,4982,6013,6014,
    6026,6035,6029,6012,6058,6068,6070.6118,6138,6149; Vi 23033, 23026.
RED NORVO: Br 6906.
JACK PETTIS: OK 41410, 41411, Vo 15703, 15761.
BEN POLLACK: Vi 20394,20408,20425,20461,21184,21437,21716,21743,21858,21857,
    21827,21941,21944,22071,22074,22147,22089,22101,22106,22252,22158,22267;
    Or 2193,3208,1998,2000,2214; Re 10057
RADIOLITES
GIL RODIN: Re 8813.
ADRIAN ROLLINI: Me 12815,12829,12855; De 265, 359.
SLIM AND HOT BOYS: Vi 38044.
BEN SELVIN: Co 2400, 2463, 2575.
BESSIE SMITH: OK 8945, 8949.
JACK TEAGARDEN: Pe 15361; Br 6993, 7652; BrE 01913.

TEN BLACK BERRIES: Ro 976, 1453; Re 10145.
TEN FRESHMEN: Pat 37054.
UNIVERSITY BOYS: Ro 1668.
VARSITY EIGHT: Ca 9098.
VENUTI BLUE SIX: CoE 686, 708.
VENUTI-LANG: Vo 15858, 15864.
JOHNNY WALKER: Co 2404.
ETHEL WATERS: Co 2409, 2481, 2826, 2853.
TED WHITE: Or 1544.
WHOOPEE MAKERS: Pe 15126, 15194, 15217, 15223.
TEDDY WILSON: Br 7498, 7501, 7736, 7739, 7781, 7789, 7824, 7859, 7940, 7943.
JACK WINN: Vo 15860

GOODMAN, BENNY (clarinet solos with Mel Stitzel, piano; Bob Conzelman, drums; Chicago,--BW): June 13, 1928
Vo 15705. That's a Plenty(e7398)   -Me 12073
 "   Clarinetitis(e7397)   BrF 500202,

BENNY BOYS (Benny Goodman, clarinet; Jimmy McPartland, cornet; Glenn Miller, trombone; Vic Briedis, piano; Dick Morgan, guitar; Harry Goodman, tuba; Bob Conselman, drums and vibes): Jan. 23, 1928
Vo 15656. A Jazz Holiday(c1652)   -Br 80027
 "   Wolverine Blues(c1654)   -HRS,

(Add Fud Livingston, clarinet and sax; sub. Ben Pollack, drums; Goodman, baritone and alto sax):*   June 4, 1928
Br 3975. Blue(e27640)*   -BrF 500202, BrF 7815, Br 80030
 "   Shirt Tail Stomp(e27643)

(Goodman, cornet*; sub. Ray Bauduc, drums):
Br 4013. Room 1411(e27639)/Jungle Blues(e27638)*-BrF 500201, BrF 7839, Br 80029

(Wingy Mannone, trumpet; Benny Goodman, clarinet; Bud Freeman, tenor sax; Joe Sullivan, piano; banjo; Harry Goodman, bass; Bob Conselman, drums): Aug. 1929
Br 4968. Muskrat Ramble(c4036)/After Awhile(c4035)
                                              -BrF 500318, BrE 1264, Br 80028

BENNY GOODMAN AND HIS ORCHESTRA (featuring Benny Goodman, clarinet; Jack Teagarden or Glenn Miller, trombone; Larry Binyon, Sid Stoneberg, saxes; Eddie Lang, guitar): 1930-31
Me 12023. And When Your Lips Met Mine(e35343)/He's Not Worth Your Tears
Me 12024. Linda(e35342)/Overnight(e35344)   (e35341)
Me 12079. Falling in Love Again(e35158)/If You Haven't Girl(e35924) Jan. 14, 1931
Me 12100. Mine Yesterday, His Today(e35838)/99 Out of a 100(e35836) Feb. 5, 1931
Me 12120. We Can Live on Love(e35834)/When Your Lover Has Gone(e35835)
Me 12138. I Wanna Be Around My Baby(e36464)/What Have You Got to Do Tonight
                                                      (e36481) Mar. 18, 1931
Me 12149. Little Joe(e36482)/It Looks Like Love(e36483)
Me 12205. Slow But Sure(e36835)/You Can't Stop Me From Lovin' June 20, 1931
Me 12208. Pardon Me Pretty Baby(e36874)/What Am I Gonna Do for Lovin(e36875)

Co 2542. Not That I Care(151794)/Help Yourself to Happiness(151795)

(Manny Klein, Charlie Teagarden, trumpets; Jack Teagarden, trombone; Bennie Goodman, clarinet; Arthur Karl, tenor sax; Joe Sullivan, piano; Dick McDonough, guitar; Artie Bernstein, bass; Gene Krupa, drums): Oct., 1933
Co 2835. Ain'tcha Glad(265165)/Gotta Right to Sing the Blues(265164)
                                                      (-Co 3168, CoE 692
(Sub. Frank Froeba, piano):
Co 2845. Dr. Heckle & Mr. Jibe(265166)/Texas Tea Party(265167)-Co 3167, CoE 712

(Sub. Shirley Clay, trumpet, for Klein; Joe Sullivan, piano):
Co 2856. Your Mother's Son-in-Law(152568), Billie Holiday, vocal -CoE 786
 "   Tappin' the Barrel(152574)   -CoE 5014
Co 2867. Keep on Doin' What You're Doin'(152599)
 "   Riffin' the Scotch(152650), Billie Holiday, vocal   -CoE 5014
Co 2871. Love Me or Leave Me(152651)   -CoE 5016
 "   Why Couldn't It Be Poor Little Me(152652)

(Manny Klein, Charlie Margulis, trumpets; Sonny Lee, trombone; Benny Goodman, clarinet; Coleman Hawkins, tenor sax; Arthur Schutt, piano; Krupa, Bernstein, McDonough, Mildred Bailey, vocals):
Co 2892. Junk Man(152702)
 "   Ol' Pappy(152703)   -CoE 730
CoE 730. Junk Man (different master)
Co 2907. Georgia Jubilee(152701)/Emaline(152704)   -CoE 759

(Charlie Teagarden, George Thow, trumpets; Jack Teagarden, trombone; Bennie Goodman, clarinet; Harry Ross, tenor sax; Teddy Wilson, piano; Bennie Martel, guitar; Harry Goodman, bass; Ray McKinley, drums):

22

```
Co  2923. I Ain't Lazy I'm Just Dreamin'(152736)/As Long As I Live(152737)
Co  2927. Moon Glow(152738)                                          -CoE 788
     "    Breakfast Ball(152739)                                     -CoE 5005

        (Sam Shapiro, Russ Case, Jerry Neary, trumpets; Jack Lacey, Red Ball-
        ard, trombones; Benny Goodman, clarinet; Ben Kantor, Hymie Schertzer,
        alto saxes; Arthur Rollini, tenor sax; Claude Thornhill, piano; Van
        Eps, guitar; Hank Wayland, bass; Sam Weiss, drums.--HD):           1934
Co  2947. Take My Word(15641)/It Happens to the Best of Friends(15642)
Co  2958. Nitwit Serenade(15643)                                     JoE 1003
     "    Bugle Call Rag(15644)                                -Br 7644,    "

        (Pee Wee Irwin, Art Sylvester, Jerry Neary, trumpets; add Dick Clark,
        tenor sax; sub. Toots Mondello, alto for Kantor; Frank Froeba, piano;
        Harry Goodman, bass.--HD):
Co  2988. I'm 100 Per Cent for You/Like a Bolt from the Blue    -CoE 1023
Co  3005. Blue Moon
     "    Throwin' Stones at the Sun                            -CoE 1037
Co  3011. Cokey(16365)
     "    Music Hall Rag(16367)                                 -CoE 5011
Co  3015. Clouds(16888)                                         -CoE 1050
     "    Night Wind(16890)                                     -CoE 5002
Co  3018. I Was Lucky                                           -CoE 1064
     "    Singin' a Happy Song
Co  3033. The Dixieland Band(16638)                             -Br 7644
     "    Down Home Rag(16641)                                  -CoE 5011

        (Sub. Ralph Muzzillo, trumpet, for Sylvester; Alan Reuss, guitar; Gene
        Krupa, drums; Helen Ward, vocals):                        March, 1935
Vi 25009. Hunkadola(89516)
     "    Dixieland Band(89519)                                 -BB 10851, HMV 183
Vi 25011. Hoorah for Love(89518)
     "    Livin' in a Great Big Way(89517)                      -HMV 284
Vi 25021. You're Heavenly(89567)/Restless(89568)                -HMV 182
Vi 25024. Japanese Sandman(89566)                               -BB 10459, HMV 48
     "    Always(89569)                                         -BB 10799,   "

        (Sub. Bunny Berigan, Nate Kazebier, trumpets, for Irwin, Neary):
Vi 25081. Get Rhythm in Your Feet(92520)
     "    Ballad in Blue(92521)                                 -BB 10851, HMV 8389
                                                          New York, July 1, 1935
Vi 25090. Sometimes I'm Happy(92546)                            -HMV 40, HMV 8523
     "    King Porter Stomp(92547)                                "     HMV 8374
Vi 25136. Blue Skies(92522)                                     -BB 10680, HMV 8398
     "    Dear Old Southland(92523)                             -BB 10458,   "
Vi 25145. Jingle Bells(92549)/(rev., Tommy Dorsey)

        (Bunny Berigan, Ralph Muzillo, Nate Kazebier, trumpets; Joe Harris, Red
        Ballard, trombones; Benny Goodman, clarinet; Hymie Schertzer, William De-
        Pew, alto saxes; Rollini, Clark, tenors; Stacy, Reuss, Goodman, Krupa.):
Vi 25193. Yankee Doodle Never Went to Town(96500)/No Other One(96501)
Vi 25195. Eeny Meeny Miney Mo(96502)/Santa Claus Came in the Spring(97015)
Vi 25215. Sandman(96299)/Good-Bye(97016)

        (Sub. Harry Geller, trumpet, for Berigan):
Vi 25245. It's Been So Long(96567)/Goody Goody(96569)
Vi 25247. Stompin' at the Savoy(96568)/Breakin' in Pair of Shoes(96570)HMV 8427
                                                          Chicago, Apr.23,1936
Vi 25258. Basin Street Blues(96503)/When Buddha Smiles(96505)   -HMV 8461
Vi 25268. Between the Devil and the Deep Blue Sea(92548), see 25090
                                                           (-BB 10460, HMV 8389
     "    Madhouse(97017)                                       -BB 10461, HMV 8431

        (Sub Pee Wee Irwin, trumpet, for Muzillo):
Vi 25279. Get Happy(100057)                                     -BB 10461
     "    Christopher Columbus(100058)                          -BB 10460, HMV 8431
Vi 25290. If I Could Be With You(96504)                         -BB 10458
     "    I Know That You Know(100059)
Vi 25316. You Can't Pull the Wool Over My Eyes(100380)/The Glory of Love(100381)
Vi 25320. Star Dust(100319)/(Rev., Tommy Dorsey)                -HMV 8468
Vi 25329. Remember(100382)                                      -BB 10680, HMV 8493
     "    Walk Jennie Walk(100383)                              -BB 10799

        (Sub. Gordon Griffin, trumpet, for Geller; Murray McEachern, trombone
        for Harris):
Vi 25340. Sing Me A Swing Song(101257)                          -BB 10462
Vi 25350. Anything for You(101258)
     "    House Hop(101255)                                     -HMV 8569
Vi 25351. These Foolish Things(101256)                          -HMV 8523
     "    In a Sentimental Mood(102214)
Vi 25355. I've Found a New Baby(102215)/Swingtime in Rockies(102217)-HMV 8481
Vi 25363. There's a Small Hotel(102066)
```

```
              (Sub. Sterling Bose, trumpet, for Kazebier):
Vi 25387. Pick Yourself Up(97712)/Down South Camp Meeting(97713)      -HMV 8516
Vi 25391. You Turned the Tables on Me(97710)                          -HMV 5146
       "  Here's Love in Your Eyes(97711)

              (Featuring Vido Musso, tenor sax):
Vi 25406. Love Me or Leave Me(97750)/(rev., Goodman Trio)
Vi 25411. St. Louis Blues(97748)/(rev., Nick LaRocca)

              (Gordon Griffin, Zeke Zarchey, Ziggy Elman, trumpets; sub. Musso, tenor
              sax, for Clark):
Vi 25434. When a Lady Meets a Gentleman Down South                    -HMV 8516
       "  You're Giving Me a Song and Dance                           -HMV 5152
Vi 25442. Organ Grinders Swing(02101)/Peter Piper(02102)
Vi 25445. Alexander's Ragtime Band(02104)/Riffin' at the Ritz(02105)

              (Ella Fitzgerald, vocal*):
Vi 25461. Good Night My Love(02463)*                                  -HMV 8542
       "  Take Another Guess(02464)*                                  -HMV 8564
Vi 25467. Bugle Call Rag(02460)                                       -HMV 8569
Vi 25469. Tain't No Use(02459)/Did You Mean It(02465)*                -HMV 8535

              (Sub. Irving Goodman, trumpet, for Zarchey; George Koenig, alto for DePew):
Vi 25486. Gee But You're Swell(03550)/Smoke Dreams(03551)             -HMV 8547
Vi 25492. Swing Low Sweet Chariot(03552)/                             -HMV 8564
       "  When You and I Were Young Maggie(03549)                     -HMV 8691

              (Sub. Zarchey, trumpet, for Goodman):
Vi 25497. Jam Session (02461)/Somebody Loves Me(02468)

              (Sub. Harry James, trumpet, for Zarchey):
Vi 25500. Never Should Have Told You(03873)/You Can Tell She Comes from Dixie
Vi 25505. This Year's Kisses(03874)/He Ain't Got Rhythm(03872)        -HMV 8595
Vi 25510. I Want to Be Happy(04236)/Rosetta(04238)                    -BB 10760
Vi 25531. Chloe(04237)/(rev., Goodman Quartet)
                            Next six sides:   Hollywood, July, 1937
Vi 25621. Peckin'(09569)/Can't We Be Friends(09570)   -BB 10462, HMV 8615
Vi 25627. Afraid to Dream(09578)/Roll 'em(09576)                      -HMV 8631
Vi 25634. When It's Sleepy Time Down South(09577)/
       "  Changes(09579)                              -BB 11225
Vi 25678. Sugar Foot Stomp(09689)                                     -GrF 8086
       "  I Can't Give You Anything But Love(09690)
Vi 25683. Bob White(09688)/Minnie the Moocher's Weddin' Day(09691)
Vi 25708. I've Hitched My Wagon to a Star(15537)/Let That Be a Lesson(15535)
Vi 25717. Loch Lomond(17041)/Camel Hop(17042)
Vi 25720. You Took the Words Right Out of My Mouth(17039)/Mama That Moon is
                                              (Here Again(17040)  -GrF 8126
Vi 25726. Life Goes to a Party(17044)/If Dreams Come True
Vi 25727. Thanks for the Memory(17453)/It's Wonderful(17452)
Vi 25792. Don't Be That Way(19831)/One o'clock Jump(19832)            -GrF 8102
Vi 25796. Sing Sing Sing, I & 2 (17695/96)

              (Harry James, Ziggy Elman, Gordon Griffin, trumpets; Red Ballard, Vernon
              Brown, trombones; Benny Goodman, Hymie Schertzer, Dave Matthews, Babe
              Rusin, Lester Young, saxes; Jess Stacy, piano; Fred Green, guitar; Wal-
              ter Page, bass; Lionel Hampton, drums):
Vi 25808. Oooo-oh-Boom(21129)/Always and Always(21130)
Vi 25814. T-Pi-Tin(21128)/Please Be Kind(21127)                       -GrF 3127

              (Bud Freeman, Noni Bernardi, Dave Matthews, Art Rollini, saxes; same
              brass; Dave Tough, drums; Stacy; Harry Goodman, bass; Benny Heller, gui-
              tar):
Vi 25827. Lullaby in Rhythm/That Feeling Is Gone
Vi 25840. Feelin' High and Happy/I Let a Song Go Out of My Heart
Vi 25846. It's the Dreamer in Me/Why'd Ya Make Me Fall in Love?

Vi 25867. Don't Wake Up My Heart/Saving Myself for You
Vi 25871. The Flat Foot Floogee/Big John Special
Vi 25878. Little Kiss at Twilight/What Goes on Here
Vi 25880. My Melancholy Baby/Wrappin' It Up
Vi 26000. Could You Pass in Love?/I've Got a Date With a Dream
Vi 26021. Blue Interlude/When I Go a-Dreamin'
Vi 26053. What Have You Got That Gets Me?/You're Lovely Madame
Vi 26060. Margie                                                      -BB 10973
       "  Russian Lullaby                                             -BB 11226
Vi 26071. I Have Eyes/You're A Sweet Little Headache
Vi 26082. I Had to Do It/Is That the Way to Treat a Sweetheart?
Vi 26087. Ciribiribin/Bumble Bee Stomp
Vi 26088. Blue Room/Make Believe(same personnel as Vi 25808)

              (Sub. Milt Yaner, sax, for Bernardi):
Vi 26089. Sweet Sue Just You/I Never Knew
```

```
              (Sub. Bernardi for Yaner):
Vi 26095. Farewell Blues                                      -BB 10973
       "  My Honey's Lovin' Arms                              -BB 11056
Vi 26099. This Can't Be Love/Sing for Your Supper
Vi 26107. Smoke House Rhythm/Topsy (Lionel Hampton, drums)
Vi 26110. I Must See Annie Tonight/Kinda Lonesome
Vi 26125. It Had to Be You                                    -BB 11056
       "  Louise

              (Sub. Jerry Jerome, saxes, for Freeman; Buddy Schutz, drums):
Vi 26130. Bach Goes to Town/Whispering
Vi 26134. Undecided/We'll Never Know
Vi 26159. Shut Eye/Good for Nothing But Love
Vi 26170. And the Angels Sing/Sent for You Yesterday
Vi 26175. Cuckoo in the Clock/Home in the Clouds
Vi 26187. I'll Always Be in Love With You/Estrellita(Sub.Schertzer for Matthews)
Vi 26211. Show Your Linen Miss Richardson/The Lady's in Love With You
Vi 26230. Rose of Washington Square/The Siren's Song
Vi 26263. You and Your Love/Who'll Buy My Bublitchki?
Vi 36205. Sing Sing Sing,I & 2(09571/72), see Vi 25500

              (Personnel unknown):
Co 35201. Rendezvous Time in Paree/Comes Love
Co 35210. There'll Be Some Changes Made/Jumpin' at the Woodside
Co 35211. Blue Orchids/What's New
Co 35241. Scatter Brain/One Sweet Letter from You
Co 35289. Faithful Forever(wco26201)/Bluebirds in Moonlight(wco26204),M.Bailey
Co 35301. Let's Dance(wco26202)/Boy Meets Horn(la1952),Chris Griffin,trumpet
Co 35313. I Thought About You/Make With the Kisses

              (Toots Mondello, Buff Estes, Buss Bassey, Jerry Jerome, saxes; Ziggy El-
              man, Johnny Martel, Corky Cornelius, trumpets; Vernon Brown, Red Ballard,
              trombones; Fletcher Henderson, piano; Charles Christian, guitar; Nick Fa-
              tool, drums; Artie Bernstein, bass):
Co 35319. Honeysuckle Rose(wco26290)/Spring Song(la1962), Gordon Griffin, trum-
              pet, instead of Martel;Arnold Covarubias,buitar;add B.Squires,trom.
Co 35331. Darn That Dream/Peace Brother                       (bone

              (Sub. James Maxwell, trumpet, for Cornelius; add Ted Vesely, trombone;
              Johnny Guarnieri, piano):
Co 35356. Busy As a Bee(wco26366)/Zaggin' With Zig(wco26368)
Co 35362. Opus Local 802(wco26365)/Stealin' Apples(la1951),see Co 35319 'B'
Co 35374. What's the Matter With Me?/What'll They Think of Next?
Co 35389. All Star Strut/King Porter Stomp

              (Sub. Irving Goodman, trumpet, for Martel):
Co 35391. How High the Moon(wco26491)/Fable of the Rose(wco26493)
Co 35396. Board Meeting(wco26367),Martel,trumpet/Let's All Sing Together
                                                              (wco26492)
Co 35410. Beyond the Moon(wco26289),See 35319 'A'/Night and Day(la1964), Martel,
                                         trumpet; Fletcher Henderson, piano)
              (Arnold Covarubias, guitar; Guarnieri, piano):
Co 35420. The Sky Fell Down(wc2974)/It Never Entered My Mind(wc2975)
Co 35426. Be Sure/Shake Down the Stars
Co 35445. Yours Is My Heart Alone/Down by Old Mill Stream, see Co 35319 'B'

              (Sub. Les Robinson, alto, for Estes ; Christian, guitar):
Co 35461. Devil May Care(wco26715)/Ev'ry Sunday Afternoon(wco26741)
Co 35472. I'm Nobody's Baby(wco26716)/Buds Won't Bud(wco26714)
Co 35487. I Can't Love You Any More/The Moon Won't Talk
Co 35497. Mister Meadowlark(wco26810)/Crazy Rhythm(wco26742)
Co 35517. Who Cares(wco26807)Just Like Taking Candy from a Baby(wco26809),Fred
Co 35527. Cocoanut Grove(wco26717)/The Hour of Parting(wco26740)  (Astaire,voc.
Co 35543. Can't You Tell(wco26418),see Co 35410/Once More(wc2976),see Co 35420
Co 35574. I Can't Resist You/Dreamin' Out Loud
Co 35594. Nostalgia/Li'l Boy Love

              (Benny Goodman, clarinet; Skippy Martin, Gus Bivona, Bob Snyder, George
              Auld, Jack Henderson, saxes; Lou McGarity, Red Gingler, trombones; Alex
              Fila, Jimmy Maxwell, Cootie Williams, Irving Goodman, trumpets; Bernie
              Layton, piano; Mike Bryan, guitar; Arthur Bernstein, bass; Harry Yaeger
              drums):
Co 35820. Nobody(co29062)/Henderson Stomp(co29064), Henderson, piano
Co 35839. Moonglow/Why Couldn't It Be Poor Little Me? (reissue)
Co 35863. Frenesi(co29179)/Hard to Get(co29180)
Co 35869. Taking a Chance on Love(co29177)/Cabin in the Sky(co29178)

              (Omit Williams, trumpet; sub. Bob Cutshall trombone, for Gingler):
Co 35910. These Things You Left Me(co29255)/Yes My Darling Daughter(co29262)
Co 35916. I'm Always Chasing Rainbows(co29274)/Somebody Stole My Gal(co29275)
              (Add Cootie Williams, trumpet;sub.Wilson,piano;Tough,drums):  (Henderson
Co 35937. I Left My Heart in Your Hand/I Hear a Rhapsody
Co 35944. This Is New/Bewitched
```

```
Co 35962. Perfidia(co29578)/Let the Door Knob Hitcha(co29502),vocal, C.Williams
Co 35977. You're Dangerous/Birds of a Feather
Co 35992. The Mem'ry of a Rose(co29532)/Corn Silk(co29505)
Co 36002. It's Always You/You Lucky People You

         (Sub. Pete Mondello, Les Robinson, saxes, for Martin,Henderson):
Co 36012. Lazy River(co29774)/Oh Look at Me Now(co29862)
Co 36022. I'm Not Complainin'/My Sister and I
Co 36050. Amapola                                              -PaE 2802
    "     Intermezzo

         (Johnny Guarnieri, piano):
Co 36067. Take It/Yours                                        -PaE 2805
Co 36109. Bugle Call Rag/The Dixieland Band (reissue)
Co 36136. I Found a Million Dollar Baby(co30422)/Good Evenin' Good Lookin'
                                                   (co30419), see below
Co 36180. Scarecrow(co29775)/Time on My Hands(co29530), Martin, Henderson,
                                             saxes; Teddy Wilson, piano
Co 36219. Soft As Spring(co30649)/Down Down Down(co30650), see La Rosita

         (Sub. Skippy Martin, Jimmy Howath, saxes, for Snyder, Bivona; Billy
         Butterfield, trumpet, for Fila; Teddy Wilson, piano; Jo Jones, drums):
Co 36254. Air Mail Special(co30421)/Tuesday at Ten(co30648), See La Rosita

         (Sub. Gene Kinsey, sax, for Howath; omit Goodman, trumpet; Mel Powell,
         piano, Charles Christian, guitar; Walter Looss, bass; Sidney Catlett,
         drums):
Co 36284. La Rosita(co30651)/Smoke Gets in Your Eyes(co30599), sub. Gordon
         Griffin, trumpet, for Maxwell; Teddy Wilson, piano; J.C. Heard,
                                                                  (drums).
         (Personnel unknown):
Co 36305. Anything/From One Love to Another
Co 36359. Elmer's Tune(co3950)/The Birth of the Blues(co3951)
Co 36379. The Count/I See a Million People
Co 36411. I'm Here/Caprice XXIV Paganini
Co 36421. Pound Ridge/I Got It Bad
Co 36429. Shady Lady Bird(co31426)/Buckle Down Winsocki(co31427)
Co 36580. Not Mine/If You Build a Better Mouse Trap
Co 36588. Jersey Bounce
Co 36590. I Threw a Kiss in the Ocean(32601)/Full Moon(32603)
Co 36613. Take Me(co32796)/Idaho(co32924)
Co 36617. All I Need Is You/(rev., by Goodman Sextet)
Co 36622. Serenade in Blue/I've Got a Gal in Kalamazoo
Co 36641. Dearly Beloved/I'm Old Fashioned
Co 36652. Why Don't You Do Right?/Six Flats Unfurnished
Co 36680. It's Always You/Mission to Moscow
Co 36684. Solo Flight(co29865),Christian,guitar/(rev., Goodman Quartet)
Co 36699. After You've Gone/At the Darktown Strutters Ball

         (Cootie Williams, trumpet):
Co 36754. My Old Flame/How Deep Is the Ocean
Co 36755. Fiesta in Blue/(rev., Sextet)
Co 55001. Benny Rides Again(xco29065),see 35820/The Man I Love(xco29063, omit
Co 55002. More Than You Know(xco29257),see 35910/Superman(xco29256) (Williams

         (Unknown personnel)
OK  6474. Let's Do It(31367)/The Earl
OK  6497. That Did It/Somebody Else Is Taking My Place
OK  6516. Winter Weather/Everything I Love
OK  6534. Someone's Rocking My Dream Boat(31942)/You Don't Know What Love Is
OK  6544. Clarinet a la King/How Long Has This Been Going On?    (31946)
OK  6580. Lamp of Memory/When the Roses Bloom Again
OK  6590. Jersey Bounce(32238)/A string of Pearls(32383)
OK  6562. Let's Give Love a Chance/Somebody Nobody Loves
OK  6606. My Little Cousin/Zoot Suit
OK  6644. Before/We'll Meet Again

BENNY GOODMAN TRIO (Benny Goodman,clarinet; Teddy Wilson,piano;Gene Krupa, drums):
                                                             July 13,1935
Vi 25115. After You've Gone(92704)/Body and Soul(92705)     -HMV 8381
Vi 25181. Who(92706)/Someday Sweetheart(92707)              -HMV 8402, GrF 7650

                                                       Chicago, April, 1936
Vi 25333. Lady Be Good(100500)                          -HMV 8462, GrF 7752
    "     China Boy(100390)                             -HMV 8467,    "
Vi 25324. Too Good to Be True/All My Live
Vi 25345. Nobody's Sweetheart                           -BB 10723, HMV 8462
    "     More Than You Know                                "      HMV 8467
Vi 25406. Exactly Like You/(rev., Goodman Orchestra)            -HMV 8503
Vi 25711. Silhouetted in the Moonlgith                          -HMV 8735
Vi 25725. Where or When, Oct.29,1947/(rev., Goodman Quartet)    -HMV 9017
```

```
             (Lionel Hampton, drums):                    Mar.25,1938
   Vi 25822. Sweet Lorraine/(rev., Goodman Quartet)
                                                          Oct.12,1938
   Vi 26090. I Must Have That Man/(rev., Goodman Quartet)  -HMv 9166
   Vi 26139. I Know That You Know(J.Kirby,bass;12/29)/(Quint) -HMV 8895,BB 10459
             (Goodman; Wilson; Morey Feld, drums):                    1945
   Co 36781. Body and Soul/(rev., Goodman Sextet)
```

BENNY GOODMAN QUARTET (Benny Goodman, clarinet; Teddy Wilson, piano; Lionel Hampton, vibraphone; Gene Krupa, drums):   Hollywood, August, 1936
```
   Vi 25398. Dinah                                -GrF 8085.  HMV 8503
      "     Moon Glow                                        -HMV 8568
                                                  New York, Nov.18,1936
   Vi 25473. My Melancholy Baby                              -HMV 8533
      "     Sweet Sue                                        -HMV 8531
                                                             Dec.2,1936
   Vi 25481. Tiger Rag                                       -HMV 8531
      "     Whispering                                       -HMV 8533
   Vi 25521. Vibraphone Blues(Aug.26,1936)                   -HMV 8563
      "     Stompin' at the Savoy
                                                             Feb.3,1937
   Vi 25529. Tea for Two                                     -HMV 8563
      "     Runnin' Wild                                     -HMV 8568
   Vi 25531. Ida/(rev., Goodman Orchestra)
                                                  Hollywood, July 30,1937
   Vi 25644. Avalon/The Man I Love                 -GrF 7991, HMV 8617
                                                  Hollywood, Aug.2,1937
   Vi 25660. Liza                                            -HMV 8630
      "     Smiles                                 -GrF 8085,    "
   Vi 25705. Hand Full of Keys                     -GrF 8068, HMV 8689
      "     Vieni Vieni                                          "
                                                  New York, Dec.2,1937
   Vi 25725. I'm a Ding Dong Daddy/(rev., Goodman Trio)-BB 10903,GrF 8068,HMV 8734
   Vi 25751. Bei Mir Bist du Schon, I & 2(Elman,trumpet,pt.2)   -GrF 8058

             (Sub. Dave Tough, drums):             New York, Mar.25,1938
   Vi 25822. Dizzy Spells/(rev., Goodman Trio)               -GG 10903
   Vi 26044. Blues in My Flat/Blues in Your Flat             -HMV 8872
                                                  Chicago,Oct.12,1938
   Vi 26090. 'S Wonderful/(rev., Goodman Trio)               -HMV 9166
   Vi 26091. Opus ½/Sweet Georgia Brown                      -HMV 8851
   Vi 26240. Sugar/Opus 3/4(sub.J.Stacy,piano;B.Schuta,drums;5/6/39)  -HMV 8957
   Co 36684. World Is Waiting for the Sunrise(32594)/(rev.,Goodman Orchestra)
```

BENNY GOODMAN QUINTET (Goodman, Wilson, Hampton, Schutz, Kirby):New York,12/29/38
```
   Vi 26139. I Cried for You/(rev., Goodman Trio)            -HMV 8895
   Vi 26166. Pick-a-Rib, 1 & 2

             (Goodman, Wilson; Red Norvo, vibraphone; Sid Weiss, bass; Morey Feld,
             drums):                                                     1945
   Co 36767. Ev'ry Time We Say Goodbye,vocal,Peggy Mann/Only Another Boy and Girl,
                                                       (vocal,Jane Harvey
```
BENNY GOODMAN SEXTET (Benny Goodman, Charlie Christian, Arthur Bernstein, Fletcher Henderson, Nick Fatool, Lionel Hampton):
```
   Co 35254. Flying Home(wco26132)                           -Co 36721
      "     Rose Room(wco26133)                              -Co 36720
   Co 35320. Memories of You/Soft Winds                      -PaE 2761

             (Sub. Johnny Guarnieri, piano):
   Co 35349. Seven Come Eleven(wco26286)/Shivers(wco26354)

             (Count Basie, piano):
   Co 35404. Till Tom Special(wco26494)/Gone With What Wind(wco26495)  -PaE 2752
   Co 35466. Poor Butterfly(wco26719)                        -PaE 2753, Co 36722
      "     The Sheik

             (Guarnieri, piano):
   Co 35482. I Surrender Dear(wco26743)                      -PaE 2757
      "     Boy Meets Goy(wco26744) "Grand Slam"             -Co 36722

             (Dudley Brooks, piano):                         June 20,1940
   Co 35553. Six Appeal(wco26940/These Foolish Things(wco26941)  -PaE 2770

             (Benny Goodman, clarinet; Cootie Williams, trumpet; Georgie Auld, tenor
             sax; Count Basie, piano; Charlie Christian, guitar; Arthur Bernstein,bass;
             Harry Jaeger, drums):                           Dec.,1940
   Co 35810. Wholly Cats(co29027)/Royal Garden Blues(co29028)  -PaE 2787
   Co 35901. As Long As I Live(co29029)                      -Co 36723
      "     Benny's Bugle(co29030)

             (Jo Jones, drums):                              Feb.,1941
   Co 35938. On the Alamo(co29513)/Gone With What Draft(co29519)  -PaE 2798
   Co 36039. Breakfast Feud(co29512)/I Found a New Baby(co29514)  -Co 36721
```

```
                (Guarnieri, piano; Dave Tough, drums):           Mar.22,1941
Co 36099. A Smo-o-oth One(co29942)                                -PaE 2816
       "  Good Enough to Keep(Air Mail Special)(co29943)          -Co 36720
Co 36594. The Way You Look Tonight
       "  Wang Wang Blues(32593)                                  -Co 36723
Co 36617. On the Sunny Side of the Street/(rev., Goodman Orchestra)

          (Kenny Kersey, piano):
Co 36755. I Can't Give You Anything But Love/(rev., Goodman Orchestra)

             (Goodman; Teddy Wilson, piano; Morey Feld, drums; Slam Stewart, bass;Red
             Norvo, vibraphone; Mike Bryan, guitar):                           1945
Co 36781. After You've Gone/(rev., Trio)

          (Unknown personnel):
OK  6486. If I Had You(co31609)/Limehouse Blues(co31610)
OK  6533. Where or When/Blues in the Night
```

GOODNER, LILLIAN (with her Jazzin' Trio):
Ajax 1720. Chicago Blues(31026-2)/No One Can Toddle Like My Cousin Sue(31027-2)

GOODY AND HIS GOOD TIMERS (Benny Goodman and The Whoopee Makers):
```
Pat 36902. Diga Diga Do                                           -Pe 15083
Pat 36903. Star Dust                                              -Pe 15084
Pat 36924. Now I'm in Love                                        -Pe 15105
Pe 15094. The Melody of Life Is Love
```

GOOFUS FIVE (Collective personnel: Jimmy Dorsey, Frankie Trumbauer, Bobby Davis,
Bobby Fallon, Sam Ruby, Adrian Rollini, Spencer Clark, saxes; Red Nichols, Chelsea Quealey, Henry Levine, trumpets; Miff Mole, Al Philburn, trombones; Jack Rusen, Arthur Schutt, pianos; Tom Felline, banjo; Herb Weil, drums,--RR):   1925-28
```
OK 40179. Tessie! Stop Teasin' Me(s72745b)/Them Ramblin' Blues(s72746b)
OK 40208. Go Emmaline(s72848b)/Hey Hey and Hee Hee(s72849b)
OK 40233. Go Long Mule/Choo Choo
OK 40244. Everybody Loves My Baby(72998c)/Oh How I Love My Darling(72999b)
OK 40261. Oh Mabel/I Ain't Got Nobody to Love
OK 40292. Deep Blue Sea Blues/Alabama Bound
OK 40314. You Better Keep the Home Fires Burning(s73159b)/Hot Tamale Molly
OK 40340. I Had Someone Else/I Like You Best of All             (s73160a)
OK 40423. Yes Sir That's My Baby/Honey I'm in Love With You
OK 40442. She's Driving Me Wild/Gonna Charleston Back to Charleston
OK 40464. Loud Speaking Papa/Are You Sorry?
OK 40474. Sweet Man
OK 40500. Clap Hands Here Comes Charley(73742b)/I Wonder Where My Baby Is To-
OK 40534. That Certain Party(73861b)/(rev.,Red Hotters)       (night(73743c)
OK 40624. Poor Papa(74168b)/I Wonder What's Become of Joe(74169b)
OK 40641. Ya Gotta Know How to Love(74198b)/(rev.,Jack Glassner)
OK 40643. Where'd You Get Those Eyes?(74199b)/(rev.,Melody Sheiks)
OK 40661. Mary Lou(74236b)/Someone Is Losin' Susan(74227b)
OK 40687. Crazy Quilt/Sadie Green
OK 40757. Sister Kate/Farewell Blues
OK 40817. Arkansas Blues/Wang Wang Blues                          -Vo 3138
OK 40886. Clementine/I Left My Sugar Standing in the Rain
OK 40940. Blue Baby/Is She My Girl Friend?
OK 40962. St. Louis Blues/Hesitating Blues (acc. Al Bernard)
OK 40997. Nothin' Does Does Like It Used to(81208b)/Where the Cot-Cot-Cotton
OK 41069. I Can't Give You Anything But Love(400834b)/Ready for (Grows(81773c)
OK 41110. Mamma's Grown Young(400722c)/Right or Wrong(400723c)
OK 41113. All of the Time/Vaniteaser
OK 41138. Sonny Boy/My Blackbirds Are Bluebirds Now
OK 41169. Sweetheart of Dreams(401451a)/That's How I Feel About You(401453a)
OK 41177. Rambling Wreck from Georgia Tech(401493a)/Alma Mater Georgia Tech
OK 41220. Deep Night/(rev., Dorsey Brothers)                    (401494c)
```

GOOSBY, FANNIE (vocal with Clarence Williams, piano; Thomas Morris, cornet):
OK 8095. Grievous Blues/I've Got the Blues That's All

          (acc. by Eddie Heywood,Sr., piano):
OK 8121. All Alone Blues/Goosby Blues
OK 8128. I Blieve My Man Is Got a Rabbit's Leg/I've Got a Do Right Daddy Now

          FANNIE MAE GOOSBY (with piano and cornet):
Br 7030. Fortune Teller Blues/Stormy Hight Blues

          GOOSBY AND HARRIS (vocal duet):
Br 7029. Can't Use You Blues/Dirty Moaner Blues
               (See also: Viola Baker, OK 8141)

GORDON, BOBBY AND HIS RHYTHM (Casa Loma Orchestra):
Vo 2926. Lady from St. Paul(la1008)/Loveless Love(la1009)

GORDON, JIMMIE (Peetie Wheatstraw's Brother), vocals:
```
De  7007. Bed Springs Blues
De  7020. Mean Mistreatin' Blues/Yo Yo Mamma Blues
De  7043. Black Gal Blues/Gone Gal Blues
De  7099. Bed Springs Blues, No. 2/Soon in the Morning
De  7230. She Sells Good Meat/Don't Take Away My P.W.A.
De  7250. Mother Blues/I'd Rather Drink Muddy Water
De  7268. Think You Need a Shot/C.C. & St. Louis Blues
De  7264. Jacksonville Blues, 1 & 2
De  7282. Big Four Whistle Blues/Drunken Woman Blues
De  7301. Graveyard Blues/Little Red Dress
De  7322. Good As I Bean to You
De  7334. Drive Me Away Blues/Playing in the Grass
```

GORDON AND HIS VIP VOP BAND, JIMMIE (some featuring Pete Brown, alto sax):
```
De  7322. You're Bound to Look Like a Monkey
De  7373. I Believe I Been Hoodooed/Plenty Trouble on Your Hand
De  7409. Rattlesnake Bite/She Wants to Rattle Me All the Time
De  7474. Fast Life/She's Doin' It Now
De  7490. Lonesome Bedroom Blues/Alberta Alberta
De  7519. Crying My Blues Away/Sail With Me
De  7536. Number Runner's Blues/Bleeding Heart Blues
De  7555. Me and My Gin/Whip It to a Jelly
De  7592. Delhia/St. Peter Blues
De  7611. Do That Thing/Get Your Mind Out of the Gutter
De  7624. If the Walls Could Talk(65499a)/Keep Your Nose Out of Other People's
De  7661. Boogie Man/Ease It to Me                              Business(63762a)
De  7702. Henpecked Man/Mojo Blues
```

GORDON AND HIS ORCHESTRA, RALPH:
```
Vi 26033. Two Left Feet/Fun in a Boiler Factory
Vi 26041. Arabian Nightmare/Twelve o'Clock in Jolopi
```

GOTHAM STOMPERS (Cootie Williams, trumpet; Sandy Williams, trombone; Barney Bigard, clarinet; Johnny Hodges, alto sax; Harry Carney, baritone, guitar; Billy Taylor, bass; Chick Webb, drums; Ivie Anderson, vocal.--HD):
```
Vr  541. Did Anyone Ever Tell You?(m302)/Where Are You?(m304)
Vr  629. My Honey's Lovin' Arms(m301)/Alabamy Home(m303)
```

GOTHAM TROUBADOURS:
```
OK 40992. Chloe(400051c)/Sunshine(400094a)
```

GOWANS' RHAPSODY MAKERS, BRAD (Brad Gowans, cornet* and clarinet#; Teddy Raph, trombone; Herman Drewes, cornet; Frank Cornwell, vocals; et al):   Dec.,1926
```
Ge  3408. Fly to Hawaii*/(rev., Felix Ferdinando)
```

  (Gowans, Drewes, Cornwell; Arnold Starr, violin; Frank Signorelli, piano; Eddie Edwards, trombone; Jim Moynahan, clarinet and sax; Fred Moynahan, drums; "Mate", tuba):   Mar., 1927
```
Ge  6039. Sunny Hawaii*/I'm Looking Over a Four Leaf Clover#
```

GOYER, EMMA (acc. by Horace Henderson, piano):
```
Pat 021060. Oh Daddy Blues
```

GRACE, TEDDY (vocals):
```
De  1398. Rock It for Me/I'm Losing My Mind Over You
De  1419. I'm So in Love With You/Dispossessed by You
De  1524. Tears in My Heart/Good-Bye Jonah
```

  (Bobby Hackett, cornet, included):
```
De  1602. I'll Never Let You Cry/I've Taken a Fancy to You
```

  (acc. by Billy Kyle, piano; Jack Teagarden, trombone; Dave Barbour, guitar; Delmar Kaplan, bass; O'Neill Spencer, drums):
```
De  2050. Love Me or Leave Me(64493a)/Crazy Blues(64495a)
De  2128. Down Hearted Blues/Monday Morning
```

  (Omit Teagarden; add Buster Bailey, clarinet):
```
De  2602. Betty and Dupree(65557a)/Arkansas Blues(65558a)
```

  (Omit Bailey; Sonny Lee, trombone):
```
De  2603. Mama Doo-Shee/Down Home Blues
De  2604. Hey Lawdy Papa/Low Down Blues
De  2605. Gulf Coast Blues/You Don't Know My Mind
De  2606. Oh Daddy Blues/Graveyard Blues
```

  (Unknown accompaniment):
```
De  3202. Let There Be Love/Left All Alone With the Blues
De  3203. Thunder in My Heart/I Love You Much Too Much
```

GRANT AND WILSON, LEOLA B. (COOT) and WESLEY (KID):
Para 12272. Crying Won't Make Him Stay(10052),Coot/Rock Aunt Dinah Rock(10053),
(duet
(Duets acc. by Fletcher Henderson Orchestra: Louis Armstrong, cornet;
Charlie Green, trombone; Buster Bailey, clarinet; Henderson, piano;
Charlie Dixon, banjo; Kaiser Marshall, drums.--HD):
Para 12317. Come on Coot Do That Thing(2280-2)   -UHCA 80, JI 6
"   Have Your Chill(2281-2)
Para 12324. You Dirty Mistreater(2279-1)/Speak Now or Hereafter Hold Your Peace
(2283-1), Joe Smith, cornet; Henderson, piano
Para 12337. Find Me at the Greasy Spoon(2282-1)/When Your Man Is Going to Put
(You Down(2284-1), Smith, Henderson only

(Acc. by piano and guitar):
Para 12831. Big Trunk Blues(352a)/Ain't Gonna Sell You None(499a)   -QRS 7085

(Unknown accompaniment):
Para 12379. Scoop It/Stevedore Man
Co 14363. Rasslin' Till the Wagon Comes/Keyhole Blues

(acc. by Whoopee Makers):   -Ro 819
Ca 9015. Ducks(3489b)
"   Mama Didn't Do It(3490a)   -Pat 7540, Pe 140,   "

(Unknown accompaniment):
OK 8944. Do Your Duty/Keep Your Hands Off My Mojo   -Vo 03121

COOT GRANT (with instrumental accompaniment):
Ro 1042. Stevedore Blues(3492-1)/(rev., Ozie Ware)
Co 14649. Get Off With Me/Deceiving Man Blues

GRANT AND WILSON (acc. by Sidney Bechet, soprano sax and clarinet; Char-
lie Shavers, trumpet; Teddy Bunn, guitar; Sam Price, piano; Wellman
Braud, bass; O'Neill Spencer, drums):   May 26,1938
De 7500. Uncle Joe(63873a)/Blue Monday on Sugar Hill(63876a)
Unissued. Toot It Brother Armstrong (63875)/I Am a Woman

GRAPPELLY, STEPHANE, violin (See Quintet of Hot Club of France.)

GRAVES, BLIND ROOSEVELT and Brother (guitar & cornet):
Para 12820. New York Blues/Guitar Boogie
Para 12891. Staggering Blues(1665)/Low Down Woman(1666)

GRAY, EDDIE (acc. by Henderson Novelty Orchestra):
BS 2011. Why Did You Make a Plaything of Me(p118)/I Like You(p119)

(acc. James P. Johnson's Harmony Eight):
BS 2020. You've Got What I've Been Looking For(p159)/Ukelele Blues(p160)

GRAY AND THE CASA LOMA ORCHESTRA, GLEN (Joe Hostetter, Frank Martinez, Bobby Jones,
trumpets; Pee Wee Hunt, Russell Rauch, trombones; Glen Gray, Clarence Hutchenrider,
Pat Davis, saxes; Mel Jensen, violin; Joe Hall, piano; Gene Gifford, guitar; Stan-
ley Dennis, bass; J. Briglia, drums.--HD):   1933
Vi 24222. Hey Young Fella(74906)
Vi 24224. Sittin' by the Fire With You(74904)/Where Are You(74905) -BB 6365
Vi 24254. Going Going Gone(75255)   -HMV 4969
"   Black Eyed Susan Brown(75257)
Vi 24256. Dardanella(75256)
"   Casa Loma Stomp(75260)   -HMV 4969
Vi 24338. Lazy Bones(76379)   -HMV 6382
"   Sophisticated Lady(76382)   -HMV 4980
Vi 24340. My Imaginary Sweetheart(76380)   -HMV 6382
"   The Night We Met(76381)

(Bobby Jones, Grady Watts, Sonny Dunham, trumpets; add Kenneth Sargent,
sax; rest same, except Jack Blanchette, guitar.--HD):
Br 6337. I Never Knew
"   Indiana   BrE 01755, BrF 500197
Br 6397. One Little Word Led to Another/After Tonight
Br 6402. Why Can't I Find Somebody to Love?/Mighty River
Br 6463. Rhythm Man/Thanksgivin'   -BrE 1451
Br 6486. New Orleans/Lady from St. Paul
Br 6494. Why Can't This Night Go On/If You Don't Want to be Sweethearts
Br 6513. Blue Prelude   -BrE 01560, BrF 0406
"   Dance of the Lame Duck   -BrE 01620,   "
Br 6584. Love Is the Thing/Under a Blanket of Blue
Br 6588. Buji   -BrE 01620
"   Whild Goose Chase   -BrE 01560
Br 6602. River's Takin' Care of Me   -BrE 01583
"   Trouble in Paradise
Br 6606. For You/I Love You Truly
Br 6611. Blue Jazz   -BrE 1365, BrE 01657, BrF 500197

Br	6618.	Mississippi Basin	
"		Louisiana Lullaby	-BrE 01598
Br	6626.	That's How Rhythm Was Born	-BrE 01596
"		It's the Talk of the Town	
Br	6628.	The Moment I Looked in Your Eyes/Music from Across the Sea	
Br	6642.	This Is Romance/My Love	
Br	6647.	Weep No More My Baby	
"		Savage Serenade	-BrE 01671
Br	6660.	Sweet Madness(14051)/Me for You Forever(14015)	
Br	6666.	And So Goodbye/Goodbye Love	
Br	6679.	Heat Wave(14199)/Not for all the Rice in China(14200)	
Br	6708.	We Were the Best of Friends/You're Gonna Lose Your Gal	
Br	6726.	Tired of It All/Dixie Lee	
Br	6738.	You Have Taken My Heart/Shadows of Love	
Br	6764.	Lullaby in Blue(14773)/That's Love(14775)	
Br	6775.	Carolina/A Hundred Years from Today	
Br	6791.	Infatuation/Love Me	
Br	6800.	I Got Rhythm	-BrE 02074, BrF 9614
"		Ol' Man River	-BrE 1755. "
Br	6858.	The House Is Haunted/Champagne Waltz	
Br	6870.	Moon Country(15081)/Ridin' Around in the Rain(15080)	
Br	6886.	Dallas Blues/Limehouse Blues	-BrE 01833, BrF 9580
Br	6910.	Spellbound/Don't Let It Happen Again	
Br	6922.	Milenberg Joys(15185)	-BrE 01866
"		Out of Space(15186)	
Br	6927.	I Never Had a Chance/Long May We Love	
Br	6932.	Jungle Fever	-BrE 01835
"		I Never Slept a Wink Last Night	
Br	6937.	You Ain't Been Living Right/Moon Glow	
Br	6964.	Learning/Out in the Cold Again	
Br	6945.	Pardon My Southern Accent(15459)/Say It(15461)	
Br	6954.	Two Cigarettes in the Dark/Here Come the British	
Br	6983.	How Can You Face Me	
Br	7320.	I Still Want You/Breakin' the Ice	
Br	7321.	Narcissus/Nocturne	-BrE 01984
Br	7325.	Linger awhile	-BrE 01866
"		Panama	
Br	7427.	Corinne Corrina	-BrF 500477
"		San Sue Strut	
Br	7532.	Avalon	
"		China Girl	-BrF 500477

(Frank Zullo, Grady Watts, Walter Smith, trumpets; Billy Rauch, Pee Wee Hunt, Fritz Hummel, trombones; Clarence Hutchenrider, clarinet; Art Ralston, Danny D'Andrew, Kenneth Sargent, Pat Davis, saxes; Joe Hall, piano; Jack Blanchette, guitar; Stanley Dennis, bass; Tony Briglia, drums.--HD):

1935-37

De	192.	A New Moon Is Over My Shoulder/I'm in Love	
De	193.	You're a Builder Upper(38717)/Judy(38718)	
De	199.	Chinatown My Chinatown	-De 3524
"		When Will I Know	
De	200.	P.S. I Love You	
"		Nagasaki	-De 813, BrE 02236
De	286.	Irresistible	
"		Stompin' Around	-De 813, BrE 02236
De	287.	Maybe I'm Wrong Again/I've Got an Invitation to a Dance	
De	298.	The Object of My Affection(39133a)/Two in a Dream(39131b)	
De	312.	Where There's Smoke There's Fire/Blue Moon	
De	334.	I Woke Up Too Soon/You Took Advantage of Me	
De	339.	In My Country That Means Love/Just a Fair Weather Friend	
De	349.	When I Grow Too Old to Dream/The Night Is Young	
De	352.	In a Blue and Pensive Mood/Fare Thee Well Annabelle	
De	375.	Things Might Have Been So Different/Ain't It Just Too Bad	
De	379.	Little Man With the Hammer/Who's Sorry Now	
De	386.	Here Comes Cookie/My Heart Is an Open Book	
De	387.	My Dance	
"		Love and a Dime	-BrE 326
De	405.	Love Passes By	
"		You're Walking in My Sleep	-BrE 326
De	430.	Once Upon a Midnight	
"		Two Heads Against the Moon	-BrE 02155
De	463.	Cotton/Chant of the Jungle	
De	552.	Without a Word of Warning	-BrE 309
"		Takes Two to Make a Bargain	
De	553.	I Wish I Were Aladdin/The Devil's Afraid of Music	-BrE 310
De	603.	Yankee Doodle Never Went to Town	-BrE 02155
"		Love Will Find a Way	
De	652.	Lovely Lady/With All My Heart	
De	688.	Moonburn/My Heart and I	-BrE 02148
De	696.	Let Yourself Go	
"		I'd Rather Lead a Band	-BrE 02138
De	869.	Bugle Call Rag/Rose of the Rio Grande	-BrE 02262
De	986.	Shades of Hades	-BrE 02386
"		Royal Garden Blues	-BrE 02516

De	1046.	Copenhagen	-BrE 02386
"		Jungle Jitters	
De	1126.	You're Laughing at Me	
"		I've Got My Love to Keep Me Warm	
De	1129.	Please Keep Me in Your Dreams	
"		Swing High Swing Low	
De	1158.	Too Marvelous for Words	
"		Sentimental and Melancholy	
De	1159.	Study in Brown	-BrE 02410
"		Whoa, Babe	"
De	1179.	I'd Be a Fool Again/You're Here You're There	
De	1180.	Love Is Good For Anything That Ails You/Was It Rain	
De	1211.	Never in a Million Years/There's a Lull in My life	
De	1246.	One Two Three Little Hours/Would You Like to Buy a Dream	
De	1368.	Yours and Mine/I'm Feelin' Like a Million	
De	1396.	Swing Low Sweet Chariot/Let 'er Go	
De	1312	Zig Zag/Goblin Band	
De	1412.	Casa Loma Stomp/For You	
De	1473.	Alway/Smoke Rings	
De	1519.	In the Mission by the Sea/Farewell My Love	
De	1520.	I'd Rather Be Right/Have You Met Miss Jones?	
De	1530.	I Remember/I've Got My Heart Set on You	
De	1540.	You Took the Words Right Out of My Mouth/The Waltz Lives On	
De	1541.	Thanks for the Memory/Mama That Moon Is Here Again	
De	1575.	Bei Mir Bist du Schon/Let's Make It a Life Time	
De	1597.	I Could Use a Dream/Sweet as a Song	
De	1607.	I Can Dream, Can't I?/Two Dreams Got Together	
De	1608.	I See Your Face Before Me/You Have Everything	
De	1634.	Did An Angel Kiss You?/Girl of My Dreams	
De	1650.	This Night Is My Night to Dream/My Heart Is Taking Lessons	
De	1672.	Memories of You(62827)/Nutty Nursery Rhymes(63181)	
De	1679.	Old Apple Tree/You Better Change Your Tune	
De	1755.	Malady in F Minor/My Bonnie Lies Over the Ocean	
De	1783.	Daddy's Boy/You Go to My Head	
De	1864.	I Cried for You/Time on My Hands	
De	2010.	At Long Last Love(dla1410)/You Never Know(dla1409)	
De	2031.	Mindin' My Business/Song of India	
De	2144.	What Is This Thing Called Love?Yours All Yours	
De	2281.	Hoboken Bucket/Last Night a Miracle Happened	
De	2292.	Could Be/I Won't Believe It	
De	2307.	I Promise You/Shut Eye	
De	2308.	Honolulu/This Night	
De	2321.	Heaven Can Wait(65037)/Sunrise Serenade(65035),piano Frankie Carle	
De	2388.	You Grow Sweeter as the Years Go By/Tears from My Inkwell	

(Sub. Sonny Dunham, trumpet, for Walter Smith; Murray MacEachern, trombone, for Hummel; Hoaby Carmichael, vocals):

De 2394. Little Old Lady(65064)/Washboard Blues(65063)

(Louis Armstrong, trumpet* or vocal#):

De 2395. Rockin' Chair(65045a)*/Lazybones(65046a)#

(Kenny Sargent, vocals):

De 2396. Star Dust(65180)/One Morning in May(35181)

(With the Merry Macs, vocals):

De 2397. Moon Country(65066)/Lazy River(65065)

(Instrumentals):

De	2398.	In the Still of the Night(65182)/Riverboat Shuffle(64962)	
De	2399.	Georgia on My Mind(65183)/Boneyard Shuffle(64963)	
De	2437.	Ay-Ay-Ay(with Louis Armstrong)/If I Had My Way	
De	2709.	Love Grows on the White Oak Tree(66079)/Prelude in C Sharp Minor(66076)	
De	2748.	Beautiful Love/Shadows (with Frankie Carle, piano)	
De	2777.	Through/Tumbling Tumbleweeds	
De	2802.	Blue Rain/Out of Space	
De	2903.	Midnight Lullaby(66750)/Shine on Harvest Moon(66748)	
De	2968.	My Wild Irish Rose/When Irish Eyes Are Smiling	
De	3006.	I Concerntrate on You/Last Night's Gardenias	
De	3016.	Watching the Clock/Wouldst Could I But Kiss Thy Hand Oh Babe	
De	3053.	Lover's Lullaby/Hours Is My Heart Alone	
De	3068.	Fable of the Rose/Save Your Sorrow	
De	3082.	Castle of Dreams/You've Got Me Out on a Limb	
De	3089.	No Name Jive, 1 & 2	
De	3121.	Charming Little Faker/Polka Dota and Moonbeams	
De	3122.	Sierra Sue/Soft Winds	
De	3163.	April Played the Fiddle/I Haven't Time to Be a Millionaire	
De	3164.	Meet the Sun Half Way(67518)/Pessimistic Character(67515)	
De	3193.	Rock Island Flag Stop	-De 4205
"		Under a Blanket of Blue	
De	3201.	Beautiful Dreamer/I Dream of Jeanie With the Light Brown Hair	
De	3216.	Clear Out of This World/Latin Tune, a Manhattan Moon and You	

```
De  3232. I Touched a Star/Temptation
De  3261. Coral Sea(67681)/When Buddha Smiles(67562)
De  3303. Big Bad Bill/Jimtown Blues
De  3348. Come and Get It/Mirage
De  3415. Our Love Affair/We Three
De  3426. Moon Over Burma/When You Awake
De  3471. Cottonwood Corners/Head on My Pillow
De  3572. I Do, Do You?/You Say the Sweetest Things
De  3573. Magic Mountain/Not So Long Ago
De  3610. Blow the Smoke Away/I'd Rather Dream
De  3639. Bye Bye Blues(68144)/Margie(68142)
De  3667. I'd Love to Live in Loveland/World Is Waiting for the Sunrise
De  3845. As If You Didn't Know/Boogie Woogie Man
De  3875. Swing Tonic/Woodland Symphony
De  4048. City Called Heaven/I Found You in the Rain
De  4067. Bells of San Raquel/Memory Lane
De  4114. Autumn Nocturne/Moonlight Cocktail
De  4156. Bottom Man on the Totem Pole, 1 & 2
De  4166. Darling How You Lied/I'll Never Forget
De  4170. Angels of Mercy/(rev., Jimmy Dorsey)
De  4292. It's the Talk of the Town/Until the Stars Fall Down
De  4298. Here You Are/Oh the Pity of It All
De  4299. Mem'ry of This Dance/One Dozen Roses
De 18322. Dear Old Pal of Mine/Till We Meet Again
De 18465. Southwind/Yesterday's Gardenias
De 18468. I Came Here to Talk for Joe/You're in Love With Someone Else
De 18471. Happy Mood/Lullaby of the Rain
De 18479. Don't Do It Darling/Don't Get Around Much Any More
De 18481. Rock-a-Bye Baby/I'm Old Fashioned
De 18508. Purple Moonlight/Moonlight Mood
De 18525. Carry Me Back to the Lone Prairie/Tall Grows the Timber
De 18546. Just Friends/I'm Through With Love
De 15035. Paramour/I May Be Wrong
De 15042. Drifting Apart/Sleepy Time Gal
          (See also: Casa Loma Orchestra)
```

GRAY AND HIS ORCHESTRA, RUSSELL (Unknown cornet; Billy Rank, trombone; Don Murray, clarinet; Frankie Trumbauer, Doc Ryker, alto saxes; Adrian Rollini, bass sax; Joe Venuti, violin; Eddie Lang, guitar; Arthur Schutt, piano; Chauncey Moorehouse, drums):
```
  OK 40938. Sugar(81575b)/(rev., Texans)                    -PaE 3489*
           *Issued under name of Frankie Trumbauer
```

GREAT DAY NEW ORLEANS SINGERS (Directed by Jimmy Johnson and Clarence Williams):
```
  OK  8755. You've Got to Be Modernistic(403533)/Shout On(403534)
```

GREEN, EDDIE and BILLIE WILSON:
```
  Para 12226. I'm Leaving You/I'm Sorry for It Now
```

GREEN AND HIS ORCHESTRA, JOHNNY (Featuring Benny Goodman, clarinet):
```
  Br  6797. Cocktails for Two/Live and Love Tonight        -BrE C1799
  Br  6855. Easy Come Easy Go/Repeal the Blues             -BrE 01757
```

GREEN, LEE (vocals with piano and guitar):
```
  Vo   1401. Railroad Blues/No. 44 (piano only)
  Vo   1422. The Way I Feel Blues/All My Money Gone Blues
  Vo   1441. Little Eddie Jones/Bad Man Napper
  Vo   1467. Dud-Low Blues(piano solo)/If I Get Drunk
  Vo   1485. Running Drunk Blues/Death Cell Blues
  Vo   1501. Memphis Fives/Bootleggin' My Jelly
  Vo   1510. Wash Day and No Soap/Don't Care If the Boat Don't Land
  Vo   1533. Gamblin' Man Blues/Down on the Border
  Vo   1562. Pork Chop Blues/Maltese Cat Blues
  Vo   1566. Death Alley Blues/Train No. 44
  Vo   1648. Five Minute Blues/Better Bring It Right Away
  Para 12865. Down in Death Valley Blues/Five Minute Blues
  De   7016. Forty-Four Blues/Memphis Fives
  De   7032. Doctorin' Fool Blues/Southern Blues
  De   7062. 'Round the World Blues/Blues About My Black Gal
  De   7346. Way I Feel/You May Be Beautiful but You Got to Die
  De   7368. Sealskin Black Woman/I'm Gonna Geat Your Bread
  De   7437. Country Gal Blues/Whip It Up and Down
```

GREEN, LIL (with instrumental accompaniment):
```
  BB  8464. Cherry Tree Blues/Just Rockin'
  BB  8524. Romance in the Dark/What Have I Done
  BB  8640. Give Your Mama One Smile/My Mellow Man
  BB  8659. Knockin' Myself Out/I Won't Sell My Love
  BB  8754. What's the Matter With Love
  BB  8790. How Can I Go On
```

```
BB  8865. Hello Babe
BB  8895. Let's Be Friends
BB  8949. Don't Know What I Do
BB  8985. If I'm a Fool
BB  9010. You Got Me to the Place
BB  9030. 99 Blues
```

GREEN, RUTH (vocals accompanied by Morris Rouse, piano):   New Orleans, 1924
   OK 8140. Sad and Lonely Blues/Mama's Got Something I Know You Want

GREEN, SLIM (with instrumental accompaniment):
   De 7104. Cocktails for Two/With Every Breath I Take
   De 7105. It's Easy to Remember/I'm Gonna Sit Right Down and Write Myself a
   De 7120. Shine(39844)/What's the Reason(39842)   (Letter
   De 7151. Accent on Youth/Cheek to Cheek

GREER AND HIS MEMPHIS MEN, SONNY (Arthur Whetsel, Freddie Jenkins, Cootie Williams, trumpets; Joe Nanton, Juan Tizol, trombones; Barney Bigard, clarinet;Johnny Hodges, alto sax; Harry Carney, baritone sax; Duke Ellington, piano; Fred Guy,guitar; Wellman Braud, bass; Sonny Greer, drums):   1930
   Co 1868. Beggars Blues(148641)/Saturday Night Function(148642) -Co 2833,Vo3012

      SONNY GREER AND HIS REXTET (Rex Stewart, cornet; Lawrence Brown, trombone; Harry Carney, baritone sax; Jimmy Hamilton, clarinet; Marlowe Morris,piano; Teddy Walters, guitar; Sonny Greer,drums; Oscar Pettiford, bass): 5/16/44
   Apollo . Sleepy Baboon/Ration Stomp
   Apollo . Kansas City Caboose/Helena's Dream

GROSS, WALTER (piano solos):
   BB 10795. I'm Always Chasing Rainbows/A Slight Case of Ivory
   BB 10937. Improvisation in Several Keys/Creepy Weepy

GRIFFIN, TOMMY (vocal acc. by Eddie Hill, piano):
   Vo 1479. Bell Tolling Blues/Ball Playing Blues

   (unknown accompaniment):
   BB 7194. Young Heifer Blues/(rev., Washboard Sam)

GRIMES QUINTETTE, TINY (Tiny Grimes, guitar and vocal; Clyde Hart, piano; Charlie Parker, alto sax; Harold West, drums; Jimmy Butts, bass):   Sept.15,1944
   Savoy 532. Red Cross/I'll Always Love You Just the Same

GUARNIERI'S ALL STAR ORCHESTRA, JOHNNY (Billy Butterfield, trumpet; Lester Young, tenor sax; Hank D'Amico, clarinet; Johnny Guarnieri, piano; Dexter Hall, guitar; Cozy Cole, drums; Billy Taylor, bass):   Apr.18,1944
   Savoy 509. Basie English/Exercise in Swing
   Savoy 511. Salute to Fats/These Foolish Things Remind Me of You

      GUARNIERI TRIO (Sammy Weiss, drums; Johnny Guarnieri, piano; Slam Stewart, bass):   Sept.20,1944
   Savoy 530. Gliss Me Again/Bowin' Singin' Sam
   Savoy 533. Deuces Wild/Deuces Mild

GUESNON, GEORGE (Acc. by Wingy Carpenter, trumpet; Edward J. Allen, piano, Jimmy Shirley, guitar; Bob Warren, drums):
   De 7740. Iberville and Franklin/Goodbye Good Luck to You
   De 7792. Black Woman Blues/Mississippi Town

GULF COAST SEVEN (Perry Bradford or Johnny Dunn group):
   Co 3916. Fade Away Blues(81021)/Daybreak Blues(81022)
   Co 3978. Papa Better Watch Your Step(81168)/Memphis Tennessee(81169)
   Co 14107. Keep Your Temper/Santa Claus Blues
   Co 14373. Georgia Is Always on My Mind/Daylight Saving

GULF COAST SPASM BAND:
   Or   204. Stale Bread Blues(3190)/(rev., Piccadilly Orchestra)

GULF COAST TRIO:
   Bu 8041 Gallopin' Dominoes/Grand Opera Blues

GUNN AND HIS ORCHESTRA, JIMMIE: 1936
   BB 6469. Star Dust/My Blue Heaven
   BB 6500. I Found a New Baby/To My Levee Home
   BB 6508. Slatt's Shuffle(rev., Bob Pope)
   BB 6578. Operator's Special/(rev., Tampa Red)

H

BOBBY HACKETT

For records under other names see:
ALL STAR JAM BAND: Com 528.
ANDREWS SISTERS: De 1562.
PETE BROWN: De 18118.
EDDIE CONDON: Com 500, 502, 515.
BUD FREEMAN: Com 507, 508.
FRANK FROEBA: De 1500, 1545, 1525.
TEDDY GRACE: De 1602.
HORACE HEIDT: Co 35250, 35446.
JAM SESSION AT COMMODORE: Com 505, 1500, 1501, 1502.
GLENN MILLER
MIFF MOLE: Com 1518.
DICK ROBERTSON: De 1487, 1498, 1585, 1619, 1620, 1599, 1601, 1675, 1125, 1181, 1283, 1367, 1415, 1707, 1726, 1823, 2364, 2765.
ADRIAN ROLLINI: De 1638.
MAXINE SULLIVAN: Vi 25895.

HACKETT AND HIS ORCHESTRA, BOBBY (Bobby Hackett, cornet; George Brunis, trombone; Pee Wee Russell, clarinet; John Blowers, drums; Dave Bowman, piano; Clyde Newcomb, bass; Eddie Condon, guitar; Lola Bard, vocals):   Feb., 1938
Vo 4047. At the Jazz Band Ball(756)/If Dreams Come True(755)
Vo 4142. That Da Da Strain(757)/You and Especially You(754), Bud Freeman, sax

(Sub Brad Gowans, trombone and alto sax; Andy Picardi, drums; add Ernie Caceres, baritone sax):   Sept., 1938
Vo 4499. Poor Butterfly(918)/Blue & Disillusioned(916), v. Linda Keene
Vo 4565. Ghost of a Chance(m917)/Doin' the New Low Down(m919)

(Sterling Bose, Bobby Hackett, trumpets; Gowans, Troupe, Pee Wee Russell Caceres, Billings, Condon, Bowman, Jacobs, Carter):   Apr., 1939
Unissued. King Arthur/World's Fair Shuffle

(Add Thompson and Columbo):   June 1939
Vo 4806. That's How Dreams Should End(wm1017)/Sunrise Serenade(wm1019)
Vo 4877. Ain't Misbehavin'(wm1018)/Embraceable You(wm1020)

(Personnel unknown):
Vo 5198. Ja Da(wm1051)/I Surrender Dear(wm1053), v., Claire Martin
Vo 5375. Bugle Call Rag(wm1050)/Dardanella(wm1052)

(Bobby Hackett, cornet; Frankie Carle, piano; Bob Knight, guitar; Bernie Mattison, drums; Eddie McKinney, bass; Jerry Borshard, trombone; Bob Riedel, clarinet; George Dessinger, tenor sax; Jimmy DeMeo, baritone sax):
Vo 5493. Clarinet Marmalade(la2126)/Singin' the Blues(la2129)   1940

(Vocals by Tempo Twisters)
Vo 5620. That Old Gang of Mine(la2124)/After I Say I'm Sorry(la2125)

HAID'S CUBS, BILL:
Bwy 1206. Crazy Rhythm/I Can't Give You Anything But Love

HAITIAN ORCHESTRA (Sidney Bechet, soprano sax and clarinet; Kenneth Roane, trumpet; Willie "The Lion" Smith, piano; O. Alderholt, bass; Leo Warney, drums.--JI 11/22/40)   1939
Bald 1012. Ti Ralph(581)/Meringue de Amour(582)
Bald 1013. Diane(576)/Nana(577)
Vs 8360. Baba/Tropical Moon
Vs 8399. Magic Isle/Mayonne
Vs 8405. Rose Rhumba/Sous Les Palmiers

HALF WAY HOUSE ORCHESTRA (Abbie Brunies, trumpet; Charles Cordella, tenor sax and clarinet; Bill Eastwood, banjo; Joe Loyacano, trombone; Leon Rappolo, alto sax; Mickie Marcour, piano; Monk Hazel, drums)   New Orleans, 1924
OK 40318. Pussy Cat Rag(8890a)/Barataria(8891a)

HALFWAY HOUSE DANCE ORCHESTRA (Abbie Brunies, trumpet; Charles Cordella, clarinet and tenor sax; Mickie Marcour, piano; Bill Eastwood, banjo; Emmett Rogers, drums)   1925
Co 476. Maple Leaf Rag(140998)/Let Me Call You Sweetheart(140999)
Co 541. Squeeze Me(140997)/New Orleans Shuffle(141000)

(Sub. Red Long, piano; Chink Martin, bass; Sidney Arodin, clarinet; Angelo Palmisano, banjo):   1926

35

```
Co    681. Since You're Gone(142007)/I'm in Love(142009)
Co   1041. Snookum(142006/It Belongs to You(142008), v., Red Long

        (Add alto sax):
Co   1263. When I'm Blue(145010)/I Want Somebody to Love(145011)

        ALBERT BRUNIES AND HIS HALFWAY HOUSE ORCHESTRA (same personnel):   1927
Co   1542. Love Dreams(146205)/Tell Me Who(146219), v., John Saba
Co   1959. Just Pretending(147658)/If I Didn't Have You(147659)
```

HALL, ADELAIDE (acc. by Lew Leslie's Blackbirds Orchestra):
Br   4031. Baby/I Must Have That Man

        (With Duke Ellington's Orchestra):
Br   6518. I Must Have That Man(12773)/Baby(12774)

EDMOND HALL

For other records see:
  RED ALLEN: De 18092; OK 6281, 6357
  SID CATLETT: Delta 10-3, 10-4.
  IDA COX: Vo 05258, 05298, 05336; OK 6405.
  BILL DAVISON: Com 549.
  DePARIS BROTHERS: Com 552; BN 40, 41.
  LENORD FEATHER: Com 547, 548.
  LIONEL HAMPTON: Vi 26557, 26608.
  W.C.HANDY: Vs 8162, 8163.
  BILLY HICKS: Vr 601.
  ART HODES: BN 34, 35.
  BILLIE HOLIDAY: Vo 3593, 3605.
  CLAUDE HOPKINS: Many Co, Br, De.
  EDDY HOWARD: Co 35771, 35915.
  FRANK NEWTON: Vr 518, 550, 571, 616, 647.
  ROSS DE LUXE SYNCOPATORS: Vi 20952, 20961, 21077.
  ZUTTY SINGLETON: De 18093.
  JOE SULLIVAN: Vo 5496, 5531; OK 5647.
  ART TATUM: De 8526.
  MARY LOU WILLIAMS: Asch 1002, 1003, 1004.

HALL CELESTE QUARTET, EDMOND (Edmond Hall, clarinet; Meade Lux Lewis, celeste;
Charlie Christian, guitar; Israel Crosby, bass):   1941
  BN   17. Profoundly Blue(r3461)/Celestial Express(r3462a-2)
  BN   18. Jamming in Four(r3459a)/Edmond Hall Blues(r3460)

        EDMOND HALL'S BLUE NOTE JAZZ MEN (Edmond Hall, clarinet; Sidney de Paris,
        trumpet; Vic Dickenson, trombone; James P. Johnson, piano; Arthur Shirley,
        guitar; Israel Crosby, bass; Sidney Catlett, drums):   Nov.29,1943
  BN   28. High Society(901)/Blues at Blue Note(903)
  BN   29. Night Shift Blues(905)/Royal Garden Blues(907)

        EDMOND HALL'S ALL STAR QUINTET (Edmond Hall, clarinet; Red Norvo, vibra-
        phone; Teddy Wilson, piano; Carl Kress, guitar; John Williams,bass):
  BN   30. Rompin' in '44(908-2)/Smooth Sailing(910-2)   Jan.25,1944
  BN   31. Blue Interval(909)/Seein' Red(911)

        EDMOND HALL'S SWINGTET (Edmond Hall, clarinet; Benny Morton, trombone;
        Harry Carney, baritone sax; Don Frye, piano; Everett Barksdale, guitar;
        Alvin Raglin, bass; Sidney Catlett, drums):
  BN   36. Big City Blues/Steamin' and Beamin'

        EDMOND HALL SEXTET (Edmond Hall, clarinet; Emmett Berry, trumpet; Vic
        Dickenson, trombone; Eddie Heywood, piano; Billy Taylor, bass; Sid Cat-
        lett, drums):   Dec.18,1943
  Com   550. The Man I Love(a4703-1)/Coquette(a4706)
  Com 1512. Downtown Cafe Boogie(a4704)/Uptown Cafe Blues(a4705)

        ED HALL AND THE BIG CITY JAZZMEN (Charlie Shavers, trumpet; Frankie So-
        colow, tenor sax; Edmond Hall, clarinet; Eddie Heywood, piano; Sid Catlett,
        drums; Oscar Pettiford, bass):   May 1,1944
  Delta 101. Sweet Georgia Brown/Blues in Room 920.

HALL AND HIS SUGAR BABIES, FRED (trumpet; clarinet; violin; guitar; banjo; tu-
ba; drums, goofus):
  OK 40410. My Sugar/Look Who's Here
  OK 40891. Is It Possible?/Some Day You'll Say
  OK 40986. Look in the Mirror/Plenty of Sunshine
  OK 41026. Waitin' for Katy/Sweetheart of Six Other Guys
  OK 41065. Constantinople/Chilly Pom Pom Pee
  OK 41088. It's Baloney/The Grass Grows Greener
  OK 41112. Butternut/On the Night We Did the Boom Boom
  OK 41183. She Only Laughs at Me/I Faw Down and Go Boom
  OK 41239. Here's That Party Now In Person(401531)/I Got a Code in My Doze
                                                                       (401808)

```
OK 41269. There's a Four Leaf Clover/It Ain't No Fault of Mine
OK 41310. Sophomore Prom/I Lift Up My Finger
OK 41369. Tain't No Sin
Ha    19. Say Arabella
```

HALL AND HIS COLLEGIANS, SLEEPY:
```
Me 12022. Sing Song Girl/The Song of the Fool
Me 12066. Just a Gigolo/It Must Be True
Me 12155. Bubbling Over/Fiesta
Me 12204. At Your Command/How the Time Can Fly
Me 12211. Little Hunka Love/Parkin' in the Moonlight
Me 12256. Life Is Just a Bowl of Cherries
Me 12299. Of Thee I Sing
Me 12311. Dancing on the Ceiling
Me 12439. It's About Time/The One Note Trumpet Player
Me 12442. I'll Never Be the Same(12105)/That Night Beside the Sea(12099)
Me 12500. Old Fashioned Love/You're Telling Me
Polk 9073. This Is the Missus
Vr   606. Lonely Serenade/Alice Blue Gown
```

HAM GRAVY, (blues vocals):
```
Vo 03275. Mama Don't Allow It/Who Pumped the Wind in My Do-Nut
```

LIONEL HAMPTON

For other records see:
```
LOUIS ARMSTRONG: OK 41442, 41448, 41463, 41468, 41478, 41486; Co 2688; De 914.
EDDIE CONDON: Com 515.
IDA COX: Vo 05258, 05298, 05336.
BENNY GOODMAN ORCHESTRA: Vi 25814, 25808, 26107,
BENNY GOODMAN QUARTET
BENNY GOODMAN QUINTET: Vi 26139, 26166.
BENNY GOODMAN SEXTET: Co 35254, 35320, 35349, 35404, 35466, 35482, 35553.
PAUL HOWARD: Vi 22660, 23354, 23420, 38068, 38070, 38122.
TEDDY WILSON: Br 7739, 7736.
```

HAMPTON AND HIS ORCHESTRA, LIONEL (Ziggy Elman, trumpet; Hymie Schertzer, George Koenig, alto saxes; Arthur Rollini, Vido Musso, tenor saxes; Jess Stacy, piano; Allan Reuss, guitar; Harry Goodman, bass; Gene Krupa, drums; Lionel Hampton, vibraphone):
```
Vi 25527. The Mood I'm In                                Feb.8,1937
     "    My Last Affair                                 -HMV 8639
Vi 25535. Jiving the Vibes(04583)                        -HMV 8651
     "    Stomp(04585), Hampton on drums                 -HMV 8615
```

(Cootie Williams, trumpet; Lawrence Brown, trombone; Mezz Mezzrow, clarinet; Johnny Hodges, alto sax; Jess Stacy, piano; Allan Reuss, guitar; John Kirby, bass; Cozy Cole, drums; Lionel Hampton, vibes & vocals):
```
                                                         Apr.14,1937
Vi 25575. Whoa Babe(07793)/Buzzin' Round with the Bee(07792)-HMV 8581,GrF 8040
Vi 25601. Stompology/(rev.,Quintette of Hob Club of France  -HMV 8651
```

(Buster Bailey, clarinet; Johnny Hodges, alto sax; Jess Stacy, piano; Allan Reuss, guitar; John Kirby, bass; Cozy Cole, drums; Lionel Hampton, vibes, piano* and drums#):
```
                                                         Apr.26,1937
Vi 25586. Rhythm Rhythm(07865)/China Stomp(07866)*
Vi 25592. On the Sunny Side of the Street                -HMV 8597
     "    I Know That You Know#                          -HMV 8639
```

(Jonah Jones, trumpet; Eddie Barefield, clarinet; Clyde Hart, piano; Bobby Bennett, guitar; Mack Walker, bass; Cozy Cole, drums; Lionel Hampton, vibes):
```
                                                         Aug.16,1937
Vi 25658. Drum Stomp(9645), Hampton, drums)
     "    Confessin'(9644)                               -HMV 8800
Vi 25666. I Surrender Dear(9647)
     "    Piano Stomp(9646), Hampton, pf.                -HMV 8800
```

(Ziggy Elman, trumpet; Vido Musso, clarinet; Arthur Rollini, tenor sax; Jess Stacy, piano; Johnny Miller, bass; Cozy Cole, drums; Lionel Hampton, vibes and vocal):
```
                                                    Hollywood, Sept.5,1937
Vi 25674. Baby Won't You Please Come Home(9682)/After You've Gone(9684)
Vi 25682. Everybody Loves My Baby(9683)/I Just Couldn't Take It(9685)
Vi 25699. The Object of My Affection(9680)/Judy(9681)
```

(Lionel Hampton, vibraphone and vocal; Johnny Hodges, alto sax; Edgar Sampson, tenor sax; Cootie Williams, trumpet; Billy Taylor, bass; Allan Reuss, guitar; Jess Stacy, piano; Sonny Greer, drums): N.Y., Jan.18,1938
```
Vi 25771. The Sun Will Shine Tonight(18336)/You're My Ideal(18335)
```

(Lionel Hampton, vibraphone; Harry James, trumpet; Benny Carter, Dave
Matthews, Hershal Evans, Babe Rusin, saxes; Billy Kyle, piano; John Kir-
by, bass; Joe Jones, drums): July 21,1938
Vi 26011. I'm in the Mood for Swing -HMV 8928
" Shoe Shiner's Drag -HMV 23
Vi 26017. Muskrat Ramble
" Ring Dem Bells(1/18/38 personnel) -HMV 8928
Vi 26039. Any Time At All/(rev., Nick LaRocca)

(Lionel Hampton, vibraphone; Omer Simeon, alto sax and clarinet; A. John-
son, R. Crowder, tenor saxes; George Oldham, alto sax; Walter Fuller,
trumpet; Alvin Burroughs, drums; Spencer Adams, piano; Jess Simpkins,
Bass): Chicago, Oct.11,1938
Vi 26114. Down Home Jump/Rock Hill Special
Vi 26173. Fiddle Diddle/Don't Be That Way(1/18/38 personnel)

(Lionel Hampton, vibraphone; Hymie Schertzer, Russell Procope, alto saxes;
Chu Berry, Jerry Jerome, tenor saxes; Irving Randolph, trumpet; Milton
Hinton, bass; Cozy Cole, drums; Allen Reuss, guitar; Clyde Hart, piano):
Vi 26209. High Society/Sweethearts on parade(see 4/5, plus Hart)N.Y.,Apr.3,1939

(Hampson, piano; Berry; ...ole; Reuss): Apr.5,1939
Vi 26233. Denison Swing/Wizzin' the Wiz
Vi 26254. Shufflin' at the Hollywood(Hart)/It Don't Mean a Thing(4/3 personnel;
Vi 26296. Big Wig in the Wigwam/Stand By for Announcements

(Harry Carney, sax; Lawrence Brown, trombone; Rex Stewart, trumpet; Clyde
Hart, piano; Lionel Hampton, vibraphone; Bill Taylor, bass; Sonny Greer,
drums): June,1939
Vi 26304. Memories of You/The Jumpin' Jive
Vi 26343. Johnny Get Your Horn(4/3 pers.)/I Can Give You Love(4/3 pers.)
Vi 26362. 12th Street ...(Hampton,pf)/Ain't Cha Comin' Home(4/3 personnel, ex-
cept Ziggy Elman, trumpet; Danny Barker, guitar -HMV 9088

(Lionel Hampton, vibraphone; L.Lee, Coleman Hawkins, Chu Berry, Ben Web-
ster, saxes; C. Gillespie, trumpet; M. Hinton, bass; Charlie Christian,
guitar; Clyde Hart, piano; Cozy Cole, drums): Sept.11,1939
Vi 26371. Hot Mallets -HMV 18
" When Lights Are Low
Vi 26393. One Sweet Letter from You/Early Session Hop -HMV 9027

(Lionel Hampton, vibraphone; Slick Jones, drums except in first title
where Hampton plays; Jerry Jerome, Toots Mondello, Ben Webster, saxes;
Ziggy Elman, trumpet; Arthur Bernstein, bass; Al Casey, guitar; Clyde
Hart, piano): Oct.30,1939
Vi 26423. Gin for Christmas/Heebie Jeebies Are Rockin' the Town(042943; see Vi
(26476 for personnel)
Vi 26447. Four or Five Times/I've Found a New Baby -HMV 9130
Vi 26453. The Munson Street Breakdown -HMV 9137
" I Can't Get Started -HMV 9152

(Lionel Hampton, vibraphone; Earl Bostic, sax; Henry Allen, trumpet; J.C.
Higginbotham, trombone; Charlie Christian, guitar; Arthur Bernstein,bass;
Clyde Hart, piano; Sidney Catlett, drums): Oct.,1939
Vi 26476. I'm on My Way from You(042941)/Haven't Named It Yet(042942)

(Lionel Hampton, vibraphone; Edmond Hall, clarinet; Coleman Hawkins, ten-
or sax; Benny Carter, trumpet; Joe Sullivan, piano; Freddy Green, guitar;
Arthur Bernstein, bass;Zutty Singleton,drums): Dec.21,1939
Vi 26557. Dinah/Singin' the Blues -HMV 9063

(Lionel Hampton, vibraphone; Toots Mondello, Bud Johnson, Buff Estes,Jer-
ry Jerome, saxes; Ziggy Elman, trumpet; Arthur Bernstein, bass; Ernie
Ashley, guitar; Spencer Odon, piano; Nick Fatool, drums):
Vi 26595. Flying Home/Save It Pretty Mama
Vi 26604. Till Tom Special/Shades of Jade
Vi 26608. Tempo and Swing/My Buddy(See Vi 26557 for personnel)

(Lionel Hampton, vibraphone, piano* or drums#; King Cole, piano; Oscar
Moore, guitar; Wesley Prince, bass; Al Spiedlock, drums, except in first
title): July 17,1940
Vi 26652. Jack the Bellboy#/Central Avenue Breakdown*
Vi 26696. Dough-Ra-Me(v.,Hampton Rhythm Boys)/Ghost of a Change(v.Helen Forrest)
Vi 26724. Jivin' With Jarvis -HMV 9137
" Blue

(Lionel Hampton, vibraphone; Marlowe Morris, piano; Teddy Bunn, electric
guitar; Douglas Daniels, guitar; Hayes Alvis, bass; Kaiser Marshall,
drums): Aug.21,1940
Vi 26739. Charlie Was a Sailor(v.,Daniels) -HMV 9152
" Martin on Every Block
Vi 26793. Pig Foot Sonata/Just for Laffs

38

```
            (Personnel unknown):
   Vi 27278. Smart Aleck/Lost Love(voc., Lee Young and Rhythm Girls)

            LIONEL HAMPTON AND HIS SEXTETTE (personnel unknown):
   Vi 27316. Altitude/I Nearly Lost My Mind
   Vi 27341. Bogo Jo/Open House
   Vi 27364. Fiddle Dee Dee/Bouncing at the Beacon
   Vi 27409. Three-Quarter Boogie/Give Me Some Skin
   Vi 27529. Now That You're Mine/Chasin' With Chase

            LIONEL HAMPTON AND HIS ORCHESTRA (Karl George, Ernest Royal, Joe Newman,
            trumpets; Fred Beckett, Luther Graven, Harry Sloan, trombones; Marshall
            Royal, Raymond Perry, Illinois Jacquet, Dexter Gordon, Jack McVea,saxes;
            Milton Buckner, piano; Irving Ashby, guitar; Vernon Alley, bass; Shadow
            Wilson, drums; Hampton, vibraharp-EW):
   De 18265. Just for You(70100)/My Wish(70102)
   De 18285. Nola/Southern Echoes
   De 18394. Flying Home/In the Bag
   De 18535. Now I Know(70771)/Half a Love Is Better Than None(70772)

            (Cat Anderson, Lamar Wright,Jr., Roy McCoy, Joe Morris, trumpets; Al
            Hayes, Michael Wood, Fred Beckett, trombones; Earl Bostic, Gus Evans,
            altos; Al Sears, Arnette Cobbs, tenors; Charles Fowlkes, baritone sax;
            Milt Buckner, piano; Eric Miller, guitar; Fred Radcliffe, drums; Vernon
            King bass; Hampton, vibes and drums.--Esquire):          March,1944
   De 18613. Hamp's Boogie Woogie/Chop Chop
   De        Flying Home/Loose Wig

            SEXTET WITH DINAH WASHINGTON (Joe Morris, trumpet; Arnette Cobbs, tenor
            sax; Rudy Rutherford, clarinet; Milton Buckner, piano; Fred Radcliffe,
            drums; Vernon King, bass; Dinah Washington, vocals; Lionel Hampton,piano*
            or drums#):                                              Dec.29,1943
   Key    605. Evil Gal Blues(lhsl)/Homeward Bound(4)*
   Key    606. I Know How to Do It(2)#/Salty Papa Blues(3)

HANDY'S ORCHESTRA OF MEMPHIS (Edward Alexander, William Tyler, Darnell Howard,vi-
olins; Charles Hillman, piano; Wilson Townes, sax and clarinet; Charles Harris,A.
R. Poole, saxes; Nelson Kincaid, clarinet; Henry Graves, cello; Archie Walls,bass;
Jasper Taylor, xylophone and drums; Sylvester V. Bevard, trombone; W.C. Handy,
trumpet.--W.C. Handy):                                                      1918
   Co  2417. Sweet Child/The Old Town Pump
   Co  2418. Moonlight Blues(77369),waltz/A Bunch of Blues(77373)
   Co  2419. That Jazz Dance(77367)/Livery Stable Blues(77377)
   Co  2420. Ole Miss Rag(77362)/The Hooking Cow Blues(77371)
   Co  2421. Fuzzy Wuzzy Rag(77356)/The Snaky Blues(77361)

            HANDY'S MEMPHIS BLUES BAND (trumpet; trombone; clarinet: sax; bass; vio-
            lin; piano; drums):
   BS   2053. St.Louis Blues(970)/Yellow Dog Blues(971)         -Pu 11098
   Para 20112. Muscle Shoals Blues/She's a Mean Job             -Ba 1053, Pu 11112

            HANDY'S ORCHESTRA (clarinet; sylophone and drums; two saxes; trombone;
            piano; banjo; bass; trumpet):
   OK  4789. Aunt Hagar's Blues(s71150a)/Louisville Blues(s71151b)   -OK 8046
   OK  4880. Farewell Blues/Gulf Coast Blues
   OK  4886. Sundown Blues/Florida Blues
   OK  4896. Memphis Blues/St. Louis Blues
   OK  8059. Panama(s71349b)/Down Hearted Blues(s71372a)
   OK  8066. Mama's Got the Blues(s71373c)/My Pillow and Me(s71469b)
   OK  8110. Darktown Reveille/Ole Miss Blues
                (See also: Sara Martin, OK 8061, 8064)

            W. C. HANDY AND ORCHESTRA (Edmond Hall, clarinet; Luis Russell,piano;
            Bingie Madison, tenor sax; J.C. Higginbotham, trombone; Sidney Catlett,
            drums; Pop Foster, bass; W.C. Handy, trumpet and vocals):   Dec.26,1939
   Vs   8162. Loveless Love(usl224)/Way Down South Where the Blues Begin(usl226)
   Vs   8163. St.Louis Blues(usl223)/Beale Street Blues(usl225)

HANNAH, GEORGE (vocals):
   Para 12786. The Snitcher Blues

            (Acc. by Meade Lux Lewis, piano):
   Para 13024. The Boy in the Boat(561)/Freakish Blues(562)
   Para 13048. Molasses Sopper Blues(560)/Alley Rat Blues(563)

HANSHAW, ANNETTE (Accompaniment possibly includes Eddie Lang, guitar and Joe Ven-
uti, violin.--RR, also DB 6/1/41):
   Me 12471. We Just Couldn't Say Goodbye (12199)/Love Me Tonight(12209)-Pana 25270
   Me 12551. I'm Sure of Everything(12670)/Fit As a Fiddle(12671)       -Pana 25413
   Pana 25324. Say It Isn't So/You'll Always By the Same Sweetheart
   Pana 25469. Moon Song/Twenty Million People
```

```
        OK 41292. Lovable and Sweet/                                    -PaE 477
         "        Moanin' Low                                           -PaE 850
        OK 41327. The Right Kind of Man(403080)/If I Can't Have You(40381)  -PaE 546
        PaE  642. When I'm Housekeeping for You/I Have to Have You
        PaE  654. Cooking Breakfast for the One I Love/When a Woman Loves a Man
        PaE  697. Just Can't Be Bothered With Me/With You
        PaE  967. Ho Hum/Moonlight Saving Time
              (Acc. by the New Englanders):
        Ve  1706. I Can't Give You Anything But Love/I Must Have That Man
        Ve  1859. Precious Little Thing Called Love/Mean to Me
        Ve  1981. True Blue Lou/Here We Are
        Ve  2066. Aren't We All/If I Had a Talking Picture of You
        Ve  2178. If I Had a Girl Like You/My Future Just Passed
        Di  2915. I've Got a Feeling I'm Falling(148489)/The One in the World(148490)
```

MISS ANNETTE HANSHAW AND THE RED NEADS (A String band, not Nichols):
Pe 12296. I'm All Alone in a Palace of Stone/If You Can't Tell the World

HAPPY HARMONISTS (Curtis Hitch, piano; Fred Rollison, cornet; Arnold Habbe, banjo; Maurice May, sax; Harry Wright, clarinet; Haskell Simpson, bass; Earl McDowell, drums; Neal, trombone):   1924
        Ge 5286. Cruel Woman(11616)/Home Brew Blues(11617)
        Ge 5402. Baptistown Crawl(11763)/Ethiopian Nightmare(11764)
        Ge 5518. Steady Steppin' Papa(11762a)/(Rev., Bucktown Five) -Clax 40353
              (See also Hitch's Happy Harmonists)

HARDWAY'S ORCHESTRA, LIL:
        Vo 1252. Milenberg Joys/(rev., Wynn's Creole Jazz Band)

              DIAMOND LIL HARDAWAY AND HER GEMS OF RHYTHM (trumpet; sax; piano; guitar;
              bass; drums):
        De 7193. Back in the Country(90660)/You Know I Know (90661)

HARDMAN AND HIS HAMMOND FIVE, GLENN (Glenn Hardman, Hammond organ; Lee Castle, trumpet; Jo Jones, drums; Freddy Green, guitar; Lester Young, tenor):
        Vo 4971. Exactly Like You(sc2637)/Who(wc2640)
        Co 35263. Upright Organ Blues(wc2639)/Jazz Me Blues(wc2641)
        Co 35341. China Boy(wc2636)/On the Sunny Side of the Street(wc2638)

HARDY, LUCIUS:
        Para 12598. Mr. Blues/Jelly Bean Man

HARDY'S ALABAMIANS, MARION (Eddie Mallory, Elisha Herbert, trumpets; Hy Clark, trombone; Marion Hardy, sax and clarinet; Warner Seals, Artie Starks, saxes;Ralph Anderson, piano; Leslie Corley, guitar; Charlie Turner, bass; Jim McEndree, drums; --JI 9/6/40):
        Co 2034. Song of the Bayou/Georgia Pines

HARLAN AND HIS ORCHESTRA, EARL:
        Pe 15789. Smoke Rings(12358/Mills Blue Rhythm Band)   -Me 12739, Do 128
                  Sophisticated Lady(13284/Don Redman)   "   "
        Me 12867. Keep on Doin' What You're Doing/Tired of it All

HARLEM FOOTWARMERS (Duke Ellington Orchestra: Arthur Whetsol, Freddie Jenkins, Cootie Williams, trumpets; Sam Nanton, Juan Tizol, trombones; Barney Bigard, clarinet; Johnny Hodges, alto sax; Harry Carney, baritone sax; Duke Ellington, piano; Fred Guy, banjo; Wellman Braud, bass; Sonny Greer, drums):   1930
        OK 8720. Jungle Jamboree(402551c)   -PaE 1946
         "   Snake Hip Dance(402553b)   -PaE 2303
        OK 8746. Blues of the Vagabond(403287b)/Syncopated Shuffle(403288b) -PaE 1535
        OK 8760. Lazy Duke(403286b)/(rev., Luis Russell)   -PaE 1549
              (Whetsol, Nanton, Bigard, rhythm, next 3 sides):
        OK 8836. Big House Blues(404482c)   -Co 14670, PaE 1044, Co 35682
         "   Rocky Mountain Blues(404483b)   PaE 1449,   "
        OK 8840. Mood Indigo(480023b)   - PaE 866
         "   Sweet Chariot(404522b)   -Co 14670,   -PaE 1615
        OK 8869. Old Man Blues(404521b)   -PaE 942
         "   Rookin' in Rhythm(404804a)   -PaE 924
              (See also: Harlem Music Masters, Lonnie Johnson's Harlem Footwarmers)

HARLEM HAMFATS (Herbert "Kid" Morand, trumpet; Odell Rand, supplemented by Buster Bailey in some titles, clarinet; Horace Malcoom, piano; Pearlis Williams or Fred Flynn, drums; Joe McCoy, guitar; Charles McCoy, mandolin or guitar; John Lindsey or Ransom Knowling, bass.--Jazz Quarterly Summer 1944):   1937
        De 7182. Lake Providence Blues/Oh Red
        De 7196. Live and Die for You/She's Gone Again
        De 7205. Let's Get Drunk and Truck/What You Gonna Do
        De 7206. Sales Tax on It/You Done Tore Your Playhouse Down
        De 7218. Move Your Hand/New Oh Red

```
De  7229. Garbage Man/Southern Blues
De  7234. Little Girl(90912b)/Week Smoker's Dream(90915a)
De  7245. I Fell Like a Millionaire/Bad Luck Blues
De  7251. If You Want to Live/My Daddy Was a Lovin' Man
De  7262. Hamfat Swing/She's a Mellow Mother for You
De  7266. I Don't Want You Lovin' Me/Keep It Swinging Round and Round
De  7283. Growling Dog/Ooh Wee Babe
De  7299. Hallelujah Joe Ain't Preaching No More/What's My Baby Doing
De  7310. Baby Don't You Tear My Clothes/You Drink Too Much
De  7312. It Was Red/Jam Jamboree
De  7326. Empty Bed Blues/We Gonna Pitch a Boogie Woogie
De  7339. I Feel Like Going to Town/I'm So Glad
De  7351. Down in Shady Lane(91126a)/I'm Cuttin' Out(91200a)
De  7367. Hoodooin' Woman/I Love That
De  7382. Tempo de Bucket(62657a)/You Got the Devil to Pay(62658a)
De  7395. Rampart and Gravier Blues/Broken Hearted Blues
De  7406. Toodle oo Blues/You Got to Be Satisfied
De  7426. My Old Lady Blues/What's on Your Mind
De  7439. Root Hog or Die/Black Gal You Better Use Your Head
De  7454. I'd Rather Be With You/Time's a-Wastin'
De  7466. Let Me Feel It/Don't Start No Stuff
De  7484. Mellow Little Devil(63662a)/The Barefoot Boy(63663a)
De  7515. It Will Never Happen Again/Trading Old Love for New
De  7530. I'm in So Much Trouble Now(63638a)/I Believe I'll Make a Change
De  7761. Little Girl/(rev., Ollie Shepard)                         (63639a)
Vo 04813. Ruin Your Beauty Spot/Sun Goes Down in Harlem
Vo 04870. Bartenders Blues/Ready for the River
Vo 05136. When My Love Has Come Down/You Can't Win in Here
Vo 05179. Oh Babe/You Brought Me Everything
Vo 05233. You Done Turned Salty/Rockin' Myself to Sleep
Vo 05287. Business Is Gone Away(wc 2721; voc.,Lil Allen)/Take Me in Your Alley
       (See also; Half Pint Jaxon, Rosetta Howard)                  (wc2725)

HARLEM HANNAH AND HER HOT BOYS:
  BB 5051. My Handy Man/Keep Your Nose Out of Mama's Business
  BB 5069. Easy Rider/A Guy That Takes His Time

       HANNAH'S HOT SHOTS:
  BB 6414. Handy Man/Why Should I

HARLEM HARLEY AND HIS HARLEM BAND:
  De 7574. Kitchen Mechanic Blues/It's You That Taught It to Me
  De 7603. The Bo De o-o de o-do(65081a)/My Only Passion(65084a)

       HARLEM HARLEY AND HIS WASHBOARD BAND:
  De 7492. Best Ever Did It/Hold It
  De 7505. Life Goes On and On/Mama Come on Home

HARLEM HARMONY KINGS (Trumpet; trombone; sax; violin; banjo; tuba; piano; drums):
  Para 12003. Hard Time Blues(a104)/John Henry Blues(a105)

HARLEM HOT CHOCOLATES (Duke Ellington Orchestra: Bubber Miley, Arthur Whetsol,
Freddie Jenkins, trumpets; Barney Bigard, clarinet and tenor sax; Joe Nanton, trom-
bone; Johnny Hodges, alto and soprano sax; Harry Carney, alto and baritone sax;Juan
Tizol, trombone; Ellington, Guy, Braud, Greer, rhythm):                     1929
  HoW 1045. Sing You Sinners(o23) (paper base; cut on only one side)
  HoW 1046. St. James' Infirmary(c36) (paper base; cut on only one side)

HARLEM HOT SHOTS (Blue Rhythm Band: Wardell Jones, Shelton Hemphill, Edward Ander-
son, trumpets; Harry White, Henry Hicks, trombones; Theodore McCord, Crawford
Wethlington, Castor McCord, saxes; Edgar Hayes, piano; Benny James, banjo; Hayes
Alvis, bass; Willie Lynch, drums.--HD):                                     1931
  Pe 15481. Black and Tan Fantasy(10601)/Sugar Blues(10625)   -Ro 1651, Or 2284

       (Wingy Mannone, trumpet and vocals; Matty Matlock, clarinet; Eddie Mill-
       er, tenor sax; Gil Bowers, piano; Nappy Lamare, guitar; Harry Goodman,
       bass; Ray Bauduc, drums;:                                   Dec.,1934
  Pe 16081. The Blues Have Got Me(16571)/Breeze(16573)   -Me 13323,Or 3098,VoE 17
                                                                   Feb.,1935
  Pe 16085. March Winds and April Showers(16798)        -Me 13333,Or 3103,  VoE 3
       "   Love is Just Around the Corner(16800)           "        "    Rex 8475
  Pe 16095. Dust Off That Old Pianna(16799)             -Me 13353,Rex 8475
       "   House Rent Party Day(16801)                     "

       (Personnel unknown):
  BB  5253. My Galveston Gal/Can This Be the End of Love
  BB  5481. Somebody Stole My Gal/Old Fashioned Love
  Elec 1931. St. Louis Blues/I Ain't Got Nobody

HARLEM HOUSE RENT STOMPERS (trumpet; guitar; piano):
  Br  7120. Gravel Pit Stomp/(rev., Rhythm Aces)
```

HARLEM MUSIC MASTERS (Ellington Orchestra; same personnel as Harlem Footwarmers):
  OK 41468. Ring Dem Bells(404519a)/(rev., Louis Armstrong)   -PaE 849

HARLEM STOMPERS:
  De 7600. Monkey Swing/My Understanding Man
  De 7616. Jammin' in Georgia/Serenade to a Jitterbug

HARLEM TRIO (George McClennon, clarinet; piano; banjo):
  OK 8158. The Funny Blues(s72668a)/The Poor Man's Blues(s72669a)
  OK 8189. Bass Clarinet Blues(s72922a)/Meddlin' With the Blues(s72923b)
       (See also: Mamie Smith)

HARLEM WILDCATS:
  Vs 6012. The Call of the Freaks/Mouth Full of Jam
  Vs 6013. Jazz Pie/Goin' to Town
  Vs 6014. Yeah Man/Zombie
  Vs 6015. Scat Song(cl745)/How Am I Doing(cl743)

HARLEM SERENADERS:
  Vs 6004. Let's Have a Party/Day Dreams
  Vs 6005. Dixieland(cl981)/Get Cannibal(cl777)

HARLEY, JOSIE (blues with piano):
  Para 12025. I'm Through With You/2 A.M. Blues

HARMANIAC FIVE:
  Para 20476. Harmaniac Blues

HARMONY HOUNDS:
  Co 14119. I've Got a Gal and She Ain't No Good/Done Got De Blues
  Co 14131. That Dog o' Mine/Up North Blues

HARRIS BROTHERS TEXANS:
  Br 4644. Gut Bucket Shuffle/Louisiana That's My Home
  Vo 15747. The Payoff/Somebody Stole My Gal

HARRIS, LILLIAN (with the Original New Orleans Jazz Band):
  Ba 1173. Four o'Clock Blues/Sugar Blues   -Re 9445
  Ba 1212. Baby Won't You Please Come Home/Mama's Got the Blues
  Ba 1224. Gulf Coast Blues/Down Hearted Blues   -Re 9510

HARRIS, MAE (with piano; cornet; trombone):
  Do 413. The Basement Blues/(rev., Bessie Williams)

HARRIS, MAGNOLIA AND HOWLING SMITH):
  Vo 1602. Mama's Quttin' and Leavin', I & 2

HARRISON, JIMMY, trombone: See following:
  CHOCOLATE DANDIES: PaE 882, 963, 1273; Co 2543.
  CONNIES INN ORCHESTRA: Cr 3093, 3107, 3180, 3191, 3212.
  DIXIE STOMPERS: Ha 407-974.
  DUKE ELLINGTON: Ge 3291.
  FLETCHER HENDERSON: Vo 1079, 1092; Br 3460, 4119; Vi 20944; Co 1002, 1059, 1543
     1913, 2329, 2352, 2586, 2414, 14392 and odd labels of this period.
  CHARLES JOHNSON: Vi 21712.
  CHICK WEBB: Vo 1607, Br 6898.

HARRY'S RECKLESS FIVE (Frank Melrose, piano; Herb Morand, trumpet; Tommy Taylor, drums and Frisco whistle; sax and clarinet.--Jazz Miscellany):
  Bwy 1355. St.James Infirmary(21470)/Wailing Blues(21469)   -Para 12898*
       *Issued on Paramount under name of Kansas City Frank & His Footwarmers

HARRY'S HAPPY FOUR (two trumpets, banjo, piano):
  OK 8229. Swingin' the Swing(73501a)/A St.Louis Chant(73502a)

HARTMAN AND HIS ORCHESTRA, GEORGE (George Hartman, trumpet; Roy Zimmerman, piano; John Casteing, drums; Lloyd Dantin, guitar; Julian Laine, trombone; John Bell, bass; Leonard Centobie, clarinet):   New Orleans, 1941
  Key 601. Jazz Me Blues(gh2a)/Tin Roof Blues(gh4a)
  Key 602. Diga Diga Doo(gh1a)/Muskrat Ramble(gh3a)

COLEMAN HAWKINS

See also following records:
  ALLEN-HAWKINS: All.
  BALTIMORE BELL HOPS: Co 2449.
  COUNT BASIE: Ok 6180, 6244.
  BENNY CARTER: VoE 81, 94, 104, 110, 118, 126; Vo 5399, 5458, 5420, 5508, OK 6001.
  CHOCOLATE DANDIES: Ok 8728; PaE 882, 963, 1273; 1138, 1645; Com 533, 1506.

CLUB WIGWAM: Do 3458.
COZY COLE: Savoy 512.
CONNIE'S INN: Vi 22698, 22721, Me 12145, 12216, 12239, 12340, Cr 3093, 3107, 3180, 3191, 3212.
LEONARD FEATHER: Com 547, 548.
BENNY GOODMAN: Co 2907, 2892, CoE 730.
LIONEL HAMPTON: Vi 26371, 26393, 26557, 26608.
FLETCHER HENDERSON: All 1922 to 1934.
HORACE HENDERSON: De 18171, 18172.
SPIKE HUGHES: DeE 3563, 3606, 3639, 3717, 3836, 3972, 5101.
JACK HYLTON: HMV.
MAGGIE JONES: Co 14074.
McKINNEY'S COTTON PICKERS: Vi 38097, 38102, 38133, 38112, 38118, 38142, 22736.
METRONOME ALL STAR BAND: Vi 27314.
MOUND CITY BLUE BLOWERS: OK 41515, 41526; Vi 38100.
JACK PURVIS: OK 8782, 8808.
VARSITY SEVEN: Vs 8135, 8147, 8173, 8179.
CLARENCE WILLIAMS: Co 14287.

HAWKINS, COLEMAN, tenor sax (acc. by Buck Washington, piano): **1934**
PaE 1825. I Ain't Got Nobody(265173)   -De 18252
  "   On the Sunny Side of the Street(265175)
PaE 1837. It Sends Me(265172-2)/(rev., Buck Washington)

      (acc. by Stanley Black, piano; Albert Harris, guitar; Tiny Winters,bass;
PaE 2007. Lullaby(e6739)/Lady Be Good(e6740)   London, 1934

      (Stanley Black, piano):
PaE 2041. Lost in a Fog(e6741)   -De 18252
  "   Honeysuckle Rose(e6742-1)   -De 3881,De 3358

      (Acc. by The Ramblers: William Poppink, Andre Van Der Oudera, saxes;Henk
      Hinrichs, trumpet; Marcel Thielemans, trombone; Theo Masman,pf; Jack Pet,
      guitar; Kees Kranenburg, drums):   Holland, 1935
DeE 5457. I Wish I Were Twins(151)/(rev., Swinging Rascals)
DeE 5581. Some of These Days(148)/After You've Gone(149)
DeE 42050. Hands Across the Table(153)/I Only Have Eyes for You(150)
                                                                    1936
DeE 5775. Netcha's Dream(am180)   -De 661, De 3881
  "   What Harlem Is to Me(am179)   -De 742
DeE 5937. Meditation(am178)   -De 742
  "   Chicago(am177)   -De 661
                                                                    1937
DeE 6407. Original Dixieland One Step/Consolation
DeE 6445. A Strange Fact/Smiles
DeE 6502. I Wanna Go Back to Harlem/Something Is Gonna Give Me Away

      (Acc. by Freddy Johnson, piano):
DeE 6597. Devotion/Lamentation
PanD 1045. Star Dust(401)/Well All Right Then(402)   -De 18251

      (Acc. by Freddy Johnson, piano; Maurice van Kleef, drums): Holland,1937
PanD 1046. When Buddha Smiles   -VoE 210
   "   Way Down Yonder in New Orleans   -VoE 218
PanD 1047. Blues Evermore   -VoE 218
   "   Dear Old Southland   -VoE 210
PanD 1048. Swinging in the Groove/I Know That You Know   -VoE 222

      (Acc. by Michael Warlop's Orchestra: Arthur Briggs, Noel Chiboust, Pierre
      Allier, trumpets; Paquinet, trombone; Andre Ekyan, Charles Lisee, Alix
      Combelle, saxes; Stephane Grappelly, piano; Django Rheinhardt, guitar;
      D'Hellemmes, bass; Maurice Haillou, drums.):   Paris, 1935
GrF 7455. Blue Moon(346)   -HMV 8388, HMV 4497
  "   What a Difference a Day Made(348)   -HMV 8494, HMV "
GrF 7527. Avalon(347)   -HMV 8388, HMV 4496
  "   Star Dust(349), p,g,b & d   -HMV 8420,   "

      (Acc. by The Berrys):   Switzerland, 1936
PaS 35512. Sorrow/Love Cries   -PaE 658
PaS 35513. It May Be Not True/Tiger Rag

HAWKINS AND HIS ORCHESTRA, COLEMAN (Henry Allen, trumpet; J.C. Higginbotham, trombone; Hilton Jefferson, clarinet and alto sax; Coleman Hawkins, tenor sax; Horace Henderson, piano; Bernard Addison, banjo; John Kirby, bass; Walter Johnson, drums):
                                                                Oct.,1933
PaE 1685. The Day You Came Along(265143-2)
  "   Jamaica Shout(265144-2)   -De 3358, OK 41566
PaE 1766. Heartbreak Blues(265145-2)/(rev., Horace Henderson)   -OK 41566

      COLEMAN HAWKINS AND HIS ALL STAR JAM BAND (Coleman Hawkins, Alix Combelle,
      tenor saxes; Benny Carter, Andre Ekyan, alto saxes; Stephane Grappelly,
      piano; Django Rheinhardt, guitar; D'Hellemmes, bass; Tommy Benford,drums):

```
                                                                    Paris. 1937
   Sw    1. Honeysuckle Rose(0la1742)/Crazy Rhythm(ola1743)  -Vi 26219, HMV 8754
   HMV 8812. Out of Nowhere/Sweet Georgia Brown

           COLEMAN HAWKINS AND HIS ORCHESTRA (Joe Guy, Tommy Lindsey, trumpets;Earl
           Hardy, trombone; Jackie Fields, Eustace Moore, altos; Coleman Hawkins,
           tenor sax; Gene Rodgers, piano; William Oscar Smith, bass; Arthur Herbert,
           drums):                                                        Oct.11,1939
   BB 10477. Meet Doctor Foo/She's Funny That Way(voc.,Thelma Carpenter)-HMV 9046
   BB 10523. Fine Dinner                                          -HMV 9046
        "   Body and Soul

           COLEMAN HAWKINS' ALL STAR OCTET(Coleman Hawkins, tenor sax; Danny Polo,
           clarinet; Benny Carter, trumpet; J.C. Higginbotham, trombone; Gene Rod-
           gers, piano; Lawrence Lucie, guitar; Johnny Williams, bass; Walter John-
           son, drums):                                                   Jan.3,1940
   BB 10693. When Day Is Done(046156)/Bouncing With Bean(046159)    -HMV 9087
   BB 10770. The Shiek of Araby(046157)                             -HMV 9151
         "  My Blue Heaven(046158)

           COLEMAN HAWKINS AND HIS ORCHESTRA (personnel unknown):
   OK  6284. Passin' It Around(27850)/Rocky Comfort(27852)
   OK  6347. Serenade to a Sleeping Beauty(27851)/Forgive a Fool(27853)

           (Coleman Hawkins, tenor sax; Ellis Larkins, piano; Jimmy Shirley, guitar;
           Max Roach, drums; Oscar Pettiford, bass):                      Dec.18,1943
   Sig 28101. Hawkins' Barrel House/Voodte (see personnel below)

           (Bill Coleman, trumpet; Andy Fitzgerald, clarinet; Al Casey, guitar;
           Shelly Manne, drums; Hawkins, Larkins, Pettiford):             Dec.9,1943
   Sig 28102. How Deep Is the Ocean(t1906-1)/Stompy(t1908)

           COLEMAN HAWKINS' SWING FOUR (Coleman Hawkins, tenor sax; Eddie Heywood,
           piano; Pettiford, Manne):                                      Dec.23,1943
   Sig 28104. Crazy Rhythm(t1923)/Get Happy(t1924)
   Sig 90001. The Man I Love/Sweet Lorraine

           COLEMAN HAWKINS' ORCHESTRA (Leo Parker, Leonard Lowry, altos; Coleman
           Hawkins, Don Byas, Ray Abramson, tenors; Al Johnson, baritone sax; Dizzy
           Gillespie, Vic Coulsen, Ed Vanderver, trumpets; Clyde Hart, piano; Max
           Roach, drums; Pettiford:                                       Feb.,1944
   Apo  751. Woodyn' You(r1000)/Rainbow Mist(r1005)
   Apo  752. Yesterdays/Bu-Dee-Daht
   Apo  753. Disorder at the Border(r1003)/Feeling Zero(r1004)

           HAWKINS QUINTET (Coleman Hawkins, tenor sax; Roy Eldridge, trumpet;Teddy
           Wilson, piano; Cozy Cole, drums; Billy Taylor, bass):          Jan.31,1944
   Key  609. 'S Wonderful/I Only Have Eyes for You
   Key  610. I'm in the Mood for Love/Bean at the Met

           COLEMAN HAWKINS QUARTET (Coleman Hawkins, tenor sax; Teddy Wilson,piano;
           Cozy Cole, drums; Israel Crosby, bass):                        Feb.17,1944
   Key  611. Flamethrower/Night and Day
   Key  612. Imagination/Cattin' at Keynote

           COLEMAN HAWKINS AND HIS SAX ENSEMBLE (Tab Smith, alto; Coleman Hawkins,
           Don Byas, tenors; Harry Carney, baritone; Johnny Guarnieri, piano; Sid
           Catlett, drums; Al Lucas, bass):                               May 24,1944
   Key 1308. Louise/On the Sunny Side of the Street

HAWKINS AND HIS 'BAMA STATE COLLEGIANS, ERSKINE (S. Lowe, W. Bascomb, M.Green,
Erskine Hawkins, trumpets; E. Sims, R. Range, trombones; W. Johnson, J.Mitchelle,
altos; P.Bascomb, tenor; H.Henry, baritone sax; A.Parrish, piano; W.McLemore, gui-
tar; J.Morrison, drums; S. Fields, bass):                                 1936-37
   Vo  3280. Until the Real Thing Comes Along/I Can't Escape
   Vo  3289. It Was a Sad Night in Harlem(19578)/Without a Shadow of a Doubt
   Vo  3318. Coquette/Big John Special                                    (19581)
   Vo  3336. Swinging in Harlem/A swingy Little Rhythm
   Vo  3545. Uproar Shout
         "  If You Leave Me                                        -VoE 117
   Vo  3567. Dear Old Southland                                    -VoE 117
         "  Swanee River
   Vo  3668. I Found a New Baby/Red Cap
   Vo  3689. I'll Get Along/I'll See You in My Dreams
   Vo  4072. Carry Me Back/Who's Sorry Now

           (Sub. Julius Dash, saxes, for Paul Bascomb):                   1938
   BB  7810. I'm Madly in Love With You/Miss Hallelujah Brown
   BB  7826. Let This Be a Warning to You/Rockin' Rollers Jubilee
   BB  7839. Weary Blues/King Porter Stomp
   BB 10012. What Do You Know About Love(voc.,Ida James)/Strictly Swing
   BB 10019. Because of You (voc., Jimmie Mitchelle)/Do You Want to Jump Children
```

```
BB 10029. A Study in Blue/Easy Rider
BB 10218. Let the Punishment Fit the Crime(voc.,Mitchelle)/I the Living I
BB 10224. Swing Out/Raid the Joint                              (voc.,Ida James)
BB 10287. Polka Dotty(voc.,Jimmie Mitchelle)/Big Wig in the Wigwam("  "   "  )
BB 10292. No Soap/Swingin' on Lenox Avenue
BB 10364. Weddin' Blues/Hot Platter
BB 10409. Gin Mill Special/Tuxedo Junction
BB 10456. Rehearsal in Love(voc.,Dolores Brown)/Satan Does the Rhumba
BB 10504. More Than You Know(voc.,Dolores Brown)/Uptown Shuffle
BB 10540. Cherry(voc.,Jimmie Mitchelle)                         -BB 30-0819
       "  You Can't Escape From Me
BB 10565. I Hadn't Anyone Till You/Baltimore Bounce
BB 10571. Gabriel Meets the Duke/Whispering Grass(voc., Mitchelle)
BB 10709. Midnight Stroll/Fine and Mellow
BB 10756. Saboo/You Bring Me Down
BB 10790. Junction Blues/Ashes in the Tray
BB 10812. Dolomite/Too Many Dreams
BB 10854. Five o'Clock Whistle/Sweet Georgia Brown
BB 10879. After Hours/Song of the Wanderer
BB 10932. Norfolk Ferry/Put Yourself in My Place
BB 10979. Nona/I Know a Secret
BB 11001. Soft Winds/S'posin'(voc.,Dolores Brown)
BB 11049. Keep Cool Fool/No Use Squawkin'
BB 11161. Tonight You Belong to Me/Rifftime
BB 11192. Who's Beatin' My Time With You/Blackout
BB 11218. Night After Night/Shipyard Ramble
BB 11277. Hey Doc/Someone's Rocking My Dream Boat
BB 11372. Uncle Bud
BB 11419. I Love You Truly(James,Mitchelle,Cap, Bob)/Blue Sea
BB 11439. Sometimes(v.Mitchelle)/I Don't Want to Walk Without You(James)
BB 11485. Wrap Your Troubles in Dreams(Mitchelle)/So Long Shorty(James)
BB 11547. Jumpin' in a Julep Joint/Bicycle Bounce
BB 11564. Tain't No Good/Knock Me a Kiss
BB 30-0813. Bear Mash Blues/Don't Cry Baby
BB 30-0819. Country Boy/(rev., see BB 10540)
```

HAYES' LOUISVILLE STOMPERS, CLIFFORD (Clifford Hayes, trombone; sax; violin; banjo or guitar; piano possibly Earl Hines in some numbers):
```
OK  8269. Get It Fixed Blues(also see Clifford's Louisville Jug Band)
Vi 20955. Blue Guitar Stomp/(rev., Benny Moten)                 -BB 6204
Vi 21489. Bye Bye Blues(42380)/Barefoot Stomp(42392)
Vi 21583. Blue Harmony/(rev., McKinney Cotton Pickers)
Vi 21588. Petter's Stomp/(rev., Benny Moten)
Vi 23346. Tippin' Through/Tenor Guitar Fiend
Vi 23407. Shady Lane Blues/Automobile Blues
Vi 38011. Clef Club Stomp/Blue Trombone Stomp                   -BB 6428
Vi 38514. Frog Hop/Shoe String Stomp
Vi 38529. Everybody Wants My Tootelum/You're Ticklin' Me
Vi 38557. Hey! Am I Blue?/Dance Hall Shuffle
          (See also: Kentucky Jazz Babies)
```

HAYES AND HIS ORCHESTRA, EDGAR (Leonard Davis, Bernard Flood, Henry Goldwin,trumpets; David James, Robert Horton, Clyde Bernhardt, trombones; Rudy Powell, Roger Boyd, Crawford Wethlington, Joe Garland, saxes; Edgar Hayes, piano; Andy Jackson, guitar; Elmer James, bass; Kenneth Clark, drums.--HD):   **1937**
```
Vr   586. Manhattan Jam(m201)/(rev., Johnny Hodges              -Vo 3773
De  1338. Caravan/Edgar Steps Out               -BrE 02448, BrF 505101
De  1382. High Wide and Handsome(62451)/Satan Takes a Holiday(62452)-BrE 02482
De  1527. Old King Cole                         -BrE 02574, BrF 505132
      "   Queen Isabella                        -BrE 02540
De  1416. Stomping at the Renny/Laughing at Life               -BrE 02520
De  1665. Let's Love(62678)/Swingin' in the Promised Land(63159)
De  1748. Sophisticated Swing/Fugitive from a Harem            -BrE 02596
De  1882. Star Dust/In the Mood                                -BrE 02620
De  1940. Barbary Coast Blues                   -BrE 02574, BrF 505132
      "   Meet the Band
De  2048. Shindig(62677)                        -BrE 02540
      "   You're My First Thought Every Morning(63296)
De  2193. Help Me/Without You
```

          EDGAR HAYES QUINTET (Edgar Hayes, piano; Rudy Powell, clarinet; Kenny
          Clark, vibraphone; Andy Jackson, guitar; Elmer James, bass; Bill Darnell, vocals):
```
De  1444. Love Me or Leave Me(62573)                           -BrE 02556
      "   So Rare(62575)                                       -BrE 02495
De  1509. I Know Now(62679)                                    -BrE 02495
      "   When You And I Were Young Maggie(62681)              -BrE 02556
De  1684. Blue Skies/Sweetheart
```

HAYMES AND HIS ORCHESTRA, JOE (Partial suggested personnel for period 1933-34: Toots Mondello, Bud Freeman, D'Andrea   , saxes and clarinet; George Irwin, Roy Wager, Sterling Bose, trumpets; Joe Yukl, Ward Silloway, trombones; Charlie Bush, drums.--RR):

```
Vi 24038. It's About Time
Vi 24353. Cast Your Sins Away/Get Cannibal
HMV 4947. He's a Curbstone Cutie/He's the Life of the Party Now
HMV 4941. Hot Jazz Pie                                            -RZ 806
HMV 6248. My Long White Robe                                      -RZ 773
       "  Pray for the Lights to Go Out
RZ   774. Hell's Bells/One Note Trumpet Player
RZ   805. Let's Have a Party/Rain Rain Go Away
RZ   806. I'm a Ding Dong Daddy
BB  5116. Louisville Lady/Gotta Go                                -Elec 2026
BB  5133. Limehouse Blues/Shine on Harvest Moon
BB  5119. Modern Melody
BB  5178. I Never Knew I Could
BB  5220. Ain't Gonna Grieve No More
BB  5918. The Lady in Red/My Melancholy Baby
BB  5920. Now I'm a Lady/Honeysuckle Rose
BB  6376. Pray for the Lights to Go Out/(rev., Britt Orchestra)
Co  2704. Let's Have a Party/The Old Man of the Mountain
Co  2716. When I Put on My Long White Robe/Ain't Gonna Pay No Toll
Co  2739. Jazz Pie/One Note Trumpet Player
Co  2781. I Cover the Waterfront/Uncle Joe's Music Store
Co  2784. Just Give Me the Girl/I Ain't Gonna Grieve No More

        (Leo White,clarinet; Edward Sarason, alto sax; Ben Harrod, baritone sax;
        Freddy Fallensby, tenor sax; Zeke Zarchey, Gordon Griffin, Cliff Weston,
        trumpets; Mike Michaels, Frank Llewelyn, trombones; Billy Miller, piano;
        Felix Giobbe, bass; Jack Maisel, drums.--RR):                1935-36
Vo  3369. St. Louis Blues/Should I                                -VoE 21
Vo  3307. That's a Plenty/Sister Kate                             -VoE C0001
Vo  3335. Doin' the Suzy-Q/The Wedding of Mr. and Mrs. Swing
Ba 33439. The Lady in Red(17282; voc.,Cliff Wetterau)/To Call You My Own(17284;
Ba 351007. Nana/Oh You Sweet Thing                          (voc.,S.Palmer)
Ro  2547. Lost Motion/Swingin' for the King                       -Me 13451
Cq  8552. I'm on a See Saw/The Gentleman Doesn't Believe
Me 13067. Dames/Rolling in Love
Me 13108. Have a little Dream on Me/The Bathtub Ran Over Again
Me 13305. Squeeze Me(15356)/Goblin Market(16160)
Me 60207. Music Goes 'Round and 'Round/Rhythm in My Nursery Rhymes
Me 60211. I Wanna Woo/Polly Wolly Doodle
Me 60305. On the Alamo/I Love to Ride the Horses
Me 60404. Wah Hoo(18581; voc.,Cliff Weston & Headliners/I'm Gonna Clap My Hands
Me 60405. Am I Gonna Have Trouble/That Never To Be Forgotton Moment
Me 60508. No Greater Love(18805;voc.,Jane Dover/I'll Stand By(18807;voc.,J.Dover)
Me 60509. Christopher Columbus/I'se a Muggin'
Me 60611. You Better Play Ball With Me(18948)/I've Got a Heavy Date(18951;voc.,
Me 60612. All Right All Right/Tormented                     (Skeeter Palmer)

        (Clyde Rogers, Nick Ciazza, Hank Haupt, John Langford, saxes; Max Herman,
        Dave Frankel, Sid Felstein, trumpets; Mike Michaels, Ronny Chase, trom-
        bones; Charles Bush, drums; Dick Newman, bass; Max Chieckes, guitar;
        Frank Cohen, piano; Barbara Burns, vocals):                 1937
Me 60801. Small Town Gal/You Can't Pull the Wool Over My Eyes
Me 60806. River Man/No Regrets
Me 61013. Bye Bye Baby/Without a Shadow of a Doubt
Me 61105. Organ Grinders Swing/Papa Tree Top Tall
Me 61112. Sitting on the Moon/Lost in My Dreams
Me 61211. You're Too Sure of Me/Moon Is Grinning at Me

        (Sub. Hawk Kogan, sax, for Ciazza; Charlie Zimmerman, Glenn Taft, trum-
        pets for Herman, Felstein; Kappy Crouse, trombone; Max Goodman, bass;Sam-
        my Parker, drums; Conrad Launave, piano; Chieckes doubling on trombone):
Me 70207. One Two Button Your Shoe/Right or Wrong                 1938
Me 70213. Will You/Call to Arms
Me 70514. Slap That Bass/Let's Call the Whole Thing Off
Me 70803. Got a Pair of New Shoes(21067)/Sun Showers(21230)voc.,Clyde Rogers

        HAYMES HARLEM SYNCOPATORS (Unknown personnel):
BS  2059. You Ought to See My Baby/Lantern of Love

HAYTON'S BLUE FOUR, LEONARD:
Vo 15705. Old Fashioned Girl/Anytime Anyday Anywhere

        LENNIE HAYTON AND HIS ORCHESTRA:
Vo  5421. One Cigarette for Two/I Love You Too Much
Vo  5471. Times Square Scuttle/AC DC Current
De  1284. Carelessly/It Looks Like Rain in Cherry Blossom Lane
De  1267. I Know Now/You Can't Run Away from Love
De  1268. Lady Who Wouldn't Be Kissed/Night Over Shanghai
De  1341. What a Beautiful Beginning/Gone With the Wind
De  1348. Can I Forget You/Folks Who Live on the Hill
De  1354. Lovely One/That Old Feeling
De  1437. Make a Wish/So Many Memories
De  1443. Morning After/Once in a While
```

HAZEL AND HIS BIENVILLE ROOF ORCHESTRA, MONK (Sharkey Bonano, trumpet and leader; Freddie Neumann, piano; Hal Jordy, sax; Joe Capraro, guitar; Monk Hazel, drums; Luther Lamar, bass; Sidney Arodin, clarinet):   New Orleans,1928
Br 4181. Sizzling the Blues/High Society
Br 4182. Ideas(mellophone by Monk Hazel)/Git-Wit-It

HEGAMIN AND THE DIXIE DAISIES, LUCILLE
Ca 254. I've Got What It Takes/Can't Get Lovin'
Ca 270. Aggravatin' Papa/Beale Street Mama
Ca 287. Papa Papa/He May Be Your Man
Ca 343. Waitin' for the Evening Mail/Now You've Got
Ca 354. Wet Yo Thumb/Two Time Dan
Ca 366. Syncopating Mama/Your Man
Ca 461. You May Be Fast But Mama's Gonna Slow You Down/If You Don't Give Me
Ca 777. My Sugar/I'd Someone Else   (What I Want

    LUCILLE HEGAMIN AND HER BLUE FLAME SYNCOPATORS:
BS 2049. He May Be Your Man/I've Got the Wonder Where He Want Blues -Ba 1048
BS 2032. Arkansas Blues/Jazz Me Blues   -Ba 1014
Arto 9053. I'll Be Good/Arkansas Blues
Arto 9058. He's My Man/Mama Whip Mama Spank
Arto 9105. Washboard Blues/Mississippi Blues
Arto 9129. He May Be Your Man/You've Had Your Day

    LUCILLE HEGAMIN (acc. by Clarence Williams Band):
Co 14164. Senorita Mine/Nobody But My Baby

HEIDT AND HIS MUSICAL KNIGHTS, HORACE (Bobby Hackett, Warren Lewis, Frank Strassek, Jerry Borshard, trumpets; Wayne Webb, trombone; Bob Riedel, George Dessinger, Jimmy DeMeo, Jerry Kasper, saxes; Henry Russell, novachord; Frankie Carle, piano; Bernie Mattinson, drums; Eddie McKinney, bass; Bob Knight electric guitar;Beatrice Perron, Virginia Drane, Mary Drane, violins):
Co 35250. Can I Help It(wco26161)/Last Night(wco26162) voc., Larry Cotton
Co 35446. Little Curly Hair in a High Chair/A Lover's Lullaby, voc., L.Cotton

HENDERSON, ALMA (vocal with piano and guitar):
OK 8489. Mine's As Good As Yours/Soul and Body

HENDERSON, BERTHA (vocal with Will Ezell,piano; D.C.Nelson, cornet):
Para 12511. Black Bordered Letter(794)/Six Thirty Blues(795)

    (Guitar by Blind Blake):
Para 12645. Terrible Murder Blues(20557-2)/So Sorry Blues(20550-1)
Para 12655. Lead Hearted Blues/Let Your Love Come Down
Para 12697. Leavin' Gal Blues/Lonesome

    (With Leonard Davis Trio and Charley Lawson):
OK 8265. Discouraged Blues/Jamboree Blues

HENDERSON, EDMONIA (vocal accompanied by Lovie Austin and Her Blues Serenaders: Tommy Ladnier,trumpet; Jimmy O'Bryant, clarinet; Lovie Austin, piano):
Para 12084. Black Man Blues(1601)/Worried 'Bout Him Blues(1603)

    (Add saxaphone):
Para 12095. Brownskin Man(1689)/Traveling Blues(1690)
Para 12097. If You Sheik on Your Mama/(rev., Ida Cox)
Para 12203. Mama Don't Want Sweet Man Anymore(1691)/Hateful Blues(1692)
Para 12239. Jelly Roll Blues(1897)/Lazy Daddy Blues(1905; add trombone; banjo)

    (Acc. by Johnny Dodds, clarinet; piano.--EW):   April 20,1926
Vo 1015. Nobody Else Will Do(e2881-82w)/Who's Gonna Do Your Loving?(e2879-80w)

    (Jelly Roll Morton, piano; cornet; tenor sax.--EW):   July 21,1926
Vo 1043. Dead Man Blues(e3576-77w)/Georgia Grind(e3574-75w)

FLETCHER HENDERSON

For records under other names see:
BALTIMORE BELL HOPS: Co 2449.
FAE BARNES: Para 12209.
AMANDA BROWN: Co 3901.
BESSIE BROWN: Co 3975.
GLADYS BRYANT: Para 12031.
CARROLL CLARK: Co 128.
CLUB ALABAM: Do 354, 370, 371, 426.
CLUB WIGWAM: Do 3458.
CONNIE'S INN ORCHESTRA: Vi 22698, 22721; Me 12145, 12216, 12239, 12340;Cr 3093, 3107, 3180, 3191, 3212.
IDA COX: Para 12251, 12258, 12263; Vo 05298, 05258.

BIG NEWS

from

BASIN STREET

DOWN where jazz was born, things are happening NOW! Organized in the summer of 1944, the NATIONAL JAZZ FOUNDATION invites you to be among the first to share in a movement of prime importance to jazz enthusiasts everywhere.

Its purpose is to establish a National Museum of Jazz, to preserve and develop the history of jazz, to immortalize its creators, to foster and encourage contemporary jazzmen and their music.

You may become a sustaining member NOW by sending in the coupon below—or you may write for brochure with complete details. If you are a member of a jazz club in your community, have it affiliated with the Foundation. WRITE US TODAY!

NATIONAL JAZZ FOUNDATION, INC.
610 HIBERNIA BLDG.,   NEW ORLEANS 12, LA.

Here is my check for $3.00, for sustaining membership during the fiscal year 1944-45.

Name ....

Address ....

KATIE CRIPPEN: BS 2003, 2018.
DIXIE JAZZ BAND: Or 1100, 10⁻¹.
DIXIE STOMPERS: All.
BENNY GOODMAN: Co 35319, 35410, 35820, 35916.
BENNY GOODMAN SEXTET: Co 35254, 35320.
GRANT AND WILSON: Para 12317, 12324, 12337.
EDDIE GRAY: BS 2011.
HORACE HENDERSON: De 18171, 18172; some Vocalions and Okehs.
ROSA HENDERSON: Vi 19124, 19157; Vo 14635, 14682, 14708, 14795, 14821, 14825, 14831, 14832, 14852; Br 2589, 2612; Co 3958.
EDNA HICKS: Vo 14650, Para 12090.
SAM HILL: Or 303, 347, 374.
ALBERTA HUNTER: BS 2008; Para 12021, 12018, 12036, 12017, 12043, 12065.
MARY JACKSON: Pat 21059.
MAGGIE JONES: Co 14050, 14055, 14059, 14063, 14074, 14139.
EMMA LEWIS: Vi 19158.
LOUISIANA STOMPERS: Para 12550.
VIOLA McCOY: Br 2591.
OZIE McPHERSON: Para 12355, 12362.
HAZEL MEYERS: Vo 14709, 14725.
JOSIE MILES: Ge 5359.
JULIA MOODY: BS 14122.
NEWPORT SYNCOPATORS: VD 81879.
MA RAINEY: Para 12238, 12252, 12332, 12338, 12357, 12374, 12352, 12364.
INEZ RICHARDSON: BS 2023.
ROSELAND DANCE ORCHESTRA: Apex 8716, Do 3445.
SAVANNAH SYNCOPATORS: Br 6176.
BESSIE SMITH: Co 3900, 3936, 3939, 3942, 13007, 14075, 14133, 14158, 14115, 14137, 14147, 14158, 14172, 14179, 14197, 14219, 14232, 14209, 14569, 14292, 14304, 14312, 14324, 14338.
CLARA SMITH: Co 3966, 3943, 3991, 4000, 14058, 14062, 14077, 14073, 12-D.
TRIXIE SMITH: Para 12208, 12211, 12232, 12249, 12256, 12262, 12330, 12336.
SOUTHAMPTON SOCIETY ORCHESTRA: Pe 14395.
SOUTHERN SERENADERS: Ha 4, 5.
STOKERS OF HADES: Co 2615.
CHARLIE STRAIGHT: Br 3224.
HANNAH SYLVESTER: Majestic 1520; Para 12033, 12034.
ETHEL WATERS: BS 2010, 2021, 2038, 14117, 14120; Co 379, 14093.
LULU WHITBY: BS 2005.
HAL WHYTE: Do 3444.
GEORGE WILLIAMS: Co 3974, 14002, 14046, 14015, 14017.
DUKE WILSON: Pe 15603, 15753.
LENA WILSON: Vo 14631, 14651; BS 14129.

<u>HENDERSON, FLETCHER</u> (piano solos):
  BS 2026. Unknown Blues(p148)/(rev., James P. Johnson)
  BS ⁻116. Chimes Blues/I Want To   -Para 12143

(Special Note: Because of so many concurrent recordings on different labels, the Fletcher Henderson section can not be handled as a strictly numerical list. Rather, the following should be considered as several lists, grouped more or less according to personnel changes and recording dates):

HENDERSON AND HIS CLUB ALABAM ORCHESTRA, FLETCHER (Howard Scott, Elmer Chambers trumpets; Charlie Green, trombone; Buster Bailey, clarinet and alto sax; Don Redman, alto sax; Coleman Hawkins, tenor sax; Fletcher Henderson, piano; Charlie Dixon, banjo; Bob Escudero, bass; Kaiser Marshall, drums.--HD):   1922
  BS 2022. Fancies(154)/My Oriental Rose(138)
  BS 2025. Gypsy Blues(15121)/Sweet Lady(15124)
  BS 2034. Shake It and Break It(838)/Aunt Hagar's Children Blues(837)
  BS 2043. The Sheik of Araby(956)/Who'll Be the Next(906)
  BS 2055. Strut Miss Lizzie/Home Again Blues
  BS 2100. Tomorrow/Baby Girl
  BS 10075. Blue Bamboo/Bamboo Isle
  Em 10713. Mam's Gonna Slow You Down(42526)/Oh Sister Ain't That Hot(42534)
  Em 10714. Steppin' Out(42525)
  Em 10744. Chattanooga/Ghost of the Blues

      FLETCHER HENDERSON AND HIS ORCHESTRA:
  Ed 51276. Shake Your Feet
  Ed 51277. Linger Awhile(9267)/(rev., Stevens Trio)
  Maj 1434. Down By the River   -Olympic 1434
  Para 20226. Beale Street Mama(1392
        "   Don't Think You'll Be Missed(1393)   -Pu 1393, Bwy, Tri 11247
  Para 20235. Down Hearted Blues(1406)/Gulf Coast Blues(1413)   -Tri "
  Para 20251. My Sweetie Went Away(1459)
  Para 20339. I Can't Get the One I Want   -Pu, Na 12251
  Bu 11255. When You Walked Out(1414)   -Max 1515
      "   Walking   -Pu 11239, Tri 11255

NEW • USED • OUT OF PRINT • ORIGINALS • REISSUES OF HOT JAZZ CLASSICS • SEND YOUR WANT LIST • SET PRICES ON ALL ITEMS • PHOTOGRAPHS • MAGAZINES • BOOKS •

the jazz man
RECORD SHOP
1221 VINE STREET
HOLLYWOOD 38, CALIFORNIA
MARILI MORDEN • PROPRIETOR

```
Vo 14636.  Gulf Coast Blues(11662-3)/Down Hearted Blues(11664-5)    June 28,1923
Vo 14654.  Dicty Blues(11817-9)/Do Doodle Oom(11820-2)               Aug.9,1923
Vo 14691.  Just Hot(12079-81)/Down South Blues(12088-9)              Oct.5 and 6,1923
                                                                     Oct.27 and Nov.30,1923
Vo 14726.  You've Got to Get Hot(12197-99)                           -Gu 7000
    "      Charleston Crazy(12376)
Vo 14740.  Potomac River Blues(12484-5)/Old Black Joe's Blues(12482-3)Dec.22,1923
Vo 14759.  Lots o' Mama(12654-5)/Cotton Picker's Ball(12651-3)       Jan.29,1924
Vo 14788.  Chicago Blues(12930-32)/Feeling the Way I Do(12933-35)    Mar.25,1924
                                                                     Apr.15,1924
Vo 14800.  Mobile Blues(13025-7)                                     -Gu 7000
    "      Tea Pot Dome Blues(13023-4)
Vo 14828.  Strutter's Drag(13233-4)/I Don't Know(13230-32)           May 21,1924
Vo 14838.  Do That Thing(13273-5)/Broken Busted Blues(13276-8)       May 28,1924
Vo 14859.  Gouge of Armour Ave.(13446-8)/Hard Hearted Hannah(13449-51)July 31,1924
                                                                     Aug.29,1924
Vo 14880.  Meanest Kind o' Blues(13631-2)                            -Gu 7007
    "      New Kind of Man(13629-30)
Vo 14892.  Forsaken Blues(13756-8)/Cold Mammas(13759-61)
Br  2592.  Sud Bustin' Blues/War Horse Mama
Aj 17011.  Dicty Blues/(rev., Seven Brown Babies)
Aj 17016.  Bull Blues/Lonesome Journey Blues
Aj 17017.  Chattanooga/I'm Gonna See You
Aj 17022.  Old Black Joe's Blues/Mistreatin' Daddy
Aj 17023.  House Rent Ball(31508)/Darktown Has a Gay White Way(31510)
Aj 17030.  I'm Crazy Over You/Mama Papa and You
Gu  7007.  Savannah/(rev., See Vo 14880, above)
Im  1332.  Oh Eva(5566)                                              -Ba 1375
Rad 1173.  Down Hearted Blues
Re  8441.  On a Night Like This                                      -Do 4063
Re  8442.  There's a Rickety Rackety Shack                -Im 1858, Do 4062
Re  8455.  Sorry(7638)/(rev., Fred Rich)                  -Ap 8716, Do 4075
Re  9655.  Jimminy Gee/(rev., Sam Lanin)
Re  9658.  Feeling the Way I Do(5497)                                -Ap 8194
    "      Red Hot Mama(5498)
Re  9668.  You Know Me Alabam'(5535)/(rev.,Nathan Glantz)            -Ba 1372
Re  9673.  Wait Till You See My Gal(5533)                            -Ba 1373
    "      Jealous(5532)                                             -Ba 1372
Re  9680.  Charley My Boy(5570)/(rev.,Missouri Jazz Band)-Ba 1383,Im 1321,Ap 8250
Re  9681.  Hard Hearted Hannah(5554)/(rev., Sam Lanin)    -Im 1329, Ba 1383
Re  9682.  I Can't Get the One I Want(5534)/(rev.,6 Black Diamonds)  -Ba 1384
Re  9683.  The Grass Is Always Greener(5562)                         -Ba 1388
Re  9684.  Where the Dreamy Wabash Flows(5561)/(rev.,Lanin) -Ap 8230, Ba 1388
Pat 036027. Shake Your Feet(105030)/Swanee River(105031)             -Pe 14208
Pat 036042. Old Black Joe's Blues                         -Ro 837, Pe 14223
    "      31st Street Blues                                         "
Pat 036069. Chicago Blues(105120)/Why Put the Blame 'on You(105121)  -Pe 14250
Pat 036083. After the Storm(105289)/(rev., Casino Orchestra)         -Pe 14264
Pat 036084. I Wish I Could Make You Cry(105221)
    "      Say Say Sadie                                             -Pe 14265
Pat 036090. Driftwood(105290)/(rev., Piedmont Orchestra)             -Pe 14271
Co  3951.  Gulf Coast Blues(81019)/Midnight Blues(81071)
Co  3995.  Dicty Blues(81211)/Do Doodle Oom(81212)
Co   126.  My Papa Doesn't Two Time No Time(81691)/Somebody Stole My Gal(81692)
Co   164.  Muscle Shoals Blues(81839)/Houston Blues(81838)
Co   202.  That's Georgia(81948)/You'll Never Get to Heaven(81949)
Co   209.  He's the Hottest Man in Town(81981)/I Never Care 'Bout Tomorrow
                                                                     (81982)
```

(ADD LOUIS ARMSTRONG, TRUMPET)

```
Co   228.  Manda(140092)/Go 'Long Mule(140093)                       Oct.7,1924
Co   249.  The Meanest Kind of Blues(140138)/Naughty Man(140139)     Oct.14,1924
Co   292.  Bye and Bye(140356)/Play Me Slow(140357)                  Jan.23,1925

           (Russell and Joe Smith, Armstrong, trumpets):             May 19,1925
Co   383.  I'll Take Her Back(140616)                                -Co 35669
    "      Money Blues(140617)
                                                                     May 29,1925
Co   395.  Sugar Foot Stomp(140639)                       -Vo 3322, Co 35668
    "      What-Cha-Call-'em Blues(140640)                -Vo 3323,      "
Co   509.  T N T (141170)/Pensacola(141171)                          Oct.21,1925

           (Armstrong, trumpet; dates unknown):
Para 20367. Prince of Wails                                          -Pu 11367
    "      Mandy Make Up Your Mind(1974)                  -Max 1517,
Re  9739.  How Come You Do Me Like You Do(5728-1)/(rev.,N.O.Jazz Band) -Ba 1443
Re  9753.  One of These Days(5712)                                   -Ba 1457
Re  9767.  My Dream Man(5713-1)/(rev.,Imperial Jazz Band)            -Ba 1475
Re  9770.  Why Couldn't It Be Poor Little Me(5811)                   -Ap 8316
Re  9774.  Everybody Loves My Baby(5748-3)/(rev.,Sam Lanin) -Aj 17109, Im 1476
Re  9775.  Araby(5731-1)
    "      I'll See You in My Dreams(5810-1)              -Im 1454, Aj 17114
```

51

```
Re   9789. Alabama Bound(5835)                                    -Im 1420, Ba 1488
Re   9803. Swanee Butterfly(5836-2)/(rev.,Moulin    e)            -Ba 1508, Do 3475
Ap   8309. Alabamy Bound(21045b)
Pat 036156. My Rose Marie(105605-1)/(rev., Sam La   )             -Pe 14337
Pat 036157. Tell Me Dreamy Eyes(105604-1)/Shanghai Shuffle(105607-1) -Pe 14338
Pat 036213. Me Neenyah(105831-1)                                  -Pe 14364
Pat 036214. Poplar Street Blues(105829)/12th Street Blues(105830) -Pe 14395*
              *Issued under name of Southampton Society Orchestra
Vo  14926. Copenhagen(two masters)/Words(13924-25-26)             Oct.20,1924
Vo  14935. Shanghai Shuffle(13949-50-51)/Naughty Man(13952-53-54) Nov.7,1924
Vo  15030. Memphis Bound/When You Do What You Do                  Dates unknown
```

(OMIT ARMSTRONG)

```
Vo  15174. Hay Foot Straw Foot/Peaceful Valley
Vo  15204. Dinah/I Want You to Cheer Me Up
Vo  15205. I Want to See a Little More/Let Me Introduce You       -Br 3026
Para 12486. Swamp Blues(2827)/Off to Buffalo(2828)                -Re 8360?
Ge   3285. When Spring Comes Peeping Through
Ge   3286. Honey Bunch
Re   9948. Sleepy Time Gal(6293)                                  -Ba 1639, Do 3613, Ap 8419
Re   9961. Then I'll Be Happy(6297)                               -Ba 1654, Do 3625, Ge 10094?
Ca   9033. Old Black Joe's Blues
  "        All By Yourself                                        -Li 3491, Ro 837
Ca   9175. Raisin' the Roof(3799)                                 -Li 3202, Ro 977
Ro    976. Freeze and Melt(3798)                                  -Li 3201
Co    532. Nobody's Rose(141410)/Pensacola(141411)
```

        (Russell Smith, Joe Smith, Rex Stewart, trumpets; Charlie Green,trombone;
        Buster Bailey, clarinet; Don Redman, alto sax; Coleman Hawkins, tenor
        sax; Fats Waller or Fletcher Henderson, piano; Charlie Dixon, banjo;
        June Coles, bass; Kaiser Marshall, drums.--   :   1926
```
Co    654. The Stampede(142205)
  "        Jackass Blues(142206)                                  -Co 35669
```

        (Sub. Tommy Ladnier, trumpet, for Stewart):
```
Co    817. The Henderson Stomp(142902)
  "        The Chant(142903; Waller, organ)                       -CoE 4421, CoE 5030
Co    854. Sweet Thing(143125)
  "        I Need Lovin'(143126)                                  -CoE 4417
Co    970. Tozo(143345)
  "        Rocky Mountain Blues(143344)                           -CoE 4421, CoE 5030
```

        (Add Jimmy Harrison, trombone):
```
Co   1002. P.D.Q. Blues(144063)                                   -CoE 4560
  "        Livery Stable Blues(144064)           -PaE 2283,           "
Co   1059. Whiteman Stomp(144132)/I'm Comin' Virginia(144133)     -CoE 4561
                                                                  Apr.27,1927
Vi  20944. St. Louis Shuffle(38496)/Variety Stomp(38497)          -BB 10246
```

        (Next two sides without Harrison):   Dec. 8,1926
```
Vo   1065. Clarinet Marmalade(e4182-83w--e20988-89)
                             (-Vo 15497, Br 3406, BrF 500388, BrE 2634
  "        Hot Mustard(e4184-85w--e20990-91)
                             (-Vo 15497, Br 3406, BrF 500388, BrE 2001
                                                                  Jan.22,1927
Br   3460. Stockholm Stomp(e21421-22)/Have It Ready(e21423-24; Waller, pf)
                                                                  (-Vo 15532
                                                                  Jan.19,1927
Vo   1079. Some of These Days(e4397-98-99w)/Baby Won't You Please Come Homr
                                                                  (e4394-95-96w)
                                                                  Mar.19,1927
Vo   1092. Fidgety Feet(e22024-25)/Sensation(e22027-28-29)  -UHCA 22/21,Vo 2710
Br   3521. Fidgety Feet(e22026), same coupling
```

        (Sub. Don Pasquall, sax, for Redman):   Chicago,Sept.14,1928
```
Br   4119. Hop Off(o2315)/(rev., Broadway Broadcasters)
```

        (Sub. Bobby Stark, trumpet, for Ladnier; Carmello Jejo,clarinet,for Bailey):
```
Co   1543. King Porter Stomp(145763)/D Natural Blues(145764)
Co  35670. Hop Off(144955)                                        Nov.4,1927
```

        (Sub. Rex Stewart, trumpet, for Joe Smith; Benny Morton, trombone, for
        Green; Benny Carter, alto, for Redman; omit Bailey):
```
Co   1913. Blazin'(148540)                                        -Vo 3323
  "        Wang Wang Blues(148541)                                -Vo 3360
Co  14392. Come On Baby(147421)/Easy Money(147422)
```

        (Sub. Claude Jones, trombone, for Morton; add Harvey Boone, alto sax;
        Clarence Holiday, guitar,; John Kirby, bass; Walter Johnson,drums.--HD):

```
                                                                    1930
Co  2329. Chinatown My Chinatown(150857)                    -PaE 1399
     "    Somebody Loves Me(150858)
Co  2352. Keep a Song in Your Soul(150997)/What Good Am I Without You(150998)
Co  2414. I've Found What I Wanted in You(151274)
     "    Sweet and Hot(151277)                             -PaE 1478

        (Sub. Benny Morton for Harrison; Russell Procope for Carter):
Co  2513. Clarinet Marmalade(151441)/Sugar Foot Stomp(151442)   -CoE 367

        (Sub. Edgar Sampson, alto sax, for Boone; J.C. Higginbotham,trombone,for
        Jones):
Co  2559. Blues in My Heart(151847)                          -CoE 132
     "    Sugar(151848)                           -PaE 1311,
Co  2565. Singin' the Blues(151845)/It's the Darnedest Thing(151846) -CoE 139

        (See Co 2329 for personnel, next two sides):
Co  2586. My Gal Sal(151275)                     -Vo 3360, CoF 847, PaE 1196
     "    My Pretty Girl(151276)                           "   , PaE 1139

        (Sub. Sandy Williams, trombone, for Morton; guitar unknown): Dec.9,1932
Co  2732. Honeysuckle Rose(152324)/Underneath the Harlem Moon(152326) -CoE 584
OK 41565. New King Porter Stomp(152325)                    -CoE 701, Co 35671

        (Russell Smith, Bobby Stark, Henry Allen, trumpets; Claude Jones, Dicky
        Wells, trombones; Hilton Jefferson, Russell Procope, Coleman Hawkins,
        Saxes; Fletcher or Horace Henderson, piano; Bernard Addison, guitar; John
        Kirby, bass; Walter Johnson, drums):                          1932
CoE  678. Queer Notions(265135)                               -De 18169
     "    It's the Talk of the Town(265136)         -Co 2825, De 18253
CoE  727. Night Life(265137)                                  -De 18254
     "    Nagasaki(265138)                         -Vo 3322, Co 2825, De 18253
CoE  701. I've Got to Sing a Torch Song(265155)               -De 18254
PaE 1717. Ain't Cha Glad(265154)/(rev., Chocolate Dandies)
PaE 1743. I'm Rhythm Crazy Now(265151)/(rev., Chocolate Dandies)  -De 18171
PaE 1766. Ol' Man River(265152)                               -De 18172
PaE 1792. Happy Feet(265150)/(rev., Chocolate Dandies)        -De 18172
PaE 2031. Minnie the Moocher's Wedding Day(265153)            -De 18171

        (Russell Smith, Bobby Stark, Rex Stewart, trumpets; Benny Morton, Claude
        Jones, trombones; Russell Procope, Coleman Hawkins, Edgar Sampson, saxes;
        Fletcher Henderson, piano; Clarence Holiday, guitar; John Kirby, bass;
        Walter Johnson, drums; Dick Robertson, vocals.--HD):          1931
Vi 22775. Sweet Music(70141)                                -GrF 6390
     "    Malinda's Weddin' Day(70143)             -HMV 4911, BB 5518
Vi 22786. Oh It Looks Like Rain(70140)
     "    My Sweet Tooth Says I Wanna(70142)                 -HMV 4911
Vi 22955. Strangers(71938; voc., John Dickens)
     "    I Wanna Count Sheep(71942; voc., H. Lattimore)
Vi 24008. Take Me Away from the River(71939)
     "    Poor Old Joe(71943)                                -BB 5518

        (Sub. Joe Thomas, Henry Allen, trumpets, for Rex Stewart, Stark; Keg
        Johnson, trombone, for Morton; Hilton Jefferson, sax, for Sampson, add
        Buster Bailey, clarinet and sax; Bernard Addison, guitar; John Kirby
        bass; Vic Engle, drums):                          New York,Mar.6, 1934
Vi 24699. Phantom Fantasie(81788)/Harlem Madness(81789)     -HMV 6515
BB  5682. Hocus Pocus(81787)                                -BB 10247
     "    Tidal Wave(81790)                                 -HMV 6562

        (Richard Vance, Joe Thomas, Roy Eldridge, trumpets; Ferdinand Arbello,
        Edward Cuffee, trombones; Buster Bailey, clarinet and alto sax; Omer
        Simeon, Elmer Williams, Chu Berry, saxes; Fletcher or Horace Henderson,
        piano; Bob Lessey, guitar; Israel Crosby, bass; Sidney Catlett, drums):
                                                          Chicago,Apr.9,1936
Vi 25297. Moonrise on the Lowlands(100361)/I'm a Fool for Lovin' You(100360)
Vi 25317. Jangled Nerves(100365)                            -HMV 4470
     "    I'm Always in Love With You(100362)               -HMV 8449

        (Sub. Jerome Pasquall, alto sax, for Simeon):
Vi 25334. Do You or Don't You Love Me(100558)/Where There's You There's Me
                                                       (100557  -HMV 8654
Vi 25339. Grand Terrace Rhythm(100559)                      -HMV 8649
     "    Riffin'(100560)                                   -HMV 8470

        (Sub. Walter Johnson, drums):
Vi 25373. Until Today(100884)
     "    Knock Knock(100885)                               -HMV 8491
Vi 25375. Sing Sing Sing(100883)                            -HMV 8649
     "    Shoe Shine Boy(100882)                            -HMV 8491
Vi 25379. Jimtown Blues(100886)/You Can Depend on Me(100887) -HMV 8647
```

(Russell Smith, Bobby Stark, Henry Allen, trumpets; Sandy Williams, Dicky Wells, trombones; Hilton Jefferson, Russell Procope, Coleman Hawkins, saxes; Horace Henderson, piano; Bernard Addison, guitar; John Kirby, bass; Walter Johnson, drums):

Vo	2527. Yeah Man(13827)	-BrE 01659,	BrF 500377
"	King Porter Stomp(13828)	-BrE 01758,	"
Vo	2583. Queer Notions(13829)	-BrE 01758,	BrF 500387
"	Can You Take It(13830)	-BrE 01659,	"
Co	35671. Can You Take It(second master)		

(Russell Smith, Irving Randolph, Henry Allen, trumpets; Keg Johnson, Claude Jones, trombones; Hilton Jefferson, Russell Procope, Buster Bailey Ben Webster, saxes; Fletcher or Horace Henderson, piano; Lawrence Lucie, guitar; Elmer James, bass; Walter Johnson, drums.--HD): **1934**

De	157. Limehouse Blues(38598)	-BrE 01985
"	Wrappin' It Up(38604)	-BrE 02039
De	158. Shanghai Shuffle(38599)	-BrE 01904
"	Memphis Blues(38605)	-BrE 02119
De	213. Tidal Wave(38602)	-BrE 02119
"	Down South Camp Meeting(38603)	-BrE 01904
De	214. Big John's Special(38600)	-BrE 01985
"	Happy As the Day Is Long(38601)	-BrE 02039

(Add Benny Carter, alto sax):

De	342. Rug Cutter's Swing(38724)	-BrE 01974
"	Wild Party	-BrE 02511
De	555. Hotter than 'ell(38725a)	-BrE 01974
"	Liza(38728a)	

(Richard Vance, Joe Thomas, Roy Eldridge, trumpets; Ferdinand Arbello, Edward Cuffee, trombones; Buster Bailey, clarinet and alto sax; Scoops Carey, alto sax; Elmer Williams, Chu Berry, tenors; Horace Henderson, piano; Bob Lessey, guitar; John Kirby, bass; Sidney Catlett,drums.--HD): **1936**

Vo 3211. Christopher Columbus(c1331)/Blue Lou(c1333) -BrE 02190, BrF 500651

(Fletcher Henderson, piano):

Vo 3213. Stealing Apples/Grand Terrace Swing -BrE 02238, BrF 500652

(Russell Smith, Richard Vance, Emmett Berry, trumpets; George Washington, J.C. Higginbotham, Edward Cuffee, trombones; Jerry Blake, Hilton Jefferson, Elmer Williams, Chu Berry, saxes; Fletcher Henderson, piano; Lawrence Lucie, guitar; Israel Crosby, bass; Walter Johnson,drums):**Mar,1937**

Vo	3485. Slummin' on Park Avenue(20754)/What Will I Tell My Heart(20752)	
Vo	3487. It's Wearin' Me Down(20753)	
"	Rhythm of the Tambourine(20755)	-VoE 90
Vo	3511. Back in Your Own Back Yard(20858)	-VoE 88
"	Rose Room(20859)	-VoE 167, BrF 500705
Vo	3534. Stampede(20857)	-VoE 90, BrF 500705
"	Great Caesar's Ghost(20860)	-VoE 86

(Sub. Albert Wynn, John McConnell, trombones, for Higginbotham, Washington; Pete Suggs, drums):

Vo	3627. If You Ever Should Leave	
"	Posin'	-VoE 109
Vo	3641. Chris and His Gang	-VoE 109
"	All God's Chillun Got Rhythm	

(Omit Chu Berry):

Vo	3713. Worried Over You	
"	Let 'er go	-VoE 129
Vo	3760. What's Your Story	-VoE 129
"	Trees	
Vo	3850. If It's the Last Thing I Do(21940)/You're in Love With Love(21942)	
Vo	4125. Sing You Sinners/Laughing Boy Blues	
Vo	4154. Saving Myself for You/It's the Little Things That Count	
Vo	4167. There's Rain in My Eyes/What Do You Hear	
Vo	4180. Don't Let the Rhythm Go to Your Head(c2231)/Moten Stomp(c2236)	

(Personnel unknown):

Co 36214. Let's Go Home(co30307)/I Like My Sugar Sweet(co30310)
Co 36289. A Pixie from Dixie(co30308)/We Go Well Together(co30309)

HENDERSON AND HIS ORCHESTRA, HORACE (Dalbert Bright, Willie Randall, Elmer Williams, Dave Young, saxes; Peewee Jackson, Ray Nance, Emmett Berry, trumpets; Edward Fant, Nat Atkins, trombones; Horace Henderson, piano; Hurley Rawey, guitar; Oliver Coleman, drums; Jesse Simpkins, bass; Fletcher Henderson, conductor):

Vo	5433. Oh Boy I'm in the Groove(sc2964; voc.,Jefferson)/Kitty on Toast(wc2965)	
Vo	5518. Shufflin' Joe(wc2963)/(Got Rhythm(wc2966; voc.,Viola Jefferson)	
Vo	5579. Honeysuckle Rose	
Vo	5606. You're Mine You(wc3048; voc.,Viola Jefferson)/Swingin' & Jumpin'	
OK	5632. Chloe(wc3050)/(rev., John Kirby)	(wc3051)
OK	5748. When Dreams Come True(wc3270)/Flinging a Whing Ding(wc3273)	
OK	5841. I Still Have My Dreams(wc3271)/Coquette(wc3274)	

          (Harold Johnson, Emmett Berry, Joe Keyes, trumpets; Howard Johnson, Bob
          Dorsey, Dalbert Bright, saxes; Horace Henderson, piano; Israel Crosby,
          bass; Debo Mills, drums; and others):
OK 5900. Smooth Sailing(28959)/Ain't Misbehavin'(28960)
OK 5953. You Don't Mean Me No Good(28958)/I'll Always be in Love With You
                                                                       (28961)
          (Original personnel):
OK 5978. Ginger Belle(wc3187)/Do Re Mi(wc3188)
OK 6026. Sultan Serenade(wc3186)/Turkey Special(wc3272)
          (For Deccas 18171, 18172, see Fletcher Henderson, PaE 1745, 1766, 1792,
          2031)

HENDERSON, KATHERINE (vocal with Clarence Williams and His Orchestra):
QRS 7032. Lonesome Lovesick Blues(256a)/Have You Ever Felt That Way(257a)
QRS 7041. Do It Baby/If You Like Me

HENDERSON, ROSA (vocal with jazz band):
Vi 19084. Good Woman's Blues/I'm Broke
Vi 19124. Midnight Blues/(rev., Lizzie Miles)
Vi 19157. Low Down Papa/Struttin' Blues

          (Fletcher Henderson, piano)
Co   3958. Afternoon Blues(81127)/I Need You(81128)
Co 14130. Talk About My Sweetie/Mama Is Waiting for You
Pe   138. Police Blues/Never Let Your Left Hand Know

          (Acc. by Fletcher Henderson's Jazz Five):
Br   2589. I'm a Good Gal/Papa Will Be Gone
Br   2612. Clearing House Blues/West Indies Blues

          (Fletcher Henderson, piano):
Vo 14627. Doggone Blue/Can't Be Bothered
Vo 14635. Where/Down South Blues
Vo 14652. If You Don't Give Me What I Want/So Long to You and the Blues

          (Henderson, piano; Coleman Hawkins, sax):
Co 14682. Every Woman's Blues/It Won't Be Long Now

          (Henderson, piano):
Vo 14708. He May Be Your Dog/I Want My Sweet Daddy
Vo 14770. Do Right Blues/Hey Hey and He He
Vo 14795. My Papa Doesn't Two Time/How Come You Do Me Like You Do
Vo 14831. Barrelhouse Blues/My Right Man

          (With clarinet, trombone and piano):
Vo 14995. Nobody Knows the Way I Feel/Penitentiary Bound Blues
Vo 15215. And I Don't Mean If/You Can't Be

          ROSA HENDERSON AND THE THREE HOT ESKIMOS (vocal with piano, clarinet and
          cornet):
Vo   1021. Chicago Policeman Blues/Here Comes Baby

HENKE, MEL (piano solos):   1939
CI   100. Henke Stomp/Lady Be Good

          (With Joe Kahn, drums):   Feb.12,1940
CI   103. Mrs. Abernathy's Piano/It's Purely Coincidental

HENRY, LENA (Acc. by piano and cornet):
Vo 14902. Sinful Blues/Family Skeleton Blues

HENRY'S LUCKY SEVEN, HOT:
Vs   5002. Brown Sugar(12195)/(rev., Mobile Melody Men)

HERMAN AND HIS ORCHESTRA, LEN (See Ken Kenny)

HERMAN AND HIS ORCHESTRA, WOODY (Tentative personnel: Woody Herman, tenor sax and
clarinet; Murray Williams, Don Watt, altos; Saxie Mansfield, Bruce Wilkens, tenors;
Clarence Willard, Kermit Simmons, trumpets; Joe Bishop, fluegelhorn; Neal Reed,
trombone; Horace Diaz, piano; Chick Reeves, guitar; Walter Yoder, bass; Frank Carl-
son, drums; Nick Hupfer, violin):   1937
De   1056. Wintertime Dreams/The Goose Hangs High
De   1057. I Can't Pretend/Someone to Care for Me
De   1064. Old Fashioned Swing/Now That Summer Is Gone
De   1079. Mr.Ghost Goes to Town(61447)/Better Get Off Your High Horse(61448)
                                                                  (-BrE 02376
De   1288. It Happened in Dixieland
       "   Dupree Blues   -BrE 02558, De 3500
De   1307. Doctor Jazz
       "   Trouble in Mind

De 1385. Lady from Fifth Avenue/Stardust on the Moon
De 1397. Don't You Know or Don't You Care/Double or Nothing
De 1523. I Double Dare You/Why Talk About Love
De 1535. My Fine-Feathered Friend/You're a Sweetheart
De 1570. Let's Pitch a Little Woo/Loch Lomond
De 1583. I Wanna Be in Winchell's Column/Broadway's Gone Hawaii

    (Jack Ferrier, Pete Johns, altos; Saxie Mansfield, Ray Hofner, tenors; sub. Malcolm Crane, trumpet, for Simmons; Tommy Linehan, piano; Ollie Matthewson, guitar):   1938
De 1801. Twin City Blues/Laughing Boy Blues
De 1839. Carolina in the Morning/Saving Myself for You
De 1879. Calliope Blues   -De 3500
  "   Flat Foot Floogee
De 1900. Don't Wake Up My Heart/Lullaby in Rhythm
De 2250. Blue Evening
  "   Indian Boogie Woogie   -De 3383
De 2440. Woodchoppers Ball/Big Wig in the Wigwam

    (Steady Nelson, Willie Willard, Mac McCorquodale, trumpets; Neal Reed, trombone; Joe Bishop, fluegelhorn; Woody Herman, clarinet; Saxie Mansfield, Joe Estren, Ray Hofner, Pete Johns, saxes; Tommy Linehan, piano; Hy White, guitar; Walter Yoder, bass; Frank Carlson, drums.--JRB):   1939
De 2508. Blues Downstairs(65382)/Blues Upstairs(65383; voc., Woody Herman)
De 2539. Paleface(65634)/The Sheik of Araby(63635)
De 2582. Casbah Blues(65636)/Farewell Blues(65637)
De 2629. Riverbed Blues/Dallas Blues
De 2658. Love With a Capital "You"/Still the Bluebird Sings
De 2664. Jumpin' Blue/Big Morning
De 2728. Love Me(66050; voc.,Mary Ann McCall)/Rosetta(66051; voc.,Steady Nelson)
De 2762. For Tonight/Put That Down in Writing
De 2772. Blue Dawn/If I Knew Then

    (Sub. Cappy Lewis, Bob Price, trumpets, for Willard, McCorquodale; Herb Tompkins, Bill Vitale, altos; Mickey Folus, tenor for Extren,Hofner, Johns; add Bud Smith trombone.--JRB):   1940
De 2817. Midnight Echoes(65979)/I'm Comin'Virginia(66673; voc.,Steady Nelson)
De 2914. It's My Turn Now/This Changing World
De 2933. Blues on Parade   -De 3501
  "   Love's Got Me Down
De 2939. Peace Brother/The Rhumba Jumps
De 2955. Smarty Pants/Careless
De 2970. It's a Blue World/Would Ja Mind?
De 2971. Thank Your Stars/Do I Love You?
De 2979. Say Si Si/Pick a Rib
De 2993. On the Isle of May/East Side Kick
De 3008. Give a Little Whistle
  "   Peach Tree Street   -De 3501
De 3017. Sky Fell Down/Blue Prelude

    (Joe Bishop leaves in late 1940)
De 3081. Blue Ink/Can This Be Love?
De 3140. Cousin to Chris/Fine and Dandy
De 3187. Get Your Boots Laced Papa, 1 & 2
De 3200. I'll Pray for You/Where Do I Go from You
De 3217. You Think of Everything/Mister Meadowlark
De 3231. End of the Rainbow/(rev., Judy Garland
De 3272. Jukin'   -De 3664
  "   Herman at the Sherman   -De 3861
De 3332. Deep Night/Whistle Stop
De 3380. Music by the Moon/Bessie's Blues
De 3396. Million Dreams Ago/Rhumboogie
De 3397. I Wouldn't Take a Million/Looking for Yesterday
De 3427. Frenesi/Song of Old Hawaii
De 3436. Golden Wedding/Five o'Clock Whistle
De 3454. Beat Me Daddy Eight to a Bar/There I Go
De 3461. Dream Valley/Whatever Happened to You?
De 3528. Love of My Life/You're the One
De 3544. I Should Have Known You Years Ago/Th... rs Remain
De 3617. Boogie Woogie Bugle Boy/Bounce Me Brother With a Solid Four
De 3630. Oh Look at Me Now/Sorrento
De 3643. Fur Trappers Ball/Blue Flame
De 3693. Everything Happens to Me/Sleepy Serenade
De 3712. Chloe/Let's Get Away from It All
De 3738. Intermezzo/My Mom
De 3745. G'Bye Now/Until Tomorrow
De 3751. Dancing in the Dark/Time Changes Everything
De 3813. Lazy Rhapsody/You'll Never Know
De 3874. Loveliness and Love/Don't Cry Cherie
De 3889. Hey Doc/Night Watchman
De 3894. There Goes That Song Again/You Call It Madness But I Call It Love
De 3955. Love Me a Little Little/Prisoner of Love

```
De   3972. Bishop's Blues(dla2675)/Woodsheddin' With Woody(dla2676)
De   3973. I Love You More, More Every Day/Concerto No.1,B Flat Minor,Op.23
De   4016. I'd Love You Again/My Foolish Heart and I
De   4024. Misirlou/By-u By-o
De   4030. Blues in the Night/This Time the Dream's on Me
De   4076. Three Ways to Smoke a Pipe/Don't Be Blue Little Pal
De   4095. I Guess I'll Be on My Way/'Tis Autumn
De   4113. Someone's Rocking My Dream Boat/Rose O'Day                    1942
De   4135. I'll Remember April/I Think of You
De   4176. Las Chiapanecas/String of Pearls
De   4188. Fooled/You Can't Hold a Memory in Your Arms
De   4198. Night of Nights/Skylark
De   4253. Lamplighter's Serenade/Even Steven
De   4372. Singing Sands of Alamosa/Gotta Get to St. Joe
De  18314. There Are Rivers to Cross/We'll Meet Again(Billie Rogers, trumpet)
De  18315. A Soldier Dreams/She'll Always Remember
De  18356. Just Plain Lonesome/Story of a Starry Night
De  18346. Amen/Deliver Me to Tennessee
De  18357. Don't Tell a Lie About Me Dear/Whisper That You Love Me
De  18364. Ooch Ooch a Goon Attach/(rev., Herman Woodchoppers)
De  18469. Please Be These/There Will Never Be Another You
De  18506. I Dood It/Be Not Discouraged
De  18512. Jingle Bells/Santa Claus Is Comin' to Town
De  18526. Four or Five Times/Hot Chestnuts
De  18544. Ten Day Furlough/Down Under

             (Woody Herman, clarinet; Flip Phillips, tenor sax; Bill Harris, trombone;
             Bama Warwick, trumpet; Ralph Burns, piano; Billy Bauer, guitar; Dave
             Tough, drums; Chubby Jackson, bass; and others):                    1945
Co  36785. I Wonder/Laura

             WOODY HERMAN'S FOUR CHIPS (Woody Herman, clarinet; Tommy Linehan, piano;
             Walter Yoder, bass; Frank Carlson, drums):
De   3577. Chips' Boogie Woogie(68057)                                   -De 3833
      "    Chips' Blues(68058)
De   4353. Elise/Yardbird Shuffle

             WOODY HERMAN AND HIS WOODCHOPPERS (Woody Herman, clarinet; Hy White,gui-
             tar; Tommy Linehan, piano; Walter Yoder, bass; Frank Carlson, drums; Cappy
             Lewis, trumpet; Neil Reed, trombone):
De   3761. South(68699)/Fan It(68700)
De   4293. Fort Worth Jail/Too Late
De  18364. Three Little Sisters/(rev., Herman Orchestra)
             (See also; Isham Jones Juniors)
```

HERTH, MILT (organ solos):
```
De    911. Madam Swings It/Stompin' at the Savoy
De   1183. Hell's Bells/Memphis Blues
De   1300. How Come You Do Me Like You Do/Put on Your Old Grey Bonnet
De   1344. Basin Street Blues
      "    Twelfth Street Rag                                            -BrE 02294
De   1445. Satan Takes a Holiday/Somebody Loves Me

             MILT HERTH TRIO (Milt Herth, organ; Willie The Lion Smith, piano; O'Neil
             Spencer, drums):                                                    1938
De   1553. Dipsy Doodle/That's Plenty                                    -BrE 02548
De   1612. Big Dipper/Bei Mir Bist du Schon
De   1699. Josephine
      "    Lost in the Shuffle                                           -BrE 02585
De   1727. Jazz Me Blues
      "    Sissy                                                         -BrE 02600
De   1736. The Campbells Are Swinging(63280)                             -BrE 02585
      "    Pop Corn Man(63445)                                           -BrE 02600
De   1800. Looney Little Tooney/Flat Foot Floogee(add Teddy Bunn, guitar)
De   1816. Toy Trumpet                                                   -BrE 02613
      "    Three Blind Mice
De   1966. Copenhagen/La De Doody Do(Quartet)
De   2046. Lambeth Walk/Rockin' in Rhythm
De   2087. Minuet in Jazz/Home Cooking Mama With the Frying Pan(Quartet)
De   2227. Goblins in the Steeple/Jump Jump's Here(Quartet)
De   2336. Whistler and His Dog/Annabelle
De   2572. Shoemaker's Holiday/In an 18th Century Drawing Room
De   2632. Everybody Loves My Baby/Spider and the Fly(Quartet)
De   2818. Church Mouse on a Spree/Scatter Brain
De   2907. Boy Scout in Switzerland/Peach Tree Street
De   2964. At a Georgia Camp Meeting/Monkeys Have No Tails in Pago Pago
De   3032. Blue Danube Swing/Hezekiah
De   3158. Girl With the Light Blue Hair/Honky Tonk Train Blues
De   3171. Slow Freight/Eep-Ipe
De   3251. Goofus/Bummel Petrus
De   3284. Dardanella/Down South
De   3393. Black and Tan Fantasy/Creole Love Call
De   3561. Huckleberry Duck/Worried Mind
```

For Complete Catalog Write to
BLUE NOTE RECORDS
767 LEXINGTON AVENUE, NEW YORK CITY

BLUE NOTE
PRESENTS
ART HODES
AND HIS CHICAGOANS

```
MAX KAMINSKY .................... Trumpet
RAY CONNIFF ..................... Trombone
ROD CLESS ....................... Clarinet
ART HODES ....................... Piano
JACK BLAND ...................... Guitar
BOB HAGGART ..................... Bass
SID JACOBS ...................... Bass
DANNY ALVIN ..................... Drums
```

● No. 505 **MAPLE LEAF RAG**
　10 Inch **YELLOW DOG BLUES**

● No. 506 **SHE'S CRYING FOR ME**
　10 Inch **SLOW 'EM DOWN BLUES**

● No. 507 **DOCTOR JAZZ**
　10 Inch **SHOE SHINER'S DRAG**

● No. 508 **THERE'LL BE**
　10 Inch 　　**SOME CHANGES MADE**
　　　　CLARK AND RANDOLPH

Set of 4 Records — and 8x10 Photo of Band — $4.24 incl. Excise Tax, F.O.B. New York City. Add 20 cents for Packing.

THE musicians on these records were all renowned masters of the Chicago style during the Prohibition era with its small band vogue, but unlike so many of their contemporaries, they do not today maintain a self-conscious, backward-looking style. Neither have they made an obvious and mechanical compromise with the popular technical style.

For one thing, these records issue from mutually exchanged ideas and suggestions, and they reveal their players' common approval of the ensemble, rather than the individual musician, as the driving force of their projected music. In this important sense, the records are a landmark. In a band dominated by the ensemble mode of feeling, every participant with his own musical thought, abstracted from the collective playing at any moment of time, is the soloist. The drummer, for example, is as articulate a soloist as the trumpeter or pianist.

Although the ensemble relationship is always felt, there are outstanding solos by the group's personalities: Art Hodes, who has achieved identity with the genuine blues consciousness; the late Rod Cless (his recent death was a severe shock), whose sensitive and tremulous musical line revives and continues the spirit once embodied in Johnny Dodds; Max Kaminsky, whose lyrical strophes are deeply evocative; and Ray Conniff, whose clear-cut trombone phrases have forceful assurance.

The selections offered on these records date back a decade or two, or even more. Most of the pieces are usually associated with traditional blues-inspired playing, while the two pieces by Hodes (**Slow 'Em Down Blues** and **Clark and Randolph**) rise frankly from the same source. Their performance is in consistently good taste, and therefore, is full of high distinction. Out of the independent, horizontal movement of the instruments in ensemble, there is a particular effectiveness to the fluid lyricism of Cless, the fine rhetoric of Kaminsky, the singing figures of Conniff, the ardent moodiness of Hodes. The collective quality of the ensemble is as effectively defined by the drums of Danny Alvin, the guitar of Jack Bland, and the bass of Bob Haggart and Sid Jacobs respectively. Note, among the numerous virtues of these records, that Kaminsky leads, but does not weight or overbalance the others. Note the continuous presence of the trombone; and note the exemplary solos of Cless in pieces as different as **Doctor Jazz** and **She's Crying for Me**. Especially note the eloquent expressiveness of the four slow pieces. —MAX MARGULIS

De 3664. Down Home Rag/Hoity Toity
De 3704. Anvil Chorus/Corn Silk
De 3740. Toy Piano Minuet/Play Play Tina
De 3757. Jessie/Friendly Tavern Polka
De 4118. Whistler's Mother-in-Law/Canadian Capers
De 4180. Pretty Little Busy Body/The Nadocky
De 4285. Jersey Bounce/Pennsylvania Polka
De 4370. Sleepy Town Train/I Wanna Go Back to West Virginia

    MILT HERTH QUARTET (Add Teddy Bunn, guitar):
De 1868. Egyptian Ella/Shoot the Likker to Me John Boy

HEYWOOD, EDDIE (Sr.) (Piano solos):
OK 8094. The Mixed Up Blues/The Black Bottom Blues

    EDDIE HEYWOOD AND HIS JAZZ SIX:
OK 8402. Trombone Moanin' Blues/Let's Start Over Again

HEYWOOD AND HIS ORCHESTRA, EDDIE (Jr.) (Eddie Heywood, piano; Doc Cheatham, trumpet; Vic Dickenson, trombone; Lem Davis, alto sax; Al Lucas, bass; Jack Parker, drums):
Com 554. T'ain't Me(a4722-1)/Save Your Sorrow(a4734-1)
Com 1514. Begin the Beguine(a4728-1)/I Cover the Waterfront(a4729-1)

HICKS AND HIS SIZZLIN' SIX, BILLY (Billy Hicks, trumpet; Fernando Arbello, trombone; Edmond Hall, clarinet; Cyril Haynes, piano; Leroy Jones, guitar; Alfred Hall, bass.):   July,1937
Vr 601. Fade Out/Joe the Bomber

HICKS AND HIS TAPROOM BOYS, CURLY (vibraphone; bass; accordion):
BB 10715. Limehouse Blues/Hindustan
BB 10757. Russian Rag/Scotch Twist
BB 10781. Joyous Companions/Four Leaf Clover
BB 10922. That's a Plenty/Allah's Holiday
BB 10977. Harvest Time/American Polka

HICKS, EDNA (blues, acc. by piano):
Vi 19083. I'm Goin' Away/(rev., Lizzie Miles)

    (Porter Grainger, piano):
Ge 5195. Sad 'n Lonely Blues(8436)/Bleeding Hearted Blues(8437)

    (Lemuel Fowler, piano):
Ge 5234. Tin Roof Blues(8470)/Oh Daddy Blues(8471)
Ge 5252. Satisfied Blues/No Name Blues

    (Acc. probably by Elmer Chambers, trumpet; Buster Bailey, clarinet; F. Henderson, piano):
Para 12023. Hard Luck Blues(1629)/I Don't Love Nobody(1630)

    (Charles A. Watson, piano):
Para 12069. Kansas City Man Blues(1549)/Uncle Sam Blues(1550)

    (Porter Grainger's Sawin' Three: trumpet; sax; piano):
Para 12089. Cemetery Blues(1631)/Poor Me Blues(1632)

    (Henderson's Trio):
Para 12090. Where Can That Somebody Be(1633)/If You Don't Give Me What I Want (1634)

    (Clarence Johnson, piano):
Br 2463. Gulf Coast Blues/Down Hearted Blues
Vo 14650. Walking and Talking Blues/You've Got Everything a Sweet Mama Needs
    (acc. Henderson Orchestra)
    (Lemuel Fowler, piano):
Vo 14659. Wicked Fives/Squawkin' the Blues
Co 14001. No Name Blues/Save Your Man and Satisfy Your Soul

    (Unknown accompaniment):
Aj 17008. Mistreatin' Daddy/Save Your Man

J. C. HIGGINBOTHAM

For records under other names see:
HENRY ALLEN: Vi 38073,38080,38088,38107,38121,38140; Vo 2997,2998,3097,3098, 3214,3215,3244,3245,3261,3262; OK 6281,6357.
LIL ARMSTRONG: De 2234, 2542.
LOUIS ARMSTRONG: OK 8669,8680,8756,8774,41350,41375; De 1347,1353,1369,1408, 1560,1635,1636,1653,1661,1822,2230,1841,1842,2267,2405,2480, 2538, 2615, 2729,2934,3011,3092,3105,3283,3204,3235.

BUSTER BAILEY (CHOCOLATE DANDIES): Vo 2887.
SIDNEY BECHET: Vi 27337, 27386.
BENNY CARTER: CoE 698, 720.
CHOCOLATE DANDIES: OK 8728.
CONNIE'S INN ORCHESTRA: Cr 3191, 3212; Me 12340, Pe 15603.
IDA COX: Vo 5258, 5298, 5336; OK 6405.
COLEMAN HAWKINS: PaE 1685, 1766; BB 10693, 10770.
LIONEL HAMPTON: Vi 26423, 26476.
W. C. HANDY: Vs 8162, 8163.
FLETCHER HENDERSON: CoE 584, 701; Co 2565, 2559, 2732; Vo 3485,3487,3534,3511.
JUNGLE TOWN STOMPERS: OK 8686.
JIMMY JOHNSON: Vo 4768, 4903.
LOU AND GINGER SNAPS: Ba 6536, 6540.
MEZZ MEZZROW: Vi 25612, 25636.
METRONOME ALL STARS: Vi 27314; Co 36499.
MILLS BLUE RHYTHM: Co 2963,2994,3020,3038,3044,3071,3078,3083,3087,3111,3135,
  3134,3147,3148,3156,3157,3158,3162; Br 7534.
JELLY ROLL MORTON: Vi 23402, 23334, 23484.
KING OLIVER: Vi 38034,38039,38049,38521.
PORT OF HARLEM: BN 3, 6, 7, 14.
JACK PURVIS: OK 8782,8808; PaE 890, 1669.
LUIS RUSSELL: OK 8656, 8760, 8734, 8766, 8780, 8811, 8830, 8849; Vo 1579;Me 12000.
ARTIE SHAW: Vi 27509.
VICTORIA SPIVEY: Vi 38546, 38570.
STOKERS OF HADES: Co 2615.
EVA TAYLOR: Me 13228.

HIGGINBOTHAM AND HIS SIX HICKS, J.C. (Henry Allen, trumpet; J.C. Higginbotham,
trombone; Charlie Holmes, alto sax; Luis Russell, piano; Pop Foster, bass; Paul
Barbarin, drums; Will Johnson, guitar):   March.1930
  OK 8772. Give Me Your Telephone Number(403736b)   -PaE 2799, OdE 067, HRS 14
   "   Higginbotham Blues(403737c)   -PaE 2799, Co 36011,   "

        J. C. HIGGINBOTHAM QUINTET (J.C. Higginbotham, trombone; Meade Lux Lew-
    is, piano; Teddy Bunn, guitar; John Williams, bass; Sidney Catlett,drums):
  BN   7. Basin Street Blues(gm532b)/(rev., Port of Harlem)   1939
  BN 501. Weary Land Blues(gm513a-5)/(rev., Frank Newton)

HIGH SOCIETY SEVEN:
  Mad 8004. For a Little While
  Or   226. Charley My Boy

HIGHTOWER'S HIGHT HAWKS (Fred Paham, clarinet; Johnny Lindsay, trombone; Willie
Hightower, trumpet; Bud Scott, banjo; Rudy Richardson, drums; Richard M. Jones,
piano.--DB 8/1/40);   1924
  Black Patti 8045. Squeeze Me/Boar Hog Blues

HILL, ALEX (piano solos, with traps):
  Vo 1270. Stompin' 'em Down/Tack Head Blues   -Br 80034

        ALEX HILL AND HIS ORCHESTRA (Alex Hill, piano; Jabbo Smith,trumpet; Omer
    Simeon, clarinet; George James, alto sax, and others.--EW):
  Vo 1465. St. James Infirmary(c5273-4)/South Bound(c5275)   -Sup 2237
  Unissued. Dyin' With the Blues(c5035)   Chicago,Dec.20, 1929
  Vo 1493. Toogaloo Shout(c5036)/Dyin' With the Blues(c5276-7; see 1st Coupling)

        ALEX HILL'S HOLLYWOOD SEPIANS (Benny Carter, Joe Thomas, Herman Autrey,
    trumpets; Claude Jones, trombone; Albert Nicholas, clarinet; George James
    alto sax; Eugene Cedric, tenor sax; Alex Hill, piano; Eddie Gibbs, gui-
    tar; Billy Taylor, bass; Harry Dial, drums):
  Vo 2826. Functionizin'(15880)/Ain't It Nice(15879)   -BrF 500495

    (Garnet Clark, piano):
  Vo 2848. Song of the Plow(16141)   -BrE 02078, BrF 500511
   "   Let's Have a Jubilee(16142)   -VoE 20
              (See Hokum Trio)

HILL, BERTHA (CHIPPIE) (contralto, acc.by Louis Armstrong, trumpet; Richard M.
Jones, piano):
  OK 8273. Low Land Blues(9456a)/Kid Man Blues(9457a)
  OK 8312. Trouble in Mind(9510b)/Georgia Man(9511a)   -Me 61270, Vo 04379
  OK 8339. Lonesome All Alone and Blue(9509a)/(rev., Mary Mack)

    (Acc. by Richard M. Jones Jazz Wizards: Jones, piano; Albert Nicholas,
    clarinet; Shirley Clay, trumpet; sax; drums; trombone):
  OK 8367. Leavenworth Blues(9710a)/Panama Limited Blues(9719a)

    (Acc. by Jones, Armstrong):   1927
  OK 8420. Pleadin' for the Blues(9949a)
   "   Pratts City Blues(9950a)   -HRS Div
  OK 8437. Mess Katie Mess(9951a)/Street Walker Bl(9720a; duet with R.M.Jones,
  OK 8453. Lovesick Blues(9971a)/Lonesome Weary bl(9972a) (Jazz Wizards,above)

```
              (Acc. by Richard M. Jones Jazz Wizards: Jones, piano;trumpet;clarinet;
           banjo):
    OK  8473. Do Dirty Blues(80881a)/Sport Model Mama(80882a)

              (Acc. by piano and Tampa Red, guitar):
    Vo  1224. Weary Money Blues/Christmas Man Blues(duet with Tampa Red)

              (Piano; cornet and clarinet):
    Vo  1248. Trouble in Mind/Hangman Blues

              (Piano; guitar):
    Vo  1264. Some Cold Rainy Day/Hard Time Blues(duet with Tampa Red)

              (Add bull fiddle):
    Vo  1406. Pratt City Blues/I Ain't Gonna Do It No More
```

HILL, HONEY (Piano solos):
   De 7604. Boogie Woogie   -De 3387
     "   Set 'em

HILL, KING SOLOMON (Blind Lemon's Buddy):
   Cr 3325. Whoopee Blues/Down on My Bended Knee

HILL, LETHIA (acc. by piano and cornet):
   Vo 14874. Old North State Blues/Never Again(by Alta Cates)

HILL AND HIS ORCHESTRA, SAM (Fletcher Henderson and His Orchestra, including Armstrong):
   Or   303. Everybody Loves My Baby(5748)
   Or   347. Alabama Bound(5835)
   Or   374. One of These Days(5712)

HILL AND HIS ORCHESTRA, TEDDY (Bill Dillard, Bill Coleman, Roy Eldridge, trumpets; Dicky Wells, trombone; Russell Procope, Howard Johnson, Teddy Hill, alto saxes;Chu Berry, tenor sax; Sam Allen, piano; John Smith,guitar; Richard Fullbright, bass; William Beason, drums.--HD):   1935
```
    Me 13351. Here Comes Cookie(16923-1)        -Cq 8521, Ba 33384, Or 3114
     "        Got Me Doin' Things(16924-1)
    Me 13364. When the Robin Sings His Song(16925-1)
     "        When Love Knocks at Your Heart(16926-1)

              (Sub. Frank Newton, Shad Collins, trumpets, for Eldridge, Coleman; Cecil
           Scott, sax, for Berry):
    Vo  3247. At the Rug Cutter's Ball(19175)                       -VoE 30
     "        Blue Rhythm Fantasy(19176)                            -VoE 97
    Vo  3294. Uptown Rhapsody(18911)                                -VoE 30
     "        Passionette(19177)                                    -VoE 97

              TEDDY HILL AND HIS NBC ORCHESTRA (Same):
    BB  6897. The Love Bug Will Bite You/Would You Like to Buy a Dream -GrF 7937
    BB  6898. Where Is the Sun/Marie                                -GrF 7938
    BB  6908. The Harlem Twister/Big Boy Blue
    BB  6941. China Boy/The You and Me That Used to Be
    BB  6943. Twilight in Turkey/A study in Brown
    BB  6954. I Know Now
     "        The Lady Who Couldn't Be Kissed                       -HMV 5254

              (Sub. John Gillespie, trumpet, for Newton; Robert Carroll, tenor sax,for
           Scott):
    BB  6988. King Porter Stomp/San Anton'
    BB  6989. Blue Rhythm Fantasy/I'm Happy Darling Dancing With You
    BB  7013. Yours and Mine/I'm Feeling Like a Million
```

EARL HINES

```
For other records see:
   LOUIS ARMSTRONG: OK 8597, 8609, 8631, 8641, 8649, 8657, 8669, 8680, 8690, 8703,
      41454; Co 36376.
   SIDNEY BECHET: Vi 26746, 27204, 27240.
   LILLIE DELK CHRISTIAN: OK 8596, 8607, 8650, 8660.
   COZY COLE: Key 1300, 1301.
   LOIS DEPPE: Ge 20021, 20022.
   DEPPE'S SERENADERS: Ge 20012.
   JOHNNY DODDS: Br 3567; Vo 15632.
   CLIFFORD HAYES: ?
   JIMMIE NOONE: Vo 1184, 1185, 1188,1207,1215,1229; Br 6192, 6174.
   CHARLIE SHAVERS: Key 1304, 1305.
   OMER SIMEON: Br 7109.
   WALLER MEMORIAL: Sig. 1, 2.
   STOVEPIPE JOHNSON: Vo 1211
```

HINES, EARL (piano solos):
```
    QRS  7036. Blues in Thirds(287)                                                 -HRS 21
          "   Off Time Blues(288a)                                                  -HRS 19
    QRS  7037. Chicago High Life                                                    -HRS 11
          "   A Monday Date                                                         -HRS 19
    QRS  7038. Stowaway(291)                                                        -HRS 20
          "   Chimes in Blues(292a)                                                 -HRS 21
    QRS  7039. Panther Rag(293)                                                     -HRS 20
          "   Just Too Soon(294a)                                                   -HRS 11
                                                                             Dec.,1928
    OK   8653. I Ain't Got Nobody(402218a)           -Co 2800, Co 35875.   PaE 510
          "   57 Varieties(402220a)                                           "     PaE 540
    OK   8832. Caution Blues(402210c)                          -Co 35876     PaE 878
          "   A Monday Date(402211a)                 -Co 2800,     "         PaE 1862
                                                                                 1932
    Br   6403. Love Me Tonight(12079a)/Down Among the Sheltering Palms(12080a)
                                                                              (12080a)
    BN      5. Th Father's Getaway(gm301x-3)/Reminiscing at Blue Note(gm302x-2)1940
    BB  10555. Rosetta(Oct.21,1939)/Glad Rag Doll(Feb.25,1929)
    BB  10642. Child of a Disordered Brain/Body and Soul
    Vi  27562. My Melancholy Baby/On the Sunny Side of the Street         Apr.3,1941
```

HINES AND HIS ORCHESTRA, EARL (George Mitchell, Shirley Clay, trumpets; William
Franklyn, trombone; Toby Turner, Lester Boone, Cecil Irwin, saxes; Earl Hines, piano and vocal; Claude Roberts, banjo; Hayes Alvis, bass; Buddy Washington, drums.
--HD):   1929
```
    Vi 22683. Sister Kate(48888)/(rev., McKnney Cotton Pickers)
    Vi 22842. Sweet Ella May(48883)
    Vi 38042. Everybody Loves My Baby(48884)                              -BB 7040
         "   Chicago Rhythm(50511)
    Vi 38043. Good Little Bad Little You(48885)                           -BB 7768
         "   Beau Koo Jack(48887)                                  -BB 7040,   "
    Vi 38048. Have You Ever Felt That Way(48886)/(rev., Bennie Moten)
    Vi 38096. Grand Piano Blues(57322)/Blue Nights(57325)                 -BB 6744
```

(Charlie Allen, George Dixon, Walter Fuller, trumpets; James Young, Louis
Taylor, William Franklyn, trombones; Omer Simeon, clarinet and also sax;
Darnell Howard, alto sax and violin; James Mundy, Cecil Irwin, tenor
saxes; Earl Mines, piano; Lawrence Gibson, guitar; Quinn Williams bass;
Wallace Bishop, drums):   1932
```
    Br   6345. Oh You Sweet Thing(12074a)                  -BrE 1464, BrF 500186
          "   Blue Drag(12075a)                            -BrE 1388,       "
    Br   6379. I Love You Because I Love You(12076a)       -BrE 1388
          "   Sensational Mood(12078a)                     -BrE 1366, BrF 500189
                                                                          June 28, 1932
    BrE 1464. Deep Forest(11993a)/(rev., see Br 6345)      -Co 35878, BrF 500189
                                                                          Feb.13,1933
    Br   6541. Rosetta(13060b)                             -BrE 01559
          "   Cavernism(13063a)                                "    , BrF 500236
    Co  35878. Rosetta (13060a)                                       Dates unknown
    BrF 500431. Swing Down                                            -Vo 3392
          "   Darkness(15007a)                                        -Vo 3379
    Br   6710. Bubbling Over(645-1)/I Want a Lot of Love(646-1)       -BrE 01682
    BrF 500236. Why Must We Part?/(rev., see Br 6541, above)
    BrF 500432. Madhouse(15003a)/(rev., see Br 6771, below)           -Vo 3379
    Br   6771. Take It Easy                                           #BrF 500432
          "   Harlem Lament                                -BrE 02075
    Br   6872. Blue(15002a, voc.;Herb Jeffries)            -BrE 01796
          "   Julia(15006a, voc., Walter Fuller)                 "
    Br   6960. Just to Be in Caroline/We Found Romance
    BrG  9407. Maybe I'm to Blame
```

(Sub. Warren Jefferson, trumpet, for Allen; Kenneth Stewart, trombone,
for Franklyn; Albert Johnson, tenor sax, for Irwin):   1934-36
```
    De   182. Sweet Georgia Brown                                    -BrE 01995
          "  That's a Plenty                                         -BrE 01928
    De   183. Angry(9475)/Cavernism(9478)
    De   218. Fat Babes                                              -BrE 01928
          "  Maple Leaf Rag                                          -BrE 01995
    De   337. Rosetta                                    -De 3517, -BrE 02286
          "  Copenhagen
    De   389. Disappointed in Love(39356a)
          "  Rhythm Lullaby(39357a)                                  -BrE 02131
    De   577. Rock and Rye
          "  Wolverine Blues                                         -BrE 02286
    De   654. Japanese Sandman(39358a)                               -BrE 02131
          "  Julia(39361a, voc., Walter Fuller)
    De   714. Bubbling Over/Blue
```

(George Dixon, Ray Nance, Walter Fuller, trumpets; William Randall, Leon
Washington, tenor saxes; Stewart, Taylor, James Young, trombones; Darnell
Howard, alto sax and violin; Omer Simeon, clarinet; Earl Hines, piano;
Gibson, Wilson, Bishop; Ida Mae James, vocals):   1937

```
Vo   3392. You're the Only One in My Dreams/Swingin' Down
Vo   3467. Rhythm Sundae(o1816)/I Can't Believe(o1818)    -OK 6250, VoE 78
Vo   3501. Flanny Doodle Swing                            -BrF 500706,VoE 83
 "         Pianology                                              "
Vo   3586. Inspiration                                                -VoE 83
 "         Honeywuckle Rose(Wimeon,Johnson,Hines,Bishop)
Vo   4008. Please Be Kind/Good Night Sweet Dreams
Vo   4032. Jezebel/Dominick Swing
Vo   4143. Solid Mama/Tippin' at the Terrace
```

(Walter Fuller, Milton Fletcher, Edward Simms, trumpets; George Dixon, trumpet, alto and baritone sax; Edward Burke, John Ewing, Joe McLewis, trombones; Albert Johnson, Robert Crowder, tenor saxes; Omer Simeon, LeRoy Harris, altos; Hines; Wilson; Claude Roberts, guitar; Alvin Burroughs, drums.--JRB): 1939-40

```
BB  10351. Grand Terrace Shuffle/Ridin' and Jivin'
BB  10377. Piano Man/Father Steps In
BB  10391. Indiana/G . T. Stomp
BB  10467. Me and Columbus, voo.,Laura Rucker/After All I've Been to You, voo.,
BB  10531. Riff Medley/ X Y Z                              (Walter Fuller
BB  10674. Number 19/Boogie Woogie on St. Louis Blues
BB  10727. Deep Forest/Lightly and Politely
BB  10763. 'Gator Swing/My Heart Beats for You
```

(Sub. Shirley Clay, trumpet, for Fletcher):
```
BB  10792. You Can Depend on Me, voo., Walter Fuller/Tantalizing a Cuban
BB  10835. Call Me Happy/Blue Because of You, voo., Leroy Harris
BB  10870. Ann, voo., Billy Eckstein/Topsy Turvy, voo., Walter Fuller
```

(Harry Jackson, Rostell Reese, Leroy White, trumpets; Ed Fant, trombone, for Burke; Scoops Carey, alto, for Simeon; Franz Jackson, tenor, for Crowder; Hurley Rawey, guitar; Truok Parham,bass.--JRB): 1941
```
BB  10985. Wait 'Till It Happens to You/Easy Rhythm
BB  11036. In Swamp Lands/Everything Depends on You
BB  11065. I'm Falling for You/Jelly Jelly
BB  11126. Jersey Bounce/Sally Won't You Come Back
BB  11199. Julia, voo., Eckstein/Comin' in Home
BB  11237. Southside/Up Jumped the Devil
BB  11308. It Had to Be You/Yellow Fire
BB  11329. Water Boy, Eckstein/Windy City Jive
BB  11374. I Got It Bad and That Ain't Good/Straight to Love
BB  11394. You Don't Know What Love Is,voo.,Eckstein/Boy With the Wistful Eyes
```

HITCH'S HAPPY HARMONISTS (Also see Happy Harmonists; Curtis Hitch, piano; Fred Rollison, cornet; Arnold Habbe, banjo; Maurice May, sax; Harry Wright, clarinet; Haskell Simpson, bass; Earl McDowell, drums; Neal, trombone, Hoagy Carmichael, piano, in first two titles only): 1925
```
Ge   3066. Bone Yard Shuffle(12245)/Wash Board Blues(12246)
Ge   5633. Cataract Rag Blues(12128)/Nightingale Rag Blues(12129)
```

HITE AND HIS ORCHESTRA, LES (Paul Campbell, Walter Williams, Forrest Powell, trumpets; Britt Woodman, Allen Durham, trombones; Les Hite, Floyd Teernham, Judillis Martyn, Rodgers Hurd, Sol Moore, saxes; Nat Walker, piano; Frank Pasely, guitar; Al Morgan, bass; Oscar Bradley, drums.--JRB): 1940-41
```
BB  11109. Board Meetin'/World Is Waiting for the Sunrise
BB  11210. T-Bone Blues/That's the Lick
Vs   8373. Board Meeting/World Is Waiting for the Sunrise
Vs   8391. T-Bone Blues/It Must Have Been a Dream
```

HITTER'S BLUE KNIGHTS, RICHARD (Elmer Schoebel group): 1925
```
Ge   3149. Stomp Off Let's Go(9725)/Hot Aire(9726)
```

RICHARD HITTER'S CABINEERS:
Everybody 1063. Riverboat Shuffle/Breakin' the Leg

ART HODES

See also:
CHICAGO RHYTHM KINGS: Sig 104, 105.
WINGY MANNONE: Vo 15797.

HODES, ART (Piano solos): 1939
```
SA  12007. Ross Tavern Boogie/South Side Shuffle(2198)
SA  12007. South Side Shuffle(2199)                                   1940
Sig  9001. A Selection from the Gutter(150laa)/Organ Grinder Bl(1502aa)-Com 545
BW      1. Snowy Morning Blues(54rs)/Four or Five Times(55rs)
BW      2. Art's Boogie/St. Louis Blues
JR   1002. Bed Rock Blues(hsl202)/You've Got to Give Me Some(hsl203)
```

ART HODES BLUE THREE(Hodes,piano;Rod Cless,clarinet;Jimmy Butts,bass):
Sig 101. I've Found a New Baby/Four or Five Times   1940
Sig 102. Diga Diga Doo/Tin Roof Blues   -Jazz 101

ART HODES COLUMBIA QUINTET (Art Hodes, piano; George Brunis, trombone;
Duke DuVal, trumpet; Rod Cless, clarinet; Joe Grauso, drums): Dec.1940
JR 1001. 103rd Street Boogie(hsl201)/Royal Garden Blues(hsl201)
JR 1003. At the Jazz Band Ball(hsl204)/Farewell Blues(hsl205-1)

ART HODES AND HIS ORCHESTRA (Sidney de Paris, trumpet; Brad Gowans,trombone; Rod Cless, clarinet; Art Hodes, piano; Eddie Condon, guitar; Earl
Murphy, bass; Zutty Singleton, drums):   1943
De 18438. Indiana(70521b)/Get Happy(70522a)
De 18437. Georgia Cake Walk/Liberty Inn Drag

ART HODES' BLUE NOTE JAZZ MEN (Max Kaminsky, trumpet; Vic Dickenson,trombone; Edmond Hall, clarinet; Art Hodes, piano; Arthur Shirley, guitar;
Sid Weiss, bass; Danny Alvin, drums):   1941
BN 34. Sugar Foot Stomp(979-1)/Sweet Georgia Brown(977)
BN 35. Squeeze Me/Bugle Call Rag

ART HODES AND HIS CHICAGOANS (Max Kaminsky, trumpet; Ray Conniff, trombone; Rod Cless, clarinet; Art Hodes, piano; Jack Bland, guitar; Bob
Haggart, bass; Danny Alvin, drums):   Mar.18,1944
BN 505. Maple Leaf Rag(960)/Yellow Dog Blues(962)
BN 506. She's Crying for Me(961)/Slow 'em Down Blues(963-2)
BN 507. Doctor Jazz(964-2)/Shoe Shiner's Drag(965)   Mar.22,1944
BN 508. There'll Be Some Changes Made(966-4)/Clark and Randolph(967)

ART HODES TRIO (Hodes, piano; Mezz Mezzrow, clarinet; Danny Alvin, drums):
Se 10-007. Feather's Lament(162)/Mezzin' Around(163)
(See also Mezz Mezzrow Trio)

JOHNNY HODGES

See also:
MILDRED BAILEY: PaE 2201, 2257.
DUKE ELLINGTON: All from early 1928.
GOTHAM STOMPERS: Vr 541, 629.
SONNY GREER: Co 1868.
LIONEL HAMPTON: Vi 25575, 25586, 25592, 25601, 25771
HARLEM FOOTWARMERS: OK 8720, 8746, 8760, 8840, 8869.
HARLEM HOT CHOCOLATES: HoW 1045, 1046.
HARLEM MUSIC MASTERS: OK 41468.
JUNGLE BAND: Br 4238,4309,4345,4492,4705,4760,4776,4783,4887.
REX STEWART 52nd STREET STOMPERS: All.
JOE TURNER: Co 1813.
COOTIE WILLIAMS RUG CUTTERS: All but Vo 3890,3922.

HODGES AND HIS ORCHESTRA, JOHNNY (Cootie Williams, trumpet; Johnny Hodges, Otto
Hardwicke, alto saxes; Barney Bigard, clarinet; Harry Carney, baritone sax; Duke
Ellington, piano; Fred Guy, guitar; Hayes Alvis, bass; Sonny Greer, drums): 1937
Vr 576. Foolin' Myself(21186)/You'll Never Go to Heaven(21188) -Vo 3771
Vr 586. A Sailboat in the Moonlight(21187)/(rev.,Edgar Hayes) -Vo 3773
Vo 3948. My Day(m727)/Silvery Moon and Golden Sands(m728)

(Omit Hardwicke, Bigard, Guy; sub. Billy Taylor, bass; add Lawrence Brown,
trombone):   1938
Vo 4046. If You Were in My Place(m794)/I Let a Song Go Out of My Heart(m795)
Vo 4115. Jeep's Blues(m793)/Rendezvous With Rhythm(m796)
Vo 4213. You Walked Out of the Picture(m852)/Empty Ballroom Blues(m854)
Vo 4242. Pyramid(m853)/Lost in Meditation(m855)
Vo 4309. A Blues Serenade(m872)/Jitterbug's Lullaby(m875)
Vo 4335. Love in Swingtime(m873)/Swingin' in the Dell(m874)
Vo 4351. There's Something About an Old Love(m888)/Krum Elbow Blues(m890)
Vo 4386. Prelude to a Kiss(m887)/The Jeep is Jumpin'(m889)
Vo 4573. Hodge Podge(m951)/Wanderlust(m953)
Vo 4622. I'm in Another World(m950)/Dancing on the Stars(m952)
Vo 4710. Like a Ship in the Nighg(m974)/Swingin' on the Campus(m976)
Vo 4849. Mississippi Dreamboat(m975)/Dooji Wooji(m977)
Vo 4917. Kitchen Mechanic's Day(wml026)/You Can Count on Me(wml028)
Vo 4941. Dance of the Goon(wml003)/Home Town Blues(wml029)
Vo 5100. Rent Party Blues(wml002)/The Rabbit's Jump(wml072)
Vo 5170. Savoy Strut(wml001)/Good Gal Blues(wml004)
Vo 5330. My Heart Jumped Over the Moon(wml027)/Truly Wonderful(wml074)
Vo 5353. Dream Blues(wml075)/I Know What You Do(wml097)
Vo 5533. Skunk Hollow Blues(wml096)/Tired Socks(wml099)
OK 5940. Moon Romance(wml073)/Your Love Has Faded(wml098)

```
                (Sub. Jimmy Blanton, bass; Ray Nance, trumpet;):    Chicago, Nov.2,1940
     BB 11021.  Day Dream(053603)/Junior Hop(053606)
     BB 11117.  Good Queen Bess(053604)/That's the Blues Old Man(053605)
                                                                 Hollywood, July 3, 1941
     BB 11447.  Squatty Roo(061346)/Things Ain't What They Used to Be(061348)
     Vi 20-1545.  Passion Flower(061347)                              -BB 30-0817
     BB 30-0817.  Going Out the Back Way(061349)/(Rev.,see Vi 20-1545, above)
```

HOKUM BOYS (vocal with piano and guitar):
```
     Para 12714.  Selling That Stuff(21035-3)/Beedle Um Bum(21036-3)
     Br  7070.  We Don't Sell It Here No More/You Ain't Livin' Right
     OK  8747.  Gin Mill Blues/The Folks Downstairs
                   (Piano, bass and guitars* or clarinet#):
     Vo 03406.  Something Good(c1633)*/You Can't Have None of That(c1653)#
```

HOKUM TRIO (piano, clarinet and banjo, directed by Alex Hill):
```
     Ve  7073.  I'm Havin' My Fun(150379)/He Wouldn't Stop Doing It(150381)
```

HOLDEN AND HIS DISCIPLES OF RHYTHM, LOU:
```
     De  3260.  Ferryboat Serenade/Maid With the Slight Swiss Accent
     De  3281.  The Lion and the Mouse(93040)/A Windy Day on the Outer Drive(93041)
     De  3408.  Yankee Doodle Polka/Swiss Bellringer
     De  3444.  It's the End of My World/Red Wagon
```

HOLIDAY AND HER ORCHESTRA, BILLIE (Bunny Berigan, trumpet; Artie Shaw, clarinet;
Joe Bushkin, piano; Dick McDonough, guitar; Pete Peterson, bass; Cozy Cole, drums;
Billie Holiday, vocals.--HD):   1936
```
     Vo  3276.  Did I Remember?/No Regrets                          -VoE  24
     Vo  3288.  Summer Time(19537)                                  - VoE 130
                Billie's Blues(19538)

                (Sub. Irving Fazola, clarinet; Clyde Hart, piano; Artie Bernstein, bass):
     Vo  3333.  A Fine Romance(19971)                               -VoE  38
                I Can't Pretend(19972)
     Vo  3334.  Let's Call a Heart a Heart/One Two Button Your Shoe -VoE  47

                (Jonah Jones, trumpet; Edgar Sampson, alto sax; Ben Webster, tenor sax;
                Teddy Wilson, piano; Allan Reuss, guitar; John Kirby, bass; Cozy Cole,
                drums):
     Vo  3431.  I've Got My Love to Keep Me Warm
         "      One Never Knows Does One                            -VoE  60
     Vo  3440.  Please Keep Me in Your Dreams                       -VoE  60
         "      If My Heart Could Only Talk

                (Eddie Tomkins, trumpet; Buster Bailey, clarinet; Joe Thomas, tenor sax;
                Teddy Wilson, piano; Carmen Mastren, guitar; John Kirby, bass; Alphonse
                Steele, drums):
     Vo  3520.  They Can't Take That Away from Me                   -VoE  95
                Let's Call the Whole Thing Off
     Vo  3543.  I Don't Know If I'm Coming or Going/Where Is the Sun -VoE  93

                (Buck Clayton, trumpet; Edmond Hall, clarinet; Lester Young, tenor sax;
                James Sherman, piano; Freddie Green, guitar; Walter Page, bass; Jo Jones,
                drums):
     Vo  3593.  Me Myself and I/Without Your Love                   -VoE 106
     Vo  3605.  A Sailboat in the Moonlight/Born to Love

                (Benny Morton, trombone; Teddy Wilson, piano; Clayton, Young, Green, Page,
                Jones):
     Vo  3748.  Traveling All Alone/He's Funny That Way
     Vo  3947.  On the Sentimental Side/Now They Call It Swing

                (Personnel unknown):
     Vo  4029.  Back in Your Own Back Yard/When a Woman Loves a Man
     Vo  4126.  The Moon Looks Down and Laughs/You Go to My Head
     Vo  4238.  I Wish I Had You/I'm Gonna Lock My Heart
     Vo  4396.  I've Got a Date With a Dream(23469)/You Can't Be Mine(23470)
     Vo  4457.  The Very Thought of You/I Can't Get Started

                (Included Chu Berry, tenor?):
     Vo  4631.  That's All I Ask of You/Dream of Life
     Vo  4834.  Why Did I Always Depend on You?/You're Too Lovely to Last
     Vo  5021.  Some Other Spring(w24877)/Them There Eyes(w24879)

                (Includes Frank Newton, trumpet):
     Vo  5129.  Swing Brother Swing/Our Love Is Different

                (Joe Sullivan, piano; Freddie Green, guitar; Jo Jones, drums; Walter Page,
                bass; Earl Warren, Lester Young, Jack Washington, saxes; Harry Edison, Buck
                Clayton, trumpets):
     Vo  5302.  You're Just a No Account(w26343)/You're a Lucky Guy(w26344)
     Vo  5377.  Night and Day(w26341)/The Man I Love(w26342)        -Cq 9457
```

        (Kermit Scott, James T. Powell, Carl Frye, saxes; Roy Eldridge, trumpet;
        Sonny White, piano; Lawrence Lucie, guitar; Johnny Williams, bass; Harold
        Went, drums):
Vo 5481. Body and Soul/What Is This Going to Get us?
Vo 5719. Tell Me More/Laughing at Life
Vo 5809. Falling in Love Again/Ghost of Yesterday

        (Teddy Wilson, piano; Roy Eldridge, trumpet; Al Hall, bass; John Collins,
        guitar; Kenneth Clarke, drums; George Auld, Don Redman, Don Byas, Jimmy
        Hamilton, saxes):
Vo 5806. The Same Old Story(28619)/Practice Makes Perfect(28620)
OK 5831. I'm All for You(28617)/I Hear Music(28618)

        (Personnel unknown):
OK 5991. I'm Pulling Through(w26900)/Time on My Hands(w26903)

        (Orchestra directed by Benny Carter):
OK 6064. St. Louis Blues(28874)/Loveless Love(28875)

        (Unknown):
OK 6214. All of Me/Romance in the Dark
OK 6270. God Bless the Child/Solitude
OK 6369. Love Me or Leave Me/Jim
OK 6451. Gloomy Sunday/I'm in a Low Down Groove

        (Sonny White, piano; Kenneth Holton, tenor sax; Jimmy McLin, guitar; John
        Williams, bass; Eddie Dougherty, drums):
Com 526. Strange Fruit(wp24403b)/Fine and Mellow(wp24405a; see below)

        (Add Frank Newton, trumpet; Tab Smith, Alto; Stanley Payne, tenor sax):
Com 527. I Gotta Right to Sing the Blues(wp24406b)/Yesterdays(wp24404a; first
                                                                              (personnel
        (Eddie Heywood, piano; Teddy Walters, guitar; Doc Cheatham, trumpet; Lem
        Davis, alto sax; Vic Dickenson, trombone; John Simmons, bass; Sid Catlett
        drums):
Com 553. I'll Get By(4744-1)/I'll Be Seeing You(4750-1)
        (See also Teddy Wilson)

HOLLYWOOD SHUFFLERS:
Vo 15837. Low Down Rhythm/Gotta Feeling for You
Vo 15841. Bigger and Better Than Ever/(rev., Louisiana Rhythm Kings)

HOMETOWN SKIFFLE (Blind Lemon Jefferson, Blind Blake, Will Ezell, Charlie Spand,
Hokum Boys, Charlie Jackson):
Para 12886. Hometown Skiffle, 1 & 2 (921453/54)

HONEY DRIPPER (Roosevelt Sykes) blues singing:
De 7011. D-B-A Blues/Ethel Mae Blues
De 7160. Dirty Mother for You/She Left Me Cold in Hand
De 7164. Honey Dripper/Second Floor Blues
De 7173. Soft and Mellow/D-B-A Blues No. 2
De 7188. Cannon Ball/Jet Black Snake
De 7197. Sugar Hill Blues/Take Off Box
De 7252. Barrel House Man/Driving Wheel Blues
De 7280. Mister Sykes Blues/New Highway 61 Blues
De 7324. Little and Low/Night Time Is the Right Time
De 7352. Monte Carlo Blues/Bread Pan
De 7381. Let Me Hang My Stocking in Your Xmas Tree/Love Lease Blues
De 7401. Hospital Heaven or Hell/Sad Yas Yas Yas
De 7411. Night Gown Blues/My Baby's Background
De 7432. Hard Lead Pencil/Drunken Gambler
De 7438. Mistake in Life/Night Time Is the Right Time No. 2
De 7458. She's Long Gone/The Dog in a Man
De 7483. Down on My Knees/Train Is Coming
De 7586. 44 Blues/Have You Seen Ida B?
De 7597. Bitter Cup Blues/Love Will Wear You Down
De 7612. Papa Low/Shoe Shiner's Moan
De 7622. Journey from the Germs/You Can't Fix It Back
De 7642. Get Your Bow Out/Under Eyed Woman
De 7655. New Mistake in Life/We Will Never Make the Grade
De 7680. Unlucky Blues/I've Made a Change
De 7708. Concentration Blues/New Style Blues
De 7747. Yellow Yam Blues/Ups and Downs Blues
De 7785. Pistol Shootin' Blues/She's Got What It Takes

        (With bass and Sid Catlett, drums):
De 7796. Right Now/Essie May Blues
De 7843. Low As a Toad/Doin' the Sally Long

HONEY SWAMP STOMPERS:
Di 2856. Wipin' the Pan/Betty

HOPKINS AND HIS ORCHESTRA, CLAUDE (Albert Snaer, Sylvester Lewis, Ovie Alston, trumpets; Fernand Arbello, trombone; Gene Johnson, Edmond Hall, Bobby Sands, saxes; Claude Hopkins, piano; Walter Jones, guitar; Henry Turner, bass: Pete Jacobs, drums):

```
Co   2665. Anything for You                         -PaE 1479
      "    Mad Moments                              -PaE 1670
Co   2674. Mush Mouth                               -PaE 1329
      "    How'm I Doin'
Co   2741. California Here I Come                   -PaE 2083
      "    Look Who's Here
Co   2747. He's a Son of the South                  -PaE 1522
      "    Canadian Capers
Co   2880. Ain't Misbehavin'                        -PaE 2134
      "    Harlem Rhythm Dance                      -PaE 2283
Co   2904. Minor Mania                              -CoE 5019
      "    Marie                                    -PaE 1815
```

(Add Fred Norman, trombone; Bill Sauls, sax):

```
Br   6750. Washington Squabble(14437a)/Mystic Moan(14438a)   -BrE 01779
Br   6864. My Gal Sal/Three Little Words    -BrF 500445, BrE 01996
Br   6891. I Can't Dance                    -BrF 500444, BrE 01838
      "    Don't Let Your Love Go Wrong     -BrF 500443,    "
Br   6916. Everybody Shuffle(15161)         -BrF 500443, BrE 02025
      "    Margie(15164)                    -BrF 500444,
De    184. In the Shade of the Old Apple Tree
      "    King Porter Stomp                          -BrE 02120
De    185. Just You Just Me(38670)                   -BrE 01941
      "    Who (38673; voc., Orlando Roberson)
De    270. Sweetheart o' Mine/Walking the Dog        -BrE 02295
De    353. Mandy                                     -BrE 01976
      "    Do You Ever Think of Me                   -BrE 02120
De    374. Trees/Love in Bloom
De    441. June in January                           -BrE 01941
      "    Chasing All the Blues                     -BrE 01976
De    674. Monkey Business
      "    Zozoi
```

(Shirley Clay, Lincoln Mills, Jabbo Smith, trumpets; Floyd Brady, Fred Norman, Vic Dickenson, trombones; Chauncey Haughton, Gene Johnson, Bobby Sands, Ben Smith, saxes; Claude Hopkins, piano; Walter Jones, guitar; A. Baker, bass; Pete Jacobs, drums; Baby White, vocal):

```
De   1153. Sunday/Swingin' Down the Lane             -BrE 02397
De   1286. June Night/Church Street Sobbin' Blues    -BrE 02447
De   1316. Honey(62140)/My Kinda Love(62143)         -BrE 02464
```

(Albert Snaer, Russell Jones, Herman Autrey, trumpets; Ray Eogan, Norman Green, Bernard Asdier, trombones; Howard Johnson, Norman Thornton, Bobby Sands, Benny Waters, saxes; Walter Jones, guitar; Elmer James, bass; Walter Johnson, drums; Hopkins, piano; O.Roberson, vocals.--JI 3/8/40):

```
Ammor  115. Out to Lunch/What's the Matter with Me        Feb., 1940
Ammor    . I Believe You/A Little Rain Must Fall
Ammor    . The Singing Hills/Yacht Club Swing
```

HORSE AND THE MILK MEN, JOE:
```
Vr    553. Riverboat Shuffle/Shake It and Break It
```

HORSEY'S HOT FIVE (cornet, trombone, clarinet, piano, violin):   Feb., 1929
```
Ge   6722. Weeping Blues/Waitin' for You
```

HOT AIR MEN (First coupling under name of Seven Hot Air Men: Manny Klein, trumpet; Le Fleur, trombone; Benny Goodman, clarinet and alto sax; Rube Bloom, piano; Stanley King, drums; bass; guitar.--HD):   1929
```
Co   1850. Gotta Feelin'for You(148617)/Low Down Rhythm(148618)  -CoE 5562
```

(Sub. Phil Napoleon, trumpet; Jimmy Dorsey, clarinet and sax):   1930
```
Co   2092. Harlem Madness(149746)/Navy Blues(149747)    -CoE  53
Co   2175. Red Hot Chicago(150154)/Chinnin' and Chattin' With May(150155)
```

HOT AND HEAVY:
```
Pe    110. Memphis Rag/Louisiana Breakdown
```

HOT CLUB SWING STARS (Phillippe Brun, Pierre Allier, Baurice Moufflard, trumpets; Danny Polo, Max Blanc, alto saxes; Alix Combelle, Noel Chiboust, tenors; Louis Richardet, piano; Roger Chaput, guitar; Louis Vola, bass; Pierre Fouad, drums):
```
Sw     48. Morning Feeling(osw51)/Every Tub(osw51)
```

HOTSY TOTSY GANG (Jimmy McPartland, cornet; Fud Livingstone, clarinet; Dudley Fosdick, mellophone; Jack Pettis, tenor sax; Vic Briedis, piano; Eddie Lang, guitar; Harry Goodman, bass; Ben Pollack, drums; Elizabeth Welsh, vocals.--DB 1/1/43):
```
Br   4014. Digga digga do/Doin' the New Low Down                    1928
Br   4044. Don't Mess Around With Me/(rev., Washingtonians)
```

```
              (Jack Teagarden, trombone; Benny Goodman, sax and clarinet; one other
           sax; Dick McPartland, guitar; Briedis, Pollack, H.Goodman; Jimmy Mc-
           Partland and one other, trumpets; violin; Milton Irving, vocals):
     Br 4112. I Couldn't If I Wanter to/(rev., Meyer Davis)
     Br 4122. Since You Went Away(e28358; Oct.16,1928/(rev., Ellington)
     Br 4200. Out Where the Blues Begin/Futuristic Rhythm
              (See also; Irving Mills & Hotsy Totsy Gang)
HOTTENTOTS:
     Para 12359. Lots o' Mama(2519)/(rev., Austin Ambassadors)
     Vo  15161. Camel Walk/Down and Out Blues
     Vo  15234. Bass Ale Blues/Chinese Blues
HOUDINI, WILMOTH (acc. by Gerald Clark's Night Owls; Walter Bennett, cornet; Wal-
ter Edwards, clarinet and sax; Berry Baro, piano; Joshy Paris, guitar; Charlie Vin-
cento, banjo; Al Morgan, bass; Wilmoth Houdini, vocals.--EW):       Feb.16,1931
     Br  7192. No Mo'Bench and Board/The Cooks in Trinidad     -Me 12906, Pe 728
     Br  7201. Sweet Papa Willie/Honey I'm Bound to Go         -Me 12905, Pe 727
                                                                    Aug.1,1941
     Br  7219. Arima Tonight/Black But Sweet                  -Me 12904, Pe 726
     Br  7224. I Need a Man/Stop Coming and Come              -Me 12903, Pe 725

HOUND HEAD HENRY (vocals accompanied by Cow Cow Davenport, piano):
     Vo  1208. Freight Train Special(o2170)                         Aug.1,1928
            "  Steamboat Blues(c2189)                               Aug.9,1928
     Vo  1209. Rooster Crowin' Blues(c2455)                         Oct. 9,1928
            "  Hound Head Blues(c2169)                              Aug. 1,1928
     Vo  1210. Cryin' Blues(c2274)/Laughin' Blues(o2275)            Aug.29,1928
     Vo  1288. My Silver Dollar Mama(c2452)/Low Down Hound Blues(c2451) Oct.17,1928
HOWARD AND HIS ORCHESTRA, BOB (Collective personnel: Bob Howard, vocals and piano;
Buster Bailey or Barney Bigard, alto sax and clarinet; Ben Webster, tenor sax;Ben-
ny Carter, saxes and clarinet; Rex Stewart(?),trumpet; Teddy Wilson, piano;Clarence
Haliday, guitar; Elmer James or Billy Taylor,bass; Cozy Cole, drums;others.--RR):
     De  343. You Fit into the Picture                         -BrE 02111
          "  Throwin' Stones at the Sun                        -BrE   221
     De  347. It's Unbelievable                                -BrE 02097
          "  Whisper Sweet                                     -BrE   221
     De  400. The Ghost of Dinah(39387a)
          "  Pardon My Love(39388a)                            -BrE   244
     De  407. Breakin' the Ice/On the Night of June the Third
     De  439. Stay Out of Love(39390a)                         -BrE   229
          "  I'll Never Change(39391a)                         -BrE   244
     De  460. Ev'ry Day
          "  Porter's Love Song to a Chambermaid
     De  484. Corrine Corrina(39518a)                          -BrE 02042
          "  I Can't Dance(39521a)                             -BrE 02042
     De  504. If the Moon Turns Green                          -BrE 02097
          "  Lulu's Back in Town
     De  513. In a Little Gypsy Tea Room/Lost My Rhythm
     De  524. I'm Painting the Town Red/I Never Saw a Better Night
     De  598. Sugar Plum(60074a)
          "  It's Written in the Stars(60075a)                 -BrE 02111
     De  627. It's Funny What a Kiss Can Do
          "  Give Me a Break Baby                              -BrE 02192

          (Bunny Berigan, trumpet, next two sides):
     De  689. Whose Big Baby Are You/You Hit the Spot          -BrE 02158
     De  720. Spreadin' Rhythm Around                          -BrE 02192
          "  Wake Up and Sing
     De  722. Much Too Much/Garbo Green                        -BrE 02191
     De  839. The Best Things Happen at Night(60939a)/Let's Not Fall in Love(60981a)
     De  862. Public Weakness, no.1/If Love Is Blind
     De  917. Sing Baby Sing                                   -BrE 02323
          "  Bojangles of Harlem                               -BrE 02296
     De  927. Mendel's Son's Swing Song(61256a)                -BrE 02296
          "  Swingin' on the Moon(61258b)                      -BrE 02323
     De  983. You're Giving Me a Song and a Dance/Hop Skip Jump
     De  990. Copper Colored Girl(61311a)/That's What You Mean to Me(61312a)

          (Bob Howard, vocal; Marty Marsala, trumpet; Syd Trucker, clarinet; Frank
          Froeba, piano; Dave Barbour, guitar; Haig Stephens, bass; Stanley King,
          drums):
     De  1195. Spring Cleaning(62037)/You're Just a Little Diff(62039)
     De  1205. Me Myself and I/You Can't Take It With You

          (Babe Rusin,tenor sax and clarinet; Slats Long,clarinet; Frank Victor
     De  1293. You're Precious to Me(62204a)/Fan My Brow(62205a)    (guitar):
     De  1306. Formal Night in Harlem(62206a)/He's a gypsy from Poughkeepsie(62207a)
     De  1357. Easy Living(62348a)/Sing and Be Happy(62350a)
     De  1372. Penny Wise Pound Foolish(62351)/I'll Take the Key and Lock You Up
     De  1489. Beat It Out/She's Tall She's Tan She's Terrific         (62349)
     De  1605. I'm Sorry I Made You Cry(62634a)/What Do You Want to Make Those Eyes
                                                              (at Me For(62635a)
```

```
                (Howard, vocal; Frank Froeba, piano; Teddy Bunn, guitar; Haig Stephens,
           bass; O'Neil Spencer, drums):
     De  1698. Raggedy But Righ/If You're a Viper
     De  1721. Baby and It Must Be Love/There Ain't Gonna Be No Doggone After While
     De  1790. Just About the Time/Talk to Me
     De  1869. Toodle-oo/In My Miz
     De  1958. Southern Casey Jones/Dapper Dan
     De  2056. I Used to Love You/Beale Street Mama
     De  2112. Kentucky Sure As You're Born(64347a)/Any Rags(64348a)
     De  2263. Sweet Emmalina/On Revival Day
     De  2356. I Can Tell By Looking in Your Eyes/Bundle of Love
     De  2730. You Better Come Back(64232a)/Keepin'Out of Mischief Now(64344a)
```

HOWARD, DARNELL, saxes and clarinet, see:
    ALABAMA RASCALS:
    JIMMY BERTRAND: Vo 1280.
    EARL HINES
    KING OLIVER: Brunswick and Vocalion.
    LUIS RUSSELL: OK 8424, 8454.
    RICHARD M. JONES: Se 12006, 12007.

HOWARD, EDDY (vocal acc. by Lou Adrian Orchestra: Jimmy McPartland, Lloyd Whalen, trumpets; Floyd Bean, piano; Larry Bauer, John Read, Bob Gebbart, trombones; Mike Simpson, clarinet and tenor sax; Hans Muenzer, Irving Kaplan, Adrian Freiche, Norman Stone, violins; Art Sandley, guitar; Paul Liddell, bass; Oscar Lluelman, drums):
```
     Co 35455. The Singing Hills/Where Was I
     Co 35471. Say It/Mements in the Moonlight
     Co 35511. Fools Fall in Love(wc3053)/The Nearness of You(wc3054)
     Co 35599. I'll Never Smile Again/Now I Lay Me Down to Dream
     Co 35747. How Deep Is the Ocean/Jealous
```
            (Acc. by Teddy Wilson Orchestra: Edmond Hall, clarinet; Bill Coleman, trumpet; Bud Freeman, tenor sax; Benny Morton, trombone; Teddy Wilson, piano; Charles Christian, guitar; Billy Taylor, bass; Yank Porter, drums):
```
     Co 35771. Old Fashioned Love(co28794)/Stardust(co28795)
     Co 35915. Exactly Like You(co28796)/Wrap Your Troubles in Dreams(co28797)
```
            (Personnel unknown):
```
     Co 35794. Whatever Happened to You/When it's Christmas on the Range
     Co 35868. Mean to Me/Or Have It
     Co 35949. Among My Souvenirs/Tonight You Belong to Me
     Co 36104. You Lucky People You/I Forgive But Can't For---
     Co 36074. Do I Worry/My Sister and I
     Co 36183. I Tried/Some Must Win
     Co 36303. Yours/I Want Out of My Way
     Co 36330. Harbor of Dreams/I'm Still Without a Sweetheart
```

HOWARD, JANE (vocal with piano and cornet):
     Or 1032. Hard Hearted Papa(1121)/Peepin' Jim Blues(1124)

HOWARD'S QUALITY SERENADERS, PAUL (Paul Howard, tenor sax; Charlie Lawrence, alto and clarinet; Lloyd Reese, alto sax; George Orndorff, Earl Thompson, trumpets; Lawrence Brown, trombone; Lionel Hampton, drums; Harvey Brooks, piano: James Jackson, bass; Thomas Valentine, banjo.--DB 11/38):
```
     Vi 22001. Overnight Blues/Charlie's Idea              -Vi 38070
     Vi 22660. New Kinda Blues(rev.,Benny Moten)           -HMV 6291
     Vi 23354. Harlem/California Swing
     Vi 23420. Cuttin'Up/Gettin' Ready Blues
     Vi 38068. Moonlight Blues
         "     The Ramble                                  -BB 5804
     Vi 38122. Quality Shout
         "     Stuff                                       -BB 5804
```

HOWARD, ROSETTA (blues singing with orchestra):
```
     De 7370. Rosetta Blues/If You're a Viper
     De 7392. Let Your Linen Hang Low/Worried Mind Blues
     De 7410. It's Your Turn/Let's Fall in Love Again
     De 7447. Harlem Jamboree/You Got to Go
     De 7459. How Long Baby/Stay on It
     De 7515. It Will Never Happen Again/Trading Old Love
     De 7531. All on Account of You/Oh Rider
     De 7551. Candy Man/Stay Away from My Door
     De 7618. Jive Is Here/Men Are Like Street Cars
     De 7627. Come Easy Go Easy(65756)/Plain Lenox Avenue(65811)
```
            (Acc. by Harlem Blues Serenaders: Charlie Shavers, trumpet; Buster Bailey clarinet; Lil Armstrong, piano; Wellman Braud, bass; O'Neil Spencer, drums; Ulysses Livingston, guitar):
```
     De 7658. He's Mine All Mine/Hog Wild Blues
     De 7640. Stomp It Out Gate/My Blues Is Like Whiskey
     De 7687. Delta Bound/My Downfall
```

HOWELL, BERT (with Fats Waller, organ):
   Vi 21062. Bye Bye Florence

HOWELL, PEG LEG (vocal with guitar):
   Co 14177. New Prison Blues/Fo' Day Blues
   Co 14194. Coal Man Blues/Tishimingo Blues
   Co 14210. New Jelly Roll Blues/Beaver Slide
   Co 14238. Sadie Lee/Papa Stobb
   Co 14320. Low Down Rounder/Rock and Gravel
   Co 14473. Skin Game Blues/Doin' Wrong

          PEG LEG HOWELL AND EDDIE ANTHONY:
   Co 14382. Turkey Buzzard Blues/Banjo Blues

          PEG LEG HOWELL AND HIS GANG
   Co 14270. Hobo Blues/Moanin' and Groanin'
   Co 14298. Peg Leg Stomp/Too Tight Blues

YOUR HELP IS NEEDED

No one person could profess to be an expert on all the records which will be inclosed in this list in its final form. There are many gaps in personnels; data are missing altogether on hundreds of records. This is only the basic list; the rest is up to collectors, all of whom are asked to share in perfecting a complete and accurate index to jazz. Send your corrections and additions to Orin Blackstone, 1016 Eleonore Street, New Orleans 15, Louisiana.

PAGE NO.	RECORDING GROUP	LABEL	SERIAL NUMBER	WAS SHOWN:	SHOULD HAVE BEEN SHOWN:

HUDSON AND HIS ORCHESTRA, DEAN:
    OK   6148. Can't You Tell(29881)/Red River Valley(29880)

HUDSON AND HIS ORCHESTRA, WILL:
    Br   8113. Travelin' Down the Trail/(rev., Sidney Phillips)
    Br   8147. China Clipper/Why Pretend
    Br   8156. One I Love Belongs to Somebody Else/On the Alamo
    Br   8164. There's Something About an Old Love/The Flat Foot Floogee
    Br   8177. Hangover in Hong Kong/Lady of the Night
    Br   8191. The Night Is Filled With Music/May I Have My Heart Back
    Br   8195. The Corrigan Hop/Miracle at Midnight
    Br   8213. I Haven't Changed a Thing(m858)/(rev., Ellington)

HUDSON-DeLANGE ORCHESTRA (George Bohn, Ted Duane, Hugh Hibbert, Pete Brendel, saxes and clarinet; James O'Connell, Steve Lipkin, Ralph Hollenbeck, trumpets; Edward Kolyer, trombone; Mark Hyams, piano; Clifford Rausch, guitar; Edward Goldberg, bass; Edward O'Hara, drums; Ruth Gaylor, vocals.--RR):   1936
    Br   7598. It's a Lot of Idle Gossip(18504)
     "   Tormented(18506)   -BrE 02199
    Br   7618. Eight Bars in Search of a Melody   -BrE 02199
     "   Hobo on Park Avenue   -BrE 02260
    Br   7656. Organ Grinders Swing/You're Not the Kind   -VoE 508
    Br   7637. Monopoly Swing/(rev., Ellington)   -BrE 02260
    Br   7700. It Seems I've Done Something Wrong Again/The Moon Is Grinning at Me
    Br   7708. When It's Sleepy Time Down South/I Never Knew

         (Sub. Wilbert Sieloff, trumpet, for Lipkin, Hollenbeck):
    Br   7715. Mint Julep/Mr. Ghost Goes to Town   -VoE 525
    Br   7727. What the Heart Believes/Looking Down at the Stars
    Br   7743. Grab Your Partner and Swing(19689)/Cross Country Hop(19690)
    Br   7785. Remember When/I'll Never Tell You I Love You
    Br   7795. If We Never Meet Again/Midnight at the Onyx
    Br   7809. How Was I to Know/Am I Intruding
    Br   7828. Love Song of a Half Wit, 1 & 2
    Br   7991. Sophisticated Swing/The Maid's Night Off   -Mal03
    Br   7998. Back in Your Arms/You're My Desire
    Ma   112. Wake Up and Live(m220)/Never in a Million Years(m222)
    Ma   125. Star Dust/Bugle Call Rag   -Br 7996
    Ma   138. Yours and Mine(m543)/I'm Feelin'Like a Million(m544) -Br 8002

         (Joe Bauer, Charles Mitchell, Howard Schaumburg, trumpets; Jack Andrews;
         Ed Collier, trombones; Ted Duane, George Bovina, tenor saxes; Pete Brendel, Gus Bivona, altos; Mark Hyams, piano; Ed Goldberg, bass; Bus Etri, guitar; Bill Exner, drums):
    Br   8007. Goin' Haywire/Popcorn Man
    Br   8016. If I Could Be With You/Magnolia
    Br   8023. Rockin' the Town/My Heaven on Earth
    Br   8040. Error in the News/College Widow
    Br   8049. Strictly Formal/You're Out of this World
    Br   8071. Definition of Swing/Off Again on Again
    Br   8077. Doin' the Reactionary/Sunday in the Park
    Br   8081. At Your Beck and Call/Mr. Sweeney's Learned to Swing
    Br   8090. I Know That You Know/I Never Knew

HUGHES AND HIS NEGRO ORCHESTRA, SPIKE (Shad Collins, Leonard Davis, Bill Dillard, trumpets; Dicky Wells, Wilbur de Paris, George Washington, trombones; Benny Carter, Howard Johnson, altos; Coleman Hawkins, tenor sax; Rodriguez, piano; Lawrence Lucie, guitar; Ernest Hill, bass; Kaiser Marshall, drums.--HD):
    DeE 3563. Nocturne(13257)   -De 18170
     "   Someone Stole Gabriel's Horn(13258)

         (Sidney Catlett, drums):
    DeE 3606. Pastoral(13259)/Bugle Call Rag(13260)

         (Sub. Henry Allen, trumpet, for Collins; Luis Russell, piano; add Chu
         Berry, tenor sax; Wayman Carver, alto sax and flute):
    DeE 3639. Arabesque(13352)   -De 18170
     "   Fanfare(13353)

         (Rodriguez, piano):
    DeE 3717. Donegal Cradle Song(13360)/Firebird(13361)
    DeE 3836. Music at Sunrise(13362)/Music at Midnight(13355; Russell piano)

         (Allen, Wells only, brass):
    DeE 3972. Sweet Sue Just You(13356)/How Come You Do Me Like You Do(13363)

         (Previous personnel):
    DeE 5101. Air in D Flat(13359)/Sweet Sorrow Blues(13354; Russell piano)
    De   191. Sirocco/Six Bells Stampede

HUMES, HELEN (vocal with piano and/or guitar):
  OK 8467. Black Cat Moan/A Worried Woman's Blues
  OK 8529. Alligator Blues/Everybody Does It Now
  OK 8545. Do What You Did/If Papa Has Outside Loving
  OK 8674. Garlic Blues/Nappy Headed Blues
  OK 8825. Cross Eyed Blues(81872)/Race Horse Blues(81882)

HUNTER, ALBERTA (voc., acc. by Henderson Novelty
  BS 2008. How Long Sweet Daddy How Long(121-2)/Bring Back the Joys(124-2)

    (Acc. by Ray's Dreamland Orchestra):
  BS 2019. He's a Darn Good Man(120-1,2)/Some Day Sweetheart(125-3)

    (Unknown orchestra accompaniment):
  Para 12001. Daddy Blues/Don't Pan Me When I'm Gone
  Para 12005. Down Hearted Blues(1105)/Gonna Have You(1107)
  Para 12006. Jazzin' Babies Blues/I'm Going Away
  Para 12007. Lonesome Monday Morning Blues(1181)/(rev., Sissel and Blake)
  Para 12014. Come on Home(1316)/Aggravatin' Papa(1325)
  Para 12016. If You Want to Keep Daddy/Tain't Nobody's Biz-ness

    (Fletcher Henderson, piano):
  Para 12017. Chirping the Blues(1321)/Someone Else Will Take Your Place(1322)
  Para 12018. Bring It With You When You Come
  Para 12020. Vamping Brown/You Can Take My Man

    (Henderson's orchestra):
  Para 12021. You Shall Reap Just What You Sow(1317)/Bleeding Hearted Blues(1320;
                                                                     (acc. by Original Memphis 5)
  Para 12036. Michigan Water Blues(1425)/Down South Blues(1426)

    (Henderson, piano):
  Para 12043. Mistreated Blues(1420)/I'm Going Away(1111; duet w. Eubie Blake)
  Para 12065. Experience Blues/Sad 'n Lonely Blues

    (Lovie Austin, piano):
  Para 12066. Miss Anna Brown(1530)/Maybe Someday(1531; J.Oubrigant, cornet)

    (Acc. by guitar and piano):
  Vi 19159. Love Me/Potomac River Blues

    (Fats Waller, organ):
  Vi 20771. Beale Street Blues/Sugar

    (Guitar and piano):
  Co 14450. Gimme All the Love You Got(148822)/My Particular Man(148823)

    (Acc. by Perry Bradford's Mean Four):
  OK 8268. Your Jelly Roll Is Good(73830b)/Take That Thing Away(73831b)
  OK 8315. I Don't Want It All(73905b)/Empty Cellar Blues(73920b; sax,cornet,
                                                                                                     (piano)
    (Clarence Williams, piano):
  OK 8365. If You Can't/You for Me

    (Perry Bradford's Mean Four):
  OK 8393. Wasn't It Nice/I Didn't Come
  OK 8409. Don't Forget to Mess Around(74333a)/I'm Tired Blues(74322b; piano &
                                                                                                           (trumpet)
    (Joe Oliver, cornet; Lil Armstrong, piano,--DB 7/15/43):
  -- -----. Dead Man Blues
  -- -----. Some Day Sweetheart

    (Acc. by Charlie Shavers, trumpet; Lil Armstrong, piano; Buster Bailey,
    clarinet; Wellman Braud, bass):   1939
  De 7633. Fine and Mellow/Yelpin' the Blues
  De 7644. Chirpin' the Blues(66104)/I'll See You Go(66106)
  De 7727. Downhearted Blues/Someday Sweetheart

    (Unknown accompaniment):
  BB 8485. Boogie Woogie Swing/I Won't Let You Down
    BB 8539. My Castle's Rocking/The Love I Have for You

HUNTER'S SERENADERS (Lloyd Hunter's orchestra directed by Victoria Spivey; including Joe Jones, drums):   1931
  Vo 1621. Sensational Mood/I'm Dreaming 'Bout My Man

HYMAN'S BAYOU STOMPERS, JOHN (John Hyman, cornet; Elry Maser, clarinet; Alvin Gau-
treaux, harmonica; Horace Diaz,piano;Hilton Lamare, guitar; Monk Hazel,drums;Chas.
Hartman, trombone):
  Vi 20593. Alligator Blues/Ain't Love Grand

I

IDAHO, BERTHA (vocal with piano acc.):
   Co 14355. Graveyard Love(146321)/You've Got the Right Eye(146322)

     (Acc. by cornet and piano):
   Co 14437. Move It on Out of Here/Down on Pennsylvania Avenue

IDEAL SERENADERS:
   Co 1131. Dawning/Shady Tree

INDIANA FIVE (Possibly Red Nichols, trumpet; Miff Mole, trombone; Eddie Lang, guitar; Vic Berton, drums; Arthur Schutt, piano; Fud Livingstone, clarinet.--See JI, 7/26/40):
   Ro   577. Nobody's Sweetheart(2895)/Where Will I Be(2896)
   Chal 591. Where Will I Be (1365)
               - - -
   Re 8337. Some of These Days   -Ba 6006
      (See also:Original Indiana Five, different band)

IPANA TROUBADOURS (Directed by Sam Lanin and sometimes reputedly featuring Benny Goodman, clarinet; the Dorsey brothers and others):
   Co   595. Sunny/Who
   Co   662. Roses Remind Me of You/When the Red Red Robin Comes
   Co   696. Baby Face/Why Do You Want to Know Why
   Co   738. Mary Lou(142603)/In a Little Garden(142604)
   Co 1009. Wherever You Go/Side by Side
   Co 1098. Give Me a Night in June/Are You Happy
   Co 1188. Dream Kisses(/rev., Ben Selvin)
   Co 1212. There's One Little Girl/(rev.; Leo Reisman)
   Co 1213. 'S Wonderful/(rev., Clicquot Club)
   Co 1283. Four Walls(145549)/In the Sing Song Sycamore Tree(145551)
   Co 1308. Sunshine/After My Laughter Came Tears
   Co 1412. Dixie Dawn/I'm Riding to Glory
   Co 1463. Nagasaki/Down Where the Sun Goes Down
   Co 1638. Glorianna/Do You
   Co 1694. I'll Get By(voc., Bing Crosby)/Rose of Mandalay(voc., Bing Crosby)
   Co 2006. Sweeter Than Sweet/My Strongest Weakness
   Co 2117. Kickin' a Hole in the Sky/Cooking Breakfast for the One I Love
   Co 2174. Blue Is the Night/Whippoorwill
   Co 2271. I Don't Mind Walkin' in the Rain/My Bluebird Was Caught in the Rain
   Co 2340. Blue Again/Button Up Your Heart
   Co 2541. You're My Only Sweetheart(waltz)/When It's Sleepy Time Down South

IRVIN, KITTY (voc., acc. by piano,possibly Mel Stitzel, and clarinet, possibly Volly de Faut.--DB 9/15/41):   1924
   Ge 5592. Daddy Do(85044a)/Copenhagen(85045b)   -Clax -----*
      *(Issued under name of Trixie Wallace)

IRVING AND THE BOYS, REX (Willis Kelly, trumpet; Sidney Perlmutter, clarinet; Sidney Peltyn, mellophone; Sam Shoobe, bass; Irving Riskin, piano; Henry Ross, tenor sax; Milton Schlesinger, drums):
   Roy 1787. Swing March(usl062)/Toy Department(usl065)
   Roy 1797. They're Off(usl063)/Dance Henry(usl064)

     (Peltyn doubles on trumpet):
   Roy 1845. Elegy to a Jitterbug(usl336)/The Acrobat(usl338)

IRWIN, PEE WEE (trumpet) see:
   HENRY ALLEN: Pe 15933, 15948, 16071, 16080.
   BROADWAY BANDITS: RZ 1733.
   TOMMY DORSEY: Vi 25544 to 26097; 26163 to 26356; 26508 -
   DORSEY CLAMBAKE SEVEN: Vi 25568 to 26370.
   BENNY GOODMAN: Co 2998 to 3033; Vi 25009 to 25024; 25279 to 25411.

J

JACK O' DIAMONDS:
 Para 12786.

JACKSON'S PLANTATION ORCHESTRA, ALEX:
   Ge 6296. Missouri Squabble/I Call You Sugar
   Ge 6249. Jack Ass Blues/(rev., State Street Ramblers)
JACKSON, BESSIE (Lucille Bogan), accompanied by piano (Walter Roland or Walter Scott):
   Pe 0197. Black Angel Blues/Tricks Ain't Walkin'

```
Pe   0198. Sloppy Drunk Blues(c5562)/Alley Boogie(c5563)        -Me 12484, Ro 5122
Pe   0253. Troubled Mind(13605)/Seaboard Blues(13589)                 -Me 12763
Pe   0281. New Muscle Shoals Blues(13609)/Red Cross Man(13548)        -Ro 5342
Pe   0295. Down in Boogie Alley(15508)/Sweet Man Sweet Man(15506)     -Me 13116
Pat 350913. That's What My Baby Likes(16965)/Man Stealer Blues 16997)
Pe   0308. Reckless Woman(15507)/Tired As I Can Be(15505)             -Me 13280
Pe   0329. Skin Game Blues(17014)/Stew Meat Blues(17013)              -Me 13415
Pe   0332. Shave 'em Dry(61972)/Barbecue Bess(16984)                  -Me 13442
Pe  60463. Lonesome Midnight Blues/You've Got to Die Some Day
Me  12485. Roll and Rattler/Groceries on the Shelf
Me  12774. T.N. & O. Blues/House Top Blues
Me  12899. My Baby Come Back/Superstitious Blues
Me  13021. Baking Powder Blues(13569)/Mean Twister(13604)
Me  13342. My Man Is Boogan Me(15487)/Pig Iron Sally(15490)
Me  51258. Jump Steady Daddy(16993)/B.D. Woman's Blues(16991)
Me  60264. I Hate That Train Called the M & O(15491)/Changed Ways Blues(15519)
```

<u>JACKSON, BO WEAVIL</u> (singing with guitar):
Para 12389. Pistol Blues(2675)/You Can't Keep No Brown(2678)

<u>JACKSON'S SWANEE SERENADERS, BUD</u> (Alto sax and clarinet; tenor sax; trumpet;trombone; piano; drums; banjo):
Br   3351. Messin' Around/Heebie Jeebies

<u>JACKSON, (PAPA) CHARLIE</u> (vocal blues, with banjo, guitar or ukelele accompaniment):
```
Para 12219. Papa's Lawdy Lawdy Blues(1850)/Airy Man Blues(1851)
Para 12236. Salt Lake City Blues(1892)/Salty Dog Blues(1893)
Para 12259. The Cats Got the Measles(10019)/I Got What It Takes(10020)
Para 12281. Shake That Thing(2120)/The Faking Blues(2121)
Para 12289. Drop That Sack/I'm Alabama Bound
Para 12296. Take Me Back Blues(2208)/Mama Don't Allow It(2223)
Para 12305. Mama Don't You Think I Know/Hot Papa Blues
Para 12422. Fat Mouth Blues/Gay Cattin'
Para 12501. Skoodle-um-Skoo/Sheik of Deslaines Street
Para 12553. Look Out Papa/Baby Don't Be So Mean
Para 12574. Blue Monday Morning Blues/Bright Eyes
Para 12602. I'm Looking for a Woman/Long Gone Lost John
Para 12660. Ash Tray Blues/No Need of Knockin' on the Blind
Para 12721. Corn Liquor Blues(21046-1)/Jungle Man Blues(21045-2)
Para 12736. Don't Break Down on Me/Baby Please Loan Me Your Heart
```

<u>JACKSON AND HIS CRAZY KATS, CLIFF</u> (Mel Herbert, Henry Goodwin, trumpets; Rudy Powell, alto and clarinet; Earl Evans, alto; Horace Langhorne, tenor; Cliff Jackson, piano; Andy Jackson, banjo; Chester Campbell, tuba; Percy Johnson, drums.--JI 9/6/40):   1930
    VD   923. Horse Feathers
    VD 81842. Torrid Rhythm (and eight other sides)

    CLIFF JACKSON QUARTET (Cliff Jackson, piano; Pee Wee Russell, clarinet;
    Bob Casey, bass; Jack Parker, drums):   Mar.4,1944
    B&W   3. Quiet Please/Squeeze Me

    CLIFF JACKSON (piano solos):   July 16,1944
    B&W   8. It Had to Be You(qc2563-1)/(rev., Black and White Quartet)

    CLIFF JACKSON'S VILLAGE CATS(Sidney de Paris, trumpet; Wilbur de Paris,
    trombone; Sidney Bechet, soprano sax and clarinet; Gene Sedric, tenor sax
    and clarinet; Cliff Jackson, piano; Everett Barsdale, guitar; Wellman
    Braud, bass; Eddie Dougherty, drums):
    B&W 1204. Quiet Please/Walking and Talking to Myself
    B&W 1205. Cliff's Boogie Blues/Jeepers Creepers

<u>JACKSON'S PEACOCK ORCHESTRA, DEWEY</u> (Dewey Jackson, cornet; Albert Snaer, trumpet; W.Luper, trombone; Willie Humphrey, tenor sax; Thornton Blue, alto sax and clarinet; Cliff Cochran, alto; Floyd Campbell, drums; Burroughs Lovingood, piano; Pete Robinson, banjo; Pop Foster, string bass; Cecil White, tuba.--DB 4/1/41):
                                                              St.Louis,June 21,1926
    Vo 1039. Go'won to Town/What Do You Want Poor Me to Do(voc. by Campbell,acc.
                                                       (by Jackson and Lovingood
    Vo 1040. Capitol Blues
         "   She's Cryin' for Me   -Br 80039

<u>JACKSON'S SERENADERS, DUKE</u> (Alto sax,; trumpet; trombone; piano; drums; banjo;bass):
    Ge 6124. Pewee Blues/Now Cut Loose   1927

<u>JACKSON AND HIS MUSICAL CHAMPIONS, EARL</u> (Duke Ellington's Orchestra, first two sides same session as Ellington Br 6093):   1932
    Me 12080. Is That Religion?   -BrE 01226
         "   Peanut Vendor
    Me 12093. Black and Tan Fantasy/Rockin' Chair   -Po 9006

(Wardell Jones, Shelton Hemphill, Edward Anderson, trumpets; Harry White, Henry Hicks, trombones; Theodore McCord, Crawford Wethlington, Castor McCord, saxes; Edgar Hayes, piano; Benny James, banjo; Hayes Alvis, bass; Willie Lynch, drums.--HD):
Me 12164. Red Devil   -BrE 01226, Me 12662, Po 9004
"   Minnie the Moocher   -Pe "
Pe 15332. Song of the Congo/The Kiss Waltz

JACKSON AND HIS ORCHESTRA, EDDIE:
Vo 2652. Dancing in the Moonlight/Little Dutch Mill

JACKSON AND HIS JACKSONIANS, FRANZ (Franz Jackson, tenor sax; Ken Kersey, piano and others):
De 7730. Boogie Woogie Camp Meeting   -De 3833
"   Summer Rhapsody
De 7779. Elephant Swing/You're the Maker of the Rain in My Heart

JACKSON AND HIS THUMPERS, FRISKY FOOT:
Ch 40043. Maxwell Street Stomp/Good Time Mama

JACKSON, JIM (vocal with guitar):
Vo 1144. Jim Jackson's Kansas City Blues, 1 & 2
Vo 1155. Jim Jackson's Kansas City Blues, 3 & 4
Vo 1164. I'm a Bad Bad Man(649)/I'm Gonna Start Me a Graveyard(651)

(Add Piano):
Vo 1284. Hey Mama it's Nice Like That, 1 & 2
                                                      May 9,1931
Vo 1295. Foot Achin' Blues(c3499)/Love Sick Blues(c3500) -Su 2214
Vo 1413. Ain't You Sorry Mama, 1 & 2
                                                      Sept,24,1929
Vo 1428. Jim Jackson's Jamboree, 1 & 2 (m204/205; with Georgia Tom, Tampa Red,
                                                      (Speckled Red)
(With guitar):
Vi 21387. I Heard the Voice of a Pork Chop(41802)/Old Dog Blue(41827)
Vi 21671. I'm Gonna Move to Louisiana, 1 & 2
Vi 38003. This Morning She was Gone/This Ain't No Place for Me
Vi 38525. I'm Wild About My Lovin'/Goin' Round the Mountain

JACKSON, LULU (vocal with guitar):
Vo 1193. You're Going to Leave the Old Home   -Su 2227
"   Careless Love Blues

(Add piano):
Vo 1242. Lost Lover Blues/Blue Ridge Blues
Vo 1278. Little Rosewood Casket/You're Going to Leave the Old Home No.2

JACKSON, MARY (vocal with Fletcher Henderson, piano):
Pat 21059. Miss Liza Jackson/I Don't Let No One Man Bother Me

(Acc. by Perry Bradford Jazz Phools):
Pe 12092. All the Time/Who'll Get It When I'm Gone

JACKSON'S UPTOWN BAND, PRESTON (Preston Jackson, trombone; Shirley Clay, trumpet; Art Stocks or Starks, clarinet and alto sax; George Reynolds, piano; Frank Brasil, guitar; drums.--JI 7/26/40)
Para 12400. It's Tight Jim(2647)/Harmony Blues(2649)
Para 12411. Yearning for Mandalay (2648)/
"   West End Blues   -Chal 803*
           *Issued under name of Golden Melody Men

JACKSON, SADIE (vocal):
Co 14181. Nobody Worries 'Bout Me/Original Black Bottom

JACKSON AND HIS RED ONIONS, SMOKE (Same as Zack Whyte on Gennett and Eddie Walker on Supertone):
Ch 15714. It's Tight Like That   -Ch 40016*
"   West End Blues
Ch 15905. Mandy/Hum All Your Troubles Away
           *Issued under name of Chuck Nelson

JACKSON, WILLIE (vocal, first coupling with Steve Lewis, piano):
Co 14136. Willie Jackson's Blues(142025)/Old New Orleans Blues(142027)
Co 14165. Who'll Chop Your Suey When I'm Gone(142588; with Buddy Christian, banjo)/Charleston Hound(142591; C.Williams, pf)
Co 14284. Kansas City Blues(145560)/T.B. Blues(145561), guitar & piano acc.
Co 14432. Long Time Men(145299)/Corn and Bunion Blues(145400), sax & piano acc.

JACOBSON'S JUNGLE KINGS, BUD (Carl Rinker, cornet; Bud Jacobson, clarinet; Bud Hunter, tenor sax; Frank Melrose, piano; Joe Rushton, bass sax; Earl Wiley, drums):
Sig 103. Opus No.1 Sans Melody/I Can't Believe   Chicago, early 1941
Sig 106. Laughing at You/Clarinet Marmalade

```
    Jazz    102. Clarinet Marmalade(1608)/Opus No.1 Sans Melody(1611)
    Sig     904. Laughing at You(1609)/I Can't Believe(1610)

JAFFE, NAT (piano with Sid Jacobs, bass):                              1945
    Sig 28111. Black and Blue(fl006)/Zonky(fl007)
    Sig 28112. How Can You Face Me(fl004)/Keepin' Out of Mischief Now(fl005)

JAM SESSION AT COMMODORE NO. 1 (Bobby Hackett, cornet; Pee Wee Russell, clarinet;
Bud Freeman, tenor sax; George Brunis, trombone; Jess Stacy, piano; Eddie Condon,
guitar; George Wettling, drums; Artie Shapiro, bass):
    Com  1500. Carnegie Drag(xp22308)/Carnegie Jump(xp22309)

            JAM SESSION NO. 2 (sub. Jack Teagarden, trombone):
    Com  1501. Embraceable You(xp22830)/Serenade to a Shylock(xp22833)

            JAM SESSION NO. 3 (Muggsy Spanier, Max Kaminsky, cornets; Miff Mole,Brad
            Gowans, trombones; Joe Marsala, alto sax; Russell,Freeman,same rhythm):
    Com  1504. A Good Man Is Hard to Find, 1 & 2 (76329/31)
    Com  1505. A Good Man Is Hard to Find, 3 & 4 (76332/30)

            JAM SESSION NO. 4 (See Eddie Condon Com 1510)

            JAM SESSION NO. 5 (Max Kaminsky, trumpet; Pee Wee Russell, clarinet; Ben-
            Morton, trombone; Eddie Condon, guitar; Joe Bushkin, piano; Bob Casey,bass;
            Sid Catlett, drums):
    Com  1513. Basin Street Blues(a4689)/Oh Katharina(a4690-1)

JAM SESSION AT VICTOR (Bunny Berigan, trumpet; Tommy Dorsey, trombone; Fats Waller,
piano; Dick McDonough, guitar; George Wettling, drums.):              1937
    Vi 25559. Honeysuckle Rose/Blues                       -HMV 8580, GrF 7921

JAMES AND HIS ORCHESTRA, BILLY:
    Vs   6001. Come on In/Where Did You Stay Last Night
    Vs   6002. Champagne Charlie Is My Name/Depression Gone from Me Blues
```

HARRY JAMES

```
See also:
    ALL STAR BAND: Vi 26144.
    DEAN AND HIS KIDS: Vo 3342.
    BENNY GOODMAN: Vi 25500 to 36205.
    LIONEL HAMPTON: Vi 26011, 26017, 26039.
    BEN POLLACK: Br 7747, 7751, 7764; Vr 504, 556.
    TEDDY WILSON: Br 7884, 7893, 7940, 7943, 7964, 7973, 7954, 7960.

JAMES, HARRY and the Boogie Woogie Trio(Pete Johnson, piano; Eddie Dougherty,drums;
Johnny Williams, bass):
    Br   8318. Boo Woo(b24060)/Woo Woo(b24061; Albert Ammons,pf)     -Co 35958
    Br   8350. Home James(b24062)/Jesse(b24063; Albert Ammons,pf)

            HARRY JAMES AND HIS ORCHESTRA (Harry James, Buck Clayton, trumpets; Eddie
            Durham, trombone; Earl Warren, Jack Washington, Herschel Evans, saxes;
            Walter Page, bass; Jess Stacy, piano; Jo Jones, drums; Helen Humes,voc.):
    Br   8035. Life Goes to a Party/When We're Alone
    Br   8038. Can't I                                               -VoE 155
         "    Jubilee                                                -VoE 136

            (Sub. Vernon Brown, trombone):
    Br   8055. One o'Clock Jump(b22252)                              -Co 36233
         "    It's the Dreamer in Me                                 -VoE 155
    Br   8067. Texas Chatter/Song of the Wanderer                    -VoE 146

            (Harry James, Ziggy Elman, trumpets; Vernon Brown, trombone; Dave Matt-
            hews, Arthur Rollini, Harry Carney, saxes; Jess Stacy, piano; Dave Tough,
            drums; Therman Teague, bass):
    Br   8136. Lullaby in Rhythm/Out of Nowhere
    Br   8178. Little White Lies/Wrap Your Troubles in Dreams

            (Unknown personnel):
    Br   8327. Ciribiribin(bw24514)/Sweet Georgia Brown(bw24515)
    Br   8337. 'Tain't What You Do(bw24193; voc.,Jack Berg)
         "    Two o'Clock Jump(bw24194)                              -Co 36232
    Br   8355. And the Angels Sing(wb24346;voc.Bernice Byres)/Got No Time(wb24348)
    Br   8406. I Found a New Baby(wb24691)/Fannie May(wb24692)
    Br   8366. Indiana(wb24347)/King Porter Stomp(wb24349)
    Br   8443. From Bottom of My Heart(b25057;voc.,F.Sinatra)/Melancholy Mood(b25059)
    Vs   8194. Tuxedo Junction(usl361)/Palms of Paradise(usl363; voc.Fran Heines)
    Vs   8201. Headin' for Hallelujah(usl360)                        -El 5034
         "    Alice Blue Gown(usl362)
    Vs   8221. How High the Moon/You've Got Me Out on a Limb
```

```
Vs  8231. Hodge Podge(us1437)                                    -El 5028
     "    Carnival of Venice(us1440)
Vs  8264. Secrets in the Moonlight/Fools Rush In
Vs  8298. Four or Five Times                                     -El 5028
     "    Flight of the Bumble Bee
Vs  8349. It's the Last Time(us1805)                             -El 5027
     "    Orchids for Remembrance(us1807)
Vs  8382. A Million Dreams Ago

          (Harry James, Jack Palmer, Claude Bowen, Jake Schaeffer, trumpets; Truett
          Jones, Dalton Rizzotto, Bruce Squires, trombones; Dave Matthews,alto sax;
          Drew Page, clarinet and alto; Claude Lakey, tenor; Jack Gardner, piano;
          Red Kent, guitar; Thurman Teague, bass; Mickey Scrima, drums):      1939
Co 35209. It's Funny to Every One But Me(b25215; voc.,F.Sinatra)/Vol Vistu Gai-
                                               (ly Star(b25213; voc.,J.Palmer)

          (Add Bill Luther, sax):                                             1940
Co 35227. Here Comes the Night(co25285; voc.,Sinatra)/Feet Draggin' Bl(co25287)
Co 35242. My Buddy(co25212;voc.,Sinatra)/Willow Weep for Me(co25286)
Co 35261. Who Told You I Cared
     "    On a Little Street in Singapore                        -Co 36700
Co 35316. Ciribiribin (voc.,Sinatra)/Avalon
Co 35340. Concerto for Trumpet(la2051)/I'm in the Market for You(la2053)
Co 35456. Back Beat Boogie/Night Special
Co 35531. Cross Country Jump(la2045)
     "    Every Day of My Life(la2047; voc.,Sinatra)             -Co 36700
Co 35587. All or Nothing at All(co25288; voc.,Sinatra)/Flash(la2044)

          (Vido Musso, Claude Lakey, Chuck Gentry, John Mezey, saxes; Dalton Riz-
          zotto, Hoyt Bohannon, Harry Rodgers, trombones; James, Claude Bowen, Al
          Stearns, Nick Buono, trumpets; Ben Heller, guitar; Mickey Scrima, drums;
          Thurman Teague, drums; Al Lerner, piano):                           1941
Co 35932. Music Makers/Montevideo
Co 35947. Flatbush Flanagan                                      -Co 36698
     "    I Never Purposely Hurt You
Co 35979. A Little Bit of Heaven(co29544)/Eli Eli(co29586)

          (Sam Rosenblum, Stam Stanchfield, William Schuman, George Koch, violins,
          added):
Co 36004. Carnival of Venice/Flight of the Bumble Bee

          (Previous personnel):
Co 36023. Ol' Man River(co29543; voc.,Dick Haymes)/Answer Man(co29545)

          (Unknonw personnel):
Co 36069. Dolores/Walkin' By the River
Co 36081. Braggin'/For Want of a Star
Co 36146. Don't Cry Cherie/La Paloma

          (First side: Previous personnel with violins; second, same trombones and
          rhythm, with Vido Musso, Claude Lakey, Sam Morowitz, Chuck Gentry, saxes;
          Claude Bowen, Al Stearns, trumpets; Glenn Herzer, Leo Zorn, Sam Rosen-
          blum, Alex Pevsner, violins; Al Friede, cello):
Co 36160. Trumpet Rhapsody, 1 & 2 (co30056/co29729)

          (Unknown personnel):
Co 36171. Aurora/Daddy
Co 36190. Jeffrie's Blues(co30331)/Sharp As a Tack(co30332)
Co 36222. Lament to Love(co30627; voc.,Dick Haymes/Dodgers' Fan Dance(co30628)
Co 36246. It's So Peaceful in the Country/Yes Indeed
Co 36255. I Guess I'll Have to Dream the Rest/I'll Never Let a Day Pass By
Co 36285. I'll Get By(co30195; voc.,Dick Haymes)                 -Co 36698
     "    Lost in Love(co30641; voc.,Dick Haymes)
Co 36296. You Made Me Love You/A Sinner Kissed an Angel
Co 36339. Don't Take Your Love from Me/Duke's Mixture
Co 36390. Minka/Misirlou
Co 36399. Record Session/Nothin'
Co 36412. You've Changed/Nobody Knows the Trouble I've Seen
Co 36430. Rancho Pillow(co31250; voc.,Dick Haymes)/Man With Lollypop Song(co31411)
Co 36434. My Melancholy Baby/My Silent Love
Co 36446. Make Love to Me/You Don't Know What Love Is
Co 36455. He's 1A in the Army/Day Dreaming
Co 36466. The Devil Sat Down and Cried/Wait Till the Sun Shines Nellie
Co 36478. B-19/I Don't Want to Walk Without You
Co 36487. J.P.Dooley, III/Jughead
Co 36500. All for Love/Blues in the Night
Co 36518. I Remember You/Last Night I Said a Prayer
Co 36533. The Clipper/Skylark
Co 36545. Crazy Rhythm/Easter Parade
Co 36549. Sleepy Lagoon/Trumpet Blues
Co 36566. One Dozen Roses/You're Too Good for Good-for-Nothing Me
Co 36579. Strictly Instrumental/When You're a Long Long Way from Home
```

```
Co 36599. But Not for Me/The Mole
Co 36614. He's My Guy/You're in Love With Someone Else
Co 36623. I Cried for You/Let Me Up
Co 36644. Daybreak/Manhattan Serenade
Co 36650. Mister Five by Five/That Soldier of Mine
Co 36659. I Had the Craziest Dream/A Poem Set to Music
Co 36668. I've Heard That Song Before/Moonlight Becomes You
Co 36672. Velvet Moon/Prince Charming
Co 36677. I Heard You Cried Last Night/James Session
Co 36683. Cherry/Jump Town
Co 36729. Estrellita/My Beloved Is Rugged
Co 36713. Sleepy Time Gal(wc2800)/Memphis Blues(hco913)
Co 36758. I'm Beginning to See the Light/The Love I Long for
Co 36778. Guess I'll Hang My Tears Out to Dry/I Don't Care Who Knows It
Co 36784. I Should Care/Cry and You Cry Alone
```

HARRY JAMES QUINTET:
Co 36773. Confessin'/When Your Lover Has Gone

JAMES AND HER SYNCO JAZZERS, JEANNETTE:
Para 12470. Down Hearted Mama/Midnight Stomp

JAMES AND HIS FEWSICIANS, JELLY:
Ge 6045. Georgia Bo Bo/Make Me Know It

JAMES, MADELYN (vocal with piano):
Br 7155. Long Time Blues/Stinging Snake Blues

JAMES, SKIP:
Ch 50031. If You Haven't Any Hay/22-20 Blues

JAXON, FRANKIE HALF PINT (vocal, acc. by Jasper Taylor, washboard and drums;
Blanche Smith Walton, piano):   Nov.,1926
BP 8040. I'm Gonna Steal You/Can't You Wait
BP 8048. Willie the Weeper/Corinne

        (Acc. by cornet and Cow Cow Davenport, piano.--JI 10/4/40):   1928
Vo 1226. Down at Jasper's Bar-B-Que/Wit Ta Ditty Low Down

        (With Davenport, piano, only):
Vo 1257. How Can I Get It?/Fan It

        (Piano, saxophone and banjo):
Vo 1285. Let's Knock a Jug/Can't You Wait?

        (Piano, cornet and traps):
Vo 1424. Take It Easy/Corinne Blues(piano and clarinet)

        (With Punch's Delegates of Pleasure):
Vo 1472. Down Home in Kentucky/You've Got to Wet It

        (Unknown accompaniment):
Vo 1539. It's Heated/Jive Man Blues
Vo 1583. Scuddlin'/Chocolate to the Bone

        FRANKIE HALF PINT JAXON AND HIS HOT SHOTS (Bob Schoffner, George Mitch-
        ell, Guy Kelly, trumpets; Preston Jackson, trombone; Dalbert Bright,David
        Young, Kenneth Anderson, saxes; Jerome Carmington, piano; John Frazier,
        bass; Tubby Hall, drums; Jaxon, vocals.--HD):
Vo 2553. Fan It/My Baby's Hot
Vo 2603. Mama Don't Allow It/Fifteen Cents   -BrE 01719

        FRANKIE HALF PINT JAXON AND HARLEM HAMFATS:
De 7286. She Brings Me Down/Wet It
De 7304. Dirty Dozens/Take It Easy Greasy
De 7345. You Certainly Look Good to Me(62426)/She Sends Me(62427)
De 7360. Chocolate to the Bone/No Need Knockin' on the Blind
De 7482. Riff It/She Loves So Good
De 7523. I Knocks Myself Out/They Put the Big Britches on Me
De 7548. Some Sweet Day/I'm Gonna Steal You

        (Next four sides: Barney Bigard, clarinet; Wellman Braud, bass; Sid Cat-
        lett, drums; Lil Armstrong, piano):
De 7619. Callin' Corinne/You Can't Put That Monkey on My Back
De 7638. Don't Pan Me(65607)/Fan It Boogie Woogie(65610)

        (Henry Allen, trumpet; Rupert Cole, clarinet; Lil Armstrong, piano; Wal-
        ter Martin, washboard):
De 7733. Wasn't It Nice(67273)/You Know Jam Don't Shake(67274)
De 7742. When They Play Them Blues/Something's Goin' on Wrong

De 7786. Be Your Natural Self/Let Me Ride Your Train
De 7795. Take Off Them Hips/Gimme a Pit's Foot
De 7806. You Can't Tell/Turn Over
        (See also: Tampa Red Vo 1228,1237,1254,1274,1281)

JAZZ HARMONIZERS (Bix Beiderbecke cornet; George Johnson, tenor sax; Jimmy Hartwell, clarinet; Dick Voynow, piano; Bob Gillette, banjo; Min Leibrook, bass; Vic Moore, drums.--HD): 1924
  Clax 40339. Riverboat Shuffle(11854)/Susie(11855)
  Clax 40366. Oh Baby(11852)/Copenhagen(11853)

        (Add George Brunis, trombone):
  Clax 40375. Sensation(9079)/Lazy Daddy(9080b)
        (Above are reissues of Wolverine Orchestra from Gennett masters)

JAZZ MASTERS:
  BX 2109. Sweet Lovin' Mama/Bees Knees
                (See also: Ethel Waters)

JAZZBO'S CAROLINA SERENADERS (Original Memphis Five):
  Ca 232. Hopeless Blues(197a)/Lonesome Mama Blues(198a)   -Mu 232
  Ca 257. Hot Lips
  Ca 258. Yankee Doodle Blues/Cuddle Up Blues
  Ca 269. Sister Kate(260c)/Achin' Hearted Blues(267c)
  Ca 284. Way Down Yonder in New Orleans/Chicago
  Ca 481. Hootin' the Hoot(153)/I Want to See My Tennessee

JEFFRIES AND HIS NIGHT OWLS, SPEED:
  Su 2755. South African Blues/Tiger Moan

JEFFERSON, BLIND LEMON (blues singer):
  Para 12347. Dry Southern Blues/Booster Blues
  Para 12354. Got the Blues/Long Lonesome Blues
  Para 12373. Chock House Blues/Jack o' Diamonds Blues
  Para 12394. Beggin' Back(361)/Old Rounders Blues(360)
  Para 12407. Black Snake Moan(381-3067-2)/Stockin' Feet Blues(382,3066)
  Para 12425. Wartime Blues(422-1)/Booger Rooger Blues(423-2)
  Para 12443. Bad Luck Blues/Broke and Hungry Blues
  Para 12454. Rabbit Foot Blues/Shuckin' Sugar Blues
  Para 12487. Teddy Bear Blues/Rising High Water Blues, George Perkins, piano)
  Para 12510. Black Snake Dream Blues/Right of Way Blues
  Para 12541. Struck Sorrow Blues/Rambler Blues
  Para 12551. Deceitful Brownskin Blues/Chinch Bug Blues
  Para 12593. Lonesome House Blues/Sunshine Special Blues
  Para 12608. See That My Grave Is Kept Clean/'Lectric Chair Blues
  Para 12622. Lemon's Worried Blues/Prison Cell Blues
  Para 12639. Lemon's Cannon Ball Moan(20401-1)/Change My Luck(20387-2)
  Para 12650. Piney Woods Money Mama/Low Down Mojo Blues
  Para 12666. Blind Lemon's Penitentiary Blues/Long Lastin' Lovin'
  Para 12679. Lockstep Blues/Hangman's Blues
  Para 12685. How Long How Long/(rev., Tampa Red)
  Para 12692. Christmas Eve Blues/Happy New Year Blues
  Para 12712. Maltese Cat Blues(20820)/D B Blues(20821)
  Para 12728. Competition Bad Blues/Sad News Blues
  Para 12899. Southern Woman Blues/Mosquito Moan
  OK   8455. Match Box Blues/Black Snake Moan

JELLY WHIPPERS:
  Herwin 501. S O B Blues/Goose Grease

JENKINS AND HIS HARLEM SEVEN, FREDDIE (Freddie Jenkins and one other, trumpets; Albert Nicholas, clarinet; Joe Turner, piano; Bernard Addison, guitar; Joe Watts, bass; Adrian Rollini, drums.--JI 9/26/39, 9/20/40): Aug.26,1935
  BB 6129. Nothin' But Rhythm/Old Fashioned Love
  BB 6193. Swinging 'em Down/(rev., Little Ramblers)
        (See also: Bernard Addison and His Rhythm)

JENNEY AND HIS ORCHESTRA, JACK (Jack Jenney, Bob Jenney, Jack Bigelow, trombones; Red Solomon, Charlie Zimmerman, Don Sprague, trumpets; Toots Mondello, Art Dollinger, Frank Meyers, Johnny Pepper, saxes; Gil Bowers, piano; Gene Krupa, drums; Chick Reeves, guitar):
  Vo 5223. Moon Ray(w26183; voc.,Meredith Blake)/High Society(w26184)
  Vo 5304. Cuban Boogie Woogie/Stardust
  Vo 5407. The World Is Waiting for Sunrise(25717)/What Is There to Say(w26186)
  Vo 5494. I'll Get By/After I Say I'm Sorry

JEROME AND HIS CATS AND JAMMERS, JERRY (Jerry Jerome, tenor sax; George Wettling, drums; John Guarnieri, piano; Yank Lawson, trumpet; Ray Coniff, trombone; Bob Haggart, bass):

```
Asch   500. Girl of My Dreams(601)/Rainbow Blues(603)
Asch   501. When I Grow Too Old to Dream(605a)/Arsenic and Old Face(608)

       (Jerry Jerome, tenor sax; Charles Shavers, trumpet; Bill Stegmeyer, clar-
       inet; Bill Clifton,piano; Specs Powell, drums; Sid Weiss, bass):
Asch   503. Walkin' With Jerry/Jammin' With Jerry
Asch   504. Rose of Washington Heights/People Will Say We're in Love
```

JESSUP AND HIS MELODY MAKERS, RED:
  Vo 3477. You're Here You're There/I'll Never Tell You I Love You

JIM JAM (vocal with inst. acc.):
  Vs 6044. Thirty-Eight/Diamond Ring Blues
  Vs 6054. Where You Been So Long/Window Pane Blues

JIMMIE'S BLUE MELODY BOYS (Jimmie Noone):
  Vo 1439. Love Me/Love

JOE'S HOT BABIES:
  Para 12783. Beans and Greens/Dry Bones

JOHNSON'S ALL STAR ORCHESTRA:
  BS 2102. Suez(1411a)/Cock a Doodle Doo(1412a)

JOHNSON'S CRACKERJACKS, EDDIE:
  Vi 23329. Duck's Yas Yas Yas/Good Old Bosom Bread   -BB

JOHNSON'S JAZZERS (vocal with piano and trumpet):
  Co 14247. Skiddle de Scow(144621)/Can I Get It Now(144622)

JOHNSON, BERT (trombone, acc. by Sam Price, piano):
  Br 7136. Nasty But Nice/(rev., Sammy Price)

JOHNSON'S LOUISIANA JUG BAND, BILL:
  Br 7067. Don't Drink It In Here/Get the "L" on Down the Road

JOHNSON, BLIND WILLIE (vocal):
  Co 14276. I Know His Blood Can Make Me Whole/Jesus Make Up My Dying Bed
  Co 14303. Dark Was the Night/It's Nobody's Fault But Mine
  Co 14343. Mother's Children Have a Hard Time/If I Had My Way   -Vo 3021
  Co 14391. I'm Gonna Run to the City of Refuge/Jesus Is Coming Soon
  Co 14425. Lord I Just Can't Keep from Crying/Keep Your Lamp Trimmed & Burning
  Co 14490. Let Your Light Shine on Me/God Don't Ever Change
  Co 14520. Take Your Burden to the Lord/God Moves on the Water
  Co 14545. Praise God I'm Satisfied/When War Was On
  Co 14556. Can't Nobody Hide from God/If It Had Not Been for Jesus
  Co 14597. Everybody Ought to Treat a Stranger Right/Go With Me to That Land
  Co 14624. Sweeter As the Years Roll By/Take Your Stand

JOHNSON AND HIS BAND, BUDDY:
  De 7684. Jammin' in Georgia/Stop Pretending
  De 7700. Reese's Idea/When You're Out With Me
  De 8507. Please Mister Johnson(68292;voc.,Ella Johnson)/Swing Along With Me
  De 8518. Southern Echoes/You Won't Let Me Go   (68293;voc.,Mack Sisters)
  De 8546. Boogie Woogie's Mother-in-Law/I'd Be Ever So Grateful
  De 8555. In There/New Please Mister Johnson
  De 8562. Troyon Swing(69117)/Southern Exposure(69118)
  De 8573. I'm My Baby's Baby/It's the Gold
  De 8599. I'm Stepping Out/Toodle-Oodle-oo
  De 8611. You'll Get Them Blues/I Wonder Who's Boogiein'My Woogie Now
  De 8616. Without the One You Love/Deep Down in the Miz
  De 8632. Baby Don't You Cry/Stand Back and Smile
  De 8640. I Ain't Mad With You/My Lonely Cabin
  De 8647. I Done Found Out(71270;voc.,Warren Evans)/Let's Beat Out Somw Love
                                                  (71271; voc.,B.Johnson)

JOHNSON'S ORIGINAL SUPERIOR BAND, BUNK (Bunk Johnson, trumpet; George Lewis, clari-
net; Jim Robinson, trombone; Lawrence Marrero, banjo; Austin Young, bass; Walter
Decou, piano; Ernest Rogers, drums):   New Orleans, June,1942
  JM   8. Down by the River(133)/Panama(140)
  JM   9. Weary Blues(135)/Moose March(137)
  JM 10. Storyville Blues(134)/Bunk's Blues(136).
  JM   . Pallet on the Floor(138)/Ballin' the Jack(139)
  JM limited edition 1. Talking by Bunk Johnson(141/143)
  JM limited edition 2. Talking(142)/Yes Lord I'm Crippled(132;personnel above)

      BUNK JOHNSON'S JAZZ BAND (Bunk Johnson, trumpet; Albert Warner, trombone;
      George Lewis, clarinet; Walter Decou, piano; Lawrence Marrero, banjo;
      Chester Zardis, bass; Edgar Mosley, drums):   New Orleans,Fall,1942
  JI 11. The Thriller Rag(4660-4a)/When I Leave the World Behind(4662-6a)
  JI 12. Franklin Street Blues(4659-3a)/Weary Blues(4667-11a)

```
JI   13. Big Chief Battle Axe(4657-1b)/Blue Bell's Goodbye(4664-8a)
JI   14. Dusty Rag(4658-2a)/Sobbin' Blues(4661-5b)
JI   15. Shine(4665-9a)/Yaaka Hula Hickey Dula(4666-10a)
JI   16. Sobbin' Blues No. 2(4661-5a)/Sometimes My Burden Is So Hard to Bear
                                                                    (4663-7a)
     BUNK JOHNSON'S BAND (includes Bunk Johnson, trumpet; Jim Robinson, trom-
     bone; George Lewis, clarinet; Lawrence Marrero, banjo; bass; drums):
AM   251. Tiger Rag(213)/See See Rider(415)         New Orleans,July,1944
AM   252. St. Louis Blues(211)/When the Saints Go Marching In(402)
AM   253. Low Down Blues(110)/Yes Yes in Your Eyes(506)
         (See also Jim Robinson's Band, George Lewis)
```

JOHNSON, CAROLINE (Blues, acc. by Fats Waller, piano):
   Ge   3307. Ain't Got Nobody to Grind Ma Coffee   -Bu 8034
     "   Mama's Losing a Mighty Good Chance   -Bu 8033

JOHNSON'S PARADISE TEN, CHARLES (Cliff Brazzington, Jabbo Smith, Sidney de Paris,
trumpet; Charlie Irvis, trombone; Ben Whittet, clarinet; Benny Carter, alto sax;
Ben Waters, tenor sax; Charles Johnson, piano; Bobby Johnson, banjo; Cyrus St.
Clair, tuba; George Stafford, drums.--JRB)?   1927
   Vi 21247. You Ain't the One(41639)/Hot Tempered Blues(41641)
   Vi 21491. Charleston Is the Best Dance After All(41640)/(rev.,Lloyd Scott)
   Em 10854. Meddlin' With the Blues
   Em 10856. Don't Forget You'll Regret(2623)
         CHARLIE JOHNSON AND HIS PARADISE BAND (Leonard Davis, Sidney de Paris,
         trumpets; sub. Jimmy Harrison, trombone, for Irvis; Edgar Sampson, alto
         sax, for Carter):   New York,Sept.19,1928
   Vi 21712. The Boy in the Boat(47531)/Walk That Thing(47532)   -BB 10248
         CHARLIE JOHNSON AND HIS ORCHESTRA (Add Gus Atkins,trumpet; Sub.George
         Washington, trombone; Billy Taylor, bass):   1929
   Vi 38059. Hot Bones and Rice   -HMV 57
     "   Harlem Drag(51298)
                 (See also: Small's Paradise Orchestra)

JOHNSON, EASY PAPA (Roosevelt Sykes) vocal and piano):   Nov.3,1930
   Me 12086. Cotton Seed Blues(c6474)/No Good Woman Blues(c6475) -Po 9010
   Me 12048. Drinkin'Woman Bl(c6476)/Papa Sweetback bl(c6477) -Vo 02697, Po 9011

JOHNSON, EDITH (vocal with Roosevelt Sykes, piano):
   Para 12823. Honey Dripper Blues/Nickel's Worth of Liver(add Ike Rodgers,trombone;
                                                              (Baby Jay,cornet)
   Para 12864. Good Chib Blues(1562-15559; Sykes,Rodgers)/Can't Make Another Day
                                                 (1563-15560; Sykes and Baby Jay)
         (Unknown acc.):
   OK 8748. Heart Achin' Blues/Ain't No More to Be Said

JOHNSON, EDNA (vocal with violin and guitar):
   Si 4046. I'm Drifting from You Blues(8703)/A Woman Gets Tired of One Man(8704),
                                                                       (piano
JOHNSON, ELIZABETH (vocal with piano and cornet):
   OK 8593. Empty Bed Blues, 1 & 2(400828b-29b)

         (With Her Turpentine Tree-o):
   OK 8798. Sobbin' Woman Blues/Be My Kid Blues

JOHNSON AND HER BEALE STREET FIVE, FLO (vocal with trumpet, trombone, clarinet,
piano and drums):
   Ca   318. Four o'Clock Blues(413-a2)/(rev., Blanche Klaise)
   Ca   319. Sugar Blues/Keep Off My Shoes

JOHNSON AND HIS ORCHESTRA, FREDDY (Arthur Briggs, Bobby Jones, trumpets; Billy
Burns, trombone; Peter Ducongé, clarinet and alto sax; Alcide Castellanos, alto
sax; Frank Big Boy Goodie, tenor sax; Freddy Johnson, piano; Sterling Conway,
guitar; Juan Fernandez, bass; Billy Taylor, drums.--HD):   Paris,1933
   BrF 500277. Sing About the Swanee(6459); voc.,Spencer Williams)/My Baby's Bone(6460)
   BrF 500278. Foxy and Grapesy(6462)/Sweet Georgia Brown(6461) voc.,Louis Cole

         (Arthur Briggs, trumpet; Johnson, piano):
   BrF 500262. I Got Rhythm(6433)/Nobody's Sweetheart(6431) voc.,Louis Cole
   BrF 500263. Japanese Sandman(6434)/Grabbin' Blues(6432)

         FREDDY JOHNSON AND HIS HARLEMITES(Sub. reeds: Booker Pittman, clarinet
         and alto sax; Cle Saddler, alto sax; Roy Butler, alto and baritone sax;
         Alfred Pratt, tenor sax):
   BrF 500340. Harlem Bound(6575)/Sweet Madness(6574;H.Flemming,trombone) -DeE 3810
   BrF 500341. I Got Rhythm(6576;Flemming,trombone)/Riger Rag(6646)   -DeE 5110

         FREDDY JOHNSON AND LEX VAN SPALL AND THEIR ORCHESTRA (Ralph Goldstein,
         trumpet; Jack Green,trombone; Lex Van Spall,alto sax & guitar;Jascha Tra-
         bsky,tenor sax & clarinet;Freddy Johnson,piano; Jacques Mirgorodsky,gui-
         tar;Al Weisbard,bass;Lew Galkin,drums;Rosie Poindexter,voc.--HD):

```
DeH 42045. I Want to Dance(am124)/Haarlem Hot Club Stomp(am125)     Holland,1935
DeH 42046. Jungle Fever(am127)/You Took Advantage of Me(am126)
```

JOHNSON, GLADYS (vocal with cornet and piano):
   Va 5048. Some Day You'll Come Back to Me(111a-1)/Slow Up Papa(199a-1)

JOHNSON AND HIS FIVE HOT SPARKS, J. C. (Omer Simeon, clarinet and sax; trumpet; trombone; banjo; piano; drums):
   QRS 7064. Crying for You(347)/Red Hot Hottentot(348)

JAMES P. JOHNSON

See also:
  PERRY BRADFORD: Vo 15165.
  ALICE LESLIE CARTER: Hy 86, 95, 96, 112.
  IDA COX: Vo 05336.
  ROSETTA CRAWFORD: De 7567, 7584.
  ROY EVANS: Co 1559.
  EDDIE GRAY: BS 2020.
  GREAT DAY: OK 8755.
  ED HALL: BN 28, 29.
  MAX KAMINSKY: Com
  LONNIE JOHNSON: OK 8291, 8358, 8411, 8340, 8376.
  LOUISIANA SUGAR BABES: Vi 21346, 21348.
  MEZZ MEZZROW: BB 10085, 10088.
  FRANKIE NEWTON: BB 10176, 10186, 10216.
  McKINNEY'S COTTON PICKERS: Vi 22511, 23000, 23012, 23031, 23035, 38097, 38102,
  PEE WEE RUSSELL: HRS 17, 1000, 1001, 1002.   (38133
  BESSIE SMITH: Co 14195, 14232, 14260, 14464, 14476, 14487, 14527.
  RUBY SMITH: Vo 4903.
  CLARA SMITH: Co 14536, 14592.
  TRIXIE SMITH: BS 2044.
  ETHEL WATERS: Co 14353, 14380, 14411; BS 14154.
  CLARENCE WILLIAMS: Co 14341.
  LAVINIA TURNER: Pat 020627.

JOHNSON, JAMES P. (Piano solos):
```
  BS   2026. The Harlem Strut(pl51-1)/Rev.,F.Henderson)
  Vi  19123. Bleeding Hearted Blues/You Can't Do What My Last Man Did
  OK   4495. Keep Off the Grass(s70259d)/Carolina Shout(s70260c)
  OK   4937. Scouting Around(s71741a)/Toddlin'(s71742a)
  OK   8770. Riffs(401565)/Feelin' Blue(401566)
  Co   3950. Weeping Blues(81099)/Worried and Lonesome Blues(81100)
  Co  14204. All That I Had Is Gone(143531)/Snowy Morning Blues(143532)

       (With Clarence Williams, piano duet):
  Co  14502. How Could I Be Blue(149951)/I've Found a New Baby(149952)

       (Solos):
  Br   4712. Crying for the Carolines/What Is This Thing Called Love
  Br   4762. Jingles(E31959)/You've Got to Be Modernistic(E31958)   -Br 80032
  Asch 3503. Snowy Morning Blues(322)/(rev., Peck's Bad Boys)
  Asch 5511. Euphonic Sounds(mal250)/(rev., Johnson Orchestra)
  Asch 1001. Boogie Woogie Stride(300-1)/Impressions(301)
  Sig 28105. Blueberry Rhyme(t1914)/Blues for Fats(t1915)
  BN     24. J.P.Boogie(777)/Gut Stomp(870)
  BN     25. Back Water Blues/Carolina Balmoral
  BN     26. Improvisations on Pine Top's Boogie Woogie(784)/Caprice Rag(783)
  BN     27. Mule Walk(781)/Arkansaw Blues(782)
```

JOHNSON HARMONY SEVEN (or EIGHT), JAMES P.:
```
  BS   2044. Long Lost Weary/You Missed a Good Woman
  OK   4504. Dear Old Southland(s70350b)/Bandana Days(s70351c)
  Pe  12034. He Took It Away from Me/If I Were Your Daddy
```

    JIMMY JOHNSON AND HIS ORCHESTRA:
```
  Co   2448. Go Harlem(151457)/Just a Crazy Song(151460)
  Co  14334. Chicago Blues(146539)/Mournful Tho'ts(146540)
  Co  14417. Put Your Mind Right on It(148015)/Fare Thee Honey Blues(148108)
  Co  14668. A Porter's Love Song/(rev., N.O. Wildcats)
  Vi  38099. You Don't Understand/You've Got to Be Modernistic
```

    (Henry Allen, trumpet; J. C. Higginbotham, trombone; James P. Johnson; piano; Gene Cedric, tenor sax; Al Casey, guitar; Johnny Williams, bass; Sid Catlett, drums):
```
  Vo   4768. Harlem Woogie(w24205); voc.,Anna Robinson)/After Tonight(w24209)
  Vo   4903. Back Water Blues(w24207)/He's Mine All Mine(w24208) voc.,Roby Smith
```

```
                JAMES P. JOHNSON BLUE NOTE JAZZ MEN (Sidney de Paris, trumpet; Vic Dick-
                enson, trombone; Ben Webster, tenor sax; James P. Johnson, piano; Arthur
                Shirley, guitar; John Simmons, bass; Sidney Catlett, drums):
     BN         32. Blue Mizz(950-1)/Victory Stride(951-3)
     BN         33. After You've Gone(953)/Joy-Mentin'(952)

                JAMES P. JOHNSON NEW YORK JAZZ ORCHESTRA (James P. Johnson, piano; Frank
                Newton, trumpet; Pops Foster, bass; Al Casey, guitar; Eddie Dougherty,
                drums):                                                        1944
     Asch  5511. The Dream(mal247)/(rev., Johnson solo)
     Asch  5512. Four o'Clock Groove(mal246)/Hesitation Blues(mal242)
     Asch  5513. The Boogie Dream(mal243)/Hot Harlem(mal248)

     JOHNSON, LIL (vocal, acc. by Charles Avery, piano):
       Vo   1299. Never Let Your Left Hand Know/You'll Never Miss Your Jelly

                (Add guitar):
       Vo   1410. House Rent Scuffle/Rock That Thing

                (Unknown accompaniment):
       Vo   3199. Press My Button/Hot Nuts
       Vo   3241. Get 'em from the Peanut Man/Sam the Hot Dog Man
       Vo   3251. Rug Cutter Function/My Stove's in Good Condition
       Vo   3266. Two Timin' Man/Was I

                LIL JOHNSON AND HER CHICAGO SWINGERS:
       Vo   3312. Let's Get Drunk and Truck/Hottest Gal in Town

                (Lee Collins, trumpet; piano and bass):
       Vo   3331. Ramblin' Man Blues/Can't Read Can't Write
       Vo   3374. Black and Evil Blues/You're Just a Cream Puff

                (Unknown accompaniment):
       Vo   3397. I'll Take You to the Cleaners/Crazy About My Rider
       Vo   3428. New Shave 'em Dry/Grandpa Said Let's Susie Q
       Vo   3455. River Hip Papa/If You Don't Give Me What I Want
       Vo   3562. Meat Balls/Little Red Wagon
       Vo   3600. Goofer Dust Swing/Take It Easy Greasy No. 2
       Ch  50002. Hot Nuts/Anybody Want to Buy
       Me  60356. If you Can Dish It/I'm Bettin' on You
       Me  60552. Take It Easy Greasy/Bonus Done Gone Through

                (James Wiggins, piano; guitar and bass):
       BB   6112. Keep on Knocking/I Lost My Baby                      -BB 8251
```

LONNIE JOHNSON

See also:
   TEXAS ALEXANDER: OK 8563, 8578, 8591, 8624, 8603, 8658, 8673, 8801.
   LOUIS ARMSTRONG: OK 8535, 8551, 8566, 8669, 8680; Vo 3055.
   CHOCOLATE DANDIES: OK 8627, 8668.
   CHARLES CREATH: OK 8257, 8280, 8477.
   JOHNNY DODDS: De 18094.
   BLIND WILLIE DUNN: OK 8637, 8689, 8743.
   DUKE ELLINGTON: OK 8623.
   McKINNEY'S COTTON PICKERS. Vi 22736, 38133.
   JIMMY NOONE: De 18095.
   VICTORIA SPIVEY: OK 8634, 8652, 8626.
   CLARENCE WILLIAMS: OK 8645

```
     JOHNSON, LONNIE (vocal):                                          1925-26
       OK   8253. Mr. Johnson's Blues(9435a)/Falling Rain Bl(9436a) John Arnold,pf &
       OK   8282. Love Story Blues/Very Lonesome Blues                  (fiddle

                (with James P. Johnson piano):
       OK   8291. Sun to Sun Blues/Bed of Sand
       OK   8309. Lonesome Jail Blues/When I Was Lovin' Changed My Mind Blues(with James
                                              (Johnson,fiddle, and De Loise Search,pf)
                (with James P. Johnson, piano, self, guitar):
       OK   8358. A Woman Changed My Life/Good Ole Wagon

                (Organ, violin):
       OK   8391. Oh Doctor/I'm Gonna Dodge the Blues

                (James P. Johnson, piano):
       OK   8340. Good Happy Home/Baby You Don't Know My Mind
       OK   8376. There's No Use of Lovin'/Baby Please Tell Me
       OK   8411. Lonnie's Got the Blues(9674)/I Have No Sweet Woman Now(9689)
       OK   8417. Five o'Clock Blues/Johnson's Trio Stomp
```

```
            (Piano and fiddle):                                        1927
   OK  8435. Ball and Chain Blues(74268a)/Sweet Woman See for Yourself(74274a)
   OK        You Don't See into the Blues Like Me/You Drove a Good Man Away

            (Guitar and vocal):                                   April,1927
   OK  8466. South Bound Water(80742)/Back Water Blues(80831; with piano)
   OK  8484. Treat 'em Right(80743)/Baby Won't You Please Come Home(80745)
   OK  8497. Mean Old Bed Bug Bl(81214)/Roaming Gambler Bl(81220) New York 8/5/27
   OK  8505. Lonesome Ghost Blues(81215)/Fickle Mama Blues(81216)
   OK  8512. St.Louis Cyclone Blues(81503;Oct,1927)/Sweet Woman You Can't(81190)
   OK  8524. Tin Can Alley Blues(81588)/Bittin'Fleas Blues(81797)
   OK  8537. Kansas City Blues, 1 & 2
   OK  8557. Life Saver Blues(81801)/Blue Ghose Blues(81802)  Chicago,Feb.,1928
   OK  8558. Playing With the Strings(400277)/Stompin''em Along Slow(400278) solos
   OK  8575. Away Down in the Alley Blues(400279)/Blues in G(400280) solos
   OK  8574. Away Down That Lonesome Road(400490)/Crowing Rooster Blues(400491)
   OK  8586. Bed Bug Blues No. 2/Sweet Potato Blues              April,1928
   OK  8601. A Broken Heart That Never Smiles/Wrong Woman Blues
   OK  8618. Broken Levee Blues/Stay Out of Walnut Street Alley

            (Duet with Victoria Spivey; piano acc.):
   OK  8626. The New Black Snake Blues, 1 & 2

            (Singing with guitar):                              Nov.16,1928
   OK  8635. When You Fall for Someone That's Not Your Own(401336)/Careless Love
   OK  8709. New Fallin' Rain Blues(402442: with violin & piano)      (401337)
   OK  8722. You Can't Give a Woman Everything/Make Whoopee at home(piano & guitar)

            (Duets with Victoria Spivey):
   OK  8733. You Done Lost Your Good Thing Now, 1 & 2(402491/92)
   OK  8744. Toothache Blues, 1 & 2(401243/47; Clarence Williams, piano)

            (Guitar and vocal):
   OK  8754. Sun Down Blues(402438)/Baby Won't You Please Come Home(402441)
   OK  8786. I Got the Best Jelly Roll in Town,No.1/Headin' for the Southland
   OK  8796. I Got the Best Jelly Roll in Town,No.2/Don't Drive Me from My Door
   OK  8822. Deep Sea Blues/Long Black Train Blues
   OK  8831. No More Troubles Now(404437)/Sam You Can't Do That to Me(404438)
   OK  8839. You Had Too Much(404523)/Don't Wear It Out(404524) with Violet Green
   OK  8846. Got the Blues for Murder Only/Let All Married Wimmin Alone
   OK  8875. The Blues Is Only a Ghost/Just a Roamin' Man
   OK  8886. Another Woman Booked Out and Bound to Go/I Just Can't Stand These
   OK  8898. Beautiful But Dumb/From a Washwoman on Up                  (Blues
   OK  8909. I Have to Do My Time/Southland Is All Right With Me
   OK  8916. Not the Chump I Used to Be(404968)/The Best Jockey in Town(404969)
   OK  8926. Sleepy Water Blues(405098)/Uncle Ned Don't Use Your Head(405099)
   OK  8937. Sam You're Just a Rat/Man Get Wise to Yourself
   OK  8946. I'm Nuts About That Gal(152259)/Racketeers' Blues(152260)
   OK 40695. To Do This You Got to Know How(80075a; guitar solo)/Nile of Genago
                                                    (73944a; with James Johnson)
   Co 14667. Home Wreckers Blues/Hell Is a Name for All Sinners         1932
   Co 14674. Unselfish Love/My Love Don't Belong to You
                                        - - -
   De  7388. Hard Times Ain't Gone Nowhere/Something Fish
   De  7397. Flood Water Blues/I'm Nuts Over You
   De  7427. It Ain't What You Usta Do/Swing Out Rhythm(guitar solo)
   De  7445. Got the Blues for West End(guitar solo)/Man Killing Broad
   De  7461. New Falling Rain Blues/South Bound Backwater
   De  7487. Devil's Got the Blues/Friendless and Blue
   De  7509. I Ain't Gonna Be Your Fool/Mr. Johnson Swing
   De  7537. Blue Ghost Blues/Lap Legged Drunk Again
   BB  8322. Nothing But a Rat/She's My Mary
   BB  8338. Four-o-Three Blues/The Loveless Blues
   BB  8363. Why Women Go Wrong/She's Only a Woman
   BB  8387. Trust Your Husband/Jersey Belle Blues
   BB  8530. Get Yourslf Together/Don't Be No Fool
   BB  8564. Be Careful/I'm Just Dumb
   BB  8684. Somebody's Got to Go/She Ain't Right
   BB  8748. Lazy Woman Blues/In Love Again
   BB  8779. I Did All I Could/Chicago Blues
   BB  8804. Crowing Rooster Blues/That's Love Blues
   BB 34-0708. Fly Right Baby/Rambler's Blues
```

```
          LONNIE JOHNSON AND BLIND WILLIE DUNN (guitar duets):
   OK  8695. Bull Frog Moan(401866d)                            -PaE 1496
       "    A Handful of Riffs(401869a)
   OK  8711. Guitar Blues(401865)/Blue Guitar(401870)
   OK  8818. Midnight Call Blues(403042)/Blue Room(403044)

          LONNIE JOHNSON AND SPENCER WILLIAMS (vocal duets with guitar and piano):
   OK  8664. It Feels So Good, 1 & 2(401622/23)                      1929
   OK  8677. Lowland Moan/So Tired of Livin' All Alone
   OK  8691. Death Is on Your Track(401730)/I Want a Little Some o'That(401670;
   OK  8697. It Feels So Good, 3 & 4(401981/82)        with Jimmy Foster)
   OK  8762. Monkey and the Baboon(403597)/Wipe It Off(403598; with Clarence Wms)
   OK  8768. She's Making Whoopee in Hell Tonight(403594)/Death Valley Is Just
                                                             Half Way Home(403668)
   OK  8775. She Don't Know Who She Wants(403672)/The Dirty Dozen(403749;Cl. Wms)
   OK  8802. Bull Frog and the Toad(404041)/Monkey and the Baboon,II(404042)
   OK  8812. Once or Twice(403596)/Keep It to Yourself(403750)

          LONNIE JOHNSON'S HARLEM FOOTWARMERS (Same as Harlem Footwarmers, except
          Lonnie Johnson, guitar):
   OK  8638. Move Over(401176b)/Harlem Twist(400032a; Otto Hardwicke,sax, instead
                                                                    (of Hodges)
JOHNSON, LOUISE (blues singer with piano):
   Para 12992. Long Ways from Home/All Night Long Blues
   Para 13008. On the Wall(L419)/By the Moon and the Stars(L420)

JOHNSON, MARGARET (vocal with Clarence Williams Blue Five, including Sidney Bechet):
   OK  8107. If I Let You Get Away With It Once(71972)/E Flat Blues(71973)

          (With Clarence Williams' Harmonizers):
   OK  8162. Nobody Knows the Way I Feel This Mornin'(s72790b)/Absent Minded
                                                                  (Blues(s72791b)
          (Acc. by Louis Armstrong, cornet; Aaron Thomson, trombone; Buddy Chris-
          tian, banjo; Clarence Williams, piano.--JRB)?                  1924
   OK  8185. Papa Mama's All Alone Blues(72996)/Changeable Daddy of Mine(72997)

          (Acc. including Bubber Miley, cornet; Charlie Irvis, trombone; Bechet,
          clarinet and soprano sax):
   OK  8193. Who'll Chop Your Suey(s73081a)/Done Made a Fool Out of Me(s73082b)

          (With Clarence Williams, piano):
   OK  8220. Death House Blues/Nobody's Blues But Mine
   OK  8230. I Love You Daddy(with Williams Harmonizers)/I'm a Good Hearted Woman
   OK  8506. Stinging Bee Blues/Best Friend Blues

          (With Black and Blue Trio):
   Vi  20333. When a 'gator Hollers/Grayson Street Blues
   Vi  20982. Dead Drunk Blues/What Kind of Love

JOHNSON, MARY (vocal and piano):
   Para 12931. Mean Black Man Blues(L172)/Dream Daddy Blues(L173)

          (With Ike Rodgers, trombone; and unknown piano):
   Para 12996. Key to the Mountain Blues(L177)/Barrel House Flat Blues(L176)
   Br   7081. Western Union Blues/Black Men Blues(piano acc.)
   Br   7093. Muddy Creek Blues/Room Rent Blues

          (Unknown accompaniment):
   Br   7153. Dawn of Day Blues/Three Months Ago Blues
   Br   7160. Death Cell Blues/Friendless Gall Blues
   Br   7175. No Good Town Blues/Morning Sun Blues
   De   7012. Peepin' at the Rising Sun/Those Black Man Blues
   De   7014. Black Gal Blues/Deceitful Woman Blues

          SIGNIFYING MARY JOHNSON
   De   7305. Delmar Avenue/I Just Can't Take It

JOHNSON, PETE (piano solos):
   SA  12004. How Long How Long(rl26)/Climbin' and Screamin'(rl27)
   SA  12005. Pete's Blues(rl29)/Let 'em Jump(rl30)
   SA  12006. Buss Robinson Blues(rl24)/B & O Blues
   SA  12008. Buss Robinson Blues(rl28)
   SA  12010. Shuffle Boogie/Pete's Blues No.2
   BN     12. Holler Stomp(rs658-6)/You Don't Know My Mind(rs662-10)

          (With string bass and drums):
   De   3384. Blues on the Down Beat/Kaycee on My mind
   De   3630. Basement Boogie/Death Ray Boogie
   De   8582. Just for You(69159)/Pete's Mixture(69160)
```

PETE JOHNSON AND HIS BOOGIE WOOGIE BOYS (Pete Johnson, piano; Lips Page, trumpet; Lawrence Lucie, guitar; Eddie Dougherty, drums; Buster Smith, alto sax; Abe Bolar, bass): 1939
Vo 4607. Roll 'em Pete/Goin' Away Blues
Vo 4997. Cherry Red(25023)/Baby Look at You(25024) voc., Joe Turner
Vo 5186. Lovin' Mama Blues/(rev., Ammons, Lewis, Johnson)
(See also: Albert Ammons, Vo 4606)

PETE JOHNSON BLUES TRIO (Pete Johnson, piano; Ulysses Livingston, guitar; Abe Bolar, bass): 1940
BN 10. Barrelhouse Breakdown(rs659-7)/Kansas City Farewell(rs660-8)
BN 11. Vine Street Bustle(rs653a-1)/Some Day Blues(rs655-3)

PETE JOHNSON'S BAND (Don Stovall, Don Byas, saxes; Eddie Barefield, clarinet; Hot Lips Page, trumpet; Pete Johnson, piano; John Collins, guitar; Abe Bolar, bass; A.G.Godley, drums):
De 18121. 627 Stomp(68332)/(rev.. Joe Turner)

JOHNSON, PORKCHOP (vocal with piano):
Ch 15796. Washboard Rub/Pork Chop Stomp

JOHNSON, ROBERT (blues vocal):
Vo 03475. Dead Shrimp Blues/I Believe I'll Dust My Broom
Vo 03519. Cross Road Blues/Ramblin' on My Mind
Vo 03563. They're Red Hot/Come on in My Kitchen
Vo 03601. Sweet Home Chicago/Walkin' Blues

JOHNSON'S HAPPY PALS, ROY:
OK 8723. Savoy Rhythm(402598)/Happy Pal Stomp(402599)

JOHNSON, RUTH (vocal with Cassino Simpson, piano; and guitar):
Para 13060. Rockin' Chair(815)/Careless Love(816)

JOHNSON, STELLA (with Dorothy Scott's Rhythm Boys):
De 7217. Don't Come Over/Hot Nuts Swing
De 7284. Mama Don't You Want No More

JOHNSON, STOVEPIPE (with Earl Hines, piano; Jimmie Noone, clarinet):
Vo 1211. I Ain't Got Nobody/Don't Let Your Mouth Start Nothing(unknown piano, clarinet, guitar)

JOHNSON, STUMP (vocal with piano):
Para 12842. The Ducks Yas Yas Yas(1488)/The Snitchers Blues(1489)   -QRS 7049

(With trumpet, guitar, piano):
Para 12862. Would You Do What I Asked You To(1558)/Kind Babe Blues(1559;no guitar)

(Banjo and piano):
Para 12906. Soaking Wet Blues(1732)/Transom Blues(1733)
Para 12938. Baby B Blues(L156;piano acc.)/You Buzzard You(L157;guitar acc.)
Vi 23327. Sail on Black Sue/Barrel of Whiskey Blues

JOHNSON, TOMMY (vocal with guitar):
Vi 21279. Cool Drink of Water Blues/Big Road Blues
Vi 21409. Maggie Campbell Blues/Bye Bye Blues

JOHNSON AND SMITH (vocal and guitar):
Ch 40074. Stove Pipe Stomp/Brown Skin Shuffle

JOHNSTON'S REBELS, JIMMY:
Pu 11449. Poor Papa/Horses

(Vocals by Tom Stacks):
Pu 11461. I Wonder What's Become of Joe(2572)/(rev.,Arthur Hall)   -Bwy 1019
Para 20452. Show That Fellow the Door(2530)/What a Man(2531)

JOLLY JIVERS (piano jive):
Vo 02532. Jookit Jookit/Watcha Gonna Do
Vo 25015. Piano Stomp(13583)/Hungry Man's Schuffle(13606)

JONES, ALBERTA and the Ellington Twins:
Ge 3403. Lucky Number Blues/I'm Gonna Put You Right in Jail

(Acc. by Roy Banks, piano):
Ge 3444. Home Alone Blues/Sud Bustin' Blues

(Acc. by Boyd, piano):
Bu 8033. It Must Be Hard/(rev., Caroline Johnson)

JONES, ANNA (acc. by Fats Waller, piano):
   Para   . You Can't Do What My Last Man Did(1469)
   Para 12052. Sister Kate/Trixie Blues

JONES AND HIS SOCK FOUR, CLARENCE:
   Para 12716. I've Got It All/Mid the Pyramids
   Para 12747. Hold It Boy/(rev., Beverly Syncopators)

JONES, COLEY (vocal with guitar):
   Co 14288. Traveling Man/Army Mule in No Man's Land

JONES, CURTIS (blues with inst. acc.):
   Vo 03756. You Got Good Business/Lonesome Bedroom Blues
   Vo 03990. Highway 51 Blues/Let Me Be Your Playmate
   Vo 05071. Heavy Hip Mama/Private Talk Blues
   OK 05996. Down Town Blues/Cradle Rockin' Blues
   OK 05744. Blue and Lonesome/Bosom Friend Blues
   OK 05834. Blue Memories/Heart Breaking Blues
   OK 05907. Day and Night Blues/Moonlight Lover Blues
   OK 05947. Love Land Blues/Treat Me Like I Treat You
   OK 06069. Dream Land Blues/Love Valley Blues
   OK 06105. Worryin' Away My Heart for You/Itty Bitty Jitter Bug
   OK 06140. Low Down Worried Blues/Mean Old Blues
   BB 8412. Gold Digger Blues/Love in a Loving Way
   BB 8455. Sugar Bowl Blues/Solid Jive

JONES, ETTA (acc. by Barney Bigard and His Orchestra: Bigard, clarinet; Joe Thomas,
trumpet; George Auld, tenor and alto saxes; Leonard Feather, piano; Chuch Wayne,
guitar; Stan Levey, drums; Billy Taylor, bass):
   B&W   9. Salty Papa Blues/Blue Top Blues
   B&W 10. Evil Gal Blues/Long Long Journey

JONES' JUNIORS, ISHAM (Woody Herman, Sonny Lee, C.Qualey, et al):
   De 770. I've Had the Blues So Long/Tormented
   De 834. Fan It/Nola

JONES AND THE GOLD FRONT BOYS, JAKE:
   Br 7130. Southern Sea Blues/Monkeyin' Around

JONES, JULIA (vocal with Parry Bradford, piano):
   Ge 5177. Liza Johnson Got Better Bread(8400a)/That Thing Called Love(84C1a)
   Ge 5233. Deceitful Blues(8467)/Here's Your Opportunity(8468b)

JONES, LITTLE HAT (vocal with guitar):
   OK 8712. Two String Blues/New 216 Blues
   OK 8815. Kentucky Blues/Bye Bye Baby Blues

JONES, MAGGIE (vocal with Lemuel Fowler, piano):
   Ge 5193. ---
   Co 14044. Four Flushing Papa/Jealous Mama Blues

       (Unknown accompaniment):
   Co 14047. Western Union Blues/Box Car Blues

       (Louis Armstrong, cornet; Fletcher Henderson, piano):
   Co 14050. Poor House Blues(140171)/Thunderstorm Blues(140175)
   Co 14055. Screamin' the Blues(140188)
       "   Good Time Flat Blues(140191)   -HRS Div
   Co 14059. If I Lose Let Me Lose(140187)/Early Every Morn'(140193),trombone
   Co 14063. Anybody Here Want to Try My Cabbage(140174)/You May Go But You'll
                                       (Come Back Some Day (140192; trombone)

       (Unknown accompaniment)
   Co 14070. Suicide Blues/Dangerous Blues

       (Acc. by Henderson's Hot Six;Joe Smith, trumpet; Charlie Green, trombone,
   Buster Bailey, clarinet; Coleman Hawkins, tenor sax; Fletcher Henderson,
   piano; Charlie Dixon, banjo; Kaiser Marshall, drums.--HD)
   Co 14074. Cheatin' on Me(140583)/Mamma(140584)

       (Acc. by St.Louis Rhythm Kings: Trumpet, trombone, clarinet, piano,drums):
   Co 14081. He's Just a Horn-Tootin'Fool(140662)/Go Get 'emCaroline(140663)

       (Trombone and piano):
   Co 14092. North Bound Blues/Undertaker Blues

       MAGGIE JONES AND HER BAND (Personnel unknown):
   Co 14102. Single Woman's Blues/Never Tell a Woman Friend
   Co 14114. Dallas Blues/South Street Blues
   Co 14127. I'm a Backbiting Mama/Never Drive a Beggar from Your Door
   Co 14139. I'm a Real Kind Mama/I'm leaving You
   Co 14243. Man I Love Is Oh So Good/You Ain't Gonna Feed in My Pasture Now
   Pat 021062. You Can't Do That/Don't Never Tell Nobody

JONES AND HER JAZZBO SERENADERS, MAUDE:
 Med 8286. Ever Lovin' Blues/(rev., Willie Brown)

JONES, RICHARD M. (Piano solos):
 Ge 5174. Jazzin't Babies Blues(11492)/12th Street Rag(11493)

See also:
 BABY MACK: OK 8313;
 LILLIE DELK CHRISTIAN: OK 8475.
 JOHNNY DODDS: De 18094.
 HIGHTOWER: BP 8045.
 BERTHA HILL: OK 8273, 8312, 8318, 8420, 8437, 8453;
 BLANCHE CALLOWAY: OK 8279.
 THELMA LaVIZZO: Para 12208.
 SAM ROBINSON: OK 8321.
 CALLIE VASSAR: Ge 5172.
 NOLAN WELSH: OK 8372.

RICHARD JONES AND HIS WASHBOARD FOUR:
 Para 12705. Hot and Ready/It's a Low Down Thing
 Para 20929. ---

    RICHARD M. JONES THREE JAZZ WIZARDS (Richard M. Jones, piano; Albert
 Nicholas,clarinet; Johnny St. Cyr, banjo.--JI 4/26/40)
 OK 8260. Spanish Dream(9447a)/29th and Dearborn(9448a)
 OK 8290. New Orleans Shags(9446a)/Wonderful Dream(9449a)

    RICHARD M. JONES' JAZZ WIZARDS (Shirley Clay, trumpet; Preston Jackson,
 trombone; Stomp Evans, clarinet and sax; Jones, piano; banjo):
 OK 8349. Kin to Kant Blues(9721a)/Mush Mouth Blues(9772a)
 OK 8390. Baby o' Mine(9773a)/(rev., Cookie's Gingersnaps)
 OK 8431. Dusty Bottom Blues(9960a)/Scagmore Green(9961a)

    (Shirley Clay, Jimmy McLery, Dave Nelson, trumpets; Billy Franklin,trom-
 bone; Artie Starks, alto sax; Omer Simeon, clarinet and alto sax; Emmett
 Hardy, tenor sax; Richard M. Jones, piano; Ikey Robinson, banjo; Bert
 Cobb, tuba, or Quinn Wilson, string bass; Walter Bishop, drums.--JI 4/26
 /40):
 Vi 20812. Hollywood Shuffle/Dark Alley
 Vi 20859. Smoked Meat Blues/Good Stuff
 Vi 21203. Jazzin' Baby Blues/Boar Hog Blues
 Vi 21345. African Hunch(40821)/(rev., Jelly Roll Morton

    (Roy Palmer, trombone):
 Vi 38040. Novelty Blues/Tickle Britches   -BB 6627

    (Jones, vocal and piano; Lee Collins, trumpet):
 BB 6569. Black Rider
 "   Trouble in Mind   -BB 6963

    JONES JAZZ WIZARDS (Two trumpets, trombone, two altos, one tenor, guitar,
 bass, drums, piano):   1935
 De 7051. Blue Reefer Blues/Bring it on Home to Grandma
 De 7064. I'm Gonna Run You Down(9847a)/Muggin' the Blues(9846a)

    RICHARD M. JONES JAZZMEN (Richard M. Jones, piano; Bob Schoffner, trum-
 pet; Preston Jackson, trombone; Darnell Howard, clarinet; John Lindsay,
 bass; Baby Dodds, drums):   Chicago,March 23,1944
 Se 12006. 29th & Dearborn(154c)/New Orleans Hop Scop Blues(155b)
 Se 12007. Jazzin' Babies Blues(156a)/Canal Street Blues(157a)

JONES' CHICAGO COSMOPOLITANS:
 De 7115. Joe Louis Chant(90323a;voc.,Geo.D.Washington)/Baby o'Mine(90324a)

JONES AND COLLINS ASTORIA HOT EIGHT (Lee Collins, cornet; Sidney Arodin,clarinet;
 Theodore Purnell, alto sax; David Jones, tenor sax; Joseph Robichaux, piano; Rene
 Hall, banjo; Al Morgan, bass; Albert Martin, drums):   New Orleans,Nov.15,1929
 Vi 38576. Duet Stomp/Astoria Strut   -BB 8168
 BB 10952. Damp Weather/Tip Easy Blues

JONES PARAMOUNT CHARLESTON FOUR:
 Para 12279. Old Steady Roll/Homeward Bound Blues

JONES-SMITH, INCORPORATED (Carl Smith, trumpet; Lester Young, tenor sax; Count
Basie, piano; Walter Page, bass; Joe Jones, drums.--HD):
 Vo 3459. Boogie Woogie(cl659;voc.,James Rushing)
 "   Lady Be Good(cl660)   -VoE 68
 Vo 3441. Shoe Shine Swing(cl657)
 "   Evenin'(cl658)   -VoE 68

JORDAN, CHARLEY (blues singing):
   Vo 1551. Gasoline Blues/Running Mad Blues
   De 7015. Rolling Moon Blues/It Ain't Clean
   De 7065. Lost Air Ship Blues/Tight Times Blues
   De 7130. Christmas Christmas Blues/Christmas Tree Blues (with Verdi Lee)

JORDAN, JIMMY (vocal):
   Co 14655. Winnie the Wailer/There Is No Justice

JORDAN'S TEN SHARPS AND FLATS, JOE:
   Co 14144. Senegalese Stomp(142170)/Morocco Blues(142171; voc., Clarence Williams)

JORDAN AND HIS TYMPANY FIVE, LOUIS:
   De 7556. Barnacle Bill the Sailor/Honey in the Bee Ball
   De 7590. Doug the Jitterbug/Flatface Blues
   De 7609. Keep a-Knockin' Blues/At the Swing Cats' Ball
   De 7623. Sam Jones Done Snagged His Britches/Swinging in the Cocoanut Tree
   De 7675. Honeysuckle Rose(66872a)/But I'll Be Back(66874a)
   De 7693. You Ain't Nowhere/Fore Day Blues
   De 7705. Hard Lovin' Blues/You Run Your Mouth and I'll Run My Business
   De 7719. You're My Meat/Jake What a Snake
   De 7723. June Tenth Jamboree(67111a)/I'm Alabama Bound(67113b)
   De 7729. After School Swing Session/You Got to Go When the Wagon Comes
   De 7777. Penthouse in the Basement/Never Let Your Left Hand Know
   De 8500. Pompton Turnpike(68170a)/Do You Call That a Buddy(68171a)
   De 8501. A Chicken Ain't Nothing But a Bird(68169a)/I Know You(68172a)
   De 8525. Pinetop's Boogie Woogie(68621aa)/T-Bone Blues(68623aa)
   De 8537. Two Little Squirrels(68622a)/Pan Pan(68624a)
   De 8560. Brotherly Love/Saxa-Woogie
   De 8581. Boogie Woogie Came to Town(68909a)/Saint Vitus Dance(68905a)
   De 8593. Knock Me a Kiss/I'm Gonna Move to the Outskirts of Town
   De 8605. Green Grass Grows All Around/How 'Bout That
   De 8627. Mama Mama Blues/Small Town Boy
   De 8638. I'm Gonna Leave You on the Outskirts/It's a Low Down Dirty Shame
   De 8645. Chicks I Pick are Slender Tender and Tall/What's the Use of Getting Sober
   De 8653. Five Guys Named Moe(71132a)/That'll Just About Knock Me Out(71129a)·
   De 3253. Don't Come Cryin' on My Shoulder/Bounce the Ball
   De 3360. Oh Boy I'm in the Groove/Waiting for the Robert E. Lee
   De 4204. Waiting for the Robert E. Lee(Sax solo by Louis Jordan)

JORDAN AND THE MOB, TAFT (Taft Jordan, trumpet; Ward Silloway, trombone; Johnny Mince, clarinet; Elmer Williams, tenor sax; Teddy Wilson, piano; Bobby Johnson, guitar; John Kirby, bass; Eddie Dougherty, drums.--HD):   1935
   Pe 16094. Night Wind(16906-2)   -Me 13352, VoE 1
      "   If the Moon Turns Green(16907-2)   -Cq 8476, Me "   "
   Pe 16102. Devil in the Moon(16914-2)/Louisiana Fairy Tale(16915-2)
                                        (-Me.13365, VoE 15

JOY'S ST. ANTHONY HOTEL ORCHESTRA, JIMMIE:
   OK 40251. Milenberg Joys/Mama Will Be Gone
   OK 40329. Clarinet Marmalade/(rev., Scranton Sirens)
   OK 40381. Indian Dawn(9109a)/China Girl(9111b)
   OK 40388. Riverboat Shuffle(9108a)/Memphis Bound(9107a)
   OK 40420. Wild Jazz/Be Yourself
   OK 40494. Red Hot Henry Brown(9371a)/Fallin' Down(9373a)
   OK 40504. Hay Foot Straw Foot(9374b)/Everybody Stomp(9375a)
   OK 40539. My Sweet Gal(9372b)/St. Louis Blues(9377a)
   OK 40627. Stomp It Mr. Kelly(9378b)/(rev., Charlie Troutt)

       JIMMY JOY AND HIS ORCHESTRA
   Br 3905. From Monday On(vbc.,Orville Andrews)/The Yale Blues
   Br 3960. Today Is Today/Chilly Pom Pom Pee
   Br 3959. I Got Worry/You're the First Thing I Think Of
   Br 4640. Harmonica Harry/Can't You Understand

JOYNER, HOWARD (vocal and piano):
   Co 14623. I'm Through With Love/I Wanna Sing About You
   Co 14650. All of Me/You Rascal You
   Co 14678. Underneath the Harlem Moon/Virginia L. Armstrong

JUNGLE BAND (Duke Ellington's Orchestra: Freddie Jenkins, Arthur Whetsol, Bubber Miley, trumpets; Joe Nanton, Juan Tizol, trombones; Johnny Hodges, Barney Bigard, Harry Carney, reeds; Ellington, piano; Fred Guy, banjo; Wellman Braud, bass; Sonny Greer, drums):   1929
   Br 4238. Tiger Rag, 1 & 2   -BrF 500169, BrE 1338
   Br 6510. Tiger Rag, 1 & 2 (28940a/41a) -- Under Ellington
   Br 4309. Paducah/Harlem Flat Blues   -BrF 500248,BrE 02003
   Br 4345. Doin'the Voom Voom(28939)   -Br 6807, BrF 500249, BrE 02365
      "   Rent Party Blues(29381)   "   "   "

```
            (Next two sides only: Chick Webb Orchestra):
    Br  4450.  Jungle Mama/Dog Bottom

            (Previous Ellington personnel, except Cootie Williams,trumpet for Miley):
                                                                              1930
    Br  4492.  Jungle Jamboree/Black and Blue          -Br 6809,   BrF 500250
    Br  4705.  Jolly Wog                       -BrE 02299, Br 6810, BrF 500251
      "        Jazz Convulsions                -BrE 01827,
    Br  4760.  When You're Smiling                     -Br 6811,   BrF 500158
      "        Sweet Mama
    Br  4776.  Maori                                   -Br 6812,   BrF 500158
      "        Admiration
    Br  4783.  Accordion Joe                           -Br 6846
      "        Double Check Stomp                                  BrF 500170
    Br  4887.  Wall Street Wail/Cotton Club Stomp                  -BrF 500159

            (Cab Calloway Orchestra):
    Br  4936.  Gotta Darn Good Reason Now
      "        St. Louis Blues                                     -Br 80016

            (Whetsol, Nanton, Bigard and rhythm section):
    Br  4952.  Dreamy Blues                        -BrE 1068, Br 6682, BrF 500139
      "        Runnin' Wild                                   , Br 6732,    "
    Br  6003.  Home Again Blues                                    -BrF 500140
      "        Wang Wang Blues                     -BrE 1088            "
    Br  6038.  Rockin' in Rhythm(E35801a)          -BrE 1105,
      "        12th Street Rag(E35802a)            -BrE 1573'         BrF 9042

JUNGLE KINGS (Frank Teschemacher, clarinet; Mezz Mezzrow, tenor sax; Muggsy Span-
ier, cornet; Joe Sullivan, piano; Eddie Condon, banjo; Jim Lannigan, bass; Gene
Krupa, drums; Red McKenzie, vocal):                                Chicago,1927
    Para 12654. Friars Point Shuffle(20563)                         -UHCA 3
      "         Darktown Strutters Ball(20564)                      -UHCA 4

JUNGLE TOWN STOMPERS (Louis Metcalf, trumpet; J.C. Higginbotham, trombone;Albert
Nicholas, clarinet; Charlie Holmes, alto sax; Theo Hill, tenor sax; Clarence Wil-
liams or James P. Johnson, piano; Will Johnson, guitar; Moore, tuba; Paul Barbarin,
drums):                                                         April 15,1929
    OK  8686.  African Jungle(401797c)/Slow As Molasses(401798b)
```

K

```
KAHN AND HIS ORCHESTRA, ROGER WOLFE (Featuring Miff Mole, trombone; Eddie Lang,
guitar; Joe Venuti, violin; Manny Klein, trumpet; Arthur Schutt, piano, and others):
    Vi 20059. Somebody's Lonely/(rev., Aaronson)                   1927-32
    Vi 20231. Jersey Walk
    Vi 20464. Delilah/(rev., Nat Shilkret)
    Vi 20466. Yankee Rose/(rev., Jean Goldkette)
    Vi 20493. A Little Birdie Told Me So/(rev., Jean Goldkette)
    Vi 20573. I Can't Believe That You're in Love With Me/Following You Around
    Vi 20634. Just the Same/(rev., Nat Shilkret)
    Vi 20717. Where the Wild Wild Flowers Grow/Calling
    Vi 20828. All By My Ownsome/(rev., Paul Whiteman)              -HMV 5366
    Vi 20599. Sometimes I'm Happy/(rev., Nat Shilkret)             -HMV 5312

            (Next side only, featuring Jack Teagarden, trombone):  March,1928
    Vi 21326. She's a Great Great Girl(43358)/(rev.,All Star Orchestra) -HMV 5514
    Vi 21368. Crazy Rhythm/Imagination                             -HMV 5535
    Vi 21082. You Came Along
    Vi 21510. You're a Real Sweetheart(45826)/Lonely Little Bluebird(45827)
    Vi 21801. Room With a View/Dance Little Lady
    Vi 21897. You're the Only One/Shady Lady
    Br 4374.  Heigh-Ho Everybody(voc.,D.Robertson)/Pretty Little Thing(voc.,F.Munn)
    Br 4479.  Do What You Do/Liza
    Br 4571.  Then You've Never Been Blue/Through
    Br 4583.  Why Was I Born/Here Am I
    Br 4600.  Without a Song/Great Day
    Br 4614.  Don't Ever Leave Me/'Twas Not So Long Ago
    Br 4699.  Cooking Breakfast for the One I Love/When a Woman Loves a Man
    Br 4742.  Exactly Like You/On the Sunny Side of the Street
    Br 4750.  Montana Call/The Moon Is Low
    Br 4811.  Into My Heart/Dark Night
    Br 4826.  Cheer Up/(rev., Isham Jones)
    Co 2653.  Lazy Day/My Silent Love
    Co 2695.  I Can't Believe It's True/You've Got Me in the Palm of Your Hand
    Co 2697.  Sheltered by the Stars/Another Night Alone
    Co 2722.  A Shine on Your Shoes/It Don't Mean a Thing
    Co 2726.  Fit as a Fiddle/Just a Little Home for the Old Folks
```

KALEY, CHARLES (acc. including Eddie Lang, guitar):
Co   886. Muddy Water/High on a Hill Top

       (With cornet and piano accompaniment):
Co   910. Alabama Stomp(143543)/Who Do You Love(143298; guitar and piano)

       (Unknown acc.):
Co   1385. Strolling in the Moonlight(145858)/Sweetheart I'm Sorry(145857)

MAX KAMINSKY

See also:
ADRIAN'S RAMBLERS: Br 6877, 6889.
CHOCOLATE DANDIES: PaE 1717, 1743, 1792, 1815.
EDDIE CONDON: BrF 500328,500406;De 18040,18041;Com 530,531,542,551,1509,1510.
TOMMY DORSEY: Vi 25284 to 25535.
BUD FREEMAN: De 18064, 18065,18066,18067,2781,2849;BB 10370,10386; Co 35853-56.
JAM SESSION AT COMMODORE: Com 1504, 1505, 1513.
MEZZ MEZZROW: Br 6778, 7551; Vi 25019, 25202.

KAMINSKY AND HIS JAZZ BAND, MAX (Max Kaminsky, trumpet; Rod Cless, clarinet;
Frank Orchard, trombone; Jack Lesberg, bass; Mac McGrath, drums; James P. John-
son, piano):   1944
Com   . Love Nest/Eccentric
Com   . Everybody Loves My Baby/Guess Who's in Town

KANSAS CITY FIVE (Bob Fuller, clarinet; Jack Frazier, trombone, and others):
Pe 14356. Get Yourself a Monkey Man
Aj 17072. Louisville Blues/Temperamental Blues
Pat 36335. Get It Fixed/Dark Gal Blues
Pat 36366. Growin' Old Blues/Jake's Weary Blues   -Pe 14547

       KANSAS CITY SIX (Eddie Durham, trombone and electric guitar; Freddie
       Green, guitar; Walter Page, bass; Jo Jones, drums; Lester Young, clari-
       net and tenor sax; Buck Clayton, trumpet):
Com   509. Countless Blues(p23422-1)/I Want a Little Girl(p23424-1)

       (Without Young: Kansas City Five):
Com   510. Laughing at Life(22580-1)/I Know That You Know(22582-1)

       (Six):
Com   511. Them There Eyes(p23423-2)/Good Mornin' Blues(22581-1; K.C. Five)
Com   512. Way Down Yonder in New Orleans(p23421-2)/Pagin' the Devil(p23425-1)

       (Lester Young, tenor sax; Dicky Wells, trombone; Bill Coleman, trumpet;
       Joe Bushkin, piano; John Simmons, bass; Jo Jones, drums):
Com   555. I Got Rhythm(a4748-1)/Jo Jo(a4747-1)

       KANSAS CITY SEVEN (Buck Clayton, trumpet; Lester Young, tenor sax; Dicky
       Wells, trombone; Count Basie, piano; Freddie Green, guitar; Jo Jones,
       drums; Rodney Richardson, bass):   Mar.22,1944
Key 1302. After Theatre Jump(21)/Lester Leaps Again(23; Young & rhythm section
Key 1303. Destination K.C.(24-1)/Six Cats & a Prince(22)   (as Kansas City 5)

KANSAS CITY FRANK (Frank Melrose, piano, with traps):
Br   7062. Pass the Jug/Jelly Roll Stomp   -Br 80031

       KANSAS CITY FRANK AND HIS FOOTWARMERS (Frank Melrose, piano; Herb Morand,
       trumpet; Tommy Taylor, drums and Frisco whistle; sax; clarinet.--KH):
Para 12898. St. James Infirmary(21470)/Wailing Blues(21469)   -Bwy 1355*
       *Broadway issue under Harry's Reckless Five)

KANSAS CITY KITTY and Georgia Tom (vocal with piano, and guitar by Tampa Red):
Vo   1508. The Doctor's Blues/You Got That Stuff

KANSAS CITY STOMPERS (Frank Melrose, piano; Jimmy Bertrand, xylophone; trumpet;
clarinet; mass sax; drums; bass):
Br   7091. Shanghai Honeymoon/Good Feelin' Blues

       KANSAS CITY TIN ROOF STOMPERS (Melrose and others):   Mar.15,1929
Br   7066. Aunt Jemima Stomp(c3127)   -Br 4965
     "   St. Louis Bound(c3128)

KANSAS JOE AND MEMPHIS MINNIE (Blues duet with guitar):
Vo   1550. North Memphis Blues/What's the Matter With the Mill

KARLE AND HIS BOYS, ART (Art Karle, tenor sax; Mezz Mezzrow, alto sax and clarinet;
Frank Newton, trumpet; Joe Bushkin, piano; Ted Tonisen, guitar; Bass Thompson, bass;
George Stafford, drums.--RR):   1936

```
Vo  3146. Moon Over Miami(18496)/I Feel Like a Feather in the Breeze(18497)
Vo  3147. Susannah(18498)/Lights Out(18499)
```

KEATING AND HIS ORCHESTRA, LLOYD (Some of these supposedly include Benny Goodman, clarinet, and/or Jimmy and Tommy Dorsey, alto sax and trombone):
```
Ha   1177. Where Can You Be(100400)/Old New England Moon
Ha   1364. Waiting for the Moon/Little Hunka Love
Ha   1372. Kiss Me Goodnight/Can't You See
Ha   1383. I'm for You 100 Per Cent/It's Love
Ha   1411. Auf Wiedersehen/Carolina's Callin' Me
Ve   2145. Across the Breakfast Table/My Future Just Passed
Ve   2181. I Love You So Much/You Can't Take My Mem'ries
Ve   2189. Here Comes the Sun(100406)/Should I Be Sorry
Ve   2467. You Try Somebody Else/(rev., Groetsch)
Vo  10501. An Evening in Caroline(236006)/Why Did It Have to Be Me
Ve  10504. Just Friends(236014)/Was That the Human Thing to Do
De   3226. I'm Yours/(rev., Leighton)
Cl   5082. Language of Love/(rev., Hotel Pennsylvania Orch.)
Cl   5103. I'll Be Blue Just Thinking of You(150907)
Cl   5350. When Yuba Plays the Rhumba/I'm Keepin' Company
Cl  11000. Tom Boy/Birthday of a Kiss
Cl  11502. Ooh That Kiss/Freddy the Freshman
```

KEGHOUSE (vocal with Jay Bird, piano):
```
Vo   1239. Sock It Blues/Canned Heat Blues
```

KELLY, WILLIE (blues singing with piano):
```
Vi  23259. Kelly's Special/Don't Put the Lights Out
Vi  23285. As True as I've Been to You/Don't Squeeze Me
Vi  23299. Nasty But It's Clean(piano solo)/You so Dumb
Vi  38608. Kelly's 44 Blues/I Love You More and More
Vi  38619. 32-20 Blues/Give Me Your Change
```

KEMP AND HIS ORCHESTRA, HAL (Reputed personnel for early 1930 period: Bunny Berigan, Mickey Bloom, trumpets; Jimmy James, trombone; Hal Kemp, Saxie Dowell, Ben Williams, Joe Gillespie, reeds; John Trotter, piano; Paul Weston, bass; Olly Humphries, banjo; Skinny Ennis, drums and vocals.--RR):
```
Br   3937. Lovable/I Don't Care
Br   3954. Get Out and Get Under the Moon/Oh Baby
Br   4078. Washington and Lee Swing/High Up on a Hill Top
Br   4212. My Lucky Star/You Wouldn't Fool Me Would You
Br   4307. That's What I Call Heaven/Things That Were Made for Love
Br   4388. When My Dreams Come True/To Be in Love
Br   4424. In the Hush of the Night/Where Are You Dream Girl
Br   4612. A Little Kiss Each Morning/I Love You Believe Me
Br   4674. H'lo Baby/(rev., Irving Mills)
Br   4676. Navy Blues/Romance
Br   4805. I Remember You from Somewhere/Washin' the blues from My Soul
Br   4807. Give Yourself a Pat on the Back/If I Had a Girl Like You
Br   4988. Fraternity Blues
Br   4992. Them There Eyes
```
        (There are many other Brunswicks and Victors)

KEENE, LINDA (vocal with Henry Levine's Band, for which see personnel):
```
Vi  27829. Embraceable You/(rev., Henry Levine)
Vi  27830. Way Down Yonder in New Orleans/Georgia on My Mind
Vi  27831. Somebody Loves Me/(rev., Henry Levine)
Vi  27832. Someone to Watch Over Me/Mound Bayou
```

   (Acc. by Joe Marsala's Orchestra: Marsala, clarinet; Joe Thomas, trumpet; Leonard Feather, piano; Chuck Wayne, guitar; Irv Lang bass; Buddy Christian, drums):   Nov.29,1944
```
B&W 1203. Lucky Woman/Blues in the Storm
```
        (See Also: Joe Marsala B&W 1201, 1202)

KENNEDY AND HIS RHYTHM ORCHESTRA, JOE: 1935
```
BB   6062. That's What You Think/Double Trouble
BB   6080. I'll Just Keep on Dreaming/Rosetta
BB   6102. Song of the Wanderer/I Never Knew
BB   6233. Rhythm Is Our Business/Chinatown My Chinatown
BB   6249. You Can Depend on Me/Confessin'
```

KENNY AND HIS ORCHESTRA, KEN (Red Norvo):   1936
```
Ch  40100. Let Yourself Go/If You Love Me(under name of Len Herman)
Ch  40101. Misty Islands of the Highlands/Life Begins When You're in Love(Herman)
Ch  40107. You Started Me Dreaming/What's the Name of That Song
```

KENTON AND HIS ORCHESTRA, STAN:
```
De   4037. The Nago/This Love of Mine
De   4038. Adios/Taboo
De   4254. Lamento Gitano(70316)/Concerto for Doghouse(70318; bass solo by Howard
De   4319. El Choclo/Reed Rapture                                    (Rumsey)
De  15063. Gambler's Blues/(rev., Langford)
```

```
            (Eddie Myers, Stan Getz, Dave Matthews, Chester Ball, Maurice Beeson,
            reeds; Marion Childers, John Carroll, Karl George, Dick Morse, trumpets;
            George Faye, Harry Forbes, Batty Varsalona, William Atkinson, trombones;
            Robert Ahern, guitar; Eugene Englund, bass; Jesse Price, drums; Stan Ken-
            ton; piano):
   Cap        . Artistry in Rhythm/Eager Beaver
   Cap     145. Do Nothin' Till You Hear from Me(1111)/Harlem Folk Dance(113)
   Cap     166. Her Tears Flowed Like Wine/How Many Hearts Have You Broken
   Cap     178. Sweet Dreams Sweetheart/Gotta Be Gettin'
   Cap     187. Ev'ry Time We Say Goodbye/Are You Livin' Old Man
```

KENTUCKY GRASSHOPPERS (Jimmy McPartland, cornet; Jack Teagarden, trombone; Benny
Goodman, clarinet; Gil Rodin, Larry Binyon, saxes; Vic Briedis, piano; Dick Mor-
gan, banjo; Harry Goodman, bass; Ray Bauduc, drums.--HD):   1929
   Ba 6295. Four or Five Times(2061)/It's Tight Like That(2062)
   Ba 6360. Makin' Friends(2170-4)/(rev., Fred Rich)
   Ba 6355. Shirt Tail Stomp(2187)/Tiger Rag(2186)
   Ba 6358. Sweet Liza(2191)/(rev., Lanin)
   Ba 6441. Twelfth Street Rag/After You've Gone(2335)
   Ba 6483. It's So Good
           (See also: Lou Conner,Dixie Jazz Band,Jimmy Bracken,Whoopee Makers,etc.)

KENTUCKY BLOWERS:
   Ge 5602. Choo Choo/(rev., Dixie Hod Carriers)

KENTUCKY HOT HOPPERS (Red Nichols, trumpet; Miff Mole trombone; Fud Livingston,
clarinet; Arthur Schutt, piano; Eddie Lang, guitar; Vic Berton, drums.--HD): 1928
   Pat 36841. Red Head Blues (2833)/The Drag(2834)   -Pe 15022
           (See Alabama Red Peppers)

KENTUCKY JAZZ BABIES
   Vi 38616. Old Folks Shake/No More Blues

KENTUCKY JUG BAND:
   Vo 1564. Walking Cane Stomp/Hard Hustlin' Blues

KENTUCKY SERENADERS (Trumpet; trombone; clarinet; sax; piano; drums;banjo):
   Re 9134. Shake It and Break It(41924)/Aunt Hagar's Children Blues(41925)
   Re 9139. My Sunny Tennessee(42045)/(rev., Manhattan Specialty Orch.)

FREDDIE KEPPARD

See also:
   JAMES BLYTHE: Para. 12376.
   DOC COOK: Ge 5360, 5373, 5374; Co 727, 813, 862
   COOKIE'S GINGERSNAPS: OK 8639, 8390, 40675.
   WILBUR SWEATMAN:

KEPPARD'S JAZZ CARDINALS, FREDDIE (Freddie Keppard, cornet; Eddie Vincent or Honore Dutrey, trombone; Johnny Dodds, clarinet; Arthur Campbell, piano; Jasper Taylor, wood blocks):   1926
   Para 12399. Stock Yards Strut(2651 1a)/Salty Dog(2653-2a) voc.,Charlie Jackson
                                                            (-UHCA 73/74, JI 4
   Para 12399. Salty Dog(2653-1), voc., Charlie Jackson

KID AND COOT (Coot Grant and Kid Wilson, q.v.):
   Co 14363. ---

KIMBROUGH, SYLVESTER (vocal):
   Br 7135. Bird Liver Blues/Garbage Can Blues

KING, FRANCES (vocal with piano and Ed Lang, guitar):
   OK 40854. She's Got It(80942a)/Oh Gee Jennie It's You(80943a)

KIRBY AND HIS ORCHESTRA, JOHN (Charlie Shavers, trumpet; Buster Bailey, clarinet;
Russell Procope, alto; Billy Kyle, piano; John Kirby, bass; O'Neil Spencer,drums):
   Vo 4624. It Feels Good(23935)/Effervescent Blues(23936)   1939-41
   Vo 4653. The Turf(23937)/Dawn on the Desert(23938)
   Vo 4890. Anitra's Dance(w24677)/Drink to Me Only With Thine Eyes(w24679)
   Vo 5048. I May be Wrong/Opus 5
   Vo 5187. Royal Garden Blues(w24946)/Blue Skies(w24996)
   Vo 5520. Front and Center(w24945)/Nocturne(wc2782)
   Vo 5542. Minute Waltz(w24680)/You Go Your Way(w26759)
   Vo 5570. Impromptu(w24995)/Little Brown Jug(wc2781)
   Vo 5605. One Alone(wc2783)/Humoresque(wc2784)
   OK 5632. Chloe/(rev., Horace Henderson)
   OK 5661. Jumpin' in the Pump Room(w26757)/Temptation(w26854)
   OK 5705. Frasquita Serenade(w28001)/Sextet from Lucia(w28002)
   OK 5761. On a Little Street in Singapore(w26856)/Zooming at the Zombie(w28004)

```
OK   5805. Blues Petite/Andiology
Co  35920. Milumbu/Can't We Be Friends
Co  35998. Bounce of the Sugar Plum Fairy(co29508)/Double Talk(co29510)
Co  35999. Then I'll Be Happy(w26999)/Coquette(w28003)
Co  36000. Rose Room(w24997)/20th Century Closet(w26760)
Co  36001. Sweet Georgia Brown(w24678)/Serenade(wc2785)
Co  36165. Cutting the Campus/I Love You Truly
De   2216. From A Flat to C                                           -De 4206
  "        Undecided
De   2367. Rehearsin' for a Nervous Breakdown(64708)/Pastel Blue(64710)
Vi  27568. Close Shave/Bugler's Dilemma
Vi  27598. Fifi's Rhapsody/It's Only a Paper Moon
Vi  27667. Night Whispers/Tweed Me
Vi  27890. Keep Smilin'/Comin' Back
```

KIRK AND HIS TWELVE CLOUDS OF JOY, ANDY (Gene Prince, Harry Lawson, trumpets; Allen Durham, trombone; Lawrence Freeman, John Williams, John Harrington, saxes; Claude Williams, violin; Mary Lou Williams, piano; William Dirvin, banjo; Andy Kirk, bass; Edward McNeill, drums; Billy Massey, vocal.--HD):   1927-28

```
Br   4653. Cloudy/Casey Jones Special
Br   4694. Mess-a-Stomp(591)/Blue Clarinet Stomp(592)     -BrF 500162, Vo 3255
Br   4803. I Lost My Gal from Memphis/Loose Ankles
Br   4863. Mary's Idea/Once or Twice
Br   4878. Snag It/Sweet and Hot
Br   4893. Corky Stomp/Froggy Bottom                       -BrE 1211, BrF 8825
Br   4981. Honey Just for You/Traveling That Rocky Road    -BrE 1054
Br   6027. Saturday/Sophomore
Br   6129. Dallas Blues/(rev., Noble Sissle)
```

(Paul King, Earl Thomson, Harry Lawson, trumpets; Theo Donelly, trombone; Dick Wilson, John Williams, John Harrington, saxes; Claude Williams, violin; Andy Kirk, baritone sax; Mary Lou Williams, piano; Ted Brinson, guitar; Booker Collins, bass; Ben Thigpen, drums and vocal; Pha Terrell, vocal.--HD):   1936-37

```
De    729. Christopher Columbus/Froggy Bottom              -CoE 5000
De    744. All the Jive Is Gone
  "        I'se a Muggin'                                  -CoE 5004
De    772. Blue Illusion                                   -CoE 5021
  "        Corky
De    809. Walkin' and Swingin'(60852)                     -CoE 5023
  "        Until the Real Thing Comes Along(60972)         -CoE 5004
De    853. Give Her a Pint                                 -CoE 5029
  "        Moten Swing (60853)                    -De 3517,-CoE 5015
De    931. Git(60861-c)                                    -CoE 5021
  "        Steppin' Pretty(60867)                          -CoE 5023
De   1046. Bearcat Shuffle
  "        Lotta Sax Appeal                       -De 3883, CoE 5015
De   1085. Lady Who Swings the Band
  "        What Will I Tell My Heart                       -BrE 02377
De   1146. Fifty-second Street                             -BrE 02377
  "        Dedicated to You
De   1208. Cloudy
  "        Puddin' Head Serenade                           -CoE 5027
De   1261. Foolin' Myself/In the Groove                    -BrE 02441
De   1303. Wednesday Night Hop(61598)/Worried Over You(62133)  -BrE 02519
De   1349. Skies Are Blues/I'll Get Along Somehow          -BrE 02469
De   1422. Better Luck Next Time(62448)/I Went to a Gypsy(62456)
De   1477. Why Can't We Do It Again/With Love in My Heart
De   1531. Downstream(61950)                               -BrE 02483
  "        I'm Glad for Your Sake(62135)
```

(Omit violin; add Earl Miller, alto sax; Henry Wells, trombone):

```
De   1579. A Mellow Bit of Rhythm(62446)                   -BrE 02483
  "        In My Wildest Dreams(62447)
```

(Sub. Clarence Trice, trumpet, for King):

```
De   1606. Bear Down/Big Dipper                            -BrE 02587
De   1663. Lover Come Back to Me/Poor Butterfly            -BrE 02575
De   1710. Key to My Heart                                 -De 3385
  "        Little Joe from Chicago
De   1827. It Must Be True/What's Mine Is Yours
De   1916. I'll Get By/I Surrender Dear
De   2081. How Can We Be Wrong/How Much Do You Mean to Me
De   2127. Toadie Toddle(64642)/I Won't Tell a Soul(64643)
De   2204. Bless You My Dear(64613)/Messa Stomp(64615)
De   2226. Jump Jack Jump(64694)/Ghost of Love(64696)
De   2261. Breeze(64695)/Sittin' Around and Dreamin'(64698)
De   2277. But It Didn't Mean a Thing/What Would People Say
De   2326. Honey(64777)/Mary's Idea(64783)
De   2383. Julius Caesar(64780)/You Set Me on Fire(65188)
De   2407. Close to Five(65190)/I'll Never Fail You(65251)
```

(Omit John Williams; add Don Byas, tenor sax; sub. Floyd Smith, guitar.--JRB):   1939

De 2483. Twinkin'(63256; previous personnel)/Floyd's Guitar Blues(65191)
De 2510. I'll Never Learn(65189)/S'posin'(65250)
De 2570. Clouds(64779; previous personnel)/Goodbye(64782; pervious personnel)
De 2617. September in the Rain/What a Life
De 2723. Dunkin'a Doughnut(64781;prev.personnel)/Then I'll Be Happy(65249;voc.
De 2774. Say It Again/Why Don't I Get Wise to Myself   (June Richmond)
De 2915. Ghost of a Chance(66878)/Big Jim Blues(66880)
De 2957. I'm Getting Nowhere With You/It Always Will be You
De 2962. Love Is the Thing/Wham
De 3033. Please Don't Talk About Me When I'm Gone/Why Go on Pretending
De 3282. Fifteen Minute Intermission/Fine and Mellow
De 3293. Scratchin' in the Gravel(67894)/Take Those Blues Away(67896; voc.,
De 3306. Now I Lay Me Down to Dream/What's Story Morning Glory (June Richmond)
De 3350. Midnight Stroll/No Greater Love

    (Sub. Rudy Powell, alto sax, for Miller; Ed Inge, for Byas; Harold Baker,
    trumpet, for Thompson):   1941-42
De 3491. Little Miss(67920)/When I Saw You(68319; voc., Henry Wells)
De 3582. If I Feel This Way Tomorrow(68363;voc.,Wells)/Or Have I(68364)
De 3619. A Dream Dropped In(68547; voc., Wells)/Is It a Sin(68548;voc.,Wells)
De 3663. Cuban Boogie Woogie/Ring Dem Bells
De 4042. Big Time Crip/47th Street Jive
De 4141. I'm Misunderstood(69521;voc.,Wells)/No Answer(69522;voc.,Wells)
De 4366. Hip Hip Hooray/Take It and Git
De 4381. Boogie Woogie Cocktail/Worried Life Blues
De 4405. Hey Lawdy Mama/McGhee Special
De 18123. The Count(68317)/12th Street Rag(68318)
    (See also: John Williams Memphis Stompers; Seven Little Clouds of
    Joy; Mary Lou Williams; Blanche Calloway Joy Boys)

KLEIN AND HIS ORCHESTRA, MANNIE (Mannie Klein, Charles Margulis, Ruby Weinstein,
trumpets; Jack Lacey, Jack Jenny, trombones; Toots Mondello, Artie Shaw, Paul
Ricci, Jess Carneol, saxes; Sam Shapiro, violin; Frank Signorelli, piano; Tony
Colucci, guitar; Artie Bernstein, bass; Chauncey Morehouse, drums; Beatrice Wain
and the Bachelors, vocals.--RR):   1936
Br 7605. I'm in Love/Ringside Table for Two
Br 7606. Hot Spell/Juba

    (With Andy Iona and His Islanders):
Co 35524. Hawaiian Drinking Song/Hawaiian War Song

    MANNIE KLEIN AND HIS SWING-A-HULAS:
Vo 4114. Melihini Mele/Moonlight in Waikiki
Vo 4170. Dreamy Hawaiian Moon/Hoohihi Oe Ke Ike Mai

    MANNY KLEIN'S HAWAIIANS:
BB 10505. Rainbows Over Paradise/Makalapua O Kamakaeha
BB 10807. Maori Brown Eyes/Ulili Hula

KOKOMO ARNOLD (blues singing):
De 7026. Milk Cow Blues/Old Original Kokomo Blues
De 7044. Sagefield Woman blues/Back to the Woods
De 7050. Sissy Man Blues/Old Black Cat Blues
De 7059. Biscuit Roller Blues/Milk Cow Blues No. 2
De 7069. Black Money Blues/Chain Gang Blues
De 7070. How Long How Long Blues/Things 'Bout Coming My Way
De 7083. Twelve/Feels So Good
De 7092. Black Annie/Slop Jar Blues
De 7103. Cause You're Dirty/Tonic Head Blues
De 7116. Milk Cow Blues No. 3/Big Leg Mama
De 7133. Monday Morning Blues/You Should Not 'a Done It
De 7139. Southern Railroad Blues/Busy Bootin'
De 7147. Policy Wheel Blues/Traveling Rambler Blues
De 7156. Front Door Blues/Back Door Blues
De 7163. Down and Out Blues/Milk Cow Blues No. 4
De 7165. Desert Blues/I Can't Get Enough of That Stuff
De 7172. I'll Be Up Some Day/Sundown Blues
De 7181. Doin't the Doopididy/Stop Look and Listen
De 7191. Bo Weavil Blues/Let Your Money Talk
De 7198. Model T Woman Blues/Mule Laid Down and Died
De 7212. Bull Head Woman Blues/Shake That Thing
De 7242. Coffin Blues/Running Drunk Again
De 7261. Lonesome Road Blues/Mister Charlie
De 7267. Cold Winter Blues/Salty Dog
De 7275. Fool Man Blues(91069)/Sister Jane Cross the Hall(91073)
De 7285. Laugh and Grin Blues/Wild Water Blues
De 7306. Backfence Picket Blues/Long and Rall
De 7319. Black Mattie/Grandpa Got Drunk
De 7347. Mean Old Twister/Red Beans and Rice
De 7361. Big Ship Blues/Set Down Gal
De 7390. Back on the Job/Shine on Moon

```
De  7417. Broke Man Blues/Head Cuttin' Blues
De  7431. Crying Blues/Neck Bone Blues
De  7449. Buddy Brown Blues/Rocky Mountain Blues
De  7464. Kid Man Blues/Tired of Runnin' from Door to Door
De  7485. Goin' Down in Galilee/Something's Hot
De  7510. Your Ways and Actions/Midnight Blues
De  7540. Bad Luck Blues/My Well Is Dry
```

KRESS, CARL and Dick McDonough, guitar duets: 1934
```
Br  6917. Danzon/Stage Fright                              -BrE 01808
Br  7885. Heat Wave/Chicken a la Swing
```

    CARL KRESS, (guitar solos):
```
De 23136. Afterthoughts, 1, 2 & 3
De 23137. Love Song/Peg Leg Shuffle
De 23138. Helena/Sutton Mutton
```

KRUGER AND HER KNIGHTS OF RHYTHM, JERRY:
```
Vr   666. The Bed Song/So You Won't Sing
```

GENE KRUPA

See also:
ADRIAN: Br 6786.
BIX BEIDERBECKE: Vi 23008, 23018.
CLEO BROWN: De 409,410,486,512.
HOAGY CARMICHAEL: Vi 38139.
CHARLESTON CHASERS: Co 2415.
CHICAGO RHYTHM KINGS: Br 4001.
EDDIE CONDON: OK 41142, PaE 2932.
REGINALD FORESYTHE: Co 3012, 3060.
BUD FREEMAN: OK 41168.
BENNY GOODMAN: Co 2835,2845,2856,2867,2871,2907,2892; most Victors.
LIONEL HAMPTON: Vi 25527, 25535.
JACK JENNEY: Vo 5223, 5304, 5407, 5494.
JUNGLE KINGS: Para 12654.
LOUISIANA RHYTHM KINGS: Br 4845, 4908, 4923, 4938, 4953.
WINGY MANNONE: Vo 15728.
McKENZIE-CONDON: OK 40971, 41011.
MIFF MOLE: OK 41445, HRS 15.
MOUND CITY BLUE BLOWERS: Co 1946; Vi 38087, 38100.
NEW ORLEANS RHYTHM KINGS: De 388, 401.
RED NICHOLS: Br 4363,4373,4701,4724,4839,4877,4885,4925,4944,4957,4982,6014,
    6026,6029,6035,6068,6070,6118,6133; Vi 23033,23026.
RED NORVO: Co 3026,3059,3079.
JESS STACY: PaE 2187, 2233.
FRANK TESCHEMACHER: UHCA 61.
FATS WALLER: Vi 38086, 38568.
TEDDY WILSON: Br 7736,7739,7762,7768.

KRUPA'S SWING GANG, GENE (Roy Eldridge, trumpet; Benny Goodman, clarinet; Chu Berry, tenor sax; Jess Stacy, piano; Allen Reuss, guitar; Israel Crosby, bass; Gene
Krupa, drums; Helen Ward, vocal):   1935
```
Vi 25263. Mutiny in the Parlor(100013)                       -HMV 8432
       "  I'm Gonna Clap My Hands(100014)                    -HMV 8429
Vi 25276. I Hope Gabriel Likes My Music(100012)   -BB 10705, HMV 8429
       "  Swing Is Here(100015)                           "., HMV 8432
```

    GENE KRUPA AND HIS CHICAGOANS (Nate Kazebier, trumpet Joe Harris, trombone; Benny Goodman, clarinet; Dick Clark, tenor; same rhythm):   1936
```
PaE 2224. Three Little Words(c90462aa)/Blues Of Israel(c90463b)   -De 18114
PaE 2268. The Last Round-Up(c90460a)/Jazz Me Blues(c90461e)       -De 18115
```

    GENE KRUPA AND HIS ORCHESTRA (Tom di Carlo, Tom Gossling, Dave Schultze, trumpets; Bruce Squires, Charles McCamish, trombones; Murray Williams, George Sirauo, altos; Vido Musso, Carl Biesacker, tenors; Milton Raskin, piano; Ray Biondi, guitar; Horace Rollins, bass; Gene Krupa, drums.--HD):   1938
```
Br 8123. One More Dream/I'm Feelin' High and Happy
Br 8124. I Know That You Know/Grandfather's Clock
Br 8139. Fare Thee Well Annie Laurie/Prelude to a Stomp
Br 8161. There's Honey on the Moon Tonight(b23009)/If It Rains Who Cares(b23006)
Br 8166. What Goes on Here
      "  Wire Brush Stomp                                         -OK 6106
Br 8188. Meet the Beat of My Heart/Nagasaki
Br 8198. Rhythm Jam/You're As Pretty As a Picture
Br 8211. Jam on Toast(b22867)/Tutti Frutti(b23324;voc., Leo Watson)
Br 8249. Bye Bye Blues(c2357,voc.,Irene Daye)/After Looking at You(c2358)
Br 8253. Walkin' and Swingin'(c2360)/Since My Best Gal Turned Me Down(c2361)
Br 8274. Wait Until My Heart Finds Out(LA1754:voc.,Daye)/Lightly and Politely
                                                                      (LA1757)
```

Br	8280.	Jeepers Creepers(voc.,Leo Watson)/Say It With a Kiss
Br	8284.	Bolero at the Savoy(LA1758), voc.,Irene Daye)/Murdy Purdy(LA1759)
Br	8289.	Never Felt Better,Never Had Less(LA1762)/Do You Wanna Jump Children
Br	8296.	Ta-ra-ra-boom-der-e(LA1760)/Apurksody(LA1764) (LA1765,voc.,Watson)
Br	8335.	Quiet and Roll 'em(LA1815)/The Madam Swings It(LA1816)
Br	8340.	The Lady's in Love With You(LA1813)/Some Like It hot(LA1814),voc.,
Br	8361.	Cracula(WB24545)/Foo for Two(WB24548) (Irene Daye
Br	8382.	Swanee River/I Dream of Jeanie
Br	8400.	You Taught Me to Love Again(WC2587;voc.,Daye)/Jungle Madness(WC2589)
Br	8412.	Challenger Hop(WC2576)/Don't Be Surprised(WC2586)
Br	8448.	You and Your Love(WB24924)/Moonlight Serenade(WB24925) voc.,I.Daye
Br	8451.	Guess I'll Go Back Home(WB24923)/Whisper While We Dance(WB24927)
Co	35205.	Old Black Joe(WB24926)/My Old Kentucky Home(WB24929)
Co	35262.	On the Beam(CO25368)/Hodge Podge(WC2574)
Co	35237.	All Dressed Up Spic and Spanish/I Like to Recognize the Tune
Co	35324.	Drummin' Man/I'd Love to Call You My Sweetheart
Co	35361.	I've Got My Eyes on You/A Lover Is Blue
Co	35366.	I've Got No Strings/The Rhumba Jumps

(Sam Donahue, Bob Snyder, Clint Neagley, Sam Musiker, saxes; Floyd O'Brien, Al Sherman, Rod Ogle, trombones; Corky Cornelius, Torg Halten, Nate Kazebier, trumpets; Milt Raskin, piano; Biddy Bastien, bass; Remo Biondi,guitar; Gene Krupa, drums): **1939**

| Co | 35387. | Symphony in Riffs(CO25369)/Marcheta(WC026377; sub. Al Jordan, Sid Grantley, trombones,for Ogle,Sherman;Tony D'Amore,piano,for Raskin) |

(Sub. Shorty Cherock, trumpet, for Kazebier): **1940**

Co	35408.	The Woodpecker Song(WC026505;voc.,Irene Daye)/Say Si Si(WC026535)
Co	35415.	A Lover's Lullaby(WC026506)/Boog It(WC026508;voc.,Irene Daye)
Co	35423.	So Long(CO27026;voc.,Irene Daye)/Tuxedo Junction(CO27027)
Co	35429.	It Happened in Kaloha(voc.,Howard DuLany)/I Love You Much(voc.,Daye)
Co	35444.	Manhattan Transfer/Moments in the Moonlight
Co	35490.	Chop Chop Charlie Chan/Love in My Heart
Co	35454.	Sierra Sue/Tiger Rag
Co	35508.	No Name Jive(CO27323)/Six Lessons from Madame LaZonga(CO27324)
Co	35520.	All This and Heaven Too/When the Swallows Come Back to Capistrano
Co	36591.	Deliver Me to Tennessee/Knock Me a Kiss
Co	36621.	That's What You Think/All Those Wonderful Years
Co	36726.	Bolero at the Savoy(31801)/Side by Side(32310) voc.,Anita O'Day
OK	5627.	Blue Rhythm Fantasy, 1 7 2 (WCO 26379/80)
OK	5643.	I'll Never Smile Again/Maybe
OK	5672.	Blueberry Hill/Orchids for Remembrance
OK	5686.	Only Forever/Love Lies
OK	5701.	And So Do I/I Am An American
OK	5715.	Never Took a Lesson in My Life/Tonight
OK	5747.	Looking for Yesterday(W26954)/Drummer Boy(WC3209) voc.,Irene Daye
OK	5760.	I'm Waiting for Ships That Never Come In/The World Is in My Arms
OK	5788.	Old Old Castle in Scotland/Rhumboogie
OK	5802.	I Hear Music/A Nightingale Sang in Berkeley Square
OK	5814.	Moon Over Burma/You're Breaking My Heart All Over Again
OK	5826.	Down Argentina Way/Two Dreams Met
OK	5836.	I'd Know You Anywhere/Like the Fella Once Said
OK	5859.	Somewhere(28752)/You Danced With Dynamite(28888) voc., Du Lany
OK	5872.	Oh They're Making Me All Over in the Army/When You Awake
OK	5883.	High on a Windy Hill/It All Comes Back to Me Now
OK	6909.	Blues Krieg/Yes My Carling Daughter

(Sub. Rudy Novack, trumpet, for Sherock;Baby Wagner, Jay Kellerher, trombones, for O'Brien, Brantley; Walter Bates, sax, for Donahue): **1940**

OK	5921.	Feelin' Fancy(WC026768;prev.personnel)/Washington and Lee Swing(27616)
OK	5935.	Isn't That Just Like Love/You Are the One
OK	5961.	Deep in the Blues/You Forgot About Me
OK	5985.	He's Gone(WC026765)/The Sergeant Was Shy(W26967)

(Sub. Pat Virgadamo, trombone, for Jordan; Bob Kitsis, piano, for D'Amore. --JRB): **1941**

OK	6021.	There'll Be Some Changes Made(c3528;voc.,Daye)/There Things You Left
OK	6034.	The Big Do/Boogie Woogie Bugle Boy (Me(C3531;voc.,DuLany)
OK	6070.	Sweet Georgia Brown(28968)/Down By the Old Mill Stream(WC2588)
OK	6106.	Hamtramck(28891; see 6009 personnel)/Wire Brush Stomp(b23007;reissue)

(Sub. Norman Murphy, Graham Young, trumpets, for Novak, Cornelius.--JRB)

OK	6118.	Georgia on My Mind/Alreet	**1941**
OK	6143.	The Things I Love/Little Man With a Candy Cigar
OK	6154.	Slow Down/Fool Am I
OK	6165.	Maria Elena/Rendezvous in Rio

(Sub.Roy Eldridge,trumpet,for Sherock;John Grassi,trombone,for Virgadamo. --JRB):

| OK | 6210. | Let Me Off Uptown/Flamingo |
| OK | 6278. | After You've Gone |

```
OK  6411. Stop, the Red Light's On/Who Can I Turn To
OK  6438. Come Be My Love/The Walls Keep Talking
OK  6498. Coppin' a Plea/Violets for Your Furs
OK  6563. Ball of Fire/All Through the Night
OK  6607. Harlem on Parade/Skylark
OK  6619. Me and My Melinda/Pass the Bounce
OK  6635. Night of Nights/Fightin' Doug MacArthur
OK  6695. Massachusetts/Murder He Says
```

KXYZ NOVELTY BAND (Houston, Tex., studio band):   1935
```
BB  5831. Avalon/Shiek of Araby
BB  5832. I Never Knew/Basin Street Blues
BB  5852. Bugle Call Rag/That's a Plenty
BB  5868. Indiana/I've Found a New Baby
```

KYLE, BILLY (Piano with rhythm):
```
De  2740. Between Sets/Finishin' Up a Date
```

    BILLY KYLE AND HIS SWING CLUB BAND (Charlie Shavers, trumpet; Eddie Williams, clarinet; Tab Smith, alto sax; Harold Arnold, tenor sax; Billy Kyle, piano; David Barker, guitar; John Williams, bass; O'Neil Spencer, drums.--HD):   1937
```
Vr   531. Margie/Big Boy Blues                                        -Vo 3615
Vr   574. Havin' a Ball/Sundays Are Reserved
```

    (Omit Williams; sub. Fran Marx, drums.--HD):
```
Vr   617. Can I Forget You/All You Want to Do Is Dance                -Vo 3778
Vr   659. Girl of My Dreams/Handle My Heart With Care                 -Vo 3843
```

L

LADD'S BLACK ACES (Apparently a Sam Lanin group using personnel from Original Memphis Five):   1922-25
```
Ge  4762. Aunt Hagar's Children's Blues(7577a)/Shake It and Break It(7578)
Ge  4794. Gypsy Blues(7666b)/I'm Just Too Mean to Cry(7667a)
Ge  4806. Brother Lowdown(7685)/Gotta Have My Daddy Blues(7678)
Ge  4809. She's a Mean Job/I Got It You'll Get It
Ge  4843. Virginia Blues(7782a;voc.,Cliff Edwards)/(rev.,Mardi Gras Sextette)
Ge  4856. My Honey's Lovin' Arms(7810)/Satanic Blues(7811)
Ge  4869. Muscle Shoals Blues/Black Eye Blues
Ge  4886. Hopeless Blues/Lonesome Mamma Blues
Ge  4938. You Can Have Him I Don't Want Him(8005a)/Sister Kate(8006a)
Ge  4995. Yankee Doodle Blues(8091)/Stop Your Kidding(8092a)
Ge  5018. Great White Way Blues(8145)/Railroad Man(8146)
Ge  5023. Aggravatin' Papa(6153b)/Sweet Lovin' Mamma(6154a)
Ge  5035. You've Got to See Mama Every Night(8172a)/Runnin Wild(8173a)
Ge  5060. Laughin Crying Blues/Aggravatin' Papa
Ge  5075. Beale Street Mamma(8255)/Sugar Blues(8256)
Ge  5125. I'm a Harmony Baby/If Your Man Is Like Mine
Ge  5127. Papa Blues(8324)/Louisville Lou(8325a)
Ge  5142. T'ain't Nobody's Business/Papa Better Watch Your Step
Ge  5150. Long Lost Mamma(8353a)/Two Time Dan(8354)
Ge  5164. Ain't Never Had Nobody Crazy Over Me(8376)/Sittin' on the Inside(8377)
Ge  5187. Bad New Blues(8415)/Broken Hearted Blues(8416)          -Starr 9426
Ge  5272. All Wrong/I've Got a Song for Sale
Ge  5366. Lots o'Mama ('728)/Nine o'Clock Sal(8729b)
Ge  5422. Nobody's Sweetheart/Unfortunate Blues
Ge  5521. Anyway the Wind Blows(9019)/Morning Won't You Ever Come(9020)
```

TOMMY LADNIER

See also:
  LOVIE AUSTIN: Para 12255,12277,12278,12283,12300,12313,12361,12380,12391.
  SIDNEY BECHET: Vi 23358,23360,24150.
  CLARA CARY: Vs 6067.
  ROSETTA CRAWFORD: De 7567,7584.
  IDA COX: Para 12044,12063,12064,12085,12086,12087,12212,12202,12220,12228,
    12237,12251,12258,12263,12318.
  JULIA DAVIS: Para 12248.
  DIXIE STOMPERS:
  EDMONIA HENDERSON: Para 12084,12095,12097,12203,12239.
  FLETCHER HENDERSON: Co 817,854,970,1002,1059; Vi 20944; Vo 1065,1079,1092;
    Br 3460,3521,4119.
  MEZZ MEZZROW: BB 10085,10087,10088,10090.
  OLLIE POWERS: Para 12059.
  MA RAINEY: Para 12081,12082,12080,12083,12200,12257,12215,12227

LADNIER AND HIS ORCHESTRA, TOMMY (Tommy Ladnier, trumpet; Mezz Mezzrow, tenor sax and clarinet; Sidney Bechet, soprano sax and clarinet; Elmer James, bass; Manzie Johnson, drums; Teddy Bunn, guitar; Cliff Jackson, piano): Nov.28,1938
  BB 10086. Ja Da(030318)/Weary Blues(030321)
  BB 10089. Really the Blues(030319)/When You and I Were Young Maggie(030320)

LAMAR AND HIS SOUTHERNERS, SLIM (Al Famularo, Pinky Gerbrecht, trumpets; Ton Catalano, clarinet and alto sax; Jim Rush, clarinet and sax; Hilton Lamare, **guitar**; Charles Hartman or Ellis Stratakos, trombone; Benny Bottle, bass; Bob **Zurke**, piano; Slim Lamar, leader; and others):
  Vi 21710. Happy/Goofus
  Vi 40093. I've Got a Brand New Gal/Nancy
    (See also: Slim and His Hot Boys)

EDDIE LANG

(Eddie Lang was one of the most prolific of recording artists; the following is only an approximation of his work):
ALABAMA RED PEPPERS: Ro 494; Ca 8109,8129,8130,8132,8204,8205.
TEXAS ALEXANDER: OK 8658, 8673,8688,8801.
ALL STAR RHYTHM: Ha 1346.
LOUIS ARMSTRONG: OK 8703.
BIX BEIDERBECKE: Vi 23008, 23018.
GLADYS BENTLEY: Uncertain.
BOSWELL SISTERS: Br 20110.
HOAGY CARMICHAEL: Vi 22864, 23013, 25371, 38139.
CHARLESTON CHASERS: Co 446,861,909,1076,1335,1539,1891.
NORMAN CLARK: Vo 15142.
COTTON PICKERS: Br 4404, 4440.
WILTON CRAWLEY: OK 8479, 8492, 8589, 8619, 8718.
BING CROSBY:
VAUGHAN DE LEATH: OK 40844.
DORSEY BROTHERS: OK and Co.
TOM DORSEY: OK 41178, 41422.
RUSSELL DOUGLAS: OK 40747, 40801.
BLIND WILLIE DUNN: OK 8633, 8637, 8743.
DUNN'S GINN BOTTLE FOUR: OK 8689.
SEGER ELLIS: OK 41077.
PEGGY ENGLISH: Vo 15504.
RUTH ETTING: Uncertain.
SAMMY FAIN: Uncertain
FOUR INSTRUMENTAL STARS: Pat 11485.
SID GARY: Uncertain.
IRENE GIBBONS: Co 14362.
JEAN GOLDKETTE: Vi 19947 to 20994.
BENNY GOODMAN: Melotone.
RUSSELL GRAY: OK 40938.
ANNETTE HANSHAW:
HOTSY TOTSY GANG:
LONNIE JOHNSON: OK 8695, 8711, 8818.
CHARLES KALEY: Co 886.
ROGER WOLFE KAHN:
KENTUCKY HOT HOPPERS: Pat 36841
FRANCES KING: OK 40854.
HAROLD LEW: OK 41465.
RED McKENZIE: OK 40893, 41071.
EMMETT MILLER: OK 41062,41095,41135,41136,41182,41205,41280,41438,41305,41342, 41377.
RAY MILLER:
HILLS HOTSY TOTSY GANG:
MIFF MOLE: OK 40758,40784,40846,40890,40932,40984,41232.
LEE MORSE:
MOUND CITY BLUE BLOWERS: Br 2908,2804,2849.
PHIL NAPOLEON: Vi 38057, 38069.
RED NICHOLS: Br 3407,3477,3490,3550,3597,3855,3955,3961,3989,4243,4286,6198, 6234,20070,20091,20092, BrG 5081.
PETTIS: Re 8243, 8463; Ba 1907. 1908.1911,1927,1929,1940,1942; Vo 15703,15761. Do 4094.
SONNY PORTER:
ALMA ROTTER: OK 40889.
BOYD SENTER: Pe 14451; Vi 21912; OK 40755,40777,40819,40836,40861,40888,40949, 41018,41059,41115.
VICTORIA SPIVEY: OK 8615.
BESSIE SMITH: Co 14427, 14435.
JOHNNY SYLVESTER: Ge 6099.
TEN FRESHMEN: Pat 37054.
FRANKIE TRUMBAUER: OK 40772-41286 et seq.; Vi 21864, 22010, 22303.
JOE VENUTI: All up to 1933.
PAUL WHITEMAN:
CLARENCE WILLIAMS: OK 8789, 8645.

LANG, EDDIE (guitar solos; first two sides with Arthur Schutt, piano):
OK 40807. Eddie's Twister(80692a)   -PaE 3338
           "   April Kisses(80693a)   -PaE 2317,   "

   (Frank Signorelli, piano):
OK 40936. Melody Man's Dream(81559)/Perfect(81560)   -PaE 3468

   (Rube Bloom, piano):
OK 40988. Losing You/Mine All Mine

   (Without accompaniment):
OK 40989. Prelude(80940)
           "   A Little Love, a Little Kiss(80941)   -OdF 165333, PaE 2317
                                                                "

   (Frank Signorelli, piano):
OK 41134. Jeannine(401158c)
           "   Add a Little Wiggle(400183b)
PaE 208. Rainbow Dreams(400182b)   -PaE 1778
PaE 1778. I'll Never Be the Same(401161a)   -PaE 2646

   (Acc. by Carl Kress, guitar):
Br 6254. Pickin' My Way(11134a)/Feeling My Way(11309a) -BrF 500177, BrE 1282

LANG AND HIS ORCHESTRA, ED (Leo McConville, trumpet; Tommy Dorsey, trombone and trumpet; Jimmy Dorsey, clarinet and alto sax; Arthur Schutt, piano; Eddie Lang, guitar; Joe Tarto, bass; Stanley King, drums.--RR):
OK 8696. Freeze and Melt(401959b)   -OK 41253, PaE 448, PaF 22429
         Hot Heels(401960c)   "   , PaE 596,   "
OK 41410. Bugle Call Rag(401958c)/(rev., Jack Pettis)   -PaE 510

   (Andy Secrest, Charlie Margulies, trumpets; Bill Rank, trombone; Izzy Friedman, clarinet and tenor sax; Bernie Bailey, frankie Trumbauer, saxes; Henry Whiteman, violin; Hoagy Carmichael, piano; Eddie Lang, guitar; Geo. Marsh, drums; Mike Trafficante, bass.--HD):
PaE 840. What Kind o' Man Is You(403031; voc., Mildred Bailey)

   (Joe Tarto, bass):
OK 41344. Walkin' the Dog(403032c)   -OdF 238010, PaE 740
           "   March of the Hoodlums(403033b)   "   PaE 1157

EDDIE LANG-JOE VENUTI AND THEIR ALL STAR ORCHESTRA (Joe Venuti, violin; Charlie Teagarden, trumpet; Jack Teagarden, trombone; Benny Goodman, clarinet and saxes; Eddie Lang, guitar; Neil Marshall, drums; Frank Signorelli, piano; Ward Lay, bass.--EW):   Oct.22,1931
Vo 15858. Farewell Blues(E37271a)
                              -Me 12277,BrF 500167,DeE 5884,Pan 25151,UHCA 106
           "   Someday Sweetheart(E37272a)
                              -Me 12277,   "   ,DeE 5883,   "   "
Vo 15864. Beale Street Blues(E37269a)
                              -Me 12294,BrF 500161,DeE 5883,Pan 25168,UHCA 108
           "   After You've Gone(E37270a)
                              -Me 12294,   "   ,DeE 5884,   "   "

LANIN AND HIS ORCHESTRA, SAM (Arcadians, Famous Players, etc.; such instrumentalists as the Dorsey Brothers, Manny Klein, trumpet; Benny Goodman, clarinet; Jack Teagarden, trombone; and others may be heard in some of these recordings):
Ge   4796. Wabash Blues/Leave Me With a Smile
Ge   4823. Ty Tee/All That I Need Is You
Ge   4820. The Sheik/ Just a Little Love
Ge   4877. Queen of the Orient
Bell   97. St. Louis Blues/Mama Blues
Bell 125. Just a Little Love Song/April Showers
Bell 412. Lonesome and Sorry/Bye Bye Blackbird
Pat 020634. Aunt Hagar's Children Blues/Shake It and Break It
Pat 021021. Dreamy Melody/(rev., Biltmore Orchestra)
Pat 036156. Some Other Day/(rev., F. Henderson)
Pat 036454. ----/(rev., Five Birmingham Babies)
Pat 036579. Forgive Me/I Want Somebody to Love
Pat 036718. The Song Is Ended/Sweetheart Memories
Pe 14115. Carolina Mammy/By the Shalimar
Pe 14227. Hugo
Pe 14256. Nobody's Sweetheart/Unfortunate Blues
Pe 14384. Alabamy Bound/I'll See You in My Dreams
Pe 14593. Blinky Moon Bay/(rev., Stillman's Orioles)
Pe 14631. I'd Give a Lot of Love/(rev., Brillhardt Orchestra)
Pe 14658. Out of My Arms/I'm Walking Around in Circles
Pe 14837. ----/(rev., Golden Gate Orchestra)
Pe 15107. If I Had You/(rev., Levee Loungers)
Pe 15345. Maybe It's Love/Confessin'
Pe 15491. Makin' Faces at the Man in the Moon/June One More Chance
Pe 15508. I Apologize(10765-2)/Me(10766-1)   -Ro 1672

```
Ca   1244. Just Once Again/(rev., Wanderers)                                    -Ro 475
Ca   2578. Someday Sweetheart
Ca   8228. Who Wouldn't Be Blue(3126)/(rev., Broadway Broadcasters)              -Ro 650
Ca   8343. Avalon Town/(rev., Mills Merry Makers)
Ca   9062. Precious Little Thing Called Love/Bad Little You
Ca   9095. Wedding of the Painted Doll(3686)/(rev.,Cliff Roberts)                -Ro 897
Ca   9103. Mean to Me
Ro    315. The Sphinx
Rc    649. Sweet Sue/(rev., Broadway Broadcasters)
Ro    653. My Pet/(rev., Dixie Daisies)
Ro    657. I Can't Give You Anything But Love(3166)/(rev., Caroliners) -Li 2882
Ro    670. That's My Weakness/Nobody Cares
Ro    671. That's Just My Way/(rev., Bob Haring)
Ro    749. The Jazz Singer(3267)/(rev., Dixie Daisies)
Ro   1225. Mona/(rev., Willie Creager)
Ro   1673. Many Happy Returns/(rev., Cherwin)
GG   1162. Who's Sorry Now/Saw Mill River Road
Ap   8134. Got a Song for Sale/Take Those Lips Away
Hytone 77. My Man/Frankie and Johnny
Je   6159. To Whom It May Concern/You're the One I Care For
HoW  1116. Maybe It's Love
HoW  1125. Something to Remember You By
HoW  1151. Ho Hum
Re   9150. The Sheik(42068)/(rev.,Rudy Wiedoeft)
Re   9191. Eddie Leonard Blues/Satanic Blues
Re   9200. Virginia Blues/Doo Dah Blues
Re   9472. Who's Sorry Now
Re   9655. ----/(rev., Fletcher Henderson)
Re   9681. He's a New Kind of Man(5549-2)/(rev., Fletcher Henderson)
Re   9684. Maytime(5548-1)/(rev., Fletcher Henderson)
Re   9774. Goo! Goo! Goodnight Dear(5664-4)/(rev., Fletcher Henderson)
Na  12222. Aunt Hagar's Children Blues/(rev., California Ramblers)
Ba   1351. Limehouse Blues
Do   3976. Gonna Get a Girl/(rev., Six Hottentots)
Co    325. Egyptian Echoes(140413)/Hungaria(140414)
Co    438. Stop Flirting(140798)/Cecilia(140799)
Co    632. For Heaven's Sake/I Found
Co    738. Mary Lou/In a Little Garden
Co    772. Give Me a Ukelele/Just a Bird's Eye View
Co   1779. Wake Up Chillun/Old Fashioned Love
OK   4986. Last Night on the Back Porch/Roamin' to Wyoming
OK  40014. Mama Goes Where Papa Goes/(rev., Ace Brigode)
OK  40037. I'm Somebody Nobody Loves/(rev., Guyon's Paradise)
OK  40053. A Smile Will Go a Long Long Way/(rev., Finzel)
OK  40069. Lonely Little Wallflower/(rev., Finzel)
OK  40084. It Had to Be You(s72413b)/Innocent Eyes(s72414b)
OK  40111. Big Boy/Oh Baby
OK  40170. Somebody Loves Me/Bagdad
OK  40200. When I Was the Dandy/My Best Girl
OK  40219. Some Other Day/I Want to See My Tennessee
OK  40257. Honest and Truly/(rev., Frankie Quartell)
OK  40740. In a Little Spanish Town(38028lb)/Moonlight on the Ganges(w80282c)
OK  40810. Side by Side/It's a Happy Old World
OK  40863. Just Once Again(81122b)/(rev., Justin Ring)
OK  40902. Somebody Lied About Me(81505; waltz)/Diane(81506; waltz)
OK  40990. Together/Ramona
OK  40933. There Must be Somebody Else
OK  41063. Don't Keep Me in the Dark/Sorry for Me
OK  41159. Everybody Loves You/Sweethearts on Parade
OK  41188. If I Had You(voc.,Bing Crosby)/(rev., Dorsey Brothers)
OK  41228. Susianna(voc., Bing Crosby)/I'm Crazy Over You(voc.,Bing Crosby)
OK  41257. When My Dreams Come True/This Is Heaven
OK  41368. Blue Is the Night/(rev., Ed Lloyd)
OK  41383. Cooking Breakfast for the One I Love/When I'm Looking at You
OK  41385. Mona
Cl   5191. Crying Myself to Sleep(100448)/(rev., Wally Edwards)
```

LANIN'S RED HEADS (Sam Lanin group featuring Red Nichols,trumpet;Joe Venuti,violin):
```
Co    327. Jimtown Blues(140397)/King Porter Stomp(140398)
Co    376. If You Hadn't Gone Away(140579)/Flag That Train(140580)
Co    483. I'm Gonna Hang Around My Sugar(141155)/Five Foot Two,Eyes of Blue
                                                                        (141156)
```

LA ROCCA AND THE ORIGINAL DIXIELAND FIVE, NICK (See Original Dixieland Jazz Band)

LASKA AND HIS ORCHESTRA, HAL (Casa Loma Orchestra):
```
PaA 34034. Romance
PaA 34038. Sweepin' the Clouds Away
PaA 34040. Sweepin' the Clouds Away (vocal)
PaA 34041. Any Time's the Time
PaA 34064. When the Little Red Roses
PaA 34070. Exactly Like You
PaA 34072. Dust
PaA 34074. On the Sunny Side of the Street
```

LATTIMORE, HARLAN (vocal):
Co 2671. Strange As It Seems/I'm Still Without a Sweetheart

HARLAN LATTIMORE AND HIS CONNIE'S INN ORCHESTRA (Don Redman's Orchestra:
Langston Curl, Shirley Clay, Sidney DeParis, trumpets; Quentin Jackson,
Claude Jones, Bennie Morton, trombones; Edward Inge, Don Redman, Rupert
Cole, Robert Carroll, saxes; Horace Henderson, piano; Talcott Reeves,
banjo; Bob Ysaguire, bass; Manzie Johnson, drums; Harlan Lattimore,voc.
--HD): <u>1932</u>
```
Co  2675. Chant of the Weeds(152217)                    -PaE 2134
     "   Got the South in My Soul(152219)               -PaE 1297
Co  2678. I Heard(152218)                               -PaE 1311
     "   Reefer Man(152220)                             -PaE 1329
```

LAVAL AND HIS WOODWINDY TEN, PAUL (Paul Lavel, clarinet and bass clarinet; Milton Cassell, flute, piccolo, oboe, English horn, clarinet, bassoon; Henry Wade, clarinet and bass clarinet; Rudolf Adler, oboe, English horn, clarinet; Alfred Evans, clarinet and bass clarinet; Angel Barnes Rattina, trumpet; Mario Janarro, piano and celeste; Antonio Collucci, guitar; Harry Patent, bass; Nat Levine,drums):<u>1941</u>
Vi 27303. Runnin' Wild/Dinah's Blues(voc.,Dinah Shore)
Vi 27304. Shoemaker's Holiday/(rev., Henry Levine)
(See also: Dinah Shore, Vi 27302)

LA VERE'S CHICAGO LOOPERS (Charles LaVere, piano; Joe Venuti, violin; Billy May, trumpet; Matty Matlock, clarinet; Floyd O'Brien, trombone; Artie Shapiro, bass; Nick Fatool, drums): <u>Hollywood,July 22,1944</u>
Jump   1. Baby Won't You Please Come Home(j2-3)/Subdivided in F(j3-1)
Jump   2. Sunday(j1-2)/I'm Coming Virginia(j4-2)

(Omit Venuti; sub. Joe Yukl, trombone; add George Van Eps,guitar)
Jump   3. Very 8 'n Boogie/Lazy River   <u>Nov.1,1944</u>

LA VIZZO, THELMA (blues acc. by Richard M. Jones, piano):
Para 12206. Trouble in Mind Blues(1756)/Fire in the Mountain Blues(1757)

LAWRANCE AND HIS QUARTET, BRIAN (Brian Lawrence, violin and vocals; Frank Gregori, accordion; Jim Easton, baritone sax; Harold Hood, piano; Mark Sheridan, guitar; Harry Wilson, bass.--JI 12/22/39):
```
Ch 40034. Ain't She Sweet
     "   Somebody Stole My Gal(gb7045)                  -De 5930
Ch 40046. Singin' in the Rain(gb6770)                   -De 5924
     "   Shine(gb6922)                                  -De 5930
Ch 40058. Tiger Rag
     "   Dinah(gb5921)                                  -De 5924
```

BRIAN LAWRANCE AND LANSDOWNE SEXTET:
Ch 40095. Everybody Loves My Baby/Miss Annabelle Lee
Ch 40114. I'll Take the South/China Boy
De 1010. Broken Doll/If You Were the Only Girl in the World

YANK LAWSON

See also:
E. BUTTERFIELD De 8543, 8551.
BOB CROSBY BOB CATS: De 1593-2108, 18355-18373.
BOB CROSBY ORCHESTRA: De 478-2151; De 15064, 18355, 18369.
TOM DORSEY: Vi 26105-26154, 26259-
JERRY JEROME: Asch 500, 501.

LAWSON'S JAZZ BAND, YANK (Yank Lawson, trumpet; James P. Johnson, piano; Rod Cless, clarinet; Miff Mole, trombone; George Wettling, drums; Bob Haggart, bass):<u>Jan,1944</u>
Sig 28103. Squeeze Me/The Sheik of Araby
Sig   . Blues/When My Dreamboat Comes Home

(Lawson, trumpet; Will Bradley, trombone; Ray Ekstrand, clarinet; James P. Johnson, piano; Carl Kress, guitar; Chauncey Moorehouse, drums; Sid Weiss, bass): <u>June 7,1944</u>
Sig   . I Found a New Baby/Jazz Me Blues
Sig   . Note Worthy Blues/Lady Be Good

(Yank Lawson, trumpet; Bill Stegemeyer, clarinet; Lou McGarity, trombone; Bob Haggart, bass; John Blowers, drums; Dave Brown, piano):
Sig 28108. Wang Wang Blues/That's a Plenty

LAZY LEVEE LOUNGERS (Henry Allen, trumpet; J.C. Higginbotham, trombone; Albert Nicholas, clarinet; Charlie Holmes, Teddy Hill, saxes; Luis Russell, piano; Bill Johnson, banjo; Pop Foster, bass; Paul Barbarin, drums; Andy Razaf, vocals):
Co 2243. If I Could Be With You(150612)/Shout Sister Shout(150613)<u>Summer,1930</u>

LEADBELLY (Huddie Ledbetter. vocal and guitar):
```
Pe    314. Out and Down/Packin' Trunk                           -Me 13326
Pe    315. Four Day Worry/Black Snake Moan                      -Me 13327
Me  60455. Pig Meat Papa
BB   8550. Don't You Love Your Daddy No More/Sail on Little Girl Sail on
BB   8559. Alberta/T.B. Blues
BB   8570. Easy Rider/Worried Blues
BB   8709. Red Cross Store Blues/Roberta
BB   8750. You Can't Lose Me Cholly/N.Y.C. Blues
BB   8981. Last Go Round/(rev., Hot Lips Page Trio)
```
         (With Golden Gate Quartet):
```
Vi  27266. The Midnight Special/Ham an' Eggs
Vi  27267. Grey Goose/Stewball
Vi  27268. Pick a Bale of Cotton/Alabama Bound
```
         (Sinful songs with 12-string guitar):
```
Mu    223. Frankie and Albert, 1 & 2
Mu    224. Looky Looky Yonder; Black Betty; Yellow Woman's Door Bell
   "       Ain't Goin' Down to the Well No Mo'; Go Down Old Hannah
Mu    225. Poor Howard; Green Corn/Fannin' Street
Mu    226. The Boll Weevil/De Kalb Blues
Mu    227. The Gallis Pole/The Bourgeois Blues
```
         (Play Party Songs):
```
Asch       . Ha Ha This-a-Way/Sally Walker
Asch       . Red Bird/Skip to Me Lou
Asch       . You Can't Lose-a-Me Cholly/Christmas Song
```
         (Songs by Lead Belly, acc. by Sonny Terry, harmonica):
```
Asch 3431. Good Morning Blues/How Long Blues
Asch 3432. Ain't You Glad/Irene
Asch 3433. John Henry/On a Monday
```

LEE AND HIS BLUE RHYTHM BAND, BARON (Wardell Jones, Shelton Hemphill, Edward Anderson, trumpets; Harry White, Henry Hicks, trombones; Charlie Holmes, Crawford Wethlington, Joe Garland, saxes; Edgar Hayes, piano; Hayes Alvis, bass; O'Neil Spencer, drums):   1932
```
Pe  15605. Cabin in the Cotton(11751-1)            -Me 12381, Ba 32445, Or 2464
   "       The Scat Song(11651a)                   -Me 12366,  "      DeF 3434
Pe  15606. Heat Waves(11363-1)   -BrF 500460,Me 12366, Or 2469, Ba 32444,ErE 01325
   "       Minnie the Moocher's Wedding Day              "        "       "
Pe  15621. The Growl(11767-1)    -BrF 500193,Me 12381,Ro 1862, Ba 32465,BrE 01325
   "       Mighty River                                 "      "         "
Pe  15629. Rhythm Spasm(11823)   -BrF 500193,Me 12418,Ro 1874,          BrE 1401
   "       White Lightning       -BrF 500192,Me 12414,  "               BrE 1463
Pe  15634. Doin'the Shake(11364)                                -Ba 32493,
   "       Wild Waves(11826)                       -Me 12414,         "   BrE 1463
```
         (Sub. Joe Garland, Eugene Mikell, saxes, for McCord, Holmes, saxes; Geo. Washington, trombone, for White):
```
Pe  15652. Sentimental Gentleman from Georgia(12181)
                                   -Me 12480,Or 2535, Ba 32531,BrE 01365
   "       You Gave Me Everything But Love(12182)
                                   -Me 12464,              "       "
Pe  15676. Old Yazoo(12203-1)                  -Me 12480,          BrE 1401
   "       Reefer Man(12204)                   -Me 12464
Pe  15696. Jazz Cocktail(12357)-BrF 500461,Me 12515,     Ba 32608,BrE 02077
   "       Smoke Rings(12358)             "       "        "       "
Pe  15822. Jazz Martini(13930)  -BrF 500376,Me 12793,             BrE 01742
   "       Feelin' Gay(13931)        "          "                    "
```
         (Under name of Blue Rhythm Band only):
```
VoE     6. Harlem After Midnight .
           (See also Mills Blue Rhythm Band)
```

LEE, CHAUNCEY C. (banjo solo, acc. Chester Meyers, piano):
```
OK 40321. Banjo Rag(8952a)/(rev., Clarence Williams Blue Five)
```

LEE AND HER JAZZ BAND, ELIZA CHRISTMAS:
```
Ge  4801. I Ain't Givin' Nothin' Away/Arkansas Blues
```

LEE AND HIS ORCHESTRA, GEORGE E. (Jesse Stone, director; Sam Auderbach, Harold Knox, trumpets; Jimmy Jones, trombone; Herman Walder, Clarence Taylor, Albert "Bud" Johnson, reeds; Julis Lee, piano; Charles Russo, guitar; Clint Weaver, bass; Pete Woods, drums.--JI 6/14/40):
```
Br     4684. Ruff Scufflin'/St. James Infirmary
Br     4761. Won't You Come Over to My House/He's Tall Dark and Handsome(voc.
Br     7132. If I Could Be With You/Paseo Strut              (Julia Lee)
Meritt 2206. Down Home Syncopated Blues(578)/Meritt Stomp(579)
```

LEE, MARY (acc. by Bob Crosby's Bob Cats):
  De 4346. I Hung My Head and Cried/You're My Darling
  De 4380. End of the World/I Don't Care Any More
  De 4402. I'll Never Cry Over You/It Makes No Never Mind
  De 4422. I Told You So/You Broke My Heart Little Darlin'

LEE, RUTH (acc. by Mutt Carey, cornet; Kid Ory, trombone; Dink Johnson, clarinet; Fred Washington, piano; Ed Garland, bass; Ben Borders, drums.--JI 8/9/40, 11/22/40):
                                                                                Los Angeles,1921
  Nor 3002. That Sweet Something/Maybe Someday   -Su 3002
    (See also: Spikes Seven Pods of Pepper, Ory's Sunsine Orchestra, Roberta Dudley)

LEE, WINTHROP AND HIS ORCHESTRA (Fred Gardner):
  PaA 34124. Loveless Love
  PaA 34148. Daniel's Blues

LEE'S BLACK DIAMONDS (Windy Rhythm Kings):
  Bwy 1294. South African/Piggly Wiggly

LEIGHTON AND HIS SOPHOMORES, CHESTER (Joe Venuti, violin, Eddie Lang, guitar; the Dorsey Brothers, and Benny Goodman, clarinet, have been mentioned as appearing on some of these):
  Ha 1215. You're Lucky to Me/Memories of You
  Ha 1232. I Am the Words
  Ha 1233. A Peach of a Pair
  Ha 1248. Satan's Holiday
  Ha 1320. Star Dust
  Ha 1370. Guilty/How That You're Gone   -Cl 5319
  Ha 1340. Without That Gal(351045)/On the Beach With You(351042)   -Ve 2415
  Ve 2220. Wasting My Love on You(150812)/(rev.,Hotel Pennsylvania Music)
  Cl 5125. Cheerful Little Earful(100439)/(rev., Lou Gold)
  Cl 5244. Heartaches(100481)/(rev., Ford Britten)

LEM, HAROLD (acc. reputedly including Lang, Venuti, Dorsey Brothers):
  OK 41465. I Got Rhythm/My Love for You

LEONARD AND HIS ROCKETS, HARLAN (Edward Johnson, William H. Smith, James Ross, trumpets; Richmond Henderson, Fred Becket, trombones; Harlan Leonard, Darwin Jones, Henry Bridges, James Keith, saxes; William S. Smith, piano; Effergee Ware, electric guitar; Winston Williams, bass; Jessie Price, drums; Ernest Williams, director):   1940
  BB 10586. Contact/Rockin' With the Rockets
  BB 10625. My Gal Sal/Hairy Joe Jump
  BB 10736. I'm in a Weary Mood/Parade of the Stompers
  BB 10823. My Pop Gave Me a Nickel/400 Swing
  BB 10883. Rock and Ride/Snaky Feelin'
  BB 10899. A la Bridges/Please Don't Squabble
  BB 10919. Skee/I Don't Want to Set the World on Fire
  BB 11032. Ride My Blues Away/My Dream
  BB 11302. Keep Rockin' /Dig It
  BB 11544. Too Much/Mistreated

LEROY'S BUDDY (Bill Gaither, blues singing, often acc. by Honey Hill, piano):
  De 7141. Tired of the Same Stuff All the Time/Georgia Woman Stomp
  De 7179. After the Sun's Gone Down/Naptown Stomp
  De 7180. Strange Woman/Pains in My Heart
  De 7194. You Done Lost Your Swing/Which One I Love the Best
  De 7202. Bad Luck Child/Pins and Needles
  De 7223. Stoney Lonesome/You Done Showed Your D.B.A.
  De 7233. Who's Been Here Since I Been Gone/Just the Wrong Man
  De 7246. Gravel in My Bread/L & N Blues
  De 7258. How Long Baby How Long/Tired of Your Line of Jive
  De 7271. Tee-Nincey Mama/Curbstone Blues
  De 7298. Evil Hearted Me/You Done Showed Your D.B.A. #2
  De 7308. Morning Dream/Too Many Women
  De 7335. New Little Pretty Mama/You're a Mean Mistreater
  De 7356. I Just Keep on Wooryin'/New Bad Luck Child
  De 7374. Orneriest Girl in Town/Sunrise Blues
  De 7394. Jiving Man Blues/I'm Wise to Your Sweet Line of Jive
  De 7404. 'Bout the Break of Day/New Evil Hearted Blues
  De 7420. Black Street Blues/Do Like You Want to Do
  De 7434. In the Wee Wee Hours/Rocky Mountain Blues
  De 7460. Tired of Sleeping By Myself/Won't You Tell Me Baby
  De 7476. Champ Joe Louis/It's Coming Back Home to You
  De 7497. You Done Lost Your Swing No. 2/Babyfield Ways Girl
  De 7512. New Pains in My Heart/Do Like I Want to Do
  De 7542. It's Grieving Me/Old Coals Will Kindle
  De 7563. Old Model A Blues/If I Was the Devil
  De 7576. So Much Trouble/Thousand Years and a Day
  De 7606. Mean Old World to Live in/Right Hand Friend

```
De  7625. Noah's Dove/I Got Your Water On
De  7637. Sweet Mama/Too Late Too Late
De  7647. Kentland Blues/Army Bound Blues
De  7659. Changing Blues/Jungle Man Blues
De  7668. Another Big Leg Woman/Lazy Woman Blues
De  7690. New So Much Trouble/Cheatin' Blues
De  7720. When My Woman's Lovin' Someone Else/Old Fashioned Woman
De  7724. Evil Yalla Woman/It's Too Late Now
```

LEROY'S DALLAS BAND:
```
Co 14402. Gone Away Blues/Tampa Shout
```

LESLIE AND HIS ORCHESTRA, NATE:
```
Vo  3584. Shake Yo' Bones/Shaggin' at the Shore
```

LEVEE SERENADERS (Jelly Roll Morton, piano; trumpet; trombone; banjo; clarinet; sax; drums; tuba; Frances Hereford, vocals):   Jan. 27 1928
```
Vo  1154. Midnight Mama(E7058c)/Mr. Jelly Lord(E7060c)        -Br 80040*
       (*Issued under name of Jelly Roll Morton and His Levee Serenaders.
       Original master nos. C1630 & 1632; dub masters incorrectly marked
       C7058C & C7060C; E numbers are Vocalion transfers ,--EW)
```

LEVEE LOUNGERS:
```
Pe 14818. The Devil Is Afraid of Music(107531)/(rev., Earl Gresh)
Pe 14926. My Melancholy Baby/Lovely Little Silhouette
Pe 14979. Get Out and Get Under the Moon/(rev., Bert Dolan)
Pe 15107. I'd Rather Be Blue/(rev., Sam Lanin)
```

LEVINE AND HIS BAREFOOTED DIXIELAND PHILHARMONIC, HENRY (Henry Levine, trumpet; Alfred Lewis Evans, clarinet; Rudolf Adler, tenor sax; Jack Epstein, trombone; Mario Janarro, piano; Tony Collucci, guitar; Harry Patent, bass; Nat Levine, drums):   1941
```
Vi 27304. Basin Street Blues/(rev., Paul Laval)

       (Dixieland Jazz Group, directed by Henry Levine):
Vi 27542. Memphis Blues/St. Louis Blues (voc., Lena Horne)
Vi 27543. Joe Turner Blues/Beale Street Blues(voc., Lena Horne)
Vi 27544. East St. Louis Blues/Aunt Hagar's Blues(voc., Lena Horne)
Vi 27545. John Henry Blues/Careless Love(voc., Lena Horne)
```

HENRY LEVINE AND HIS STRICTLY FROM DIXIE JAZZ BAND:
```
Vi 27829. Strictly from Dixie/(rev., Linda Keene)
Vi 27831. Shine/(rev., Linda Keene)
```

LEWIS, EMMA (vocal acc., by Fletcher Henderson, piano):
```
Vi 19158. I Don't Let No One Man Worry Me
```

LEWIS, FURRY (vocals with guitar):
```
Vo  1111. Rock Island Blues/Everybody's Blues
Vo  1133. Big Chief Blues/Falling Down Blues
Vi 23345. Cannon Ball Blues/Dry Land Blues
```

LEWIS AND HIS NEW ORLEANS STOMPERS, GEORGE (George Lewis, clarinet; Kid Howard, trumpet; Jim Robinson, trombone; Lawrence Marrero, banjo; Edgar Mosley, drums; Chester Zardis, bass#; Jim Little, tuba*):   New Orleans, May 16,1943
```
Cli  101. Climax Rag(cd105)#/Deep Bayou Blues(cd123)#
Cli  102. Two Jim Blues(cd104)*without Howard/Milenberg Joys(cd118)#
Cli  103. Just a Closer Walk With Thee(cd107)#/Just a Little While to Stay Here
Cli  104. Dauphine Street Blues(cd113)#/Fidgety Feet(cd119)#        (cd114)#
Cli  105. Careless Love Blues(cd111)#/Don't Go 'Way Nobody(cd122)#

       GEORGE LEWIS (Clarinet solo with Marrero, banjo; Slow Drag, bass):
AM   254. Burgundy Street Blues(95)/(rev., Jim Robinson's Band)     July 1944
```

LEVY DUO, JOHN (John Levy, bass; Jimmy Jones, piano):   1944
```
Se 10011. Improvisations
Se 10012. Improvisations
```

MEADE LUX LEWIS

See also:
ALBERT AMMONS: Vo 4606, 5186.
SIDNEY BECHET: BN 6.
EDMOND HALL: BN 17, 18.
GEORGE HANNAH: Para 13024, 13048.
J. C. HIGGINBOTHAM: BN 7, 501.
PORT OF HARLEM: BN 6,7,14.
ROB ROBINSON: Para 13028, 13030, 13064.

LEWIS, MEADE LUX (piano solos): 1929
  Para 12896. Honky Tonk Train Blues(20246)/(rev.,Chas. Avery) -Bwy 5063*, Sig 65
           *Under name of Hatch Seward.
                                                                         1936
  PaE 2187. Honky Tonk Train Blues(90469) -De 18110
  BrE 02176. Mr. Freddie Blues(90564) -De 3831, BrF 505053
      "   I'm in the Mood for Love(celeste) "
  De   819. Celeste Blues(90562; celeste) -De 3831, BrE 02243
      "   Yancey Special -De 3387, "
                                                   Chicago, May 7,1936
  Vi 25541. Honky Tonk Train Blues/Whistling Blues -BB 10175, HMV 8579
  SA 12002. Messin' Around/(rev., Albert Ammons) 1939
  SA 12003. Deep Fives/Blues de Luxe
  SA 12004. Far Ago Blues/Closin' Hour Blues

  BN   1. Solitude(443-12)/Melancholy(444-11) 1940
  BN   4. Twos and Fews(GM 537; with Albert Ammons, piano)
  BN   8. The Blues, I, II(486a-1/2)
  BN   9. The Blues, III,IV(488a-3/489a-4)
  BN 15. Honky Tonk Train Blues(rs791b)/Tell Your Story(rs794a)
  BN 16. Bass on Top(rs792c)/Six Wheel Chaser(rs793a)

      (Harpsichord. Variations on a Theme):
  BN 19. Nineteen Ways of Playing a Chorus(rs934b)/Self Portrait(rs937a)
  BN 20. School of Rhythm(rs935b)/Feelin' Tomorrow Like I Feel Today(rs938a)

      (Piano solos):
  BN 22. Rising Tide Blues(bn639)/Tell Your Story No. 2(rs794b)
  BN 39. Chicago Flyer(bn1202)/Blues Whistle(bn1203)
  Vo 4608. Bear Cat Crawl(23893)/(rev., Albert Ammons) -Co 35961
  Asch 3521. Boogie Tidal(729)/Yancey's Pride(732) 1945
  Asch 3522. Denapas Parade(728)/Glendale Glide(746)
  Asch 3523. Randini's Boogie(730)/Lux's Boogie(731)

LEWIS, SAMMIE (acc. by Mandy Randolph, piano):
  Ge 5147. Cootie Crawl/Crazy Over Daddy

      SAMMIE LEWIS AND THE BAMVILLE SYNCOPATORS:
  Vo 1030. There'll Come a Time/Arkansas Shout

LEWIS AND HIS BAND, TED (Ted Lewis and Don Murray or Jimmy Dorsey, clarinets and
saxes; Sam Shapiro, Sol Klein, violins; Dave Klein, trumpet; George Brunis, Harry
Raderman, trombones; Jack Aaronson, piano; Tony Gerardi, banjo and guitar; Harry
Barth, bass; John Lucas, drums.--RR)?
  Co 1391. Start the Band/Oh Baby
  Co 1428. I Ain't Got Nobody/A Good Man Is Hard to Find
  Co 1485. King for a Day(waltz)/Moonlight Madness
  Co 1525. A Jazz Holiday(145953)/Jungle Blues(145954)
  Co 1573. Clarinet Marmalade/Shimeshawabble -Me 13379
  Co 1656. She's Funny That Way/Wear a Hat With a Silver Lining
  Co 1709. When the Curtain Comes Down(147417)/Glad Rag Doll(147423)
  Co 1789. Roses of Picardy/Limehouse Blues
  Co 1854. I'm Walkin' Around in a Dream(148559)/Maybe Who Knows(148562)
  Co 1882. I'm the Medicine Man for the Blues(148560)/Wouldn't It Be Wonderful
                                                                              (148561)
      (Add Muggsy Spanier, trumpet): 1929
  Co 1916. Lewisada Blues/(148568)/I Love You(148578) -CoE 5608
  Co 1957. Through(148933)/Lonely Troubadour(148936)
  Co 1999. Lady Luck(148932)/My Little Dream Boat(146742)

      (Frank Teschemacher, clarinet, next two sides):
  Co 2029. Farewell Blues(148930) -OK 41580
      "   Wabash Blues(148931) -OK 41579

      (Omit Frank Teschemacher): 1930
  Co 2088. You've Got That Thing(149613)/Harmonica Harry(149734)
  Co 2113. San(149783) -CoE 63
      "   Aunt Hagar's Blues(149784) -CoE 64
  Co 2144. On the Sunny Side of Street(150043)/Singing Vagabond Song(150050)
  Co 2181. The Lonesome Road(149758) -CoE 63
      "   Dinah(149911) -CoE 64
  Co 2217. The Yellow Dog Blues(150482)/Sobbin' Blues(150490) -CoE 189
  Co 2246. World Is Waiting for the Sunrise(150460)/Three o'Clock in the Morning
                                                                          (150467)
  Co 2336. Somebody Stole My Gal(150478)/Someday Sweetheart(150479) -CoE 460

      (Benny Goodman, clarinet): 1931
  Co 2378. Headin' for Better Times(151196) -CoE 304
      "   Just a Gigolo(151206)

```
Co  2408. At Last I'm Happy(151197)
     "    Truly(151306)                                                    -CoE 281

     (*Add Fats Waller and Bud Freeman):
Co  2428. Egyptian Ella(151395)*/Crazy 'Bout My Baby(151396)*
Co  2452. One More Time(151514)                                            -CoE 351
     "    Ho Hum(151517)                                                   -CoE 304
Co  2467. Dip Your Brush in Sunshine(151513)/Little Church in Valley(151518)
Co  2527. Dallas Blues(151397)*/Royal Garden Blues(151398)*
Co    "   I'm all Dressed Up With A Broken Heart(151662)/I Love You in the Same
Co  2560. Old Playmate(151864)/Evening in Caroline(151865)  (Sweet Way(151663)

     (Omit Benny Goodman):                                                 1932
Co  2635. My Woman(152136)/Somebody Loves You(152141)
Co  2652. A Shanty in Old Shanty Town(152137)/Sweet Sue(152140)
Co  2748. Buy American(152362)/Try a Little Tenderness(152365)
Co  2753. There's a New Day Comin'(152360)/Have You Ever Been Lonely(152363)
Co  2758. There's a Ring Around My Rainbow(152361)/All Aboard for Dreamland
Co  2774. Moonlight Millionaires(152394)/Stormy Weather(152400) (152364; waltz)
Co  2775. The Gold Diggers Song(152393)/It's Sunday Down in Caroline(152401)
Co  2777. In a Garden in Old Kalua(152399)/An Old Old Man With an Old Old Pipe
Co  2786. Lazybones(152420)/Rhythm(152423)                                 (152402)
Co  2799. In the Vine Covered Church(152422)/Here You Come With Love(152454)
Co  2807. Ten Thousand Years Ago(152453)/Little Locket of Long Ago(152455)
```

LEWIS AND HIS ENTERTAINERS, WILLIE (Bobby Martin, Bill Coleman, trumpets; Billy
Burns, trombone; Benny Carter, trumpet and alto sax; Willie Lewis, George Johnson,
alto saxes; Joe Haymes, tenor sax; Herman Chittison, piano; John Mitchell, guitar;
June Coles, bass; Ted Fields, drums.--HD):   1935
```
PatF  803. I've Got a Feelin' You're Foolin'(opt2450)/Rhythm Is Our Business
PatF  816. Stay Out Of Love(opt2451)/Just a Mood(opt2453)        (opt2452)
PatF  817. All of Me(opt2454)/Star Dust(opt2455)
```

     (Omit Martin; sub. Frank 'Big Boy' Goodie, tenor sax, for Carter; Louis
     Vola, bass):   1936
```
PatF  898. Stompin' at the Savoy(opt2630)/Christopher Columbus(opt2631)
PatF  914. I'm Shooting High(opt2649; voc.,Adelaide Hall)/Lost(opt2650)
PatF  915. Alone(opt2651; voc.,Alice Man)/Say You're Mine(opt2652; voc.,Adelaide
PatF 1030. Sweet Sue(opt2904)/Organ Grinders Swing(opt2905)       (Hall)
PatF 1295. Swing Time/Swing Brothers Swing
PatF 1297. Ol' Man River/Basin Street Blues
```

LEWIS BRONZEVILLE FIVE:
```
BB   8445. Mississippi Fire Blues/Natchez Mississippi Blues
BB   8460. Low Down Gal Blues/Linda Brown
```

LILL'S HOT SHOTS (Louis Armstrong, trumpet and vocal; Kid Ory, trombone; Johnny
Dodds, clarinet; Lil Hardin Armstrong, piano; John St. Cyr, banjo):   May 28,1926
```
Vo  1037. Georgia Bo Bo(E3156)       -OrE 1009,BrF 500319,ErE 02065*
     "   Drop That Sack(E3157)          "        "        "
Vo  1037. Drop That Sack(E3158)
```
         *Foreign Brunswicks under Armstrong's name.

LINCOLN, CHARLIE (vocal with guitar):
     Co 14475. Mojo Blues/Country Breakdown

LINDLEY, DONALD (trumpet solos with piano):
     Co 546. Trumpet Blues(141450)/Sweet Stuff(141451)

          DONALD LINDLEY AND HIS BOYS (Donald Lindley, trumpet; Hank Winston,piano;
          Pierre Olker, bass; Phil Wing, alto sax; Howard Grantham, trombone; Mutt
          Hayes, tenor sax; Julian Davidson, banjo.--DB 4/15/42):
     Co 1443. Nothin' Doin'/Slidin' Around

LION AND THE CUBS, THE (Willie The Lion Smith, piano; Max Kaminsky, trumpet, Rod
Cless, clarinet; Frank Orchard, trombone; Jack Lesberg, bass; Mac McGrath, drums):
     B&W . Let's Mop It/How Could You Put Me Down
     B&W . Bugle Call Rag/Muskrat Ramble

LISTON, VIRGINIA (vocals acc. by Clarence Williams, piano):
```
OK  8092. Bed Time Blues/You Thought I Was Blind
OK  8115. You Don't Know My Mind Blues(s71862d)/Sally Long Blues(s71863d)
OK  8122. Shreveport Blues(s72102b)/Jail House Blues(s72265a;guitar acc. by
                                                             ("Sidney Bechet")
OK  8126. You Can Have It(s72232b)/Just Take One Long Last Look(s72233b) duet
OK  8134. House Rent Stomp/Happy Shout                       (with Sam Gray)
OK  8138. I Don't Love Nobody(acc.inst.trio)/Tain't a Doggone Thing But the
OK  8151. Don't Agitate Me Blues/I Never Knew What Blues Were  (Blues(trio)
OK  8160. Mississippi Blues/San Francisco Blues
```

```
           (Acc. by Clarence Williams Blue Five: Louis Armstrong, trumpet; Sidney
           Bechet, clarinet and soprano sax; Charlie Irvis, trombone; Clarence
           Williams piano; Buddy Christian, banjo):
OK   8173. You've Got the Right Key But the Wrong Keyhole(s72916b)
       "  Bill Draw(s72935a; piano only)
OK   8187. Early in the Morning(s72915b)/Give It to Me Good(s72934b;no Armstrong)

           (Acc. by Clarence Williams, piano):
OK   8175. Weeping Willow Blues/Pineland Blues

           (Clarence Williams, piano; Sidney Bechet, clarinet):
OK   8196. Night Latch Kay Blues(s72938b)/Any Day the Sun Don't Shine(s72939b)

           (Clarence Williams, piano):
OK   8218. Papa De Da Da(s73387a)/You Can Dip Your Bread in My Gravy(s73391a)
OK   8234. I'm Sick of Fattenin' Frogs(organ)/Ain't Gonna Play No Second Fiddle
OK   8247. Monkey Jungle Bl(s72937b)/Make Me a Pallet(s73390a;mandolin) (organ)

           (Unknown accompaniment):
Vo   1032. Rolls Royce Papa/I'm Gonna Get Me a Man
```

LITTLE ACES (Reissue of Chocolate Dandies, OK 8627):
  OK 41136. Four or Five Times(401221a)/(rev., Big Aces)

LITTLE BROTHER (Eurreal Montgomery, piano solos):   1929
  Para 13006. Vicksburg Blues(L501)/No Special Rider(L502)

```
       E. MONTGOMERY:                                       Jan.5,1931
Vo  02706. Louisiana Blues(c6879a;plus guitar & voc.)
       "   Frisco Hi-Ball Blues(c6880b)                     -Me 12548

           (Blues singing with piano, dates unknown):
BB   6072. Vicksburg Blues No. 2                            -BB 7970
       "   Mama You Don't Mean Me No Good
BB   6073. Loveless Love
BB   6658. Chinese Man Blues/Something Keeps a-Worryin' Me
BB   6697. Louisiana Blues No. 2/Vicksburg Blues No. 3

           (Piano solos):                                   Oct.16,1936
BB   6733. Shreveport Farewell/Crescent City Blues          -BB 10953

           (Vocal with piano):
BB   6766. Tantalizing Blues/The First Time I Met You       -MW 7112
BB   6788. Deceived Blues/Workhouse Blues, (voc., Annie Turner)
BB   6811. Santa Fe Blues/A & V Railroad Blues
BB   6825. Never Go Wrong Blues/(rev., Tampa Red)
BB   6894. Farish Street Jive(piano solo)/(rev., Mack and Mack)
BB   6916. Leaving Town Blues/Out West Blues
BB   7178. West Texas Blues/Mistreatin' Woman Blues
BB   7806. Misled Blues/One Arm Slim
```

LITTLE CHOCOLATE DANDIES (See Chocolate Dandies)

LITTLE DAVID (Alexander) (Blues singing):
```
De   7211. Original Sweet Patunia/Standing By a Lamp Post
De   7270. Ramblin' Mind Blues/New Sweet Patunia
```

LITTLE JAZZ TRUMPET ENSEMBLE (Joe Thomas, Emmett Berry, Roy Eldridge, trumpets;
Johnny Guarnieri, piano; Cozy Cole, drums; Israel Crosby, bass): Jan.24,1944
```
Key   607. St. Louis Blues/Don't Be That Way
Key   608. Fiesta in Brass/I Want to be Happy
```

LITTLE PILGRIMS:
  Dandy 5241. First Love Memories

LITTLE RAMBLERS (Largely interchangeable with California Ramblers. Featuring in
some titles. Red Nichols, trumpet; Jimmy Dorsey, clarinet and alto sax; Adrian
Rollini, bass sax; Tommy Dorsey, trombone, and others):
```
Co    175. Arkansas Blues/Them Ramblin' Blues
Co    203. Tessie/Hard Hearted Hannah                       -Co 1443
Co    217. Deep Blue Sea Blues(140070)/I'm Satisfied Beside That Sweetie(140071)
Co    346. Don't Bring Lulu/Cross Words
Co    248. Panama Mamas/Prince of Wails
Co    423. Deep Elm/Melancholy Lou
Co    403. Look Who's Here(140644)/Got No Time(140645)
Co    524. I Love My Baby(141343)/In Your Green Hat(141354)
Co    535. Fallin' Down/Tomorrow Mornin'
Co    628. Could I/Here Comes Malinda
Co    679. Hot Henry/I Wonder What
Co   1103. Swamp Blues/Play It Red
```

```
        (From Adrian's Tap Room Gang):
   BB  6043. Loveless Love/Gretna Green
   BB  6045. Cotton/Truckin'
   BB  6077. What a Night/(rev., California Ramblers)

        (Ward Pinkett, cornet and vocal; Albert Nicholas, clarinet; Adrian Roll-
        ini, vibraphone; Jack Rusin, piano; Danny Barker, guitar; Joe Watts,bass;
Sammy Weiss, drums.--JI 9/20/40):                                    Oct.5,1935
   BB  6130. I'm on a See Saw/I'm Painting the Town Red
   BB  6131. Red Sails in the Sunset/Tender as the Night
   BB  6144. Everything Is Okey Dokey/(rev., Bernard Addison)
   BB  6193. Tap Room Special/(rev., Freddie Jenkins)

        (Unknown personnel):
   BB  6189. A Little Bit Independent/(rev., California Ramblers)
   BB  6191. You Hit the Spot/(rev., California Ramblers)
   BB  6192. I'm the Fellow Who Loves You/Life Begins at Sweet Sixteen

        (Bill Dillard, cornet; Albert Nicholas, clarinet; Adrian Rollini, vibra-
        phone; Jack Rusin, piano; Danny Barker, guitar; Joe Watts, bass; Weiss,
        drums.--JI 9/20/40):                                         Dec.27,1935
   BB  6220. The Music Goes 'Round and Around/I'm Shooting High
   BB  6232. I'm Building Up to an Awful Letdown/I've Got My Fingers Crossed

        (Personnel unknown):
   BB  6237. The Day I Let You Get Away/Rhythm in My Nursery Rhymes
   BB  6238. Too Much Imagination/(rev., California Ramblers)

LOCKE BROTHERS RHYTHM ORCHESTRA:
   BB  6287. Betty Dupree/Don't You Tear My Clothes
   BB  6332. Sweet Sue/China Boy
```

CRIPPLE CLARENCE LOFTON

```
See also:
   SAMMY BROWN: Ge 6337
   BUMBLE BEE SLIM: Vo 02995, 03090.
   RED NELSON: De 7155, 7171.

LOFTON, CRIPPLE CLARENCE (vocal with piano & guitar*):
Vo 02951. Strut That Thing(c947b); traps)/Monkey Man Blues(c948a)*
Me 61166. Brown Skin Girls(c1074a)*/You Done Tore Your Playhouse Down(c1075a)
                                                                     -Cq 8758
        (Piano solos,):
   SA 12003. Streamline Train/Had a Dream                                1939
   SA 12009. Pine Top's Boogie Woogie/I Don't Know
   Se 10002. The Fives(129)/South End Boogie(130)                       1944
   Se 10006. In de Mornin'(140)/Early Blues(141)
   Se 12005. I Don't Know(142)/Streamlined Train(143)

LOFTON, POOR BOY (blues singing with guitar):
   De  7010. Poor Boy Blues/It's Killin' Me
   De  7049. Dirty Mistreater/Rainy Day Blues
   De  7076. Jake Leg Blues/My Mean Baby Blues

LOMAX, LAWRENCE (acc. by Clarence Williams Orch.):
   OK  8132. Nobody Loves Me But My Mother(s72353b)/She'll Be There Mother Mine
   OK  8165. Without You Dear/Sweetheart Mine                          (s72354b)

LoSCALZO & HIS DIXIELAND WOODSHEDDERS, MIKE (Phil Napolean, trumpet; Brad Gowans,
valve trombone; Leonard Centobie, clarinet; Mike LoScalzo, piano; Chuck Wayne,gui-
tar; Jack Lessberg, bass; Toney Spargo, drums and kazoo):       New York,May,1945
   B&W 1212. Tin Roof Blues/Muskrat Ramble
   B&W 1213. Indiana/Sister Kate
   B&W 1214. Royal Garden Blues/Jazz Band Ball
   B&W 1215. Some Day Sweetheart/That's a-plenty

LONGSHAW, FRED (piano solos):
   Co 14080. Chili Pepper(140657)/Tomato Sauce(140658)

LOU AND HIS GINGER SNAPS (Luis Russell's Orchestra: Henry Allen, Bill Coleman,
trumpets; J.C. Higginbotham, trombone; Albert Nicholas, clarinet and alto sax;
Charlie Holmes, alto sax; Theo Hill, tenor sax; Luis Russell, piano; Will John-
son, guitar; Pop Foster, bass; Paul Barbarin, drums):                    1929
   Ba  6536. Broadway Rhythm(2525-1)/(rev., Dick Cherwin)            -Ca 9319
   Ba  6540. The Way He Loves Is Just Too Bad(2533-4169)/(rev., Fred Rich
                                                           ↙Ro 1108, Ca 9320
        (See also: Dixie Jazz Band: Or 1726, 1728)
```

LOUIS' HARLEM STOMPERS (Casa Loma Orchestra):
Co 2615. Casa Loma Stomp/(rev., Fletcher Henderson Stokers of Hades)

LOUISIANA FIVE (Alcide Nunez, clarinet; Anton Lada, drums; Charles Panelli, trombone; Joe Cawley, piano; banjo):
Co 2742. Just Another Good Man Gone Wrong(78376)/Yelping Hound Blues(78377)
Co 2768. The Alcoholic Blues(78523)/(rev., Wilbur Sweatman)
Co 2775. I Ain't Got No Time to Have the Blues(78522)/(rev., Sweatman)
Co 2857. You Can't Get Lovin'/(rev., Ted Lewis)
Co 2949. Slow and Easy/Dance o' Mania
Em   501. Yelping Hound Blues(503-3)/High Brown Babies Ball(504-1)
Em 1026. Thunderbolt/Dixie Blues
Em 1076. Viginia Blues/Lead Me to It
Em 1078. Summer Days
      "   Golden Rod   -Med 8139
Em 1083. Ringtail Blues(4486)   -Med 8139
      "   Blues My Naughty Sweetie Gives to Me(4487)
Em 9150. Orange Blossom Rag
Em 9178. Rainy Day/(rev., Emerson Dance Orch.)
Em 9179. Yama Yama Blues/Church Street Sobbin' Blues
Em 10116. Weary Blues/Down Where the Rajah
Em 10172. Big Fat Ma(4697)/Weeping Willow Blues(4737)
Em 10229. Sunshine Girl/Be Happ-E
Em 10241. Town Topic Rag/I'll Get Him Yet

LOUISIANA JOE AND SLIM (piano and drums):
Ch 50063. Memphis Rhythm/Crossing Beale Street

LOUISIANA RHYTHM KINGS (Personnel unknown):   Chicago,Jan.31,1928
Vo 15657. Mississippi Mud/Nobody's Sweetheart

    (Next coupling scheduled but not issued, really by Chicago Rhythm Kings:
    Muggsy Spanier, cornet; Frank Teschemacher, clarinet; Mezz Mezzrow, sax;
    Joe Sullivan, piano; Jim Lannigan, tuba; Gene Krupa, drums; Eddie Condon,
    guitar and vocal):   April 28,1928
Vo 15692. Baby Won't You Please Come Home(c1907a,b)/Friar's Point Shuffle
                                                                   (c1909a,b)
    (Personnel and recording date unknown):
Vo 15710. I Can't Give You Anything But Love/(rev., Duke Ellington)
Vo 15716. When You're Smiling/Dusky Stevedore   Chicago,July 21,1928
Vo 15729. Skinner's Sock/Hallucinations

    (Red Nichols, trumpet; Glenn Miller, trombone; Jimmy Dorsey or Fud Livingston, clarinet; and others):   New York,Feb.20,1929
Vo 15779. Futuristic Rhythm(E29319)/Out Where the Blues Begin(E29320)
Vo 15784. That's a Plenty(E29321)/(rev., Wolverines)

    (See personnel for Vo 15828"B", below):
Vo 15810. I'm Walking Through Clover(E29691)/(rev., Original Memphis Five)

    (Red Nichols, trumpet; Jack Teagarden, trombone; Pee Wee Russell,clarinet; Bud Freeman, tenor sax;Joe Sullivan,piano;Dave Tough,drums):
                                                                   June 11,1929
Vo 15815. Last Cent(E30031)/Basin St.Blues(E30030;voc.,Teagarden) -BrE 02506
Vo 15828. That Da Da Strain(E30029)   -HRS 7
      "   Ballin'the Jack(E29689;with Goodman,clarinet;Mole,trombone) -HRS 15

    (Earlier personnel with Jimmy Dorsey):   Sept.10,1929
Vo 15833. Waiting at the End of the Road(E30544)/Marianne(E30546)
Vo 15841. Little by Little(E30545)/(rev.,Hollywood Shufflers)

    (Red Nichols, trumpet; Glenn Miller, trombone; Jimmy Dorsey, clarinet;
    Babe Rusin, tenor Sax; Adrian Rollini, bass sax; Jack Rusin,piano; Gene
    Krupa, drums; Eddie Condon, guitar):   Jan.20,1930
Br 4706. Oh Lady Be Good(E31945)/I Have to Have You(E31948)   -Br 6829
Br 4845. Meanest Kind of Blues(E31947)
      "   Swanee(E31943)   -BrF 500325
                                                                   Jan.27,1930
Br 4908. Karavan(E31913)/O'er the Billowy Sea(E31911)   -Br 6837
Br 4923. Lazy Daddy(E31912)/There's Egypt in Your Dreamy Eyes(E31916)-Br 6838
Br 4938. Pretty Baby(E31914)   -Br 6840
      "   Tell Me(E31915)   -BrF 500325
Br 4953. Sweet Sue Just You(E31946)/Squeeze Me(E31944)   Jan.20,1930

LOUISIANA RHYTHMAKERS (Duke Ellington Orchestra: Reissues of JUNGLE BAND: Br 6038 and Br 4952):
Me 12445. Rockin' in Rhythm(e35801a)/Twelfth Street Rag(E35802a)   -Pe 15650
Me 12468. Runnin' Wild(e34927a)/Dreamy Blues(e34928a)

LOUISIANA STOMPERS (Fletcher Henderson Orchestra):
Para 12550. Hop Off/Rough House Blues

LOUISIANA SUGAR BABES (Jabbo Smith, trumpet; Garvin Bushnell, clarinet, alto sax
and bassoon; James P. Johnson, piano; Fats Waller, organ.--Jl 1/26/40):   1927
    Vi 21346. Thou Swell(42568)/Persian Rug(42569)
    Vi 21348. Willow Tree(42566)/'Sippi(42567)

LOUISVILLE RHYTHM KINGS (Benny Goodman, clarinet; Gil Rodin, Larry Binyon, saxes;
Jack Teagarden, trombone; Al Harris, Jimmy McPartland, trumpets; Eddie Bergman,
violin; Vic Briedis, piano; Dick Morgan, banjo; Harry Goodman, bass; Vic Moore,
drums):
    OK 41189. Let's Sit and Talk About You(401535)/In a Great Big Way(401559)
    PaF 22305. Shout Hallelujah Cause I'm Home(401558)

LOVIN' SAM FROM DOWN IN BAM (Sam Theard; blues singing; accompaniment by Cow Cow
Davenport, piano, likely, at least in some titles):
    Br 7073. She's Givin' It Away/State Street Blues
    Br 7075. She Skuffles That Ruff/What You Gonna Do
    Br 7090. Get Your Mind On It/Doodle It Back
    Br 7094. Hot Dog Man/I Ain't No Ice Man
    Br 7096. The Lover and the Beggar/You Rascal You
    Br 7117. Huggin' and Kissin' and Gwine On/I'm Goin' Back and Get Some More
    Br 7131. Ain't Nobody Got Nothin'/Get it in Front
    Br 7167. Can You Imagine That/You Rascal No. 2
    Br 7183. Ugly Child/Bring It on Home to Your Grandma
    Br 7198. Three Sixes/She Can Love So Good

    LOVIN' SAM AND JOHN OSCAR (two pianos):
    Br 7208. High Yellow and Seal Skin Brown/You Can't Get That Stuff No More

LOWN AND HIS LOUNGERS, BERT (Sherry Magee, Lou Bode, Paul Mason, reeds; Frank
Cush, Eddie Farley, trumpets; Glenn Miller, trombone; Chauncey Gray, piano; Buddy
Falco, violin; Tom Felline, banjo; Ward Lay, bass; Stanley King, drums.--RP):
    Ha 892. Here Comes My Ball and Chain(148179)/(rev., Arthur Ross)
    Ha 920. Big City Blues(148178)/(rev., Lou Gold)   -Di 2920
    Ha 974. Jazz Me Blues/(rev., Dixie Stompers)   -Vo 1974, Di 2974

    BERT LOWN AND HIS ORCHESTRA):
    Co 2258. Bye Bye Blues
    Vi 22603. To Whom It May Concern/(rev., Duke Ellington)   -HMV 5981
    HMV 5958. You're Simply Delish/You're the One I Care For
    HMV 6005. By My Side

LUCAS AND THE STATE STREET FOUR, JANE:
    Vo 03314. Dreaming of You/I Can't Last Long

LUMBERJACKS (Another pseudonym used to cover various Mills recording units; first
title, however, is by Duke Ellington's orchestra):
    Ca 8352. Black Beauty(3411)   -Li 3000

    (Following sides apparently by Jack Pettis):
    Ca 8365. I'm Looking for Tulips(3418)/(rev., Broadway Broadcasters) -Li 3013
    . Spanish Dream(3409)/(rev., Mississippi Music Makers)   -Ro 779
    . Since You Went Away(3420)/(rev., Detroiters)   -Ro 791
    . Oh Boy It's a Pleasure(3456)/(rev., Varsity Eight)   -Li 3036
    Ca 9020. I Found My Sunshine in the Rain   -Ro 824

    (Jimmy McPartland, cornet; Jack Teagarden, trombone; Benny Goodman, clarinet; Gil Rodin, Larry Binyon, saxes; Vic Briedis, piano; Dick Morgan, banjo; Harry Goodman, bass; Ray Bauduc, drums.--HD):
    Ca 9030. Whoopee Stomp(3514)/(rev., Caroliners)   -Ro 834

    (Personnel unknown):
    Ca 9041. Blue Little You(3579)/(rev., Bob Haring)   -Ro 845
    . Let Me Be Alone With You(3588)/(rev., Vincent Richards)   -Ro 849
    Ca 9063. Makin' Whoopee(3615)/(rev., Joe Green)   -Ro 867
    Ca 9084. I've Never Been Loved by Anyone Like You
    Ca 9147. Would You Be Happy(3767)/(rev., Harry Salter)   -Ro 949
    . Will You? Won't You?(3842)/(rev., Detroiters)   -Ro 973

LUNCEFORD AND HIS CHICKASAW SYNCOPATORS, JIMMIE (See also Chickasaw Syncopators;
preaching by Moses Allen in first title):   1931
    Vi 38141. In Dat Mornin'/Sweet Rhthm   -BB 5330

    JIMMIE LUNCEFORD AND HIS ORCHESTRA (Eddie Tomkins, Sy Oliver, Tommy Stevenson, trumpets; Henry Wells, Russell Bowles, trombones; Willie Smith, Earl Carruthers, Joe Thomas, saxes; Edwin Wilcox, piano; Al Norris, guitar; Moses Allen, bass; James Crawford, drums):   1934-35
    Vi 24522. Jazznocracy(81325)   -BB 5713, HMV 6476
    "   Chillun Get Up(81326)   "
    Vi 24586. White Heat(81324)   -BB 5713, HMV 6493
    "   Leaving Me(81327)   "
    Vi 24601. Breakfast Ball(82219)   -BB 6133, HMV 135
    "   Here Goes(82220)   "

Vi	24669.	Swingin' Uptown(82218)	-HMV 120, HMV 6
"		Remember When(82221)	"
De	129.	Unsophisticated Sue	-BrE 01948
"		Sophisticated Lady	
De	130.	Nana(38541)/Miss Otis Regrets(38542)	-BrE 01883
De	131.	Mood Indigo(38532)/Rose Room(38533)	
De	299.	Stratosphere(38535)	-BrE 01965
"		Solitude(38969)	-BrE 02112
De	369.	Star Dust	-BrE 01948
"		Rhythm Is Our Business	-BrE 01965
De	415.	Rain/Because You're You	
De	453.	Since My Best Gal Turned Me Down	
"		Black and Tan Fantasy	-BrE 02112

(Sub. Paul Webster, trumpet, for Stevenson; Elmer Crumbley, Eddie Durham, Russell Bowles, trombones; add Laforet Dent, Dan Grisson, saxes.--HD):

De	503.	Runnin' Wild(39554)	-BrE 02277
"		Four or Five Times(39556)	-De 3515
De	572.	Rhythm in My Nursery Rhymes	-BrF 505040, BrE 02052
"		Call It Anything(previous personnel)	
De	576.	Babs	-BrF 505055, BrE 02170
"		Thunder	
De	628.	Charmaine	-De 3514
"		Oh Boy	
De	639.	Bird of Paradise(39552)	-BrE 02133
"		Rhapsody, Jr.(39553)	-BrE 02052
De	668.	Avalon	-BrF 505040, BrE 02297
"		Swanee River	-BrE 02391
De	682.	I'm Nuts About Screwy Music(60275)	-BrF 505055, BrE 02170
"		I'm Walking Through Heaven With You(dla2447)	
De	712.	My Blue Heaven	-De 3520, BrE 02244
"		Stomp It Off(previous personnel)	
De	765.	Hittin' the Bottle(60016)	-BrE 02133
"		Dream of You(38915; previous personnel)	
De	788.	The Best Things in Life Are Free(60276)	
"		Jealous(39171; previous personnel)	
De	805.	I'll Take the South	-BrE 02244
"		The Melody Man	-BrE 02277
De	908.	Sleepy Time Gal(39551)	
"		Organ Grinder's Swing(61246)	-BrE 02288
De	915.	On the Beach at Bali Bali	
"		Me and the Moon	-BrE 02288
De	960.	Living from Day to Day(61249)	-BrE 02345
"		Tain't Good(61250)	-BrF 505071, BrE "
De	1035.	This Is My Last Affair	-BrF 505094
"		Running a Temperature	
De	1128.	He Ain't Got Rhythm(61550)/Slumming on Park Ave.(61553)	-BrE 02457
De	1219.	Muddy Water	-BrF 505112
"		Honest and Truly	-BrE 02418
De	1229.	Count Me Out	
"		Linger a While	-BrE 02418
De	1318.	I'll See You in My Dreams	-BrF 505094, BrE 02449
"		The Merry Go Round Broke Down	"
De	1340.	Coquette(62259)/For Dancers Only(62263)	
De	1355.	Posin'(62344)	-De 3514, BrE 02476
"		Honey Keep Your Mind on Me(62346)	
De	1364.	Ragging the Scale(62261)	
"		The First Time I Saw You(62345)	-BrF 505112
De	1506.	Hell's Bells	-De 3515
"		Put on Your Old Grey Bonnet	-BrE 02476

(Sub. James Young, trombone, for Durham):

De	1569.	Annie Laurie/Frisco Fog	-BrF 505126, BrE 02549
De	1617.	Margie(63133)/Like a Ship at Sea(dla1011)	BrE 02570
De	1659.	Pigeon Walk(dla1010)/I'm Laughing Up My Sleeve(63135)	
De	1734.	Love Nest/Teasin' Tessie Brown	
De	1808.	My Melancholy Baby/By the River Sainte Marie	
De	1927.	Down by the Old Mill Stream(63585)/Sweet Sue Just You(63587)	

(additional Decca records below)

(Sub. Ted Buckner, sax, for Dent):

Vo	4754.	You're Just a Dream(24052)/I've Only Myself to Blame(24055)
Vo	4582.	'Tain't What You Do(23905)/Cheatin' on Me(23906)
Vo	4595.	Rainin'(23904)/Le Jazz Hot(23907)
Vo	4667.	Baby Won't You Please Come Home(24051)/Blue Blazes(24086)
Vo	4712.	You Set Me on Fire(24054)/Shoemaker's Holiday(24085)
Vo	4831.	The Lonesome Road(24053)/Mandy(w24350)
Vo	4875.	What Is This Thing Called Swing(24083)/Ain't She Sweet(w24352)
Vo	4887.	Time's a-Wastin'(23908)/Well All Right Then(w24644)
Vo	4979.	Oh Why Oh Why(w24643)/I Love You(w24646)
Vo	5033.	You Let Me Down(w24966)/I Want the Waiter(w24968)
Vo	5116.	Who Did You Meet Last Night(w24965)/Sassin' the Boss(w24967)
Vo	5207.	Belgium Stomp(w26066)/Think of Me Little Daddy(w26068)
Vo	5276.	I Used to Love You(w24969)/Liza(w26069)

(Eugene Young, Gerald Wilson, Webster, trumpets): **1940**
Vo 5326. Wham/Lunceford Special
Vo 5362. Put It Away(25749)/Uptown Blues(25755)
Vo 5395. I'm in an Awful Mood(25752)/Blues in the Groove(w26398)
Vo 5430. Pretty Eyes(25754)/It's Time to Jump and Shout(w26400)
Co 35453. I Wanta Hear Swing Songs(w26399)/Sonata by Beethoven(la2166)
Co 35484. Easter Parade(w24351)/I'm All Alone With You(25750)
Co 35510. I Got It(wo3067)/What's Your Story Mornin'Glory(la2163)
Co 35547. Bugs Parade(w26397)/Chopin's Prelude #7(wo3068)
Co 35567. Monotony in Four Flats(wo3071)/I Ain't Gonna Study War No More(woo26938)
Co 35625. Watcha Know Joe(woo28005)/Please Say the Word(woo28008)
Co 35700. Minnie the Moocher Is Dead(woo26937)/Pavanne(woo26939)
Co 35725. Swingin' on C(wo3069)/Let's Try Again(wo3070)
Co 35782. Red Wagon(woo28006)/You Ain't Nowhere(woo28007)
Co 35860. Rock It for Me(25751)/Barefoot Blues(woo26936)
Co 35919. Mixup(24084)/Blue Afterglow(co29295)
Co 35967. Flight of the Jitterbug(co29294)/Okay for Baby(co29293)
Co 36054. Dinah, 1 & 2 (la2164/65)
De 3718. Twenty-four Robbers(68875)/I Had a Premonition(68876)
De 3807. Battle Axe(68877)/Chocolate(69036)
De 3892. Blue Prelude(68874)/Peace and Love for all(69035)
De 3931. Flamingo(dla2449)/Siesta at the Fiesta(dla2450)
De 4032. Hi Spook(69681)/Yard Dog Mazurka(69682)
De 4083. Gone(69680)/Impromptu(69683)
De 4125. Blues in the Night, 1 & 2
De 4289. I'm Losing My Mind/Life Is Fine
De 18324. I'm Gonna Move to the Outskirts of Town
De 18504. Keep Smilin' Keep Laughin'/ It Had to Be You
De 18463. Strictly Instrumental/Knock Me a Kiss
De 18534. Easy Street/You're Always in My Dreams

(Melvin Moore, Bob Mitchell, William Scott, Russell, trumpets; John Ewing Russell Bowles, Fernando Arbello, Earl Hardy, trombones; Chauncey Jarrett, alto; Omer Simeon, alto, tenor and clarinet; Joe Thomas, tenor, Ernest Purce, alto, tenor, baritone; Jock Carruthers, baritone, alto; Ed Wilcox, piano; Al Norris, guitar; Joe Marshall, drums; Truck Parham, bass):
De 18594. Back Door Stuff, 1 & 2 (71756/57) **Feb.8,1944**
De 18618. Jeep Rhythm/I Dream a Lot About You

LYTELL, JIMMY (clarinet solos):
Pat 36584. Messin' Around/Coney Island Washboard -Pe 14765
Pat 36741. Stockholm Stomp/Be Blue
Pat 36717. Sugar/Headin' for Harlem
Pe 106. Two Faced Man
Pe 14749. Old Folks Shuffle/Red House
Pe 14846. Zulu Wail/Fakir's Rhythm
Pe 14956. Davenport Blues/Missouri Squabble
Pe 15005. Yellow Dog Blues/Sweet Emmalina

JIMMY LYTELL AND HIS ALL STAR SEVEN (Jimmy Lytell, clarinet; Carmen Mastren, guitar; Russ Case, trumpet; Chauncey Morehouse, drums; Will Bradley trombone; Frank Signorelli, piano; Haig Stephens, bass; Savannah Churchill, voc.):
Bea 104. He's Commander in Chief of My Heart(13569)/Fat Meat Is Good Meat(13571)
Bea 106. Tell Me Your Blues/Two Faced Man

#

ASCH RECORDS
HOT JAZZ

MARY LOU WILLIAMS TRIO

JAMES P. JOHNSON

ART TATUM TRIO

MEADE LUX LEWIS

★ ★ ★

JOHN KIRBY & ORCH.　　　　BLUES

COLEMAN HAWKINS　　　　LEADBELLY

STUFF SMITH TRIO　　　　JOSH WHITE

YANK LAWSEN JAZZ BAND

★ ★ ★

FOLKSAY

WOODY GUTHRIE　　　　BURL IVES

LANGSTON HUGHES

ASCH RECORDS
117 West 46th Street, New York 19, N.Y.

INDEX TO JAZZ
VOLUME III

PUBLISHED BY THE RECORD CHANGER, FAIRFAX, VA.

Commodore Announces

The first records by the

JAZZ MEN OF TOMORROW

BOB WILBER'S WILD CATS

PERSONNEL

Bob Wilber, Clarinet; **Johnny Glasel**, Cornet; **Dick Wellstood**, Piano;
Charlie Traeger, Bass; **Denny Strong**, Drums

C-583 Willie the Weeper   C-584 Blues for Fowler
       Mabel's Dream   Wild Cat Rag

Two 10-Inch Records—$1.05 Each

THREE FINE JAZZ ALBUMS

Disc Album No. 632	Pee Wee Russell Jazz Ensemble With Muggsy Spanier	$3.15
Disc Album No. 701	Joe Sullivan Jazz Quartet With Sidney Bechet	$3.93
Disc Album No. 709	Baby Dodds Drum Solos	$2.89

The Hard-To-Get
"COMES JAZZ" ALBUM NOW IN STOCK

		Price
Columbia Set C-40	BUD FREEMAN AND HIS FAMOUS CHICAGOANS	$3.57
Set C-29	BIX BEIDERBECKE	$3.57
Set C-31	BESSIE SMITH	$3.57

		Price
Columbia Set C-126	NEW ORLEANS JAZZ ALBUM BY KID ORY'S CREOLE JAZZ BAND	$3.57

As Always, We Have a Complete Stock of Jazz Labels Including

CRESCENT	CIRCLE	JAZZ INFORMATION	JAZZ MAN	PACIFIC
CENTURY	EXNER	BLUE NOTE	KING JAZZ	WEST COAST

WHILE THEY LAST!

Charles Delaunay's Famous HOT DISCOGRAPHY $2.50

—also—

JAZZ RECORD BOOK	JAZZ CAVALCADE	THE REAL JAZZ
JAZZMEN	HORN OF PLENTY	$2.50
$3.50 Each	REALLY THE BLUES	SHINING TRUMPETS
	$3.00 Each	$5.00

—and others—

If you're looking for a rare record, drop us a line. We may have that particular record, and at a price far below the Auction market.

When in New York, drop into our Collectors' Department, or send us your name and address and you will be promptly placed on our mailing list. Careful and individual attention paid to all Mail Orders. All prices include tax. Shipments made via Railway Express Collect for Shipping Charges ONLY

Commodore Music Shop

136 East 42d Street, N.Y.C.

RECORDS

Shipped Anywhere By Our

MAIL ORDER DEPARTMENT

★

We specialize in rare labels and always stock the latest releases, as well as new and used items, current or cutout

★

The RECORD SHACK

11800 Wilshire Blvd., Los Angeles 25, Calif., U.S.A.
Open Evenings and Sundays • Telephone ARizona 92681

Introduction

Publication of Volume III of the INDEX TO JAZZ calls for an apology, both for the unseemly delay in its appearance and for my inability to acknowledge, so far, many of the contributions from various correspondents.

It also calls for reassurances that the first draft of the INDEX will now be finished in short order, with the complete revision, incorporating the data supplied by collectors the world over, to follow as soon as possible.

Major gaps in the work, such as missing master numbers and dates, are being filled so rapidly that it seems certain that the ultimate goal,—chronological arrangement of each artist's recordings,—will be achieved without too much difficulty. A plan is also being worked out to supply a serial number key by which a given record may be quickly traced to its proper position in the more lengthy sections.

This certainly will permit a more orderly grouping of personnels and dates, and at the same time should satisfy those collectors who want a numerical guide of some sort.

Although I hope eventually to answer all letters, I want to acknowledge without further delay, the assistance given so far by the following collaborators:

John S. Abercrombie, Jeff Aldam, C. I. Alexander, Walter C. Allen, J. E. Alschuler, Joe Ames, Arthur Appelbaum, George Avakian, Harry Avery.

Sol Babits, Dick Bachrach, Bruce Baker, Monte Ballou, James G. Barlow, H. C. Barringer, E. T. Batchelder, J. D. Bates, Larry Beals, Lari Behrman, Buck Bemis, Arthur Bergonzone, Edward H. Bilderback, George Blaine, Rudi Blesh, Morton H. Blumberg, William E. Bonnet, Robert Y. Bodine, Sharkey Bonano, Bill Bowden, Paul Braverman, James M. Broadus, D. C. Brown, Jr., Ken Brown, Marvin Brown, Tom Brown, Abbie Brunies, W. H. Buck, Kay Buckmaster, Berney Burleson.

Ann Cagle, James Causey, Oscar Celestin, Jack Chamberlain, Theodore Chandler, Jr., Gordon R. Chapman, Richard Christy, Clyde H. Clark, Bill Cleland, Alan M. Cohn, Dexter G. Cook.

Ralph Damelio, Stanley F. Dance, J. R. T. Davies, George C. Davis, Gordon Darrah, Robert Dean, Chip Decker, Charles Delaunay, Paul De Mane, Jr., Leon Demeuldre, Dave Dexter, John L. Dow, Louis Dumaine, John J. Durkota, Frank Dutton.

H. M. Easterling, Sanford M. Edelstein, Nesuhi Ertegun, William H. Evans.

Jack Farrell, Art Feher, Charlie Flander, Rudi A. Fehr, Edwin W. Foy, Wallace Fry.

Harry H. Galbraith, Fred Garber, W. M. Garland, Jr., H. Gellatly, John Gildersleeve, Robert T. Greer, Thurman and Mary Grove, Don Gunnison.

M. J. Hall, John Hammond, Merrill M. Hammond, Jr., Horace Meunier Harris, James Havel, Monk Hazel, Will Roy Hearne, John G. Heinz, Olle Helander, Wallace T. Herrell, Jr., Fred H. Higginson, Bob High, Howard K. Hilton, George Hoefer, H. H. Hollis, Kenneth Hulsizer, John Hyman.

Henry F. Ivey, Thomas C. Jackson, W. A. Jackson, Irving L. Jacobs, Robert A. Jobe, Henry D. Johnson, Cliff Jones, Max Jones.

Ben Kaplan, Jerry Kawakami, George W. Kay, Faith and Bob Kelsey, R. D. Kempner, Carl A. Kendziora, Jr., Jan Kindler, J. H. King, Edward Kinsel, James E. Kirby, Andrew Kirchner, Ed Kohr, Eric E. A. Krans, Gus Kuhlman.

Milton C. Laidlaw, Francis T. Laney, Jimmy Laney, George and Phyllis Laufer, Dick Leekley, N. Marc Levine, Oscar Levine, Harry Lim, Alfred Lion, Ernest L. Little, Jr., Al Loewenson, John R. Logan, Cliff E. Longanecker, E. C. Loud, William C. Love.

J. T. MacLean, George Malcolm-Smith, Joseph Madison, Dick Madtes, Daniel L. Mahony, Richard D. Mallow, M. Mannogian, J. J. Martin, Henry T. Maserow, Frank Mayer, Vincent Mazzella, C. T. McCaffrey, Jr., Albert J. McCarthy, James H. McCarthy, Bob McCormick, C. W. McKinney, F. C. McKnight, James P. McKune, Stewart L. Medill, Ed Meikel, Edward J. Mello, Sam Meltzer, Irwin C. Miller, Jim Moynahan, Edward Mullener.

Tod New, H. H. Niesen, Jr., Thomas J. O'Donnell.

Tony Parenti, Emerson R. Parker, William Hewitt Parry, Al Pearson, Howard E. Penny, P. A. Phillippi, Jr., Edward A. Podesta, Ned Polsky, Mario A. Toscano Pouchan, Larry Quilligan.

Fred Ramsey, Jr., Jack L. Rankin, George Rarpinsky, Jay Reeder, Ray Reid, Bill Riddle, Dick Ridlon, Lloyd M. Ritter, Frank A. Ritz, William L. Rogers, Herman Rosenberg, W. M. Rudder, Norman N. Ruetenik, Jim Rush, Ross Russell, William Russell, Brian A. L. Rust, Jim Robinson.

Robert B. Sales, M. R. Salvin, Dr. Daniel B. Salzberg, Arthur L. Schawlow, Sigmund Schechter, Kenneth Schram, Abe Schulman, Harry Schuster, Dick Sears, Norman Shacker, P. H. Shaw, Ronald Shores, William T. Sigafoose, Bill Shearer, P. L. Sipp, Jr., Bob Smith, Jr., Earl S. Smith, Earl T. Smith, Harrison Smith, Steve Smith, Vernon Smith, Muggsy Spanier, Lee Stafford, John Steiner, Derrick Stewart-Baxter, Dave Stoneback, Ralph J. Sturges, William H. Sturrup.

Peter Tanner, Lois and Gene Tate, Peter J. Taylor, Herbert Thrune, Don Townsend, John H. Treudley, Frank Trolle.

Warren Vache, Julian Van Hecke, Ralph Venables, G. E. Vickers, Joseph F. Voeglein, Jr.

W. Wallden, Robert Waller, Theodore F. Watts, Leslie Webb, W. C. Wenzel, Lloyd C. Whaley, Benjie White, Bozy White, Bert Whyatt, Eugene Williams, Les Zacheis.

copyright, 1947, Gordon Gullickson.

ABBREVIATIONS – RECORDS

Ae	Aeolian Vocalion	JI	Jazz Information
Aj	Ajax	JM	Jazz Man
AM	American Music	JR	Jazz Record
Ap	Apex	Key	Keynote
Au	Autograph	KJ	King Jazz
Ba	Banner	Li	Lincoln
BB	Bluebird	Ma	Master
Bea	Beacon	Mad	Madison
BN	Blue Note	Man	Manhattan
BP	Black Patti	Max	Maxsa
Br	Brunswick	Me	Melotone
BrE	English Brunswick	Mu	Musicraft
BrF	French Brunswick	MW	Montgomery Ward
BrG	German Brunswick	Na	National
BS	Black Swan	Nor	Nordskog
Bu	Buddy	OdF	French Odeon
B&W	Black and White	OdG	German Odeon
Bwy	Broadway	OK	Okeh
Ca	Cameo	Or	Oriole
Cap	Capitol	OrE	English Oriole
Cen	Century	PaA	American Parlophone
Ch	Champion	PaE	English Parlophone
Chal	Challenge	PaF	French Parlophone
Ci	Circle	PaS	Spanish Parlophone
CI	Collectors Item	Pana	Panachord
Cl	Clarion	PanD	Dutch Panachord
Cli	Climax	Para	Paramount
Clax	Claxtonola	Pat	Pathe
Co	Columbia	PatA	Pathe Actuelle
Com	Commodore	PatF	French Pathe
Cont	Continental	Pe	Perfect
Cq	Conquer	Ph	Philharmonic
Cr	Crown	Po	Polk
Crs	Crescent	Pu	Puritan
De	Decca	Rad	Radiex
DeE	English Decca	Re	Regal
DeF	French Decca	Ro	Romeo
DeH	Dutch Decca	Roy	Royale
Di	Diva	RZ	Regal Zonophone
Do	Domino	Sa	Salabert
Ed	Edison	Sav	Savoy
El	Elite	SA	Solo Art
Elec	Electradisk	SD	Steiner-Davis
Em	Emerson	Se	Session
Ex	Excelsior	Si	Silvertone
FR	Firestone	Sig	Signature
Ge	Gennett	Su	Sunshine
GG	Grey Gull	Sup	Supertone
Gl	General	Sw	Swing
GrF	French Gramophone	Tele	Telefunken
Gu	Guardsman	Tri	Triangle
Ha	Harmony	UHCA	United Hot Clubs
Harmo	Harmograph	Ul	Ultraphone
Her	Herwin	VD	Van Dyke
HMV	His Master's Voice	Ve	Velvet Tone
HoW	Hit of Week	Vi	Victor
HRS	Hot Record Society	Vo	Vocalion
Hy	Hytone	VoE	English Vocalion
Im	Imperial	Vr	Variety
Je	Jewel	Vs	Varsity

SOURCES

DB	Down Beat (George Hoefer)	JI	Jazz Information
Dis.	Discography (British magazine)	JM	Jazz Music (British magazine)
		JR	Jazz Record
EW	Eugene Williams	JRB	Jazz Record Book
HD	Hot Discography	JT	Jazz Tempo
HJ	Hot Jazz	RC	Record Changer
JAZZ	Magazine (W. C. Love)	RR	Rhythm on Record
	Te	Tempo	

M

MACK, BABY (acc. by Louis Armstrong, cornet: Richard M. Jones, piano):
   OK 8313. You've Got to Go Home on Time(9512)/What Kind o'Man Is That(9513)

MACK, BILLY AND MARY (Vocal duet, acc. by Punch Miller, cornet; possibly Steve Lewis or Morris Rouse, piano.--DB 1/15/41)   **New Orleans, 1924**
   OK 8195. My Heartbreakin' Gal(8897b)/Black But Sweet, Oh God(8892a)

      (Unknown acc.):
   OK 8296. You Don't Know Much/How Could My Man(Mary Mack, solo)

      MARY MACK (Baby Mack?), acc. by Chicago Black Swans:
   -- -----. You Drink Too Much(c1770-2)

      (Acc., piano, trombone, banjo):
   OK 8339. Oh Me, Oh My Blues(73906b)/(BERTHA "CHIPPIE" HILL)

      (Unknown acc.):
   BB 8131. I Vouch for My Man/Stingaree Man
          (See also: Baby Mack)

MACK, IDA MAY (Singing with piano):
   Vi 38030. Elm Street Blues/Good Bye Rider
   Vi 38532. Mr. 49 Blues/Wrong Doin' Daddy

MACON ED (Vocal with violin and guitar):
   OK 8676. Worrying Blues(402290B)/Wringing That Thing(402289a),w.Tampa Joe

MAGEE AND HIS DIXIELANDERS, SHERRY (Gus Fetterer, clarinet: Harman Drewes, trumpet; William Drewes, trombone: Harry Ford, piano; Fred J. Bauer, drums; Arnold Fishkind, bass; Henry Schnier, tenor sax):   **1939**
   Vo 5281. Tin Roof Blues/Shake It and Break It
   Vo 5436. Satanic Blues(25691)/Bluin' the Blues(25693)

MALNECK AND HIS ORCHESTRA, MATTY:
   De 2060. Sing You Sinners/Hearts and Flowers
   De 2182. St. Louis Blues/Humoresque
   De 2616. By the Waters of Minnetonka/Lazy Rhapsody
   Co 35212. Park Avenue Fantasy/Then I Wrote the Minuet in G
   Co 35299. Carnival of Venice/William Tell Overture
   Co 35308. Song of India/Meditation
   Co 36140. An American in Paris/Anvil Chorus
   Co 36174. Green Eyes/I Take to You
   Co 36184. Little Girl Blue/Hurry Back to Sorrento

MANLEY, HELENA (vocal acc. by piano):
   OK 8111. Red Head Stepchild Blues/Loving Blues

MANNING, SAM (vocal, acc. by his Blue Hot Syncopators(Trumpet, alto sax, clarinet, banjo, drums):
   OK 8302. Keep Your Hands Off That(74031b)/Go,I've Got Somebody Sweeter Than
                                                         You(74032b)

      (West Indian singing, acc. by Cole Jazz Trio):
   OK 65004. The Bargee/Mabel, See What You've Done
   OK 65005. Camilla/Sweet Willie

      (Acc. by Cole Jazz Orchestra):
   Co 14110. Bungo/Let Go My Hand

      (Unknown):
   Br 7026. Bouncing Baby Boy/Woman's Sweeter Than Man

      MANNING AND FREEMAN:
   Br 7027. Goin' Back to Jamaica/Nothin'But a Double-Barreled Shotgun's Gonna
   Br 7028. American Woman and West Indian Man, I & 2   (Keep Me Away from You

      SAM MANNING (with Felix Krazy Kats):
   De 182567. Papa Don't Want No Fish and Rice Again/Go Back to You Ma
   De 18256. Sweet Willie/Salt Lane Gal
   De 18259. Looking for Me Santa Claus/Medley of West Indian Songs
   De 18260. Gambia Talk/Iron Bar

WINGY MANONE

See also:
   ADRIAN: Vi 25072, 25085, 25208.
   ARCADIAN SERENADERS: OK 40272, 40378, 40440.
   BARBECUE JOE: Ge 7320, Ch 16192.
   CELLAR BOYS: Vo 1503, Br 80066.
   GENE GIFFORD: Vi 25041, 25065.
   BENNY GOODMAN: Br 4968.
   HARLEM HOT SHOTS: Pe 16081, 16085, 16095.

RAY MILLER
RUSS MORGAN: Co 3067.
RED NICHOLS: Br 6013, 6058.
NEW ORLEANS RHYTHM KINGS: De 161, 162, 229, 464.
NAPPY LAMARE: Capitol 10025.

MANNONE'S HARMONY KINGS, JOE (Joe Mannone, trumpet and vocal· Hal Jordy, clarinet and alto: Bob Sacks, tenor· Johnny Miller, piano· Steve Brou or Brue, guitar; John Ryan, drums Arnold Loyacana, bass.--JR 10/44, 1/45):   April, 1927
Co 1044. Up the Country Blues(143951)/Ringside Stomp(143952)
Co 14282. Sadness Will be Gladness(143949)v.c.,Earl Warner/(Cat's Head(143950)

    JOE 'WINGY' MANNONE AND HIS CLUB ROYALE ORCHESTRA (Featuring Mannone, trumpet· Wade Foster, clarinet Jack Gardner, piano: Gene Krupa, drums, Bud Freeman, tenor sax):   1928
Vo 15728. Downright Disgusted/Fare Thee Well

    (Mannone, trumpet and vocal; Frank Teschemacher, clarinet; "Snurps", tenor sax: Art Hodes, piano: Ray Biondi, guitar: Augie Schellange, drums):   1929
Vo 15797. Isn't There a Little Love   -HRS 13
   "   Trying to Stop My Crying   -Br 80064, HRS 3

    (Correction for BARBECUE JOE AND HIS HOT DOGS: Wingy Mannone, trumpet & vocal: George Walters, clarinet; Maynard Spencer, piano; Dash Burkis, drums; unknown tenor sax):   1929
Ch 16153. Tar Paper Stomp(16951)/Tin Roof Blues(17059)
                                      -Ch 40005, De 7425, BrE 7807
    (Mannone, trumpet and vocal; Miff Frink, trombone; George Walters, clarinet and tenor sax; Maynard Spencer, piano: Orville Haynes, tuba; Dash Burkis, drums; unknown banjo):
Ch 16127. Up the Country(17058)   -Ch 40054, Ge 7320, De 7366
   "   Weary Blues(17060)   -Ch 40055,   "   , De 7415
    (Add Bob Price, Ed Camden, trumpets):
Ch 16192. Big Butter and Egg Man(17061)   -Ch 40055, De 7415
   "   Shake That Thing(16950) see 1st personell-Ch 40054, De 7366, BrE 02504

    WINGY MANNONE AND HIS ORCHESTRA (Wingy Mannone, trumpet and vocal; Matty Matlock, clarinet; Eddie Miller, tenor sax· Gil Bowers, piano; Nappy Lamare, guitar: Harry Goodman, bass; Ray Bauduc, drums):   May, 1934
Br 6911. No Calling Card(B15150a)   -BrE 01818, BrF 500462
    "   Strange Blues(15151a)   -PaE 2875,   "   "
Br 6940. Send Me(B15152a)   -BrE 02007, PaE 2875, BrF 500463
    "   Walkin' the Streets(B15153a)   -BrE 02055, Vo 4464,   "

    (Wingy Mannone, trumpet: Santa Pecora, trombone; Sidney Arodin, clarinet; Terry Shand, piano; Benny Pottle, bass; Ray Bauduc, drums):   Oct.,1934
OK 41569. Just One Girl(16087)/She's Crying for Me(16088)   -Co 35685
OK 41570. Royal Garden Blues,(16086)/Zero(16089)

    (Wingy Mannone, trumpet and vocal; Matty Matlock, clarinet; Eddie Miller tenor sax; Gil Bowers, piano; Nappy Lamare, guitar and vocal; Harry Goodman, bass; Ray Bauduc, drums):   December, 1934
OK 41573. Nickel in the Slot(C016572)/Swing Brother Swing(CO16574)
                                                       -Vo 3171, PaE 2126
                                                             March, 1935
Vo 2913. Isle of Capri(17005)   -Vo 4464,BrE 254
    "   I Believe in Miracles(17006)   -Pana 25748
Vo 2914. Fare Thee Well Annabelle(17007)
    "   On the Good Ship Lollypop(17008)   BrE 254
Vo 2933. You're an Angel(17258)/I'm in Love All Over Again(17259) April, 1935
Vo 2934. About a Quarter to Nine(17257)   -BrE 02064
    "   Let's Spill the Beans(17260)   -BrE 02055
                                                             June, 1935
Vo 2963. Every Little Moment(17638)   -BrF 02064
    "   Black Coffee(17639)   -BrE 02055
Vo 2972. Sweet and Slow(17640)/Lulu's Back in Town(17641)

    (Wingy Mannone, trumpet and vocal· Joe Marsala, clarinet: Bud Freeman, tenor sax: Gil Bowers, piano· Carmen Mastren, guitar; Sid Weiss, bass; Ray Bauduc, drums):   July, 1935
Vo 2989. A Little Door, a Little Lock, a Little Key(17783)-BrE 02073, BrG 9879
    "   Love and Kisses(17784)
Vo 2990. Let's Swing It(17782)
    "   Rhythm Is Our Business(17785)   -BrE 02073

    (Sub. Mattlock, clarinet; Tony Zimmers, tenor sax):   August, 1935
Vo 3023. From the Top of Your Head(18021)/Takes Two to Make a Bargain(18022)
                                                         -BrG 9878
Vo 3058. A Smile Will Go a Long Long Way(18020)/I'm Gonna Sit Right Down and
                           (Write Myself a Letter (18023)

7

(Wingy Mannone, trumpet and vocal: Jack Teagarden, trombone: Mattlock, clarinet; Bowers, piano; Mastren, Weiss, Bauduc):   Sept.,1935
Vo 3070. I've Got a Feeling(18134)/You Are My Lucky Star(18135)
Vo 3071. Every Now and Then(18133)/I've Got a Note(18136)
Vo 3071. I've Got a Note(second master)

(Mannone, Marsala, Bowers, Mastren, Weiss, Bauduc):   Dec.,1935
Vo 3134. I'm Shooting High(18403)/The Music Goes Round and Around(18404)
Vo 3135. You Let Me Down(18405)/I've Got My Fingers Crossed(18406)

(Add George Brunies, trombone):   Jan.,1936
Vo 3158. Rhythm in My Nursery Rhymes(18596)/The Broken Record(18598)
Vo 3159. Ol' Man Mose(18597)   -BrE 02196, BrG 9989
" Please Believe Me(18599)

(Wingy Mannone, trumpet and vocal; Ward Silloway, trombone; Joe Marsala,clarinet; Eddie Miller, tenor sax; Bowers, piano; Lamare, guitar; Bob Haggart, bass; Bauduc, drums):   March,1936
Vo 3191. Is It True What They Say About Dixie(18797)
" Goody Goody(18798)   -BrE 02196
Vo 3192. Shoe Shine Boy(18795)/West Wind(18796)

(Wingy Mannone, trumpet and vocal; Matlock and Marsala, clarinets; Miller, tenor: Conrad Lanoue, piano: Lamare: Bauduc; Artie Shapiro, bass)Apr.,1936
BB 6359. You Started Me Dreaming(101197)/Tormented(101198)   -HMV 8451
BB 6360. It's No Fun(101300)/Rhythm Saved the World(101301)
BB 6375. Dallas Blues(101199)/Swingin' at the Hickory House(101302)

(Wingy Mannone, trumpet and vocal; Murray Williams, clarinet; Tom Mace, alto; Eddie Miller, tenor: Lanoue; Mastren; Shapiro, Weiss):   May,1936
BB 6393. Isn't Love the Strangest Thing(101576)/Every Once in a While(101577)
BB 6394. Sing Me a Swing Song(101574)/Hesitation Blues(101575)
BB 6411. Basin Street Blues(101573)   -RZ 2301
" Panama(101578)

(Mannone; Mike Viggiano, clarinet; Mace, alto: Jimmy Lemaire, tenor sax; Jack Lemaire, guitar; Abby Fisher, drums: Lanoue; Shapiro):   Aug.,1936
BB 6472. I've Just Made Up With That Old Girl of Mine(102378)/You're Not the
BB 6473. Summer Holiday(102375)/No Regrets(102376)   (Kind(102379)
BB 6483. River Man(102374)
" Afterglow(102377)   -RZ 2301

(Omit Mace; sub. Marsala, clarinet; Weiss, drums; add Al Mastren, trombone):
BB 6536. It Can Happen to You(0216)/Cottage by the Moon(0218) Oct.,1936
BB 6537. Fancy Meeting You(0220)   -RZ 2367
" A Good Man Is Hard to Find(0221)
BB 6549. It's the Gypsy in Me(0217)/And They Said It Wouldn't Last(0219)
BB 6616. In the Groove(0551)/(AMANDA RANDOLPH)   Nov.,1936
BB 6618. Let Me Call You Sweetheart(0552)/Easy Like(0553)
BB 6605. Floatin' Down to Cotton Town(0555)/(CHARLIE BARNET)
BB 6606. I Can't Pretend(0554)/A Fine Romance(0556)

(Mannone; Brunis; Matlock; Marsala: Lanoue: Shapiro; Danny Alvin,drums):
BB 6804. You Showed Me the Way(04568)/I Can't Lose Longing(04569) Feb.,1937
BB 6806. Boo Hoo(04567)   -RZ 2414
" Oh Say Can You Swing(04570)   -RZ 2438
BB 6816. Formal Night in Harlem(04565)   -RZ 2438
" Sweet Lorraine(04566)

(Unknown personell):   May,1937
BB 7002. Don't Ever Change(010247)/You're Precious to Me(010249)
BB 7003. The Image of You(010246)/Life Without You(010248)
BB 7014. It Must Be Religion(010250)/The Prisoner's Song(010251)

(Babe Rusin, tenor sax: Marsala; Mannone; Lanoue; Shapiro; Alvin; Jack Lemaire):   Sept.,1937
BB 7197. Everything You Said Came True(013882)
" Getting Some Fun Out of Life(013883)   -RZ 264
BB 7198. I Ain't Got Nobody(013880)/Jazz Me Blues(013884)
BB 7214. I've Got My Heart Set on You(013881)/Laugh Your Way Through Life
                                         (013885) -RZ 2659
(Sub. Chu Berry, tenor sax):   Jan.,1938
BB 7389. Annie Laurie(018321)/Loch Lomond(018322)   -RZ 2732
BB 7391. Down Stream(018323)/Where's the Waiter(018324)
BB 7395. My Mariaccia Take a Steamboat(018325)
" In the Land of the Yamo Yamo(018326)   -RZ 2850

(Wingy Mannone, trumpet and vocal: Brad Gowans, trombone Al Kavich, sax & clarinet; Wilder Chase, piano: Bob Bennett, guitar: Sid Jacobs, bass;Danny Alvin, drums):   July,1938
BB 7621. Martha(023417)/Flat Foot Floogee(023419)   -RZ 2812
BB 7622. Heart of Mine(023415)/Little Joe from Chicago(023420)
BB 7633. Mannone Blues(023418)
" Let's Break the Good News(023416)   -RZ 2850

THIS IS NOT THE LAST WORD

This is no bible of jazz music. Collectors who examine this list will find corrections to make, additions and deletions to suggest. This is only the rough draft of what is intended to be a co-operative effort of the entire jazz collecting world, a complete and objective guide to hot records. Please send your notes to Orin Blackstone, 1016 Eleonore St., New Orleans 15, Louisiana. Credit will be given each month in the Record Changer to all who contribute to the final list.

PAGE NO.	RECORDING GROUP	LABEL	SERIAL NUMBER	WAS SHOWN:	SHOULD HAVE BEEN SHOWN:

PAGE NO.	RECORDING GROUP	LABEL	SERIAL NUMBER	WAS SHOWN:	SHOULD HAVE BEEN SHOWN:

(Mannone; Buster Bailey, clarinet: Chu Berry: Lanoue; Zeb Julian, guitar;
Jules Cassard, bass: Cozy Cole, drums):   April,1939
BB 10296. Downright Disgusted(036534)/Boogie Woogie(036539)
BB 10266. Corrine Corrina(036535)   -HMV 9352
  "   I'm a Real Kinda Poppa(036536)
BB 10289. Jumpy Nerves(036537)   -HMV 9352
  "   Casey Jones(036538)   -HMV 9360

(Sub. Danny Barker, guitar):   June 19,1939
BB 10331. Royal Garden Blues(037729)
  "   In the Barrel(037731)   -HMV 9360
BB 10401. Beale Street Blues(037730)   -HMV 9155
  "   Farewell Blues(037732)
BB 10432. Fare Thee My Baby Fare Thee Well(037733)/Limehouse Blues(037734)

(Mannone; Buck Scott, trombone Gus Fetterer, clarinet; Chu Berry, tenor;
Ernie Hughes, piano: Zeb Julian, guitar: Sid Jacobs, bass: Cozy Cole,drums):
BB 10560. Sudan(041972)/When the Saints Go Marching In(041974)   Sept.,1939
BB 10749. Blue Lou(041971)/How Long Blues(041973)
BB 300801. My Honey's Lovin'Arms(041975)/When My Sugar Walks Down the Street
                                        (041976)   -HMV 9313
(Mannone; Scott; Phil Olivala, clarinet: Lanoue; Julian: Jacobs; Alvin):
                                                 Jan.15,1940
BB 10604. South With the Boarder(045935)   -HMV 9155
  "   Put on Your Old Grey Bonnet(045937)
BB 10773. She's Crying for Me(045934)/The Mosquito Song(045936)

(Mannone; Archie Rosati, clarinet; Babe Bowman, tenor: Stan Wrightsman,
piano; Russell Soule, buitar; Bill Jones, bass: Dick Cornell,drums)Sept.1940
BB 10844. Rhythm on the River(049980)/Ain't It a Shame About Mame(049981)
BB 10909. Dinner for the Duchess(049982)/When I Get You Alone Tonight(049983)

(Mannone; George Brunis, trombone· Joe Marsala, clarinet: Mel Powell,piano:
Al Morgan, bass; Zutty Singleton, drums: Carmen Mastren,guitar):March,1941
BB 11107. Mama's Gone Goodbye(062859)/Stop the War(062861)
BB 11298. Orchi Chornya(062858)/The Boogie Beat'll Getcha(062860)

WINGY MANNONE AND HIS BAND (With Eddie Marr)   Aug.,1941
De 18325. Jam and Jive, 1 & 2 (2693/4)
De 18326. Jam and Jive, 3 & 4 (2695/6)
De 18327. Jam and Jive, 5 & 6 (2697/8)

WINGY MANNONE AND HIS ORCHESTRA:
JD 7777. O Sole Mio/Shake the Blues Away

WINGY MANNONE'S DIXIELAND BAND (Wingy Mannone, trumpet: Matty Matlock, clar-
inet; Nappy Lamare, guitar; Stan Wrightsman, piano; Jake Flores, Floyd O'-
Brien, Abe Lincoln, trombones; Phil Stephens, bass: Zutty Singleton,drums):
Cap 10024. Tailgate Ramble(215-5B)   Hollywood,March 7,1944
  "   Sister Kate(218-2A), omit O'Brien, Lincoln

WINGY MANNONE'S JUMP JAMMERS: (Wingy Manone; Marvin Ashbaugh; Ray Bauduc;
Andy Kelly; Joe Yukl; Roy Hol; Matty Mattlock):

Gilt Edge 536. Hot Peanuts/Salt Pork West Virginia
Gilt Edge 539. Bedroom Blues/Whiffle Diffle Bird
Gilt Edge 535. Big Leg Mama Blues/Last Call for Alcohol

(Personnel uncertain):
4-Star 1066. I must Be Dreaming/My Blue Heaven(Gloria Wood,vc)
4-Star 1074. Cement Mixer/I'm Confessin'
4-Star 1075. Git It Got It and Gone/When It's Sleepy Time Down South
4-Star 1116. Isle of Capri/What Good Is You
4-Star 1125. Sugar(426)/Black Market Blues(428)

ARA 143. The General Jumped at Dawn/(BOB CROSBY)
ARA 145. Tin Roof Blues(9793-1A)/If I Could Be With You(9794-2D),Kay Starr,vc

MANOR ALL STARS (Ray Turner, tenor sax: Roy Stevens, trumpet: Freddy Otis,piano;
Manor 2000.Mervel Falls In/Never Go There   (et al);

MANSFIELD AND HIS BAND, ANDY:
Ch 15438. Sh-h, Here Comes My Sugar/Third Rail
              (See Cotton Pickers,Gennett 6380)

FATE MARABLE'S SOCIETY SYNCOPATORS (Sidney Desvignes, Amos White, trumpets; Harvey Lankford, trombone; Norman Mason, Bert Bailey, Walter Thomas, saxes; Marable,
piano; Willie Foster, guitar; Henry Kimble, bass; Zutty Singleton,drums):
JI 8/9/40):   New Orleans, 1924
OK 40113. Pianoflage/Frankie and Johnnie

11

MAPLE CITY FOUR (Vocal, acc. by piano, washboard, whistle, jug):
Me 12699. Tiger Rag(C548-3)/Oh Monah(C549-2)
(See Windy City Four)

PAUL MARES AND HIS FRIARS SOCIETY ORCHESTRA (Paul Mares, trumpet; Santo Pecora, trombone; Omer Simeon, clarinet; Boyce Brown, alto sax; Jess Stacy, piano; Marvin Saxbe, guitar; Pat Pattison, bass; George Wettling, drums): 1935
  OK 41574. Nagasaki(C870)   -Co 35880
   " Maple Leaf Rag(C872)   -Co 35686
  OK 41575. Reincarnation(C871)   -Co 35686
   " The Land of Dreams(C873)   -Co 35880
(See also: Friars Society Orchestra & New Orleans Rhythm Kings)

MARINERS (vocal trio with Eddie Lang, guitar):
  OK 41433. Happy Feet/Down the River of Golden Dreams(with Red McKenzie)
  OK 41449. I Don't Mind Walkin'/Just a Little Dance

FRANKLYN MARKS:
  Ma   121. Jammin'/Turn Off the Moon

MARLBOROUGH MELODY SYNCOPATORS:
  Clover 1581. Yellow Dog Blues

RUDY MARLOWE AND HIS ORCHESTRA (The following reputedly features Jack Teagarden, trombone and other Marlowe records may have hot soloists) --DB 9/1/42):
  Ha 1062. Dixie Jamboree

SYLVIA MARLOWE (harpsichord):
  Ge 4406. Honky Tonk Train/Yancey Special

DODO MARMAROSA TRIO (Dodo Marmarosa, piano; Ray Brown, bass; Jackie Mills, drums)
  At   225. Mellow Mood/How High the Moon   1946
  At   226. Dodo's Blues/I Surrender Dear

ALAMO 'PIGMEAT' MARKHAM (blues singer with Oliver(Rev.) Mesheux's Blue Six: Oliver Mesheux, trumpet; Sandy Williams, trombone; Vivian Smith, piano; Jimmy Shirley, guitar; Israel Crosby, bass; Tommy Benford, drums):
  BN   48. Blues Before Sunrise(254-2)/How Long How Long Blues(256)
  BN 509. See See Rider(257-1)/You've Been a Good Ole Wagon(255-1)

JOE MARSALA

See also:
  ADRIAN: Vi 25072, 25085, 25208.
  ALL STAR JAM BAND: Com 528.
  PETE BROWN: De 18118.
  DANDRIDGE: Vo 3291, 3304, 3315, 3351, 3352.
  JAM SESSION: Com 1504, 1505.
  DELTA FOUR: De 737.
  FEATHER: Vo 4062.
  LINDA KEENE: BW 1203.
  WINGY MANNONE: Vo 2989, 2990, 3134, 3135, 3158, 3159, 3191, 3192; BB 6359, 6360, 6375, 6536, 6537, 6549, 6616, 6618, 6605, 6606, 6804, 6806, 6816, 7197, 7198, 7214, 7389, 7391, 7395, 11107, 11298.
  SHARKEY: Vo 3400, 3410, 3450, 3470.
  GEORGE WETTLING: De 18044, 18045.

JOE MARSALA AND HIS CHICAGOANS: (Joe Marsala, clarinet; Marty Marsala, trumpet; Ray Biondi, violin; Adele Girard, harp; Eddie Condon, guitar; Joe Bushkin, piano; Danny Alvin, drums; Art Shapiro, bass):
  Vr   565. Wolverine Blues(M412)/Jazz Me Blues(M414)

    JOE MARSALA AND HIS DELTA FOUR (Bill Coleman, trumpet and vocal; Carmen Mastren, guitar; Gene Traxler, bass; Pete Brown, alto sax; Joe Marsala, clarinet):
  Gl 1717. Wandering Man Blues(2796-2)/Salty Mama Blues(2797-3)   1940
  Gl 3001. Three o'Clock Jump(2798-2)/Reunion in Harlem(2799-2)

    JOE MARSALA AND HIS ORCHESTRA (Joe Marsala, clarinet; Marty Marsala, trumpet; Ray Biondi, violin; Joe Bushkin, piano; Jack Lemaire, guitar; Art Shapiro, bass; Buddy Rich, drums):
  Vo 4168. Hot String Beans/Mighty Like the Blues
  Vo 4116. Woo Woo/Jim Jam Stomp

    JOE MARSALA AND HIS DELTA SIX (Joe Marsala, clarinet; Benny Carter, trumpet; Pete Brown, alto sax; Billy Kyle, piano; Bobby Hackett, guitar; Cozy Cole, drums; Hayes Alvis, bass):
  De 18111. Twelve Bar Stampede(65437a), Brown, Hackett also on trumpets; Carter
   "   Feather Bed Lament(65438a)   (on alto sax

    JOE MARSALA AND HIS ORCHESTRA:
  De 3715. Bull's Eye(68854a)/Slow Down(68857a)

```
De   3764. I Know That You Know(68856a)/Lower Register(68855a)      -BrE 03245
     (Joe Marsala, clarinet and alto; George Brunies, trombone; Dick Cary,piano;
     Zutty Singleton,drums; Eddie Condon,guitar.--DB 2/11/46):
OdA-----. Walkin' the Dog/Lazy Daddy

        JOE MARSALA'S ALL TIMERS (Bobby Hackett, cornet: Joe Marsala, clarinet;Frank
        Orchard, trombone; Gené Schroeder,piano; Eddie Condon,guitar· Rollo Laylan,
        drums; Bob Casey, bass):                                    March 23,1944
Sav 10001. Tiger Rag/Clarinet Marmalade
Sav      . Joe's Blues/Village Blues

     (Marsala, clarinet; Pete Brown, alto; Charlie Shavers,piano and trumpet;Al
     Casey, guitar and drums; Specs Powell, piano and drums; Al Matthews, bass
     and violin.):                                              July 21,1944
Sig      . Blues Before Dawn/Escapade
Sig      . Roses of Picardy/When the Moon Comes Over the Mountain

        JOE MARSALA SEPTET (Joe Marsala, clarinet: Chuck Wayne, guitar; Joe Thomas,
        trumpet; Adele Girard, harp; Charlie Queener,piano; Irving Lang, bass;Bud-
        dy Christian, drums):                                   Nov.29,1944
BW  1201. Zero Hour/Romance
BW  1202. Joe Joe Jump/Don't Let It End

        (Sub. Sid Weiss, bass):                                 May 4,1945
Mu   328. Gotta Be This or That/Southern Comfort
Mu   329. Lover(5285-1)/Don't Let It End(5286-1)

     (Joe Marsala, clarinet; Marty Marsala, trumpet: Adele Girard,harp; Chuck
     Wayne, guitar; Gene di Novi, piano):
Mu   344. East of the Sun/Slightly Dizzy

     (Joe Marsala, clarinet; Dizzy Gillespie, trumpet: Cliff Jackson, piano;
     Chuck Wayne, guitar; Irving Lang, bass):
BW    18. My Melancholy Baby/Cherokee

GILBERT MARSH ORCHESTRA (Miff Mole reissues):
  PaA 34038. Navy Blues(no vocal)/Sweeping the Clouds Away
  PaA 34040. Navy Blues (vocal)
  PaA 34041. Lucky Little Devil

CARL MARTIN (blues singer, acc. by Chuck Segar, piano):
  Ch 50074. I'm Gonna Have My Fun(90635)/High Water Flood Blues(instrumental)

DAISY MARTIN (vocal):
  Ge  4712. Royal garden Blues/Spread Yo' Stuff
  Re  9548. Feelin' Blue/What You Was
  OK  8001. Play 'em for Mama Sing 'em for Me/I Won't Be Back 'Till You Change
                                                                   (Your Ways
     (Acc. by Tampa Blue Jazz Band):
  OK  8027. Brown Skin (duet with Clarence Williams)/If You Don't Wang Me

SARA MARTIN (voc. acc. by Clarence Williams, piano):
  OK  4904. Where Can That Somebody Be(s71629A)/Goin' Down to the Levee(s71655B)
  OK  8009. How Long/I Didn't Start
  OK  8041. Sugar Blues(s70935D)/Achin' Hearted Blues(s70990B)

     (Acc. by Thomas Waller, piano):
  OK  8043. 'Tain't Nobody's Bus'ness If I Do(s71068c)
       "   You Got Ev'rything a Sweet Mama Needs(s71069B)
  OK  8045. Mama's Got the Blues(s71105B)/Last Go Round Blues(s71106B)

     (Clarence Williams, piano):
  OK  8058. Joe Turner Blues(s71391B)/(ESTHER BIGEOU)
  OK  8060. Keeps on a-Rainin'(s71390B)/Michigan Water Blues(s71398B)

     (Acc. W.C. Handy's Orchestra):
  OK  8061. Come Home Papa Blues/It Takes a Long Time to Get 'em
  OK  8064. Laughin' Cryin' Blues/Sweet Baby Goodbye(acc.Cry Baby Godfrey,piano)

     (Clarence Williams, piano):
  OK  8062. Original Blues/I Got What It Takes(duets with Shelton Brooks)
  OK  8063. If Your Man Is Like My Man(s71399B)/Cruel Backbitin'Blues(s71449A)
  OK  8065. Leave My Sweet Daddy Along/(ESTHER BIGEOU)
  OK  8067. Monkey Man Blues(s71455B),duet with Clarence Williams/Yodeling Blues
           (371465A),duet with Eva Taylor and cornet obligato by Thomas Morris
  OK  8078. Nobody in Town Can Bake Sweet Jelly Roll Like Mine/If You Don't Like
                                                              (it Leave it
     (Duet with Eva Taylor: piano, Clarence Williams; Cornet obligato, Thomas
  OK  8082. Hesitation Blues/That Free and Easy Papa o' Mine       (Morris):
```

(Clarence Williams, piano):
OK 8083. Ye Shall Reap Just What You Sow/You Just Can't Have no One Man
OK 8084. Just Thinkin' Blues(s71630A)/Tired o' Waitin' Blues(s71653B)
OK 8085. New Orleans Hop Scop Blues(s71669B)/Uncle Sam Blues(s71670B)
OK 8086. Mistreated Mama Blues/Runnin' 'round With the Blues
OK 8087. Jelly's Blues/My Good Man's Blues
OK 8088. Sweet Man Was the Cause of it All(s71696B)/Sympathizing Bl(s71697B)

(Acc. by Clarence Williams Blue Five: Thomas Morris, cornet; Charlie Irvis, trombone; Buddy Christian, banjo; Clarence Williams, piano; Sidney Bechet, soprano sax.--JI 11/22/40):
OK 8090. Blind Man Blues(s71711B)/Atlanta Blues(s71712B)

(Clarence Williams Harmonizing Four):
OK 8099. Graveyard Dream Blues(s71961B)/A Green Gal Can't Catch on(s71962B)
(Unknown accompaniment):
OK 8093. Trouble Blues/I'm satisfied
OK 8097. Blue Gum Blues/Slow Down Sweet Papa Mama's Catchin' Up

(Acc. by Sylvester Weaver, guitar):
OK 8104. I've Got to Go and Leave My Daddy Behind(s71981A)/Roamin' bl(s71998A)
OK 8117. Longing for Daddy Blues(s71980A)/Goodbye Blues(s71999B)
OK 8136. Everybody's Got the Blues(8582A)/My Man Blues(8583A)

(Duet with Clarence Williams):
OK 8108. I'm Cert'nly Gonna See 'Bout That(s71984B)/Squabbling Bl(s71985B)

(Sylvester Weaver, guitar):
OK 8146. Every Woman Needs a Man/Got to Leave My Home Blues

(Williams' Harmonizers):
OK 8154. He's Never Gonna Throw Me Down(72587)/Too Late Now to Get Your Baby
(Back(72592),piano acc.,Williams
(Wylvester Weaver, guitar):
OK 8161. Pleading Blues/If I Don't Find My Brown I Won't Be Back

(Acc. by Sara Martin's Jug Band):
OK 8166. Jug Band Blues(s72825B)/Don't You Quit Me Daddy(s72832B)
OK 8176. I Got the Crying Blues(s72833B)/Blues Please Go Away(s72835B)
OK 8188. Blue Devil Blues/Jug Band Blues

(Acc. Clarence Williams, piano):
OK 8172. Cage of Apes/Sobbin' Hearted Blues
OK 8191. I'd Rather Be Blue Than Green(s72855B)/What Kind'a Man Is You
(s72846B,piano, Lemuel Fowler
(Acc. Clarence Williams Blue Five):
OK 8203. Eagle Rock Me Papa/Things Done Got Too Thick

(Sara Martin's Jug Band):
OK 8211. I'm Gonna Be a Lovin' Old Soul/I Ain't Got No Man
OK 8214. Strange Lovin' Blues(acc.string trio)/Can't Find Nobody to Do Like
My Old Daddy Do(acc. guitar-banjo)
OK 8226. Some Blues(acc. piano)/Poor Me Blues(acc.Sylvester Weaver)
OK 8231. Papa Papa Blues/Come Back Daddy and Ease My Aching Heart
OK 8237. I Can Always Tell When a Man Is Treatin' Me Cool(9030A; string trio)
Daddy Ease This Pain of Mine(9025A; acc. guitar-banjo)

(Clarence Williams, piano):
OK 8249. Old Fashioned Sara Blues(s72853B)/I'm Sorry Blues(9024A,banjo-guitar)

(Acc. Harry's Happy Four):
OK 8262. Yes Sir That's My Baby(73799B)/Alabamy Bound(73780B)

(Duet with Clarence Williams; acc. by Williams Blue Five: June Clark, cornet; Jimmy Harrison, trombone; Len Fields, sax; Williams,piano.--JI 11/41):
OK 8270. I'm Gonna Hoodoo You(73773B)/You Going Ain't Giving Me the Blues
(73774B)
(Solo, with same accompaniment):
OK 8283. What More Can a Monkey Woman Do(73775B)/Down at the Razor Ball
(73753B),trombone,cornet & Piano
(Unknown accompaniment):
OK 8292. Forget Me Not Blues/Some of These Morns
OK 8304. Give Me a Little/Nobody Knows and Nobody Cares
OK 8308. That Dance/The Last Time

(Acc. Clarence Williams Blue Five):
OK 8325. Brother Ben(74072A)/Careless Man Blues(74074B)
OK 8336. What's the Matter Now/I Want Every Bit of It
OK 8374. Some Sweet Day/Late Last Night

(Clarence Williams, piano):
OK 8394. A Glass of Beer, a Hot Dog and You(74335B)/Look Out Mr.Jazz(74336B)
OK 8412. Shipwrecked Blues(74338B)/Numbers on the Brain(74337B)

14

```
        (Unknown accompaniment):
   OK  8427. Georgia Stockade Blues/Mournful Blues
   OK  8442. How Could I Be Blue/Prisoners Blues

        (Clarence Williams Blue Five):
   OK  8461. Cushion Foot Stomp(80712B)/Take Your Black Bottom Ourside(80713B)
   OK  8513. Ornery Blues/Loving Is What I Need

        (Acc. by Clarence Williams Orchestra, possibly including King Oliver,cornet):
   QRS 7042. Death Sting Me Blues(278A)/Mistreating Man Blues(306   -Para 12841
```

BILLY MASON AND HIS ORCHESTRA (Billy Mason, piano: Duncan Whyte, trumpet; Buddy
Featherstonhaugh, tenor; David Shand, clarinet and alto; Alan Ferguson, guitar;
George Elrick, drums; Bill Busby, bass):   England, May,1935
   DeE 5564. Don't Be Angry(TB-1790)/If You Knew Susie(TB-1789)   -Ch 40035
   DeE 5773. My Mammy/Paradise

MASON-DIXON ORCHESTRA (Frank Trumbauer, Charles Strickfadden, saxes; Izzy Friedman, clarinet; Andy Secrest, Charles Margulies, cornets: Joe Venuti, violin;Len-
nie Hayton, piano; Eddie Lang, guitar; Stanley King, drums; Min Leibrook,bass):
   Co   1861. Alabammy Snow(148538)/What a Day(148537)

MATSON'S CREOLE SERENADERS, CHARLIE:
   Ed 51222. 'Tain't Nobody's Business If I Do
   Ed 51224. I Just Want a Daddy

EMMETT MATTHEWS AND HIS ORCHESTRA
   Vo 3226. There's Always a Happy Ending/I'll Stand By
   Vo 3228. You Can't Pull the Wool Over My Eyes/Take a Good Look at Mine
   Vo 3317. The Way You Look Tonight/Bojangles of Harlem
   Vo 3332. You Came to My Rescue/Night in Manhattan

TINY MAYBERRY (blues singing with orchestra):
   De 7496. Oh That Nasty Man/Someday Someday
   De 7520. Evil Hearted Woman/Mayberry Blues
   De 7593. I Got a Feeling for You/Mailman Blues

NORRIDGE MAYHAM AND HIS BARBECUE BOYS:
   Vo 03429. Ash haulin' Blues/Enuff to Run You
   Vo 03465. Wrap Your Troubles in Dreams/If I Had My Way

BERT MAYS (blues singing with piano):
Para 12614. Mam's Mind Blues/Toublesome Mind Blues
Para 12632. Oh Oh Blues/Midnight Rambler Blues

TOMMY McCLENNAN (blues singer):
   BB 8347. You Can't Mistreat Me Here/New Shake em on Down
   BB 8373. Whiskey Head Woman/Bottle It Up and Go
   BB 8408. Baby Don't You Want to Go/Cotton Patch Blues
   BB 8444. Brown Skin Girl/Baby Please Don't Tell on Me
   BB 8499. New Highway No. 51/I'm Goin' Don't You Know
   BB 8545. My Baby's Doggin' Me/She's a Good Looking Woman
   BB 8605. She's Just Good Huggin' Size/My Little Girl
   BB 8669. My Baby's Gone/It's Hard to Be Lonesome
   BB 8853. Classy Mae Blues/Des'e My Blues
   BB 8897. Cross Cut Saw Blues/You Can't Read My Mind
   BB 8957. I'ma Guitar King/Travelin' Highway Man
   BB 9005. It's a Cryin' Pity/Deep Blue Sea Blues
   BB 9015. Mozelle Blues/Mo. So and So Blues
   BB 340706. Blue As I Can Be/Roll Me Baby
   BB 340716. I Love My Baby/Shake It Up and Go

GEORGE McCLENNON'S JAZZ DEVILS (George McClennon, clarinet; probably Eddie Hey-
wood, Sr., piano; et al):
   OK 8143. Box of Blues(s72512B)/Dark Alley Blues(s72513B)
   OK 8150. New Orleans Wiggle(s72524B)/Michigan Water Blues(s72525B)
   OK 8236. Anybody Here Want to Try My Cabbage/Home Alone Blues
                  (See also: Harlem Trio):

CHARLES McCOY (vocal):
   Br 7141. Last Time Blues/(WALTER VINCENT)
   Br 7156. Your Valves Need Grinding/It's Hot Like That(with Walter Vincent)
   Br 7165. Blue Heaven Blues/Glad Hand Blues

     McCOY AND THE MISSISSIPPI HOT FOOTERS:
   Br 7118. It Ain't No Good, I & 2
   OK 8773. You Gonna Need Me/Always in Love
   OK 8881. I've Been Blue/So Good #2

        (with Bo Carter):
   OK 8853. Mississippi I'm Longin' for You/Northern Starvers Are Returning Home

```
            (Unknown accompaniment):
      Vo  1726. Bottle It Up
      De  7037. Motherless and Fatherless Blues

VIOLA McCOY (vocal):
      Ge  5108. If You Want to Keep Your Daddy Home/Laughing Crying Blues
      Ge  5128. Midnight Blues/Triflin' Blues

            (Acc. Bob Ricketts' Band):
      Ge  5151. Gulf Coast Blues/Tired o' Waitin'

            (Acc. Porter Grainger, piano):
      Ge  5175. Long Lost Mama(8389A)/Wish I Had You(8390)

            (Unknown accompaniment):
      Vo 14633. Bleeding Hearted Blues/If You Want to Keep Your Daddy Home
      Vo 14632. Sad and Lonely Blues/Just Thinking
      Vo 14801. It Makes No Difference Now/West End Blues

            (Duet with Billy Higgins: acc. piano & cornet):
      Vo 14912. Deep on Going                               -Aj 17066, Si 3019
           "    Get Yourself a Monkey Man                        "

            (Unknown accompaniment):
      Vo 15245. Shake That Thing/Stomp Your Blues

            (Acc. Fletcher Henderson Jazz Five):
      Br  2591. If Your Good Man Quits You Don't Wear Black/I ain't Gonna Marry
                     Ain't Gonna Settle Down
            (Acc. Kansas City Five):
      Ed 51478. Memphis Bound(98600-12)

            (Cornet and piano accompaniment):
      Ro   302. I'm Savin' It All for You(2219-C2)/Papa If You Can't Do Better(2220-B2)
      Ro   374. Git Goin'(110-A1)/Some Day You'll Come Back to Me(111-A2)  -Ca 1097
      Ro   375. Slow Up Papa/Fortune Teller Blues
      Ro   385. Black Snake Blues(2447-C1)/Soul and Body(2448-B2)
      Co 14395. If You Really Love Your Baby(147773)/I Want a Good Man(147772)

McCOY AND JOHNSON (singing with guitar)
      Vi 23313. Don't Want No Woman/I Never Told a Lie

HATTIE McDANIEL (acc. by Lovie Austin's Blues Serenaders):
      OK  8434. I Wish I Had Somebody/Boo Hoo Blues
      OK  8569. I Thought I'd Do It/Just One Sorrowing Look

            (Acc. piano and cornet):
      Para 12751. Dentist Chair Blues, 1 & 2
      Para 12790. Any Kind of Man/New Love Maker

            (Acc. by Louis Armstrong, trumpet: Earl Hines, piano; Boyd Atkins, soprano
            sax; Stomp Evans, baritone sax; Honore Dutrey, trombone: Rip Bassett, ban-
            jo):                                                    May 10,1927
      OK(unissued) Sam Henry Blues(80852)/Poor Boy Blues(80853)

HELEN McDONALD (acc. by Lemuel Fowler, piano):
      Ge  5193. Squawkin' the Blues(8431)/You Got Everything(8432)

EARL McDONALD'S ORIGINAL LOUISVILLE JUG BAND:
      Co 14255. She's in the Graveyard Now/She Won't Quit But Slow Down
```

DICK McDONOUGH

```
See also:
   MILDRED BAILEY: Vo 3056, 3057.
   CHARLESTON CHASERS: Co 446, 861,909,1076,1229,1260,1539,1891,1925,2415.
   DORSEY BROTHERS: All Brunswicks
   CLIFF EDWARDS: Pe 11637.
   GENE GIFFORD: Vi 25041, 25065.
   BENNY GOODMAN: Co 2835,2845,2856,2867,2871,2892,2907· CoE 730.
   BILLIE HOLIDAY: Vo 3276, 3288, 3333, 3334.
   JAM SESSION: Vi 25559.
   CARL KRESS: Br 6917, 7885.
   JOHNNY MERCER: De 142.
   GLENN MILLER:
   RED NICHOLS: Br 3626, 3627.
   RED NORVO: Br 6906.
   ADRIAN ROLLINI: De 265, 359; VoE 191.
   JACK TEAGARDEN: Co 2558.
   JOE VENUTI: CoE 637, 686, 708: Co 2783.
```

DICK McDONOUGH AND HIS ORCHESTRA (Artie Shaw, Adrian Rollini, Chauncey Morehouse, Larry Binyon, Claude Thornhill are featured on some of these records, which have not been sorted out. Bunny Berigan is said to play on those marked with an asterisk):
(In most cases, Melotone numbers are interchangeable with Perfect and/or Oriole)
   Me 60807. Take My Heart/Stars in My Eyes
   Me 60808. The Scene Changes/On the Beach at Bali Bali
   Me 60907. I'm Greateful to You(19467)/Summer Holiday(19466)
   Me 60908. Dear Old Southland*/Way Down Yonder in New Orleans*
   Me 61101. South Sea Island Magic/Afterglow
   Me 61102. In a Sentimental Mood/It Ain't Right
   Me 61104. Midnight Blue/When the Moon Hangs High
   Me 61202. I'm One Step Ahead of My Shadow(19891)/Now or Never(19892)
   Me 61203. You're Giving Me a Song and Dance/Love What Are You Doing to My Heart
   Me 70107. With Thee I Swing*/I'm in a Dancing Mood*   -Cq 8761
   Me 70111. Tea on the Terrace/There's Frost on the Moon
   Me 70204. Dardanella*/Between the Devil and the Deep Blue Sea*   -VoE 0004
   Me 70311. The Girl on the Police Gazette/He Ain't Got Rhythm
   Me 70312. I Can't Lose That Longing for You/The Goona Goo
   Me 70502. The Mood That I'm In
   Me 70518. Shall We Dance/Beginner's Luck
   Me 70603. Spring Cleaning/I'm Never Blue Where the Grass Is Green
   Me 70614. All God's Chillun Got Rhythm
   Me 70707. You're Looking for Romance/And Then They Called it Love
   Me 70716. Two Hearts Are Dancing/Don't Ever Change
   Me 70908. Public Melody No. 1/Cabin of...
   Me 71004. Have You Got Any Castles Baby/Love Is on the Air Tonight
   Me 71102. That Old Feeling*/The Big Apple*
   Me 71111. You and I Know/An Old Flame

CHARLIE McFADDEN (singing acc. by Dobby Bragg, piano):
 Para 12928. People People Blues(L154-1)/Groceries on the Shelf(L155-1)
 Para 13076. Yellow Woman Blues/Groceries on the Shelf #2

   (vocal duet with Dobby Bragg):
 Para 13093. St. Louis Tricks Woman/You Got That Thing

   SPECKS McFADDEN:
 De 7315. People People/Groceries on My Shelf

REV. F. W. McGEE (sermons with singing):
 OK 8438. I'm Glad My Lord Saved Me
 Vi 20858. He Is a Saviour for Me
 Vi 38028. Crucifision of Jesus
 Vi 38583. I've Seen the Devil/Holes in Your Pocket
 BB 5261. Babylon Is Falling Down/Jonah in the Belly of the Whale
 BB 5345. Nothing to Do in Hell/Fifty Miles of Elbow Room

BROWNIE McGHEE (Blind Boy Fuller No. 2: vocal blues with instrumental acc.):
 OK 05785. Picking My Tomatoes/Night Rambling Woman(with Fuller)
 OK 05812. Let Me Tell You 'Bout My Baby/My Barkin' Bulldog Blues
 OK 05881. Not Guilty blues/Poison Woman Blues
 OK 05923. Me and My Dog Blues (BLIND BOY FULLER)
 OK 06007. Back Door Stranger/I'm Callin' Daisy
 OK 06056. Be Good to Me/Born for Bad Luck

HOWARD McGHEE (trumpet, acc. by two tenor saxes and rhythm):
 Philo 115. Stardust
 Philo 116. Lifestream
 Philo 117. Intersection
 Philo 118. Mop Mop

   HOWARD McGHEE AND HIS ORCHESTRA (McGhee, trumpet; Vernon Bittle, piano: Charles Mingus, bass; Teddy Edwards, tenor sax; Nat McFay, drums; Stanley Morgan, guitar):
 Mod 111. Deep Meditation/(HADDA BROOKS)
 Mod 120. Play Boy Blues(Pearl Traylor, vc)/11:45 Swing
 Mod 124. Around the Clock, 1 & 2 (Pearl Traylor, vc)
 Mod 125. Gee I'm Lonesome(Pearl Traylor,vc)/Call It the Blues(Estelle Edison,vc)
 Mod 136. McGhee Special/McGhee Jumps

JIMMY McHUGH'S BOSTONIANS (featuring Benny Goodman, clarinet; Jack Teagarden, trombone; Jimmy McPartland, cornet):
 Ha 736. I Don't Care(147062)/(THE HARMONIANS)   -Ve 1763
 Ha 795. Baby(147495)/(JERRY MASON)   -Ve 1795
 Ha 823. In a Great Big Way(147761)/Let's Sit and Talk About(147760)-Ve 1823
 Ha 836. The Whoopee Stomp(147497)/Futuristic Rhythm(147759)   -Ve 1836
 Ha 899. Remember I Love You(147496)*
    *Issued as Sunny Clapp and Band o' Sunshine

ARTHUR McKAY (blues singing):
 De 7068. Central Limited Blues/Heavy Stuff Blues
 De 7364. She Squeezed My Lemon/Somebody's Been Ricin' My Black Gal

McKENZIE'S CANDY KIDS (Red McKenzie, vocals; Jack Bland, banjo; Dick Slevin, kazoo):
- Vo 14977. Panama/When My Sugar Walks Down the Street
- Vo 14978. Best Black/Stretch It, Boy
- Vo 15088. Morning After Blues/Happy Children
- Vo 15166. Hot Honey/If You Never Come Back
- Vo 15539. Nervous Puppies/What Do I Care What Somebody Said   -BrE 02507

RED McKENZIE AND HIS MUSIC BOX (with Eddie Lang, guitar; Joe Venuti, violin):
1927
- OK 40893. There'll Be Some Changes Made(81037B)/My Wyncopated Melody Man(81038C)
  -PaE 3382, OdF 165194
  (Add Eddie Condon, guitar):   1928
- OK 41071. My Baby Came Home(400720)/From Monday On(400721)   -PaE 184

RED McKENZIE AND THE SIX SPIRITS OF RHYTHM (Teddy Bunn, Leo Watson, Wilbur and Douglas Daniels, vocals and guitars; Virgil Scoggins, traps: Wilson Myers, bass):   1934
- De 186. From Monday On   -BrE 01891
- "   Way Down Yonder in New Orleans   -BrE 01997
- De 243. It's All Forgotten Now/What's the Use of Getting Used to You
- De 302. As Long As I Live   -BrE 01891
- "   I've Got the World on a String   -BrE 01997

RED McKENZIE AND HIS RHYTHM KINGS (McKenzie, vocal: Slats Long, clarinet; Mike Riley, trombone: Ed Farley, trumpet: Conrad Lanoue, piano: George Yorke, bass; Eddid Condon(?), guitar; Stan King(?), drums): 1935
- De 507. Let's Swing It
- "   Murder in the Moonlight   -BrE 02088
- De 521. That's What You Think   -BrE 02157
- "   Double Trouble   -BrE 02088
- De 587. Monday in Manhattan(60097A)
- "   Every Now and Then(60098A)   -BrE 02105
- De 609. Wouldn't I Be a Wonder
- "   Georgia Rocking Chair   -BrE 02105

(McKenzie, vocal; Babe Rusin, tenor sax: Bunny Berigan, trumpet; Frank Signorelli, piano; Carmen Mastren, guitar: Sid Weiss, bass; Stan King, drums):
1936
- De 667. Sing an Old Fashioned Song   -BrE 02181
- "   I'm Building Up to an Awful Letdown   -BrE 02167

(Sub. Paul Ricci, tenor; add Al Philburn, trombone):
- De 721. Don't Count Your Kisses   -BrE 02157
- "   I Don't Know Your Name   -BrE 02181
- De 734. Moon Rose(60447B)
- "   When Love Has Gone(60445A)   -BrE 02167
- De 790. I Can Pull a Rabbit Out of My Hat/I Can't Get Started With You

RED McKENZIE AND HIS ORCHESTRA (Unknown personnel, except Bunny Berigan on on first record):
- Vr 520. Wanted(M137)/Sweet Lorraine(M136)
- Vr 589. I Cried for You/the Trouble With Me Is You
- Vo 2534. It's the Talk of the Town/This Time It's Love
- Vo 3898. Georgiana/Out of This World
- Co 2556. Just Friends/Time on My Hands
- Co 2587. I'm Sorry Dear/I Found You
- Co 2620. Can't We Talk It Over/There's Something in Your Eyes
- Co 2645. Lovable/Dream Sweetheart

RED McKENZIE (with orchestra directed by Ernie Caceres, baritone sax; Billy Butterfield, trumpet; Lou McGarity, Buddy Morrow, Frank D'Annolfo, trombones; Jess Stacy, piano; Red Norvo, vibraphone: Carl Kress, guitar: George Wettling, drums; Bob Casey, bass):   Oct.5,1944
- Com 562. It's the Talk of the Town(A4827-1)/Wherever There's Love(A4829-2)
- Com 572. Sweet Lorraine/Through a Veil of Indifference
          (See also: Mound City Blue Blowers)

McKENZIE AND CONDON'S CHICAGOANS (Jimmy McPartland, cornet Frank Teschemacher, clarinet; Bud Freeman, tenor sax; Joe Sullivan, piano; Eddie Condon, banjo; Jim Lannigan, bass; Gene Krupa, drums):   Dec.16,1927
- OK 40971. Nobody's Sweetheart(82082B)   -UHCA 11, Co 35952, PaF 85378, PaE 643
- "   Liza(82083A)   -UHCA 12, Co 35952, PaF 85377, PaE 379
- OK 41011. Sugar(82030A)/China Boy(82031B)-UHCA 10,Co 35951, PaF 85363, PaE 2379

McKENZIE AND CONDON'S BOYS (Frank Teschemacher, clarinet: Eddie Condon, banjo; probably Joe Sullivan, piano; Krupa, drums: Mezz Mezzrow, tenor sax; possibly Muggy Spanier, cornet,--JI 3/21/31):   Chicago, March 27, 1928
- Br(unissued). Jazz Me Blues (C1808 & C1809)/Singing the Blues (C1810 & C1811)

(Teschemacher, clarinet & alto; Rod Cless, alto; Mezzrow, tenor; Sullivan; Condon; Krupa):   April 28,1928
- Br(unissued). Singin' the Blues(C1905A & B)/Jazz Me Blues(C1906B)
- UHCA 61. Jazz Me Blues(C1906A) issued from test pressing under name of
           Frank Teschemacher's Chicagoans. (See also: Chicago Rhythm Kings)

McKENZIE, WILLIE MAE (blues singing):
Vo 3552. Papa Don't Hold Out on Me/I'm Getting Even With You

McKENZIE AND CRUMP (vocals with piano):
Para 12857. Who's Gonna Do Your Jelly Rollin'(1536)/That's a Married Man's Weak-
(ness (1537)
McKINLEY'S JAZZ BAND, RAY (Ray McKinley, drums; Skeets Herfurt, clarinet; George
Thow, cornet; Joe Yukl, trombone: Joe Sullivan, piano: Jim Taft, bass):
De 1019. Love in the First Degree   -BrE 02374
  "   New Orleans Parade   -De 3685,   "
De 1020. Shack in the Back(DLA 330A)/Fingerwave(DLA 331A)

    RAY McKINLEY & FREDDIE SLACK (drums and piano):
Co 35963. Southpaw Serenade(CO 29526)/(WILL BRADLEY ORCHESTRA)

    RAY McKINLEY QUARTET (McKinley, drums: Slack, piano: Peanuts Hucko, tenor;
    D. Goldberg, bass):
Co 36101. Tea for Two/(WILL BRADLEY ORCHESTRA)   -PaE 2849
        (See also: All Will Bradley recordings)

McKINNEY'S COTTON PICKERS (Don Redman,George Thomas,Milton Senior,saxes; Prince
Robinson,tenor sax and clarinet: John Nesbit,Langston Curl,trumpets: Claude
Jones,trombone; Todd Rhodes,piano: Cuba Austin,drums: Dave Wilborn,banjo; Robert
Escudero,tuba):   July 11-12,1928
Vi 21583. Four or Five Times(46093)/(CLIFFORD HAYES
Vi 21611. Milenberg Joys(46096)   -BB 10954
  "   Shimme-sha-wabble(46402)   -Vi 400114
Vi 21730. Cherry(46098)   -Vi 400114, BB 6304
  "   Some Sweet Day(46401)
Vi 38000. Crying and Sighing(46095)   -HMV 6287,HMV 4892
  "   Nobody's Sweetheart(46400)   -BB 5728,HMV 4892
Vi 38025. Put It There(46094)
  "   Stop Kidding(46099)

    (Sub. James Dudley,alto,for Senior):   Chicago, Nov.23,1928
Vi 38013. It's Tight Like That(48619)
  "   There's a Rainbow 'Round My Shoulder(48620)

    (NOTE: Masters 48617 and 48618, attributed to Jean Goldkette on Victor
    21805, may be McKinney sides: also master 46097, a Goldkette release on
    Vi 21590. See DB 11/15/43)

                                                              1929
Vi 38051. It's a Precious Little Thing Called Love(51084)
  "   Do Something(51205)
Vi 38052. Beedle Um Bum(51204)   -BB 6595
  "   Sellin' That Stuff(51206)   "
Vi 38061. Save It Pretty Mama(51085)   -BB 7695
  "   I Found a New Baby(51086)   "
Vi 22932. Will You Won't You Be My Baby(51087)
  "   (For reverse, see next to final personnel)
Vi 38118. If I Could Be With You One Hour(58545)   -HMV 6335
  "   Zonky(59140; Feb. 3, 1930)   -Vi 400115,BB 5728
Vi 38142. I'll Make Fun for You(58543)   -HMV 4907
  "   Then Someone's in Love

    (Don Redman,Benny Carter, Coleman Hawkins, saxes: Joe Smith, Sidney De-
    Paris, Rex Stewart, trumpets: Claude Jones, trombone; James P. Johnson,
    piano; Kaiser Marshall, drums; Billy Taylor, bass; ----banjo or guitar):
Vi 22736. Wherever There's a Will Baby(57140; Lonnie Johnson,guitar)
                                                -BB 10249,HMV 135
Vi 38097. Plain Dirt(57064; Nov. 5, 1929)   -Vi 400115,HMV 4990
  "   Gee, Ain't I Good to You(57065)   -BB 10249,HMV 4967
Vi 38102. Miss Hannah(57068)   -BB 10232,HMV 4901
  "   The Way I Feel Today(57067)   HMV 6204
Vi 38133. Peggy(57139; Lonnie Johnson, guitar) -BB 10706
  "   I'd Love It(57066; Fats Waller,piano)   "   ,HMV 6947

    (Don Redman, George Thomas, saxes: Prince Robinson, tenor and clarinet:
    Cuffee Davidson, Quentin Jackson, trombones; James P. Johnson, piano;
    Smith, Nesbit, Stewart, trumpets: Wilborn; Austin; Taylor):
                                                     July 28-29,1930
Vi 23000. Okay Baby(64004)   -HMV 4837
  "   I Want a Little Girl(64007)   BB 10954

```
       Vi 23012. Just a Shade Corn(64002)                        -HMV 4931
              "  Cotton Picker's Scat(64008)                         "
       Vi 400116. Blues Sure Have Got Me
       Vi 22511. Baby Won't You Please Come Home(64003)    -Vi 400116
              "  Hullabaloo(64006)                               -HMV   24
       Vi 22683. I Want Your Love(63195)/(EARL HINES)
       Vi 23031. Hello(63196)
              "  (For coupling, see next personnel)
                 (Sub. Edward Inge, alto, for Thomas):
       Vi 23031. You're Driving Me Crazy(64056)            -HMV 6286
       Vi 23035. To Whom It May Concern(64055)
              "  Come a Little Closer(64058)
                                                                Nov.4,1930
                 (Sub. Buddy Lee, trumpet, for Nesbit; add Benny Carter, sax; Todd Rhodes,
                 piano):
       Vi 22640. Talk to Me(64605)/(BLANCHE CALLOWAY)      -HMV 487C,HMV 6087
       Vi 23020. Never Swat a Fly(64608)                   -Vi 400117, HMV 24
              "  Laughing at Life(64607)
       Vi 23024. After All You're All I'm After(64609)     -HMV 6262
              "  I Miss a Little Miss(64610)
       Vi 22932. Rocky Road(64606)                         -Vi 400117,HMV 4914
       Vi 22628. She's My Secret Passion(67935)
              "  It's a Lonesome Old Town(67934)
                 (Sub. Adolphus Cheatham, trumpet, for Lee· Jimmie Dudley, Wilton Jeffer-
                 son, saxes, for Redman, Thomas):
       Vi 22811. Do You Believe in Love at Sight(68300)
              "  Wrap Your Troubles in Dreams(70495)

McKINNEY, SADIE (Acc. by cornet and piano):
       Vi 2Q565. Brownskin Flapper/Rock Away Blues
```

Down in New Orleans

•

There's a new place for collectors to meet . . . The crescent city's first exclusive phonograph record store, featuring all the current labels—plus a large stock of collectors items . . . Write for auction list now available, and when in New Orleans visit Orin Blackstone at the . . .

•

New Orleans Record Shop

439 Baronne Street   New Orleans 13, La.

McLEAN AND HIS RHYTHM ORCHESTRA, CONNIE
BB   6474. Without a Shadow of a Doubt/Sing Sing Sing
BB   6482. High Falutin' Stomp(Alex Miller, v.c.)
  "   All I Want In This World Is You(Alex Miller & Chubby Wright, v.c.)
BB   6485. Breeze Ray Breeze(Ludwick Brown,v.c.)/How Can You Face Me(Chubby
                                                              (Wright,v.c.)
    CONNIE McLEAN AND HIS RHYTHM BOYS:
De   7175. I Can't Use That Thing/Rockin' My Troubles
De   7176. Shylock Blues/Sissy Man Blues
De   7189. When the Breath Bids the Body Goodbye/You Done Lost Your Good
                                                              (Thing Now

JIMMY McPARTLAND

See also
  ALL STAR ORCHESTRA: Uncertain.
  JIMMY BRACKEN: Re 8723, 8768, 8813, 8826: Do 4274: Ba 6295.
  BROADWAY BROADCASTERS: Ca 1149,8228,9008,9023,9130,9152; Ro 1043.
  CAROLINERS: Ca 9042.
  EDDIE CONDON: OK 41142.
  LOU CONNOR: Or 1483.
  COTTON PICKERS: Ca 9048, 9207.
  DIXIE DAISIES: Ca 9004, 9035: Ro 887: Li 3169.
  DIXIE JAZZ BAND: Or 1396, 1363, 1515, 1536, 1537, 1624, 1668, 1690.
  JEAN GOLDKETTE: Many
  BENNY GOODMAN: Vo 15656, Br 3975, 4013.
  GOODY AND HIS GOOD TIMERS: Pat 36902, 36903, 36924.
  GRANT AND WILSON: Ca 9015.
  HOTSY TOTSY GANG: Br 4014, 4044, 4112, 4122, 4200.
  EDDY HOWARD: Co 35455, 35471, 35511, 35599, 35747.
  KENTUCKY GRASSHOPPERS: Ba 6295, 6360, 6355, 6358, 6441, 6483.
  LOUISVILLE RHYTHM KINGS: OK 41189, PaF 22305.
  LUMBERJACKS: Ca 9030.
  IRVING MILLS:
  McKENZIE-CONDON: OK 40971, 41011.
  JIMMY McHUGH: Ha 763, 795, 823, 836, 899.
  NEW ORLEANS RAMBLERS: Me 12133, 12230.
  BEN POLLACK:
  JACK PETTIS: HMV 4893.
  GIL RODIN: Re 8813, Ba 6483.
  VARSITY EIGHT:
  WHOOPEE MAKERS:
  WOLVERINES: Br and Vo. Ge 5620.

McPARTLAND'S SQUIRRELS, JIMMY (Jimmy McPartland, trumpet: Joe Harris, trombone;
Rosy MacHargue, clarinet: Dick Clark, tenor sax; Jack Gardner, piano Dick Mc-
Partland, guitar; Country Washburn, tuba; George Wettling, drums): Chicago, 1936
HRS 1003. I'm All Bound 'Round With the Mason-Dixon Line   -De 18441
  "   Eccentric   -De 3363
HRS 1004. Panama   -De 3363
  "   Original Dixieland One Step   -De 18441
    JIMMY McPARTLAND AND HIS ORCHESTRA (Jimmy McPartland, trumpet· Floyd Bean,
    piano; Boyce Brown, alto sax; Bud Jacobson, clarinet: Dick McPartland, gui-
    tar; Jim Lannigan, bass; Hank Isaacs, drums):   1939
De 18042. Jazz Me Blues(91832A)/Chiha Boy(91833A)   -BrE 03057
De 18043. The World Is Waiting for Sunrise(91834A)/Sugar(91835A) -BrE 03058

    McPARTLAND'S V-CORPS SEXTETTE (McPartland, cornet: Tony Barbaro,clarinet;
    Johnnie Savina, alto: Charlie Patrick, piano: Johnny McKenna, bass; Tommy
    Hubbard, drums.--DB 9/15/45)   Brussels, May 1,1945
-- -----. Basin Street Blues/Georgia on My Mind
-- -----. Jazz Me Blues/Blues

McPHERSON, OZIE (vocal blues, acc. Fletcher Henderson's Orchestra):
  Para 12355. Nobody Rolls Their Jelly Roll Like Mine(2455-3)
    "   I'm So Blue Since My Sweetie Went Away(2456-3)
  Para 12362. Down to the Bottom Where I Stayed(2422)/I Want My Lovin'(2453)

        (Acc. Lovie Austin's Blues Serenaders):
  Para 12327. Outside of That(287)/You Gotta Know How(288)
  Para 12350. Standing on the Corner Blues(2423)/He's My Man(2424)

McSHANN, JAY (piano solos, with singing by Walter Brown*):
  De   8570. Vine Street Boogie/Swingmatism(orchestra)
  De   8607. One Woman's Man*(orchestra)/So You Won't Jump
  De   8595. Red River Blues*/New Confessin' the Blues*
  De   8623. Baby Heart Blues*/Cryin' Won't Make Me Stay*
  De   8635. 'Fore Day Rider/Hootie's Ignorant Oil

    JAY McSHANN AND HIS ORCHESTRA:
  De   4387. Lonely Boy Blues(70993A)/Sepian Stomp(70996A)

(Harold Bruce, Bernard Anderson, Orville Minor, trumpets: Joe Baird, trombone; Bob Mabane, Charles Parker, John Jackson, Harry Ferguson, saxes; McShann, piano; Eugene Ramey, bass: Gus Johnson, drums):
De 8559. Hootie Blues(93731A)/Confessin' the Blues(93734A)
De 8583. Dexter Blues(93732A) -BrE 03401
" " Hold 'em Hootie(93735A), piano, bass, drums
De 4418. Jumpin' Blues/Get Me on Your Mind

JAY McSHANN'S KANSAS CITY STOMPERS (Jay McShann, piano: Oliver Todd, trumpet; Tommy Douglas, alto sax: Claiborne Graves, tenor sax; Efferge Ware, guitar; Walter Page, bass: Baby Lovett, drums; Julia Lee, vocalist):
Cap 10030. Come on Over to My House(F-346B-1)/Trouble in Mind(F347B-1)
Cap 10039. Moten Swing(345B-1)/On the Sunny Side(348A-1) Kansas City,11/1/44

JAY McSHANN AND HIS JAZZ MEN(Cleophus Curtis, tenor sax; Raymond Taylor, bass; Albert Wichard, drums; McShann,piano: E.Gregor*,alto:Major Evans*, trumpet):
Philo 108. Walking/Confessing the Blues*
Philo 109. When I've Been Drinking/Hard Working Man's Blues*
Philo 110. Merry-Go-Round/Bad Tale

JAY McSHANN AND HIS ORCHESTRA:
Mer 8002. Hootie Boogie/Garfield Avenue Blues

McTELL, BLIND WILLIE (vocal with Curly Weaver, guitar):
De 7810. Cold Winter Day/Lay Some Flowers on My Grave

McVEA'S ALL STARS, JACK (Cappie Oliver, trumpet: Jack McVea, tenor; Bob Mosley, piano; Frank Clark, bass; Rabon Tarrant, drums):   Hollywood, Aug.7,1945
Melo 109. Silver Symphony/Scrub Sweep and Mop
Melo 110. New Deal/Fightin' Mama Blues

(M. Royale, clarinet; J.Perdie, trumpet; J. Shackelford, piano; F. Clark, bass; R. Tarrant, drums; J. McVea, tenor):
B&W 750. Bartender Boogie(BW 115-1)/Ooh Mop(BN 114-1)
B&W 751. Frisco Blues/Wine-o
B&W 762. Play It Over(BW 167)/My Business Is C.O.D. (BW169-1)
B&W 763. House Party Boogie/Baby Make Up Your Mind
B&W 767. Jack's Boogie/F Minor Boogie
B&W 768. Jam Boogie/Frantic Boogie
Ap 367. Oo' Wee Baby, oo' Wee/Wiggle Wiggle Woogie

McVEA-BAILEY ORCHESTRA:
Rhythm 502/509. Rainy Day Blues/I'll Be True

MELODY SHEIKS:
OK 40307. Florida/Stepping in Society

FRANK MELROSE

See also:
BEALE STREET WASHBOARD BAND: Vo 1403.
BROADWAY RASTUS: Para 12764.
CELLAR BOYS: Vo 1503; Br 80066.
HARRY'S RECKLESS FIVE: Bwy 1355.
BUD JACOBSON: Sig 103, 106, 904; Jazz 102.
KANSAS CITY FRANK: Br 7062: Para 12898.
KANSAS CITY STOMPERS: Br 7066, 7091.
AL MILLER: Br 7063.
STATE STREET RAMBLERS: Ch 40009, 40007.

MELROSE, FRANK (piano solos, with drums): Feb.19,1929
Ge 6774. Jelly Roll Stomp(14802)/Pass the Jug(14803)
ARC tests.Piano Breakdown (9608) New York,1928-29
"   "   Market Street Jive(9602)
"   "   Distant Moan(9620)
"   "   Whoopee Stomp(9609)
-- ----- 403 Blues   Chicago; privately recorded for Frank Lyons
-- ----- Grandpa's Spells
-- ----- Hammond Boogie
Vs 7---- Carmichael's Cosmics
Vs (test).Josephine (12-inch) Chicago, 1939

(Melrose, piano; Sleepy Caplin, drums: Pete Daley,trumpet; Duney Ward,clarinet; Jack Daley, banjo; Bill Moore, bass):
Vs (test).Sugar Foot Strut
Vs (test).You Viper You
Vs (test).(Untitled)

MEMPHIS FIVE (see Original Memphis Five)

MEMPHIS HOT SHOTS (Duke Ellington Orchestra):
  Ha 1377. I Can't Realize That You Are in Love With Me(100549)   -Ve 2455
  "   I'm So in Love With You(100550)   "

  (Unidentified):
  Ha 1368. Shout Sister Shout(100547)/Baby Won't You Please Come Home(100548)
                                                                              (-Cl 5381
MEMPHIS JAZZERS (None of the many titles issued under this name has any known interest to jazz collectors, except those below, which are believed to feature King Oliver, cornet.--DB 10/1/43):
  VD 7801. Close Fit Blues(3394)*
  "   Moanin' Low   -Rad 1763
  Rad 1804. In Harlem's Araby(3744A)
            *Issued on VD 77038 as New Orleans Pepsters

MEMPHIS JOE (with piano):
  Vo 1277. Plenty Gals Blues/(TAMPA RED)

MEMPHIS JUG BAND:
  OK 8955. Jazzbo Strut/Ruckus Juice and Chittlins
  OK 8956. Tear It Down/Boodie Bum
  OK 8958. Gator Wobble/Business Ain't Right
  OK 8959. Insane Crazy Blues/Bottle It
  OK 8960. Mary Ann/Memphis Shakedown
  OK 8963. Love Is Cold/She Sold It
  OK 8966. Little Green Slippers/Jug Band Quartette
  Vi 20552. Stingy Women/Sun Brimmers
  Vi 20675. Newport News/Memphis Jug
  Vi 21066. Beale Street Mess Around/I'll See You in the Spring
  Vi 20781. I'm Looking for the Bully of the Town/Sunshine Blues
  Vi 20809. Memphis Boy/Sometimes I Think
  Vi 21185. Kansas City Blues/State of Tennessee Blues
  Vi 21278. Papa Long Blues/Coal Oil Blues
  Vi 21412. Bob Lee Jr. Blues/I Packed My Suitcase
  Vi 21524. She Stays Out All Night Long/Snitchin' Gambler
  Vi 21657. Evergreen Money/Peaches
  Vi 21740. Sugar Pudding/Lindberg Hop
  Vi 23251. 4th Street Mess Around/Papa's Got Your Bath
  Vi 38015. On the Road Again/Black Woman Is Like Black Snake
  Vi 38504. Stealin' Stealin'/Whitewash Blues
  Vi 38537. Jug Band Waltz/Mississippi River Waltz
  Vi 38551. What's the Matter/I Can't Stand It
  Vi 38558. Kansas City Moan/Memphis Yo Yo Blues
  Vi 38586. Tired of You/I Can Beat You Plenty
  Vi 38578. I Whipped My Woman With a Singletree
  Vi 38599. Bumble Bee Blues/Everybody's Talking
  Vi 38605. Cave Man/Ambulance Man
  Vi 38620. It Won't Act Right/Cocaine Habit

MEMPHIS MINNIE:
  Co 14439. When the Levee Breaks/That Will
  Vo 1476. I'm Talkin' About You/Bumble Bee
  Vo 1606. Garage Fire Blues/Grandpa and Grandma Blues
  Vo 03046. Joe Louis Strut/In the Ring
  Vo 03187. Minnie's Lonesome/Nobody Home
  Vo 03222. Hoodoo Lady/Ice Man
  Vo 03612. Down in the Alley/Look What
  OK 04797. Bad Outside Friends
  "   Low Down Man Blues   -Cq 9275
  OK 05670. Boy Friend Blues/Nothing in Gambling
  OK 05728. It's Hard to Please My Man
  "   Lonesome Shark Blues   -Cq 9764
  OK 6733. When You Love Me/Love Come and Go
  Cq 9282. Call the Fire Wagon
  Cq 9763. Ma Rainey
  De 7037. Keep It to Yourself/Moaning the Blues
  De 7048. You Can't Give It Away/Dirty Mother for You
  De 7019. Banana Man Blues/Chickasaw Train Blues
  De 7084. Sylvester and His Mule Blues/When You're Asleep
  De 7102. Down in New Orleans/Reachin' Pete

MEMPHIS MOSE (vocal blues):
  Br 7102. Pig Meat Papa/Hear Me Beefin' at You
  Br 7134. Tomorrow Blues/Blue Moanin'
  Br 7143. Billie the Grinder/(AL MILLER BOYS)

MEMPHIS NIGHT HAWKS (Probably Darnell Howard, clarinet; James Blythe, piano: trumpet; trombone· guitar; tenor sax; bass; drums.--DB 9/15/44):   March-April, 1932
  Vo 1736. Jockey Stomp(11622-2)/Sweet Feet(11633-1)
  Vo 1744. Biscuit Roller(11613-2)/Come on In Baby(11627-2)
  Vo 2593. Shanghai Honeymoon(11615-1)/Wild Man Stomp(11623-1)
  Unissued. Slow Drag Blues(11613). Baby If You Can't Do Better(11614). Beedle
     "   um Bum(11616). M. & O Blues(11624). Weary Way Blues(11634).

MEMPHIS SLIM (vocal blues):
    BB 8584. Beer Drinking Woman/Grinder Man Blues
    BB 8615. Empty Room Blues/You Didn't Mean Me No Good
    BB 8645. I See My Great Mistake/Shelby County Blues
    BB 8903. Old Taylor/I Believe I'll Settle Down
    BB 8945. You Gonna Worry Too?/Whiskey and Gin Blues
    BB 8974. This Life I'm Living/Caught the Old Coon at Last

MEMPHIS STOMPERS
    Vi 21270. Hold It Still(41841)/Kansas City Blues(41882)
    Vi 21641. Memphis Stomp(41840)/Goofer Feathers Blues(41883)
    Vi 21709. Yea Alabama/Washington and Lee Swing
    Vi 22737. I'm Blue But Nobody Cares/(EUBIE BLAKE)
    Vi 23371. Gettin' the Bird/Stompin' Away
    Me 12210. Just One More Chance/That's the Time
    Vo 1453. Lotta Sax Appeal/(WILLIAM STOMPERS)
         (See also: Snooks and His Memphis Stompers)

MEMPHIS STRUTTERS:
    Ch 15415. Canned Heat Blues/(ALABAMA FUZZIE WUZZIES

MERCER, JOHNNY (vocal, acc. by orchestra including Jack Teagarden, trombone;Sterling Bose, trumpet, and Dick McDonough, guitar):
    De   142. Lord I Give You My Children(38417)/The Bathtub Ran Over Again(38419)
         (Acc. Frankie Trumbauer's Orchestra):
    Co 18002. Sizzling One Step Medley/Medley of Isham Jones Hits
         (Acc. Eddie Miller's Orchestra):
    Cap 164. Duration Blues/Sam's Got Him

MEROFF AND HIS ORCHESTRA, BENNY (Featuring Wild Bill Davison, trumpet):   #
    Br 4709. Happy Days Are Here Again/The Talk of the Town

         (Actually Frankie Trumbauer's Orchestra: Bix Beiderbecke, Ray Ludwig, trumpets; Bill Rank, trombone: Don Murray, clarinet: Frankie Trumbauer, Doc Ryker, Adrian Rollini, saxes: Joe Venuti, Matty Malneck, Henry Whiteman, violins; Eddie Lang, guitar: Arthur Schutt, piano: Chauncey Morehouse,drums):
    OK 40912. Just an Hour of Love(81499)/I'm Wonderin' Who(81500)   -PaE 3463

         (Wild Bill Davison, trumpet; personnel otherwise unknown):
    OK 40967. Lonely Melody(81889C/When You're With Somebody Else(81919B)
    OK 41171. Smiling Skies(402202C)/Me and the Man in the Moon(402203C)

METRONOME ALL STAR BAND (Toots Mondello, Benny Carter, Coleman Hawkins, Tex Beneke, saxes; Benny Goodman, clarinet; Harry James, Ziggy Elman, Cootie Williams, trumpets; Tommy Dorsey, J.C. Higginbotham, trombones: Count Basie, piano: Charles Christian,   #
guitar; Artie Bernstein, bass; Buddy Rich, drums):   Jan.16,1941
V   Vi 27314. One o'clock Jump/Bugle Call Rag   -HMV 9195

         (Charlie Spivak, Ziggy Elman, Harry James, trumpets: Jack Teagarden, Jack Jenney, trombones: Toots Mondello, Benny Carter, Eddie Miller, Charlie Barnet, saxes; Benny Goodman, clarinet: Gene Krupa, drums; Charlie Christian, guitar; Jess Stacy, piano: Bob Haggart, bass):   1940
    Co 35389. King Porter Stomp(WC026489A)   -PaE 2746

         (ALL STAR NINE) Carter, Christian, Stacy, Teagarden, Goodman, Haggart, James, Miller, Krupa):
    Co 35389. All Star Strut   -PaE 2746

         (Benny Goodman, clarinet: Toots Mondello, Benny Carter, also saxes; Vido Musso, Tex Beneke, tenor saxes: Harry James, Roy Eldridge, Cootie Williams, trumpets: J.C.Higginbotham, Lou McGarity, trombones: Count Basie, piano; Freddie Green, guitar; Doc Goldberg, bass: Gene Krupa, drums):
    Co 36499. Royal Flush(32079)
         (ALL STAR LEADERS: Goodman,Krupa,Basie,Carter,Williams,Higginbotham:Barnet; Alvino Rey, guitar: John Kirby, bass :
    Co 36499. I Got Rhythm

MEYERS, ANNA and the Original Memphis Five:
    Pe 12038. Evil Minded Blues/Last Go 'Round Blues

MEYERS, HAZEL (vocal):
    Vo 14688. Low Down Papa

         (Acc. Joe Smith, cornet; Fletcher Henderson, piano):
    Vo 14709. Awful Moanin' Blues/He's Never Gonna Throw Me Down
    Vo 14725. Chicago Bound Blues/Mason Dixon Blues

         (Acc. Fats Waller, piano.--JI 11/22/40):
    Vo 14861. When Your Troubles/Maybe Someday

         (Unknown accompaniment):
    AJ 17054. Lonesome for That/You Never Have No

         (Acc. Starks Hot Five):
    OK 8364. Blackville After Dark(9766a)/Heart Breaking Blues(9767a)

MEZZ MEZZROW

See also:
CHICAGO RHYTHM KINGS: Br 4001.
EDDIE CONDON: OK 41142.
ROSETTA CRAWFORD: De 7567, 7584.
EDDIE'S HOT SHOTS: Vi 38046.
LIONEL HAMPTON: Vi 25575, 25601.
ART HODES: Se 10-007.
JUNGLE KINGS: Para 12654.
ART KARLE: Vo 3146, 3147.
TOMMY LADNIER: BB 10086, 10089.
FRANKIE NEWTON: BB 10176, 10186, 10216.
TESCHEMACHER'S CHICAGOANS: UHCA 61.
FATS WALLER: Vi 24737, 24738, 24742.

MEZZROW AND HIS ORCHESTRA, MEZZ (Mezz Mezzrow, clarinet and alto sax;Benny Carter, alto and trumpet; Max Kaminsky, Freddie Goodman, Ben Gusick, trumpets;Floyd O'Brien, trombone; Johnny Russell, tenor sax: Teddy Wilson, piano; Jack Sunshine, guitar; Pop Foster, bass; Jack Maisel, drums):   1933
 Br 6778. Swingin' With Mezz(14274A) -PaE 2881,BrF 500370, BrE 01762
 "   Love You're Not the One for Me(14275a) " " "
 Br 7551. Free Love(B 14272A) -BrF 9527,BrF 500369,
 "   Dissonance(B 14273A) " " BrE 02509

(Mezz Mezzrow, clarinet and alto sax: Benny Carter, alto sax; Bud Freeman, tenor sax; Max Kaminsky, Renald Jones, Chelsea Quealey, trumpets; Floyd O-Brien, trombone: John Kirby, bass: Willie 'The Lion' Smith, piano: **Chick** Webb, drums): New York, May 7, 1934
Vi 25019. Apologies(82393)/Sending the Vipers(82394) -HMV 8403, BB 10250
Vi 25202. Old Fashioned Love(82392)/35th & Calumet(82395) -HMV 8408, BB 10251

MEZZ MEZZROW AND HIS SWING BAND (Mezz Mezzrow, clarinet; Frank Newton, trumpet: Bud Freeman, tenor sax: Willie Smith, piano; Albert Casey, guitar; Wellman Braud, bass; George Stafford, drums): 1936
BB 6320. A Melody from the Sky(99772)/Lost(99773) -GrF 7753
BB 6319. Mutiny in the Parlor(99774)/The Panic Is On(99775) -GrF 7771
BB 6321. I'se a-Muggin'(99776-7)

MEZZ MEZZROW ORCHESTRA(Mezz Mezzrow, clarinet: Sy Oliver,trumpet; J.C.Higginbotham,trombone; Happy Caldwell,tenor sax: Bernard Addison,guitar: Pop Foster,bass; Sonny White,piano: James Crawford,drums):New York,June 14,1937
Vi 25612. The Swing Session's Called to Order/Hot Club Stomp -GrF 8100,HMV 8846
Vi 25636. Blues in Disguise/That's Hoe I Feel Today -GrF 8028,HMV 8656

(Mezzrow,clarinet; Tommy Ladnier,Sidney DeParis,trumpets: Teddy Bunn,guitar; Elmer James,bass; James P.Johnson,piano: Zutty Singleton,drums):
    New York,Nov.21,1938
BB 10085. Comin' on With the Come On, 1 & 2 -Sw 47
BB 10088. Revolutionary Blues/Gettin'Together(Quintet,see below) -Sw 78

MEZZROW-LADNIER QUINTET(Mezzrow: Ladnier; Pop Foster,bass; Teddy Bunn,guitar; Manzie Johnson,guitar): New York,Dec.19,1938
BB 10087. Royal Garden Blues/If You See Me Comin' -Sw 57
BB 10090. Averybody Loves My Baby/Ain't Gonna Give Nobody None of My Jelly
 (Unknown personnel): (Roll
Victor Test. Swingin' for Mezz(028991-1) Dec.21,1942

 MEZZROW-BECHET QUINTET (Mezzrow; Bechet: Fitz Weston,piano; Pop Foster, bass; Kaiser Marshall,drums):
KJ 140. Gone Away Blues/De Luxe Stomp
KJ 141. Bowin' the Blues/Old School
KJ 142. Out of the Gallion/Ole Miss

 MEZZROW BECHET SEPTET (Mezzrow: Bechet: Hot Lips Page, trumpet; Jimmy Blythe, Jr.,piano; Danny Barker,guitar; Pop Foster,bass; Sidney Catlett,drums):
KJ 143. Blood on the Moon/House Party
KJ 144. Levee Blues/Saw Mill Man Blues(vocals by Pleasant Joseph)

 MEZZ MEZZROW TRIO (Art Hodes,piano; Mezz Mezzrow, clarinet; Danny Alvin, drums): 1944
Se 10008. Really the Blues(160)/Milk for Mezz(F-161)

MICHALL AND HIS NEW ORLEANS BOYS, ERNEST (Ernest "Mike" Michall,clarinet; alto sax; guitar; piano; violin):
 BP 8046. Toledano Street Blues/Sidewalk Blues(clarinet solo, with piano)

MIDNIGHT AIRDALES(featuring Bud Freeman, tenor sax):
 Co 1981. Swanee Shuffle(149002)/I Gotta Have You(149003)

25

MIDNIGHT RAMBLERS (Possibly a Jimmy Blythe group):
  Vo 03395. Out With the Wrong Woman/(STATE STREET SWINGERS)

MIDNIGHT ROUNDERS (Rhythm quartet probably led by Jimmy Blythe, piano):
  Vo 1218. Shake Your Shimmy/(ALBERT WYNNE GUT BUCKET FIVE)
  Vo 1237. Bull Fiddle Rag/(TAMPA RED)

MIDNIGHT SERENADERS (Harry Tropper,leader,tuba and string bass: Benny Sans,piano;
Stanley Norris,sax; Andy Pedulla,Bill Mach,trumpets. Art Cope,violin; Eddie Obermiller,clarinet; Tony Monico,drums: Frank Lhotak,trombone.--DB 12/15/42): Chicago
  Para 20657. When Sweet Susie Goes Stepping By(20765-2)
        "   Tin Roof Blues(20789-7)   -Bwy 1216

MIDNIGHT STOMPERS:
  Edison Bell Winner 4874. Riverboat Blues(11555)/Tiger Rag11556)

MIDWAY DANCE ORCHESTRA (Murphy Steinberg,cornet: Jesse Barnes,trombone: Art Kassel,saxes; Elmer Schoebel,piano; Lew Black,banjo; Steve Brown,bass: Bobby De Lee,
drums; Leon Rappolo is mentioned as clarinet, but this seems doubtful.--JT #13):
  Co   33. Lots o' Mamma(81311)/The Black Sheep Blues(81312)   Chicago, 1923
  Co   51. Cotton Pickers' Ball'81313)
        "   Buddy's Habits(81383): Roy Kramer,clarinet.   -ReE 8148

MIDWAY GARDEN ORCHESTRA
  Para -----. Sobbin' Blues/Lots o' Mamma   -Clax 40273
  Para 20272. Black Sheep Blues/(YOUNG'S CREOLE JAZZ BAND)   -Clax 40272

MILES, JOSIE (vocal with piano):
  Ge 5261. Baby's Got the Blues/Kansas City Man Blues
  Ge 5292. He's Never Gonna Throw Me Down(8572A)/Graveyard Dream Blues(8573A)

   (Fletcher Henderson, piano):
  Ge 5307. He Went Away and Left Me Blues(8607A)/I Want My Sweet Daddy(8608A)
  Ge 5339. He's My Man, Your Man(8661A)/Awful Moanin' Blues(8662A)

   (Joe Smith, cornet: Henderson, piano):
  Ge 5359. War Horse Mamma(8708A)/You Don't Know My Mind Blues(8709A)
  Ge 5391. Pipe Dream Blues/31st Street Blues

   JOSIE MILES AND THE CHOO CHOO JAZZERS:
  Aj 17057. Lovin' Henry Blues(31641)/Freight Train Blues(31644)

   JOSIE MILES (Acc. by Kansas City Five):
  Ed 51476. Sweet Man Joe(9762B)

   (Acc. by Henderson and Snowden):
  BS 14121. When You're Crazy Over Daddy/Please

   (Acc, by orchestra):
  BS 14136. Four o'clock Blues/How I've Got Dem Twilight Blues
  BS 14139. Low Down Bama Blues/Love me in Your Old Time Way   -Para 12160

MILES, LIZZIE (vocal with orchestra):
  OK 8031. Muscle Shoals Blues(s70496B)/She Walked Right Up and Took My Man
  OK 8032. State Street Blues/Virginia Blues
  OK 8037. Wicked Blues/He May Be Your Man But He Comes to See Me Sometimes
  OK 8039. Please Don't Tickle Me Babe/Lonesome Monday Morning Blues   (Away(s70497B)
  OK 8040. Hot Lips/Take It Cause It's All Yours
  OK 8048. Sweet Smellin' Mama/He Used to Be Your Man But He's My Man Now
  OK 8049. The Trixie Blues/(EVA TAYLOR)
  OK 8050. The Black Bottom Blues/(EVA TAYLOR)
  OK 8052. The Yellow Dog Blues/(KITTY BROWN)

   (Acc, piano and cornet):
  OK 8456. Grievin' Mama Blues/Slow Up Papa

   (Acc. Clarence Johnson, piano):
  Br 2462. My Pillow and Me(10858)/Black Man(10864),Spencer Williams,piano
  Co 3897. Haitian Blues/Sweet Smellin' Mama
  Co 3920. Triflin' Man Blues/Family Trouble Blues
  Vi 19083. Messin' Around/(EDNA HICKS)
  Vi 19124. Cotton Belt Blues/(ROSA HENDERSON)

   Accompaniment unknown):
  Vi 23281. My Man of War Blues
  Vi 23306. Electrician Blues/Done Throwed the Key Away

   (Jelly Roll Morton, piano):   1929
  Vi 38571. I Hate a Man Like You/Don't Tell Me Nothin' 'Bout My Man

   (Uncertain accompaniment):
  Vi 38607. Good Time Blues/(LEE AND SMITH

```
        (Acc. piano and clarinet):
   Do  4055. Mean Old Bedbug Blues/(MISS FRANKIE)

        (Unknown accompaniment):
   Co 14435. My Different Kind of Man/You're Such a Cruel Papa

        LIZZIE MILES AND HER CREOLE JAZZ HOUNDS:
   Em 10586. Four o'Clock Blues/Aggravatin' Papa

        LIZZIE MILES AND HER MELROSE STOMPERS:
   Vo 05165. That's All Right Daddy(wc2775A)                    -Cq 9357
      "     Keep Knockin', No. 2(wc27777A)
   Vo 05260. He's My Man(wc2774A)/Mellow Rhythm(wc2773A, instrumental only)
   Vo 05325. Hold Me, Parson(wc2776A)/He's Red Hot to Me(wc2780A)
   Vo 05392. Twenty Grand Blues/Stranger Blues
```

BUBBER MILEY

```
See also:
   HOAGY CARMICHAEL: Vi 38139.
   DUKE ELLINGTON: Many early recordings.
   HARLEM HOT CHOCOLATES: HoW 1045, 1046.
   MARGARET JOHNSON: OK 8193.
   JUNGLE BAND: Br 4238, 4309, 4345.
   KING OLIVER: Vi 22298, 38124, 38137.
   LEO REISMAN: Vi 22244, 22306, 22282, 22746, 22836, et al.
   SUSIE SMITH (Monette Moore): Para -----.
   TEXAS BLUES DESTROYERS: Vo 14914: Pe 14341; Pat 036160.
```

MILEY AND HIS MILEAGE MAKERS, BUBBER (Bubber Miley, trumpet: Charlie Irvis,trombone; Earl Fraser,piano; Bernard Addison,guitar; Hilton Jefferson,alto: Happy
Caldwell,tenor; drums: bass.--DB 6/15/41):   1930
```
   Vi 38138. I Lost My Gal from Memphis(62232)/Without You Fmaline(62233)
   Vi 38146. Black Maria(63108)/Chinnin' and Chattin' with May(63109)

        (Unknown personnel)
   Vi 23010. Loving You the Way I Do(63645)/The Penalty of Love(63646)
```

MILLER AND HIS MARKET STREET BOYS, AL (Most of the following have piano, guitar
and mandolin, with some additionally featuring bass and drums. All have vocals.
Frank Melrose is believed to be the pianist on the first coupling, and probably
others. See JR 6/46):   1929 et seq.
```
   Br 7063. I Would If I Could(3083)                             -Vo 02700
      "    Somebody's Been Using That Thing(3080)
   Br 7084. It Ain't Killed Nobody Yet/Maybe You'd Feel That Way Too
   Br 7088. I Found Your Key Hole/Don't Be a Fool
   Br 7097. It Must Be Good/Let Me Put My Shoes Under Your Bed
   Br 7105. Somebody's Been Using That Thing No.2/Thirty-first and State
   Br 7140. Bone Blues/That Stuff You Sell
   Br 7143. Gimme a Li'l Taste/(MEMPHIS MOSE)

        AL MILLER AND HIS SWING STOMPERS(Vocals: clarinet: bass: guitar):
   Ch 50072. Juicy Mouth Shorty(90600A)/Ain't That a Mess(90608A)

MILLER, EDDIE (vocal):
   Br 7133. Freight Train Blues/Good Jelly Blues
```

EDDIE MILLER

```
See also:
   ALL STAR BAND: Vi 26144.
   BUNNY BERIGAN: PaE 2316, 2327.
   BILLY BUTTERFIELD: Capitol Gershwin Album
   CAPITOL JAZZMEN: Cap 10011, 10012.
   BOB CROSBY BOB CATS: All.
   BOB CROSBY ORCHESTRA: All pre-war.
   WINGY MANNONE: Br 6911, 6940; OK 41573: Vo 2913, 2914, 2933, 2934, 2963,2972,
      3191, 3192: BB 6359, 6360, 6375, 6393, 6394, 6411.
   MOUND CITY BLUE BLOWERS.
   METRONOME: Co 35389
   JOHNNY MERCER: Cap 164.
   HARLEM HOT SHOTS: Pe 16081, 16085, 16095.
   GLENN MILLER: CoE 1150: Co 3051.
   NEW ORLEANS RHYTHM KINGS: De 388, 401.
   BEN POLLACK: Vi 24284: Co 2870, 2879.
   LOUIS PRIMA: Br 7376, 7471, BrF 02077, DeE 5621.
   CLARK RANDALL: Br 7415, 7466, 7436.
   GIL RODIN: Or 3130: Cr 3017, 3045, 3046, 3016.
   JESS STACY: Vs 8060, 8076, 8132, 8140.
   JACK TEAGARDEN: Cr 3051.
   JIMMY WAKELEY: De 18728.
```

MILLER AND HIS ORCHESTRA, EDDIE (Eddie Miller, Arthur Rando, Ray Lundale, Matty
Matlock, Clyde Rogers, reeds; Charles Griffard, Bob Goodrich, Bruce Hudson, trum-
pets; Abe Lincoln, Elmer Smithers, Eddie Kuczborski, trombones; Nappy Lamare,
guitar; Stan Wrightsman, piano; Art Shapiro, bass; Hick Fatool,drums):
 Cap 170. Yesterdays(205A)/Stomp Mr. Henry Lee(206B) Hollywood,Feb.4, 1944
 Cap 10040. Our Monday Date(204A)/(STAN KENTON)

  EDDIE MILLER'S CRESCENT CITY QUARTET (Eddie Miller, clarinet; Stan Wrightsman,piano; Ray Bauduc,drums; Nappy Lamare,guitar; Irvin Verret,vocal):
 Cap 10023. Cajun Love Song(567-3B)/(ZUTTY SINGLETON) Hollywood,Jan.27,1945

MILLER, EMMETT (comic dialogue with Roy Cowan; piano accompaniment):
 OK 40976. Thousand Frogs on a Log(400015A)/Brother Bill(400016B)

  (Comic dialogue, accompanied by E.Payson Re and His University Five):
 OK 41005. Sam and His Family(400037B)/Hungry Sam(400038A)

  (Most of the following are syled EMMETT MILLER AND HIS GEORGIA CRACKERS,
  signifying vocals accompanied by Dorsey Brothers group including Eddie
  Lang, guitar):
 OK 41062. I Ain't Got Nobody(400782C)/Lovesice Blues(400783B)
 OK 41095. Any Time(401060)/St.Louis Blues(401061)
 OK 41135. Take Your Tomorrow(401116)/Dusky Stevedore(401117)
 OK 41182. She's Funny That Way(401510)/You're the Cream in My Coffee(401548)
 OK 41205. Lion Tamers(400784)/You Lose(401511)
 OK 41280. I Ain't Gonna Give You None of My Jelly Roll(401509) -PaE 2163
  " Right or Wrong(401546)
 OK 41305. Loving Sam(402932)/Big Bad Bill(402933)

  (Jack Teagarden, trombone, on 402948,402949 and 402950):
 OK 41342. Ghost of St.Louis Blues(402934)/Sweet Mamma(402948)
 OK 41377. Pickaninnies' Paradise(402949)
  " The Blues Singer from Alabam(402950) -PaE 1115

  (Previous personnel):
 OK 41438. God's River Blues(400781)/That's the Good Old Sunny South(401547)

  (Dialogue, with piano):
 OK 41462. Licker Taster/Sam and Bill at the Graveyard

  (Unknown personnel):
 BB 6577. Any Time/The Gypsy

GLENN MILLER

See also:
 CHARLESTON CHASERS: Co 2415.
 DORSEY BROTHERS: All OK and Columbia.
 BENNY GOODMAN: Vo 15656; Br 3975, 4013; Melotones.
 LOUISIANA RHYTHM KINGS: Vo 15779, 15784, 15810, 15833, 15841; Br 4706, 4845,
  4908, 4923, 4938, 4953.
 BERT LOWN:
 MOUND CITY BLUE BLOWERS: Vi 38100.
 RED NICHOLS: Many.
 BEN POLLACK: Vi 20394, 20408, 20425, 20461, 21184, 21437.
 FRANKIE TRUMBAUER: HMV 119, 158.
 WOLVERINES: Vo and Br.

MILLER AND HIS ORCHESTRA, GLENN (Bunny Berigan, Charlie Spivak,trumpets: Ray Bau-
duc,drums; Eddie Miller,tenor sax: Johnny Mince,clarinet & alto: Claude Thornhill,
piano; Glen Miller,trombone: Delmar Kaplan,bass: Fredo Prospero,Nick Pisani,Danny
D'Andrea,violins.--JRB):   April 25,1935
 CoE 1150. In a Little Spanish Town(17381)   -Co 35881
  " Solo Hop(17382)
 Co 3051. Blues Serenade(17379)/Moonlight on the Ganges(17380)

  (George Siravo,alto: Hal McKintyre,alto and clarinet; Jerry Jerome,Carl
  Biesecker,tenors; Charles Spivak,Manny Klein,Sterling Bose,trumpets: Jesse
  Ralph,Harry Rogers,trombones: Howard Smith,piano; Dick McDonough,guitar;
  George Simon,drums; Ted Kotsaftis,bass):
 De 1239. Moonlight Bay/How Am I to Know
 De 1284. Wistful and Blue/Anytime Anyday Anywhere
 De 1342. Peg o' My Heart/I'm Sitting on Top of the World
 Br 7915. I Got Rhythm   -Vo 5051
  " Time on My Hands
 Br 7923. Sleepy Time Gal   VoE 127, Vo 5051
  " Community Swing

  (Miller,Ralph,Bud Smith,trombones: George Irwin,Bob Price,Ardelle Garrett,
  trumpets: Jerome,Biesecker,tenors: Tony Viola, McIntyre,altos; Irving Fazola,clarinet and alto; Rolly Bundock,bass; Carmen Mastren,guitar; Chummy
  MacGreggor,piano; Doc Cenardo,drums):

```
Br   8034.  My Fine Feathered Friend/Silhouetted in the Moonlight
Br   8041.  Sweet Stranger/Every Day's a Holiday
Br   8062.  Doin' the Jive                                          -Vo 5131
      "     Humoresque(B22080)                                      -Vo 4449
Br   8152.  Why'd Ya Make Me Fallin Love/Don't Wake Up My Heart
Br   8173.  Dipper Mouth Blues                                      -Vo 5131
      "     Sold American                                           -Vo 4449

      (Tex Beneke, tenor sax, and other unidentified changes in personnel): 1938
BB   7853.  My Reverie/King Porter Stomp
BB   7870.  My the Waters of the Minnetonka
BB  10201.  And the Angele Sing(Ray Eberle,vc)/The Chestnut Tree(Marion Hutton,vc)
BB  10214.  Sunrise Serenade
      "     Moonlight Serenade                                      -Vi 201566
BB  10219.  Three Little Fishies/Wishing Will Make It So
BB  10229.  My Last Goodbye/The Lady's in Love With You

      (Bob Price,Dale McMickle,Lee Knowles,trumpets· Glenn Miller,Al Mastren,
      Paul Tanner,trombones; Hal McIntyre,Tex Beneke,Wilbur Schwartz,Stanley
      Aronson,Al Klink,saxes: Chummy MacGregor,piano; Arthur Enns or Alan Reuss,
      guitar;Rowland Bundock,bass: Maurice Purtill,drums.--JRB):    1939
BB  10269.  Runnin' Wild/But It Didn't Mean a Thing(M.Hutton,vc)
BB  10276.  Stairway to the Stars/To You
BB  10286.  Little Brown Jug                                        -Vi 201566
      "     Pavanne
BB  10290.  The Lamp Is Low/Blue Evening
BB  10299.  I'm Sorry for Myself/Back to Back
BB  10303.  Cinderella/Moon Love
BB  10317.  Guess I'll Go Back Home(Beneke,vc)/Slip Horn Jive
BB  10352.  Sold American/Pagan Love Song
BB  10358.  The Man With the Mandolin/The Little Man Who Wasn't There
BB  10366.  Over the Rainbow/Ding Dong the Witch Is Dead
BB  10372.  Blue Orchids/Baby Me
BB  10388.  Twilight Interlude(Ray Eberle,vc)/Glen Island Special
BB  10399.  My Isle of Golden Dreams/Wham
BB  10404.  Blue Moonlight/My Prayer

      (Sub. Clyde Hurley,trumpet, for Price; Harold Tennyson,sax, for Aronson;
      Richard Fisher,guitar):
BB  10416.  In the Mood                                             -Vi 201565
      "     I Want to Be Happy
BB  10438.  Out of Space(Ray Eberle,vc)/So Many Times
BB  10465.  Faithful Forever/Bluebirds in the Moonlight
BB  10486.  Blue Rain/Who's Sorry Now
BB  10495.  Farewell Blues/Indian Summer(Ray Eberle,vc)
BB  10498.  It Was Written in the Stars(Eberle,vc)/Johnson Rag
BB  10507.  Oh Johnny/Ciribiribin
BB  10520.  Careless/Vagabone Dreams
BB  10526.  On a Little Street in Singapore/This Changing World
BB  10536.  Faithful to You(Ray Eberle,vc)/It's a Blue World
BB  10553.  In an Old Dutch Garden/Starlit Hour
BB  10561.  Ooh! What You Said/I Beg Your Pardon
BB  10570.  When You Wish Upon a Star/The Gaucho Serenade
BB  10580.  Give a little Whistle/The Sky Fell Down
BB  10587.  Missouri Waltz/Beautiful Ohio
BB  10598.  The Woodpecker Song/Let's All Sing Together
BB  10605.  Too Romantic/Sweet Potato Piper

      (Sub. J.Abato,sax,for Tennyson: add John Best,trumpet· sub T.Mack,trombone,
      Mastran: add Frank D'Annolfo,trombone):
BB  10612.  Tuxedo Junction                                         -Vi 201552,Vi 201565
      "     Danny Boy
BB  10622.  Imagination/Say Si Si
BB  10631.  My My/Say It
BB  10638.  Sierra Sue/Moments in the Moonlight
BB  10657.  Polka Dots and Moonbeams/What's the Matter With Me
BB  10665.  Star Dust                                               -Vi 201567
      "     My Melancholy Baby(Tex Beneke,vc)
BB  10673.  The Rumba Jumps(Hutton,Beneke,vc)/I'll Never Smile Again(Eberle,vc)
BB  10684.  Hear My Song Violetta/Starlight and Music
BB  10689.  Shake Down the Stars(Eberle,vc)/Boog-It(Marion Hutton,vc)
BB  10694.  April Played the Fiddle/I Haven't Time to a Millionaire
BB  10701.  Alice Blue Gown/Wonderful One
BB  10717.  Devil May Care/I'm Stepping Out With a Memory Tonight
BB  10728.  Fools Rush In/Yours Is My Heart Alone

      (Sub. Jim Priddy,trombone,for Mack; Ernie Caceres,sax,for Abato):  1940
BB  10740.  Slow Freight/Bugle Call Rag
BB  10745.  The Nearness of You/Mister Meadowlark
BB  10754.  Pennsylvania 6-5000                                     -Vi 201567
      "     Rug Cutter's Swing
BB  10768.  Blue berry Hill/A Million Dreams Ago
BB  10776.  When the Swallows Come Back to Capistrano/A Cabana in Havana
BB  10796.  Angel Child/Be Happy
```

(Sub. Jack Lathrop,guitar):
BB 10832. Crosstown(Jack Lathrop,vc)/What's Your Story, Morning Glory
BB 10845. The Call of the Canyon/Our Love Affair
BB 10860. I Wouldn't Take a Million/Fifth Avenue
BB 10876. Beat Me Daddy Eight to the Bar/Falling Leaves
BB 10893. A Handful of Stars/Yesterthoughts
BB 10900. Shadows on the Sand/Five o'Clock Whistle
BB 10906. I'd Know You Anywhere/You've Got Me This Way
BB 10913. Make Believe Ballroom Time(Modernaires,vc)/Old Black Joe
BB 10931. Nightingale Sang in Berkeley Square/Boodbye Little Darlin'(Eberle,vc)
BB 10936. Do You Know Why/Isn't That Just Like Love
BB 10959. Somewhere/Fresh As a Daisy
BB 10970. Along the Santa Fe Trail(Fberle,vc)/Yes My Darling Daughter(Hutton,vc)

(Sub. Billy May,Ray Anthony,trumpets,for Hurley,Knowles; Herman Alpert,bass, for Bundock):
BB 10982. Anvil Chorus, 1 & 2
BB 10994. Frenesi/My Blue Heaven
BB 11001. The Mem'ry of a Rose/Prairieland Lullaby
BB 11020. I Do Do You/You Are the One
BB 11029. Song of the Volga Boatmen   -Vi 201564
  "   Chapel in the Valley
BB 11042. You Stepped Out of a Dream/Ring Telephone Ring
BB 11063. I Dreamt I Dwelt in Harlem/A Stone's Throw from Heaven(Eberle,vc)
BB 11069. A Little Old Church in England/When That Man Is Dead and Gone
BB 11079. It's Always You(Eberle,vc)/Ida Sweet as Apple Cider(Beneke,vc)
BB 11095. Perfidia/Spring Will Be SoSAd
BB 11110. The One I Love/Sun Valley Jump
BB 11135. The Spirit Is Willing/The Air Minded Executive
BB 11163. Boulder Buff/The Booglie Wooglie Piggy
BB 11183. Don't Cry Cherie/Sweeter Than the Sweetest
BB 11187. I Guess I'll Have to Dream the Rest/Take the "A" Train
BB 11203. Peekaboo to You/Cradle Song
BB 11215. You and I/The Angels Came Thru
BB 11219. Under Blue Canadian Skies/Adios
BB 11230. I Know Why/Chattanooga Choo Choo
BB 11235. The Cowboy Serenade/Below the Equator
BB 11263. It Happened in Sun Valley/The Kiss Polka
BB 11274. Elmer's Tune/Delilah
BB 11287. From One Love to Another(Fberle,vc)/I'm Thrilled(Eberle,vc)
BB 11299. The Man in the Moon(Fberle,vc)/Ma Ma Maria(Fberle & Modernaires)
BB 11315. This Time the Dream's on Me(Fberle,vc)/Says Who Says You Says I(Hutton, Beneke & the Modernaires, vc)
BB 11326. Dear Arabella(Hutton,Beneke,Modernaires)/Orange Blossom Lane(Fberle,vc)
BB 11342. Dreamsville,Ohio(Eberle & Modernaires)/Papa Niccolini(Eberle,Beneke,
BB 11353.Jingle Bells(Beneke,Caceres,Modernaires/(ALVINO REY)   (Modernaires)
BB 11365.Ev'rything I Love/Baby Mine(Eberle & choir,vocals)
BB 11369.Humpty Dumpty Heart(Eberle)/This is No Laughing Matter(Eberle)

(Sub.Alec Fila,trumpet,for Anthony: Babe Rusin,sax,for McIntyre: add Bobby Hackett,guitar and/or trumpet: sub.E.Goldberg,bass):
BB 11382. Day Dreaming
  "   A String of Pearls   -Vi 201552
BB 11386. Moonlight Sonata(MacGregor,piano)/Slumber Song
BB 11397. The White Cliffs of Dover/We're the Couple in the Castle(Fberle)
BB 11401. Happy in Love/Moonlight Cocktail
BB 11416. Fooled(Ray Fberle)/It Happened in Hawaii(Eberle & Modernaires)
BB 11429. The President's Birthday Ball/Angels of Mercy
BB 11438. When the Roses Bloom Again(Eberle)/Always in My Heart(Eberle)
BB 11443. Dear Mom(Fberle & Modernaires)/Keep 'em Flying
BB 11450. Let's Have Another Cup of Coffee/Chip Off the Old Block
BB 11462. The Story of a Starry Night/Skylark
BB 11474. The Lamplighter's Serenade/Don't Sit Under the Apple Tree
BB 11480. On the Old Assembly Line/When Johnny Comes Marching Home
BB 11493. She'll Always Remember(Eberle,Modernaires)/Shhh, It's a Military
          Secret(Marion Hutton, Beneke, Modernaires)
Vi 27873. American Patrol   -Vi 201564
  "   Soldier Let Me Read Your Letter
Vi 27879. Sleep Song/Sweet Eloise
Vi 27894. Knit One Purl Two/Lullaby of the Rain
Vi 27933. The Humming Bird/Yesterday's Gardenias
Vi 27934. At Last/Kalamazoo
Vi 27935. That's Sabotage/Serenade in Blue
Vi 27943. Long Tall Mama/Conchita Marquita Lilita Pepita Rosita Juanita Lopez
Vi 27953. Dearly Beloved/I'm Old Fashioned
Vi 201509. Sleepy Town Train/Juke Box Saturday Night
Vi 201520. Moonlight Mood/Moonlight Becomes You
Vi 201523. That Old Black Magic/A Pink Cocktail for a Blue Lady
Vi 201529. Rhapsody in Blue/Along the Santa Fe Trail
Vi 201536. Blue Rain/Caribbean Clipper
Vi 201546. It Must Be Jelly/Rainbow Rhapsody
Vi 201563. Here We Go Again/Long Time No See Baby
Vi 201585. Basket Weaver/On a Little Street in Singapore
Vi 201600. Helpless/When Johnny Comes Marching Home

MILLER, JIM (vocal with guitar and harmonica):
  Vo 1737. Next Door Man/Joker Man Blues

MILLER'S NEW ORLEANS FROLICKERS, JOHNNIE (Johnnie Miller,piano: Chink Martin,bass;
Sidney Arodin,clarinet; Sharkey Bohano,trumpet: Leo Adde,drums; Steve Brou,banjo:
Hal Jordy,saxophone):   New Orleans,1927
  Co   1546. Panama(146193)/Dipper Mouth Blues(146194)

MILLER, LUELLA (vocals):
  Vo 1044. Pretty Man Blues/Dago Hill Blues
  Vo 1234. Chicago Blues(orch. acc.)/Wee Wee Daddy Blues(piano acc.)

PUNCH MILLER

See also:
  JIMMY BERTRAND: Vo 1280.
  FRANKIE FRANKO: Me 12009.
  HALF PINT JAXON: Vo 1472.
  MACK & MACK :OK 8195.
  TINY PARHAM:
  AL WYNNE: Vo 1218, 1220.
  JIMMY WADE: Vo 1236 (vocal)

MILLER AND HIS SOUTH SIDE STOMPERS, PUNCH (Punch Miller,trumpet: Artie Starks,
clarinet; Richard M.Jones,piano: John Lindsay,bass; Clifford Jones,drums):
  Se 12014. West End Blues(F178)/Boy in the Boat(F181)   Chicago,June 12,1941
  Se 12015. Sugar Foot Stomp(F179)/Muscle Shoals Blues(F180)

MILLER AND HIS ORCHESTRA, RAY (Personnel of Miller's recording bands has included
Frankie Trumbauer and Jimmy Dorsey,saxes: Tommy Dorsey and Miff Mole,trombones:
Joe Venuti,violin: Eddie Lang,guitar; and Muggsy Spanier,trumpet*):
  Br 3676. Blue Baby/Yep, Long 'Bout June
  Br 3677. Weary Blues/I Ain't Got Nobody   -BrE 3716
  Br 4077. Anything You Say/If I Have You
  Br 4131. Rose of Mandalay
    "   Who Wouldn't Be Jealous of You*   -BrG 8139
  Br 4194. Mississippi Here I am*   -BrG 8140
    "   No One in the World But You
  Br 4223. In a Great Big Way/Let's Sit and Talk About You
  Br 4224. That's a Plenty*/Angry*   -BrG 8153, 3947, 81267
  Br 4233. My Angeline/Cradle of Love
  Br 4352. Moonlight and Roses/In My Garden of Memory
  Br 4425. You Want Lovin'/Someone's Falling in Love
  Br 4579. On Iowa/Go U Northwestern
  Br 4669. My Victory/Blue Butterfly
  Br 4675. Finesse/Funny Dear What Love Can Do
  Br 4682. That's Where You Come In/In a Kitchenette
  Br 4687. Nobody's Using It.Now/Hoosier Hop
  Br 4692. Ain't You Baby/Harlem Madness
  Br 4704. There Will Never Be Another Mary/(LLOYD HUNTLEY)
  Br 4735. Kiss Me With Your Eyes/When It's Springtime in the Rockies
  Br 4857. Beneath Montana Skies/Montana
  BrE 2606. Come on, Red
  BrE 3132. Stomp Your stuff
  BrE 3328. Mercy Percy
  BrE 3731. Sister Kate
  BrE 3749. My Honey's Lovin' Arms

MILLER, SODARISA (vocal acc. by James Blythe, pianist, on Para 12231,12276,12306,
and probably others):
  Para 12231. Hot Springs Water Blues(240)/Who'll Drive My Blues Away(241)
  Para 12243. Down By the Rever/Don't Dog Me
  Para 12261. Confessin' Blues/Broadway Daddy Blues
  Para 12276. Sunshine Special/Be Yourself
  Para 12293. Nobody Knows/Fighting Blues
  Para 12306. Midnight Special(2225)/Reckless Don't Care Mama Blues(2227)
            - - -
  Vi 20404. Lonesome Room Blues/I Keeps My Kitchen Clean

MILLINDER AND HIS ORCHESTRA, LUCKY (See also Mills Blue Rhythm Band):
  De 3956. Slide Mr.Trombone(69438A)/Rock Daniel(69440A; Rosetta Tharpe,vc)
  De 4041. Big Fat Mama(69706A)/Trouble in Mind(69437A, Rosetta Tharpe)-BrE 03295
  De 4099. Let Me Off Uptown/How About That Mess
  De 4146. Hey Huss/Ride Red Ride
  De 4261. Fightin' Doug MacArthur/We're Gonna Have to Slap the Dirty Little
  De 18353. Savoy/Rock Me (Rosetta Tharpe,vc)   (Jap
  De 18386. Shout Sister Shout(Tharpe)/I Want a Tall Skinny Papa(Tharpe)
  De 18496. When the Lights Go On Again/That's All(Tharpe)
  De 18529. Apollo Jump/Are You Ready
  De 18569. Don't Cry Baby/Sweet Slumber
  De 18609. I Can't See for Lookin'/Hurry Hurry
  De 18674. Who Threw the Whiskey in the Well/Shipyard Social Function
  De 18867. Some Day/Shorty's Got to Go

MILLS BROTHERS (John, Herbert, Harry and Donald, vocalists; John Mills, guitar):
```
Br   6179. Tiger Rag                                          -BrE 1229,1415,02020
      "    Nobody's Sweetheart                                             "
Br   6225. You Rascal You/Baby Won't You Please Come Home     -BrE 1255
Br   6269. I Heard                                            -BrE 1283
      "    How'm I Doin'                              -Me 13179,           "
Br   6278. Rockin' Chair                                      -BrE 1296, 02062
      "    Goodbye Blues                              -Ro 2381,   ", BrE 1415
Br   6305. Loveless Love                                      -BrE 1305
      "    Chinatown                                  -Me 13182,BrE 1331
Br   6330. Sweet Sue                                  -Me 13181,BrE 1305
      "    St. Louis Blues                            -Pe 13057,Ba 33211,BrE 1331
Br   6357. Bugle Call Rag                             -Me 13182,BrE 1346
      "    Old Man of the Mountain
Br   6430. Dirt Dishing Daisy                         -Pe 13082,BrE 1419
      "    Git Along                                                       "
Br   6485. Shine                                              -BrE 1316, 1424
      "    Dinah                                              -BrE 1271,   "
Br   6517. Doin' the New Low Down(with Cab Calloway's Orchestra) -BrE 01518
Br   6519. I Can't Give you Anything But Love                 -BrE 01520
      "    Diga diga Do (With Ellington)
Br   6525. My Honey's Lovin' Arms                             -BrE 1469
      "    Smoke Rings                                -CoE 1959,BrF 1497
Br   6785. Jungle Fever                               -CoE 2010,Me 13177,BrE 01766
      "    I've Found a New Baby                              -CoE 2001,BrE 01761
Br   6913. Sleepy Head                                -Me 13177,BrE 01766
      "    Put on Your Old Grey Bonnet                        -BrE 01761
Br   6894. Swing It Sister/Money in My Pocket                 -BrE 01756
Br  20102. Gems from George White's Scandals(with Boswell Sisters) -BrE 105
Br  20112. OK America (with Boswell Sisters)
Pe  13057. Coney Island Washboard                     -Ba 33211, BrE 1363
Pe  13082. Fiddlin' Joe                               -CoE 2010, BrE 1497
De    165. My Gal Sal/Ida Sweet As Apple Cider                -BrE 01863
De    166. Miss Otis Regrets                                  -BrE 01887
      "    Old Fashioned Love                                 -BrE 01943
De    167. Rockin' Chair                                      -BrE 02062
      "    Tiger Rag                                          -BrE 02020
De    176. Lazybones                                          -BrE 01800
      "    Nagasaki                                           -BrE 01800
De    228. Some of These Days                                 -BrE 02020
      "    I've Found a New Baby
De    267. Limehouse Blues                                    -BrE 01943
      "    Sweeter Than Sugar                                 -BrE 01987
De    380. Sweet Georgia Brown                                -BrE 01987
      "    There Goes My Headache
De    402. What's the Reason                                  -BrE 01999
      "    Don't Be Afraid to Tell Your Mother                -BrE 02035
De    497. Moanin' for You                                    -BrE 02062
      "    Sweet Lucy Brown                                   -BrE 02035
De    617.(See Bing Crosby)
De    961. Shoe Shine Boy                                     -BrE 02245
      "    Rhythm Saved the World
De   1082. London Rhythm/Solitude                             -BrE 02284
De   1147. Swing for Sale/Pennies from Heaven                 -BrE 02367
De   1148. (See Ella Fitzgerald)
De   1227. The Love Bug Will Bite You/Rockin' Chair Swing     -BrE 02415
De   1245. (See Louis Armstrong)
De   1360. 'Long About Midnight                               -BrE 02298
      "    Old Folks at Home(Armstrong)                       -BrE 02461
De   1495. Since We Fell Out of Love                          -BrE 01999
      "    In the Shade of the Old Apple Tree(with Armstrong) -BrE 02461
De   1876. Caravan/The Flat Foot Floogee(Armstrong)           -BrE 02622
De   1892. (See Louis Armstrong)
De   1964. Julius Caesar/Sixty Seconds Got Together           -BrE 02642
De   2008. The Yam                                            -BrE 02679
      "    The Lambeth Walk                                   -BrE 02648
De   2029. Juniculi Funicula                                  -BrE 02709
      "    Just a Kid Named Joe                               -BrF 02679
De   2285. Sweet Adeline(64934)                       -De 23623, BrE 02932
      "    You Tell Me Your Dream(64948)                      -De 23623
De   2441. Goodbye Blues                                      -BrE 03002
      "    Sweet Sue Just You                                 -BrE 02764
De   2599. Side Kick Joe                                      -BrE 03002
      "    Way Down Home(64949)                               -De 23627
De   2804. Asleep in the Deep                                 -BrE 02709
      "    Meet Me Tonight in Dreamland
De   2982. It Don't Mean a Thing                              -BrE 02782
      "    Put on Your Old Grey Gonnet                        -BrE 02832
De   3132. Swanee River/Old Black Joe
De   3225. My Gal Sal(67341)                          -De 23624, BrE 03042
      "    Just a Dream of You,Dear(67380)                    -De 23624
De   3291. Sleepy Time Gal                                    -BrE 03042
      "    Marie (with Louis Armstrong)
```

```
De   3151. (See Louis Armstrong)
De   3180. (See Louis Armstrong)
De   3331. On the Banks of the Wabash(67367)              -De 23626
      "   Moonlight Bay(67340)                            -De 23626
De   3381. Once Upon a Dream
      "   When You Were Sweet Sixteen(67382)              -De 23627
De   3455. Can't Yo Heah Me Callin' Caroline(67366)       -De 23625
      "   Love's Old Sweet Song
De   3486. Bird in the Hand/When You Said Boodbye
De   3567. How Did She Look/
      "   Did Anyone Call                                 -BrE 03150
De   3545. See Benny Carter)
De   3688. Georgia on My Mind                             -BrE 02892
      "   Shine                                           -BrE 02844
De   3705. Break the News to Mother/Darling Nelly Gray
De   3763. Rig a Jig Jig/Down, Down, Down
De   3789. Brazilian Nuts/I Yi Yi Yi Amigo
De   3901. The Very Thought of You(69017A)/If It's True(69016A)
De   4070. Bells of San Raquel/I Guess I'll Be on My Way
De   4108. Delilah/Window Washer Man
De   4187. Lazy River/627 Stomp
De   4251. Dreamsville, Ohio/Beyond the Stars
De  18318. I'll Be Around/Paper Doll
De  18473. I Met Her on Monday/In Old Champlain
De  18599. Till Then/You Always Hurt the One You Love
De  18663. I Wish/Put Another Chair at the Table
De  18753. Never Make a Promise in Vain(73170)/Don't Be a Baby,Baby(72804)
De  18834. I Don't Know Enough About You/There's No one But You
De  23638. Too Many Irons on the Fire(73629)/I Guess I'll Get the Papers(73628)
CoE  2001. Any Time Any Day Anywhere
BrE 02093. Lulu's Back in Town/Sweet and Low
BrE 02399. Big Boy Blue/Dedicated to You
BrE 02460. Let Me Dream/Organ Grinder's Swing
BrE 02542. Little Old Lady/Caravan
BrE 92725. Jeepers Creepers/Stop Beatin' Around the Mulberry Bush
BrE 02741. You'll Have to Swing It/Stardust
BrE 02782. Smoke Rings
BrE 02800. Three Little Fishies/Strawberry Fair
BrE 02823. South of the Border/And the Angels Sing
BrE 02832. F.D.R. Jones
BrE 02844. Basin Street Blues
BrE 02892. Ain't Misbehavin'
```

MILLS BLUE RHYTHM BAND

(Special Note: The following should be substituted for, and used interchangeably with, the summary printed under the name of the BLUE RHYTHM BAND in Vol.I. Several mistakes were made in the original listing, notably the inclusion of the Earl Jackson, Me 12080, which is actually an Ellington record: and the crediting of Vo 1617 and 1646 to Baron Lee, whereas both are "Chocolate Dandies" items by the King Oliver band. Some of the Baron Lee records also appeared on other labels under the name of Billy Banks)
```
  BLUE RHYTHM BOYS: Br 6143, 6299.
  BLUE RHYTHM BAND: VoE 6.
  BILLY BANKS: Pe 15505.
  BLUE RIBBON BOYS: Pe 15468.
  KING CARTER: Co 2439, 2504, 2638.
  HARLEM HOT SHOTS: Pe L5481.
  EARL JACKSON: Pe 15332, Me 12164.
  BARON LEE: Pe 15605,15606,15621,15629,15634,15652,15676,15696,15822.
  MILLS BLUE RHYTHM BAND: As below.
  MILLS BLUE RHYTHM BOYS: Br 6156, 6199.
  CHUCK RICHARD: Vo 2877, 2867; BrE 02009.
```

MILLS BLUE RHYTHM BAND (Theodore McCord, Crawford Wethlington, Castor McCord,saxes; Wardell Jones, Shelton Hemphill, Edward Anderson,trumpets; Harry White,Henry Hicks, trombones; Edgar Hayes,piano; Benny James,banjo: Hayes Alvis,bass; Willie Lynch, drums):   1931
```
Vi 22763. Heebie Jeebies(69978)                          -HMV 6290, 4881
      "   Minnie the Moocher(69960)                      -HMV 6087, 4871
Vi 22800. Moanin'(69963)/(DUKE ELLINGTON)
```
(Sub. George Washington,trombone,for White: Joe Garland,Gene Michael,Crawford Wethlington,saxes: O'Neil Spencer,drums):   1933
```
BB  5688. The Growl/The Stuff Is Here
Vi 24442. Harlem After Midnight                          -HMV 8433
      "   Love's Serenade                                -HMV 6487
Vi 24482. Break It Down(78093)                           -HMV 103, 4983
      "   Kokey Joe(78094)
PaE 2366. Weary Traveller
CoE  734. Buddy's Wednesday Outgin(265076)/Ridin' in Rhythm(265074)
```

```
          (Sub. Henry Allen,trumpet,for Anderson; J.C. Higginbotham,trombone,for Hicks;
          Add Buster Bailey,clarinet: Lawrence Lucke,guitar) Lucky Millender, leader
Co  2963. Out of a Dream/Let's Have a Jubilee                               1934
Co  2994. Solitude/Keep Rhythm Going
Co  3020. Back Beats/Spitfire                                      -CoE 1055
Co  3038. Swingin' in E Flat(C016035A)                             -PaE 2381
     "    African Lullaby(C016271)
Co  3044. Dancing Dogs(C016273)
     "    Brown Sugar Mine(C016702; Chuck Richards, voc.)          -PaE 2366
Co  3071. Harlem Heat(C017760)                                     -PaE 2392
     "    There's Rhythm in Harlem(C017797)
Co  3078. Cotton/Truckin'                                          -CoE 1153
Co  3083. Dinah Lou/Waiting in the Garden
Br  7534. Once to Every Heart(C017761; Chuck Richards,v)/Tallahassee(C017798)
Br  7853. When Lights Are Low

          (Sub. Tab Smith,alto sax,for Bailey):                             1936
Co  3087. Ride Red Ride/Congo Caravan                    -PaE 2145,OK 6119
Co  3111. Broken Dreams of You(C018421)Chuck Richards,voc)/Yes Yes(C018422)
Co  3135. St.Louis Wiggle Rhythm/Red Rhythm                        -CoE 5024
Co  3134. Jes Naturally Lazy/Ev'rything Is Still Okay
Co  3147. Until the Real Thing Comes Along/Merry Go Round
Co  3148. Carry Me Back to Green Pastures/In a Sentimental Mood
Co  3156. Balloonacy                                                -PaE 2392
     "    Barrelhouse

          (Sub. Billy Kyle,piano, for Hayes; John Kirby,bass,for Alvis):
Co  3157. The Moon Is Grinning at Me
     "    Showboat Shuffle                                         -PaE 2381
Co  3158. Mr.Ghost Goes to Town/Algiers Stomp
Co  3162. Callin' Your Bluff/Big John Special                      -PaE 2337

          (Charlie Shavers,Carl Warwick,Harry Edison,trumpets; Sandy Watson,Wilbur
          DeParis,trombones; Tab Smith,Eddie Williams,Ronald Haymes,Harold Arnold,
          saxes: Billy Kyle,piano; David Barker,guitar: John Williams,bass; O'Neil
          Spencer,drums.--HD):  Chappie Willet,vocals                       1937
Vr   503. Blue Rhythm Fantasy/Harlem Madness                        -Vo 3808
Vr   546. Prelude to a Stomp/Rhythm Jam                             -Vo 3817

          (Sub. Alfred Cobbs, trombone, for Watson: Ben Watson, sax,for Haymes):
Vr   604. The Image of You/The Lucky Swing
Br   624. Camp Meeting Jamboree/When Irish Eyes Are Smiling
Vr   634. Let's Get Together/Jammin' for the Jackpot
```

<u>MILLS CAVALCADE ORCHESTRA</u> (George Brunis,trombone and leader: Norman Conley, Althea Conley, trombones; Florence Dieman,Elvira Rohl Battista,trumpets; Jules Harrison,Marie Carpenter,Evelyn Pennak and Herbie Haymer,saxes; Henrietta Borchard, Rudy Berson,Sid Sidney,violins: Gladys Mosier,piano; Jessie Moore,bass: Frank Carlson,drums): -RR   1935
```
Co  3066. Rhythm Lullaby/Liza Lee                                   -CoE 219
```

<u>MILLS AND HIS HOTSY TOTSY GANG, IRVING</u> (Featuring Phil Napoleon,trumpet; Miff Mole,trombone; Larry Binyon,sax: JoeTarto,bass; Sten King,drums.--DB 1/1/43):
```
Br  4482. Sweet Savannah Sue/Can't We Get Together
Br  4498. Some Fun                                                 -BrF 1037

          (Napoleon,Leo McConville,trumpets; Tommy Dorsey,trombone; Jimmy Dorsey,Binyon,saxes; Benny Goodman,clarinet; Tarto: King: Hoagy Carmichael):
Br  4559. Harvey/March of the Hoodlums
Br  4587. Star Dust

          (Omit Goodman: add Matty Malneck,violin):
Br  4641. Manhattan Rag/What Kind of Man Is You                    -BrG 8645
Br  4674. My Little Honey and Me                                   -BrG 8594

          (Napoleon and Sterling Bose,trumpets: Benny Goodman,clarinet: Harry Goodman,
          bass; Jack Pettis,sax; Al Goering,piano; Gene Krupa,drums; Malneck,violin):
Br  4838. Railroad Man/Crazy 'Bout My Gal                  -BrE 03297,BrF 500147

          (Napoleon,Bose,Dorsey Broghers,Carmichael,Tarto,Krupa; Babe Rusin,sax; Joe
          Cornell):
Br  4920. High and Dry/Barbaric                            -BrE 1023,BrG 8883

          (Red Nichols,trumpet: Jack Teagarden,trombone; Goodman: Malneck; Krupa;Jack
          Rusin; Min Liebrook):
Br  4983. Strut Miss Lizzie/Deep Harlem                            -BrF 500091

          (Dorsey Brothers; Goodman; Cornell; Goering; Malneck; Bill Moore,trumpet;
          D.Ober,drums):
Br  4998. What a Night/I Wonder What My Gal Is Doin'
```

BILL ROBINSON, tap dancer, accompanied by Irving Mills and His Hotsy Totsy Gang:
```
Br  4535. Ain't Misbehavin'/Doin' the New Low Down
              (See also: Hotsy Totsy Gang)
```

IRVING MILLS AND HIS ORCHESTRA:
Vi 22669. So Sweet/Doin' the Rhumba
Vi 38105. At the Prom/(JACK PETTIS)
Br 8163. It's a Long Long Way to Your Heart/The Lonesome Trail Ain't Lonesome
Br 8183. Manhattan Holiday/Dream of Me   (Anymore

MILLS MERRY MAKERS (Benny Goodman,clarinet; Jack Teagarden,trombone; Jimmy Mc-
Partland,trumpet; probably Larry Binyon,tenor sax: et al.--JI 11/41):
Ve 7121. Farewell Blues(149955)
Ha 1099. When You're Smiling(149954)/(JULIE WINTZ)   -Di 3099
Ha 1104. St.James Infirmary(149953)   Ve 2104, Di 3104

(McPartland*, Goodman#, and Teagarden% may be heard in the following, as
indicated):
Pat 36961. Honey(See also Broadway Broadcasters,Ca 9130)*#   -Pe 15142
Pe 15183. This Is Heaven
Ca 8334. Do You Wonder That I love You(3362)/(DIXIE BAISIES)
Ca 8336. I'm Talking About My Wonderful Gal(3363)   -Ro 759
Ca 8373. I'm Rollin' in Love(3428)   -Ro 796
Ca 9000. Bad Girl(3430-2)   -Li 3029, Ro 804
Ca 9170. In a Great Big Way   -Ro 972
   "   Love Me or Leave Me   -Ro 943
Ca 9203. Milwaukee Walk
Ca 9235. Moanin' Low   -Ba 6472,Pe 15208
Ca 9005. My Honey's Lovin' Arms/Let's Do It
Ro 1003. You Oughta Know(3891)/(CLIFF ROBERTS)
Ro 1073. Satisfied
Ro 1082. Look What You've Done to Me(4112)/(DIXIE DAISIES)
Li 3233. The Junior-Senior Prom(3900)%/(BROADWAY BROADCASTERS) -Ca 9206

MILLS MUSIC MASTERS (Personnel unknown):
Me 12059. Little Spanish Dancer/I'm So in Love With You
Me 12091. Please Don't Talk About Me When I'm Gone/They Satisfy

MILLS MUSICAL CLOWNS (Jack Teagarden,trombone: Benny Goodman,clarinet; et al):
Pat 36930. Railroad Man/Baby   -Pe 15111
Pat 36944. Futuristic Rhythm/Out Where the Blues Begin
Pat 36955. Sweetest Melody   -Pe 15136
Pat 36974. Wipin' the Pan   -Pe 15155
   "   I Used to Love Her

MILLS SWINGPHONIC ORCHESTRA (Charlie Spivak, Manny Feinstein, trumpets: Larry
Binyon, alto sax; Babe Rusin, tenor: Paul Ricci,clarinet; Sam Weiss,drums; Artie
Bernstein,bass; Carl Kress,guitar; Franklyn Marks,piano):
Ma 126. Merry Widow on a Spree(366)/Dear Dear What Can the Matter Be(367)
--   ---. At a Cuban Cabaret

MILLS TEN BLACKBERRIES (Duke Ellington's Orchestra):
Ve 7088. Sweet Mama(150584)/Double Check Stomp(150586)
Ve 7082. Hot and Bothered(150585)/Black and Tan Fantasy(150590)-Di 6056,Cl 5331

MILLS AND HIS BLUES SERENADERS, WARREN (Featuring an interpolation by Duke Ellington and His Orchestra):
Vi 35962. Gems from Blackbirds of 1928/St. Louis Blues

MIRANDA AND HIS MEANDERERS, JACK (Jack Miranda,clarinet; Buddy Featherstonehaugh,
tenor sax; Norman Payne,trumpet; Felix King,piano; Eddie Freeman,guitar; Al Burke,
bass; Ronnie Gubertini,drums):   1935
PaE 2149. Bread and Jam/Ida Sweet as Apple Cider(Pat Dodds,piano)

MISS RHAPSODY (Rhapsody Underhill,vocal; Emmett Berry,trumpet: Walter Thomas,
alto and tenor sax; June Cole,piano; Cozy Cole,drums; Billy Taylor,bass):
                                                             July 6,1944
Sav 5511. Hey Lawdy Mama/Groovin' the Blues

MISSISSIPPI JOOK BAND (Piano, tambourin, guitar):
Me 61165. Hittin' the Bottle Stomp(HAT 139)/Skippy Whippy(HAT 145)
Me 61271. Dangerous Woman(HAT 141)/Barbecue Bust(HAT 145)
MISSISSIPPI MAULERS (jazz band with vocals by Roy Evans):
Co 1545. My Angeline(146755)/Don't Mess Around With Me(146756)

MISSOURI JAZZ BAND (Unidentified, although some of the records sound like Red Ni-
chols groups):
Ba 1399. San/(SAM LANIN)
Ba 1662. Spanish Shawl
Ba 1778. Breezin' Along With the Breeze(6629-2)
Ba 1999. How I Hate That Desert Song/(GOLDEN GATE)
Ba 3857. Clap Yo' Hands/Do Do do
Ba 3935. South Wind
Ba 6030. Miss Annabelle Lee
Ba 6099. Who's Got the Blues for You Now
Ba 7003. Mary Ann/(IMPERIAL DANCE ORCHESTRA)
Ba 7007. Four Walls

```
      Do  3605. Angry(16137)
      Do  3952. Stomp Off Let's Go
      Do  4089. Keep Sweepin'the Cobwebs/Whether It Rains Whether It Snows
      Re  8352. I'm Comin' Virginia/(LUCKY TEN)
      Re  9514. Bugle Call Rag(5162)/My Sweetie Went Away(5198)
      Re  9525. Big Blond Mama/Slow Poke
      Re  9568. Walk Jenny Walk/Mama Loves Papa
      Re  9578. Doo Wacka Doo
      Re  9586. Somebody Nobody Loves
      Re  9710. Too Tired                                            -Ba 1412
      Re  9855. The Farmer Took Another Load Away
      Pu 11478. Sadie Green(378)/(IRWIN ABRAM)
      Or   521. When a Blonde Makes Up Her Mind
      Or   537. My Darling Della/The Tricky Ten
      Or  1769. I'm Gonna Count My Sheep(19098-3)/(VINCENT LOPEZ)
      Pe 15273. The Man from the South/Nobody's Sweetheart
      Pe 15283. Sing You Sinners                                    -BrIm 2309
```

MISSOURI JAZZ HOUNDS:
```
      Ba  1200. Yes We Have No Bananas/Oh Harold
      Re  9470. Nothin' But
      Re  9490. That Red Head Gal/(SAM LANIN)
```

MISSOURIANS, THE (Cecil Scott,clarinet and tenor sax; William Blue,Andrew Brown, altos; Walter Thomas,tenor; R.Q.Dickerson and Reuben Reeves or Lamar Wright, trumpets; De Priest Wheeler,trombone; Jimmie Prince,piano: LeRoy Maxey,drums; J. F. Smith,tuba; Charles Stamps or Morris White,banjo):
```
      Vi 38067. Market Street Stomp                                 -HMV 16, 19
       "        Missouri Moan
      Vi 38071. Ozark Mountain Blues                                -HMV 19
       "        You'll Cry for Me, But I'll Be Gone(Cab Calloway,voc.?)
      Vi 38084. 400 Hop                                             -BB 6084
       "        Scotty Blues
      Vi 38103. I've Got Someone/Vine Street Drag
      Vi 38120. Prohibition Blues/Stoppin' the Traffic
      Vi 38145. Two Hundred Squabble/Swingin' Dem Cats              -HMV 21
               See also: Cab Calloway; Cotton Club Orchestra.
```

MITCHELL, GEORGE (trumpet. See following):
   ADA BROWN: Vo 1009.
   JOHNNY DODDS: Br 3568, 3997.
   EARL HINES: Vi 22683,22842,38042,38043,38048,38096.
   HALF PINT JAXON: Vo 2553, 2603.
   JELLY ROLL MORTON: Vi 20221,20296,20252,20405,20415,20431,20772,20948,21345;
      BB 10252,10254,10255,10256.
   NEW ORLEANS BOOTBLACKS: Co 14337,14465.
   NEW ORLEANS WANDERERS: Co 698,735.
   LUIS RUSSELL: Vo 1010.
   MA RAINEY: ?
      (Note; The listing of George Mitchell among the personnel of the Dixie Washboard Band, in Vol. I, appears to be incorrect in the light of subsequent information)

MOBILE MELODY MAKERS:
   Rad 1225. A Little Bit of Jazz/(COTTON BLOSSOM ORCHESTRA)

   MOBILE MELODY MEN:
   Vr 5002. Me Too(2078)/(HOT HENRY)

MOBILE REVELERS (vocals with guitar and piano):
   VD 5122. St.Louis Blues(3764B)   -VD 74287*
           *Issued under "Alabama Harmonizers".

MODERNISTS, THE (Benny Goodman's Orchestra; Goodman,clarinet: Hymie Schertzer, Ben Kantor,Arthur Rullini,saxes; Sam Shapiro,Russ Case,Jerry Neary,trumpets; Jack Lacey,Red Ballard,trombones; Claude Thornhill,piano: George Van Eps,guitar: Sam Weiss,drums; Harry Goodman,bass):   1934
   Pe 16002. I'm Getting Sentimental Over You(15884-1)/Solitude(15883-1)
                                       -Ba 33192,Me 13159,Or 2990,VoE 3/12

MIFF MOLE

See also:
   ALABAMA RED PEPPERS: Ro 494; Ca 8109,8129,8130,8132,8204,8205.
   ARKANSAS TRAVELERS: Ha 332,383,421,459,505,601.
   CHARLESTON CHASERS: Co 446, 861, 909, 1076, 1229, 1260, 1335, 1539, 1891, 1925,
   COTTON PICKERS: Br 2292 through 3001.   (1989.
   GOOFUS FIVE: Uncertain.
   INDIANA FIVE: Uncertain.
   JAM SESSION: Com 1504, 1505.
   JAZZBO'S CAROLINA SERENADERS:
   ROGER WOLFE KAHN:

LADD'S BLACK ACES:
YANK LAWSON: Sig 28103.
LOUISIANA RHYTHM KINGS: Vo 15828.
RED NICHOLS: Br 3477 through 4456, except 4363, 4373.
NICHOLS STOMPERS: All.
NICK'S DIXIELAND JAZZ BAND: Man 10-1,2,3.
ORIGINAL MEMPHIS FIVE: Most.
RED HEADS: Most.
RED AND MIFF'S STOMPERS: All.
SIOUX CITY SIX: Ge 5569.
SIX HOTTENTOTS: All.
MUGGSY SPANIER: Com 1519.
TENNESSEE TOOTERS: All.
WABASH DANCE ORCHESTRA:
MILT SHAW: OK 41158.

MOLE AND HIS LITTLE MOLERS, MIFF (Miff Mole,trombone: Red Nichols,trumpet: Jimmy Dorsey,clarinet; Arthur Schutt,piano; Eddie Lang,guitar:Vic Berton,drums):
                                                           1st,2nd,5th sides,Jan.26,1927
OK 40758. Alexander's Ragtime Band(80338A)   -Co 36280,PaE 3320,0dF 165090
  "   Some Sweet Day   " , PaE 2508
OK 40784. A Hot Time in the Old Town   -PaE 3326
  "   The Darktown Strutters Ball   "   "
OK 40846. Hurricane(80340)   -PaE 3362,0dG 189176
  "   Davenport Blues(80501)   "   "

  (Sub. Fud Livingston,clarinet; Add Adrian Rollini,bass sax):   1927
OK 40890. Imagination(81296)   -PaE 2286,3420,0dF 165192
  "   Feelin' No Pain(81297)   -PaE 3420,0dF 165192
OK 40932. Original Dixieland One Step(81298B)
                                       -Co 36010,PaE 3530,0dF 165276,Br 8243
  "   My Gal Sal(81413B)   "   "   "
OK 40984. Honolulu Blues(81414B)/The New Twister(81415C)-PaE 3441,0dF 165328

  (Nichols; Mole; Frank Teschemacher,clarinet: Joe Sullivan,piano; Eddie Con-
  don,banjo; Gene Krupa,drums):   July 6,1928
OK 41445. Shim-me-sha-wabble(400850A)
                       -Ha 1427*,Co 35953,UHCA 23,0dF 238185,PaE 2506
  "   After You've Gone(different personnel; see below)
                       *On Harmony as Tennessee Music Men
HRS   15. Windy City Stomp(400849C)*/(LOUISIANA RHYTHM KINGS)
                       *Reissued on Co 35953 as "One Step to Heaven"

  (Red Nichols,Phil Napoleon,trumpets; Miff Mole,trombone; Fud Livingston,
  clarinet and tenor sax; Arthur Schutt,piano; Stanley King,drums; guitar*;
  tuba, mellophone*):
OK 41098. Crazy Rhythm(400895B)*   -PaE 230,0dF 165412
  "   You Took Advantage of Me(400896A)*   "
OK 41153. You're the Cream in My Coffee(401394B)-PaE 368,PaF 22230,0dF 165546
  "   Wild Oat Joe(401395B)   -PaE 2328,   "   "

  (For another record from this session see Milt Shaw, OK 41158)

  (Sub. Jimmy Dorsey,clarinet and alto sax; Eddie Lang,guitar; no bass): 1929
OK 41232. I've Got a Feeling I'm Falling(401815C)   -PaE 2355
  "   That's a plenty(401816B)

  (Carl Kress,guitar; no Nichols):
OK 41273. Birmingham Bertha(402529C)   -PaE 432, 0dF 165273
  "   Moanin' Low (402530C)   -PaE 849,   "

  (Add Adrian Rollini,bass xax; Joe Tarto,bass):
OK 41371. Navy Blues(403740A)   -PaE 701
  "   Lucky Little Devil(403741B)   -PaE 702

  (Babe Rusin,tenor sax; omit Rollini):
PaE 647. You Made Me Love You(402986)
OK 41445. After You've Gone(402987C),no bass -UHCA 24,0dF 238185,PaE 1063
  "   Shim-me-sha-wabble(see 7/6/28 session above)

  (Miff Mole,trombone; Paul Ricci,clarinet and sax; Frank Signorelli,piano;
  Tony Tortomas,trumpet; Sam Weiss,drums; Carl Kress,guitar):
Br 7842. How Could You   -VoE 87
  "   On a Little Bamboo Bridge
Vo 3468. I Can't Break the Habit of You(20692)   -VoE 87
  "   Love and Learn(20693)   "

  MIFF MOLE & HIS NICKSIELAND BAND(Mole,trombone; Bobby Hackett,trumpet; Pee
  Wee Russell,clarinet; Ernie Cacares,baritone sax; Eddie Condon,guitar;Gene
  Schroeder,piano; Bob Casey,bass; Joe Grauso,drums):
Com 1518. Peg o' My Heart/St. Louis Blues

MONARCH JAZZ QUARTET:
  OK 8736. Four or Five Times/What's the Matter Now
  OK 8761. I ain't Got Nobody/Somebody's Wrong

MONDELLO AND HIS ORCHESTRA, TOOTS (unknown personnel):
  Br 8031. Let That Be a Lesson to You/Thanks for the Memory
  Br 8061. Naughty, Naughty/You're in Love With Love
  Br 8094. I Love You Just Because/Let Me Day Dream
  Br 8105. At Sundown/I'll See You in My Dreams

        (Toots Mondello,alto sax; Carl Kress,guitar: Jerry Jerome,tenor; Al Kendis,
        drums; Noni Bernardi,alto; Joe Swarzman, bass; Arthur Rollini,tenor; Ziggy
        Elman,trumpet; Claude Thornhill,piano):
  Vs 8110. Sweet Lorraine(US 1100-1)/Beyond the Moon(US 1101-1)
  Vs 8118. St.Louis Gal(US 1098-1)/Louisiana(US 1099-2)

        MONDELLO, (saxophone solo, with Claude Thornhill,piano; Nick Fatool,drums):
  Roy 1817. Here's Your Change(US 1177-1)/Burnin' Sticks(US 1180-2) Dec.18,1939
  Roy 1823. Sunset Lullaby/Shades of Jade

MONKEY JOE (vocals):
  Vo 05166. Just Give Some Away/Carry My Business On
  Vo 05274. You Don't Have to Tell Me/That Same Cat
  Vo 05348. Bitin' on Me/Mountain Baby Blues
  OK 5685. Bad Luck Man Blues/We Can't Get Along
  OK 06153. McComb City Blues/Old Man Blues

MONTGOMERY, EURREAL (pianist, see "Little Brother")

MONTGOMERY, J. NEAL AND HIS ORCHESTRA):
  OK 8682. Atlanta Low Down(402313B)/Auburn Avenue Stomp(402314B)

MOODY, JULIA (voc., acc. by Joe Smith's Jazz Band):
  BS 14122. The Cootie Crawl/Jada Blues

        (Orchestra accompaniment):
  BS 14140. Starvin' for Love/Laughin'Cryin' Blues

        (With cornet; clarinet; trombone):
  Re 9765. Worried Blues/Broken Busted Blues

  Co 14087. Strivin' Blues/Last Night Blues

        (Acc. Edgar Dowell's Chicago Waddlers):
  Co 14103. Police Blues/Midnight Dan

        (Acc. by the Dixie Wobblers):
  Co 14121. He'll Do You Wrong/That Chicago Wiggle

MOONLIGHT REVELERS (New Orleans style band, variously listed as King Oliver or
Louis Armstrong possibility):
  GG 1775. Alabama shuffle (3606)   -VD 71775*
  GG 1767. Baby Knows How(3608)
                    *Issued as by Five Hot Chocolates

MOORE, ALEX (blues singing with piano, guitar):
  Co 14496. West Texas Woman/It Wouldn't Be So Hard
  De 7288. Blue Bloomer Blues/Come Back Baby
  De 7552. Bull Cow Blues/Hard Hearted Woman

MOORE, ALICE (vocals with trombone and piano):
  Para 12471. Serving Time Blues/Loving Heart Blues
  Para 12819. Black and Evil Blues/Broadway Street Woman Blues

        (Henry Brown,piano; Ike Rodgers,trombone):
  Para 12868. My Man Blues(1577)/Prison Blues(1576)
  Para 13107. Lonesome Dream Blues(L170-2)/Kid Man Blues(L-171-2)

        LITTLE ALICE FROM ST. LOUIS:
  De 7028. Riverside Pusher(9318)/Black Evil Blues(9317)
  De 7056. Lonesome Woman Blues/Trouble Blues
  De 7109. Just Sitting Here Wondering/Death Valley Blues
  De 7132. Tomorrow Blues(90184)/Blue Black and Evil Blues(90183)
  De 7153. S.O.S. Blues(90177)/Daddy Calling Mamma(90178)
  De 7190. Grass Cutter Blues/Telephone Blues
  De 7227. Dark Angel/Money Tree Man
  De 7253. Three Men(90754)/I'm Going Fishing Too(90752)
  De 7293. New Blue Black and Evil Blues/Just a Good Girl Treated Wrong
  De 7327. Tired of Me Blues/Midnight Creepers
  De 7369. Too Many Men/Don't Deny Me Baby
  De 7380. Doggin' Man Blues/Hand in Hand Woman
  De 7393. Unlucky Play Blues/Push Cart Pusher

MOORE, GERRY (piano solos):
  PaE 2223. Gerry Building/May Write Blues
        GERRY MOORE AND HIS CHICAGO BRETHREN:
  DeE 6347. Oh Lady Be Good(TB2853-1)/Honeysuckle Rose(TB2854-1)

38

MOORE AND HIS NEW ORLEANS BLACK DEVILS, GRANT:
Vo 1622. Original Dixieland One Step/Mama Don't Allow No Music In Here

MOORE, KID PRINCE (blues singing):
De 7475. Bear Meat Blues/Single Man Blues
De 7514. Ford V-8 Blues/Sally Long
De 7539. Talkin' 'Bout the Snuff/That's Lovin' Me

MOORE, MONETTE (blues singer, with various accompaniments believed to include Rex Stewart, cornet, on some records):
Para 12015. Sugar Blues/Best Friend Blues
Para 12030. Gulf Coast Blues/Down Hearted Blues

(Naomi Carew, piano):
Para 12067. Muddy Water Blues/Treated Wrong Blues

(James Cassino,piano; Wyatt Houston,violin,first side: James Blythe,piano, second side):
Para 12210. Rocking Chair Blues(8074)/Friendless Blues(8077)

(Piano and cornet):
Vo 14903. I Wanna Jazz Some More/Texas Man Blues
Vo 14911. Heart Broken Mama/Death Letter Blues
Co 14105. Take It Easy(141153)/Get It Fixed(141154)

(Orchestra accompaniment):
Vi 20356. If You Don't Like Potatoes/Somebody's Been Lovin' My Baby

MONETTE MOORE AND HER SWING SHOP BOYS:
De 7161. Rhythm for Sale/Two Old Maids in a Folding Bed

MOORE, DWIGHT 'GATEMOUTH" (acc. by Dallas B   v and His Small Town Boys):
Na 6001. I Ain't Mad at You Pretty Bab   It Ain't None of Me(59)
Na 6002. I'm Going Way Back Home/Did   Love a Woman

(Acc. by Bud Johnson's All Stars: Budd Johnson,sax: Harry Carney,sax; Jimmy Hamilton,clarinet; Dick Vance,trumpet· Sam Benskin, piano; Al Hall,bass;J. C. Heard,drums):
Na 4004. Walking My Blues Away(85)/Bum Dee Dah Ra Dee(86)

MORAND, HERB (trumpet: see following):
BEALE STREET WASHBOARD BAND: Vo 1403.
HARLEM HAMFATS: All.
HARRY'S RECKLESS FIVE: Bwy 1355.
ROSETTA HOWARD: Deccas.
HALF PINT JAXON: Deccas.
KANSAS CITY FRANK: Para 12898.

MOREHOUSE AND HIS SWING SIX, CHAUNCEY (Chauncey Morehouse,drums and vibraphone; Claude Thornhill,piano; Aftie Bernstein,bass; Charlie Spivak,trumpet: Jimmy Lytell,clarinet; George Brunis,trombone):
Vr 608. Blues in B Flat(M513)/On the Alamo(M513)
Vr 638. My Gal Sal(M512)/(JOHNNY WILLIAMS)

CHAUNCEY MOREHOUSE AND HIS ORCHESTRA(Morehouse,Stan King,drums; Felix Giobbe, bass; Jack LeMaire,guitar; Fulton McGrath,piano; Ralph Muzzillo,Toots Camareta,Chelsea Quealey,trumpets; Larry Alpeter,Andy Russo,trombones; Milton Yaner,Slats Long,altos; Carl Biesecker,Tony Zimmers,tenor saxes):
Br 8122. Maži-Pani/Plastered in Paris
Br 8142. Ku-Li-A/Oriental Nocturne

MORGAN AND HIS ORCHESTRA, RUSS (Personnel is said to contain Wingy Mannone,trumpet, in this and possibly other titles):
Co 3067. Sliphorn Sam

MORGAN'S JAZZ BAND, SAM (Jim Robinson,trombone: Sam Morgan,trumpet; Ike Morgan, trumpet; Andrew Morgan,tenor and clarinet; Earl Foucher,alto and soprano saxes; Johnny Davis,banjo; Shine Nolan,drums; Sidney Brown,bass; Walter Decou,piano):
Co 14213. Everybody's Talking About Sammy(143976)   New Orleans,Sept.,1923
"   Sing On(143978)   -Co 14539
Co 14258. Steppin' on the Gas/Mobile Stomp
Co 14267. Down by the Riverside
"   Over in the Glory Land   -Co 14539
Co 14351. Short Dress Gal(145000)/Bogalousa Strut(145001)

MORRIS PAST JAZZ MASTERS, THOMAS (Thomas Morris,cornet: Happy Caldwell,tenor sax; possibly Buster Bailey,clarinet: Clarence Williams,piano; Ed Allen,trumpet,and others):   1926
OK 4867. Lonesome Journey Blues(S71531C)/When the Jazz Band Starts to Play
OK 4940. Beaucoupe de Jazz/Those Blues   (71532B)
OK 8055. Original Charleston Strut/E Flat Blues No. 2
OK 8075. The Bull Blues(E Flat No. 1)/Just Blues That's All
         (See also: Fannie Goosby: OK 8095)

THOMAS MORRIS AND HIS SEVEN HOT BABIES:
Vi 20179. Ham Gravy/Jackass Blues
Vi 20180. Georgia Grind/Charleston Stampede
Vi 20316. Who's Dis Heah Stranger/(NEW ORLEANS BLUE FIVE)
Vi 20330. Blues from the Everglades/P.D.Q. Blues
Vi 20364. The Mess/(NEW ORLEANS BLUE FIVE)
Vi 20483. The Chinch/Lazy Drag
     (See Thomas(Fats) Waller for Vi 20776,20890,21127,21202,21358)

MORSE, LEE (Benny Goodman, clarinet, and Eddie Lang, guitar, are among those mentioned as having accompanied this vocalist on various records. The band in most of the Columbias is called "Her Blue Grass Boys" or "Her Southern Serenaders"):
Pat 36546. Everything's Peaches/(WILLARD ROBISON)
Pe 11216. In Old Madrid/Juanita
Pe 11580. Yes Sir That's My Baby
Pe 11582. Dallas Blues
Pe 11602. I Love My Baby/Deep Wide Ocean Blues
Pe 11604. Nobody Else/Garland of Old Fashioned Roses
Pe 11636. Jersey Walk
Pe 12180. Better Shoot Straight With Your Mama(105692)/Everybody Loves My Baby
Pe 12181. Lee's Lullaby/All Alone   (103693)
Co 939. Ain't He Sweet/Mollie Make Up Your Mind
Co 974. Side by Side/My Idea of Heaven
Co 1011. I'd Love to Be in Love/Where the Wild Wild Flowers Grow
Co 1063. What Do I Care What Somebody Said/I Hate to Say Goodbye
Co 1082. We(My Honey and Me)/Rosita
Co 1149. Dawning/I've Looked All Over for a Girl Like You
Co 1199. Did You Mean It/Old Fashioned Romance
Co 1276. Give Me a Good Night Kiss/Keep Sweeping the Cobwebs Off the Moon
Co 1303. Let a Smile Be Your Umbrella/There Must Be a Silver Lining
Co 1328. After We Kiss/Poor Butterfly Waits for Me
Co 1381. I'm Lonely/In the Sing Song Sycamore Tree
Co 1434. Lonesome for You/When I Lost You
Co 1466. Be Sweet to Me/Don't Keep Me in the Dark Bright Eyes
Co 1497. Shadows on the Wall/Mother
Co 1584. Mississippi Mud/I must Have That Man
Co 1621. Old Man Sunshine/Don't Be Like That
Co 1659. If You Want a Rainbow/Let's Do It
Co 1716. You're My Own/Where the Shy Little Violets Grow
Co 1752. Susianna(147397)/Main Street(146989)
Co 1866. I'm Doin' What I'm Doin' for Love/He's a Good Man to Have Around
Co 1896. Miss You/In the Hush of the Night
Co 1922. Sweetness/Moanin' Low
Co 1972. Love Me/Sweethearts' Holiday
Co 2012. Look What You've Done to Me/If I Can't Have You
Co 2037. My Fate Is in Your Hands/Too Good to Be Forgotten
Co 2063. I Love You/A Little Kiss Each Morning
Co 2101. Blue Turning Grey Over You/Until Love Comes Along
Co 2136. Tain't No Sin/I'm Following You
Co 2165. Sing You Sinners/Cooking Breakfast for Two
Co 2225. Swingin' in a Hammock/Seems to Me
Co 2248. Little White Lies/Nobody Cares If I'm Blues
Co 2270. Just You and I/I still Get a Thrill
Co 2308. When the Organ Played at Twilight/Just a Little While
Co 2333. Loving You the Way I Do/Wastin' My Love on You
Co 2348. You're Drivin' Me Crazy/My Secret
Co 2388. Blue Again/I'm One of God's Chillun
Co 2417. Walkin' My Baby Back Home/I've Got Five Dollars
Co 2436. By My Side/The Tune That Never Grows Old
Co 2474. Let's Get Friendly/I'm Through With Love
Co 2497. It's the Girl/I'm an Unemployed Sweetheart
Co 2650. Lawd You Made the Night Too Long/When the Lights Are Soft and Low
Co 2705. Something in the Night/Moonlight on the River
  (Acc. Eddie Duchin's Orchestra)
Co 18001. One Hour With You(Medley)/Paradise (Waltz medley)

BENNY MORTON

See Also:
HENRY ALLEN: De 18092.
ALLEN-HAWKINS: Pe 15815,15858.
BALTIMORE BELL HOPS: Co 2449.
COUNT BASIE: De 1581, 1965, 2004, 2030, 2212, 2224, 2249, 2284, 2325; Co 35321, 35338, 35357.
BENNY CARTER: Vo 2870, 2898; OK 6001; BB 10962, 10998, 11090.
CONNIE'S INN: Vi 22698,22721;Me 12145,12216,12239,12340;Cr 3092,3107,3180.
ED HALL: BN 36.
FLETCHER HENDERSON: Co 1913,2513,2559,2565,14392;Vi.22775,22786,22955,24008.
BILLIE HOLIDAY: Vo 3748,3947,4029.
EDDY HOWARD: Co 35771, 35915.
JAM SESSION: Com 1513.
HARLAN LATTIMORE: Co 3675, 2678.

```
      BEN POLLACK; Co 2870, 2879.
      DON REDMAN: All Br, Me, Vo.
      JOE SULLIVAN: Vo 5496,5531,5556; OK 5647.
      TEDDY WILSON: Br 7550, 7554, 7640, 7729, 8053, 8259, 8265, 8270.
```

MORTON AND HIS ORCHESTRA, BENNY (Benny Morton,trombone: Henry Allen,trumpet; Edward Inge,Jerry Blake,alto sax and clarinet: Teddy McRae,tenor sax; Don Kirkpatrick,piano; Bobby Johnson,guitar; Billy Taylor,bass; Manzie Johnson,drums): <u>1934</u>
```
      Co   2902. Get Goin'(152717; J.Blake,voc)/Fare Thee Well to Harlem(152718)
      Co   2924. Tailor Made(152719)/Gold Digger's Song(152720,Allen,voc.) (-CoE 746
```

BENNY MORTON AND HIS TROMBONE CHOIR(Benny Morton,Bill Harris,Vic Dickenson, Claude Jones,trombones: Johnny Guarnieri,piano; Cozy Cole,druma; Alix Hall, bass): <u>May 30,1944</u>
```
      Key 1309. Liza(HL38-1)/Once in Awhile(HL39)
      Key 1315. Sliphorn Outing/Where or When
```

BENNY MORTON AND HIS ORCHESTRA(Morton,trombone: Eddie Dougherty,drums; Sammy Benskin,piano; Jimmy Butts,bass; Robert Stark,trumpet: Prince Robinson, clarinet):
```
      Asch 506. Boogie/Williphant
      Asch 507. Star Dust/Chicken at the Chester
```

BENNY MORTON'S ALL STARS (Morton,trombone; Barney Bigard,clarinet: Ben Webster,tenor sax; Sammy Benskin,piano; Israel Crosby,bass: Eddie Dougherty, drums):
```
      BN   46. The Sheik of Araby(221)/Conversing in Blue(220)
      BN   47 . Limehouse Blues(222)/My Old Flame(219)
```

JELLY ROLL MORTON

See also:
```
   WILTON CRAWLEY: Vi 38116, 38136.
   JOHNNY DUNN: Co 14306, 14358.
   LEVEE SERENADERS: Vo 1154.
   LIZZIE MILES: Vi 38571.
   DAVE NELSON: QRS ?
   NEW ORLEANS RHYTHM KINGS: Ge 5217, 5219, 5220, 5221.
   BILLIE YOUNG: Vi 23339.
```

MORTON, FERDINAND 'JELLY ROLL' (Piano solos):   <u>Richmond,Ind.,1923-24</u>
```
   Ge  5218. Grandpa's Spells(11544)/Kansas City Stomp(11545)
   Ge  5289. King Porter Stomp(11537)/Wolverine Blues(11546)
   Ge  5323. The Pearls(11547)/(SOL WAGNER ORCHESTRA)
   Ge  5486. New Orleans Joys(11538)/Perfect Rag(11917)              -Si 4041
   Ge  5515. Bucktown Blues(11913)/Tom Cat Blues(11914)              -Si 4040
   Ge  5552. Jelly Roll Blues(11911)/Big Fat Ham(11912)              -Si 4038
   Ge  5590. Shreveport Stomp(11908)/Stratford Hunch(11915)
   Ge  5632. Tia Juana(11907)/Mamamita(1191)                   -Ge 3043,Si 4028
                                                                   Chicago, 1924
   Rialto 535. London Blues                                              -Se  3
   Para 12216. Mamamita(8071)/35th Street Blues(8072)         -Pu 12216,SD 101

       (with King Oliver, cornet):
   Au   617. King Porter(685)/Tom Cat(687                                -Se  1

       (with clarinet and kazoo):
   Au   623. My Gal/Wolverine Blues(Volly de Faut,clarinet)

       (Solos):                                                      about 1925
   SD  103. Frog-i-more Rag
                                                                          1926
   Vo  1019. Sweetheart o' Mine/Fat Meat and Greens                 -Br 80068
   Vo  1020. King Porter Stomp/The Pearls                      -OrE 1007,Br 80067
                                                             Camden,N.J.,July 8,1929
   Vi 38527. Seattle Hunch(49449)/Freakish(49451)                   -Vi 27565
   Vi 38627. Pep(49448)/Fat Frances(49450)                          -BB 10257

       (Solos,--with vocals*):                                 New York,Dec.,1939
   Gl  4001. Original Rags(R2561)/Mamie's Blues(R2573)*
   Unissued. Sportin' House Rag(R2560)
   Gl  4002. The Naked Dance(R2571)/Michigan Water Balues(R2579)*
   Unissued. Naked Rag(R2563)
   Gl  4003. The Crave(R2562)/Buddy Bolden's Blues(R2570)*
   Gl  4004. Mister Joe(R2564)/Winin' Boy Blues(R2566)*
   Unissued. Animule Dance(R2567)
   Gl  4005. King Porter Stomp(R2565)/Don't You Leave Me Here(R2572)*
                                                              Washington,D.C.,1939
   JM    11. Winin' Boy Blues(MLB147)/Honky Tonk Music(MLB149)
   JM    12. Finger Buster(MLB145)/Creepy Feeling(MLB146)
   Unissued. Honkey Tonk Music No. 2(MLB148)
```

41

"THE AUTOBIOGRAPHY OF JELLY ROLL MORTON"
(The following are Library of Congress recordings, all made at Washington, D.C., in 1938, some of which are now being released to the public on the Circle label.--JR 3/46):   with vocals*

```
1638 A & B.   Alabama Bound*
1639 A & B-1. King Porter Stomp*
1639 B-2.     You Can Have It, I Don't Want it*
1639 B-3.     Monologue on Stolen Jazz Tunes and Why They Weren't Spoken
1640 A & B.   Monologue on His Ancestry, Early Life and First Music Lessons
1641 A & B.   -----
1642 A-1.     Sammy Davis' Ragtime Style*
1642 A-2.     Pretty Baby*
1642 B.       Monologue on Tony Jackson*
1643 A-1.     Tony Jackson's Naked Dance
1643 A-2.     Monologue on Sportin' Life in New Orleans
1643 B.       Honky Tonk Blues*
1643 B-1.     Pretty Baby*
1644 A-1.     Monologue on New Orleans Honky Tonks
1644 A-2.     Levy Rambler Blues*
1644 B.       Monologue on Aaron Harris
1645 A.       Aaron Harris Was a Bad Bad Man*
1645 B.       Monologue on Aaron Harris, Madame Papa Loos, Sheep One, and Robert
1646 A & B.   Robert Charles' Story*                                    (Charles
1646 B-2.     Game Kid Blues*
1647 A.       Monologue on Game Kid and Buddy Carter
1647 B.       Monologue on New Orleans Death Customs and Food*
1648 A & B-1. Monologue on New Orleans Funeral Customs and Beginnings of Jazz*
1649 A & B.   Monologue on Beginnings of Jazz*
1650 A & B.   Monologue on Origins of Jazz and Styles of Playing*
1651 A & B.   Monologue on Breaks and Riffs in Jazz, on Swing, and on His Theory
1652 A.       Monologue on Bill Johnson, Early Jazz Bands & Leaders*  (of Jazz*
1652 B.       If I Was Whiskey and You With a Drink*
1653 A.       They Call Her Frivolous Sal*
1653 B.       Maple Leaf Rag
1654 A&B.     Monologue on St. Louis Ragtime*
1655 A & B.   Lowdown Blues*
1656 A & B.   The Winin' Boy*
1657 A & B.   The Animule Dance*
1658 A & B.   Monologue on Early Blues and Buddy Bolden*
1659 A.       Mr. Jelly Lord*
1659 B.       Monologue on Jelly Roll Blues and Origin of His Nickname*
1660 A.       Jelly Roll Blues*
1660 B.       Monolobue on New Orleans Honky Tonks
1661 A & B.   Monologue on New Orleans Tough Characters*
1662 A & B.   See See Rider*
1663 A & B.   Monologue on New Orleans Clubs, Parades and Fights*
1664 A & B.   Monologue on His Early Experiences*
1665 A.       Monologue on His Travels*
1665 B.       Monologue on Saloons and Piano Players of Beale Street and Memphis*
1666 A.       Monologue on Bad Sam and Bum Frenchy*
1667 A & B.   Make Me a Pallet on the Floor*
1668 A & B.   -----
1669 A.       The Dirty Dozen*
1669 B.       The Murder Ballad*
1670 A.       Now Let Me Tell You*
1670 B.       I Know You've Got My Man*
1671 A.       They Brought That Gal to the Prison Gates
1671 B.       Gal When I Get Through You Think I Am a Man*
1672 A.       Ask My Sister, Please Don't Be Like Me*
1672 B.       Goodbye to the World, I know I'm Gone*
1673 A.       Fickle Fay Creep
1673 B.       Jungle Blues
1674 A.       King Porter Stomp
1674 B.       Sweet Peter
1675 A.       Hyena Stomp
1675 B.       Wolverine Blues
1676 A.       -----
1676 B.       State and Madison
1677 A & B.   The Pearls
1678 A.       Bert Williams
1678 B.       Freakish
1679 A.       Pep
1679 B.       Monologue on the Georgia Skij Game*
1680 A.       -----
1681 A.       Indian Songs at the Mardi Gras*
1681 B.       New Orleans Blues
1682 A-1.     Dialogue on Jaaz and Blues*
1682 A-2.     La Paloma into Blues
1682 B.       Creepy Feeling
1683 A.       -----
1684 A.       Mama Nita
1684 B-1.     Can Can*
1684 B-2.     If You Don't Shake Don't Get No Cakes*
1685 A.       Spanish Swat
```

42

```
1685 A.      Spanish Swat
1685 B.      Misbehavin'*
1686 A.      I Hate a Man Like You*
1686 B.      Michigan Water Blues*
1687 A&B.    Wining Boy*
1688 A-1.    Mamie Desdume's Blues*
1688 B-1.    Boogie Woogie Blues
1688 B-2.    Albert Carroll Blues
1688 B-3.    Dialogue
2487-2489.   New Orleans Street Bands
```

MORTON'S JAZZ BAND. JELLY ROLL (Natty Dominique,cornet: Zue Robertson,trombome;
Jelly Roll Morton,piano; Horace Eubanks,clarinet; drums):   Chicago,Dec.,1923
OK 8105. Some Day Sweetheart(8498A)/London Blues(8499A)

    JELLY ROLL MORTON'S STOMPS KINGS(Morton,piano; Jasper Taylor,drums; Dom-
inique,cornet; Townes,clarinet and alto; Roy Palmer,trombone):Chicago,1924
Para 12050. Big Fat Ham(1434)
Para 20251. Muddy Water Blues(1435-2)   -Pu 11251, Na 12251
Para 20332. Mr.Jelly Lord(8065-2: listed as by "JRM's Steamboat Four) -Pu 11332
  "   Steady Roll(8066-1)   "

    JELLY ROLL MORTON'S KINGS OF JAZZ (Morton,piano: Lee Collins,trumpet;Roy
Palmer,trombone;Balls Ball,clarinet;others unknown):   Chicago, 1924
Au 606. Fish Tail Blues(635)/High Society(636)   -Se 2
Au 607. Weary Blues/Tiger Rag   -Se 4

    JELLY ROLL MORTON'S INCOMPARABLES(Unknown personnel):   1925
Ge 3259. Mr. Jelly Lord(12467)/(FESS WILLIAMS)

    JELLY ROLL MORTON'S RED HOT PEPPERS(Morton,piano: Andrew Hilaire,drums;
John Lindsay,bass; John St.Cyr,banjo; Omer Simeon,clarinet; George Mitch-
ell,trumpet; Kid Ory,trombone.--JM 2/3/44)   Chicago,Sept.15,1926
Vi 20221. Black Bottom Stomp(36239)   -BB 10253, HMV 3164
  "   The Chant(36241)   "   "
Vi 20296. Smoke House Blues(36240)   -BB 8372, HMV 3164
     (Coupling see below)

    (Add Barney Bigard and Darnell Howard, clarinets): Chicago,Sept.21,1926
Vi 20252. Sidewalk Blues(36283)   -Vi 400118, HMV 5212
   "   Dead Man Blues(36284-1)   "   "
Vi 20252. Dead Man Blues(36284-2)
Vi 20296. Steamboat Stomp(36285)   -BB 8372

    (Omit Bigard,Howard):   Chicago,Dec.16,1926
     Vi 20405. Someday Sweetheart(37254; two violins)/Original Jelly Roll
     BB 10255. Original Jelly Roll Blues(37256-2)   (Blues(37256-1)
Vi 20415. Doctor Jazz(37257)/(DIXIELAND JUG BLOWERS)   -BB 10255
Vi 20431. Grandpa's Spells(37255-2)/Cannon Ball Blues(37258-1)
BB 10254. Grandpa's Spells(37255-3)/Cannon Ball Blues(37258-2)

    (Morton,piano; Baby Dodds,drums; Quinn Wilson,tuba; John St.Cyr,banjo;
Johnny Dodds,clarinet; Stomp Evans,alto sax; Collins or Mitchell,trumpet;
George Bryant,trombone):   Chicago,June 4,1927
Vi 20772. Hyena Stomp(38627)/Billy Goat Stomp(38628)
Vi 21345. Jungle Blues(38630-2)/(RICHARD M. JONES)
BB 10256. Jungle Blues(38630-3)/Wild Man Blues(38629)
                                                       June 10,1927
Vi 20948. Beale Street Blues(38661)   -BB 10252
   "   The Pearls(38662-2)
BB 10252. The Pearls(38662-3)

    (Clarinet, piano, drums from above personnel):
Vi 21064. Wolverine Blues(38663)/Mr.Jelly Lord(38664)   -BB 10258

    (Morton,piano; Tommy Benford,drums; Bill Benford,tuba; Lee Blair,banjo;
Omer Simeon,clarinet; Ward Pinkett,trumpet; Geechy Fields,trombone):
                                                  New York,June 11,1928
Vi 21658. Shoe Shiner's Drag(45621)   -BB 5707, BB 7725
   "   Shreveport(45623-1)(clarinet,piano,drums)-HMV 9220 " BB 7710
Vi 21658. Shreveport(45623-2: clarinet,piano,drums)
Vi 38010. Kansas City Stomps(45620)   -BB 5109, BB 7757
   "   Boogaboo: (45622)   -BB 6031, BB 7725
Vi 38024. Georgia Swing(45619)   -BB 5109, 8515, HMV 10, 9221
   "   Mournful Serenade(45624-1; trom.cl.,pf.,ds) -BB 6601, 8515, HMV 9221
Vi 38024. Mournful Serenade(45624-2)
   Unissued. Honey Babe(45625)/Sidewalk Blues(45626) trumpet,piano,drums; both
                                                                    (sides.

43

(Morton,piano; Manzie Johnson,drums; Bass Moore,bass; Lee Blair,guitar;
Russell Procope,clarinet and alto; Joe Garland,tenor; Paul Barnes, sopra-
no sax; Edwin Swayzee, Ed Anderson, possibly Lee Collins,trumpets; Billy
Cato,trombone):   New York,Dec.6,1928
Unissued. Everybody Loves My Honey Now(48433)/You Oughta See My Girl(48436)
Vi 38055. Deep Creek(48435)   -BB 5333, HMV 10, 9220, Vo 400119
"   Red Hot Pepper(48434)   -BB 6601   "

           (Morton,piano; ___ Alexander,drums; Bass Hill,tuba; Barney ___,banjo; Geo.
           Baquet,clarinet; Walter Thomas,Joe Thomas,Paul Barnes,saxes; ___ Brisco,
           'Horsecollar' Draper,trumpets; Charlie Irvis,trombone):
                                                          Camden,N.J.,July 9,10,12,1929
Vi 38075. Burnin' the Iceberg(49452)   -Vi 400120
"   Tank Town Bump(49459)   -HMV 56
Vi 38078. Pretty Lil(49454)   -Vi 400120
"   New Orleans Bump(49456)
Vi 38093. Courthouse Bump(49453)/Sweet Aneta Mine(49455)
Vi 38113. Down My Way(49457)/Try Me Out(49458)

           (Morton,piano; Paul Barbarin,drums: Pops Foster,bass: Will Johnson,banjo;
           Albert Nicholas,clarinet; Henry Allen,trumpet;J.C.Higginbotham,trombone):
Vi 23402. Sweet Peter(57080)/Jersey Joe(57081)   New York,Nov.13,1929
Vi 23334. Mint Julep(57083)/(For reverse, see fifth personnel below)
Vi 23424. Mississippi Mildred(57082)/(For reverse,see fourth personnel below)

           JELLY ROLL MORTON TRIO(Morton,piano; Barney Bigard,clarinet; Zutty Sing-
           leton or Paul Barbarin, drums):   New York,Dec.17,1929
Vi 38108. Smilin' the Blues Away(57784)/Turtle Twist(57785)   -BB 10194
Vi 38601. My Little Dixie Home(57786)/That's Like It Ought to Be(57787)

           RED HOT PEPPERS(Morton,piano: Cozy Cole,drums: Billy Taylor,tuba; Bernard
           Addison,banjo; Eddie Barefield,clarinet; Ward Pinkett,one other,trumpets;
           Wilbur deParis,trombone):   New York,March 5,1930
Vi 23004. I'm looking for a Little Bluebird(59507)/(See 3rd personnel below)
Vi 23019. That'll Never Do(59506)/(See fourth personnel below)   -HMV 4836
Vi 23321. If Someone Would Only Love Me(59505)/(See 2nd personnel below)
Vi 23351. Each Day(59504)/(See 3rd personnel below)

           (Morton,piano; Tommy Benford,drums: Bill Benford,tuba; Bernard Addison,
           guitar: unknown banjo; Eddie Barefield,clarinet; Ward Pinkett,Bubber Miley,
           trumpets; Wilbur DeParis. trombone):   New York,March 19-20,1930
Vi 38125. Fussy Mabel(59643)
"   Ponchatrain(59644)   -Vi400121
Vi 38135. Little Lawrence(59532)   -Vi 400121
"   Harmony Blues(59532)

           (Morton,piano; Cozy Cole,drums; Billy Taylor,tuba; Lee Blair,banjo; Eddie
           Barefield,Joe Thomas,Walter Thomas,reeds; Ward Pinkett,one other,trumpets;
           Geeche Fields,trombone):   New York,June 2,1930
Vi 23307. Crazy Chords(62184)/(See 2nd personnel below)
Vi 23321. Oil Well(62182)
Vi 23424. Primrose Stomp(62185)
Vi 23429. Load of Coal(62183-1)
Vi 23429. Load of Coal(62183-2)

           (Morton,Tommy Benford; Pete Briggs,tuba; Howard Hill,guitar; Albert
           Nicholas, clarinet: Pinkett; Fields):   New York,July 14,1930
Vi 22681. Blue Blood Blues(62341)   -BB 8201
Vi 23004. Mushmouth Shuffle(62342)   -BB 8201
Vi 23334. Low Gravy(62339)   -BB 8302
Vi 23351. Strokin' Away(62340)   -BB 8302

           (Morton; Addison; Pinkett; Bill Beason,drums; Bill Taylor,tuba; Sandy
           Williams,trombone; unknown clarinet):   New York,Oct.9,1930
Vi 23019. Fickle Fay Creep(64314)   -HMV 4837
Vi 23307. Gambling Jack(64313)

           JELLY ROLL MORTON'S NEW ORLEANS JAZZMEN (Sidney Bechet,soprano sax; Al-
           bert Nicholas,clarinet; Happy Caldwell,tenor sax: Sidney DeParis, trum-
           pet; Claude Jones,trombone; Wellman Braud,bass; Zutty Singleton,drums;
           Lawrence Lucie,guitar; Morton,piano):   New York,Sept.14,1939
BB 10429. Didn't He Ramble(041456)/Winin' Boy Blues(041459)   -HMV 9217
BB 10434. High Society(041457)/I Thought I Heard Buddy Bolden(041458) -HMV 9216

           (Omit Bechet; sub. Fred Robinson,trombone,for Jones)New York,Sept.28,1939
BB 10442. West End Blues(041362)/Climax Rag(041360)   -HMV 9219
BB 10450. Don't You Leave Me Here(041361)/Ballin'the Jack(041363) -HMV 9218

           JELLY ROLL MORTON SEVEN (Morton,piano; Red Allen,trumpet; Albert Nicho-
           las, clarinet; Zutty Singleton,drums; Wellman Braud,bass; Joe Britton,
           trombone; Eddie Williams,sax):   New York,Jan.4, 1940
Gl 1703. Sweet Substitute(R2582)/Panama(R2583)
Gl 1704. Good Old New York(R2584)/Big Lip Blues(R2585)

44

```
            THE MORTON SEXTET (Omit Britton,trombone):        New York,Jan.23,1940
     Gl 1706. Why(2621)/Get the Bucket(2622)
     Gl 1707. If You Knew(2623)/Shake It(2624)

          . THE MORTON SEVEN(Add Claude Jones,trombone):      New York,Jan.30,1940
     Gl 1710. Mama's Got a Baby(2634)/My Home Is in a Southern Town(2635)
     Gl 1711. Dirty,dirty,dirty(2632)/Swinging the Elks(2633)

MORTON'S ORCHESTRA, TOM (Featuring the Original Indiana Five):
     Di 2930. Anything to Hold You Baby(148606)/Birmingham Bertha (148607)
     Ha  937. Broadway Baby Dolls(148608)/(GOLDEN GATE ORCHESTRA

MOSBY AND HIS DIXIELAND BLUE BLOWERS, CURTIS (Two trumpets, three sax: trombone;
banjo; tuba; drums; violin):
     Co 1191. Weary Stomp(144761)/In My Dreams(144763)
     Co 1442. Blue Blowers/Hardee Street

MOSELY'S BAND, SNUB (Mosely,trombone; Bob Carroll,trumpet; Willard Brown, sax;
Lloyd Phillips,piano; Vernon King,bass; A.Godley,drums):
     De 7728. Swinging With Mose/Man With the Funny Little Horn

            (Call Cobbs,piano; Fred Clarke,bass):
     De 8586. Sing a Little Ditty/Hey Man Hey Man(with the Tampa Boys)
     De 8614. Between You and the Devil
         "    Blues at High Noon                              -BrE 03462
     De 8626. Case of the Blues/'Deed I Do
     De 8636. Snub's Blues
         "    Swampland                                       -BrE 03449

MOSS, BUDDY (vocal blues with guitars):
     OK 04380. Undertaker Blues/Oh Lordy Mama No. 2
     OK 05589. Misery Man Blues/Some Day Baby
     OK 05626. Jinx Man Blues/Oh Lordy Mama
```

BENNIE MOTEN

See also:
   MARY BRADFORD: OK 8102, 8123.
   ADA BROWN: OK 8101, 8123.

MOTEN'S KANSAS CITY ORCHESTRA, BENNIE (Bennie Moten, piano; Thamon Hayes, trombone; Lamar Wright, cornet; Woodie Walder, clarinet; Sam Tall, banjo; Willie
Hall, drums.---Pickup #12):
                                                              St.Louis,1923-24
     OK 8100. Elephant's Wobble(8459A)
         "   Crawdad Blues(8460A)

            (Add Harry Cooper, cornet; Harlan Leonard, tenor):
     OK 8184. Tulsa Blues(8771A)
         "   Goofy Dust(8772A)

     OK 8194. South(8769B)
         "   Vine Street Blues(8770A)

     OK 8213. Baby Dear(8774A)
         "   As I Like It(9121A)

     OK 8242. Things Seem So Blue to Me(9123A)   June, 1925
         "   18th Street Strut(9124A)

     OK 8255. She's Sweeter Than Sugar(9118A; William Little, Jr., voc.)
         "   South Street(9119A)

     OK 8277. Sister Honky Tonk(9120A)
         "   Kater Street Rag(9125A)   -PaE 3256

            (Ed Lewis, Lamar Wright, cornets: Thamon Hayes, trombone; Harlan Leonard,
       alto; Jack Washington, alto and baritone; Woodie Walder, tenor; Bennie
       Moten, piano; Sam Tall, banjo; Abe Bolar, bass; Willie Hall, drums):
                                                              Dec.,1926
     Vi 20406. Harmony Blues(37233)
         "   Thick Lip Stomp(37232)   -HMV 5302
                                                                  "
     Vi 20422. Missouri Wobble
         "   Midnight Mama

     Vi 20485. Kansas City Shuffle(37234)
         "   Yazoo Blues(37235)

```
Vi 20811. Muscle Shoals Blues
    "     White Lightning Blues

    (Sub. Leroy Berry, banjo; Walter Page, bass; Willie McWashington,
    drums):                                              June, 1927
Vi 20855. Sugar(38677)                                   -HMV 5430
    "     Dear Heart(38668)
Vi 20946. Baby Dear(38670)
    "     12th Street Rag(38671)
Vi 20955. Moten Stomp(38674)                             -HMV 6204
    "     (CLIFFORD HAYES)
Vi 21199. Ding Dong Blues(38673)
    "     Pass Out Lightly(38672)
Vi 21584. The New Tulsa Blues(38669)
    "     (CLIFFORD HAYES)

    (Sub. Booker Washington, trumpet, for Wright; Add LaForest Dent, sax):
                                                         March, 1928
Vi 21693. Get Low Down(42933)                            -HMV 17
    "     Kansas City Breakdown(42929)
Vi 21739. Justrite(42924)
    "     Trouble in Mind(42930)
Vi 38012. Slow Motion(42926)                             -HMV 17
    "     Hot Water Blues(42931)
Vi 38021. She's No Trouble(42934)                        -Vi 24893
    "     South(42935)                                     "
Vi 38037. Tough Breaks(42927)                            -BB 6638
    "     It's Hard to Laugh or Smile(42925)             -BB 8228
Vi 38048. Sad Man Blues(42928)
    "     (EARL HINES)

    (Add Ira "Buster" Moten, accordion):                 August, 1929
Vi 38072. Moten's Blues(55424)
    "     Let's Get It(55421)
Vi 38081. Terrific Stomp(55420)                          -BB 6304
    "     That's What I'm Talkin' About(55425)
Vi 38091. Kansas City Squabble(55422)
    "     New Goofy Dust Rag(55430)
Vi 38104. That Certain Motion(55426)
    "     Rite Tite(55423)
Vi 38123. It Won't Be Long(55427)
    "     Loose Like a Goose(55428); Buster and Bennie Moten, piano, clarinet
                                                         (and traps)
Vi 38132. When Life Seems So Blue(42932)
    "     Just Say It's Me(55429)

    (Joe Keyes, Dee Stewart, Hot Lips Page, trumpets; Dan Minor, Eddie Dur-
    ham, trombones; Eddie Barefield, Jack Washington, Ben Webster, saxes;
    Count Basie, piano; Berry; Page; McWashington; James Rushing, vocals):
                                                         Nov.,1929, and Aug.,1930
Vi 38114. Mary Lee(57313)                                -BB 6638
                                                         -BB 6851

Vi 38144. Boot It(57312)
    "     Every Day Blues(57305)
Vi 22660. As Long As I Love You(62926)                   -HMV 4912
    "     (PAUL HOWARD)
Vi 22680. Ya Got Love(53012)                             -HMV 4889
    "     I Wanna Be Around My Baby(68900)
Vi 22734. When I'm Alone(62924)
    "     I Wish I Could Be Blue(62910)
Vi 22793. That Too, Do(62912)/(LUIS RUSSELL)             -HMV 4912
Vi 22958. Oh Eddie(62911)                                -HMV 4986
```

```
Vi 23007.  New Vine Street Blues(57315)
     "     Band Box Shuffle(57303)                       - BB 6710
Vi 23023.  Liza Lee(62921)                                    "
     "     Get Goin'(62922)
Vi 23028.  Won't You Be My Baby(62909)                   -BB 6711
     "     Somebody Stole My Gal(62927)                  -BB 5481
Vi 23030.  Bouncin' Around(62929)
     "     New Moten Stomp(62925)                        -BB 6709
Vi 23037.  Rumba Negro(57301)/(DON JOSE)                 -HMV 4845
Vi 23342.  Small Black(57304)
     "     Rit-Tit Day(57314)
Vi 23357.  Jones Law Blues(57302)

           (Sub. Leonard for Washington; add Buster Smith, sax):   Dec.13,1932
Vi 23384.  Moten Swing(74847)              -BB 10259,BB 6032,HMV 6377
     "     Toby(74846                  -HMV 4986,    "       "   HMV 6425
Vi 23393.  Prince of Wails(74854)                        -BB 6851
     "     Two Times(74855)
Vi 23391.  The Count(62916)                              -BB 6719
     "     Here Comes Marjorie(62915)
Vi 23429.  Professor Hot Stuff(62923)

Vi 24216.  New Orleans(74850)              -BB 10955,BB 6218
     "     Lafayette(74853)                -BB 10955 BB 6390,HMV 4953
Vi 24381.  Milenberg Joys(74852)                  BB 5585,HMV 4953
     "     Blue Room(74848)                          "    HMV 4990

BB  6711.  Now That I Need You(62928)
```

MOUND CITY BLUE BLOWERS (Red McKenzie,vocals and comb; Dick Slevin,kazoo; Jack
Bland, banjo):   (See also· McKenzie's Candy Kids)   1924-27
   Br 2581. Blue Blues/Arkansaw Blues
   Br 2602. San(with Frankie Trumbauer,alto sax)/Red Hot(with Trumbauer,alto)
   Br 2648. Barb Wire Blues/You Ain't Got Nothin' I Want

           (Add Eddie Lang, guitar):
   Br 2804. Tiger Rag/Deep Second Street Blues
   Br 2849. Gettin' Told/Play Me Slow
   Br 2908. Wigwam Blues/Blues in F

           (Eddie Condon,banjo; Gene Krupa,drums; McKenzie; Bland,guitar):
   Co 1946. Indiana(148895)/Fire House Blues(148896) ·

           (Red McKenzie, comb and vocal: Jack Teagarden,trombone: Al Morgan,bass;
           Frank Billings,drums; Jack Bland,guitar; Eddie Condon,banjo):
                                                            New York,Sept.25,1929
Vi 38087. Tailspin Blues(56151)   -BB 10209,GrF 6951,HMV 6252
     "   Never Had a Reason to Believe in You(56152)
                                             -BB 6270,BB 10209,GrF 6951, HMV 187

           (Sub. Glenn Miller,trombone: Gene Krupa,drums: add Coleman Hawkins,tenor
           sax; Pee Wee Russell,clarinet):   New York,Nov.14,1929
Vi·38100. One Hour(57146)   -HMV 6150,GrF 6501,BB 10037
     "   Hello Lola(57145)   -BB 6270,HMV 6163,   "   "

           (Sub.Jimmy Dorsey,clarinet; omit trombone: add Muggsy Spanier,cornet;
           Jack Rusin,piano):
OK 41515. Georgia on My Mind(404966C)   -UHCA 51,PaF 85104,PaE 1003
     "   I Can't Believe That You're in Love With Me(404967B)
                                               -UHCA 52,   "   "   "
OK 41526. Darktown Strutters Ball(404994A)   -Co 36281, PaF 85184,PaE 1044
     "   You Rascal You(404995A)   "   "   CoE 5007
           (Some or all of the above were issued on Harmony under the
            name of "Tennessee Music Men)

           (Red McKenzie,comb; Yank Lawson,trumpet; Eddie Miller,tenor sax; Nappy
           Lamare,guitar & voc., Bob Haggart,bass; Ray Bauduc,drums): Nov.8,1935
Ch 40059. Thanks a Million/I'm Sittin' High
Ch 40060. On Treasure Island(60139A)/Red Sails in the Sunset(60137A)

           (Eddie Miller,tenor & clarinet: Yank Lawson,trumpet: Lamare,guitar: Pete
           Peterson,bass; Ray Bauduc,drums):

```
    Ch 40073.  Eeny Meeny Miney Mo(60219A)/A Little Bit Independent(60220A

    Ch 40076.  I'm Shootin' High/I've Got My Fingers Crossed
    Ch 40081.  The Music Goes'Round and Around(60296A)/The Broken Record(60295A)

            (Featuring Bunny Berigan, trumpet):                         1936
    Ch 40082.  I'm Gonna Sit Right Down and Write Myself a Letter(60311A)
         "     Rhythm in My Nursery Rhymes(60313A)                -DeE 5905
    Ch 40091.  Mama Don't Allow It                                -DeE 5905
         "     I Hope Gabriel Likes My Music

            (Sterling Bose, trumpet):
    Ch 40098.  You Hit the Spot(60481A)                           -DeE 5926
         "     Spreadin' Rhythm Around (60482A)
    Ch 40099:  Wah-Hoo                                            -DeE 5949
         "     Saddle Your Blues to a Wild Mustang                -DeE 5926

            (Eddie Miller,tenor sax and clarinet: Yank Lawson,trumpet; Nappy Lamare,
            guitar; Pete Peterson,bass; Ray Bauduc,drums):
    Ch 40103.  High Society Blues(60223)                          -De 1274
         "     I'm Gonna Clap My Hands(60485A; previous personnel)
    De  1274.  Muskrat Ramble(60224)

            (Bunny Berigan,trumpet; Eddie Miller,tenor and clarinet featured):
    Vo  2957.  What's the Reason(17515)/She's a Latin from Manhattan(17516)
    Vo  2973.  You've Been Taking Lessons in Love/Indiana         -BrF 500562

MOYER, GOOF
    Pe 14692.  Mellophone Stomp/(BLACK DIAMOND SERENADERS)

MUD DAUBER JOE
    De  7008.  I Got to Have a Little More/Someday I'll Be in the Clay
    De  7009.  Meat Cutter Blues
    De  7087.  Going Back Home Blues

MUFF, MAE
    Vs  6053.  Big Gun Blues/Grasshopper Papa

MUNDY AND HIS ORCHESTRA, JIM:
    Vr   598.  I Surrender Dear/Ain't Misbehavin'

            (Frank Galbreath,Bobby Moore,Leroy Hill,trumpets; Ed Johnson,Jon McConn-
            ell, Norman Green,trombones; Ted Barnett;Al Gibson,James Hamilton,Skippy
            Williams,saxes; Bill Doggett,piano; Connie Wainwright,guitar; Rossiere
            Wilson,drums; Jack Jarvis,bass):
    Vs  8136.  Little Old Lady from Baltimore(US 1182)/A Lover Is Blue(US 1184)
    Vs  8148.  Sunday Special(US 1181)/All Aboard(US 1183)

MURPHY AND HIS ORCHESTRA, SPUD (Stanley Wilson,Sid Feldstein,Barney Zudecoff,trum-
pets; Morrell Crouse,Sam Genuso,trombones; Ted Duane,Pete Brundel,Charle Brosen,
saxes; Mark Hyams,piano; Nichael Storme,bass; Nat Polen,drums.--JRB):       1939
    De  1853.  Transcontinental/My Little Girl
    De  2040.  Quaker City Jazz(DLA1264A)/Cherokee(DLA1265A)
    De  2109.  Ecstasy/Dancing With a Debutante

            LYLE 'SPUD' MURPHY AND HIS ORCHESTRA(Sub.Frank Berardi,Frank Wysochanski,
            trumpets,for Feldstein,Zudecoff: Bill Heathcock,Bill Abel,trombones for
            Crouse,Genuso; Clyde Rogers,sax,for Duane; Spud Murphy,sax; Ken Einford,
            guitar; Ed O'Hara,drums, for Polen):
    BB 10157.  Hold Out for Love/Just a Phrase
    BB 10539.  Booly Ja-Ja/Dance of the Doinks
    BB 10875.  Pinetop Breakaway/Sand Dune

MUSICAL MANIACS:
    Vo  3691.  Down By the Old Mill Stream(21432)/Am I Blue(21434)

MUSICAL STEVEDORES (Elmer Snowden,banjo or guitar· Charles Holmes and/or Charlie
Grimes,alto and clarinet; Henry 'Bud' Hicks,trombone: trumpet; tuba; Cliff Jack-
son,piano.---Personnel given by Jackson through Wallace Fry):
    Co 14406.  Happy Rhythm(147899)/Honeycomb Harmony(147900)

MUSICAL VOYAGERS (Dorsey Brothers Orchestra):
    PaA 34152. Can This Be Love/I Can't Make a Man

MUSSO'S ALL STARS, VIDO: (Musso,tenor sax: Kai Winding, Gene Roland,trombones:
Safranski,bass):
    Sav  599.  Moose on a Loose/Vido in a Jam

            (Vido Musso,tenor sax solo, with Safranski's All Stars):
    Sav  601.  Spellbound
```

N

PHIL NAPOLEON

See also:
CHARLESTON CHASERS: Co 1229-2309.
COTTON PICKERS: Br 2292-2879, 4325-4447.
EMPERORS: Ha 362, 383.
EMPERORS OF JAZZ: Swan 7506, 7507, 7508, 7509.
HOT AIR MEN: Co 2092, 2175.
JAZZBO CAROLINA SERENADERS:
LADD'S BLACK ACES:
MIKE LO SCALZO: BW 1212-1215.
IRVING MILLS: Br 4482, 4498, 4559, 4587 4641, 4674, 4838, 4920.\
MIFF MOLE: OK 41098-41445.
NEW ORLEANS BLACK BIRDS: Vi 38027.
RED NICHOLS:
ORIGINAL MEMPHIS FIVE: Most.
JOE VENUTI:

NAPOLEON AND HIS ORCHESTRA, PHIL (Phil Napoleon, trumpet; Frank Signorelli,piano;
George Bohn,alto sax and clarinet, and others.--RR):
  Vi 20605. Go Joe Go/Take Your Finger Out of Your Mouth   -HMV 5331
  Vi 20647. Clarinet Marmalade/(CHARLES DORNBERGER)

    NAPOLEON'S EMPERORS (Napoleon,trumpet; Tom Dorsey,trombone; Jimmy Dorsey,
    sax and clarinet; Signorelli,piano; Eddie Lang,guitar: Ted Napoleon,
    drums: violin):
  Vi 38057. Mean to Me/My Kinda Love
  Vi 38069. You Can't Cheat a Cheater   -HMV 120
   "   Anything   -HMV 4955

    PHIL NAPOLEON AND HIS ORCHESTRA:
  Ed 51908. Go Joe Go(11394B-12)/Tiger Rag(11395C-13)
  Ed 52021. Rubber Heels(11594A-13)/Clarinet Marmalade(11595A-12)
  Fd -----. Five Pennies(18028C-14)
  Vr   656. Blue Bayou/Love Me
  Vr   669. That's a Plenty/Swing Patrol

NASH QUINTET, TED (Ted Nash,tenor sax; Joe Thomas,trumpet; Jess Clarkson,piano;
J.C.Heard,drums; Trigger Alpert,bass):
  Key   628. I've Got a Pocketful of Dreams(Marie Bryant,vc)/The Girl in My
                                           (Dreams Tries to Look Like You

NAYLOR'S SEVEN ACES (Oliver Naylor,leader; Jules Bauduc,banjo: Ray Bauduc,drums:
Pinky Gerbrecht,cornet; Charles Hartman,trombone: Jerry Richel,sax):
  Ge 5375. Hugo(8743A)/You(8746A)
  Ge 5392. High Society(8740A)/31st Street Blues(8747A)
  Ge 5393. Ringleberg Blues(8742)/Ain't That Hateful(8748)
  Ge 5643. Bye Bye Baby/You and I

    OLIVER NAYLOR'S ORCHESTRA:
  Vi 19688. Sweet Georgia Brown/(BENSON ORCHESTRA)   -HMV 2078
  HMV 2079. Slowin' Down Blues

NELSON AND HIS BOYS, CHUCK (Zack Whyte's band, whose records also were issued
under the names of Smoke Jackson and Eddie Walker):
  Ch 40016. West End Blues(14837)/(PAUL'S NOVELTY ORCHESTRA)

NELSON AND THE KING'S MEN, DAVE (Dave Nelson,Melvin Herbert,trumpets; Wilbur de
Paris,trombone: Buster Bailey,Glyn Pacque,Charlie Frazier,Wayman Carver,saxes;
Sam Allen,piano; Arthur Taylor,guitar: Simon Marrero,bass: Gerald Hobson,drums.
JI 8/9/40. In JR 5/46, Nelson himself indicates Danny Barker,guitar; mentions
an additional trombonist, Clarence Berton: says nothing of Wayman Carver. Pacque,
in RC 9/46, is quoted as giving Jack 'Paducah' Bradley, also sax, in addition to
those mentioned in JI):
  Vi 22639. I Ain't Got Nobody(64849)   -BB 5029
   "   When Day Is Done(64850)
  Vi 23039. Some of These Days(64851)/(JOE VENUTI)   -BB 5029

    (Harrison Smith says Nelson made the following, and possibly other titles,
    with Jelly Roll Morton, piano):
  ORS -----. Tomboy Sue/Kidney Feet

NELSON, JEWELL (vocal with rhythm accompaniment):
  Co 14390. Jet Black Snake Blues(147614)/Beating Me Blues(147615)

NELSON AND HIS ORCHESTRA, OZZIE (Harry Johnson,trumpet, is featured in the following and possibly other Nelson records):
  Br 7426. I'll Never Say 'Never Again' Again/I'm Just an Ordinary Human

        (Jack Teagarden,trombone, supposedly on this):
  Br -----. Dream a Little Dream of Me

NELSON, RED (Blues singer acc. by Charles Avery,piano;unknown guitar):   1935
  De 7136. Grand Trunk Blues(90465A)/Slave Man Blues(90466AA)
  De 7154. Detroit Special(90468)/Long Ago Blues(90467)

        (Cripple Clarence Lofton,piano):
  De 7155. Sweetest Thing Born(90605A)/When the Soldiers Get Their Bonus(90606A)
  De 7171. Cryin' Mother Blues(90597A & AA)/Streamline Train(90598A & B)

        (Piano; guitar; bass; saxophone):
  De 7185. Empty Bed Blues(90690A)/What a Time I'm Havin'(90689A)

        (Piano; guitar; bass):
  De 7256. Gambling Man(90857A)/Who Put Those Jinx on Me(90859A)
  De 7263. The Girl I Left Behind(90858B)/Gravel in My Bed(90856A)

NELSON, ROMEO (Piano and singing* or talking):
  Vo 1447. Head Rag Hop(C4300C)   -Br 80021, HRS 8
       "   Gettin' Dirty Just Shakin' That Thing*
  Vo 1494. Dyin' Rider Blues*/1129 Blues*

NELSON, BLUE COAT TOM:
  OK 8838. Blue Coat Blues/J.C. Johnson's Blues

NEW FRIENDS OF RHYTHM (Sylvan Shulman,violin; Louis Kievman,viola; Anthony Coluc-
ci,guitar; Harry Patent,bass; Zelly Smirnoff,violin; Alan Shulman,cello; Laura
Newell,harp):
  Vi 26229. The Droschky Drag/When Johnny Comes Marching Home
  Vi 26256. Capriciousness No.24/Barbers' Hitch
  Vi 26315. Bach Bay Blues/Fable in Sable
  Vi 26425. Shoot the Schubert to Me Hubert/Goulash
  Vi 26503. Foster Chile/High Voltage

        (Add Buster Bailey,clarinet: sub.Harry Glickman,violin,for Smirnoff):
  Vi 26647. Heavy Traffic on Canal Street/Mood in Question
  Vi 27412. Coo, Dinny Coo/Sweet Sue, Just You(no Bailey)

NEW JERSEY DANCE ORCHESTRA (Pseudonym for British Guardsman reissues of Original
Memphis Five, Fletcher Henderson, Tennessee Tooters and others)

NEW MAYFAIR ORCHESTRA (See Ray Noble)

NEW ORLEANS BLACK BIRDS (Bill Moore, Mannie Klein,trumpets: Tommy Dorsey,trombone;
Dick Stabile,clarinet: Jack Pettis, C melody sax; Fulton McGrath,piano; Carl
Kress,guitar; Merle Klein,bass: Dillon Ober,drums.--JS 5-6/46):   Nov.6,1928
  Vi 38026. Honolulu Blues(48128)/Baby(48129)

        (Phil Napoleon,trumpet; Tommy Dorsey,trombone; Jimmy Dorsey,alto sax &
        clarinet; Matt Malneck,violin; Dick McDonough,banjo; Frank Signorelli,
        piano; Joe Tarto,bass; Ted Napoleon,drums):   Dec.11,1928
  Vi 38027. Playing the Blues(49249)/Red Head(49248)

NEW ORLEANS BLUE FIVE:
  Vi 20316. King of the Zulus/(THOMAS MORRIS)
  Vi 20364. My Baby Doesn't Squawk/(THOMAS MORRIS)
  Vi 20653. South Rampart Street Blues/(CHARLES JOHNSON)

NEW ORLEANS BLUE NINE:
  GG 1263. John Henry Blues(A105-2)/(OLYMPIC DANCE ORCHESTRA)
  GG 1282. Yellow Dog Blues/(OLYMPIC DANCE ORCHESTRA)
  GG 1290. Always Got the Blues

NEW ORLEANS BLUES BAND:
  Vs 6029. Big Blues(G16005)/Small Blues(G16006)

NEW ORLEANS BOOT BLACKS (George Mitchell,cornet; Johnny Dodds,clarinet: Kid Ory,
trombone; Lil Armstrong,piano; Johnny St.Cyr,banjo; Baby Dodds,drums; Stump Evans
(?), alto sax):   1927
  Co 14337. Flat Foot(142438)/Mad Dog(142439)
  Co 14465. Mixed Salad(142436)/I Can't Say(142437)
              (See also: New Orleans Wanderers)

NEW ORLEANS FEETWARMERS (See Sidney Bechet)

NEW ORLEANS FIVE (Probably Original Memphis Five):
  Ro   371. Some of These Days(2407D-2)/The Memphis Blues(2408C-1)

50

NEW ORLEANS JAZZ BAND (Eddie Edwards,trombone· Frank Christian,cornet; Johnny Stein,drums; Achille Bacquet,clarinet; Jimmy Durante,piano.--Needle 12/44, JR 2/46):
   Ge 4508. Ja-Da Medley/He's Had No Lovin' for a Long Long Time

        (Essentially the same personnel is believed to be on the following, except clarinet by Sidney Arodin, Brad Gowans* or Jim Moynahan):
Do 335. It Had to Be You/My Papa Doesn't Two Time Any More
Do 338. Limehouse Blues/Down Where the South Begins
Re 9739. Copenhagen(5680-1)/(FLETCHER HENDERSON)
Re 9852. My Sweet Louise(6007-1)/(BAR HARBOR SOCIETY ORCHESTRA)   -Ba 1556
Re 9923. Camel Walk*/Sweet Man   -Ba ?
Ba -----. Melancholy Baby*
        (See also: Lillian Harris)

NEW ORLEANS LUCKY SEVEN (Bix Beiderbecke,cornet: Bill Rant,trombone: Don Murray, clarinet; Adrian Rollini,bass sax; Frank Signorelli,piano; Howdy Quicksell, banjo; Chauncey Morehouse,drums):   Oct.5; Oct.25,1927
   OK 8544. Royal Garden Blues(81519B)   -Co 35664,PaE 2580,PaE 3465
      "   Goose Pimples(81568B)   -Co 35664,PaE 127,PaE 2465

NEW ORLEANS OWLS (Billy Burton,leader,violin: Earl Crumb,drums; Pinky Vidacovich, Benjie White,alto saxes; Lester Smith,tenor sax; Bill Padron,cornet: Frank Netto, trombone; Rene Jelpi,banjo; Dan LeBlanc,bass; Zefried Christensen,piano):
Co 489. Stomp Off Let's Go(140992)/Oh Me Oh My(140993)
Co 605. Owl's Hoot(140994)/(WARNER'S SEVEN ACES)
Co 688. West End Romp(142023)/Tampekoe(142020)
Co 823. Brotherly Love(143114)/Blowin' Off Steam(143110)
Co 862. White Ghost Shivers(143112)/(COOK'S DREAMLAND ORCHESTRA)
Co 943. Eccentric(143115)/Nightmare(143113)
Co 1045. Pretty Baby(142022)/Dynamite(142021)
Co 1158. Meat on the Table(143982)/Piccadilly(142019)

        (Sub.Hilton Lamare,banjo; Red Bowman,cornet; Mose Ferrer,piano, for 145022,145023,145024):
Co 1261. Goose Pimples(145023)/Throwin' the Horns(145024)
Co 1547. That's a Plenty(143981)/The New Twister(145022)

NEW ORLEANS PEPSTERS (First title believed to feature King Oliver,cornet):
VD 77038. Close Fit Blues(3394B)   -GG 1718
    "   Desdemona Blues(3246)
VD 81843. -----/(BAYSTATE BROADCASTERS)   -GG 1843
        (See Memphis Jazzers)

NEW ORLEANS RAMBLERS (Jimmy McPartland,cornet: Jack Teagarden,trombone; Benny Goodman,clarinet; Jack Pettis,sax, and others):
Me 12133. I'm One of God's Children
Me 12230. That's the Kind of Man for Me/(THE TRAVELERS)

NEW ORLEANS RHYTHM KINGS (Paul Mares,trumpet; George Brunies,trombone; Leon Rappolo,clarinet; Mel Stitzel,piano; Frank Snyder,drums):   Richmond,Ind., 1923
Ge 5102. Wolverine Blues(11357a)
   "   Weary Blues(11355b)   --Bu 8003
Ge 5104. Sweet Lovin' Man(11352)   -BrE 02210
   "   Maple Leaf Rag(11358b)   -UHCA 45,BrE 02209
Ge 5104. Sweet Lovin' Man(11352a)
Ge 5105. That's a Plenty(11353)   -UHCA 88
   "   Tin Roof Blues(11359)   -BrE 02208,UHCA 87
Ge 5105. That's a Plenty(11353a)   -BrE 02208
   "   Tin Roof Blues(11359a)   -Bu 8001
Ge 5105. That's a Plenty(11353b)
   "   Tin Roof Blues(11359b)
Ge 5106. Da Da Strain(11356)
   "   Shimmeshawabble(11354)
Ge 5106. Shimmeshawabble(11354a)

        (Jelly Roll Morton* or Kyle Pierce,piano· add Jack Pettis,Glen Scoville, saxes: Lew Black,banjo: Steve Brown,bass: sub. Ben Pollack,drums.--JQ II, 1):   Late 1923
Ge 5217. Marguerite(11536a)/Milenberg Joys(11551a)*
Ge 5217. Milenberg Joys(11551c)*
Ge 3076. Milenberg Joys(11551)*
Ge 5219. Sobbin' Blues(11535a)*   -Bu 8003
   "   Angry(11539)
Ge 5219. Angry(11539a)
Ge 5220. Clarinet Marmalade(11540)/My Jelly Lord(11541a)*
Ge 5220. Clarinet Marmalade(11540a)   -BrE 02209
   "   Mr. Jelly Lord(11541c)
Ge 5221. London Blues(11550)*/Mad(11552a)

```
                (Mares; Rappolo, Santa Pecora,trombone: Charles Cordella,tenor sax; Red
                Long,piano; Chink Martin,bass; Bill Eastwood,banjo; Leo Adde,drums):
                                                            New Orleans,Jan.,1925
     OK 40327.  She's Cryin' for Me(8904A)/Golden Leaf Strut(8905a)    -PaE 3254
     OK 40422.  Baby(8902a)
         "      I Never Knew What a Gal Could Do(8903b)                -HRS    6

                (Cordella,clarinet; omit Rappolo):                March 26,1925
     Vi 19645.  She's Cryin' for Me(32125)                            -BB 10956
         "      Everybody Loves Somebody Blues(32126)                      "

                (Wingy Mannone,trumpet; George Brunies,trombone; Sidney Arodin,clarinet;
                Terry Shand,piano; Barney Pottle,bass; Bob White,drums.--JR 10/44):9/34
     De   161.  San Antonio Shout(38608)                              -BrE 02040
         "      Tin Roof Blues(38609)                    -De 3523, BrE 01910
     De   162.  Panama(38610)                                         -BrE 01910
         "      Jazz It Blues(38611)                                  -BrE 02040
     De   229.  Ostrich Walk(38735)                                   -BrE 01988
         "      Original Dixieland One Step(38736)                         "
     De   464.  Bluin' the Blues(38734A)                              -BrE 02337
         "      Sensation(38737A)                                          "

                (Muggsy Spanier,cornet; Eddie Miller,clarinet: Gene Krupa,drums; rest
                same): Red McKenzie,vocals):                         Feb.20,1935
     De   388.  Dust Off That Old Pianna(39380B)                      -BrE 02008
         "      Since We Fell Out of Love(39381A)                     -BrE 02008
     De   401.  Baby Brown(39378A)                                    -BrE 03447
         "      No Lovers Allowed(39379A)                             -BrE 02510
     De   401.  Baby Brown(no vocal)

     NEW ORLEANS SEVEN ORCHESTRA (Reissues of the Varsity Seven: Benny Carter,trumpet
     and alto sax; Coleman Hawkins, tenor sax; Danny Polo,clarinet; George Wettling,
     drums; Jos Sullivan,piano; Ulysses Livingston,guitar; Artie Shapiro,bass; Jeanne
     Burns and Ulysses Livingston,vocals*: Joe Turner#):
          El  5032.  Easy Rider(1159-1)*/How Long How Long Blues(1284-1)#

     NEW ORLEANS WANDERERS (Same Personnel as New Orleans Bootblacks):
          Co   698.  Perdido Street Blues(142426)/Gate Mouth(142427)       -UHCA 16/15
          Co   735.  Too Tight(142428)/Papa Dip(142429)

     NEW ORLEANS WILD CATS:
          Co 14599.  Wild Cats on Parade(151497)/Harlem Baby(151499)
          Co 14662.  Baby Mine/(BENNETT SWAMPLANDERS)
          Co 14668.  Wild Cat Stomp/(JIMMY JOHNSON)

     NEW YORK STOMPERS (Pseudonymn for British Mayfair issues of Venuti-Lang Vocalions,
     Melotones)

     NEW YORK SYNCOPATORS (California Ramblers group including Dorsey Brothers; also
     used as pseudonym for reissues on Odeon and Parlophone of various Armstrong,
     Venuti, etc., recordings):
          OK 40965.  Mary(81858C)/Cobblestones(81926A)
          OK 41162.  Sweet Dreams(401299B)/Dreaming of the Day(401428A)
          OK 41202.  Carressing You/Dream Train
          OK 41264.  Now I'm in Love/The One That I Love Loves Me
          OK 41434.  It Seems to Be Spring(404212C)/Beware of Love(404213A)
          OK 41472.  Baby's Birthday Party/Wedding of the Birds

     NEWPORT SOCIETY ORCHESTRA:
          Di  2511.  Are You Lonesome Tonight(144835)/I'm Walkin' on Air(144837)
          Di  2579.  In the Sing Song Sycamore Tree(145482)/There Must Be a Silver Lining
                                                                             (145559)
     NEWPORT SYNCOPATORS (Fletcher Henderson Orchestra):                   1926-1928
          VD 81879.  The Terror.
```

FRANK NEWTON

```
     See also:
          BUSTER BAILEY: Vr 668; Vo 4089, 4564, 5510.
          CHARLIE BARNET: Vr 627, 633.
          STELLA BROOKS: Disc 5030, 5031, 5032.
          TEDDY HILL: Vo 3247, 3294; BB 6897-6954.
          BILLIE HOLIDAY: Vo 5129; Com 527.
          J.P. JOHNSON: Asch 5511, 5512, 5513.
          ART KARLE: Vo 3146, 3147.
          MEZZ MEZZROW: BB 6319, 6320, 6321.
          PORT OF HARLEM: BN 3, 6, 7, 14.
          CECIL SCOTT: Vi 38098, 38117.
          BESSIE WMITH: OK 8946, 8949.
          WILLIF SMITH: De 1366-1957.
          MARY LOU WILLIAMS: Asch 1002, 1003, 1004.
          TEDDY WILSON: Br 7640, 7729.
```

NEWTON AND HIS UPTOWN SERENADERS, FRANKIE (Frank Newton,trumpet; Edmond Hall, clarinet; Pete Brown,alto sax; Cecil Scott,tenor sax; Don Frye,piano; John Smith, guitar; Dick Fulbright,bass; Cozy Cole,drums): 1937
Vr 518. You Showed Me the Way(174)/Please Don't Talk About Me When I'm Gone (175)

(Add Russell Procope,alto sax):
Vr 550. There's No Two Ways About It(404)/'Cause My Baby Says It's So(405)
Vr 571. I Found a New Baby(402)/The Brittwood Stomp(403)

(Omit Procope; sub. John Kirby,bass; O'Neil Spencer, drums):
Vr 616. Easy Living/Where or When   -Vo 3777
Vr 647. The Onyx Hop(559)/Who' Sorry Now(175; first personnel)   -Vo 3839

FRANK NEWTON AND HIS CAFE SOCIETY ORCHESTRA (Newton,trumpet; Tab Smith, Stanley Payne,alto saxes; Ken Hollon,tenor sax; Sid Catlett,drums; Ulysses Livingston,guitar: Ken Kersey,piano: Johnny Williams,bass):
Vo 4321. Tab's Blues(W24365A)/Frankie's Jump(W24367A)   -PaE 2708
Vo 4851. Jitters(W24366A)/Jam Fever(W24368A)
Vo 5410. Vamp(25203)/Parallel Fifths(B25204)

FRANKIE NEWTON AND HIS ORCHESTRA (Newton,trumpet; Mezz Mezzrow,clarinet; Pete Brown,alto sax; John Kirby,bass; Cozy Cole,drums; James P. Johnson, piano; Albert Casey,guitar):   Jan.13,1939
BB 10176.Rosetta   -Sw 53
  "   The World Is Waiting for the Sunrise
BB 10186.Romping   -HMV 8927, Sw 68
  "   Minor Jive   -Sw 53
BB 10216.Who   -HMV 8927, Sw 68
  "   The Blues My Baby Gave to Me

ALBERT NICHOLAS

NICHOLAS, ALBERT, clarinet, see:
  BERNARD ADDISON: BB 6144, 6174.
  HENRY ALLEN: Vi 23006, 23338, 38073, 38080, 38088, 38107: BB 10702: Vo 2997,2998.
  LOUIS ARMSTRONG: OK 8669,8680:Vo 3055;OK 8756,8774,41350,41375; De 1347-1661,
  BECHET-NICHOLAS: BN   (2267.
  ADA BROWN: Vo 1009.
  CHICAGO HOTTENTOTS(possibly): Vo 1008.
  LILLIE DELK CHRISTIAN: OK 8475.
  DIXIE JAZZ BAND: Or 1726, 1728.
  BABY DODDS TRIO: Circle 1001, 1002.
  ALEX HILL: Vo 2826, 2848.
  BERTHA HILL: OK 8367, 8437.
  FREDDIE JENKINS: BB 6129, 6193.
  RICHARD M. JONES: OK 8260, 8290.
  JUNGLE TOWN STOMPERS: OK 8686.
  LAZY LEVEE LOUNGERS: Co 2243.
  LITTLE RAMBLERS: BB 6130, 6131, 6144, 6193, 6220, 6232.
  LOU AND HIS GINGER SNAPS: Ba 6536, 6540.
  JELLY ROLL MORTON: Vi 23402, 23334, 23424, 22681, 23004, 23351; BB 10429, 10434, 10442, 10450; Gl 1703-1711.
  KING OLIVER: Vo 1007, 1014, 1033.
  LUIS RUSSELL: Vo 1010; OK 8656, 8734, 8760, 8766, 8780, 8811, 8830, 8849;Vo 1579;
    Me 12000; Vi 22789; 22793, 22815.
  FATS WALLER: Vi 38110, 38119.

NICHOLS AND HIS FOUR TOWERS ORCHESTRA, RAY:
  BB 5902. Who's Sorry Now/Rosetta
  BB 5904. Sugar Foot Stomp(Connie's Inn Orchestra)
  BB 5548. Rollin' Home/The Very Thought of You
  BB 6013. Black Coffee

RED NICHOLS

See Also:
  ALABAMA RED PEPPERS:
  ARKANSAS TRAVELERS: Some OK; all Harmony.
  BOSWELL SISTERS: Br 20107, 20110.
  ARNOLD BRILLHARDT (possibly): Pe 14631.
  CALIFORNIA RAMBLERS:
  CAPTIVATORS:
  CAROLINA WANDERERS: Ge ?
  CHARLESTON CHASERS: Co 446-1539.
  COTTON PICKERS: Br 2937, 2981, 3001.
  CLIFF EDWARDS:
  PEGGY ENGLISH: Vo.15504.
  GOLDEN GATE ORCHESTRA:
  GOOFUS FIVE:

BLUE NOTE PRESENTS
ART HODES' HOT FIVE

SIDNEY BECHET

ART HODES

WILD BILL DAVISON

POPS FOSTER

FRED MOORE

- No. 531 SAVE IT PRETTY MAMA
  DARKTOWN STRUTTERS' BALL

- No. 532 SHINE
  MEMPHIS BLUES

- No. 533 ST. JAMES INFIRMARY
  WAY DOWN YONDER
  IN NEW ORLEANS

BLUE NOTE ALBUM 103
3 — 10" RECORDS $3.75   Excl. of Taxes

FOR COMPLETE CATALOG WRITE TO

BLUE NOTE RECORDS
767 LEXINGTON AVENUE   NEW YORK 21, N. Y.

SIDNEY BECHET ON BLUE NOTE

BN-6 SUMMERTIME (Featuring SIDNEY BECHET)
SIDNEY BECHET QUINTET

POUNDING HEART BLUES
PORT OF HARLEM SEVEN

SIDNEY BECHET	Soprano Sax and Clarinet	MEADE "LUX" LEWIS	Piano
FRANK NEWTON	Trumpet	TEDDY BUNN	Guitar
J. C. HIGGINBOTHAM	Trombone	JOHN WILLIAMS	Bass
		SIDNEY CATLETT	Drums

BN-7 BASIN STREET BLUES
(Featuring J. C. HIGGINBOTHAM)
J. C. HIGGINBOTHAM QUINTET

BLUES FOR TOMMY
PORT OF HARLEM SEVEN

SIDNEY BECHET ....Soprano Sax   MEADE "LUX" LEWIS........Piano
FRANK NEWTON ....Trumpet   TEDDY BUNN ....Guitar
J. C. HIGGINBOTHAM Trombone   JOHN WILLIAMS ....Bass
        SIDNEY CATLETT ....Drums

BN-13 LONESOME BLUES
DEAR OLD SOUTHLAND

SIDNEY BECHET'S BLUE NOTE QUARTET

SIDNEY BECHET ....Clarinet   TEDDY BUNN ....Guitar
    and Soprano Sax   GEORGE "POP" FOSTER ....Bass
        SIDNEY CATLETT ....DRUMS

BN-43 BLUE HORIZON (Featuring SIDNEY BECHET)
MUSKRAT RAMBLE

BN-44 ST. LOUIS BLUES
JAZZ ME BLUES

SIDNEY BECHET'S BLUE NOTE JAZZ MEN

SIDNEY DE PARIS ....Trumpet   ART HODES ....Piano
VIC DICKENSON ....Trombone   GEORGE "POPS" FOSTER ....Bass
SIDNEY BECHET ....Clarinet &   MANZIE JOHNSON ....Drums
    Soprano Sax

BN-502 SATURDAY NIGHT BLUES
BECHET'S STEADY RIDER

SIDNEY BECHET'S BLUE NOTE QUARTET

SIDNEY BECHET ....Clarinet   GEORGE "POP" FOSTER ....Bass
TEDDY BUNN ....Guitar   SIDNEY CATLETT ....Drums

BN-517 QUINCY STREET STOMP
WEARY WAY BLUES

BECHET-NICHOLAS BLUE FIVE

SIDNEY BECHET ....Soprano Sax   ART HODES ....Piano
    & Clarinet   GEORGE "POPS" FOSTER ....Bass
ALBERT NICHOLAS ....Clarinet   DANNY ALVIN ....Drums

IDEAL SERENADERS: Co 1131.
INDIANA FIVE: ?
ALLAN JONES: Vi 119040.
CHARLES KALFY: Co 910.
KENTUCKY HOT HOPPERS: Pat 36841.
LANIN'S RED HEADS: All.
LITTLE RAMBLERS:
LOUISIANA RHYTHM KINGS: Vo 15779,15784,15810,15815,15828,15833,15841:All Br.
IRVING MILLS: Br 4983.
MISSOURI JAZZ BAND: ?
MIFF MOLE: OK 40758-41232.
RED AND MIFF'S STOMPERS: Ed 51854,51878; Vi 20778, 21183, 21397.
RED HEADS:
SIX HOTTENTOTS:
DON VOORHEES: Co 1123, 1124, 1126, 1129, 1131, 1180, 1229, 1260.
WABASH DANCE ORCHESTRA:
WE THREE:

NICHOLS AND HIS FIVE PENNIES, RED: (Red Nichols,trumpet; Jimmy Dorsey,alto and
clarinet; Ed Lang,guitar; Artie Schutt,piano; Vic Berton,drums.--"Re-Minting the
Pennies," Venables and White, 1942): Dec.20,1926
  Br 3407. Washboard Blues(20993)-Vo1069,15498,BrE 01801,BrG 222,Br 6814,Br 80072
    "   That's No Bargain(20994) "   "   "   "   "
  BrE 01801. That's No Bargain(20995)   -BrG 222,   Br 80072

    (Add Miff Mole,trombone):
  Br 3477. Buddy's Habits(21594) -Vo 15573,BrE 01802,BrG 358,Br 6815,Br 80071
    "   Boneyard Shuffle(21597)   "   "   "   "   "

    (Add Joe Venuti,violin):   March 3,1927
  Br 3490. Bugle Call Rag(21718)   -BrE 01803,BrG 7556,Br 6816
    "   Back Beats(21721)   "   "   "

    (Omit Venuti):
  Br 3550. Hurricane(21984)   -Vo 15566,BrE 01804,BrG 456,Br 6817
    "   Alabama Stomp(22981)   "   "   "   "   "

    (Add Phil Napoleon,second trumpet:Adrian Rollini,bass sax): June 20,1927
  BrE 01805. Cornfed(23666)   -BrG 7543
  Br 3597. Cornfed(23667)   -Vo 15602,   Br 6818
    "   Mean Dog Blues(23755)   "   ,BrE 01805,BrG 7543,   "

    (Nichols,Napoleon,trumpets: Mole,trombone; Fud Livingston,clarinet and
    tenor; Adrian Rollini,bass sax and goofus; Dick McDonough,banjo; Schutt,
    piano; Berton,drums):   Aug.15,1927
  Br 3626. Ida(24232)   -Vo 15622,BrE 01536,BrG 7559,Br 6819,Br 80069
    "   Feelin' No Pain(24235)   "   "   "   "   "
  Br 3627. Riverboat Shuffle(24225)-BrF 500400,BrE 01806,BrG 7601,Br 6820.
    "   Eccentric(24228)

    (Omit Rollini; Dudley Fosdick,mellophone; Carl Kress,guitar):Feb.27,1928
  Br 3854. Avalon(26693)   -BrF 50042,BrE 01569,BrG 7707,Br 6681,Br 80070
    "   Nobody's Sweetheart(26749: Mar.1,1928)   - ditto -
  Br 3855. Japanese Sandman(26695)   -BrE 01851,   Br 6821
    "   Five Pennies(23668: personnell as of 6/20/27) -BrE 01851, Br 6821

    (Add Jimmy Dorsey,alto sax):
  Br 3955. There'll Come a Time(27606)   -BrE 3850,BrG 7849,Br 6822
    "   Whispering(27623; Venuti,violin: no guitar)
                                             -BrE 3850,BrG 7849,Br 6822
  Br 3961. Panama(27605)
    "   Margie(27625)
Unissues. I Can't Give You Anything But Love(27624)
  Br 3989. Imagination(27626)   -BrE 01855,   Br 6823
    "   Original Dixieland One-Step(27627)   "   "

    (Augmented orchestra; Scrappy Lambert, vocal):
  Br 20062. Poor Butterfly(26772)   -BrE 20066,BrG 5004
    "   Can't You Hear Me Calling Caroline(26775)"   "

    (Includes Venuti and Lang):   May 31,1928
  Br 20070. Dear Old Southland(27621)   -BrE 125
    "   Limehouse Blues(27622)   "   ,BrG 5081
  BrG 5081. Dear Old Southland(no vocal)

    (Red Nichols,Mannie Klein,trumpets. Miff Mole,trombone; Dudley Fosdick,
    Mellophone; Fud Livingston,clarinet; Jimmy Dorsey,alto sax; Adrian Rol-
    lini,bass sax; Carl Kress,guitar; Arthur Schutt,piano; Vic Berton,drums):
                                                                    Oct.2,1928
  Br 4456. A Pretty Girl Is Like a Melody(28326)
                                     -BrF 1033,BrE 01854,BrG 8337,Br 6826,BrF 8337
    (See coupling below)

UNISSUED. I Must Have That Man(28327)

    (Benny Goodman, clarinet; omit Lovingston,Dorsey):
Br 4243. I Never Knew(29209)   -BrE 02356
"   Who's Sorry Now(29210)

    (Add Livingston,tenor; omit Mole; probably Lennie Hayton,piano):Feb.5/29
Br 4363. Chinatown My Chinatown(29222)
    (See coupling below)   -Br 6825,BrE 01856,BrF 1029,500403,BrG 8298
Unissued. On the Alamo(29223)

    (Nichols,Klein,Mole,Fosdick,Dorsey,Livingston,Rollini,Kress,Schutt,King):
Br 4456. Alice Blue Gown(29294)   -Br 6826,BrF 1033
BrE 01856. Alice Blue Gown(different master)   -BrF 8337,BrG 8337
Br 4286. Allah's Holiday(29295)-Br 6824,BrE 01853,BrF 1002,   BrG 8264
"   Roses of Picardy(29296)   "   "   "   "

    (Red Nichols, Leo McConville,trumpets; Jack Teagarden,Glenn Miller,trombones; Goodman,clarinet; Babe Rusin,tenor; Jack Rusin,piano; Carl Kress, guitar; Gene Krupa,drums):   April,1929
Br 4373. Indiana(29708)   -Br 6718,BrE 01591,BrF 500404,BrG 9206
"   Dinah(29709)   "   "   "   " ,Br 80006
Br 80006. Indiana(29708B)
Br 4363. On the Alamo(29710) -Br 6825,BrE 01856,BrF 1029,BrF 500403,BrG 8298
BrE 5019. On the Alamo(29711; voc.,Scrappy Lambert)

    (Nichols,one other, trumpet: Teagarden,Miller: Jimmy Dorsey,alto and clarinet; Larry Binyon,tenor and flute; Eddie Bergman and Al Beller,violins; Bill Schumann,cello and oboe; Schutt,Kress,Krupa):
Br 20091. I'll See You in My Dreams(29995)/Some of These Days(29996)
Br 20092. It Had to Be You(29994)/Sally Won't You Come Back(29997)   -BrE 101

    (Same brass; Pee Wee Russell,clarinet; Bud Freeman,tenor sax; Jack Rusin, piano; Eddie Condon,banjo; Art Miller,bass; Dave Tough,drums; Red McKenzie,vocals):
Br 4778. Who Cares(30056)   -Br 6831
"   Rose of Washington Square(30057)   -BrE 1204,BrF 500200,   "

    (Same brass; Goodman,clarinet; Livingston,tenor; Bergman,Beller,violins; Schumann,cello; Rusin,piano; Condon,banjo; Harry Goodman,bass;Tough,drums):
Br 4500. I May Be Wrong(30503; S.Lambert,voc.)   -Br 6753
"   The New Yorkers(30504: Red McKenzie,voc.)

    (Nichols,trumpet; Teagarden,Miller,trombone· Jimmy Dorsey,clarinet and alto; Goodman,clarinet; Rusin,piano; Condon,Miller,Tough): Sept.9,1929
Br 4790. Nobody Knows(30538)   -BrE 02505,BrF 8744,BrG 8744,Br 6832
"   Smiles(30540)   "   "   "   "
Unissued. Nobody Knows(30539)

    RED NICHOLS AND HIS ORCHESTRA:
Br 4651. They Didn't Believe Me(30712)   -Br 6827,BrG 8655
"   Say It With Music(31270)   "

    (Featuring Nichols,Dorsey and Rusinbrothers, Krupa):
Br 4695. Strike Up the Band(31883)   -Br 6753, BrG 8659
"   Soon(31884)   "

    (Nichols,one other,trumpets; Dorsey,trombone; Livingston,clarinet; Rusin, tenor sax; Rollini,bass sax; Jack Rusin,piano; Kress; Krupa):
Br 4701. Sometimes I'm Happy(31903)   -Br 6828, BrG 8673
"   Hallelujah(31904)   "   "

    (Nichols,Ruby Weinstein,trumpets: Teagarden,Miller,trombones; Jimmy Dorsey,alto and clarinet; Teg Brown,banjo or guitar: Rusin brothers, Rollini, Krupa):
Br 4839. I'm Just Wild About Harry(31923)   -Br 6833, BrE 1121
"   After You've Gone(31924: Teagarden,voc.)   "   BrE 1104
Br 4724. I Want to Be Happy(32040)   -BrF 8832,Br 6830,BrE 1032
"   Tea for Two(32041)   -BrF 8832,Br 6830, BrE 1032

    (Add Charlie Teagarden,trumpet; sub.Benny Goodman,clarinet,Sid Stoneberg, alto,for Dorsey; Joe Sullivan,piano; Artie Miller,bass,for Rollini):
                                                                           July,1930
Br 4877. Peg o' My Heart(33304)-BrF 1019,BrF 8962,BrG 9862,Br 6839
"   China Boy(33306)   "   "   "   " , Br 80004
Br 80004. Peg o' My Heart(33304B)
Br 4885. Shimmeshawabble(33334)-BrE 1204,BrF 500200,BrG 8866,Br 6836
"   Sheik of Araby(33333) -BrE 1104,BrF 500403   "   " ,Br 80005
Br 80005. Shimmeshawabble(33334B)
Br 4944. Sweet Georgia Brown(33305)   -BrE 1048,BrF 8997,BrG 8997,Br 6841

57

(Omit Weinstein; sub. Bud Freeman,tenor,for Stoneberg and Rusin; Rollini, for Miller; omit Brown):
                                                                       Aug.27,1930
Br 4944. By the Shalimar(34112)   -Br 6841,BrE 1048,BrF 8997,BrG 8997
Unissued. How Come You Do Me Like You Do(34110)
Br 4925. Carolina in the Morning(34109)/Who?(34111)   -Br 6839, BrE 1062

(Same brass; Goodman,clarinet; Rusin brothers; Miller; Krupa):
Br 6026. On Revival Day, 1 & 2 (34626/27)   -Br 6843, BrE 1087

(Nichols,Weinstein,Teagarden,trumpets: Teagarden,Miller,trombones; Goodman,clarinet; Stoneberg,alto: Binyon,tenor and flute; Ed Bergman,Ed Solinsky,violins; Jack Rusin,piano; Teg Brown,guitar; Artie Miller; Krupa):
Br 4957. Embraceable You(34958)   -BrF 8963, BrG 8966
    "   I Got Rhythm(34959)   -BrE 1300, Br 6711, "   "
Br 4982. Linda(35214)/Yours and Mine(35215)   -BrF 9003, BrG 9003
Br 6029. You Said It(35167)   -BrF 9007, BrG 9007
    "   Sweet and Hot(35168)   -BrE 1300,Br 6711, "   "
Br 6068. Things I Never Knew Till Now(36108)   -BrF 9032
    "   Keep a Song in Your Soul(36111)   -Br 6845,   "
Br 6070. Teardrops and Kisses(36109)/Were You Sincere(36110)   -BrG 9046

(Sub. Georgie Stoll,trombone,for Teagarden; Fulton McGrath,piano,for Rusin):
Br 6118. Love Is Like That(36730)   -BrG 9055
    "   You Don't Know What You're Doin'
Br 6191. It's the Darnesdest Thing(36728)   -BrE 1275
    "   Singin' the Blues(36729)   -Br 6845,   "

(Red Nichols,Charlie Teagarden,Wingy Mannone,trumpets; Glenn Miller,trombone; Jimmy Dorsey,alto and clarinet; Babe Rusin,tenor; Joe Sullivan, piano; Art Miller,bass; Gene Krupa,drums):
Br 6012. My Honey's Lovin' Arms(35618)   -BrE 1121,BrF 9005, BrG 9005.
    "   Rockin' Chair(35619)   -BrE 01852   "   "

(Sub. Goodman,clarinet and baritone,for Dorsey: Jack Rusin,piano, for Sullivan):
Br 6058. Bug-a-boo(35733)/Corrine Corrina(35734)-BrE 1120,BrF 9024,BrG 9024
Br 6149. How Come You Do Me Like You Do   -BrE 1180, BrF 9099
    "   Moan You Moaners(36832: next full personnel below) "   "

RED NICHOLS ORCHESTRA,(featuring Goodman):
Br 6014. Blue Again(35738)   -BrE 1082, BrF 9002
    "   When Kentucky Bids the World Good Morning(35739) "   "

(Featuring Nichols,Teagarden,Goodman,Krupa):
Br 6035. The Peanut Vendor(35954)/Sweet Rosita(35955)   -BrE 1076, BrF 9000

(Featuring Jimmy Dorsey,alto and clarinet):
Br 6138. Slow But Sure(36855)/Little Girl(36856)   -BrF 9094
Br 6164. How the Time Can Fly(36857)/(THE NEW YORKERS)

RED NICHOLS AND HIS FIVE PENNIES(Nichols,trumpet; Miller,trombone;Jimmy Dorsey,clarinet; Babe Rusin,tenor; Jack Rusin,piano; Perry Botkin,guitar; Artie Miller,bass; Gene Krupa,drums):
Br 6133. Just a Crazy Song(36830)/You Rascal You(36831) -BrF 1163, BrF 9090
Br 6160. How Long Blues(36877)/Fan It(36878)   -BrF 1213, BrF 9117

(Nichols; Jimmy Dorsey; Joe Venuti,violin; Ed Lang,guitar· Fulton McGrath,piano; Vic Berton):
Br 6198. Oh Peter(37204)/Honolulu Blues(37205)   -BrE 1223,BrF 9170

(Red Nichols,Johnny Davis,Don Moore,trumpets:Will Bradley,trombone; Jimmy Dorsey,alto and clarinet; Russ Lyon,alto: Babe Rusin,tenor; McGrath,piano; Tony Starr,banjo and vocal; Artie Bernstein,bass; Vic Engle,drums):
Br 6219. Junk Man Blues(37234)   -BrE 1125, BrG 9192
    "   Get Cannibal(37233)   -BrE 1281,   "

(Nichols, Jimmy Dorsey, Venuti, Lang, Schutt, Berton):
Br 6234. Yaaka Hula Hickey Dula(37438)/Haunting Blues(37439)BrE 1262, F 9199

(Red Nichols, Johnny Davis: Will Bradley; Jimmy Dorsey,Babe Rusin; McGrath, Bernstein, Engle):
Br 6421. 21 years(37462)/My Sweetie Went Away(37463)   -BrE 1293, BrG 9203

(Omit Davis; reinstate Starr: sub. Jack Rusin):
Br 6767. Slow and Easy(37456)/Waiting'for Evening Mail(37437)   -BrE 1312

(Reinstate Davis; sub. Larry Binyon, tenor and flute,for Rusin; Dick McDonough,guitar; Stan King,drums: add Harry Hoffman,violin; Connee Boswell, Art Jarrett, vocals):

Br 20110. New Orleans Medley, 1 & 2 (11427)/(11283)   -BrE 118
Unissued. New Orleans Medley, 1 (11282)

    (Nichols,Dorsey,Babe Rusin,McGrath,McDonough,Bernstein,Engle):
Br 6266. Clarinet Marmalade(11314)/Sweet Sue(11315)
                                                         -BrE 1301,PaE 2598,BrF 500176
    (Sub. Jack Rusin,piano):
Br 6312. Goin' to Town(11868)/Goofus(11869)   -BrF 9269
Br 6348. Our Home Town Mountain Band 1 & 2(11870/71)   -BrE 1343, BrG 9267

    (Red Nichols,Johnny Davis; Dorsey and Rusin brothers; Binyon,Venuti,Mc-
    Donough,Bernstein,King; Sid Garry,Art Jarrett,Boswell Sisters,Chick Bull-
    ock,vocals):
Br 20107. California Medley,1 & 2(11432)/(11569)   -BrE 108, BrF 5112

    RED NICHOLS AND HIS ORCHESTRA (Personnel unknown)
Br 6451. Love and Nuts and Noodles(8825)/Heat Waves(8830)   -BrG 9372
Br 6461. Everybody Loves My Baby(8826)
  "   I'm Sorry I Made You Cry(8827)   -BrE 1441
Br 6534 .Sugar(8829)
  "   Dinah Lou(8831)   -BrE 1441
Unissued. I'll Be Ready When the Great Day Comes(14358)

NOTE: Br 6829, 6834, 6837, 6838, 6840 are reissues of Louisiana Rhythm Kings sides, under Red Nichols' name.

    (Red Nichols,Ray McCosh,George Schmidt,trumpets; Buford Trevor, Buck
    Weaver,trombones; Gilbert Schweser,Howard Jenkins,Don Purviance,saxes;
    King Harvey,guitar; Mannie Strand,piano; Bill Lower,bass; Paul Collins,
    drums):
Br 7358. When You And I Were Young(15932)/Dardanella(15933)
Br 7460. Three Little Words(15930)/Harlem(15931)

    RED NICHOLS' STOMPERS (Featuring Red Nichols,trumpet; Miff Mole,trombone;
    Frankie Trumbauer, sax; Fud Livingstone, clarinet: Adrian Rollini, bass
    sax; Chauncey Morehouse,drums):
Vi 21056. Sugar(40512)/Make My Cot Where the Cot-Cot-Cotton Grows(40513)
                                                           -HMV 5433
    (No Rollini or Trumbauer):
Vi 21560. Harlem Twist(45814)/Five Pennies(45815)

    RED NICHOLS AND HIS FIVE PENNIES (Unknown personnel):
Br 545. Love's Old Sweet Song/Troublesome Trumpet
BB 5547. Jungle Fever/Rockin' in Rhythm
BB 5553. Shine/Runnin' Wild

    (Bobby Jones,Billy Sheperd,H.Yolonsky,R.Schultz,saxes; Red Nichols, D.
    Stevens, J.Wood,trumpets; M.Croy,R.Gebhart,trombones; W.Maxted,piano;
    Tony Colucci,guitar: F.Ray,bass; Vic Engle,drums):   June,1939
BB 10179. Our Love/You're So Desirable
BB 10190. The King Kong/The Hour of Parting
BB 10360. Hot Lips/Parade of the Pennies   -HMV 8980
BB 10408. Wail of the Winds/Davenport Blues   -HMV 9028

    (Sub. C.Humphrey for Yolonsky,Schultz;S.Wilbur for Gebhart: Mike Bryan,
    guitar; Harry Jaeger,drums):   Oct.2,1939
BB 10522. A Pretty Girl Is Like a Melody/Poor Butterfly   -HMV 9038
BB 10451. You're the Greatest Discover/I love Again

    FIVE PENNIES (Nichols,Sheperd,Jones,Jaeger,Bryan,Ray):
BB 10593. My Melancholy Baby/Robins and Roses
BB 10683. She Shall Have Music/Let Me Dream

    (Conn Humphrey,Heinie Beau,Bobby Jones,Ray Schultz,saxes; Al Mastren,
    Jack Knaus,trombones: Doug Wood,Hilton Brockman,Red Nichols,trumpets;
    Bill Maxted,piano; Frank Ray,bass; Merritt Lamb,guitar; Harry Jaeger,
    drums):   June 11,1940
OK 5676. Lowland Blues(WC026919A)/Beat Me Daddy(WC026921A)   -PaE 2777
OK 5648. Overnight Hop(WCO 26918A)/Meet Miss Eight Beat(WC026920A)

    (Nichols,cornet; Heinie Beau,clarinet: Don Lodice,tenor sax: Floyd O'
    Brien,trombone; Earl Sturgis,piano; Gene Englund,bass; Frank Carlson,
    drums):   Hollywood.Oct.18,1944
Cap 10029. Royal Garden Blues(433-3A)/I'm in the Mood for Love(434-3A)

    (Omit O'Brien):
Cap   If I Had You/Little By Little

    (Sub. Herbie Haymer,tenor; Paul Leu,piano: Thurman Teague,bass; Rollie
    Colver,drums):   June 28,1945

```
         Cap      . You're My Everything
         Cap      . When You Wish Upon a Star
         Cap      . Love Is the Sweetest Thing
         Cap      . Can't Help Lovin' Dat Man

              RED NICHOLS AND HIS FIVE PENNIES:
    University 506. Memphis in June/Stop Look and Listen
    University 507. Perfidia/I'm on Your Waiting List
              RED NICHOLS AND HIS ORCHESTRA (Nichols,Beau, Haymer; Bud Wilson,trombone;
         George Van Eps,guitar; D.Whiting,bass; Stan Wrightsman,piano; Nick Fatool,
              drums):
         Mercury 8015. You Satisfy(306-2)/Battle Hymn of the Republic(307-2)

    NICHOLSON, FREDDIE 'REED' (vocal with piano):
         Br  7152. You Gonna Miss Me Blues/Dirty No Gooder
         Br  7204. Freddie's Got the Blues/I Ain't Sleepy

              (J. H. Shayne, piano):
         Br  7220. The Rollers Rub/You Don't Know My Mind

    NICKERSON, BOZO (vocal with piano):
         Vo  1525. Bozo's Blues, 1 & 2

    NICK'S DIXIELAND JAZZ BAND (Muggsy Spanier,cornet: Miff Mole,trombone: Pee Wee
    Russell,clarinet; Charles Carroll,drums; Gene Schroeder,piano; Jack Lesberg,bass):
         Man    101. Dixieland One Step/I Can't Give You Anything But Love      1945
         Man    102. Three Little Words/Livery Stable Blues
         Man    103. I'm Sorry I Made You Cry/Miff's Blues

              (Muggsy Spanier,cornet; Carl Kress,guitar: Lou McGarrity,trombone; Pee
              Wee Russell,clarinet; Joe Grauso,drums· Gene Schroeder,piano: Bob Casey,
              bass):
         Man    201. Muskrat Ramble/Tin Roof Blues

              (Sub. Charles Carroll,drums: Bob Haggart,bass; add Ernie Caceres,bari-
              tone sax):
         Man    202. Feather Brain Blues/Lucky to Me

              (Nick Rongetti,piano, on first side):
         Man    203. That's a Plenty/Bugle Call Rag

              (Spanier,Kress,McGarrity,Russell,Grauso,Schroeder,Casey):
         Man    301. Indiana/Jelly Roll

              (Personnel as for"Feather Brain"):
         Man    302. Clarinet Marmalade/Mama's in the Groove
         Man    303. Fidgety Feet/My Honey's Lovin' Arms

    NOBLE, GEORGE (vocal with piano):
         Me 70675. The Seminole Blues(C897)/If You Lose Your Good Gal Don't Mess With
                                                                          (Mine(C919)
    NOBLE AND HIS ORCHESTRA, RAY (Ray Noble,leader and arranger: Max Goldberg, Bill
    Shakespeare, trumpets; Lew Davis,Tony Thorp,trombones; Laurie Payne,Freddie
    Gardner,Bob Wise,George Smith,saxes; Jean Pougnet,Eric Siday,Harry Berley, Reg
    Pursglove,violins; Harry Jacobson,piano; Bert Thomas,guitar; Tiny Winters,bass;
    Bill Harty,drums): -- Clef 3-5/46
              Includes discs labeled New Mayfair Dance Orchestra. Recorded in London,
              a few without strings and some with an augmented orchestra):    1929-34
         Vi 22667. Say a Little Prayer for Me
         Vi 22745. Puzzle Record, 1 & 2
         Vi 22953. Got a Date With an Angel
         Vi 22964. Live, Laugh and Love/Just Once for All
         Vi 24004. Beside a Dutch Canal/Lights of Paris
         Vi 24022. The Punter's Lament/Pick the Winner
         Vi 24034. Hold My Hand/Pied Piper of Hamelin                -HMV 6112
         Vi 24064. Goodnight Vienna/Living in Clover
         Vi 24090. Twentieth Century Blues                           -HMV 4001
         Vi 24128. Sailing on the Robert E. Lee                      -HMV 6176
            "      With All My Love
         Vi 24149. There's a Ring Around the Moon/In the Bushes
         Vi 24211. Brown Bird Singing/Bird Songs at Eventide
         Vi 24212. Looking at the Bright Side/We've Got the Moon and Sixpence
         Vi 24226. Bedtime Story
         Vi 24263. Try a Little Tenderness                           -HMV 6284
         Vi 24276. Balloons/Say Yes to Mr. Brown
         Vi 24278. Love Tales
            "      Have You Ever Benn Lonely                         -HMV 6319
         Vi 24279. Ich Liebe Dich, My Dear
         Vi 24296. Butterflies in the Rain/Roll Along Kentucky Moon
         Vi 24297. Lying in the Hay/Wanderer                         -HMV 6306
         Vi 24308. A Letter to My Mother/Standing on the Corner
```

```
Vi 24314.  Brighter Than the Sun
    "      What More Can I Ask                                    -HMV 6302
Vi 24333.  I'll Do My Best to Make You Happy/Love Is the Sweetest Thing
Vi 24341.  My Heart's to Let                                      -HMV 6323
Vi 24347.  Three Wishes
Vi 24357.  Old Spinning Wheel/Hang Out the Stars in Indiana
Vi 24388.  Seven Years With the Wrong Woman
Vi 24396.  Less Than the Dust/Temple Bells
Vi 24427.  Turkish Delight, 1 & 2
Vi 24485.  Love Locked Out/On the Other Side of Lovers' Lane
Vi 24499.  Lady of Spain
Vi 24513.  There's Something About a Soldier
Vi 24556.  Peter, Peter
Vi 24575.  On a Steamer Coming Over/You Ought to See Sally
Vi 24577.  Japanese Sandman/Tiger Rag                             -HMV 6425
Vi 24594.  Who Walks In When I Walk Out                           -HMV 6453
Vi 24599.  Spanish Eyes/That's What Life Is Made Of
Vi 24603.  Oceans of Time                                         -HMV 6450
    "      The Sun is 'Round the Corner
Vi 24619.  Not Bad
    "      Repeal the Blues                                       -HMV 6471
Vi 24624.  Mademoiselle
    "      My Hat's on the Side                                   -HMV 6421
Vi 24657.  I'll Be Good/The Very Thought of You
Vi 24700.  An Hour Ago This Minute                                -HMV 6470
    "      Midnight the Stars and You
Vi 24711.  What Now                                               -HMV 6470
Vi 24713.  Goodnight Little Girl/Sweetheart in My Dreams          -HMV 6146
Vi 24720.  Over My Shoulder                                       -HMV 6504
    "      When You've Got Springtime
Vi 24724.  It's All Forgotten/Lady of Madrid
Vi 24749.  I'll Follow My Secret Heart/Nevermore
Vi 24752.  How Could I Be Lonely/I'm Telling the World
Vi 24771.  Grinzing/Isle of Cpri
Vi 24806.  Blue Danube/I Love You Truly
Vi 24850.  Dreaming a Dream
Vi 24865.  Clouds/Flowers for Madame
Vi 24872.  How Can We Be Wrong/It's Band for Me                   -HMV 6396
Vi 24884.  My Kid's a Crooner
Vi 25003.  Roll Along Covered Wagon
Vi 25006.  Driftin' Tide
    "      Fxperiment                                             -HMV 6408
Vi 25016.  Goodnight Sweetheart                                   -HMV 5984
    "      Time on My Hands                                       -HMV 5983
Vi 25020.  Mad About the Boy/Younger Generation
Vi 25190.  I'm the Fellow/Life Begins at Sweet Sixteen
Vi 25200.  I Built a Dream/Somebody Ought to Be Told
Vi 25262.  Rock Your Cares Away
    "      Roll Up the Carpet                                     -HMV 6380
Vi 36063.  Cat and the Fiddle Selections
Vi 36080.  Casanova Selections
Vi 36141.  Evergreen Selections
Vi 36163.  Kern's Melodies
Vi 36194.  Ray Noble Medley
HMV  5660. Do Something
HMV  5717. Copper Blues
HMV  5740. Baby You've Got the Right Idea
HMV  5819. You've Got to Be Modernistic/Crazy Feet
HMV  5826. High Society Blues
HMV  5936. Put Your Worries Through the Mangle/Hunting Tigers in India,Yah
HMV  5983. I'm Glad I Waited
HMV  5984. Shout for Happiness
HMV  6031. Lazy Day
HMV  6040. Roll on Mississippi Roll on
HMV  6088. Speedboat Bill
HMV  6130. Meet Me Tonight in the Cowshed/Must It End Like This
HMV  6131. By the Fireside                                        -Vi 25141
    "      Put Your Arms Around Me
HMV  6147. Blues in My Heart                                      -Vi 25141
    "      It's Great to Be in Love                               -Vi 25232
HMV  6157. My Girl Don't Love Me Anymore/With Love in My Heart
HMV  6241. There's Another Trumpet in the Sky, 1 & 2
HMV  6284. Always in My Heart
HMV  6321. Look What You've Done
HMV  6323. When You've Fallen in Love
HMV  6331. Hustlin' and Bustlin' for Baby
HMV  6337. No More Love
HMV  6347. It's Within Your Power
HMV  6366. I Only Want One Girl/Fools in Love
HMV  6375. I've Got to Sing a Torch Song/Pettin' in the Park
HMV  6408. Snowball
HMV  6411. I Was in the Mood
HMV  6421. This Town's Too Quiet
HMV  6422. And So Goodbye/This Is Romance
```

```
HMV  6438. My Song Goes 'Round the World/Song Without Words
HMV  6478. One Morning in May
HMV  6485. After All You're All I'm After
HMV  6508. All I Do Is Dream of You

      (Collective personnel for American Victor recordings; Nick Pisani, Fred
      Prospero, Dan D'Andrea,violins; Milt Yaner,Johnny Mince,Jin Cannon,Bud
      Freeman,saxes: Charlie Spivak,Pee Wee Irwin,trumpets; Will Bradley,
      Glenn Miller,trombones: Claude Thornhill,piano; George Van Eps,guitar;
      Delmar Kaplan,bass; Bill Harty,Dave Tough,droms; possibly Mike Doty,
      Toots Mondello,Johnny Van Eps,saxes; Sterling Bose,trumpet, in some
      titles.--RR):                                                    1935-36
Vi 24891. Allah's Holiday                                         -HMV   173
      "   Relicario
Vi 25040. Paris in Spring/Bon Jour
Vi 25070. Chinatown My Chinatown/Let's Swing It                   -HMV    49
Vi 25082. Way Down Yonder in New Orleans/St. Louis Blues          -HMV   263
Vi 25094. Top Hat White Tie and Tails/The Piccolino               -HMV   247
Vi 25104. I Wished on the Moon/Why Dream                          -HMV   211
Vi 25105. Double Trouble/Why Stars Come Out
Vi 25187. Where Am I/Dinner for One
Vi 25209. With All My Heart/Beautiful Lady in Blue
Vi 25223. Bugle Call Rag/Dinah
Vi 25240. If You Love Me/We Saw the Sea
Vi 25232. My Sweet
Vi 25241. Let Yourself Go/Let's Face the Music
Vi 25277. The Touch of Your Lips/Yours Truly is Truly Yours
Vi 25313. The Moment I Saw You/(RUXY VALLEE)
Vi 25346. Big Chief De Sota/Empty Saddles
Vi 25422. Easy to Love/I've Got You Under My Skin
Vi 25448. Now/Little Old Lady

      (Acc. to Al Bowlley, vocals):
Vi 25007. Basin Street Blues/My Melancholy Baby
Vi 25142. Red Sails in the Sunset/Roll Along Prairie Moon

      (Personnel unknown):
Br  8076. You Couldn't Be Cuter/Just Let Me Look at You
Br  8079. The Moon of Manakoora/I Hadn't Anyone Till You
Br  8098. Vilia/Crazy Rhythm
Br  8153. Now It Can Be Told/My Walking Stick
Br  8180. Alexander's Ragtime Band/Marching Along With Time
Br  8262. You're So Desirable(B23573)/You That I Loved(B23572)
Br  8351. Friday Night at the Harty's(LA1799A)/Saturday Night at the Nobles
Co 35258. Iroquois/Comanche War Dance                              (LA1800A)
Co 35311. When Irish Eyes are Smiling/Till I Kissed You Goodbye
Co 35335. Katie Went to Haiti/Chico's Love Song
Co 35346. Where Was I/In the Heart of the Dark
Co 35392. Sweet Potato Piper/Captain Custard
Co 35507. Louisiana Purchase/Outside of That I Love You
Co 35557. Sleepy Time Gal/Seminole
Co 35577. If I Had My Way/Carolina in the Morning
Co 35596. Maybe/I'll Never Smile Again
Co 35646. A Prairie Fairy Tale(SC3252A)/The Moon Over Madison Square(WC 3253A)
Co 35733. We Three/A Nightingale Sang in Berkeley Square
Co 35708. From Oakland to Burbank(CO3250B)/Harlem Nocturne(WC3251A)
Co 35775. Along the Santa Fe Trail/An Handful of Stars
Co 35804. Arise My Love/Moon Over Burma
Co 35814. Isola Bella/Red Roof Cottage
Co 35850. Sioux Sue/Far Away
Co 36005. A Little Old Church in Fngland/Walkin' Through Mocking Bird Lane
Co 36116. By the Waters of Minnetonka/Cherokee
Co 36162. A Little Bit of Blarney/My Wild Irish Rose
Co 36212. Swing Low Sweet Chariot/On the Alamo
Co 36256. Kiss the Boys Goodbye/Is That Good
Co 36271. If It's You/Harbor of Dreams
Co 36467. It Isn't a Dream Anymore/The magic of Magnolias
Co 36479. While My Lady Sleeps/By the Light of the Silvery Moon
Co 36546. Goodnight Sweetheart/The Very Thought of You
Co 36765. Sweet Dreams Sweetheart/How Bright the Stars
Co 36822. The Charm of You/What a Sweet Surprise
Co 36834. So-o-o-o in Love/The Wish That I Wish Tonight
Co 36883. Cuddles/Walkin' with My Honey
Co 36893. It Might As Well Be Spring/Full Moon and Fmpty Arms

NOLAN, DIXIE (and Johnnie Hardge, vocals with guitar and piano):
Vi 38556. Worried Love, 1 & 2
```

JIMMIE NOONE

See Also:
CAPITOL JAZZMEN: Cap 10009-10
LILLIE DELK CHRISTIAN: OK 8356, 8536, 8596, 8607, 8650, 8660.

```
CLUB AMBASSADOR: Br 7096.
COOK'S DREAMLAND ORCHESTRA: Ge 5360,-5373,.5374.
COOKIE'S GINGERSNAPS: OK 8369, 8392, 40675.
STOVEPIPE JOHNSON: Vo 1211.
KING OLIVER: Co 13003, 14003.
OLLIF POWERS: Para 12059.
SAVANNAH SYNCOPATORS: Br 7124.
JIMMIE'S BLUE MELODY BOYS: Vo 1439.
```

NOONE'S APEX CLUB ORCHESTRA, JIMMIE (Jimmie Noone,clarinet; Joe Poston,alto sax;
Earl Hines,piano; Buddy Scott,banjo; Johnny Wells,drums.--JI 11/8/40):   May,1928
```
Vo  1184.  Sweet Sue(C1938c)                                          -Br 80024
      "    I know That You Know(C1937C)                                  "
Vo  1185.  Four or Five Times(C1939C)                                 -BrF 500320
      "    Every Evening(C1940C)                                      -Br 80025
Me 12543.  Four or Five Times(C1939B)                                 -Br 80025
      "    Every Evening(C1940B)
Vo  1188.  Ready for the River/Forevermore

           (Add Lawson Buford, tuba):                                   Aug.,1928
Vo  1207.  Apex Blues(C2258B)                                         -Br 80023
      "    Sweet Lorraine(C2268)                                      -BrF 500320

Br 80023.  Sweet Lorraine(C2268B)
Vo  1215.  Oh Sister Ain't That Hot
      "    Blues My Naughty Sweetie Gives to Me(C2260C)               -Br 80026
Vo  1229.  Monday Date(C2259C)                                        -Br 80026,UHCA 41
      "    King Joe                                                   -HRS 13

           JIMMIE NOONE AND HIS APEX CLUB ORCHESTRA (Noone,clarinet; Poston, alto;
           Alex Hill,piano; Junie C. Cobb,banjo; Bill Newton,tuba; Johnny Wells,
           drums: George Mitchell,trumpet):                              1927-28
Vo  1238.  It's Tight Like That/Let's Sow a Wild Oat
Vo  1240.  She's Funny That Way/Some Rainy Day

           (Omit trumpet):                                               1928
Vo  1267.  Chicago Rhythm/I Got a Misery
Vo  1272.  Love Me or Leave Me/Wake Up Chillun Wake Up

           (Sub. Zinky Cohn,piano; Wilbur Gorham,guitar; May Alix,vocal):  1929
Vo  1296.  Am I Blues/Birmingham Bertha

           (Mitchell,Poston,Cohn,Gorham,Newton,Wells; Fats Williams,trombone):
Vo 15819.  Ain't Misbehavin'/Off Time

           (Reissue of Club Ambassadors, Br 7096):
Vo  2779.  Apex Blues/My Daddy Rocks Me

           (Omit Newton,Mitchell,Williams):
Vo 15823.  Anything You Want/That Rhythm Man

           (Add Newton, tuba):                                            1930
Vo  1415.  'Sposin'(vocal,Elmo Tanner)/True Blue Lou
Unissued.  Serenading the Moon(Tanner, vocal)
Vo  1416.  Satisfied/Through
Vo  1436.  I'm Doin' What You're Doin'/He's a Good Man to Have Around
Vo  1439.  Love/Love Me (Issued as Jimmie's Blue Melody Boys)
Vo  1466.  Have a Little Faith in Me(Tanner,voc.)/Cryin' for the Carolines
Vo  1471.  Should I/I'm Following You
Vo  1490.  Deep Trouble/El Rado Shuffle
Vo  1497.  I Lost My Gal from Memphis/When You're Smiling(Georgia White,voc.)
Vo  1506.  On Revival Day/I'm Driftin' Back to Dreamland
Vo  1554.  Three Little Words(May Alix,voc.)/Something to Remember You By(Alix,
Vo  1580.  He's Not Worth Your Tears/Trav'lin' All Alone(M.Bailer,vocs.)  (voc.)

           (Sub. Eddie Pollack,alto and baritone, for Poston):
Vo  1518.  Virginia Lee/So Sweet
Vo  1531.  Little White Lies/Moonlight on the Colorado
Vo  1584.  You Rascal You/Bring It on Home to Grandma

           (Noone,Pollack; Earl Hines,piano; John Henley,guitar; Quinn Wilson,bass;
           Benny Washington,drums;Art Jarrett,vocals):                    1931
Br  6174.  When it's Sleepy Time Down South/I Need Lovin'  -BrE 1234, BrF 9134
Br  6192.  It's You/River Stay 'Way from My Door                      -BrF 9135

           (Sub. Clarence Browning,piano; omit Jarrett):
Vo  2619.  Inka Dinka Doo                                             -DeE 3904
      "    Like Me a Little Bit Less
Vo  2620.  Dixie Lee(C686-1)                                          -DeE 3904
      "    Delta Bound(C688-1)
```

```
        (Add Jimmy Cobb,trumpet; Sub. John Lindsay, bass♢):
   Vo  2862. I'd Do Anything for You(C859A)              -BrF 500513
    "      Liza(C861A)                                   -BrF 500514
   Vo  2888. A Porter's Love Song                        -BrF 500513
    "      Shine                                         -BrF 500514
   Vo  2907. Soon(C903B)                                 -Pana 25720
    "      It's Easy to Remember(C906A)                      "
   Vo  2908. Lullaby of Broadway(C904A)                  -Pana 25749
    "      Here Comes Cookie(C905A)                      -Pana 25768
        (Guy Kelly,trumpet; Preston Jackson,trombone; Jimmie Noone,clarinet; Fran-
        cis Whitby,tenor sax; Gideon Honore,piano; Israel Crosby,bass; Tubby Hall,
        drums):                                                              1937
   PaE 2281. Way Down Yonder in New Orleans(90576A)/Sweet Georgia Brown(90578A)
                                                         -De 18440
   PaE 2303. He's a Different Type of Guy(90575A)/The Blues Jumped a Rabbit(90577A)
                                                         -De 18439
        (Charlie Shavers,trumpet; Jimmie Noone,clarinet; Pete Brown,alto sax;
        Frank Smith,piano; Teddy Bunn,guitar; Wellman Braud,bass. O'Neil Spencer,
        drums):                                                              1938
   De  1584. Bump It(Apex Blues)                         -De 3519, BrE 03303
    "      I Know That You Know                          -De 3863
   De  1621. Four or Five Times(62833A)                  -BrE 03303
    "      Japansy(62837A)
   De  1730. Call Me Darling,Call Me Sweetheart(62835B)/I'm Walkin' This Town
   De  7553. Sweet Lorraine(62830A)/Hell in My Heart(62834A)        (62836A)
        (Richard M. Jones,Piano; Nat Dominique,trumpet; Preston Jackson, trom-
        bone; Jimmie Noone,clarinet; Lonnie Johnson,guitar; John Lindsay, bass;
        Tubby Hall,drums):                                                   1940
   De 18095. New Orleans Hop Scop Blues(93030A)          -BrE 03169
    "      Keystone Blues(93031A)                             "
        JIMMIE NOONE TRIO(Noone,clarinet: Gideon Honore,piano; John Simmons,
        bass♢):                                                              1941
   BB  8609. Moody Melody/They Got My Number Now
   BB  8649. I'm Going Home/Then You're Drunk

NORSINGLE, BEN (vocals):
   Br  7043. Black Cat Blues/Motherless Blues
   Br  7041. Red River Bottom Blues/Rover's Blues

NORTH, HATTIE (vocal with piano):
   Vo  1433. Honey Dripper Blues/Living That Man Blues

NORTHWEST MELODY BOYS:
   Ge  6278. Sugar Foot Stomp(FRANK BUNCH)
```

RED NORVO

```
See also:
   MILDRED BAILEY: Most Vocalion; all Crown.
   HOAGY CARMICHAEL: Vi 24505, 24627.
   BENNY GOODMAN:
   ED HALL: BN 30, 31.
   KEN KENNY: All.
   STEW PLETCHER: all.
   TEDDY WILSON: Br 7964, 7973.
   SLAM STEWART QUINTET: Cont 10001, 10002.
                                                                             1933
NORVO, RED (xylophone solos):
   Br  6562. Hole in the Wall/Knockin' on Wood      -BrE 01563,BrF 9417,BrG 9419
        (Acc. by Benny Goodman,bass clarinet; Dick McDonough,guitar; Artie Bern-
        stein,bass):
   Br  6906. In a Mist(B14361A)/Dance of the Octopua(B14362A)-Br 8236, BrE 01686
        RED NORVO AND HIS SWING SEPTET (Jack Jenney,trombone; Artie Shaw,clari-
        net; Charlie Barnet,tenor sax; Teddy Wilson,piano; Bobby Johnson,guitar;
        Hank Wayland,bass; Bill Gussack,drums; Norvo,xylophone.--JRB):       1934
   Co  2977. I Surrender Dear(16022)                     -Co 35688, CoE 5012
    "      Tomboy(16033)                                 -PaE 2110
   Co  3026. The Night Is Blue(16034)                    -PaE 2088
    "      With All My Heart and Soul(16709),octet, see personnel below-PaE 2110
   Co  3059. Old Fashioned Love(16021A)                  -Co 35688, CoE 5012
    "      Honeysuckle Rose(16703: octet)                -PaE  211
```

RED NORVO AND HIS SWING OCTET (Bunny Berigan,trumpet; Jack Jenney, trombone; Johnny Mince,clarinet; Chu Berry,tenor sax; Teddy Wilson,piano; George Van Eps,guitar: Artie Bernstein,bass; Gene Krupa,drums; Norvo, xylophone):
Co 3079 Blues in E Flat(16711)/Bug House(16710)   -Co 36158

RED NORVO AND HIS SWING SEXTETTE (Stew Pletcher,trumpet; Eddie Sauter, mellophone and arranger; Donald McCook,clarinet; Herbie Haymer,tenor sax; Dave Barbour,guitar; Pete Peterson,bass; Bob White,drums; Norvo, xylophone):   1936
De 670. Polly Wolly Doodle/The Wedding of Jack and Jill
De 691. Gramercy Square(60300A)/Decca Stomp(60315A)

(Add Howard Smith,piano; omit Sauter; sub. Maurice Purtill,drums, for White):
De 779. I Got Rhythm/Lady Be Good   -BrE 02255
Unissued. Thou Swell
Unissued. My Heart Stood Still
Unissued. I'll Never Be the Same
Unissued. A Pretty Girl Is Like a Melody

RED NORVO AND HIS ORCHESTRA (Stew Pletcher,Bill Hyland,trumpets; Leo Moran,trombone: Frank Simeone; alto sax; Herbie Haymer,tenor sax;Slats Long,sax and clarinet; Joe Liss,piano; Dave Barbour,guitar; Pete Peterson,bass; Purtill,drums: Norvo,xylophone; Mildred Bailey,vocals):
Br 7732. It All Begins and Ends With You/Picture Me Without You
                                                (-VoE 36,BrF 500676
Br 7744. A Porter's Love Song/I Know That you Know   -VoE 32,BrF 500691

(Sub. Hank D'Amico,clarinet, for Long; Al Mastren,trombone):
Br 7761. When Is a Kiss Not a Kiss
     "   It Can Happen to You   -VoE 43
Br 7767. Now That Summer Is Gone(B20093)   -VoE 43
     "   Peter Piper(B20095)

(Sub. Bill Miller,piano; Red McGarvie,guitar):
Br 7813. Slumming on Park Ave.(C1735)   -VoE 102
     "   I've Got My Love to Keep Me Warm(C1736)   "
Br 7815. Smoke Dreams   -VoE 59,BrF 500709
     "   A Thousand Dreams of You   "   "
Br 7868. I Would Do Anything for You   -VoE 84
     "   Liza   -VoE 85
Br 7896. Jiving the Jeep/Remember   -VoE 91
Br 7928. Posin'/Every One's Wrong But Me

(Stew Pletcher,George Wendt,Luis Mucci,trumpets: Al Mastren,trombone; Hank D'Amico,Charlie Lamphere,L.Goldstein,saxes· Herbie Haymer,tenor sax; Bill Miller,piano;McGarvie,Peterson,Purtill,Norvo)':
Br 7932. The Morning After/Do You Ever Think of Me   -VoF 108
Br 7975. Russian Lullaby/Clap Hands Here Comes Charlie   -VoE 121
Br 7970. Tears in My Heart/Worried Over You   -VoE 132

(Zeke Zarchey,Jimmy Blake, Barney Zudecoff,trumpets; Weis Hein,trombone; D'Amico,Goldstein,Lamphere,Jerry Jerome,saxes: Alan Hanlon,guitar; Geo. Wettling,drums; Miller, Peterson, Norvo; Mildred Bailey,vocals):
Br 8068. I Was Doing All Right/Love Is Here to Stay
Br 8069. Always and Always(B22322)   -VoE 156
     "   It's Wonderful(B22324)
Br 8085. More Than Ever   -VoE 142
     "   Serenade to the Stars
Br 8088. The Week End of a Private Secretary(B22407)/Please Be Kind(B22408)
Br 8089. How Can You Forget/There's a Boy in Harlem
Br 8145. Savin' Myself for You/Daydreamin'

(Bailey,vocal*; uncertain as to other personnel):
Br 8103. Tea Time/Jeannine
Br 8135. You Leave Me Breathless*   -PaE 2552
     "   Says My Heart*
Br 8171. After Dinner Speech/A Cigarette and a Silhouette
Br 8182. Put Your Heart in a Song/The Sunny Side of Things
Br 8194. Wigwammin'/How Can I Thank You
Br 8202. Graden of the Moon/Jump Jump's Here
Br 8227. You're a Sweet Little Headache(B23456)/I Have Eyes(B23457)
Br 8230. This Is Madness(B23454)*/Who Blew Out the Flame(B23455)*
Br 8240. Just You Just Me(B23294)/You Must Have Been a Beautiful Baby(23517)
Br 8288. Undecided(B23809)/Thanks for Everything(B23814)
Vo 4738. Toadie Toddle/There'll Never Be Another You   -PaE 2706
Vo 4648. I Get Along Without You Very Well(24091)/Kiss Me With Your Eyes
Vo 4698. Cuckoo in the Clock(24093)*/We'll Never Know(24173)   (24092)
Vo 4785. You're So Desirable(24176)/Three Little Fishies(WB24345C)*

65

```
        Vo  4818. Yours for a Song(W24344D)/I Can Read Between the Lines(W24342C)
        Vo  4833. Rehearsin' for a Nervous Breakdown(24175)/Blue Evening(W24343A)
        Vo  4953. In the Middle of a Dream(24802)/My Love for You(24803)
        Vo  5009. Some Like It Ho/Have Mercy

              RED NORVO'S QUARTET (Norvo; Stuff Smith,violin; Remo Palmieri,guitar;
              Clyde Lombardi, bass):                                 April 5,1944
        SD      . Confessin'
        SD      . Red's Stuff
        SD      . Rehearsin'
        SD      . A Fawn Jumped at Dawn

              RED NORVO'S ALL STAR SEXTET (Norvo,vibraharp; Teddy Wilson,piano; Slam
              Stewart,bass; Eddie Dell,drums; Remo Palmieri,guitar; Aaron Sachs, clar-
              inet)* or SEPTET (omit Palmieri; add Joe Thomas,trumpet; Vic Dickenson,
              trombone; sub. Specs Powell for Dell; Hank D'Amico for Sachs)#:    1944
        Key 1310. Subtle Sextology(HL-49)*/Russian Lullaby(HL-61)#
        Key 1314. The Man I Love*/Seven Come Eleven*
        Key 1319. Blues a la Red*/I Got Rhythm#

              RED NORVO'S SELECTED SEXTET (Dizzie Gillespie,trumpet; Charlie Parker,alto
              sax; Flip Phillips,tenor sax; Teddy Wilson,piano; Slam Stewart,bass; J.C.
              Heard,drums; Norvo, vibraharp):
        Comet 6. Slam Slam Blues/Hallelujah
        Comet 7. Congo Blues(15)/Get Happy(14)

NOVELTY BLUE BOYS:
        GG  7026. Loveless Love/Deep River Blues

NUBIAN FIVE (with Lena Wilson):
        Pe 20910. Memphis Tennessee/He Used to Be Your Man
```

FLOYD O'BRIEN

```
See also:
        CHOCOLATE DANDIES: PaE 1792, 1717, 1743; Co 2875.
        EDDIE CONDON: BrF 500328, 500406, Co 35680.
        BOB CROSBY BOB CATS:
        BUD FREEMAN: OK 41168.
        GENE KRUPA:
        CHARLIE LA VERE: Jump 1,2,5.
        CHUCK MACKEY: Ju 10, 11.
        WINGY MANNONE: Cap 10024.
        MEZZ MEZZROW: Br 6778, 7551, Vi 25202, 25019.
        RED NICHOLS: Cap 10029.
        FATS WALLER: Vi 24737, 24738, 24742.
        GEORGE WETTLING: De 18044, 18045.
```

O'BRIEN'S STATE STREET SEVEN, FLOYD (Chuck Mackey,trumpet; Joe Rushton,bass sax;
Matty Matlock,clarinet; Charles LaVere,piano; George Van Eps, guitar; Nich Fatool,
drums; Artie Shapiro,drums):   Hollywood,Feb.24,1945
        Jump 4. Carolina in the Morning(J9-2)/Royal Reserves Blues(J-10-2)

JIMMY O'BRYANT

```
See also:
        LOVIE AUSTIN: Para 12255, 12277, 12278, 12283.
        IDA COX: Para 12044, 12063, 12064, 12085, 12086, 12087, 12097, 12202, 12212,
            12220, 12228, 12237.
        JULIA DAVIS: Para 12248.
        EDMONIA HENDERSON: Para 12084, 12095, 12097, 12203, 12239.
        MA RAINEY:
```

O'BRYANT'S WASHBOARD BAND (Jimmy O'Bryant,clarinet: Jimmy Blythe,piano; Jasper
Taylor, washboard. First coupling below issued under name of Jimmy O'Bryant,
"clarinet wizard"; Broadway issue under name of Jimmy Bryant".):
```
        Para 12246. Drunk Man's Strut(679A)/Red Hot Mama (677A)            -Bwy
        Para 12260. Skoodlum Blues(A758)/Midnight Strutters(A759)
        Para 12265. Washboard(10036-2: 253)/Brand New Charleston(10037-2: Ruth Coleman,
        Para 12277. Georgia Breakdown/Pickin' Blues                        (voc.)
        Para 12287. Clarinet Getaway/Back Alley Rub
        Para 12288. Blue Eyed Sally(252:10079-2)/Washboard Blues(253;10036-2: reissue of
        Para 12294. Three J Blues/Steppin' on the Gas         ("Washboard" above)
```

```
           (Add Bob Shoffner,cornet, on three sides*):
  Para 12297. The Joys*/Switch It Miss Mitchell
  Para 12312. Everybody Pile*/Charleston Fever*
  Para 12308. Down to the Bricks(2233-1)/I Found a Good Man After All(2234-2)
  Para 12321. Sugar Babe/Milenberg Joye
  Para 12329. Chicago Skiffle/My Man Rocks Me
  Para 12346. Shake That Thing(2435)/(BLYTHE'S SINFUL FIVE)

O'HARE'S SUPER ORCHESTRA, HUSK:
  Ge  4850. Boo Hoo Hoo/Tiger Rag
  Ge  4921. Clover Blossom Blues/Night
  Ge  4983. Swanee Smiles/You Give Me Your Heart
  Ge  5009. San(11068)/(FRIARS SOCIETY ORCHESTRA
  Vo 15646. Milenberg Joys/My Daddy Rocks Me

OHIO NOVELTY BAND(Originally issued on Vocalion under the name of McKenzie's
Candy Kids,q.v.):
  Aco 16033. If You Never Come Back
  Br   3484. Nervous Puppies/What Do I Care What Somebody Said

O.K. RHYTHM KINGS (Pseudonym for the Casa Loma Orchestra, q.v. for personnel):
  PaE   890. Casa Loma Stomp
  PaE   934. San Sue Strut
  PaF   982. Alexander's Ragtime Band
  PaF  1072. Royal Garden Blues

OKEH MELODY STARS:
  OK  8382. Look Out for Jazz/Glass of Beer

OLD SOUTHERN JUG BAND:
  Vo 14958. Hatchet Head Blues/Blues Just Blues
```

KING OLIVER

```
See also:
  ELIZA BROWN:?
  BUTTERBEANS AND SUSIE: OK 8163, 8182.
  CHOCOLATE DANDIES: Vo 1610, 1617.
  DIXIE SYNCOPATORS: Pe 15685.
  BLIND WILLIE DUNN: OK 8689.
  ALBERTA HUNTER:?
  ELIZABETH JOHNSON: OK 8593.
  MARLBOROUGH MELODY SYNCOPATORS: ?
  MEMPHIS JAZZERS: VD 7801; Rad 1804.
  MISSISSIPPI TRIO: VD 77039.
  MOONLIGHT REVELLERS: GG 1775, 1767.
  JELLY ROLL MORTON: Au 617.
  SAVANNAH SYNCOPATORS: Br 3245, 3361, 3373, 6046.
  SIPPIE WALLACE: OK 8205, 8206.
  CLARENCE WILLIAMS:?
  JACK WINN: Me 12064.

OLIVER, KING (cornet solo, with Jelly Roll Morton, piano):
  Au    617. King Porter(685)/Tom Cat(687)                            -Se 1

OLIVER'S JAZZ BAND, KING (King Oliver,Louis Armstrong,cornets: Honore Dutrey,
trombone; Johnny Dodds,clarinet; Stomp Evans,sax; Lil Hardin,piano; Bill Johnson,
banjo; Baby Dodds, drums):                                              1923
  Para 12088. Southern Stomps(1623-1)/(YOUNG CREOLE BAND)
  Para 12088. Southern Stomps(1623-2)                              -Cen 3011

  Para 20292. Mabel's Dream(1622-1)        -BrE 03575,Clax 40292,Pu 11292
         "    Riverside Blues(1624-2)      -BrE 03575,Clax 40292, Sig 905
  Para 20292. Mabel's Dream(1622-2)                                -Sig 905

         KING OLIVER'S CREOLE JAZZ BAND(Same personnel):
  Ge  5132. Weather Bird Rag(11388)             -JI 5,UHCA 75,BrE 02202
        "   Dipper Mouth Blues(11389B)     -Ge 3076,JI 10,UHCA 77,BrE 02200
  Ge  5133. Just Gone(11383B)                                -BrE 02202
        "   Canal Street Blues(11384B)         -JI 1,UHCA 67,BrE 02200
  Ge  5134. Mandy Lee Blues(11385C)             -JI 2,UHCA 70,BrE 02201
        "   I'm Going Away to Wear You Off My Mind(11386C)    -BrE 02201
  Ge  5135. Chimes Blues(11387A)                -JI 1,UHCA 68
        "   Froggie Moore(11390B)               -JI 2,UHCA 69
  Ge  5184. Snake Rag(11391)                    -JI 5,Uhca 76

         (King Oliver,Louis Armstrong,cornets· other personnel uncertain):
  Ge  5274. Alligator Hop(11633B)/Krooked Blues(11638)          Late 1923
  Ge  5275. Zulus Ball(11635A)/Workingman Blues(11636B)
  Ge  5276. If You Want My Heart/That Sweet Something Dear
```

KING OLIVER'S JAZZ BAND (Original personnel):
OK 4906. Sweet Lovin' Man(8392B)/Sobbin' Blues(8394B)
OK 4918. Where Did You Stay Last Night(8401A)/
"   Dipper Mouth Blues(8402A)   -HRS 4,Br 8223
OK 4933. Snake Rag(8391A)/   -HRS 12
"   High Society Rag(8393B)
OK 4975. Jazzin' Babies' Blues(8403A)/(CLARENCE WILLIAMS BLUE FIVE)
OK 40000. Buddy's Habit(8#75B)
"   Tears(8476B)   -HRS 12
OK 40034. Riverside Blues(8484A)
"   Working Man Blues(8486B)   -OdG 3197
OK 8148. I Ain't Gonna Tell Nobody(8477B)   -IRSM 2
"   Room Rent Blues(8478A)   -OdG 3198, IRSM 1
OK 8235. Sweet Baby Doll(8485A)   -IRSM 4
"   Mabel's Dream(8487A)   -IRSM 3

         (Probably Jimmie Noone, clarinet):
Co 13003. Chattanooga Stomp(81300)/New Orleans Stomp(81304)
Co 14003. London (Cafe) Blues(81302)/Camp Meeting Blues(81303)

         KING OLIVER AND HIS DIXIE SYNCOPATORS (King Oliver,Bob Shoffner,trumpets:
         Kid Ory,trombone: Albert Nicholas,clarinet and alto sax; Barney Bigard,
         tenor sax; one other,possibly Darnell Howard,sax; Luis Russell,piano; Bud
         Scott,banjo; Bert Cobb,tumba; Paul Barbarin,drums.--Eugene Williams in the
         Record Changer, 9/44):   Chicago, March 11, 1926
         (Brunswick recordings* were issued under name of "Savannah Syncopators")
Vo 1007. Too Bad(E2632-33W)   -Br 80082
"   Snag It(E2634-35W)   -Vo 15503,Br 80039

         (Georgia Taylor,vocal#):   April 21-23,1926
Vo 1014. Deep Henderson(E2891-92W,E19678-79)   -Br 3245*
"   Jackass Blues#(E2913-14-15W, E19675-6-7)   "
                                                      May 29,1926
Vo 1033. Sugar Foot Stomp(E3178-79W)   -Vo 15503,Br 3361*
"   Wa Wa Wa(E3180-81W, E20636-37)   -Br 3373*
Unissued. The Hobo's Prayer(E3182-83W)

         (Darnell Howard, sax and clarinet):   July 23,1926
Unissued. Someday Sweetheart(E3553W)
"   Messin' Around(F3554W)
Vo 1049. Tack Annie(E3555-56W)
"   New Wang Wang Blues(E3846-47W, E20255,56), see next date

         (Johnny Dodds reportedly clarinet on first side):   Sept.17,1926
Vo 1059. Someday Sweetheart(F3842-43W,E20251-52,E20638-39)
                                 -Vo 15493,Br 3373*,Me 12064,Br 80082
"   Dead Man Blues(E3844-45W,E20253-54)   -Vo 15493
Br 3361*. Snag It(E3848-49W,E20257-58,E20591-92)   -Br 80081

         (King Oliver,Thomas 'Tick' Gray,trumpets: Kid Ory,trombone, Omer Simeon,
         Darnell Howard,Barney Bigard,reeds; Lawson Buford,tuba; Russell,Scott,
         Barbarin):   April 22,1927
Vo 1112. Willie the Weeper(F5167-68W, E22737-38)   -Br 80079
"   Black Snake Blues(E5169-70-71W)
Vo 1113. (cancelled) Doctor Jazz(F5172-73-74W, E22729-30-31)
Vo 1114. Showboat Shuffle(E5175-76-77W, EE22732-34, E26316-18)   -Br 3998
"   Every Tub(E5178-79W, E22735-36, E26314-15)   "

         (Unknown personnel)   New York,July 8,1927
Unissued. Aunt Jemima(E23879-80)
                                                      Oct.13,14,1927
Unissued. Sobbin' Blues(E6655-57W)
"   Tin Roof Blues(E6658-60W)
"   Aunt Hagar's Blues(E6667-68W)
"   Farewell Blues(E6669-70W)
                                                      Nov.18,1927
Vo 1152. Farewell Blues(E6806-07W,E25352-53)   - Br 3741
"   Sobbin' Blues(E6810-11-w,E25354-55)   "
Unissued. Tin Roof Blues(E6808-09W)   Feb.25 & March 3,1928
"   Tin Roof Blues(E7172-73W)
"   Aunt Hagar's Blues(E7174-75W)
"   Who Threw That Rug(E7184-85W)
"   Crab House Blues(E7186-87W)
                                                      June 11,1928
Vo. 1189. Tin Roof Blues(E7388A-B, E27684A-B)
"   West End Blues(E7389A-B, E27685A-B)
Vo 1190. Sweet Emmaline(E7390A-B, E27686A-B)
"   Lazy Mama(E7391A-B, E27687A-B)

```
            (Probably including Omer Simeon, clarinet):            Aug.13,1928
   Br  4028. Got Everything(E28055A-B)
        "   Four or Five Times(E28056A-B)                       Sept.10 & 12,1928
   Vo  1225. Speakeasy Blues(E28185A-B)                             -Br 80080
        "   Aunt Hagar's Blues(E28186A-B)                               "
   Vo  4469. I'm Watching the Clock(E28203A-B)
        "   Slow and Steady(E28757A-B)                             Nov.14,1928
   Unissued. Janitor Sam(E28204A-B)

            KING OLIVER AND HIS ORCHESTRA (Probably including Ward Pinkett,trumpet;
            Br 6046* issued under name of "Savannah Syncopators"):     Jan.9,1931
   Br  6053. Papa De Da(E35910A-B)/Stop Crying(E35912A-B)
   Br  6046*.Who's Blue(E35911A-B)/Honey That Reminds Me:(Luis Russell Orch.)
   Br  6065. Sugar Blues(E36102A-B)/I'm Crazy About My Baby(E36103A-B)Feb.18,1931
   Unissued. Where That Ol' Man River Flows(E36101A-B)

            (Probably Louis Metcalf,King Oliver,trumpets; J.C.Higginbotham, trombone;
            Charlie Holmes,alto sax; Teddy Hill,tenor sax; Luis Russell,piano; Will
            Johnson,guitar; Bass Moore,tuba; Paul Barbarin,drums):    Jan.16,1929
   Vi 38034. West End Blues(49650)/(DUKE ELLINGTON)
   Vi 38521. Freakish Light Blues(49649)/I've Got That Thing(49651)
                                                                     Feb.1,1929
   Vi 38039. Call of the Freaks(48333)           -BB 6546,BB 7705,HMV 36
        "   The Trumpet's Prayer(48334)                "         "   "
                                                                    Feb.25,1929
   Vi 38049. Can I Tell You(50523)/My Good Man Sam(50525)

            (Personnel uncertain; includes J.P.Johnson; Glyn Paque,sax; Dave Nelson):
   Vi 38090. What You Want Me to Do(56756)/Too Late(56758)
   Vi 38101. Sweet Like This(56757)/I Want You Just Myself(57528)
   Vi 23029. I Can't Stop Loving You(57529)                        -HMV 4844
        "   I'm Lonesome Sweetheart(57527)
   Vi 38109. Frankie and Johnny(58339)/Everybody Does It in Hawaii(58338)
   Vi 23388. New Orleans Shout(58340)/Nelson Stomp(64013: last session below)

            (Bubber Miley,Henry Allen,trumpets; James Archey,trombone; Bobby Holmes,
            clarinet; Glyn Paque,alto: unknown tenor; Don Frye,piano; Fred Moore,
            drums; Clinton Walker,tuba; Arthur Taylor,guitar.--RC Sept.1946):
   Vi 22298. When You're Smiling(58528)/St.James Infirmary(58527)    -BB 5466
   Vi 38124. I Must Have It(59525)/You're Just My Type(59527)

            (Oliver, Dave Nelson, trumpets: Archey,trombone: Glyn Paque,Hilton Jeff-
            erson,altos; Walter Wheeler,tenor; same rhythm):
   Vi 38137. Edna(59747)/Rhythm Club Stomp(59526; session above)
   Vi 38134. Mule Face Blues(59749)/Boogie Woogie(59748)

            (Same brass; Bobby Holmes,Glyn Paque,Hilton Jefferson,Charles Frazier,
            sexer; Eric Franker,piano; Gerald Hobson,drums; Clint Walker,bass; Arthur
            Taylor,guitar):
   Vi 23001. Struggle Buggy(62236)/Don't You Think I Love You(62237)   -HMV 4930
   Vi 22681. Olga(62238)                                               -HMV 4870
   Vi 23011. What's the Use of Living Without Love(63134)
        "   Passing Time With Me(63135)

            (Uncertain, possibly including Henry Allen,trumpet):
   Vi 23009. Shake It and Break It(63639)/Stingaree Blues(63640)       -BB 10707

ORIGINAL COTTON CLUB ORCHESTRA (see Cotton Club Orchestra)

ORIGINAL CREOLE STOMPERS (Wooden Joe Nicholas,trumpet; Albert Burbank,clarinet;
Jim Robinson,trombone; Baby Dodds,drums; Lawrence Marrero,banjo; Slow Drag,bass):
   AM   513. Eh La Bas/Up Jumped the Devil              New Orleans,summer,1945

ORIGINAL CRESCENT CITY JAZZERS (Wingy Mannone,cornet; John Riddick,piano; Avery
Loposer,trombone; Cliff Holman,clarinet and alto; Eddie Powers,tenor sax: Felix
Guarino,drums):                                              New Orleans,1924
   OK 40101. Sensation Rag(8566A)/Christine(8567A)

ORIGINAL DIXIE RAG PICKERS:
   Globe  1341. Dinah
   Nadsco 1278. Charleston Rhythm(3622B)/(HIGH SOCIETY SEVEN)
   Radiex 1289. Waiting for the Moon(3650A)/(HIGH SOCIETY SEVEN)
   Radiex 1292. I'm in Doubt
   Radiex 1296. Strut Your Jonas/Cecelia
   Radiex 1467. I'll Be With You Dixie Lou(2580B)
   Supreme.1321. I'm Music Mad(3781)
   Supreme 1346. Tentin' Down in Tennessee(3867)
       GG 1298. I'm Gonna Charleston Back to Charleston(3691B)
       BB 7019. Beale Street Blues/(COTTON BLOSSOM ORCHESTRA)
```

ORIGINAL DIXIELAND JAZZ BAND

ORIGINAL DIXIELAND JASS BAND (Dominick J. LaRocca,trumpet; Larry Shields,clarinet;
Eddie Edwards,trombone; Henry Ragas,piano; Tony Sbarbaro(Spargo),drums):   1917
  Vi 18253. Dixieland Jass Band One-Step/Livery Stable Blues
  Co 2297. Darktown Strutters Ball(77086)/Indiana(77087)   -CoE 2903
  Ae 1205. At the Jass Band Ball/Barnyard Blues
  Ae 1206. Tiger Rag   -BrE 02500
  "   Ostrich Walk
  Ae 1242. Look at 'em Doing It Now
  "   Reisenweber Rag   -BrE 02500
  Ae 12097. Oriental Jazz/(DABNEY'S BAND)

    ORIGINAL DIXIELAND JAZZ BAND (Same personnel):   1918
  Vi 18457. At the Jazz Band Ball/Ostrich Walk   -HMV 1021
  Vi 18472. Skeleton Jangle/Tiger Rag
  Vi 18483. Bluin' the Blues/Sensation Rag   -HMV 1022
  Vi 18513. Mournin' Blues/Clarinet Marmalade   1919
  Vi 18564. Fidgety Feet/Lazy Daddy

    (Unknown personnel; may be Memphis Five):
  Hy   140. Gypsy Blues/My Honey's Loving Arms

    (Emile Christian,trombone; J.Russell Robinson,piano; LaRocca,Shields,
    Sbarbaro):   England,1919-1921
  CoE 735. At the Jazz Band Ball/Barnyard Blues
  CoE 736. Ostrich Walk/Sensation Rag
  CoE 748. Tiger Rag/Look at 'em Doing It Now
  CoE 759. Satanic Blues/Lasses Candy
  CoE 804. Tell Me/Mammy o' Mine
  CoE 805. My Baby's Arms/I'm Forever Blowing Bubbles
  CoE 815. I've Got My Captain Working for Me Now/I Lost My Heart in Dixieland
  CoE 824. Alice Blue Gown/Sphinx
  CoE 829. Sudan

    (Add Bennie Krueger,saxes: sub. Edwards,trombone):   U.S.A.
  Vi 18717. Margie/Palesteena   -HMV 1199
  Vi 18722. Broadway Rose/Sweet Mamma(Papa's Getting Mad)   -HMV 1216
  Vi 18729. Home Again Blues/Crazy Blues   -HMV 1227
  Vi 18772. St.Louis Blues(Al Bernard,vocal)
  "   Jazz Me Blues   -HMV 1257
  Vi 18798. Dangerous Blues/Royal Garden Blues(Al Bernard, vocals)
  Vi 18850. Bow Wow Blues/(BENSON ORCHESTRA)

    (LaRocca,trumpet; Eddie Edwards,trombone: Artie Seaberg,clarinet; Don
    Parker,saxes; Henry Vaniselli,piano; Tony Sbarbaro,drums):   1924
  OK 4738. Some of These Days(s71043-F)/Toddlin' Blues(s71044-B)
  OK 4841. Tiger Rag(s71429-B)/Barnyard Blues(s71430-B)

    ORIGINAL DIXIELAND FIVE (LaRocca,Edwards,Shields,Robinson,Sbarbaro):1936
  Vi 25502. Original Dixieland One Step/Barnyard Blues   -HMV 8648
  Vi 25524. Skeleton Jangle/Tiger Rag   -HMV 8642
  Vi 25525. Bluin' the Blues/Clarinet Marmalade

    NICK LA ROCCA AND THE ORIGINAL DIXIELAND JAZZ BAND(Augmented group):
  Vi 25403. Bluin' the Blues/Tiger rag
  Vi 25411. Clarinet Marmalade(BENNY GOODMAN)
  Vi 25420. Did You Mean It/Who Loves You
  Vi 25460. Ostrich Walk/Toddlin' Blues
  Vi 25668. Fidgety Feet/(MUNRO'S ORCHESTRA)
  Vi 26039. Old Joe Blade/(LIONEL HAMPTON)

    (Personnel unknown):
  BB 7444. In My Little Red Book/Goodnight Sweet Dreams
  BB 7454. Drop a Nickel in the Slot/Jezebel
  Vo 3099. You Stayed Away Too Long/Slippin' Through My Fingers

ORIGINAL GEORGIA FIVE:
  Olympic 1434. Down Among the Sleepy Hills of Tennessee

ORIGINAL INDIANA FIVE (Some collectors believe earlier recordings of this group
include Red Nichols and Miff Mole, but the band is more likely to have a personnel
similar to that given below for the Harmony issues. George Zack is reported to
have been the pianist on the Gennetts. The Oriole issues were principally under
the name of the Dixie Jazz Band):
  Ba 1931. Coffee Pot Blues(682)   -Or 828
  Ba 6006. Some of These Days   -Ca 1138
  Ba 6031. Rarin' to Go/(MISSOURI JAZZ BAND)
  Ba 7027. My Melancholy Baby(982)

```
   Ba   7084. Moten Stomp(1366)
   Ca   1138. Memphis Blues
   Ro    577. Nobody's Sweetheart(2895)/Where Will I Be(2896)
   Bell  456. My Baby Knows How/Heebie Jeebies
   Bell  463. Brown Sugar/There Ain't No Maybe
   Bell  547. Low Down Sawed Off Blues
   Pu  11146. Sister Kate/When All Your Castles              1925-26
   Ge   3060. Seminola/Everything is Hotsy Totsy Now
   Ge   3083. Cuckoo(9618)/Say Arabella(9619)
   Ge   3093. Two Tired Eyes/(BAILEY LUCKY SEVEN)
   Ge   3059. Sweet Georgia Brown
   Ge   3121. Oh Boy What a Girl/(HAPPY COLLEGIANS)          -Se 4003
   Ge   3148. I'm Goin' Out If Lizzie Comes In(9739)/(RED SANDERS)
   Ge   3182. Everybody's Doin' the Charleston Now
   Ge   3183. No Man's Mama(9812)/(JACK STILLMAN)
   Ge   3218. Pensacola/Song of the Vagabond
   Pe  14173. Mean Mama/Stavin' Change
   Pe  L4200. St. Louis Gal/Tin Roof Blues
   Pe  14225. Back o' Town Blues/Jubilee Blues
   Pe  14558. I'd Rather Be Alone(106537)
   Pe  14560. Lo Nah/(FIVE BIRMINGHAM BABIES)                -Pat 36379
   Pe  14601. Too Bad(106728)/Sittin' Around
   Pe  14609; Hard to Get Gertie                             -Pat 36428
   Apex 8890. Where Will I Be

         (Tom Morton, director):
   OK  40456. Oh Boy What a Girl(73586b)/Indiana Stomp(73587B)
   OK  40599. Hard to Get Gertie(74092B)/Pensacola(74093B)

         (Sam Castin,trumpet; Michael Fucillo,trombone; Nick Vitalo,clarinet; Tom
         Morton,drums, et al.--JI 6/14/40; JT #9):
   Ha    47. Everybody Stomp(141103)/I'm Gonna Hang Around My Sugar(141104)
   Ha    58. Everybody's Doin' the Charleston Now/(ORIGINAL MEMPHIS FIVE)
   Ha   101. I'd Rather Be Alone(141489)/Pensacola(141491)
   Ha   134. Running After You(141490)/(UNIVERSITY SIX)
   Ha   179. So Is Your Old Lady(141944)/(DIXIE STOMPERS)
   Ha   217. Spanish Mamma(142219)/Deep Henderson(142221)
   Ha   245. I'd Leave Ten Men Like Yours(142220/(UNIVERSITY SIX)
   Ha   267. Hangin' Around(141942)/Florida Low Down(141943)  -Ve 1267
   Ha   327. Delilah/(BROADWAY BELL HOPS)
   Ha   432. Play It Red/One Sweet Letter from You
   Ha   387. The Chant/Stockholm Stomp
   Ha   459. Struttin' Jerry(144227)/(ARKANSAS TRAVELLERS)
   Ha   501. Someday Sweetheart(144805)/I'm Coming Virginia(144806)  -Di 2501
   Ha   510. Clementine/(UNIVERSITY SIX)
   Ha   632. Junkman's Dream/What Can a Poor Fellow Do
   Ha   930. Anything to Hold You,Baby(148606)/Birmingham Bertha(148607)

ORIGINAL JAZZ HOUNDS(Personnel includes Johnny Dunn,trumpet; Perry Bradford,piano;
Garvin Bushell,clarinet and sax):
   Co  14086. Fo' Day Blues(140760)/1620 to 1865(Uncle Eph's Dream)(140761)
   Co  14094. I Ain't Gonna Play No Second Fiddle(140840)/Slow Down(140841)
   Co  14124. Cannon Ball/Lucy Long
```

ORIGINAL MEMPHIS FIVE

See also:
```
   COTTON PICKERS: Br 2292-2532.
   ALBERTA HUNTER: Para 12021.
   JAZZBO'S CAROLINA SERENADERS: Cameos.
   LADD'S BLACK ACES: Gennetts.
   ANNA MEYERS: Pe 12038, Pat 20870.
   NEW ORLEANS FIVE: Ro 371.
   LEONA WILLIAMS.
   JACK WINN.
```

ORIGINAL MEMPHIS FIVE (Phil Napoleon,trumpet; Vincent Grande or Miff Mole,trombone; Jimmy Lytell,clarinet; Frank Signorelli,piano; Jack Roth,drums: unknown
banjo on some sides):   1922
```
   Vo  14461. Stop Your Kidding/That Barking Dog, Woof Woof
   Vo  14506. Four o'Clock Blues/Aggravatin' Papa
   Vo  14527. Great White Way Blues/Loose Feet
   GG   1140. Sister Kate
   GG   1200. Mindin' My Business                            -Or 175
   GG   1188. That Teasin' Squeezin' Man                     -Nadsco 7013
   GG   1206. My Papa Doesn't Two Time
   GG   1247. Take Me(3522)/Madrid Blues(3511)
   Nadsco 7013. Four o'Clock Blues
   Bell 149. Lonesome Mama Blues/Cuddle Up
   Bell 153. Sister Kate/Pacific Coast Blues
   Bell 168. Got to Cool My Doggies Now/Chicago
   Bell 185. Wicked Dirty Fives/Stop Your Kiddin'
   Bell 199. Hot and Cold/Whoa Tillie Take Your Time
```

```
Bell    257. Oh Sister Ain't That Hot
Bell    262. Your Mamma's Gonna Slow You Down/Steppin' Out
Para  20131. Lonesome Mama Blues(1057)/Those Longing for You Blues(1058)-Pu 11131
Para  20142. I'm Going to Wear You Off My Mind(1091)/Don't Pan Me(1090)
Para  20161. Struttin' at the Strutters Ball(1168)/Sister Kate(1169)
Para  20192. Four o'clock Blues(1265)           -Harmo 775,Pu 11265,Bwy  1119
   "         Haunting Blues(1266)                            "          "
Para  20281. St.Louis Gal/Back o' Town Blues
Bwy   11445. Meanest Blues/Nobody Knows
Tr    11400. Red Hot Mamma/You Know Me Alabam'
Ca      478. Sweet Papa Joe(752)
Rad    1184. Sad News Blues/(PENNSYLVANIA SYNCOPATORS)
Ed    51204. The Great White Way Blues(9077A)/Shufflin' Mose(9078B)
Ed    51246. The Jelly Roll Blues(9173B)/A Bunch of Blues(9174B)
Pat   20825. Got to Cool My Doggies Now/Sister Kate             -Pe 14051
Pat   20842. Ji Ji Boo/You Can Have Him Blues
Pat   20855. He May Be Your Man/Stop Your Kiddin'       -Pe 14067,Davega 5057
Pat   20870. That Da Da Strain/Tain't Nobody's Biz-ness If I Do  -Davega 5067
Pat   20877. Evil Minded Blues/Last Go Round Blues
Pat   20888. Railroad Man                                       -Pe 14081
   "         Great White Way Blues(5091)                        -Re 9455
Pat   20893. Four O'Clock Blues/(SYNCO JAZZ BAND)               -Pe 14087
Pat   20900. Aunt Hagar's Blues/Ivy
Pat   20920. Farewell Blues
Pat   20921. Sweet Lovin' Mama/That Eccentric Rag               -Pe 14105
Pat   20939. That Red Head Gal/I Never Miss the Sunshine        -Pe 14121
Pat   20977. Papa Blues(5090)                              -Re 9455,Ba 1178
   "         Keep It Under Your Hat
Pat   20981. Memphis Glide/(GOLDEN GATE ORCHESTRA)              -Pe 14132
Pat   20995. Hen Pecked Blues/Papa Better Watch Your Step
Pat   21031. Struttin' Jim                                      -Pe 14155
Pat   36043. That Teasin' Squeezin' Man/Snuggle Up a Bit        -Pe 14224
Pat   36061. Red Hot                                            -Pe 14242
Pat   36072. Blue Grass Blues/Sioux City Sue                    -Pe 14253
Pat   36095. Shine                                              -Pe 14275
Pat   36138. Mamma's Boy/Emmaline                               -Pe 14349
Pe    14298. Africa/Superstitious Blues
Pe    14315. I'm Going Back
Pe    14322. How Come You Do Me Like You Do/Somebody Stole My Gal
Pe    14332. Evening/Choo Choo
Pe    14389. Meditation
Pe    14565. Throw Down Blues
Pe    14804. Wistful and Blues/What do I care
PatE  11097. Indiana Stomp(106677)/Military Mike(106678)
PatE  11471. Play It Red/Nothin'
Sal     246. Jacksonville Gal
Re     9325. Beedle Beedle Bum/Buzz Mirandy
Re     9395. Bee's Knees(1220)/Stop your Kiddin'(1221)           -Ba 1132
Re     9365. Sister Kate/Pacific Coast Blues                     -Ba 1104
Re     9407. Runnin' Wild/Loose Feet  *                          - Ba 1143
Re     9543. Bad News Blues/That Teasin' Squeezin' Man o' Mine
Re     9573. House of David Blues(5314)/Oh Sister Ain't That Hot(5315) -Ba 1282
Re     9615. May Be/(NEW ORLEANS JAZZ BAND)
Re     9583. Steppin' Out/Dancing Dan
Re     9588. Mama's Gonna Slow You Down/Lovey Come Back
Re     9656. Big Boy
Ba     1110. Struttin' at the Strutters Ball
Ba     1193. Shufflin' Mose/Memphis Glide
Ba     1309. Shake Your Feet/That Bran' New Gal o' Mine
Im     1305. Maybe She'll Phone Me
Em    10439. Aunt Hagar's Blues/Shake It and Break It
Em    10725. Lots o' Mamma/Mindin' My Business
Em    10740. Sioux City Sue/My Papa Doesn't Two Time
Em    10741. 31st Street Blues
Em    10782. Red Hot Mamma/Wait Till You See My Gal

        (Vincent Grande,trombone,--JT #10):              May 25,1923
Co     3924. Pickles(81036)/(LANIN ORCHESTRA)
                                                         Sept.27,1923
Co        7. Walk Jenny Walk(81242)/Last Night on the Back Porch(81243)
Co       37. More(81379)/She Wouldn't Do What I Asked Her to(81380)  Dec. 4,1923
Co       50. St.Louis Gal(81393)/Shufflin' Mose(81394)               Dec.11,1923
Co       74. Why Should I Weep(81500)/Since Ma Is Playing Mah Jng(81501) Jan.25,1924
Co      155. Ain't Gonna Rain No Mo'(81804)/Red Hot Mama(81805)       June 4,1924
Co      186. The Grass Is Always Greener(81885)/Sioux City Sue(81886)July 25,1924
Co      260. Mobile Blues(140163)/How Come You Do Me Like You Do(140164) Dec.4,1924
Co      308. Doo Wacka Doo(140337)/Nobody Knows What a Red-Head Mama Can Do(140338)
                                                                   /(Feb.10,1925
        (Sub. Miff Mole,trombone):                                Sept.25,1925
Co      480. Indiana Stomp(141050)/Throw Down Blues(141051)
Co      502. Jacksonville Gal(141193)/Tain't Cold(141194)         Oct.26,1925
Ha       56. Tain't Cold(141195)/Hot Air(141197)
Ha       58. Jacksonville Gal(141196)/(ORIGINAL INDIANA FIVE)
```

```
                                              Dates unknown
                                                 -HMV 1633
Vi 19052. Who's Sorry Now/Snakes Hips
Vi 19170. Tin Roof Blues/I've Gotta Song for Sale
Vi 19480. Meanest Blues/How Come You Do Me Like You Do
Vi 19594. Sob Sister Sadie/Throw Down Blues
Vi 19805. Bass Ale Blues/Military Mike
Vi 20039. Tampeekoe/Static Strut
Br  3039. Chinese Blues/Tain't Cold
Br  3630. Lovey Lee/How Come You Do Me Like You Do         -Vo 15623
Vo 15712. I'm More Than Satisfied/My Angeline
Vo 15761. Fireworks/(JACK PETTIS)
Vo 15805. Beale Street Blues/Memphis Blues
Vo 15810. Kansas City Kitty/(LOUISIANA RHYTHM KINGS)
```

(Phil Napoleon,trumpet; Tommy Dorsey,trombone: Jimmy Dorsey,clarinet;
Frank Signorelli,piano; Ted Napoleon,drums):   Nov.24,1941
```
Co  2577. St.Louis Gal(151888)/My Honey's Loving Arms(151890)
Co  2588. Jazz Me Blues(151887)/Anything(151889)
```

(Phil Napoleon*, or Chris Griffin,trumpet· Frank Signorelli,piano; Al
Philburn,trombone; Sal Franzella,clarinet: Nick Caiazza,tenor sax; Haig
Stephens,bass; Chauncey Morehouse,drums):   1946
```
Stinson 365-1. Limehouse Blues/Between the First Hello and the Last Goodbye
Stinson 365-2. Darktown Strutters Ball*/Sour Puss Hannah
Stinson 365-3. Memphis Blues*/Saxophone Joe
```
(Napoleon and Signorelli are also featured on recent Swan issues
under the name of "Emperors of Jazz")

ORIGINAL MEMPHIS MELODY BOYS(Elmer Schoebel,piano: Murphy Steinberg,cornet;
"Wingy"____,clarinet; et al):
```
Ge  5123. Wonderful Dream(11378A)/Made a Monkey Out of Me(11380A:Billy Meyers,
Ge  5157. There's No Gal Like My Gal(11377B)/Blue Grass Blues(11379A)  (voc)
Bu  8005. Creole Washboard Blues
```

ORIGINAL MIDNIGHT RAMBLERS ORCHESTRA:
```
Au   ?  Midnight Ramblers Stomp
Au   ?  Owl Strut
Au   ?  Midnight Ramblers Blues
Au   ?  Bowling Green
```

ORIGINAL NEW ORLEANS JAZZ BAND (See New Orleans Jazz Band)

ORIGINAL ST. LOUIS CRACKERJACKS:
```
De  7235. Good Old Bosom Bread/Swing Jackson
De  7236. Blue Thinking of You/Crackerjack Stomp
De  7248. Echo in the Dark/Fussin'
De  7265. Lonesome Moments/Chasing the Blues Away
```

ORIGINAL TUXEDO JAZZ ORCHESTRA (Oscar Celestin,Shots Madison,trumpets; William
Ridgely,trombone: Emma Barrett,piano; Thomas Benton,guitar: Simon Marrero,bass;
clarinet; drums):   New Orleans,1924
```
OK  8198. Careless Love(8907A)/Black Rag(8908A)
OK  8215. Original Tuxedo Rag(8906A)/(WILLIAMS BLUE FIVE)
```

ORIGINAL WOLVERINES (See Wolverine Orchestra)

ORIGINAL ZENITH BRASS BAND OF NEW ORLEANS (Including George Lewis,clarinet; Kid
Howard and Peter Bocage,trumpets: Jim Robinson,trombone; Baby Dodds,Lawrence
Marrero,drums):   New Orleans,1945
```
Ci  1005. Salutation March/If I Ever Cease to Love
Ci  1006. Bugle Boy March/Tain't Nobody's Biz-ness If I Do
Ci  1007. Fidgety Feet/Shake It and Break It
```

KID ORY

See also:
```
LOUIS ARMSTRONG: Ok 8261-8566; Vi 202087,202088.
BENNETT SWAMPLANDERS: Co 14557.
CHICAGO FOOTWARMERS: OK 8599, 8613, 8792.
JOHNNY DODDS.
RUTH LEE: Nor 3008.
ROBERTA DUDLEY: Nor 3007.
LILL'S HOT SHOTS: Vo 1037.
JELLY ROLL MORTON: Vi 20221, 20296, 20252, 20405, 20415, 20431.
NEW ORLEANS BOOTBLACKS: Co 14337, 14465.
NEW ORLEANS WANDERERS: Co 698, 735.
KING OLIVER: Vocalion and Brunswick.
LUIS RUSSELL: Vo 1010.
SPIKES PODS OF PEPPER: Nor 3009.
SIPPIE WALLACE: OK 8470, 8499.
```

ORY'S SUNSHINE ORCHESTRA (Mutt Carey,cornet: Kid Ory,trombone: Dink Johnson,clarinet; Fred Washington,piano; Ed Garland,bass; Ben Borders,drums):
<u>Santa Monica,Calif.,1921</u>
  Su 3003* Ory's Creole Trombone/Society Blues
          *(Original issue: Nordskog 3009, Spikes Seven Pods of Pepper)

      KID ORY'S CREOLE JAZZ BAND (Mutt Carey,trumpet; Kid Ory,trombone; Omer Simeon,clarinet; Buster Wilson,piano: Bud Scott,guitar; Ed Garland,bass; Alton Redd,drums): <u>Aug.,1944</u>
Crs 1. South(CPM1033-1A)/Creole Song(CPM 1035-2A)
Crs 2. Blues for Jimmy/Get Out of Here

      (Sub. Darnell Howard,clarinet: Minor Hall,drums): <u>1945</u>
Crs 3. Maryland/Oh Didn't He Ramble
Crs 4. Down Home Rag/1919

      (Simeon,clarinet): <u>Aug.,1945</u>
Crs 5. Do What Ory Say(1010)/Careless Love(1009)
Crs 7. Panama(1006)/Under the Bamboo Tree(1011)

      (Howard,clarinet): <u>Nov.,1945</u>
Crs 6. Ory's Creole Trombone(1025-2)/Original Dixieland One-Step(1022)
Crs 8. Maple Leaf Rag(1023-4)/Weary Blues(1024-2)

      (Original personnel, with Joe Darensbourg,clarinet,in place of Simeon):
Exner 3. Dippermouth Blues(FX 5-3A)/Savoy Blues(EX 6-2A) <u>Feb.12,1945</u>
Exner 4. High Society(FX 7-2A)/Ballin' the Jack(FX 8-2A)

      (Barney Bigard,clarinet: Carey,Ory,Wilson,Scott,Garland,Hall): <u>1947</u>
Co 37274. Bucket Got a Hole in It/Tiger Rag
Co 37275. Eh La Bas/Joshua Fit de Battle of Jericho
Co 37276. Bill Bailey Won't You Please Come Home/Creole Bo Bo
Co 37277. The World's Jazz Crazy, Lawdy So Am I/Farewell to Storyville

OSCAR'S CHICAGO SWINGERS:
De 7186. I Wonder Who's Boogiein' My Woogie Now/New Rubbing on the Darned Old
De 7201. My Gal's Been Foolin' Me/Try Some of That   (Thing

OSCAR, JOHN (vocal):
Br 7080. In the Gutter/Mama Don't Allow No Easy Riders Here

OTIS AND HIS ORCHESTRA, JOHNNY (Teddy Buckner,Billy Jones,Loyal Walker,Par Jones, trumpets; Lorenzo Cocker,Eli Robinson,John Pettigrew,Jap Jone,trombones; Rene Black,James Von Streeter,Paul Quinechette,Bob Harris,Leon Beck,saxes; Curtis Counce,bass; Bernie Cobbs,guitar; Bill Doggett,piano; James Rushing,vocals):
Ex 141. My Baby's Business/Preston Love's Mansion
Ex 142. Jimmy's Round the Clock Blues/Harlem Nocturne
Ex 152. Omaha Flash/Jeff-Hi Stomp
Ex 156. Miss Mitchell/Ultra Violet
Ex 157. Sergeant Barksdale, 1 & 2

OWENS, BIG BOY GEORGE (vocal with guitar): <u>1927</u>
Ge 6006. Kentucky Blues/The Coon Crap Game

HOT LIPS PAGE

See also:
Albert AMMONS: Com 1516.
CHU BERRY: Vr 532, 587; Com 541, 1508.
IDA COX: Vo 05258, 05298, 05336.
EDDIE AND SUGAR LOU.
PETE JOHNSON: De 18121, Vo 4997, 5186.
MEZZROW-BECHET: KJ 143, 144.
BENNIE MOTEN.
WALTER PAGE: Vo 1463.

PAGE AND HIS ORCHESTRA, HOT LIPS (Oran 'Hot Lips' Page,trumpet and vocal; probably Jim Reynolds,piano; Sam Davis,Buster Smith,Jimmy Powell,saxes; Abe Bolar,bass; Ed Connery,drums):
De 7433. Old Man Ben/Down on the Levee   -VoE 197
De 7451. Good Old Bosom Bread(63393A)/He's Pulling His Whiskers(63394A)VoE 206
De 7699. I Would Do Anything for You(67091A)/I Won't Be Here Long(67100A)
De 7714. Gone With the Gin/I Ain't Got Nobody
De 7757. A Porter's Love Song to a Chambermaid(67093A)/Walk It to Me(67099A)

      (Hot Lips Page,Eddie Mullens,Bobby Moore,trumpets; George Stevens,Harry White,trombones; Ben Waters,Ben Smith,Ernie Powell,Ulysses Scott,saxes; Jim Reynolds,piano; Connie Wainright,guitar: Abe Bolar,bass; Alfred Taylor,drums): <u>1938</u>
BB 7567. I Let a Song Go Out of My Heart(22928)
     "   Rock It for Me(22926)   -HMV 9369
BB 7569. Feelin' High and Happy(22924)/at Your Beck and Call(22925)

```
BB   7583. Jumpin'(22923)                                              -HMV 9369
  "       Skullduggery(22927)
          (Sub. Ben Williams,sax, for Scott: Dave Page,trumpet,for Mullens):
BB   7680. Will You Remember Tonight Tomorrow(23737)/And So Forth(23733)
BB   7682. The Pied Piper(23734)/I'm Gonna Lock My Heart(23736)
BB   7684. If I Were You(23732)/Small Fry(23735)

          HOT LIPS PAGE TRIO(Page,trumpet; Ernest Hill,bass: Teddy Bunn,guitar and
          vocal):
BB   8634. Evil Man's Blues/Do It, If You Wanna
BB   8660. My Fightin' Gal/Just Another Woman(Page,vocal and mellophone)

          HOT LIPS PAGE AND HIS BAND (Don Stovall,Don Byas,Eddie Barefield,saxes;
          Page,trumpet; Pete Johnson,piano: John Collins,guitar: Abe Bolar,bass;
          A.G.Godley,drums):                                               1941
De  18124. Lafayette(68334A)/South(68335A)

          (Unknown personnel):
De   8531. Harlem Rumbain' the Blues(68435A)/No Matter Where You Are(68436A)

          (Page,trumpet and vocal; Don Byas,tenor sax: Earl Bostick,B.G.Hammond,
          altos; Clyde Hart,piano; Al Lucas,bass; Jack Parker,drums):      1944
Com   558. Fish for Supper/You Need Coachin'
Com   574. These Foolish Things/Six, Seven, Eight or Nine

          (Page,trumpet and vocal; Lucky Thompson,tenor sax; Lem Johnson,tenor;
          Ace Harris,piano; John Simmons,bass; Sid Catlett,drums):
Com   571. You'd Be Frantic Too/Rockin' at Ryan's

          (Page,trumpet and mellophone; Don Byas,tenor; George Johnson,Floyd Will-
          iams,altos; Clyde Hart,piano; Sid Catlett,drums; John Simmons,bass):
Sav   520. Uncle Sam Blues(S5463-C)/Pagin' Mr. Page(S5464)         June 14,1944
Sav   605. Dance of the Tambourine(S5462)/I Keep Rollin' ON(S5465)

          (Page,trumpet; Vic Dickenson,trombone· Lucky Thompson,sax; Hank Jones,
          piano; Sam Allen,guitar; Jesse Price,drums):Carl Wilson,bass):
Cont 6002. Gee Baby Ain't I Good to You/Lady in Bed                 Nov.30,1944
Cont 6003. Big D Blues/It Ain't Like That

          (Featuring Ben Webster,Don Byas,saxes; Benny Morton,trombone):
Cont 6015. Lady in Debt(W3397)/Sunset Blues(W3400)
Cont 6017. Florida Blues(W3403)/They Raided the Joint(W3399)

PAGE TRIO, MILT (featuring Oscar Pettiford, bass):
Manor 1000. It's Only a Paper Moon/Soda Pop

PAGE, STAR (Blues vocals):
  Para 12684. Georgia Blues/Ain't Puttin' Out

PAGE BLUE DEVILS, WALTER (James Simpson,Hot Lips Page,James LuGrand,trumpet;
Walter Page,bass; Reuben Lynch,guitar; Alvin Burroughs,drums; Count Basie,piano;
Dan Minor,trombone: Ted Manning,Buster Smith,altos; Rubin Roddy,tenor; James
Rushing,vocal.--DB 6/15/43):                                    Kansas City,1927
  Vo  1463. Blue Devil Blues/Squabblin'

PALMER,SYLVESTER (vocal with piano):
  Co 14524. Do it Sloppy(403304)/Broke Man Blues(403305)

PANASSIE AND THE SWING CLUB BAND, HUGUES (Hugues Panassie,clarinet: assisted by
players of the Hot Club of Zurich, Switzerland):                    Zurich,1942
  Fl  4092. Seefeld Stomp/Angi's Blues

          (Under name of Bond Street Swingers):
  Fl  4090. Blue Moon/China Boy

PAPA EGG SHELL (L.Casey. Vocal and guitar):
  Br  7095. Far From Home/Whole Soul Blues
  Br  7082. I'm Going Up the Country, 1 & 2

PAPA TOO SWEET
  OK  8651. Big Fat Mama/Tight Like That(with Harry Jones)

PAPALIA AND HIS ORCHESTRA                                            New Orleans
  OK 40347. Cross Word Mama you're puzzling Me(8898A)/Sometime When You're Alone
                                                                         (8899A)
PARAMOUNT PICKERS (Johnny Dodds,clarinet· with guitar and piano):       1928-29
  Para 12779. Steal Away(21184-1)                                     -Cen 3010
       "     Salty Dog(21185-2)

PARENTI, TONY (clarinet solo, with Vic Breidis,piano):
  Ca  0180. Old Man Rhythm(18744-5)/(EDDIE PEABODY)              -Je 5836,Or 1836
```

```
          ANTHONY PARENTI'S FAMOUS MELODY BOYS (Parenti,clarinet; Henry Knecht,
          trumpet; Vit Lubowski,piano; George Triay,drums; Mario Finazzo,bass; Tony
          Papalia,sax; Mike Holloway,banjo; Russ Papalia,trombone):New Orleans,1924
OK 40308. That's a Plenty(8895A)/Cabaret Echoes(8896A)

          (Sub. Leon Prima, trumpet):
Vi 19647. Creole Blues/12th Street Blues
Vi 19697. Dizzy Lizzy/French Market Blues
Vi 19698. La Vida Medley(Ida; Gypsy Love Song)/Be Yourself

          PARENTI'S LIBERTY SYNCOPATORS (Original personnel, except Ray Bauduc,
Co   545. Midnight Papa(140988)/Cabaret Echoes(140990)           (drums):
Co   836. Up Jumped the Devil(142000)/New Crazy Blues(142004)
Co  1264. Weary Blues(142003)/African Echoes(142005)

          TONY PARENTI'S NEW ORLEANIANS (John Hyman,cornet: Ellis Stratakos,trom-
          bone; Parenti,clarinet and sax; Buzzy Williams,piano; Jack Cohen,guitar;
          Monk Hazel,drums and mellophone):
Co  1548. In the Dungeon(146221; voc.Hazel)/When You and I Were Pals(146222;
                                                                  (voc.,Cohen)
          (Unknown personnel):
Br  4184. You Made Me Like It Baby/Gumbo
```

TINY PARHAM

```
See also:
   ARDELL BRAGG: Para 12398, 12458.
   JOHNNY DODDS: Para 12471, 12483
   CHARLIE ENGLISH: Para 12610
   PICKETT-PARHAM: Para 12441.
   JASPER TAYLOR: Para 12409(?)

PARHAM AND HIS FORTY-FIVE (Tiny Parham,piano; rest of personnel unknown):
Para 12586. Jim Jackson's Kansas City Blues                      -Cen 3005
     "      A Little Bit Closer

          TINY PARHAM AND HIS MUSICIANS(Some of these feature Punch Miller,trumpet):
Vi 21553. The Head Hunter's Dream(46037)/Cuckoo Blues(46041)
Vi 21659. Clarice/Snake Eyes
Vi 22778. Now That I've Found You/Sud Buster's Dream
Vi 22842. Rock Bottom/(EARL HINES)
Vi 23027. Blue Moon Blues/Doin' the Jug Jug
Vi 23386. Memphis Mamie/Nervous Tension
Vi 23410. Pig's Feet and Slaw/Steel String Blues
Vi 23426. Bombay/Golden Lily
Vi 23432. After All I've Done for You/My Dreams
Vi 38009. Jogo Rhythm/Stuttering Blues                           -BB 8130
Vi 38041. Subway Sobs
     "    Blue Island Blues                                      -BB 7005,BB 10044
Vi 38047. That Kind of Love/Blue Melody Blues
Vi 38054. Voodoo/Skag-a-lag
Vi 38060. Tiny's Stomp/Stompin' on Down
Vi 38076. Washboard Wiggles                                      -BB 6570
     "    Echo Blues
Vi 38082. Lucky 3-6-9/Jungle Crawl
Vi 38111. Dixieland Doin's/Cathedral Blues
Vi 38126. Fat Man Blues
     "    Black Cat Moan                                         -BE 6570

          TINY PARHAM'S FOUR ACES:
De  7780. Frogtown Blues(93027A)/Spo-De-O-Dee(93029A; with Sam Theard,voc.)
```

CHARLIE PARKER

```
See also:
   DIZZY GILLESPIE: Manor 5000; Gu 1001,1002,1003.
   TINY GRIMES: Sav 532.
   CLYDE HART: Cont 6013.
   HOWARD McGHEE: Dial 1007.
   JAZZ AT THE PHILHARMONIC: Disc 2002, 2003, 2004, 2005.
   RED NORVO: Comet 6, 7.
   TRUMMIE YOUNG: Cont 6005.

PARKER QUINTET, CHARLIE (Charlie Parker,alto sax; Tiny Grimes,guitar and vocal;
Clyde Hart,piano; Harold West,drums: Jimmy Butts,bass):        Sept.15,1944
   Sav  541. Red Cross (originally issued under Tiny Grimes)/Tiny's Tempo
   Sav  613. Romance Without Finance(5712)/I'll Always Love You Just the Same
                                                            (5711;see Grimes)
          (Unknown personnel):
   Sav  573. Billie's Bounce/Now's the Time
```

```
        (Solo):
   Sav  597. Koko/(DON BYAS)

        CHARLIE PARKER SEPTET(Parker,alto: Dodo Marmarosa,piano; Lucky Thompson,
        tenor sax; Miles Davis,trumpet; VicMcMillan,bass; Roy Porter,drums; Arvin
        Garrison,guitar):
   Dial 1002. Nigh in Tunisia/Ornithology
   Dial 1003. Yardbird Suite/(GILLESPIE SEXTET)
   Dial 1004. Moose the Mooche/(GILLESPIE SEXTET)
   Dial 1006. Bird Lore(1012)/Bird Lore(1013)
   Dial 1007. Lover Man(alto solo: 1022A; acc.H.McGhee,trumpet: Jimmy Bunn,piano;
                                                                  (bass; drums)
   PARKER AND HIS ORCHESTRA, ED:
     OK 41466. Too Late/Between the Devil and the Deep Blue Sea
     OK 41533. Old Playmate/River Stay 'Way from My Door

        (Reputedly featuring Benny Goodman,clarinet):
     OK 41537. Now's the Time to Fall in Love/When I Wore My Daddy's

   PARKER, SHORTY BOB (blues singing with guitar, piano):
     De 7470. Death of Slim Green/I'm Through With Love
     De 7488. Ridin' Dirty Motorsickle/Tired of Being Drug Around
     De 7526. Rain and Snow/So Cold in China

   PARRISH, TURNER (Piano):
     Ch 50046. Trenches                                          -De 3832
        ".    The Fives

        (Vocal and piano):
     Ch 16509. Four Day Blues/My Own Lonesome Blues
     Ch 16629. Graveyard Blues/Ain't Gonna Be Your Day

   PARRY'S RADIO RHYTHM CLUB SEXTET, HARRY (Harry Parry,clarinet: George Shearing,
   piano; J.Deniz,guitar; B.Edwards,drums; T.Bromley,bass; R.Marsh,vibes):
                                                        England,Jan.28,1941
   PaE 2786. I've Found a New Baby/Black Eyes
   PaE 2789. Softly As in a Morning Sunrise/Boog It

        (Sub. S. Molyneuax,bass):                                 May 3,1941
   PaE 2793. Dim Blues/Parry Opus
   PaE 2804. It Don't Count/I'm Young and Healthy
   PaE 2808. Don't Be That Way/Bounce Me Brother With a Solid Four
   PaE 2817. Champagne/Honeysuckle Rose                          July 19,1941

        (Parry; J.Deniz,guitar; L.Caton,solo guitar; R.March,vibraphone; T. Poll-
        ard,piano; T.Bromley,bass: B.Midgley,drums):              Oct.19,1941
   PaE 2822. The Java Joint/Oceans and Notions(Deniz,Bromley,Marsh)
   PaE 2826. My Melancholy Baby/I May Be Wrong

        (Sub.A.Slavin,guitar: C.Short,bass; B.Richards,drums; add R.Dare,tenor
        sax):                                                     Jan.17,1942
   PaE 2832. Blues for Fight/Thrust and Parry
   PaE 2834. Sheik of Araby/Someday Sweetheart

        (Parry,Dare,Marsh,Pollard,Caton,Short,Richards):          March 27,1942
   PaE 2840. Basin Street Ball/Blue Prelude
   PaE 2842. Sweet Georgia Brown/Doggin' Around

        (Sub. S.Raymond,drums; omit Marsh):                       June 5,1942
   PaE 2844. Crazy Rhythm/Angry
   PaE 2846. Rose Room/My Blue Heaven

        (Parry,clarinet; K.Oldham,tenor sax; D.Wilkins,trumpet; Y.deSousa,piano;
        J.Deniz,guitar; S.Molyneaux,bass; S.Raymond,drums):       Aug.14,1942
   PaE 2851. I Can't Dance/Rock It Out
   PaE 2854. Potomac Jump/Who's Sorry Now

        (Omit Deniz):                                             Nov.11,1942
   PaE 2857. Jingle Bells/Blues Aroun' My Bed
   PaE 2860. Bogi/Ain't Misbehavin'
   PaE 2866. Time on My Hands/Lady Be Good                       Dec. 8,1942
   PaE 2867. Travelin' Blues/Alexander's Ragtime Band

        (Add D. Neville,alto, baritone):                          Dec.10,1942
   PaE 2863. Mr. Five by Five/I Never Knew
   PaE 2870. Stardust/Darktown Strutters Ball                    March 23,1943
   PaE 2873. You Are My Lucky Star/Blue Train Blues
   PaE 2878. Polly Put the Kettle On/Dr. Heckle and Mr. Jibe     June 21,1943
   PaE 2879. St.Louis Blues/Body and Soul

        (Parry, Neville, Oldham; S.Roderick,trumpet; deSousa,Molyneuax;Raymond):
   PaE 2882. 100 Years from Today/Tea for Two                    July 22,1943
   PaE 2885. Runnin' Wild/Basin Street Blues(personnel next above)
   PaE 2889. Ida/Rosetta (personnel as for Aug.19,1943)
   PaE 2894. No Gin Blues/Hallelujah (personnel as for October 23,1943)
```

PATTON, CHARLEY (vocal with guitar):
  Para 12854. Down the Dirt Road Blues(1524)/It Won't Be Long(1525)
  Para 12877. Pea Vine Blues/Tom Rushen Blues

PAYNE AND HIS ORCHESTRA, ART:
  Ge 5631. Oh Maud/You Can't Make a Woman Change

PEARSON, BILL (vocal with guitar):
  Br 7053. Detroit Blues/Good Stuff

PEARSON, DAVID (vocal):
  OK 8847. Friendless Blues

SANTO PECORA

See also:
  WINGY MANNONE: OK 41569, 41570.
  PAUL MARES: OK 41574, 41575.
  NEW ORLEANS RHYTHM KINGS: OK 40327, 40422; Vi 19645.
  SHARKEY: Vo 3353, 3380.

PECORA AND HIS BACK ROOM BOYS, SANTO (Santo Pecora,trombone; Shorty Sherock,trumpet; Meyer Weinberg,clarinet; Stan Wrightsman,piano; Frank Frederico,guitar;Thurman Teague,bass; Riley Scott,drums and vocal): New York,April 22,1937
  Co 36159. Magnolia Blues(MH 1006)/I Never Knew What a Gal Could Do(MH 1007)

PEE WEE, ZUTTY AND JAMES P. (See Pee Wee Russell):

PEEPLES, ROBERT (vocal with Henry Brown,piano):
  Para 12995. Wicked Devil's Blues(L-182)/Fat Greasy Baby(L-183)

PERRY'S HOT DOGS:
  Ba 1641. I'm Gonna Hang Around My Sugar/Has Been Blues
  Re 8007. Give Me Just a Little Bit of Your Love(6424)/(MISSOURI JAZZ BAND)

PERRYMAN, RUFUS (See Speckled Red)

PERSON, ALICE (Vocal blues, acc. by F. Coates,piano):
  Para 12523. Third Street Blues/Greyhound Blues

PERTUM, CHARLES 'SPECK' (vocal and piano):
  Br 7128. Broken Down Blues/Weak Eyed Blues
  Br 7146. Harvest Moon Blues/Gambler's Blues

PETERS, TEDDY (vocal accompanied by Johnny Dodds,clarinet, and unknown pianist on first side and by saxophone,piano,banjo and two cornets, probably including King Oliver, on second): March 11,1926
  Vo 1006. What a Man/Georgia Man

PETTIS, ARTHUR (vlues with piano and guitar):
  Br 7182. Good Boy Blues/That Won't Do
  Br 7209. Revenue Men Blues/Quarrelin' Mama Blues

JACK PETTIS

See also:
  BALTIMORE SOCIETY ORCHESTRA: Or 569.
  JACK BINNEY: PaA 34076.
  DIXIE JAZZ BAND: Or 1127, 1131.
  FRIARS SOCIETY ORCHESTRA: All Gennett.
  HOTSY TOTSY GANG: Br 4014, 4044.
  LUMBERJACKS:
  MILLS HOTSY TOTSY GANG: Br 4838.
  MILLS MUSICAL CLOWNS:
  NEW ORLEANS BLACKBIRDS: Vi 38026.
  NEW ORLEANS RAMBLERS: Me 12133, 12230.
  NEW ORLEANS RHYTHM KINGS: Ge 5217 - 5221.
  TEN FRESHMEN: Pat 37054.
  JOE VENUTI: OK 41192, 41263.

PETTIS AND HIS BAND, JACK (Jack Pettis, tenor sax: Bill Moore,trumpet; Joe Venuti,violin; Eddie Lang,guitar; et al):
  Ba 1907. Stockholm Stomp(6998)/(SAM LANIN)   -Re 8229
  Ba 1908. St.Louis Shuffle(6997)   -Re 8221
  Ba 1911. He's the Last Word(6996)/(BILL PERRY)   -Re 8225
  Ba 1927. It All Depends on You(7040-2)/Muddy Water(7041-2)
  Ba 1929. I Gotta Get Myself Somebody to Love(7043)/(CREAGER) -Do 3895
  Ba 1940. I'm Back in Love(7105)
  Ba 1942. That's My Hap-Hap-Happiness(7106-3)/Ain't She Sweet(7107-2)-Do 3914

  (Omit Venuti; sub. Dick McDonough,guitar):

Re 8463. Candied Sweets(7669)/Let a Smile Be Your Umbrella
Do 4091. Once Over Lightly(7689)/Steppin' It Off(7690)

  JACK PETTIS AND HIS PETS(Bill Moore,trumpet; Jack Pettis,tenor; Ed Lang,
   guitar; Al Goering, piano: et al):   July 3,1928
Vi 21559. Spanish Dream(45672)/Doin't the New Low Down(45674)
Vi 21793. Bag o'Blues(45673)/Freshman Hop(48127; next date)

  (Moore, Pettis, et al):
Unissued. Nobody's Sweetheart(48126)   Nov.6,1928

  (Moore; Pettis; Goering; Jack Teagarden,trombone; Dick Stabile,clarinet;
   et al):   May 9,1929
Vi 38105. Bugle Call Blues(51694)/(IRVING MILLS)   -HMV 6288
Unissued. Companionate Crawl(51691)
  " Campus Crawl(51692)
  " Wild and Wooly Willy(51693)

  (Moore, Teagarden, Pettis, McDonough, Goering; Benny Goodman,clarinet;
   D. Ober,drums: et al):
OK 41410. Bag o' Blues(401596)/(ED LANG)
OK 41411. Freshman Hop(401594)
  " Sweetest Melody(401595)   -PaE 673

  (Probably similar):
Vo 15703. Hot Heels/Dry Martini
Vo 15761. Broadway Stomp/(ORIGINAL MEMPHIS FIVE)
Vr 558. Hawaiian Heat Wave(1003)/Swing Session in Siberia(1004)

PETWAY, ROBERT (blues singer with instrumental acc.):
BB 8987. Hollow Log Blues/Boogie Woogie Woman

PHILADELPHIA MELODIANS (Duke Ellington Orchestra; 1930 personnel):
PaE 883. Three Little Words(480028E)
   (While this was the only issue of the above record, at least one
   Louis Armstrong disc was reissued in England under the Philadelphia
   Melodians pseudonym)

FLIP PHILLIPS

See also:
 BILL HARRIS: Key 618, 626.
 J.C. HEARD: Key 623.
 WOODY HERMAN: Columbia.
 CHUBBY JACKSON: Key 616.
 RED NORVO: Comet 6, 7.

PHILLIPS AND HIS FLIPTET, FLIP (Neil Hefti,trumpet: Bill Harris,trombone; Flip
Phillips,tenor sax; Aaron Sachs,clarinet· Marjorie Hyams,vibraphone; Ralph Burns,
piano; Billy Bauer,guitar; Dave Tough,drums; Chubby Jackson,bass): Oct.2,1944
Sig 28106. Pappilloma(S-2)/Skyscraper(S-1)

  (Phillips, Burns, Jackson, Bauer,Shelly Manne):
Sig 28117. Why Shouldn't I(101B-2A)/Swingin' for Popsie(102-2A)
Sig 28119. Stompin' at the Savoy(1001A)/A Melody from the Sky(S-3; orig.pers.)

  (Bill Shine,clarinet: Phillips, Hefti, Burns, Bauer, Jackson, Tough):
Sig 90003. Bob's Belief(RHT-5)/Sweet and Lovely(RHT-6: solo with Burns)

PIANO KID EDWARDS (See Edwards,Piano Kid)

PICHON, WALTER (Singing with Henry "Red" Allen,trumpet; Teddy Bunn,guitar):
Vi 38544. Yo Yo/Doggin' That Thing   1928-29

  WALTER "FATS" PICHON (piano and vocal)   New Orleans,1945
Raymac 1101. Fat and Greasy(A-3361)/Deep South Boogie(A-3362)
   (See also: QRS Boys)

PICKETT, CHARLIE (blues singing with guitar):
De 7707. Down the Highway/Let Me Squeeze your Lemon

PICKETT-PARHAM APOLLO SYNCOPATORS (Tiny Parham, piano; Leroy Pickett,leader):
Para 12441. Alexander Where's That Band(457)/Mojo Strut(458)

PIEDMONT DANCE ORCHESTRA (Fletcher Henderson?):
Pat 36203. I'll See You in My Dreams/Alabamy Bound

PIERCE AND HIS ORCHESTRA, CHARLES (Muggsy Spanier,Dick Fiege,cornets; Frank
Teschemacher,clarinet:Ralph Rudder,Charles Pierce,saxes; Dan Lipscomb,piano;
Stuart Branch,banjo; Johnny Mueller,bass; Paul Kettler,drums): Chicago,1927
Para 12619. Bull Frog Blues(20399)   -UHCA 1
  " China Boy(20400)   -UHCA 2

```
            (Omit Fiege; and Jack Ried,trombone):           Nov.8,1927
     Para 12616. Nobody's Sweetheart(20534)               -Bwy 1174,Co 35950

            (Charlie Altiere,cornet: Morry Bercov,clarinet):
     Para 12640. Jazz Me Blues(20469)                      -BrE 02502,UHCA 71
          "     Sister Kate(20470)                         -Co 35950 ,UHCA 72
                 (See also: Jungle Kings)

PINETOP (Aaron Sparks; vocal with piano and guitar):
     BB  6041. Workhouse Blues/Tell Her About Me
     BB  6125. Every Day I Have the Blues
     BB  6202. Got the Blues About My Baby

            PINETOP AND LINDBERG:
     Vi 23330. East Chicago Blues                          -BB 10177
        "      4 X 11 = 44
     Vi 23359. Louisiana Bound/I Believe I'll Make a Change

PINEWOOD TOM (vocals):
     Pe   318. Mean Mistreater/D.B.A. Blues
     Pe   323. Cherry Picker/Tweet Tweet Mama
     Pe   328. Prodigal Son/Homeless and Hungry
     Pe   334. Black Man/Gone Dry Blues
     Me 13328. Black Gal/Milk Cow Blues

PINKETT, WARD (trumpet; see):
     JUNGLE BAND: Br 4450
     LITTLE RAMBLERS: BB 6130, 6131, 6144, 6193.
     JELLY ROLL MORTON.
     KING OLIVER.
     JOE STEELE.
     CLARENCE WILLIAMS: Pe 15403.

PIRON'S NEW ORLEANS ORCHESTRA (A.J.Piron,violin; Peter Bocage,trumpet: John Lindsay,
trombone; Lorenzo Tio,Jr.,clarinet and tenor sax: Louis Guarine,alto; Charlie Bo-
cage,banjo; Clarence Seguirre,tuba; Louis Cottrelle,drums: Steve Lewis,piano):
     Vi 19233. Mamma's Gone Goodbye/New Orleans Wiggle                    1924
     Vi 19255. Do Doodle Oom/West Indies Blues
     Vi 19646. Do Just As I Say/Red Man Blues
     OK 40021. Bouncing Around(S72132B)/Kiss Me Sweet(S72133D)
     OK 40189. LOuisiana Swing(S72320B)/Sittin' on the Curbstone Blues(S72322B)
     Co    99. Ghost of the Blues/Bright Star Blues
     Co 14007. Sud Bustin' Blues(81435)/West Indies Blues(81436)
                 (See also: Ester Bigeou: OK 8118; Lela Bolden: OK 8139).

PLANTATION SERENADERS:
     Ch 15386. Missouri Squabble/When Eurastus Plays Hos Old Kazoo

PLETCHER AND HIS ORCHESTRA, STEW (Pete Peterson,bass: Maurice Purtill,drums; Dave
Barbour,guitar; Don McCook,clarinet; Herbie Haymer,tenor sax; Red Norvo,vibes and
piano; Stew Pletcher,trumpet & vocals.--DB 4/1/44):
     BB  6343. The Touch of Your Lips                       -HMV 8453
         "     I Hope Gabriel Likes My Music
     BB  6344. I Don't Want to Make History/Will I Never Know?
     BB  6345. You Never Looked So Beautiful/You

PODS OF PEPPER (Ikey Robinson,vocals; kazoo; mandolin; piano; traps):
     Co 14590. You've Had Your Way(151278)/Get Off Stuff(151279)
     Co 14664. I Was a Good Loser/Gee I Hate to Lose That Gal
```

BEN POLLACK

```
See also:
     BEN'S BAD BOYS: Vi 21971.
     CONNEE BOSWELL: De 1160, 1161, 1420, 1421, 1433, 1434, 1862.
     DEAN AND HIS KIDS: Vo 3342.
     DIXIE DAISIES: Ca 9004.
     BENNY GOODMAN: Br 3975.
     HOTSY TOTSY GANG: Br 4014, 4044, 4112.
     NEW ORLEANS RHYTHM KINGS: Ge 5217-5221.
     SHARKEY: Vo 3353, 3380.

POLLACK AND HIS CALIFORNIANS, BEN (Harry Greenberg,Al Harris,cornets: Glenn
Miller,trombone: Benny Goodman,clarinet; Gil Rodin,alto: Fud Livingston,tenor;
Vic Briedis,piano; Lou Kessler,banjo; Harry Goodman,bass: Ben Pollack,drums.--
DB 1/14/46):                                                Sept.14,1926
     Unissued. I'd Love to Call You My Sweetheart(36237)/Sunday(36238)

            (Add Victor Young,Al Beller,violins):           Dec.9,1926
     Vi 20394. When I First Met Mary(37218; Joey Ray,voc.)/(GEORGE OLSEN)
     Vi 20408. 'Deed I Do(37219; Pollack,voc.)              -HMV 5281
```

(Omit violins):   Dec.17,1926
Vi 20425. He's the Last Word(37261: Williams Sisters, voc.)
Vi 20461. You're the One for Me(37260; Ilomay Bailey, voc.)
Unissued. That's What I Think of You(39058)/Who Is Your Who?(39059)June 24,1927
Unissued. Honey Do(3909)/I Ain't That Kind of a Baby(39091)   July 7,1927

   (Jimmy McPartland,Frank Quartell,cornets; Glenn Miller,trombone; Benny
   Goodman,clarinet; Gil Rodin,alto: Larry Binyon,tenor; Vic Briedis,piano;
   Dick Morgan,banjo; Harry Goodman,bass; Ben Pollack,drums):   Dec.7,1927
Vi 21184. Waitin' for Katie(41342)/Memphis Blues(41343)
Unissued. California Medley(41344)

   (Sub. Al Harris,cornet; for Quartell; Bud Freeman,tenor sax,for Binyon;
   add strings):   April 6,1928
Unissued. Singapore Sorrows(43540; Pollack,voc.)
Vi 21437. Sweet Sue(43541)/Singapore Sorrows(43540;Pollack,voc., remade on
                                                                        (April 26,1928.
   BEN POLLACK AND HIS PARK CENTRAL ORCHESTRA (McPartland,Harris,cornets:
   Jack Teagarden,trombone: Goodman,clarinet; Rodin,alto; Binyon,tenor and
   flute; Al Beller,Ed Bergman,violins; Bill Schumann,cello; Breidis,piano;
   Morgan,guitar; Harry Goodman,bass; Pollack):   Oct. 1,1928
Vi 21716. Forever(47577; waltz)/(TROUBADOURS)   -HMV 5587
Unissued. You're Gone(47576)

   (Vocals by Belle Mann):   Oct.15,1928
Vi 21743. Buy Buy for Baby(47742)/She's One Sweet Show Girl(47743) -HMV 5596
Vi 21827. Then Came the Dawn(49220; D.Robertson,voc.)/Sentimental Baby(49221;
                                             (Gene Austin,voc. -Dec.3,1928
Unissued. Let's Sit and Talk About You(48286)   Dec.24,1928
Vi 21858. Futuristic Rhythm(48287; Pollack,voc.)/Let's Sit and Talk About You
                      (48286;Burt Lorin,voc.),remade Jan.29,1929
Vi 21857. Sally of My Dreams(48302; Burt Lorin,voc.)/WARING'S PA.)Jan.24,1929

   (Sub.Ruby Weinstein,trumpet,for Harris: Dick McPartland,guitar, for Mor-
   gan; Ray Bauduc,drums):   Mar.1,1929
Vi 21941. Louise(50905;Chas.Roberts,voc.)/Wait 'Til You See Ma Cherie(50906)
Vi 21944. My Kinda Love(50912;Pollack,voc.)/On With the Dance(50913;Pollack,v)
Vi 22252. I'd Like to Be a Gypsy(53517;Lorin,voc.)/(TED FIO RITO)
Unissued. Finding the Long Way Home(53518; Lorin,voc.)
Vi 22071. In Hush of Night(53947;Lorin,v.)/Who't Cha(53948;Lorin,v)July 25/29
Vi 22074. Bashful Baby(53949; Lorin,voc.)/OHMAN-ARDEN ORCHESTRA)

   Charlie Teagarden,Ruby Weinstein,trumpets: Jack Teagarden,trombone; Mat-
   ty Matlock,clarinet; Gil Rodin,alto; Larry Binyon,tenor and flute; Ed
   Bergman,Ed Solinsky,violins; Schumann,cello and oboe; Briedis, Morgan,
   Goodman, Bauduc):   Aug.15, 1929
Vi 22089. True Blue Lou(53991; Lorin,voc.)/(COON-SANDERS)
Vi 22106. Where the Sweet Forget-Me-Nots Remember(53989;Lorin,voc.)/(SHILKRET)
Vi 22147. Song of the Blues(53990;Lorin,voc.)/(SMITH BALLEW)
Vi 22101. Sweetheart,We Need Each Other(56105;Lorin,voc.)   -HMV 5729
   "   You're Always in My Arms(56106;Lorin,voc.)   "
Vi 22158. You Made Me Happy Today(56721;C.Roberts,v.)   Sept.27,1929
   "   From Now On(56722; Chas.Roberts,voc.)
Vi 22267. Keep Your Undershirt On(57637;Lorin,voc.)/(HIGH HATTERS)Nov.29,1929
Unissued. Reaching for the Moon(57638;Lorin,voc.)/.

   BEN POLLACK AND HIS ORCHESTRA(Sub. Babe Russin,tenor,for Binyon; Gil Bow-
   ers,piano; Nappy Lamare,guitar):   Feb.,1930
HoW 1026. I'm Following You
HoW 1027. Crying for the Carolines

   (Add Sterling Bose,cornet):   Sept.,1930
Pe 15325. If I Could Be With You(9819-1,21314),Teagarden,voc.)
           -Ro 1363,Or 1998,Re 10054,Do 4588,Je 5998,Ba 0747,CMS 103
   "   There's a Wah Wah Gal in Agua Caliente(9820-2,3)
                                  -Ba 0752,Re 10057,Im 2338

   (Sub. Eddie Miller,tenor, for Russin):   Feb.,1931
Pe 15434. Sing Song Gal(10378;Ted Bancroft,voc.)   -Or 2193,Ro 1561
   "   Fall in Love(10379; Bancroft,voc.)   "   "
Pe 15428. You Didn't Have to Tell Me(10380;Teagarden,voc.)   -Or 2208,CMS 103
                                                                 March, 1931
Pe 15341. I've Got Five Dollars(10416:Pollack,voc.)   -Ro 1576
   "   Sweet and Hot(10417: Pollack,voc.)   "
Pe 15432. I'm a Ding Dong Daddy(10418;Pollack,voc.)   -Or 2214,Ro 1577

   (Sterling Bose,Charlie Spivak,trumpets; Jack Teagarden,trombone; Matlock,
   Rodin,Miller,reeds; Ed Bergman,Al Beller,Barney Winston,violins; Bill
   Schumann,cello and oboe; Bowers,Lamare,Goodman,Bauduc):   March,19,1933
Vi 24284. Linger a Little Longer(75409;Doris Robins,voc.)
   "   Two Tickets to Georgia(75412; Lamare,voc.)
Unissued. I Bring a Song(75410)/Low Down Upon the Harlem River(75411)

(Yank Lawson,Charlie Spivak,Shirley Clay,trumpets; Joe Harris,Benny Morton,trombones; Matlock,clarinet: Rodin,alto; Dean Kincaid,alto; Miller, tenor: Al Beller,Ray Cohan,violins; Lamare,Bowers,Goodman,Bauduc)

Co 2870. Got the Jitters(152662; Lamare,voc.)   Dec.28,1933
"   I'm Full of the Devil(152665; Pollack,voc.)
Co 2879. Deep Jungle(152663)/Swing Out(152664)   -CoE 5036

(Omit Clay, Morton):   Jan.23,1934
Co 2886. My Little Grass Shack(152693)
"   Going to Heaven on a Mule(152694)   -PaE 1800
Unissued. I Wanna Be Loved(152692)
    Feb.23,1934
Co 2901. Dancing in the Moonlight(152721)   -RZ 1298
"   Ole Mammy Ain't Gonna Sing(152723; Joe Harris,voc.)
Co 2905. Here Goes(152724)
"   The Beat of My Heart(152725)   -RZ 1305
Co 2906. Voo-Doo(152722)/(MADRIGUERA)   -RZ 1305
Co 2910. Alone on the Range(152726)/(H. HALL)
Co 2929. Night on the Desert(152755)/Sleepy Head(152756)   May 29,1934
Co 2931. Freckle Face,You're Beautiful(152757)/I've Got a Warm Spot for You
    (152758)

(Harry James,Shorty Sherock,trumpets; Bruce Squires,trombone; Opie Cates, saxes; Irving Fazola,clarinet; Al Beller,Ray Cohan,violins; Freddie Slack,piano; Joe Price,guitar; Thurman Teague,bass; Sammy Taylor,drums):

Br 7747. Through the Courtesy of Love/Now or Never   1936
Br 7751. I Couldn't Be Mad at You/I'm One Step Ahead of My Shadow
Br 7764. Song of the Islands(B19882)   -Cc 36325,VoE 113
"   Jimtown Blues(B19889)

(Unknown personnel):
Vr 504. Deep Elm(B4373)/The Moon Is Grinning at Me(B4375)   -Vo 3760
Vr 556. Peckin'/In a Sentimental Mood   -Vo 3819

(Muggsy Spanier,cornet; Bob Goodrich,Ray Woods,trumpets; Galen Lloyd,trombone; Art Quenzer,Jack Stacy,M.Carlton,E.Kanter,saxes; Al Beller,violin; Bob Lane,piano; Garry McAdams,guitar; F.Palmer,bass; Ben Pollack,drums; Frances Hunt,vocals):   1937

De 1424. Song of the Islands/Yours for the Asking
De 1435. If You Ever Should Leave(DLA868-A)/I'm Dependable(DLA870-A)
De 1476. Have You Ever Been in Heaven(DLA866-A)/Mama I Wanna Make Rhythm(DLA869-B)

(Don Anderson,Bob Goodrich,Andy Secrest,trumpets: Joe Yukl,trombone: Opie Cates,M.Carlton,Morton Friedman,Alan Harding, saxes; Al Beller,violin; Bob Lane,piano; Bob Hemphill,guitar; Jim Taft,bass; Graham Stevenson, drums; Paula Gayle,vocals):   1938

De 1815. You'Ll Be Reminded of Me(DLA1231-A)/There's Rain in My Eyes(CLA1233-A)
De 1891. Everybody's Doin' It/This Is the Life--International Rag
De 2057. After You've Gone/Looking at the World Through Rose Colored Glasses

(Sub. George Thow,Clyde Hurley,trumpets,for Goodrich,Secrest; Earl Hagen trombone: Peyton Legare,George Hill,saxes,for Carlton,Harding;Carroll Thompson,guitar: Jim Lynch,bass):

De 2005. Meet the Beat of My Heart/What Are You Doing Tonight
De 2006. As Long As I Live/Sing a Song of Sixpence
De 2012. Naturally/So Unexpected

BEN POLLACK'S PICK A RIB BOYS(Muggsy Spanier,cornet,with clarinet,tenor sax and rhythm): Peggy Man, vocals

De 1458. My Wild Irish Rose(DLA912-A)   -Br 3686
"   Can't You Hear Me Calling,Caroline(DLA915-a)
De 1465. If It's the Last Thing I Do(DLA945-A)   -BrE 02538
"   You Made Me Love You(DLA947-A)   "
De 1488. I'm in My Glory(DLA946-A)
"   The Snake Charmer(DLA948-A)   -BrE 02557
De 1517. Boogie Woogie(DLA910-A)/California Here I Come(DLA911-A)
De 1546. Alice Blue Gown(DLA913-A)
"   Cuddle Up a Little Closer(DLA914-A)   -De 3526,BrE02557

(Omit Muggsy Spanier):
De 1851. Morocco(DLA1201-A)/Nobody's Gonna Take You From Me(DLA1204-A)

DANNY POLO

See also:
EMBASSY RHYTHM EIGHT: DeE 5435, 5467.
JEAN GOLDKETTE: Vi 20588.
COLEMAN HAWKINS: BB 10693, 10770.
HOT CLUB SWING STARS: Sw 48, 55.
SPIKE HUGHES: DeE 1690,1703,1710,1709,1730.
SEXTET OF RHYTHM CLUB OF LONDON: BB 10529, 10557.
JOE SULLIVAN: Vo 5496, 5531, 5556; OK 5647.
VARSITY SEVEN: Vs 8135, 8147, 8173, 8179.
GEORGE WETTLING: De 18044, 18045.

```
     DeE  6578. Money for Jam/Mr. Polo Takes a Solo

           DANNY POLO AND HIS SWING STARS (Danny Polo,clarinet; Tommy McQuarter,
           trumpet; Eddie Macauley,piano; E.Freeman,guitar; D.Barber,drums; Dick
           Bass):
     DeE  6518. Stratton Street Strut
            "    More Than Somewhat(TB3249-1)                          -De 1718
     DeE  6550. Blue Murder(TB3250-1)                                  -De 1718
            "    That's a Plenty(TB3251)

           (Add George Chisholm,trombone; Sidney Raymond,alto sax; sub.Norman Brown,
           guitar):                                                         1938
     DeE  6604. Don't Try Your Jive on Me/Mozeltov
     DeE  6615. Jazz Me Blues(TB3483-2)/If You Were the Only Girl in the World
                                                                       (TB3486-1)
           (Phillippe Brun,trumpet; Alix Combelle,tenor; Garland Wilson* or Una Mae
           Carlisle,piano; Oscar Aleman,guitar; Louis Vola,bass; Jerry Mengo,drums):
     DeE  6989. Montparnasse Jump(4862)/Doing the Gorgonzola(4861)*    Paris,1939
     DeE 59001. Polonaise*/China Boy

           DANNY POLO AND GARLAND WILSON (clarinet and piano, with Mengo,drums):
     DeE  7039. You Made Me Love You/Montmarte Moan

POPE AND HIS BAND, BOB:
     De   8509. Stop Teasing Me/When You Got to Go You Got to Go
     De   8519. That's All I Ask of You(68133;Joan Lee,voc.)/(WINGY CARPENTER)
     BB   6508. Madhouse/(JIMMIE GUNN)

POPE, JENNY (vocals with piano):
     Vo   1438. Whiskey Drinking Blues/Doggin' Me Around
     Vo   1522. Blue Frog Blues/Tennessee Workhouse Blues

PORT OF HARLEM JAZZ MEN (Frank Newton,trumpet; J.C. Higginbotham,trombone; Albert
Ammons,piano; Teddy Bunn,guitar; John Williams,bass; Sidney Catless,drums):
     BN     3. Mighty Blues(516-2)/Rocking the Blues(517-1)         .

           PORT OF HARLEM SEVEN(Sidney Bechet,clarinet and soprano sax; Meade Lux
           Lewis,piano: Newton; Higginbotham; Bunn; Williams; Catlett):
     BN     6. Pounding Heart Blues/(SIDNEY BECHET)
     BN     7. Blues for Tommy(532X-12)/(J.C.HIGGINBOTHAM QUINTET)

           PORT OF HARLEM JAZZ MEN (Original personnel):
     BN    14. Port of Harlem Blues(515A-5)/(FRANK NEWTON QUINTET)

PORTER ALL STARS, DICK (Clyde Hart,piano; John Kirby,bass; Jonah Jones,trumpet;
Cozy Cole,drums; Bobby Bennett,guitar; Edgar Sampson, sax and clarinet; Dick
Porter,vocals):
     Vo   3355. Sweet Thing/Swingin' to a Swing Tune
     Vo   3469. May I Have the Next Romance(20683)/There's No Two Ways About It
     Vo   3478. Swing Boy Swing/Poor Robinson Carusoe                 (20684)

PORTER, SONNY (vocals with Ed Lang,guitar; piano):
     Co  14366. How Long Blues(147107)/Deck Hand Blues(147108)

POTTER, NELLIE (blues with cornet, trombone acc.):
     Ba   1483. A Good Man Is Hard to Find

POWELL'S JAZZ MONARCHS (J.R. Powell,director; recorded in St. Louis):
     OK   8333. Laughing Blues(9683)/Chauffeur's Shuffle(9682)

POWELL AND HIS ORCHESTRA, MEL (Billy Butterfield,trumpet; Lou McGarity,trombone;
Benny Goodman,clarinet; George Berg,tenor sax; Mel Powell,piano; Al Morgan,bass;
Kansas Fields,drums):
     Com   543. When Did You Leave Heaven(76986A)/Blue Skies(76988A)
     Com   544. The World Is Waiting for the Sunrise(76987A)

POWELL AND HIS HI DE HO BOYS, TOMMY:
     De   7231. Hi De Ho Swing/That Cat Is High
     De   7255. Got the Blues for Harlem/Just About the Time

POWERS' HARMONY SYNCOPATORS, OLLIE (Alex Calamese,first cornet; Tommy Ladnier,
second cornet; Eddie Venson,trombone; Jimmie Noone,clarinet: Horace Diemer,alto
sax; Glover Compton,piano; "Dago", banjo; "Bass" Moore,tuba; Ollie Powers,drums):
.--JI 11/8/40)
     Para 12059. Play That Thing(1502-1,2,3,4)     -Para 20263,Clax 40263,Pu 11263
            "    Jazzbo Jenkins(1538; vocal recording by "Ollie Powers with the Har-
                                                            (mony Syncopators")
PREER AND THE COTTON CLUB ORCHESTRA, ANDY (Probably Reuben "River" Reeves,R.Q.
Dickerson,trumpets; DePriest Wheeler,trombone; Bill Blue,Andy Brown,Cecil Scott,
Walter Thomas,saxes: James Prince,piano; Charley Stamps,banjo; Smith,bass; LeRoy
Maxey,drums.--Dis.,Dec,1943):                                         March,1927
     Ge   6056. I Found a New Baby(/JOHNNY SILVESTER)
              (See also: Missourians; Original Cotton Club Orchestra:
                         Cab Calloway)
```

PREVIN TRIO, ANDRE (Andre Previn,piano; Dave Barbour,guitar: John Simmon,bass):
Su 10057. Blue Skies(SRC-120-7)/Good Enough to Keep(SRC-119-3)

      (Previn; I.Ashby,guitar; Red Callender,bass):
Su   . Subtle Slough/Warm Valley
Su   . Main Stem/Something to Live For
Su   . I Got It Bad/Take the "A" Train

SAM PRICE

See also:
BLUE LU BARKER: Decca.
PETE BROWN: De 8613, 8625.
JAMES BLYTHE: JR; KJ 145.
COW COW DAVENPORT: De 7462, 7486, 7813.
JIMMIE GORDON: De 7474, 7490, 7519, 7624.
GRANT AND WILSON: De 7500.
TRIXIE SMITH.
ROSETTA THARPE: De 48013.

PRICE AND HIS FOUR QUARTERS, SAMMY:
  Br 7136. Blue Rhuthm Stomp/Nasty But Nice(Bert Johnson,trombone; Price,piano)

     SAM PRICE AND HIS TEXAS BLUSICIANS (Eddie Mullins,Joe Brown,trumpets; Don
     Stovall,alto; Ray Hill,tenor; Sam Price,piano; Duke Jones,bass; Wilbur
     Kirk,drums.--JRB):   1940
De 7732. Cow Cow Blues/Swing Out in the Groove
De 8505. Oh Red/How 'Bout That Mess

     (Unknown personnel):
De 8515. Jumpin' the Boogie/Thinking
De 8547. The Goon Drag(68920)/I Lost Love(68954)

     (Shad Collins,trumpet; Lester Young,tenor: and others.--JRB):
De 8557. Just Jivin' Around/Things About Coming My Way

     (Chester Boone,trumpet; Floyd Brady,trombone: Don Stovall,alto; Skippy
     Williams,tenor; Sam Price,piano; Ernest Hill,bass; Herb Cowans,drums):
De 8566. Valetta/I Know How to Do It   1941

     (Unknown personnel):
De 8575. Do You Dig My Jive(69365)/Boogie Woogie Moan(69368)
De 8609. Harlem Gin Blues(70030; Ruby Smith,voc.)/Why Don't You Love Me Any-
De 8624. Blow Katy Blow(70190)/Match Box Blues(70032)(more(70029;R.Smith,voc)
De 8642. Teed-Up/Frantic
De 8649. Lead Me Daddy Straight to the Bar(68922)/It's All Right Jack(70189)

PRIMA, LOUIS (trumpet, with Dave Rose piano: Norman Gast,violin):
  BB 5758. Dinah/Chinatown, My Chinatown

     LOUIS PRIMA AND HIS NEW ORLEANS GANG(Louis Prima,trumpet and vocal;Sid-
     ney Arodin,clarinet; George Brunis,trombone; Claude Thornhill,piano;
     George Van Eps,guitar; Art Shapiro,bass: Stan King,drums):   1936
Br 7320. I Still Want You(B16288)
"   Breakin' the Ice(B16289-A)   -DeE 5459
Br 7335. 'Long About Midnight(C016025-A)/Star Dust(C016026-A)
Br 7394. Sing It Way Down Low(B16150)   -DeE 5777
"   Let's Have a Jubilee(B16286)   -DeE 5499
Br 7524. That's Where the South Begins(C016023)
"   Jamaica Shout(C016024)   -DeE 5429

     (Sub. Eddie Miller,clarinet and tenor sax; Nappy Lamare,guitar; Ray Bau-
     duc,drums):
Br 7376. House Rent Party Day(B16540)
"   Bright Eyes(B16543)   -DeE 5499
Br 7419. Put on An Old Pair of Shoes/I'm Livin' in a Great Big Way
Br 7431. Sugar Is Sweet and So Are You/Swing Me With Rhythm
Br 7471. It's the Rhythm in Me(B16541A)/Worry Blues(B16542A)

     (Prima; Brunis; Pee Wee Russell,clarinet; Frank Pinero,piano; Garrett Mc-
     Adams,guitar; Jack Ryan,bass; Sam Weiss,drums):   1935
Br 7448. The Lady in Red(B17612)
"   Chasing Shadows(B17614)   -DeE 5621
Br 7456. Chinatown My Chinatown(B17613)
"   Basin Street Blues(B17615)   -DeE 5626
Br 7479. In a Little Gypsy Tea Room(B17739)/Let's Swing It(B17740)
Br 7499. Plain Old Me(B17762)   -DeE 5777
"   Weather Man(B17764)
Br 7531. How Am I Doin'(B17763)/Solitude(B17761)   -BeE 5692

```
                (Prima; Russell; Joe Catalyne,tenor sax; Pinero; McAdams; Ryan; George
                Pemberty,drums):                                                   1936
     Br    7586. I'm Shooting High(1079)/I've Got My Fingers Crossed(1081)
     Br    7596. Sweet Sue(1078)/I Love You Truly(1080)               -DeE 5911
     Br    7628. It's Been So Long(1101)/Sing Sing Sing(1106)
     Br    7657. Alice Blue Gown(1102)
           "     Darktown Strutters Ball(1105)                        -DeE 6001
     Br    7666. Dinah(1103)                                          -DeE 6001
           "     Lazy River(1104)

                (Augmented group):
     Br    7680. Cross Patch/Swing Me a Lullaby
     Br    7709. Confessin'/Let's Have Fun
     Br    7740. Let's Get Together and Swing/The Stars Know

                (Louis Prima,trumpet and vocals; Meyer Weinberg,clarinet and sax; Frank
                Pinero,piano; Frank Frederico,guitar; Louis Mascinter,bass; Godfrey Hirsch,
                drums):
     Vo    3376. Pennies from Heaven(C1676)/What Will Santa Claus Say(C1678)
     Vo    3388. The Goose Hangs High/Mr. Ghost Goes to Town
     Vo    3506. The Love Bug Will Bite You/Fifty-Second Street
     Vo    3628. Afraid to Dream/Danger, Love at Work
     Vo    3657. You Can't Have Everything(LA1378A)/Tin Roof Blues(LA1379A)
     Vo    3921. I Can't Believe You're in Love With Me/Rhythm on the Radio

                LOUIS PRIMA AND HIS BAND (Same Personnel):                         1938
     De    1618. Yes There Ain't No Moonlight Tonight/Rosalie
     De    1674. Where Have We Met Before/Now They Call It Swing
     De    1871. Nothing's Too Good for You/You Call It Madness
     De    1953. Doin' the Serpentine/Why Should I Pretend

                (Sub. John Castaing, drums):
     De    2242. Jitterbugs on Parade/Show Me the Way to Go Home
     De    2279. Exactly Like You(DLA1638-A)/Now and Then(DLA1640-A)
     De    2660. A Good Man Is Hard to Find(65952-A)/If I Could Be With You One Hour
     De    2749. Of Thee I Sing/Sweet and Lowdown                     (65953-A)

PRIME, ALBERTA (blues duet with Sonny Greer.  Piano accompaniment Duke Ellington?):
     Blu-Disc 1007. Parlor Social Deluxe/It's Gonna Be a Cold Winter

PROCTOR, HELEN (blues singing with orchestra including Henry Allen,trumpet):
     De    7666. Blues at Midnight/Cheatin' on Me
     De    7703. Let's Call It a Day/Take Me Along With You

PROFIT, CLARENCE (piano solos):
     Co   35378. Body and Soul(WC026308-B)/I Didn't Know What Time It Was(WC026396-A)

                CLARENCE PROFIT TRIO:
     De    8503. Times Square Blues(68080-A)/Hot and Bothered(68081-A)
     De    8527. Dark Eyes(68079-A)/Azure(68082-A)

PULLUM, JOE (blues singing with piano):
     BB    5459. Black Gal/(ROB COOPER)
     BB    5534. C.W.A. Blues(Rob Cooper,piano)/Dows See That Train Comin'(Cooper,pf.)
     BB    5592. Woman Oh Woman/Houston Blues
     BB    5947. Black Gal No.4/(ROB COOPER)
     BB    6426. Bedroom Blues/Hattie Green

PUNCH'S DELEGATES OF PLEASURE( Punch Miller,trumpet, and leader; see Frankie Half
Pint Jaxon: Vo 1472).
```

JACK PURVIS

```
Also recorded:
     FRANK FROEBA: Co 3110, 3131, 3151, 3152.
     WHITEY KAUFMAN: Victor

PURVIS, JACK (cornet solos, rhythm accompaniment):
     OK  41404. Copyin' Louis(403522-B)/Mental Strain at Dawn(403523-A)

                JACK PURVIS AND HIS ORCHESTRA(Jack Purvis,cornet; J.C. Higginbotham,trom-
                bone; Coleman Hawkins,tenor sax; Adrian Rollini,bass sax; Frank Froeba,
                piano; Will Johnson,guitar; Charles Kegley,drums):          March,1930
     OK    8782. Poor Richard(403892-A)                                     -PaE  992
           "     Down Georgia Way(403893-B)                                 -PaE  698
     OK    8808. Dismal Dan(403891-A)/(See coupling below)                  -PaE 1449

                (Sub.Greely Walton,sax,for Hawkins):                        April,1930
     OK    8808. Be Bo Bo(403994-A)                                         -PaE 1252
     PaF    890. When You're Feeling Blue(403993-A)/(O.K.RHYTHM KINGS)      -PaA 36093
     PaF   1669. What's the Use of Cryin' Baby(403992-B)/(LUIS RUSSELL)     -PaA 36093
```

Q

Q.R.S. BOYS (Walter "Fats" Pichon,piano; Robert Cloud,tenor sax; Bennie Nawahi,
guitar.---Personnel from Harrison Smith):   1929
   QRS 7062. Wiggle Yo Toes(338)/I've Seen My Baby(339)
   QRS ----. Bourbon Street
   QRS ----. Dime Song
   QRS ----. Downtown
   QRS ----. Black Boy Blues
   QRS ----. Dad Blame Blues

QUEBEC QUINTET, IKE (Ike Quebec,tenor sax; Roger Ramirez,piano; Tiny Grimes,guitar; Milton Hinton,bass; J.C. Heard, drums):
   BN   37. Blue Harlem/Tiny's Exercise
   BN   38. She's Funny That Way/Indiana

      IKE QUEBEC'S SWINGTET(Jonah Jones,trumpet: Tyree Glenn,trombone; Ike Quebec,tenor sax; Roger Ramirez,piano; Tiny Grimes,guitar; Oscar Pettiford, bass; J.C. Heard,drums;
   BN   42. Mad About You(991)/Facin' the Face(992-1)
   BN 510. If I Had You/Hard Tack

      IKE QUEBEC'S SWING SEVEN (Buck Clayton,trumpet; Keg Jonnson,trombone; Grachan Moncur,bass; Quebec; Ramirez; Grimes; Heard):
   BN 515. Topsy/Cap-Mute Clayton

      IKE QUEBEC'S QUINTET (Quebec; Dave Rivera,piano; Napoleon Allen,guitar; Milton Hinton,bass; J.C. Heard,drums):
   BN 516. Dolores/Sweethearts on parade

      (Quebec; Johnny Guarnieri,piano; Bill d'Arango,guitar; Milton Hinton, bass; J.C.Heard,drums):
   Sav 570. I.Q. Blues(5831)/Jim Dawgs(5829)

QUINTETTE OF THE HOT CLUB OF FRANCE (Django Reinhardt, Joseph Reinhardt, Roget Chaput, guitars, Stephane Grappelly,violin; Louis Vola,bass):   Paris,1934
  U1 1422. Dinah(P77161)   -Roy 1753
        "   Oh,Lady Be Good(P77163)   -Roy 1754
  U1 1423. Tiger Rag(77162)   -Roy 1753
        "   I Saw Stars(77164)
  U1 1444. Lily Belle May June(P77240; Jerry Mengo,voc.)   -De 23004
        "   Sweet Sue(P77241; Mengo,voc.)   -Roy 1780
  U1 1443. Confessin'(77243)   -Roy 1788
        "   Continental(77243; Mengo,voc.)
  U1 1479. Blue Drag(77351)
        "   Swanee River(77352)   -Roy 1785
  U1 1484. Your Sweet Smile(77353)   -Roy 1807
        "   Ultrafox(77354)   -De 23003,Roy 1785

      (Sub. Pierre Ferret,guitar, for Chaput; add Pierre Allier,Alphonse Cox, Arthur Briggs,trumpets; D'Hellemmes,trombone):
  U1 1512. Avalon(77434)   -De 23002,Roy 1780
        "   Smoke Rings(77435)   -Roy 1788

      (Omit brass):
  U1 1511. Clouds(77440)   -De 23002
        "   Believe It Beloved(77441)
  U1 1547. Chasing Shadows(77537)   -Roy 1798
        "   I've Had My Moments(77538)   "
  U1 1548. Some of These Days(77539)   -De 23004
        "   Djangology(77540)   -De 23003

      (The Decca reissues above, as well as the originals below, appeared under the name of STEPHANE GRAPPELLY AND HIS HOT FOUR):
  De 23021. Limehouse Blues(2035)/(for coupling, see below)   -DeE 5780
  DeE 5780. I Got Rhythm(2036)
  De 23032. St.Louis Blues(2009)/(for coupling see below)   -DeE 5824

      (Sub. Rovira, bass):
  De 23021. I've Found a New Baby(2079)   -DeE 5943
  DeE 5943. It Was So Beautiful(2080)
  De 23031. China Boy(2081)   -DeE 5824
        "   Moonglow(2082)   -DeE 5831
  De 23032. It Don't Mean a Thing(2083)   -DeE 5831

      (Sub. Lucien Simoens, bass):   1936
  GrF 7704. I'se a Muggin(OLA1057; Freddy Taylor,voc.)
        "   Oriental Shuffle(OLA1059)   -Vi 26506,HMV 8474
  GrF 7706. Limehouse Blues(OLA1062)   -Vi·25511,HMV 8463
        "   I Can't Give You Anything But Love(OLA1058; Taylor,voc.) -HMV 8463

86

```
GrF  7707. After You've Gone(OA1060; Taylor,voc.)        -Vi 25511,HMV 8479
     "    Are You in the Mood(OLA1061)                    -Vi 26506,      "

     (Vola, bass):
GrF  7843. Nagasaki(OLA1290)                              -Vi 25558,HMV 8518
     "    Sweet Chorus(OLA1295)                                           "
GrF  7790. Georgia on My Mind(OLA1292; Taylor,voc.)       -Vi 26578,HMV 8532
     "    Shine(OLA1293; Taylor,voc.)                     -Vi 25558,HMV 8534
GrF  7898. Swing Guitars(OLA1291)                         -Vi 25601,HMV 8532
     "    In the Still of the Night(OLA1294)              -Vi 26578,HMV 8534

     (Sub. Marcel Bianchi,guitar,for Joseph Reinhardt):                 1937
HMV  8598. Body and Soul(1710)/A Little Love, a Little Kiss(1716)
HMV  8606. You're Driving Me Crazy(1704)                  -Vi 26733
     "    Mystery Pacific(1717)
HMV  8614. Miss Annabelle Lee(1714)/Runnin' Wild(1712)
HMV  8669. Solitude(1706)/When Day Is Done(1711)
HMV  8690. Hot Lips(1707)/Ain't Misbehavin'(1708)
HMV  8718. Tears(1705)/Rose Room(1709)
HMV  8629. Exactly Like You(1702)                         -Vi 26733
     "    In a Sentimental Mood(1718)
HMV  8737. The Shiek of Araby/Liebestraum No. 3
Sw      2. Chicago/Charleston

          (Stephane Grappelly,violin; Django Reinhardt, Joseph Reinhardt,Eugene
          Vees,guitars; Louis Vola,bass; plus brass section on first side and
          violin section on second):
GrF  1046. Mabel/Bolero

          (Omit brass and violins):
Sw     23. Minor Swing/Viper's Dream                      -Vi 26218
Sw     77. My Serenade/Younger Generation(different personnel, see Sw 128)
Sw     40. Paramount Stomp(OLA1995; Warlop,violin)/Swinging With Django(OLA1994)
                                                          --Vi 27272
          (Grappelly,violin;Django Reinhardt, Pierre Ferret, Jean Ferret, guitars;
          Emmanuel Soudieux, bass):
Sw    128. Stockholm

          (Grappelly,; Django Reinhardt; Chaput; Vees; Vola):  London, 1938
DeE  6675. Sweet Georgia Brown                            -De 23065
     "    Black and White                                 -De 23067
DeE  6616. Night and Day                                  -De 23067
     "    Stompin' at Decca                               -De 23066
DeE  6639. Honeysuckle Rose                               -De 23066
     "    Souvenirs                                       -De 23065
DeE  9428. My Sweet
De  23152. Daphne

          (Sub. Joseph Reinhardt for Chaput: Roger Grasset, bass,for Vola):
DeE  9433. The Lambeth Walk                               -De 23077
     "    The Flat Foot Floogee
De  23077. Why Shouldn't I?

          (Recorded in Paris):
DeF  6899. Swing from Paris
     "    Them There Eyes                                 -De 23262
DeE  6875. Direct Appeal                                  -De 23261
     "    Three Little Words                              -De 23264
De  23263. Love Letters

          (Grappelly; Django and Joseph Reinhardt; Pierre Ferret; Soudieux):
DeE  7027. Jeepers Creepers
     "    Swing 39                                        -De 23262
DeE 59023. Hungaria
     "    Twelve Years                                    -De 23264
DeF 59019. I Wonder Where My Baby Is Tonight              -De 23152
     "    Time on My Hands
DeE 59006. Tea for Two
     "    Japanese Sandman                                -De 23263
De  23261. My Melancholy Baby
DeE 59018. Undecided(vocal Beryl Davis)/Don't Worry About Me(Garppelly,piano)
DeE 59045. H.C.Q.Strut/The Man I Love(Grappelly,piano)

          DJANGO REINHARDT AND THE NEW HOT CLUB QUINTETTE(Reinhardt,solo guitar;
          Hubert Rostaing,clarinet; Joseph Reinhardt,guitar; Francis Lucas,bass;
          Pierre Fouad,drums):                                          1940
Sw     83. Blues/Futuristic Rhythm
```

```
         (Sub. Tony Rovira,bass):
   Sw    88. Les Yeux Noirs/Nuages(add Alix Combelle,clarinet)
         Sw   103. Petits Mensonges/Oiseaux des Iles(Combelle,tenor sax)
   Sw   118. Sweet Sue/Exactly Like You(Combelle,tenor sax)
   Sw    95. Swing 41 (Combelle,clarinet)
   Sw   123. Vendredi 13/(for coupling see below)
   Sw   137. Mabel/(for coupling see below)

         (Django Reinhardt,Hubert Rostaing,Eugene Vees,Emmanuel Soudisux,Pierre
         Fouad):                                                            1942
   Sw   123. Crepuscule
   Sw   137. Swing 42
   Sw   146. Dinah/Lentement,Mademoiselle(Andre Jourdan,drums)
   Sw   162. Belleville(Jourdan,drums)

         (Django Reinhardt,solo guitar; Andre Lluis,Gerard Leveque,clarinet;
         Eugene Vees,guitar; Jean Storme,bass; Gaston Leonard,drums):
   Sw   158. Oui/Manoir de Mes Reves

         STEPHANE GRAPPELLY'S HOT FOUR (Grappelly and Warlop,violins; Django Rein-
         hardt and Roger Chaput,guitars):
   Sw    74. You Took Advantage of Me
            (See also Django Reinhardt)
```

QUINTONES, THE (vocal group, accompanied by Buck Ram's Orchestra(Buck Clayton,
         trumpet;George Koenig,clarinet; Carl Galehouse,tenor; Les Burness,piano;
         Walter Page,bass; Joe Jones,drums):
   Vo 5172. When My Sugar Walks Down the Street/Fool That I Am
            (See also: Barney Bigard Orchestra, Vo 4928)

R

RADIOLITES, THE (orchestra sometimes featuring Benny Goodman,clarinet, and Jack
Teagarden,trombone?):
   Co   793. If I'd Only Believed in You/Sunday
   Co   903. Ain't She Sweet/Song of Shanghai
   Co 1067. The Sphinx
   Co 1114. Dancing Tambourine
   Co 1123. The Calinda(144623)/(DON VOORHEES)
   Co 1150. Everybody Loves My Girl/There's a Cradle in Caroline
   Co 1209. There Must Be Somebody Else
   Co 1301. I Still Love You
   Co 1326. Forever and Ever/Rain or Shine
   Co 1375. That's My Mammy
   Co 1468. Cheerio/One Step to Heaven
   Co 1432. Sweet Lorraine/If I Can't Have You
   Co 2347. And Then Your Lips Met Mine(150957)/(KNICKERBOCKERS)

         (Pseudonym for Benny Goodman's Orchestra, probably including Charlie Tea-
         garden, trumpet):   New York,Sept.15,1931
   Co 2540. Love Letters in the Sand(151796)/I Don't Know Why(151797)

RAEBURN AND HIS ORCHESTRA, BOYD (Including Dizzy Gillespie,trumpet; Johnny Both-
well,alto sax; Oscar Pettiford,bass):
   Guild 107. Interlude(542)   -Mu 489
      "   I Didn't Know About You
   Guild 111. Summertime(549)
      "   March of the Boyds(543)   -Mu 489

         (Tom Allison,trumpet solos; Bothwell; Trummie Young,trombone):
   Guild 133. You Came Along from Out of Nowhere
      "   Boyd's Nest(579)   -Mu 490
   Mu   490. Blue Prelude(580)

         (Including Dodo Marmarosa,piano: Ray Linn,trumpet: Hal McKusick,alto sax;
         Frankie Socolow,tenor; Jackie Miles,drums):
   Jewel 10000. Tonsilectomy/Forgetful
   Jewel 10001. Yerza/Rip Van Winkle
   Jewel 10002. Boyd Meets Stravinsky/I Only Have Eyes for You
   Jewel 10003. The Man With the Horn/Hip Boyds
   Jewel 10004. Prelude to the Dawn/Duck Waddle
   Jewel Album, D-1. Little Boyd Blue. Temptation. Blue Echoes. Body and Soul.
            Dalvatore Sally. Over the Rainbow.

RAGON AND HIS ORCHESTRA, IKE:
   Vo 03513. Maple Leaf Rag/Slap That Bass
   Vo 03547. Truckin' on the Old Camp Ground(HS53)/Harlem Blues(HS54)

RAINBOW DANCE ORCHESTRA (Broadway Broadcasters item with Benny Goodman,clarinet):
   Ro   366. St. Louis Blues(2357)

MA RAINEY

RAINEY, MADAME "MA" (blues singer, accompanied by Lovie Austin and Her Blues Serenaders:--Tommy Ladnier,cornet; Jimmy O'Bryant or Buster Bailey,clarinet; Lovie Austin,piano; Jasper Taylor or Kaiser Marshall,drums .--JI 9/6/40; "Jazz in New Orleans"): Chicago, 1923
Para 12080. Bo-Weavil Blues(1597)-2)/Last Minute Blues(1609)-2)
Para 12081. Bad Luck Blues(1596)-2)/Those All Night Long Blues(1599)-2)
Para 12082. Barrel House Blues(1598)-2)/Walking Blues(1613)-2)
Para 12083. Moonshine Blues(1608)-2)/Southern Blues(1612)-2)

    (Acc. by the Pruitt Twins, guitars):
Para 12098. Lost Wandering Blues(1698)-2)/Dream Blues(1699)-1)

    (Previous personnel):
Para 12200. Honey Where Have You Been So Long(1701)/Ma Rainey's Mystery Record
Para 12215. Those Dogs of Mine(1703-1)/Lucky Rock Blues(1704-2)   (1759)

    (Acc. by guitar):
Para 12222. Shave 'em Dry(1824)/Farewell Daddy(1825)

    (Acc. by Her Georgia Jazz Band, same personnel):
Para 12227. South Bound Blues(1741-1)/Lawd Send Me a Man Blues(1758-2)
Para 12257. Ya-da-do(1702-2)/Cell Bound Blues(10001-2)

    (Acc. by Her Georgia Jazz Band: Louis Armstrong,cornet; Charlie Green, trombone; probably Buster Bailey,clarinet; Austin; Marshall):
Para 12238. Jelly Bean Bl(1926-2)/Countin' the Blues(1927-2) -JI 8, UHCA 83/84
Para 12252. See See Blues(1925-1)
Para 12252. See See Rider Blues(1925-2)   -JI 9, UHCA 86

    (Probably Howard Scott, cornet):
Para 12252. Jealous Hearted Blues(1924-2)   -JI 9, UHCA 85
Para 12242. Booze and Blues(1922)/Toad Frog Blues(1923)

MA RAINEY AND HER GEORGIA BAND(Trumpet,clarinet,piano,banjo,drums,frisco whistle. NOTE: George Mitchell,Shirley Clay and Henry Mason,trumpets, have said that they recorded separately with Ma Rainey on various unidentified discs):
Para 12284. Army Camp Harmony Blues(2136)-1)/Explaining the Blues(2137)-2)
Para 12290. Louisiana Hoo Doo Blues(2138-1)/Goodbye Daddy Blues(2139-1)

    (Trumpet, sax, piano, banjo, drums):
Para 12295. Stormy Sea Blues(2209-1)/Levee Camp Moan(2212-2)
Para 12303. Night Time Blues(2211)/Four Day Honory Scat(2213)
Para 12311. Rough and Tumble Blues(2210)/Memphis Bound Blues(2214)

    (Acc. by Her Georgia Band: Joe Smith,trumpet; Charlie Green,trombone; Buster Bailey,clarinet; Fletcher Henderson,piano; Charlie Dixon,guitar; Kaiser Marshall,drums; unknown bass sax): January, 1926
Para 12332. Slave to the Blues(2369-2)/Oh My Babe Blues(2374-1)
Para 12338. Chain Gang Blues(2372-2)/Wringing and Twisting Blues(23752)
Para 12357. Yonder Come the Blues(2370-1)/Stack o' Lee Blues(2376-2)
Para 12374. Titanic Man Blues(2371)/Bessemer Bound Blues(2373)

MA RAINEY AND HER GEORGIA BAND (Al Wynn,trombone: Thomas Dorsey,piano; Cedric Odom,drums; --- Fuller,trumpet; unknown sax.--DB 5/20/46):
Para 12352. Seeking Blues(2452-1)/Mountain Jack Bl(2466-3; Jas.Blythe,piano acc.)
Para 12364. Broken Hearted Blues(2448-1)/Jealousy Blues(2451-4)

    (With Her Georgia Band: Trumpet, trombone, clarinet, piano, drums, frisco
Para 12384. Sissy Blues(2628-1)/Broken Soul Blues(2629-2)   (whistle):
Para 12395. Down in the Basement(2627-1)/Trust No Man(2631-1; Lillian Henderson, (piano acc.)

    (Acc. by two violins and guitar):
Para 12419. Little Low Mamma Blues(403: 4019-2)/Grievin' Hearted Blues(404;4020-2)

    (B.T. Wingfield,cornet: unknown clarinet and piano):
Para 12438. Soon This Morning(451)/Don't Fish in My Sea(462; James Blythe,piano)
Para 12455. Weepin' Woman Blues(407)-2)/Morning Hour Blues(405:guitar,piano acc.)

    (Trumpet, trombone, piano, banjo, tuba):
Para 12508. Misery Blues(734;4707-1)/Dead Drunk Bl(773;4708-2; Hop Hopkins,piano)
Para 12526. Slow Driving Moan(857)/Gone Daddy Blues(858)
Para 12548. Big Boy Blues(889)/Damper Down Blues(890)
Para 12566. Blues oh Blues(948; 4683-2)/Oh Papa Blues(949;4692-1)

    (Add clarinet):
Para 12590. Ma Rainey's Black Bottom(20229-2)/Georgia Cake Walk(20232-1)
Para 12603. New Bo-Weavil Blues(20233-1)/Moonshine Blues(20234-2)
Para 12647. Blues the World Forgot I(20228)/Blues the World ForgotII (20230)

MA RAINEY'S GEORGIA BAND(Prof.C.M.Russell,director; instrumental):
Para 12612. Hellish Rag(20231-2)/Ice Bag Papa(20235-3)

MA RAINEY AND HER TUB JUG WASHBOARD BAND(unknown personnel):
Para 12668. Heah Me Taling to You(20663)/Prove It on Me Blues(20665)
Para 12687. Black Cat Hoot Owl Blues(20661)/Victim of the Blues(20667)
Para 12706. Traveling Blues(20667)/Deep Moaning Blues(20668)
Para 12804. Log Camp Blues(20662)/Hustling Blues(20664)

(Acc. Tampa Red,guitar: and piano):
Para 12760. Sleep Taling Blues(20879)/Blame It on the Blues(20881)

(piano accompaniment):
Para 12735. Tough Luck Blues(20880)/Screech Owl Blues(20885)

(Duet with Papa Charlie Jackson; banjo acc.):
Para 12718. Ma and Pa Poorhouse Blues(20921)/Big Feeling Blues(21044)

(Guitar and piano accompaniment):
Para 12902. Runaway Blues(20883-3)/Leaving This Morning(20897-1)
Para 12926. Sweet Rough Man/Black Dust Blues
Para 12963. Daddy Goodbye Blues(20878-1)/Black Eye Blues(20898-2)

(NOTE: Ma Rainey is reported to have recorded also for Okeh,
possibly under a pseudonym, with Kid Ory,trombone, and
Louis Armstrong,cornet, in the accompaniment)

RAM AND HIS ORCHESTRA, BUCK (Frankie Newton,Shad Collins,trumpets; Tyree Glenn,
trombone; Earl Bostic,alto sax: Don Byas,tenor· Ernie Caceres,baritone; Red Norvo,vibraphone; Teddy Wilson,piano; Remo Palmieri,guitar: Cozy Cole,drums; Slam
Stewart,bass): Sept.18,1944
 Sav 572. Twilight in Teheran(S-5714)/Swing Street(S-5716)
 Sav   . Ram Session/Morning Mist

RAMBLERS, THE (Bob Hamilton,organ; Billy Kyle,piano; Teddy Bunn,guitar; O'Neil
Spencer,drums,vocals):
 De 2470. 'Tain't What You Do/Money Is Honey
 De 2499. Honey in the Bee Ball(65490-A)/Lonesome Railroad(65493-A)

(This is also the name of a Dutch dance orchestra which has recorded
extensively with Coleman Hawkins and Benny Carter,q.v.,and in its own
right)
ORIGINAL RAMBLERS (Theo Masma,piano; William Poppink,alto,baritone,clarinet; Dreese,tenor; Eddy Meenk,trumpet; Gerard Spruyt,trombone; Jack Pet,
guitar; Kees Kranenburg,drums.--RR): 1929
HMV 4820. Every Morn/Hot Lips
HMV 4821. Alabamy Snow/High Tension
Od 164112. Broadway Medley/Haven't I
Od 164116. Down Among the Sugar Cane/When I Tip Toe Through the Tulips
Od 164117. Avalon/Down Among the Sugar Cane

THE RAMBLERS(Add Jack Dememint,alto and clarinet; sub.Andre Van Der Ouderaa,tenor sax,clarinet and violin,for Dreese; add Sid Buckman,trumpet;
J.Hilarius,bass): London,1932
DeE 40308. Business in F/Music in My Fingers
DeE 40309. Chinatown My Chinatown/Lazy Feet
DeE 40310. Erratic Rhythm/My Blue Heaven

(Sub. Rinus van Zelm,alto,for Dememint; Sam Dasberg,Jules Hagenaar,trum-
DeE 3583. Who's Sorry Now/Jig Walk   (pets):
DeE 3588. Decca Stomp/Vladivostock
DeE 3620. 13th December Stomp
DeE 3655. Everybody Loves My Baby/Way Down Yonder in New Orleans

(Masman,piano; William Poppink,Joop Huisman,Andre van der Ouderaa,saxes;
Eddy Meenk,Henk Hinrichs,George Helvoirt,trumpets: Marcel Thielemans,
Heinz Lachman,trombones; Jack Pet,guitar; Gerard Spruyt,bass; Kees Kranenburg,drums):
DeF 5407. Dancing Dogs/Ohio Serenade
DeE 42011. Alabama Swing/By the Shalimar
DeE 42012. Duke's Holiday/Manhattan Shuffle
DeE 42020. Sittin' on a Backyard Fence/Shanghai Lil
DeE 42029. White Heat/Farewell Blues

(George Van Helvoirt,Jack Bulterman,Ferry Barendse,trumpets; Marcel Thielmans,trombone; William Poppink,Andre van der Ouderaa,Frits Reinders,Fred
van Ingen,saxes; Theo Masman,piano; Jac Pet,bass; Kees Kranenburg,drums):
DeB 8814. Aurora/Oh Aha 1942
DeB 9004. At the Ramblers Ball/De Plein Fouet
DeB 9069. Ping Pong/Banco
DeB 9070. Triple Sec, 1 & 2 (drum solos, with orchestra)
DeB 9071. Au Revoir/Chasse a Courre
DeB 9072. La Chaise a Bascule/Orient Express

```
DeB  9119.  Emotion/Obsession
DeB  9120.  Jubileum/Studio 10
DeB  9122.  In Spanning/Hilversum Express
DeB  9170.  In Zie de Zon/Angelina
```

RAMONA AND HER GANG (Ramona Davies,piano and vocal; Jack Teagarden,trombone;
Charlie Teagarden,trumpet; John.Cordaro,sax and clarinet: Dick McDonough,guitar;
Arthur Miller,bass; Larry Gomar,drums.--RR):   1935
```
Vi 25138.  Every Now and Then                          -HMV 8406
    "      No Strings                                  -HMV 4563
Vi 25156.  Barrel House Music                          -HMV 4563
    "      I Can't Give You Anything But Love
```

RAMPART STREET WASHBOARD BAND (see Beale Street Washboard Band)

RAMSEY AND LEE (vocals with George Ramsey,piano):
Para 13067. Sittin' on Top of the World

RANDALL AND HIS ORCHESTRA, CLARK (Phil Hart,Yank Lawson,trumpets; Art Foster,trombone; Matty Matlock,clarinet,alto sax; Gil Rodin,alto; Eddie Miller,tenor; Dean Kincaid,tenor; Gil Bowers,piano; Hilton Lamare,guitar· Bob Haggart,bass; Ray Bauduc,drums; Frank Tennille(Clark Randall), vocals):   March, 1935
```
Br  7415.  Troublesome Trumpet(B17047; Lamare,voc.)/When Icky Morgan Plays the
Br  7466.  Jitterbut(B17160)/If You're Looking for Someone(17161)(Organ(B17048)
Br  7436.  Drifting Tide(17218)/Here Comes Your Pappy With the Wrong Kind of
                                                        (Load(B17219; Lamare,voc.)
```
(See also: Gil Rodin's Orchestra)

SLATS RANDALL AND HIS ORCHESTRA (personnel unknown):
```
Br  4331.  Bessie Couldn't Help It/I Get the Blues When It Rains
Br  4562.  I'd Do Anything for You/Blame It on the Moon
Br  4568.  Got a Great Big Date/Let's Don't 'n' Say We Did
Br  4719.  Sweetheart Trail/What a Perfect Night for Love
Br  4779.  Skirts/I'm a Ding Dong Daddy
Br  6304.  Hello Gorgeous/My Mom
```

RANDOLPH AND HER ORCHESTRA, AMANDA (Bunny Berigan,trumpet, and the Dorsy brothers?):
```
BB  6616.  ----/(WINGY MANONE)
BB  6617.  He May Be Your Man/For Sentimental Reaons
BB  6619.  ----/(CHARLIET BARNET)
```

RANGER, JACK (vocal with guitar and piano):
```
OK  8795.  Thieving Blues(402767)/T.P. Window Blues(402768)
OK  8847.  Lonesome Grave Blues
```

RAPPOLO, LEON (clarinet, see):
FRIARS SOCIETY ORCHESTRA: All.
HALFWAY HOUSE ORCHESTRA: OK 40318(alto)
NEW ORLEANS RHYTHM KINGS: Gennett and Okeh.

RAY AND HIS ORCHESTRA, FLOYD:
```
De  2337.  Three o'clock in the Morning(65055-A)/Comin' on With the Blues(65056-A)
De  2500.  Love Is Simply Grand(65057-A)/Firefly Stomp(65394-A)
De  2618.  Jammin' the Blues(65058-A)/Side By Side(65393-A)
De  2923.  My Little Dream Girl(65392-A)/Blues at Noon(65395-A)
```

REARDON, CASPER (harp, with orchestra):
```
Schirmer 511.  Easy to Love/I Can't Give You Anything But Love
Schirmer 512.  I Got Rhythm/They Didn't Believe Me
Liberty  199.  You'll Have to Swing It/Summertime
Liberty  218.  Washboard Blues/What Is This Thing Called Love
---      113.  Misbehavin'/Sentimental
```

REB'S LEGION CLUB 45's:
Hollywood ---. My Mammy's Blues/Sheffield Blues

RED DEVILS:
Co 14568. Tiger Rag/Dinah

RED AND HIS BIG TEN(Red Nichols,Ruby Weinstein,trumpets: Glenn Miller,Tommy Dorsey,trombones; Benny Goodman,clarinet; Sid Stoneberg,Pete Pumiglio,saxes; Roy Bargy,piano; Carl Kress,guitar; Gene Krupa,drums):   1931
```
Vi 23026.  I'm Tickled Pink With a Blue Eyed Baby/That's Where the South Begins
Vi 23033.  At Last I'm Happy/If You Haven't Got a Girl
```

RED AND MIFF'S STOMPERS (Nichols,cornet; Miff Mole,trombone: Jimmy Dorsey,clarinet and alto sax; Arthur Schutt,piano: Vic Berton,drums):
```
Ed 51854.  Alabama Stomp(11245)/Stampede(11246)
Ed 51878.  Hurricane(11291)/Black Bottom Stomp(11292)
Vi 20778.  Delirium(37768)/Davenport Blues(37769)
```

(Sub. Fud Livingston, clarinet):
```
Vi 21183.  Feelin' No Pain(40169)
Vi 21397.  Slippin' Around(40168)/(COON-SANDERS)
```

RED HEADS (Red Nichols, cornet: Miff Mole,trombone: Jimmy Dorsey,clarinet; Arthur Schutt,piano; Vic Berton,drums):
  Pat 36347. Nervous Charlie(106041-1)/Headin' for Louisville(106402-2)-Pe 14528
  Pe 14565. Fallen Arches(106400)

  (Dorsey,alto sax; add Fud Livingston,clarinet; Fred Morrow,alto; Howdy Quicksell,banjo; sub. Rubs Bloom,piano):
  Pat 36387. Poor Papa(106602-2)/(MIKE SPECIALE)   -Pe 14568
  Pe 14600. Hangover(106604)/'Tain't Cold(106603)

  (Nichols; Mole; Bloom; Berton; Eddie Lang,guitar: Bobby Davis,clarinet
  PatA 11134. Jig Walk(106690)   (and sexes):

  (Nichols; Mole; Dorsey; Schutt; Berton):
  Pe 14673. Wild and Foolish(106746)
  PatA 11376. You Should See My Tootsie
  PatA 11515. How Come You Do Me Like You Do
  Pat 36458. Hi Diddle Diddle(106787-2)/Dynamite(106788-2)   -Pe 14639

  (Add Fud Livingston,clarinet; Eddie Lang,guitar; Leo McConville,trumpet):
  Pat 36527. Alabama Stomp(107094-2)/Brown Sugar(107096-2)   -Pe 14708
  Pe 14617. Hurricane(107095)

  (Sub. Brad Gowans,cornet (?), for McConville; omit Livingston):
  Pat 36557. Heebie Jeebies(107205-1)/Black Bottom Stomp(107206B) -Pe 14738
  Pat 36576. That's No Bargian(107204-1)/(ORIGINAL MEMPHIS FIVE) -Pe 14757

  (Nichols; Mole; Dorsey; Bloom):
  Pat 36583. Here or There(107351C)/Tell Me Tonight(107350D)   -Pe 14764

  (Nichols; Mole; Schutt; Berton; possibly Pee Wee Russell,clarinet):
  Pat 36701. Baltimore(107784)/Good Man Is Hard to Find(107782) -Pe 14882
  Pat 36707. Nothin'Does Does Like It Used to Do Do Do/(GOLDEN GATE) -Pe 14888

  (See Red Nichols: Br 6058):
  Me 12495. Bug-a-Boo(35733-A)/Corrine Corrina(35734-A)   -Or 2574

RED ONION JAZZ BABIES (Louis Armstrong,cornet; Aaron Thomson,trombone; Buster Bailey,clarinet; Buddy Christian,banjo: Lil Armstrong,piano):   Nov.,1924
  Ge 5607. Terrible Blues(9206-C)   -HRS 31,Br 80062,Si 4032
       "   Santa Claus Blues   "   "
  Ge 5627. Of All the Wrongs You've Done to Me(9177)   -HRS 31,Si 4029
  (Sub. Sidney Bechet,clarinet; Charlie Irvis,trombone):
  Ge 5267. Cake Walking Babies(9248-A)   - Si 4029
  (See also: Josephine Beatty)

  (The following is actually Johnny Sylvester's Orchestra):
  Si 4031. Brotherly Love

RED HOT SYNCOPATORS):
  Bell 445. Jack Ass Blues/Gettin' the Blues

DON REDMAN

See also:
  LOUIS ARMSTRONG: OK 8649, 8657, 8669, 8680, 8690, 8703.
  BIG ACES: OK 41136.
  BOSWELL SISTERS: Br 20109.
  PERRY BRADFORD: Vo 15165.
  CHOCOLATE DANDIES: OK 8627, 8668, 8728.
  CLUB WIGWAM: Dom 3458 (reissue Henderson)
  DIXIE STOMPERS.
  DUKE ELLINGTON: Ge 3291.
  FLETCHER HENDERSON: To 1928.
  BILLIE HOLIDAY: OK 5831, 5806.
  HARLAN LATTIMORE: Co 2675, 2678.
  McKINNEY'S COTTON PICKERS:
  VIOLA McCOY: Br 2591.
  BESSIE SMITH: Co 14260, 14569.

REDMAN AND HIS ORCHESTRA, DON (Henry Allen,Langston Curl,Leonard Davis,trumpets; Fred Robinson,George Washington,trombones: Don Redman,Rupert Cole,Edward Inge, Bobby Carroll,saxes; Horace Henderson,piano; Talcott Reeves,banjo; Bob Escudero, bass; Manzie Johnson,drums):   1931
  Br 6211. Chant of the Weed(E37225-A)   -Br 80036,BrE 1244
       "   Shakin' the African(E37291-A)   "   "
  Br 6233. I Heard/Trouble, Why Pick on Me   -BrE 1280

  (Shirley Clay,Langston Curl,Sidney DeParis,trumpets: Benny Morton,Claude Jones,Fred Robinson,trombones: rest same):

```
Br   6273. How Am I Doin'/Try Gettin' a Good Night's Sleep        -BrE 1320
Br   6344. You Gave Me Everything But Love                        -BrE 1366
 "         It's a Great World, After All
Br   6354. I Got Rhythm(B12007-A)                      -Me 51104,BrE 1344
 "         Tea for Two                                           -BrE 1389
Br   6368. If It's True(B11194-A)                                -BrE 1389
 "         Hot and Anxious(B12006-A)                             -BrE 1344
Me  12417. Got the South in My Soul

           (Sub. Quentin Jackson,trombone, for Robinson):
Br   6401. Underneath the Harlem Moon(B12444-A)/Ain't I the Lucky One(B12445-A)
Me  12739. Smoke Rings                                          (-BrE 1427
Br   6412. Pagan Paradise(B12306-A)                              -BrE 1400
 "         Two Time Man(B12307-A)                    -Co 35689,     "
Br   6429. Doin' What I Please(B12446-A)                         -BrE 1498
 "         Nagasaki(B12447-A)                          -Me 51104,    "

           (Sub. Don Kirkpatrick,piano):                            1933
Br   6523. How Ya Feelin'                                       -BrE 02076
 "         Mommy I Don't Want to Go to Bed                      -BrE 01989
Br   6517. Doin' New Low Down(with Mills Bros., Calloway)
BrE 01989. How Can I Hi-De-Hi(with Mills Bros., Calloway)
Br   6520. Doin' New Los Down(12810; with Bill Robinson)
Br   6560. Sophisticated Lady                        -Me 12739,BrE 01541
 "         That Blue Eyed Baby fro Memphis                           "
Br   6520. Shuffle Your Feet(13007; with Mills Brothers)
Br   6585. I Won't Tell/It's All Your Fault

           (Omit Claude Jones, trombone):
Br   6622. Lazybones(B13694-A)                                  -BrE 01589
 "         Watching the Knife and Fork Spoon(B13695-a)
Br   6684. I Found a New Way to Go to Town/That Dallas Man      -BrE 01638
Br   6935. Lonely Cabin(14181-A)/You Told Me But Half the Story(B14180-A)/
BrF 500331. She's Not Too Bad                                  (-BrE 01843

           (Add Henry Allen,trumpet: Jerry Blake,sax and clarinet):
Br   6745. I Wanna Be Loved(B14536-A)/Got the Jitters(B14559-A)

           (Clay; DeParis; Ronald Jones,trumpets; Jackson; Morton,Gene Simon,trombone;
           Inge, Redman, Cole, Harvey Boone, sexes; Kirkpatrick; Escudero; Johnson;
           Clarence Holiday,guitar):                                1936
Me  60709. Lazy Weather(19293)                                   -VoE 10
 "         Moonrise on the Lowlands(19204)                       -VoE C002
Me  60802. A Little Bit Later On(19202)                          -VoE 10
 "         I Gotcha(19205)                                       -VoE 18

           (Sub. Howard Baker,Otis Johnson,trumpets, for Clay and DeParis: Sidney
           Catlett, drums):
Vo   3354. Bugle Call Rag/Too Bad                      -Me 61218, VoE 45
VoE  C007. We Don't Know from Nothing/Who Wants to Sing My Love Song

           (Bob Lessey,guitar; add Eugene Porter,sax):              1937
Vr    580. Exactly Like You/On the Sunny Side of the Street      -Vo 3823
Vr    605. Stormy Weather/Sweet Sue                              -Vo 3829
Vo   3836. The Naughty Waltz/The Man on the Flying Trapeze

           (Otis Johnson,Tommy Stevenson,Al Killian,trumpets;Claude Jone,Gene Simon,
           trombones; Scoville Brown,Edward Inge,Tapley Lewis,Bob Carroll,Don Redman,
           saxes; Nick Rodriguez,piano; Manzie Johnson,drums; Escudero; Lessey):
BB  10061. Margie/Down Home Rag
BB  10071. I'm Playing Solitaire/Milenberg Joys
BB  10081. Sweet Leilani/'Deed I Do
BB  10095. I Got Ya/Auld Lang Syne
BB  10305. Three Little Mainds/The Flowers That Bloom in the Spring
BB  10615. You Ain't Nowhere/About Rip Van Winkle
BB  10765. Shimme-Sha-Wabble/Chant of the Weed
Vi  26206. Jump Session/Class will Tell
Vi  26258. Chew-Chew-Chew/Igloo
Vi  26266. Baby Won't You Please Come Home/Ain't I Good to You
```

RUBEN REEVES

See also:
   CAB CALLOWAY: Br 6020-6321
   COTTON CLUB ORCHESTRA: All
   MISSOURIANS: All.
   ANDY PREER: Ge 6056.

REEVES AND HIS RIVER BOYS, RUBEN 'RIVER' (Ruben Reeves,trumpet; DePriest Wheeler, trombone; William Blue, Andrew Brown,saxes: Jimmy Prince,piano: Charley Stamps, banjo; LeRoy Maxey,drums; ---- Smith,bass):
Vo 1292. Parson Blues/River Blues
Vo 1297. Papa Skag Stomp/Bugle Call Blues
Vo 1407. Moanin' Low/Black and Blue
Vo 1411. Blue Sweets/Texas Spacial Blues
Vo 15838. Head Low/Have You Ever Felt That Way
Vo 15839. Do I Know What I'm Doing?/Shoo Shoo Boogie Boo

  (Ruben Reeves,James Tate,Cicero Thomas,trumpets; Gerald Reeves,John Thomas, trombone; Frank Johnson,Fred Brown,Norvell Morton,saxes: Eddie King,piano; Elliott Washington,banjo; Sudie Reynaud,bass; Jasper Taylor,drums): **1934**
Vo 2636. Yellow Five/Screws, Nuts and Bolts
Vo 2723. Mazie/Zuddan

DJANGO REINHARDT

See also:
PIERRE ALLIER: Sw 89, 108.
P.BRUN: Sw 15, 26, 34, 44, 54, 80.
BENNY CARTER: Sw 20, 36.
GARNET CLARK: GrF 7618, 7645.
BILL COLEMAN: Sw 14, 32. 42.
ALEX COMBELLE: Ul 1544; Sw 73,81,93,84,85,96,117.
ELLINGTONIA: HRS 1003, 1004.
NOEL CHIBOUST: Sw 86, 97, 119
ANDRE EKYAN: Sw 4, 67, 98, 202, 127
FESTIVAL SWING: Sw 91, 129.
FRANK GOODIE: Ul 1527
S. GRAPPELLY: Sw 21,69,74; De 23079.
COLEMAN HAWKINS: GrF 7455, 7527; Sw 1; HMV 8812
HUBERT ROSTAING: Sw 87.
EDDIE SOUTH: Sw 8, 12, 18, 45, 4, 31.
DICKIE WELLS: Sw 6, 16, 27.
CHRISTIAN WAGNER: Sw 102.
MICHEL WARLOP: GrF 7314; Pol 512736, 512737, 512738; Sw 13, 28, 43.
QUINTETTE OF THE HOT CLUB OF FRANCE.

REINHARDT, DJANGO (guitar solos):
HMV 8587. Parfum(1740)/Improvisation(1739)

 (Acc. by Louis Gaste,guitar; D'Hellemes,bass):
Sw 7. St.Louis Blues/Bouncin' Around

 (Acc. by Stephane Grappelly,piano):
Sw 35. Sweet Georgia Brown/You Rascal You(Acc.Louis Vola,bass)
DeE 6935. I've Got My Love to Keep Me Warm/Improvisation No.2(solo)
DeE 6828. Louise/Please Be Kind
DeE 7009. If I Had You/Nocturne   -De 23098

 (Unaccompanised):
Sw 65. Naguine/Echoes of Spain

 (Acc. by Yvon de Bie, piano):
Rhy 5016. Vous et Moi/Distraction
Rhy 5017. Blues en mineur/Studio 24

 (Acc. Stan Brenders Orchestra):
Rhy 5500. Nuages/Djangology
Rhy 5026. Divine Biguine/Chez Moi a Six Heures
Rhy 5025. Django Rag/Dynamite
Rhy 5024. Eclats de Cuivre/Tons d'Ebene

 (Acc. Fud Candrix and His Orchestra):
Rhy 5018. Mixture/Bei Dir War es Immer so Schone
Rhy 5030. Place de Brouckere/Seul ce Soir
Sw 162. Belleville
Sw 166. Melodie au Crepuscule/Place de Brouckere

 (DJANGO'S MUSIC: Phillippe Brun,Pierre Allier,Alex Renard,Piguillem,trumpets; G.Paquinet,G.Moat,P.Deck,trombones; Alix Combelle,baritone sax; Charlies Lewis,piano; Reinhardt,guitar; Pierre Ferret,guitar; E.Soudeiux, bass):
Sw 79. Tears/At Jimmy's Bar(Brun; Renard; Combelle; Lewis: Reinhardt; Soudeiux,
                        (only)
 (Add Andre Ekyan, alto sax):
Sw 82. Limehouse Blues/Daphne (without Piguillem; Moat· Deck)
 (Pierre Allier,Aime Barelli,Christian Bellest,Severin Luino,trumpets; Christian Wagner,Max Blanc,Jacquemont,Noel Chiboust,Alix Combelle,saxes; Hubert Rostaing,clarinet; Djanto and Joseph Reinhardt,guitars;Tony Rovira,bass; Pierre Fouad,drums): **1941**
Sw 95. Stockholm/(QUINTETTE OF HOT CLUB OF FRANCE)

REISMAN AND HIS ORCHESTRA, LEO (Bubber Miley,trumpet, is featured in records indicated by asterisk(*). There are scores of other Reisman records of no jazz interest):
  Vi 22282. What Is This Thing Called Love?*/She's Such a Comfort to Me
  Vi 22306. Puttin' on the Ritz*/(NAT SHILKRET)
  Vi 22398. Happy Feet*/I Like to Do Things for You
  Vi 22746. Without that Gal*/When the Moon Comes Over the Mountain
  Vi 22757. Take It From Me*/It's the Girl
  Vi 22794. Have a Heart*/Tonight or Never
  Vi 24011. If It Ain't Love*/Night Shall Be Filled With Music
  Vi 24048. Got the South in My Soul*(Lee Wiley,vocl.)/(RUBY NEWMAN)
  Vi 24126. After Tonight*/As Long As Love Lives On

REMUE AND HIS NEW STOMPERS, CHARLES (Charles Remue,clarinet and saxophone; Mike Eugelen,guitar; Tuur Peeters,bass; Chaitrain,trumpet: et al):
  Ed Bell 0153. Ain't She Sweet/High Fever
  Ed Bell 0163. Dr. Jazz(10926)/Pamplona(10923)
  Ed Bell 0164. Bridge of Avignon/Far Away Bells
  Ed Bell 0162. Roll Up the Carpet/Sha-Wan-Da-Moo
  Ed Bell 0160. Vladivostock/Slow Gee-Gee
  Ed Bell 0161. Slippery Elm/Tampeekoe
  Ed Bell 0154. Allahabad/Lucky Day

RENA'S JAZZ BAND, KID (Henry 'Kid' Rena,trumpet: Louis Nelson,Alphonse Picou, clarinets; Jim Robinson,trombone: Willie Santiago,guitar; Albert Glenny,bass; Joe Rena,drums):   New Orleans, 1940
  Delta 800. Panama/
  Delta 804. High Society Rag
  Delta 801. Gettysburg March/
  Delta 803. Lowdown Blues
  Delta 802. Milenberg Joys/
  Delta 805. Clarinet Marmalade
  Delta 806. Weary Blues/
  Delta 807. Get It Right

RENEAU, GEORGE (vocal with piano and guitar):
  Vo 14946. Got the Railroad Blues/Birmingham

RENDLEMAN AND THE ALABAMIANS, DUNK: 1928
  Ge 6322. Mean Dog Blues/(TRIANGLE HARMONY BOYS)

RHODES, DORIS (vocals, acc. by Joe Sullivan,piano; Sidney Catlett,drums: Billy Taylor,bass; Eddie Condon,guitar: Bud Freeman,tenor sax; Pee Wee Russell,clarinet; Max Kaminsky,trumpet; Brad Gowans,trombone):   1940
  Co 35449. Let There Be Love/Sierra Sue
  Co 35548. My Melancholy Baby(C027093)/Lorelei(C027095)

RHYTHM ACES (Jabbo Smith,trumpet: Omer Simeon,clarinet; Ike Robinson,banjo; Hayes Alvis,bass; Fraser,piano):
  Br 4244. Jazz Battle/(WALTER BARNES)   -UHCA 44

  (Add G. James,alto sax):
  Br 7120. I Got the Stinger/(HARLEM HOUSE RENT STOMPERS)
    (See also: Jabbo Smith's Rhythm Aces)

RHYTHM KINGS (See the Five Rhythm Kings)

RHYTHM MAKERS:
  Vo 15763. Wabash Blues/(WHOOPEE MAKERS)

RHYTHM MANIACS (featuring Irving Fazola,clarinet):
  Vo 3655. Pagan Love Song(21433)/Somebody Stole My Gal(21435)

RHYTHM WRECKERS:
  Vo 3341. Sugar Blues/She'll Be Coming Around the Mountain
  Vo 3390. Alice Blue Gown(19919)/Wabash Blues(19918)
  Vo 3523. Never No Mo' Blues/12th Street Rag
  Vo 3608. Marie/September in the Rain

RHYTHMAKERS, THE (Henry Allen,trumpet; Jimmy Lord,clarinet: Pee Wee Russell,tenor sax; Fats Waller,piano; Eddie Condon,banjo; Jack Bland,guitar: Pops Foster, bass; Zutty Singleton,drums; vocals by Billy Banks):   July 26, 1932
  Ba 32502. Mean Old Bed Bug Blues(12120-1)   -Me 12457,Or 2554,VoE 20,CMS 105
  "   Yellow Dog Blues(12121-3)   -Me 12481,Or 2554, "   CMS 107
  Co 35882. Mean Old Bed Bug Blues(12120-2)/
  "   Yellow Dog Blues(12121-2)
  Ba 32530. I'd Do Anything for You(12119-1) -Me 12457,Or 2534,BrE 02508,CMS 105
  "   Yes Suh(12122-2)   -PaE 2810,Mel2481,   "   BrE 02078,CMS 107

RICH AND HIS ORCHESTRA, FRED (This recording orchestra has used various jazz players at intervals, including Jimmy Dorsey, Will Bradley, Benny Goodman, Jack Teagarden, Dick McDonough, Arthur Schutt, et al., especially in the later Columbias):

```
Ba    6477. Sweetness(2412)/(DUBIN'S DANDIES)
Ba    7104. Laugh Clown Laugh(1512)/(HOLLYWOOD DANCE ORCHESTRA)
Ge    6001. Don't Take Your Black Bottom Away
Ca     938. Betty(1892)/(BROADWAY BROADCASTERS)
Ca    1019. I Can't Get Over/(SEVEN POLAR BEARS)
Do    3893. Take Your Finger(17038)/(SAM LANIN)
Ha      90. Don't Wake Me Up(141419)/Someone's Stolen(141421)
Ha     112. In the Middle of the Night(141590)/(BAR HARBOR ORCH.)
Ha     119. Bell Hoppin' Blues/Poor Papa
Ha     136. Could I(141783)/Gimme a Little Kiss(141785)
Co     706. On the Riviera/Barcelona
Co     734. Moonlight on the Ganges/Play Gypsies Dance Gypsies
Co     777. When Day Is Done/All Alone Monday
Co     802. Clap Yo' Hands/Do Do Do
Co     871. Crazy Words Crazy Tune/High High High Up in the Hills
Co     900. It All Depends on You/Somebody Else
Co    1108. Lucky in Love/Good News
Co    1160. Together We Two
Co    1235. I Fell Head Over Heels in Love
Co    1241. Man I Love/(LEO REISMAN)
Co    1299. I'm Walkin' on Air
Co    1389. Do I Hear You Saying/You Took Advantage of Me
Co    1740. Wedding Bells(147969)/(JAN GARBER)
Co    1838. Singin' in the Rain(148502)/Nobody But You(148503)
Co    1878. Why Can't You(148426)/Used to You(148427)
Co    1965. Revolutionary Rhythm(148973)/Until the Real Thing Comes Along(148974)
Co    1979. Until the End(148692)/I Don't Want Your Kisses(148857)
Co    2043. He's So Unusual(149429)/Dixie Jamboree(149430)
Co    2099. What Is This Thing(149738)/What Would I Care(149739)
Co    2195. Dream Avenue(150463)/For You(150464)
Co    2328. Embraceable You(150883)/I Got Rhythm(150885)

         FREDDIE RICH AND HIS ORCHESTRA (Benny Carter, Sid Perlmutter, Babe Rusin,
         Sid Stoneburn, Frank Chase, Stafford Simon, saxes; Nate Natalie, Red Solo-
         mon, Roy Eldridge,trumpets; Larry Altpeter,trombone; Clyde Hart,piano; Ken
         Binford,guitar; Hayes Alvis, bass; Johnny Williams,drums):            1940
Vo    5420. How High the Moon(W26517)/A House With a Little Red Barn(W26515)
Vo    5507. I'm Forever Blowing Bubbles(W26516)/Till We Meet Again(W26514)

RICHARD, CHUCK (Acc. by the Blue Rhythm Band):
Vo    2867. Love's Serenade/Like a Bolt from the Blues          -BrE 01983
Vo    2877. Blue Interlude/Devil in the Moon                    -BrE 01990
BrE 02009. Rainbow Filled With Music

RICHARDSON, INEZ (acc. by Fletcher Henderson Orch.):
BS    2023. -----

RICHARDSON ORCHESTRA, DICK (Joe Venuti's Orchestra):
PaA 34092. Promises

RICHARDSON, MOOCH (blues singer):
OK    8555. Mooch Richardson's Low Down Barrel House Blues, #1/T. & T. Blues
OK    8611. Mooch Richardson's Low Down Barrel House Blues, #2/Helena Blues

RICHMOND, JUNE (acc. by Johnny Warrington Orch):
Mer   2033. Don't Worry 'Bout That Mule(170)/Don't Jive Me Like That(172)

RIDLEY, ETHEL (blues vocals):
Aj  17126. Get It Fixed(31813; acc.Choo Choo Jazzers)/Low Down Daddy Blues
                                                     (31814; piano & clarinet)
         (Acc. Perry Bradford's Jazz Phools):
Vi  19111. Memphis Tennessee/If Anybody Here Wants a Real Kind Mama

         (Perry Bradford, piano):
Co    3941. Liza Johnson's Got Better Bread(81067)/Here's Your Opportunity
                                                                (Blues(81068)
RILEY AND HIS ORCHESTRA, MIKE:
De    1263. I'm Hatin' This Waitin' Around/Spending All My Time With the Blues
De    1271. Jammin'/That's Southern Hospitality
De    1655. You're Giving Me the Run-Around/Oh Boom
De    1662. Cachita/Oh Dear What Can the Matter Be

         RILEY-FARLEY AND THEIR ORCHESTRA:
De     578. Music Goes Round and Around                         -De  3364
       "    Lookin' for Love
De     619. I Never Knew/South
De     641. Wabash Blues/Blue Clarinet Stomp
De     683. I'm Gonna Clap My Hands                             -De  3364
       "    Not Enough
De     684. I Wish I Were Aladdin/You're Wicky-You're Wacky- You're Wonderful
De     994. High Hat a Piccolo and a Cane/Trouble Don't Like Music
De    1031. Jingle Bells/Santa Claus Is Comin' to Town
De    1041. With Thee I Swing/Hey Hey
```

RINGER'S ROSEMONT ORCHESTRA, JOHNNY: 1927
    Ge 6199. Swamp Blues/Rubber Heels

RINGGOLD, ISSIE (cornet and piano acc.):
    Co 14509. Be on Your Merry Way(149798)/He's a Good Meat Cutter(149797)

RITCHIE AND HIS BOYS, BUD):
    Ch 40010. Slappin' the Bass(17164-B)/Rockin' Chair(17162)

ROBECHAUX AND HIS NEW ORLEANS RHYTHM BOYS, JOSEPH (Joseph Robichaux,piano; Ward
Crosby,drums: Eugene Ware,trumpet: Eugene Porter,tenor sax; Alfred Gishard,alto
sax; Walter Williams,guitar; Rene Hall(?),banjo):   New York, 1932
    Vo 2539. St.Louis Blues(13852-2)/King Kong Stomp(13855-1)
    Vo 2540. Lazybones/Stormy Weather
    Vo 2545. You Keep Me Always Living in Sin/Jig Music
    Vo 2575. Ring Dem Bells/Forty-Second Street
    Vo 2592. The Riff(13859-1)/Shake It and Break It(13886-2)
    Vo 2610. After Me the Sun Goes Down(13860-2)/Why Should I Cry for You(13885-2)
    Vo 2646. Zola(13853-2)/I Would Do Anything for You(13877-1)
    Vo 2796. Foot Schuffle(13854-1)/Saturday Night Fish Fry Drag(13857-1)
    Vo 2827. Every Tub/She Don't Love Me
    Vo 2881. Sleep, Come On and Take Me(13875-1)/Just Like a Falling Star(13876-1)

ROBERTS, SALLY (acc. by Sylvester Weaver,guitar):
    OK 8500. Useless Blues/Black Hearse Blues

ROBERTS, SNITHCER (vocals with piano acc.):
    OK 8750. The Ducks Yas Yas Yas/Low Moanin' Blues(with piano and guitar)
    OK 8781. Your Heart Is Right Blues/Snitchers Blues(with piano and violin)

ROBERTSON AND HIS ORCHESTRA, DICK (Bunny Berigan,trumpet: Al Philburn,trombone;
Paul Ricci,clarinet: Frank Signorelli,piano; Carmen Mastren,guitar; Sid Weiss,
bass; Stan King,drums; Dick Robertson,vocals. . Panachord issues under name of
'Jack North's Orchestra').--"Hot Jazz":   March 16,1936
    Pan 25856. Lost(60900)   -DeE 5976
        "   Touch of Your Lips(60904)   -DeE 5950
    Pan 25860. Is It True What They Say About Dixie(60905)   -DeE 5967
    Pan 25865. Hills of Old Wyoming(60903)
    Pan 25871. It's a Sin to Tell a Lie(60902)
    Unissues. Welcome Stranger(60901) Note:--This title and "Lost"(see above),
              were coupled on American Decca 752 under the name of Benny Fields,
              but master numbers are lacking to establish whether they are
              Robertson items.
        (Personnel unknown):
    De 1099. Waltz You Saved for Me/Three o'clock in the Morning
    De 1125. Happy Days Are Here Again/Mardi Gras
    De 1131. Goodnight My Love/When My Dreamboat Comes Home
    De 1169. Marie(62030)/May I Have the Next Romance With You(62028)
    De 1181. When the Poppies Bloom Again(62027-A)/Wanted(62029-A)

        (Andy McKinney,trumpet; Russ Genner,trombone: Slats Long,clarinet; Herbie
        Haymer,tenor sax; Red Norvo,piano; Pete Peterson,bass: Maurice Purtill,
        drums):
    DeE 5995. I'll Bet You Tell That to All the Girls/On the Beach at Bali Bali

        (Bobby Hackett,cornet; Al Philburn,trombone: Paul Ricci,clarinet; Frank
        Froeba,piano; Frank Victor,guitar; Haig Stephens,bass; Sam Weiss,drums):
    De 1209. Little Old Lady(62074-A)
        "   Too Marvelous for Words(62075-A)   -Pan 25928
    De 1215. My Little Buckaroo(62076)   -Pan 25919
        "   September in the Rain(62077)   -Pan 25920

        (Sub. Sid Trucker,clarinet: Frank Signorelli,piano: Stan King,drums):
    De 1260. You'll Never Go to Heaven(62168)
        "   Toodle-oo(62169)   -Pan 25929
    De 1283. It Looks Like Rain in Cherry Blossom Lane(62170)   -Pan 25920
        "   On a Little Dream Ranch(62171)   "
    De 1334. Good Morning(62284)
        "   The Merry Go Round Broke Down(62286)   -Pan 25928
    De 1335. Gone With the Wind(62287-A)   -Pan 25942
        "   The Miller's Daughter Marianne(62285-A)

        (Sub. Johnny McGee,trumpet: Buddy Morrow, trombone):
    De 1367. Sailboat in the Moonlight(62418)
        "   Strangers in the Dark(62419)   -Pan 25942
    De 1374. My Cabin of Dreams(62420)   -Rex 9146
        "   Heaven Help This Heart of Mine(62421)

        (Johnny McGee, Ralph Muzzillo,trumpets: Philburn; Trucker; Froeba; Victor;
        Stephens; King):

97

De	1407.	Egg Tide(62559)	-Pan 25960
"		Carolina Town(62560)	
De	1415.	You Can't Stop Me from Dreaming(62561)	-Pan 25960
"		Blossoms on Broadway(62562)	-Pan 25953
De	1436.	Sidewalks of New York(62563)/Come Josephine in My Flying Machine	
			(62564)

(Sub Hackett, Johnny Carlson,trumpets; Don Watt,clarinet· Signorelli,pf):

De	1511.	In My Merry Oldsmobile(62666)	
"		Daisy Bell(62667)	-DeF 6845
De	1487.	Roses in December(62668)	-Pan 25953
"		Getting Some Fun Out of Life(62669)	

(Sub. Morrow, trombone: Froeba,piano):

De	1498.	Rollin' Plains(62696-A)	-DeE 6876
"		I Want You for Christmas(62697-B)	
De	1512.	Shanty in Old Shanty Town(62698)/I Wonder Who's Kissing Her Now(62700)	
De	1536.	That Old Gang of Mine(62703)/Won't You Come Over to My House(62704)	
De	1675.	Two Little Girls in Blue(62702)	-DeE 6844
"		I Wonder What's Become of Sally(63164)	"
De	1735.	My Gal Sal(62705)	-DeE 6817
"		Take Me Out to the Ball Game	
De	1758.	Sweet Rosie O'Grady(62701)	-DeE 6845
"		In the Good Old Summer Time	
De	1952.	That's How I Need You(62705)	-DeE 6816
"		Oh How I Miss You Tonight	
De	1979.	When It's Springtime in the Rockies(62699)/El Rancho Grande	

(McGee, Muzillo,trumpets; Philburn,trombone: Watt,clarinet: Signorelli, piano; Dave Barbour,guitar; Stephens,bass; King,drums):
Unissued. Somebody's Thinking of You Tonight(62859)

De	1585.	Ten Pretty Girls(62860)	
"		Little White Lighthouse(62861)	-Pan 25974

(Sub. Hackett,trumpet,for McGee):

De	1599.	House on the Hill(62892)/Sail Along,Silv'ry Moon(62895)	
De	1601.	Rhythm of the Snowflakes(62891)/Let's Waltz for Old Time's Sake	
DeF	6846.	Three o'clock in the Morning(62894)	(62893)
De	1619.	You're a Sweetheart(63162)	-Rex 9268
"		Somebody's Thinking of You Tonight(63165)	
De	1620.	Bob White(63161)/You Started Something(63163)	

(Jack Teagarden,trombone: McGee,Muzillo,trumpets: Tony Zimmers,sax and clarinet; Froeba;Barbour;Stephens;Weiss):

De	1706.	Drop a Nickel in the Slot(63355)	
"		You Went to My Head(63356)	-Pan 26003
De	1707.	Goodnight Angel(63353)	-Pan 25977
"		Let's Sail to Dreamland(63354)	-Pan 25984

Unknown personnel):

De	1726.	Oh mama(63375)/Cry Baby Cry(63374)
De	1823.	Dust/Teacher's Pet
De	1847.	Ferdinand the Bull/Mr. Wu, Chinese Laundry Blues
De	1914.	Hi-Yo Silver/When Mother Nature Sings Her Lullaby
De	2022.	Indiana Moonlight/No Wonder
De	2023.	All American Girl/You Gotta Be a Fottball Hero
De	2059.	Tutti Frutti/You're the Only Star
De	2146.	Memories/You're the Very Last Word in Love.
De	2260.	Gardenias/I Cried for You
De	2276.	Kermit the Hermit/My Melancholy Baby
De	2354.	I Promise You/Penny Serenade
De	2364.	I'm a Lucky Devil/I'm Building a Sailboat of Dreams
De	2419.	It Makes No Difference Now/Little Skipper
De	2497.	Pippinella/Where Do You Work-a John
De	2541.	Ain't Cha Comin' Out/Maybe

(Bobby Hackett,trumpet, included):

De	2765.	Baby Me/What Good Will It Do
De	2807.	I Only Want a Buddy Not a Sweetheart(66612A)/Who Did You Meet Last
		(Night(65606)

(Unknown personnel):

De	2782.	Night Before Christmas/That's What I Want for Christmas
De	2827.	Are You Havin' Any Fun/Comes Love
De	2828.	Hello Mister Kringle/Somebody Told Me They Loved Me
De	2845.	Lilacs in the Rain/O Johnny O Johnny
De	2920.	Ma/She Had to Go and Lose It at the Astor
De	2926.	As 'Round and 'Round We Go/Put Your Little Foot Right Out
De	2973.	Boomps-a-Daisy/Playmates
De	3031.	All Alone/Row Row Row
De	3124.	Little Girl/Ain't You Ashamed
De	3125.	I Wish I Had Died in My Cradle/Wreck of the Old '97
De	3141.	If I Could Be With You/I Want a Girl

```
De  3189.  Gang That Sang Heart of My Heart/Guy Needs a Gal
De  3304.  Goodbye Little Darlin Goodbye/I'll Never Smile Again
De  3305.  Ferryboat Serenade/On a Simmery Summery Day
De  3323.  I Am an American/You're a Grand Old Flag
De  3349.  Breaking My Heart to Keep Away from You/When I Get You Alone Tonite
De  3378.  Darling How Can You Forget So Soon/My Greatest Mistake
De  3410.  Hello Little Girl of My Dreams/It's a Mighty Pretty Night for Love
De  3462.  Connie's Got Connections in Connecticut/Mickey
De  3558.  Oh How I Hate to Get Up in the Morning/They're Making Me All Over in
De  3559.  I Used to Love You/San Antonio Rose                  (the Army
De  3607.  Go Home Little Girl Go Home/So You're the One
De  3632.  Many Happy Returns of the Day/My Greenwich Village Sue
De  3659.  Sidewalk Serenade/Wise Old Owl
De  3669.  Blues/Somebody Stole My Gal
De  3707.  It's a Sin to Tell a Lie/Waltz Was Born in Vienna
De  3791.  Be Honest With Me/Goodbye Dear I'll Be Back in a Year
De  3792.  G'Bye Now/Just a Little Bit South of North Carolina
De  3908.  Answer to You Are My Sunshine/$21 a day--Once a Month
De  3961.  Got a Letter from My Kid Today/What's the Good of Moonlight
De  3981.  I Don't Want to Set the World on Fire/I'm Alone Because I Love You
De  4031.  Till We Meet Again/Wedding Bells
De  4060.  The Only Thing I Want for Christmas/Under the Mistletow
De  4116.  I May Stay Away a Little Longer/Goodbye Mamma
De  4117.  We Did It Before/Everyone's a Fighting Son of That Old Gang
De  4129.  When Your Old Wedding Ring was New/I Had Someone Else Before I Had
De  4144.  You're a Sap Mister Jap/Remember Pearl Harbor              (You
De  4151.  One for All All for One/I Paid My Income Tax Today
De  4167.  Daddy You've Been a Mother to Me/Dear Mom
De  4189.  On the Street of Regret/Walking the Floor Over You
De  4233.  I Hate to Lose You/Twenty-one years
De  4283.  I'm in Love With the Girl I Left Behind Me/Keep 'em Flying
De  4294.  She Don't Wanna/One Dozen Roses
De  4308.  Wings Over the Navy/Eyes of the Fleet
De  4318.  Hats Off to MacArthur/This Time
De  4330.  You Gotta Quit Cheatin' on Me/Uncle Eph's Got the Coon
De  4365.  Ching/Isabella Kissed a Fella
De  4373.  Under a Strawberry Moon/Oh Pardon Me
```

ROBERTSON, JIM (blues singer)
  BB 8686. Brother Henry/Birmingham Woman

ROBERTSON, ZUE (trombone. See Jelly Roll Morton: OK 8105.)

ROBINSON, ELZADIE (vocal):
Para 12420. Humming Blues/Houston Bound

    (Acc. by Will Ezell, piano):
Para 12417. Barrelhouse Man(400)/Sawmill Man(399)
Para 12509. Whiskey Blues(736)/Back Door Blues(735)
Para 12544. Tick Tock Blues/Hour Behind the Sun
Para 12573. St.Louis Cyclone Blues(Bob Call,piano)/Santa Claus Crave(Bob Call)

    (Johnny Dodds(?), clarinet):
Para 12635. Elzadie's Policy Blues(20534)/Pay Day Blues(20528)

    (Will Ezell, piano):
Para 12689. Wicked Daddy/It's Too Late Now
Para 12701. Arkansas Mill Blues(20910-3)/Gold Mansion Blues(20911-1)
Para 12724. Rowdy Man Blues(20912)/Going South Blues(20913)
Para 12768. Cheatin' Daddy/Your Last Night
Para 12795. My Pullman Porter Man/Ain't Got Nobody

ROBINSON AND HIS BULL FIDDLE BAND, BANJO IKEY (Jabbo Smith,trumpet, is reported
to play in the first record below):
  Br 7057. Ready Hokum/Got Butter on It
  Br 7059. Rock Me Mama/My Four Reasons
  Br 7068. You've Had You Way/Without a Dime(vocal only)

    (Vocal only):
  Br 7052. Pizen Tea Blues/Rockpile Blues

      BANJO IKEY ROBINSON AND HIS WINDY CITY FIVE:
  Ch 40011. Scrunch-Lo(90057-A)/Swing It(90060-A)   -De 7430
  Ch 50073. Sunshine(90058-A)/"A" Minor Stomp(90059-A)   -De 7650
           (See also: Pods of Pepper)

ROBINSON, JIM (trombone; see):
  BUNK JOHNSON: All but Jazz Information.
  GEORGE LEWIS NEW ORLEANS STOMPERS: All.
  SAM MORGAN: All.
  ORIGINAL CREOLE STOMPERS: AM 513.
  ORIGINAL ZENITH BRASS BAND: Ci 1005, 1006, 1007.
  KID RENA: All Delta

```
         JIM ROBINSON'S BAND (Jim Robinson,trombone; George Lewis,clarinet; Law-
         rence Marrero,banjo; Slow Drag,bass: Baby Dodds,drums):     July,1944
   AM    254. Ic Cream/(GEORGE LEWIS)
```

ROBINSON, MABEL (with Sam Price's Blusicians):
   De 8601. Me and My Chauffeur(70187-A)/I've Got Too Many Blues(70188-A)

ROBINSON, ROB (vocals,acc. by Meade Lux Lewis,piano):
   Para 13028. I Got Some of That(608)/The Preacher Must Get Some Sometime(609)
   Para 13030. Don't Put That Thing on Me(610)/Sittin' on Top of the World(611)
   Para 13064.

         BOB ROBINSON AND HIS BOB CATS (with Meade Lux Lewis):
   BB   6929. Makin' a Fool Out of Me/She's a Mellow Thing

ROBINSON AND MACK (Sam Robinson and Mary Mack) vocals acc.Richard M.Jones,piano):
   OK   8259. Don't Lose Your Head/I Beg to Be Excused
   OK   8298. It's All the Same to Me/Make Room for Someone Else

         SAM ROBINSON (acc. by Richard M. Jones,piano):
   OK   8321.

ROBINSON AND HIS ORCHESTRA, WILLARD):
   Pat 36630. At Sundown/(LUCKY DEVILS)   -Pe 14811
   Pat 36631. Hallelujah/(LUCKY DEVILS)   -Pe 14812
   Pat 36640. Harlem Blues/(LOU GOLD)   -Pe 14821
   Pe 14847. Blue Baby Why Are You Blue(MIKE SPECIALE)
   Pat 36668. Blue River/New Hampshire   -Pe 14849
   Pat 36655. Flapperette/Lotus Land

         (Featuring Bix Beiderbecke,cornet; Frankie Trumbauer,sax; Don Murray,clar-
         inet; Arthur Schutt,piano; Carl Kress,guitar; Vic Berton,drums):   1926
   Pe 14905. I'm More than Satisfied(1)/(PALCE GARDEN ORCHESTRA)
   Pat 36724. I'm More Than Satisfied(2)/(PALACE GARDEN ORCHESTRA)

         (Featuring Schutt,piano):
   Pe 14925. The Man I Love/Thou Swell

         (Unknown personnel):
   Vi 21651. Deep River/'Tain't So Honey Tain't So
   Vi 21866. If I Had You
   Co   1772. Blue Hawaii/A Garden in the Rain
   Co   1818. Head Low/Peach of Mind
   Co   1948. Beale Street Blues/Harlem Blues
   Co   2268. Tall Timber/In the Wilderness

RODGERS, GENE (piano):
   JD   8888. Rhapsody Boogie/Poet and Peasant Boogie

IKE RODGERS

See also:
   HENRY BROWN: Para 12825, 12934.
   EDITH JOHNSON: Para 12823, 12864.
   MARY JOHNSON: Para 12996; Br 7081, 7093.
   ALICE MOORE: Para 12819, 12868, 13107.

RODGERS, IKE (trombone solo, acc. by Henry Brown,piano):
   Para 12816. It Hurts So Good/Screenin' the Blues   -Cen 3003

         IKE ROGERS AND HIS BIDDLE STREET BOYS:
   Br   7086. Malt Can Blues/(HENRY BROWN)

GIL RODIN

See also:
   BEN'S BAD BOYS.
   BRACKEN
   BROADWAY BROADCASTERS.
LOU CONNOR: Or 1483.
   COTTON PICKERS: Ca 9048, 9207.
   BOB CROSBY.
   DIXIE JAZZ BAND: Or 1624, 1668, 1690.
   KENTUCKY GRASSHOPPERS: All.
   LOUISVILLE RHYTHM KINGS: OK 41189, PaF 22305.
   LUMBERJACKS: Ca 9030.
   BEN POLLACK: Vi, Pe, HoW, Co.
   CLARK RANDALL:
   GRANT AND WILSON: Ca 9015.
   TEN BLACKBERRIES:
   UNIVERSITY BOYS:
   TED WHITE:
   WHOOPEE MAKERS

RODIN AND HIS ORCHESTRA, GIL (Jack Teagarden,trombone and vocal; Sterling Bose, cornet; Jimmy Dorsey,clarinet; Gil Rodin,alto sax; Eddie Miller,tenor sax; Vic Brledis or Gil Bowers,piano; Ray Bauduc,drums: Hilton Lamare,guitar; Harry Goodman,bass): 1931
  Cr 3016. If I Could Be With You(1011)-2B)/FRANK NOVAK)
  Cr 3017. Beale Street Blues(1010; Eddie Gale, vocal)
  Cr 3045. 99 Out of a Hundred Wanna Be Loved(1117-1A)/(BOB REYNOLDS)
  Cr 3046. Hello Beautiful(1118-3B)/(JACK ALBIN)

    (Same personnel as for Clark Randall Orch.):
  Me 13377. Restless(17050)/What's the Reason(17049)   - Or 3130

    (Unknown personnell):
  Me 13376. Right About Face/Love's Serenade

ROGERS' RED PEPPERS, RODNEY:
  3744. Milenberg Joys/Chili Blues

ROLAND, WALTER (piano (and vocal?):
  Pe 0293. Collector Man Blues/C.W.A. Blues
  Pe 0322. Screw Worm/School Boy Blues
  Cq 8491. Dices Blues/Early in the Morning
      (See also: Lucille Bogan; Bessie Jackson)

ADRIAN ROLLINI

See also:
  BERNARD ADDISON: BB 6144, 6174.
  ADRIAN'S RAMBLERS: Br 6786, 6877, 6889; Vo 2675.
  ADRIAN'S TAP ROOM GANG: Vi 25072, 25085, 25208.
  ALL STARS: Vi 26144.
  BIX BEIDERBECKE: OK 40923, 41001.
  RUBE BLOOM: Co 2103, 2186, 2218.
  JEAN BURNS: BrE 02095, 02342.
  CALIFORNIA RAMBLERS.
  CAROLINA WANDERERS.
  CORNELL: OK 41386.
  DUBIN'S DANDIES(?)
  CLIFF EDWARDS: Pe 11566, 11626.
  FRED ELIZALDE.
  FIVE BIRMINGHAM BABIES.
  FOUR INSTRUMENTAL STARS: Pat 11485.
  GOLDEN GATE.
  GOOFUS FIVE.
  RUSSELL GRAY: OK 40938.
  GORDON GRIMES: Ch 15322.
  FRED HALL.
  FREDDIE JENKINS: BB 6129, 6193.
  LITTLE RAMBLERS:
  LOUISIANA RHYTHM KINGS: Br 4706, 4845, 4908, 4923, 4938, 4953.
  DICK McDONOUGH:
  BENNY MEROFF: OK 40912.
  MIFF MOLE: OK 40890, 40932, 40984, 41371.
  NEW ORLEANS LUCKY SEVEN: OK 8544.
  RED NICHOLS:
  JACK PURVIS.
  FRANKIE TRUMBAUER.
  JOE VENUTI.

ROLLINI AND HIS ORCHESTRA, ADRIAN (Mannie Klein,trumpet; Tommy Dorsey,trombone; Benny Goodman,clarinet; Jimmy Dorsey,clarinet and alto; Art Rollini,tenor sax; Arthur Schutt,piano; Dick McDonough,guitar; Adrian Rollini,bass sax; and others,-- Discobraphy, 9/15/43): April, 1933
  PaE 2515. Blue Prelude(265131)/Mississippi Basin(265132)
  Unissued. Charlie's Home(265133)
  Co 2785. Happy As the Day Is Long(265134)

    (Sub. Fulton McGrath,piano; Ed Lang,guitar; omit Goodman; add Joe Venuti,
    violin; Jack Cornell,accordion; Art Miller,bass):
  Pe 15736. You've Got Me Cryin'Again(13050)   -Me 12630,DeE 3158
    "   Hustlin' & Bustlin' for baby(13051)   -Im 2846,Me "   "

    (Bunny Berigan,trumpet; Al Philburn,trombone; Pee Wee Russell,clarinet;
    Art Rollini,tenor; Adrian Rollini,bass sax; McDonough; Miller; Herb Weil,
    drums and vocal; Red McKenzie, vocal*):
  Pe 15799. Ah But Is It Love(13663)   -Me 12756,DeE 3702
    "   I've Gotta Get Up and Go to Work*(13664)   "
  Pe 15805. If I Had Somebody to Love/Dream On   -Me 12766
  Pe 15817. By a Waterfall(13999)   -Me 12788,Or 2757,Ro 2130,Cq 822-
    "   Backyard Fence(14000)   -DeE 3827, "   "   "   "
  Pe 15819. I'll Be Faithful(14001)   -Me 12790
    "   Beloved(14002)   -DeE 3848,   "

```
            Goodman, clarinet; McGrath, piano):
                                                                     -Me 12815
   Pe 15831.  You've Got Everything(14147)
      "       And So Goodbye(14148)                    -DeE 3796,       "
   Pe 15839.  Sweet Madness(14152;Herb Weil,voc.)      -Or 2784,Me 12829
      "       Savage Serenace(14153;Clay Bryson,voc)   -DeE 3827,   "      "
   Me 12855.  Sittin' on a Log(14380; Jane Vance)      -Or 2803,DeE 3848
      "       I Raised My Hat(14381; Herb Weil,voc.)          "
   Me 12866.  Song of Surrender(14378)/Coffee in Morning(14379) howard Phillips,voc.
   Me 12892.  On the Wrong Side of the Fence(14565)/Ol' Pappy(14566)
   Me 12893.  Who Walks In(14567)/Got the Jitters(14568)       -Or 2829

            (Bunny Berigan,Manny Klein,trumpets; Fulton McGrath,piano; Arthur Rollini,
            tenor sax; Adrian Rollini, bass sax; Benny Goodman,clarinet: George Van
            Eps,guitar; Jack Teagarden,trombone: Artie Bernstein,bass; Stan King,
            drums):                                                      1934
   De   265. Sugar(38875-A)                                      -BrE 01942
      "      Riverboat shuffle(38878-A)                          -BrE 02510
   De   359. Davenport Blues(38876)                      -De 3862,BrE 01942
      "      Somebody Loves Me(38877)                    -De 3525,BrE 03447

            (Personnel as for Pe 15831):
   Vo  2672. A Thousand Good Nights(14995)                       -DeE 3989
      "      Butterfingers(14996)                                -DeE 3967
   Vo  2673. Waitin' at the Gate for Katy(14997)    -DeE 5009, Edison Winner 126
      "      Little Did I Dream(14998)                           -DeE 5009
   Vo  2675. How Can It Be a Beautiful Day(14999)                -DeE 3967

            (Featuring Irving Goodman,trumpet: Art Dollinger,tenor,clarinet: Adrian
            Rollini,bass sax and vibraphone: Jack Rusin,piano: Gwynn Hestor,guitar;
            George Hnida,bass; Phil Silman,drums):                       1936
   De   787. Tap Room Swing(60906)                                -CoE 5006
      "      Lessons in Love(60909)
   De   807. Swing Low(60907)                                     -CoE 5006
      "      Stuff, Etc.(60908)                                   -CoE 5024

            (Jonah Jones,trumpet; Sid Stoneberg,clarinet: Art and Adrian Rollini; Mc-
            Grath; McDonough; Hnida; Al Seidel,drums):
   Ma   114. Slap That Bass(322)/Let's Call the Whole Thing Off(323)

            ADRIAN ROLLINI TRIO(Rollini,vibraphone,with Frank Victor,guitar; Haig
            Stephens,bass):                                              1937-8
   De  1132. Vibrollini(61455)                                    -BrE 02380
      "      Jitters(61508)                                       -BrE 12404
   De  1157. Driftin'(61456)                                      -BrE 02380
      "      Rebound(61507)                                       -BrE 12404

            ADRIAN ROLLINI QUINTET (Bobby Hackett,cornet; Frank Victor,guitar; Frank
            Clark,bass; Buddy Rich,drums; Rollini,vibes: Sunny Skylar,vocals):  1938
   De  1638. Bei Mir Bist Du Schon(63174)/(for coupling see Orchestra below)
   De  1639. Josephine(63175)
      "      You're a Sweetheart(63176)                           -BrE 02579
   De  1654. True Confession(63177)                               -BrE 02579
      "      I've hitched my wagon to a Star(63178)

            ADRIAN ROLLINI AND HIS ORCHESTRA (Johnny McGee,trumpet: Paul Ricci,clari-
            net; Adrian Rollini,bass sax; Al Duffy,violin; Jack Rusin,piano; Victor;
            Clark; Rich; Pat Hoke,vocals):
   De  1638. Bill(63138)                                          -VoE 191
   De  1973. Singin' the Blues(63139)                             -VoE 191
      "      The Sweetest Story Ever Told(63140)

            QUINTET (Same personnel as previously):
   Vo  4212. Ten Easy Lessons(23147)/Small Fry(23148)             -CoE 2057
   Vo  4257. I Wish I Had You(23149)/Bumpy Road to Love(23150)

            TRIO: (Rollini; Victor; Clark):                              1939
   Vo  5621. I Can't Believe You're in Love With Me(1084)/Dardanella(1088)
   Vo  5435. Fstrellita(1083)/Dark Eyes(1087)
   Vo  5376. Stardust--Solitude(1085?)/Diga Diga Do(1086?)
   Vo  5200. Moonglow(1089)/Pavanne(1090)
   Vo  5582. Honky Tonk Train Blues(1147)/Martha(1149)            1940.
   OK  5979. Isle of Capri/The Girl With the Light Blue Hair

            (Unknown Personnel ):
   Feature 1005. Lili Marlene/First Class Private Mary Brown
   Feature 1006. Hesitation Blues/Is You Is Or Is You Ain't My Baby
```

ROSE AND HIS ORCHESTRA, VINCENT (Benny Goodman's Orchestra: Sam Shapiro, Russ
Case, Jerry Neary,trumpets; Jack Lacey, Red Ballard, trombones; Benny Goodman,
clarinet; Ben Kantor, Hymie Schertzer, altos; Arthur Rollini,tenor; Claude
Thornhill,piano; George Van Eps,guitar; Harry Goodman,bass; Sam Weiss,drums;
Tony Sacco,vocals): <u>Sept.11.1934</u>
    Pe 16001. Learning(15881)/Stars Fell on Alabama(15882)   -Me 13158, Or 2989

ROSELAND DANCE ORCHESTRA (Fletcher Henderson's Orchestra with Louis Armstrong
  Do 3445. I'll See You in My Dreams(original issue: Re 9775)   (trumpet):

ROSENKRANTZ AND HIS BARONS, TIMMIE (Red Norvo,vibraphone; Charlie Venturo,Otto
Hardwicke, Johnny Bothwell, Harry Carney,saxes; Jimmy Jones,piano; Specs Powell,
drums; J.O. Levey, bass):
  Cont 6012. Blues at Dawn(W-3345)/Bouncy(W-3344)

ROSENTHAL AND HIS ORCHESTRA, HARRY (Benny Goodman's Orch.:See Broadway Bandits):
  Co 2986. You're the Top(16347)/All Through the Night(16348)

ROSS DE LUXE SYNCOPATORS (Cootie Williams,Melvin Herbert,trumpets; Eddie
Williams,trombone; Edmond Hall,Robert Cloud,Earl Evans,reeds; Alonzo Ross,piano;
Casper Tower,banjo; Dick Fulbright,bass; Frank Houston,drums.--JI 8/9/40): <u>1927</u>
  Vi 20952. Mary Bell/Lady Mine
  Vi 20961. Skad-o-lee/Florida Rhythm
  Vi 21077. Monia/Baby Stop Teasin' Me
  Unissued. Don't You Wanta Know/Believe Me Dear

ROSS, DOLLY (vocals):
  Br 7005. He Don't Know/Hootin' Owl Blues

ROSS, LOUISE (vocals):
  Co 14118. Can't Fool Me Blues/No Home Blues

ROSS, OLLIE, (vocals):
  Br 7045. Broad Road Blues/Ox-Meat Blues

ROUNDERS, THE (Whoopee Makers issue):
  Re 8831. Lovable and Sweet(108929-3)

RUCKER, LAURA (vocals acc. by Cassino Simpson,piano):
  Para 13075. St.Louis Blues/Little Joe
  Para 13087. St. James Infirmary/Upside Down

      LAURA RUCKER AND HER SWING BOYS:
  De 7260. Something's Wrong/Swing My Rhythm

LUIS RUSSELL

See also:
  ADA BROWN: Vo 1009.
  HENRY ALLEN: All Victor; Pe 16071, 16080.
  LOUIS ARMSTRONG: OK 8669,8680, 8756, 8774, 41350, 41375; De 579-685; 797-866;
    De 1347-1842; 2267-3105; 3204-18091.
  WILTON CRAWLEY:
  DIXIE JAZZ BAND: Or 1726, 1728
  HANDY: Vs 8162, 8163.
  HIGGINBOTHAM: OK 8772.
  SPIKE HUGHES: DeE 3639, 3836, 5101.
  LAZY LEVEE LOUNGERS: Co 2243.
  LOU AND HIS GINGER SNAPS: Ba 6536, 6540.
  KING OLIVER: Vo, Br, and some Vi.
  SAVANNAH SYNCOPATORS: Br 6046.

RUSSELL'S HOT SIX (George Mitchell,trumpet; Kid Ory,trombone; Albert Nicholas,
clarinet and alto sax; Barney Bigard,tenor sax; Luis Russell,piano; Paul Barbarin,drums; bass; guitar.--JI Dec.20,1940):
  Vo 1010. Sweet Mumtaz/29th and Dearborn   -OrE 1003

      LUIS RUSSELL'S HEEBIE JEEBIE STOMPERS(Bob Shoffner,trumpet; Preston Jack-
    son,trombone; Darnell Howard,alto sax; Barney Bigard,tenor sax; Luis Russell,
    piano; John St.Cyr,guitar; Paul Barbarin,drums): <u>1926</u>
  OK 8424. Plantation Joys(9903-A)/Please Don't Turn Me Down(9904-A)
  OK 8454. Sweet Mumtaz(9905-A)/Dolly Mine (9906-A)

      LUIS RUSSELL AND HIS BURNING EIGHT (Louis Metcalf,trumpet; J.C.Higgin-
    botham,trombone; Charlie Holmes,alto sax; Teddy Hill,tenor; Albert Nich-
    olas,clarinet; Russell,piano; Will Johnson,guitar; J. Moore,tuba; Paul
    Barbarin,drums): <u>Jan 5,1929</u>
  OK 8656. Call of the Freaks(401533-B)/It's Tight Like That(401534-A)
  OK 8760. Savoy Shout(401532)   -Vo 3480,PaF 2523
      LUIS RUSSELL AND HIS ORCHESTRA (Henry Allen, Bill Coleman,trumpet; Higg-
    inbotham; Nicholas; Holmes; Hill; Russell; Johnson; Barbarin; Pops Foster,
    bass): <u>Sept.,1939</u>
  OK 8734. The(New) Call of the Freaks(402938-C)   -Co 35960,PaF 1645
    "   Jersey Lightning(402940-B)   " PaE 740

```
    OK  8766. Feeling the Spirit(402939-C)/(see below for coupling)   -PaE 1882

        (Sub.Otis Johnson,trumpet,for Coleman):                        Jan.2,1930
    OK  8766. Doctor Blues(403524-C)                      -Vo 3480, PaE 1273
    OK  8780. Saratoga Shout(403680-A)                              -PaE 2225
     "        Song of the Swanee(403682-C)                          -PaE 1669

        (Allen, Higginbotham, Holmes, Nicholas, Hill, Russell, Johnson, Foster,
        Barbarin):                                                   June,1930
    OK  8811. Louisiana Swing(404047)                                -PaE  795
     "        On Revival Day(404049)                                 -PaE 2186
    OK  8830. Poor Li'l Me(404048-C)/

        (Sub. Greely Walton,tenor,for Hill):                         Sept.1930
    OK  8830. Mugging Lightly(404428-B)                              -PaE  934
    OK  8849. Panama(404429)                                         -PaE  963
     "        High Tension(404430)                                   -PaE 1064
    Vo  1579. Saratoga Drag(E35758-C)                   -Br 80038,BrE 02503
     "        Case on Dawn(E35759-C)                        "       BrE 02002
    Me 12000. I Got Rhythm

        (Henry Allen,Robert Cheeks,Gus Atkins,trumpets: Dickie Wells,trombone:
        Albert Nicholas,clarinet and alto: Henry Jones,alto: Greely Walton,tenor;
        Luis Russell,piano; Pops Foster,bass· Paul Barbarin,drums):       1931
    Vi 22789. Goin' to Town(70196)/Say the Word(70197)            -HMV 4907
    Vi 22793. You Rascal You(70195)/(BENNIE MOTEN)                -HMV 4881
    Vi 22815. Freakish Blues(70198)/(SNOOKS)                      -HMV 4897

        (Leonard Davis,Rex Stewart,Gus Atkins,trumpets: Nathaniel Story,James
        Archey,trombones; Henry Jones,Charlie Holmes,Bingie Madison,Greely Wal-
        ton,saxes: Luis Russell,piano: Pops Foster,bass; Barbarin,drums):    1934
    Pe 15995. Ol' Man River(15576-1)               -Me 13146,Ba 33179,VoE 13
     "        At the Darktown Strutters Ball(15571-1)      "    "   VoE 009
    Pe 16086. Hokus Pokus(15574-1)/Ghost of the Freaks(15573-1) -Me 13334, VoE  2
    Pe 16103. Primitive(15575)                            -Me 13366, VoE 13
     "        My Blue Heaven(15572)                         "       VoF 009
        (Unknown personnel):
    Manor 1006. Boogie in the Basement/You Taught Me to Smile Again
    Manor 1022. After Hour Creep/Garbage Man Blues
    Ap  1012. Sad Lover Blues
    Ap  1020. Don't Take Your Love From Me/Sweet Memory
    Ap  1022. I've Got a Gal/1280 Jive
    Ap  1035 . All the Things You Are/My Silent Love
```

PEE WEE RUSSELL

See also:
BILLY BANKS: Pe 15615,15620,15642; HRS 17.   CLIFF JACKSON: BW 3, 4.
VIC BERTON: Vo 2944,2964,2974.   JAM SESSION: Com 1500,1501,1504,
JACK BLAND: Pe 15689, 15694, Co 35841.   1505,1513.
GEORGE BRUNIX: Com 546,556.   LOUISIANA R.KINGS: Vo 15815,15828.
CARMICHAEL: Vi 22864, 23013.   MOUND CITY BLUE BLOWERS:Vi 38100.
BUDDY BLACK: Vs 8230, 8233.   RED NICHOLS: Br 4778.
EDDIE CONDON: BrF 500328,500406; Co 35680;   NICK'S: All Manhattan.
De 18040,18041; Com 500,502,515,530,531,   PRIMA: Br 7448-7666.
535,536,542,551,1509, 1510.   ADRIAN ROLLINI.
WILD BILL DAVISON: Com 1511   MUGGSY SPANIER: Com 576; Disc 6030,
BUD FREEMAN: Com 507,508; De 2781,2849;   6031, 6032.
18064-18067: BB 10370,10386;Co 35853-35856. THE THREE DEUCES: Com 537, 539.
TEDDY GRACE.   LEE WILEY: Liberty.
BOBBY HACKETT:Vo 4047,4142,4499,4565,4806,   TEDDY WILSON: Br 8112, 8116.
                                  (4877.

RUSSELL'S RHYTHMAKERS, PEE WEE(Max Kaminsky,trumpet; Dickie Wells,trombone; Pee
Wee Russell,clarinet; Al Gold,tenor sax; James P.Johnson,piano; Freddie Green,gui-
tar; Wellman Braud,bass; Zutty Singleton,drums):   1938
   HRS 1000. Dinah/Baby Won't You Please Come Home
   HRS   17. Baby Won't You Please Come Home(second master)
   HRS 1001. There'll Be Some Changes Made(23392)/Horn of Plenty Blues(23393)
            (See also: Pee Wee, James P. and Zutty)

        PEE WEE RUSSELL'S JAZZ ENSEMBLE(Pee Wee Russell,clarinet; Muggsy Spanier,
        cornet; Cliff Jackson,piano; Joe Grauso,drums; Vic Dickenson,trombone;
        Bob Casey or Francis Palmer,bass):   1946

   Disc Album 632. Muskogee Blues
         "   I'd Climb the Highest Mountain
         "   Since My Best Gal Turned Me Down
         "   Rosie
         "   Take Me to the Land of Jaz
         "   Red Hot mama

RECORD RELEASE DATES
Compiled by Arthur H. Feher

The tabulation below shows the dates at which records were put on sale by various recording companies. This is a chart of *release dates* not of recording dates.

The figures presented are the serial numbers of the first records to be released in the respective years. Generally speaking the record companies did follow a numerical sequence in making their releases, but on each label there are some numbers that were withheld a week or two or as long as two months in some cases.

BA	BB	BN	BR	YEAR	CA	CO	CQ	DE		
	340738	48	80073	1946		36865		8672	18725	23467
	340718	300830	40	80060	1945	36760		4450	8670	18635	23370
	340708	300819	24	80050	1944	36690		4425	8655	18575	23280
	340701	300803	NONE	80000	1943	36665		4400	8645	18530	
	8900	11410	21		1942	36480	9900	4110	7880	8590	18200	23245
	8600	10990	17		1941	35900	9560	3540	7700	8500	18100	23195
	8330	10550	13	8480	1940	35330	9250	2920	7670			23100
	7960	10080		8280	1939		9050	2200	7550			23075
80101	7340			8040	1938		8920	1580	7390			23060
70101	6730			7790	1937		8720	1050	7260			23010
60101	6210			7550	1936	3110	8550	620			
33310	5780			7330	1935	2980	8400	310			
32920	5330			6690	1934	2860	(RACE)	8200	DF	DO	GE	HA.
32655				6450	1933	2740	14675	8030				
32330				6220	(RACE) 7230	1932	2580	14635	7870			
32000				4980	7180	1931	2340	14570	7550	3250			1250
6380				4550	7120	1930	9300	2040	14480	6350	3060			1060
6200				4160	7010	1929	8360	1660	14380	7100	2790	4220	6700		790
6120				3750		1928	1260	1220	14270		2550	4060	6310		550
1860				3380		1927	1030	830	14175		2310	3830	6000		310
1635				3020		1926	810	530.	14110			3600	5750	3410	70
1440				2760		1925	610	280	14050			410	5600	3180	
1275				2540		1924	420	20	14000			240	5300		

ME	OK	OR	PARA	PAT	YEAR	PE	RE	RO	SI	VE	VI	VO	
					1946						201750		
	6730				1945						201615		
	6715				1944						201550		
	6700				1943						201510		
	6525				1942				650		27710		
	5955				1941				500		27260		
					1940						26440	5270	
					1939						26125	4550	
80101					1938	80101					25720	3810	
70101			70101		1937	70101		70101			25480	3400	
60101			60101		1936	60101		60101			25210	3125	
13270			3065		1935	16040		2440			24820	2875	
12875			2820		1934	15870		2190			24460	2620	(RACE)
12565		(RACE)	2620		1933	15710		1980			24195	23375	1730
12285	41535	8925	2390		1932	15545		1750			22865		1675
12040	41475	8845	2150		1931	15375	10190	1510	9630		22580	23025	1565
	41340	8745		12865	37070	1930	15250		1090			22210	38100	1450
	41160	8645	1300		36885	1929	15066	8660	830	9220	1790	21770	38000	15740	1230
	40950	8525	1000		36710	1928	14890	8440	500		1550	21070		15640	1160
	40720	8415			36544	1927	14725	8170	330		1310	20330		15450	1005
	40520	8280	510	12325	036359	1926	14540	9940	190			19860		15150	
	40200	8165	320	12230	036161	1925	14342	9740		4000		19520		14900	
	4040	8090	165	12080	036011	1924	14192	9570		2300		19205		14690	

105

Authentic Jazz

ON UNBREAKABLE

VINYLITE PRESSINGS

- NEW ORLEANS STOMPERS
- IDA COX
- KING OLIVER
- LOVIE AUSTIN
- TOMMY LADNIER
- NORK
- BIX
- YOUNG'S CREOLE JAZZ BAND
- BARREL HOUSE 5
- JIMMY BLYTHE
- JELLY-ROLL MORTON
- JOHNNY DODDS
- MUGGSY SPANIER
- CLARENCE WILLIAMS
- ETC.

For Complete Catalog Write To

VINYLITE JAZZ
211 East 15th Street, New York City 3

the jazz man
RECORD SHOP
6420 Santa Monica Boulevard
HOLLYWOOD 38, CALIFORNIA

• NEW • USED • OUT OF PRINT • ORIGINALS • REISSUES OF HOT JAZZ CLASSICS • SEND YOUR WANT LIST • SET PRICES ON ALL ITEMS • PHOTOGRAPHS • MAGAZINES • BOOKS •

VOLUME FOUR

INDEX TO JAZZ

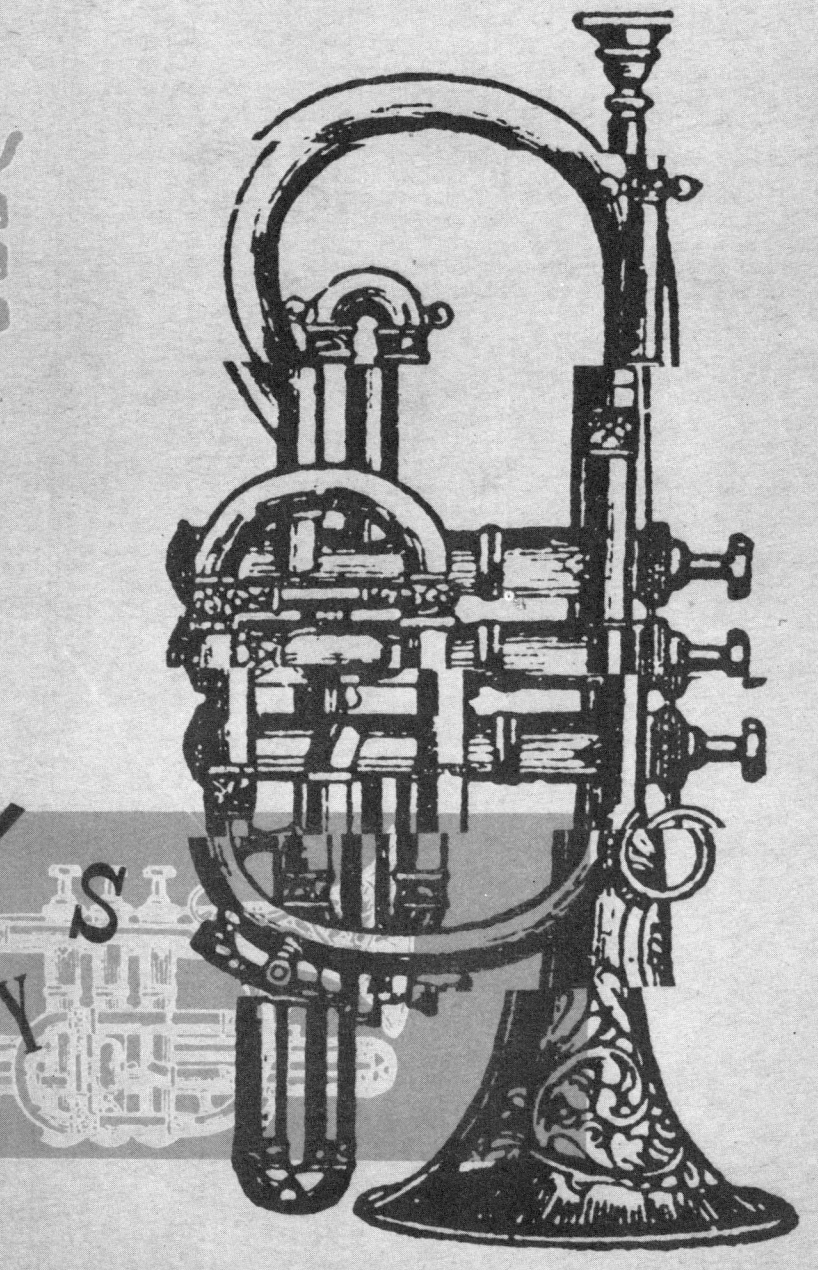

BY ORIN BLACKSTONE

ABBREVIATIONS — RECORDS

Ae	Aeolian Vocalion	JI	Jazz Information
Aj	Ajax	JM	Jazz Man
AM	American Music	JR	Jazz Record
Ap	Apex	Key	Keynote
Au	Autograph	KJ	King Jazz
Ba	Banner	Li	Lincoln
BB	Bluebird	Ma	Master
Bea	Beacon	Mad	Madison
BN	Blue Note	Man	Manhattan
BP	Black Patti	Max	Maxsa
Br	Brunswick	Me	Melotone
BrE	English Brunswick	Mu	Musicraft
BrF	French Brunswick	MW	Montgomery Ward
BrG	German Brunswick	Na	National
BS	Black Swan	Nor	Nordskog
Bu	Buddy	OdF	French Odeon
B&W	Black and White	OdG	German Odeon
Bwy	Broadway	OK	Okeh
Ca	Cameo	Or	Oriole
Cap	Capitol	OrE	English Oriole
Cen	Century	PaA	American Parlophone
Ch	Champion	PaE	English Parlophone
Chal	Challenge	PaF	French Parlophone
Ci	Circle	PaS	Spanish Parlophone
CI	Collectors Item	Pana	Panachord
Cl	Clarion	PanD	Dutch Panachord
Cli	Climax	Para	Paramount
Clax	Claxtonola	Pat	Pathe
Co	Columbia	PatA	Pathe Actuelle
Com	Commodore	PatF	French Pathe
Cont	Continental	Pe	Perfect
Cq	Conquer	Ph	Philharmonic
Cr	Crown	Po	Polk
Crs	Crescent	Pu	Puritan
De	Decca	Rad	Radiex
DeE	English Decca	Re	Regal
DeF	French Decca	Ro	Romeo
DeH	Dutch Decca	Roy	Royale
Di	Diva	RZ	Regal Zonophone
Do	Domino	Sa	Salabert
Ed	Edison	Sav	Savoy
El	Elite	SA	Solo Art
Elec	Electradisk	SD	Steiner-Davis
Em	Emerson	Se	Session
Ex	Excelsior	Si	Silvertone
FR	Firestone	Sig	Signature
Ge	Gennett	Su	Sunshine
GG	Grey Gull	Sup	Supertone
Gl	General	Sw	Swing
GrF	French Gramophone	Tele	Telefunken
Gu	Guardsman	Tri	Triangle
Ha	Harmony	UHCA	United Hot Clubs
Harmo	Harmograph	Ul	Ultraphone
Her	Herwin	VD	Van Dyke
HMV	His Master's Voice	Ve	Velvet Tone
HoW	Hit of Week	Vi	Victor
HRS	Hot Record Society	Vo	Vocalion
Hy	Hytone	VoE	English Vocalion
Im	Imperial	Vr	Variety
Je	Jewel	Vs	Varsity

Copyright 1948, Gordon Gullickson

THE GIANTS OF JAZZ!

COLUMBIA RE-ISSUES THE ORIGINAL RECORDS THAT MADE JAZZ HISTORY

Twenty-two colorful albums! Not only a comprehensive collection of the famous soloists, groups and specialists, but a living demonstration of the vitality, versatility and virtuosity of the creators and innovators of Jazz styles! Your dealer has them in stock now.

LOOK AT THIS LIST

LOUIS ARMSTRONG
Columbia C-28

BIX BEIDERBECKE
Columbia C-29

FLETCHER HENDERSON
Columbia C-30

BESSIE SMITH, Vol. 1
Columbia C-31

DUKE ELLINGTON
Columbia C-38

BUD FREEMAN
Columbia C-40

EARL HINES
Columbia C-41

FRANK TESCHEMACHER
Columbia C-43

BOOGIE WOOGIE
Columbia C-44

HOT TROMBONES
Columbia C-46

DORSEY BROTHERS
Columbia C-51

LOUIS ARMSTRONG HOT FIVE, Vol. 1 Columbia C-57

TEDDY WILSON—BILLIE HOLIDAY Columbia C-61

HOT TRUMPETS
Columbia C-66

LOUIS AND EARL
Columbia C-73

KID ORY
Columbia C-126

ELLINGTON SPECIAL
Columbia C-127

BOOGIE WOOGIE, Vol. 2
Columbia C-130

BILLIE HOLIDAY, Vol. 1
Columbia C-135

LOUIS ARMSTRONG HOT FIVE, Vol. 2 Columbia C-139

BESSIE SMITH, Vol. 2
Columbia C-142

BIX AND TRAM
Columbia C-144

HEAR THE GREAT ARTISTS AT THEIR BEST ON

Columbia Records

Trade-marks "Columbia" and ⓜ Reg. U. S. Pat. Off.

Introduction

The first draft of the INDEX TO JAZZ has been finished. This, the fourth and final volume, completes the framework for an alphabetical guide to all jazz and blues artists and their recordings.

Several hundred collectors and researchers have been engaged, since the first section was published, in fitting the body to this framework. By their corrections and additions, they have turned the light on some dark corners and have succeeded in polishing various rough edges.

From the first, the project was regarded as a cooperative one. Everyone who possessed information of value not contained in the first draft was asked to submit the missing data and to point out any inaccuracies otherwise. In short, collectors were asked to consider the INDEX TO JAZZ as their own project, and to help perfect it for their mutual benefit.

This call for help was answered by jazz collectors over the world. The names of these who had assisted up to that time were listed in the introduction to Volume III. Additional collaborators are named at the end of this foreword. It had been intended to acknowledge this kind of assistance in the monthly issues of The Record Chagner, but this did not work out.

Some correspondents pointed out the omission of important records, or supplied missing master numbers and dates here and there. Others went into the greatest and most helpful detail. Their willingness to devote so much time and effort to the undertaking was greatly appreciated, of course.

It was promised that this cooperative effort would lead ultimately to the production of a revised edition that would incorporate all this new information and would be, presumably, the most complete and accurate encyclopedia of recorded jazz that could de devised. This purpose is now reaffirmed. If before there had been any doubt of the wisdom of continuing toward this end, the material that has been accumulated imposes the obligation that it be used.

Sponsors of the INDEX TO JAZZ felt that there was a need for more than one approach to the subject of recorded jazz, and that an alphabetical guide was the most serious lack. They were also of the opinion that the great body of blues recordings constituted a cornerstone of jazz that should be fully documented, and that various types of recordings on the border-line should not be neglected either. We took a step in that direction in the first draft, and the revised edition will contain all the pertinent listings that are obtainable.

So a one-volume corrected edition will be published. While it will be attempted without waste of time, it is necessary to say that it will not be accomplished speedily. Much of the material is already at hand; but it has to be sifted and authenticated, and in final form the book will have to be carefully checked for accuracy in many ways.

For the time being, primary attention will be given to the collecting of further data and shaping it for use. Later will come the problems of physical production. The permanent edition undoubtedly will be printed in fairly large type, and it may come out in loose-leaf form, so that supplemental or corrected pages may be supplied at intervals to keep it up to date.

This will be definitely decided later, after all the advantages and disadvantages have been considered. Suggestions as to the proper format will be welcomed.

It had been hoped that a sample page could be reproduced in this volume to indicate how the printed book will look, but sufficient time has not been available to prepare this. It can be stated, however, that whereas only one line was used generally for each record to save space in the first draft, the uniform policy for the revision will be a separate line for each side. There will be other changes too, principally toward improving the presentation of each main artist's work in chronological order, and in one spot, although cross-references will be maintained and extended.

Various specialists have been or will be consulted on the question of serving as section editors. This is in line with the basic cooperative scheme, and suggestions and corrections will be welcomed from all sources just as much as ever.

Having spent approximately five years assembling this material, the writer is well aware of the work that is involved in tracing and verifying record data, even in the limited field of an individual collector's specialty. I do hope, however, that those who are willing to undergo some of this mental punishment will continue to send information, and not slacken their efforts because of the fear that they will be duplicating someone else's efforts.

I have found that there are not too many duplications among the various amendments offered so far. Even so, one bit of information in a set of corrections might be the key to the solution of a difficult problem.

The willingness of so many collectors to cooperate, in fact, was a very large factor in driving me through to completion of this first draft. The remainder of the responsibility rests with Gordon Gullickson, who caused me to undertake the project in the first place and who gave me encouragement to continue, at times when I had my doubts. To him, thanks for so many kindnesses, and patience.

To the following new collaborators, thanks for assistance since the publication of Volume III:

Jack Baylis, Payson Clark, George W. Cleary, J. L. Dixon, Joseph DuMontier, Bob Fiedler, Richard G. Holbrook, Cornelius W. Hauck, L. M. Hurvich, Leni Kesl, Robert Parent, P. Sondheim, Bill Stamm, and Fred Trescott.

—ORIN BLACKSTONE.

S

SABLON, JEAN (vocals, acc. by Garland Wilson, pianO):
    Co 4174. Un Seul Couvert Please James(CL 5651)/Ces Petites Choses(with Orch.)
    Co 4175. Si Tu M'Aimes/Le Chant des Tropiques(with Orch,)

    (Wilson, piano and Django Reinhardt, guitar):
    Co 4178. La Derniere Bergere/Un Paiser

    (Add clarinet):
    Co 4191. Je Sais que Veus Etes Jolie/Par Correspondance

    (Reinhardt present; Wilson uncertain):
    CoF 1406. Le Jour ou Je Te Vix/Prenez Garde au Grande Mechant Loup
    CoF 1191. Le Meme Coup/Je Suis Sex-Appeal

    (Wilson, Reinhardt):
    CoF 1672. Cortinental/Miss Otis Regrets

SAFRANSKI'S ALL STARS, EDDIE (Lem Davis, alto: Vido Musso, tenor; Sanford Gold, piano; Eddie Safranski, bass; Denzil Rest, drums):
    Sav 601. Lem Me Go(5893)/Spellbound(5892: omit Davis)

ST. LOUIS BESSIE:
    Vo 1559. Sugar Man Blues; 1 & 2
    Vo 1615. Meat Cutter Blues/He Treats Me Like a Dog

ST. LOUIS JIMMY:
    BB 8889. Going Down Slow/Monkey Face Blues
    BB 8933. Come Day Go Day/Lost Ball Blues
    BB 9016. Can't Stand Your Evil Ways/Soon Forgot You
    BB 340718. Back on My Feet Again/Nothing But Blues
    BB 340727. One More Break/Strange Women

ST. LOUIS RED MIKE:
    BB 7744. Hell Ain't But a Mile and a Quarter/Red Mike Blues

ST. LOUIS RHYTHM KINGS (Mickey Bloom,trumpet: Pete Palletsi,trombone; Louis Maesto,clarinet· Nick Moleri,piano: Christia Maesto,drums):
    Co 349. Papa De Da D-(140495)/She's My Sheba(140494)
    (See Maggie Jones: Co 14081)

SALLY SAD (vocals, acc. by trumpet):
    Vs 6033. Daddy What You Going to Do(15719)/Don't Say Goodbye(15718)

    (Piano acc.):
    Vs 6040. Shadow Blues(14982)/Gin House Blues(14987)
    Vs 6058. Mistreated Mama(14990)/Jelly Roll Mill(18804)
    Vs 6066. Gypsy Woman Blues/Good Hearted Woman
    (Different singers were assigned the name "Sally Sad" on the records above; Ivy Smith may have been one of them.)

SAMPSON, DERYCK (piano solos)
    Bea 7004. Canal Street Boogie Woogie/Homeless on the Range
    Bea 7005. Kansas City Boogie Woogie/Chinese Boogie Woogie
    Bea 7006. Monday's Wash/Blackberry Jam
    Bea 7015. Boogie Express/Erin Go Boogie
    Bea 7016. Table Top Boogie/Basin Street Boogie

SAMPSON AND HIS ORCHESTRA, EDGAR:
    Vo 4942. Don't Try Your Jive on Me(WM 1023)/Pick Your Own Lick(WM 1024)

SAVAGE, HELEN (vocals, acc. by the Dixie Syncopators: Omer Simeon,clarinet; William Barbee,piano; trumpet: tuba· drums):
    Br 4536. For Just a Little Love from You/It's Bad for Your Soul

SAVANNAH SIX:
    Ha 56. Hot Aire/Tain't Cold

SAVANNAH SYNCOPATORS (First seven sides were recorded by King Oliver's Dixie Syncopators and five were originally issued under that name on Vocalion: see Oliver section for details):
    Br 3245. Jackass Blues/Deep Henderson (originally Vo 1014)
    Br 3361. Sugar Foot Stomp(originally Vo 1033)/Snag It(original issue this no.)
    Br 3373. Wa Wa Wa(originally Vo 1033)/Someday Sweetheart(originally Vo 1059)
    Br 6046. Who's Blue(original issue this number)/Honey That Reminds Me(This side by Luis Russell's Orchestra)

(The following is by Fletcher Henderson's Orchestra: Rex Stewart, Russell Smith, Bobby Stark,trumpets; Benny Morton,Claude Jones,trombones; Coleman Hawkins, Russell Procope,Edgar Sampson, saxes: Henderson,piano; Clarence Holiday,guitar; John Kirby,tuba; Walter Johnson,drums):July/31
Br   6176. Radio Rhythm(E36927A)   -Br 80037, BrF 500134, BrE 1205
 "   Low Down on the Bayou   "   BrE 1227

(Jimmie Noone's Orchestra: George Mitchell,trumpet; Fats Williams,trombone; Noone,clarinet; Joe Poston,alto; Zinky Cohn,piano; Wilbur Gorham, guitar; Bill Newton,tuba; Johnny Wells,drums; Helen Savage,vocal in first side.--JI 11/8/40):   1928
Br   7124. After You've Gone/My Melancholy Baby

SAVOY BEARCATS (Probably Fletcher Henderson's Orchestra of 1926-27):
Vi 20182. Nightmare/Senegalese Stomp
Vi 20307. Bearcat stomp/How Could I Be Blue
Vi 20460. Hot Notes/Stampede

SAVOY DICTATORS (Hal Mitchell,Chippie Outcalt,trumpets; Bobby Plater,alto; Count Hastings,tenor; Howard Scott,trombone; Clem Moorman,piano; Al Henderson, bass; Willie Johnson,guitar; Danny Gibson,drums):
Sav   100. Rhythm and Bugs(L-1a)/Tricks(L-1)
Sav   101. Heyfuss-Geyfuss(10001)/Jam and Crackers(444)

SCARE CROW (vocals, acc.by trumpet, sax, piano, banjo, drums on first and third sides):
Vs   6041. Want Your Ashes Hauled(16612)/Ornery Blues(16976; piano acc.)
Vs   6046. Traveling Blues(16609)/I'm Long Gone(16965; piano acc.to duet)

SCHOEBEL AND HIS FRIARS' SOCIETY ORCHESTRA, ELMER (Dick Feigie,trumpet; Jack Read,trombone; Frank Teschemacher,clarinet; Floyd Town,tenor; Schoebel,piano; Charlie Barger,guitar; John Kuhn,tuba; George Wettling,drums):   Oct.,1929
Br   4652. Copenhagen(C4559D)   -Br 80065, BrE 03309, UHCA 17
 "   Prince of Wails(C4560C)   "   "   UHCA 18

SCHROEDER, GENE (piano solos, acc. by Bob Casey,bass; Joe Grauso,drums):
BW   5. Tea for Two/Sweet Georgia Brown
BW   33. Liza(25)/I Ain't Got Nobody(26)

ARTHUR SCHUTT

For other records by this pianist see: Alabama Red Peppers, Arkansas Travelers, Arnold Brillhardt, Charleston Chasers (All but Co 2219), Chicago Loopers, Cotton Pickers, Denza Dance Band, Dixie Jazz Band(Or 1022), Dorsey Brothers, Tommy Dorsey(OK 41178), Cliff Edwards, Bob Effros(Br 4620), Peggy English(Vo 15504), The Georgians, Benny Goodman (Co 2892, 2907), Goofus Five, Roger Wolfe Kahn, Kentucky Hot Hoppers, Eddie Lang(Ok 40807, 8696, 41410), Sam Lanin, Benny Meroff(OK 40912), Miff Mole, Red Nichols, Red and Miff, Red Heads, Fred Rich, Willard Robison, Adrian Rollini, Boyd Senter, Six Hottentots, Frankie Trumbauer, Joe Venuti, Don Voorhees, Wabash Dance Orchestra, We Three.

SCHUTT, ARTHUR (piano solos)
OK 41243. Lover Come Back to Me   -PaE 412
 "   Piano Puzzle
Ha   860. Jack in the Box/Rambling in Rhythm   -De 2860

(Duets with Jack Cornell):
BrF 1134. Canadian Capers/Flapperette

(Duets with Marlene Fingerle):
De 29121. Bolero, 1 & 2 (Ravel)
De 29130. 'By Jupiter' Medley/'You Were Never Lovelier' Medley

ARTHUR SCHUTT AND HIS ORCHESTRA:
OK 41345. Take Everything But You(403276A)/(SPARTEN SYNCOPATORS) -PaE 594
OK 41346. My Fate Is In Your Hands   -PaE 587
 " .   If I'm Dreaming(waltz)
OK 41359. Have a Little Faith(403584A)/Crying for Carolines(40358B)PaE 619
OK 41360. I'm Following You/(CAROLINA CLUB ORCH.)   -PaE 587
OK 41391. Montana Call/The Moon Is Low
OK 41392. It Must Be You(waltz)/(ED LLOYD)
OK 41400. Eleven Thirty Saturday Night/(THE SERENADERS) -PaE 672

SCORPION WASHBOARD BAND:
Vs 6003. Dinah/Yeah Man

7

SCOTT AND HIS BLUE BOYS, BLUE:
   BB 6520. Rubbin' Rubbin'/I Can Dish It

SCOTT AND HIS BRIGHT BOYS, CECIL (Bill Coleman,Frankie Newton,trumpets; Dicky Wells,trombone: John Williams,Harold McFarren,altos; Cecil Scott,clarinet & baritone; Don Frye,piano; Rudolph Williams,banjo; Mack Walker,bass; Lloyd Scott,drums):   1929
      Vi 38098. Lawd,Lawd(57709)/In a Corner(57710)   -HMV 14425, BB 8276

   CECIL SCOTT AND HIS ORCHESTRA (Same personnel):
      Vi 38117. Bright Boy Blues(57711)/Springfield Stomp(57712)
      (See also Lloyd Scott and His Orchestra)

SCOTT, EFFIE (vocal with piano and guitar):
   Vo 1416. Lonesome Hut Blues/Sunshine Special

SCOTT, GENEVIA (vocal acc. by Fletcher Henderson,piano):
   Fat 021005. Gulf Coast Blues/Michigan Water Blues   -Pe 12064

SCOTT, LEONARD:
   Vo 03311. You Done Tore Your Playhouse Down/She's Got Something

SCOTT, HAZEL (piano solos, with drums):
   De 18127. Ritual Fire Dance(68482A)/Two Part Invention,A Minor(68484AA)
   De 18128. Prelude in C Sharp Minor(68483AA)/Country Gardens(68481AA)
   De 18129. Hungarian Rhapsody #2(68485A)/Minute Waltz(68480A)

   (Acc. by J. C. Heard, drums):
   De 18340. Hazel's Boogie Woogie/Blues in B Flat
   De 18341. Embraceable You/Three Little Words
   De 18342. Dark Eves/Hallelujah

   (Vocal with orchestra):
   De 23429. The Man I Love/Fascinating Rhythm(voc. & piano)
   De 23551. Take Me in Your Arms(72790-T6A)/I'm Glad There is You(72849A)

   (Piano solos):
   Sig 15023. I Guess I'll Have to Change Plans(199-1B)/Valse in C#(SRC 196-1C)
   Sig 15024. Fantasie Impromptu(201-1A)/Nocturne in B Flat min.(SRC 202-1A)
   Sig 15025. A Rainy Night in G(SRC 198-1D)/How High the Moon(SRC 197-1B)
   Sig 15026. Sonata in C Minor(200-1E)/Idyll(203-1B)
   Sig 15073. On the Sunny Side of the Street/I've Got the World on a String
   Sig 15126. Butterfly Kick/Ich Vil Sich Spielen

SCOTT AND HIS ORCHESTRA, LLOYD (Bill Coleman, Jabbo Smith, Gus McCullen, trumpets; Dicky Wells, trombone: Cecil Scott,John Williams,Fletcher Allen, clarinets and saxes; Don Frye,piano; Hubert Mann,banjo: Lloyd Scott,drums; bass): -- RC Nov.1946)   1926
   Vi 20495. Symphonic Scrcrch(37530)/Happy Hour(37531)
   Vi 21491. Harlem Shuffle(37529)/(CHARLES JOHNSON)

SCOTT, MAE (vocal acc. by Lemuel Fowler, piano):
   Para 12048. Squawkin' the Blues/I'll Get Even

SCOTT QUINTETTE, RAYMOND (Raymond Scott,piano: Dave Harris,tenor: Pete Pumiglio,clarinet; Dave Wade,trumpet: Louis Shoobe,bass Johnny Williams,drums):
                                                                                        1938
   Ma 108. Minuet in Jazz(M117)/Twilight in Turkey(M118)-Br 7992, Co 36107
   Ma 111. The Toy Trumpet(M119)
    "   Powerhouse(M120)   -Br 7993, Co 36311
   Br 8000. Dinner Music for a Pack of Hungry Canibals   -Co 36258
    "   Reckless Night on Board an Ocean Liner   "

   (Ted Harkins,bass):
   Br 8058. War Dance for Wooden Indiana/The Penguin   -Co 36316
   Br 8144. The Happy Farmer/Egyptian Barn Dance   -Co 36277

   (Russ Case,trumpet):
   Br 8452. Siberian Sleighride(WB24744A)/Tobacco Auctioneer(24935B)Co 36121
   Co 35247. The Girl With Light Blue Hair/New Year's Eve in Haunted House
   Co 35347. In an 18th Century Drawing Room/Boy Scout in Switzerland
   Co 35585. Bumpy Weather Over Newark/Peter Tambourine

   RAYMOND SCOTT AND HIS ORCHESTRA (Pete Pumiglio,clarinet & alto; Dave Harris,Art Drellinger,tenors, Reggie Merrill,alto; Chris Griffin,Mike Meola,Willie Kelly,trumpets: Irvin Sontag,Joe Vargas,trombones;Walter Gross,piano; Vince Maffei,guitar; Lou Shoobe,bass:John Blowers,drums):
                                                                                        1940
   Co 35363. Huckleberry Duck(WCO 26315B)   -PaE 2744
    "   Just a Gigolo(WCO 26178A)   -PaE 2781

```
Co 35364. Business Men's Bounce(WCO 26357A)           -PaE 2744
    "    The Peanut Vendor(WCO 26180C)                -PaE 2781

     (B.Lagasse,D.Long,S.Webb,H.Winterhalter,aaxes; Lindsey DeLory,C.McCam-
ish,trombones; S.E.Market,L.Stearns,B.LeMar,trumpets; A.Picard,drums;
Art Ryerson,guitar; B.Lazaroff,piano: Stewart Jackson,bass)June 17,1940
Co 35565. Four Beat Shuffle(WCO 26928A)/Birdseed Special(WCO26930B)
                                                      (-PaE 2776
     (Unknown personnel):
Co 35623. And So Do I/Now I Lay Me Down to Dream
Co 35745. Yesterthoughts/Stranger
Co 35803. Nice Day in the Country
    "     Pretty Little Petticoat                     -Co 36226
Co 35864. All Around the Christmas Tree/Happy Birthday to You
Co 35911. Eagle Beak/Copyright 1950
Co 35940. Petite(CCO 3516)/When Cootie Left the Duke(CCO 3514)
Co 35980. Evening Star/Blues My Girl Friend Taught Me
Co 36083. I Understand/The Things I Love
Co 36090. Let's Get Away from It All/The Band Played On
Co 36103. In the Hush of the Night/Just a Little Bit South of North Carolina
Co 36149. Where You Are/Keep Cool, Fool
Co 36161. Do You Care/I Touched a Star
Co 36211. In a Subway Far from Ireland/Mexican Jumping Bean
Co 36288. Beau Night in Hotchkiss Corners/The Merry Caroussel
Co 36410. Key West/On the Jersey Side

     RAYMOND SCOTT QUINTETTE:
Co 37359. The Girl at the Typewriter(WB24883-B)/Get Happy(WCO26181-A;Orch.)
Co 37360. The Quintet Plays Carmen(WB24943-B)/Little Bit of Rigoletto
Co 37361. Manhattan Minuet(WB24914-B)/Moment Musical(WB24488-B)(WB24937-B)
Co 37362. Two Way Stretch(F34046)/At Arabian House Party(WCO26929-A;Orch.)

     RAYMOND SCOTT AND HIS ORCHESTRA
De 18264. Symphony Under the Stars/Caterpillar Creep  -BrE 03345
De 18276. Eight Letters in the Mailbox/Kodachrome     -BrE 03367
De 18377. Pan American Hot Spot/Secret Agent
De 18422. Careful Conversation at a Diplomatic Function/Carrier Pigeon

     (Featuring Charlie Shaver,trumpet: Milt Yaner,alto: Johnny Guarnieri,
piano; Cliff Leeman,drums):
Son  3003. Enchanted Forest(SR 525)/Toonerville Trolley(SR 34049)
Son  3008. Magic Garden(SR 527-2)/Mr Basie Goes to Washington(SR 526-2)

     (Unknown personnel):                                       1947
MGM 10006. Manhattan Serenade/We Knew It All the Time
MGM 10067. Tired Teddy Bear/Huckleberry Duck

SCOTT, ROOSEVELT (vocal with inst. acc.):
Vo 05137. You Call That Right/Send Me
Vo 05206. Black Gal Blues/Brown Skin Woman Swing
Vo 05415. Panama Special/Look Up and Down
Vo 05502. Be My Baby/Doctor Bill Blues

SCOTT, SONNY (vocals):
Vo 25013. Working Man's Moan/Early This Morning

     (Guitar accompaniment):
Vo 25017. Hard Luck Man/Red Rooster Blues

SCOTT AND HIS DOWN BEAT CLUB SEPTET, TONY (Including Dizzy Gillespie,
trumpet; Bill Simon,clarinet; Ben Webster,tenor):
Gotham 105. Ten Lessons With Timothy/All Too Soon(Sarah Vaugh,vocal)

SCRANTON SIRENS ORCHESTRA (Recorded in New Orleans)
OK 40297. Why Should I Believe in You(8909-A)/(JOHN TOBIN'S MIDNIGHT SERE-
OK 40329. Common Street Blues/(JIMMIE JOY)                  (NADERS)

SCRUGGS, IRENE (vocal with cornet):
Vo  1017. Home Town Blues/Sorrow Valley

     (Acc. Clarence Williams, piano):
OK  8142. Everybody's Blues(S-72486B)/Why He Left Me I Don't Know(S-72487B)
     (Acc. Little Brother Montgomery, piano):              1929
Para 13023. Must Get Mine in Front/Good Meat Grinder
Para -----. St.Louis Woman Blues/Borrowed Love Blues

SEARCY TRIO(DeLoise Searcy,piano· Clifford King,cornet·Edgar Green,clarinet):
                                                       St.Louis,1926
OK  8360. Kansas Avenue Blues(9665A)/East St. Louis Stomp(9666A)
```

SEATTLE HARMONY KINGS (Including Rosy McHargue,clarinet   Joe Hooven,trumpet.
A Benson organization directed by Eddie Neibaur):
    Vi 19772. If I Had a Girl Like You/Darktown Shuffle
    Vi 20142. Breezin' Along With the Breeze/(ART LANDRY)
    Vi 20133. How Many Times/(TED WEEMS)

SEDRIC AND HIS HONEY BEARS (Eugene Sedric,tenor; Jimmy Powell,Fred Skarret,
clarinets and altos; Herman Autrey,trumpet; Henry Duncan,piano; Slick Jones,
drums; Albert Casey,guitar; Cedric Wallace,bass):   1939
    Vo 4552. Choo Choo(M934; voc.,Sedric)/The Wail of the Scromph(M935)
    Vo 4576. Off Time/The Joint Is Jumpin'

SEGAR, CHARLIE (piano solos):   Chicago,1934
    De 7027. Cuban Villa Blues(C-9432B)/Southern Hospitality(C-9433B)
    De 7075. Cow Cow Blues(9643A)
    "   Boogie Woogie(9646A)   -De 3832

    (Piano and vocal, acc. drums):   Chicago,1940
    Vo 05441. Stop and Fix It Mama(WC 2958)/Key to the Highway(WC 2957)
    Vo 05539. Lonesome Graveyard Blues(WC 2959A)/Dissatisfied Blues(WC2960A)
    (Segar reputedly may be heard on Mississippi Mudder De 7207, and
     on records under the name of Georgia Pine Boy)

SEIDEL AND HIS ORCHESTRA, EMIL (Same personnel as for Hoagy Carmichael and
His Pals, Ge 6311):
    Ge 6309. -----

SELVIN AND HIS ORCHESTRA, BEN (As recording director and house leader for
several companies, Selvin has issued scores of records under his name. His
Columbias only, some of which feature Benny Goodman,clarinet*, Tommy Dorsey,
trombone, Jack Teagarden, trombone, and Ed Lang,guitar, are listed here):
    Co 1133. Wherever You Are/Play Ground in the Sky
    Co 1188. Among My Souvenirs/(IPANA TROUBADOURS)
    Co 1274. We'll Have a New Home/When You're With Somebody Else
    Co 1285. Oh Gee Oh Joy/Say So
    Co 1321. Tell Me You're Sorry/When
    Co 1337. In My Bouquet of Memories/Ramona
    Co 1341. Speedy Boy(145776)/(MAL HALLETT)
    Co 1399. I'm Afraid of You/Indian Cradle Song
    Co 1426. Chilly Pom Pom Pee/Just a Night for Meditation
    Co 1538. Lady Whippoorwill(146936)/Right Out of Heaven(146937)
    Co 1635. Carmen(146940)/My Inspiration is You(147394)
    Co 1719. Carolina Moon/If I Had You
    Co 1738. Broadway Melody/(BROADWAY NITELITES)
    Co 1739. Redskin(147956)/(COLUMBIANS)
    Co 1875. Miss You/Junior
    Co 1964. The Web of Love(148984)/I'm in Love With You(148987)
    Co 2077. Why(149699)/Cross Your Fingers(149700)
    Co 2096. Funny Dear What Love Can Do(149736)/Tain't No Sin(149737)
    Co 2116. Happy Days Are Here Again/The One Girl
    Co 2206. Dancing With Tears in My Eyes/When It's Springtime in Rockies
    Co 2255. Why Have You Forgotten Waikiki(150621)/East to Fallin Love
    Co 2287. I'm Yours(150723)/Dixiana(150724)   (150622)
    Co 2323. My Man from Caroline(150900)/Still I Love Her(150902)
    Co 2345. Song of the Fool(150952)/Who's Calling You(150954)
    Co 2356. I Miss a Little Miss(151117)/Cheerful Little Earful(151118)
    Co 2367. On a Little Balcony in Spain(151178)/Lady Play Your Mandolin
    Co 2421. Smile Darn Ya(151365)/One Man Band(151367)   (151179)
    Co 2400. 99 Out of a Hundred(151285*·Helen Rowland,v.)/Love for Sale
    Co 2366. Yours and Mine*/Little Spanish Dancer   (151287)
    Co 2381. Would You Like to Take a Walk/He's Not Worth Salt of Tears
    Co 2438. Soldier on the Shelf/Two Hearts in Three-Quarter Time
    Co 2463. Now You're in my Arms(151548; Helen Rowland,voc)/Poor Kid
    Co 2473. Dancing in the Dark/High and Low   (151547)
    Co 2499. Do the New York/Hikin' Down the Highway
    Co 2491. Sing Another Chorus Please/(PAUL WHITEMAN)
    Co 2501. Nobody Loves Baby*/My Sweet Tooth
    Co 2515. This Is the Mrs./My Song
    Co 2524. Trees/Yours Is My Heart Alone
    Co 2537. I Don't Want Love(Eddie Lang, solo)
    Co 2554. Little Mary Brown(151850*)/Charlie Cadet(151838)
    Co 2562. She Didn't Say Yes/Try to Forget
    Co 2575. Bend Down Sister*/Now's the Time*
    Co 2592. Oh What a Thrill/Goodnight Moon
    Co 2585. All of Me/I Found You
    Co 2596. When We're Alone/You're My Everything
    Co 2604. Was That the Human Thing to Do/Delishious
    Co 2618. Dancing on the Ceiling/Just Friends
    Co 2628. Too Many Tears/My Mom

```
Co  2654. Lullaby of the Leaves/Whistle and Blow Your Blues Away
Co  2661. Crazy People/Is I in Love
Co  2669. Hummin' to Myself/Cabin in the Cotton
Co  2676. Holding My Honey's Hand/Sleep Come on and Take Me
Co  2731. Young and Healthy/You're Getting to Be a Habit With Me
Co  2734. Street of Dreams(152334)/A White House of Our Own(152333)
Co  2778. Sweetheart Darlin'/Adorable
Co  2789. Morning Noon and Night/Reflections in the Water
Co  2813. Emperor Jones/Dinner at Eight
Co  2834. You're My Past Present and Future/(JOE VENUTI)
Co  2844. My Dancing Lady/(BERNIE CUMMINS)
Co  2854. Build a Little Home/(MEYER DAVIS)
Co  2935. Rollin' Home/The Prize Waltz
Co  2936. I Only Have Eyes for You/Born to Be Kissed
Co 18000. 'Face the Music' Medley/'Hot-Cha' Medley
```

SEMINOLE SYNCOPATORS: Recorded in Atlanta
```
 OK 40228. Blue Grass Blues(S-72484A)/Sailing on Lake Pontchartrain(8741A)
```

SENTER, BOYD (clarinet):
```
 Para 20341. Mobile Blues(228)/(CHICAGO DE LUXE ORCHESTRA)
 Para 20364. Fat Mamma Blues/Gin Houn' Blues
 Pat  36256. It's Time to Keep Away from you/Slippery Elm     -Pe 14437
 Pat  36270. Gertie/Craving                                    -Pe 14451
 Pat  36528. Beef Stew/(GOOF MEYER)                            -Pe 14709
 Pe   14517. Shake Your Dogs/Wake 'em Up
 Pat  36285. Bucktown Blues/You've Broken My Heart
```

        (Acc. by Arthur Schutt, piano: Ed Lang, guitar):
```
 OK 40745. New St.Louis Blues                        -Cl 5112, PaE 3321
        "  Bad Habits                     -PaE 3321, Vo 3030, Ve 7060
 OK 40777. Bluin' the Blues                          -PaE 3329, Vo 2937
        "  Clarinet Tickle                                "   Vo 2936
 OK 40819. Christine(80315B)                         -PaE 3351, Vo 3075
        "  Someday Sweetheart(80325A)                      "   Vo 3014
 OK 40836. Not Maybe(80985B)                         -PaE 3384, Vo 2937
        "  Beale Street Blues(80987A)                -PaE 107,  Vo 2936
 OK 40861. Sigh and Cry Blues(80988B)                -PaE 3411, Vo 3031
        "  I Ain't Got Nobody(81004B)   -Ve 7060, PaF 3411, Vo 3030
 OK 40949. Wabash Blues(80313B)                      -PaE 3505, Vo 3075
        "  The Boss of the Stompe(81002B)            -PaE 168,  Vo 3061
 OK 41059. Fniale Blues                              -PaE 283,  Vo 3061
        "  Somebody's Wrong                                     -Vo 3031
 OK 40888. Hot Lips                                  -PaF 3384
        "  The Grind Out                             -PaE 3505
 PaF   168. Tain't Clean
```

        BOYD SENTER AND HIS SENTERPEDES (Probably Mickey Bloom, trumpet: Dorsey
        Brothers: Lang: Schutt: Stan King):
```
 OK 41115. Original Stack o'Lee Blues(400647B) -PaE 501, Vo 3015, Di 6044
        "  Downhearted Bl(81001B:Schutt,Lang only)-PaE 107, Vo 3014, Di 6044
 OK 41018. Sister Kate(400168A)                    -Vo 3015, Cl 5194
        "  Just So So(400155B:Schutt,Lang only)    -Vo 3116, PaE 283
 OK 41163. Original Chinese Blues(400653B)                  -PaE 143
        "  Prickly Heat(400645D; with Schutt and Lang only)
 PaF   143. Mobile Blues
 PaF   501. No More
```

        (Approximately the same group, with Fud Livingston, tenor: Lang and
        Schutt probably replaced):
```
 Vi 21864. Goin' Back to Tennessee                          -BB 6203
        "  Wabash Blues                                     -BB 5455
 Vi 22010. I'm in the Jailhouse Now/Rich Man Poor Man
 Vi 21912. Shine/Doin' You Good                             -HMV 4493
 Vi 22812. A Good Man Is Hard to Find
        "  Waterloo                                         -BB 5376
 Vi 23032. Smiles
        "  Give It to Me Right Away                         -BB 5376
```

        (Mezzrow, tenor, possibly on next two):
```
 Vi 22303. Copenhagen(57032)/Beale St. Blues      -BB 6050, HMV 4488
 Vi 22464. No One(57033)/Sweetheart Blues                   -HMV 4913
```

SEPIA SERENADERS (Clarence Grimes, alto and clarinet: Cliff Jackson, piano:
Elmer Snowden, banjo: George Gray, vocals): -- RR   1935
```
 BB 6770. Ridiculous Blues/Name less blues
 BB 5782. Breakin' the Ice/Baby Brown
 BB 5803. Dallas Blues/Alligator Crawl
```

II

SESSION SIX (Eddie Johnson, tenor; Nat Jones, alto; Jesse Miller, trumpet: John Levy, bass; Alvin Burroughs, drums; Jimmy Jones, piano):   April 2, 1944
  Se 12009. Yesterdays/In the Act
  Se -----. Big Oaks/I Wished on the Moon

SEVEN ACES (Ralph Bennett organization):
  Co 816. Don't Take That Black Bottom Away(143007)/That's My Girl(143013)

SEVEN HOT AIR MEN (See Hot Air Men)

SEVEN BROWN BABIES (Fletcher Henderson group):
  AJ 17011. Charleston Crazy/Dicty Blues

SEVEN GALLON JUG BAND (Clarence Williams group):
  Co 2087. Wipe 'em Off/What If I Do

SEVEN LITTLE CLOUDS OF JOY (Andy Kirk group):
  Br 7180. Gettin' Off a Mess/You Rascal You

SEVEN LITTLE POLAR BEARS:
  Ca 915. Horses/Someone Is Losing Susan
  Ca 952. Animal Crackers/I Love Her
  Ca 1019. Girl Has Eye Trouble/(FRED RICH)
  Ca 8188. Mississippi Mud/(THE WASHINGTONIANS)

SEVEN MISSING LINKS:
  Pe 14486. Angry/Milenberg Joys

SEWARD, HATCH (Meade Lux Lewis, piano solo):
  Bwy 5063. Honky Tonk Train Blues(20246)*
    *(Reissue of Paramount 12896)

SEXTET OF THE RHYTHM CLUB OF LONDON (Danny Polo, clarinet; Pete Brown, alto; Hazel Scott, piano; Albert Harris, guitar; Arthur Herbert, drums; Pete Barry, bass):   Dec.1, 1939
  BB 10529. Calling All Bars/Mighty Like the Blues
  BB 10557. Why Didn't William Tell/You Gave Me the Go-By   -HMV 9062

SHARKEY'S NEW ORLEANS BOYS (Sharkey Bonano, trumpet & vocal; Julian Laine, trombone; Meyer Weinberg, alto and clarinet; Dave Weinstein, tenor: Armand Hugg, piano; Bill Bourgeois, guitar; Ray Bonitas, bass; Augie Schellange, drums):
                                                             1936
  De 1014. Yes She Do No She Don't(60843)   -BrE 02513
    "   Everybody Loves My Baby(60842)

  (SHARKEY AND HIS SHARKS OF RHYTHM (Sharkey Bonano, trumpet and vocal: Irving Fazola, clarinet; Santo Pecora, trombone; Clyde Hart, piano; Ben Pollack, drums; Frank Frederico, guitar: Thurman Teague, bass):
                                            New York, Oct.7, 1936
  Vo 3353. Mudhole Blues(20015)/Swing In Swing Out(20016)   -VoE 44
  Vo 3380. I'm Satisfied With My Gal(20013)   -VoE 178
    "   High Society(20014)   -PaE 2825,   "

  (Sharkey, trumpet and vocal; Buddy Morrow, trombone; Joe Marsala, clarinet; Joe Bushkin, piano; Eddie Condon, guitar: Art Shapiro, bass; George Wettling, drums):
  Vo 3400. Mr. Brown Goes to Town(20366)   -VoE 112
    "   When You're Smiling(20368)
  Vo 3410. Blowing Off Steam(20365)   -VoE 61
    "   Wash It Clean(20367)

  (Sharkey, trumpet and vocal; George Brunies, trombone; Joe Marsala, clarinet; Joe Bushkin, piano; Fred Wayland, bass; Eddie Condon, guitar; Al Sidell, drums):
  Vo 3450. Old Fashioned Swing(20599)   -VoE 112
    "   Big Boy Blue(20600)
  Vo 3470. Swingin' on Swanee Shore(20598)/Swing Like a Rusty Gate(20601)
                                                      (-VoE 80

CHARLIE SHAVERS

See also:
  GEORGE AULD: Ap 754, 755.
  BUSTER BAILEY: Vs 8333, 8337, 8358, 8365.
  MILDRED BAILEY:
  BLUE LU BARKER: De 7648 - 7709.
  CHARLIE BARNET: BB 10210.
  SIDNEY BECHET: Vi 27600 - 27904.
  TINY BRADSHAW:
  SID CATLETT: Delta 10 - 4, 10 - 3.

COZY COLE: Cont 6000, 6001, 6004.
JOHNNY DODDS: De 1676, 2111, 7413.
TOMMY DORSEY:
BEA FOOTE: De 7457, 7535, 7554.
TEDDY GRACE: De 2604, 2605, 2606.
GRANT AND WILSON: Do 7500.
ED HALL: Delta 10-1.
HERBIE HAYMER:
ROSETTA HOWARD: De 7658, 7640, 7687, 7801.
ALBERTA HUNTER: De 7633, 7644, 7727.
JERRY JEROME: Asch 503, 504.
JOHN KIRBY:
BILLY KYLE: Vr 531, 574, 617, 659.
MILLS BLUE RHYTHM BAND: Vr 503, 546, 604, 624, 634.
JIMMIE NOONE: De 1584, 1621, 1730, 7553.
BILLIE HOLIDAY:
RED NORVO:
KEYNOTERS: Key 1313.

SHAVERS QUINTET, CHARLIE (Charlie Shavers,trumpet: Earl Hines,piano: Tab
Smith,alto: Jo Jones,drums; Al Lucas, bass):   April 15,1944
  Key 1304. Mountain Air/Rosetta
  Key 1305. Curry in a Hurry/Stardust

     CHARLIE SHAVERS AND HIS ALL AMERICAN FIVE (Shavers,trumpet; Coleman
     Hawkins,tenor; Teddy Wilson,piano; Billy Taylor,bass; Denzil Best,
     drums):   Oct.18,1944
  Key 619. My Man(HL 68)/El Salon de Gutbucket(HL 69)

ARTIE SHAW

See Also:
  MILDRED BAILEY: Vo 3367, 3378.
  BUNNY BERIGAN: VO 3224, 3225.
  BOSWELL SISTERS:
  BILLIE HOLIDAY: Vo 3276, 3288.
  MANNY KLEIN:
  DICK McDONOUGH:
  RED NORVO: Co 2977, 3026, 3059.
  JACK TEAGARDEN: Co 2802, 2913.
  FRANKIE TRUMBAUER: Br 7663, 7665.

SHAW AND HIS ORCHESTRA, ART (Artie Shaw,clarinet; Tony Zimmers,tenor; Willie
Kelly,trumpet; Mark Bennett,trombone: Fulton McGrath,piano: Wes Vaughn,gui-
tar; Hank Wayland,bass; Sam Weiss, drums: two violins,viola, cello):   1935
  Br 7688. Japanese Sandman(B19434)/A Pretty Girl Is Like a Melody(B19435)
  Br 7698. No Regrets(B19437)/Used to Above Love(B19436) (-Vo 4465,VoE 25
  Br 7721. South Sea Island Magic/It Ain't Right   -Vo 4637, VoE 13
  Br 7741. Darling Not Without You/You're Giving Me Song & Dance -VoE 18
  Br 7750. Let's Calla Heart a Heart/One Two Button Your Shoe

     (Shaw,clarinet; Tony Pastor,tenor: Lee Castle,trumpet Mike Michaels,
     trombone; Joe Lippman,piano; Gene Stone,guitar; Ben Ginsberg,bass; Sam
     Weiss,drums; plus strings):   1936
  Br 7735. Sugar Foot Stomp   -VoE 48
   "   Thou Swell   -VoE 54

     (Add Zeke Zarchy,trumpet: strings are: Jerry Gray,Frank Siegfield,
     violins; Sam Rosenblum,viola; William Schuman,cello):
  Br 7771. The Skeleton in the Closet   -VoE 48
   "   There's Frost on the Moon

     (Sub. Buddy Morrow,trombone: Tony Gatuzzi,guitar; George Wettling,
  Br 7778. There's Something in the Air/Take Another Guess (drums):
  Br 7787. Love and Learn   -VoE 79
   "   Moon Face
  Br 7794. The Same Old Line(B20344)   -Vo 4514, VoE 54
   "   You Can Tell She Comes from Dixie(B20345)   "   VoE 543
  Br 7806. Cream Puff/Sobbin' Blues   -VoE 63
  Br 7827. Copenhagen(B20449)   -Vo 4336, VoF 67
   "   My Blue Heaven(B20451)   -PaE 2686,   "   VoE 79
  Br 7835. Moonlight and Shadows(B20680)   -VoE 543
   "   No More Tears
  Br 7841. Was It Rain/Love Is Good for Anything That Ails You   -VoE 548

     ART SHAW AND HIS STRINGS (Omit tenor and brass):
  Br 7852. Streamline/Sweet Lorraine   -Vo 4598, VoE 56

13

ART SHAW AND HIS NEW MUSIC (Shaw,clarinet: Art Masters,Les Robinson,altos; Tony Pastor,Fred Petry,tenors; John Best,Malcolm Crane,Tom DiCarlo, trumpets; Harry Rodgers,George Arus,trombones; Les Burness,piano; Al Avola,guitar; Ben Ginsberg,bass; Cliff Leeman,drums): 1936

Br 7895.	All God's Chillun Got Rhythm/It Goes to Your Feet	-VoE 566
Br 7899.	All Alone/Because I Love You	-VoE 105, PaE 2661

(Sub. Harry Freeman,alto, for Masters):

Br 7907.	Blue Skies	-VoE 111, PaE 2676
"	I surrender Dear	-VoE 114, "
Br 7914.	Someday Sweetheart	-VoE 114, PaE 2661
"	Night and Day	-VoE 111
Br 7934.	Afraid to Dream/If You Ever Should Leave	
Br 7936.	Sweet Adeline	-Vo 4182, VoE 131
"	How Dry I am	

(Sub. Jules Rubin, tenor, for Petry):

Br 7942.	Am I in Love/Please Pardon Us We're in Love	
Br 7947.	The Blues A & B(B21462)/(B21463)	-Vo 4401, PaE 2790,VoE 124
Br 7952.	The Chant	-Vo 4539
"	Fee Fi Fo Fum	-VoE 131, "
Br 7965.	Nightmare	-Vo 4306, VoE 120, PaE 2554
"	It's a Long Long Way to Tipperary	"
Br 7976.	Shoot the Likker to Me John Boy/Free Wheeling	-Vo 4198
Br 7971.	If It's the Last Thing I Do/I've a Strange New Rhythm in Heart	
Br 7986.	Let 'er Go	-Vo 4438
"	Strange Loneliness	-PaE 2554
Br 8010.	I'm Yours(B21898)	Vo 4865
"	Just You	
Br 8019.	Monsoon/Free for All	

ART SHAW AND HIS ORCHESTRA (Shaw,clarinet: Les Robinson,Hank Freeman, altos; Tony Pastor, Ronny Perry,tenors: Chuck Peterson,John Best,Claude Bowen,trumpets: George Arus,Ted Vesely,Harry Rodgers,trombones; Les Burness,piano; Al Avola,guitar; Sid Weiss,bass: Cliff Leeman,drums): 1938

BB 7746.	Begin the Beguine(24079)-Vi 27546, Vi 201752, HMV 8906,GrF 8343	
"	Indian Love Call(24080)	-HMV 8869,GrF 8296
BB 7772.	Comin' On (24081)	-GrF 8336
"	I Can't Believe(24084)	-HMV 8948
BB 7759.	Back Bay Shuffle(24082)	-Vi 27547, GrF 8327
"	Any Old Time(24083; Billie Holiday, voc.)	

ARTIE SHAW AND HIS ORCHESTRA (Sub. Russ Brown,trombone, for Vesely; George Koenig,alto, for Les Robinson):

BB 7875.	Nightmare(27229)	-Vi 201752, HMV 8869, GrF 8296
"	Non Stop Flight(27230)	-HMV 8925, GrF 8391
BB 7889.	You're Sweet Little Headache(27233: Helen Forrest,voc.)	
"	I Have Eyes(27234)	
BB 10001.	Yesterdays(27231)/What Is This Thing Called Love(27232)	

(Les Robinson back):

BB 10046.	Deep in a Dream(28975: H.Forrest,v.)/Day After Day(28976)	
BB 10054.	Softly As in a Morning Sunrise(28977)	
"	Copenhagen(28978)	-HMV 8880,GrF 8336
BB 10055.	Between a Kiss and a Sigh(28973)/Thanks	

(Shaw,clarinet· Hank Freeman,Les Robinson,altos; Tony Pastor,George Auld,tenors; Bernie Privin,Chuck Peterson,John Best,trumpets; George Arus,Les Jenkins,Harry Kitsers,trombones; Bob Kitsis,piano; Al Avola, guitar; Sid Weiss,bass: George Wettling,drums): Dec.,1938

BB 10075.	A Room With a View(3073L:H.Forrest,v.)/They Say(30733;Forrest)	
BB 10079.	Say It With a Kiss(30732)/Took Million Years(30734)Forrest vocs.	
BB 10091.	Jungle Drums(30735)	-HMV 8894
"	It Had to Be You(30736)	-HMV 8948

(Buddy Rich,drums): 1939

BB 10124.	Carioca(31827)	-HMV 8893, GrF 8327
"	Bill(31825; H.Forrest,voc.)	
BB 10125.	The Donkey Serenade(31824)	-HMV 8893
"	My Heart Stood Still(31492)	
BB 10126.	Lover Come Back to Me(31491)	-HMV 8937
"	Rosalie(31493)	
BB 10127.	Zigeuner(31826)	-HMV 8937
"	Supper Time(31494; H.Forrest,voc.)	
BB 10128.	The Man I Love(31823)	-HMV 8949
"	Vilia(31495)	

14

```
BB 10134. Delightful Delirium(31869;Pastor,v.)/I Want My Share of Love
BB 10141. This Is It(31868)/It's All Yours(31867)    (31866;Forrest,V)
BB 10148. Alone Together(31864)
     "    Rose Room(31865)                                    -HMV 8949
                                                         Mar.12,1939
BB 10178. Deep Purple(32964;Forrest,voc.)                -HMV 8906
     "    Pastel Blue(32966)
BB 10188. I'm in Love With the Honorable Mr. So & So(32962)   -GrF 8391
     "    Prosschai(32963)                                    -HMV 8925
BB 10195. You Grow Sweeter As the Years Go By(32999)
     "    If You Ever Change Your Mind(35302: H.Forrest, voc.)
BB 10202. One Night Stand(35303)                         -HMV 8936
     "    One Foot in the Groove(35304)
HMV  8936. Why Begin Again
BB 10215. You're So Indiff'rent(35300)/Snug As Bug in a Rug(35301)
BB 10307. I Poured My Heart into a Song(36238; H.Forrest,voc.)
     "    When Winter Comes(36239)                       -HMV  8958
BB 10319. All I Remember Is You(36240;Forrest,v.)/Octoroon(36237)
BB 10320. Out of Nowhere(36241)/I'm Cominb Virginia(32965)-HMV8997,GrF 8467
BB 10324. Can't Afford to Dream(36264)/Comes Love(36265: H.Forrest,voc.)
BB 10334. Moonray(36293)/Melancholy Mood(36294) Helen Forrest,vocals
BB 10345. I'll Remember(36292)/Easy to Say(36291; H.Forrest,voc.)
BB 10347. Go Fly a Kite(36266)/A Man and His Dream(36267)     -HMV 8979
BB 10385. Traffic Jam(36268)                      -Vi 27548, HMV 9006
     "    Serenade to a Savage(36269)             -Vi 27549,     "

     (Sub. Harry Geller,trumpet, for Best):                Aug.27,1939
BB 10406. Day in Day Out(42606; Forrest,v.)/Put That Down in Writing(42605)
BB 10412. Last 2 Weeks in July(42608)/2 Blind Loves(42607)-HMV 9017, 8483
BB 10430. Oh Lady Be Good(42609)/I Surrender Dear(42610)     -HMV 9018
BB 10446. Many Dreams Ago(42755;HF,v.)/If What you Say(42757) Late 1939
BB 10468. Table in a Corner(42756)/Without a Dream to My Name(42758) HF,v.
BB 10482. You're a Lucky Guy(43319)/Love is Here(43316; Forrest,voc.)
BB 10492. All in Fun(43317; Forrest,voc.)
     "    All the Things You Are(43318; Forrest,voc.)       -Vo 201561

     (Sub. Dave Barbour, guitar):
BB 10502. Shadows(43367)/I Didn't know What Time It Was(43368)
BB 10509. Do I Love You(43369)/When Love Beckoned(43370) Forrest, vocals

     Artie Shaw,clarinet; Blake Reynolds,Bud Carleton,Dick Clark,Jack Stacy,
     saxes; Norton Raderman,flute; Phil Nemoli,oboe; Joe Drechter,bass clar-
     inet; Charlie Margulies,Manny Klein,George Thow,trumpets; Randall Mill-
     er,Bill Rank,Babe Bowman,trombones; Jack Cane,French horn; Mark Levant,
     Harry Bluestone,Peter Eisenberg,Robert Barene,Sid Brokaw,Dave Cracov,
     Jerry Joyce,Alex Law,violins; David Sturkin,Stanley Spiegelman, Jack
     Gray,violas; Jules Tannenbaum, Irving Lipschultz,cellos: George Denaut,
     bass; Stan Wrightsman,piano; Bobby Sherwood,guitar: Carl Maus,drums):
                                                      Hollywood,Mar.3,1940
                                                        -Vi 27546, HMV 9079
Vi 26542. Frenesi(42546)
     "    Adios Mariquita Linda(42547)
Vi 26563. Gloomy Sunday(42548)/Don't Fall Asleep(42551)      -HMV 9116
Vi 26614. My Fantasy(42549)/Mister Meadowlark
Vi 26642. Dreaming Out Loud                                  -Vi 201537
     "    Now We Know

     (Shaw,clarinet: B.Kanter,L.Bowen,H.Lawson,Jack Stacy,saxes; sub. Gell-
     er,trumpet,for Margulies; Cane,French horn; Bluestone,Cracov,Joyce, M.
     Russell,B.Bower,B.Morrow,violins; Sturkin,S.Freed,violas; C.Bernard,
     cello; L.Henderson,piano; Sherwood,guitar: J.De Naut,bass; S.Prinz,
     drums):                                                May 13,1940
Vi 26654. April in Paris/King for a Day                      -HMV 9105
Vi 26760. Old Old Castle in Scotland/If It's You
Vi 26790. A Handful of Stars/Love of My Life
Vi 27230. Star Dust/Temptation
Vi 27256. You Forgot About Me/Whispers in the Night
Vi 27315. Beau Night in Hotchkiss Corners/The Calypso

     (Shaw,clarinet; G.Wendt,J.Cathcart,Billy Butterfield,trumpets; Jack
     Jenny,Vernon Brown,trombones: H.Plumb,C.Bassey,altos; Les Robinson,
     Jerry Jerome,tenors: T.Boardman,T.Klages,B.Brower,B.Morrow,A.Beller,E.
     Lamas,violins; A.Harshman,K.Collins,violas; F.Goerner,cello; Johnny
     Guarnieri,piano; Al Hendrickson,guitar: Jud De Naut,bass; Nick Fatool,
     drums):                                                Sept. 1940
Vi 27335. Dancing in the Dark/(GRAMERCY FIVE)      -Vi 201554, Vi 27548
Vi 27343. Pyramid                                            -HMV 9197
     "    This is Romance
Vi 27354. Danza Lucumi                                       -HMV 9197
     "    Chantez Les Bas
```

```
Vi 27362. I Cover Waterfront(add Ray Coniff,trombone)/Marinela   -HMV 9214
Vi 27385. Alone Together/Who's Excited?
Vi 27411. Blues, 1 & 2
Vi 27405. Moonglow(Coniff,trombone)/(GRAMERCY FIVE)             -Vi 27549
```

ARTIE SHAW AND HIS GRAMERCY FIVE (Shaw,clarinet: Billy Butterfield,
trumpet: Johnny Guarnieri,harpsichord: Al Hendrickson,guitar: Jud de
Naut,bass: Nick Fatool,drums):   Late 1940
```
Vi 26762. Special Delivery Stomp                               -HMV 9146
    "     Keepin' Myself for You
Vi 26763. Summit Ridge Drive(no guitar)                        -HMV 9146
    "     Cross Your Heart
Vi 27289. Dr.Livingstone I presume/When Quail Come Back to SQ  -HMV 9207
Vi 27335. Smoke Gets in Your Eyes
Vi 27405. My Blue Heaven
```

ARTIE SHAW AND HIS ORCHESTRA (Unknown personnel):
```
Vi 27432. What Is There to Say/Prelude in C Major
Vi 27499. Georgia on My Mind/Why Shouldn't I
```

(Shaw,clarinet; Henry Allen,trumpet; J.C.Higginbotham,trombone; Benny
Carter,alto; Sonny White,piano; Jim Shirley,guitar: Billy Taylor,bass;
drums; eight violins; two violas; two cellos; harp: Lena Horne,vocals):
June 26,1941
```
Vi 27509. Love Me a Little Little(066147)                      -HMV 9322
    "     Don't Take Your Love from Me(066149)    -Vi 201593, HMV 9322
Unissued. Confessin'(066146)/Beyond the Blue Horizon(066148)
```

(Unknown personnel):
```
Vi 27536. It Had to Be You                                     -Vi 201593
    "     If I Had You
Vi 27609. This Time the Dream's on Me/Blues in the Night(fea.Hot Lips Page,
Vi 27641. Is It Taboo/Beyond the Blue Horizon         (vocal & trumpet)
Vi 27664. If I Love Again/Rockin' Chair
Vi 27703. Nocurne/Through the Years
Vi 27705. Solid Sam/Make Love to Me
Vi 27719. I Ask the Stars/Take Your Shoes Off,Baby(Hot Lips Page,voc.)
Vi 27746. Someone's Rocking My Dreamboat/I Don't Want to Walk Without You
Vi 27779. Absent Minded Moon/Not Mine
Vi 27798. Hindustan/Somebody Nobody Loves
Vi 27806. Just Kiddin' Around/Sometimes I feel like Motherless Child(Hot
Vi 27838. To a Broadway Rose/Deuces Wild              (Lips Page,voc.)
Vi 27860. Carnival/Needlenose                                  -HMV 9291
Vi 27895. St.James Infirmary Blues,1 & 2(Hot Lips Page,trumpet) -HMV 9307
```

(Shaw,clarinet; Les Clarke,Tommy Mace,altos; John Walton,Herb Steward,
tenors: Chuck Gentry,baritone; Tony Fase,Roy Eldridge,Ray Linn,George
Schwartz,trumpets· Ray Conniff,Pat McNaughton,Skip Morr,Harry Rodgers,
trombones; Dodo Marmarosa,piano; Barney Kessel,guitar: Morey Rayman,
bass: Lou Fromm,drums):
```
Vi 201612. Ac-cent-chu-ate the Positive/Jumpin' on the Merry Go Round
Vi 201620. Lady Day/Let's Take the Long Way Home
Vi 201638. 'S Wonderful/I'll Never Be the Same
Vi 201668. Little Jazz/September Song
Vi 201696. Bedford Drive/Tabu
Vi 201716. That's for Me/Yolanda
```

ARTIE SHAW AND HIS GRAMERCY FIVE (Shaw,clarinet; Roy Eldridge,trumpet;
Dodo Marmarosa,piano; Barney Kessel,guitar; Morris Rayman,bass: Lou
Fromm,drums):   Jan.,1945
```
Vi 201647. Sad Sack/Grabtown Apple
Vi 201800. Mysteriose/Hop Skip and Jump
Vi 201929. The Gentle Grifter/Scuttlebut
```

ARTIE SHAW AND HIS ORCHESTRA:
```
Vi 201930. These Foolish Things/Time on My Hands
Vi 201931. They Didn't Believe Me/Can't Help Lovin' Dat Man
Vi 201932. Lament/Kasbah
Vi 201933. I Could Write a Book/A Foggy Day
Vi 201934. I Can't Get Started/Easy to Love
Vi 201935. Just Floatin' Along/No One But You
Vi 201936. I Can't Escape from You/Keepin' Myself for You
Vi 201937. Thrill of a Lifetime/Lucky Number
```

(12-inch records: dates and personnel unavailable):
```
Vi 36383. Concerto for clarinet, 1 & 2
Vi 280405. Suite No. 8/Evensong
Vi 280406. Summertime/Maid With the Flaccid Air
```

```
Mu   357. Let's Walk(5408)/Ghost of a Chance(5417A)              1946
Mu   365. Along With Me/I Got the Sun in the Morning
Mu   389. Night and Day/Get Out of Town
Mu   390. In the Still of the Night/What Is This Thing Called Love
Mu   391. Begin the Beguine(withdrawn)Love for Sale(substitute)/You Do
Mu   392. I've Got You Under My Skin/Heart Belongs to Daddy   (Something
Mu   409. The Hornet/How Deep Is the Ocean
Mu   378. The Glider(5419-?)/Love of My Life(5416C)
Mu   412. Changing My Tune(5635)/For You For Me Forevermore(5629)
Mu   428. Anniversary Song/Guilty
Mu   441. They Can't Convince Me(5467)/And So to Bed(5650)
Mu   445. Connecticut/Don't You Believe It Dear
Mu 5004-05-06. The Pied Piper of Hamelin(narrated by Harry Von Zell,with
              original music by Artie Shaw
```

SHAW, JESSIE (vocals):
```
Ro   303. I Couldn Stand a Little Lovin'/Don't Take
Ro   372. I Haven't Told Her/I Ain't Got Nobody
```

SHAW AND HIS ORCHESTRA, JOEL:
```
Cr  3244. Who's Your Little Who-Zis(1566-2B)
     "    One More Kiss, Then Goodnight(1567-1A)
Cr  3271. Sweet Violets
     "    Business in F (C1628)                               -Vs 8035
Cr  3285. Some of These Days/Alexander's Ragtime Band
Cr  3304. Oh Monah
    "3304. Business in Q(C1691)                               -Vs 8035
Cr  3312. Call of the Freaks/Mouthful of Jam
Cr  3319. The Darktown Strutters Ball/Dinah
Cr  3332. Minnie the Moocher's Weddin' Day/When You're Getting Along With
Cr  3333. The Scat Song/How'm I Doin'                         (Your Gal
Cr  3352. That's a Plenty/Let's Have a Party
Cr  3362. Get Cannibal/Basin Street Blues
Cr  3381. Sing(1851-2A)/This Is the Chorus of a Song(1852-1B)
Cr  3382. Avalon/Margie
Cr  3413. White Zombie/The Old Man of the Mountain
Cr  3414. Jazz Pie/Yeah Man
Cr  3423. Goin' to Town/Reefer Man
Cr  3444. Original Dixieland One-Step(1981-2B)/Ida(1980-3A)
Cr  3451. Indiana/One-Man Woman
Vs  8029. Tiger Rag/Clarinet Marmalade
Vs  8041. Tony's Wife/Sweet Muchacha
          (See also: Harlem Wildcats)
```

SHAW AND HIS DETROITERS, MILT
```
Me 12040. Blue Again/To Whom It May Concern
Me 12098. Walkin' My Baby Back Home/Running Between the Rain Drops
Vo 15697. Poor People/That's My Weakness Now
```

   (Red Nichols,Phil Napoleon,trumpets: Miff Mole,trombone; Fud Livingston,clarinet and tenor: Arthur Schutt,piano: Stan King,drums; violin;
   tuba):
```
OK 41158. Where Shy Little Violets Grow(401392)/(DORSEY BROS.)-OdG 189226
OK 41172. On the Alamo(401393C)/(RAYMOND DANCE BAND)
          (See Miff Mole,OK 41153 for two other sides cut at same time)
```

   (Unknown personnel):
```
OK 41196. A Precious Little Thing Called Love(401580)/Mia Bella Rosa(401581B)
Co  1811. Walking With Susie(148158)/Breakaway(148159)
Cr  3002. What's the Use of Living Without Love(1031)
Cr  3005. My Baby Just Cares for Me(1029-2A)/Don't Tell Her(1030-3)
```

SHAWNE AND HIS ORCHESTRA, TED (Pseudonym for Louis Armstrong on American
                                                           (Parlophone)
SHAYNE, HARRY 'FREDDIE' (Piano and vocals):   Chicago, 1936
```
De  7663. Mr. Freddy Blues(90533A)/Lonesome Man Blues(90534A)  Ch 50061
```

   J.H. 'MR. FREDDIE' SHAYNE (Shayne,piano; John Lindsay,bass; Baby Dodds,
   drums):
```
Ci  1011. Mr. Freddy's Rag(C-3A-4)/Chestnut Street Boogie(C-6-4)
          (See also: Priscilla Stewart, Para 12224; Redd Nicholson, Br 7220)
```

SHELLY'S TRIO (Johnny Hodges,alto: Eddie Heywood,piano; Shelly Manne,drums):
```
Sig 90003. Flamingo/Night and Day                            May 26,1944
Sig 90004. On the Sunny Side of the Street/Time on My Hands
```

SHELTON, EZRA HOWLETT (piano rag solo):
```
Au   724. Dearest Darling                                     -Se  3
```

SHEFTER AND HIS RHYTHM OCTET, BERT (Bert Shefter and V. Brenner,pianos;
Toots Mondello, Paul Ricci, saxes: Dave Wade,trumpet: Herb Quigley,drums;
Adrian Rollini,vibraphone: K.Binford,guitar: Art Bernstein,bass):
  Vi 25614. S.O.S./Locomotive
  Vi 25622. Chopin's Ghost/(BUNNY BERIGAN ORCH.)
  Vi 25632. Burglar's Revenge

    BERT SHEFTER AND HIS ORCHESTRA (Bert Shefter,piano; Nat Brown,sax;
    Al Raxon,clarinet; Al Philburn,trombone: Hymie Rosenbaum,trumpet;
    Phil Kraus,vibraphone; Richard Von Holberg,bass; Sam Weiss,drums):
  De 2525. Monkey on a String/Trammin' at the Fair
  De 2584. Farmer in a Delemma(65566-A)/Deserted Desert(65569-A)
  De 2653. Toast to Paganini's Ghost/Wig Wag

SHEPARD AND HIS KENTUCKY BOYS, OLLIE:
  De 7384. If It Ain't Love/It's a Low Down Dirby Shame
  De 7400. Honey Bee/Sweetheart Land
  De 7408. No One to Call You Dear/She Walks Like a Kangaroo
  De 7435. Drunk Again/One Woman Blues
  De 7448. S-B-A Blues/Brown Skin Woman
De 7463. What's Your Guess/Good Woman
  De 7480. Biscuit Rolling Time/Hope You Haven't Forgotten Me
  De 7493. This Place Is Leaping/Solid Jack
  De 7508. Little Pigmeat/Frankenstein Blues
  De 7541. Pee Wee Pee Wee/At Your Mercy
  De 7585. Numbers Blues/New Low Down Dirty Shame
  De 7613. Outdoors Blues/My Blood Dripping Blues
  De 7602. Sugar Woman Blues/Shepard Blues
  De 7629. Sweetest Thing Born/Jelly Roll
  De 7639. Blues 'Bout My Gal/ Oh Maria
  De 7651. Li'l Liza Jane/Don't You Know
  De 7665. Baby It's My Time Now/King of All Evil
  De 7716. Hell Is So Low Down/Octabia Blues

SHEROCK AND HIS ORCHESTRA, SHORTY (Sherock,trumpet; Willie Smith,alto;
Corky Corcoran,tenor; Arnold Ross,piano; Allen Reuss,guitar: Dave Coleman,
drums; Ed Mihelich,bass):   Hollywood,Jan.31,1945
  Sig 28113. Meandering(SRC 1945-1)/Talk of the Town(SRC 1945-3)
  Sig 28118. Snafu(LS 1945-2)/The Willies(LS 1945-4)

SHERWOOD AND HIS ORCHESTRA, BOBBY:
  Cap 107. The Elks Parade/I Don't Know Why
  Cap 123. Harlem Butterfly/Moonlight Becomes You
  Cap 161. Arkansas/Swingin' at the Semloh
  Cap 231. Snap Your Fingers(794-4A)/Cotton Tail(795-4A)
  Cap 286. Sherwood's Forest/Least That's My Opinion

    (Bobby Sherwood,conductor and arranger: Eddie Greene,Bob Burns,Don
    Anderson,William Waddilove,trumpets; Bob Leaman,Bert Johnson,Al Thompson,trombones: Joe McAnarney,Bob Graetlinger, Herbie Haymer,Harry
    Schuchman,Eddie Lucas,saxes; Basil Hutchinson,guitar; Fritz Becker,
    piano; Don Tonti,bass; John Cyr,drums):   Hollywood,Dec.4,1944
  Cap 10037. In the Dark(499-2A)/(BILLY BUTTERFIELD)

SHOFFNER, BOB (trumpet) see:
  HALF PINT JAXON: Vo 2553, 2603.
  JIMMY O'BRYANT: Para 12297, 12312.
  KING OLIVER:
  LUIS RUSSELL: OK 8424, 8454.

SHORT, TONY (piano solos, recorded in England):
  DeF 8525. Dipper Mouth Blues(DR 9012-2)/Milton Street Moan(DR 9018-2)

SHORTY GEORGE (vocals)
  Br 7106. Jones Law Blues/My Babe Blues

SHREVEPORT SIZZLERS (Trumpet: trombone: saxes: rhythm):
  OK 8918. Railroad Rhythm(405106A)/Zonky(405107A)
SIGNORELLI AND HIS ORCHESTRA, FRANK (Including Frank Signorelli,piano; probably Red Nichols,trumpet, and others):
  Pe 14699. She's Still My Baby(107072-2)/(McLAUGHLIN'S MELODIANS)
  Pe 14704. Don't Be Angry With Me/(LOU GOLD ORCHESTRA)

OMER SIMEON

See also:
  HARRY DIAL: Vo 1594.
  DIXIE RHYTHM KINGS: Br 7115, 7127
  LIONEL HAMPTON: Vi 26114, 26173.

FLETCHER HENDERSON: Vi 25297, 25317.
ALEX HILL: Vo 1465, 1493.
EARL HINES: Br 6345 through BB 10870.
J.C. JOHNSON: QRS 7064.
R.M.JONES: Victors.
JIMMIE LUNCEFORD:
PAUL MARES: OK 41574, 41575.
JELLY ROLL MORTON:
KING OLIVER:
KID ORY: Crs 1,2,5,7.
RHYTHM ACES: Br 4244, 7120.
JABBO SMITH:
EVA TAYLOR: ?
TINY PARHAM:
JIMMY MUNDY: Vr.

<u>SIMEON, OMER</u> (clarinet solos, acc. by Earl Hines,piano; Claude Roberts, banjo; Wallace Bishop,drums): <u>1930</u>
  Br 7109. Beaukoo Jack/Smoke House Blues

    OMER SIMEON TRIO, The Carnival Three: Simeon,clarinet; James P.Johnson, piano; George 'Pops' Foster,bass): <u>New York,Feb.22,1945</u>
  Disc 6001. Lorenzo's Blues(D205)/Harlem Hotcha(D206)
  Disc 6002. Bandanna Days(D207)/Creole Lullaby(D208)

<u>SIMPSON, COLETHA</u> (vocal acc. by James Williams,piano):
  Br 7089. Riverside Blues/Lonesome Lonesome Blues(with piano & guitar)

    (Acc. by Cass Simpson,piano):
  Br 7112. Black Man's Blues/Down South Blues

<u>SIMPSON, CASSINO</u> (piano, see):
  MADLYN DAVIS: Para 12498, 12528.
  RUTH JOHNSON: Para 13060.
  LAURA RUCKER: Para 13075, 13087.
  COLETHA SIMPSON: Br 7112.
  ARTHUR SIMS: OK 8373, 40675.

<u>SIMS AND HIS CREOLE ROOF ORCHESTRA, ARTHUR</u> (Bernie Young,trumpet; Preston Jackson,trombone; Arthur Sims,alto and clarinet; Cassino Simpson,piano; Bill Williams,bass; Cliff Jones,drums): <u>Chicago,1926</u>
  OK 8373. How Do You Like It Blues(9763A)/Soapstick Blues(9765A)
  OK 40675. As Long As I Have You(9764)/(COOKIE'S GINGERSNAPS) -PaE 5711

<u>SIMS, HENRY</u> (vocal acc. by violin and guitar):
  Para 12940. Tell Me Man Blues(L65-1)/Be True Be True Blues(L66-2)

<u>SIMS, LEE</u> (piano; many with trumpet or other acc.)
  Br 3202. Tenderly/Talking to the Moon
  Br 3266. I'd Climb the Highest Mountain/Adorable
  Br 3320. Pal of My Lonesome Hours
        What's the Use of Cryin' -BrE 1025
  Br 3551. Falling in Love With You/Song of the Wanderer
  Br 3617. Me and My Shadow/I'm Coming Virginia
  Br 3754. Let's Misbehave/Mine All Mine
  Br 3758. The Song Is Ended/Among My Souvenirs
  Br 3764. Some of These Days/Meditation
  Br 3799. Indian Love Call/Deep in My Heart, Dear
  Br 3800. Are You Thinking of Me Tonight/Diane
  Br 4010. If I Lost You/When Summer Is Gone
  Br 4152. I Can't Give You Anything But Love/Sonny Boy
  Br 4339. Caressing You/If I Had You
  Br 4422. Love Me or Leave Me/Lover Come Back to Me
  Br 4572. Pagan Love Song/I'm Just a Vagabond Lover
  Br 4639. Don't Ever Leave Me/Why Was I Born
  Br 4650. Gotta Feelin' for You/Ain't Misbehavin'
  Br 4780. St. Louis Blues/I Wish I Could Shimmy Like My Sister Kate
  Br 6040. Body and Soul/Something to Remember You By -BrE 1092
  Br 6132. Rockin' Chair/Star Dust -BrE 1153
  Br 6212. Blues in My Heart/Sweet and Lovely -BrE 1248
  Br 6649. Don't Blame Me/Lazybones -BrE 01604
  BrE 01679. Did You Ever See a Dream Walking/Everything I Have Is Yours
  Br 20069. Contrasts/Improvisation
  De 875. Take My Heart/There's a Small Hotel
  De 879. These Foolish Things Remind Me of You/When Did You Leave Heaven

<u>SINGLETON AND HIS ORCHESTRA, ZUTTY</u> (Lil Armstrong,piano; Red Allen,trumpet; Benny Morton,trombone; Edmond Hall,clarinet; Bernard Addison,guitar; George 'Pops' Foster,bass; Zutty Singleton,drums): <u>1940</u>
  De 18093. King Porter Stomp(67841A)/Shim-me-sha-wabble(67842A)

```
          ZUTTY SINGLETON'S TRIO (Barney Bigard,clarinet: Fred Washington,piano;
          Zutty Singleton,drums):                         Hollywood,June 30,1944
     Cap 10022. Lulu's Mood(265-1B)/Barney's Bounce(264-2A)

          ZUTTY SINGLETON'S CREOLE BAND (Bigard,clarinet; Norman Bowdwn,trumpet;
          Shorty Houghton,trombone: Fred Washington,piano; Bud Scott, guitar; Ed
          Garland,bass; Zutty Singleton,drums):           Hollywood,June 30,1944
     Cap 10023. Crawfish Blues(263-3A)/(EDDIE MILLER)

SIOUX CITY SIX (Bix Beiderbecke,cornet; Miff Mole,trombone; Frankie Trumbauer,
alto; Rube Bloom,piano; Min Leibrook,bass: Vic Moore,drums):        Dec.,1924
     Ge  5569. Flock o' Blues(9119A)/I'm Glad(9120C)            -BrE 02207, Se 7

SISSLE, NOBLE (vocals with orchestra, probably led by Jim Europe):
     Pat 22284. I'm Just Simply Full of Jazz/Ain't Cha Coming Back, Mary Ann
     Pat 22357. Jazz Baby's Ball/Melodious Jass

          (With Eubie Blake, vocal and piano):
     Vi  19494. Manda/Dixie Moon
     Vi  19086. Down Hearted Blues/Waitin' for the Evening Mail
     Med  8252. Crazy Blues/(ARTHUR FIELDS)
     Para 12007. Crazy Blues(156)/(ALBERTA HUNTER)
     Re   9158. Doggone Struttin' Fool/Red White and Blues

          (Acc. by Rube Bloom, piano):
     OK  40877. Broken Hearted(81226C)/Just Once Again(81227C)
     OK  40882. A Night in June/Are You Happy

          NOBLE SISSLE AND HIS SIZZLING SYNCOPATORS (Unknown personnel):
     Em  10296. St. Louis Blues/Broadway Blues
     Em  10357. Loveless Love/Boll Weevil Blues
     Em  10365. Long Gone(41700)/Low Down Blues(41699)
     Em  10367. Royal Garden Blues(41636)/My Mammy's tears(41701)
     Em  10385. Baltimore Buzz(41783)/Honeysuckle Time(41784)

          (Buster Bailey,Rudy Jackson,Ramon Usera,saxes; Juice Wilson,Roseman,
          violins; Pike Davis,Demus Dean,trumpets: Jim Reevy,trombon; Pinckney,
          piano; Henry Edwards,bass: Jesse Baltimore,drums):
     PaF   125. Just Give the Southland to Me/Sunny Skies          London, 1929
     PaF   126. Love Lies/Again
     PaF   259. Colombo/Shout Hallelujah
     HMV  5709. Camp Meetin' Day/Miranda
     HMV  5731. Kansas City Kitty/I'm Crooning a Tune About You
     HMV  5723. Recollections/You Want Lovin' and I want Love

          (Sub. Arthur Briggs,Tommy Ladnier,trumpets; Billy Burn,trombone; Frank
          Goodie,sax, for Bailey; Edward Coles,bass; Jack Carter,drums; omit
          violins; add Frank Ethridge,guitar):
     CoF   192. Daughter of the Latin Quarter/Sunny Sunflower Land
     CoF   193. You Can't Get to Heaven That Way/Confessin'

          NOBLE SISSLE AND HIS ORCHESTRA (Tommy Ladnier,Arthur Briggs,trumpets;
          Billy Burns,trombone; Sidney Bechet,soprano and bass sax; Ramon Usera,
          Ralph DeChesney,Rudy Jackson,saxes; Pinckney,piano; Frank Ethridge,gui-
          tar; Edward Coles,bass: Jack Carter,drums):            New York,1930
     Br   6073. Loveless Love       -Me 12444*,Pe 15649, BrE 1117, BrF 9049
      "         Got the Bench Got the Park                "       "       "
                *Under "Georgia Syncopators"

     Br   6111. Roll on Mississippi, Roll on/Wha'd Ya do to Me -BrF 1158,BrF 9073
     Br   6129. Basement Blues/(ANDY KIRK)                       -BrF 500124

          (Wendell Culley,Demus Dean,Clarence Brereton,trumpets: Chester Burrill,
          trombone; Sidney Bechet,soprano and clarinet; James Tolliver,Ramon
          Usera,Harvey Boone,saxes: Oscar Madera,violin; Harry Brooks,piano;
          Howard Hill,guitar; Edward Coles,bass: Jack Carter,drums.--JI 11/22/40):
     De    153. Under Creole Moon(9295: Sissle,voc.)/Polka Dot Rag(9298)Chicago/34
     De    154. The Old Ark Is Moverin'(9296; Billy Banks,voc.)   -BrE 01851
      "         Loveless Love(9297; Lavada Carter, voc.)                 "

          (Sub. Chauncey Haughton,sax, for Boone):                     New York
     De    766. I Wonder Who Made Rhythm(60890:Banks, voc.)           -CoE 5032
      "         Tain't a Fit Night Out for Man(60891; Sissle,voc.)    -CoE 1493
     De    778. That's What Love Did to Me(60888: Lena Horne,voc.)
      "         You Can't Live in Harlem(60889; Banks, voc.)
     De    847. I Take to You(60892; Lena Horne,voc.)               -CoE 5032
      "         Rhythm of the Broadway Moon(60893: Sissle, voc.)    -CoF 1493

          (Sub. Gil White, sax, for Tolliver; Jimmy Miller, guitar: Jimmy Jones,
          bass; Wilbur Kirk, drums; Tolliver on piano):           New York,1937
```

Vr   552. Bandana Days(398)/I'm Just Wild About Harry(399)
Unissued. Dear Old Southland/St.Louis Blues

    NOBLE SISSLE'S SWINGSTERS (Bechet, Miller, Jones, Kirk):
Vr   648. Okey Doke(406)/Characteristic Bl(407; Billy Banks,voc.)-Vo 3840
    (See also: Sidney Bechet and Noble Sissle's Swingsters)

SIX BLACK DIAMONDS:
  Ba 1265. Sobbin' Blues(5292-2)/Easy Melody(5296-1)
  Ba 1188. Nothin' But
  Ba 1181. Farewell Blues
  Ba 1656. Steppin' Fool(6284-2)/(NEWPORT SOCIETY ORCHESTRA)   -Do 3633
  Ba 1540. Charleston/Sweet Georgia Brown
  Ba 6167. Chloe/(MISSOURI JAZZ BAND)
  Ba 6318. Dixiana/(CAMPUS BOYS)
  Re 8149. Susie Oh Susie/Mary Lou
  Re 8706. I Never Care About Tomorrow
  Re 9527. Oh Min/Rubetown Frolics
  Re 9612. Lots o' Mamma(5425-2)/Mindin' My Business(5426-2)
  Re 9682. Charleston Cabin(5560-1)/(FLETCHER HENDERSON)

SIX BLUE CHIPS (Pee Wee Irwin,trumpet: Joe Marsala, clarinet: Frank Signorelli,piano; Carmen Mastren,guitar: Art Shapiro,bass: Stan King,drums):
  De   740. Steel Roof(60356)/Cheatin' Cheech   (--Tempo,Jan.1940

SIX HOTTENTOTS (Red Nichols,trumpet: Miff Mole,trombone· Jimmy Dorsey,clari-
net; Arthur Schutt,piano; Vic Berton,drums: Joe Tarto,bass.--JI 2/16/40):
  Ba 1964. I'm in Love Again(7173-2)/(MISSOURI JAZZ BAND)-Re 8289, Do 3935
  Ba 1986. Memphis Blues(7241)   -Re 8335, Do 3956
  Ba 6009. Hurricane(7265-1)   -Re 8335, Do 3976
    "   Melancholy Charlie(7264)   -D6 3975
  Ba 6008. Sometimes I'm Happy(7174-3)/(INDIANA FIVE)   -Do 3975
  Do 3956. St. Louis Blues
  Do 3931. Rosy Cheeks(7175-1)   -Re 8289,Max 1622
  (Note: The last title also was issued on Oriole 883 under the
  name of the Dixie Jazz Band)

SIX JOLLY JESTERS (Duke Ellington's Orchestra):   1930
  Vo 1449. Oklahoma Stomp(E31372)/(JUNIE C. COBB)
  Vo 15843. Six or Seven Times(E31301)/Goin' Nuts(E31371)--Last side may not
                                                    (be Ellington)
SIX MEN AND A GIRL (Earl Thompson,trumpet; Mary Lou Williams,piano; Dick
Wilson,tenor; Floyd Smith,guitar; Buddy Miller,alto and clarinet; Booker
Collins,bass; Ben Thigpen,drums):   New York,Jan.26,1940
  Vs 8190. Scratchin' the Gravel(US 1318-1)/Zonky(US 1319-1)
  Vs 8193. Mary Lou Williams Blues(US 1316-1)/Tea for Two(US 1317-1)

SKILES AND HIS VINE STREET BOYS, DUDE:
  vr   516. I Can't Give You Anything But Love/My Girl
  Vr   . Blackberry Jam/Farewell Blues

SKILLET DICK AND HIS FRYING PANS:
  Ch 40086. Rock and Gravel/Jelly Bean Rag

SLACK AND HIS EIGHT BEATS, FREDDIE:
  De 4043. Boogie Woogie on Kitten on the Keys(DLA 2469)
    "   That Place Down the Road Apiece(DLS 2471A; trio)
  De 4130. Pig Foot Pete/Strange Cargo

    FREDDIE SLACK AND HIS ORCHESTRA:
  Cap 102. Here You Are(14A)/Cow Cow Boogie(16A) Ella Mae Morse,voc.
  Cap 113. Doll Dance/He's My Guy
  Cap 115. Mister Five by Five/The Thrill Is Gone
  Cap 122. I Lost My Sugar in Salt Lake City/The Wreck of the Old '97
  Cap 126. That Old Black Magic/Hit the Road to Dreamland
  Cap 129. Riffette/(JOHNNY MERCER)
  Cap 133. Get on Board Little Chillun/Old Rob Roy
  Cap 137. Waitin' for the Evening Mail/(PAUL WHITEMAN)
  Cap 146. Furlough Fling/Silver Wings in the Moonlight

    (Karl Leaf,Lee Baxter,Neeley Plumb,Clyde Hylton,Ralph Lee,Barney
    Bigard,reeds: William Morris,Charlie Griffard,George Wendt,trumpets;
    Gerald Foster,Bill Lower,Jimmy Skiles,trombones; T-Bone Walker,guitar;
    Phil Stephens,bass: Henry Coleman,drums; Freddi Slack,piano):
  Cap 160. Ain't That Just Like a Man/Swingin' on Star Hollywood,Mar.9,1944
  Cap 172. Cuban Sugar Mill/Small Batch o' Nod
  Cap 203. A Kiss Goodnight/Gee Chi Love Song

    (Unknown personnel):
  Cap 251. House of Blue Light/Hey Mr. Postman

```
        (Slack and Ella Mae Morse,voc., with rhythm section):
   Cap   278. Pig Foot Pete(1088-2)/Your Conscience Tells You So(1087-3)

        (With T-Bone Walker,vocal and guitar):
   Cap 10033. I Got a Break,Baby/Mean Old World

          FREDDIE SLACK EIGHT BEATS BY FOUR (Slack,piano: Remo Palmieri,guitar;
          Clyde Lombardi,bass; Irving Kluger,drums):
   Cap 20029. Behind the Fight Beat(372-2A1)/Rib Joint(371-2A2)

          FREDDIE SLACK AND HIS ORCHESTRA:
   Cap 20030. Southpaw Serenade(377-3A1)/Strange Cargo(379-3A1)
   Cap 20031. Blackout Boogie(solo: 380-4A1)/Cat's 9th Life(8 Beats;369-2A1)
   Cap 20032. Kitten on the Keys(378-3A1)/Bashful Baby Blues(253-4A)
```

SLIM AND HIS HOT BOYS (Slim Lamar,George Schilling,Jimmy Rush,saxes; Irwin
Kunz,Tony Almerico,trumpets; Ellis Stratakos,trombone; Dee Larreque,piano;
Von Gammon,drums; Benny Pottle,drums; Jack Cohan,guitar and vocal):
   Vi 38044. Mississippi Stomp/That's a Plenty

SLIM AND SLAM (Slim Gaillard,guitar; Slam Stewart,bass, and others):
   Vo 3981. Tip-i-Tin   -PaE 2542
         " That's What You Call Romance
   Vo 4021. Flat Foot Floogee   -PaE 2542
         " Chinatown
   Vo 4110. Dancing on the Beach/Ferdinand
   Vo 4225. Look-a-There/Tutti Frutti   -PaE 2594
   PaE 2567. Lady Be Good/8,9 and 10
   Vo 4346. Vol Vist du Gaily Star/Jump Session
   Vo 4461. Laughin' in Rhythm/Humpty Dumpty

          (Slim Gaillard,guitar and vocal; Slam Stewart,bass and vocal: K.Hollen,
          tenor; S.Allen,piano; S. Dobson,drums):
   Vo 4521. Dopey Joe(23683)/Buck Dance Rhythm(23686)   -PaF 2634
   Vo 4594. Sweet Safronia(23684)/It's Gettin' Kinda Chilly(23685)-PaE 2707
          (See also: Slim Gaillard)

SLOKE AND IKE (blues singing):
   De 7315. Chocolate Candy Blues/Raggedy But Right
   De 7375. Say Pretty Mama/Slocum Blues

SLOPPY HENRY (vocal with piano by Eddie Heywood,Sr.):
   OK 8178. Tom Cat Rag/Cannon Ball Blues

          (Acc. by guitar and violin):
   OK 8630. Long Tall Disconnected Mama/Canned Heat Blues

          (Piano and cornet. King Oliver?):
   OK 8683. Hobo Blues(402281)/The Best Cheap Car in the Market Is a Ford
                                                                    (402282)
          (Acc. Porter Grainger, piano; cornet):
   OK 8805. Some Sweet Rainy Day/Say I Do It(acc.Lonnie Johnson,guitar)
   OK 8845. Jomo Man Blues/Royal Palm Blues(acc. by Grainger only)

SMALL, PAUL (vocals featuring accompaniment by Joe Venuti,violin and Eddie
   CoE 1050. Till Tomorrow(265000)/Remember Romance(265001)   (Lang,guitar):
   CoE 1070. Baby(265003)/Just a Little Home(265022)
   CoE 1096. Hold Me(265019)/Sidewalk Waltz(265035)
   CoE 1136. Just a Little Flower Shop(265101)/I Can't Remember(265103)

          PAUL SMALL'S COLLEGIANS:
   Cr 3196. Guilty(1472)/Who Am I(1474)

SMITH AND LEE (vocals acc. by Johnny Dodds,clarinet: Baby Dodds,drums; Lil
Armstrong,piano):
   Vi 38607. If I Could Be With You/(LIZZIE MILES)

BESSIE SMITH

SMITH, BESSIE (vocals, acc. by Clarence Williams,piano)--Vocal Jazz
                                                    New York,Feb.15-16,1923
   Co 3844. Down Hearted Blues(80863)/Gulf Coast Blues(80864)
   Co 3898. 'Tain't Nobody's Biz-Ness If I Do(80862)/Keeps on A-Rainin'
                                                                    (80865)
          BESSIE SMITH AND HER DOWN HOME TRIO (Clarinet: banjo: Clarence Williams,
          piano):   April 11,1923
   Co 3877. Aggravatin' Papa(80949)/Beale Street Mamma(80950)

          (Clarence Williams,piano):
   Co 3888. Baby Won't You Please Come Home Blues(80952)/Oh Daddy Blues(80953)

```
          (Fletcher Henderson,piano):                       April 28,1923
Co  3900. Mama's Got the Blues(80995)/Outside of That(80996)
Co  3936. Bleeding Hearted Blues(81075)/Midnight Blues(81080)June 14-15,1923
Unissued. Sittin' on the Curbstone Blues(81074)
Co  3939. Lady-Luck Blues(81078)/Yodling Blues(81079)
Co  3942. If You Don't I Know Who Will(81092)              June 21,1923
      "   Nobody in Town Can Bake a Sweet Jelly Roll Like Mine(81093)
Unissued. Play 'em for Mamma(81091)

          (Irving Johns,piano):                            Sept.20,1923
Co  4001. Jail-House Blues(81226)
      "   Graveyard Dream Blues(81237  Jimmy Jones,piano)  Sept.26,1923
Unissued. Dot 'em Down Blues(81225)

          (George Baquet,clarinet: Irving Johns,piano):    Sept.27,1923
Co 13000. Whoa,Tillie,Take Your Time(81224)/My Sweetie Went Away(81245)

          (Jimmy Jones,piano):                             Sept.26,1923
Co 13001. Cemetery Blues(81241)
      "   Any Woman's Blues(81283: Fletcher Henderson,piano)  Oct.16,1923
Unissued. Blue Bessie(81238)

          (Johns and Jones,pianos):                        Sept.24,1923
Co 13005. St. Louis Gal(81231)/Sam Jones' Blues(81232: Johns only)

     BESSIE SMITH AND CLARA SMITH(Fletcher Henderson,piano):  Oct.4,1923
Co 13007. Far Away Blues(81261)/I'm Going Back to My Used to Be(81262)

     BESSIE SMITH (Acc. by clarinet; Fletcher Henderson,piano):  Dec.4,1923
Co 14000. Chicago Bound Blues(81391)/Mistreatin' Daddy(81392)

          (Piano and guitar):                              Jan.8-10,1924
Co 14005. Frosty Mornin'Blues(81464)/Easy Come Easy Go Blues(81470)

          (Piano and clarinet):
Co 14010. Haunted House Blues(81466)/Eavesdropper's Blues(81469)

          (Piano and guitar):
Unissued. Rampart Street Blues(81471)/Lawdy Lawdy Blues(81472)

          (Irving Johns,piano):                            April 7-9,1924
Co 14018. Boweavil Blues(81671)/Moonshine Blues(81676)

          (Violin and guitar* or piano#):                  April 4-8,1924
Co 14020. Sorrowful Blues(81664)*/Rocking Chair Blues(81669)#
Co 14023. Hateful Blues(81672)#/Frankie Blues(81675)#
Co 14025. Pinchbacks,Take'em Away(81668·Irving Johns,piano)
      "   Ticket Agent Ease Your Window Down(81670)#

          (Unknown acc.):                                  April 23,1924
Unissued. Banjo Blues(81720)/Four Flushing Papa(81721)

          (Also sax: Fletcher Henderson,piano):            July 22,1924
Co 14031. Lou'siana Low-Down Blues(81881)/Mountain Top Blues(81882)

          (Charlie Green,trombone: Henderson,piano):       July 23,1924
Co 14032. Work House Blues(81883)/House Rent Blues(81884)  July 31,1924
Co 14037. Salt Water Blues(81893)/Rainy Weather Blues(81907) Aug.8,1924

          (Joe Smith,cornet: Green,trombone: Henderson,piano):  Sept.26,1924
Co 14042. Weeping Willow Blues(140062)          -Co 3172, PaE 2479
      "   The Bye Bye Blues(140063)

          (Two clarinets: Fred Longshaw,piano):            Dec.6,1924
Co 14051. Sing Sing Prison Blues(140170)
      "   Dying Gambler's Blues(140176; sub. Green,trombone,for clarinets)

          (Fred Longshaw,piano):                           Dec.11,1924
Co 14052. Follow the Deal on Down(140161)
      "   Sinful Blues(140162)

          (Clarinets and Fred Longshaw,piano):             Dec.12,1924
Co 14060. Woman's Trouble Blues(140166)
      "   Love Me Daddy Blues(140167)

          (Louis Armstrong,cornet: Fred Longshaw,organ* or piano#):  Jan.14,1924
Co 14056. Reckless Blues(140242)*                -Co 3172, PaE 2476
      "   Sobbin' Hearted Blues(140249)#
Co 14064. The St.Louis Blues(140241)*    -Co 3171, PaE 2344, PaE 2476
      "   Cold in Hand Blues(140250)#    -Co 35672, PaE 2344
Co 14079. You've Been a Good Ole Wagon(140251)#         -Co 35672
      "   Dixie Flyer Blues(140607; Charlie Green,trombone:piano;clarinet
                                                          (April 15,1924
          (Green,trombone; piano and clarinet*):          April 14-15,1924
Unissued. Ragtime Dance(140600)
Unissued. Careless Love Blues(140604)*
Unissued. He's Gone Blues(140605)*
Unissued. Nashville Woman Blues(140606)*                     -PaE 2482
Co 14075. Soft Pedal Blues(140601)        acc. by Henderson's Hot Six, see
      "   The Yellow Dog Blues(140586:                (below)-Co 3175, PaE 2480
```

(Acc. Henderson's Hot Six: Joe Smith,cornet; Charlie Green,trombone;
Buster Bailey,clarinet: Coleman Hawkins,tenor; Fletcher Henderson,
piano; Charlie Dixon,banjo: Kaiser Marshall,drums):   May 5,1925
Co 35673. Cake Walking Babies(140585)   -CoS 342
Co 14075. The Yellow Dog Blues(140586)

(Louis Armstrong,cornet· Charlie Green,trombone· Longshaw,piano)
                                                    May 26-27,1925
Co 14083. Careless Love Blues(140626)   -Co 3172, PaE 2479
   "   He's Gone Blues(140717: Longshaw only)
Co 14090. Nashville Woman's Blues(140625)
   "   I Ain't Goin' to Play Second Fiddle (140630)
Co 14095. J. C. Holmes Blues(140629)
   "   I Ain't Got Nobody(140858; sax,piano,banjo)   Aug.19,1925

(Acc. by sax, piano, banjo):   Aug.19,1925
Co 14098. Nobody's Blues But Mine(140857)
   "   My Man Blues(140890: duet with Clara Smith, acc.by piano)9/1/25
Unissued. Down Old Georgia Way(140889: with Clara Smith)

(Clarence Williams,piano):   Nov.17,1925
Co 14109. New Gulf Coast Blues(141276)
   "   Florida Bound Blues(141277)
Unissued. I Wish I Could Shimmy Like My Sister Kate(141275)

(Joe Smith,cornet; Charlie Green,trombone; Fletcher Henderson,piano):
Co 35842. At the Christmas Ball(141283)   Nov.18,1925
Unissued. Telephone Blues(141284)
Co 14115. I've Been Mistreated and I Don't Like It(141285)
   "   Red Mountain Blues(141293; clarinet & piano) Nov.20,1925

(Alto* or cornet and piano):   Nov.20-Dec.9,1925
Co 14123. Golden Rule Blues(141294)*
   "   Lonesome Desert Blues(141370)
Unissued. At the Christmas Ball(141369)
Unissued. Squeeze Me(141373)

(Clarence Williams,piano):   March 5,1926
Co 14129. What's the Matter Now(141769)
   " ·   I Want Ev'ry Bit of It(141770)
Co 14133. Squeeze Me(141768)
   "   Jazzbo Brown from Memphis Town(141819· piano and clarinet)

(Joe Smith,cornet; Henderson,piano):   May 4,1926
Co 14137. Money Blues(142146)   -Co 3174, PaF 2478
   "   Hard Driving Papa(142148)
Co 14147. Baby Doll(142147)   -Co 35674,UHCA 5
   "   Them 'Has Been' Blues(141767; Clarence Williams,piano)
Co 14158. The Gin House Blues(141820; piano,clarinet)   March 18,1926
   "   Lost Your Head Blues(142149)

BESSIE SMITH AND HER BLUE BOYS (Joe Smith,cornet: Buster Bailey,clarint;
Fletcher Henderson,piano):   Oct.25-26,1926
Co 14172. One and Two Blues(142876)   -HRS 2,Co 36281
   "   Honey Man Blues(142875: Henderson only)
Co 14179. Young Woman's Blues(142878)   -Co 35673, UHCA 6, CoS 342
   "   Hard Time Blues(142874; Henderson only)

(Jimmy Johnson, piano):   Feb.17,1927
Co 14195. Preachin' the Blues(143490)   -Co 35842, PaF 2483
   "   Back Water Blues(143491)   -PaE 2481

BESSIE SMITH AND HER BAND (Joe Smith,cornet; Charlie Green or Jimmy
Harrison,trombone; Buster Bailey,clarinet*; Fletcher Henderson,piano;
Charlie Dixon,banjo):   March 2-3,1927
Co 14197. After You've Gone(143567)*
   "   Muddy Water(143569)*   -Co 3174, PaF 2478
Co 14209. Send Me to the 'lectric Chair(143576)
   "   Them's Graveyard Words(143583)
Co 14219. Alexander's Ragtime Band(143568)*   -Co 3173, PaE 2477
   "   There'll Be a Hot Time in Town Tonight(143570)
Co 14232. Trombone Cholly(143575)   -Co 3176, PaE 2480
   "   Lock and Key(143736; Jimmy Johnson, piano):

(Piano and guitar):   Sept.27,1927
Co 14250. Mean Old Bed Bug Blues(144796)
   "   A Good Man Is Hard to Find(144797)
Co 14260. Sweet Mistreater(143735; Johnson,piano):
   "   Homeless Blues(144800: Alto and piano)
Co 14569. Lookin' for My Man Blues(144801; Alto, piano)
   "   Hot Springs Blues(143584: see March 3, 1927)

(Tommy Ladnier,trumpet· Fletcher Henderson,piano: June Coles,tuba):
                                                        Oct.27,1927
Co 14273. Dyin' By the Hour(144918)   -CoS 346
   "   Foolish Man Blues(144919)   "

24

```
          (Trumpet; Charlie Green,trombone: piano):           Feb.9,1928
Co 14292. Thinking Blues(145626)                                -PaE 2483
   "      I Used to Be Your Sweet Mamma(145628)                 -PaE 2482
Co 14304. Pickpocket Blues(145627)
   "      I'd Rather Be Dead and Buried in My Grave(145650; clarinet,pf.)
Unissued. Hit Me in the Nose Blues(145651; clarinets, piano)

          (Charlie Green,trombone; Porter Grainger,piano):   March 20,1928
Co 14312. Empty Bed Blues, part 1 (145785)  -Co 35675, Vo 3286, CoS " 349
   "      Empty Bed Blues, part 2 (145786)                      "       "
Co 14324. Put It Right Here(145787)
   "      Spider Man Blues(145783; clarinets, piano)
Unissued. Tombstone Blues(145784; clarinets, piano)

          (Trumpet: Charlie Green,trombone; piano):           Feb.21,1928
Co 14338. Standin' in the Rain Blues(145670)
   "      It Won't Be You(145671)
Unissued. I'm a Cheater(145672)

          (Varying accompaniments, including saxes,clarinet,trombone,piano):
Co 14354. Yes Indeed He Do(146887)                           Aug.24,1928
   "      Devil's Gonna Git You(146888)
Co 14375. Washwoman's Blues(146893)
   "      Please Help Me Get Him Off My Mind(146896)
Co 14384. Slow and Easy Man(146894)
   "      Me and My Gin(146897)
Co 14399. You Ought to Be Ashamed(146889)
   "      Poor Man's Blues(146895)

          (Eddie Lang,guitar: Clarence Williams,piano):      May 8,1929
Co 14427. I'm Wild About That Thing(148485)
   "      You've Got to Give Me Some(148486)
Co 14435. Kitchen Man(148487)

          (Ed Allen,cornet: Cyrus St.Clair,tuba; Clarence Williams,piano)
Co 14435. I Got What It Takes(148533)                        May 15,1929
Co 14451. Nobody Knows You When You're Down and Out(148534)
                                          -Co 3176, PaF 2481, Co 37577
   "      Take It Right Back(148854: Williams only)
Unissued. What Makes Me Love You So(148855: Williams, piano)

          (Jimmy Johnson,piano):                              Aug.20,1929
Co 14464. He's Got Me Goin'(148902)
   "      It Makes My Love Come Down(148904)
Unissued. My Sportin' Man(148901)
Unissued. When My Baby Comes(148905)
Co 14476. Wasted Life Blues(149074)                           Oct.1,1929
   "      Dirty No Gooder's Blues(149075)
Co 14487. You Don't Understand(149136)                        Oct.11,1929
   "      Don't Cry Baby(149137)
Co 14527. Blue Spirit Blues(149134)
   "      Worn Out Papa Blues(149135)

          (Louis Bacon,trumpet; Charlie Green,trombone; Garvin Bushell,clarinet;
          Clarence Williams,piano):                          March 27,1930
Co 14516. Keep It to Yourself(150131)
   "      New Orleans Hop Scop Blues(150132)

          (Charlie Green,trombone; Clarence Williams,piano):  April 12,1930
Co 37576. See If I'll Care(150458)
   "      Baby Have Pity on Me(150459)

          (Acc. by Bessemer Singers):                          June 9,1930
Co 14538. On Revival Day(150574)
   "      Moan You Mourners(150575)

          (Trumpet and piano):                                July 22,1930
Co 14554. Hustlin' Dan(150657)
   "      Black Mountain Blues(150658)

          (Cornet; Charlie Green,trombone: Clarence Williams,piano; Floyd Casey,
          drums):                                             June 11,1931
Co 14611. In the House Blues(151594)                          -PaE 2329
   "      Blue Blues(151596)
Co 14663. Long Old Road(151595)
   "      Shipwreck Blues(151597)

          (Acc. by piano):                                    Nov.20,1931
Co 14634. Need a Little Sugar in My Bowl(151883)
   "      Safety Mama(151884)

          (Acc. by Buck and His Band: Frank Newton,trumpet; Jack Teagarden,trom-
          bone; Benny Goodman,clarinet: Chu Berry,tenor: Buck Washington,piano;
          Billy Taylor,bass; Bobby Johnson,guitar):            Nov.24,1933
OK  8945. Do Your Duty(152577)             -UHCA 47, Co 37575, PaF 1793
   "      I'm Down in the Dumps(152580)    -UHCA 48,    "        "
OK  8949. Gimme a Pigfoot(152578)          -UHCA 49, Co 37574, PaF 2146
   "      Take Me for a Buggy Ride(152579) -UHCA 50,    "        "
```

SMITH, BESSIE MAE (vocal with piano by Wesley Wallace):
Para 12922. St. Louis Daddy(duet with Wallace)/Farewell Daddy Blues

CLARA SMITH

SMITH, CLARA (acc. by Fletcher Henderson, piano):
Co 3943. Every Woman's Blues/I Got Everything a Woman Needs
Co 3961. Down South Blues/Kind Lovin' Blues
Co 3966. All Night Blues(81153-3)/Play It(81154-2)
Co 3991. I Want My Sweet Daddy Now(81183)/Irresistible Blues(81184)
Co 4000. I Never Miss the Sunshine(81202)/Awful Mornin' Blues(81210)
Co 12. Uncle Sam Blues(81253)/Kansas City Man bl(81222;S.Miller,pf.)
Co 13002. Don't Never Tell Nobody(81198)/Waitin' for Evenin' Mail(81250)
Co 13007. (See Bessie Smith)

    CLARA SMITH AND HER JAZZ BAND (Including Stanley Miller, piano):   1924
Co 14006. It Won't Be Long Now(81476)/Hot Papa(81477)
Co 14009. Chicago Blues(81513)/31st Street Blues(81514)

    CLARA SMITH AND HER JAZZ TRIO:
Co 14013. I'm Gonna Tear Your Playhouse Down(81495)/You Don't Know My Mind
                                                  (81509;acc.by piano and sax)
    (Unknown acc.):
Co 14019. West Indiex Blues/Clearing House Blues
Co 14016. I Don't Love Nobody/My Doggone Lazy Man

    (Acc. clarinet and piano):
Co 14021. War Horse Mama(81683)/Cold Weather Papa(81684)

    (Guitar and ukelele):
Co 14022. Back Woods Blues(81694)/Mean Papa Turn in Your Key(81697; guitar
    (Clarinet* or ukelele and piano):   (and piano)
Co 14026. Good Looking Papa Blues(81508)*/Don't Advertise Your Man(81722)

    (Saxophone and piano):
Co 14034. Deep Blue Sea Blues(81931)/Texas Moaner Blues(81932)
Co 14039. Basement Blues/Mama's Gone Goodbye

    (Clarinets and piano):
Co 14041. Freight Train Blues(140064)/Done Sold My Soul to Devil(140076)

    (Unknown acc.):
Co 14045. Death Letter Blues/Prescription for the Blues
Co 14049. San Francisco Bl(140091;piano,clarinets)/(GEORGE WILLIAMS)
Co 14053. Steel Drivin' Sam/He's Mine All Mine

    (Louis Armstrong,cornet: Charlie Green,trombone: Fletcher Henderson,
    piano):   Jan.,1925
Co 14058. Nobody Knows the Way I Feel Dis Mornin'(140226)
   "   If You Only Knowed(140230; violin, piano)
Co 14062. Broken Busted Blues(140227)
   "   You Better Keep the Home Fires Burning(140231; piano, violin)

    (Harmonica and guitar):
Co 14069. My Good for Nuthin'Man(140459)/When I Steps Out(140470; Lemuel
                                                                (Fowler,piano)
    (Louis Armstrong,cornet; unknown piano):
Co 14073. Court House Blues(140492)/The L.& N. Blues(140471;Fowler,piano)
Co 14077. Shipwrecked Blues(140491)/My John Blues(140493; trombone added)

    CLARA SMITH AND HER JAZZ BAND:
Co 14085. Different Way Blues(140750)/Down Home Bound Blues(140752)
Co 14097. My Two Timing Papa(140859)/Kitchen Mechanic Blues(140860)
Co 14098. (See Bessie Smith)
Co 14104. Alley Rat Blues/When My Sugar Walks Down the Street
Co 14108. The Market Street Blues/It Takes the Lawd to Tell What's on My
Co 14117. I'm Tired of Bein' Good/Onery Blues   (Mind
Co 14126. You Get Mad/Disappointed Blues
Co 14138. Look Where the Sun Done Gone(142117)/Rock Church Rock(142118)

    (Fletcher Henderson,piano):   1926
Co 14143. Salty Dog(142252)/My Brand New Papa(142253)

    (Lemuel Fowler,piano):
Co 14150. How'm I Doin'(142250)/Whip It to a Jelly(142251)
Co 14202. Percolatin' Blues(143140)/Ease It(143141)
Co 14183. Livin' humble(143142-2)/Get on Board(143143-1)

    (Unknown acc.):
Co 14192. You Don't Know who's Shakin' Your Tree(143230)
   "   Cheatin' Daddy(143155; with sax and piano):
Co 14160. Separation Blues/Ain't Nothin' Cooking
Co 14223. Black Woman's Blues/That's Why Undertakers are Busy(144249)

```
         (Acc. by Five Black Kittens):
Co 14240. Strugglin' Woman's Blues(144528)/Black Cat Moan(144527)
         (Unknown Acc.):
Co 14256. You Can't Get It Now(144001:clarinet,piano)/Troublesome Blues
Co 14294. Race Track Blues/Jelly Bean Blues(142137)    (144000:sax,piano)
Co 14319. Jelly Look What You Done Done/It's All Coming Home to You
Co 14344. Steamboat Man Blues(146324)/Sobbin' Sister Blues(146325)
Co 14368. Wanna Go Home(146636:organ,cello)/Ain't Got Nobody to Grind My
                                                        (Coffee(146828)
Co 14398. It's Tight Like That/Daddy Don't Put That Thing on Me Blues
Co 14409. Tell Me When/Empty House Blues
Co 14419. Gin Mill Bl(146311;piano,Lem Fowler)/Get My Mind on That Thing
Co 14462. Tired of the Way You Do/Papa I Don't Need You Now    (146507)
Co 14497. Let's Get Loose
Co 14536. Oh Mr. Mitchell/Where Is My Man  (James P. Johnson,piano)
Co 14553. Don't Fool Around on Me/Down in Mouf' Blues
Co 14568. Getting Old on Your Job/What Makes You Act Like That
Co 14580. Woman to Woman/Low Land Moan  (Piano,trombone)
Co 14592. I Want a Two Fisted Papa/Good Times
Co 14619. Unemployment Papa/Ol' Sam Tages  (Asbestos Burns, piano)
Co 14633. For sale(151810)/You Dirty Dog(151811)  piano acc.
Co 14645. Street Department Papa/Pictures on the Wall
```

SMITH, CLEMENTINE (vocal: acc. clarinet):
PatA 032067. Hard Luck Blues/Strange Man   -Pe 12146

SMITH, ELIZABETH (vocal with orchestra):
Vi 21539. Police Done Tore My Playhouse Down/(ALBERTA HUNTER)

SMITH, FABER (vocal with Jimmy Yancey, piano):
Vo 05464. I Received a Letter/Fast St.Louis Blues

SMITH AND HIS RHYTHM KINGS, FATS:
Vo 03528. Music Makes Me Fell That Way/If I had You

SMITH, HAZEL (vocal with piano and trumpet. King Oliver?):
OK 8620. Get Up Off Your Knees/West End Blues

SMITH, IVY (vocals acc. by Cow Cow Davenport,piano, and LeRoy Pickett,violin):
Para 12436. My Own Man Blues(445)/Rising Sun Blues(446; Davenport and B.T.
Para 12447. 3rd Alley Bl(480)/Sad & Blue(479;. Davenport,only) (Wingfield,cornet)
      IVY SMITH AND HER BUDDIES (Including Davenport):
Ge 7040. Doin' That Thing/(BYRD AND GLOVER)
         (Piano acc.):
Sup 9515. Gin House Blues/No Good Man Blues
Vs 6027. Save My Jelly(originally on BP 8008 under name of Lil Brown)
         (See also Cow Cow Davenport)
                                                                      *
SMITH AND HIS RHYTHM ACES, JABBO (Jabbo Smith,trumpet; Omer Simeon,clarinet;
Joe Fraser,piano; Ikey Robinson,banjo; Hayes Alvis,tuba; alto,supposedly
George James, may be heard on those marked #):
Br 4244. See the Rhythm Aces)
Br 7058. Little Willie Blues*/Sleepytime Blues*
Br 7061. Sweet 'N Low Blues*/Take Your Time*
Br 7065. Sau Sha Stomp/Let's Get Together
Br 7069. Michigander Blues#/(HILDA ALEXANDER & MAMIE McCLURE)
Br 7071. Ace of Rhythms*/Take Me to the River
Br 7078. Decautr Street Tutti/Till Times Get Better
Br 7087. Lina Blues#(including trombone. Smith?)/Croonin' the Blues#
Br 7101. Boston Skuffle#   -UHCA 44
"   Tanguay Blues#
Br 7111. Moanful Blues#/Band Box Stomp#
Br 7120. (See Rhythm Aces)
      JABBO SMITH AND HIS ORCHESTRA (Jabbo Smith,trumpet; Ben Smith,Les
      Johnikings,altos; Sam Simmons,tenor; Jim Reynolds,piano; Connie Wain-
      wright,guitar; Elmer James,bass; Alfred Raylor,drums):
De 1712. Absolutely(63219A)/How Can Cupid Be So Stupid(63221A)
De 1980. Rhythm in Spain(63218A)/More Rain More Rest(63220A)

SMITH AND HIS SEPIANS, JIMMY:
De 8591. I Ain't Got Nobody to Love(69818A)/Big Chump Blues(69820A)

SMITH, JOE (trumpet: see:
  IDA COX.
  DIXIE STOMPERS.
  GRANT AND WILSON: Para 12324, 12337.
  FLETCHER HENDERSON.

ROSA HENDERSON.
ALBERTA HUNTER.
MAGGIE JONES.
McKINNEY COTTON PICKERS.
HAZEL MEYERS: Vo 14709, 14725.
JOSIE MILES: Ge 5359, 5391.
JULIA MOODY.
MA RAINEY.
BESSIE SMITH.
TRIXIE SMITH.
ETHEL WATERS.

SMITH, JULIA (vocals):
  Or 771. Crap Shootin' Papa/Nobody But

SMITH, KATE (acc. by the Charleston Chasers, q.v.):
  Co 911. I'm Gonna Meet My Sweetie Now/One Sweet Letter from You

SMITH, LAURA (Acc. by Clarence Williams' Harmonizers):
  OK 8157. Has Anybody Seen My Man(S72724-B)/Texas Moaner Blues(S72719B)
  OK 8186. I'm Gonna Get Myself a Real Man/My Best Friend Stole My Man
                                                                                                 (with piano only)
  (Acc. by clarinet, piano, banjo):
  OK 8169. I Can Always Tell When My Man Don't Want Me 'Round(S72897-B)
    "   Two-Faced Woman Blues(S72896-B; acc.by Clarence William,piano)
  OK 8179. Lake Pontchartrain Blues(S72898-B0/Gravier St.Blues(S72899-B)

  (Acc. by Perry Bradford's Mean Four):
  OK 8246. Humming Blues/Disgusted Blues

  (Acc. by violin, piano, banjo):
  OK 8252. Face to Face(73663-B)/Take Me Home Heavenly Father(73664-B)
  (Clarence Williams, piano):
  OK 8331. Jackass Blues(80045-B)/Them Has Been Blues(80046-B)

  (Perry Bradford's Mean Four):
  OK 8316. -----
  (Unknown acc.):
  Vi 20945. Red River Blues/Fightin' Blues

SMITH AND HIS ORCHESTRA, LE ROY (John Long,violin; Frank Nelt,Charlie Gains, Pike Davis,trumpets; LeRoy Williams,trombone; Emerson Harper,alto,clarinet, oboe; Stanley Peters,tenor and bassoon; Harold Henson,alto,cello and bass; Harry Brooks,piano; Sam Speede,banjo: Fred Peters,bass: unknown drums.-- Herman Rosenberg, JI 8/9/40):
  Vi 21472. St. Louis Blues/I'm a Broken Hearted Blackbird

SMITH'S GUTBUCKETEERS, LLOYD (reputedly including Jabbo Smith, trumpet):
  Vo 1560. Rub Me Some More/Wak Up Sinners
  Vo 1573. That's My Stuff/I'm Going Away
        (See also: Chocolate Dandies)

SMITH AND HER JAZZ HOUNDS, MAMIE (Mamie Smith,vocal, and instrumental group including at different times Johnny Dunn,Bubber Miley,trumpets: Coleman Hawkins,tenor: Buster Bailey,clarinet; Perry Bradford,Porter Grainger,piano; LeRoy Parker,Sam Walker,George Bell,violins; Dope Andrews: Jake Green,trombones; Stickie Elliott, Bob Fuller,clarinets, and others):
  OK 4113. That Thing Called Love(S7275-E)/You Can't Keep a Good Woman Down
  OK 4169. Crazy Bl(S7529-C)/It's Right Here for You(S7539-B)   (S7276-D)
  OK 4194. Fare Thee Honey Blues(S7589-C)/The Road Is Rocky(S7590-B)
  OK 4228. Mem'ries of You Mammy(S7642-B)/If You Don't Want Me(S7643-B)
  OK 4253. Don't Care Blues(S7658-F)/Lovin' Sam from Alabam'(S7659-C)

MAMIE SMITH'S JAZZ HOUNDS (No vocal):
  OK 4254. Royal Garden Blues(S7724-B)/Shim-me-King's Blues(S7725-B)

  MAMIE SMITH AND HER JAZZ HOUNDS:
  OK 4295. Jazzbo Ball(S7788-B)/"U" Need Some Loving Bl(S7795-A)
  OK 4296. Old Time Blues/That Thing Called Love
  OK 4305. You Can't Keep a Good Man Down/Baby You Made Me Fall For You
  OK 4351. What Have I Done(S7789-C)/Dangerous Blues(S7959-C)

  MAMIE SMITH AND HER JAZZ BAND
  OK 4416. Daddy Your Mama Is Lonesome(S70075B)/Sax-o-Phoney Bl(S70101-C)
  OK 4427. Mamma Whip! Mamma Spank!/I'm Free,Single,Disengaged,Looking for
  OK 4445. The Want Wang Blues/Get Hot   (Someone to Love
  OK 4446. Down Home Blues(S70127-E)/Arkansas Blues(S70141-A)
  OK 4471. Stop Rest Awhile/Weepin'
  OK 4511. Sweet Man o'Mine(S70102-B)/Let's Agree to Disagree(S70246-B)
  OK 4542. Sweet Cookie/Oh Joe Please Don't Go
  OK 4578. Doo Dah Blues(S70479-C0)/Wabash Blues(S70481-B)

OK 4600. A-Wearin'Away the Bl(S70122-B)/There's Only One Man(S70480-B)
OK 4623. I Want a Jazzy Kiss/A Little Kind Treatment
OK 4630. Lonesome Mama Blues(S70654-B)/New Orleans(S70655-B)
OK 4631. Mean Daddy Blues(S70650-B)/Dem Knock-Out Blues(S70651-B)
OK 4658. Alabama Blues/Mamie Smith Blues
OK 4670. Got to Cool My Doggies Now/You Can Have Him I Don't Want Him
OK 4689. Wish That I Could But I Can't Forgive You Blues(S70809-A)
"   That Da Da Strain(S70825-B)
OK 4752. I Ain't Gonna Give Nobody None of This Jelly Roll(S71079-B)
"   Don't Mess With Me(S71080-B)
OK 4767. The Darktown Flappers Ball/Sigin' Around With the Blues
OK 4781. I'm Gonna Get You(S71112-B)/You've Got to See Mamma(S71161-C)
OK 4856. Frankie Blues/Mean Man
  (Acc. by the Harlem Trio, including Sidney Bechet, soprano; banjo,
  probably Porter Grainger,piano):
OK 4926. Lady Luck Blues(71725)/Kansas City Man Blues(71726)
  (Clarence Williams,piano):
OK 4935. Good Looking Papa/You Can't Do What My Last Man Did
  (Porter Grainger, piano):
OK 4960. Plain Old Blues(S71727-A)/Mistreatin' Daddy Blues(S71759-A)
OK 40019. My Mammy's Blues/Do It Mr. So and So
  MAMIE SMITH'S JAZZ HOUNDS (Featuring Hawkins; no vocal):
OK 8024. Cubanita/Rambling Blues
OK 8030. The Decatur Street Blues(S70468-B)/Carolina Blues(S70469-B)
OK 8036. Stuttering(S70777-B)/Strut Your Material(S70792-A)
OK 8072. Those Longing for You Blues/(HARLEM TRIO)
OK 8915. Jenny's Ball   -PaE 1195
"   Golfing Papa
  (Acc. by Choo Choo Jazzers):
Aj 17068. What You Need Is Me(piano,cornet)/My Sweet Man (piano)
  (Unknown acc.):
Vi 20210. Goin' Crazy With the Blues/I Once Was Yours
Vi 20233. What Have You Done to Make Me Feel This Way/Sweet Virginia Blues

SMITH, PINE TOP (piano with vocal):   1928-29
Vo 1245. Pine Top's Boogie Woogie/Pine Top Blues   -Br 80008, UHCA 113
Vo 1256. Big Boy They Can't Do That/Nobody Knows You When You're Down and
                                                    (Out(duet with Reynolds)
Vo 1266. I'm Sober Now(C2797-C)   -Br 80009
"   I Got More Sense Than That
Vo 1298. Jump Steady Blues(2799-A)   -UHCA 65
"   Now I Ain't Got Nothin' at All
Br 80009. Jump Steady Blues(2799-B)

SMITH, RUBY (vocals):
BB 7864. Hard Up Blues/'Lectric Chair Blues
  (Acc. by Henry Allen,trumpet; J.C.Higginbotham,trombone; James P.John-
  son,piano; Gene Sedric,tenor; Al Casey, guitar; Johnny Williams,bass;
  Sid Catlett,drums):
Vo 4903. Back Water Blues(w24207)/He's Mine All Mine(w24208)

SMITH, SIX CYLINDER (vocal with guitar):
Para 12968. Oh Oh Lonesome Blues(L-213-1)/Pennsylvania Woman Bl(L214-2)

SMITH AND HIS ONYX CLUB BOYS, STUFF (Stuff Smith,violin & vocal; Jonah Jones,
trumpet; Raymond Smith,piano; Bobby Bennett,guitar; Mack Walker,bass; John
Washington, drums):   1936
Vo 3169. I'se a Muggin,1 & 2(18654/18655) Musical numbers game -BrE 02182
Vo 3170. I'm Puttin' All My Eggs in One Basket/I Hope Gabriel Likes My
                                                                (Music
  (Sub. James Sherman,piano; Cozy Cole,drums):
Vo 3200. I Don't Want to Make History   -VoE 28
"   Tain't No Use
Vo 3201. After You've Gone/You'se a Viper
Vo 3234. I've Got a Heavy Date/Robins and Roses   -VoE 72
Vo 3270. It Ain't Right/Old Joe's Hittin' the Jug
Vo 3300. Knock Knock   -VoE 37
         Bye Bye Baby   -VoE 37
Vo 3314. Serenade to a Wealthy Widow
"   Man With the Jive
  (Add Buster Bailey,clarinet; Sub.Clyde Hart, piano):
De 1279. Onyx Club Spree   -BrE 02450
"   Twilight in Turkey   -BrE 02450
De 1287. Where is the Sun
"   Upstairs

29

STUFF SMITH AND HIS ORCHESTRA (Jonah Jones,trimpet: George Clark,tenor;
Sam allen,piano; Bernard Addison,guitar; John Brown,bass: Herbert Coll-
ens,drums; Stuff Smith,electric violin):
Vs 8063. Sam the Vegetable Man(7793-3-9)/When Paw Was Courtin'(7795-3-10)
Vs 8081. My Blue Heaven/My Thoughts

(Sub. Fric Henry,piano: Luke Stewart,guitar):
Vs 8242. I've Got You Under My Skin(US 1507-1)/Crescendo in Drums(US1508-1)
Vs 8251. It's Up to You(US 1506-1)/Joshua(US 1509-1)

STUFF SMITH TRIO (Smith,violin; Jimmy Jones,piano: John Levy,bass):
Asch 3531. Look at Me/Midway   Sept.1,1944
Asch 3532. Don't You Think/Great Big Eyes
Asch 3533. Desert Sand/Skip It
Mu   367. Time and Again(Sarah Vaughan,voc.)/Is Is

SMITH, SUSIE (Monette Moore, acc. by the Choo Choo Jazzers: Piano,clarinet,
Aj 17073. Rainy Weather Blues/Salt Water Blues   (trombone):

(Duet with Billy Higgins; acc. piano,cornet):
Aj 17095. How Can I Miss You/You Ain't Nothin' to Me
(NOTE: Some Paramount sides are reported to have been released
under this name with accompaniment consisting of Bubber Miley,
June Clark,cornets: Bob Fuller,clarinet; Buddy Christian, guitar.--
DB 2/1/42)

SMITH AND HIS ORCHESTRA, TAB (Frank Humphries,trumpet; Tab Smith,alto; Mike
Hedley,tenor: Raymond Tunia,piano; Walter Johnson,drums; Al McKibbins, bass
Trevor Baconvocals):   May,1944
De 8661. You Lovely You/I'll Live True to You
De   . All Night Long/Brown Skin Gal

TAB SMITH'S ORCHESTRA
Harlem 1008. Tab's Purple Heart(In-88-B)/(BILL JOHNSON)   -Queen 4171

SMITH'S RHYTHM ACES, TED:
Gh 40006. Boogie Woogie(17967)/Jig Time(17968)

WILLIE (The Lion) SMITH

See also:
SIDNEY BECHET: Vi 27600-27904.
JOE BUSHKIN: Com 520.
MILT HERTH TRIO.
LION AND HIS CUBS: BW 6, 24.
MEZZ MEZZROW: Vi 25019, 25202, BB 6319-20-21.
HAITIAN ORCHESTRA.
CLARENCE WILLIAMS.

SMITH, WILLIE (THE LION), piano solos:
De 2269. Passionette(63141A)/Morning Air(63142A)
Com 518. What Is There to Say/Tea for Two
Com 519. Stormy Weather/I'll Follow You
Com 521. Echoe of Spring/Fading Star
Com 522. Rippling Waters/Finger Buster
Com 523. Passionette/Morning Air
Com 524. Concentrating/Sneakaway
Com 525. The Boat and the Boat/The Devil and the Deep Blue Sea

(With Joe Bushkin* and Jess Stacy#, pianos):
Com 520. The Lion and the Lamb*/ Three Key Boards*#

WILLIE (THE LION) SMITH AND HIS CUBS (Ed Allen,trumpet; Cecil Scott,
clarinet and tenor: Smith,piano; Willie Williams,washboard):   1936
De 7073. There's Gonna Be the Devil to Pay(39489A)/What Can I Do With a
                                    (Foolish Little Girl Like You(39491B)
BrE 02389. What Can I Do...(39491-A)   -De 1144, BrE 02513
De 7074. Harlem Joys(39492)   "   BrE 02659
     "   Streamline Gal(39490)
De 7086. Breeze/Sittin' at the Table
De 7090. Echo of Spring(39535)
     "   Swing Brother Swing(39537)   -BrE 02659
BrF 02388. Echo of Spring(35935-a)

(Dave Nelson,trumpet: Buster Bailey,clarinet; Robert Carroll,tenor;
Smith,piano; James McLin,guitar; Ellsworth Reynolds,bass; Eric Henry,
drums):   1936
De 1291. The Swampland Is Calling Me/I Can See You all Over -BrE 02458
De 1308. More Than That(61935A)/I'm All Out of Breath(61936A)-BrE 02463

(Frank Newton,trumpet; Buster Bailey,clarinet; Pete Brown,alto,Smith,
piano;McLin;John Kirby,bass;O'Neil Spencer,drums):   1937

```
De  1366.  Peace Brother Peace/Knock Wood
De  1380.  The Old Stamping Ground/Get Acquainted With Yourself
De  1503.  Achin' Hearted Blues(62596A)/Honeymooning on a Dime(62596A)
De  1957.  I've Got to Think It Over/Blues,Why Don't You Let Me Alone
```

    WILLIE (THE LION) SMITH AND HIS ORCHESTRA (Sidney de Paris,trumpet;
Jimmy Lane,Johnny Mullins,Stony Smith,saxes; Smith,piano; Bernard
Addison,guitar; Dick Fulbright,bass; Puss Johnson,drums):   1940
```
Gl  1712.  Noodlin'/Peace on You
Gl  1713.  Rushin'/Won'tcha Do It to Me
```

SMITH SIX, WILLIE (Willie Smith,alto; Vido Musso,tenor; Buddy Childers,trumpet; Eddie Safranski,bass; Lee Young,drums; Andre Previn,piano):
```
Sunset 7560.  I Found a New Baby/All the Things You are
```

SMITH, TRIXIE (vocals with the Jazz Masters:
```
BS  14127.  Give Me That Old Slow Drag/My Man Rocks Me    -Para 12164
BS  14114.  Pensacola Blues/He May Be Your Man
BS  14132.  Take It Daddy It's All Yours/Through With You -Para 12165
BS  14138.  2 A.M. Blues/I'm Gonna Get You
```
    (Acc. by James P. Johnson's Harmony Eight):
```
Para 12162.  Long Lost Weary Blues/You Missed a Good Woman
Para 12167.  Voodoo Blues/Log Cabin Blues
```
    (Acc. by Fletcher Henderson's Orchestra):
```
Para 12208.  I Don't Know and I Don't Care Blues(1766)/Sorrowful Bl(1780-2)
```
    TRIXIE SMITH AND HER DOWN HOME SYNCOPATORS(Fletcher Henderson's Orch.):
```
Para 12211.  Freight Train Bl(1767-1)/Don't Shake It No More(1807-1)
Para 12211.  Freight Train Blues(1767-2)/
Para 12232.  Praying Blues(1886-2)/Ada Jane's Blues(1887-1)
Para 12245.  Choo Choo Blues/Ride Jockey Ride
Para 12249.  Everybody Loves My Baby(1995-6)/How Come You Do Me Like You Do
                                                                 (1996-6)
```
    (Including Louis Armstrong,cornet; Charlie Green,trombone; Buster
Bailey,clarinet):   1925
```
Para 12256.  You've Got to Beat Me to Keep Me(2015-2)/Mining Camp Bl(2016-1)
Para 12256.  Mining Camp Blues(2016-2)
Para 12262.  The World's Jazz Crazy and So Am I(2063-1)/Railroad Bl(2064-1)
Para 12262.  The World's Jazz Crazy and So am I(2063-2)    -Ji 7, UHCA 81
     "       Railroad Blues(2064-2)                           ", UHCA 82
```
    TRIXIE SMITH (with Fletcher Henderson's Orchestra: Joe Smith,cornet;
Charlie Green,trombone; Buster Bailey,clarinet; Fletcher Henderson,
piano; Charlie Dixon,banjo; bass):   1926
```
Para 12330.  Everybody's Doing That Charleston Now(2362-2)
     "       Love Me Like You Used to Do(2365-1)
Para 12336.  He Likes It Slow(2363-1)/Black Bottom Hop(2364)
Para 12336.  He Likes It Slow(2363-2)
```
    (Acc. by Charlie Shavers, trumpet; Sidney Bechet,soprano and clarinet;
Sam Price,piano; Teddy Bunn,guitar· Richard Fulbright,bass: O'Neil
Spencer,drums):   New York,May 26,1938
```
De  7469.  Trixie Blues(63867-A)                           -VoE 217
     "     My Daddy Rocks Me(63868-A)
De  7489.  Freight Train Blues(63866)                      -VoE 217
     "     My Unusual Man(63877)
De  7528.  He May Be Your Man(63870)/Jack I'm Mellow(63871)
De  7617.  My Daddy Rocks Me, No.2(63869)/No Good Man
```

SMOLEV AND HIS SYNCOPATORS, MARVIN (Melvin Herbert,Henry Goodwin,trumpets; unknown trombone; Rudy Powell,alto and clarinet; Earl Evans,alto; Horace Langhorne,tenor; Cliff Jackson,piano: Andy Jackson,banjo; Chester Campbell, tuba, Percy Johnson,drums):   1930
```
GG   1850.  There's a Ring Around the Moon(3926)
GG   1853.  We'll Be Married in June(3927)
Rad   934.  The Terror(3935)                                -VD 81879
      "     Waiting Through the Night(3934)
Rad   938.  Apart from You(3933)
Rad   945.  Desert Blues(3931)
Rad   947.  She's Just the Baby(3928)/Because I'm Lonesome(3932)
              (See also: Cliff Jackson)
```

SNEED AND HIS SNEEZERS, JACK (blues singing):
```
De  7522.  Big Joe Louis/Numbers Man
De  7566.  Sly Mongoose/West Indies Blues
De  7621.  Old Chris/Paul Revere
De  2529.  Jamaica Mama/Sissy in the Barn
```

SNOOKS AND HIS MEMPHIS RAMBLERS (Al Muller, Walter Ashby, Elly Bellare,saxes; and clarinets; James Migliore,Estes Manasco,trumpets; Ken Herlin, trombone; Rupe Biggadike,piano; Bob Cooke,banjo;Chuck Jordan,bass: Snooks Friedman, drums.--RR):

```
Vi 22629. Love Is Like That/I'm Happy When You're Happy
Vi 22662. Smile Darn You Smile/Crazy 'Bout My Baby
Vi 22684. Bon Soir/(SONNY CLAPP)
Vi 22704. Building a Home/You Don't Need Glasses
Vi 22720. Dip Your Brush in Sunshine/Let a Little Pleasure Interfere with
Vi 22737. I'm Blue But Nobody Cares/(EUBIE BLAKE)                (Business
Vi 22779. Sweet Georgia Brown/Some Other Time
Vi 22813. Kissable Baby/The Cutest Kid in Town
Vi 22815. Japanese Sandman/(LUIS RUSSELL)                    -HMV 6303
Vi 22895. Nothin' to Do But Love/Why Did It Have to Be Me
Vi 23038. Hello Beautiful/Wha'd Ja Do to Me
Pe 15479. That's My Desire                                   -Ro 1647
    "     One More Time
Me 12203. Makin' Faces
Me 12259. When It's Sleepy Time Down South
```

SNOWDEN, Q. ROSCOE (piano solos):
OK 8119. Deep Sea Blues(S71919-D)/Misery Blues(S71920-D)

SOCOLOW AND THE DUKE QUINTET, FRANKIE (Socolow,tenor: Freddy Webster,trumpet, and others):
Duke 112. Reverse the Charges/The Man I Love
Duke 115. September in the Rain/Blue Fantasy

SOPER, TUT (piano, with Baby Dodds, drums):   Chicago,Jan.31,1944
SD 5000. Oronics(9132A)/Stardust Stomp(9134A)
SD 5001. Thou Swell(9133A)/It's a Ramble(9135A)

SOPHISTICATES (Matty Malneck,violin; Mannie Klein,trumpet; Milt Delugg,accordion; Bobbie Van Eps,piano; Marshall Fisher,guitar; Louis Chicco,harp; Arthur Bernstein,bass: Ralph Hansell,drums):
De 1883. Dark Eyes(DLA 1245A)/Song of the Volga Boatmen(DLA 1246A)
De 1818. Liebestraum/Swing Low Sweet Chariot

SOUTH AND HIS ALABAMIANS, EDDIE (Eddie South,violin; Henry Crowder,piano;
Romy Burke,drums; guitar):   1927
Vi 21151. La Rosita(40997)/By the Waters of Minnetonka(41356)
Vi 21155. The Voice of the Southland(40998)/My Ohio Home(41357)
Vi 21605. That's What I Call Keen(45134)/(ALL STAR ORCHESTRA)

    (Add clarinet and sax):   Paris, 1928
GrF 5628. Two Guitars/Doin' the Racoon

    EDDIE SOUTH AND HIS ORCHESTRA (South: Crowder: Everett Barksdale,guitar; Milton Hinton,bass; Jimmy Bertrand,drums):
Vi 22847. Hejre Kati/Marcheta   -HMV 4984
Vi 24324. Old Man Harlem(75495)   -BB 10120,   "
    "   No More Blues(75496)   "
Vi 24343. Gotta Go(75864)/My! Oh My!(75862) -GrF 7029, HMV 193
Vi 24383. Nagasaki(75497)   -BB 10120
    "   Mama Mockingbird (75863)

    EDDIE SOUTH (acc. by Django Reinhardt,guitar):
Sw   8. Eddie's Blues(OLA 2145-1)   -Vi 26222, HMV 8778
     " Sweet Georgia Brown(OLA 2146-1: add Wilson Myers,bass) "   "

    (Eddie South, Stephane Grapelly,violins; Django Reinhardt, Roger Chaput, guitars; Myers, bass):
Sw 12. Dinah/Daphne

    (Omit Chaput and Myers)
Sw 18. Swing Interpretation of Bach Concerto/Improvisation on Bach Con-
                                                                    (certo
    (Add Michel Warlop,violin; Chaput, Myers):
Sw 45. Oh Lady Be Good/Fiddle Blues(without Warlop,Chaput,Myers)

    (South and Reinhardt):
Sw 31. Somebody Loves Me/I Can't Believe You're in Love with Me(add
                                                    (Paul Cordonnier,bass)
    EDDIE SOUTH AND HIS ORCHESTRA (South,violin: Stanley Facey,piano; Eugene Fields,guitar; Doles Dickens,bass: Gordon Powell,drums):   1941
Co 35633. Pardon, Madame/A Pretty Girl Is Like a Melody
Co 35634. Zigeuner/Melodie in A
Co 35635. Para Viga Me Voy/La Cumparsita
Co 35636. Hejre Kati/Praeludium and Allegro
Co 36193. Stompin' at the Savoy/Oh Lady Be Good

SOUTH MEMPHIS JUG BAND:
Vo 02585. Policy Rag(13726-2)/Doctor Medicine(13732-L)

SOUTH STREET RAMBLERS(Same as Barrel House Five, Para 12875):
QRS 7019. Endurance Stomp(1595)/Some Do and Some Don't(1596)

SOUTHAMPTON SERENADERS:
Pe 14772. Moonbeam/All I Want Is You

SOUTHAMPTON SOCIETY ORCHESTRA (Fletcher Henderson's Orchestra, featuring Louis Armstrong, trumpet):
  Pe 14395. Poplar Street Blues(105829-1)/12th St. Blues(105830-1)-Pat 0316214
  (Unknown personnel):
  Pe 14838. Me and My Shadow/Meet Me in the Moonlight

SOUTHERN MELODY ARTISTS:
  OK 41129. Forever(401164),waltz/My Window of Dreams(401163)waltz,Seger El-
  OK 41198. My Angeline, waltz   (lis,voc.)
  OK 412L6. When the World Is at Rest(401750)/Some Sweet Day(401751)
  OK 41229. Dear, When I Met You, waltz
  OK 45285. You Can't Take My Mem'ries from Me(401422)/Tennessee(401423)

SOUTHERN NIGHT HAWKS (See Jimmy Bracken, Do 4274):
  Cr 81092. It's Tight Like That(8541)

SOUTHERN RAG-A-JAZZ BAND (Will Marion Cook orchestra, featuring Sidney Bechet, soprano sax.--JI 11/41):   London,1920
  Winner 3592. Do You Ever Think of Me(6984)/My Mammy(6985)
  Winner 3607. Tiger Rag(6986)/When My Baby Smiles at Me(7002)
  Winner 3625. Coal Black Mammy(7003)/Crooning(7004).

SOUTHERN SERENADERS:
  Muse   301. Runnin' Wild   -Ca 310
     "   You've Got to See Mama Every Night
  Li   2540. Feelin' Kinda Blue
  OK 41456. Always in All Ways/Body and Soul

  (Fletcher Henderson's Orchestra, featuring Louis Armstrong,trumpet):
  Ha   4. I Miss My Swiss(140819)/(MANHATTAN DANCE MAKERS)
  Ha   5. Alone At Last(140820)/(MANHATTAN DANCE MAKERS)

SOUTHERN TRIO (Clarinet and alto; piano; banjo):
  Mad 1921. Yellow Dog Blues(2869A)/Loveless Love Blues(2910A)

SOUTHLAND SIX (Trumpet; trombone: clarinet: piano; banjo· drums):
  Vo 14476. Ivy(10397)/Runnin' Wild(10393)

SOUTHLAND SYNCOPATORS:
  Vo 15544. Brown Sugar/(KENSINGTON SERENADERS)

SPAND, CHARLIE (Piano and vocal, with guitar):
  Para 12790. Fetch Your Water(1291)/Soon This Morning(1292)
  Para 12817. Back to the Woods Blues/Good Gal (no guitar)
  Para 12856. Ain't Gonna Stand for That(1534)/Moanin' the Blues(1535)
  Para 12863. Hastings St.(1561; with Blind Blake,guitar)/(BLIND BLAKE)
    (-Co 37336, Sig 65101
  Para 12887. In the Barrel Blues(21455-7)/Levee Camp Man(21456-2)
  Para 12917. Mississippi Blues(L34-2)/Got to Have My Sweetbread(L36-3)
  Para 12930. Room Rent Blues(102)/45th Street Blues(L35)
  Para 13005. She's Got Good Stuff(506)/Big Fat Mama Blues(509)
  Para 13047. Thirsty Woman Blues(507)/Dreamin' the Blues(498)
  Para 13022. Mistreatment Blues/Soon This Morning
  Para 13101. Evil Woman Spell/Georgia Mule Blues
  Para 13112. Hard Times Blues/Tired Woman Blues
    (See also: HOMETOWN SKIFFLE, Para 12886)

  (Voc. with inst.acc.):
  Vo 05699. Alabama Blues/Rock and Rye
  Vo 05757. Gold Tooth Mama/Hoodoo Woman Blues
  Vo 05894. Big Alley Rat Blues/She's a Squabblin' Woman
  Vo 05946. Soon This Morning No.2(WC 3153-A)/Lone Mother Blues(WC 3175AA)

SPANGLER, ROY (piano solo):
  Rex 5342. Red Onion Rag/(M. J. O'CONNELL)

MUGGSY SPANIER

See also:
  DANNY ALTIER: Vo 15740.
  BECHET-SPANIER: all.
  BENSON ORCHESTRA ?
  CONNIE BOSWELL.
  BUCKTOWN FIVE: All.
  CHICAGO RHYTHM KINGS: Br 4001.
  BING CROSBY.
  DORSEY BROTHERS: Pe 15265, 15269.
  SEGER ELLIS: Br 6022.
  JUNGLE KINGS: Para 12654.
  TED LEWIS: Co 1916 - 2807.

RAY MILLER: Br 4194, 4224, 4131.
MOUND CITY BLUE BLOWERS: OK 41515, 41526.
NEW ORLEANS RHYTHM KINGS: De 338, 401.
NICK'S DIXIELAND BAND: Manhattan,
CHARLES PIERCE: Para 12619, 12616.
BEN POLLACK: De 1424, 1435, 1476.
POLLACK'S PICK-A-RIB BOYS: All but De 1851.
PEE WEE RUSSELL: Disc 632.
JAM SESSION AT COMMODORE: Com 1504-1505.
LEE WILEY: Com 1507.

SPANIER AND HIS RAGTIME BAND, MUGGSY (Muggsy Spanier,trumpet; George Brunies, trombone: Rod Cless,clarinet; Ray McKinstry,tenor; Pat Pattison,bass; Marty Greenberg,drums; Bob Casey,guitar: George Zack,piano): July 7,1939
(Note: HMV pressings are reported to have been made from different masters)
BB 10384. Someday Sweetheart(040261)   -HMV 9008
 "   That Da Da Strain(040263)   "
BB 10417. Big Butter and Egg Man(040260)   -HMV 9033
 "   Eccentric(040262)   "

(Sub. Bernie Billings,tenor: Joe Bushkin,piano: Don Carter,drums; Casey
bass):   Nov.10,1939
                                                                -HMV 9047
BB 10506. Sister Kate(043376)   -HMV 9033
 "   Dipper Mouth Blues(043377)   -HMV 9042
BB 10518. At the Jazz Band Ball(043375)   "
 "   Livery Stable Blues(043378)

(Sub. Nick Cai-zza,tenor):   Nov.22,1939
                                                                -HMV 9147
BB 10532. Riverboat Shuffle(043894)   "
 "   Relaxin' at the Touro(043895)
BB 10719. At Sundown(043896)   -HMV 9092
 "   Bluin' the Blues(043897)   "

(Sub. Al Sidell,drums):   Dec.12,1939
                                                                -HMV 9067
BB 10682. Dinah(045746)   "
 "   Black and Blue(045747)
BB 10766. Lonesome Road(045745)   -HMV 9103
 "   Mandy, Make Up Your Mind(045748)   "

MUGGSY SPANIER AND HIS ORCHESTRA (Spanier,Ralph Muzillo,Frank Bruno, Red Schwartz,trumpets; Vernon Brown,Bud Smith,trombones; Irving Fazola, clarinet; Benny Goodman,Joe Herde,altos: Nick Caiazza,John Smith,tenors, Dave Bowman,piano; Ken Broadhurst,guitar; Jack Kelleher,bass; Don Cart- er,drums.--RGVV in "Discography")   Jan.2,1942
De 4168. Can't We Be Friends(70125A)/Chicago(70126A)   -BrE 03330
De 4271. Little David Play Your Harp(70124A)/Hesitating Blues(70127B; Mug-
         gsy Spanier and His Ragtimers: Muggsy, Fazola, Brown, Caiazza,
         Bowman, Kelleher, Broadhurst, Carter)   -BrE 03373

(Muggsy Spanier,cornet; Ruby Weinstein,Leon Schwartz,Elmer O'Brien, trumpets: Vernon Brown,Ford Leary,trombones: Joseph Herde,Karl Kates, altos: Nick Caiazza,Joseph Forcheti,tenors· Edward Caine,baritone: Charles Queener,piano: Ken Broadhurst,guitar; Jack Kelleher,bass; Al Hammer,drums: Dottie Reid, Ford Leary,vocals):   June 1,1942
De 4328. American Patrol(70802)/More Than You Know(70804)   -BrE 03397
De 4336. Wreck of the Old '97(70801)/Two o'clock Jump(70803)

MUGGSY SPANIER AND HIS RAGTIMERS (Spanier,cornet; Pee Wee Russell,clar- inet; Ernie Caceres,baritone; Eddie Condon,guitar: Dick Cary,piano; Sid Weiss, bass; Joe Grauso,drums):   April,1944
Com 1517. Sweet Lorraine/September in the Rain

(Spanier,cornet; Miff Mole,trombone; Russell, clarinet; Dick Cary,piano; Condon,guitar; Tony Spargo,drums: Bob Casey,bass):   April 15, 1944
Com ----- . Angry
Com ----- . Weary Blues
Com ----- . Snag It
Com ----- . Alice Blue Gown

(Spanier,cornet; Russell,clarinet; Mole,trombone: Boomie Richmond,ten- or; Condon,guitar; Gene Schroeder,piano; Bob Haggart,bass; George Wettling,drums):
Com 586. Riverside Blues/Rosetta
Com 1519. Memphis Blues/Sweet Sue Just You

(Sub. Lou McGarity,trombone; Joe Grauso,drums; omit Richmond): Dec.'44
Com 576. Whistlin' the Blues(A4838-#)/The Lady's in Love(A4837-1)

(Muggsy Spanier and His Orchestra: Spanier,cornet: Pee Wee Russell, Clarinet· Nick Caiazza,tenor: Vernon Brown,trombone:Schroder,Haggart):
Disc 6030. Am I Blue/How Come You Do Me Like You Do
Disc 6031. You're Driving Me Crazy/Sentimental Journey
Disc 6032. Pee Wee Squawks/Muggsy Special

SPARKS, AARON (see Pinetop)

SPARTON SYNCOPATORS:
  OK 41345. I'll Still Go on Wanting You/Take Everything But You

SPECKLED RED (Rufus Perryman, piano and vocal):   Sept.,1929
  Br 7116. The Dirty Dozen(M187-C)   -Br 80020
       "   Wilkins Street Stomp(piano; M188-D)   -Br 80021
  Br 7137. House Dance Blues/(BOB CALL)
                                                          April,1930
  Br 7151. The Dirty Dozen, No.2(C5584-C)
       "   The Right String
  Br 7164. Speckled Red Blues/Lonesome Mind Blues
  Br 7200. We Got to Get That Thing Fixed/(JIM THOMPKINS)

       SPECKLED RED (piano: guitar; mandolin):
  BB 7985. Do the Georgia/St.Louis Stomp
  BB 8012. Try Me One More Time/Louise Baltimore Blues
  BB 8036. Take It Easy/You Got to Fix It
  BB 8069. Welfare Blues/Early in the Morning
  BB 8113. What Makes You Treat Me Mean/Down on the Levee
             (See also: Jim Jackson, Vo 1428)

SPENCER TRIO (Billy Kyle,piano: Buster Bailey,clarinet: O'Neil Spencer,drums):
  De 1873. John Henry(63779A)/Afternoon in Africa(63781A)
  De 1941. Lorna Doone Short Bread/Baby Won't You Please Come Home

SPENCER AND HIS ORCHESTRA, EARLE
  BW   799. E.S. Boogie(385)/Spencerian Theory(389)
  BW   800. E.S.Boogie II(384)/Spencerian TheoryII(391)
  BW   801. Rhapsodie in Boogie(387)/Rhapsodie in BoogieII(390)
  BW   828. Gangbusters/Five Guitars in Flight
  BW   843. Soft and Warm/Amber Moon

SPIKES SEVEN PODS OF PEPPER (Mutt Carey,cornet: Kid Ory,trombone; Dink Johnson,clarinet; Fred Washington,piano: Ed Garland,bass: Ben Borders,drums):
  Nor 3009. Ory's Creole Trombone/Society Blues Santa Monica,Calif.,1921
           (Also issued on Sunshine 3003 under name of ORY'S SUNSHINE ORCHESTRA:
           same group accompanied Ruth Lee on Nor 3008, Sun 3002: Roberta Dudley on Nor 3007, Sun 3001)

SPIKES MAJORS AND MINORS, RFB:
  Co 1193. Fight That Thing(144766)/My Mammy's Blues(144765)

SPIRITS OF RHYTHM (Leo Watson,vocals: Teddy Bunn,guitar and vocal: Leonard Feather,piano; Ulysses Livingston,guitar: George Vann,drums and vocals: Red Callender,bass):   Hollywood,Jan.24,1945
  BW   21. Suspicious Blues/Coquette
  BW   22. Honeysuckle Rose/Last Call Blues
  BW   23. Scattin' the Blues/She Ain't No Saint
     SPIRITS OF RHYTHM (vocal and instrumental):
  De   160. Dr. Watson and Mr. Holmes/Junk Man

SPIVEY, VICTORIA (vocal with piano):
  OK 8338. Black Snake Blues(9651A)/No More Jelly Bean Blues(9679A: acc. by
                              (DeLloyd Barnes,piano;Pierce Gist,cornet)
  OK 8351. Dirty Woman's Blues/Long Gone Blues
  OK 8370. Hoodoo Man Blues/Spider Web Blues
     (Acc. by Erby's Fidgety Five):
  OK 8389. Humored and Petted Blues(74264A)/Blue Valley Blues(74275B)
     (Piano acc.):
  OK 8410. It's Evil Hearted Me(74262A)/Santa Fe Blues(74263A)
     (Piano and guitar):
  OK 8464. Steady Grind(80766B)/Idle Hour Blues(80767B)
  OK 8481. The Alligator Pond Went Dry/Arkansas Road Blues
  OK 8494. No. 12 Let Me Roam(80770B)/T-B Blues(80771B)
  OK 8517. Gartersnake Blues/Christmas Morning Blues
  OK 8531. Dope Head Blues(81585A)/Blood Thirsty Blues'81589A)
  OK 8550. Jelly Look What You Done/Red Lantern Blues
  OK 8565. A Good Man Is Hard to Find/Your Worries Ain't...
  OK 8581. Nightmare Blues(81590A)/Murder in the First Degree(81596B)
           (Acc. by Clarence Williams Blue Five,including Eddie Lang,guitar)
  OK 8615. My Handy Man(401114)/Organ Grinder Blues(401115)
     VICTORIA SPIVEY AND LONNIE JOHNSON, (vocal duet with piano & guitar):
  OK 8626. New Black Snake Blues, 1 & 2 (401222/23A)
  OK 8652. Furniture Man Blues, 1 & 2
     (Piano acc.):
  OK 8634. No Papa No(401242B)/Mosquito Fly and Flea(401246B)

```
              (Acc. by Louis Armstrong,trumpet; Fred Robinson,trombone; Jimmy Strong,
          tenor; Gene Anderson,piano; Mancy Cara,guitar; Zutty Singleton,drums):
   OK  8713. Funny Feathers(402525C)/How Do You Do It That Way(402526A)
                                                                      (-PaF 2177
          VICTORIA SPIVEY AND LONNIE JOHNSON (duet with piano and guitar):
   OK  8733. You Done Lost Your Good Thing Now, 1 & 2
   OK  8744. Tootache Blues, 1 & 2
          VICTORIA SPIVEY (acc. by Henry Allen,trumpet: J.C.Higginbotham,trombone;
          Charlie Holmes,alto; Pop Foster,bass; Will Johnson,guitar):    Nov.,1929
   Vi 38546. Moanin' the Blues(56734)                                -BB 8619
          "     Telephoning the Blues(56735)
   Vi 38570. Bloodhound Blues(56732)                                 -BB 8619
          "     Dirty T.B. Blues(56733)
              (Acc. piano and guitar):
   Vi 38584. New York Blues/Showered With the Blues
   Vi 38598. Haunted With the Blues/Lonesome With the Blues
              (Duet with HAROLD GREY, piano and guitar acc.):
   Vi 38609. Gotta Have What It Takes, 1 & 2
          VICTORIA SPIVEY (piano and guitar acc.):
   Vo  1606. Nebraska Blues(Charles Avery,piano)/He Wants Too Much
   Vo  1640. Lowdown Man/Don't Trust Nobody
                 (See also; Hunter Serenaders, Vo 1621)
          VICTORIA SPIVEY AND THE CHICAGO FOUR (Lee Collins,trumpet; plus piano,
          bass,clarinet):
   Vo 03366. Any Kinda Man/I Ain't Gonna Let You See My Santa Claus
   Vo 03405. Hollywood Stomp(C1567)/Detroit Moan(C1568)
   Vo 03639. Good Cabbage/From One to Twelve
          SWEET PEAS SPIVEY (with Dot Scott's Rhythm Dukes):
   De  7203. Black Snake Blues/I'll Never Fall in Love Again
   De  7204. Grievin' Me (90786A)/Double Dozens(90787C)
   De  7222. Sweet Peace/T.B's Got Me
   De  7237. 410 Blues/You Weren't True
                 (See also: SWEET PEAS)
```

JESS STACY

```
   See Also:
     DANNY ALTIER: Vo 15740.
     BUDDY CLARK: Vs 8230, 8233.
     EDDIE CONDON: Com 500, 502, 505.
     BOB CROSBY.
     ZIGGY ELMAN.
     BUD FREEMAN: Com 501, 514.
     BENNY GOODMAN.
     LIONEL HAMPTON: Vi 25527,25535,25575,25601,25586,25592.
     JAM SESSION: Com 1500,1501,1504,1505.
     HARRY JAMES.
     GENE KRUPA: Vi 25263, 25276, PaF 2224, 22268.
     PAUL MARES: OK 41574, 41575.
     RED McKENZIE: Com 562, 572.
     METRONOME: Co 35389.
     WILLIE (THE LION) SMITH: Com 520.
     JACK TEAGARDEN: Com 505.
     GEORGE WETTLING: De 18044, 18045.
     LEE WILEY: Com 1507; Maj 7258-59.
     PEE WEE RUSSELL FOUR: Com 596.

   STACY, JESS (piano solos: with Israel Crosby,bass: Gene Krupa,drums):  1936
   PaF  2187. Barrelhouse(C-90446A)/(MEADE LUX LEWIS)              -De 18119
   PaF  2233. In the Dark; Flashes(C-90445A)                       -De 18119
          "     The World Is Waiting for the Sunrise(C-90447A)     -De 18110
                                                                         1939
              (Piano solos):
   Com   506. Ramblin'(22828-2)/Complainin'(P-23990-2)
   Com   517. Candlelights(P-23989-1)/Ain't Goin' Nowhere(P-23991-1)
   Com   529. She's Funny That Way(R-2126); with Bud Freeman,tenor sax)
          "     You're Driving Me Crazy(R-2127)
   Com  1503. Ec-Stacy/The Sell Out
              JESS STACY AND HIS ALL STARS (Billy Butterfield,trumpet; Les Jenkins,
          trombone; Eddie Miller,tenor; Hank D'Amico,clarinet; Jess Stacy,piano;
          Allen Hanlon,guitar; Don Carter,drums; Sid Weiss,bass);
   Vs  8064. What's New(1: voc.Carlotta Dale)/Melancholy Mood(2;C.Dale,voc.)
   Vs  8076. Noni(3)/Jess Stay(4)
              (Sub. Irving Fazola,clarinet; omit Hanlon):
   Vs  8121. Breeze(US 1110-1)/Breeze(US 1111-1)
```

```
     Vs  8132. I Can't Believe That You're in Love With Me(US 1112-2)
      "        Clarinet Blues(US 1114-1)
     Vs  8140. A Good Man Is Hard to Find(US 1113-2)
            JESS STACY AND HIS ORCHESTRA (Including Billy Butterfield, trumpet;
            Bob Haggart,bass, and others, with Lee Wiley,vocals):
     Vi 201708. Daybreak Serenade/It's only a Paper Moon

STAFFORD AND HER JAZZ BAND, MARY (Including Ernest Elliott,clarinet & alto):
     Co  3365. Royal Garden Blues(79628)/Crazy Blues(79629)
     Co  3390. Down Where They Play the Blues(79776)/I'm Gonna Jazz My Way
                  (Right Straight Thru Paradise(79775)
     Co  3418. Strut Miss Lizzie/If You Don't Want to Send Me
     Co  3426. Wild Weeping Blues/I've Lost My Heart to the Meanest Girl
     Co  3493. Arkansas Blues/Blind Man Blues

STATE STREET BOYS (violins,piano,bass with vocals probably by Big Bill
     OK  8962. Don't Tear My Clothes/She Caught the Train      (Broonzy):
     OK  8964. Midnight Special/Crazy 'Bout You
     OK  8965. Sweet to Mama(C 889)/The Dozen(C 893)           -Vo 03049

STATE STREET RAMBLERS (Johnny Dodds,clarinet; Natty Dominique,trumpet; prob-
ably Jimmy Blythe,piano: Jimmy Bertrand,washboard):           Nov.,1927
     Ge  6232. Cootie Stomp/The Weary Way Blues
     Ge  6249. There'll Come a Day/(ALEX JACKSON)

       (See Blythe's Blue Boys for reissues of the above, and some of the
       following, on Champion.  Also a few of those below were reissued on
       Decca under the name of the Blue Jay Boys.  Personnel: Blythe,piano;
       Dominique, cornet; Bertrand,washboard; O'Bryant,clarinet; Stump Evans,
       sax*; unknown bass):                                    1926-27
     Ge  6454. Pleasure Mad(13688)/My Baby* (no cornet)
     Ge  6485. Tack It Down(13691)/Shanghai Honeymoon
     Ge  6552. Some Do and Some Don't(13690)/Endurance Stomp(14065*: no cornet)
     Ge  6569. Brown Skin Mama(14067*;no cornet):How Would You Like to Be Blue*
     Ge  6589. Tell Me Cutie*(no cornet)/Tuxedo Stomp*(no cornet)  (no cornet)
     Ge  6641. Yearning and Blue*(no cornet)/Some Day You'll Know Blues*(no ")
     Ge  6692. Oriental Man(13687)/St.Louis Nightmare

       (Frank Melrose,piano, is reported to play on those marked*, and Roy
       Palmer,trombone on some#):
     Ch 40007. Barrel House Stomp(17620)*#/Kentucky Blues(17623)*#
     Ch 40009. Richmond Stomp(17631)*/Georgia Grind(17621)*#
     Ch 40070. Sic 'em Tige(17627)#/South African Blues(17625)
     Ch 40086. Tiger Moan(17619)*/Careless Love(17622)
     Sav   503. Kentucky Blues/Tiger Moan

STATE STREET SWINGERS (Trumpet; clarinet; bass; clarinet; vocals by Washboard
     Vo 03319. Oh Red/Whippin' That Jelly                      (Sam):
     Vo 03364. Swing Cat Swings(C1568)/Oh Red No. 2(C1564)
     Vo 03395. -----/(MIDNIGHT RAMBLERS)
     Vo 03462. Don't Tear My Clothes/You Drink Too Much

STEELE AND HIS ORCHESTRA, JOE (Including Ward Pinkett,trumpet):
     Vi 38066. Top and Bottom/Coal-Yard Shuffle

STEVENSON, JOSEPHINE (voc.acc. by June Clark,trumpet; Willie(The Lion) Smith,
piano): -- JI 11/41
     OK  -----  Bleeding Moon/Love's Lament

STEWART, PRISCILLA (vocals acc. by James Blythe, Piano):
     Para 12205. You Ain't Foolin' Me (1760-2)/True Blues(1761-2)
     Para 12224. Mecca Flat Blues(239)/Mr. Freddie Blues(J.H.Shayne,piano)
     Para 12240. I Never Call My Man's Name(1916-1)/Delta Bottom Blues(244: alto
                                                  (sax by Stump Evans)
     Para 12253. Tall Brown Blues(9085; add Jimmy O'Bryant,clarinet)
       "         The Woman Ain't Born(9086-4)
     Para 12286. I Was Born a Brownskin(2090)/Priscilla Blues(2091)
     Para 12360. It Must Be Hard/Somebody's Chewin'
     Para 12402. Biscuit Roller(2643-2: plus cornet)/Jefferson County(2659-2)
     Para 12465. Someday Sweetheart/P.D.Q. Blues

       (Unknown acc.):
     Para 12740. A Little Bit Closer(21042)/I Want to See My Baby(21043)
     Para 12999. Goin' to the Nation/Switch It Miss Mitchell
```

REX STEWART

See also:
   BALTIMORE BELL HOPS: Co 2449.
   SIDNEY BECHET: Vi 26746,27204,27240.

BARNEY BIGARD.
CHOCOLATE DANDIES: OK 8728.
CONNIE'S INN.
DIXIE STOMPERS.
DUKE ELLINGTON: 1935 - 1945.
ELLINGTONIA:
SONNY GREER: Ap 354-55.
LIONEL HAMPTON: Vi 26304, 26343, 26362.
FLETCHER HENDERSON.
McKINNEY COTTON PICKERS.
MONFTTE MOORE.
LUIS RUSSELL.

STEWART AND HIS ORCHESTRA, REX (Rex Stewart,trumpet; George Stevenson,trombone: Bingie Madison,tenor; Rudy Powell,clarinet; Roger Ramirez,piano; Billy Taylor,bass; Jack Maisel,drums):   1935
Vo 2880. Stingaree(16410-1)   -BrF 500519, DeE 5458
     "   Baby, Ain't You Satisfied(16411-1)

REX STEWART AND HIS 52nd STREET STOMPERS (Rex Stewart; Lawrence Brown, trombone; Johnny Hodges,alto and soprano; Harry Carney,baritone; Duke Ellington,piano; Ceele Burke,electric guitar; Billy Taylor,bass; Sonny Greer,drums):   1937
Va   517. Rexatious(B4369)/Lazy Man's Shuffle(B4370)   -Vo 3810

(Add Freddie Jenkins,trumpet; sub. Brick Fleagle,guitar;Jack Maisel, drums):
Va   618. The Back Room Romp(M 549)/Tea and Trumpets(M 552) -Vo 3831
Va   664. Love in My Heart(M 550)/Sugar Hill Shim Sham(M 551) -Vo 3844

REX STEWART AND HIS ORCHESTRA (Stewart,trumpet: Joe Nanton,trombone; Barney Bigard,clarinet; Ellington,piano; Taylor,bass: Greer,drums):
Vo 5448. I'll Come Back for More(WM995: Louis Bacon,voc.) March 20,1939
     "   "Fat Stuff" Serenade(WM 996)
Vo 5510. San Juan Hill(WM 994)/(BUSTER BAILEY)

REX STEWART AND HIS FEETWARMERS (Rex Stewart,cornet: Barney Bigard,clarinet; Billy Taylor,bass: Django Reinhardt,guitar):   Paris,1938
Sw   56. Solid Old Man/Montmarte(Django's Djump)
Sw   70. Finesse(Night Wind)/I Know That You Know
        (NOTE: The above titles,except 'Low Cotton' instead of 'Solid Old Man' were originally issued on HRS 1003, 1004, under 'Improvisations in Ellingtonia'. The same numbers were retained for HRS reissues, with the titles reading 'Low Cotton','Django's Djump', 'Night Wind','Solid Rock' and credited to Rex Stewart's Big Four)

REX STEWART'S BIG SEVEN (Rex Stewart,cornet: Barney Bigard,clarinet; Lawrence Brown,trombone; Billy Kyle,piano; Frick Fleagle,guitar; Wellman Braud,bass: Dave Tough,drums):   1940
HRS 2004. Diga Diga Do/Cherry
HRS 2005. Solid Rock/Bugle Call Rag

REX STEWART AND HIS ORCHESTRA (Stewart,cornet; Lawrence Brown,trombone; Ben Webster,tenor; Harry Carney,baritone; Duke Ellington,piano; Jimmy Blanton,bass: Sonny Greer,drums):   Chicago,Nov.2,1940
BB 10946. Without a Song(053607)   -HMV 9208
     "   My Sunday Gal(053608)
BB 11057. Mobile Bay(053609)   -HMV 9208
     "   Linger Awhile(053610)   Hollywood,July 3,1941
BB 11258. Some Saturday(061342)/Subtle Slough(061343)

REX STEWART'S BIG EIGHT(Stewart,cornet: Tab Smith,alto; Harry Carney, baritone; Lawrence Brown,trombone; Johnny Guarnieri,piano; Brick Fleagle, guitar; Cozy Cole,drums: Sid Weiss,bass):   June 5,1944
Key 1306. I'm True to You/Swamp Mist
Key 1307. Little Goose/Zaza
       (Stewart,cornet: Al Sears,tenor; Carney;Brown:Eddie Heywood,piano; Ulysses Livingston,guitar; Keg Purnell,drums: Junior Raglin,bass):
Cap 10035. Dutch Treat(561-3A)/Rexercise(552-4A)   Hollywood,Jan.25,1945
Cap -----. Tain't Like That/Blue Jay(Joya Sherrill,voc.)

STEWART'S TEN KNIGHTS OF SYNCOPATION,SAMMY:
Para 20340. Manda(1862-2)/My Man Rocks Me(1863-1)
        (See also: Florence Cole Talbert)

SAMMY STEWART AND HIS ORCHESTRA:
Vo 15734. Crazy Rhythm/Wob-a-ly Walk

STEWART, SLAM (bass, with Mike Bryan,guitar: Hal West,drums: Erroll Garner,
Sav 537. Play Fiddle Play(5780-A)/Dark Eyesky(5781)   (piano):
     SLAM STEWART QUINTET (Slam Stewart,bass: Red Norvo,vibraharp; Johnny Guarnieri,piano: Bill deArango,guitar;Morey Feld,drums): May 28,1945

```
Cont 10000. Mood to Be Stewed/Slammin' the Gate
Cont 10001. The Voice of the Turtle(W3330)/Time on My Hands(W3334)
Cont 10002. A Bell for Norvo(3335)/On the Upside Looking Down(W3333)
Cont 10003. Jingle Bells/Honeysuckle Rose
```

SLAM STEWART QUARTET:
```
Mu   367. Dr. Foo/Oh Me Oh My Oh Gosh
Mu   396. Coppin' Out/Blues Collins
```

STOKERS OF HADES: (Fletcher Henderson's Orchestra: Russell Smith,Bobby Stark, Rex Stewart,trumpets; J.C.Higginbotham,Benny Morton,trombones;Fussell Procope, Edgar Sampson,altos: Coleman Hawkins,tenor; Henderson,piano: John Kirby,bass; Walter Johnson,drums; guitar):   1932
```
   Co  2615. Business in F(151851)                    -CoF 156, PaE 1196
```

STOKES, RAY (piano solos):
```
   Sw    76. South of the Border/A Pretty Girl Is Like a Melody
```

RAY STOKES TRIO (Stokes,piano; Wilson Meyers,bass; Buddy Christian,drums)
```
   BW    11. Stokin'the Boogie(59)/Preadin'Bl(61;Meyers,v.)New York,Jan.3,1945
   BW    12. Blues for Clarence Profit(60)/The Little Goose(62)
```

STOMP SIX (Muggsy Spanier,cornet: Volly de Faut,clarinet: Guy Carey,trombone; Marvin Saxbe,guitar; Mel Stitzel,piano: Joe Gish,tuba):   1924
```
   Au   626. Why Couldn't It Be Poor Little Me/Everybody Loves My Baby -Se 5
```

STOMPIN' SIX:
```
   Sunset 1098. Jimtown Blues/Roamin' Around
   Sunset 1099. Down and Out Blues/Creole Blues
```

STONE'S BLUES SERENADERS, JESSE:
```
   OK  8471. Boot to Boot/Starvation Blues
   Vr   521. Snaky Feeling/Windstorm
```

STRAIGHT AND HIS ORCHESTRA, CHARLEY: (Chicago group; nothing known of person-
```
   Br  3076. Sweet Southern Breeze/Talking to the Moon             (nel):
   Br  3136. What a Man/Hi Diddle Diddle
   Br  3203. That's Why I Love You/Her Beaus Are Only Rainbows
   Br  3224. Hobo's Prayer/Deep Henderson
   Br  3324. What's the Use of Cryin'/Tell Me Tonight
   Br  3516. Side by Side/Nesting Time
   Br  3899. Persian Rug/That's What I Call Keen
   Br  3900. Sweet Sue Just You/Sentimental Baby
   Br  3797. My Ohio Home/Everywhere You Go
   Br  3944. Midnight Till Dawn/Last Night
   Br  4026. Do You Don't You/Waiting and Dreaming
   Para 20244. Buddy's Habits/Henpecked Blues
```

STRAINE, MARY (vocals, acc. by Joseph Smith's Jazz Band):
```
   BS 14123. Sister Kate/Last Go Round Blues
   BS 14150. Chirpin' the Blues/Down Hearted Blues  (F.H.Henderson,piano):
```

STRANGE, JIMMIE (vocals):
```
   De  7226. Yas Yas Yas
   De  7284. Yas Yas Yas, No.2
```

STRATAKOS AND HIS JUNG HOTEL ORCHESTRA, ELLIS (John Hyman,Howard Reed,trumpets; Ellis Stratakos,trombone; John Reininger,Joe Loyancano,altos: Eddie Powers, Von tenor; Joe Wolf,piano; Fred Lyacano,guitar and vocal; Dave Fridge,bass: Von Gammon,drums):   **New Orleans,1928**
```
   Vo 15792. Precious Little Thing Called Love/Weary River
```

STRAUSS, JOHNNIE (blues singing):
```
   De  7035. Old Market Street Blues/St.Louis Johnnie Blues
   De  7081. Hard Working Woman/Radio Broadcasting Blues
```

STREAMLINE MAE:
```
   OK 06045. Streamline Blues/Romance in the Dark
   OK 06093. Blue Blues/School Boy Blues
```

STURGIS, RODNEY (blues singing):
```
   De  7550. Gal That Wrecked My Life/Toodle Loo on Down
   De  7579. Away from you/So Good
```

JOE SULLIVAN

See also:
```
   LOUIS ARMSTRONG: OK 8703.
   BILLY BANKS: Pe 15615, 15620, 15642, Co 35841, HRS 17.
   CAPITOL JAZZMEN: Cap 10009-10.
   CHICAGO RHYTHM KINGS: Br 4001.
   EDDIE CONDON: OK 41142, PaE 2932, BrF 500328, Co 35680, De 18040, 18041,
        Com 542, 1509,1510.
```

BING CROSBY: De 617.
BOB CROSBY.
EDDIE'S HOT SHOTS: Vi 38046, BB 10168.
BENNY GOODMAN: Br 4968, Co 2835, 2856, 2867, 2871.
LIONEL HAMPTON: Vi 26557.
BILLIE HOLIDAY: Vo 5302-5377.
JUNGLE KINGS: Para 12654.
LOUISIANA RHYTHM KINGS: Vo 15815, 15828.
McKENZIE-CONDON: OK 40971, 41011.
FRANK TESCHMACHER: UHCA 61.
RAY McKINLEY: De 1019, 1020.
MIFF MOLE: OK 41445, HRS 15.
NEW ORLEANS SEVEN (Varsity Seven)
RED NICHOLS.
DORIS RHODES: Co 35449, 35548.
VARSITY SEVEN.
THREE DEUCES: Com 537, 539.

SULLIVAN, JOE (piano solos):   1933
  Co 2876. Gin Mill Blues(265140)/Honeysuckle Rose(265139)PaE 1686,UHCA 31/32
  Co 2925. Onyx Bringdown(265142)/(BUCK WASHINGTON)   -PaE 2006,UHCA 34
  PaE 2006. Little Rock Getaway(265141)   UHCA 33
                                                                            1935
  De 600. Just Strolling(DLA 226)   -BrF 505038, BrE 02136
  " "   Little Rock Getaway(DLA 225)   -BrF 505027, BrE 02099
  BrF 505038. My Little Pride and Joy(DLA 224)   -BrE 02130
  BrF 505027. Minor Mood(DLA 227)   -BrE 02099
  Com 538. Forevermore(R 4060-1)/Del Mar Rag(R 4054-2A-1)   1941
  Com 540. Andy's Blues(R 4053)/Summertime(R 4061)
  Sunset 10053. The Bass Romps Away(SRC 100)/24 Hours at Booths'(SRC101)Mar'44

    JOE SULLIVAN AND HIS CAFE SOCIETY ORCHESTRA (Eddie Anderson,trumpet;
  Benny Morton,trombone; Edmond Hall,clarinet; Danny Polo,clarinet and
  tenor; Sullivan,piano: Freddie Green,guitar; Henry Turner,bass; John-
  ny Wells,drums):   1940
  Vo 5496. Oh Lady Be Good(WCO 26501A)/I Can't Give You Anything But Love
                                            (WCO 26503A;Joe Turner,voc.-PaE 2773
  Vo 5531. Low Down Dirty Shame(WCO 26502A; Joe Turner,voc.) -PaE 2773
  " "   Solitude(WCO 26500A)
    (Sub. Billy Taylor,bass,for Turner; Wells,drums; omit Green,guitar):
  Vo 5556. I Cover the Waterfront (Helen Ward,voc.)/Pom Pom

    JOE SULLIVAN QUINTETTE (Joe Sullivan,piano: Archie Rosate,clarinet;
  Zutty Singleton,drums; Ulysses Livingston,guitar; Artie Shapiro,bass):
  Sunset 10050. Heavy Laden/Night and Day   Oct.7,1944
  Sunset 10052. Brushin' Off the Boogie(SRC 104)/High Dudgeon(SRC 103)

    JOE SULLIVAN JAZZ QUARTET (Sullivan,piano; Sidney Bechet,soprano and
  clarinet; Pops Foster, bass; George Wettling,drums):
  Disc 6003. Sister Kate/Fidgety Feet
  Disc 6004. Panama/Joe's Chimes
  Disc 6005. Got It and Gone/Timothy

SULLIVAN,MAXINE, (vocals acc. by Claude Thornhill,piano; Frank Newton,trum-
pet; Babe Rusin,tenor; Buster Bailey,clarinet; Pete Brown,alto: O'Neil Spen-
cer,drums; John Kirby,bass):
  Vo 3654. Loch Lomond/I'm Coming Virginia   -VoE 116, CoE 5045, PaE 2901
  Vo 3679. Annie Laurie/Blue Skies   -VoE 122, CoE 5042, PaE 2899
  Vo 3848. Nice Work If You Can Get It/Easy to Love

    (Charlie Shavers,trumpet;Brown: Bailey; Kirby, Spencer, Thornhill):
  Vo 3885. Darling Nellie Gray/Folks Who Live on Hill -CoE 5046, PaE 2902
  Vo 3993. It's Wonderful/You Want to My Head
  Vo 4015. Dark Eyes/(CHARIOTEERS)   -CoE 5044, PaF 2900
  Vo 4068. Brown Bird Singing/(CHARIOTEERS)   -CoE 5044, PaF 2900

    (Acc. Charlie Shavers,trumpet; Buster Bailey,clarinet: Russell Procope,
  alto; Billy Kyle,piano; John Kirby,bass; O'Neil Spencer,drums):1938-39
  De 3954. Loch Lomond/Just Like a Gypsy   -BrE 03246
  De 4154. My Blue Heaven/St.Louis Blues   -BrE 03316
  De 4307. Beside the River Clyde/How Do I Know It's Real
  De 18349. Kentucky Babe/Ma Curly-Headed Baby
  De 18555. MY Ideal/When Your Lover Has Gone   -BrE 03440
  Co 35710. Molly Malone(CO 27768)/Barbara Allen(CO 27769)
    (Acc. by orchestra):
  Vi 25802. Moments Like This/Please Be Kind
  Vi 25810. It Was a Lover and His Lass/Dark Eyes

    (Bobby Hackett,cornet: Eddie Powell,flute: Jimmy Lytell, Paul Rickey,
  Bernie Kaufman, Babe Rusin,saxes: Claude Thornhill,piano; John Kirby,
  bass: Buddy Rich,drums):   1938

```
Vi 25894. Spring Is Here/Down the Old Ox Road
Vi 25895. St.Louis Blues                                    -HMV 8789
     "    L'Amour Toujours L'Amour
Vi 26124. Kinda Lonesome/Say It With a Kiss                 -HMV 8875
Vi 26132. Night and Day/It Ain't Necessarily So             -HMV 8911
```

(Lloyd Reese,trumpet; Leo Travvel,clarinet: Floyd Turnham,alto; Ulysses Banks,tenor; Eddie Beal,piano; George Callender,bass: Oscar Bradley, drums.--JRB):   1939
```
Vi 26237. Corn Pickin'/I'm Happy About the Whole Thing
Vi 26260. I Dream of Jeanie With the Light Brown Hair/Drink to Me Only
                                                           (With Thine Eyes
```
(Acc. by Cedric Wallace Orchestra):
```
JD  7420. Behavin' Myself for You/I Carry the Torch for You
```

SUMMERFORD, ANNIE (acc. by Eddie Heywood's Black Bottom Ramblers):
```
OK  8174. Fo-Day Blues/Low-Down Blues
```

SUPERIOR JAZZ BAND:
```
Bell 144. Georgia/Virginia Blues
```

SWAN AND LEE (vocal duet):
```
OK  8732. Fishy Little Thing/It Sure Is Nice
```

SWANEE SWINGERS (Including Woody Herman,clarinet: Neil Reid,trombone): 1936
```
De  1022. Take It Easy/Slappin' the Bass
```

SUTTON, BUDDY (vocal with inst. acc.):
```
Ch 15654. Mama I Don't Need You Now/You'll Come Back to Me
```

SWEATMAN'S ORIGINAL JAZZ BAND, WILBUR
```
Co  2548. Regretful Blues/Everybody's Crazy About the Doggone Blues
Co  2596. The Darktown Strutters Ball(77856)/Goodbye, Alexander(77857)
Co  2663. Has Anybody Seen My Corinne(78016)/Dallas Blues(78096)
Co  2682. Ringtail Blues(78191)/Bluin' the Blues(78192)
Co  2707. Rainy Day Blues(78255)/Ja Da (78256)
Co  2721. A Good Man Is Hard to Find(78292)/That's Got 'em(78294)
Co  2752. I'll Say She Does(78373)/Lucille(78374)
Co  2768. Kansas City Blues(78366)/(LOUISIANA FIVE)
Co  2775. Slide Kelly Slide(78367)/(LOUISIANA FIVE)
Co  2818. Hello Hello(78588)/I Ain't Gonna Give Nobody None o'This Jelly
Co  2994. But(79257)/Think of Me Little Daddy(79277)       (Roll(78692)
Co  2611. Indianola/Oh You La La
Co  2645. Rock a Bye Your Baby/Those Draftin' Blues
```
(Clarinet solos, with piano and banjo):
```
Vi 23254. Got 'em Blues/Battleship Kate
Vi 38597. Breakdown Blues/Sweat Blues
```
    WILBUR SWEATMAN'S JAZZ BAND:
```
Vo  2945. Florida Blues/Battleship Kate
Vo  2983. Hooking Cow Blues/Watcha Gonna Do
Pat 20167. Joe Turner Blues/Bag of Rags
```

SWEET PEAS (Victoria Spivey, acc. by Henry Allen,trumpet: Charlie Holmes, alto; Luis Russell,piano; Will Johnson,guitar):
```
Vi 23361. Leavin' You Baby/Day Breakin' Blues
Vi 38565. Longin' for Home/Heartbreakin' Blues
```

SWIFT'S JAZZ BAND, SAMMY:
```
BS  2042. Blue Danube Blues/Have You Forgotten
```

SYKES, ROOSEVELT (piano and vocals, occasionally plus guitar. Big Bill
```
OK  8702. Boot That Thing/44 Blues                         (Broonzy?):
OK  8727. All My Money Gone Blues/The Way I Feel Blues
OK  8742. Henry Ford Blues/I'm Tired of Being Mistreated
OK  8749. Skeet and Garret(403312)/Home of Your Own Blues(403321)
OK  8776. Roosevelt's Blues/Ten and Four Blues
OK  8787. Black River Blues/Poor Boy Blues
OK  8819. Bury That Thing/Lost All I Had Blues
OK  6709. Sugar Babe Blues/Training Camp Blues
```
    ROOSEVELT SYKES AND HIS TRIO:
```
BW   100. Tenderhearted Woman/This Tavern Boogie
```
    ROOSEVELT SYKES (vocal and piano):
```
BB 340721.I Wonder Mellow Queen
BB 340729.Honeysuckle Rose/Jivin' the Jive
BB 340737.The Honeydripper/High Price Blues
BB 340745.Little Sam/Any Time is the Right Time
Vi 201906.Sunny Road/That's My Gal
```
    (See also: The Honey Dripper, Easy Papa Johnson and Edith Johnson)

SYLVESTER, HANNA (acc. by Fletcher Henderson Orchestra):
  Para 12033. Farewell Blues(1403-2)/Midnight Blues(1407-2)
  Para 12034. The Wicked (Dirty) Fives/(MONETTE MOORE)
    (Henderson, piano):
  Majorie 1520. Papa Better Watch Your Step/Seven Eleven
    (Unknown acc.):
  Pat 32007. I Want My Sweet Daddy/Down South Blues

SYLVESTER AND HIS PLAYMATES, JOHNNY:
  Ge 6026. A Blues Serenade
  Ge 6095. Wherever You Go Whatever You Do/Mine
    (Featuring Eddie Lang, guitar):
  Ge 6099. St. Louis Blues

SYNCO JAZZ BAND:
  PatA 020665. Dangerous Blues/Mysterious Blues
  PatA 020770. Hot Lips/State Street Blues
  PatA ------. Carolina Blues/Gin Gin Ginny Shore
  Pe   14043. Chicago/Clover Blossom Blues
  Co   2783. Breeze/(WALDORF-ASTORIA ORCH.)

    NEW SYNCO JAZZ BAND:
  Pat 021076. Black Sheep Blues
  Pat 036016. Do Doodle Oom/Land of Cotton Blues
  Pat 20778. Haunting Blues
  Pat 22207. Old Joe Blues/Hunkatin

T

TALLAHASSEE EIGHT:
  Pe 0272. Black Gal/Screaming Woman

TAMPA BLUE JAZZ BAND
  OK 4405. Mule Blues(S-70064-C)/Bad Land Blues(S-70065-A)
  OK 4425. I've Got the Joys(S-70093-B)/(SAMUEL'S JAZZ BAND)
  OK 4499. Down Home Blues(S-70313-B)/Every Day(S-70314-B)
  OK 4522. Uncle Bud/Atta Baby
  OK 4544. Rock Blues/Hurry Back Home
  OK 4595. West Texas Blues(S-70575-C)/Ain't Got Nothin' Blues(S-70574-C)
  OK 4663. Hot Lips(S-70773-C)/(JOSEPH SAMUEL'S JAZZ BAND)
  OK 4671. Haunting Blues/(MARKELS ORCHESTRA)
  OK 4773. Loose Feet(S-71141-A)/Four o'Clock Blues(S-71140-B)
  OK 4777. At the Weeping Widow's Ball/(MARKEL'S ORCHESTRA)
  OK 4791. The Fives/The Cootie Crawl
  OK 4803. Sunny Jim(S-71248-B)/(GLANTZ AND HIS ORCHESTRA)
  OK 4816. Railroad Man/Keep Off My Shoes
  OK 4826. Maxie Jones/(MARKELS ORCHESTRA)
  Apex 4397. Dangerous Blues/Get Hot
    (See also Daisy Martin, OK 8027)

TAMPA KID (vocals):
  De 7278. Baby Please Don't Go/Keep on Trying

TAMPA RED (guitar and vocals):
  Vo 1216.(See Georgia Tom)
  Vo 1224.(See Chippie Hill)
  Vo 1264.(See Chippie Hill)

    TAMPA RED'S HOKUM JUG BAND (with vocals by Half Pint Jaxon):
  Vo 1228. It's Tight Like That/How Long How Long Blues
  Vo 1237. You Can't Come In/(MIDNIGHT ROUNDERS)
  Vo 1254. Good Gordon Gin/Down the Alley
  Vo 1274. Boot It Boy/My Daddy Rocks Me
  Vo 1281. Sho Is Hot/Mess Katie Mess

    TAMPA RED AND GEORGIA TOM (vocals with guitar and piano):
  Vo 1244. No.2 It's Tight Like That/Chicago Moan Blues
  Vo 1246. (See Georgia Tom)
  Vo 1251. Jelly Whippin' Blues/Train Time Blues
  Vo 1268. Uncle Bud/Juicy Lemon Blues
  Vo 1277. The Ducks Yas Yas Yas/(MEMPHIS JOE)
  Vo 1286. Pat That Bread/(HENRY THOMAS)
  Vo 1294. It's So Nice/Voice of the Blues
  Vo 1409. What You Gonna Do/Givin' It Away
  Vo 1418. No.3 It's Tight Like That/Strange Woman Blues
  Vo 1426. What Is It That Tastes Like Gravy/You Better Tighten Up on It
  Vo 1429. Mama Don't Allow No Easy Riders Here/Strewing Your Mess

TAMPA RED (guitar solos):
Vo 1258. How Long How Long Blues/It's Tight Like That
Vo 1404. Prison Bound Blues/You Got to Reap What You Sow
Vo 1572. Broken Love/Dying Mercy Blues

TAMPA RED'S HOKUM JUG BAND:
Vo 1420. I Wonder Where My Easy Rider's Gone/Come on Mama Do That Dance
Vo 1430. Mama Don't Allow No Easy Riders Here/Saturday Night Scrontch

TAMPA RED (with Georgia Tom, vocals with guitar and piano):
Vo 1450. Corrine Corrina/Kunjine Baby
Vo 1491. Friendless Blues/Dying Mercy Blues
Vo 1596. Jinx Doctor Blues/Jealous Mama Blues
Vo 1608. Bear Cat's Kittens/Unhappy Blues
Vo 1628. Call It Boogie Woogie/Toogaloo Blues
Vo 1654. Georgia Hound Blues/New Stranger's Blues
Vo 02720. That Stuff Is Here/Sugar Mama Blues, No.1

TAMPA RED (vocals and guitar):
BB 6211. Drinkin' My Blues Away/Dark and Stormy Night
BB 6166. You Missed a Good Man/When I Take a Vacation
BB 6353. Let's Get Drunk and Truck/Maybe It's Someone Else You Love
BB 6443. When You Were a Gal of Seven/(JESSE'S STRING FIVE)
BB 6425. Nutty and Buggy Blues/Stormy Sea Blues
BB 6498. She Don't Know My Mind No.2/(WALTER DAVIS)
BB 6532. You Got Me Worryin'/All Night Blues
BB 6681. I Need You By My Side/Blue and Evil Blues
BB 6620. I Hate Myself/You Stole My Heart
BB 6755. One and Only/Stop Truckin' and Susie-Q
BB 6787. If It Wasn't for You/My Za Zu Girl
BB 6825. Some Day I'm Bound to Win/(LITTLE BROTHER)
BB 6832. Cheatin' on Me/Right or Wrong
BB 6968. You Got to Learn to Do It/(BOOTS'BUDDIES)
BB 7010. My Gal Is Gone/When the One You Love Is Gone
BB 7091. When Love Comes In/(SONNY BOY NELSON)
BB 7115. I'm Takin' It and Make My Getaway
BB 7225. Harlem Swing/You're More Than a Palace
BB 7236. I'm Gonna Get High/(BOOTS BUDDIES)
BB 7269. Oh Baby Oh Baby/(BOOTS BUDDIES)
BB 7499. Most of Us Do/That May Get It Now
BB 7538. Gonna Get High Together/Heck of a How Do You Do
BB 7591. Lie in My Heart/Happily Married
BB 7793. Sweetest Gal in Town/Now That You're Gone
BB 7822. Love With a Feeling/When I Had a Good Woman
BB 7879. Crazy With the Blues/When Bad Luck Is on You
BB 7961. My Baby Said Yes/Keep on Dealin'
BB 8046. Forgive Me Please/Blues for My Baby
BB 8086. She Got the Best in Town/Hellish Old Feeling
BB 8179. You Say It's Love/Please Don't Throw Me Down
BB 8205. You Got to Give Me Some/Poor Old Gal Blues
BB 8238. No Good Woman Blues/Nobody Knows How Bad I Feel
BB 8266. Booze Head Woman/If I Had Known
BB 8291. Sad Letter Blues/Bessemer Blues
BB 8327. Sweet Mellow Woman Blues/Don't Forget It
BB 8353. I'll Try to Forget/Ready for Rhythm
BB 8368. My Two Women/I Got a Big Surprise for You
BB 8407. Dangerous Woman Blues/I'm Bettin' on You
BB 8454. I Don't Care No More/Nobody's Sweetheart Now
BB 8475. The Way to Get the Low Down/You Say We're Through
BB 8575. What Am I Going to Do/Baby Take a Chance With Me
BB 8635. Tired of Your Reckless Ways/It Hurts Me Too
BB 8654. Don't You Lie to Me/Anna Lou Blues
BB 8890. No Baby No/You Better Be Ready to Go
BB 8919. Georgia Georgia Blues/It's a Low Down Shame
BB 8962. She's Love Crazy/So Far So Good
BB 8991. Don't Deal With the Devil/I Got a Right to Be Blue
BB 9009. Don't Jive Me Mama/Gin Head Woman
BB 9024. Mean and Evil Woman/She Want to Sell My Monkey
BB 340700. Let Me Play With Your Poodle/My First Love Blues
BB 340711. You Gonna Miss Me When I'm Gone/It Ain't Fur It
BB 340724. Lula Mae/The Woman I Love
BB 340731. Detroit Blues/Sure Enough I Do

(Big Maceo Meriweather, piano: Tyrell Dixon, drums):
BB 340740. Mercy Mama/Getter Let My Gal Alone

TARRANT, RABON (Vocals with Jack McVea and His All Stars):
Apo 365. I Live True to You/Naggin' Woman Blues
Apo 366. We're Together Again/Listen Baby Blues
Apo 370. Tarrant Blues/It Never Should Have Been This Way
Apo 377. Blues This Morning/Opus Boogie

43

TATE'S VENDOME ORCHESTRA, ERSKINE (Freddie Keppard,James Tate,trumpets;
Fayette Williams,trombone: Alvin Fernandez,clarinet: Norval Morton,tenor;
Buster Bailey,alto: Erskine Tate,banjo: .Jimmy Bertrand,drums: Adrian Robi-
inson,piano.--DB 12/38):   1923
   OK   4907. Cutie Blues(8399-A)/Chinaman Blues(8400-A)

     (Louis Armstrong,James Tate,trumpets Fayette Williams,trombone; Stomp
     Evans,alto and baritone: Norval Morton,tenor: Alvin Fernandez,clarinet:
     Teddy Weatherford,piano; Jimmy Bertrand,drums: John Hare,bass; Frank
     Fthridge,banjo):   May,1926
   Vo   1027. Stomp Off Let's Go(F3142)-Vo 15372, OrE 1004, BrF 183, Br 80061
   "   "   Static Strut(F3140)   "   "   "   "   "

TANNER'S RHYTHM KINGS, FRANK
   BB   6667. You Don't Love Me/Magnolias in the Moonlight
   BB   6686. Wrappin' It Up/Time for One More
   BB   6690. Sailor Man Rhythm
   BB   6750. A Texas Teaser

TATUM, ART (piano solos):
   Br   6543. St. Louis Blues/Tiger Rag   -BrE 01516, BrF 500265
   Br   6553. Sophisticated Lady/Tea for Two   -BrE 01554, BrF 500337
   De   155. Moonglow   -BrE 01877
   "   Emaline   -BrE 01862
   De   156. Cocktails for Two
   "   Love Me   -BrE 02015
   De   306. Star Dust   -BrE 02015
   "   Beautiful Love
   De   468. After You've Gone   -BrE 01862, BrF 500515
   "   The Shout   -BrE 01877,   "
   De   741. I Ain't Got Nobody(38428-C)   -BrE 01978
   "   When a Woman Loves a Man(38389-A)
   De   1373. Anything for You   -BrE 02015
   "   Liza(38432-A)
   BrF 02489. Liza(38432-D)
   BrE 02051. Ill Wind
   De   1603. Gone With the Wind/Stormy Weather
   De   2052. Sheik of Araby/Chloe
   De   2456. Deep Purple/Tea for Two
   De   8502. Begin the Beguine/Rosetta
   De   8550. St.Louis Blues/Back Home Again in Indiana
   De 18049. Elegie/Humoresque
   De 18050. Sweet Lorraine/Get Happy
   De 18051. Tiger Rag/Lullaby of the Leaves
   Asch   3561. Fine and Dandy/It Has to Be You
   Asch   3562. Ja Da/Where or When
   Asch   3563. Sweet and Lovely/Danny Boy
   ARA   . Hallelujah/Memories of You
   ARA   . Poor Butterfly/Lover
   ARA   . Yesterdays/Runnin' Wild
   ARA   . Song of the Vagabonds/Kerry Dance

     ART TATUM AND HIS SWINGSTERS (Art Tatum,piano: Lloyd Reese,trumpet; Mar-
     shall Royal,clarinet: Bill Perkins,guitar; Joe Bailey,bass: Oscar Brad-
     ley,drums):   1937
   De   1197. Body and Soul   -BrE 02518
   "   What Will I Tell My Heart   -BrE 02417
   De   1198. I've Got My Love to Keep Me Warm   -BrE 02518
   "   With Plenty of Money and You   -BrE 02417

     ART TATUM AND HIS BAND (Joe Thomas,trumpet· Edmond Hall,clarinet; Art
     Tatum,piano; John Collins,guitar: Billy Taylor,bass; Eddie Dougherty,
     drums):   1941
   De   8526. Battery Bounce (68608-AA)   -BrE 03430
   "   Wee Baby Blues(Joe Turner,voc.;68605-A)
   De   8536. Last Goodbye Blues(Joe Turner,voc.)/Stompin' at the Savoy
   De   8563. Lonesome Graveyard(69359-A:J.Turner,voc.)   -BrE 03462
   "   Corrine Corrina(69358-A; J.Turner,voc.)
   De   8577. Lucillee   -BrE 03430
   "   Rock Me Mama

     ART TATUM AND HIS TRIO (Tatum,piano: Slam Stewart,bass: Tiny Grimes,
                                                                                       (guitar):
   Comet   1. The Man I Love/Dark Eyes
   Comet   2. Body and Soul/I Know That You Know
   Comet   3. On the Sunny Side of the Street/Flying Home
   Asch 4521. Boogie/If I Had you
   Asch 4522. Soft Winds/Topsy

TAYLOR'S BIG EIGHT, BILLY (Johnny Hodges,alto: Harry Carney,baritone: Emmett
Berry,trumpet: Vernon Brown,trombone· Johnny Guarnieri,piano; Billy Taylor,
bass; Brick Fleagle,guitar: Cozy Cole,drums):   Aug.1,1944
   Key   615. Carney-val in Rhythm(CC-2)/Night Wind(CC-4)

TAYLOR'S DIXIE SERENADERS:
Vi 23277. Wabash Blues/Everybody Loves My Baby

TAYLOR, EVA (vocals accompanied by Clarence Williams, piano):
OK 4740. Sister Kate(S71056-B)/Baby Won't You Please Come Home(S71057-B)
OK 4805. 12th Street Rag/Down Hearted Blues
Ed 14046. Have You Ever Felt That Way(N-1049-C-1-4)/West End Bl(N-1050-A)

(Acc. by Clarence Williams' Blue Five: Sidney Bechet, clarinet:Clarence Williams,piano; trumpet: trombone; banjo): 1923
OK 4927. Oh Daddy Blues(S71747-B: duet with C.Williams)
 " I've Got the Yes We Have No Bananas Blues(S71748-B)

(Acc. Clarence Williams, piano):
OK 8047. Down Hearted Blues(S71162-C)
 " You Missed a Good Woman When You Picked All Over Me(S71163-B)
OK 8049. 12th Street Rag(S71260-A)/(LIZZIE MILES)
OK 8050. You Can Have My Man/(LIZZIE MILES)
OK 8051. My Pillow and Me/I'm Going Away Just to Wear You Off My Mind
OK 8067. (See Sara Martin)
OK 8068. I'm Gonna See You When Your Troubles Are Just Like Mine
 " You'll Never Have No Luck By Quittin' Me
OK 8069. From Now on Blues(S71512-B)/Church St.Sobbin' Blues(S71513-B)
OK 8082. (See Sara Martin)

(Acc. by Clarence Williams Blues Five: Sidney Bechet, soprano,clarinet; possibly King Oliver,trumpet. Charlie Irvis,trombone: Clarence Williams, piano; Buddy Christian,banjo):
OK 8073. Barefoot Blues(71538)/Do It a Long Time Papa(71539)
OK 8089. Original Charleston Strut/If You Don't I Know Who Will

EVA TAYLOR AND LAWRENCE LOMAX (duets with orchestra):
OK 8114. Old Fashioned Love/Open Your Heart

EVA TAYLOR (with Clarence Williams Trio: Bechet,Williams,Christian):
OK 8129. Irresistible Blues(S71910-C)/Jazzin' Babies Blues(S71911-B)

(Acc. Clarence Williams' Harmonizers):
OK 8145. Ghost of the Blues/When You're Tired of Me

EVA TAYLOR-CLARENCE WILLIAMS (duets with cornet and banjo acc.):
OK 8183. Arkansaw Blues/Terrible Blues

EVA TAYLOR (accompanied by Clarence Williams' Blue Five; Louis Armstrong, cornet; Sidney Bechet,soprano and clarinet: Charlie Irvis,trombone; Clarence Williams,piano; Buddy Christian,banjo): 1925
OK 8342. You Can't Shush Katie(73739-B)/(BUDDY CHRISTIAN)
OK 40330. Pickin' on Your Baby(S73084-B)/Cast Away(S73204-A)

EVA TAYLOR (acc. by Clarence Williams,piano: Buddy Christian,banjo):
OK 8228. Far As I'm Concerned/Get Off My Money Blues

(Acc. Clarence Williams' Morocco Five):
OK 8407. Nobody But(74388-B)/Morocco Blues(74389-B)

(Acc. Clarence Williams' Blue Seven):
OK 8414. Candy Lips(80214-A)/Scatter Your Smiles(80215-A)   -OK 40715

(Acc. Clarence Williams's Blue Five,incl.Jabbo Smith,trumpet.--JM 1,2,3):
OK 8444. If I Could Be With You/I Wish You Would

EVA TAYLOR (vocals with piano and cello):
OK 8518. May We Meet Again(81786-B)/She's Gone to Join the Song-Birds in
(Heaven(81787-B)
(Unknown acc.):
OK 8585. Chloe/Back in Your Own Back Yard

(Acc. Clarence Williams' Orchestra):
OK 8665. Happy Days and Lonely Nights(401469-A)/If You Want the Rainbow
OK 40671. When the Red Red Robin(74243-B)/Virginia(74244-B)   (401470-B)

(Acc. piano and cornet):
Vi 38575. What Makes Me Love You So/You Don't Understand

EVA TAYLOR'S BOY FRIENDS (Probably Ed Allen,cornet: J.C.Higginbotham, trombone; Cecil Scott,clarinet; Willie Smith,piano: John Kirby,bass):1934
Me 13228. Crazy Blues/The Stuff Is Here and It's Mellow   -Ba 33261

TAYLOR AND HIS SWING MEN FROM HARLEM, FREDDY (Freddy Taylor,Charlie Johnson, trumpet; Chester Lanier,Fletcher Allen,saxes. John Ferrier,piano; Oscar Aleman,guitar; D'Hellemes,bass; William Diemer,drums):   Paris,1935
Ul 1489. Blue Drag   -Ul 11251,-Or 105, Ro 1778
    "   Viper's Dream

TAYLOR'S ORCHESTRA, JACKIE (with the Boswell Sisters):
Vi 22500. When Love Come/We're on the Highway to Heaven

TAYLOR'S STATE STREET BOYS,JASPER (Natty Dominique,trumpet; Johnny Dodds,clarinet; Eddie Ellis,trombone. Tiny Parham,piano: Jasper Taylor,washboard.--DB 6/15/41):

Para 12409. Stomp Time Blues(2770-2)/It Must Be the Blues(2771-2)

TAYLOR, MONTANA (piano with the Jazoo Boys,vocals): 1928
  Vo 1275. Whoop and Holler Stomp/Hayride Stomp

  (Piano solos):
  Vo 1419. Indiana Avenue Stomp -UHCA 66
  "   Detroit Rocks
  Ci . Indiana Avenue Stomp/In the Bottom 1946
  Ci . Low Down Bugle/I Can't Sleep
  Ci . Sweet Sue/Fo' Day Blues

TAYLOR, 'BIG ROAD' WEBSTER (vocals with guitar):
  Vo 1271. World in a Jug/Sunny Southern Blues

JACK TEAGARDEN

See also:
ALL STAR ORCHESTRA: Vi 26144.
LOUIS ARMSTRONG: OK 8703, Vi 202378.
BAYSTATE BROADCASTERS: VD 81843.
BEN'S BAD BOYS: Vi 21971.
JIMMY BRACKEN.
BROADWAY BROADCASTERS:
CAPITOL JAZZMEN: Cap 10009, 10010.
HOAGY CARMICHAEL: Vi 22864, 23013, 25371.
CAROLINERS.
CHARLESTON CHASERS: Co 2415.
CLOVERDALE: OK 41551.
EDDIE CONDON: OK 41142, De 23393, 23430, 23432, 23718.
LOU CONNOR: Or 1483.
COTTON PICKERS: Ca 9048, 9207, Ro 997.
BING CROSBY: De 3970.
DIXIE DAISIES:
DIXIE JAZZ BAND: Or 1515, 1536, 1537, 1624, 1668, 1690.
EDDIE'S HOT SHOTS: Vi 38046, BB 10168.
BUD FREEMAN: Co 35853-56.
BENNY GOODMAN.
TEDDY GRACE: De 2050, 2128.
HOTSY TOTSY GANG: Br 4112, 4122, 4200.
JAM SESSION: Com 1501.
ROGER WOLFE KAHN: Vi 21326.
KENTUCKY GRASSHOPPERS:
LANG-VENUTI: Vo 15858, 15864.
SAM LANIN.
LOUISIANA RHYTHM KINGS: Vo 15815, 15828.
LOUISVILLE RHYTHM KINGS: OK 41189, PaE 340.
LUMBERJACKS: Ca 9030.
WINGY MANNONE: Vo 3070, 3071.
RUDY MARLOWE.
JIMMY McHUGH: Ha 763, 795, 823, 836, 899.
JOHNNY MERCER: De 142.
METRONOME ALL STAR BAND: Co 35389.
EMMETT MILLER: OK 41342, 41377.
MILLS HOTSY TOTSY GANG: Br 4983.
MILLS MERRYMAKERS: Ve 7121, Ha 1099, 1104, Li 3233.
MILLS MUSICAL CLOWNS:
MOUND CITY BLUE BLOWERS: Vi 38087.
OZZIE NELSON.
NEW ORLEANS RAMBLERS: Me 12133, 12230.
RED NICHOLS.
JACK PETTIS: OK 41410, 41411, Vi 38105, Vo 15703, 15761.
BEN POLLACK.
RAMONA AND HER GANG: Vi 25138, 25156.
GIL RODIN.
ADRIAN ROLLINI: De 265, 359.
BESSIE SMITH: OK 8946, 8949.
TEN BLACK BERRIES:
TEN FRESHMEN:
THREE T's: Vi 25273.
FRANKIE TRUMBAUER:
UNIVERSITY BOYS:
VARSITY EIGHT:
JOE VENUTI:
FATS WALLER: Vi 38086, 38119.
TED WHITE.
PAUL WHITEMAN.
WHOOPEE MAKERS.
JACK WINN: Vo 15860.

TEAGARDEN AND HIS TROMBONE, JACK (acc. by Bobby Hackett,cornet; Pee Wee Russell,clarinet; Bud Freeman,tenor: Jess Stacy,piano: Eddie Condon,guitar; Geo. Wettling,drums; Artie Shapiro,bass): 1938
  Com   505. Diane(22832-2)/(EDDIE CONDON)

TEAGARDEN AND HIS ORCHESTRA, JACK (Jack Teagarden,trombone; Jimmy McPartland, cornet; Benny Goodman,clarinet; and others): -See Whoopee Makers 1930
  Pe 15361. You're Simply Delish(10102)   -Do 4649
  Pe 15363. Son of the Sun

    (Jack Teagarden,trombone and vocal: Sterling Bose,trumpet: Jimmy Dorsey, clarinet; Eddie Miller,tenor; Gil Rodin,alto: Vic Breidis,piano; Hilton Lamare,guitar; Harry Goodman,bass: Ray Bauduc,drums): See Gil Rodin Orch 1931
  Cr 3051. Rockin' Chair(1119)/
  "   Loveless Love(1120-1)   -HRS 5
  Cr 3051. Loveless Love(1120-2)   -HRS 5

    (Jack Teagarden,Tommy Dorsey,trombones; Charlie Teagardem.Sterling Bose, trumpets: Pee Wee Russell,clarinet and alto: Bud Freeman,tenor; Max Farley,baritone; Fats Waller,piano; Stan King,drums; Artie Bernstein,bass; Dick McDonough,guitar): Oct.14,1941
  Co 2558. You Rascal You(151839)   -CoE 424
  "   That's What I Like About You(151840)

    JACK TEAGARDEN AND HIS CHICAGOANS (Jack Teagarden,trombone and vocal; Charlie Teagarden,trumpet; Bud Freeman,tenor; Dave Rose,piano and others): 1933
  Co 2802. Shake Your Hips(152458)   -PaE 1670
  "   Someone Stole Gabriel's Horn(152459)
  Co 2913. I've Got 'It'(152456)/Plantation Moods(152457)

    JACK TEAGARDEN (vocal and trombone: acc. by Charlie Teagarden,trumpet; Jimmy Dorsey,clarinet and alto·Hilton Lamare,guitar; Artie Bernstein, bass, and others: 1934
  Br 6716. A Hundred Years from Today(B14296-B)   -BrE 01683, BrF 500392
  "   Just Couldn't Take It Baby(B14297-A)PaE 2599, " "
  Br 6741. Blue River(B14295)/Love Me(B14294)   -BrE 01703, BrF 500398
  Br 6780. Fare Thee Well to Harlem(B14877)/Ol'Pappy(B14878)
                                            (-BrE 01746, BrF 500427
    JACK TEAGARDEN AND HIS ORCHESTRA (Teagarden,trombone and vocal; Benny Goodman,clarinet; Frankie Trumbauer,C melody: Bill Rank,Jack Fulton, trombones; Casper Reardon,harp:Charlie Teagarden,trumpet: Art Tatum, piano; Artie Bernstein,bass: Larry Gomar,drums):
  Br 6993. Stars Fell on Alabama(15939)   -BrE 01913, BrF 500482
  "   Your Guess Is As Good as Mine(15940)   -BrE " "
  Br 7652. Junk Man(B15938-A)/(CASA LOMA) -PaE 2599, BrE 01979, BrF 500512

    (Charlie Spivak,Karl Garvin, Alex Fila,trumpets; Jack Teagarden,Mark Bennett,Red Bone,Joe Gutierrez,trombones; Ernie Caceres,Clint Garvin, Art St.John,John Van Eps,Hub Lytle,saxes: John Anderson,piano; Allen Reuss,guitar: Art Miller,bass: Clois Teagarden,drums; Meredith Blake,* vocals): 1939
  Br 8370. Persian Rug(WB 24375- A)   -PaE 2694
  "   The Sheik of Araby(WB 24376-A)*
  Br 8373. Class Will Tell(WB 24377-A)/If It's Good(WB 24450-A)
  Br 8378. Cinderella,Stay in My Arms(WB 24451-B
  "   That's Right I'm Wrong(WB 24453-A; Jean Arnold,voc.)
  Br 8397. I Gotta Right to Sing the Blues(WB 24452-A)   -OK 6272
  "   Yankee Doodle(WB 24454-A; Jean Arnold,voc.)
  Br 8388. Octoroon/White Sails
  Br 8401. Pickin' for Patsy(WB 24484-A)/Undertow(WB 24485-A)   -PaE 2856

    (Karl Garvin,Frank Ryerson,Lee Castle,trumpets: Eddie Dudley,Mark Bennett, Joe Gutierrez,Jack Teagarden,trombones; Ernie Caceres,Clint Garvin, John Van Eps,Art St.John,Hub Lytle,saxes: Jack Rusin,piano: Bonnie Pottle,bass; Dave Tough,drums: Allan Reuss,guitar: 1940
  Br 8431. Especially for You(WC 2624-A; Linda Keene,voc.)   -PaE 2721
  "   You're the Moment in My Life(WC 2626-2; L.Keene,voc.)
  Br 8435. You Know(WC 2625-A)/The Little Man Who Wasn't There(WC 2627-A)
  Br 8454. Puttin' and Takin'(WC 2654-A)/Blues to the Dole(WC 2656-A)
  Co 35206. I swung the Election(WV 2655-A)/Aunt Hagar's Blues(WC 2657-A)
  Co 35215. One Hundred to One/I'll Remember
  Co 35224. I Wanna Hat With Cherries/I'm Taking My Time With You
  Co 35233. Two Blind Loves/Hawaii Sung Me to Sleep
  Co 35245. Stop Kiddin' My Heart/You Could Say Hello
  Co 35252. So Many Times/A Table in the Corner
  Co 35297. Muddy River Bl(WC026164-a)/Wolverine Bl(WC026165-a)   -PaE 2739
  OK 6272. United We Swing(WCO 26167-A)
  Co 35323. Beale St.Bl(WC026243-A)/Swingin' on the Teagarden Gate(WC026245A)
  Co 35727. Rippling Waters(WC2658-A)/Peg O'My Heart(WC026023-A) (PaE 2735
  Co 35450. Red Wing/Somewhere a Voice Is Calling

(John Fallstich,Sid Feller,Tommy Gonsolin,trumpets: Jack Teagarden,Joe Gutierrez,Joe Ferrell,Seymour Goldfinger,trombones; Tony Antonelli,Jack Goldie,Larry Walsh,Art St.John,Joe Ferdinando,saxes; Nat Jaffe,piano; Frank Perri,guitar; Ed Naquin,drums; Arnold Fishkind,bass):
Vs 8196. You You Darlin'/The Moon and the Willow Tree
Vs 8202. Love for Sale(US 1364-1:Kitty Kallen,voc.)/Wham(US1367-1)
Vs 8209. If I Could Be With You(US1356-1)/My Melancholy Baby(US1357-1)
Vs 8218. Can't We Talk It Over(US 1358-1)/The Blues(US 1359-1)
Vs 8278. Night on the Shalimar/The Devil May Care
Vs 8388. And So Do I/Wait Till I Catch You in My Dreams
Vs 8273. I Hear Bluebirds/Fatima's Drummer

JACK TEAGARDEN'S BIG EIGHT(Jack Teagarden,trombone & vocal; Rex Stewart,trumpet; Barney Bigard,clarinet; Ben Webster,tenor; Billy Kyle,piano; Brick Fleagle,guitar; Billy Taylor,bass; Dave Tough,drums):<u>1940</u>
HRS 2006. St. James Infirmary/Shine
HRS 2007. The Big Eight Blues/The World Is Waiting for the Sunrise

JACK TEAGARDEN AND HIS ORCHESTRA (John Fallstich,Pokey Carriere, Sid Feller,trumpets: Jack Teagarden,Joe Gutierrez,Joe Ferrell,Seymour Goldfinger,trombones; Joe Ferdinando,alto: Danny Polo,alto and clarinet; Tony Antonelli,Art Moore,tenors; Art Beck,baritone: Ernest Hughes,piano; Arnold Fishkind,bass: Paul Collins,drums): <u>1941</u>
De 3642. Prelude in C Sharp Minor(68637-A)   -BrE 03238
 "   Blues to the Lonely(68639-A)
De 3701. Dark Eyes(68636-A)   -BrE 03365
 "   Chicks Is Won'erful(68638-A)
De 3844. St.James Infirmary(DLA 2414-a)   - BrE 03264
 "   Black and Blue(DLA 2415-A)
De 4071. Blue River(DLA 2413-A)   -BrE 03323
 "   A Rhythm Hymn(DLA 2506-A)
De 4317. A Hundred Years from Today   -BrE 03365
 "   Nobody Knows the Trouble I've Seen
De 4409. Blues Have Got Me/Prelude to the Blues

(With Bing Crosby and Mary Martin,acc. by orchestra):
De 3970. The Waiter and the Porter and the Upstairs Maid

(Unknown acc.):
Viking 103. Frenesi/Here's My Heart
Viking 104. Accidentally on Purpose/It All Comes Back

(Acc. by Paul Whiteman Orchestra):
Cap 137. The Old Music Master

JACK TEAGARDEN'S CHICAGOANS (Jack Teagarden,trombone and vocal; Billy May,trumpet: Heinie Beau,clarinet; Dave Matthews,tenor: Dave Barbour, guitar; Joe Sullivan,piano: Art Shapiro,bass: Zutty Singleton,drums):
Cap 10027. 'Deed I Do(110-A)/Stars Fell on Ala(109-A)<u>Hollywood,Nov.16,1943</u>

JACK TEAGARDEN AND HIS ORCHESTRA (Unknown personnel)
Tea 11224. Basin Street Blues/Martian Madness

JACK TEAGARDEN AND HIS SWINGIN' GATES (Teagarden,trombone; Max Kaminsky,trumpet: Ernie Caceres,clarinet: Norma Teagarden,piano; Pops Foster,bass: George Wettling,drums):   <u>Dec.,1944</u>
Com 592. Chinatown My Chinatown(A-4839-2)/Big T Blues(A-4840)
Com 1521. Rockin'Chair(Teagarden,Wingy Mannone,voc.)/Pitchin'a Bit Short

TEMPLE, JOHNNIE (blues singing with guitar):   <u>1935</u>
Vo 02987. The Evil Devil Blues/Jacksonville Blues
Vo 03068. Lead Pencil Blues/Big Boat Whistle
De 7244. New Vicksburg Blues(C90980)   <u>Chicago,1936-37</u>
 "   Louise Louise Blues(C90981)   -De 48002
De 7316. Peepin' Through Keyhole(C91249)/E.St.Louis Blues(C91251)
De 7337. So Lonely and Blue(C91247)/New Louise Louise Blues(C91248)
De 7416. Snapping Cat(C91246)/Mama's Bad Luck Child(C62655); acc. by Harlem
De 7444. Pimple Blues(C91250)/Mean Baby b1(62656)   (Ham Fats,see below)

(Acc. by Harlem Ham Fats: Herb Morand,trumpet; Odell Rand,clarinet; Horace Malcolm,piano; Fred Flynn,drums; John Lindsay,bass; Joe McCoy, guitar; Charles McCoy,guitar):   <u>Oct.6,1937</u>
De 7385. Gimme Some of That Yum Yum(62653-A)/Hoodoo Women(62654-A)

(Sub, Buster Bailey,clarinet):   <u>Apr.22,1938</u>
De 7456. What Is It That Smells Like Gravy(63670)/County Jail Bl(63674)
De 7495. Every Dog Must Have His Day(63671-A)/Fare You Well(63672- A)
De 7532. Stavin' Chain(63673)/Gonna Ride 74(63675: no trumpet)

(Unknown acc.):   <u>1938-39</u>
De 7547. Big Leg Woman   -De 48002
 "   Between Midnight and Dawn
De 7564. When the Breath Bids Your Girl Friend's Body Goodbye/Mississippi
De 7573. What a Fool I've Been(91521)/Jelly Roll Bert(65203) (Woman's Bl
De 7583. Grinding Mill(91522)/Better Not Let My Good Gal Catch You Here
De 7599. Getting Old Blues(65205)/If I Could Holler(65208)
De 7632. Up Today and Down Tomorrow(65204)/The Sun Goes Down in Blood
                                                        (65206)

```
        (Acc. John Robinson,clarinet; Sam Price,piano; John Lindsay,bass: Lon-
     nie Johnson,guitar):                                         Sept.13,1939
De   7643. Good Suzie(91758)/Down in Mississippi(91759)
De   7660. Streamline Blues(91757)/Evil Bad Woman(91760)
De   7678. Cherry Ball((1761)/Let's Get Together(91762)

        Buster Bailey,clarinet; Sam Price,piano; Herb Cowans,drums; Al Casey,
     guitar):                                                    April 4,1940
De   7735. Good Woman Blues(67489-A)/Sugar Bowl Blues(67495-A)
De   7750. Skin and Bones Woman(67490)/Stick Up Woman(67496)
De   7772. I'm Cuttin' Out(67491)/Lovin' Woman Blues(67493)
De   7782. Fireman Blues(67492)/Roomin' House Blues(67494)

        (Acc. trumpet; clarinet: piano; drums):.                 Sept.23,1940
De   7809. Jive Me Baby(68138)/Fix It Up and Go(68141)
De   7825. Baby Don't You Love Me No More(68136)/Corrine Corrina(68139)
De    .    My Pony(68137)/Bow Leg Woman(68140)

        (Unknown accompaniment):                                         1941
BB   8913. Jinks Lee Blues/Sundown Blues
BB   8968. Big Woman Blues/What Is That She Got

TEMPO JAZZMEN (Dizzy Gillespie,trumpet; Lucky Thompson,tenor; Milt Jackson,
vibraharp; Ray Brown,bass: Stan Levey,drums; Al Haig,piano):
Dial 1001. Dynamo A(1003-A)/Dynamo B(1003-B)          Hollywood,Feb.5-6,1946
Dial 1004. When I Grow Too Old To(1004-B)/(CHARLEY PARKER)
Dial 1005. Diggin' for Diz/(HOWARD McGHEE)
Dial 1008. Confirmation(1001-E)/(RALPH BURNS)

TEMPO KING AND HIS KINGS OF TEMPO (Marty Marsala,trumpet; Joe Marsala,clari-
net; Queenie Ada Rubin or Bulim,piano; Eddie Condon or Ray Biondi,guitar;
Martin Stuhlmaker or George Yorke,bass: Stan Kind,drums.--Pickup 1,10):1936-37
BB   6533. Bojangles of Harlem/Organ Grinder's Swing           -RZ 2267
BB   6534. William Tell/I Would Do Anything for You
BB   6535. I'll Sing You a Thousand Love Songs
           Papa Treetop Tall                                   -RZ 2269
BB   6560. Alabama Barbecue                                    -RZ 2460
     "     That's What You Mean to Me
BB   6563. Sweet Adeline/We Can Huddle at Home
BB   6575. A High Hat a Piccolo and a Cane/You're Giving Me a Song & Dance
BB   6637. To Mary With Love
     "     Through the Courtesy of Love                        -RZ 2322
BB   6642. You've Got Something There/One Hour for Lunch
BB   6643. Swingin' the Jinx Away                              -RZ 2322
     "     I Was Saying to the Moon                            -RZ 2302
BB   6684. You Turned the Tables on Me                         -RZ 2323
     "     Keepin' Out of Mischief Now
BB   6687. Hey Hey Hey/Hallelujah Things Look Rosy Now
BB   6688. Something Happened to Me/An Apple a Day
BB   6721. Nero/Pennies from Heaven
BB   6725. Someone to Care for Me                              - RZ 2396
BB   6758. Slumming on Park Avenue/He Ain't Got Rhythm         -RZ 2503
BB   6768. There's a Ranch in the Sky                          -RZ 2439
     "     Moonlight on the Prairie
BB   6770. My Last Affair
     "     Gee But You're Swell                                -RZ 2426
BB   6780. Swing High Swing Low                                -RZ 2439
     "     Floating on a Bubble                                -BZ 2426
Vo   3630. Folks Who Live on the Hill/High Wide and Handsome
Vo   3653. Alligator Crawl/Riding on the Old Ferris Wheel
Vo   3671. Am I Dreaming/All or Nothing at All
Vo   3682. On With the Dance
Vo   3716. Cryin' Mood/Our Love Was Meant to Be
Vo   3899. The One Rose/I Can Always Dream
Vo   4073. If I Look Like I Feel/I Want You to Sing
Vo   4156. I Got a Notion/That's the Way It Goes

TEN BLACK BERRIES (Duke Ellington Orchestra):                         1930
Ba   0594. St.James Infirmary(9319-?)  -Or 1849, Ro 1209, Re 8941, Do 4498
     "     Rent Party Blues(9321-1)            "                    -Cq 7486
Pe   15272. St.James Infirmary(9319-1)
VoE  0006. Rent Party Blues(9321-3)
Ca   0207. When You're Smiling(9320-1) -Or 1862, Ro 1218, Do 4498, Re 8941
Pe   15272. When When You're Smiling(9320-1)
Ba   0598. Jungle Blues(9322-1)/(HOLLYWOOD ORCH.) -Or 1854,Je 5854,Ro 1215
VoE  0006. Jungle Blues(9322-2)

        (Whoopee Makers group: Jimmy McPartland,cornet; Jack Teagarden,trombone;
     Benny Goodman,clarinet; Gil Rodin,alto; Bud Freeman,tenor; Vic Breidis,
     piano; Dick Morgan,banjo; Harry Goodman,bass; Ray Bauduc,drums):
Ro    839. Bugle Call Rag
Ro    976. Dirty Dog/The Sorority Stomp
Ro   1453. St.Louis Bl(2357-5)/Tiger Rag(8476-3) -Ba 0839,Or 2089,Re 10145
```

49

TEN BLACK DIAMONDS (Whoopee Makers group,similar to above and Ten Freshmen
    Ro 1125. Freshman Hop(9103-?)/(FRED RICH)   (below):

TEN FRESHMEN (Whoopee Makers group,including Teagarden,Goodman and Jack
    Pat 37054. Freshman Hop(108645)/Bag o'Blues(108647)   (Pettis,tenor):

       (Unknown personnel):
    Pe 15224. Rio Rita
    Do 4430. Perhaps

TENNESSEE HAPPY BOYS:
    Je 5573. Love Me a Little Bit Every Day(2171-2)/(UNIVERSITY BOYS)
    Or 1724. Happiness Lane

TENNESSEE MUSIC MEN (Originally issued as Mound City Blue Blowers):
    Ha 1375. Georgia on My Mind/Can't Believe That You're in Love   Ve 2453
    Ha 1378. Darktown Strutters Ball/You rascal you   -Ve 2456, Cl 5392
       (Frankie Trumbauer's Orchestra, q.v.):
    Ha 1415. Deep Harlem/Bugle Call Rag(reissue of Ed Lang Orch.)
    Ha 1420. Choo Choo/(ALL STAR RHYTHM BOYS:Venuti)   -Ve 2527
       (Fred Garnder's Texas University Troubadours):
    Ha 1406. Loveless Love
    Ve 2529. No Trumps/Baby Won't You Please Come Home(Trumbauer)
       (Miff Mole Orchestra*; or Joe Venuti#):
    Ha 1427. Shimmeshawabble*/Raggin' the Scale#

TENNESSEE TEN:
    Vi 19094. Gulf Coast Blues; Sugar Blues/Down Hearted Blues
    Vi 19105. Long Lost Mamma/(THE COLLEGIANS)
    Vi 19073. You Gotta See Mamma Every Night
    Vi 19109. Waitin' for the Evenin' Mail/'Tain't Nobody's Biz-ness If I Do
    Vi 19130. That Big Blonde Mamma/(BENSON ORCHESTRA)

TENNESSEE TOOTERS (Cotton Pickers groups,featuring Phil Napoleon - Miff Mole
et al through Vo 15004 and Red Nichols-Mole in the remainder; see Cotton
Pickers, many of the following titles having originally appeared under that
name on Brunswick, for full personnels):
    Vo 14952. Prince of Wails/I Ain't Got Nobody
    Vo 14967. Hot Hot Hottentot/How Come You Do Me Like You Do
    Vo 14985. Everybody Loves My Baby/Jacksonville Gal
    Vo 15004. Those Panama Mammas/Red Hot Henry Brown
    Vo 15022. Kansas City Stomps/Jimtown Blues
    Vo 15068. Milenberg Joys/What-Cha-Call 'em Blues
    Vo 15086. Charleston/If I Had a Sweet Mamma
    Vo 15109. Sweet Man/deep Elm
    Vo 15135. Everybody Stomp/I Ain't Got Nobody Blues
    Vo 15169. Back Home in Illinois/Hot Aire
    Vo 15201. Fallin' Down
    Vo 15388. Miner Gaff/Hobo's Prayer
    Vo   144. Chattanooga/Ground Hog Blues

TERRY, SONNY (Harmonica and vocal, with OH RED, washboard):
    Vo 05538. Harmonica Stomp/Harmonica and Washboard Blues

       SONNY TERRY (harmonica and vocals):
    OK 05864. Blowing the Blues/Forty-Four Whistle Blues
       (See also: Leadbelly Asch Album 343: Folksay Asch Album 432;
        Blues Asch Album 550)

TERRY AND HER PLAY BOYS, THELMA:
    Co 1390. Lady of Havana(145853)/The Voice of the Southland(145854)
    Co 1532. Starlight and Tulips/(GUY LOMBARDO)

       (Including Bob Zurke,piano):
    Co 1588. Dusky Stevedore/When Sweet Susie Goes Stepping by

    Co 1706. Mama's Gone Goodbye(145852)/(FULCHER)

FRANK TESCHEMACHER

See also:
    CELLAR BOYS: Vo 1503, Br 80066.
    CHICAGO RHYTHM KINGS: Br 4001.
    EDDIE CONDON: PaE 2932.
    JAN GARBER: Co 2115.
    JUNGLE KINGS: Para 12654.
    TED LEWIS: 6o 2029.
    WINGY MANNONE: Vo 15797.
    McKENZIE-CONDON: OK 40971, 41011.

MIFF MOLE: OK 41445, HRS 15.
CHARLES PIERCE: Para 12619, 12616.
ELMER SCHOEBEL: Br 4652.

TESCHEMACHER'S CHICAGOANS, FRANK (Frank Teschemacher,clarinet and alto; Rod Cless,alto,; Mezz Mezzrow,tenor; Joe Sullivan,piano; Eddie Condon,banjo;Gene Krupa,drums): Chicago,April 28,1928
UHCA 61. Jazz Me Blues(C1906-A)
Unissued. Jazz Me Blues(C1906-B)/Singing the Blues(C1905-A,B)

   FRANK TESCHEMACHER, with the Chicago Rhythm Kings (name changed from Louisiana Rhythm Kings): Muggsy Spanier,cornet,; Frank Teschemacher, clarinet; Mezz Mezzrow,tenor: Joe Sullivan,piano; Eddie,Condon,banjo; Jim Lannigan,bass:' Gene Krupa,drums): Chicago,'May 2, 1928
Br 80064. Baby Won't You Please Come Home(C 1907,E 7348W)
   (See also: Chicago Rhythm Kings,Louisiana Rhythm Kings,McKenzie-
                                                            (Condon)

TEXAS BLUES DESTROYERS (Bubber Miley,trumpet, with organ accompaniment):
Vo 14913. Lenox Ave.Shuffle/Down in the Mouth Blues -Pe 14341, Pat 036160

TEXAS TOMMY (Tom Dorsey, vocal and guitar, acc. by piano):
Br 7044. Jail Break Blues/Trinity River Bottom Blues
Vs 6035. Ridin' Papa(15306)/It's All Over(15307)
Vs 6039. New Using That Thing(15308)/Broke and Hungry(15309)

THARPE, SISTER ROSETTA (vocals with guitar):
De 2243. The Lonesome Road/Rock Me
De 2328. I Looked Down the Line/God Don't Like It
De 2503. My Man and I/That's All
De 2558. Bring Back Those Happy Days/This Train
De 3254. Beams of Heaven/Saviour Don't Pass Me By
De 3956. Rock Daniel!(acc.Lucky Millinder Orch.)/(MILLINDER)
De 4041. Trouble in Mind(acc.Lucky Millinder Orch.)/(MILLINDER)
De 8538. Sit Down/End of My Journey
De 8548. Stand By Me/There Is Something Within Me
De 8594. I'm in His Care/Just a Closer Walk With Thee
De 8610. Nobody's Fault But Mine/Precious Lord Hold My Hand
De 8634. I Want Jesus to Walk Around My Bedside/Pure Religion
De 8639. All Over This World/What He Done for Me
De 18386. I Want a Tall Skinny Papa/Shout Sister Shout(acc.L.Millinder Orch.)
De 8657. Sleep on Darling Mother/I Want to Love So God Can Use Me
De 8669. Two Little Fishes/Strange Things Happening Every Day -De 48009
De 8672. Singing in My Soul/I Claim Jesus First
De 11002. When I Move to the Sky/Don't Take Everybody to Be Your Friend
                                                            (-De 48025

THEARD, LOVIN' SAM (blues singing):
De 7025. Rubbin' on the Darned Old Thing/That Rhythm Gal
De 7146. Till I Die
   (See also: Lovin' Sam from Alabam')

THOMAS' DEVILS:
Br 7064. Boot It Boy/Sho Is Hot
   THOMAS' MUSCLE SHOALS DEVILS:
OK 8225. Morning Dove Blues/Wash Woman Blues

THOMAS, EARL (blues singing):
De 7195. Burying Ground/Sugar Girl Blues
De 7221. Bonus Men/Rent Day Blues

THOMAS, GEORGE (vocals,first coupling under name of Ramblin' Thomas, with guitar acc.):
Para 12616. Sawmill Moan(20337)/Ramblin' Mind Blues(20339)

   (Piano and guitar acc.):
Para 12826. Fast Stuff Blues(1426)/Don't Kill Him in Here(1427)

THOMAS, 'RAGTIME TEXAS' HENRY (vocals with guitar):
Vo 1094. John Henry/Cottonfield Blues
Vo 1137. The Fox and the Hounds/Red River Blues
Vo 1197. Don't Ease Me In/Texas Easy Street Blues
Vo 1230. Bull Doze Blues/Old Country Stomp
Vo 1249. Texas Worried Blues/Fishing Blues
Vo 1443. Railroadin' Some/Don't Leave Me Here
                                                           Chicago

THOMAS, HERSAL (piano solos):
OK 8227. Suitcase Blues(8958-A)/Hersal Blues(9166-A)
   (See also: Hociel Thomas)

THOMAS, HOCIEL (vocals,with piano,clarinet and violin):
Ge 3004. I Can't Feel Frisky Without My Whiskey(MARIE GRINTER)
Ge 3006. Worried Down With the Blues/I Must Have It

```
              (Acc. by Hersal Thomas, piano):
     OK   8222. Fish Tail Dance/Worried Down by the Blues

              (Acc. by Louis Armstrong's Jazz Four: Louis Armstrong, cornet; Johnny
         Dodds,clarinet; Lil Armstrong,piano: Johnny St.Cyr,banjo):        1925
     OK   8258. Adam and Eve Had the Blues(9473-A)/Put It Where I Can Get It
     OK   8289. Gambler's Dream(9471)/Washwoman Blues(9475)           (9474-A)
     OK   8326. Sunshine Baby(9472)/I've Stopped MY Man(9476)

              (Acc. by Louis Armstrong,trumpet: Hersal Thomas, piano):
     OK   8297. Deep Water Blues(9519-A)/Lonesome Hours(9522-A)
     OK   8346. G'wan I Told You(9520)/Listen to Me(9521)
```

THOMAS AND HIS ORCHESTRA, HOWARD:
   Ch 40080. In the Shade of the Old Apple Tree/Business in F

THOMAS' BIG SIX, JOE (Joe Thomas,trumpet: Lem Davis,alto: Ted Nash,tenor;
Jimmy Jones,piano; Billy Taylor,bass: Denzil Best,drums):
   HRS 1016. Riff Street/A Touch of Blue

      (Babe Mathews, vocals):
   HRS 1017. No Better for Ya/He's Got So Much

         JOE THOMAS AND HIS ORCHESTRA (Joe Thomas,trumpet: Hilton Jefferson,alto;
      Jerry Jerome,tenor; Tyree Glenn,trombone; Bernie Leighton,piano; Leon
      Abramson,drums; Hy White,guitar; Billy Taylor, bass):
   Key   642. Black Butterfly/You Can Depend on Me

THOMAS AND HER BOYS, LILLETTE:
   Sterling 100. Blues for My Daddy/Lillette's Boogie
   Sterling 101. Variety Blues/That's What Happened to Me
   Sterling 108. Boogie Woogie Time Down South/Down It and Get from Around It
   Sterling 109. Riffs and Rhythm/Old Time Daddy Blues

THOMAS, MILLARD G. (piano solos):
   Ajax 17045. Lazy Drag/Page Your...
   Ajax 17053. Twee-Twa-Twa Blues/Hard Luck Blues
   Ajax 17074. Blue Ivories(1625)/Reckless Blues(1628)

THOMAS, SIPPIE (vocals, probably with Johnny Dodds,clarinet, in the accompaniment on the first side):
   Vi 38502. I'm a Mighty Tight Woman/You Gonna Need My Help

THOMAS AND HIS JUMP CATS, WALTER (Emmett Berry,trumpet; Walter Thomas, Ben
Webster, Bud Johnson, tenors; Clyde Hart,piano; Cozy Cole,drums; Oscar Pettiford, bass):
   Celebrity 8125. Broke But Happy/Blues on the Delta

         SIR WALTER THOMAS AND HIS ALL STARS (Hilton Jefferson,alto; Eddie Barefield,clarinet and tenor; Walter Thomas,tenor: Coleman Hawkins,tenor;
      Jonah Jones,trumpet: Clyde Hart,piano; Cozy Cole,drums: Milt Hinton,
      bass):   Oct.3,1944
   Celebrity 8128. Every Man for Himself/Look Out Jack
   Celebrity   Out to Lunch/In the Hush of the Night

         (Charlie Shavers,trumpet: Ben Webster,Ernie Caceres,Walter Thomas, tenors; Cozy Cole,drums; Billy Taylor,Slam Stewart,bass):
   JD 8129. Save It Pretty Mama/Peace Tree Street Blues
   JD 8130. For Lovers Only/The Bottle's Empty
   JD 8131. Black Maria's Blues/Dee Tee's

THOMPSON AND THE BOYS, KAY:
   Br 7560. You Hit the Spot/You Let Me Down
   Br 7564. Don't Mention Love to Me/Out of Sight Out of Mind
   Vi 25564. Carelessly/There's a Lull in My Life
   Vi 25582. Exactly Like You/It Had to Be You

THOMPSON'S ALL STARS, LUCKY (Featuring Lucky Thompson,tenor: J.J.Johnson,trombone: Karl George, trumpet):
   Ex 145. Why Not/No Good Man Blues
   Ex 146. Phace/Irresistible You

THOMPSON AND HIS ALL STARS, SIR CHARLES:
   Apollo 757. If I Had You/Takin' Off

THORNHILL AND HIS ORCHESTRA, CLAUDE (featuring Maxine Sullivan, vocal):
   Vo 2595. Harbor Lights   -VoE 125
            Gone With the Wind
   Vo 3616. Whispers in the Dark   -VoE 125
            Stop You're Breaking My Heart

         (Joe Aguano,Ralph Harden,Bob Sprentall,trumpets: Dale Brown, George
      Paulsen,clarinets; Tasso Harris,Bob Jenney,trombones:H.A.Tennyson,John

Nelson,Bill Motley,Herman Russum,saxes;Claude Thornhill,piano; Albert
Harris,guitar; Harvey Sell,bass: Sandy Graff,drums.--JRB):   1940-41
- OK 5838. The Bad Humor Man(H-19)/I've Got a One Trace Mind(H-20)
- OK 5901. The Legend of Old California/Love of My Life
- OK 5988. Alt Wien/Love Tales
- OK 6168. Stack of Barley(29904)/Hungarian Dance No.5(29906)
- OK 6178. Do I Worry(30262)/Sleepy Serenade(30263)
- OK 6202. Overnight(30369)/When the Lilacs Bloom Again(30261)
- OK 6124. O Sole Mio/Traumerei
- OK 6234. Portrait of a Guinea Farm/All I Need

(Unknown personnel):
- Br 7951. An Old Flame Never Dies/You and I Know
- Br 7957. Don't Save Your Love/Ebb Tide

(Dale Brown,Hammond Russum,John Nelson,Ted Goddard,saxes; Irving Fazola,
George Paulsen,clarinets: Conrad Gazzo,Rusty Diedrick,Bob Sprentall,
trumpet; Bob Jenney,Tasso Harris,trombones: Thornhill,piano; Harvey Cell,
bass; Gene Lemen,drums):   1941-2
- Co 36287. I'm Thrilled/Sing a Love Song
- Co 36298. You Were Meant for Me(30859)/Paradise(30861)
- Co 36268. Where or When/Snowfall
- Co 36361. Lovers in Glass Houses/Mandy Is Two
- Co 36371. Concerto for Two/Jim
- Co 36391. Moonlight Masquerade/Orange Blossom Lane
- Co 36413. Baby Mine/Miss You
- Co 36431. The Bells of San Raquel/I Found You in the Rain
- Co 36435. Autumn Nocturne/Where Has MY Little Dog Gone
- Co 36456. I Hate You Darling/Everything I Love
- Co 36458. Somebody Nobody Love/Rose O'Day

(Fazola,clarinet, left the band at about this period):
- Co 36472. Chattanooga Choo Choo/This Love of Mine
- Co 36477. We're the Couple in the Castle/I Said No
- Co 36513. Ya Lu Blu/Somebody Else Is Taking My Place
- Co 36527. Memory Lane/The Lamp of Memory
- Co 36535. Grieg's Piano Concerto/I'll Pray for You
- Co 36560. Count Me In/She'll Always Remember
- Co 36578. America I Love You/Something to Remember You By
- Co 36616. Be Careful It's MY Heart/Lullaby of the Rain
- Co 36658. Rock-a-bye Baby/I'm Getting So Tired I Can Sleep
- Co 36725. There's a Small Hotel/Moonlight Bay

THREE BARBERS:
- Pe 14595. Down Town Rag/Buggy Blues

THREE BITS OF RHYTHM (vocal with piano, bass, guitar):
- De 8553. Bronzeville Jump/The Old Blues
- De 8572. I'm Lonesome/This Is the Boogie the Woogie the Boogie

THREE BLUES CHASERS (clarinet, piano, drums):
- OK 8595. Lame Buck Blues(400777)/Nothin' But Blues(400778)

THREE DEUCES (Joe Sullivan,piano; Pee Wee Russell,clarinet: Zutty Singleton,
- Com 537. Deuces Wild(R4050-L)/Last Time I saw Chicago(R4051-2) (drums):
- Com 539. Jig Walk(R 4049)/About Face(R 4052)

THREE JACKS (instrumental):
- OK 41102. Chile Blues/Spanish Shawl

THREE JOLLY MINERS (Bob Fuller,clarinet; banjo; piano):
- Vo 1003. Pig Alley Stomp/Ridiculous Blues
- Vo 15087. Louisville Blues/Lake George Blues
- Vo 15111. Ketch Your Breath/Plain Old Blues
- Vo 15164. House Party Stomp/Grand opera Blues

THREE KEYS (Bon Bon, Slim and Bob):
- Vo 2569. You Can Depend on Me/I Found a New Baby
- Br 6411. Nagasaki(B 12424-A)/Fit As a Fiddle(B 12425-A)   -Vo 2732
- Br 6388. Jig Time/Someone Stole Gabriel's Horn   -Vo 2730
- Br 6423. Basin Street Blues/Wah-Dee-Dah
- Br 6522. That Doggone Dog/I Would Do Anything for You
- Co 2706. Somebody Loses Somebody Wins   -PaE 1409
- "   Mood Indigo   -PaE 1431

THREE MONKEY CHASERS (Bob Fuller group):
- Ha 23. Cocoanut Strut(140856)/Corn Bread Wiggle(140855)
- Ha 50. Uncle Remus Stomp/Montmarte Giggles

THREE RIFFS (vocals with orchestra):
- De 7634. Ace in the Hole/It's a Killer Mr. Miller

THREE'S A CROWD (Piano, guitar and clarinet):
   BB 10014. That's Got 'em/We Want Five
   BB 10051. Rosetta/S'posin'

THREE SHARPS AND A FLAT (vocals, with Bass, guitar, drums):
   De 2278. Skinny-Do/I'm Gettin' Sentimental Over You
   De 7561. I Ain't in Love No More/I Am I Am Am Am
   De 7569. I'm Through/Swingin' in the Candy Store
   OK 05857/Crazy and Worried Blues/Rosie in the Garden
   OK 05971. Piccolo Stomp(C3406)/That's That Rhythm(C3405)

THREE T'S: (Charlie Teagarden,trumpet; Jack Teagarden,trombone and vocal;
   Frankie Trumbauer,alto; Bud Freeman,tenor; Roy Bargy, piano; Carl Kress,guitar; Artie Miller, bass; Bob White,drums):
   Vi 25273. I'se a Muggin, 1 & 2   -HMV 5063

TIBBS' CONNIE'S INN ORCHESTRA, LE ROY:
   Co 14309. One o'Clock Blues/I Got Worry

TINSLEY'S WASHBOARD BAND (Probably same as Washboard Rhythm Kings):
   Vi 24405. Shoutin' in the Amen Corner   -HMV 8655, BB 6219
      "   I Would If I Could

TOLBERT AND HIS GENTLEMEN OF SWING, SKEETS:
   De 7630. Bouncing of Rhythm/Stuffs Out
   De 7570: Skin 'em Back(65085)/Get Up(65086)
   De 7591. I've Lost My Head Over You/This Is the End
   De 7653. Railroad Blues(65924)/I'm Blowin' My Top(65925)
   De 7669. Swing Out/Fine Piece of Meat
   De 7717. Hole Holy Roly Poly/Harlem Ain't What It Usta Be
   De 7722. I Can't Got for You/W.P.A.
   De 8506. Sugar Boogie/I'll Make It Worth Your While
   De 8516. Those Draftin' Blues/Bugle Blues
   De 8528. Jumpin' Like Mad(68192)/Hit That Jive Jack(68515)
   De 8534. Sammy's Choppin' Block/Four O'Clock Blues
   De 8565. The Rhumba Blues(69236)/Jumpin' in the Numbers(69237)
   De 8579. Big Fat Butterfly(69235)/Uncle Eph's Dream(69234)
   De 8589. Git It(69732)/Lazy Gal Blues(69731)
   De 8608. Delta Land Blues/Ride On
   De 8617. Fill Up/Because I Love My Daddy So
   De 8631. That's That Messy Boogie/What Is the Matter Now
   De 8641. Hey Man Hey Man(71198)/C.O.D. (71197)

TOO BAD BOYS:
   Para 12861. Corrine Corrina Blues/Ballin' the Jack

TOUGH QUINTET, DAVE (Joe Thomas,trumpet; Ted Nash,tenor; Bernie Leighton,
piano; Jack Lesberg,bass; Dave Tough, drums):
   Jam 906. You Were Meant for Me/East of the Sun
   Jam 907. Love Walked In/When You're Smiling

TOWEL, JIM (vocal with piano: Cow Cow Davenport):
   Br 7060. Buckwheat Cakes/I've Been Hoodooed

TRAVELERS, THE (Manny Klein,Leo McConville,trumpets; Tommy Dorsey,trombone;
Jimmy Dorsey,Alf Evans,Paul Mason,saxes; Arthur Schutt,piano; Tony Coluccio,
banjo; Hank Stern,tuba; Stan King,drums):   June,1929
   OK 41259. Am I Blue(402465)/(ED LOYD)   -PaE 426, PaE 2475
   OK 41260. Baby Oh Where Can You Be(402466)   -PaE 426
      "   Breakaway(402467)   -PaE 6197
         (Charlie Margulies,Bill Moore,Lou Garcia,trumpets; Tommy Dorsey, Glenn
         Miller,trombones: Jimmy Dorsey,Arnold Brillhardt,Bud Freeman,saxes,Ed
         Lang,guitar; Schutt; Stern; King):   Nov.,1930
   Od 36160. Can This Be Love(404543)   -Ve 2242*
         *Jerry Mason and His Californians
   OK 41471. Fine and Dandy(404544)   -PaE 993
      "   I Can't Make a Man(404545)   -PaE 882
         (Dorsey group):
   Me 12113. Sweet and Hot/You Said It
   Me 12148. I've Got.../Dream a little

TRAYLOR, PEARL (vocals):
   Mod 112. Lonesome Gal Blues/(HADDA BROOKS)
   Mod 114. Somebody's Got to Go/(HADDA BROOKS)

TRAYMORE ORCHESTRA (Duke Ellington Orchestra):
   Vo 15556. Black and Tan Fantasy
         (Originally on Brunswick as 'Washingtonians')

TREMER, GEORGE H. (piano solo):
   Ch 15436. Spirit of '49 Rag(77-C)   -De 7137

TRENT AND HIS ORCHESTRA, AL (Alphonse Trent,piano; Eddie Durham,guitar; Leo Moseley,trombone, and others):   1930
   Ge 6710. Nightmare/Black Rhapsody
   Ch 16587. I Found a New Baby   -Ch 40096
    "Clementine
   Ch 40096. After You've Gone

TRENT AND HIS DEACONS, JOE (Saxophone; banjo; drums; possibly Duke Ellington, piano.--Db 12/15/44):
   Blu Disc 1003. Deacon Jazz(T-2007-1)/Oh How I Love My Darling(T-2008-1;
                                           (Sunny and the Deacons)

RICH TRICE (vocals with guitar):
   De 7701. Come on Baby/Trembling Bed Spring Blues

TRICE, WELLY (blues singing):
   De 7358. Come on In Here Mama/Let Her Go God Bless Her

TRIO DE TROMPETTES (Bill Dillard, Bill Coleman,Shad Collins,trumpets;Dicky Wells,trombones; Django Reinhardt,guitar; Richard Fullbright,bass; Bill Beason drums):   Paris,1937
   Sw   27. I Got Rhythm(OLA 1886)/(DICKY WELLS)

TROMBONE RED AND HIS BLUE SIX:
   Co 14612. Greasy Plate Stomp(151615)/B Flat Blues(151616)

TROTTER AND HIS ORCHESTRA, JOHN SCOTT (Featuring Andy Secrest,cornet; Charlie LaVere,piano; Jack Mayhew, sax):
   De 4213. Parade of the Wooden Soldiers/March of the Toys
   De 4214. Triumphal March(Peter and the Wolf)/Prelude in G Minor
   De 4215. Danse Espagnole No.1/Tambourin Chinois
   De 4216. Kitten on the Keys/Sapphire
   De 4217. Maple Leaf Rag(DLA 2593-B)/Russian Sailors' Dance(DLA 2615-A)

TROUTT'S MELODY ARTISTS, CHARLIE:
   OK 40589. Running After You(9626-A)/Mountain City Blues(9627-A)
   Co 1030. Transportation Blues, 1 & 2 (143935/36)
   Co 1265. Transportation Blues, 3 & 4

FRANKIE TRUMBAUER

See also:
   BROADWAY BELL HOPS: Ha 504, 508.
   TOM BARKER: PaA 34119.
   BENSON ORCHESTRA
   CHICAGO LOOPERS: Pat 36729).
   COTTON PICKERS: Br 2766, 2818, 2879, 2937.
   JEAN GOLDKETTE:
   GOOFUS FIVE:
   RUSSELL GRAY: OK 40938.
   EDDIE LANG: OK 41344, PaE 840.
   LANG-VENUTI:
   SAM LANIN:
   MASON-DIXON: Co 1861.
   JOHNNY MERCER: Co 18002.
   BENNY MEROFF: OK 40912.
   RAY MILLER:
   MOUND CITY BLUE BLOWERS: Br 2002.
   RED NICHOLS: Vi 21056.
   WILLARD ROBISON: Pat 36724, Pe 14905.
   SIOUX CITY SIX: Ge 5569.
   JACK TEAGARDEN: Br 6993, 7652.
   THREE T'S: Vi 25273.
   JOE VENUTI.
   PAUL WHITEMAN:

TRUMBAUER AND HIS ORCHESTRA, FRANKIE (Bix Beiderbecke,cornet; Bill Rank,trombone; Jimmy Dorsey,clarinet; Trumbauer,alto and C melody: Doc Ryker,alto;Irving Riskin or Paul Mertz*,piano; Eddie Lang,guitar,or Howdy Quicksell,banjo#; Chauncey Morehouse,drums):   Feb.4,1927
   OK 40772. Singin' the Blues(80393) -Br 7703, PaE 1838, PaE 3323, Co 37804
     "   Clarinet Marmalade(80392-A*#)-Vo 3010,4412,PaE 3323,2304 Co 37804
   OK 40871. Trumbology(80391-C)   -Co 36280, PaE 3419, PaE 2465
     "   For No Reason at All In C(81085)ø   -PaE 3419, PaE 2532
   Co 35667. For No Reason at All in C(second master) ø
          (ø 'Tram, Bix and Lang')

```
              (Sub. Don Murray,clarinet and tenor):                May 9,1927
OK 40882. Ostrich Walk(81071-B)     -UHCA 29, PaE 3349, PaE 2492, Co 37805
    "     Riverboat Shuffle(81072-B)-UHCA 30,       "          "          "
                                                               May 13,1947
OK 40843. I'm Comin' Virginia(81083-B)-Br 7703,PaE 3361,2687,  Co 36280
    "     Way Down Yonder in New Orleans(81084-B*)
                                     (-Vo 3010, 4412,PaE 3361, Co 37806

              (Add Adrian Rollini,bass sax):                    Aug.25,1927
OK 40879. Blue River(81274-B)/Cradle in Caroline(81275-D)      -PaF 3440
OK 40903. Three Blind Mice(81273-C)/Krazy Kat(81489-B; add J.Venuti,violin)
                                                                (-PaE 105
         TRAM-BIX-LANG (Bix plays piano with short cornet in this and in B
         side of OK 40871 above):
OK 40916. Wringin' and Twistin'(81450-A)   -Vo 3150, PaE 3504, Co 37806
              (BIX BEIDERBECKE , piano solo)

         ORCHESTRA (Previous personnel, plus Joe Venuti, violin): Sept.28,1927
OK 40926. Humpty Dumpty(81488-A)/Baltimore(81490-B)

              (Possibly Pee Wee Russell,clarinet):              Oct.25,1927
OK 40966. Crying All Day(81570-C)                    -PaE 2176, Co 35956
    "     A Good Man Is Hard to Find(81571-B)        -PaE 3489,    "

              (Sub. Izzy Friedman,clarinet; Min Leibrook,bass sax; George Marsh,drums;
              Lennie Hayton,piano; Matty Malneck,violin: add Harry Goldfield,cornet;
              Harold Strickland, alto):
OK 40979. There'll Come a Time(40003-B)              -PaE 3526, PaE 2097
    "     Mississippi Mud(400034-A)                        "         "
Unissued. Two Letters from Dixie(400002)/From Monday on(400033)
OK 41044. Jubilee(400004-C)/(LARRY ABBOTT)           -PaE 161, PaE 2054

              (Omit Strickland):                                April 3,1928
OK 41019. Our Bungalow of Dreams(400188-A)                     -PaE 142
    "     Lila(400189-B)                                       -PaE 141
OK 41039. Borneo(400603-B)                                     -PaE 203
    "     My Pet(400604-C)                                     -PaE 141
              (Sub. Harry Gale,drums):                          July 5,1928
OK 41100. Bless You Sister(400989-C)                           -PaE 1882
    "     Dusky Stevedore(400990-B)                            -PaE 265
              (Roy Bargy,piano):                                Sept.20,1928
OK 41145. Take Your Tomorrow(401133-B).              -Co 37807, PaE 265
    "     Love Affairs(401134-C)
Unissued. Sentimental Baby(401135)
PaF  2645. Love Nest(401195-B)                                  Oct.5,1928
PaE  2176. The Japanese Sandman(401196-C)
OK 41128. High Up on a Hilltop(401197-A)                       -PaE 2644
    "     Sentimental Baby(401198-A)                           -PaE 298
              (Sub. Marsh,drums; Andy Secrest,cornet,for Goldfield: Bix reportedly
              does not play on first coupling below):
OK 41209. Futuristic Rhythm(401703-B)                          -PaE 2644
    "     Raisin' the Roof(401704-D)                   April 17 & 30,1928
                                                               -PaE 6208
OK 41231. Louise(401809-B)                                     -PaE 398
    "     Wait Till You See Ma Cherie(401810-C)
OK 41286. Baby Won't You Please Come Home(401811-C)  -PaF 1978, Co 37807
    "     I Like That(401841-C)                                -PaE 714
PaE   420. No One Can Take Your Place(401840-B)
              (Sub. Charlie Margulies,cornet, for Bix Beiderbecke: Stan King,drums;
              Venuti,violin; add Strickland, sax):
OK 41252. Nobody But You(401952)/I've Gotta Feelin' for You(401953)
OK 41268. Shivery Stomp(401961)                                -PaE 511
    "     Reachin' for Someone(401962)                         -PaE 420
OK 41301. Love Ain't Nothin' But the Blues(402963-B)           -PaE 644
    "     How Am I to Know(402964-A)                           -PaE 618
OK 41313. Turn on the Heat(403050)/Sunny Side Up(403052)       -PaE 499
OK 41326. My Sweeter Than Sweet(403082-A)/(CAROLINA CLUB ORCH.) -PaE 583
OK 41330. Manhattan Rag(403051:add Henry Whiteman,Matty Malneck,violins)
                                                               (-PaE 1978
    "     What Wouldn't I Do for That Man(403083)              -PaE 583

              (Add Harry Goldfield,trumpet):
OK 41421. Happy Feet(404007)                                   -PaE 701
    "     I Like to Do Things for You(404008)                  -PaE 702
OK 41431. Get Happy(404009-D)/Deep Harlem(404010-B)

              (Previous personnel, without Venuti, and with Bernie Bailey in place
              of Strickland):
OK 41437. What's the Use(404268)/Hittin' the Bottle(404269)    -PaE 1013
OK 41450. Bye Bye Blues(404433)                                -PaE 796
    "     Choo Choo(404434)                                    -PaE 821
```

```
        (Unknown personnel):
Co  2710. Business in 3/I Think You're a Honey
Co  2729. The Newest St. Louis Blues(152284)/Between the Devil and the
                                                        (Deep Blue Sea(152285)
Co  2897. Cinderella's Wedding Day                          -CoE 542
    "     Bass Drum Dan                                     -CoE 580
        (Nat Natoli,trumpet; Bill Rank,trombone: Rosie McHargue,Frankie Trum-
        bauer,saxes; Matty Malneck,violin: Dave Rose,piano; John Tobin,banjo;
        Dan Gaybe,bass; Bob Conselman,drums):
BrE 01225. Bass Drum Dan
Br  6146. Crazy Quilt/In the Merry Month of Maybe·          -BrE 01261
Br  6159. Georgia on My Mind/Honeysuckle Rose               -BrE 01192
        (Nat Natoli,Charlie Tegarden,trumpets· Jack Teagarden,trombone; Frankie
        Trumbauer,Bennie Benaccio,Harold Strickland,John Cordaro,saxes; Mischa
        Russell,violin; Roy Bargy,piano; Dick McDonough,guitar; Artie Miller,
        bass; Herb Quigley,drums):                                    1934
Br  6763. Juba/Break It Down
Br  6788. Emaline(B 14849-A)/'Long About Midnight(B14851-A) -BrE 01767
Br  6912. China Boy                                         -BrE 01812
    "     Break It Down
Br  6997. In a Mist
        (Nat Natoli,Bunny Berigan,trumpets; Glenn Miller,trombone: Artie Shaw,
        clarinet and alto; Jack Shore,Frankie Trumbauer,Larry Binyon,saxes;Roy
        Bargy piano; Lionel Hall,guitar; Artie Bernstein,bass; Jack Williams
        drums):                                                       1935
Vi 24812. Blue Moon(86219)/Down to Uncle Bill's(86821)     -HMV  119
Vi 24834. Troubled(86222)                                  -HMV 158, HMV 4454
    "     Plantation Moods(86220)
        (Ed Wade,Charlie Teagarden,trumpets· Jack Teagarden,trombone: Frankie
        Trumbauer,alto: Johnny Mince,clarinet; Mud Hayes,John Cordaro,saxes;
        Roy Bargy,piano: George Van Eps,guitar; Artie Miller,bass: Stan King,
        drums):                                                  Feb.,1936
Br  7613. Breakin' in Pair or Shoes(B18601)/Hope Gabriel Likes My(B18630)
Br  7629. Flight of a Hay-Bay(B18600)/Announcers' Blues(B18602)-BrE 02197
        (Sub. Artie Shaw,clarinet: Carl Kress,guitar):
Br  7663. The Mayor of Alabam'(B19114)/'S Wonderful(B19116)  -BrE 02232
Br  7665. Somebody Loves Me/Ain't Misbehavin'
        (Russ Case,Charlie Teagarden,trumpets: Jack Teagarden,trombone; Frankie
        Trumbauer,John Cordaro,altos; Eddie Miller,tenor; Matty Matlock,clari-
        net; Roy Bargy,piano: Carl Kress,guitar: Artie Miller,bass· Ray Bauduc,
Br  7687. I'm an Old Cowhand(B 19442)/Diga diga Do(B 19443)     (drums):
        (Unknown personnel):
Vs  8215. Wearing of the Green: Irish Washer-Woman(US1401-1)/No Retard
Vs  8223. Jimtown Bl(US 1406-2)/Laziest Gal in Town(US1408-1)   (US1402-1)
Vs  8225. Not on the First Night Baby(US1407-1)/Walkin' th Dog(US 1421-1)
Vs  8239. I Surrender Dear(US 1404-1)/(JOHNNY McGEE)
Vs  8256. Don't Stand a Ghost of a Chance(US1403-1)/Sugar Foot Stomp
Vs  8243. Never Never Land Fantasy/National Emblem March    (US 1419-1)

TUB JUG WASHBOARD BAND:
    Para 12671. Tub-Jug Rag(20652-1)/San(20671-2)

TUCKER, BESSIE (vocals with piano):
    Vi 21708. The Dummy/Fort Worth and Denver Blues
    Vi 23385. Bogy Man/Key to the Bushes
    Vi 23392. Mean Old Master/T.B. Moan
    Vi 38536. Bessie's Moan/Penitentiary Blues
    Vi 38542. Better Boot That Thing/Katy Blues

TUCKER, SOPHIE (vocals, acc. by Miff Mole's Molers; Ted Shapiro at piano):
    OK 40813. One Sweet Letter from you(80737-B)/50 Million Frenchmen Can't
                                                          (Be Wrong(80738-A)
TUMMINIA, JOSEPHINE (vocals, acc. by Jimmy Dorsey and His Orchestra):
    De 29009. Blue Danube Waltz(DLA 757)/The Wren(DLA 731)

TURK'S ORCHESTRA, AL:
    OK  8362. Snag It/Hi Henry Stomp                        -OK 40653
    OK 40660. Shanghai Honeymoon/(JAZZ PILOTS)

TURNER, ANNIE (vocals, acc. by Little Brother Montgomery, piano):
    BB  6788. Workhouse Blues/Deceived Blues

TURNER AND HIS MEMPHIS MEN, JOE (Duke Ellington's Orchestra: Arthur Whetsel,
Freddie Jenkins,Cootie Williams,trumpets· Sam Nanton,Juan Tizol,trombones;
Barney Bigard,clarinet: Johnny Hodges,alto: Harry Carney,bariton; Ellington,
piano: Fred Guy,guitar; Wellman Braud,bass: Sonny Greer,drums): April 4,1929
```

```
Co  1813. Freeze and Melt(148171)
 "        Mississippi Moan(148172) April 28, 1929        -Co 36157
Co 36157*.ThatRhythm Man(148640)
         *Issued under Duke Ellington and His Memphis Men
```

TURNER, BIG JOE (vocals with Willie (The Lion) Smith,piano):
 De 7824. Doggin' the Dog/Rainy Day Blues
 De 7827. Jumpin' Down Blues(68396-A)/Careless Love(68395-B)

   (Unknown acc.):
 De 7856. Ice Man/Somebody's Got to Go
 De 7868. Chewed Up Grass/Nobody in Mind

   (With Freddie Slack Trio):
 De 4093. Rocks in My Bed(DLA 2738)/Goin' to Chicago Blues(DLA 2740)

   JOE TURNER AND HIS FLY CATS (Hot Lips Page,trumpet; Pete Johnson,piano;
   John Collins,guitar; Abe Bolar,bass· A.G.Godley,drums; Joe Turner,voc.):
 De 18121. Piney Brown Blues(68333-A)/(PETE JOHNSON'S BAND)

   JOE TURNER with Pete Johnson Trio (Johnson,piano: Dallas Bartley,bass;
   Ernest Ashley,guitar):   Oct.30,1944
 De 11001. Rebecca(72525-A)/It's the Same Old Story(72526-A)
 De 48042. I Got a Gal for Every Day in Week(72523-2A)/Little Bitty Gal Bl
                                                              (72524-2A)
   JOE TURNER (with Pete Johnson's All Stars: Pete Johnson,piano; Don
   Byas,tenor; Frank Newton,trumpet; Al Hall,bass; Harold West,drums;
   Leonard Ware,guitar):
 Na 9010. S.K. Blues, 1 & 2
 Na 9011. Watch That Jive/Johnson and Turner Blues

TURNER, LAVINIA (vocals acc. by piano):
 OK 8042. How Can I Be Your Sweet Mamma/Don't Cut Off Your Nose to Spite
                                                              (Your Face
     LAVINIA TURNER AND HER JAZZ BAND (Including June Clark,trumpet?):
 Pat 020572. Sweet Man o' Mine/A-Wearin'

TUXEDO ORCHESTRA:
 Vo 15395. Cryin' for the Moon/You've Got Those Wanna Go Back Again Blues
 Vo 15500. Oh How I Love You/(SIX HAYSEEDS)
 Vo 15595. Bye Bye Pretty Baby/Lock a Little Sunbeam Down in Your Heart

TUXEDO SYNCOPATORS (Cliff Jackson,pianist, is believed to be the leader of
some or all of these sides):
 Pat 22292. Dardanella/When My Baby Smiles at Me
 Pe 14305. Scotch and Soda/Please Tell Me
 Mad 5098. Horse Feathers

TWO OF SPADES:
 Co 14072. Harmonica Blues/Meddlin' With the Blues

TYUS, EFFIE AND CHARLES (duets with Clarence Williams, piano):
 OK 8133. Jazz Crazy(S-72345-A)/Omaha Blues(S-72346-A)
 OK 8149. You've Got to Prove It to Me(S-72618-B)/I Want to Go Back to the
                                                              (Farm(S-72617-A)
     EFFIE-CHARLES TYUS-HORACE GEORGE (vocal trio):
 OK 8164. Emancipation Day in Georgia/(HORACE GEORGE,clarinet)

   (Unknown acc.):
 OK 8330. You've Got to Recognize Me/Good Old Bygone Days
 OK 8459. Alibi-ing Papa/Sweet Mama Goodie

     EFFIE-CHARLES TYUS (acc. Williams Trio):
 OK 8200. I'm Funny 'Bout My Cookin' Blues/Cuddle Up Close,It's Wintertime

U

UNCLE SKIPPER (blues singing)
 De 7353. Chifferobe/Cutting My A.B.C.'s
 De 7455. Look What a Shape I'm In/Twee Twee Twa

UNDERWOOD, SUGAR (piano solos):
 Vi 21538. Davis Street Blues/Dew Drop Alley Stomp

UNIVERSITY BOYS:
 Or 1338. Sonny Boy(1765)/(BOB GREEN
 Or 1549. Honey(2178-1)   -Je 5573
 Or 1606. Rainbow Man(2292-2)/(BILLY JAMES)
 Ro 1607. Passing Fancy
 Or 1627. Singin' in the Rain/(COLLINS DANCE ORCHESTRA)

```
              (Jimmy McPartland,trumpet: Jack Teagarden,trombone: Benny Goodman,
         clarinet: Gil Rodin,alto):
    Or   1668. Lovable & Sweet(2431-3)/(DIXIE JAZZ BAND)              -Je 5685
```

UNIVERSITY SIX (California Ramblers group including Miff Mole,trombone; Adrian Rollini,bass sax: Red Nichols,trumpet: Bobby Davis,alto):
```
    Ha     36. Camel Walk/Sailor's Sweetheart
    Ha     37. Desdemona/You Told Me to Go
    Ha     71. Smile a Little Bit(141305)/Then I'll Be Happy(141306)
    Ha     73. In Your Green Hat(141339)/I Love My Baby(141341)
    Ha    106. Fallin' Down(141304)/(HARMONIANS)
    Ha    134. Dustin' the Donkey
    Ha    155. Georgianna(141838)/(MANHATTAN DANCE MAKERS)
    Ha    209. Ace in the Hole/(DIXIE STOMPERS)
    Ha    224. Tiger Rag(142195)/San(142196)
    Ha    230. I Ain't Got Nobody/Oh If I Only Had You
    Ha    245. St.Louis Hop(142490)/(ORIGINAL INDIANA FIVE)
   ·Ha    262. That's a Good Girl(142678)/Give Me a Ukelele(142679)
    Ha    296. My Baby Knows How(142899)/Lonely Eyes(142901)
    Ha    316. It Takes a Good Woman/Wait'll You See
    Ha    367. Oh Lizzie(143447)/The Cat(143448)
    Ha    382. Nobody But(143446)/It's O.K.Katy With Me(143449)
    Ha    399. So Long Pal(144021)/Rosy Cheeks(144022)
    Ha    433. Slow River/Lazy Weather
    Ha    444. Bless Her Little Heart/That's a Grand and Glorious Feeling
    Ha    474. Pastafazoola/(NIGHT CLUB ORCHESTRA)
    Ha    534. Is She My Girl Friend(144877)/The Beggar(144878)
    Ha    551. Changes(145360)/There's Something Spanish in Your Eyes(145258)
    Ha    565. When You're With Somebody Else(145454)/Mine All Mine(145455)
    Ha    570. Under the Clover Moon(145456)/(THE WESTERNERS)
    Ha    617. Lila/Stay Out of the South
    Ha    652. Chilly Pom Pom Pee
    Ha    653. Constantinople(146302*.(ERNIE GOLDEN)
    Ve   1425. Yes She Do(144023)/She's Got It(144224)
    Ve   1529. Manhattan Mary(144879)/(LOU GOLD)
    Ve   1414. Beale Street Blues/Sister Kate
    Di   2466. Roam On My Little Gypsy Sweetheart(144472)/Swanee Shore(144474)
    Di   2489. Who's That Knocking at My Door(144609)/Oh Doris Where Do You
                                                              (Live(144612)
```

V

VANT, LOUISE (vocals; June Clark,trumpet, is reported to have been among the accompanists on some of these sides):
```
    OK   8264. Save Your Sorrow(73810)/Show Me the Way to Go Home(73811)
    OK   8275. I'm Tired of Everything/If You Hadn't Gone Away

         (Acc. Perry Bradford's Mean Four):
    OK   8310. Pensacola Blues(74055-A)/New Crazy Blues(74056-A)

         (Acc. Roy Barnes, piano):
    OK   8341. The Man I Love Is Oh So Goot to Me/Daddy Don't You Try to Pull
                                                    (That Two-Time Thing on Me
```

VARIETY BOYS (Trumpet, tenor, piano, guitar, bass, violin, vibraharp,clarinet):
```
    De   8549. Harlem Fiesta(93602-A)/Tack Annie(93601-A)
    De   8564. The Chant(93603)/Uptown Jive(93600)
```

VARSITY SEVEN (Benny Carter,trumpet and alto; Coleman Hawkins,tenor: Danny Polo,clarinet: Joe Sullivan,piano; Ulysses Livingston,guitar: George Wettling, drums; Artie Shapiro,bass):
```
    Vs   8135. Scratch My Back(US 1160-1)/Save It Pretty Mama(US 1161-1)
    Vs   8147. Easy Rider(US 1159-1)/It's Tight Like That(US 1158-1)
    Vs   8173. How Long How Long Blues(US 1284-1)/Pom Pom(US 1287-1)
    Vs   8179. Shake It and Break It(US 1285-1)/A Pretty Girl Is Like a Melody
                                                                  (US 1286-1)
```

VARSITY EIGHT (California Ramblers group,including Adrian Rollini,bass sax; Dorsey brothers: Miff Mole,trombone: Red Nichols,trumpet,at various times, especially in middle and later periods):
```
    Ca    400. Last Night on the Back Porch(626)'/(BOB HARING)
    Ca    420. Oh Joe(627)/(BOB HARING)
    Ca    444. Don't Take Those Lips Away(726)/(FRANKLIN'S ORCHESTRA)
    Ca    498. Mean Blues(784)/(BROADWAY BROADCASTERS)
    Ca    480. Say It With a Ukelele(785)/(HARRY LANGE)
    Ca    505. Hula Lou
    Ca    516. Why Did I Kiss That Girl(881)/HARING HAPPY HARMONISTS)
    Ca    556. San/(HARRY LANGE)
    Ca    559. Doodle Doo Do(995)/(H. SANTREY)
    Ca    574. Knock at the Door(1066)/(BOB HARING)
    Ca    580. I Can't Find a Name
```

```
Ca    588. Hard Hearted Hannah(1099)/(H. SANTREY)
Ca    617. Tea for Two(1197)/(LOU GOLD)
Ca    605. Them Ramblin' Blues(1143)/(STATLER ORCH.)
Ca    622. Copenhagen/(BOB HARING)
Ca    633. Dear One(1216)/(LOU GOLD)
Ca    640. Beets and Turnips(1201)/(BOB HARING)
Ca    641. Doo Wacka Doo/(BOB HARING)
Ca    680. Ain't My Baby Grand/I Ain't Got Nobody to Love
Ca    695. But I Like You Best of All(1378)/(BOB HARING)
Ca    714. Nobody Knows Don't Bring Lulu
Ca    724. If You Knew Susie(1447)/(MIKE SPECIALE)
Ca    725. Cheatin' on Me(1379)/(ACE BRIGODE)
Ca    730. Sweet Georgia Brown/Lady of the Nile
Ca    732. Ah ha (1437O)/(LOU GOLD)
Ca    741. Charleston(1448)/(BOB HARING)
Ca    750. Yes Sir That's My Baby(1489)/(PAUL VAN LOAN)
Ca    753. Moonlight and Roses
Ca    780. Tryin' to Keep Away
Ca    817. Milenberg Joys
Ca    835. Freshie(1698)/(DIXIE DAISIES)
Ca   1144. New Kind o' Man
Ca   1009. I Can't Get the One I Want/You Know Me Alabam'
Ca   1255. Casey Jone/(MIKE SPECIALE)
Ca   1266. Steamboat Bill(2858)/(BROADWAY BROADCASTERS)    -Ro  578
 -     - . Vo-Do-Do-Dee-O Blues(2523)                      -Li 2697
 -     - . Chicken Reel(2857)/Farewell Blues(2859)         -Ro  564
 -     - . Talkin' to Myself(3343)                         -Ro  744
 -     - . When Summer Is Gone(3499)                       -Ro  806
Ca   9003. He Ain't Never Been to College

      (Whoopee Makers: Featuring Jimmy McPartland, trumpet; Jack Teagarden,
      trombone; Benny Goodman, clarinet):
Ca   9098. The Sorority Stomp(3698)                        -Ro  900
Ca   9174. Dirty Dog(3766)

      (Previous personnel)
Ca   9143. I Get the Blues When It Rains(3804)/(JOE GREEN) -Ro  945
Ca    - . What Do We Get from Boston(3958)                 -Ro 1035
 -    - . Send Love Through the Breeze(4034)               -Ro 1068
 -    - . Sweetheart of My Student Days                    -Ro 1466
Ba  32105. You're Driving Me Crazy/(ELLIOTT JACOBY)
```

VASSAR, CALLIE (vocals, acc. by Richard M. Jones, piano):
```
Ge   5172. Maybe Someday(11489-B)/All Night Blues(11490-B)
Ge   5173. I'm Lonesome Nobody Cares for Me(11488-B)/Original Stomps
                                                             (11491-B)
```
VAUGHN, SARA (vocals, acc. by Dizzy Gillespie,trumpet; George Auld,alto and tenor; Aaron Sachs,clarinet; Leonard Feather,piano; Chuck Wayne,guitar; Morey Feld,drums; Jack Lesberg,bass):   Dec.31,1944
```
Cont -----. East of the Sun/Night in Tunisia
Cont  6024. Signing Off/No Smokes Blues
Cont  6061. Willie Mae Willow Foot(acc. Hot Lips Page Orch.)
```
      (Gillespie,trumpet: Charlie Parker,alto: Flip Phillips,tenor; Nat Jaffe,piano; Bill de Arango,guitar; Max Roach,drums: Curly Russell,bass):
```
Cont  6008. What More Can a Woman Do/I'd Rather Have Memory*   May 25,1945
Cont  6024. Mean to Me                     *Tad Dameron, piano

Mu    494. Body and Soul/Everything I Have Is Yours
Mu    503. I Cover the Waterfront/I Don't Stand a Ghost of a Chance
Mu    504. Tenderly/Don't Blame Me
Mu    505. I've Got a Crush on You/Penthouse Serenade
Mu    499. I'm Through With Love/Lover Man(reissue of Dizzy Gillespie item)
```
           (See also: George Auld; Dizzy Gillespie; Teddy Wilson)

VENTURA SEXTETTE, CHARLIE (Ventura, tenor; Howard McGhee,trumpet; Arnold Ross, piano; Dave Barbour,guitar; Art Shapiro, bass; Nick Fatool,drums):
```
Sunset 10051. Ghost of a Chance(106)/Tea for Two(107)
Sunset 10054. I Surrender Dear(109)/C-V Jump(108)
```
      CHARLIE VENTURA QUARTET (Ventura,tenor; Arnold Ross,piano; John Levy, bass: Specs Powell,drums):
```
Sav   530. Dark Eyes(5836)/Ever So Thoughtful(5834)
Sav   632. Big Deal(5833)
```
      CHARLIE VENTURA SEXTET(Ventura,tenor: Barney Bigard,clarinet; Red Callender,bass; Barney Kessel,guitar; Harry Fields,piano; Ray de Geer,alto):
```
Lamplighter A-1. Stompin' at the Savoy, 1 & 2
Lamplighter A-1. The Man I Love , 1 & 2
```
      (Sub. Milt Raskin,piano; Allan Reuss,guitar; omit De Geer; Nick Fatool,
                                                                 (drums):
Lamplighter A-1. I Don't Know Why/Charlie Boy

```
         CHARLIE VENTURA SEXTETTE(Buck Clayton,trumpet: Ventura,tenor: Billy
         Rowland,piano; Eddie Yance,guitar: Specs Powell,drums: All Hall,bass):
BW    37. C-V Jam/Out You Go
BW    38. Tammy's Dream(T-14)/Let's Jump for Rita(T-15)

         (Red Rodney,trumpet: Ventura,tenor; Willie Smith,alto; Arnold Ross,
         piano; Billy Hadnott,bass: Barney Kessel,guitar; Nick Fatool,drums):
BW  1219. Who's Sorry Now/The Man I Love
BW  1220. Nobody Knows the Trouble I've Seen/'S wonderful

         (Charlie Kennedy,alto; Ted Napoleon,piano; Allan Reuss,guitar; Red Call-
         ender,bass):
BW  1221. Chopin's Minute Waltz/Slow Joe
BW  1222. What Is This Thing Called Love/I'm in the Mood for Love

         CHARLIE VENTURA AND HIS ORCHESTRA:
Na  7013. Misirlou(162)/Either It's Love Or It Isn't(160)
Na  7015. Please Be Kind/How High the Moon
Na  9029. Moon Nocturne, 1 & 2

         CHARLIE VENTURA SEXTET (Charlie Shavers, trumpet: Bill Harris,trombone;
         Ventura,tenor: Ralph Burns,piano; Bill De Arango,guitar; Chubby Jackson,
         bass; Dave Tough,drums):
Na  9036. Synthesis(236; Buddy Stewart, voc.)/Blue Champagne(238)
```

JOE VENUTI

```
See also:
ALL STAR RHYTHM BOYS: Ha 1346, 1420.
IRENE BEASLEY: Vi 21467.
BIX BEIDERBECKE: Vi 23008, 23018.
BROADWAY BELL HOPS.
BOSWELL SISTERS: Br 20110.
HOAGY CARMICHAEL: Vi 22864,23013,23034,25371: Vi 38139.
BING CROSBY: De 4800.
DORSEY BROTHERS.
CLIFF EDWARDS.
SEGER ELLIS.
FOUR INSTRUMENTAL STARS: Pat 11485.
JEAN GOLDKETTE.
RUSSELL GRAY: OK 40938.
ANNETTE HANSHAW.
ROGER WOLFE KAHN.
LANIN'S RED HEADS: Co 327, 376, 483.
CHARLIE LA VERE: Jump 1, 2.
CHESTER LEIGHTON.
LANG-VENUTI.
HAROLD LEM.
McKENZIE: OK 40893, 41071.
BENNY MEROFF: OK 40912.
RAY MILLER.
RED NICHOLS.
FRANKIE TRUMBAUER.
PAUL WHITEMAN.
TRAVELERS.
PAUL SMALL.
```

```
                                                                          1927
VENUTI, JOE (violin, and Eddie Lang, guitar):                       -PaE 3330
OK 40762. Wild Cat                                      -PaE 2493,
    "     Sunshine                                                  -CoE 5001
Co   914. Black and Blue Bottom(142698)                                 "
          Stringin' the Blues(142697)

         (Add Arthur Schutt, piano):                         -PaE 3352, PaE 2632
OK 40825. Doin' Things(81058)
    "     Goin' Places(81059)

         JOE VENUTI'S BLUE FOUR (Joe Venuti,violin; Eddie Lang,guitar; Arthur
         Schutt,piano: Adrian Rollini,bass sax and goofus):
                                                             -PaE 3367, PaE 2551
OK 40853. Kickin' the Cat(81118)                                       -PaE 3442
    "     Beatin' the Dog(81119)
OK 40897. Cheese and Crackers(81432-C)                       -PaE 2581,
    "     A Mug of Ale(81433-C)                              -Vo 3160, PaE  109
OK 40947. Penn Beach Blues(81822)
    "     Four String Joe(81823)          -PaE 2581,               "

         JOE VENUTI-EDDIE LANG (acc. Frank Signorelli, piano):
Vi 21561. Doing Things(45812)                                       -BB 10280
    "     Wild Cat(45813)                                              "

         JOE VENUTI'S BLUE FOUR (Venuti,violin: Don Murray, sax: Rube Bloom or
         Frank Signorelli*,piano: Eddie Lang,guitar):
                                                                    -PaE  982
OK 41025. Dinah(400178)                                             -PaE  520
    "     The Wild Dog(400179)
```

OK 41076. The Man From the South(400788-C) -PaE 607
" Pretty Trix(400789-B)* -PaE 1916

JOE VENUTI AND HIS NEW YORKERS (Featuring Eddie Lang,guitar, with full size band):
OK 41051. I Must Be Dreaming(400706-B) -PaE 182
" 'Tain't So Honey 'Tain't So(400707-A) "
OK 41056. Because My Baby Don't Mean Maybe(400767-C) -Vo 3161, PaE 201
" Just Like Melody Out of the Sky(400768B) "
OK 41087. Pickin' Cotton(400884) -PaE 309
" I'm on the Crest of a Wave(400885) "
OK 41133. Doin' Things(401193-B)
" I Must Have That Man(401194-B) -PaE 280
OK 41192. That's the Good Old Sunny South(401584-C)Weary River(401585-A)
OK 41263. Little Pal(401847)/I'm in Seventh Heaven(401848) -PaE 427
OK 41320. Chant of Jungle(403071-C)/Wonderful Something(403072-C)PaE 608

JOE VENUTI'S BLUE FOUR (Venuti,violin; Jimmy Dorsey,sax and clarinet; Rube Bloom,piano; Eddie Lang,guitar: unknown drums):
OK 41144. The Blue Room(401159) -Vo 3011, PaE 1916
" Sensation(401160) -PaE 596
OK 41251. My Honey's Lovin' Arms(401449)
" Goin' Home(401450-A) -Vo 3043

(Venuti,violin; Frankie Trumbauer,sax and bassoon; Lennie Hayton,piano; Lang,guitar):
OK 41361. Runnin' Ragged(403078) -PaE 531
" Apple Blossoms(403079) -PaE 647

Venuti,violin; Adrian Rollini,bass sax; Itsy Riskin,piano; Eddie Lang, guitar):
OK 41432. Raggin' the Scale(404005-C) -PaE 778, Vo 3043
" Put and Take(404006) -PaE 973

JOE VENUTI AND HIS NEW YORKERS(Including Jack Teagarden,trombone;Jimmy Dorsey,alto and clarinet: Venuti,violin; Lang,guitar):
OK 41427. Promises(404032-B) -PaE 776
" Dancing With Tears in My Eyes(404033-C) -PaE 744
OK 41451. Out of Breath/I'm Only Human After All

(Sub. Tommy Dorsey,trombone):
Vi 23015. My Man from Caroline(63683) -HMV 4890
" I Like a Little Girl(63684)
Vi 23018. Wasting MY love on You(63682)/(BIX BEIDERBECKE)
Vi 23039. Gettin' Hot(53506) -HMV 4890

JOE VENUTI AND HIS BLUE FOUR (Venuti,violin: Jimmy Dorsey,clarinet and saxes: Eddie Lang,guitar: piano):
Vi 23021. The Wild Dog(63700) -HMV 4940
" Really Blue(64301) -HMV 4866
OK 41469. I've Found a New Baby(404549) -PaE 924
" Sweet Sue(404550) -PaE 878
OK 41506. Pardon Me Pretty Baby(404940-B) -PaE 1003
" Little Buttercup(404942-B) -PaE 1252
Co 2488. Little Girl -PaE 1003
" Tempo di Modernage -PaE 1063

JOE VENUTI'S REHYTHM BOYS:
Co 2535. There's No Other Girl(151790) -PaE 1287
" Now That I Need You(151791)
Co 2589. Wolf Wobble(151792)/(DORSEY BROTHERS) -PaE 1071
PaF 1115. To To Blues(151793)

JOE VENUTI-EDDIE LANG BLUE FIVE (Venuti,violin; Jimmy Dorsey,trumpet, as well as clarinet and alto: Adrian Rollini,bass sax and vibraphone; piano):
Co 2765. Raggin' the Scale(265066)/(ART KASSEL) -CoE 612
CoE 601. Pink Elephants(265069)/Hey Young Fella(265067)
Co 2782. Jig Saw Puzzle Blues(265068) -CoE 612
" Vibraphonia(265117; omit Lang) -PaE 2083

(Sub. Dick McDonough,guitar):
CoF 637. Hiawatha's Lullaby/My Gypsy Rhapsody
Co 2783. Isn't It Heavenly/(BILLY COTTON)

JOE VENUTI AND HIS BLUE SIX (Joe Venuti,violin: Benny Goodman,clarinet; Bud Freeman,tenor, Adrian Rollini,bass sax; Joe Sullivan,piano: Dick McDonough,guitar: Neil Marshall,drums): 1935
Co 2834. Doin' the Uptown Lowdown(265147)/BEN SELVIN) -De 18167, CoE 708
CoE 686. The Jazz Me Blues(265148-2)/In De Ruff(265149-2) -De 18168
CoE 708. Sweet Lorraine(265146-2) -De 18167

JOE VENUTI AND HIS ORCHESTRA:
Pe 15830. I Want to Ring Bells(14077-1) -Me 12807, DeE 3803
" Gather Lip Rouge While You May(14079-1) " "
Pe 15832. You're My Past Present & Future(14076) -Me 12816, DeE 3797
" Doin' the Uptown Lowdown(14078) " "

```
    Me 12831.  Moon Glow(14080-1)                              -Ro 2309, DeE 5177
       "       Cheese and Crackers(14081)                         "
    Me 12828.  Heat Wave(14215-2)                              -Or 2783, DeE 5202
       "       Faster Parade(14216-1)                             "
    Pe 15845.  My Dancing Lady(14255-1)          -Or 2791, Me 12838, DeE 3860
       "       Everything I Have Is Yours(14256-1)        "        "     DeE 3803
    Or  2820.  One Minute to One(14488-1)/You Have Taken Heart(14489-1)-Pe15869
    Me 12839.  No More Love/Build a Little Home
    Pe 15871.  Cinderella's Fella(14501-1)/Alice,Wonderland(14502-1) -Me 12886
    BB  5293.  Fiddlesticks(78187)/Phantom Rhapsody(78190)      -Elec 2164
    BB  5520.  Everybody Shuffle(78188)/Moon Glow(78189)           -RZ 1419

        JOE VENUTI AND HIS BLUE FOUR (Joe Venuti,violin: Don Barrigo,tenor;Ar-
        thur Young,piano; Frank Viggiano,guitar; Douglas Lees,bass):
    RZ  1452.  Satan's Holiday/Hell's Bells and Hellelujah   England,Sept.1934
    RZ  1508.  Tea Time/Romantic Joe(Venuti and Young only)

        (Venuti,violin;Arthur Rollini,tenor and clarinet: Adrian Rollini, bass
        sax and vibraphone: Fulton McGrath,piano: Frank Victor,guitar; Victor
        Angle,drums):                                                    1935
    OK 41586.  Fiddlesticks/Goblin Market
    De   624.  Mello As a 'Cello                              -BrE 02018
       "       Nothing But Notes                              -BrE 02304
    De   625.  Mystery                                        -BrE 02018
       "       Tap Room Blues                                 -BrE 02304
    De   669.  Send Me/Vibraphonia, No. 2                     -BrE 02053

        JOE VENUTI AND HIS ORCHESTRA (unknown personnel):
    Co  3103.  Twenty-Four Hours a Day
       "       Eny Meeny Miney Mo(18506)                       -CoE1319
    Co  3104.  Stop Look and Listen/Yankee Doodle Never Went to Town

        JOE VENUTI (violin, Russ Morgan, piano):
    Co  3105.  Red Velvet/Black Satin

        JOE VENUTI AND HIS ORCHESTRA:
    De  2312.  Something(64951-A)/Nothing(64953-A)
    De  2313.  Flip(64950-A)/Flop(64952-A)

VICKSBURG BLOWERS:
    Ge  6089.  Twin Blues/Monte Carlo Joys

VICKSBURG TEN:
    Ch 15477.  Clarinet Marmalade/Riverboat Shuffle

VINCENT, WALTER (vocals):
    Br  7126.  Your Friends Gonna Use It Too
    Br  7141.  Overtime Blues
    De  7169.  Losin' Blues/When the Breath Bids the Body Goodbye
    De  7178.  Wrong Man/I Ain't Gonna Have It

        WALTER VINCSON (Same?): vocals
    BB  8908.  Gulf Coast Bay/She's Leaving Me
    BB  8963.  Rosa Lee Blues/Can't Get a Word in Edgeways

VINSON AND HIS ORCHESTRA, EDDIE:
    Mer 2031.  Mr. Cleanhead Steps Out(446-B)/Juice Head Baby(449-B)
    Mer 8003.  Cherry Red Blues/Somebody's Got to Go
    Mer 8009.  Just a Dream/Too Many Women Blues
    Mer 8023.  Cleanhead Blues/When a Woman Lover Her Juice
    Mer 8028.  Old Maid Boogie(636-7)/Kidney Stew Blues(634-8)
    Mer 8039.  Lazy Gal(800-1)/Bonus Pay(801-2)
    Mer 8051.  Luxury Tax Blues(921-2)/Gonna Send You Back Where I Got You
                                                              (From(923-2)
VIRGINIA CREEPERS:
    Pe 14790.  San 'n Blue/(ORLANDO'S ORCHESTRA)

VIRGINIA FOUR (blues singing)
    De  7662.  Dig My Jelly Roll/Moaning the Blues

VOORHEES AND HIS ORCHESTRA, DON (Red Nichols,Leo McConville,trumpet: Miff
Mole,trombone; Bill Trone,mellophone: Phil Gleason,Fred Morrow,Paul Cart-
wright,saxes and clarinets: Joe Raymond,violin; Dick McDonough,guitar; banjo;
Arthur Schutt,piano; Jack Hansen,bass: Vic Berton,drums):              1927
    Co   881.  Who Do You Love(143346)/Muddy Water(143347) Charles Kaley,voc.
    Co  1078.  Fantasy on St.Louis Blues, 1 & 2
    Co  1123.  Baby's Blue(144641;Frank Harris,voc.)/(RADIOLITES)
    Co  1124.  Highways are Happy Ways(144630)/When the Morning Glories Wake Up
    Co  1126.  Rain(144636)/(AL HENDLER)                (in the Morning(144637)
    Co  1129.  My Blue Heaven(144651;L.James,voc.)/Soliloquy(144629)
    Co  1180.  Clementine(144642;Frank Harris,voc.)/EDDIE THOMAS)
    Co  1225.  Worrying(144647)
```

Co 1284. Ol' Man River/Can't Help Lovin' Dat Man
Co 1824. One Alone/Riff Song
HoW 1091. Go Home and Tell Your Mother
Pe 15215. If You Believed in Me(108912)/(CASINO DANCE ORCHESTRA)

W

WABASH DANCE ORCHESTRA (Red Nichols' Orchestra: Nichols,trumpet: Miff Mole, trombone; Jimmy Dorsey,alto and clarinet; Fud Livingston, tenor and clarinet; Arthur Schutt,piano, and others):
    Duo 4001. That's My Weakness Now(28195)
    Duo 4003. Because My Baby Don't Mean Maybe Now(28226)
    Duo 4005. My Ohio Home(28199)
    Duo 4006. Chloe(21220)
    Duo 4007. She's a Great Great Girl(28225)
    Duo 4008. Ready for the River(28221)
    Duo 4009. Sweet Sue(28222)
    Duo 4012. My Pet(28220)
    Duo 4024. Get Out and Get Under the Moon(28194)

WABASH TRIO (Possibly King Oliver,trumpet: James P.Johnson,piano: unknown guitar):
    Rad 7039. Coal Black Blues(3384)/Lone Western Blues(3383)   -VD 77039*
            *Issued under name of Mississippi Trio

WADES MOULIN ROUGE ORCHESTRA (Jimmy Wade,trumpet: William Dover,trombone; Stump Evans,alto and soprano: Arnett Nelson,alto: Eddie South,Stanley Wilson violins; Teddy Weatherford,piano; Walter Wright,bass; Edwin Jackson,drums.--
JM 10):   1924
    Para 20295. Someday Sweetheart(1620-1)/Mobile Bl(1621-2)-Pu 11295, Harmo 893
    Pu 11363. You've Got Ways I'm Crazy About(1686)/So Long to You and the
                                                                (Blues(1646)
        JIMMY WADE'S ORCHESTRA (vocals by Perry Bradford).   1927
    Ge 6105. Original Black Bottom Dance/All That I Had is Gone   -BP 8019
        JIMMY WADE AND HIS DIXIELANDERS (Featuring Jimmy Wade,trumpet·
        Miller,trumpet and singing: Alex Hill, piano):   Oct.,1928
    Vo 1236. Mississippi Wobble
     "   Gates Blues(C 2429-A)   -Br 80041

WAGNER AND HIS RHYTHMASTER, LARRY (Walter Smith,trumpet: Gene Prentergast, clarinet; Hub Lytell,tenor; Adrian Rollini,vibraphone: Fulton Shoobe,bass; Murry Gaer,drums: Dave Barbour,guitar: Fulton McGrath,piano):
    Vi 25723. Autopsy on Schubert/Two Dukes on a Pier
        (Walter Smith,trumpet: Art Ralston, Pat Davis,Clarence Hutchenrider, saxes; Claude Thornhill, piano; Dave Barbour,guitar; Denny Dennis,bass; Milton Schlesinger,drums):
    Vi 25772. Hearts Without Flowers/Sneakin' a Sleep

WAKELY, JIMMY (western singer, with Eddie Miller and His Hep Dogies, featuring Miller,tenor):
    De 18728. I've Got Nuggets in My Pockets/Too Bad Little Girl Too Bad

WALKER, UNCLE BUD (vocals):
    OK 8828. Look Here Mama Blues/Stand Up Suitcase Blues

WALKER AND HIS BAND, EDDIE (Zack Whyte's Chocolate Beau Brummels,q.v. for personnel):
    Sup 9368. West End Blues/It's Tight Like That   (sonnel):
    Sup 9486. Mandy/Hum All Your Troubles Away
        (Records by this group also were issued under the names of
        Smoke Jackson and Chuck Nelson on Champion label)

WALKER AND HIS ROLLICKERS, JOHNNY (Benny Goodman,clarinet, is featured in at least the last two recordings):
    Co 2201. The Mug Song/Give Yourself a Pat on the Back
    Co 2247. Kitty from Kansas City/Betty Co-Ed
    Co 2380. Under the Spell of Your Kiss(151193)/Personally,I Love You(151218)
    Co 2404. Walkin' MY Baby Back Home/When Your Lover Has Gone

WALLACE, FRANCES, (vocals):
    Br 7076. Low Down Man Blues/Too Late Too Late Blues

WALLACE, MINNIE (vocals with orchestra):
    Vi 38547. Dirty Butter/The Old Folks Started It

WALLACE, SIPPIE (vocals, with piano by Eddie Heywood,Sr.):
    OK 8106. Shorty George Blues(8491-A)/Up the Country Blues(8490-A)

```
         (Acc. Clarence Williams, piano):
   OK  8144. Underworld Blues(S-72569-A)/Caldonia Blues(S-72568-B)
   OK  8159. Can Anybody Take Sweet Mama's Place(72579B)/Stranger's Bl(S-72580B)
   OK  8168. Mama's Gone Goodbye(S-72567-B)/Leaving Me,Daddy,Is Hard to Do
                                                                    (S-72570-A)
         (Acc. by Clarence Williams' Harmonizers: Williams,piano; Sidney Bechet,
         soprano; Buddy Christian,banjo):
   OK  8177. Wicked Monday Morning Blues/Sud Bustin' Blues

         (Acc. by Clarence Williams' Trio):
   OK  8190. He's the Cause of Me Beiing Blue(S-73018-B)/Let My Man Alone Bl
   OK  8197. I'm So Glad I'm Brownskin(73014-B)/Off & On(73015-B)(S-73019-B)

         (Acc. King Oliver,cornet;Hersal Thomas,piano):
   OK  8205. Morning Dove Blues(8964-B)/Every Dog Has His Day(8966-A)
   OK  8206. Devil Dance Blues(8965-a)/Walkin'Talkin'Blues(73013-B;acc. by
                                                          (Clarence Williams,piano)
         (Acc. by Clarence Williams' Blue Five: Louis Armstrong,trumpet:Charlie
         Irvis,trombone: Sidney Bechet,soprano:Clarence Williams,piano; Buddy
         Christian, banjo):                                            1924
   OK  8212. Baby I Can't Use You No More(73007-B)/Trouble Everywhere(73008-B)

         (Acc. by Perry Bradford's Jazz Phools):
   OK  8232. Section Hand Blues/Parlor Social De Luxe

         (Acc. Hersal Thomas,piano):  (plus clarinet and guitar* or banjo#)
   OK  8243. Murder's Gonna Be My Crime(73566-B)/Suitcase Bl(73576-A)*
   OK  8251. The Man I Love(73567-B)/I'm Sorry for It No(73575-A)#

         (Acc. Hersal Thomas,piano:Rudy Jackson,saxophone):
   OK  8276. Being Down Don't Worry Me(73557-B)/Advice Blues(73580)

         (Acc. Louis Armstrong,trumpet· Hersal Thomas,piano):
   OK  8301. A Jealous Woman Like Me(9546-A)/A Man for Every Day in the Week
   OK  8328. Special Delivery Bl(9547-A)/Jack of Diamonds(9548-A)    (9561-A)
   OK  8345. The Mail Train Blues(9559-A)/I Feel Good(560-A)

         (King Oliver,cornet: Hersal Thomas,piano):
   OK  8439. I'm a Mighty Tight Woman(9929-A)/Bedroom Blues(9930-A)

         (Acc. by Louis Armstrong,trumpet; Kid Ory,trombone; Johnny Dodds,clar-
         inet; Lil Hardin,piano; Lonnie Johnson,guitar; Pete Briggs,bass; Baby
         Dodds,drums):
   OK  8470. Lazy Man Blues(80839-B)/The Flood Blues(80840-B)
   OK  8499. Dead Drunk Blues(80837)/Have You Ever Been Down(80838)

WALLACE AND HIS CAMPUS BOYS, TED (California Ramblers,group):
   Co  1756. Mean to Me(148032)/The One That I Love Loves Me(148033)
   Co  1791. My Kinda Love(148141)/Sweet Seventeen(148142)
   Co  1833. Jericho/I've Got a Feelin' I'm Fallin'
   Co  1938. Sweetheart's Holiday/Huggable You
   Co  1984. Campus Capers
   Co  2104. What Do I Care/When You're Smiling
   Co  2140. Get Happy/Sweetheart Trail
   Co  2236. Here Comes the Sun/Absence Makes the Heart Grow Fonder
   Co  2254. Little White Lies/Hittin' the Bottle
   Co  2322. Football Freddy/Fraternity Blues
   Co  2376. Hello Beautiful(151191)/Where Have You Been(151192)
   Co  2301. Sweet Jennie Lee/My Baby Just Cares for Me
   Co  2413. One Little Raindrop(151270)/Thrill Me(151271)
   Co  2471. Star Dust/Have You Forgotten
   Co  2514. Shine on Harvest Moon/Come to Me
   Co  2523. Life Is Just a Bowl of Cherries/Guilty
   Co  2573. I Promise You/Home
   Co  2601. Starlight/How Long Will It Last
   OK  40778. Oh Lizzie/The Cat
   OK  41091. There's Something Spanish in Your Eyes
   OK  41141. Beggars of Life/Blue Shadows
   BB  6251. I'm Gonna Sit Right Down and Write Myself a Letter     -RZ 2047
        "    Mama Don't Allow It
   BB  6252. Goody Goody/Alone at a Table for Two

WALLACE, WESLEY (piano solos)
Para 12958. No. 29 (184)/Fanny Lee Blues(185)

         BESSIE MAE SMITH AND WESLEY WALLACE(vocal duet with piano acc. by
         Wallace):
Para 12922. St. Louis Daidy(L-78-1)
        "   Farewell Baby Blues(L-90-2: voc. by Bessie Mae Smith, acc. by
                                                                   (Wallace)
```

FATS WALLER

See also:
    GENE AUSTIN: Vi 22223.
    ALTA BROWNE: Ge 3318.
    JUANITA STINETTE CHAPPELLE: Vi 21062.
    CHOCOLATE DANDIES: OK 8728.
    CLOVERDALE COUNTRY CLUB: OK 41551.
    EDDIE CONDON: Com 535, 536.
    BERT HOWELL: Vi 21062.
    ALBERTA HUNTER: Vi 20771, 21539.
    JAM SESSION: Vi 25559.
    CAROLINE JOHNSON: Ge 3307.
    ANNA JONES: Para 12052, 12043.
    LOUISIANA SUGAR BABES: Vi 21346, 21348, BB 10260
    SARA MARTIN: OK 8043, 8045.
    MAUDE MILLS: Ba 6043.
    HAZEL HEYERS: Vo 14861.
    RHYTHMAKERS: Ba 32502, 32530: Co 35882.
    JACK TEAGARDEN: Co 2558.

WALLER, THOMAS (piano solos):
    OK 4757. Muscle Shoals Bl(S-70948-D)/Birmingham Blues(S-70949-D)
                                                                    1926-27
        (Pipe organ solos):   -HMV 8501
    Vi 20357. St.Louis Blues(36773)/Lenox Ave. Blues(36774)   -Vi 23260
    Vi 20470. Loveless Love
        "   Soothin' Syrup
    Vi 20492. Sloppy Water Blues/Rusty Pail
    Vi 20655. Messin' Around/Stompin' the Bug
                                                            Camden,N.J.,May 20,1927
    Vi 20890: Beale Street Blues(38047)/Fats Waller Stomp(38050;Morris H.B.)
    Vi 21525. Sugar(38044)   -Vi 23331, BB 5093
        "   Hog Maw Stomp(37820; earlier date)
                                                            Camden,N.J.,Dec.1,1927
                                                                -Vi 23331, BB 5093
    Vi 21127. I Ain't Got Nobody(40094)
        "   Red Hot Dan(40095; with Morris' Hot Babies)
    Vi 21358.The Digah's Stomp(40096)/Geechee(40097; with Morris'Hot Babies)
    Vi 23260. That's All
                                                            New York,March 1,1929
        (Piano solos):   -HMV 4347, HMV 4902, Vi 27768
    Vi 38508. Handful of Keys(49759)   "   Vi 25338
        "   Numb Fumblin'(49762)
                                                            Camden,N.J.,Aug.2,1929
                                                                    -HMV 3243
    Vi 22092. I've Got a Feeling(49494)   -BB 10263
        "   Love Me or Leave Me(49495)   -HMV 3243
    Vi 22108. Ain't Misbehavin'(49492)   -BB 10264
        "   Sweet Savannah Sue(49493)   -HMV 4
    Vi 38554. Gladyse(49496)   -BB 10263,   "
        "   Valentine Stomp(49497)   Aug.29,1929
    BB 10264. Waiting at the End of the Road   New York,Sept.24,1929
                                                            -Vi 25338, HMV 4902
    Vi 38613. Smashing Thirds(56710)
        "   My Feelin's Are Hurt(56126; earlier date)
    Vi 38568. Fate Is in Your Hands(57190)/Turn on the Heat(57191) Late 1929
                                                            New York,Mar.21,1930
        THOMAS WALLER-BENNIE PAINE (piano duet)   HMV 8496
    Vi 22371. St. Louis Blues(59720)/After You've Gone(59721)

        THOMAS 'FATS' WALLER (piano solos):
    Co 14593. I'm Crazy 'Bout My Baby(151417)   -Vo 3016, PaE 1197
        "   Draggin' My Heart Around(151418)
                                                            New York,Nov.16,1934
        FATS WALLER (piano solos):   -HMV 41, BB 10115
    Vi 24830. African Ripples(86208)   -HMV 10098
        "   Alligator Crawl(86210)   -HMV 41, HMV 8784, GrF 8176, -HMV 35
    Vi 25015. Clothes Line Ballet(86209)   BB 10133, HMV 8784, Vi 27768,
        "   Vipers Drag(86211)   New York,June 9,1937
    Vi 25618. Keepin' Out of Mischief Noe(10652)-Vi 27767, HMV 8625, BB 10099
        "   Tea for Two(10655)   -Vi 27666
    BB 10099. Star Dust(10653)
    Vi 25631. Basin St. Blues(10654)   -HMV 8636, Vi 27767, BB 10115
        "   I Ain't Got Nobody(10656)   "   Vi 27766, BB 10133
                                                            London,Aug.1938
        (Organ solos,):   -Vi 27459, GrF 8214
    HMV 8816. Deep River(OEA 6288)   -Vi 27458,   "
        "   Go Down Moses(OEA 6387)
    HMV 8818. Swing Low Sweet Chariot(OEA 6385)   -Vi 27458
        "   All God's Chillun Got Wings(OEA 6386)   -Vi 27460
    Vi 27459. Lonesome Road(OEA 6390)
    Vi 27460. Water Boy(OEA 6389)

66

```
                                              New York, May 13, 1941
      (Piano solos):
Vi 27563. Ring Dem Bells/Carolina Shout
Vi 27765. Rockin' Chair/Georgia on My Mind
```

WALLER, THOMAS, and Thomas Morris and His Hot Babies: Thomas Morris, cornet;
Charlie Irvis, trombone; Waller, piano and pipe organ; unknown guitar):
Vi 20776. Savannah Babies(38051)/Won't You Take Me Home(38052) -HMV 5417
Vi 21202. Please Take Me Out of Jail(40098)/He's Gone Away(40093)

WALLER AND HIS BUDDIES, FATS (Charlie Gains, trumpet:Charlie Irvis, trombone;
Arville Harris, clarinet and alto: Waller, piano; Eddie Condon, banjo):
                                              New York, Mar. 1, 1929
Vi 38050. The Minor Drag(49760)/Harlem Fuss(49761)   -HMV 1, BB 10185

(Henry Allen, Charlie Gains, trumpets; Jack Teagarden, trombone and vibra-
phone: Charlie Green, trombone; Albert Nicholas, Otto Hardwick, altos;
Larry Binyon, tenor: Waller, piano; Condon, banjo; Al Morgan, bass; Gene
Krupa, drums):
Vi 38086. Lookin' Good But Feelin'Bad(56727)/I Need Someone Like You(56728)

(Henry Allen, Leonard Davis, trumpets; Jack Teagarden* or J.C. Higginbot-
ham#, trombone; Otto Hardwick, clarinet and alto; Happy Caldwell, tenor;
Waller, piano; Condon, banjo; Al Morgan, bass):
Vi 38110. Lookin' for Another Sweetie Now(57929)/When I'm Alone(57926)
Vi 38119. Ridin' But Walkin'(57927)*/Won't You Get Off It Please(57928)#

FATS WALLER AND HIS RHYTHM (Herman Autrey, trumpet: Ben Whittet, clari-
net; Fats Waller, piano and vocals; Al Casey, guitar: Billy Taylor, bass;
Harry Dial, drums):   New York, May 16, 1934
Vi 24641. I Wish I Were Twins(82527)   -HMV 1
   "   Armful of Sweetness(82528)   -HMV 7
Vi 24648. A Porter's Love Song to a Chambermaid(82526)   -BB 10016
   "   Do Me a Favor(82529)   -HMV 7

(Sub. Fugene Sedric, clarinet and tenor, for Whittet):
Vi 24714. Georgia May(83699)   -HMV 12, BB 10078
   "   Don't Let It Bother You(84107)   "
Vi 24708. Then I'll Be Tired of You(84106)   -HMV 13
   "   Have a Little Dream on Me(84108)

(Add Floyd O'Brien, trombone; sub. Mezz Mezzrow, clarinet and alto):
                                              New York, Sept. 28, 1934
Vi 24737. Now Can You Face Me(84418)   -HMV 14, BB 10143
   "   Sweetie Pie(84419)   -HMV 8; BB 10262
Vi 24738. Mandy(84420)   -HMV 11
   "   You're Not the Only Oyster(84422)-HMV 11,298,BB 10261, Vi202218
Vi 24742. Let's Pretend There's a Moon(79377)   -HMV 14
   "   Serenade for a Wealthy Widow(84417)   -HMV 8, BB 10262

(Bill Coleman, trumpet; Fugene Sedric, clarinet and tenor; Waller, piano;
Albert Casey, guitar: Billy Taylor, bass: Harry Dial, drums): Nov. 7, 1934
Vi 24801. Dream Man(84923)   -HMV 117, BB 10261
   "   I'm Growing Fonder of You(84924)   "
Vi 24808. Believe It Beloved(84992)   -HMV 134, HMV 15
   "   If It Isn't Love(84925)   -HMV 4430,   "
Vi 24826. Honeysuckle Rose(84921)   -Vi 201580
   "   Breakin' the Ice(84926)

(Sub. Charlie Turner, bass):   Camden, Jan. 5, 1935
Vi 24846. Baby Brown(87083)   -HMV 45, BB 10109
   "   Because of Once Upon a Time(87085)   -HMV 134,   "
Vi 24863. I'm a Hundred Percent for You(87082)
   "   You Fit into the Picture(87087)   -HMV 5333
Vi 24853. Night Wind(87084)/
   "   I Believe in Miracles(87086)
Vi 24867. Baby Brown(no vocal)
   "   I'm a Hundred Percent for You(no vocal)

(Sub. Herman Autrey, trumpet; Rudy Powell, clarinet and alto):
                                              New York, Mar. 6, 1935
Vi 24888. I Ain't Got Nobody(88777)   -HMV 156
   "   Oh Suzanna(88787)
Vi 24889. Pardon My Love(88783)
   "   What's the Reason(88784)   -HMV 156
                                                             -HMV 45
Vi 24892. Whose Honey Are You(88789)   -BB 10156
   "   Rosetta(88781)
Vi 24898. Louisiana Fairy Tale(88776)
   "   Cinders(88786)
Vi 25026. Rosetta(88782: no vocal)
   "   I Ain't Got Nobody(88778; no vocal)   -HMV 32
Vi 25027. What's the Reason(88785; no vocal)   -HMV 32
   "   Whose Honey Are You(88780; no vocal)
                                                      Dates unknown

                              67

```
Vi 25039. You're the Cutest One(89763)              -BB 10129
         I Hate to Talk About Myself(89765)
Vi 25044. You've Been Taking Lessons in Love(89762)
 "       Gonna Sit Right Down and Write Myself a Letter(89764) -HMV 5031
Vi 25063. Lulu's Back in Town(89760)
 "       Sweet and Slow(89761)

    (Herman Autrey,trumpet; Rudy Powell,clarinet & alto; Waller,piano;James
     Smith,guitar; Charlie Turner,bass; Arnold Bolden,drums)N.Y.June 24,1935
Vi 25075. You're the Picture I'm the Frame(88991)
 "       My Very Good Friend the Milkman(88992)     -HMV 5376
Vi 25078. Take It Easy(88990)                       -HMV  519
 "       There's Gonna Be the Devil to Pay(88994)
Vi 25087. Twelfth Street Rag(88995)                 -HMV   26
 "       Sweet Sue(88988)                           -HMV   29
BB 10332. Blue Because of You(88993)
         There'll Be Some Changes Made(88996)
Vi 25471. Dinah(88989)/(See June 8,1936,session for reverse)  -HMV 504
Vi 25194. Somebody Stole My Gal(88997)              -HMV   46
 "       Sugar Blues(92916)
                                                    Dates unknown
Vi 25116. Truckin'(92915)                           -HMV  262
 "       The Girl I Left Behind Me(92920)
Vi 25120. You're So Darned Charming(92992)
 "       I'm on a See Saw(92998)
Vi 25123. Thief in the Night(94100)
 "       Got a Bran' New Suit(92997)                -HMV 5012
Vi 25131. Rhythm and Romance(92994)
 "       A Sweet Beginning Like This(92996)
Vi 25140. Woe Is Me(92993)                          -HMV 5031
 "       Loafin'(92995)
Vi 25175. Georgia Rockin' Chair(92918)
 "       Brother, Seek and We Shall Find(92919)

    (Sub. Sedric for Powell; Yank Porter for Bolden):
Vi 25196. Sweet Thing(98171)
 "       A Little Bit Independent(98175)            -HMV 5012
Vi 25211. I've Got My Fingers Crossed(98173)
Vi 25222. When Somebody Thinks You're Wonderful(98172)  -HMV 5040
 "       You Stayed Away Too Long(98176)            -Vi 202216

    (Sub. Albert Casey, guitar):
Vi 25266. The Panic Is On(98894)
 "       Sugar Rose(98895)                          -HMV 5062
Vi 25253. West Wind(98898)                          -HMV 5062
 "       Sing an Old Fashioned Love Song(99035)     -HMV 5135
Vi 25255. Oooh! Looka There(98896)                  -Vi 202218
 "       That Never-To-Be-Forgotton Night(98899)    -HMV 5062
Vi 25281. Moon Rose(98897)
 "       Garbo Green(99036)

    (Sub. Arnold Bolden,drums):
Vi 25295. Us on a Bus(101194)
 "       Christopher Columbus(101195)               -HMV 5077
Vi 25296. All My Life(101189)                       -HMV 5087
 "       It's No Fun(101192)                        -HMV 5098
Vi 25315. Cross Patch(101191)                       -HMV 5098
 "       Cabin in the Sky(101193)                   -HMV 5077

    (Sub. Slick Jones,drums):
Vi 25342. It's a Sin to Tell a Lie(101667)          -Vi 201595
 "       Big Chief DeSota(101672)
Vi 25348. Let's Sing Again(101671)                  -HMV 5098
 "       The More I Know You(101668)                -HMV 5159

    (Sub. Yank Porter,drums):                       New York,June 8,1936
Vi 25359. Black Raspberry Jam(102016)               -HMV 5376
 "       Paswonky(102019)
Vi 25430. Lounging at the Waldorf/(See Sept.9,1936,session for reverse)
Vi 25471. Latch On(102021)/(See June 24,1935, session above for reverse)
Vi 25536. Bach Up to Me(102017)                     -HMV 5431
 "       The Meanest Thing You Ever Did Was to Kiss Me(04953) (-Vi 202219

    (Sub. Slick Jones,drums):
Vi 25374. Until the Real Thing Comes Along(102402)  -HMV 5415
 "       I'm Crazy 'Bout My Baby(102400)            -HMV 5120
Vi 25388. There Goes My Attraction(102403)          -HMV 5120
 "       Bye Bye Baby(102405)                       -HMV 5116
Vi 25394. The Curse of an Aching Heart(102404)      -HMV 5116
 "       I Just Made Up With That Old Girl of Mine(102401)  -HMV 5159
                                                    Sept.9,1936
Vi 25409. Copper Colored Gal of Mine(0340)          -HMV 5133
 "       I'm at the Mercy of Love(0341)
Vi 25415. S'posin'(0339)                -Vi 202220, HMV 5135, BB 10156
 "       Floatin' Down to Cotton Town(0342)
Vi 25430. La De-De La De-Da(0343)/(See 6/8/36 above for reverse)-HMV 5150
                                                    Chicago,Nov.29,1936
Vi 25483. A Thousand Dreams of You(01807)
 "       Swingin' Them Jingle Bells(01805)          -BB 10016, Vi 201602
```

```
Vi 25478. Hallelujah Things Are Rosy Now(01801)
    "       Tain't Good(01804)
Vi 25488. Hallelujah Things Are Rosy Now(01800; no vocal)
    "       Tain't Good(01803; no vocal)
Vi 25490. A Thousand Dreams of You(01808; no vocal)      -HMV 5184
          Swingin' Them Jingle Bells(01806; no vocal)         "
Vi 25491. A Rhyme for Love(01809)
    "     I Adore You(01810)
                                                      Dates unknown
Vi 25498. Please Keep Me in Your Dreams(03843)/Nero(03845)
Vi 25499. Who's Afraid of Love(03842)/One in a Million(03844)
Vi 25505. Havin' a Ball(03840)/I'm Sorry I Made You Cry(03841)
Vi 25530. You're Laughin' at Me(04949)                   -HMV 5215
    "     I Can't Break the Habit of You(04950)
Vi 25537. When Love Is Young(04952)/Did Anyone Ever Tell You(04951)
Vi 25554. You've Been Reading My Mail(06415)/Spring Cleaning(06418)
Vi 25550. Where Is the Sun(06414)/Old Plantation(06417)  -HMV 5212
Vi 25551. Cryin' Mood(06413)/To a Sweet and Pretty Thing(06416)
                                              New York,April 9,1937
Vi 25563. Boo Hoo(07747)/The Love Bug Will Bite You(07748) -HMV 5229
Vi 25565. You Showed Me the Way(07746)/San Anton'(07750) no vocals
Vi 25571. I've Got a New Lease on Love(07753)/Sweet Heartache(07754) no
Vi 25579. You Showed Me the Way(07745)                    (vocals
    "     San Anton'(07749)                              -HMV 5215
Vi 25580. I've Got a New Lease on Love(07751)/Sweet Heartache(07755)
Vi 25779. Honeysuckle Rose/Blue Turning Grey Over You
Vi 36206. Honeysuckle Rose(07755)/Blue Turning Grey Over You(10651)-HMV 2937
                                                        June 11,1937
Vi 25604. Don't You Know or Don't You Care(10648)/Lost Love(10649)-HMV5258
Vi 25608. Smarty(10647)/I'm Gonna Put You in Your Place(10650)
                                              New York,Sept.7,1937
Vi 25671. Always in Mood for You(13348)/She's Tall,Tan,Terrific(13349)
Vi 25672. You've Got Me Under Your Thumb(13344)/Beat It Out(13345)
Vi 25679. You're My Dish(13350)
    "     More Power to You(13351)                       -HMV 5314
Vi 25681. Our Love Was Meant to Be(13346)/I'd Rather Call you Baby(13347)
Vi 25684. How Can I With You(14645)/Jealous of Me(14650)   Dates unknown
Vi 25689. The Joint Is Jumpin'(14646)                      Vi 201582
    "     A Hopeless Love Affair(14647)
Vi 25712. What Will I Do in the Morning(14648)/How Ya Baby(14649)

(Paul Campbell,trumpet: Caughey Roberts,clarinet and sax; Waller,piano
and vocal; Ceele Burke,buitar; Al Morgan,bass; Lee Young,drums):
                                                      Hollywood,1938
Vi 25749. Every Day's a Holiday(9884)                    -HMV 5333
    "     Neglected (9885)                               -HMV 5342
Vi 25753. I'm in Another World(9887)                     -HMV 5360
    "     My First Impression of You(9889)
Vi 25762. My Window Faces the South(9886)
    "     Why Do Hawaaians Sing Aloha(9888)              -HMV 5342

(Previous personnel, with Cedric Wallace,bass):        New York,1938
Vi 25806. Love to Whistle(21151)                         -HMV 5360
    "     Florida Flo(21153)
Vi 25812. You Went to My Head(21152)
    "     Lost and Found(21154)                          -HMV 5377
Vi 25817. Something Tells Me(21150)/Don't Try to Cry Your Way Back to Me
                                                            (21155)
FATS WALLER, HIS RHYTHM AND ORCHESTRA (Herman Autrey,John Hamilton,
Nathaniel Williams,trumpets: George Robinson,John Haughton,trombones;
Fugene Sedric,Samuel Simmons,William Alsop,James Powell,Alfred Skerritt,
saxes; Waller,piano and vocal; Al Casey; Wallace; Jones):
Vi 25830. Let's Break the Good News(22431)/I Simply Adore You(22433)
Vi 25834. You Had an Evening to Spare(22430)/Scrontch(22432)
Vi 25847. In the Gloaming(22429)/The Sheik of Araby(22434)
Vi 26045. Hold My Hand(22435)/Inside(22436)

FATS WALLER AND  HIS RHYTHM (Dave Wilkins,trumpet; George Chisholm,
trombone: Ian Shepherd,tenor; Alfie Kahn,clarinet and tenor; Waller,
piano, organ and vocal; Alan Ferguson,guitar; Len Harrisson,bass; Ed-
mundo Ross,drums):                                    London,Aug.,1938
HMV 5398. Music Maestro Please/A tisket a Tasket
HMV 5399. Pent Up in a Penthouse/The Flat Foot Floogee
HMV 5415. Ain't Misbehavin'                              -Vi 201581
    "     Don't Try Your Jive on Me                      -BB 10100

(Autrey, Sedric, Waller, Casey, Wallace, Jones):       New York,1938
Vi 25891. There's Honey on the Moon Tonight(23760)
    "     Fair and Square(23764)
Vi 25898. On the Bumpy Road to Love(23763)               -HMV 5431
    "     We the People(23765)
Vi 26002. If I Were You(23761)/The Wide Open Places(23762)
BB  7885. Shame Shame(27290)/Steal Me With Your Kisses(27293) Oct.13,1938
```

69

```
BB 10000.  Two Sleepy People(27289)                        -Vi 201583, HMV 5452
    "      I'll Never Forgive Myself(27291)
BB 10008.  You Look Good to Me(27292)                              -HMV 5493
BB 10035.  Yacht Club Swing(27294)/(EDDIE DeLANGE)
BB 10070.  I'd Give My Life for You(30363)/Dance at Wedding(30365) Dec.7'38
BB 10062.  Imagine My Surprise(30366)/I Won't Believe It(30367)
BB 10078.  I Wish I Had You(30364)/(reissue of 'Georgia May',Vi 24714)
BB 10149.  Patty Cake Patty Cake(30369)                            -HMV 5476
BB 10205.  The Spider and the Fly(30368)                           -HMV 5486
    "      Remember Who You're Promised To(32948)
BB 10116.  You Outsmarted Yourself(31531)                                1939
    "      Hold Tight(31534)                             -Vi 201581, HMV 5469
BB 10129.  Good for Nothin' But Love(31533)
BB 10136.  Last Night a Miracle Happened(31532)                    -HMV 5469
    "      Kiss Me With Your Eyes(31535)
BB 10143.  A Good Man Is Hard to Find/How Can You Face Me
BB 10170.  You Asked for It(32942)/Got No Time(32945)
BB 10184.  Step Up and Shake My Hand(32946)/Undecided(32947)
BB 10192.  Some Rainy Day(32943)
    "      Tain't What You Do(32944)                               -HMV 5486
           (Herman Autrey,trumpet: Chauncey Graham,sax; Waller,piano and vocal;
           John Smith,guitar; Cedric Wallace,bass: Larry Hinton,drums):
BB 10346.  Honey Hush(38207)/You Meet the Nicest People in Your Dreams(38210)
BB 10369.  I Used to Love You(38208)                     -Vi 202219, HMV 5533
    "      Anita(38211)
BB 10322.  Blue Because of You
    "      There'll Be Some Changes Made                         -Vi 202216
           (Sub.John Hamilton,trumpet; Sedric,tenor; Jones,drums):
BB 10393.  Bless You(41529)/It's the Tune That Counts(41530)
BB 10405.  Squeeze Me(41528)                                     -Vi 202217
    "      Wait and See(38209; personnel above)
BR 10419.  Abdullah(41531)/Who'll Take My Place(41532)
BB 10437.  Bond Street(41533)/What a Pretty Miss(30212; personnel above)
BB 10500.  Suitcase Susie(43347)
    "      You Feet's Too Big(43348)                             -Vi 201580
BB 10527.  It's you Who Taught It to Me(43346)
    "      You're Lettin' the Grass Grow Under Your Feet(43349)
BB 10573.  Darktown Strutters Ball(43350)                        -Vi 202220
    "      I Can't Give You Anything But Love(43351)             -Vi 201582
BB 10624.  Black Maria(44601)/The Moon Is Low(44603)
BB 10658.  Oh Frenchy(44599)                                     -Vi 201595
    "      Cheatin' on Me(44600)
BB 10744.  Mighty Fine(44602)/Fep Ipe Wanna Piece of Pie(48782)
           (Sub. Ed Smith, guitar):                                      1940
BB 10698.  Old Grand Dad(48775)/Little Curly Hair in a High Chair(48777)
BB 10730.  Send Me Jackson(48781)/Square from Delaware(48778)
BB 10779.  Too Tired/You Run Your Mouth I'll Run My Business
BB 10803.  Fat and Greasy/At Twilight
BB 10829.  Stop Pretending/Hey Stop Kissin' My Sister(051871)
BB 10841.  I'll Never Smile Again/Stayin' at Home
BB 10858.  Fats Waller's Original F Flat Blues(Swinga-Dilla St.(feat.organ)
BR 10892.  My Mommie Sent Me to the Store/Dry Bones(051868)
BB 10943.  I'm Gonna Salt Away Some Sugar/Blue Fyes
BB 10967.  Abercrombie Had a Zombie/Tain't Nobody's Biznezz If I Do
BB 10989.  Everybody Loves My Baby                               -Vi 202217
    "      Scram!
BB 11010.  Come Down to Farth My Angel/Liver Lip Jones
BB 11078.  Shortenin' Bread/Mamacita
BB 11102.  All That Meat and No Potatoes/Buckin' the Dice
BR 11115.  Let's Get Away from It All
    "      I Wanna Hear Swing Songs                                   -HMV 1028
BB 11175.  I Understand/Pantin' in the Panther Room
BR 11188.  Headlines in the News/I Repent
BB 11222.  Twenty-Four Robbers
    "      Do You Have to Go                                         -HMV 5787
           FATS WALLER, HIS RHYTHM AND HIS ORCHESTRA:
BB 11262.  Come and Get It/Chant of the Groove
BB 11296.  Sad Sap Sucker Am I/Rump Steak Serenade
BB 11324.  The Bells of San Raquel/Buck Jumpin'
BB 11518.  The Jitterbug Waltz/We Need a Little Love
           FATS WALLER AND HIS RHYTHM:
BB 11383.  Oh Baby Sweet Baby/Pan Pan
BB 11425.  Cash for Your Trash
    "      That Gets It, Mr. Joe
BB 11469.  Winter Weather/Clarinet Marmalade
BB 11539.  Don't Give Me That Jive/You Must Be Losing Your Mind
BR 11569.  Swing Out to Victory/By the Light of the Silvery Moon.
BB 300814. Up Jumped You With Love/Your Socks Don't Match
```

```
        [Benny Carter,trumpet; Alton 'Slim' Moore,trombone; Gene Porter,clari-
        net and sax; Irving Ashby,guitar; Slam Stewart,bass· Zutty Singleton,
        drums: Fats Waller,piano and vocals.--Cut from motion picture sound-
Vi 404003. Ain't Misbehavin'/Moppin' and Boppin'                    (track):

        FATS WALLER MEMORIAL (Earl Hines,piano;Al Casey,guitar; Oscar Petti-
        ford, bass):
Sig 28109. Squeeze Me(F-1003)/I've Got a Feeling I'm Falling(F-1001)
Sig 38110. Honeysuckle Rose(F-1002)/My Fate Is In Your Hands(F-1000)

        (Nat Jaffe,piano; Sid Jacobs,bass):
Sig 28111. Black and Blue(F-1006)/Zonky(F-1007)
Sig 28112. How Can You Face Me(F-1004)/Keepin' Out of Mischief Now(F-1005)

WALSH AND HIS ORCHESTRA, JACK:
   Ro   384. Four or Five Times(246-A1)/(NIGHT HAWKS)

WANDERERS, THE:
   HMV   26. Tiger Rag
   BB  5834. A Good Man Is Hard to Find/It's You I Adore
   BB  5869. I Ain't Got Nobody/Wanderer's Stomp

WARE, OZIE (vocals, acc. by 'Hot Five' group from Duke Ellington's Orchestra
including Barney Bigard,clarinet; trumpet; piano; drums; tuba):
   Vi 21777. Santa Claus Bring My Man Back to Me/I Done Caught You Blues

        (Acc. by Ellington orchestra)
Pat  7540. Hit Me in the Nose Bl(3532)/(GRANT-WILSON)          -Ca 9039
Ca   9039. It's All Coming Home to You(3533: piano acc.)
Ro   1042. He Just Don't Appeal to Me(3715)/(COOT GRANT)
```

WASHBOARD RHYTHM

(The following three groups seem to be closely related, although instrumenta-
tion varies widely. Eddie Shine, sax and clarinet, and Steve Washington,gui-
tar, have been listed usually as integral members of the bands, most of which
are fairly large combinations with brass and reed sections highlighted by
washboard rhythm):

```
        WASHBOARD RHYTHM BAND:
CoE   611. Hustlin' and Bustlin' for Baby
   "       Shuffle Off to Buffalo                               -Co 14680
Co  14680. Going Going Gone
CoF  626. Midnight Rhythm/Ghost of a Chance
CoF  642. Swing Gate/Coming of the Hi De Ho

        WASHBOARD RHYTHM BOYS:
Vi 23357. Depression Stomp/(BENNIE MOTEN)
Vi 23364. Say It' Isn't So/I'm Gonna Play
Vi 23367. Ash Man Crawl/If You Were Mine
Vi 23368. Boy in the Boat/Someone Stole Gabriel's Horn
Vi 24059. Tiger Rag/(ALEX BARTHA)                               - BB 6084
Vo  1724. It Don't Mean a Thing/Sentimental Gent.from Georgia   DeE 5176
Vo  1725. Someone Stole Gabriel's Horn/Scat Song
Vo  1729. Gotta Be Gonna Be You                                 -DeE 3781
   "       Syncopate Your Sins Away                             -BrE 01504
Vo  1730. Oh You Sweet Thing/Something's Gotta Be Done
Vo  1731. Angeline                                              -BrE 01504
   "       Yes Suh                                              -DeF 3781
Vo  1732. Blue Drag
   "       Wah-Dee-Dah
Vo  1733. Old Yazoo/I'm Gettin' Sentimental Over You
Vo  1734. Spider Crawl/Anything for You
Me 12780. I Cover the Waterfront/Learn to Croon
Me 12781. Lazybones(13840-1)/Mississippi Basin(13846-1)         -Or 2755
Me 12794. St. Louis Blues/Some of These Days
Me 12928. Old Man Blues/Dog and Cat                             -Do 177

        WASHBOARD RHYTHM KINGS
Vi 22719. A Porter's Love Song to a Chamber Maid                -BB 5042
   "       Every Man for Himself
Vi 22814. Shoot 'em                                             -BB 8228
   "       Many Happy Returns of the Day                   -BB 5042, HMV 4954
Vi 22958. Pepper Steak/(BENNIE MOTEN)
Vi 23283. Please Tell Me/Who Stole the Lock
Vi 23301  Blues in My Heart/Georgia on My Mind
Vi 23323. If You Don't Love Me/Was That the Human Thing to Do
Vi 23337. All This World Is Made of Glass                       -BB 5127
Vi 23344. I'm Her Papa/Hey Crawley Blues
Vi 23348. Just Another Dream of You/My Silent Love
Vi 23373. How Deep Is the Ocean                                 -BB 8174
   "       Underneath the Harlem Moon.
```

```
        Vi 23375. Fire                                    - BB 8174, HMV 6362
           "      Nickel for a Pickle                     - BB 8164
        Vi 23380. Ikey and Mikey
           "      Sloppy Drunk                            - BB 8164, HMV 4954
        Vi 23403. Dinah                                   - BB 5127
           "      Nobody's Sweetheart
        Vi 23405. Sophisticated Lady/Happy As the Day Is Long
        Vi 23408. Boola Boo/My Pretty Girl
        Vi 23413. Move Turtle/Kelsey's
        Vi 23415. I Want to Ring Bells/Hard Corn
        HMV 4085. Holding My Honey's Hand
        HMV 6362. I'm Gonna Play Down By the Ohio
        BB  6157. Arlena/Brownskin Mama
        BB  6278. Hot Nuts
        BB  6186. Please Come on Down/Street Walkin' Blues
        Vi 23604. Hummin' to Myself
```

WASHBOARD SAM (Robert Brown; vocals, acc. on many titles by Big Bill(Broonzy) guitar, and/or Joshua Altheimer, piano):
```
        BB  6765. Nashville, Tennessee/Razor Cuttin' Man
        BB  6870. Big Woman/Come on In
        BB  6970. The Big Boat/Easy Ridin' Mama
        BB  7001. Back Door/We Wanna Move
        BB  7048. Low Down Woman/I Drink Good Whiskey
        BB  7148. Out With the Wrong Woman/(KELLY'S BAND)
        BB  7194. You Done Tore My Playhouse Down/(TOMMY GRIFFIN)
        BB  7291. Washboard's Barrel House Song/Where Were You Last Night
        BB  7328. Ladies' Man/Beer Garden Blues
        BB  7403. Somebody's Got to Go/Second Story Man
        BB  7440. Want to Woogie Some More/(ROBERT L. McCOY)
        BB  7501. Don't Leave Me Here/Towboat Blues
        BB  7552. My Woman's a Sender/Barbecue
        BB  7601. Mountain Blues/Phantom Black Snake
        BB  7664. Yellow Black and Brown/It's Too Late Now
        BB  7732. I'm Gonna Keep My Hair Parted/Serve It Right
        BB  7780. Sophisticated Mama/I'm Gonna Pay
        BB  7834. Cruel Treatment/Policy Writer's Blues
        BB  7836. Save it for Me/Jumpin' Rooster
        BB  7906. Bucket's Got a Hole in It/When My Love Changes
        BB  7977. Walkin' in My Sleep/Washboard Swing
        BB  7993. Warehouse Blues/C.C.C Blues
        BB  8018. Gonna Kill My Baby/You Waited Too Long
        BB  8044. Hand Reader Blues/Rack 'em Back
        BB  8076. Suspicious Blues/I'll Be Up Some Day
        BB  8184. That Will Get It/I Believe I'll Make a Change
        BB  8211. Diggin' My Potatoes/Booker T. Blues
        BB  8243. I Love My Baby/Good Old Easy Street
        BB  8270. Wasn't He Bad/This Time Is My Time
        BB  8323. Has My Gal Been Here/Somebody Changed That Lock on My Door
        BB  8342. Jersey Cow Blues/Don't Fool With Me
        BB  8358. So Early in the Morning/Block and Tackle
        BB  8377. We Gonna Do Some Rug Cutting/Beauty Spot
        BB  8424. I Won't Be Sober Long/Going Back to Arkansas
        BB  8450. She Fooled Me/How Can I Play Fair
        BB  8469. Louise/ Oh Babe
        BB  8500. Sun Gonna Shine in My Door/Beale Street Sheik
        BB  8554. Digging My Potatoes No. 2/Morning Dove Blues
        BB  8525. Why Did You Do That to Me/Chiselin' Blues
        BB  8540. Oh Joe/Greyhound Bus
        BB  8569. I'm Going to St. Louis/Good Luck Blues
        BB  8599. Just Got to Hold You/Yes, I Got Your Woman
        BB  8644. Good Time Tonight/Dissatisfied Blues
        BB  8675. Ain't You Comin' Out Tonight/She's a Bad Luck Woman
        BB  8878. I'm Feelin' Low Down/I'm Not the Lad
        BB  8909. Levee Camp Blues/Life Is Just a Book
        BB  8937. She Belongs to the Devil/Brown and Yellow Woman Blues
        BB  8967. Let Me Play Your Vendor/Broadcast Blues
        BB  8997. Gonna Hit the Highway/Evil Blues
        BB  9007. I've Been Treated Wrong/Lover's Lane Blues
        BB  9018. Get Down Brother/You Stole My Love
        BB  9039. How Can You Love Me/River Hip Mama
        BB 340705. Good Old Cabbage Greens/Stop and Fix It
        BB 340710. I Get the Blues at Bed Time/I Laid M
        Vi 202162. Diggin' My Potatoes/Back Door
        Vi 202440. Soap and Water Blues/You Can't Make the Grade
```

WASHBOARD SERENADERS (Clarence Profit,piano, and Teddy Bunn,guitar, have been mentioned as members of this group):
```
        Vi 38127. Washboards Get Together                 -HMV 6114
           "      Kazoo Moan
        HMV 6289. Tiger Rag
        HMV 6303. Tappin' the Time Away
```

(Arthur Brooks,piano: Jerome Darr,guitar: Bruce Johnson,washboard and
vocal: Harold Randolph, comb and vocal, and others):   London,1935
PaF   229. Lonesome Road/Dear Old Southland
PaF   358. Black Eyes/Nagasaki
PaF   428. St. Louis Blues/Sheik of Araby

WASHBOARD WONDERS (Jimmy O'Bryant's Washboard Band):
  Si   3548. Midnight Strutters/Shake That Thing

WASHINGTON'S SIX ACES, BEN:
  OK   8269. Compton Avenue Blues/(CLIFFORD HAYES)

WASHINGTON, BOOKER T.. (vocals with piano):
  BB   8352. Death of Bessie Smith/Just Want to Think
  BB   8378. Good Time Woman/Cotton Club Blues
  BB   8413. Cozy Corner Blues/Save It All for Me
  BB   8449. Wrapped Up in Bad Luck/If I Get Lucky

WASHINGTON, FLOYD (BUCK) (piano solo):   1934
  Co   2925. Old Fashioned Love(265174-1)/(JOE SULLIVAN) -PaE 1837, De 18169

WASHINGTON SEXTETTE, DINAH (Joe Morris,trumpet: Rudy Rutherford,clarinet:
Arnette Cobbs,sax: Milt Buckner,piano: Fred Radcliffe,drums: Vernon King,bass;
Dinah Washington, vocals):
  Key   605. Evil Gal Blues/Homeward Bound
  Key   606. Salty Papa Blues(843)/I Know How to Do It(842:Hampton,drums)
                                                              (-Mer 8044
     DINAH WASHINGTON, acc. by Lucky Thompson and His All Stars(Thompson,
  Jewel Grant,Karl George,Lee Young,Gene Porter,Charles Mingus,Wilbert
  Baranco,Milt Jackson):
  Apo   368. Wise Woman Blues(S 1170-3)/No Voot No Boot(S 1172-2)
  Apo   371. My Lovin' Papa/Mellow Mama Blues
  Apo   374. Walking Blues/Rich Man's Blues

     DINAH WASHINGTON (vocals with orchestra)
  Mer 2052. Joy Juice/I Can't Get Started With You
  Mer 8010. Oo-We Walkie Talkie/When a Woman Loves a Man

WASHINGTON, LIZZIE (vocal):
  Ge   6126. Lowdown Brown/Workingman Blues
  Vo   1459. Every Day Blues/Whiskey Head Blues

WASHINGTON AND HIS ORCHESTRA, STEVE (including Benny Goodman,clarinet):
  Vo   2598. Sing a Little Low Down Tune/We Were the Best of Friends
  Vo   2609. Love Me/Blue River

WASHINGTONIANS (Probably Duke Ellington,piano: Bubber Miley,trumpet; Charlie
Irvis,trombone: Otto Hardwick,alto; Fred Guy,banjo: Sonny Greer,drums) 1924
Blu Disc 1002. Choo Choo(T2005-2)/Rainy Nights(T2006-2)   -Bwy 11437
     (Sub. Joe Nanton,trombone: Add Rudy Jackson,Harry Carney,saxes; Wellman
     Braud,bass):   1927
  Pat 36781. East St.Louis Toodle-oo(2944) -Ca 8182,Ro 612,Li 2837,Pe 14962*
    "   Jubilee Stomp(2945)   "   "   "   "   "
  Pat 36787. Take It Easy(2946)/(7 LITTLE POLAR BEARS)-Ro 618,Ca 8188,Pe 14968*
             *Perfects under name of 'Whoopee Makers'.
  Br   3526. Black and Tan Fantasy(E-22299)/Soliloquy

     (Sub. Barney Bigard,clarinet, for Jackson: add Arthur Whetsel,trumpet):
  Ha   577. Sweet Mamma(145488)/Bugle Call Rag(145490)   -Di 2577
  Ha   601. Stack o'Lee Blues(145489)/(ARKANSAS TRAVELERS)   -Di 2601

     (Sub. Johnny Hodges,alto, for Hardwick):   March,21,1928
  Br 4009. Take It Easy   -Vo 15704, BrE 01778
    "   Black Beauty   -BrE 02306
  Br 4044. Jubilee Stomp(E-27091)/(HOTSY TOTSY GANG) -Vo 15710, BrE 03878
                                                              Oct.28,1928
  Br 4122. The Mooche(E-28359)/(HOTSY TOTSY GANG)   -BrE 01235, BrF 500190
                                                              Dates unknown
  Ro   827. Hot and Bothered(3528-108447)   -Ca 9023,Pat 36915*
    "   (BROADWAY BROADCASTERS)
  Ro   836. The Mooche(3527-108446)   -Pat 36899*
  Ro   829. Move Over(3529-108448)   -Li 3054, Ca 9025, Pat 36899*
    "   (BOB HARING)
             *Pathes issued under name of 'Whoopee Makers'

     (Sub. Freddie Jenkins,trumpet, for Metcalf; add Juan Tizol,trombone):
  Ve 7072. E.St.Louis Toodle-oo/The mooche See: Mills 10 Black Berries

     (Personnel unknown: not Ellington):
  Ca 9094. Mississippi Here I Am(3613)/Tight like That(3618)-Ro 868,Li 3093

```
            (Previous Ellington personnel):
     Ca  9175. Saratoga Swing(3713)/(FLETCHER HENDERSON)          -Li 3202
     Ca  9195. Who Said It's Tight Like That(3714)/(COTTON PICKERS)  -Ro 997
     Ro  1101. Doin' the Voom Voom(4062)/Saturday Night Function(4064)
            (See also: Dixie Jazz Band and Whoopee Makers for other
             issues of the last coupling, plus Flaming Youth(4063)
             under Whoopee Makers credit).
```

WATERS, ETHEL (acc. by Cordy Williams' Jazz Masters):
     BS 2010. Oh Daddy(P-114)/Down Home Blues(P-115)
            ETHEL WATERS AND HER JAZZ MASTERS(probably including Joe Smith,cornet):
     BS 2021. One Man Nan(P-146)/There'll Be Some Changes Made(P-147)
     BS 2038. Dying With the Blues(P-149)/Kiss Your Pretty Baby Nice(P-150)

            (next coupling under name of ETHEL WATERS and Joe Smith's Jazz Masters):
     BS 14117. Jazzin' Babies Blues/Kind Lovin' Blues
     BS 14120. That Da Da Strain/Georgia Blues   -Para 12177
     BS 14128. At the New Jump Steady Ball/Oh Joe Play That Trombone
     BS 14146. Midnight Blues/Memphis Man
     BS 14151. Lost Out Blues/You Can't Do What MY Last Man Did(piano acc.)
     BS 100707.Spread Yo' Stuff/Snuggle Up   (-Para 12181

            ETHEL WATERS (acc. by Joe Smith,cornet, and L.Austin,piano):
     Para 12214. Tell 'em Bout Me(1737)/You'll Need Me When I'm Long Gone(1740)

            (Acc. by Lovie Austin's Blues Serenaders: Add Buster Bailey,clarinet,
             and a drummer to above):
     Para 12230. Black Spatch Blues(1747)/I Want Somebody All My Own(1749)
     Para 12313. Craving Blues
     Para 20302. Mindin' My Biznezz(1661)/How My Sweetie Loves Me(1662) earlier
                                                                         (group
            (Acc. by Albury's Blue and Jazz Seven):
     Cardinal 2036. The New York Glide(673)/At the New Jump Steady Ball(674)

            (Acc. by Fletcher Henderson, piano):
     Vo 14860. Back Bitin' Mamma/Pleasure Mad

            ETHEL WATERS AND HER EBONY FOUR (Joe Smith,cornet Fletcher Henderson,
            piano; probably Buster Bailey,clarinet; Coleman Hawkins,tenor,in some):
     Co   379. No One Can Love Me(140565)/Sweet Georgia Brown(140597)
     Co   433. Brother You've Got Me Wrong(140564)/Sympathetic Can(140791)
     Co 14093. Go Back Where You Stayed Last Night(140790)/Down Home Bl(140792)
     Co 14112. You Can't Do What My Last Man Did(140864)
      "   Maybe Not At All(141209)
     Co 14116. No Man's Mamma(141207)/Shake That Thing(141429: piano by Pearl
                                                                     (Wright)
            ETHEL WATERS AND HER PLANTATION ORCHESTRA:
     Co   472. Loud Speaking Papa/Pickanniny Blues
     Co   487. Sweet Man(141163)/Dinah(141164)

            (Acc. by Joe Smith,cornet· piano):
     Co   561. Tell 'em About Me(141208)/I've Found a New Baby(141542)

            (Acc. by piano):
     Co 14125. Make Me a Pallet on the Floor(141543)/Bring Your Greenbacks
     Co 14132. Throw Dirt in Your Face/Refrigerating Papa   (141544)
     Co 14134. If You Can't Hold the Man(141705)/Wonder What's Become of Joe
     Co 14146. Sugar(141707)/You'll Want Me Back(141709)   (141708)

            ETHEL WATERS AND HER JAZZ BAND:
     Co 14153. Heebie Jeebies(142476)/Everybody Mess Aroun'(142477)
     Co 14162. We Don't Need Each Other Any More/Take What You Want
     Co 14170. I'm Comin' Virginia/He Brought Joy to My Soul

            ETHEL WATERS, (Piano acc.):
     Co 14182. My Special Friend Is Back in Town(142651)/Jersey Walk(142704;
     Co 14199. After All Years/Satisfying Papa   (acc.Pearl Wright,piano)

            (Acc. by Joe Smith,cornet; saxophone· pianoO):
     Co 14214. Weary Feet(144100)/Take Your Black Borrom Outside(144103)
     Co 14297. Home(144102)/I'm Saving It All for You(141690: piano acc.)
     Co 14229. Smile(144101)/I Want My Sweet Daddy Now

            (Acc. violin and piano):
     Co 14264. Someday Sweetheart(144864)/Some of These Days(144867)

            (James P. Johnson, piano):
     Co 14353. My Handy Man(146873)/Guess Who's in Town(146872)
     Co 14380. Do What You Did Last Night(146874)/Get Up Off Your Knees(146883;
                                                        (acc. by Clarence Williams)
            (Clarence Williams,piano):
     Co 14365. Organ Grinder Blues(146882)/West End Blues(146881)
     Co 14411. My Baby Sure Knows How to Love(146884)/Lonesome Swallow(146871;
                                                        (acc.by James P.Johnson)

                                      74

```
       (Acc. by orchestra):
Co   1837. Birmingham Bertha(148531)/Am I Blue(148532)
Co   1871. True Blue Lou(148671)/Second Handed Man(148670; piano acc.)
Co   1905. Do I Know What I'm Doing(148672)/Shoo Shoo Boogie Boo(148673)
       (Acc. by Pearl Wright,piano):
Co  14458. Long Lean Lanky Mama(148804)/Better Keep Your Eye on Your Man
                                                                    (148805)
       (unknown acc.):
Co   1933. Traveling All Alone/Waiting at the End of the Road
Co   2184. Black and Blue/Porgy
Co   2222. You Brought a New Kind of Love to Me/My Kind of Man
Co   2288. You're Lucky to Me/Memories of You
Co   2346. Three Little Words/I Got Rhythm
Co  14565. Georgia Blues/I Like the Way He Does It

       (Acc. by orchestra including Benny Goodman, clarinet):
Co   2409. When Your Lover Has Gone(151298)/Please Don't Talk About Me When
Co   2431. Without That Gal/Can't Stop Me from Loving You (I'm Gone(151299)

       (unknown acc.):
Co   2511. Shine on Harvest Moon/River Stay 'Way from My Door
Co   2826. Heat Wave/Harlem on My Mind

       (Acc. by Benny Goodman's Orchestra: Charlie Teagarden,Shirley Clay,trum-
       pets; Jack Teagarden,trombone: Benny Goodman,clarinet; Art Karle,tenor:
       Joe Sullivan,piano; Dick McDonough,guitar: Artie Bernstein,bass; Gene
       Krupa,drums):                                              Oct.,1933
Co   2853. I Just Couldn't Take It Baby(152566)/A Hundred Years from Today
                                                                    (152567)
       (Acc. by Duke Ellington's Orchestra:
Br   6516. Blackbirds Medley,1 & 2(13079-80)                    -BrE 01517
Br   6517. I Can't Give You Anything But Love(B-12783A)         -Br 6758
 "         (MILLS BROTHERS, CAB CALLOWAY)                             "
Br   6521. Porgy(B-12784/St.Louis Blues(acc.not by Ellington)   -Br 6758

       (Acc. by orchestra):
Br   6564. Stormy Weather(B-13292A)/Love Is the Thing(B-13293A)  -Co 36329
Br   6617. Don't Blame Me/Shadows on the Swanee
Br   6885. You've Seen Harlem at Its Best/Come Up and See Me Sometime
De    140. Miss Otis Regrets/Moonglow
De    141. Give Me a Heart to Sing to/I Ain't Gonna Sin No More
De    234. Dinah/You're Going to Leave the Old Home, Jim?
De   1613. I'll Get Along Somehow/You're a Sweetheart
De   4410. When It's Sleepy Time Down South/How Can I Face This Wearied
                                                                    (World
       (Acc. by Ed Mallory's Orchestra):
BB  10038. You're Mine/Frankie and Johnnie
BB  10207. Y' Had It Comin' to You/What Goes Up Must Come Down
BB  10415. Bread and Gravy/Push-Out
BB  10517. I Just Got a Letter/Baby What Else Can I Do

WATTERS AND HIS YERBA BUENA JAZZ BAND, LU (Lu Watters,Bob Scobey,cornets;
Ellis Horne,clarinet: Turk Murphy,trombone: Walter Rose,piano: Clarence Hayes,
Russ Bennett,banjos: Dick Lammi,bass: Bill Dart,drums):    Hollywood,Dec.,1941
JM       1. Maple Leaf Rag(109)/Black & White Rag(119: Rose,Bennett,Hayes,
JM       2. Memphis Blues(113)/Irish Black Bottom(110)      (Dart;Mar.,1942)
JM       3. Smokey Mokes(112)/Muskrat Ramble(131-A: sub.Squire Girsback,bass;
                                                                    Mar.,1942
JM       4. At a Georgia Camp Meeting(107: Hayes,only banjo)
 "          Original Jelly Roll Blues(108: Hayes,only banjo)

       (Sub. Squire Girsback,bass):                                 Mar.,1942
JM       5. Riverside Blues(127)/Cake Walking Babies(128)
JM       6. Come Back Sweet Papa(120)/Tiger Rag(130)
JM       7. Fidgety Feet(122)/Temptation Rag(118: Rose,Bennett,Hayes,Dart)
JM      13. Milenberg Joys/Daddy Do
JM      14. London Blues(123)/Sunset Cafe Stomp(124)
JM      15. High Society(129)/Terrible Blues(121)

       (Wally Rose,piano solo):
JM      17. Hot House Rag(117: with Hayes,Bennett,Dart)/(BUNK JOHNSON)

       (Sub. Bob Helm,clarinet; Harry Mordecai,banjo):            Apr.,1946
West Coast 101. Canal Street Blues/Antigua Blues
West Coast 102. Chattanooga Stomp/Creole Belles
West Coast 103. Trombone Rag(40-A)/Sunburst Rag(36-A: Rose,Mordecai,Lammi,Dart)
West Coast 104. Big Bear Stomp(20-A)/Working Man Blues(13-a)
West Coast 105. Annie Street Rock(154)/Down Home Rag(62)          May,1946
West Coast 106. South/Richard M. Jones Blues
West Coast 107. Emperor Norton's Hunch(151-A)/Harlem Rag(74:Rose,Mordecai,
West Coast 108. That's a Plenty(103-B)/Beinville Blues(152-A)  (Lammi,Dart)
West Coast 109. I'm Goin' Hunting(75)/Friendless Blues(69)
West Coast 110. Pineapple Rag(56:Rose,Lammi,Mordecai,Dart)/Minstrels of Annie
West Coast 111. 1919 Rag(105)/Ostrich Walk(162)                   (Street(77)
```

WATSON AND HIS ORCHESTRA, LEO:
 De 2750. Man With the Mandolin/Utt Da Zay
 De 2959. It's the Tune That Counts/Ja Da

WE THREE (Red Nichols,cornet: Arthur Schutt,piano: Vic Berton,drums):
 Pe 14645. Trumpet Sobs
 Pe 14673. Plenty Off Center/(REDHEADS)

  (With Eddie Lang,guitar):
 Pat 11347. Get With/Get a Load of This

WEATHERFORD, TEDDY (piano solos):   Paris,1937
 Sw 5. Tea for Two(two masters)/Weatherbeaten Blues
 Sw 38. My Blue Heaven/Ain't Misbehavin'
 Sw 58. I Ain't Got Nobody

  (Piano, with rhythm section):   Calcutta,India
 IndCo 40164. Birth of the Blues(22063)/Darktown Strutters Ball(22064)
 IndCo 40220. Blues in the Night(22182)/St.Louis Blues(22185)
 IndCo 40225. Basin Street Blues(22183)/Memphis Blues(22184)

WEAVER, CURLEY (blues singing):
 De 7077. Early Morning Blues/Tricks Ain't Walkin' No More
 De 7664. Fried Pie Blues/Oh Lawdy Mama
 Co 14388. No No Blues(147305)/Sweet Petunia(147304)

  (With Ruth Willis):
 Ro 5204. Some Cold Rainy Day(12933)

WEAVER, SYLVESTER (guitar solos):
 OK 8109. Guitar Blues(S-71996-B)/Guitar Rag(S-71997-B)
 OK 8152. Smoketown Strut/I'm Busy and You Can't Come In
 OK 8480. Damfino Stump(80723)/**Guitar Rag(80727)**
 OK 8608. Polecat Blues/Railroad Porter Blues

  WEAVER AND BEASLEY (guitar duets):
 OK 8530. Bottle Neck Blues(81883-A)/St. Louis Blues(81884-B)

CHICK WEBB

See also:
 LOUIS ARMSTRONG: Vi 24200, 24204.
 ELLA FITZGERALD SAVOY EIGHT.
 MEZZ MEZZROW: Vi 25019, 25202.
 JIM MUNDY: Vr 598.

WEBB AND HIS ORCHESTRA, CHICK (The following two sides were issued originally under the name of the Jungle Band, and personnel probably was: Ward Pinkett,Edwin Swayze,trumpets: Robert Horton,trombone· Elmer Williams,tenor;Hilton Jefferson; Omer Simeon,altos and clarinets: Don Kirkpatrick,piano;Chick Webb,drums; Banjo; tuba)--JM 10   1929
 Br 4450. Dog Bottom   -BrE 01235
 "   Jungle Mama

  (Shad Collins, Louis Hunt,Louis Bacon,trumpets: Jimmy Harrison,trombone;
 Benny Carter,Hilton Jefferson,altos: Elmer Williams,tenor Don Kirkpatrick,piano: John Trueheart,banjo: Elmer James,bass; Chick Webb,drums)
                             1931
 Vo 1607. Soft and Sweet   -BrE 02079
 "   Heebie Jeebies   -Br 6898, BrE 01857
 Br 6898. I'm Left With the Blues in My Heart   -BrE 1857

  (Mario Bauza,Taft Jordan,Renald Jones,trumpets: Sandy Williams,trombone;
 Edgar Sampson,Pete Clark,altos: Elmer Williams,tenor: Joe Steele,piano;
 John Trueheart,guitar; John Kirby,bass: Chick Webb,drums):   1934
 CoE 741. Get Together(152687)
 "   On the Sunny Side of the Street(152658) -Co 2875, Vo 3246
 CoF 754. When Dreams Come True(152686)/Darktown Strutters Ball(152659)
 Co 2920. I Can't Dance(152733)/Imagination(152734) -CoF 5009
 Co 2926. Why Should I Beg for Love(152735)   -PaE 2117
 "   Stompin' at the Savoy(152740)   -Vo 3246, PaE 2088
                             1935
 OK 41571. True(W-152770)
 "   If It Ain't Love(W-152772)   -Vo 3100
 OK 41572. Blue Minor   -Vo 3100
 "   Lonesome Moments
 De 172. Blue Minor/On the Sunny Side of the Street -De 3318, BrE 01915
 De 173. That Rhythm Man   -BrE 02019
 "   Lona
 De 483. It's Over Because We're Through(39138-A)/Don't Be That Way
 De 494. Are You Here to Stay/Love & Kisses (39140-A)-BrE 02029

         (Sub Bobby Stark,trumpet, for Jones: add Fernand Arbello,trombone;Way-
       man Carver,tenor & flute; Jordan, Ella Fitzgerald,vocals):
De   588. Moonlight and Magnolias/Rhythm and Romance
De   640. I'll Chase the Blues Away(60056-A)   -BrE 02249
         "   I May Be Wrong(60057-A)
De   785. Down Home Rag(39615-A)/Crying My Heart Out(61000)   -BrE 02290

         (Sub. Ted McRae,tenor,for Williams; Dell Thomas,bass: sub. Claude Jones,
       trombone, for Arbello):   1936
De   830. Sing Me a Swing Song   -De 3319, BrE 02264
         "   Facts and Figures   -BrE 02375
De   831. Under the Spell of the Blues(61001-A)   -BrE 02264
         "   A Little Bit Later On(61125-A)   -De 3319,   "
De   995. Devoting MyTime to You   -BrE 02405
         "   Go Harlem   -BrE 02514
De   1065. Blue Lou
         "   Swingin' on the Reservation   -BrE 02396
De   1087. What a Shuffle(39141-A)
         "   I Got the Spring Fever Blues(61363-A)   -BrE 02396
         (Sub. Nat Story,trombone,for Jones: Louis Jordan,alto, for Sampson;
       Tommy Fulford,piano; Bobby Johnson,guitar; Beverly Peer,bass):   1937
De   1032. You'll Have to Swing It/Vot for Mister Rhythm   -BrE 02357
De   1114. There a Frost on the Moon   -BrE 02381
         "   Love You're Just a Laugh   -BrE 02419
De   1115. Gee But You're Swell
         "   Love Marches On   -BrE 02381
De   1123. When I Get Low I Get High   -BrE 02405
         "   Take Another Guess
De   1120. Clap Hands Here Comes Charley/You Showed Me the Way
De   1213. It's Swell of You   -BrE 02438
         "   Wake Up and Live
De   1273. Rusty Hinge/Cryin' Mood   -BrE 02470
De   1356. Love Is the Thing,So They Say/That Naughty Waltz
         (Sub. Bobby Johnson,guitar; Chauncey Haughton,sax,clarinet,for Clark):
De   1521. Just a Simple Melody(62725-A)/Holiday in Harlem(62728-A)
De   1586. Strictly Jive/Rock It for Me   (-BrE 02536
De   1681. I've Got a Guy/Harlem Congo
De   1716. Squeeze Me/If Dreams Come True
         (Sub. Garvin Bushell,alto, for Haughton):
De   1587. Midnight in Harlem/The Dipsy Doodle   -BrE 02569
De   15039. I Want to Be Happy/Hallelujah   -BrE 0138
         (Sub. Hilton Jefferson,alto,for Jordan; add George Matthews,trombone):
De   1840. A-Tisket A-Tasket(63693-A)/Liza(63708-A)   1938
De   1894. Pack Up Your Sins and Go to the Devil/Everybody Step -BrE 02660
De   1899. Azure/I'm Just a Jitterbug   -BrE 02631
De   2021. Wacky Dust/Spinnin' the Webb   -BrE 02669
De   2080. MacPherson Is Rehearsin'(63935-A)   -BrE 2680
         "   I Let a Tear Fall in the River(64465-A)
De   2148. Ella(63937-A)   -BrE 02687
         "   I Found My Yellow Basket(64576-A)
De   2231. Who Ya Hunchin'/Gotta Pebble in My Shoe
         (Sub. Richard Vance,trumpet, for Bauza):   1939
De   2105. F.D.R.Jones(64573-A)/I Love Every Move You Make(64574-A)
De   2309. My Heart Belongs to Daddy/It's Foxy
De   2310. Tain't What You Do/I Can't Stop Lovin' You
De   2323. Undecided(65039-A)/In the Groove at the Grove(65041-A)
         (Sub. John Trueheart,guitar):
De   2389. It's Slumbertime Along the Swanee(65095-A)/Chew Chew Chew(65097-A)
De   2468. I'm Up a Tree/Have mercy
De   2556. One Side of Me/Little White Lies
De   2665. Sugar Pie/That Was My Heart
De   2721. This Heart of Mine
De   2803. Coochi Coochi Coo

       CHICK WEBB AND HIS LITTLE CHICKS (Chauncey Haughton,clarinet: Wayman
       Carver,flute; Tommy Fulford,piano; Chick Webb,drums: Beverly Peer,bass):
De   1513. I Ain't Got Nobody/In a Little Spanish Town   -BrE 02546
De   1759. I Got Rhythm/Sweet Sue

WEBB'S DIXIELANDERS, GEORGE(Owen Bryce,cornet: Ed Harvey,trombone: Wally
       Fawkes,clarinet; George Webb,piano; Buddy Vallis,banjo; Rock Beckwith,
       drums):   For Decca,London,Jan.6,1945
Unissued. Georgia Cakewalk
Unissued. Bluin' the Blues
Unissued. Copenhagen
         (Sub. Derek Bailey,drums):   May 6,1945
Unissued. Georgia Cakewalk
Unissued. Bluin' the Blues
Unissued. Willie the Weeper

```
        (Add Reg Rigden,cornet):
    Unissued. Hesitatin' Blues

        (Bryce,Rigden,cornets; Harvey,trombone; Fawkes,clarinet; Webb,piano;
        Vallis,banjo; Art Streatfield,tuba: Roy Wykes,drums):    Dec.2,1945
    Jazz  0001. Come Back Sweet Papa/New Orleans Hop Scop Blues
    Jazz  0003. Dippermouth Blues/Riverside Blues
    Unissued. Original Dixieland One-Step/High Society

        (Same personnel: BBC Overseas Transcriptions):                1946
    Smoky Mokes; Jenny's Ball; Da Da Strain: Sugar Foot Stomp: Lewisada
    Blues; Riverside Blues; Hesitatin' Blues: When the Saints Go Marchin'
    In.

        (Same personnel· for private label):                    Sept.,1946
    Lewisada Blues; London Blues; Jenny's Ball; Weary Blues.

    DeF 8735. South(10836)/London Blues(10837)               Nov.9,1946
    Unissued. Jenny's Ball/Muskrat Ramble(Harry Brown,trombone):
```

WEBSTER QUARTET, BEN (Ben Webster,tenor; Sid Catlett,drums; John Simmons,bass
Marlowe Morris,piano):
 Se 10010. Perdido/I Surrender Dear

  BEN WEBSTER (tenor, acc. by Johnny Guarnieri,piano; Oscar Pettiford,
  bass: David Booth,drums):
 Sav 553. Honeysuckle Rose(5436)/Blue Skies(5438)
 Sav 580. I Surrender Dear(5437-1)/Kat's Fur(5439)

WELCH AND HER SWING QUARTET, ELIZABETH (Benny Carter,trumpet,alto; Gene Rodgers,piano; Ivor Mairants,guitar; Wally Morris,bass; Elizabeth Welch,vocals):
 VoF 515. The Man I Love/Drop In the Next Time You're Passing
 VoE 526. Poor Butterfly/That's How the First Song Was Born

DICKY WELLS

See also:
 HENRY ALLEN: Pe 15933, 15948; Vo 2956, 2965.
 ALLEN-HAWKINS: Pe 15802, 15808.
 COUNT BASIE.
 FREDDIE GREEN: Duke 113, 114.
 FLETCHER HENDERSON: Vo 2527, 2583: Co 35671.
 TEDDY HILL.
 SPIKE HUGHES: All.
 KANSAS CITY CIX: Com 555, 573.
 KANSAS CITY SEVEN: Key 1302, 1303.
 LUIS RUSSELL: Vi 22789-93; 22815.
 PEE WEE RUSSELL: HRS 17, 1000, 1001.
 CECIL SCOTT: Vi 38098, 38117.
 LLOYD SCOTT: Vi 20495, 21491.
 TRIO DE TROMPETTES: Sw 27.

WELLS AND HIS ORCHESTRA, DICKY (Bill Dillard,Shad Collins,trumpets; Dicky
Wells,trombone: Howard Johnson,alto: Sam Allen,piano; Roger Chaput,guitar;
Bill Beason,drums):   Paris,1937
 Sw 3. I've Found a New Baby(1894-1)   -Vi 26617
 " Hot Club Blues(1897-1; no Collins)

 (Bill Dillard,Bill Coleman,Shad Collins,trumpets: Dicky Wells,trombone;
 Django Reinhardt,guitar; Richard Fullbright,bass; Bill Beason,drums):
 Sw 6. Bugle Call Rag(1884-1)   -HMV 8799, Vi 26220
 " Between the Devil and the Deep Blue Sea(1885-1)

 (Omit Dillard and Collins):
 Sw 16. Sweet Sue(1887-1)
 " Hangin' Around Boudon(1888-1)   -Vi 26617
 Sw 27. Japanese Sandman(1889)/(TRIO DE TROMPETTES)   -HMV 8826

 (Original personnel):
 Sw 39. Dinah(1895-1)/Nobody's Blues But My Own(1896-1)

 DICKY WELLS, TROMBONE (acc. by Sam Allen,piano: Roger Chaput,guitar;
 Bill Beason,drums):
 Sw 10. Lady Be Good(1898-1)
 " Dicky Wells Blues(1899-1)   Vi 27318

 DICKY WELLS AND HIS ORCHESTRA (Bill Coleman,trumpet; Dicky Wells,trombone: Lester Young,tenor; Ellis Larkins,piano; Al Hall,bass: Freddy
 Green,guitar; Jo Jones, drums):
 Sig 90002. I Got Rhythm/I'm For It Too
 Sig 28115. Hello Babe(1919-1)/Linger Awhile(1920)

DICKY WELLS' BIG SEVEN (George Treadwell,trumpet Dicky Wells,trombone; Bud Johnson, tenor; Cecil Scott,baritone; Jimmy Jones,piano; Al McKibbon,bass; Jimmy Crawford,drums):
HRS 1018. Drag Nasty--The Walk/Opera in Blue
HRS 1019. Bed Rock/We're Through(voc.by Sarah Vaughn)

WELLS' SHIM SHAMMERS, DICKIE (This is a kazoo band, having no connection with Dicky Wells, the trombonist):
Co 2829. Baby Are You Satisfied/(WILLIAMS JUG BAND)   -PaE 2345

WELLS AND HIS ORCHESTRA, HENRY:
De 3073. Among My Souvenirs/Back in Your Own Backyard
De 3134. Garden in the Rain(67248-AA)/Home(67246-A)   -De 48017

WELLS, TUDIE (vocals, acc. by Fletcher Henderson,piano):
PatA 032006. Uncle Sam Blues/Baby's Got the Blues

WELSH, NOLAN (vocals, acc. by Louis Armstrong,cornet: Richard M. Jones,piano):
OK 8372. The Bridwell Blues(9727-A)/St. Peter Blues(9728-A)

    (Clarence Black,violin: Jones,piano):
OK 8425. Bouncing Blues(9918-A)/Nolan Welsh's Blues(9916-A)

WENDLING, PETE (piano solos):
OK 4868. Papa Blues/(HARRY JENTES)
OK 4984. Page Paderewski/(RUDY WIEDOEFT)

WETTLING'S CHICAGO RHYTHM KINGS, GEORGE (Charlie Teagarden,trumpet; Floyd O'Brien,trombone; Danny Polo,clarinet: Joe Marsala,tenor: Jess Stacy,piano; Jack Bland,guitar: Artie Shapiro,bass: George Wettling,drums):   1940
De 18044. Bugle Call Rag(67060-A)/Sister Kate(67061-A)   -BrE 03059
De 18045. I've Found a New Baby(67059-A)/Darktown Strutters' Ball(67062-B)
                                                             (-BrE 03060
    GEORGE WETTLING JAZZ TRIO (Mezz Mezzrow,clarinet: Gene Schroeder,piano; George Wettling,drums):   July 1,1944
BW   7. Everybody Loves My Baby/Some of These Days
BW   27. That's a Plenty(20)/China Boy(19-1)

    GEORGE WETTLING'S NEW YORKERS (Joe Thomas,trumpet: Jack Teagarden,trombone: Coleman Hawkins,tenor; Hank d'Amico,clarinet: Herman Chittison, piano; Billy Taylor,bass; George Wettling,drums):   Dec.12,1944
Key 1311. Home(72-1)/Too Marvelous for Words(73)
Key 1318. You Brought a New Kind of Love to Me(74)/Somebody Loves Me(75)

    GEORGE WETTLING AND HIS RHYTHM KINGS (Billy Butterfield,trumpet; Wilbur deParis,trombone: Edmond Hall,clarinet: Dave Bowman,piano: Bob Haggart,bass; George Wettling,drums):
Com 561. How Come You Do Me Like You Do(A-4802-2)/Struttin' With Some
                                                       (Barbecue(A-4802-3)
WHEATSTRAW, PEETIE (The Devil's Son-in-Law: vocals with piano & guitar):
Vo 02712. The Last Dime/Long Lonesome Drive
Vo 02783. Packin' Up Blues/Back Door Blues
Vo 03249. Kidnapper's Blues/Froggie Blues
BB 5451. Devil's Son-in-Law/Pete Wheatstraw
De 7007. Doin' the Best I Can
De 7018. Throw Me in the Alley
De 7061. Good Home Blues/These Times
De 7082. Numbers Blues/All Night Long Blues
De 7111. Whiskey Head Blues/Slave Man Blues
De 7129. Santa Claus Blues/Lonesome Lonesome Blues
De 7123. Good Hustler Blues/ C. and A. Train Blues
De 7144. Cocktail Man Blues/King Spider Blues
De 7159. Coon Can Shorty/When I Get My Bonus
De 7167. Deep Sea Love/First Shall be Last and the Last Shall Be First
De 7177. Kidnapper's Blues/Poor Millionaire Blues
De 7187. Meat Cutter Blues/Old Good Whiskey Blues
De 7200. Working Man Blues/Low Down Rascal
De 7228. Country Fool Blues/Drinking Man Blues
De 7243. False Hearted Woman/When a Man Gets Down
De 7257. Little House/I Don't Want No Pretty Faced Woman
De 7272. Beggar Man Blues/Fairasee Woman
De 7292. Crapshooter's Blues/Peetie Wheatstraw Stomp
De 7311. Working on the Project/Would You Would You Mama
De 7348. Crazy With the Blues/Ramblin' Man
De 7379. New Working on the Project/Third Street's Going Down
De 7391. Give Me Black or Brown/Peetie Wheatstraw Stomp
De 7403. Baby Lou Baby Lou/Sick Bed Blues
De 7422. Devilment Blues/I'm Gonna Cut Out Everything
De 7441. Cake Alley/Sweet Lucille
De 7453. 304 Blues/Hard Headed Black Gal
De 7465. Banana Man/Wrong Woman

```
De  7479.  What More Can a Man Do/Shack Bully Stomp
De  7498.  Saturday Night Blues/Good Little Thing
De  7529.  Truckin' Through Traffic/Sugar Mama
De  7544.  Me No Lika You/Hot Springs Blues
De  7568.  Black Horse Blues/Man Ain't Nothin' But a Fool
De  7578.  Little Low Mellow Mama/Sinking Sun Blues
De  7589.  Possum Den Blues/Road Tramp Blues
De  7605.  One to Twelve/Let's Talk Things Over
De  7641.  Working Man's Blues/Easy Way Blues
De  7657.  Beer Tavern/I Want Some Sea Food
De  7676.  Love Bug Blues/Rolling Chair
De  7692.  Confidence Man/You Can't Stop Me from Drinking
De  7738.  Big Money Blues/Five Minutes Blues
De  7753.  Big Apple Blues/Two Time Mamma
De  7778.  Pocket Knife Blues/Machine Gun Blues
De  7788.  Chicago Mill Blues/Suicide Blues
De  7798.  Cuttin' Em Slow/Jaybird Blues
De  7815.  Gangster's Blues/Look Out for Yourself
De  7823.  No 'Count Woman/What's That
De  7837.  I Don't Feel Sleepy/My Little Bit
De  7844.  You Got to Tell Me Something/Love Me With Attention
De  7857.  Seeing Is Believing/I'm a Little Piece of Leather
De  7879.  Mister Livingood/The Good Lawd's Children
De  7886.  Bring Me Flowers While I'm Living/Hearse Man Blues
De  7894.  Don't Put Yourself on the Spot/Pawn Broker Blues
De  7901.  Separation Day Blues/Old Organ Blues
De  7904.  Southern Girl Blues/(OSCAR WOODS)
```

WHEELER AND HIS SUNSET ORCHESTRA, "DOC":
```
BB 11314.  How 'Bout That Mess/Foo-Gee
BB 11389.  Big and Fat and Forty-Four/Gabby
BB 11529.  Me and My Melinda/Sorghum Switch
```

WHITBY, LULU (vocals, with Henderson Novelty Orch.):
```
BS  2005.  Home Again Blues(108)/Strut Miss Lizzie(109)
```

WHITE AND HER BLUES CHASERS, BEVERLY:
```
JD  7111.  If Things Don't Get Better/My Baby Comes First With Me
```

WHITE, BUKKA (vocals with guitars):
```
OK  05489.  When Can I Change My Clothes/High Fever Blues
OK  05526.  Special Stream Line/Strange Place Blues
OK  05588.  Black Train Blues/Fixin' to Die Blues
OK  05625.  Bukka's Jitterbug Swing/Good Gin Blues
OK  05683.  Parchman Farm Blues/District Attorney Blues
OK  05743.  Sleepy Man Blues/Aberdeen Mississippi Blues
```

WHITE, GEORGE (vocals with trumpet and guitar):
```
OK  45382.  Dust Pan Blues/Miss Moonshine
```

WHITE, GEORGIA (vocals, mostly with piano and guitar--Danny Barker?):
```
De  7072.  Your Worries Ain't Like Mine/You Done Lost Your Good Thing Now
De  7100.  Dallas Man/Dupree Blues                                  ( -De 48001
De  7122.  Freddie Blues/Honey Dripper Blues
De  7135.  Graveyard Blues/Easy Rider Blues
De  7149.  If You Can't Get Five Take Two/River Blues
De  7152.  Get 'em from the Peanut Man
De  7166.  Can't Read Can't Write/Someday Sweetheart
De  7174.  There Ain't Gonna Be No Doggone After Awhile/Rattlesnakin' Daddy
De  7183.  It Must Be Love/New Hot Nuts
De  7192.  I'll Keep Sittin' On It/Trouble in Mind
De  7199.  I Just Want Your Stingaree                              -De 48006
 "        Black Rider
De  7209.  New Dupree Blues/Pigmeat Blues
De  7216.  Was I Drunk/No Second Hand Woman
De  7252.  Tell Me Baby
De  7254.  Marble Stone Blues/Your Hellish Ways
De  7269.  Dan the Back Door Man/Sinking Sun Blues
De  7287.  Grandpa and Grandma/Little Red Wagon
De  7277.  Walking the Street
De  7309.  Toothache Blues/I'm So Glad I'm 21 Today
De  7323.  When My Love Comes Down/Daddy Let Me Lay It on You
De  7332.  Mistreated Blues/New Trouble in Mind
De  7357.  Moonshine Blues/Biscuit Roller
De  7377.  Away All the Time/Georgia Man                           -De 48006
De  7389.  Alley Boogie
 "        Red Cap Porter
De  7405.  All Night Blues/Fare Thee Honey Fare Thee Well
De  7419.  Careless Love/Strewin' Your Mess
De  7436.  Stuff Is Here/Rock Me Daddy
```

```
De  7450.  Almost Afraid to Love/I'm Blue and Lonesome
De  7477.  Tain't Nobody's Business If I Do/Too Much Trouble
De  7521.  Holding My Own/Trouble in Mind Swing
De  7534.  Dead Man's Blues/Love Sick Blues
De  7562.  Blues Ain't Nothing But/My Worried Mind Blues
De  7596.  Married Woman Blues/Way I'm Feelin'
De  7608.  When the Red Sun Turns to Gray/Fire in the Mountain
De  7620.  Beggin' My Daddy/Take Me for a Buggy Ride
De  7631.  Hydrant Love/What Have You Done to Me
De  7652.  Do It Again/How Do You Think I Feel
De  7672.  I'm Doing What My Heart Says Do/Tain't Nobody's Fault But Yours
De  7689.  Furniture Man/You Got to Drop the Sack
De  7741.  Jazzin' Babies Blues/Late Hour Blues
De  7754.  You Ought to Be Ashamed of Yourself/Sensation Blues
De  7783.  Papa Pleaser/Panama Limited Blues
De  7807.  Crazy Blues/Worried Head Blues
De  7853.  Territory Blues/When You're Away
De  7866.  Mail Plane Blues/(NORA LEE KING)
```

WHITE'S SYNCOPATORS, HAL (Fletcher Henderson's Orchestra with Louis Armstrong, trumpet: issued on Regal 9774 under Henderson's name):
```
Do  3444.  Everybody Loves My Baby(5748)
```

WHITE, JOSHUA (vocals and guitar):   1932-36
```
Pe  0208.  Bad Depression Blues/Howling Wolf Blues
Pe  0209.  Things About Coming My Way/So Sweet So Sweet
Pe  0213.  Lazy Black Snake Blues/Downhearted Man Blues
Pe  2019.  Black and Evil Blues/Little Brother Blues
Pe  0243.  Double Crossing Women/Crying Blues
Pe  0244.  Baby Won't You Doodle-Doo-Doo/High Brown Cheater
Pe  0257.  Blood Red River/Low Cotton
```

(Under the name of the Singing Christian):
```
Pe  0258.  Jesus Gonna Make Up My Dyin' Bed/Motherless Children
Pe  0263.  Pure Religion Hallilu/I Don't Intend to Die in Egyptland
Pe  0277.  You Sinner You/Down on Me
Pe  0285.  Can't Help But Crying Sometime/Lord I Want to Die Easily
Pe  0292.  Death's Coming Back After You/Four and Twenty Elders
Pe  O 311. My Father Is a Husband Man/This Heart of Mine
Pe  0324.  I Got a Home in That Rock/Paul and Silas Bound in Jail
Me  51160. Got a Key to the Kingdom/While the Blood Runs Warm in Your Veins
Me  60257. How About You/On My Way
Me  60457. Did You Read That Letter/My Soul Is Gonna Live With God
```

JOSHUA WHITE AND HIS CAROLINIANS (vocal group with guitar):
```
Co  35559. Nine Foot Shovel/Chain Gang Bound
Co  35560. Trouble/Goin' Home, Boys
Co  35561. Cryin' Who? Cryin' You, 1 & 2
Co  35562. Told My Cap'n/Jerry
```

JOSHUA WHITE (with Guitar, and Wilson Myers, bass):
```
Mu   248.  Careless Love/Prison Bound
Mu   249.  Hard Times/Monday, Tuesday, Wednesday
Mu   250.  Motherless Children, 1 & 2
```

JOSHUA WHITE TRIO (White, guitar and vocal: Sidney Bechet, clarinet; Wilson Myers, bass):
```
BN    23.  Careless Love/Milk Cow Blues
```

JOSH WHITE (vocal and guitar):
```
Key K-107. Southern Exposure:  Uncle Sam Says:  Jim Crow Train;  Bad Housing
             Blues;  Hard Times Blues;  Defense Factory Blues.
Key K-125. Strange Fruit;  John Henry;  Evil Hearted Man;  House of the
             Rising Sun;  Riddle Song;  Whatcha Goin' to Do
Disc 3004. Dupree(223)/Mean Mistreatin' Woman(220)                   1944
Disc 3005. Baby Baby(222)/Miss Otis Regrets(221)
```
(With guitar and organ):   1945
```
De 23416.  Johnny Has Gone for a Soldier(72664-A)/Beloved Comrade(72662-A)
```

(With Ed Hall's Orchestra):
```
De 23475.  I Left a Good Deal in Mobile/Did You Ever Love a Woman
```

WHITE'S COLLEGIANS, TED:
```
Or   931.  Hurricane(919-2)/Melancholy Charlie(918-1)
Or  1277.  Who Wouldn't Be Blue(1635-1)/(BILLY JAMES)
Or  1281.  That's My Weakness Now(1637-1)/(BOB GREEN)
Or  1419.  I'll Get By(1919-3)/(BOB GREEN)
Or  1477.  If I Had You                                          -Je 5511
Or  1489.  Good Little Bad Little You(2066-1)/(BILLY JAMES)
Or  1503.  Wedding Bells(2087-1)/(BILLY JAMES)
Or  1509.  You Were Meant for Me(2097-3)/(BILLY JAMES)
```

```
         (Jimmy McPartland,trumpet; Jack Teagarden,trombone; Benny Goodman,
         clarinet; Jack Pettis,tenor, and others):
      Or 1544. Shirt Tail Stomp(2187-5)/Tiger Rag(2186-3)          -Je 5577

      Or 1613. To Be in Love(2316)/(BOB GREEN)
      Or 1634. Painting the Clouds With Sunshine(2369-3)/(BILLY JAMES)
```

PAUL WHITEMAN

```
WHITEMAN'S RHYTHM BOYS, PAUL (Bing Crosby, Al Rinker, Harry Barris,vocals):
   Vi 20783. Sweet Li'l Ain't She Sweet/Mississippi Mud--I Left My Sugar
   Vi 21104. Miss Annabelle Lee/(FOUR ARISTOCRATS)            ( -Vi 24240
   Vi 21302. What Price Lyrice/From Monday On                  -Vi 24349
   Vi 24095. Bahama Mama/Lost in Your Arms
   Vi 27688. That's Grandma
   Vi 24190. Jig Time/(PICKENS SISTERS)
   Co  1455. That's Grandma/Wa Da Da
   Co  1629. Rhythm King/My Suppressed Desire
   Co  1819. Louise/Blackbirds and Bluebirds
   Co  2223. A Bench in the Park

WHITEMAN AND HIS ORCHESTRA, PAUL (Henry Busse,trumpet: Buster Johnson,trom-
bone; Gus Mueller,clarinet; Hale 'Pee Wee' Byers,saxophone; Ferde Grofe,
piano; Mike Pingitore,banjo; Sammy Heiss,bass; Hal MacDonald,drums; Paul
Whiteman,violin):                                        Camden,N.J.,1920-22
   Vi 18690. Whispering/The Japanese Sandman                  -HMV 1160
   Vi 18694. Wang Wang Blues/Anytime Anyday, Anywhere         -HMV 1178
   Vi 18758. My Man/Cherie
   Vi 18803. Say It With Music/Sweet Lady
   Vi 18824. Canadian Capers/(BENSON ORCHESTRA)               -HMV 1310
   Vi 18825. Weep No More My Mammy/April Showers
   Vi 18826. Everybody Step                                   -HMV 1318
      "     Ka-Lu-A--Blue Danube Blues
   Vi 35701. Dance of the Hours-Love in Idleness/Avalon-Just Like a Gypsy
   Vi 35703. Grieving for You-Feather Your Nest/My Wonder Girl-Coral Sea
   Vi 35744. Mandalay-Step Henrietta/Where Is That Old Girl of Mine-Driftwood
   Vi 18842. Just a Little Love Song/Ty-Tee
   Vi 18859. On the 'Gin 'Gin 'Ginny Shore/Marie
   Vi 18865. Lonesome Hours/Cute
   Vi 18872. After the Rain/Jimmy
   Vi 18879. Old Fashioned Girl/Little Grey Sweetheart of Mine
   Vi 18880. Bygones/By the Sapphire Sea
   Vi 18882. Do It Again
   Vi 18891. Some Sunny Day/(CLUB ROYAL ORCHESTRA)
   Vi 18898. Coo-Coo/(GREEN BROTHERS)
   Vi 18899. Georgie/Stumbling                                -HMV 1382

      (Sub. Ross Gorman,clarinet and saxes,for Mueller: Sammy Lewis,trombone):
   Vi 18901. You Won't Be Sorry/(CLUB ROYAL ORCHESTRA)
   Vi 18911. 'Neath the Southern Sea Moon/It's Up to You
   Vi 18923. My Rambler Rose/(CLUB ROYAL)
   Vi 18938. I'm Just Wild About Harry/(BENSON ORCHESTRA)     -HMV 1407
   Vi 18939. Tricks                                           -HMV 1407
      "     Coal Black Mammy
   Vi 18949. I'll Build a Stairway to Paradise/You Remind Me of My Mother
   Vi 18960. Just As Long as You Have Me/Blowing Bubbles All Day Long
   Vi 18962. Carolina in the Morning/(ZEZ CONFREY)            -HMV 1516
   Vi 18963. Homesick/(GREAT WHITE WAY ORCHESTRA)
   Vi 18966. Romany Love/(GREAT WHITE WAY ORCHESTRA)
   Vi 18985. Journey's End/When Hearts Are Young
   Vi 18977. The Yankee Princess/Sweetheart Lane
   Vi 18983. Crinoline Days                                   -HMV 1655
      "     Pack Up Your Sins
   Vi 18988. Until My Luck Comes Rolling Along/Just Like a Doll
   Vi 19003. I Gave You Up Just Before You Threw Me Down/Ivy
   Vi 19007. Parade of the Wooden Soldiers                    -HMV 1589
      "     Mister Gallagher and Mr. Shean
   Vi 19008. When All Your Castles Come Tumbling Down/(ZEZ CONFREY)
   Vi 19016. Lady of the Evening                              -HMV 1637
      "     Fate
   Vi 19030. Dearest                                          -HMV 1649
      "     'Way Down Yonder in New Orleans

      (Henry Busse,Tommy Gott,Frank Siegrist,trumpets: Roy Maxon,Willy Hall,
      Jack Fulton,trombones. Chester Hazlett,Ross Gorman, Hal MacLean, Rube
      Crozier,saxes; Harry Perella,Raymond Turner,pianos; Kurt Dieterle,James
      McKilltop,Paul Daven,Irving Achtel,violins; Mike Pingitore,Harry Reser,
      banjos; Herb Herdon,John Speizel,bass: Harold MacDonald,drums; Grofe,
      arranger: Whiteman,conductor):                              1924-25
   Vi 19033. Falling/Burning Sands
   Vi 19034. Crying for You/(ZEZ CONFREY)
   Vi 19035. Bambalina/(GREAT WHITE WAY ORCHESTRA)
```

Vi 19024. That American Boy of Mine/(GREAT WHITE WAY ORCHESTRA)
Vi 19043. By the Shalimar/Sweet One
Vi 19073. Nuthin' But/(TENNESSEE TEN)   -HMV 1677
Vi 19139. If I Can't Get the Sweetie I Want   -HMV 1714
    "   Last Night on the Back Porch
Vi 19145. Chansonette/What Do You Do Sunday, Mary
Vi 19155. Cut Yourself a Piece of Cake/(BENSON ORCHESTRA)
Vi 19161. Sittin' in a Corner
Vi 19162. Little Butterfly/(TROUBADOURS)
Vi 19209. Roamin' to Wyoming/(FRED WARING)
Vi 19217. Arcady/I'm Sittin' Pretty in a Pretty Little City
Vi 19191. Mama Loves Papa   -HMV 1867
    "   Every Night I Cry Myself to Sleep Over You
Vi 19229. I'm Goin' South   -HMV 1797
    "   Steppin' Out
Vi 19244. Along the Old Lake Trail/Someone Loves You After All
Vi 19252. Learn to Do the Strut
    "   So This Is Venice   -HMV 1812
Vi 19264. Limehouse Blues
Vi 19273. Don't Mind the Rain/(BROOKE JOHNS)
Vi 19283. Ain't You Ashamed   -HMV 1853
    "   Maybe
Vi 19299. Lazy/What'll I Do
Vi 19309. Love Has a Way/There's Yes Yes in Your Eyes
Vi 19330. Spain
Vi 19339. It Had to Be You
    "   The Hoodoo Man   -HMV 1938
Vi 19345. Pale Moon
Vi 19353. Where the Rainbow Ends/Paradise Alley
Vi 19381. San/I Can't Get the One I Want   -HMV 1889
Vi 19389. Dixie's Favorite Son/Walla-Walla
Vi 19391. By the Waters of the Minnetonka/Meditation from Thais
Vi 19402. The Song of Song/(TROUBADOURS)
Vi 19414. Lonely Little Melody/Somebody Loves Me
Vi 19420. Little Old Clock on the Mantel/(JACK SHILKRET)
Vi 19428. Where the Dreamy Wabash Flows
Vi 19447. Bagdad/Hard Hearted Hannah
Vi 19456. Tell Me Dreamy Eyes/My Twilight Rose
Vi 19461. Rose Marie/My Road
Vi 19462. Doo Wacka Doo/Eliza   -HMV 1937
Vi 19487. All Alone
Vi 19517. Indian Love Call/Tell Her in the Springtime
Vi 19546. Where's My Sweetie Hiding/Oh Joseph
Vi 19551. Lady Be Good/Fascinating Rhythm
Vi 19557. Call of the South/Alabamy Bound
Vi 19569. Gotta Getta Girl/(WARING'S PENNSYLVANIANS)
Vi 19584. The Only One for Me   -HMV 2007
    "   Lucky Kentucky   -HMV 2054
Vi 19641. Pozzo
    "   Whoa Nellie
Vi 19682. Tell Me More/Who Do I Love You
Vi 19692. Steppin' in Society   -HMV 2104
    "   Let Me Linger Longer in Your Arms
Vi 19694. Southern Rose/Gigolette
Vi 19719. Indian Dawn/Ogo Pogo
Vi 19720. Footloose   -HMV 2112
    "   Sing Loo
Vi 19726. Remember/Why Is Love
Vi 19721. Sonya   -HMV 2112
    "   Got No Time   -HMV 2111
Vi 19753. I Miss My Swiss/The Kinky Kids Parade
Vi 19773. I'm Tired of Everything But You
    "   The Rhythm Rag   -HMV 2175
Vi 19785. Ida--I Do   -HMV 5037
    "   Charlestonette
Vi 19790. Days of Hearts and Flowers   -HMV 2185
    "   Peaceful Valley
Vi 19862. Caprice Viennois/Hymn to the Sun
Vi 19920. That Certain Feeling
    "   Sweet and Low Down   -HMV 5109
Vi 19946. I Never Knew How Wonderful You Were   -HMV 5039
    "   Sweet Child
Vi 19902. I Wonder Where My Baby Is Tonight/Lo-Nah
Vi 19929. Poor Little Rich Girl/(INTERNATIONAL NOVELTY ORCH.)
Vi 19934. No Man's Mamma/(BUSSE'S BUZZARDS)
Vi 55225. Rhapsody in Blue, 1 & 2 (George Gershwin, piano);
Vi 55226. Suite of Serenades, 1 & 2
Vi 20017. Tentin' Down in Tennessee   -HMV 5064
    "   Georgianna   -HMV 5084
Vi 20019. No Foolin'
    "   Lulu Belle
Vi 20138. Countess Maritza/Birth of the Blues
Vi 20139. Precious/Moonlight on the Ganges

83

Vi 2009?. St.Louis Blues   -HMV 5165
   "   Hell Hoppin' Blues   -HMV 5065
Vi 20007. Valencia
   "   No More Worryin'.   -HMV 5065
Vi 20200. Cho Cho San/Song of India
Vi 20266. In a Little Spanish Town/There's a Boatman on the Volga

    (Red Nichols,Henry Busse,Bob Mayhew,trumpets: Tommy Dorsey,Willy Hall,
    Jack Fulton,trombones: Charles Strickfadden,baritone; Chester Hazlitt,
    alto; Jimmy Dorsey,alto; Rube Crozier,tenor; Max Farley,tenor; Hal
    MacLean,flute· Lloyd Turner,Harry Perella,pianos: Hal MacDonald,drums;
    Mike Pingitore,banjo; Mike Trifficante,bass; Bing Crosby,vocals*):1927
Vi 20418. Wistful and Blue(Dec.22,1926)*/Lonely Eyes
Vi 20501. I Always Knew/When I'm in Your Arms
Vi 20505. Silver Moon/Your Land and My Land
Vi 20508. Muddy Water(March 7,1927)*
Vi 20513. That Saxophone Waltz*/It All Depends on You
Vi 20514. Everything's Made for Love
Vi 20570. Song of the Wanderer/So Blue
Vi 20627. Pretty Lips*/Side By Side* (Red Nichols solo)   -HMV 5318
Vi 20646. I'm in Love Again*/Wherever You Go
Vi 20679. Love and Kisses(May 13,1927)*
   "   Magnolia(May 24,1927)* (Nichols solo)   -HMV 5317
Vi 20683. Fallen Leaf(2/10/27)/Shanghai Dream Man*(2/10/27)
Vi 20684. Like You(5/19/27)

    (Matty Malneck, violin):
Vi 20751. I'm Comin'Virginia(4/29/27*)(guitar,Gilbert Torres)/Just Once
Vi 20757. Collette(6/15/27)/Broken Hearted(5/24/27)*   (Again(6/22/27)
Vi 20784. I'll Always Remember You(5/9/27)/Who Do You Love(3/9/27)
Vi 20828. My Blue Heaven(7/6/27)*
Vi 20784. Manhattan Mary(7/13/27)/Broadway(8/16/27)
Vi 20881. Just a Memory(8/19/27)/Cheerie Beerie Bee(8/15/27)
Vi 20882. The Calinda(8/19/27)*   -HMV 5384
                                                                      Aug.16,1927
Vi 20883. It Won't Be Long Now(Jimmy Dorsey,clarinet and baritone; Tommy
              Dorsey,trombone and trumpet)/Fivestep*   -HMV 5511
Vi 20885. Shaking the Blues Away/Oooh Maybe It's You   Aug.20,1927
Vi 20972. Dancing Tambourine/Shady Tree   Sept.22,1927
Vi 20973. Beautiful Ohio/Missouri Waltz*
Vi 21119. Sensation Stomp/Whiteman Stomp   Aug.11,1927

    (Jimmy Dorsey,Charles Strickfadden,saxes; Chester Hazlitt,bass clari-
    net; Tommy Dorsey, Bruce Cullen,trombones· Bix Beiderbecke,cornet;
    Mischa Russell,Kurt Dieterle,violins; Hal MacDonald,drums; Steve Brown,
    bass; Matt Malneck,viola; vocal by Hoagy Carmichael):Chicago,Nov.18,1927
Vi 35877. Washboard Blues(40901)   -Vi 36186
   "   Among My Souvenirs (full band)   Nov.22,1927

    (Bix Beiderbecke,Charlie Margulies,Henry Busse,Bob Mayhew,trumpets:Tom-
    my Dorsey,Willy Hall,Jack Fulton,Bruce Cullen,trombones: Frankie Trum-
    bauer,Jimmy Dorsey,Rube Crozier,Charles Strickfadden,Chester Hazlitt,
    Nye Mayhew,Hal MacLean,Jack Mayhew,saxes: Matt Malneck,Kurt Dieterle,
    Mischa Russell,John Bowman,Charles Gaylord,violins: Harry Perella, Roy
    Bargy,pianos: Mike Pingitore, banjo: Mario Perry,accordion; Steve Brown,
    bass; Mike Trifficante,tuba: Min Leibrook,bass sax)   Nov.25,1927
Vi 21103. Changes(40937-A)*   -HMV 5461, HMV 8913
   "   Mary(40945)
Vi 25370. Changes(40937-B)*/Mary(40945-B)

    (Sub. Bill Rank,trombone,for Dorsey)   New York,Jan.4,1928
Vi 21214. Lonely Melody(41295-A)   -HMV 5516
   "   Ramona   -Vi 25436
Vi 25366. Lonely Melody(41295-B)/Underneath a Mellow Moon
Vi 21228. Smile(41294)/(VIRGINIANS)   -HMV 5465
Vi 21304. O Ya Ya(41296)/Parade of Wooden Soldiers(27268)   Jan.5,1928
Vi 24078. Poor Butterfly(Feb.7)*   Jan.11-27,1928
   "   San(30172-6)   -HMV 5581
Vi 25367. San(30172-7)   -Vi 25249
Vi 21218. Ol' Man River*/Make Believe*
Vi 21240. Back in Own Back Yard(41471-3)/Sunshine(Feb.13,1928)Jan.28,1928
Vi 27689. Back in Your Own Back Yard(41471-4)
Vi 21464. Sugar(see Feb.28th session)   Feb.7-8,1928
   "   There Ain't No Sweet Man(41681-A)   -HMV 5515
Vi 25675. There Ain't No Sweet Man(41681-B)
Vi 21731. Japanese Sandman/Whispering(Feb.15)
Vi 25238. Dardanella(41683)   -HMV 8931
   "   Avalon   Feb.9,1928
Vi 21599. Oriental
Vi 21796. By the Waters of the Minnetonka/Meditation from 'Thais'
Vi 24105. Love Nest(41684)/My Wonderful One   Feb.10-13,1928

                                   84

```
              (Sub. Izzy Friedman,clarinet and sax,for J.Dorsey): Feb.13-18-28,1928
Vi 21274. Mississippi Mud(41696-A)*/From Monday On(41689-A-6)*    -HMV 5492
Vi 25366. Mississippi Mud(41696-B)*
Vi 25368. From Monday On(41689-B-4)*/From Monday On(41689-3)*
Vi 21464. Sugar(43118-A)(See'There Ain't No Sweet Man',above)    -HMV 8931
Vi 21365. When You're With Somebody Else(43120-1)
Vi 25368. Sugar(43118-B)
Vi 27689. When You're With Somebody Else(43120-2)

              (Sub. Lennie Hayton,piano, for Perella):           Mar.1-2,1928
Vi 35912. 'Showboat'Selections(43123)/Ol' Man River              -HMV 1505
Vi 21301. Coquette(43125-A)                                      -HMV 5564
    "     Dolly Dimples(Jan.5,1928)
Vi 25675. Coquette(43125-B)                                      Mar.12,1928
Vi 21338. When(43138)/NAT SHILKRET)                    -Vi 25367,HMV 5493
Vi 21338. When (Second master)
Vi 21365. I'm Wingin' Home*
Vi 27687. Down in Old Havana Town
Vi 35933-34. Metropolis, 1, 2, 3 & 4                    March 14-15-16,1928
Vi 21315. Ma Belle,March of the Musketeers*
Vi 21325. When You're in Love/Little Log Cabin of Dreams
HMV  5509. Lovable(43145)*                                      -Vi 27685
Vi 21388. My Angel/In My Bouquet of Memories            April 21-22-23-25,1928
Vi 21389. My Pet(43662-2)*                                      -HMV 5504
    "     I'm Afraid of You(#4 master)*
Vi 27685. I'm Afraid of You(#3 master)*
Vi 27686. My Pet(43662-1)*/Forget Me Not
Vi 21398. You Took Advantage of Me(43670)*                      -Vi 25369
    "     Do I Hear You Sayin'?*
Vi 21431. Dancing Shadows*                                      -Vi 27687
Vi 21438. Louisiana(43667-A)*/Dixie Dawn                -HMV 5522, HMV 8913
Vi 25369. Louisiana(43667-B)*
Vi 21453. It Was the Dawn of Love(43663)*/(GOODRICH ORCH.)      -HMV 5522
Vi 21678. Grieving*

              (Dates and personnel unknown):
Vi 24104. Kammenoi Ostrow/Marche Slav

              (Bix Beiderbecke apparently is not on any of these 12-inch records):
                                                                 1927-28
Vi 35822. Rhapsody in Blue, 1 & 2 (Gershwin, piano):
Vi 35859. Mississippi Suite, 1 & 2
Vi 35883. My Heart Stood Still/Together
Vi 35921. Chloe
Vi 35952. Three Shades of Blue, 1 & 2
Vi 35992. High Water*/Midnight Reflections
Vi 36044. Sea Burial/Caprice Futuristic
Vi 36065. Wagneriana, 1 & 2
Vi 36067. Study in Blue
Co 50069. My Hero/Merry Widow
Co 50070. La Golondrina*/La Paloma*
Co 50098. Silent Night/Christmas Melodies*

              (Bix Beiderbecke,trumpet, included):               1928
Co 50068. My Melancholy Baby(98537)/The Man I Love       -CoE 9578
Co 50095. Gypsy(98579)/Jeannine
Co  1401. Last Night I Dreamed You Kissed Me(146249)/Evening Star(146250)*
Co  1402. Get Out and Get Under the Moon*/Constantinople*
Co  1441. Because My Baby Don't Mean Maybe Now(146549)*  -CoE 5007
    "     Just Like a Melody from Out of the Sky(146545)
Co  1444. 'Tain't So Honey'Tain't So(146316)*            -CoE 4981
    "     That's My Weakness Now(146542)*                -CoE 5006
Co  1448. Chiquita(146335)/Lonesome in the Moonlight(146546)*
Co  1464. Pickin'Cotton(pickup group: not Whiteman)/American Tune
Co  1465. I'm on the Crest of a Wave(146541)*/What D'Ya Say(146611:pickup
Co  1478. Mother Goose Parade(146328)              (group,not Whiteman)
    "     Felix the Cat(146334)
Co  1484. In the Evening(pickup group:not P.W.)/If You Don't Love Me(notPW)
Co  1491. Oh You Have No Idea(146327)                    -CoE 4956
    "     Georgie Porgie(146543)*                        -CoE 5040
Co  1496. Is It Gonna Be Long(146317)                    -CoE 4956
    "     I'd Rather Cry Over You(146320)*               -CoE 4980
Co  1505. Just a Little Bit o'Driftwood(146547)/Out o'Town Gal(146550)*
Co  1553. Blue Night(146329)/Roses of Yesterday(146947)

              (Beiderbecke out of band):
Co  1558. Sidewalks of New York/Good Old Summer Time
Co  1630. Where Is the Song of Songs for Me(147032)/Just a Sweetheart
                                                                 (147042)
              (Charlie Margulies,Harry Goldfield,Ed Pinder,Andy Secrest,trumpets;
              Bruce Cullen,Willy Hall,Bill Rank,Jack Fulton,trombones; Frankie Trum-
              bauer,Chester Hazlitt,Charles Strickfadden,Izzy Friedman,Rube Crozier,
```

85

Roy Maier,saxes: Kurt Dieterle,Matt Malneck,Mischa Russell,John Bowman,
violins; Roy Bargy,Lennie Hayton,pianos; Mike Pingitore,banjo; George
Marsh,drums; Mike Trifficante,Min Leibrook,basses):   1929
Co 1683. Makin' Whoopee*/I'm Bringing a Red Red Rose
Co 1701. Let's Do It*/Japanese Mammy
Co 1723. Cradle of Love(147749)/How About Me(147537)
Co 1731. Lover Come Back to Me/Marianne
Co 1736. Button Up Your Overcoat(147926)/My Lucky Star(147950)
Co 1755. Coquette(148013)*/My Angeline(147751)*
Co 1771. Louise)/Blue Hawaii

(Beiderbecke returns: Secrest replaces Pinder):
Co 1822. Reaching for Someone(148408)*/When My Dreams Come True(148407)
Co 1845. Your Mother and Mine(148422)*/Orange Blossom Time(148423)*
Co 1862. S'posin'-/Laughing Marionette
Co 1877. I'm in Seventh Heaven(148183)*/Little Pal(148184)*
Co 1945. Oh Miss Hannah(148421)*/China Boy(148409)
Co 50103. I Can't Give You Anything But Love/Sweet Sue
Co 50139-40-41. Concerto in F (Gershwin), 1, 2, 3, 4, 5, & 6

(Omit Beiderbecke):
Co 1974. Waiting at the End of the Road(148986)*/Love Me(149006)
Co 1993. When You're Counting the Stars Alone*/At Twilight*

(Add Eddie Lang,guitar; Joe Venuti,Ted Bacon,Otto Landau,violins;Bernie
Daly,sax):
Co 2010. I'm a Dreamer Aren't We All*/If I Had a Talking Picture of You*
Co 2023. Great Day*/Without a Song*
Co 2047. Should I/Bundle of Old Love Letters*
Co 2098. Nobody's Sweetheart(149123)/After You've Gone(149159)*
Co 50113. Tschaikowskiana, 1 & 2
Co 2656. Chinese Lullaby
Co 50198. Song of India/Liebestraum
Co 2163. It Happened in Monterey(149811)/Song of Dawn(149822) April,1930
Co 2164. Happy Feet(149810)*/A Bench in the Park(149825)*
Co 2170. Ragamuffin Romeo/I Like to Do Things for You*
Co 2171. You Brought a New King of Love to Me/Livin' in the Sunlight*

(Andy Secrest,Harry Goldfield,Nat Natalie,trumpets: Bill Rank,Jack Ful-
ton, Willy Hall,trombones; Frank Trumbauer,Charles Strickfadden,fud Liv-
ingston,Chester Hazlitt,saxes:Matt Malneck,Kurt Dieterle,John Bowman,
Mischa Russell,violins; Roy Bargy,piano; Mike Pingitore,guitar; Mike
Trifficante,bass; George Marsh,drums):   Fall,1930
Co 2224. Sittin' on a Rainbow/Old New England Moon
Co 2263. Song of the Congo/Wedding of the Birds
Co 2277. New Tiger Rag/Nola
Co 2289. In My Heart it's You/A Big Bouquet for You
Co 2297. Body and Soul/Something to Remember You By
Co 2491. Choo Choo

(Mildred Bailey, voc.#)   1931-32
Vi 22828. Can't You See#/When It's Sleepy Time Down South#
Vi 22883. Eleven Pounds of Heaven#/(WAYNE KING)
Vi 22913. Tango Americano
Vi 22834. Cuban Love Song/Tell Me With a Love Song
Vi 22849. When the World Was New
Vi 22870. Dance of the Little Dutch Dolls
Vi 22885. Sylvia/Vilia
Vi 22984. Lawd You Made the Night Too Long(voc.,Red McKenzie)
Vi 22998. Voice in the Old Village Choir
Vi 22827. Old Playmate/A Faded Summer Love
Vi 24017. Daybreak(voc.,Red McKenzie)/Toselli's Serenade

(Omit Frankie Trumbauer)
Vi 24088. I'll Never Be the Same#/We Just Couldn't Say Goodbye#
Vi 24089. Three on a Match(voc.,Red McKenzie)/Here's Hoping
Vi 24140. You're Telling Me/Let's Put Out the Lights
Vi 36199. A Night With Paul Whiteman at the Biltmore(voc., Red McKenzie)

(Bunny Berigan,Harry Goldfield,Nat Natalie,trumpets; Bill Rank,Jack
Fulton,Vincent Grande,trombones; Charles Strickfadden,Fud Livingston,
John Cordaro, Bob Davis,Bennie Bonnacio, saxes: Kurt Dieterle,Matt Mal-
neck,Mischa Russell,Harry Struble,violins: Roy Bargy,Ramona Davies,
pianos: Mike Pingitore,guitar and banjo: Aftie Miller,bass; Herb
Quigley,drums):   1933
Vi 24188. Willow Weep for Me/So At Last It's Come to This
Vi 24189. In the Dim Dim Dawning
Vi 24238. I'd Write a Song/You Are the Song
Vi 24285. Look What I've Got/In a Park in Paree
Vi 24364. Marching Along Together/My Moonlight Madonna
Vi 24400. Night Owl/It's Only a Paper Moon
Vi 24453. Let's Begin/Touch of Your Hand

86

Vi 36085. Night and Day/Medley of Cole Porter Tunes
Vi 24455. Smoke Gets in Your Eyes/Something Had to Happen

    (Charlie Tegarden,Nat Natalie,Harry Goldfield,trumpets: Jack Teagarden,
Bill Frank,Jack Fulton,trombones: Frank Trumbauer,John Coradro,Charles
Strickfadden,Bennie Bonaccio,saxes: Kurt Dieterle,Matt Malneck,Mischa
Russell,Harry Struble,violins:Roy Bargy,Ramona Davies,pianos; Miller;
Quigley; Pingitore):   1934
Vi 24571. Fare Thee Well to Harlem(J.Teagarden & Johnny Mercer,vocs)/(JACK
Vi 24517. If I Love Again/Wagon Wheels   (JACKSON)
Vi 24574. Bouncing Ball/Sunspots
Vi 24514. My Little Grass Shack/Old Fashioned World
Vi 24615. Christmas Night in Harlem(JT & JM, vocals)/Carry Me Back to the
Vi 24672. Love in Bloom/(RICHARD HIMBER)   (Green Pastures

    (Sub. Matt Matthewson,trombone,for Fulton):
Vi 24852. Serenade for a Wealthy Widow/Deep Forest
Vi 36131. Deep Purple/Park Avenue Fantasy
Vi 36141. Anything Goes Medley
Vi 36159. Stardust/Blue Moonlight
Vi 36175. Jubilee, 1 & 2
Vi 24769. I Get a Kick Out of You/You're the Top
Vi 24770. All Through the Night/Anything Goes
Vi 24844. The Night Is Young/When I Grow Too Old to Dream

    (Sub. Larry Gomer,drums):   1935-36
Vi 25086. Ain't Misbehavin'/Dodging a Divorcee
Vi 25091. I'm in the Mood/I Feel a Song
Vi 25113. The Duke Insists/Garden of the Weed
Vi 25134. When Love Comes Your Way/Why Shouldn't I
Vi 25135. Me and Marie/Picture Me Without You
Vi 25150. Sugar Plum/New Orleans
Vi 25151. I'm Sittin' High/Thanks a Million
Vi 25192. Darktown Strutters Ball/Farewell Blues
Vi 25197. I Dream Too Much/Jockey on a Carousel
Vi 25198. I Got Love/I'm the Echo
Vi 25251. Wheel of the Wagon/Saddle Your Blues
Vi 25252. What's the Name of That Song/Wah-Hoo
Vi 25319. Nobody's Sweetheart/Stop Look and Listen
Vi 25404. Announcer's Blues

    (Sub. Ed Wade,trumpet, for Natalie: Add Vernon Hayes,George Bamford,
saxes; Vincent Piero,accordion):   1936
Vi 25265. Everything Stops for Tea/Wake in a Dream
Vi 25269. My Romance/Little Girl Blue
Vi 25274. Gloomy Sunday/A Waltz Was Born in Vienna
Vi 25278. Look for the Silver Lining
Vi 36183. Slaughter on Park Avenue

    (Sub. Murray Cohan,sax, for Bonnacio; add Al Golladoro,alto: Sub. Char-
lie LaVere,piano, for Ramona: omit Kurt Dieterle):   1937
Vi 25552. Shall We Dance/For You
Vi 36198. All Points West, 1 & 2

    (Charlie Teagarden,Harry Goldfield,Bob Cusamano,Bob Alexy,trumpets;
Miff Mole, Jack Teagarden,Hal Matthews,trombones; Al Golladoro,Sal Fran-
zella,Frank Golladoro,Art Drelinger,Murray Cohan, Vincent Capone,George
Ford,Harold Feldman,Miles Fargarson,saxes: Roy Bargy,Frank Signorelli,
pianos; Mike Pingitore,banjo: Artie Miller,bass: Artie Ryerson,guitar;
George Wettling,drums: Al Duffy,Jules Schachter,Maurice Ancher,Kurt
Dieterle,Harry Struble,violins):   Dec.,1938
De 29051. Rhapsody in Blue, 1 & 2
De 29052. Second Rhapsody, 1 & 2
De 29053. Cuban Overture,1 & 2 (Rosa Linda,piano)
De 29054. Cuban Overture III/An American in Paris, 1
De 29055. An American in Paris, 2 & 3

    PAUL WHITEMAN AND HIS SWING WING (Charlie Teagarden,trumpet; Jack Tea-
garden,trombone: Sal Franzella,clarinet Al Golladoro,alto: Art Dreling-
er,tenor, Walter Gross,piano; Arthur Ryerson,guitar; Artie Miller,bass;
Rollo Laylan,drums):
De 2073. I Used to Be Color Blind(64619)/Peelin' the Peach(64621)
De 2074. Sing a Song of Sixpence(64620)/Jamboree Jones(64617)
De 2145. I'm Comin' Virginia(64616)/Aunt Hagar's Blues(64618)
De 2222. Mutiny in the Nursery(64792)/Jeepers Creepers(64793)
De 2283. I Go for That(64794)/Never Felt Better Never Had Less(64791)
De 2417. Now and Then/Three Little Fishies
De 2418. Step Up and Shake My Hand(65368)/Horray for Spinach(63367)
De 2696. Lazy/Mandy

    PAUL WHITEMAN'S BOUNCING BRASS(Brass section of large orchestra):
De 2466. I'm Found a New Baby(65360)/Rose Room(65361)
De 2697. Heat Wave/Home Again Blues

PAUL WHITEMAN SAX SOCTETTE (Full reed section):
De 2467. After You've Gone(65365)/I Kiss Your Hand Madama(65364)
De 2698. Blue Skies/What'll I Do
PAUL WHITEMAN'S SWINGING STRINGS(Full violin section):
De 2223. Oh Lady Be Good(64738)/Liza(64739)
De 2268. Japanese Sandman/Ragging the Scale
De 2430. Minuet in Jazz/Toy Trumpet
De 2699. A Pretty Girl Is Like a Melody/Soft Lights and Sweet Music
PAUL WHITEMAN'S WOODWINDS:
De 2694. Crinoline Days/Tell Me Little Gypsy
PAUL WHITEMAN'S FOUR MODERNAIRES(Acc. by the Swing Wing):
De 2844. Broom Dance/Piggy Wiggy Woo
De 2921. Hoiriger Schottische/Hot Gavotte
De 3038. Ragtime Cowboy Joe/Wham
De 3137. Rain/At the Story Book Ball
PAUL WHITEMAN AND HIS ORCHESTRA (Charlie Teagarden, Harry Goldfield, Cusamano,Alexy,trumpets; Miff Mole,Nat Lobovsky,Hal Matthews,trombones; Golladoro brothers,Franzella,Brown,Fargarson,Feldman,Capone,saxes; Joe Mooney,accordion;Signorelli,Ryerson,Pingitore,Bargy,Wettling;strings added for concert arrangements): Sept.,1939
De 29056-57. Concerto in F(Gershwin)
De 29058. Manhattan Serenade/Manhattan Moonlight
De 29059. Metropolitan Nocturne/Manhattan Masquerade
De 29060. Side Street in Gotham, 1 & 2
De 2075. All Ashore/My Reverie
De 2076. When I Go a Dreamin'/There's No Place Like Your Arms
De 2083. While a Cigarette Was Burning(64676)/Heart and Soul(64678)
De 2505. The June Bugs Dance(65575)/The Shoemaker's Holiday(65778)
De 2578. To You/Moon Love
De 2690. Say It With Music/Lady of the Evening
De 2691. All Alone/Remember
De 2692. Easter Parade/Say It Isn't So
De 2693. How Deep Is the Ocean/Russian Lullaby
De 2695. Alexander's Ragtime Band/Nobody Knows
De 2912. All the Things You Are/All in Fun
De 2913. Heaven in My Arms/That Lucky Fellow
De 2937. My Fantasy/Darn That Dream
De 2938. Gaucho Serenade/Creaking Old Mill by the Creek
PAUL WHITEMAN AND HIS ORCHESTRA (Pickup group):
Cap 101. I Found a New Baby/The General Jumped at Dawn
Cap 116. Trav'lin' Light(Featuring Billie Holiday)/You Were Never Lovelier
Cap 108. Serenade in Blue/I've Got a Gal in Kalamazoo
Cap 137. The Old Music Master(featuring Jack Teagarden)
(Gus Mueller,clarinet: Buster Johnson,trombone: Tommy Gott,trumpet: Mike Pingitore,banjo: Ferde Grofe,piano; Hal MacDonald,drums: Hank Stern,tuba): Hollywood,Feb.19,1945
Cap 10026. Wang Wang Blues(572-1B)
(Paul Geil,Tommy Gott,Nate Kazebier,trumpets· Allan Thompson,Elmer Smithers,trombones; Alvin Weisfeld,Harold Schaer,Irving Greenwald, Joe Rushton,Herbie Haymer,saxes; Matty Malneck,violin: Grofe,piano; Perry Botkin,guitar· Mike Pingitore,banjo; Art Shapiro,bass; MacDonald):
Cap 10026. San(571-2A)
PAUL WHITEMAN AND HIS ORCHESTRA:
Vi 27801. Well-Digger's Breakdown/A Zoot Suit(vocal by Wingie Manone and (Dolly Mitchell)
PAUL WHITEMAN AND HIS ORCHESTRA (with choral group and Earl Wild, piano soloist):
Sig GP-1. A Rhapsody in Blue, 1, 2, 3 & 4
WHITEWAY JAZZ BAND:
Para 20014. Tiger Rag/Blues My Naughty Sweetie Gave to Me
WHITMAN, ESSIE (vocals, acc. by the Jazz Masters):
BS 2036. Sweet Daddy It's You I Love(P-155)/If You Don't Believe I Love (You(P-156)

WHOOPEE MAKERS

See also:
BAYSTATE BROADCASTERS: VD 81843.
JIMMY BRACKEN: All.
BROADWAY BROADCASTERS.
CAROLINERS.
LOU CONNOR: Or 1483.
COTTON PICKERS: Ca 9049, 9207: Ro 997.

DIXIE DAISIES.
DIXIE JAZZ BAND: Or 1515, 1536, 1537, 1624, 1668, 1690.
BUDDY FIELDS: ?
GOODY AND HIS GOODTIMERS: All.
GRANT-WILSON: Ca 9015.
KENTUCKY GRASSHOPPERS: All.
LUMBERJACKS: Ca 9030.
JIMMY McHUGH: TEN BLACK DIAMONDS.
MILLS MERRY MAKERS.   TEN FRESHMEN.
NEW ORLEANS RAMBLERS: Me 12133, 12230.   UNIVERSITY BOYS: Or 1668.
JACK PETTIS.   VARSITY EIGHT: Ca 9098, 9174.
ROUNDERS: Re 8831.   TED WHITE: Or 1544.
TEN BLACK BERRIES: Ro 839, 976, 1453.

WHOOPEE MAKERS (Duke Ellington's Orchestra: Bubber Miley,trumpet;:Joe Nanton,trombone; Otto Hardwick,Rudy Jackson,Harry Carney,saxes; Duke Ellington, piano; Fred Guy,banjo; Wellman Braud,bass: Sonny Greer,drums):   1927
(See also: Washingtonians)
  Pe 14962. East St.Louis Toodle-oo(2944)/Jubilee Stomp(2945)
  Pe 14968. Take It Easy(2946)/(SEVEN LITTLE POLAR BEARS)

    (Add Louis Metcalf,Arthur Whetsel,trumpets: sub.Barney Bigard,clarinet,
    for Jackson; Johnny Hodges,alto, for Hardwick):
  Pat 36899. The Mooche(108446)/Move Over(108448)
  Pat 36915. Hot and Bothered(108447)/(BROADWAY BROADCASTERS)

    (Sub. Freddie Jenkins,trumpet, for Metcalf: add Juan Tizol,trombone):
  Pat 36923. Hottentot(108537)/Misty Mornin'(108533)   -Pe 15104
  Pat 37059. Doin' the Voom Voom(4063)/Flamin' Youth(4063)
                                    -Pe 15240,Re 8874,Do 4428,Ba 6548, Cq 7428
  Pe 15418. Rockin' Chair(10357)/Them There Eyes(10356)   -Ro 1556

    (Jimmy McPartland,cornet; Jack Teagarden,trombone; Benny Goodman,clarinet; Gil Rodin,alto; Bud Freeman,tenor; Vic Breidis,piano; Dick Morgan,banjo; Harry Goodman,bass; Ray Bauduc,drums):
  Pat 36944. Futuristic Rhythm(108565)
  Pat 36945. St.Louis Blues*/Bugle Call Rag(108515)*   -Pe 15126
  Pat 36974. Wipin' the Pan/I Used to Love Her
  Pat 37042. Dirty Dog(3766)/Sorority Stomp(108648)*   -Pe 15223
  Pat 37013. Tiger Rag(3698)/Some of These Days(3903)   -Pe 15194
  Pe 15217. Twelfth Street Rag(108931)*/It's So Good(108930)*
  Pe 15431. Sweet and Hot
  Ca 9004. Diga Diga Doo(108486)/'Cause I'm in Love

    (Unknown personnel):
  Pe 15376. Humpty Dumpty
  Pe 15507. Slow But Sure
  Co 14367. Sister Kate(147057)/Somebody Stole My Gal(147058)

    (Jimmy McPartland,cornet; Benny Goodman,clarinet, and others):
  Vo 15763. Dardanella/(RHYTHM MAKERS)
  Vo 15768. I've Never Been Loved By Anyone Like You/(WOLVERINES)
  Vo 15769. Rush Inn Blues/Freshman Hop

WHYTE'S CHOCOLATE BEAU BRUMMELS, ZACK (Otis Williams,Orlando Randolph,trumpets; Walter Williams,trombone; Chick Gordon,Joe Goff,altos; Chuck Wallace, Jimmy Cole,tenors; Bob Benson,piano; Harry Walker,Cat Glenn,guitars; Bud Washington,drums; Jack Johnson,bass.--DB 9/1/45):
  Ge 6781. Mandy/Hum All Your Troubles Away
  Ge 6798. It's Tight Like That/West End Blues
    (See also: Chuck Nelson, Smoke Jackson, Eddie Walker)

WIGGINS, JAMES 'BOODLE IT' (vocal with piano):
  Para 12662. Keep a Knockin' an' You Can't Get In(20378)/Evil Woman Blues
                                            (20379)-Bwy 5086
  Para 12860. Frisco Bound/44 Blues

WILBER'S WILD CATS, BOB (Johnny Glasel,cornet: Bob Wilber,clarinet: Dick Wellstood,piano; Charlie Traeger,bass: Denny Strong,drums):   1947
  Com 583. Willie the Weeper/Mabel's Dream
  Com 584. Blues for Fowler/Wild Cat Rag

WILDER OCTET, ALEC (Mitchell Miller,oboe,Jimmy Carroll,clarinet; Toots Mondello,bass clarinet; Eddy Powell,flute; Harold Goltzer,basson; Walter Groos, harpsichord; Frank Carroll,bass; Gary Gillis,drums):   1938-39
  Br 8294. A Debutante's Dairy(B-23861)/Neurotic Goldfish(B-23864)-CO 36319
  Br 8307. Concerning Etchings(B-23862)/Little Girl Grows Up(B-23863)-Co 36126
  Br 8410. Sea Fugue Mama(B-24749)/Japanese Sandman(WB-24752)   -Co 36323
  Co 35648. The Children Met the Train/Seldom the Sun
  Co 35988. Blue Room/Sweet Sue
  Co 36186. His First Long Pants/Her Old Man Was Suspicious
  Co 36187. Pieces of Eight*/Bull Fiddles in a China Shop
  Co 36188. Please Do Not Disturb/The House Detective Registers
  Co 36189. Kindergarten Flower Pageant/Dance Man Buys a Farm

WILEY, ARNOLD (piano solos):
  Br 7113. Arnold Wiley Rag/Windy City

WILEY, LEE (vocals, acc. by Max Kaminsky,trumpet: Bud Freeman,tenor; Joe
Bushkin,piano; Artie Shapiro,bass: George Wettling,drums):   1940
  Rabson 1. Here in My Arms/Baby's Awake Now
  Rabson 2. I've Got Five Dollars/Glad to Be Unhappy
  Rabson 3. You Took Advantage of Me/A Little Birdie Told Me So
  Rabson 4. As Though You Were There/Ship Without a Sail

    (Add Eddie Condon,guitar: and others, including Pee Wee Russell on
  some sides):
  Liberty 281. How Long Has This Been Going on/My One and Only
  Liberty 282. I've Got a Crush on You/Someone to Watch Over Me(Fats Waller,
  Liberty 283. 'S Wonderful/Sam and Delilah   (organ)
  Liberty 284. But Not for Me/Sweet and Low Down

    (Bunny Berigan,trumpet: Sid Weiss,bass; Joe Bushkin,piano; George
  Wettling,drums, featured on some of the following):
  Liberty 294. You Do Something to Me/Looking at You
  Liberty 295. Why Shouldn't I/Easy to Love
  Liberty 296. Find Me a Primitive Man/Let's Fly Away
  Liberty 297. Let's Do It/Hot House Rose

    (Acc. by Muggsy Spanier,cornet: Jess Stacy,piano):
  Com 1507. Down to Steamboat Tennessee/Sugar

    (Acc. by Orchestra):
  De 132. Motherless Child/Careless Love
  De 322. Hands Across the Table/I'll Follow My Secret Heart
  De 15034. I've Got You Under My Skin/What Is Love?

    (Acc. by Eddie Condon's Orchestra):
  De 23393. Wherever There's Love
  De 23432. The Man I Love/Someone to Watch Over Me

    (Acc. by Jess Stacy's Orchestra):
  Maj 7258. Sugar/Woman Alone with the Blues
  Maj 7259. But Not for Me/Memories

WILKINS, ROBERT (vocals with guitar):
  Br 7125. Falling Down Blues/That's No Way to Get Along
  Br 7158. Get Away Blues/I'll Go With Her Blues
  Br 7168. Nashville Stonewall Blues/Police Sergeant Blues
  Vi 23379. I Do Blues/Jailhouse Blues

WILLIAMS' COTTON CLUB ORCHESTRA:
  Vi 24083. Red Blues/Anything for You

WILLIAMS' STOMPERS:
  Vo 1453. Sumpin' Slow/(MEMPHIS STOMPERS)

WILLIAMS' WASHBOARD BAND:
  BB 5204. Kelsey's/Hard Corn

WILLIAMS, BESSIE (Viola McCoy: vocals, acc. by Fletcher Henderson, piano
or Charlie Dixon*, guitar):
  Do 362. How Come You Do Me Like You Do(5509)*/Mae Harris Blues
  Do 363. You Don't Know My Mind(5483)/Buzzin' Around(5484)*

WILLIAMS AND HIS GANG, BILL:
  Ch 15215. Make Me Know It

CLARENCE WILLIAMS

See Also:
  LIL ARMSTRONG: Co 14678.
  ANNA BELL: QRS 7008, 7009.
  HELEN BAXTER: OK 8080.
  ESTHER BIGEOU: OK 8029, 8056, 8057, 8058, 8065, 8125.
  BLUE GRASS FOOTWARMERS: Ha 206, 248.
  LAURA BRYANT: QRS 7055.
  BUTTERBEANS AND SUSIE:
  DORA CARR: OK 8130, 8250, 8306, 8284.
  BUDDY CHRISTIAN: OK 8311, 8332, 8342; Pe 118.
  ROSETTA CRAWFORD: OK 8096.
  DAVENPORT AND CARR: OK 8244.
  DIXIE WASHBOARD BAND.
  SUSIE EDWARDS: OK 8182.
  HORACE GEORGE: OK 8164.

IRENE GIBBONS: Co 3834, 3922, 1436?.
FANNIE GOOSBY: OK 8095.
GREAT DAY NEW ORLEANS SINGERS: OK 8755.
LUCILLE HEGAMIN: Co 14164.
KATHERINE HENDERSON: QRS 7032, 7041.
ALBERTA HUNTER: OK 8365.
WILLIE JACKSON: Co 14165.
J.P. JOHNSON: Co 14502.
KI KI JOHNSON: QRS 7001, 7003.
MARGARET JOHNSON: OK 8107, 8162, 8185, 8193, 8220, 8230, 8506.
JOE JORDAN: Co 14144, Co 3791.
VIRGINIA LISTON: All OK.
LAWRENCE LOMAX.
DAISY MARTIN: OK 8027
SARA MARTIN.
THOMAS MORRIS.
PINEWOOD TOM:
IRENE SCRUGGS: OK 8142.
SEVEN GALLON JUG BAND: Co 2087.
BESSIE SMITH.
LAURA SMITH: OK 8157, 8186, 8169, 8179, 8331.
MAMIE SMITH: OK 4935.
VICTORIA SPIVEY: OK 8615.
EVA TAYLOR:
EFFIE TYUS.
SIPPIE WALLACE.
ETHEL WATERS: Co 14380, 14365, 14411.

WILLIAMS, CLARENCE (vocals, acc. by orchestra):   1922
 OK 8020. If You Don't Believe I Love You(S-70210-C)/Pullman Porter Bl(S-70240-B)
 OK 8021. Roumaina Blues/(BROWN AND TERRY)
 OK 8029. The Dance They Call the Georgia Hunch/(ESTHER BIGEOU)

    (Piano solos):   1923
 OK 4893. Mixing the Blues/The Weary Blues
 OK 40172. My Own Blues(S-72706)/Gravier Street Blues(S-72707)   1924
 Co 14241. Shootin' the Pistol(vocal)/When I March in April(with vocal)   1927
 OK 8604. Organ Grinder Blues(400844)/Wildflower Rag(400845)   1928

    (Vocal with piano):   1930
 OK 8806. You Rascal You(404219-B)/Michigan Water Blues(404220-B)
 Vi 38524. A Pane in the Glass/Too Low

    (Vocal acc. by James P. Johnson,piano):
 Co 14341. My Woman Done Me Wrong(146761)/Farm Hand Papa(146762)

    (Clarence Williams, Lonnie Johnson, Spencer Williams,vocals, with piano;
    guitar, kazoo):
 OK 8762. Monkey and the Baboon(403597)/Wipe It Off(403598)   -Vo 03013
 OK 8775. She Don't Know Who She Wants(403672)/The Dirty Dozen(403749)

WILLIAMS' BLUE FIVE, CLARENCE (Thomas Morris,cornet; Charlie Irvis,trombone; Sid-
ney Bechet,soprano or clarinet; Clarence Williams,piano: Buddy Christian, banjo
or guitar.--Elliott Goldman: Clarence Williams Discography):   1923
 OK 4925. Wild Cat Blues(S-71706-B)/Kansas City Man(S-71707-B)
 OK 4966. Achin' Hearted Blues(S-71797-A)/'Taint Nobody's Bus'ness(S-71928B)
 OK 4975. New Orleans Hop Scop Blues(S-71929-B)/(KING OLIVER)

    (Vocals by Eva Taylor*):
 OK 3055. Farewell Blues*(S-71500-F)   - OK 7055
  "   Gulf Coast Blues(S-71499-A*)

    (Sub. Louis Armstrong, cornet):   1924
 OK 8171. Texas Moaner Blues(S-72914-B)/House Rent Bl(earlier date with Thomas
                                                                (Morris.S-72059-B)
 OK 8181. Everybody Loves My Baby(S-72959-B; Aaron Thompson,trombone)*
  "   Of All the Wrongs You've Done to Me(72958-B:*Aaron Thompson,trombone)
 OK 40260. Mandy,Make Up Your Mind(S-73026-B*;sarrousaphone by Bechet)-Co 35957
  "   I'm a Little Blackbird(S-73027-B*)
 OK 40321. Cake Walkin' Babies(S-73083-A*)/(CHAUNCEY LEE)   1925
 OK 8215. Papa De-Da-Da(S-73205-A*)plus Buster Bailey,soprano/(ORIGINAL TUXEDO
                                                                 (JAZZ ORCHESTRA)
    (Add Buster Bailey,clarinet):
 OK 8245. Coal Cart Blues(73694-B*, Charlie Green,trombone)   -HRS 6
  "   Santa Claus Blues(73695-B*)
 OK 8272. Just Wait Til You See My Baby(73686-B*)/Livin' High(73687-B*)
 OK 8254. Squeeze Me(73738-A*)/Santa Claus Bl(73721-A*Williams,Armstrong,Chris-
                                                                           (tian)
    (Ed Allen,trumpet; Boyd Atkins,saxophone; Bechet,clarinet; Clarence Will-
    iams,piano; Buddy Christian,banjo):
 OK 8267. Shake That Thing(73837-B*)/Get It Fixed(73838-B*)

(Sub. tuba for banjo):
OK 8286. I've Found a New Baby(73957-A*)/Pile of Logs and Stones(73959-B*)

CLARENCE WILLIAMS STOMPERS (Trumpet, trombone: two saxes; piano; banjo; tuba):
1926
OK 40541. Spanish Shawl(73893)/Dinan(73894)
OK 40598. Jackass Blues(74090-B)/What's the Matter Now(74091-B)

CLARENCE WILLIAMS' WASHBOARD FOUR (Ed Allen,trumpet: Buster Bailey,clarinet and alto; Clarence Williams: piano and vocal: Washboard Jackson, washboard):
1927
OK 8440. Nobody But/Candy Lips   -PaE 3445, PaE 2531
OK 8525. Yama Yama Blues(81864-B)/Church Street Sobbin' Blues(81865-C)

CLARENCE WILLIAMS BLUE SEVEN (Ed Allen, trumpet: Bert Socarras,clarinet; Arville Harris,soprano; Ed Cuffee,trombone: Clarence Williams,piano: Cyrus St.Clair,tuba: Floyd Casey,drums):
OK 8443. Senegalese Stomp(74443)/Wouldja(74444)
OK 8510. Baby Won't You Please Come Home(81472-A)/Close Fit Blues(81473-A)

CLARENCE WILLIAMS' WASHBOARD FIVE (Allen; Williams: Socarras; St.Clair; Willie Williams, washboard):
OK 8462. Cushion Foot Stomp(80688-F)   -PaE 3383
"   Take Your Black Bottom Outside(80689-F)   -PaE 3381

CLARENCE WILLIAMS' BLUE FIVE (King Oliver,trumpet: Bert Socarras, Cecil Scott,clarinets: Charlie Irvis,trombone; Williams: St. Clair; Casey):
OK 8465. Black Snake Blues(80728-B)/Old Folks Shuffle(80729-B)

CLARENCE WILLIAMS AND HIS NOVELTY FOUR (Oliver;Williams; Lonnie Johnson, violin and guitar: Eddie Lang,guitar; drums: Hoagy Carmichael,vocals):
OK 8645. In the Bottle Blues(401390-B)/What Ya Want Me to Do(401391-A)
(See also BLIND WILLIE DUNN)

CLARENCE WILLIAMS WASHBOARD BAND (Ed Allen: Williams; Ben Waters,clarinet; St. Clair):
Mar.8,1927
Vo 1088. Cushion Foot Stomp(E21786-7)/P.D.Q. Blues(E21788-9)   -Br 7000

CLARENCE WILLIAMS BLUE FIVE (Allen· Cecil Scott,clarinet and tenor; Charlie Irvis,trombone; Williams; Casey: Katherine Henderson,voc.):**Apr.27,1927**
Br 7017. Take Your Black Bottom Outside(E4857-8-9)   -Br 3664
"   Baltimore(E4860-1-2)   -BrE 3703, Vo 1130

CLARENCE WILLIAMS' ORCHESTRA (Featuring June Clark,trumpet: Irvis,trombone; Williams, piano):
Br 3580. Zulu Wail/Slow River   -BrE 3667

CLARENCE WILLIAMS' JAZZ KINGS (Bert Socarras, Ben Waters,clarinets: Williams; Christian; St. Clair):
Co 14193. Gravier Street Blues(143348)/Candy Lips(143349)

(Ed Allen, Ed Anderson,trumpets: Irvis,trombone; Ben Whittet,Cecil Scott,Ben Waters, saxes and clarinets: Williams; Christian; St.Clair; George Stafford,drums):
1927-31
Co 14244. I'm Going Back to Bottomland(144546)/You'Ll Long for Me(144547)
Co 14287. Dreaming the Hours Away(145521)/Close Fit Blues(145521)
Co 14314. Sweet Emmalina(145992)/Any Time(145993)
Co 14326. Red River Blues(146365)/I Need You(146366)
Co 14348. The Keyboard Express(146825)/Walk That Broad(146826)
Co 1735. If You Like Me Like I Like You(147726)/Have You Ever Felt That Way
Co 14422. Breeze(148104)/Mountain City Blues(148105)   (147928)
Co 14434. Our Cottage of Love(148638)/Them Things Got Me(148639)
Co 14447. Whoop It Up(148744)/I'm Not Worrying(148745)
Co 14460. A Pane in the Glass(148940)/Freeze Out(148941)
Co 14468. Nervous Breakdown(149056)/Railroad Rhythm(149057)
Co 14488. Zonky(149665)/You Gotta Be Modernistic(149666)
Co 14555. High Society Blues(150659)/Lazy Levee Loungers(150660)
Co 14666. Baby Won't You Please Come Home/Papa De-Da-Da

CLARENCE WILLIAMS AND HIS ORCHESTRA (King Oliver,trumpet: Ben Waters,clarinet and tenor; Charlie Irvis,trombone; Clarence Williams,piano; Buddy Christian,banjo; Cyrus St.Clair,tuba):
1928
QRS 7001. Lone Grave/Look What a Hole I'm in(Ki Ki Johnson,vocals)
QRS 7003. Wrong Woman Blues/Lady Your..
QRS 7004. Long Deep & Wide(151)/Speakeasy(152-A)   -Para 12884, Bwy 1347
QRS 7005. Squeeze Me(153)/New Down Home Blues(154-A)   -Bwy 1348
QRS 7008-09. (See ANNA BELL)

(Sub. Ed Anderson,trumpet· add Ben Whittet,alto):
QRS 7032. (See KATHERINE HENDERSON)
QRS 7033. Wildflower Rag(267)/Midnight Stomp(268)   -Para 12839
QRS 7034. Bozo(270)/Bimbo(271)
QRS 7040. I'm Through(269)/Longshoreman Blues(272)
QRS 7041. (See KATHERINE HENDERSON)

92

```
         (Sub. King Oliver, trumpet; omit Whittet):
QRS  7042. (See SARA MARTIN)
QRS  7043. Mean Tight Mama(305: Sara Martin,voc.)/Kitchen Man Bl(307;Sara Mar-
QRS  7044. Beau Koo Jack(308)/Sister Kate(309)                       (tin,voc)
         (Unknown personnel):
QRS  7035. Don't Turn Your Back on Me/Hole in the Wall(Sara Martin,vocals)
QRS  7055. Smoke House Blues/Haunting Blues (Laura Bryant,vocals)
         (Acc. Katherine Henderson,vocal):
Bwy  5034. West End Blues(235-2)/St.Louis Blues(236-A)
         (Edith Johnson,vocals; Williams,piano):
QRS  7048. You Ain't No Good Blues(311)/You Know That Ain't Right(312)
         CLARENCE WILLIAMS AND HIS ORCHESTRA (Possibly including Jabbo Smith,.
Para 12587. Shake 'Em Up(2887-2)/Jingles(2888-2)                     (trumpet):
Para 12870. Saturday Night Jug/A Pane in the Glass
         CLARENCE WILLIAMS' JUG BAND(Cecil Scott,clarinet; Putney Dandridge,piano;
         Clarence Williams,vocals and jug: Cyrus St.Clari,tuba):
Co   2087. Wipe 'em Off(149690)                                      -PaE 2339
 "         What If I Do(149691)
         (Sub. Herman Chittison,piano; Ikey Robinson,banjo,for St.Clair):
Co   2806. Shim Sham Shimmy(152463)                                  -PaE 1680
 "         High Society(152464)
Co   2829. Chizzlin' Sam(152465)/(DICKY WELLS SHIM SHAMMERS)         -PaE 1680
Co   2863. Organ Grinder Blues(152464)/You Ain't Too Old(152468)
         CLARENCE WILLIAMS' WASHBOARD FIVE (Unknown):                1928
OK   8572. Sweet Emmaline(400620)/Log Cabin Blues(400621)
OK   8584. Shake It Down(400702)/Red River Blues(400703)
OK   8629. Walk That Broad(401152)/Have You Ever Felt That Way(401153)
         CLARENCE WILLIAMS' ORCHESTRA:
OK   8592. Lazy Mama(400818)/Mountain City Blues(400819)
OK   8617. Organ Grinder Blues(401131)/I'm Busy and You Can't Come In(401132)
         (Featuring Eddie Lang,guitar):
OK   8663. Watching the Clock(401466)/Freeze Out(401467)
         CLARENCE WILLIAMS' WASHBOARD BAND:
OK   8672. Mississippi Blues(401611)/Steamboat Days(401612)
         (Ed Allen,trumpet; Ben Whittet,clarinet and alto; Clarence Williams,
         piano; Willie Williams,washboard):                          1929
OK   8706. High Society(402489)                                      -PaE 2243
 "         Whoop It Up(402490)
         (Sub. Cecil Scott for Whittet):
OK   8738. You Gotta Give Me Some(403045)                            -PaE 2147
 "         I've Got What It Takes(403046)                            -PaE 2243
OK   8752. You Don't Understand(403280)                              -PaE 2147
 "         What Makes Me Love You So(403281)
         (Allen; Charlie Irvis,trombone: Scott; Williams; St.Clair;washboard play-
                                                                           (ers):
OK   8763. Left All Alone With the Blues(403630)                     -PaE 2225
 "         I've Found a New Baby(403631)
         (Ed Allen, Louis Metcalf,trumpets: Scott; Williams: Willie Williams,wbd.):
OK   8790. Whip Me With Plenty of Love(403972)/Worn Out Bl(403973)   -PaE 2203
         CLARENCE WILLIAMS NOVELTY BAND (Scott: Williams; Chittison; Robinson):
OK   8798. He Wouldn't Stop Doing It(404034)/You're Bound to Look Like a Mon-
                                                      (key When You Get Old(404035)
         (Personnel unknown):
OK   8821. Where the Old Man River Flows(404382)/Shout Sister Shout(404383)
OK   8826. Sitting on Top of the World(404435)/Kansas City Man Blues(404436)
OK   8842. Papa De Da-Da(404547)/Hot lovin'(404548)
         CLARENCE WILLIAMS' WASHBOARD BAND:
Vi  38063. Lazy Mamma/In Our Cottage of Love
Vi  38630. Touchdown/I'm Not Worryin'
Vi  24039. Charlie Two-Step/Sleep Come On and Take Me
         CLARENCE WILLIAMS AND HIS ORCHESTRA (Ed Anderson or June Clark,trumpet;
         Harry White,trombone; Clarence Williams,piano; Cyrus St.Clair,tuba):1931
Pe  15387. Papa De-Da-Da(110200)/Baby Won't You Please Come Home(110201)
Pe  15403. Hot Lovin'(110199)/Shout Sister Shout(110276)   (-Ro 1505, Re 10199
         (Unknown personnel):
Do   3755. Boodle Um Bum(6551)/I've Found a New Baby(6552)
         CLARENCE WILLIAMS AND HIS ORCHESTRA (Ed Allen,trumpet: Cecil Scott,clar-
         inet: Clarence Williams,piano; Floyd Casey,washboard):      1933
```

Vo 25009. Black-eyed Susan Brown(13544-1)/Mama Stayed Out All Night Long
Vo 25010. High Society(13546-1)/I Like to Go Back(13547-1)   (13545-1)

    (Clarence Williams,vocal: sub. Willie Smith,piano):
Vo 2541. Beer Garden Blues(13835-1)
"   Breeze(13838-1)   -Co 37680
Co 37680. Beer Garden Blues(13835-2)
Vo 2563. You've Got the Right Key/She's Got a Little Bit Left
Vo 2584. Dispossessin' Me(13837)/Chocolate Avenue(13938: Williams,piano)

    (Sub. Williams,piano; add Jimmy McLin,guitar: Cyrus St.Clair,tuba; Chick Bullock,vocals):
Vo 2602. For Sale:Harlem Rhythm Dance
Vo 2616. Swaller-Tail Coat(14422-1)/Looka-There Ain't She Pretty(14423-2)
Vo 2629. Jimmy Had a Nickel(14611-1;voc.,Dick Robertson)/He's a Colonel from
                                                             (Kentucky(14612-1)
Vo 2736. Old Street Sweeper(14573-2)/After Tonight(13936-1; no McLin,St.Clair)
Vo 2654. New Orleans Hop Scop Blues/I Got Horses
Vo 2674. Ill Wind(14991)/As Long As I Live(14992)
Vo 2676. Mister Will You Serenade/St.Louis Blues
Vo 2689. I Can't Dance(14989)/Christmas Night in Harlem(14990)

    (Personnel unknown):   1944
Vo 2718. Pretty Baby/Won't You Come Over
Vo 2759. I'm Gonna Wash Your Sins Away/Let's Have a Showdown
Vo 2778. Bimbo/Way Down Home
Vo 2788. I Can Beat You/Trouble

    (Ed Allen,trumpet; Cecil Scott,clarinet; James P.Johnson,piano; Floyd Casey,washboard; Clarence Williams, Eva Taylor,vocals):
Vo 2854. Chizzlin' Sam/Jerry the Junker

    (Sub. Williams,piano: add Dick Fullbright,bass):
Vo 2838. Big Fat Mamma/Sashay Oh Baby
Vo 2805. Ain't Gonna Give Nobody None of My Jelly Roll(15602)
"   Sugar Blues(15847; add Pete Brown, alto)

    (Add Pete Brown,alto; Bullock vocals):
Vo 2871. Tain't Nobody's Business(15845)
"   Organ Grinder Blues(15399; from session above with Jas.P.Johnson)
Vo 2889. I'm Getting My Bonus in Love/Tell Her the Truth
Vo 2909. Jungle Crawl(15848)/Savin' Up for Baby(16840)
Vo 2899. I Saw Stars/Rhapsody in Love   1935
Vo 2927. Milk Cow Blues   -Me 13328
"   There's Gonna Be the Devil to Pay
Vo 2938. Black Gal   -Me 13328
"   Foolish Little Girl
Vo 2958. I Can See You All Over the Place/I Can't Think of Anything

    (Allen; Scott; Williams; St.Clair; Casey):
Vo 2991. Yama Yama Blues(17602)/Lady Luck Blues(17604)
Vo 3195. This Is My Sunday Off(17601)/Let Every Day Be Mother's Day(17603)

    CLARENCE WILLIAMS TRIO(Williams,organ; Don Baker,piano; Cozy Cole,drums; Connie Berry vocals):
BrG 81761. Bluer Than Blue(22978)/I'm Falling for You(22979)

    (Personnel unknown):
BB 6918. Top of the Town/More Than That
BB 6919. Turn Off the Moon(06851)   -RZ 2539
"   Jammin'(06853)
BB 6932. Cryin' Mood(06852)   -RZ 2539
"   Wanted(06854)
BB 11368. Thriller Blues/Uncle Sam, Here I Am

COOTIE WILLIAMS

See Also:
BARNEY BIGARD: Vr 515, 525.
DUKE ELLINGTON.
LEONARD FEATHER: Com 547, 548.
BENNY GOODMAN: Co 35820, 35863, 35869, 35937--
GOODMAN SEXTET: Co 35810 - 36755.
GOTHAM STOMPERS: Vr 541, 629.
SONNY GREER: Co 1868.
LIONEL HAMPTON: Vi 25575, 2560k, 25771.
HARLEM FOOTWARMERS & HARLEM MUSIC MASTERS.
JOHNNY HODGES: All Vocalion.
LONNIE JOHNSON: OK 8638.
JUNGLE BAND: Br 4492 --
METRONOME ALL STAR: Vi 27314, Co 36499.
ROSS DE LUXE SYNCOPATORS.
JOE TURNER: Co 1813, 36157.
TEDDY WILSON: Br 7867, 7877.

WILLIAMS AND HIS RUG CUTTERS, COOTIE (Cootie Williams,trumpet; Joe Nanton,trombone; Johnny Hidges,alto and soprano; Harry Carney,baritone; Duke Ellington,piano; Fred Guy,guitar; Hayes Alvis, bass; Sonny Greer,drums): March 8,1937
- Vr 527. Downtown Uproar(M-186)/Blue Reverie(M-188) -Vo 3814
- Vr 555. Digga Digga Do(M-187)/I Can't Believe That You're in Love With Me (M-185)-Vo 3818

(Sub.Juan Tizol,trombone; Billy Taylor,bass; add Barney Bigard,clarinet; Otto Hardwick,alto; omit Hodges, Guy): Oct.26,1937
- Vo 3890. Watching(M-670)/I Can't Give You Anything But Love(M-672)
- Vo 3922. Jubilesta(M-669)/Pigeons and Peppers(M-671)

(Sub. Lawrence Brown,trombone; add Hodges; omit Bigard): 1938
- Vo 3960. Lost in Meditation(M-726)/Echoes of Harlem(M-729)

(Add Bigard, tenor):
- Vo 4061. Swingtime in Honolulu(M-802)/Carnival in Caroline(M-803)
- Vo 4086. A Lesson in C(M-801)/Ol' Man River(M-804)
- Vo 4324. Blues in the Evening(M-877)/Sharpie(M-878)
- Vo 4425. Chasin' Chippies(M-876)/Swing Pan Alley(M-879)
- Vo 4574. Delta Mood(M-954)/The Boys from Harlem(M-955)
- Vo 4636. Mobile Blues(M-956)/Gal-Avantin'(M-957)

(Omit Bigard): 1939
- Vo 4726. Boudoir Benny(M-983)/Ain't the Gravy Good(M-984)
- Vo 4958. Night Song(WM-1042)/Black Beauty(WM-1045)
- Vo 5411. Beautiful Romance(M-982)/She's Gone(M-985)

(Add Bigard,tenor; sub. Jimmy Blanton,bass; omit Hardwick): 1940
- Vo 5618. Blues a Poppin'(WM-1043)/Black Butterfly(WM-1143)
- OK 5690. Dry Long So(WM-1144)/Give It Up(WM-1146)
- OK 6336. Top and Bottom(WM-1044)/Toasted Pickle(WM-1145)

COOTIE WILLIAMS AND HIS ORCHESTRA (Williams,trumpet; Lou McGarity,trombone; Artie Bernstein,bass,and others from Benny Goodman Orchestra):
- OK 6224. Ain't Misbehavin'(30424)/Blues in My Condition(30425)
- OK 6370. West End Blues(30423)/G-Men(30426)

(Cootie Williams,Emmett Berry,George Treadwell,Harold Johnson,trumpets; Ed Burke,George Stevenson,R.H.Horton,trombones: Eddie Vinson,Charlie Holmes,altos; Ed Davis,Lee Pope,tenors; Ed di Verneuil,baritone; Earl Powell,piano; Sylvester Payne,drums; Norman Keenan,bass): Jan.4-6,1944
- Hit 7084. Things Ain't What They Used to Be/Cherry Red Blues
- Hit 7075. Tess' Torch Song/Now I Know
- Hit 7108. Is You Is or Is You Ain't/Blue Garden Blues
- Hit 7119. 'Round Midnight/Somebody's Got to Go

COOTIE WILLIAMS SEXTET (Cootie Williams,trumpet; Eddie Vinson,alto; Ed Davis,tenor: Earl Powell,piano: Sylvester Payne,drums: Norman Keenan,bass):
- Hit 8087. My Old Flame/Echoes of Harlem(orchestra)
- Hit 8088. Honeysuckle Rose/Sweet Lorraine
- Hit 8089. Floogie Boo/Talk a Little Trash
- Hit 8090. Got to Do Some War Work/I Don't Know

COOTIE WILLIAMS AND HIS ORCHESTRA:
- Cap 215. House of Joy(678-2A)/Everything But You(681-1A)
- Cap 237. Juice Head Baby(664)/Salt Lake City Bounce(665)
- Cap 266. When My Baby Left Me(680)/Echoes of Harlem(909)
- Cap 289. Wrong Neighborhood(965)/Let's Do the Whole Thing or Nothing At All (969)
- Cap 314. Ain't Got No Blues Today(990)/I May Be Easy(967)
- Maj 1136. I Want to Be Loved(T-1128)/I Can't Get Started(T-1126)
- Maj 1150. Inflation Blues(T-1127)/Sound Track(T-1129)

WILLIAMS, DOUGLAS (clarinet solos, with piano, drums):
- Vi 21269. Slow Death(41813)/Roadhouse Stomp(41814)
- Vi 21695. Late Hours/Kind Daddy
- Vi 38031. Riverside Stomp/Friendless Blues
- Vi 38518. Neal's Blues/Buddy George

DOUGLAS WILLIAMS AND HIS ORCHESTRA:
- Vi 23264. Darktown Jubilee/The Beale Street Sheik
- Vi 23337. Clarinet Jiggles
- Vi 23362. Memphis Gal/Sister Ella
- Vi 38623. Three o'clock/Louisiana Hop

WILLIAMS, ELSIE (blues singing):
- De 7399. Bring It Back/You Got Something There

WILLIAMS AND HIS ROYAL FLUSH ORCHESTRA, FESS (Leroy Rutledge,John Brown,Oscar Clark,trumpets; David James,trombone; Jerome Pasqual,Craig Watson,altos; Perry Smith,tenor; Lloyd Phillips,piano; Bill Johnson,banjo and guitar; Olin Aderhold, bass; Ralph Bedell,drums.--In addition to this personnel (from RR), Bob Shoffner and Jabbo Smith,trumpets, have been mentioned as taking part in some of the records. Fess Williams, besides being the vocalist and leader, played saxes and clarinet):

```
       Ge  3336. Ya Gotta Know How/It's Breaking My Heart
       Vo  1054. Messin' Around/Heebie Jeebies                    -Br 3351*
                 *Issued as Bud Jackson Swanee Serenaders
       Vo  1058. Atlanta Black Bottom/High Fever
       Vo  1085. My Pretty Girl/White Ghost Shivers
       Vo  1117  Ozark Blues/Alligator Crawl
       Br  3596. Number Ten/Razor Edge
       Br  3632. Phantom Blues                                    -OrE1011
            "    Variety Stomp
       Ha   189. Make Me Know It/My Mamma's in Town
       Vi 23003. Just to Be With You Tonight/Everything's O.K. With Me
       Vi 23005. Ida/Dinah
       Vi 23025. All for Grits and Gravy                          -HMV 4840
            "    She's Still Dizzy                                -HMV 4839
       Vi 38056. Friction                                         -HMV   18
            "    Here 'Tis
       Vi 38062. Sell It/Betsy Brown
       Vi 38064. A Few Riffs
            "    Do Shuffle                                       -HMV   18
       Vi 38077. Hot Town                                         -BB  6431
            "    Kentucky Blues
       Vi 38085. Ain't Misbehavin'/Sweet Savannah Sue
       Vi 38095. Musical Camp Meeting/Buttons
       Vi 38106. Slide Mr. Jelly Slide/Going to Getcha
       Vi 38126. Big Shot/Snag Nasty
       Vi 38131. 'Leven Thirty Saturday Night/I'm Feelin' Devilish
       Vi 24153. Playing My Saxophone                             -HMV 4944
            "    You Can't Go Wrong                               -HMV 4991

WILLIAMS, GEORGE and Bessie Brown (vocals):
       Co  3974. Satisfied Blues/Double Crossin' Daddy

           (Acc. Fletcher Henderson, piano):
       Co 13006. Papa Don't Mean Your Mamma No Good(81348)/If Mamma Quits Papa What
                                                          (Will Papa Do(81342)
           GEORGE WILLIAMS (vocals):
       Co 14002. Gal Ain't Born/Woman Gets Tired of One Man
       Co 14030. Hard Hearted Gal/I'm Tired of Begging
       Co 14049. Chain Gang Blues/(CLARA SMITH)

               GEORGE WILLIAMS AND BESSIE BROWN (vocals, acc. by Alex Brown, piano):
       Co 14011. It Takes a Brownskin/You Ain't quittin Me Without Two Weeks Notice
       Co 14017. You Need Some(F.Henderson,piano)/He's Never..
       Co 14015. I'm Goin'(Fletcher Henderson,piano)/I Won't Stand

           (Cornet & piano acc.):
       Co 14033. No Second Handed Lovin' for Mine(81847)/If You Hit My Dog I'll Kick
       Co 14046. When you Go Huntin/I Can Do What you do(trombone) (Your Cat(81848)
       Co 14135. Hit Me/You Can't Proposition Me

WILLIAMS AND HIS ORCHESTRA, HOD:
       BB  7104. The Big Apple/Shades of Hades
       BB  7106. Lady from Fifth Avenue/Night Over Shanghai
       BB  7108. Little Fraternity Pin/My secret Love Affair

WILLIAMS, JABO (piano solos):
     Para 13127. Kokomo Blues, 1 & 2
     Para 13130. Fat Mama Blues/Polock Blues
     Para 13141. Jab Blues                                        -JI 3
            "    Pratt City Blues

WILLIAMS, JOE (blues singing, with guitar, haromínca):
       BB  8969. Break 'em on Down/Please Don't Go
       BB  9025. Highway 49/Some Day Baby

WILLIAMS' SYNCO JAZZERS, JOHN:
     Para 12457. Down in the Gallion/Goose Grease
       BP  8009. Cut Loose/Pee Wee Blues

               WILLIAMS STOMPERS AND MEMPHIS STOMPERS:
       Vo  1453. Sumpin' Slow/Lotta Sax Appeal
       Me 12210. Just One More Chance/That's the Time

WILLIAMS AND HIS BOYS, DRUMMER MAN JOHNNY:
       Vr   594. Little Old Lady/Where's My Sweetie Hiding
       Vr   638. Build a Stairway to Paradise/(MOREHOUSE)
       Vo  5213. Clarinet Marmalade(W-24954-A)/Memory Lane(W-24952-A)

WILLIAMS AND HER DIXIE BAND, LEONA:
       Co  3599. Achin' Hearted Blues(80239)/Struttin' Blues(80240)
       Co  3565. Cruel Daddy Blues/Decatur Street
       Co  3642. Got to Cool My Doggies/Makes No Difference
```

```
Co  3696. Sugar Blues(80517)/The Meanest Man in the World(80518)
Co  3713. Sister Kate/If You Don't Think I Love You
Co  3815. I'm Going Away/Bring It With You
Co  3885. Teasin' Squeezin' Man/If Your Man Is Like My Man
```

WILLIAMS, LEROY (cornet solos, acc. by piano):
```
Co 14500. Welcome Stranger(149533)/Lullaby Baby(149532)
```

   TE ROY WILLIAMS AND HIS DALLAS BAND
```
Co 14402. Tampa Shout/Going Away Blues
```

   TE ROY WILLIAMS AND HIS ORCHESTRA:
```
Ha    439. Oh Malinda(144214)/Lindbergh Hop(144215)              -Ve 1439
```

WILLIAMS, MARY LOU (piano solos):   Dec.,1930
```
Br   7178. Night Life(C-5724-C)/Drag 'em(C-5725-D)               -Br 80033
```

   (With celeste; bass; guitar; drums):
```
De    781. Mary's Special(61023-A)/
           Overhand(60878-A)                                     -De 3385
De   1021. Corny Rhythm/Isabelle
De   1155. Clean Pickin'/Swingin' for Joy
```

   (Acc. drums and bass):
```
De   2796. The Rocks(64665-A)/The Pearls(64662-A)
De   2797. Sweet Patunia(64664-A)/Mr. Freddie Blues(64663-A)
Co  37334. Little Joe from Chicago(CO-25470; piano solos)         Oct.12,1939
```

   MARY LOU WILLIAMS AND HER KANSAS CITY SEVEN (Harold Baker,trumpet; Theodore Donnelly,trombone; Dick Wilson,sax: Ed Inge,clarinet; Mary Lou Williams,piano; Booker T. Collins,bass; Ben Thigpen,drums):
```
De  18122. Baby Dear(68365-A)/Harmony Blues(68366-AA)
```

   MARY LOU WILLIAMS TRIO(Bill Coleman,trumpet; Mary Lou Williams,piano; Al
   Hall,bass):
```
Asch 3511. Blue Skies(7111)/Russian Lullaby(710)
Asch 3512. Night and Day(711)/Persian Rug(712)
Asch 3513. I Found a New Baby(715)/You Know Baby(714)
```

   MARY LOU WILLIAMS AND HER CHOSEN FIVE (Frank Newton,trumpet; Edmond Hall,
   clarinet; Vic Dickenson,trombone: Mary Lou Williams,piano; Al Lucas,bass;
   Jack Parker,drums):
```
Asch 1002. Little Joe(652)/Drag 'em(solo: 661)
Asch 1003. Roll 'em(652)/Mary's Boogie(660: solo)
Asch 1004. Lullaby of the Leaves(651)/St.Louis Blues(662: solo)
Asch  502. Satchel Mouth Baby/(JERRY JEROME)
```

   (Dick Vance,trumpet; Vic Dickenson,trombone: Claude Greene,clarinet; Don
   Byas,tenor; Mary Lou Williams,piano; Jack Parker,drums; Al Lucas,bass):
```
Asch 1005. Stardust, 1 & 2
Asch 1006. Gjon Mili Jam Session/Man o' Mine
```

   (Bill Coleman,trumpet: Coleman Hawkins,tenor; Mary Lou Williams; Parker;
   Lucas):
```
Asch 1007. Lady Be Good/Carcinoma(Coleman;Williams:Al Hall)
```

   (Add Joe Evans,alto; Claude Greene,clarinet; sub. Eddie Robinson,bass;
   Denzil Best,drums):
```
Asch 1008. Song in My Soul(1300)/This and That(1301)
```

   MARY LOU WILLIAMS(piano) & JOSH WHITE(vocals) with Bill Coleman,trumpet;
   Eddie Doughery,drums; Jimmy Butts,bass):
```
Asch 2001. Froggy Bottom(784)/The Minute Man(780)
```

   MARY LOU WILLIAMS TRIO (Williams,Parker,Lucas):
```
Asch A-620. Aries; Taurus the Bull; Leo the Lion: Virgo; Cancer: Gemini.
Asch A-621. Libra; Scorpio; Saggittarius- Capricornus; Aquarius: Pisces
```

   MARY LOU WILLIAMS (piano solos):
```
Disc 5025. How High the Moon/Cloudy
Disc 5026. Blue Skies/The Man I Love
Disc 5027. These Foolish Things/Lonely Moments
```

   MARY LOU WILLIAMS TRIO (Williams,piano; June Rotenberg,bass; Bridget O'
   Flynn,drums):
```
Vi 202025. Humoresque/Waltz Boogie
Vi 202174. It Must Be True/Harmony Grits
```

WILLIAMS AND HER JAZZ JESTERS, MIDGE:
```
Vr   519. In Shade of Old Apple Tree(M-132)/Walkin' the Dog(M-134)  -Vo 3812
Vr   670. The One Rose/An Old Flame Never Dies
Vo  3821. Let's Begin Again/Sentimental Over You
```

WILLIAMS, RUBBERLEGS (vocals, with Herbie Fields, alto):
```
Sav  564. That's the Stuff You Gotta Watch/Pointless Mama Blues
```

WILLIAMS AND HIS THREE NATURALS, SAMMY (Johnny McGhee,trumpet; Billy Kyle,piano;
Cozy Cole,drums; Sammy Williams,electric organ):
   Vo 4197. I'm Gonna Lock My Heart/All Alone
   Vo 4229. Some Sunny Day/Now It Can Be Told
   Vo 4243. My Feeling Stick

WILLIAMS' BIG EIGHT, SANDY (Joe Thomas,trumpet; Sandy Williams,trombone; Harry
Carney,baritone; Johnny Hodges,alto; Jimmy Jones,piano; Brick Fleagle,guitar; Sid
Weiss,bass; Shelly Manne,drums):
   HRS 1007. Chili Con Carney/Mountain Air
   HRS 1008. After Hours on Dream Street/Sumpin' Jumpin' Round Here

WILLIAMS, SIDNEY (piano solos):   1928
   Ge 6353. Mississippi Shivers/Barbecue Blues(Watson's Pullman Porters)

WILLIAMS, SONNY BOY (vocals with piano):
   De 8513. I Want a Little Girl/One Little Date With You
   De 8532. Poppin'/You're the One for Me
      SONNY BOY WILLIAMS AND HIS ORCHESTRA:
   De 8643. Honey It Must Be Love/Savoy Is Jumpin'
   De 8651. Reverse the Charges/Rubber Bounce

WILLIAMS, TRIXIE (vocals with piano):
   Ge 6090. Moanful Mama/Blue and All By Myself(Violet Jackson)

WILLIAMSON, SONNY BOY (vocals and harmonica, with various accompaniments, sometimes including Walter Davis,piano):
   BB 7059. Good Morning School Girl/Sugar Mama Blues
   BB 7302. Early in the Morning/Project Highway
   BB 7352. Suzanna Blues/Black Gal Blues
   BB 7404. Worried Me Blues/Frigidaire Blues
   BB 7428. Up the Country Blues/Collector Man Blues
   BB 7500. Sunny Land/My Little Cornelius
   BB 7536. I'm Tired Truckin' My Blues Away/You Can Lead Me
   BB 7576. Miss Louisa Blues/Until My Love Comes Down
   BB 7603. Moonshine/Beauty Parlor
   BB 7665. Decoration Blues/Down South
   BB 7707. Honey Bee Blues/Whiskey Headed Blues
   BB 7756. You Give An Account/You've Been Foolin' Around Downtown
   BB 7805. My Baby I've Been Your Slave/Deep Down in the Ground
   BB 7847. Lord Oh Lord Blues/Shannon Street Blues
   BB 7995. Susie-Q/Goodbye Red
   BB 8010. Little Girl Blues/Number Five Blues
   BB 8034. The Right Kind of Life/Insurance Man Blues
   BB 8094. Rainy Day Blues/Christmas Morning Blues
   BB 8237. Sugar Mama Blues/Good for Nothing Blues
   BB 8265. Bad Luck Blues/My Little Baby
   BB 8307. Doggin' My Love Around/Little Low Woman Blues
   BB 8333. Good Gravy/T.B. Blues
   BB 8357. Something Going on Wrong/Good Gal Blues
   BB 8383. I'm Not Pleasing You/New Jailhouse Blues
   BB 8403. Joe Louis and John Henry Blues/Thinking My Blues Away
   BB 8439. Lifetime Blues/Miss Ida Lee
   BB 8474. Tell Me Baby/Honey Bee Blues
   BB 8580. I Been Dealing With the Devil/War Time Blues
   BB 8610. Welfare Store Blues/Train Fare Blues
   BB 8674. Jivin't the Blues/My Little Machine
   BB 8866. I'm Gonna Catch You Soon/Million Years Blues
   BB 8914. She Was a Dreamer/Shady Grove Blues
   BB 8955. Drink on Little Girl/Springtime Blues
   BB 8992. My Black Name Blues/I Have Got to Go
   BB 9031. Broken Heart Blues/Ground Hog Blues
   BB 340701. Black Panther Blues/She Don't Love Me That Way
   BB 340736. Desperado Woman Blues/Miss Stella Brown
   BB 340744. Elevator Woman/Sonny Boy's Jump
   Vi 201875. You're an Old Lady/Early in the Morning
   Vi 202056. Shake the Boogie/Mean Old Highway
   Vi 202184. Hoodoo Hoodoo/Sonny Boy's Cold Chills
   Vi 202369. Mellow Chick Swing/G.M. and O. Blues

WILLIAMSON BEALE STREET FROLIC ORCHESTRA:
   Vi 20555. Memphis Scrontch/Bear Wallow
   Vi 21410. Scandinavian Stomp(37959)/Midnight Frolic Rag(37960)

WILSON'S T.O.B.A. BAND:
   Para 12408. Steady Roll/Backyard Blues

WILSON, CHICKEN, and Skeeter Hinton (guitar, washboard):
   QRS 7051. D.C. Rag/Myrtle Avenue Stomp

WILSON AND HIS TEN BLACK BERRIES, DUKE (Jack Teagarden,trombone; Benny Goodman,
clarinet; others unknown): 1932
  Ba 32463. Beale Street Blues -Pe 15617, Ro 1858
  "   Put on Your Old Grey Bonnet(11/40; by different group, probably
                                                  (Mills Blue Rhythm Band)
    (Probably Mills Blue Rhythm Band):
  Pe 15603. Oh Monah/How'm I Doin'
  Pe 15632. Bull Fiddle Blues/Got the South in My Soul

    (Fletcher Henderson Orchestra?):
  Ba 32733. Red Devil(E-36668)/The House of David Blues(E-36926)   -Pe 15753

WILSON, EDITH (vocals, acc. by Johnny Dunn's Original Jazz hounds, q.v.):
  Co 3479. Nervous Blues/Vampin' Liza Jane
  Co 3506. Old Time Blues(79993)/Frankie(80014)
  Co 3537. West Texas Blues/I Don't Want Nobody
  Co 3558. Birmingham Blues(80151)/Wicked Blues(80150)
  Co 3634. Take It 'Cause It's All Yours(80357)/Mammy I'm Thinking of You(80356)
  Co 3653. Rules and Regulations(80383)/He May Be Your Man(80382)
  Co 3674. Lonesome Mama Blues(80449)/What Do You Care(80450)
  Co 3746. Pensacola Blues(80555)/Evil Blues(80554)
  Co 3787. Dixie Blues(80683)/He Used to Be Your Man(80684)
    EDITH WILSON AND HER JAZZ BAND:
  Co 14008. Daddy Cange Your Mind(81478)/I Don't Know and I Don't Care(81479)

    EDITH WILSON (acc. by Alabama Joe, guitar):
  Co 14027. Muscle Shoals Blues/How Come You Do Me Like You Do
  Co 14054. Double Crossin' Papa/He's a Mean Mean Man

    (Acc. unknown):
  Br 4685. My Man Is Good for Nothing/Black and Blue

WILSON, GARLAND (piano solos): 1931
  OK 41556. Rockin' Chair   -PaE 1194
    "   Memories of You   -PaE 1862
                                           (Paris, 1933-34)
  BrF 500220. Blues in B Flat/Get Up Bessie   -BrE 1476
  BrF 500358. Mood Indigo/China Boy   -BrE01692
  BrF 500359. You Rascal You/The Way I Feel   -BrE01784
  BrE 02283. Shim Sham Drag/Your Heart and Mine   London
  BrE 03115. Just a Mood/Just One of Those Things
  Sw   19. The Blues Got Me/Bei Mir Bist du Schoen   Paris,1938
  Sw   46. Blue Morning(celeste)/The Blues I Love to Play
  Sw   61. Sweet Lorraine/You Showed Me the Way

WILSON AND HIS ORCHESTRA, GERALD:
  Ex 122. Moon Rise/Synthetic Joe
  Ex 124. Top of the Hill/Puerto Rican Breakdown
  Ex 126. Just Give Me a Man/Just One of Those Things
  Ex 149. Yenta/Come Sunday
  Ex 150. Love Me a Long Long Time/I Don't Know What That Is
  Ex 160. You Better Change Your Way of Lovin'/Skip the Gutter
  Ex 161. Ain't It a Drag/I'll String Along With You
  BW 777. Cruisin' With Cab/Pammy
  BW 778. One o'clock Jump(224)/Warm Mood(225)

WILSON, LENA (acc. by Perry Bradford's Jazz Phools):
  Para 12029. Deceitful Blues(1362)/I Don't Let No One Man Worry Me(1363)
  BS 14129. The Wicked Fives/You've Got Everything

    (Acc. by Conaway's Rag Pickers):
  Br 2590. Four-Flushin' Papa/Hula Blues
  Br 2464. Bleedin' Hearted Blues/Chirpin' the Blues

    (Acc. by Fletcher Henderson, piano):
  Si 3009. Your Time Now/I Need You to Drive My Blues Away

    (Acc. by Porter Grainger, piano):
  Vi 19085. Triflin' Blues/'Tain't Nobody's Biz-ness If I Do

    (Acc. by the Nubian Five):
  Pe 12044. Memphis Tennessee/He Used to Be Your Man

    (Unknown acc.):
  Vo 14651. Michigan Water Blues/Afternoon Blues
  Co 3915. Deceitful Blues/Memphis Tennessee
  Co 14618. My Man o' War/What's Your Price

WILSON, LEOLA B. (vocal with Blind Blake, guitar):
  Para 12392. Dying Blues(2655)/Ashley Street Blues(2656)
    (Acc. unknown):
  Co 14669. I Can't Get Enough
  Co 14675. Dirty Spoon Blues/Jive Lover

WILSON, SOCKS (vocals. See also: GRANT AND WILSON):
   Co 14541. You Rascal You/Dem Socks Dat My Pappy Wore

WILSON AND HIS ORCHESTRA, TED (Unknown; not Teddy Wilson):
   Vo 2896. Goin' Shoppin'/My Heart Is an Open Book
   Vo 2897. I Was Lucky/A Little White Gardenia
   Vo 2747. I Wish I Were Twins/Practice What You Preach
   Vo 2924. Clouds/If the Moon Turns Green

TEDDY WILSON

See also:
   HENRY ALLEN: Vo 3244, 3245.
   LOUIS ARMSTRONG: Vi 24232, 24233, 24245, 24257, 24351, 24369; BB 5363.
   MILDRED BAILEY: Vo 3056,3057,3067,3078,3431,3482; PaE 2201, 2257.
   WILLIE BRYANT: Vi.
   BENNY CARTER: CoE 698,720; Vo 2870, 2898.
   CHOCOLATE DANDIES: PaE 1717, 1743, 1792, 1815.
   BUCK CLAYTON: Me 1201, 1202.
   PUTNEY DANDRIDGE: Vo 3006 - 3269; 3399, 3409.
   BENNY GOODMAN: Co 2923, 2927; Co 35937 - 36284.
   BENNY GOODMAN TRIO: QUARTET; QUINTET: All.
   BENNY GOODMAN SEXTET: Co 36781.
   EDMOND HALL: BN 30, 31; Com 557.
   COLEMAN HAWKINS: Key 609, 610, 611, 612.
   BILLIE HOLIDAY: Vo 3431, 3440, 3520, 3543, 3748.
   BOB HOWARD.
   EDDY HOWARD: Co 35771, 35915.
   TAFT JORDAN: Pe 16094, 16102.
   MEZZ MEZZROW: Br 6778, 7551.
   RED NORVO: Co 2977, 3026, 3059, 3079; Key 1310,1314,1319; Comet 6, 7.
   BUCK RAM: Sav 572.
   CHARLIE SHAVERS: Key 619.

WILSON, TEDDY (piano solos):   1933
   Br 7543. Every Now and Then/It Never Dawned on Me   -BrE 02110
   Br 7563. Liza   -VoE 85
   "   Rosetta   -BrE 02160
   Br 7572. I Found a Dream/On Treasure Island   -BrE 02113
   Br 7599. I Feel Like a Feather in the Breeze/Breakin' in a New Pair of Shoes
   Br 8025. Don't Blame Me/Between the Devil and the Deep Blue Sea   Co 36274
   Co 36631. Smoke Gets in Your Eyes/Them There Eyes   1943
   Co 36632. These Foolish Things/Rosetta
   Co 36633. I Can't Get Started/I Know That You Know
   Co 36634. China Boy(CCO-3688)/Body and Soul(CCO-3694)
   Mu   369. Cheek to Cheek(5461)/You're My Favorite Memory(5478)   1946
   Mu   370. Strange Interlude(5464)/Hallelujah(5477)
   Mu   371. Why Shouldn't I(5463)/Sunny Morning(5462)
   Mu   372. All of Me(5476)/Long Ago and Far Away(5480)

WILSON AND HIS ORCHESTRA, TEDDY (Roy Eldridge,trumpet; Benny Goodman,clarinet;
Ben Webster,tenor; Teddy Wilson,piano; John Trueheart,guitar; John Kirby,bass;
Cozy Cole,drums; Billie Holiday,vocals):   July 2,1935
   Br 7498. What a Little Moonlight Can Do(B-17767)   -BrE 02066, Co 36206
   "   A Sunbonnet Blue(B-17769)   -   "   "
   Br 7501. I Wished on the Moon(B-17766)   -BrE 02063, Co 36205
   "   Miss Brown to You(B-17768)   -Br 8087, "   "

   (Sub. Cecil Scott,clarinet; Lawrence Lucie,guitar; add Hilton Jefferson):
   Br 7511. What a Night What a Moon, What a Girl(B-17913)   -BrE 02071
   "   It's Too Hot for Words(B-17915)
   Br 7520. I'm Painting the Town Red(B-17914)   -BrE 02072
   "   Sweet Lorraine(B-17916)   -Br 8087,   "

   (Roy Eldridge,trumpet; Benny Morton,trombone; Chu Berry,tenor; Teddy Wil-
   son,piano; Dave Barbour,guitar; Kirby; Cole; Holiday):   Oct.25,1935
   Br 7550. Yankee Doodle Never Went to Town(B-18197)   -BrE 02118
   "   Twenty-four Hours a Day(B18196)
   Br 7554. If You Were Mine(B18209)   -BrE 02160, Co 36206
   "   Eeny Meeny Miney Mo   -BrE 02141

   (Richard Clark,trumpet; Johnny Hodges,alto; Tom Macey,clarinet; Wilson,
   piano; Barbour,guitar; Grachan Moncur,bass; Cole; Holiday):
   Br 7577. These 'n' That 'n' Those(B-18316)   -VoE 23
   "   Sugar Plum(B-18317)
   Br 7581. You Let Me Down(B-18318)   -BrE 02141
   "   Spreadin' Rhythm Around(B-18319)

   (Gordon Griffin,trumpet; Theodore McRae,tenor; Rudy Powell,clarinet; Wilson; Trueheart; Cole; Moncur; Holiday):
   Br 7612. Rhythm in My Nursery Rhymes(B-18613)/Life Begins When You're in Love
                                                                    (B-18612)

(Frank Newton,trumpet; Benny Morton,trombone; McRae,tenor; Jerry Blake, clarinet,alto; Wilson; Trueheart; Stan Fields,bass; Cole; Ella Fitzgerald,vocals): March 17,1936
Br 7640. Christopher Columbus(B-18829)
" All My Life(B-18832) -Br 8116

(Roy Eldridge,trumpet; Buster Bailey,clarinet; Chu Berry,tenor; Wilson, piano; Bob Lessey,guitar; Israel Crosby,bass; Sidney Catlett,drums):
Br 7673. Mary Had a Little Lamb(C-1376)
" Too Good to Be True(C-1377) -VoE 23
Br 7684. Warmin' Up(C-1378) -PaE 2871, Co 36314, BrE 02256
" Blues in C Shar Minor(C-1379) " " "

(Jonah Jones,trumpet; Johnny Hodges,alto; Harry Carney,baritone and clarinet; Wilson; Lawrence Lucie,guitar; Kirby; Cole; Holiday): June 30,1936
Br 7699. These Foolish Things/Why Do I Lie About You
Br 7702. Guess Who
" It's Like Reaching for the Moon -VoE 33
Br 7729. I Cried for You -Co 35862, PaE 2823, VoE 33
" Melancholy Baby(18830; from 3/17 session) " , PaE 2868, VoE 76

(Gordon Griffin,trumpet; Benny Goodman,clarinet; Vido Musso,tenor; Wilson piano; Lionel Hampton,vibes; Allan Reuss,guitar; Harry Goodman,bass; Gene Krupa, drums):
Br 7736. You Turned the Tables on Me/Sing Baby Sing -VoE 35
Br 7739. You Came to My Rescue/Here's Love in Your Eyes -VoE 41

(Irving Randolph,trumpet; Vido Musso,clarinet; Ben Webster,tenor; Wilson: Reuss; Krupa; Milton Hinton,bass; Holiday):
Br 7762. Easy to Love(B-20105)/The Way You Took Tonight(B-20107)
Br 7768. With Thee I Swing/Who Loves You -VoE 53

(Jonah Jones,trumpet; Benny Goodman,clarinet; Ben Webster,tenor; Wilson; Reuss; Kirby; Cole; Holiday):
Br 7781. Sailin'/I Can't Give You Anything But Love -VoE 52
Br 7789. Pennies from Heaven/That's Life I Guess -VoE 49

(Irving Randolph,trumpet; Vido Musso,clarinet; Ben Webster,tenor; Wilson; Reuss; Kirby; Cole; Midge Williams,vocals):
Br 7797. Right or Wrong(B-20410)/Where the Lazy River Goes By(B-20411)
Br 7816. Tea for Two/I'll See You in My Dreams -VoE 73

(Buck Clayton,trumpet; Benny Goodman,clarinet; Lester Young,tenor;Wilson; Freddy Green,guitar; Walter Page,bass; Jo Jones,drums; Holiday,vocals):
Jan.25,1937
Br 7824. This Year's Kisses/He Ain't Got Rhythm -VoE 101
Br 7859. Why Way I Born -Co 36283, VoE 71
" I Must Have That Man(B-20571) -Co 36207, "

(Henry Allen,trumpet; Cecil Scott,clarinet,alto; Prince Robinson,tenor; Wilson,piano; James McLin,guitar; Kirby; Cole; Holiday):
Br 7840. My Last Affair
" You Showed Me the Way -VoE 76
Br 7844. The Mood That I'm In -VoE 89
" Sentimental and Melancholy

(Cootie Williams,trumpet; Johnny Hodges,alto; Harry Carney,baritone,clarinet; Wilson; Reuss; Kirby; Cole; Holiday):
Br 7867. Carelessly -VoE 89
" How Could You
Br 7877. Moanin' Low/Fine and Dandy -VoE 92

(Harry James,trumpet; Buster Bailey,clarinet; Johnny Hodges,alto; Wilson; Reuss; Kirby; Cole; Helen Ward,vocals):
Br 7884. It's Swell of You/There's a Lull in My Life -VoE 96
Br 7893. How Am I to Know/I'm Coming Virginia

(Buck Clayton,trumpet; Hodges; Young; Wilson; Reuss; Artie Bernstein, bass; Cole; Holiday): May,1937
Br 7903. Mean to Me(B-21120) -PaE 2868, VoE 107, Co 35926
" I'll Get By(B-21119) " " "
Br 7917. Sun Showers/Yours and Mine

(Clayton; Buster Bailey,clarinet; Young; Wilson; Holiday; Fred Green,guitar; Bernstein; Jo Jones): June 1,1937
Br 7911. Foolin' Myself(B-21217) -Co 36207
" Easy Living(B-21218) -Co 36208
Br 7926. I'll Never Be the Same/I Found a New Baby

(Harry James,trumpet; Benny Goodman,clarinet; Vido Musso,tenor; Wilson; Reuss; Harry Goodman,bass; Gene Krupa,drums):
Br 7940. Remember Me/You're My Desire
Br 7943. The Hour of Parting/Coquette

TEDDY WILSON QUARTET (Harry James,trumpet: Teddy Wilson,piano; Red Norvo, xylophone; John Simmons,bass):
Br 7964. Ain't Misbehavin'(LA-1408-C)/Honeysuckle Rose(LA-1431-A)
Br 7973. Just a Mood, 1 & 2   -PaE 2741

TEDDY WILSON AND HIS ORCHESTRA (Harry James,trumpet Archie Rosate,clarinet; Vido Musso,tenor; Wilson; Reuss; Simmons; Cole):
Br 7954. The Big Apple/You Can't Stop Me From Dreaming
Br 7960. If I Had You/You Brought a New Kind of Love to Me

(Buck Clayton,trumpet: Vido Musso,clarinet: Prince Robinson,tenor: Wilson; Reuss; Page; Krupa):
Br 8008. My Man/Can't Help Lovin' Dat Man   -Co 36113
Br 8015. Nice Work If You Can Get It/Things Are Looking Up   -VoE 128

(Clayton; Benny Morton,trombone; Lester Young,tenor; Wilson; Green; Page; Jones):
Br 8053. My First Impression of You/If Dreams Come True

(Clayton; Bailey; Young; Wilson; Green; Bernstein; Jones):
Br 8070. When You're Smiling/I Can't Believe You're in Love With Me-Co 36335
Co 36208. When You're Smiling(B-22194; second master)

(Bobby Hackett,trumpet; Pee Wee Russell,clarinet; Tab Smith,alto; Eugene Sedric,tenor; Wilson: Reuss: Al Hall,bass; Bloomer,drums; Nan Wynn,voc.):
                                                               March,1938
Br 8112. Moments Like This(22611)
 "   I Can't Face the Music(22612)   -PaE 2553
Br 8116. Don't Be That Way(B-22613)   -Co 36335, PaE 2553
 "   (reissue of Br 7640; All My Life)

(Featuring Hackett):
Br 8141. I'll Dream Tonight/You Go to My Head
Br 8150. If I Were You(B-22822)   -PaE 2569
 "   Jungle Love(B-22825)

(Jonah Jones,trumpet: Benny Carter,alto; Ben Webster,tenor: Wilson; Kirby; Cole; Wynn):
Br 8199. Now It Can Be Told(B-23305/A-Tisket A-Tasket(B-23308)   -PaE 2582
Br 8207. Laugh and Call It Love/On the Bumpy Road to Love   -PaE 2608

(Harry James,trumpet; Benny Morton,trombone: Edgar Sampson,Benny Carter, altos: Herschel Evans,Lester Young,tenors; Wilson; Al Casey,guitar; Walter Page,bass: Jo Jones,drums; Billie Holiday,vocals):
Br 8259. Everybody's Laughing(B-23642)/Here It Is Tomorrow Again(B-23643)
Br 8265. Arril in My Heart(B-23688)/I'll Never Fail You(B-23689)
Br 8270. Say It With a Kiss(B-23687)/They Say(B23690)

(Bobby Hackett,trumpet; James Young,trombone: Toots Mondello,Ted Buckner, Bud Freeman,Chu Berry,saxes; Wilson; Casey; Hinton: Cole; Holiday):
Br 8281. You're Gonna See a Lot of Me(B-23761)/Hello My Darling(B-23762)
Br 8283. Let's Dream in the Moonlight/You're So Desirable

(Roy Eldridge,trumpet; Ernie Powell,clarinet; Benny Carter,alto: Wilson; Barbour; Hinton; Cole; Holiday):
Br 8314. What Shall I Say(B-24044)/It's Easy to Blame the Weather(B-24045)
Br 8319. More Than You Know(B-24046)/Sugar(B-24047)   -Co 36117, PaE 2660

(Karl George,Adolphus Cheatham,Harold Baker,trumpets; Jake Wiley, Floyd Brady,trombones; Pete Clark,alto; Rudy Powell,alto,clarinet; Ben Webster, George Irish,tenors: Wilson; Casey; Hall; J.C.Heard,drums):   1939
Br 8438. Jumpin' for Joy(WB-24824)/The Man I Love(WB-24826)
Br 8455. Love Grows on the White Oak Tree(WB-24931)/This Is the Moment(WB24932)
Co 35220. Booly-Ja-Ja/Exactly Like You   -PaE 2726
Co 35207. Early Session Hop(WB-24933)/Lady of Mystery(WB-24934) -PaE 2732
Co 35711. Sweet Lorraine(CO-25736)/Liza(CO-25738)
Co 35232. Jumpin' on the Blacks and Whites(WCO-26058)
         The Little Things in Life Mean So Much(26059)
Co 35298. Hallelujah(WCO-26060)/Some Other Spring(WCO-26061)
Co 35354. Moon Ray/Wham

(Add Buster Harding, second piano):
Co 35372. In the Mood(WCO-2643%)/Crying My Soul Out for You(WCO-26435)
Co 35737. Cocoanut Grove(WCO-26437)/71(WCO-26438)

(Bill Coleman,trumpet: Benny Morton,trombone; Jimmy Hamilton,clarinet & sax; George James,baritone: Teddy Wilson,piano; Al Hall,bass; Eddie Gibbs, guitar; Yank Porter,drums):   Sept.,1940
Co 35905. Embraceable You(CO-29234)/I Never Knew(CO-29233)
Co 36084. Oh Lady Be Good(CO-29236)/But Not for Me(CO-29235)   -PaE 2815

(Emmett Berry,trumpet; Hymie Shertzer,Jimmy Hamilton,Babe Russin,saxes; Wilson,piano; Gene Fields,guitar; Johnny Williams,bass; J.C.Heard,drums; Billie Holiday,vocl):   Feb.10,1942

102

```
Co 37493. Until the Real Thing Comes Along(32408)
   "    I Cover the Waterfront(31003-1; Al Casey guitar)      Aug.7,1941
```

TEDDY WILSON QUINTET (Charlie Shavers, trumpet: Teddy Wilson,piano; Red Norvo,vibraphone; Al Hall,bass; Specs Powell,drums):
- Mu 316. Just You Just Me
-    "   Just for You Blues(Morey Feld,drums· Billy Taylor,bass)
- Mu 317. Every Time We Say Goodbye/This Heart of Mine (Maxine Sullivan,vocs.)
- Mu 318. Bugle Call Rag(5238)/Memories of You(5241)
- Mu 319. I Surrender Dear(5240)/Runnin' Wild(5239)

TEDDY WILSON SEXTET (Buck Clayton,trumpet· Ben Webster,tenor; Teddy Wilson; Al Casey; Al Hall: J.C.Heard):   Aug.14,1945
- Mu 332. I Can't Get Started(5297)/Stompin' at the Savoy(5298)
- Mu 336. Blues Too(5299)/If Dreams Come True(5296)

TEDDY WILSON OCTET (Clayton· S.Browne,clarinet: Don Byas,tenor: George James,baritone; Wilson: Remo Palmieri,guitar; Taylor; Heard):Aug.19,1946
- Mu 421. I Want to Be Happy(5654)/Don't Worry 'Bout Me(5653:Sara Vaughan,voc)
- Mu 446. Moonlight on the Ganges/September Song(Sara Vaughan,voc.)

(Charlie Ventura,tenor?):
- Mu 462. Time After Time(Sara Vaughan,voc.)/Moon-Faced Starry Eyed

WINDING'S NEW JAZZ GROUP, KAI (Shorty Rogers,trumpet; Kai Winding,trombone; Stan Getz,tenor; Shorty Allen,piano; Shelly Manne,drums; Iggy Shevack,bass):
- Sav 590. Grab Your Axe Max(5868)/Always(5869)

KAI'S KRAZY KATS (Same):
- Sav 602. Sweet Miss(5866)/Loaded(5867)

WINDY CITY FOUR (Vocal, acc. by piano, washboard, whistle, jug):
- Vo 1738. Tiger Rag(C-548-3)/Oh Monah(C-549-2)   -Me 12699*
   *Issued under name of MAPLE CITY FOUR)

WINDY RHYTHM KINGS (Jimmy Cobb,cornet: Junie Cobb,clarinet: Ernie Smith, sax; unknown piano; Jimmy Bertrand,drums):
- Para 12770. South African Blues/Piggly Wiggly Blues   -Cent 3009

WINN AND HIS DALLAS DANDIES, JACK (Whoopee Makers group including Jimmy McPartland,cornet: Jack Teagarden,trombone; Benny Goodman,clarinet):
- Vo 15860. Loved One(F-32948-A)
-    "   St.Louis Blues(F-29947-A: by different band, unknown personnel)
- Me 12051. Loved One (second master)

(Original Memphis Five):
- Me 12008. Lovey Lee/How Come you Do Me Like You Do

(Reissue of Johnny Dodds' Black Bottom Stompers, Br 3567: Louis Armstrong, cornet: Honore Dutrey or Kid Ory,trombone; Johnny Dodds,clarinet; Earl Hines,piano: Bud Scott,banjo: Stomp Evans, sax; Baby Dodds,drums):
- Me 12064. Melancholy(E-22728)   Apr.22,1927

(Reissue of King Oliver, Vo 1059, q.v.)
-    "   Someday Sweetheart(E-3843-W)

WINSTON, EDNA (blues singer with orchestra):
- Vi 20424. Pail in My Hand/Mama's Donna Drop Your Curtain
- Vi 20857. Rent Man Blues/'Way After One and My Daddy Ain't Come Home Yet

WISCONSIN ROOF ORCHESTRA (Probably Bernie Young,Randolph,trumpets: Preston Jackson,trombone; Inge,Bailey, Mundy, saxes: Cassino Simpson,piano; Mike McKendrick,banjo; Walker,bass; Rice,drums.--JI 2/2/40):   1928
- Para 12562. Who's That Knocking at My Door(20118-2)/Deep River Blues(20119-2)

(Probably different group; see DEVINE'S WISCONSIN ROOF ORCHESTRA):
- Para 12686. Farewell Blues(20392-1)   -Bwy 1210
-    "   Memphis Blues(20393-A)

WITTWER TRIO, JOHNNY (Johnny Wittwer,piano; Joe Darensbourg,clarinet; Keith Purvis,drums):
- Exner 1. Wolverine Blues(3890)/Joe'sBlues(3889)
- Exner 2. Come Back Sweet Papa(3892)/Tiger Rag(3891)

JOHNNY WITTWER (piano solos):   1947
- JM 18. Ragged But Right/Aunt Hagar's Blues
- JM 19. Ace in the Hole/Two Kinds of People
- JM 20. Ragtime Nightingale/Bill Bailey

THE WOLVERINES

WOLVERINE ORCHESTRA (Bix Beiderbecke,cornet: Al Gande,trombone; Jimmy Hartwell,
clarinet; George Johnson,tenor: Dick Voynow,piano: Bob Gillette,banjo; Min Leibrook,bass; Vic Moore,drums):   Richmond,Indiana,March,1924
   Ge   5408. Fidgety Feet(11751-a)   -BrE 02204, HRS 22
   "   Jazz Me Blues(11754-a)   -BrE 02203,HRS 25

       (Omit trombone):   May 15,1924
   Ge   5453. Oh Baby(11852)   -Clax 40336*, BrE 02501, HRS 25
   "   Copenhagen(11853)   BrE 02205,UHCA 46
   Ge   5454. Riverboat Shuffle(11854-C) -Clax 40339*,   HRS 9
   "   Susie(11855-a)
  Ge 20062. I Need Some Pettin'(11930-B)   Sept.,1924
   "   Royal Garden Blues(11931-C)   -BrE 02204, HRS 26
  BrE 02205. Tiger Rag(11932)   -HRS 24

       (Add George Brunies,trombone):   New York,Oct.,1924
   Ge   5542. Sensation(9079)   -Clax 40375*, HRS 23
   "   Lazy Daddy(9080-A)   -HRS 9
   Ge   5542. Lazy Daddy(9080-B)   -Clax 40375*

       (Omit Brunies):   Nov.,1924
   Ge   5565. Tia Juana(9115-B)   -HRS 26
   "   Big Boy(9116; Beiderbecke, piano)   -BrE 02203, HRS 24
       *Claxtonola issues,above, issued under name of JAZZ HARMONIZERS)

       (Sub. Jimmy McPartland,cornet):   Feb.,1925
   Ge   5620. Prince of Wails(9231-A)/When My Sugar Walks Down the Street(9218-B)

       THE WOLVERINES (Unknown personnel):
   Br   3332. Crazy Quilt/You're Burnin' Me Up

       ORIGINAL WOLVERINES (Richard Voynow, director):
   Vo 15634. The New Twister/Shim-me-sha-wabble   -UHCA 102, Br 3707
   Vo 15635. A Good Man Is Hard to Find   -UHCA 100, Br 4000
   "   Royal Garden Blues   -UHCA 101,   "
   Vo 15705. Dear Old Southland   -UHCA 100
   "   Limehouse Blues   -UHCA 101
   Vo 15732. Sonny Boy/There's a Rainbow 'Round My Shoulder
   Vo 15751. Sweethearts on Parade/I'll Get By
   Vo 15766. I Faw Down an' Go Boom/If I Had You
   Vo 15768. I'll Never Ask for More/(WHOOPEE MAKERS)
   Vo 15784. He She and Me/(LOUISIANA RHYTHM KINGS)
   Vo 15795. Some Sweet Day/My Castle in Spain Is a Shack in the Lane

WOODING AND HIS ORCHESTRA, SAM (Bobby Martin, Maceo Edwards,Tommy Ladnier,trumpets;
Herbert Fleming,trombone; Garvin Bushell,clarinet,oboe,sax: Willie Lewis,alto;
Eugene Sedric,tenor; Samuel Wooding,piano: John Mitchell,banjo; John Warren, bass;
George Howe,drums.--JI 11/41):   Berlin,Germany,1924
   Vox 1883. Shanghai Shuffle/Oh Katherina
   Vox 1891. Alabamy Bound/By the Waters of the Minnetonka

       (Sub. Adolphus Cheatham,trumpet, for Ladnier?: Jerry Blake,alto,for Bushell;
       Freddie Johnson,piano):   Barcelona, Spain
  PaSp 25420. Carrie/Tiger Rag
  PaSp 25421. Sweet Black Blues/My Pal Called Sal
  PaSp 25424. Bull Foot Stomp/Indiana Love

       SAM WOODING AND HIS ORCHESTRA (Harry Cooper,Bobby Martin,trumpets; Albert
       Wynn,Billy Burns,trombones; Willie Lewis,Ralph James,altos: Eugene Sedric,
       tenor and clarinet; Freddy Johnson,piano: Ted Fields,drums; June Cole,bass;
       John Mitchell,guitar.--RC 8/46):   Paris,France,1927-28
  PatF 8684. Downcast Blues(300482)/Weary River(4300483)
  PatF 8696. Hallelujah(300481)/Button Up Your Overcoat(300538)
  PatF 8707. Breakaway(300539)/My Sin(300540)
  Poly 521596. Singin' in the Rain(2813)/I've Got a Feeling I'm Falling(2815)
  Poly 521597. How Am I to Know(2812)/Can!t We Be Friends(2814)
  BrF 500097. Love for Sale/I Have Two Loves
  BrF 500098. Even If You Love Me/I Surrender Dear

WOODS, OSCAR (blues singing):
   De   7219. Don't Sell It--Don't Give It Away/Lone Wolf Blues

WYLIE'S GOLDEN PHEASANT ORCHESTRA, AUSTIN:
   Vo 15098. Charleston Baby of Mine/I'm Gonna Charleston Back to Charleston

WYNN'S GUT BUCKET FIVE, ALBERT (Dolly Hutchinson,trumpet; Albert Wynn,trombone;
Barney Bigard,clarinet; Jimmy Flowers,piano; Arthur Bassett,banjo, and others,--
DB 1/1/40; JI 11/8/40):   1926

```
     OK   8350. When(9789-A; Lillie Delk Christian,voc.)/That Creole Band(9790-A)

          (Punch Miller,trumpet and vocal: Albert Wynn,trombone: Lester Boone,
          clarinet,alto,baritone; Alex Hill,piano; Charlie Jackson,guitar; un-
          known drums).--JR 10/43):                              Oct.,1928
     Vo 1218. Crying My Blues Away/(MIDNIGHT ROUNDERS)
     Vo 1220. Parkway Stomp(C-2424-C)/Down By the Levee(C-2381-C; William Barbee,
                                                                     (piano)
          (Sub. William Barbee, piano):
     Vo 1252. She's Crying for Me(C-2382-C)/(LIL HARDAWAY)
```

Y

YANCEY, ALONZO (piano solos):   Chicago,April,1944
  Se 10003. Ecstatic Rag/Hobo Rag
  Se 10015. Everybody's Rag/12th Street Rag

YANCEY, JIMMY (piano solos):   Chicago,May,1939
  SA 12008. The Fives/Jimmy's Stuff
  Unissued. Sweet Patootie/Yancey's Blues/ Yancey's Stomp
  Vi 26589. Yancey Stomp/State Street Special
  Vi 26590. Tell 'em About Me/Five o'clock Blues
  Vi 26591. Slow and Easy Blues/Mellow Blues
  Vo 05490. Old Quaker Blues   Feb.23,1940
     "   Bear Trap Blues(WC-2961)   -Co 37335
  Vo 05464. (See FABER SMITH)
  BB 8630. Crying in My Sleep/Death Letter Blues(with vocals)   Sept.6,1940
  Vi 27238. Yancey's Bugle Call Rag/35th and Dearborn
  Se 12001. Yancey Special(133)/Eternal Blues(131)   1941
  Se 12002. How Long Blues(120;Estella Yancey,voc;organ acc.)/Midnight Stomp(134)
  Se 12003. Pallet on the Floor(135;Estella Yancey,voc.)/How Long Blues(117-A)
  Se 10001. Boodlin'/Jimmy's Rocks
  Se 10005. Shave 'em Dry/At the Window

YAS YAS GIRL (Merline Johnson; vocals, with some accompaniments including Big
Bill,guitar, and/or Joshua Altheimer,piano):
  Vo 03638. Blues Everywhere/I'd Rather Drink Muddy Water
  Vo 03928. Crime Don't Pay/New Drinking My Blues Away   -Co 37780
  Vo 05105. Time and Mellow/Nobody Knows How I Feel
  Vo 05180. You Can't Have None of That/I'd Rather Be Drink   -Co 37786
  Vo 05286. I Just Keep on Drinking/I Got to Have My Daddy   -Co 37685
  Vo 05219. Don't Have to Sing the Blues/I Need You By My Side
  Vo 05337. Want to Woogie Some More/I'll Try to Forget
  Vo 05382. Front Door Blues/Mama's Bad Luck Child
  Vo 05501. You Don't Know My Mind/You're a Pain in the Neck to Me
  Vo 05614. Black Gypsy Blues/I'm Not Your Fool
  Vo 05676. I Won't Sell My Love/Stop and Listen
  Vo 05870. Worried Heart Blues/Man to Man   -Co 37692
  Vo 05932. You Know It Ain't Right/Black Ghost Blues
  Vo 05984. Got the Blues for My Baby/Milk Man Blues   -Co 37693
  Vo 06032. Evil Old Nightmare/See Saw Blues
  Co 37465. Fighting Man Blues/Froggy Bottom
  Co 37471. Good Old Easy Street/Two by Four Blues

YATES, BLIND RICHARD (vocals, with piano):   1927
  Ge 6104. Sore Bunion Blues/I'm Gonna Moan My Blues Away

YOUNG'S CREOLE JAZZ BAND, BERNIE (Bernie Young,trumpet· Preston Jackson,trombone;
Happy Caldwell,clarinet; Stomp Evans,C-melody sax; Cassino Simpson,piano; Mike
McKendrick,banjo; Eddie Temple,drums.--DB 10/1/40):   1922-23
  Para 12060. Every Saturday Night/What's the Use of Lovin'
  Para 12088. Dearborn Street Blues/(KING OLIVER)
  Para 20272. Tin Roof Blues(1535-2)/(MIDWAY GARDEN ORCH) -Harmo 863, Clax 40272

YOUNG, BILLIE (vocals, acc. by Jelly Roll Morton,piano):
  Vi 23339. When They Get Lovin' They's Gone/You Done Played Out Blues

LESTER YOUNG

See also: COUNT BASIE.   Jones-Smith: Vo 3459,3441.
           UNA MAE CARLISLE.   KANSAS CITY 6:Com 509,511,512,
           BENNY GOODMAN: Vi 25808,25814. SAM PRICE:De 8557.   (555,573
           JOHNNY GUARNIERI: Sav 509, 511. KANSAS CITY 7: Key 1302, 1303.
           GLENN HARDMAN: Vo 4971,Co 35263,35341. DICKY WELLS: Sig 28115,90002.
           BILLIE HOLIDAY: Vo 3593 --   TEDDY WILSON.

YOUNG QUARTET, LESTER (Lester Young,tenor; Johnny Guarnieri,piano; Sid Catlee,
drums; Slam Stewart,bass):
  Key 603. I Never Knew/Just You Just Me
  Key 604. Sometimes I'm Happy(3)/Afternoon of a Basie-ite(4)

LESTER YOUNG TRIO(Young;tenor;King Cole,piano;Red Callender,bass):
Philo P-1. Body and Soul; I Can't Get Started; Tea for Two; Indiana
    LESTER YOUNG AND HIS BAND(Vic Dickenson,trombone:Lester Young,tenor;Dodo
    Marmarosa,piano;Red Callender,bass:Henry Tucker,drums):   1946
Philo 123. D.B. Blues/Lester Blows Again
Philo 124. These Foolish Things/Jumping at Mesners
Philo 125. He Don't Love Me Anymore/Pleasing Man Blues(Helen Humes,vocals
Philo 126. See See Rider/It's Better to Give Than Receive(Helen Humes,vocals)
    (Personnel unknown):
Alad 127. It's Only a Paper Moon/After You've Gone
Alad 128. Lover Come Back to Me/Jammin' With Lester
Alad 137. You're Driving Me Crazy/Lester Leaps-In
Alad 138. She's Funny That Way/Lester's Be Bop Boogie
Alad 162. Sunday/S.M. Blues
Alad 163. Jumping With Symphony Sid/No Eyes Blues
Alad 164. On the Sunny Side of the Street/Sax-o-Re-Bop
Alad 200. Jumping at the Woodside/One o'Clock Jump
    LESTER YOUNG (tenor,with rhythm section):
Sav 551. I Don't Stand Ghost of a Chance(5455)/Lester's Savoy Jump(5457)
Sav 581. Lester's Blues(5454)/Back Home Again in Indiana(5456)

YOUNG AND HIS ORCHESTRA,TRUMMY(Trummy Young,trombone;Harry Curtis,alto:Leo Williams,tenor;John Malchi,piano;Tommy Potter,bass;Eddie Byrd,drums):   Feb.7,1944
Se 12010.Talk of the Town/Hollywood
Se 12011. The Man I Love, 1 & 2
    (Dizzy Gillespie,trumpet;Trummy Young,trombone;Charlie Parker,alto;Clyde
    Hart,piano;Don Byas,tenor;Mike Bryan,guitar;Specs Powell,drums;Al Hall,
Cont 6005. Seventh Avenue(W-3306)/Sorta Kinda(W-3307)   (bass):
    TRUMMY YOUNG AND HIS LUCKY SEVEN(Buck Clayton,trumpet;Trummy Young,trombone & vocal;Ike Quebec,tenor;Kenneth Kersey,piano;Mike Bryan,guitar;
    Jimmy Crawford, drums: Slam Stewart, bass):   May 2,1945
Duke 110. I'm Living for Today/Good and Groovy
Cosmo 901. Rattle and Roll(4900-B)/Behind the Fight Ball(4901-B)
    TRUMMY YOUNG AND HIS ORCHESTRA(Including Young,trombone;Artie Baker, Ray
    Eckstrand,Nick Caiazza,Herbie Fields,Stanley Webb,saxes:Bill de Arango
GI 106. Tidal Wave/Try Try Again   (guitar,& others):1946
GI 107. Don't Be a Baby Baby/Lazy Lullaby

YUKL AND HIS WABASH FIVE,JOE(George Thow,cornet;Joe Yukl,trombone;Pete Legare,clarinet;Eddie Skrivanek,guitar;Stan Wrightsman,piano;Fred Whiting,bass;Graham
Ju 7. Sugar(28-2)/Body and Soul(25-2)   (Stevenson,drums):Oct,27,1945
Ju 8. Royal Garden Blues/Two Quart Blues

ZACK,GEORGE (piano & vocs., with Danny Alvin* or George Wettling,drums):
Com 566. Snowball*/Lazy River   Oct.3,1944
ZURKE AND HIS DELTA RHYTHM BAND,BOB (Nat Natalie,Sterling Bose,Chelsea Quealey,trumpets;Vincent Grande,William Pritchard,Art Foster,trombones;John Gassoway,
Chuck Dale,Larry Binyon,Noni Bernardi,Sid Stoneburn,saxes;Bob Zurke,piano;Chick
Reeves,guitar;Felix Giobbe,bass; Stan King,drums.--JRB):   1939
Vi 26317. Hobson Street Blues   -HMV 9034
        Each Time You Say Goodbye(Claire Martin,voc.)
Vi 26331. It's Me Again(Claire Martin,voc.)/Southern Exposure
Vi 26342. Honky Tonk Train/Melancholy Mood
    (Sub. Pete Peterson,bass):
Vi 26355. Between the Devil and the Deep Blue Sea   -HMV 9034
        I've Found a New Baby
Vi 26395. It's a Hap-Hap-Happy Day/Faithful Forever
Vi 26411. Cuban Boogie Woogie/On a Little Street in Singapore
Vi 26420. Fit to Be Tied(Claire Martin,voc.)/Peach Tree Street(S.Bose,voc.)
    (Sub.Jack Thompson,trumpet,for Natalie:Ray Noonan,Seymour Goldfinger,new
    trombone section; Mike Doty,Gus Ehrman,Ted Mack,John Gassoway,saxes; Noel
Vi 26446. Holy Smoke(Ehrman,voc.)/Somebody Tole me(F.Poe,voc)(Kilgren,guitar):
Vi 26467. I Want My Mama(Evelyn Poe,voc.)/Nickle Nabber Blues
Vi 26474. You Hit My Heart/Put Your Little Foot There
Vi 26526. Tom Cat on the Keys/Everybody Step
    (Sub.Wilton Hutton,trumpet,for Thompson:F.Milligan,Bob McReynolds,trombones;James Clifford,Ernie Caceres,saxes,for Doty,Mack;L.B.King,bass;Al
Vi 26561.Tea for Two/I Love You Much to Much(E.Poe,voc.)   (Sidell,drums):1940
Vi 26607. I Bought a Wooden Whistle/I'm Losing My Mind
    (Sub.Howard Gaffrey,Wayne Williams,trumpets,for Bose,Hutton;Mack Zammer,
    Hobart Simpson,trombones;Marty Berman,Art Wamser,Charles Spiro,saxes for
    Clifford,Ehrman,Caceres; Harry Cohen,bass):
Vi 26646. Rhumboogie/Cow Cow Blues
ZUTTY AND HIS BAND(Vernill York,trumpet;Horace Eubanks,clarinet & alto;Honey Gordon,piano;Mike McKendrick,guitar;Leonard Bibbs,bass;Zutty Singleton,drums): 1935
De 431. Look Over Yonder(9880-B)/Runenae Papa(9881-B)
De 432. I Would Do Anything for You(9879-A)/Clarinet Marmalade(9884-A)
De 465. Royal Garden Blues/Bugle Call Rag

106

Bibliography

CLEF MAGAZINE

DOWN BEAT (DB),
George Hoefer's "Hot Box"

DISCOGRAPHY (Dis.),
British magazine

ESQUIRE JAZZ BOOKS

HOT DISCOGRAPHY (HD),
Charles Delaunay; Paris, 1943

HOT JAZZ (HJ),
French magazine

JAZZ MAGAZINE
William C. Love

JAZZ INFORMATION (JI)

JAZZ MUSIC (JM),
British magazine

JAZZ NOTES
Australian magazine

JAZZ QUARTERLY

JAZZ RECORD (JR)

JAZZ SESSION

JAZZ RECORD BOOK (JRB),
Charles Edward Smith et al.; New York, 1942

JAZZ TEMPO (JT),
British magazine

METRONOME MAGAZINE

NEEDLE

PICKUP
British magazine

RECORD CHANGER (RC)

RHYTHM ON RECORD (RR),
Hilton R. Schleman; London, 1936

TEMPO (Te)

YEARBOOK OF POPULAR MUSIC,
by Paul Edward Miller; Chicago, 1942

AMERICAN MUSIC

BUNK JOHNSON

517 — River Shannon — Moon Over the Mt.
518 — Jada — Poor Butterfly
519 — Got To See Mamma — Beautiful Doll
520 — In the Gloaming — Kathleen

ORIGINAL CREOLE STOMPERS
(Featuring Wooden Joe Nicholas & Albert Burbank)

513 — Eh, La-Bas! — Up Jumped the Devil

DINK'S GOOD TIME MUSIC

515 — Stomp de Lowdown — Grace and Beauty
516 — So Dif'rent Blues — Take Your Time
523* — Rag Bag Rag — The Stella Blues
524* — Las Vegas Stomp — Yeah Man
525* — Jelly Roll Blues — Frisco Dreams
526* — Indian Rag — Dink's Blues

Scheduled for 1948 Release

10-inch Records — $1.05 each

BUNK JOHNSON

251 — Tiger Rag — C. C. Rider
252 — St. Louis Blues — Saints Go Marching In

12-inch Vinylite Records — $1.75 each

Ragtime piano solos by one of the original St. Louis creators,

CHARLES THOMPSON
SCHEDULED FOR 1948 RELEASE

Send for other lists.
Mail order shipments postpaid for 25c per package.

A M RECORDS

704 LEWIS STREET   CANTON, MO.